The Cambridge Handbook of Sociocultural Psychology

Sociocultural psychology is a discipline located at the crossroads between the natural and social sciences and the humanities. This international overview of the field provides an antireductionist and comprehensive account of how experience and behavior emerge from human action with cultural materials in social practices. The outcome is a vision of the dynamics of sociocultural and personal life in which time and developmental constructive transformations are crucial.

This second edition provides expanded coverage of how particular cultural artifacts and social practices shape experience and behavior in the realms of art and aesthetics, economics, history, religion, and politics. Special attention is also paid to the development of identity, the self, and personhood throughout the lifespan, while retaining the emphasis on experience and development as key features of sociocultural psychology.

ALBERTO ROSA is a professor of psychology at the Universidad Autónoma de Madrid, Spain, where he lectures on the history of psychology and cultural psychology. He has carried out research and edited books on the developmental psychology of the physically challenged, notably *Psicología de la Ceguera* (1993) and *El Niño con Parálisis Cerebral* (1993) as well as on the history of psychology, such as his *Metodología de la Historia de la Psicología* (1996) and *Historical and Theoretical Discourse* (1994, co-authored with Jaan Valsiner). His most recent book, *Hacer(se) Ciudadan@s: Una Psicología para la Democracia* (2015, co-authored with Fernanda González), is on the influence of culture and history in shaping identity and citizenship.

JAAN VALSINER is the Niels Bohr Professor of Cultural Psychology at Aalborg University, Denmark. He was the founding editor of the journal *Culture & Psychology*, and he has published and edited around 40 books, including *The Guided Mind* (1998), *Culture in Minds and Societies* (2007), and *Invitation to Cultural Psychology* (2014). He has been awarded the 1995 Alexander von Humboldt Prize and the 2017 Hans Kilian Prize for his interdisciplinary work on human development as well as the Senior Fulbright Lecturing Award in Brazil in 1995–1997. He has been a visiting professor in Brazil, Japan, Australia, Estonia, Germany, Italy, Luxembourg, the United Kingdom, and the Netherlands.

The Cambridge Handbook of Sociocultural Psychology

Second Edition

Edited by

Alberto Rosa
Universidad Autónoma de Madrid

Jaan Valsiner
Aalborg University, Denmark

CAMBRIDGE
UNIVERSITY PRESS

University Printing House, Cambridge CB2 8BS, United Kingdom

One Liberty Plaza, 20th Floor, New York, NY 10006, USA

477 Williamstown Road, Port Melbourne, VIC 3207, Australia

314–321, 3rd Floor, Plot 3, Splendor Forum, Jasola District Centre, New Delhi - 110025, India

79 Anson Road, #06-04/06, Singapore 079906

Cambridge University Press is part of the University of Cambridge.

It furthers the University's mission by disseminating knowledge in the pursuit of education, learning, and research at the highest international levels of excellence.

www.cambridge.org
Information on this title: www.cambridge.org/9781107157699
DOI: 10.1017/9781316662229

First published 2018

Printed in the United Kingdom by TJ International Ltd. Padstow Cornwall

A catalogue record for this publication is available from the British Library

ISBN 978-1-107-15769-9 Hardback
ISBN 978-1-316-61028-2 Paperback

Contents

List of Figures   *page* ix
List of Tables   xi
Contributors   xii

Editors' Introduction   1

Sociocultural Psychology on the Move   3
ALBERTO ROSA AND JAAN VALSINER

Part I Theoretical and Methodological Issues   11

1 The Human Psyche Lives in Semiospheres   13
   ALBERTO ROSA AND JAAN VALSINER

2 Cultural Psychology as the Science of Sensemaking: A
   Semiotic-cultural Framework for Psychology   35
   SERGIO SALVATORE

3 Knowledge and Experience: Interobjectivity, Subjectivity, and Social
   Relations   49
   GORDON SAMMUT, MARTIN W. BAUER, AND SANDRA JOVCHELOVITCH

4 "Mediationism" in Cognitive and Social Theory   63
   ALAN COSTALL

5 Sociocultural Psychology and Interpersonal Psychoanalysis: The
   Semiotic Space in the Consulting Room   78
   PHILIP J. ROSENBAUM

Part II Action, Objects, Artifacts, and Meaning   101

6 Spirited Psyche Creates Artifacts: Semiotic Dynamics of Experience in
   the Shaping of Objects, Agency, and Intentional Worlds   103
   ALBERTO ROSA

7 Making Social Objects: The Theory of Social Representation   130
   WOLFGANG WAGNER, KATRIN KELLO, AND ANDU RÄMMER

8 Beyond the Distinction between Tool and Sign: Objects and Artifacts
   in Human Activity   148
   REIJO MIETTINEN AND SAMI PAAVOLA

9   The Sociocultural Study of Creative Action   163
    VLAD PETRE GLĂVEANU

10 Symbolic Resources and Imagination in the Dynamics of Life   178
    TANIA ZITTOUN

    **Part III The Agent Rises a Reflective Self: Education and
    Development**   205

11 Early Infancy – a Moving World: Embodied Experience and the
    Emergence of Thinking   207
    SILVIA ESPAÑOL

12 Object Pragmatics: Culture and Communication – the Bases for Early
    Cognitive Development   223
    CINTIA RODRÍGUEZ, MARISOL BASILIO, KARINA CÁRDENAS,
    SÍLVIA CAVALCANTE, ANA MORENO-NÚÑEZ, PEDRO PALACIOS,
    AND NOEMÍ YUSTE

13 Distinguishing Two Processes of Self-reflection   245
    ALEX GILLESPIE

14 Making Memory: Meaning in Development of the Autobiographical
    Self   260
    KATHERINE NELSON

15 Mapping Dialogic Pedagogy: Instrumental and Non-instrumental
    Education   274
    EUGENE MATUSOV

16 Development and Education as Crossing Sociocultural Boundaries   302
    GIUSEPPINA MARSICO

    Part IV Institutional Artifacts for Value   317

17 Ownership and Exchange in Children: Implications for Social and
    Moral Development   319
    GUSTAVO FAIGENBAUM

18 Possessions and Money beyond Market Economy   333
    TOSHIYA YAMAMOTO AND NOBORU TAKAHASHI

    Part V Aesthetic and Religious Experiences   349

19 The Sociocultural Constitution of Aesthetic Transcendence   351
    MARK FREEMAN

20 Sociocultural Science of Religion and Natural Belief   366
    JAMES CRESSWELL

21 *Psyche* and *Religio* Face to Face: Religion, Psychology, and Modern
Subjectivity in the Mirror   380
LUIS MARTÍNEZ GUERRERO

Part VI Practices and Artifacts for Imagining Identity   397

22 Imaginative Processes and the Making of Collective Realities in
National Allegories   399
LUCA TATEO

23 National Identities in the Making and Alternative Pathways of
History Education   424
MARIO CARRETERO, FLOOR VAN ALPHEN, AND CRISTIAN PARELLADA

24 The Politics of Representing the Past: Symbolic Spaces of Positioning
and Irony   443
BRADY WAGONER, SARAH H. AWAD, AND IGNACIO BRESCÓ DE LUNA

25 Beyond Historical Guilt: Intergenerational Narratives of Violence
and Reconciliation   458
GIOVANNA LEONE

26 Psytizenship: Sociocultural Mediations in the Historical Shaping of the
Western Citizen   479
JORGE CASTRO-TEJERINA AND JOSÉ CARLOS LOREDO-NARCIANDI

Part VII Experiences Make the Person   501

27 The Human Experience: A Dialogical Account of Self and Feelings   503
JOÃO SALGADO AND CARLA CUNHA

28 Knowing Ourselves: Dances of Social Guidance, Imagination, and
Development by Overcoming Ambivalence   518
SETH SURGAN, AURORA PFEFFERKORN, AND EMILY ABBEY

29 Personal History and Historical Selfhood: The Embodied and
Pre-reflective Dimension   538
ALLAN KØSTER AND DITTE ALEXANDRA WINTHER-LINDQVIST

30 The Development of a Person: Children's Experience of Being and
Becoming within the Cultural Life Course   556
PERNILLE HVIID AND JAKOB WAAG VILLADSEN

31 The Construction of the Person in the Interethnic Situation: Dialogues
with Indigenous University Students   575
DANILO SILVA GUIMARÃES AND MARÍLIA ANTUNES BENEDITO

32 Social Identities, Gender, and Self: Cultural Canalization in
Imagery Societies   597
ANA FLÁVIA DO AMARAL MADUREIRA

33 The Experience of Aging: Views from Without and Within   615
    DIETER FERRING

General Conclusion   631

34 An Epistemological Coda: Sociocultural Psychology among
    the Sciences   633
    ALBERTO ROSA AND JAAN VALSINER

    Index   652

Figures

3.1 Psychological phenomena in the spaces between the personal–collective and the private–public dimensions. *page* 53
6.1 Triadic formalisms accounting for action, semiosis, experience, and realities. 117
6.2 Semiotic structure of the *intentional scheme*. 119
6.3 *Actuation*: Semiotic development of *intentional action* and *objects*. 120
6.4 Fractal structure of experience and behavior: Development of *symbols* and *arguments*. 122
6.5 Substitutive semioses in the dynamics of sociocultural phenomena and personal experiences. 125
7.1 An antique and a modern wheelchair. 135
7.2 Choir from Tõstamaa 1865. 140
8.1 Status of the gum disease defined in the care plan. 156
9.1 Decorated eggs at different stages. 166
9.2 The five A's framework of creativity. 167
10.1 Loop of imagination in a three-dimensional space. 182
10.2 Semiotic prism. 190
10.3 A star-like model. 193
12.1 Triadic interaction at two and four months of age. 227
12.2 Symbolic uses of objects. 230
12.3 Self-regulation with private gestures and protocanonical uses. 232
12.4 Numerical uses of objects. 234
14.1 Bounds of experiential space in an environmental event or encounter. 262
15.1 Diverse and vast terrain of dialogic pedagogy. 277
16.1 In the elevator: regulation of sociocultural, interpersonal, and inner borders. 304
16.2 "School borderscape." 310
16.3 The school border zone. 310
16.4 The border zone within a school. 311
16.5 School entrance hall as a social membrane. 312
18.1 Expanded mediational structure (EMS). 334
21.1 An eternal obsessive loop. The genealogical relationship between religion and psychology. 391
22.1 Abstraction and reification. 403
22.2 *The Triumph of Henry IV* by Peter Paul Rubens. 405
22.3 Changing configurations of distinctions and relationships. 406
22.4 *Consequences of War* by Peter Paul Rubens. 409
22.5 *Italia and Germania* by Friedrich Overbeck. 409
22.6 Female personifications of France, Russia, and Britain. 410

22.7	Demonstration against same-sex marriage in Paris.	411
22.8	Map of Sykes–Picot Agreement.	412
22.9	The imagined land.	413
22.10	Exotic at home and homeness in the exotic.	415
22.11	World War I propaganda posters advocating intervention.	416
22.12	Abstraction/reification in "umbrella revolution."	418
22.13	Schoolchildren rehearsal for the Empire Games in New South Wales, 1938.	420
23.1	Map of the Iberian Peninsula around 710. Historical map adapted from García de Cortazar, *Atlas de Historia de España*. Barcelona: Planeta, 2005.	432
23.2	Map of the Iberian Peninsula around 721.	432
23.3	Map of the Iberian Peninsula around 1212.	432
23.4	Map of the Iberian Peninsula around 1491.	432
23.5	Student drawing of the Iberian Peninsula around 710. Adapted from Lopez, Carretero & Rodriguez-Moneo (2015).	433
23.6	Student drawing of the Iberian Peninsula around 721.	433
23.7	Student drawing of the Iberian Peninsula around 1212.	433
23.8	Student drawing of the Iberian Peninsula around 1491.	433
24.1	Street art on the presidential palace wall in Cairo, June, 2013.	451
24.2	Government poster in Cairo, February 2016.	452
27.1	The three layers of the human mind: first-, second-, and third-person perspectives.	511
27.2	The triadic structure of a dialogical position.	512
27.3	A dialogical conception of feelings.	513
28.1	The openness of the sign to future meaning.	519
32.1	Social identities as boundary phenomena: from differences to inequalities, from inequalities to intolerance.	602
34.1	Psyche: dynamic processes arising from a spiral of circular reaction cycles.	634
34.2	Epistemic overlaps in the study of the developmental dynamics of psyche.	636
34.3	Argument: a semiotic sign compiling values arising from action and producing experiences.	641
34.4	Fields of sense (and culture) arising from experience and influencing behavior.	641
34.5	Crisscrossing boundaries of cultural, institutional, interpersonal, and subjective fields.	645

Tables

8.1   BIM-related software used in a Finnish construction project in 2011–2012.   *page* 158
33.1   Overview of central concepts, models, and theories on human aging.   619

Contributors

EMILY ABBEY is a professor of psychology at Ramapo College of New Jersey, USA. Working from a developmental orientation and a cultural perspective, she is curious about ambivalence, the semiotic organization of human lives, and the relationship between poetry and psychology.

SARAH H. AWAD is a PhD fellow at the Centre for Cultural Psychology, Aalborg University, Denmark. She received her MSc degree in social and cultural psychology from the London School of Economics and Political Science, UK, and her BA degree in mass communication from the American University in Cairo, Egypt. Her research interests are in the interrelations between the fields of cultural psychology, communication, and social development. She studies the process by which individuals develop through times of life ruptures and social change using signs to create alternative visions of social reality. She looks specifically at images in the urban space and their influence on identity, collective memory, and power relations within a society.

MARISOL BASILIO is a research fellow at the Faculty of Education of the University of Cambridge, UK, working as part of the Centre for Research on Play in Education, Development and Learning (PEDAL). Her research interest focuses on the interplay between communication, self-regulation, and play in children's development.

MARTIN W. BAUER is a professor of social psychology and research methodology at the London School of Economics and Political Science, UK. A former editor of *Public Understanding of Science*, he currently directs the MSc Social & Public Communication program and lectures regularly in Brazil and China. He investigates science, attitudes, and common sense through theory and indicator construction using comparative surveys, media monitoring, and qualitative inquiries.

MARÍLIA ANTUNES BENEDITO is concluding her undergraduate studies at the Institute of Psychology at the University of São Paulo, Brazil. She developed a research project in the field of cultural psychology about Amerindian identity in the urban context, which involved interviewing Amerindian undergraduate students.

IGNACIO BRESCÓ DE LUNA is currently working as an associate professor at the Centre for Cultural Psychology, Aalborg University, Denmark. He received his PhD degree from the Autonomous University of Madrid, Spain, where he worked as an associate professor until 2014. His research interests revolve around collective memory and identity, the teaching of history, positioning theory, and the narrative mediation of remembering.

KARINA CÁRDENAS, PhD, is a qualified early years teacher and developmental researcher. She is an assistant professor at the Pontificia Universidad Católica de Chile, in Villarrica. Her research interests concern the early development of communication and pedagogical interactions using material objects in early childhood education.

MARIO CARRETERO is a professor at Autonoma University of Madrid, Spain, and a researcher at the Facultad Latinoamericana de Ciencias Sociales (FLACSO), Argentina. He has carried out extensive research on history education.

JORGE CASTRO-TEJERINA is a professor of the history of psychology at the Universidad Nacional de Educación a Distancia (UNED) in Madrid, Spain. His work is oriented toward the study of the relationship between the history of psychology and sociocultural topics such as citizenship, professional identities, aesthetics, and cultural theory.

SÍLVIA CAVALCANTE, PhD, is a researcher of developmental and educational psychology at the Department of Cogntion, Development and Educational Psychology at the University of Barcelona, Spain. Her research interest focuses on early childhood development and education, especially on number development in young children, from a socio-cognitive approach.

ALAN COSTALL is a professor of theoretical psychology and deputy director of the Centre for Situated Action and Communication at the University of Portsmouth, UK. His work explores the implications of a "mutualist approach" to psychology. A serious engagement of this approach with the sociocultural should (he hopes) be able to counter the nuttiness of postmodernism.

JAMES (Jim) CRESSWELL is a cultural psychologist who is primarily interested in dialogicality and how it can enrich our understanding of psychological phenomena. This interest draws on the aesthetic theory of the Bakhtin Circle and has led him to do community engaged research with immigrants.

CARLA CUNHA, PhD, is currently an assistant professor at the University Institute of Maia (ISMAI – Instituto Universitário da Maia), Portugal, where she coordinates the Master in Clinical and Health Psychology program. Her current research interests are focused on change processes in psychotherapy, identity transformation, and the dialogical self.

SILVIA ESPAÑOL, PhD, is a researcher at the CONICET (National Council of Scientific and Technical Research), Argentina. Her area of specialty is the socio-cognitive development in early infancy. Her work is on the border between cognitive developmental psychology, psychology of music, and the area of human movement.

GUSTAVO FAIGENBAUM graduated from the University of Buenos Aires, Argentina, and obtained his PhD in philosophy at the New School University, New York, USA. He is a professor at the Universidad Autónoma de Entre Ríos, Argentina. His research focuses on social development, social cognition, ownership, and exchange.

DIETER FERRING, until his untimely death in August 2017, was a professor of developmental psychology and geropsychology at the University of Luxembourg. He was the director of the Integrative Research Unit on Social and Individual Development (INSIDE). His main research areas lie within lifespan development and aging, focusing on personal and social factors contributing to autonomy or dependence in old age.

MARK FREEMAN is a professor and chair of the Department of Psychology and Distinguished Professor of Ethics and Society at the College of the Holy Cross in Worcester, Massachusetts, USA. He is the winner of the 2010 Theodore R. Sarbin Award in the Society for Theoretical and Philosophical Psychology.

ALEX GILLESPIE is an associate professor in social psychology at the London School of Economics and Political Science, UK, and co-editor of the *Journal for the Theory of Social Behaviour*. His research focuses on communication, divergences of perspective, misunderstandings, and listening.

VLAD PETRE GLĂVEANU is an associate professor and head of the Department of Psychology and Counseling at Webster University Geneva, Switzerland, director of the Webster Center for Creativity and Innovation (WCCI), and Associate Professor II at the Center for the Science of Learning and Technology (SLATE), Bergen University, Norway. He has published extensively in the cultural psychology of creativity.

DANILO SILVA GUIMARÃES is a professor at the Institute of Psychology within the University of São Paulo, Brazil. His main focus of research is the process of symbolic elaborations out of tensional boundaries between cultural alterities, psychology, and Amerindian peoples.

PERNILLE HVIID is an associate professor at the Department of Psychology at the University of Copenhagen, Denmark. Her research focuses on developmental processes from a cultural life course perspective. Her empirical focus is on children's life and development in institutional practices and on the development of educational and managerial practices aiming at caring for and educating children.

SANDRA JOVCHELOVITCH is a professor of social psychology at the London School of Economics and Political Science, UK, where she directs the MSc program in social and cultural psychology. Her research focuses on the sociocultural psychology of representations, public spheres, and community development. Her latest research examines human development under poverty and urban segregation, focusing on trajectories of self and community in the favelas of Rio de Janeiro.

KATRIN KELLO holds an MA in history and PhD in media and communications. At the time of writing the chapter she was a researcher at the Institute of Social Studies, University of Tartu, Estonia. She currently works at the Estonian Research Council. She is interested in history of law as well as in social memory, history politics, and social representation theory.

ALLAN KØSTER is a postdoc fellow at Aalborg University, Denmark. He holds a PhD in philosophy of psychology and is trained as a clinical specialist in narrative therapy. Thematically, his research centers on the relation between selfhood, embodiment, and narrative in psychological processes as these are socioculturally embedded.

GIOVANNA LEONE is an associate professor of social psychology at Sapienza University of Rome, Italy, where she teaches social psychology, communication, political psychology, and community psychology. Her main research interests include social and collective aspects of autobiographical memory, ambivalent effects of over-helping as observed in multicultural classrooms, and relationships between changes of historical narratives on past intergroup violence and reconciliation.

JOSÉ CARLOS LOREDO-NARCIANDI is a professor of the Department of Psicología Básica I at the Universidad Nacional de Educación a Distancia (National University for Open Education) in Madrid, Spain. He currently teaches the history of psychology and epistemology. His areas of interest are the history of psychology from a genealogical point of view, constructivist traditions in the social sciences, and technologies of subjectivity.

ANA FLÁVIA DO AMARAL MADUREIRA has a PhD in psychology from the Universidade de Brasília, Brazil. She is a professor of psychology at Centro Universitário de Brasília, Brazil, and does research in psychology and education with a specific interest in the relations between social identities, diversity, and prejudice.

GIUSEPPINA MARSICO is an assistant professor of development and educational psychology at the University of Salerno (Italy), a postdoctoral researcher at the Centre for Cultural Psychology at Aalborg University (Denmark), and a visiting professor at the PhD program in psychology at the Federal University of Bahia (Brazil).

LUIS MARTÍNEZ GUERRERO has a PhD in psychology at the Universidad Autónoma de Madrid, Spain. He is an associate professor of medical anthropology at the Universidad Antonio de Nebrija, Spain. His interests include the cultural psychology of religion, the history of emotions, the technologies of the self, and the genealogy of modern subjectivity.

EUGENE MATUSOV is a professor in the School of Education at the University of Delaware, USA. His main interests are in dialogic pedagogy and in studying how to design safe learning environments for all students.

REIJO MIETTINEN is a professor emeritus of adult education at the Faculty of Educational Sciences of the University of Helsinki, Finland, and works in the Center for Research on Activity, Development and Learning (CRADLE). His research group studies scientific work, network collaboration, producer–user interaction, and learning in technological innovations.

ANA MORENO-NÚÑEZ is an assistant professor of developmental psychology at Universidad de Valladolid, Spain. She received her PhD from Universidad Autónoma de Madrid and has worked as a research fellow at the Singapore National Institute of Education at Nanyang Technological University, Singapore. Her research focuses on micro-genetic analysis of the role of adults as a guide in children's developmental processes and how their actions contribute to children outcomes at an early age, in both home and school settings.

KATHERINE NELSON is Distinguished Professor Emerita of Psychology at the Graduate Center of the City University of New York, USA. She is a fellow of the American Psychological Association and the Association for Psychological Science. She is the recipient of awards for a distinguished research career from the American Psychological Association and the Society for Research in Child Development and she also received the SRCD Book Award in 2008. Her research focuses on the development of language, memory, and cognition during the late infancy and early childhood years.

SAMI PAAVOLA is an associate professor at the Faculty of Educational Sciences at the University of Helsinki, Finland, and is affiliated with the Center for Research on Activity, Development and Learning (CRADLE). His research focuses on digitization of work and on collaborative learning and inquiry.

PEDRO PALACIOS, PhD, is a professor in the Department of Psychology at the Universidad Autónoma de Aguascalientes, Mexico. His research interest is in studying the origin and development of symbols in infants.

CRISTIAN PARELLADA is a lecturer at the Faculty of Psychology of the University of La Plata, Argentina, and researcher at the Facultad Latinoamericana de Ciencias Sociales (FLACSO), Argentina. His research interests are related to history education and national identity, particularly in relation to how historical maps are represented by both students and textbooks.

AURORA PFEFFERKORN is a graduate student at Fordham University in New York, USA. She is an interdisciplinary social historian, utilizing the study of psychology and literature in her work. She enjoys studying moments of great social upheaval and change, though specializes in medieval European history.

ANDU RÄMMER is a researcher and lecturer of sociology at the University of Tartu, Estonia. He is interested in the formation of values, diffusion of new ideas, public acceptance of new technologies, trust in science, and social representation theory.

CINTIA RODRÍGUEZ is a professor of developmental psychology at the Universidad Autónoma de Madrid, Spain. She worked in the Geneva School in the 1980s, where she developed a semiotic-pragmatic approach on objects in communicative situations. Her research area is concerned with early socio-cognitive development in natural contexts.

ALBERTO ROSA is a professor of psychology at the Universidad Autónoma de Madrid, Spain, where he lectures on the history of psychology and cultural psychology. He is interested in the history of psychology and the semiotics of experience as mediated by cultural artifacts.

PHILIP J. ROSENBAUM, PhD, is a clinical psychologist, psychoanalyst, and the director of the Counseling and Psychological Services (CAPS) at Haverford College in Pennsylvania, USA. His interests are in studying the commonalities between contemporary interpersonal analytic practice and cultural psychology.

JOÃO SALGADO, PhD, is an assistant professor at the University Institute of Maia (ISMAI – Instituto Universitário da Maia), Portugal, and the director of the PhD program in clinical psychology. His work has been mainly devoted to theoretical and empirical research on psychotherapy and on the dialogical perspective, ranging from leading clinical trials to qualitative micro-analytic studies and theoretical development.

SERGIO SALVATORE is a professor of dynamic psychology at the Department of History, Society and Humanities at the University of Salento, Italy. His scientific interests are the psychodynamic and semiotic theorization of mental phenomena and the methodology of analysis of psychological processes as field dependent dynamics. He also takes an interest in theory and the analysis of psychological intervention in clinical, scholastic, organizational, and social fields.

GORDON SAMMUT is a senior lecturer in social psychology at the University of Malta. He is interested in the negotiation and outcomes of diverse perspectives. His work explores social representations of Arabs and Muslims in Europe and support for dictatorship and democracy in Libya.

SETH SURGAN is a professor of psychology at Worcester State University, Massachusetts, USA, where he enjoys both relieving students of their confusions about how psychology constructs knowledge and deepening their confusion about the role of culture in psychological processes.

NOBORU TAKAHASHI is a professor of school education at Osaka Kyoiku University, Japan. His research interest is literacy development in cultural context.

LUCA TATEO is an associate professor in epistemology and the history of cultural psychology at the Centre for Cultural Psychology, Aalborg University, Denmark. His research interests are in the study of imagination as higher psychological function, the epistemology and history of psychological sciences in order to reflect on the future trends of psychological research, and related methodological issues.

JAAN VALSINER is currently Niels Bohr Professor of Cultural Psychology at Aalborg University, Denmark. He is a cultural psychologist with a consistently developmental axiomatic base that is brought to the analysis of any psychological or social phenomena.

FLOOR VAN ALPHEN is a postdoctoral researcher at Autonoma University, Madrid, Spain. She studies historical narratives and social identities in a cultural psychological vein with a particular interest in adolescents, cultural diversity, and human mobility.

JAKOB WAAG VILLADSEN is a PhD fellow at the Copenhagen Center of Cultural Life Course Studies at the Department of Psychology, University of Copenhagen, Denmark. His main interest is in early childhood development in educational settings, focusing on subjectivity and how it emerges, develops, and is preserved in the cultural life course of the individual – lived and shared with others.

WOLFGANG WAGNER is a professor of psychology at the University of Tartu, Estonia, and was formerly at Johannes Kepler University, Linz, Austria. He is interested in the theory and research in societal psychology, social and cultural knowledge, the popularization of science, intergroup relationships, racism, and social representation theory.

BRADY WAGONER is Professor of Psychology at Aalborg University, Denmark, and an associate editor for the journals *Culture & Psychology* and *Peace & Conflict*. He received his PhD from the University of Cambridge, UK, where he started his line of research on social and cultural psychology, remembering, social change, and the development of dynamic methodologies. His recent books include *The Constructive Mind: Bartlett's Psychology in Reconstruction* (Cambridge University Press, 2017), *The Psychology of Imagination* (2017) and

Handbook of Culture and Memory (2017). He was awarded the Early Career Award by the American Psychological Association (Division 26).

DITTE ALEXANDRA WINTHER-LINDQVIST, PhD, is an associate professor of developmental psychology at Aarhus University, Denmark. She is interested in phenomena central to the development of children and young people from a point of view of lived experience.

TOSHIYA YAMAMOTO is a director at the Developmental Research Support Center, Shizuoka, Japan. His research interest is the ontogeny of possession in a sociohistorical context.

NOEMÍ YUSTE, PhD, is an associate professor of developmental psychology at UNIR University. Her research field centers on peer interactions and first symbolic productions in school contexts.

TANIA ZITTOUN is a professor at the Institute of Psychology and Education at the University of Neuchâtel in Switzerland. She is working on the development of a sociocultural psychology of the life course with a specific focus on the dynamics of transition, imagination, and the role of institutions. Her current work examines mobile lives as well as aging persons.

Editors' Introduction

Sociocultural Psychology on the Move

Alberto Rosa and Jaan Valsiner

The first edition of this *Handbook* (Valsiner & Rosa, 2007) is now ten years old. At the time it was first published, we mentioned that its publication could be taken as a landmark of the consolidation of a discipline. Looking back now, we can say that we were right, as the notion of culture is now widely conceived and has been on the rise over the last decade (Van Belzen, 2010; Chirkov, 2016; Chiu & Hong, 2007; Glăveanu, 2016; Sullivan, 2016; Valsiner, 2007, 2014). Sociocultural psychology is one of the branches of cultural psychology and has as its focus the socially normative nature of the wider cultural context within which a person relates to the world through specific sets of meaningful actions. The focus on meaningfulness of human action – through semiosis (making and use of signs) – is shared by sociocultural psychology and cultural psychology.

During the past decade, sociocultural psychology has both consolidated and expanded in many directions. This is noticeable, first, by the publication of several handbooks on cultural psychology – indicating the interest in culture and social psychology (Kitayama & Cohen, 2007) – and, second, by the richness of various streams in cultural psychologies (Valsiner, 2012). Additionally, the field's move toward cultural historical psychology (Yasnitsky, Van der Veer, & Ferrari, 2014) summarizes perspectives of the whole field that have developed out of the historical traditions of Lev Vygotsky (Zavershneva & Van der Veer, 2017) and Alexander Luria. Some volumes have been written as textbooks aimed at students (Heine, 2008; Voestermans &

Verheggen, 2013), others as theoretical volumes aimed at scholars (Valsiner et al., 2016). This has been paralleled by a growing body of books and journals devoted to publishing theoretical and empirical contributions. The social science arena that utilizes the notion of culture in one way or another is experiencing a "booming and buzzing" creativity that may provide new breakthroughs in our understanding of human living in the tumultuous social world filled with the disappearance of knowledge into the agitation of doctrines, drone attacks under the aegis of "protection," battles against "terrorism" that feed into fears and unleash xenophobia, and – last but not least – the globalization of consumption-focused societal ideologies. The waves of social turmoil are like tsunamis in social media – making social upheaval a more complex threat than nuclear weapons have ever been. The sociocultural perspective is likely to dominate the current social favorite, the "neurosciences," which, despite their promises to cure disease, cannot alter the social pathologies of the societies in which people participate. The future is for the social sciences – given that the societal escalations of the contemporary world cross the boundary of calm tolerance and risk slipping into sectarianism.

The Birth of the Second Edition

In the present, seemingly never-ending flow of academic publications, it is a special honor if a book appears in new editions – all the more if the idea is initiated by someone other than the authors or editors. Cambridge University Press's suggestion to produce a second edition of the *Handbook of Sociocultural Psychology* came as somewhat of a surprise – but it was certainly timely. The field had grown in the decade since the first edition, and so have our understandings of it. We are now in a position to guide further development of the discipline – a task to be taken up both humbly and determinedly. We are creating a sculpture out of the clouds, a book that gives form to the flow of ever-new ideas – whether ingenious, repetitive, or mundane. Our aim is to isolate the ingenious ideas from the many others.

We decided on an overhaul of the original idea by introducing a meta-structure of ideas not yet developed 11 years ago. As a whole, this is a completely new volume. True, some of the contributions from 2007 have been preserved in altered form, but our approach to the *Handbook* as a whole is new. It now expands the views on experience and development that appeared in the first edition; at the same time, it shifts its scope by paying more attention to how particular cultural artifacts and social practices shape experience and behavior throughout the lifespan. The "socio" component of the title points toward the volume's base in cultural objects, while actions on these provide the focus for the present *Handbook*. In the wider field of social sciences, where psychology as a discipline is vanishing into the black hole of the neurosciences, this second edition of the *Handbook* preserves the sociocultural aspects of psychology through an interdisciplinary synthesis.

Real Interdisciplinary Synthesis

It is through interaction and communication in particular scenarios, often in conditions of ambiguity and ambivalence that challenge the actor to position himself or herself, that cultural artifacts (tools, symbols, images, discourses, norms) are put into use and transformed, sometimes in a creative way. Not only are these kinds of situations occasions for producing novelty but

they also show how personal experiences produce individual development and are a source of cultural transformation. This makes understanding (meaning making of subjective experiences) a key theoretical issue.

Different disciplines help one another. Semiotics and literary criticism offer explanations not only about how sign systems turn into symbols and utterances but also about how experiences can be considered signs for orienting action and canalizing actuations. A semiotic theory of human experiences and actions that addresses how actors understand and perform in situations offers formalisms capable of modeling how personal experience and behavior are linked and is instrumental in explaining how social representations are elaborated, put into use, and transformed.

This set of theories images a dynamics of sociocultural and personal life in which time and developmental constructive transformations are crucial. Education and development; mastering and transforming meditational tools through play, imagination, and art; and stabilizing changes through symbols, discourses, and practices make it possible to establish aesthetic and ethic systems of values and, with them, shared forms of feeling, knowledge, and social institutions. The mutual co-construction of psyche and sociocultural systems shapes particular forms of identity and the self, which, together with cultural systems of beliefs, produce varieties of personal experiences that cannot be ignored when considering civil and personal governance.

In This Volume

Sociocultural psychology is a discipline with blurred limits that intersects with other psychological subdisciplines, the social sciences, and the humanities. It is therefore important to chart the network of theories that informs and links its corpus of knowledge. Action, artifact, and meaning are key concepts with a long history within the sociocultural tradition. They have proved to be useful for explaining the transitions between the realm of culture to those of behavior and subjectivity. Several theories, when taken together, can provide an integrative image of how such transitions can happen without falling on any kind of dualism or reductionism.

Part I is devoted to the theoretical and methodological issues that frame the contents of the volume. It starts with a parsimonious naturalist overview of how the human psyche gets shaped in processes that begin in the bioecological domain, then produces meaning and mind, and, finally, the spirit of culture. As Rosa and Valsiner (Chapter 1) explain, human beings are a cultural species that cannot but live in a semiosphere. Such a view leads Salvatore (Chapter 2) to conceive psychology as a science of sensemaking and to present a semiotic–cultural framework for human psychology. This has far-reaching consequences in both the psychological and the epistemological realms. Sammut, Bauer, and Jovchelovitch (Chapter 3) demonstrate that what we take as objective or subjective cannot be conceived without taking into account how social communication iteratively transforms experience and coordinates social relations. Costall (Chapter 4) argues that an ecological psychological approach, even if social and semiotic, does not need to resort to a representationist kind of cognitive mediation. The general framework presented in Part I prompts Rosenbaum (Chapter 5) to discuss the similarities and differences between cultural psychology and interpersonal psychoanalysis and how the theories can benefit from one another.

Enactive autopoietic constructivism offers a dynamic view of how the co-construction of functional structures in an agent, when acting within an environment of objects, allows the production of explanations capable of transitioning from the biological to the social realm via the mediation of artifacts and sign systems. Ecological psychology, actor-network theory, and the systems of activity theory are theoretical

approaches that take into account how material and virtual objects are graspable in human action and integrated in networks of actants, institutions, and discourses, and so are able to describe how the structure of actions gets transformed and new cultural products and novel ways of social interaction appear.

In such a vein, Part II focuses on how human action in the environment simultaneously produces perception and meaning and transforms elements of the environment, producing artifacts, social conventions, symbols, and arguments. Rosa (Chapter 6) examines how the semiotic properties of behavior and experience can explain the production of artifacts and conventions and the transformation of human agency through social history and ontological development. Wagner, Kello, and Rämmer (Chapter 7) focus on how social communication produces shared social objects of many different kinds, ranging from concrete material elements to abstract entities, such as global warming or national identity. Miettinen and Paavola (Chapter 8) explore artifacts and semiotic tools as intertwined elements within the changing dynamics of systems of activity. Glăveanu (Chapter 9) discusses how sensemaking and interpretation, evaluation and use, and dialogue and perspective taking in the dynamics of the relations involving the triad of actor, artifact, and audience can expand the scope of creativity studies. Finally, Zittoun (Chapter 10) discusses how imagination and "symbolic resources" are key elements for human development, the shaping of personal life courses, and also societal changes.

Part III is devoted to education and development. Español (Chapter 11) presents a convincing argument about how early motor development and body awareness develop together in early forms of social interaction. It is on the vitality forms of movement so developed, that the child can participate in the social world of conventional symbols and arguments. Social interaction, mediated by objects (toys) in different play situations, transforms movement and body awareness into conventional cultural uses of objects and early cognitive development. In their chapter, Rodríguez et al. (Chapter 12) discuss the development of canonical uses of objects that is a pragmatic link for the later acquisition of cultural concepts. The self is one of these concepts. Gillespie (Chapter 13) conceives the self as arising from the phenomenological experience of self-reflection, when one becomes an object for oneself. As Nelson (Chapter 14) views it, meaning-making processes simultaneously develop different forms of memory and self-awareness when the child accumulates experiences while participating in different levels of human culture and related language formats and uses. Development and education are then inconceivable without being immersed in sociocultural dialogues. Matusov (Chapter 15) examines the notion of dialogue in education, distinguishing between two kinds of dialogical pedagogy: instrumental, aiming at making all students arrive at some curricular end points preset by the teacher and/or the society, and noninstrumental, expecting students to arrive at new curricular end points that cannot be predicted in advance. This movement between what already exists in the life of a person and what could come into being in the next moment prompts Marsico (Chapter 16) to conceive education and development as liminal and future oriented, constantly working on the border of the "beyond area," moving through the semiotic boundaries between social institutions.

Part IV elaborates these ideas further by focusing on how value develops within institutional settings. Faigenbaum (Chapter 17) presents a view on moral development by reviewing the development of ownership, exchange, and reciprocity in children's institutional experience. In a similar vein, Yamamoto and Takahashi (Chapter 18) explore money as a cultural tool mediating market and gift exchanges among children – examining the cultural meanings money

takes within varieties of relationships between children and parents or friends.

Part V shifts the volume's focus to the study of aesthetic and religious experiences. Artifacts, rituals, and texts of different kinds are outcomes of human action constructing the cultural landscape. They provide arguments for shaping individual experiences, the personal understanding of individual and collective life, and the position they take when experiencing events. Freeman (Chapter 19) argues that aesthetic transcendence cannot be conceived without sociocultural values, beliefs, and ideals incited by particular local objects. Cresswell (Chapter 20) challenges the idea of "natural" religion as beliefs emerging as epiphenomena of cognitive mechanisms and presents an alternative approach that addresses the givenness of religious belief without predicating on socioculturally decontextualized mechanisms. Martínez Guerrero (Chapter 21) argues that while psychology presents religion as a key cultural phenomenon for understanding the organization of people's daily experiences through the use of its symbols, rituals, and discourses, the reverse can also be said: religion played an important role in shaping both the contemporary Western individual and the psychological categories for its description. This is exemplified by examining Ignatius of Loyola's *Spiritual Exercises* as a milestone in the configuration of subjectivity and the government of emotions in the modern subject.

Part VI centers on how cultural resources shape identity, placing particular emphasis on the role historical narratives play in interpreting past and current events in conflict management and in civic life. History and historical narratives are cultural devices that provide information about the activities of a group over time and also produce aesthetic and moral feelings toward different groups. Tateo (Chapter 22) develops a theoretical model of the psychological processes that produce abstract and intangible concepts, such as "nation," "love," "faith," or "freedom," that allow for contact with particular objects in everyday experience, to act as allegorical representations of those abstract concepts. Carretero, Van Alphen, and Parellada (Chapter 23) present historical narratives as tools for scaffolding feelings of collective and personal identity and therefore also as instrumental for instilling ethnic and nationalistic ideologies, but they also argue that history education is an occasion for fostering critical reflection on social life, as a defense against ideological indoctrination. Wagoner, Awad, and Brescó (Chapter 24) explore the social–political dynamics by which the past is represented and used by differently positioned people and how alternative interpretations arise before the displayed symbolic weaponry to preserve one's own ideological position. In a similar vein, Leone (Chapter 25) highlights how historical accounts can keep conflicts alive, unless their capability for producing feelings of superiority and grievance or guilt and vengeance is defused. This requires building a narrative of reconciliation, which often needs to change the aesthetic and moral arguments on which the groups and their members' identities are conceived – not an easy task. Part VI concludes with Castro-Tejerina and Loredo-Narciandi's (Chapter 26) reflection on the role of psychology in shaping the Western idea of citizenship – what they term *Psytizenship*. As they view it, postmodernity is forging a repsychologization of the subject that is necessarily conflictive and plural.

Part VII is the final and longest part in the *Handbook*. It is devoted to examining a variety of personal experiences and the shapes they take throughout the lifespan. Salgado and Cunha (Chapter 27) offer a view of human experience as arising from a dialogue between the self and feelings. They approach the experiential mind by combining the phenomenological, sociocultural, and semiotic outlooks. As they present it, the flow of human experience combines first-, second-, and third-person perspectives, with affectivity crossing over these three layers and

therefore acting as a core element within the dynamics of the human mind for the institution of the sense of selfhood. Surgan, Pfefferkorn, and Abbey (Chapter 28) conceive experience as resulting from a future-oriented process based on overcoming the ambivalence between what is known now and what might be the case in the next moment. Their chapter focuses on the social and societal roots of ambivalence and the means of overcoming ambivalence within the process of constructing meaning when facing the quandaries of life.

The construction of the personal realm is a challenge for sociocultural psychology. Køster and Winther-Lindqvist's (Chapter 29) contribution centers on the individual dimension of personal history by distinguishing between the preverbal, prereflective embodied landscape of experience (historical selfhood) and personal history as the broader ontogenetic and existential process through which an individual continuously becomes the person he or she is. This makes embodiment the point of transfer between nature and culture, sociogenesis and ontogenesis, and also relevant for the development of individual agency. Hviid and Villadsen (Chapter 30) also claim the importance of taking into account children's development as persons. They present an empirical study on children's meaning-making processes while in dialogue with cultural elements in the living spaces where they experience events. These self-reflecting experiences, when assembled with the workings of imagination on cultural material, can be turned into tools for shaping one's own actions and, eventually, one's own self by setting a life project.

The rest of the chapters discuss how adults understand their lives and experiences when in contentious situations. Guimarães and Benedito (Chapter 31) present an empirical study on how indigenous Brazilian university students experience tensions between the way of life and ethnic–cultural values of their communities of origin and those of life in the urban context and academic institution. Madureira (Chapter 32) presents a discussion on gender identities as resulting from cultural canalization by rigid semiotic boundaries separating what is perceived as masculine from the feminine. The last chapter is a study on aging, which Ferring (Chapter 33) approaches by combining two points of view: from without and from within. It starts with a discussion on the differing qualifications that the term *aging* has received in diverse theoretical models and then goes into particular biographic narratives that highlight the importance of life events and adaptive processes within the family in the subjective construction of the self and the life course. The general conclusion (Chapter 34) elaborates on a person-centered approach in the study of human aging that takes into account how family and culture interact in shaping life in advancing age.

Conclusion: Directions in Sociocultural Psychology

Sociocultural psychology is a discipline that deals with change and diversity in social life, in collective and individual conduct, and in personal experiences. It is a disciplinary field of knowledge whose theories have to be devised in such a way as to be able to explain regularities but also account for individual variation. It is a kind of idiographic science in which the understanding of individual observation is grounded on nomothetic principles able to explain how human action in concrete settings is the result of an agency distributed in a system involving biological, social, and cultural elements.

Sociocultural psychology is a liminal field of knowledge crossing the paths of other disciplines. These disciplines feed the knowledge they produce, but this knowledge cannot simply be added together in an eclectic mass. No "big data" can solve basic problems in any science – least of all in psychology. Sociocultural psychology has to keep moving to produce integrative theories to relate new findings from the neighboring disciplines in order to develop its own research.

This is accomplished through carefully considering the complexities of methodology (Branco & Valsiner, 1997; Valsiner, 2017). Methods taken out of context of the wider methodology cycle do not guarantee meaningful knowledge, as effective theories are needed.

However, at the same time, sociocultural psychology should avoid attempting to provide definite and comprehensive accounts of the phenomena it studies. Such accounts are necessarily partial – they are meaningful from some theoretical perspectives and meaningless from others. For example, the majority of psychological data that are statistically analyzed in psychology as solid data may at best be considered "anecdotal" from any sociocultural psychology perspective. Why? There is no evidence in statements like "men were found to be different from women at the statistical criterion of conventional (P < 0.05) level" that may be based on large samples. Such evidence fits the gossip columns of journalists who are watching for socially scandalous findings from psychology, but they do not provide new insights into the phenomena under study. A careful, in-depth study of a particular man (or woman) within his (or her) immediate activities context and of the guiding framework of the social norm systems of society would provide solid evidence. Generalization in psychology is not only possible but also the rule in psychology as science (Valsiner, 2015). Consequently, psychology is similar to all other basic sciences where a phenomenon under study is unique – a comet, a planet, or an asteroid to which the human engineering genius might send a landing robot for the study of its particular qualities. Yet, the evidence of such particulars is of crucial importance for our general understanding of our universe. Such understanding is abstract and general, and it has potential for contextualizations in other particular locations.

Nevertheless, sciences of the human *psyche* transcend the disciplines that deal with physical and biological objects. A special feature of our perspective is the *self-reflective nature* of human beings – as it is reflected in sociocultural psychology. We need to keep ourselves aware that the discourses it produces are but the transitory construction of a kind of interobjective knowledge resulting from the operation of a dynamic system of distributed agencies. Scientific knowledge is itself a cultural product that results from human efforts to respond to the quandaries of life – if it does not change as the dynamics moves, it becomes stagnant and useless both for general knowledge and for practical applications in societies.

References

Branco, A. U. & Valsiner, J. (1997). Changing methodologies: A co-constructivist study of goal orientations in social interactions. *Psychology and Developing Societies*, 9(1), 35–64.

Chirkov, V. (2016). *Fundamentals of Research on Culture and Psychology: Theory and Methods*. London: Routledge.

Chiu, C.-Y. & Hong, Y-Y. (2007). *Social Psychology of Culture*. London: Psychology Press.

Glăveanu; V. P. (2016). *The Palgrave Handbook of Creativity and Culture Research*. London: Palgrave Macmillan.

Heine, D. J. (2008). *Cultural Psychology*. New York: W. W. Norton.

Kitayama, S. & Cohen, D. (2007). *Handbook of Cultural Psychology*. New York: Guilford Press.

Sullivan, D. (2016). *Cultural-Existential Psychology: The Role of Culture in Suffering and Threat*. Cambridge: Cambridge University Press.

Valsiner, J. (2007). *Culture in Minds and Societies*. New Delhi: Sage.

Valsiner, J. (Ed.). (2012). *The Oxford Handbook of Culture and Psychology*. New York: Oxford University Press.

Valsiner, J (2014). *An Invitation to Cultural Psychology*. London: Sage.

Valsiner, J. (2015). Generalization is possible only from a single case (and from a single instance). In B. Wagoner, N. Chaudhary, & P. Hviid (Eds.), *Integrating Experiences: Body and Mind Moving between Contexts* (pp. 233–244). Charlotte, NC: Information Age.

Valsiner, J. (2017). *From Methodology to Methods in Human Psychology*. New York: Springer.

Valsiner, J., Marsico, G., Chaudhary, N., Sato, T., & Dazzani, V. (Eds.). (2016). *Psychology as the Science of Human Being*. Cham, Switzerland: Springer.

Valsiner, J. & Rosa, A. (Eds.). (2007). *The Cambridge Handbook of Sociocultural Psychology*. New York: Cambridge University Press.

Van Belzen, J. (2010). *Towards Cultural Psychology of Religion: Principles, Approaches, Applications*. Dordrecht, Netherlands: Springer.

Voestermans, P. & Verheggen, T. (2013). *Culture as Embodiment: The Social Tuning of Behaviour*. Chichester, UK: John Wiley.

Yasnitsky, A., Van der Veer, R., & Ferrari, M. (2014). *The Cambridge Handbook of Cultural-Historical Psychology*. Cambridge: Cambridge University Press.

Zavershneva, E. & Van der Veer, R. (2017). *Vygotsky Notebooks*. New York: Springer.

Part I
Theoretical and Methodological Issues

1 The Human Psyche Lives in Semiospheres

Alberto Rosa and Jaan Valsiner

The spider makes operations resembling the operations of the weaver, and the bee creating its waxen cells disgraces some architects. But from the very beginning, the worst architect differs from the best bee in that before building the cell of wax, he already has built it in his head. The result, which is received at the end of the process of work, already exists in the beginning of this process in an ideal form in a representation of a person. The person does not only change the form given by nature, but in what is given by nature he, at the same time, realises his conscious purpose, which as a law determines the way and character of his actions and to which he must subordinate his will.

K. Marx

For several hundred years we humans have been considering ourselves part of nature, despite disliking the idea of being subject to a fate beyond our control. We believe we are matter – but *living* matter. That belief stops us from relating with mountains, pebbles on a beach, and water that we drink. As we move around, we accept that we are animals. Yet we are not happy to be reduced to dogs, laboratory rats, or even dinosaurs. We are *symbolic* animals who are able to imagine what is currently absent in our immediate environment and *anticipate* its potential arrival, but also *create meaning* for what is and what is not yet. We undertake risky trips to discover the western route to India only to end up with the menace of two Americas; we invent various deities only to kill one another in their name.

And on top of all of that, we create the notion of *science*. We assume the ambivalence between ordinary living and reflection about it when putting effort into building sciences that scrutinize the causes of the events we live with the intention of exercising some agency on the preparation of possible futures. We are subject to the events of nature as the matter we are, but we also believe we dwell in a world not only of matter but also of imagined entities and events

we want to achieve, avoid, or even lead. For this purpose we sometimes strain to make ourselves healthier or stronger and also cultivate our offspring and ourselves to become smarter, wiser, and, sometimes, kinder and better. And this we do by looking after the bodies, and also in what, for want of a better word, we call the *spirit*. And then we deny its importance for science – a passionate inquiry. Not only are we symbolic and sign-making animals but we are just strange animals. The self-affirming label we attach to our species – *Homo sapiens* – requires further investigation into the ways that *sapiens* operate.

Our aim here will be to present an argument that may allow us to understand how a living body can be encouraged by the spirit of a culture so that an animal may eventually turn into a moral being able to conduct himself or herself – in short, how matter, life, and culture can engender the human spirit. Arguably, then, what we will do here is sketch a sort of ontology of *psyche* – the subject matter of *psychology*. In so doing, we certainly will not assume that psyche is any kind of permanent entity with substantial features that are innate. Our purpose is purely instrumental: to demarcate the scope of the phenomenon of human experiences for psychological sciences to inquiry and, more specifically, those of particular interest for sociocultural psychology.

Answering this question is not easy. No one has seen, touched, or felt the psyche. But neither has anybody touched *gravity* or *weather*. All these are abstract concepts that translate into very concrete manifestations – things fall, and we take umbrellas with us when we see rainclouds. We know that we "have psyche" but cannot pinpoint where it is located. It is in every place in our subjective living – and yet it is nowhere. *Psyche* seems to have a ghostly nature, but not very different to that of *physis*, the subject matter of physics. If we want to avoid venturing into speculation about what that elusive creature might be, we had better choose a parsimonious track. What we will do here for this purpose is, first, look at what the practitioners of psychology said were the matters of their interest, then go into elucidating how psyche and mind can evolve from the world of matter and produce the *spirit* of culture and how we can make it a subject for the scrutiny of science, and, finally, put some order in the myriad terms like psyche, mind, or spirit that populate psychological texts.

1.1 What Is Meant by the Word *Psyche*?

At the beginning, *psyche* was just a short way of referring to life. For the ancient Greeks, *psyche* was the vital principle, as *anima* was for the Romans. Things were either animated or unanimated, because they had an *anima* or a *psyche*. Plato, as he did with everything else, decided to give substance to that principle. It was an idea that produced an entity: the soul, which was a thing that, as all others, was both vital and spiritual, embodied and ideal, perishable and transcendent; an entity that, in addition, had the desire, and capability, for reaching beauty, knowledge, and truth. So, Plato created an entity and provided it with contents and desires. Such a conception impregnated the cultures that evolved

around the three religions of the book, and also the Scientific Revolution.

Descartes laid the groundwork of modern thought, but he did so at the price of breaking psyche into halves. Some of its functions were to be explained by the material structure of the organs (lower psychological processes), while higher psychological processes (language and reason) resulted from the working of the immaterial *res cogitans*. This division of psyche has hindered psychology for centuries, even if "the discovery of time," resulting from the Enlightenment and the Industrial Revolution (Toulmin & Goodfield, 1965), deeply changed the ideas about psyche. Yet even now – in the twenty-first century – the implications of time as irreversible, while *experienced as if it is not*, has not reached the conceptual schemes of postbiological sciences. This contrast – the reality of the irreversibility of a lifetime and our depiction of it in time-freed terms – is the work of the psyche.

The German idealistic tradition (Leibniz, Wolff, Kant, Herder, Fichte, Hegel, Marx) chose to center on the *spirit*, the vital principle, leaving aside any consideration of its material basis. The spirit was capable of accumulating experiences, producing knowledge and feelings, solving problems, and conceiving entities beyond sensorial phenomena. The spirit was then able to develop the capabilities of the mind by producing new rules of action for practical reasoning. In so doing, they pointed out something important: spirit was not something to be found solely in live matter or in the workings of the mind; it was also found in social groups, laws, and institutions. It could be changed and transformed and was able to shape the fashions of individual psyches in different parts of the world, not because they were different in their biological structures, but because of the differing historical development of societies. From then on, psyche and spirit were no longer synonymous. Spirit became both social and individual and was thought to be able to percolate through skins and borders. The consequence was to make consciousness (and the unconscious) gain prominence as a central psychological issue.

The theory of evolution naturalized psyche and cast a fresh look on how to conceive its vital functions. Survival was shown to depend on the ability of organisms to act in their environments. Psyche turned into an inherently relational, functional entity. Now a new duality was to be added to that of mind and body: the organism, an enclosed space with its own dynamics, and the environment, the world of things beyond the skin. Behavior was the way of bridging the gap between the inner and the outer realms. Homeostasis, irritability, orientation, and motivation rose, then, as principles for the explanation of behavior. From that moment on, psyche could not be conceived as devoid of its biological basis.

When the new science of psychology appeared at the turn of the eighteenth century, hardly any person denied the need to take both approaches into account (Valsiner, 2012). The challenge to face at that time was scrutinizing how physical forces turned into subjective phenomena so that knowledge and will could result from the workings of the mind. The pioneering work of Herbart and Lotze, as well as Fechner's psychophysics, Brentano's focus on inherent intentionality, and Wundt's experimental psychology, resulted from this endeavor. Over the nineteenth century, the fight between *Naturwissenschaften* and *Geisteswissenschaften* resulted in the victory of the former – yet in a narrow sense. An attempt was made at the end of the nineteenth century to create what was labeled "objective" science, how subjective experience rises out of biological processes. These early attempts to create a psychology of the canonical human subject of experience were the beginning of a *third-person approach* to the study of psychological processes.

However, the development of linguistics, literary studies, and history in the nineteenth century left a footprint of a different kind on psychology. Emphasized by the *Völkerpsychologie*

movement in the second half of the nineteenth century (Diriwächter, 2004; Jahoda, 1992), the domains of language, religion, and art could not be left aside if the significance of personal experiences of individuals of flesh and blood were to be taken into account. Such significance is something that impregnates life; it is directly describable and understood, and so it seems not to be in need of explanation. It suddenly emerges as in need of explanation when it is an obstacle to the human striving toward some goal. Teleology seemed, then, indispensable to account for how a living person can turn into a person *with a biography* – embedded within the history of a community. Hence importance was given to the study of values and the emphasis on idiographic studies of individual instances. A *first-person approach* to the study of human lived experiences developed from this way of conceiving psychology.

Functional approaches of different kinds shared this exertion with different emphases. Franz Brentano, following the Aristotelian-Scholastic tradition, showed the path for a psychology aimed toward studying the ways psyche acts on the world, is affected by these encounters, and ends up producing thinking and knowledge about the world and ourselves. The Austrian and Würzburg schools and the *Ganzheit* and gestalt psychologists, influenced by phenomenology, followed this path while striving to keep the holistic outlook coming from German *Naturphilosophie*. They upheld a view of psyche as a complex dynamic totality encompassing, but also differentiating, the subjective realm and the environment (Ash, 1995; Diriwächter & Valsiner, 2008).

American pragmatists developed a different kind of functionalism. Putting the notion of usefulness up as the criterion of truth made it possible to arrive at the idea that knowledge is local and socially constructed. However, the pragmatist scholars could leave us with practically useless yet theoretically highly innovative perspectives. Charles Peirce, William James, John Dewey, and

George H. Mead took seriously the Aristotelian idea that psyche is what those living have that keeps them alive and away from damage. Psyche and consciousness (like Aristotle's *entelechy*) were natural functions that showed in the actions of organisms living in their environments.

So viewed, action (*pragma*) – what the individual actually does, overtly or in a hidden manner – came to occupy the central focus for psychological enquiry. Action was conceived as a process going on at both sides of (and crossing over) the borders between organs, organisms, and their environments, searching for an equilibrium that, if ever reached, is always shown to be transitory and dynamic. Motivation, attention, learning, thinking, and their development were then conceived as matters of interest for a psychology interested not only in describing the performances and abilities of individuals but also in how these functions develop and their efficiency improves. Consequently, these psychological processes became naturalized as biological functions.

Behaviorism took this move one step further. It kept the functional outlook but added the mechanistic explanation of British associationism. The result was that psyche was reduced to a kind of Cartesian machinery whose movements could only be explained by discrete changes in elements of its entourage, by alterations in its inner balance, and by a combination of both. The so-called cognitive revolution expanded the metaphor of the mechanical tinker-toy beyond the observed interchanges between the body and the environment. The mind was then turned into a virtual machine for processing information implemented in strings of symbols and systems of rules for problem solving. This approach reduced thinking to an effect of the syntax of sign systems, making semiotics for the explanation of processing irrelevant and consciousness a useless epiphenomenon or, in some versions, a kind of process only possible to tackle after making ad hoc adjustments. Teleology and the sense of lived experiences were

issues to be discarded or, at best, left as matters of concern for the humanities.

All these approaches, despite their discrepancies about what psychology could be, offered valuable contributions for the understanding of myriad psychological phenomena and for explaining many psychological processes. But the image of psyche that resulted was like a kind of patchwork. Psychology appeared to be a sort of kaleidoscope that showed different aspects of psyche when turned. Psyche, then, appears to be a creature that can only be conceived as an entity manufactured by psychology. Every psychological approach, therefore, shapes the conception of psyche to fit the different tasks of psychologists as they carry out their studies.

Sociocultural psychology cannot be an exception. If we believe it worthy to state a particular view of psyche, it is because we think it may provide a useful framework for better defining the scope of interest, which the phenomena considered as relevant, and to develop theories for sociocultural psychology. This is why we believe this instrumental task is worthy, even if its results are destined to be changed or discarded once they no longer serve a purpose.

1.2 Setting a Sociocultural Outlook about *Psyche*

Sociocultural psychology is a part of human psychology that "deals with psychological phenomena that happen because of the socio-cultural aspects of human lives in varied social contexts" (Valsiner & Rosa, 2007, p. 1) – a field of knowledge with fuzzy limits, made of a family of perspectives resulting from dialogue between psychology, social sciences, and the humanities (*Geisteswissenchaften*). Throughout its rather long past, several features emerged:

1 A focus on the study of action and activity – hence, transcending the limits of defining

psychology as a study of behavior or cognition, or as neuroscience

2 An emphasis on the instrumental nature of action and sign mediation of the psyche – with the result of linking psychology with semiotics

3 A time-inclusive consideration of phenomena – hence, evolutionary, historical, and developmental ideas are at the root of the sociocultural perspective

4 An interest in human experiencing and consciousness – resulting in the primacy of idiographic perspectives in generalizing science (Salvatore & Valsiner, 2010)

5 A growing attention to the study of discursive/conversational phenomena – with a focus on meaning construction through all versions of sign systems (not only verbal language)

6 Restoration of the primacy of the qualitative nature of phenomena over their quantitative aspects and, consequently, the development of qualitative methods and idiographic studies

The sociocultural perspective is a parallel and partially overlapping arena of social sciences to various versions of cultural psychology (Valsiner, 2009, 2014). The latter takes the social *Umwelt* of the persons or other social units (groups, communities, ethnic groups, etc.) into account but does not necessarily analyze these contextual features in their own terms. The sociocultural approach includes perspectives from psychology, anthropology, sociology, and history – hence it lives up to the wide and loud sociopolitical call for "interdisciplinarity."

1.2.1 A Structural-Systemic Approach

The *psyche* is based on the *soma* – there is no subjectivity without the body that is biologically ready for it. As Aaro Toomela (2015, p. 327) has put it, "body would be mindless without environment." It is when both interact that parts of one or the other show qualities that simultaneously permit and constrain the specific kinds of relationships they can have, forming altogether a higher-order structural whole. The consequence is that any change within the organism–environment system, including the actions of the body, cannot be taken to be caused solely by one particular change in one of the elements but can also be a result of the constraints and possibilities that the interrelations of the elements of the system as a whole offer.

However, the structural capabilities of the biological structure of human beings are insufficient for explaining how higher psychological processes – intentional actions oriented toward self-constructed goals – appear. The challenge is to account for how consciousness arises from encounters within a system encompassing material entities. Lev Vygotsky (1896–1934) – a literary scholar who turned to psychology in the 1920s – solved this question by focusing on the creative synthesis that human sign use makes possible (Valsiner, 2015). While analyzing the ways in which meaningful affective generalization in the process of encountering a short story or fable becomes possible, he showed how human affect can "jump" out of the immediate experience and flavor human living (Vygotsky, 1925/1971). Various objects in our lives are capable of becoming the means of operating other objects, with the added consequence of signaling to other organisms how to coordinate their activities in the environment. Communicative action thus appears, and from this a new kind of entity eventually arises: symbols. Tools and symbols are again transformed through their recursive use within the social life of a group, making another kind of (abstract) entity appear: culture. Sociocultural phenomena thus become as indispensable as biological phenomena in explaining the workings of the human psyche. The historical time frame is then added to the evolutionist and developmental approaches of functionalism.

Vygotsky took symbols to be indispensable for the development of higher psychological functions, pointing out that conventional symbols can only be acquired if individuals are immersed in a social environment where actions and interactions are mediated by practices, sign systems, and institutions. Human consciousness is thus conceived as an effect of communication first with others and then with the self taken as another. The result is that thinking gets transformed and deliberation is made possible, opening the way for the subjective realm to arise. Therefore, to leave consciousness aside would lead us to conceive of humans as zombies devoid of the ability to set distant goals and make plans, unable to set teleological structures for regulating their behavior beyond natural teleonomy.

This Vygotskian approach Toomela (2015) termed *structural-systemic*, in accordance with Bertalanffy's general systems theory (1968/1976) – a theoretical tool developed for the study of living things and social phenomena. Throughout the last decades, systemic approaches of many kinds have been developed in particular fields of knowledge. We believe that revisiting some of them could be useful for the purpose of elaborating an updated conception of how a sociocultural psyche may look for the purposes of current research in the field.

We will approach this task parsimoniously. We will start by looking at how natural phenomena – of the kind studied in the natural sciences – produce myriad structures that shape hierarchies of open systems in interaction; we will continue by examining how some kinds of individual systems are able to profit from their interactions with their environments so that they can behave intelligently; and finally, we will explore how a new kind of entity – symbols – ensues from social communication among sentient and emotional entities, forming symbolic systems of communication and causing higher psychologi-

cal functioning in consciousness, culture, and the self.

1.3 Psyche Arises from Natural Life Processes

1.3.1 From Biological Processes to Social Behavior

The first task, then, is to examine how psychological functions can develop from the biological structures of living organisms. This is what Humberto Maturana and Francisco Varela (1992) did when they developed a theory of enactive cognition that took care in keeping within the limits of biological explanations, based on the physical and chemical laws that govern the exchanges within organizational structures. Knowledge, then, is conceived as the effective actions of living organisms for keeping their existence in their particular environments – the world they live in.

Living organisms (from a cell or a paramecium to a Nobel Prize laureate) are continually and actively doing something, for example, feeding and self-producing, so that their being and doing are indistinguishable. They simultaneously are the producers and the product of their actions. This is what Maturana and Valera called the *autopoietic*[1] character of biological organization, which can be summarized as follows:

1 The components of an autopoietic unit are dynamically linked in a network of interactions (metabolism).
2 Some of these components form a border, a limit to this network of transformations: a membrane (or skin). This membrane is not just a product or a limit on the network of interactions but part of it; otherwise, the cell (or body) as a unit would disappear, and metabolism would not be possible.

3 Living organisms are characterized by their autopoietic organization. They differ in their structures, but they are similar in their organization.

4 Living beings are autonomous units, which means that what happens inside the body follows the laws derived from the structure of internal relations.

Looking within from without: The object and the descriptions of the observer. This approach seeks to explain life through the relationships between structures, but when so doing, it is also necessary to take into account that these structures and their relationships can become objects for science only when they are turned into objects to be described, explained, and discussed, and this requires an observer who puts them into language. This may seem obvious, but it is also far from trivial; it has far-reaching consequences that we will discuss later.

Levels of structural complexity. Living entities are structures of many different kinds with different levels of complexity. This leads Maturana and Varela (1992) to characterize different kinds of organization that also increase the complexity of their autopoietic processes.

A cell is a *first-order autopoietic unit* that relates with elements of its environment, which may include other cells. Their mutual contact causes structural changes in all that depend on the particular characteristics of the affected structure (the unit or environment). The result is a series of successive, mutually consistent structural changes, *structural couplings*, which will keep going for as long as both the autopoietic unit and the environment do not disintegrate. An observer could say that the history of changes resulting from these structural couplings is the *evolution* of the autopoietic unit.

Metacellular organisms are *second-order autopoietic units*. In addition to the structural couplings among first-order autopoietic units of which the organism is made, there are structural couplings between the organism as a whole and its environment beyond the skin. This causes metacellular units to have a peculiar property: first-order autopoiesis is subordinated to second-order autopoiesis; i.e., the survival of individual cells is subordinate to the survival of the organism as a whole. This is what an observer calls *adaptation*, a process that also shows in *ontogenesis*: the process through which the organism as a whole develops through autopoietic processes from an original cell.

Both organism and environment are blind to each other; i.e., the changes that happen within each are regulated by the organism's or environment's structure, which also constrains the ways in which it can be affected by external shocks. This causes these changes to have an iterative, dynamic character. The consequence is that changes within the organism or the environment cannot be taken as instructive for each other: they trigger changes but do not act as instructions for the other party to process. It is the observer who can say that the structure of the organic system is what determines its actions and also who specifies what configurations of the environment can trigger structural changes in the system. And last, but not least, *behavior* is not what the organism does by itself but the description the observer makes about the changes that happen in what he or she delimits as organism and environment when focusing on his or her encounters.

What the observer describes as behavior takes new properties in the case of metacellular organisms with a nervous system. Neurons establish sensorimotor connections and also form interneuron connections, which cause them to work as a closed network of exchanges. This network causes the nervous system to participate in the operation of an organism as a mechanism that maintains the structural changes of the body within certain limits. The plasticity of the nervous system is in its ability for constant change in line with changes in the environment. The nervous system (NS), the organism to which it belongs, and the environment operate on each other as selectors of their corresponding structural changes and therefore produce new iterative coupling processes to keep operating, or otherwise disintegrate. This is a process the observer identifies as *learning*, since it looks as if changes in the NS correspond to changes in the environment. These are *second-order structural couplings*, different from the first-order structural couplings that occur in unicellular organisms.

Some multicellular organisms are capable of establishing social relations that, among other things, are necessary for sexual reproduction and care of the offspring. Social phenomena result when organisms participate in setting up social groups, which also tend to self-preservation. These kinds of interactions among organisms is what an observer calls communicative behavior. They are *third-order structural couplings* that have novel characteristics. Mutual interference between organisms does not happen through direct physical encounters but through a mediator: a body movement, a sound, or some kind of token. Through the eyes of an observer, communication occurs without physical contact, through actions at a distance that act as intermediate structures (signs) that are simultaneously a cause and a product of this kind of mutual coupling. It then becomes vital to address the issue of how signs and symbols can arise from the action of an organism in its environment.

Each conceptual system has its limits. Maturana and Varela's (1992) theory of enactive cognition took good care in keeping within the limits of natural science. But in so doing, they also acknowledged the need to take into account the descriptions and interpretations an observer makes. Without them, intentional interpretations about the organism–environment encounters (adaptation, behavior, learning) could not have been produced. It is not only that symbols and grammar are needed to compose the observer's interpretations but also that they are a result of communicative actions of the kind referred to in the preceding paragraph. In addition, if those descriptions and interpretations are claimed to correspond to real empirical events – i.e., to hold true – signs, symbols, meaning, and concepts have to be explicated, as do the processes that cause them to develop from natural encounters. Our next move is to examine how this may be explained.

1.3.2 Signs Are Internalized Mediators for Interaction

The first decades of the twenty-first century have witnessed the production of contributions from psychology, cognitive sciences, and artificial intelligence, which – following the influence of neoconnectionism and embodied cognition – open new vistas, some of which we believe worthy to take into account for a sociocultural outlook. Of particular interest are the ways in which recursive structural couplings are presented as situated bottom-up processes capable of producing mental representations in such a way that the results are compatible with a Peircean semiotic outlook.

Sign, meaning, and knowledge. The first issue to address is what is meant by sign and meaning. Recent developments in artificial intelligence and robotics have left aside the structural conception of sign as a fixed entity and meaning as the relation between a sign and its referent. Rather, signs have turned to being conceived as the "structural couplings between *reality* and activations of an agent that arises from agent–environment interaction" (Vogt, 2002, p. 431), taking as *reality* either an object of the world or some internal state of the agent. According to this view, signs are the *form* of an interactive process, i.e., a process that Vogt relates to Peirce's conception of sign as resulting from a process of semiosis (see Rosa, 2007a). Following this pragmatist outlook, *meaning* is then conceived as the functional relation between an agent's bodily experience (the form action takes) and its relation with the subsequent consequences of action. Thus, signs and meanings are embodied and situated dynamic processes, encompassing both the agent and the elements of the environment. The question then turns to how different kinds of signs can evolve from these bodily experiences so that concepts can be conceived as developing from these couplings. Furthermore, how would these concepts orient future bodily experiences?

1.4 Psyche and Signs Make Intelligent Minds

From perception to conceptualization. Barsalou (1999) offers a theory about how particular modal perceptual systems are able to capture modality-specific states during perception and action. According to his view, when a physical entity or event is perceived, feature detectors in the relevant modality-specific areas in the brain are activated, producing a pattern of activation. Once a pattern becomes active in the brain area, conjunctive neurons in an association area store these features for later use. These association areas have an architecture organized in multiple hierarchical levels – equivalent to Damasio's (1989) "convergence zones" – and have the functional ability to reenact sensorimotor and other intraorganismic states. These reenactments most frequently are not complete, and may be distorted when reactivated, which is no obstacle for some semblance of the original state to be reinstated. Barsalou conceives these processes as underlying mental imagery, which in turn is the basis for conceptualization, comprehension, memory, and reasoning.

In Barsalou's (1999, 2003) theory, conceptualization is a process that results from the operation of two central complementary constructs – *simulators* and *simulations* – that work as follows. When different members of the same

category of objects are encountered, similar neural pattern areas are activated; this causes similar populations of conjunctive neurons to form patterns of statistically correlated features of these activations in topographically related areas. The consequence is that a multimodal representation of a category (Rosch & Mervis, 1975) is instantiated in a distributed system throughout the brain's association- and modality-specific areas. Such a distributed system is a *simulator*, a transient structure (a functional system) able to reenact subsets of neural patterns of activation as specific *simulations* tailored to the constraints of the ongoing situated action. A category, then, is conceptualized through a learning process in which conjunctive neurons integrate sensorimotor and introspective features. As situated actions proceed forward, addressing other elements in the environment, the same process works recursively as the stream of actions flows, continuously triggering goal-relevant inferences about objects, actions, mental states, and the background setting.

Conceptualization, then, is viewed as resulting from the autopoietic organization of the nervous system inserted within a second-order autopoietic structure in interaction with its environment through spiral recursive loops that also could be described as circular reactions. Conceptualization thus starts with perceptual action and, through recursive abductive inferences, turns perceptual action into a form of thinking.

Abstraction and thinking. Barsalou (2003) views abstractions as temporary online constructions derived from a loose set of property and relation simulators. Across occasions, both statistical attractors and dynamic variability characterize the abstraction process. As a category emerges, the properties and relations of its members are stored in the respective simulators and established in memory, increasing the likelihood of reinstating the abstraction later on another occasion. The resulting representations abstract the critical properties of category members and discard irrelevant ones, representing just some aspects of category members, reenacting partial information and discarding details. Abstraction, then, is more of a skill than a structure. The consequence is that simulators produce schematic prototypical representations. When viewed in this way, a simulator acts as a semiotic engine continuously producing simulations of categories resulting from indexical and iconic semiotic processes embodied in online actions (Rosa, 2007a, 2007b). Nevertheless, the system remains dynamic, such that future abstractions vary widely, each tailored to the current situation and to the statistics of the interpretive system. The recursive operation of these processes causes the number of simulators and simulation to proliferate to identify complex relational configurations of environmental and organismic states in background events. Conceptualization, then, has a hierarchical, dynamic, and systemic nature, allowing some concepts to become increasingly disengaged from environmental entities and increasingly associated with mental events.

The representations produced in this way are more a process than a static structure. They resemble Piaget and Inhelder's (1966) conception of mental images as the interiorized imitations of accommodative action that also have the capability of conceiving the permanence of an object when absent from sensorial stimulation – making it also possible to discriminate among different qualities and kinds of objects. This kind of representation could be taken as quasi-symbolic, since the steady relation with its referent results from an individual habit but not from any kind of social convention.

Proper symbols can only exist if (1) someone takes an environmental object, state, or event to be another object, state, or event and (2) this relation is recognized among different agents when acting in the same environment. This can only happen if at least two agents are performing a task in a shared environment and are successful in signaling to each other in order to coordinate their actions to reach a common goal. Movements, sounds, or some other kind of structural change could perform this function, but this would require that the internal state of one agent be made apparent to another, so that the disturbance in the environment produced by the first party could act as a signal for triggering internal processes in the second party.

1.4.1 Conventional Symbols Are a Product of Communication When Acting

How such a process starts is key to elucidating the origins of symbols, the lexicon, and language at large. Research coming from artificial intelligence robotics offers some interesting results worthy to be taken into account. Mobile robots are able to develop from scratch a shared lexicon about the objects they can detect in their environment: they can give names (produce a sequence of signals referring) to these objects and communicate those names to other parties (Steels, 1996; Vogt, 2002). Other studies have explored how a student robot learns a lexicon about the environment when imitating the actions of a teacher robot that had the lexicon preprogrammed (Billard & Hayes, 1997; Billard & Dautenhahn, 1998) and also the evolution of lexicon dynamics (Steels & McIntyre, 1999). These studies were carried out applying what Steels (1996) – inspired by Wittgenstein (1958) – calls a *language game model*. This model, in addition to the principle of self-organization – discussed in previous paragraphs – includes the principle of *cultural interaction*, which means that mechanisms are designed for exchanging parts of their vocabulary with each other while performing a joint novel task, and also the principle of *individual adaptation*, which evaluates the effect of each "speech act" in reinforcing or weakening the form-meaning connections that allow the lexicon to expand (Steels, 1996; Vogt, 2002).

These studies show impressive results. However, they are vulnerable to criticisms not only because many elements have been preprogrammed for the sake of simplicity and design elegance but also because the task agents have to perform are reduced to reach consistency in attributing a name to an object. This causes the semiotic symbols produced to be only referentially meaningful. Later research is focusing on how robots could use their lexicons to improve their learned capabilities to sustain their energy levels so that they remain usable. This is a move toward the study of artificial life and expands the use of symbols not only into considering their pragmatic value but also into exploring a different kind of semantic value: survival and life meaning (Ziemke & Sharkey, 2001; Vogt, 2002).

1.5 Psyche's Feelings Drive the Mind toward Reflection

Perceptual signs refer to objects and events of the environment, but they do not come alone. Disturbances in the environment affect the inner state of the organism. These affects are crucial for tuning the chain of systemic interactions of the diverse autopoietic units of which the organism is made and of the organism at large with its environment. But there is more. Affects are also signs of internal states that leave a trace in memory and can be reinstated later by stimulation. Thus feelings have a representational capability so that they can evoke something previously experienced (Bartlett, 1925; for comprehensive coverage, see Wagoner, 2017). This is crucial for social interaction.

Emotions are categories that emerge from bodily experiences (of general feelings) that take on the function of monitoring the internal state of the organism and arouse it for action – something that can be pictured as an internal mechanism for gathering the strength for acting. Emotions coordinate and synchronize components that are more or less dissociated in separate functions: (1) evaluation of objects and events, (2) regulation of the system, (3) monitoring of the internal state and the organism–environment interaction, and (4) production of body changes that precede motor reactions that an observer may interpret as announcing behavioral intentions (Scherer, 2004).

The coming together of perception and affection was already observed back in a nineteenth-century investigation of sensations – elementary units of the psyche – by noticing their tone of feeling (*Gefühlston*; Wundt, 1874). The act of perceiving produces signs that organize the alterities presented – objects in the environment take on forms that are co-constructed with the psyche (Kanizsa, 1979, Metzger, 2006, 2008). The affective process leads to changes in the internal state of the organism. For Russell (2003), *core affect* is an evaluation of the internal state of the agent, resulting from the iteration of previous physiological states (tiredness, stress, relaxation, etc.) and previous learning (habituation, novelty), which can be organized into two axes: valence (positive/negative) and activation (alert/relaxed). Core affect also activates attention and the search for the source of the inner changes felt. Without affect, the intentional character of signs and symbols would be devoid of the sense of value needed for desires and purposes to develop.

Feelings play the function of general presentation for the organization of responses. Feelings are both the primary physiological reaction and the semiotic outcome of earlier actuations. They are also signs for the direction of future ones. They result from appraisal processes that trigger motivational processes, giving value (life meaning) to objects, events, agents, and performances. Feelings also have the capability of acting as indexical and iconic (formal) signs of one's own agency; this makes them one of the elements on which the sense of the self could be developed (Innis, 2016; Rosa 2007a, 2016). The core of the self is intentional action.

Intentional communication. Emotions produce motor reactions that can be read as distal signs of the internal state of the organism and their readiness to act. Darwin (1872) noted that the physical manifestation of emotions could have an effect on an observer. This does not mean that emotional expressions intend to show – or communicate – an internal mood or state but simply that they can make an impression on others. What may happen is that another party may have learned how to interpret those signals. Intentional communication arises when control is achieved on the effect that these initially naïve expressions cause in an audience. It is then when emotional expressions take a communicative function, signaling to others a readiness to act (threats, submission, recognition of defeat, etc.) – what can be interpreted as a behavioral economy resulting from previous conceptualizations (maximizing gains and minimizing damage). When this happens, it can be said that there is reciprocity of perspectives.

Tactical simulation and deceit are a further development of intentional communication. Some apes are capable of pretending a false readiness to act in the presence of other members of the pack, with the effect that some others are misled to act in a way favorable to the intentions of the deceiver (Byrne & Whiten 1988). This has been taken as evidence of the existence of a "theory of mind" (Premack & Woodruff, 1978), an ability to represent mental states (intention and purposes) of other parties, which is taken as a new kind of ability: metarepresentation (i.e., a representation capable of rendering a representation). The rudiments of this can be seen in some apes, but it only develops fully in humans (see Carruthers & Smith, 1996).

Deceiving shows a new functional ability: that of changing the function of a particular pattern of motor movements, serving, then, a purpose different to that of its original function (Rivière & Sotillo, 1999). Rather than showing what one feels, one pretends to be feeling something different, so that the performance one plays fools somebody else to act in a way that may open the door to do what one really wants to do. This shows a combination of perspectives, a dissociation between means and ends, and, more importantly, a distinction between content and reference (Sonesson, 2010). But there is also something else, the beginning of an awareness of oneself as an agent among others, i.e., an early form of individual identity that shows in the capability to operate in intersubjective situations, in which some kind of represented reality is taken as shared. This is tremendously important, because this means that an awareness of the difference between experience and reality is emerging and also that what one believes to be real and true may be neither. This signals the dawn of imagination and also the beginning of the distinction between reality and fiction. The paradox is that the ability to create fictitious experiences, which opens the door to the possibility of new forms of experience and knowledge, is born from the capability to deceive and lie – something that begs true and false to develop as concepts indispensable for social life as well as the ability to distinguish between one and the other.

1.6 Psyche Goes Social, Learns to Talk, and Gives Birth to the Self

When a pattern of motor movements is dissociated from its original pragmatic function of operating on an object (unanimated or alive) and turns to be used for a different purpose, and even more, when an object is incorporated into a pattern of actions to be used as a means to operate on another object for some new purpose, an observer could say that means and ends have been dissociated and tools have been born. When an emotional expression (the result of an impression) – a shout or a pattern of motor movements – turns into a sign addressed to somebody else, and this second party acts in such a way that an observer would say it is reinstating the meaning the sign had for the first party, another kind of tool appears: a semiotic instrument, a social symbol born from intentional communication. From then on, the recursive instrumental use of these meditational means produces a cascade of events that signals the dawn of culture and humanity.

Gestures and vocal sounds first turn into deictics (here, there, I, you), and then into words designating objects and actions. These symbols eventually combine into utterances to convey commands and describe events. These utterances have the effect of causing propositional representations (internal speech) to arise from iconic and indexical forms of mental representation. Once this happens, reality is not only what is presented to the eyes or the skin but also what can be heard and imagined through symbols. When symbols operate on other symbols, new meanings arise and, with them, new kinds of entities are produced and added to the reality of the physical objects that one comes across. Now the world also dwells in language; it can be reinstated, or even invented, when talking. The result is that some forms of knowledge can be wrapped in speech and communicated from one generation to another. In short, culture simultaneously changes the environment and provides new resources and constraints for action.

Tools and symbols change the environment and produce culture and society. Tools multiply the capability of agents to extract resources and transform the environment in which they live. This also leads to changes in group activities and structure. Division of labor turns groups into organized societies, at the cost of loosening the bonds among their members. Different occupations lead to a dispersion of abilities, knowledge, interests, and values between various groups (gender, age, or lineage), producing intricate networks of power relations. New kinds of sociocultural practices and tools are then needed to counteract these centrifugal forces. Music, dance, and rituals develop to attune moods and

feelings, while stories and myths provide shared systems of collective representation that attribute causality and responsibility to natural and social events (*religio*, from *religare*, "tying together"). The result is that tools, symbols, and practices shape the beliefs, values, and experiences of individual members in a fashion particular to a society. All these elements make up a complex system of meanings, values, and morals – a rationality that gets shaped throughout the historical transformation of a particular society.

Thus societies are at once coherent and diverse. Their members may share many cultural tools, beliefs, and values, but they may also differ in their positions within the social structure, their occupations and interests, and may have followed varied patterns of upbringing. Not only is this diversity a seed for historical change but it also sets the groundwork for developing and cultivating new experiences and skills.

Higher psychological processes. Sociocultural symbols (sounds, gestures, tokens, or icons) are not only material tools that change social life. They also transform the operations of the mind. Symbols can not only refer to perceptual iconic representations and to concepts arising from individual experiences but also make meanings from the experiences of others accessible. In addition, propositional representation can improve conceptualization processes, causing new concepts to appear, as well as create new symbols that are able to represent those new meanings, which in turn can be communicated, expanding the cultural reservoir of cognitive tools. Concepts such as past, future, beyond, time, space, power, true, and false are born from these processes. The consequence is that ongoing social dialogues penetrate into individual minds, making experiences, concepts, and knowledge available well beyond what one particular individual can directly experientially live. Thus, gradually, the real (the structures with which the body couples) becomes a subset of the reality represented in symbols. Furthermore, this communication makes peripheral experiencing – observational learning – the main mechanism of the sharing of environments; for example, experiencing a panorama of the Pyrenees from a distance is a shared parallel experience between participants in a tourist group.

Social knowledge, then, becomes a heritage to be transferred over generations in similar ways. It is not the perceivable stimulus in the form of an old and shabby family heraldic sign on the wall of a run-down castle that reminds a young man that he is a member of an aristocratic – even if by now poor – family. It is the meaning of such a sign in transferring the social status independent of local conditions that matters. This can only be done through social practices in which somebody's utterances direct somebody else's conduct on the environment ("I should act as an aristocrat when I beg for donations!") at the same time that a dialogue between interlocutors develops. The conceptualization and abstraction processes triggered in the interacting parties, while tuning their operations on the environment, make it possible to reinstate social meanings in the minds of the participants, leading to a transitory intersubjectivity. Once verbal communication can direct somebody's actions in the absence of the referred object, declarative knowledge appears.

Social practices of cultural communication produce further effects on individual psychological skills. The use of different sign systems for the transfer of declarative knowledge forces thinking processes to reshape so that they can be reinstated in socially shared chains of symbols following conventional rules of communication. This changes both the structure of thinking processes and their capability for producing new concepts and knowledge. The ontopotentiality of symbols (Valsiner, 2002), the capacity of symbols to produce new symbols, and the recursive capability of language to produce utterances referring to other utterances cause thinking, sociocultural symbols, and speaking to

fuse into an alloy that transforms mental processes and gives birth to higher psychological processes (Vygotsky, 1986). Attention, imagination, and memory are then transformed, and it is no longer necessary for them to be tied to structural couplings between physical structures. Symbols liberate these processes from the tyranny of presence and lead them to dwell among the residents in the house of culture built by the group through its communicative exchanges. Then it becomes possible to imagine the absent, to prepare for what may happen, and even to plan possible futures.

1.6.1 The Self: A Character Searching for an Author

The self is one of the imagined entities born of communication, language, and culture (Martin & Gillespie, 2010; Mead, 1934). As such, it is a product of conceptualization and abstraction operating with symbols in social life.

An individual in a group must coordinate her or his actions with others when cooperating in shared activities; in doing this, the individual makes and receives commands, requests, answers, and complaints. An individual also is a member of a group (generational, gender, family, or caste) and, as such, is asked to do some things and prevented from doing others. A person must learn what to do, how, and when, as well as what not to do, and also who that person is and what is one's place. In addition, one, like everything else in the world, is given a name to which one must respond. The result is that one receives and adopts social belongings and an individual identity.

Something quite drastic happens then: human agents do more than react to environmental contingencies; they turn into actors performing social rituals inserted in sociocultural practices and activities, and they get involved in conflicts and social dramas that happen in their group. In doing so, they perform cultural scripts in varied settings, with the effect that their interpretations create new meanings. The consequence is that they also create new contingencies to direct the actions of others and themselves and therefore produce innovations that may remain for generations to come. New scenarios can then be imagined, and new ways to convert them into practical reality can be created – for better or for worse. Actors thus not only interpret the scripts they receive but may also turn into authors of their own lives and transform the cultural instruments they receive – and thereby also sociocultural life.

1.6.2 Consciousness and Personhood Arise through Cultural Means

As we have seen, the self is grounded on identity, but it goes beyond that. When receiving orders from others, one must also learn to direct oneself, so that one is not only disciplined by others but also learns how to discipline oneself. In so doing, one begins to conceive of oneself as an object among other objects in the world, as an agent and an actor among others, as somebody one can address and command, even if one also complains, to oneself. When this happens, lived events turn into "emotional episodes" (Russell, 2003), making feelings instrumental for the direction of one's actions and opening the way for will to arise from motives and desires.

Now, what is felt is something that is happening *to me*. It is not only that somebody does or says something disagreeable; it is also that it offends *me*, it is something that is against what should be, and so "I feel *angry*," and so provoked that I cannot avoid feeling that "I am ready to hit him or her," and although my monitoring system starts working immediately ("*even as I am angry, I should* stay calm"), my body still shows my anger, so that the other party might say, "*You seem to want to* hit me." All this categories-

based (emotions here operate as choice categories in terms of Mammen, 2016) self-regulation is paralleled by the abstraction of sense categories through processes of pleromatization (Valsiner, 2014) that create the atmosphere for the here-and-now setting. The laughter by him (or her) while saying "*You seem to want to* hit me" can lead to further escalation (including hitting) or diffusion of the anger (the other says, "Yes, I want to kill you" – and both laugh). Human psyche operates within – and through – hypergeneralized affective fields (Valsiner, 2014). This nature of the psyche indicates that the main modus operandi of human beings is fuzzy, general, atmospheric relating with others.

The result is that one can now talk to oneself, referring events to oneself as if one were another. Thinking, then, can turn into argumentative dialogues as one becomes able to debate what happened and how one feels affected by what happened. Now one becomes able to ponder what to do, with their pros and cons.

In sum, symbolic representation transforms how thinking proceeds. Now, it does not only work through abstractions coming from perception, affections, and emotions; there are also different systems involved, such as choice and sense categories (Mammen, 2016). Their mutual feeding-in provides the human being flexibility to move beyond the here-and-now setting and consider both future possibilities and reconstructions of the past. The human psyche that operates through signs involves generalization with subsequent specification in new encounters with the world (Stjernfeldt, 2014). Semiosis frees human beings to consider the future as well as to generalize – always from singular encounters with the world (Valsiner, 2016). *Homo sapiens* is a symbolizing and abstracting animal who dreams about – and is simultaneously apprehensive of – the future. This opens the door for imagination to conceive of entities that go beyond what is directly felt but also makes it possible to imagine oneself (and others) as an entity capable of feeling, suffering or enjoying, thinking, deciding, and acting; and what is more, one gets to acknowledge that one may – and most probably will – feel proud, regretful, or guilty of what one may do or refrain from doing. The self, reflection, autonoetic consciousness, and moral responsibility appear together in the same package, although not without pain (see Chapter 13, this volume).

Symbolic communication and culture result from human action but also lead to the production of humanity. According to the story presented above, higher psychological processes – which only appear in humans – are unthinkable without social structures and culture. But culture should be conjugated in plural. Every human group developed its own culture over time, which leads one to assume that not all forms of being human are identical. Each cultural environment shapes psyches and minds, and the experiences lived, in different fashions. It is as if the spirit of culture were imbued in the mind of each member of the group, merging with the natural psychic apparatus (Vygotsky, 1986). Each *person*, then, is an idiosyncratic unit always in a dynamic tension with an environment that is not only physical and governed by efficient causality but also symbolic and ruled by a semiotic logic, and therefore populated with imagined entities that signal possible alleys for action.

Human action cannot be conceived solely as resulting from an agent reacting to an environment, from an actor playing a script, or coming out from an author devising a plot. It is all these things at once and more. Human behavior is always situated in a moving landscape with waves and accidents the reality of which one can never be sure. That is why human personal experience cannot be left aside when trying to explain how individual behavior negotiates life. Hence sociocultural psychology cannot leave aside a first-person approach when studying psychological phenomena.

1.7 Psyche Blows the Spirit of Culture into the Mind

The world one believes one lives in is the world one experiences, even if actual behavior happens in what an omniscient observer would call "the real world." Experienced objects, events, feelings, desires, duties, regrets, goals, or plans to reach those goals cannot be communicated, thought on, and understood without symbols and arguments – and these are creatures borrowed from the reservoir of cultural resources. But what do we mean by culture?

1.7.1 Culture: The Spirit of Psyche

The word *culture* comes from the Latin verb *colere*, which means "to cultivate" in the agricultural sense (Jahoda, 1992). This agricultural metaphor, implying a taming of nature through intentional human action, is still very much with us. We keep saying someone is cultivated as a result of training or refinement of mind or taste, a use that started to appear in Western Europe from the eighteenth century onward. A related term, sometimes used as a synonym for *culture*, is *civilization* – a word coming from the Latin *cives*, meaning "city." Civilization, pronounced in singular, is sometimes used as the opposite to barbarism or savagery, making it more or less equivalent to enlightenment. To civilize, then, is "to overcome barbarism" and, when applied to individuals, refers to relieving them of their "natural savagery" to turn them into citizens. The notion of culture often marks these processes (Valsiner, 2014). Sociocultural resources – tools, symbols, rituals, practices, institutions – fuse with the surrounding landscape making up the *Umwelt* where human individuals live, turning the world understandable and providing senses for the lived experiences and so opening the way for individual lives to be taken as meaningful. In sum, a particular fashion of humanity gets embodied in the members of the group.

1.7.2 Cultural Landscapes Are the Environment for Human Action

Cultures are made of different types of elements embodied in structures of many kinds (sounds, gestures, tokens, icons, rituals, tools, practices), either transient (needing to be reenacted every time) or fixed in more or less permanent material structures. This causes the cultural dynamics of oral and literary societies to be different (Ong, 1982). Culture is not a term to denote only a reservoir of accumulated information but focuses on an organized and complex system that receives, translates, and interprets materials that take over the function of signs. These dynamics cause culture to operate as a collective memory and intelligence that are continuously reshaped.

Semiotics is the science of signs. An important contribution of the Tartu school of semiotics, built on the literary scholarship of Juri Lotman (Sonesson, 1994; see also Kull, 2011), is to translate the notion of culture into a system of texts ("modeling systems") – a network of hypertexts. For them a text is any form of symbolic production regulated by some kind of grammar. This means that texts are not to be restricted to inscriptions of natural languages; they are any kind of received information kept in whatever code or support medium.

Modeling systems, so conceived, are social communication devices that perform their functions through various processes. On one hand, they convey messages that communicate senders and recipients – the audience; they also connect to a historical tradition, fulfilling functions of collective memory, updating and forgetting some information, and so continuously enriched with new interpretations. Moreover, a text acts as a mediator for the contact of hearer or reader with herself or himself, guiding specific aspects of culture and enabling or disabling aspects of her or his personal culture and skills. When this happens, the text can exceed the role of mediator to turn into a partner for a dialogue between the reader and the voices included in the text, acting, then, as an independent intellectual formation with which one converses. Finally, the text also acts as a spokesperson, representing a cultural context, whether as a metaphor for the whole of a culture or as a metonymy of some part of it.

Translations. Texts, to be understandable for their users, have to be expressed in a code that both producers and receivers employ homogeneously. However, homogeneity is a matter of degree and depends on the nature of the code and the familiarity users have with it. Multivocal or complex codes are particularly open to ambiguities, with the result that the message information could be degraded, but this also opens it to new interpretations; consequently, new meanings can arise, and even the codes themselves could be transformed. Semiotic innovation, then, is dependent on the heterogeneity of the communities in contact.

Texts are for the guidance of action, which means that to be understood, they need to be translated from one code to another. This prompted Lotman (2005) to say that texts are a meeting place between codes and languages, between producers and consumers, sometimes coming from different times and different macrotexts as well as from different cultural traditions. Texts are inherently bilingual: it is the existence of a "border" between codes that gives texts their semiotic capacity.

1.7.3 Semiospheres, Border Irregularities, and Semiotics

Semiosphere is one of Lotman's better-known concepts and has given title to a series of volumes (Lotman, 1996, 1998, 2000). The name comes from an analogy with the concept of biosphere and refers to the space occupied by a complex system of semiotic formations. Outside this semiotic space, the aforementioned textual functions would be impossible: i.e., outside this semiotic space, no meaning is possible. Whatever kind of otherness that may exist beyond the limits of the semiosphere could only reach significance if incorporated into "texts." In other words, outside the semiosphere, there is only unfathomable chaos.

Boundaries. The concept of *boundary* is central in Lotman's culturology. It refers to the frontier between the semiotic universe and the chaos of the unknown, or among various semiospheres, which only become comprehensible through the exchanges across boundaries. It is at the borders where bilingualism, translation, negotiation, and conflict happen. It is the existence of borders that creates the demand for semiotization, and also what makes it possible. It is in border areas where hybrid phenomena, translations between codes, and dialogue between texts can generate new meanings and symbols to colonize the alien and unknown semiotically.

Semiospheres (regardless of which of them we refer to) are not homogeneous: they also have internal semiotic irregularities. In the words of Lotman (2005, p. 213):

Semiotic space is characterised by the presence of nuclear structures (frequently multiple) and a visibly organised more amorphous semiotic world gravitating towards the periphery, in which nuclear structures are immersed ... The active interaction between these levels becomes one of the roots of the dynamic processes within the semiosphere.

Irregularity is not independent of the description of the structure of the semiosphere that an observer may produce at a given time; it varies depending on the descriptive language that an observer may use. If he or she borrows the language from what he or she believes to be the core system, the description of the system appears rigid. On the contrary, if a language coming from the periphery is adopted, the system is made to look flexible. Whatever the case, the new texts that are produced come to occupy a place within the internal borders of the semiosphere, generating new changes in both its internal structure

(displacements of structures between the center and the periphery) and the rate of change (nuclear changes are slower than peripheral changes).

In short, it is irregularity that causes the existence of borders and therefore produces dialogue and information growth. As Lotman says, without otherness, neither communication nor consciousness could exist. Therefore, the existence of a plurality of semiotic formations is a prerequisite for the existence of languages, which always occur in the plural, as each requires the others to exist. Semiospheres, then, are in a continuous process of change, subject to historical development. Nevertheless, though describable and explicable, the historical change of cultures is not predictable.

1.8 Conclusion: We Understand Our Experiences from the Way the *Psyche* Leads the Self to Live

The argument here presented has been developed following the rules of parsimony. Our aim was to present a view of what the psyche of sociocultural psychology may look like. To achieve this aim, the voice of an observer was always needed, not only because descriptions of phenomena and explanations of processes had to be produced but also because the argument was aimed at explaining the kind of psychological processes the observer needed to put into play to produce his or her observations, interpretations, and explanations.

Psychology is the science in charge of the explanation of experience. This causes it to be a reflective science that can benefit from a methodological use of reflexivity (Rosa, 2015). Psychological knowledge is a product of sociocultural life that results from empirical observations of observers who abstract concepts, make inferences, and produce descriptive and explanatory utterances addressed to an audience. In sum, psychological knowledge is an outcome of the labor of psychologists, who are themselves human organisms making sense of their experiences when encountering others by using sociocultural tools and symbols. The psychological descriptions and explanations that are produced should aim to explain how psychological knowledge can result from the working of the psychologists' minds.

Sociocultural psychology aims at describing and explaining how human beings behave and make sense of their lives. It is an area of psychology that looks at human beings as persons, not only as organisms or as information-processing devices; that is why it cannot avoid taking individual experiences, understandings, and purposes into account. Cultural psychology is to be conjugated in the first, second, and third person (Varela & Shear, 1999), both in plural and singular, producing nomothetic and idiographic knowledge. It is a psychology in the third person, because it refers to how individuals behave, think, and feel; it is a psychology in the first person, because it cannot avoid referring to how each of us feels, thinks, and behaves; and it is a second-person psychology, because the utterances pronounced about psyche would not be understandable to the audience (the *you*s) if they could not resonate with their own experiences and knowledge.

Psyche is a way of referring to life in an environment; it encompasses both the organism and its surroundings and behaves when both join together. The mind is a product of psyche's behavior that ends up transforming the environment. The collective workings of minds throughout time create symbols and culture – the realm of the spirit – which shape an imagined world from which the self and the person emerges. The consequence is that each psychological subject, each person, dwells in the house of a culture – a subjective *Umwelt* – which provides the constraints and resources for the guidance of behavior, the shaping of individual experiences, and the fashioning of personal consciousness.

Psyche and psychology are inherently dialogical. Each is a product of the other and always shows a shape adapted to each circumstance. Neither is to be exhausted by any description or explanation. That is why all accounts, including the one presented here, cannot but be incomplete and transient.

Note

1 *Autopoiesis* is a neologism coined by these authors. It comes from the Greek verb *poieo*, which means "creation" and is the root of the word *poetry*. Autopoiesis, then, is the ability of living matter to transform itself.

References

Ash, M. G. (1995). *Gestalt Psychology in German Culture, 1890–1967: Holism and the Quest for Objectivity*. Cambridge: Cambridge University Press.

Barsalou. L. W. (1999). Perceptual symbol systems. *Behavioral and Brain Sciences*, 22, 577–660.

Barsalou, L. W. (2003). Abstraction in perceptual symbol systems. *Philosophical Transactions of the Royal Society*, 358, 1177–1187. DOI: 10.1098/rstb.2003.1319.

Bartlett, F. C. (1925). Feeling, imaging and thinking. *British Journal of Psychology*, 16, 16–28.

Bertalanffy, L. von (1968/1976). *General System Theory: Foundations, Development, Applications* (rev. edn). New York: George Braziller.

Billard, A. & Dautenhahn, K. (1998). Grounding communication in autonomous robots: An experimental study. *Robotics and Autonomous Systems*, 24(1–2), 71–79.

Billard, A. & Hayes, G. (1997). Robot's first steps, robot's first words. In P. Sorace & S. Heycock (Eds.), *Proceedings of the GALA '97 Conference on Language Acquisition, Edinburgh*. Edinburgh: Human Communication Research Centre.

Byrne, R. W. & Whiten, A. (1988). *Machiavellian Intelligence*. Oxford: Oxford University Press.

Carruthers, P. & Smith, P. K. (Eds.). (1996). *Theories of Theories of Mind*. Cambridge: Cambridge University Press.

Damasio A. R. (1989). Time-locked multiregional retroactivation: A systems-level proposal for the neural substrates of recall and recognition. *Cognition*, 33, 25–62.

Darwin, C. R. (1872). *The Expression of the Emotions in Man and Animals* (1st edn). London: John Murray. Retrieved from http://darwin-online.org.uk/content/frameset?pageseq=1&itemID=F1142&viewtype=text.

Diriwächter, R. (2004). Völkerpsychologie: The synthesis that never was. *Culture & Psychology*, 10(1), 179–203.

Diriwächter, R. & Valsiner, J. (Eds.). (2008). *Striving for the Whole: Creating Theoretical Syntheses.* New Brunswick, NJ: Transaction Publishers.

Innis, R. (2016). Affective semiosis: Philosophical links to a cultural psychology. In J. Valsiner, G. Marsico, G. Chaudhary, T. Sato & V. Dazzani (Eds.), *Psychology as a Science of Human Being: The Yokohama Manifesto.* Cham, Switzerland: Springer.

Jahoda, G. (1992). *Crossroads between Culture and Mind.* Cambridge, MA: Harvard University Press.

Kanizsa, G. (1979). *Organization in Vision: Essays on Gestalt Psychology.* New York: Praeger.

Kull, K. (2011). Yuri Lotman in English: Bibliography. *Sign Systems Studies*, 39(2/4), 343–356.

Lotman, I. M. (1996). *La semiosfera I: Semiótica de la cultura y del texto* (trans. from Russian by Desiderio Navarro). Madrid: Cátedra.

Lotman, I. M. (1998). *La semiosfera II: Semiótica de la cultura y del texto de la conducta y del espacio* (trans. from Russian by Desiderio Navarro). Madrid: Cátedra.

Lotman, I. M. (2000). *La semiosfera III. Semiótica de las artes y de la cultura* (trans. from Russian by Desiderio Navarro). Madrid: Cátedra.

Lotman, J. (2005). On the semiosphere. *Sign Systems Studies*, 33(1), 206–229 (trans. by Wilma Clark).

Mammen, J. (2016). Using a topological model in psychology: Developing sense and choice categories. *Integrative Psychological and Behavioral Science*, 50(2), 196–233.

Martin, J. & Gillespie, A. (2010). A neo-Meadian approach to human agency: Relating the social and the psychological in the ontogenesis of perspective-coordinating persons. *Integrative Psychological and Behavioral Science*, 44, 252–272. DOI 10.1007/s12124-010-9126-7.

Maturana, H. & Varela, F. (1992). *The Tree of Knowledge: The Biological Roots of Human Understanding.* Boston: Shambhala Publications.

Mead, G. H. (1934). *Mind, Self and Society.* Chicago: Chicago University Press.

Metzger, W. (2006). *Laws of Seeing.* Cambridge, MA: MIT Press.

Metzger, W. (2008). *Gesetze der Sehens.* Eschborn, Germany: Dietmar Klotz.

Ong, W. (1982). *Orality and Literacy: The Technologizing of the World.* London: Routledge.

Piaget, J. & Inhelder, B. (1966). *L'image mental chez l'enfant.* Paris: Press Universitaires de France.

Premack, D. G. & Woodruff, G. (1978). Does the chimpanzee have a theory of mind? *Behavioral and Brain Sciences*, 1, 515–526.

Rivière, A. & Sotillo, M. (1999). Comunicazione, suspensione e semiosi umana: Le origine edella prattica e de la comprensione interpersonale. *Metis*, 1, 45–72.

Rosa, A. (2007a). Acts of psyche: Actuations as synthesis of semiosis and action. In J. Valsiner & A. Rosa (Eds.), *Cambridge Handbook of Sociocultural Psychology* (pp. 205–237). New York: Cambridge University Press.

Rosa, A. (2007b). Dramaturgical actuations and symbolic communication: Or how beliefs make up reality. In J. Valsiner & A. Rosa (Eds.), *Cambridge Handbook of Sociocultural Psychology* (pp. 293–317). New York: Cambridge University Press.

Rosa, A. (2015). The reflective mind and reflexivity in psychology: Description and explanation within a psychology of experience. In G. Marsico, R. Ruggieri, & S. Salvatore (Eds.), *Reflexivity and Psychology* (Yearbook of Idiographic Science, vol. 6, pp. 17–44). Charlotte, NC: Information Age Publishing.

Rosa, A. (2016). The self rises up from lived experiences: A micro-semiotic analysis of the unfolding of trajectories of experience when performing ethics. In J. Valsiner, G. Marsico, N. Chaudhary, T. Sato, & V. Dazzani (Eds.),

Psychology as the Science of Human Being: The Yokohama Manifesto (pp. 105–127). Cham, Switzerland: Springer.

Rosch, E. & Mervis, C. B. (1975). Family resemblances: Studies in the internal structure of categories. *Cognitive Psychology*, 7, 573–605.

Russell, J. A. (2003). Core affect and the psychological construction of emotion. *Psychological Review*, 110(1), 145–172. DOI: 10.1037/0033–295X.110.1.145.

Salvatore, S. & Valsiner, J. (2010). Between the general and the unique: Overcoming the nomothetic versus idiographic opposition. *Theory & Psychology*, 20(6), 817–833.

Scherer, K. R. (2004). Feelings integrate the central representation of appraisal-driven response organization in emotion. In A. S. R. Manstead, N. Frijda & A. Fischer (Eds.), *Feelings and Emotions* (pp. 136–157). Cambridge: Cambridge University Press.

Sonesson, G. (1994). The concept of text in cultural semiotics. Communication to the 3rd Congress of the Nordic Association for Semiotic Studies, Trodheim. Retrieved from www.academia.edu/5424645/GÖRAN_SONESSON_The_Concept_of_Text_in_Cultural_Semiotics_1_The_Concept_of_Text_in_Cultural_Semiotics.

Sonesson, G. (2010). Here comes the semiotic species: Reflections on the semiotic turn in the cognitive sciences. In B. Wagoner (ed.), *Symbolic Transformation: The Mind in Movement through Culture and Society* (pp. 38–58). London: Routledge.

Steels, L. (1996). Emergent adaptive lexicons. In P. Maes (Ed.), *From Animals To Animats: Proceedings of the Fourth International Conference on Simulating Adaptive Behavior* (vol. 4). Cambridge, MA: MIT Press.

Steels, L. & McIntyre, A. (1999). Spatially distributed naming games. *Advances in Complex Systems*, 1(4), 301–323.

Stjernfeldt, F. (2014). *Natural Propositions: The Actuality of Peirce's Doctrine of Dicisigns.* Boston: Docent Press.

Toomela, A. (2015). Vygotsky's theory on the Procrustes' bed of linear thinking: Looking for structural–systemic Theseus to save the idea of

"social formation of mind." *Culture & Psychology*, 21: 318–339. DOI: 10.1177/1354067X15570490.

Toulmin, S. & Goodfield, J. (1965). *The Discovery of Time*. New York: Harper & Row.

Valsiner, J. (2002). Irreversibility of time and ontopotentiality of signs. *Estudios de Psicologia*, 23(1), 49–59.

Valsiner, J. (2009). Cultural psychology today: Innovations and oversights. *Culture & Psychology*, 15(1), 5–39.

Valsiner, J. (2012). *A Guided Science: History of Psychology in the Mirror of its Making*. New Brunswick, NJ: Transaction Publishers.

Valsiner, J. (2014). *Invitation to Cultural Psychology*. London: SAGE.

Valsiner, J. (2015). The place for synthesis: Vygotsky's analysis of affective generalization. *History of the Human Sciences*, 28(2), 93–102.

Valsiner, J. (2016). The nomothetic function of the idiographic approach: Looking from inside out. *Journal of Person-Oriented Research*, 2(1–2), 5–15. DOI: 10.17505/jpor:2016.02.

Valsiner, J. & Rosa, A. (2007). The myth, and beyond: Ontology of psyche and epistemology of psychology. In J. Valsiner & A. Rosa (Eds.), *Cambridge Handbook of Sociocultural Psychology* (pp. 23–39). New York: Cambridge University Press.

Varela, F. J. & Shear, J. (1999). First-person methodologies: What, why, how? *Journal of Consciousness Studies*, 6(1–2), 1–14.

Vogt, P. (2002). The physical symbol grounding problem. *Cognitive Systems Research*, 3, 429–457.

Vygotsky, L. S. (1986). *Thought and Language*. Cambridge, MA: MIT Press.

Vygotsky (1925/1971). *Psychology of Art*. Cambridge, MA: MIT Press.

Wagoner, B. (2017). *Frederic Bartlett – A Life*. Cambridge: Cambridge University Press.

Wittgenstein, L. (1958). *Philosophical Investigations*. Oxford: Blackwell.

Wundt, W. M. (1874). *Grundzüge der physiologischen Psychologie*. Leipzig, Germany: W. Engelman.

Ziemke, T. & Sharkey, N. E. (2001). A stroll through the worlds of robots and animals: Applying Jakob von Uexküll's theory of meaning to adaptive robots and artificial life. *Semiotica*, 134(1–4), 701–746.

Further Reading

Braudel, F. (1969). *Écrits sur l'histoire*. Paris: Flammarion.

Frijda, N. (2004). Emotions and action. In A. S. R. Manstead, N. Frijda, & A. Fischer (Eds.), *Feelings and Emotions* (pp. 158–173). Cambridge: Cambridge University Press.

Harnad, S. (1990). The symbol grounding problem. *Physica D*, 42, 335–346.

Harris, M. (1979). *Cultural Materialism: The Struggle for a Science of Culture*. Walnut Creek, CA: Altamira Press.

Lotman, I. M. (1990). *Cultura y explosión: lo previsible y lo imprevisible en los procesos de cambio social*. Barcelona: Gedisa.

Searle, J. R. (1980). Minds, brains, and programs. *Behavioral and Brain Sciences*, 3:417–424.

Sun, R. (2000). Symbol grounding: A new look at an old idea. *Philosophical Psychology*, 13(2), 149–172.

Valsiner, J. (1998). *The Guided Mind: A Sociogenetic Approach to Personality*. Cambridge, MA: Harvard University Press.

2 Cultural Psychology as the Science of Sensemaking: A Semiotic-cultural Framework for Psychology

Sergio Salvatore

Cultural psychology has been undergoing intense development over the last three decades. The recognition that human experience is embedded in the culture has enabled us to approach an increasing number of psychological and psychosocial phenomena with fresh eyes – e.g., ontogenesis, education, memory, imagination and creativity, life transitions, economic issues, identity, immigration, communicational exchange between people as well as social groups, work behavior, social development, and psychotherapy (for an overview, see Kitayama & Cohen, 2007; Matsumoto, 2001; Valsiner, 2012).

These developments call for another step forward: the building of cultural psychology as a *general theory of psychology*, namely, a fundamental, unifying framework for psychological science as a whole – what gestalt theory, behaviorism, psychoanalysis, and cognitivism were for twentieth-century psychology.

Psychological science is in dire need of finding new grounds on which to restore the sense of unity of its many lines of investigation. As was already recognized almost a century ago (Heidbreder, 1933), psychologists have embraced a sort of division of intellectual labor, focusing on specific processes and leaving to a remote future the task of building comprehensive models. This has made psychology into a sort of archipelago comprising a myriad of intellectual islands, each of them endowed with its own ontology, semantics, and aims (Salvatore, 2016).

The disaffection with this fragmentation emerges cyclically among scholars. The proliferation of – at best – middle range theories based on the different systems of ontological, epistemological, and methodological assumptions hampers the recognition of the metaphysical and pragmatic assumptions grounding the theories as well as their interconnections and (in)compatibilities (Henriques, 2011). It prevents constraints from being placed on the proliferation of entities and of ad hoc explicative devices, in so doing exposing the theories to the latent influence of common sense (Salvatore, 2016); and it leaves scholars unable to put the findings of the many psychological subdisciplines in mutual communication. At the level of applicative models, there is a further critical consequence of the disunity of psychological science. At this level, psychology appears to be a collection of a huge number of theories each of them focused on a specific field of experience and/or phenomenon – e.g., bullying, aggressive behavior, community membership, health behavior, psychotherapy, organizational commitment, religious fundamentalism, and so forth – studied as if it was a specific, self-contained object endowed with its own way of working, rather than reflecting a more general class of processes. Such a fragmentation weakens the validity of models and undermines the effort to improve their efficacy and effectiveness. It leaves the knowledge developed in a specific field segregated within said field, unable to be transferred and therefore further interpreted and developed according to more general conceptual frameworks.

Various efforts have been made to cope with the fragmented state of the discipline (e.g., Henriques, 2011; Kimble, 1990; Mandler, 2011; Valsiner, 2009; Salvatore, 2016). Recently, the *Review of General Psychology* (July, 2013) devoted a special issue to the topic, hosting 19 contributions that each propose an approach to the unification of psychology. Such a number and variety of contributions is a mark of the renewed interest in the integration of psychological science; yet, it is also the symptom of how divided the field is and how hard it is to build a unifying perspective within it. Most efforts (for a different approach, based on the conceptual analysis of the ontological assumption grounding current middle-scale models, see Marsh & Boag, 2014) interpret this task in terms of the importation of the paradigmatic foundation grounding other sciences (e.g., physics, evolutionary biology, genetics) – Lickliter and Honeycutt (2013), for instance, called for a revised version of the evolutionary theory as the basis for the unification of psychology. Yet such a reductionist approach has not proved productive (e.g., Green, 2015, Stam, 2004). What psychology needs is not a normative frame imposed from the outside of its language; rather, it has to develop its own framework from within – surely taking into account the development of other sciences, but not overlapping them.

I believe that this is the mission of the cultural psychology of the twenty-first century – to go beyond domain-specific theorizations, in order to provide psychological science with a unifying general semantics. In so doing, the cultural psychology will fulfill the ambition of the few pioneers (Boesch, 1991; Smedslund, 1988; Valsiner, 2001) that have seen in it something more than a collection of domain-specific models. In the following pages, I will attempt to contribute to this perspective, presenting in brief the culturally informed general theory of psychology –

namely, a metatheoretical framework providing: (a) an epistemological approach to knowledge building; (b) the definition of the object of psychology; and (c) a description of its basic way of functioning.

2.1 Psychology as a Theory-driven Science: A Call for Abstractive Generalization

This section focuses on the first aspect of the framework – I will argue for a change to a modeling approach in the discipline. According to this change, cultural psychology has to intentionally adopt the concepts as analytical categories, rather than the concepts having one specific phenomenical referentiality. This means that cultural psychology has to move from an extensional to an intensional approach to culture.[1]

2.1.1 Extensional and Intensional Categories

Most of the current approaches within cultural psychology can be seen as *psychology of culture* – that is, as a psychological view of the culture(s) and its intertwined linkage with mental processes. This means that the notion of culture is intended as a concept endowed with an ontological reference, namely, as a representation of something being (or happening) in the world. In this respect the current cultural psychologies are fully consistent with the extensional logic grounding mainstream psychology's categories. For example, concepts like "self," "emotion," "motivation," "representation," "unconscious," and so forth are considered more or less implicitly to refer to corresponding structures/mechanisms that have an ontological substantiality and capacity of producing effects. For a critical view of the ontologizing tendency of mainstream psychology, focused on the theory of emotion but easily generalizable, see Feldman-Barrett (2006).

Such an approach provides important insights, but it is unable to raise cultural psychology to the status of general theory. This is the case for two main reasons. First, the general theory is placed at the meta-empirical level: it frames the definition of the phenomena, therefore, it has to come (logically) before the datum – as its premise. Accordingly, it is void of empirical content for the very reason that it is the source of such content. An analogy with Kantian categories can be used to clarify this point. According to the German philosopher, categories of space and time (as well as quality, quantity, etc.) are not extensional categories, that is, they do not have empirical content. They represent not a certain characteristic of the world but the way we shape the experience of the world; we have empirical experience of reality because of and through such categories. The same can be said for psychological constructs, once they are approached in an *intensional*, rather than extensional way (i.e., as an analytic, modeling category, see Note 1 and below). Second, any empirical content cannot but be associated with a normative meaning, the expression of a certain language game. In other words, it is embedded within the commonsensical domain regulating the way people experience or deal with it; consequently, if the general theory had empirical content, it could not avoid being shaped by the normative meaning implied in it. And this means that the general theory would be the product of the common sense, rather than the epistemic place where common sense is understood (for a discussion of this point, see Salvatore, 2016, Introduction).

To claim that the general theory of psychology cannot but be meta-empirical is the same as saying that it has to be composed of *intensional* categories. An intensional category is a concept that is defined in terms of the semantic linkages it has with other concepts of the language to which it belongs – rather than in terms of the referential bond with the reality. A system of intensional categories, then, is a closed language that mediates the epistemic relation with the world, rather than representing it. Needless to say, intensional logic is not a way of escaping the reality; on the contrary, it is the device for empowering the capacity of understanding it. Owing to the empirical emptiness of its categories, an intensional language can enter relations with an infinite set of phenomena and bring them back to a single, basic semantics. Physics' basic categories, just like the categories of any formalized science, are instances of intensional concepts: super-strings, quarks, G constant, do not refer to things of the world; they are conceptual tools used for shaping and thus interpreting the world. As these sciences show, the adoption of intensional concepts does not mean escaping from the issue of subjecting theories to validation. Rather, the adoption of analytic categories means a doubling of the process of validation – on the one hand, any interpretation provided by any analytic category cannot but involve a certain set of empirical statements that can be tested empirically like any extensional concept.[2]

2.1.2 Intensionality and Abstractive Generalization

The view of cultural psychology as general theory involves a particular logic of generalization, different from the inductive logic grounding contemporary mainstream psychology. Indeed, meta-empirical generalization is a matter of *abstractive generalization* (Salvatore & Valsiner, 2010; Salvatore, 2016). The logic of abstractive generalization is based on the assumption of the nature of the field of psychological phenomena (Salvatore & Tschacher, 2012) (here and henceforth the term "psychological phenomena" is used just to denote the phenomena that psychologists address, without any ontological and essentialist implication): the great many phenomena of interest to psychology (i.e., memory, perception, communication, attachment, resilience, psychopathology, and so forth) are as many field instantiations of a *very limited set of fundamental dynamics*, whose modeling represents the core aim of psychological science. A dynamics is the inherent organization of a process, namely, of a certain phenomenon unfolding over time (see below; for a discussion of the organization as the unit of analysis in psychology, see Mandler, 2011). Accordingly, the dynamics can be considered as *the pattern of temporal relation of relations*.

Thus, dynamics is an abstract entity, void of any inherent empirical content. On the other hand, is should be clear that such emptiness does not equate to the lack of relation with the world – rather, it consists of the capacity of referring to a potentially infinite set of empirical contents, as many as the ones which might instantiate the second-ordered relation mapped by the dynamics.

In short, abstractive generalization is *generalization*, because it treats any set of empirical contents (i.e., any phenomenon – a behavior, an experience) as the specimen of a general class (i.e., the dynamics); it is *abstractive*, because this general class is an intensional category, namely, a conceptual object void of contingent empirical content (this view entails the notion of abstraction as pertinentization, as historically defined by Bühler, 1934/1990).

2.1.3 Conclusive Remarks

The abstractive generalization represents a different approach from those efforts to build a general theory that are aimed at attributing psychological phenomena to alleged causative mechanisms detected by more basic sciences (in particular biology, see Lickliter & Honeycutt, 2013; but also physics, see Kimble, 1990). In contrast, the abstractive generalization entails an inherently antireductionist approach. This is the case because it sees the dynamics to be modeled as an inherent quality of the phenomenon, rather than an external cause belonging to a more basic

phenomenical domain. In other words, the focus on the dynamics does not mean searching for a causal factor that affects the phenomenon from the outside (i.e., efficient cause); rather, it means modeling the phenomenon in terms of its inner constitutive organization (i.e., formal cause; see below).

In short, according to the intensional viewpoint, the issue of making cultural psychology into a general theory of psychology is to be seen as a matter of attributing the multiplicity of phenomenical forms investigated by the many psychological subdisciplines to the single meta-empirical object that psychology takes as its target.

On the other hand, even if it seems very far from mainstream psychology, such an approach has a rich, long-standing tradition in twentieth-century psychology. Piaget's work is paradigmatic of such a view. Indeed, the Piagetian theory requires a twofold level of reading. At a first level, the theory of the ontogenesis of mental structure is a domain-specific theory (i.e., a theory of how the child's cognitive system emerges and develops). Yet, through such a domain-specific theory, Piaget pursued his more general scientific aim – namely, the modeling of the fundamental cognitive dynamics characterizing living systems as a whole. Again, the notion of gestalt is an abstract model that has no empirical content and precisely for this reason it has been used for understanding several phenomenical domains (e.g., perception, thought, personality) in a unified way. The same can be said for the Vygotskian notion of mediation that is still used for modeling a plurality of phenomena (i.e., learning, work activity, rehabilitative interventions) in terms of a single basic dynamics. More recently, enactivism (Baerveldt & Verheggen, 2012) has provided an interpretation of several psychological phenomena (from perception to social representation) in terms of the abstract notions of organizational closure and structural coupling drawn from the model of autopoietic systems and its further development (Maturana & Varela, 1980; Varela, Thompson, & Rosch, 1991).

2.2 Cultural Psychology as the Science of Sensemaking

In this section, I will briefly outline three basic assumptions and their corollaries defining the ontological and epistemological pillars of the general theory, namely, the definition of the abstract object it addresses.

2.2.1 Assumption 1 – Processual Ontology

Scientific objects – that is, the object of psychology – are processes unfolding over time (Atmanspacher & Martin, 2004), rather than entities. This view has a strong tradition in psychology – just to give one example, it grounds James's pragmatist and functionalist approach to mind.

A process is intended here as a pattern of relations reproduced over time through the continuous variation of occurrences and conditions. This means that a process is *bivalent* – it is inherently transient (i.e., an ongoing change) and at the same time it is inherently invariant (i.e., a unique pattern reproduced over time). A river provides an image of process – it is always the same because it is always changing.

Needless to say, this view does not negate the phenomenological concreteness, the fact that the content of the experience has the forms of things (be they thoughts or pieces of the world), which are constrained by physical, material structures. This is the case because of the bivalence of the process: as in the case of the river, concrete contents are the ongoing emergent output of the processuality, rather than its causal source.

2.2.2 Corollary 1A – Holism

The definition of the process provided above implies that it is a *dynamic whole*. This means that elements of the process acquire their value in terms of their relation with the whole process.

It is worth adding that a fully coherent form of holism implies that it has to concern synchronic as well as diachronic relations. This form of holism has been modeled in terms of *temporal nonlocality*. Temporal nonlocality leads to overcome the view of process as a sequence of distinguishable stages associated via causal linkages: everything happens as the following instant of what has happened. Life does not recognize something like a before and an after.

Temporal nonlocality has been studied in the context of quantum physics and chaos theory (Atmanspacher & Martin, 2004). However, it is fully consistent with the view of sensemaking as a dynamic gestalt (Valsiner, 2007) as well as the theory of affective semiosis based on the interplay between symbolic and embodied signs (Salvatore & Freda, 2011; Salvatore & Zittoun, 2011; see below).

2.2.3 Corollary 1B – Organizational Closure

The bivalence of process entails that it has an inherent identity, what Maturana and Varela call *organization* – "the relations that define a system as a unity, and determine the dynamics of interaction and transformations which it may undergo as such a unity" (Maturana & Varela, 1980, p. 137). Accordingly, the process continuously changes its structure – i.e., the way elements interact with each other – as the way of enacting its organization (for a discussion of the relation between organization and structure, see Baerveldt & Verheggen, 2012). And this means that a process is endowed with organizational closure – namely, it works within the constraints and in terms of its own organization.

In what follows, I adopt the term *dynamics* to denote the form of such organization that provides the process with its identity. Accordingly, the dynamics can be seen as the set of constraints on the selection of the process' structural transformations.

2.2.4 Corollary 1C – Immanent Formal Causation

The definition of the process as endowed with organizational closure implies the adoption of the notions of constitutiveness and formal causation. Molecules of water are not something different from the river. The river does not come after the molecules, as its consequence (*efficient causation*). Rather, molecules *are* the river, their dynamic reciprocal linkages (formal causation) is what makes up the river (for a discussion of the interpretation of psychosocial processes in terms of constitutiveness, see Heft, 2013). Thus, to understand the process means to understand its immanent dynamics, namely, the way its organization constrains its structural changes.

This corollary is particularly relevant in psychology (and generally in the social sciences), because it enables the *post hoc–propter hoc fallacy* to be avoided. Indeed, most – if not all – psychological phenomena concern relations among mental states (feelings, ideas, perceptions) and between mental states and behaviors. To consider such relations in terms of efficient causal linkages means assuming that there is a transference of energy between the antecedent (*explanans*) and the subsequent (*explanandum*) – an assumption that can hardly be held in the case of mental states (unless they are considered brain states – but in that case one would cease psychological modeling). For a discussion of this point, based on the recognition that the linkages between mental states are hermeneutic and linguistic (i.e., the following state of mind is a way of interpreting the previous, rather than the effect of it), we highlight in particular the work of Smedslund (e.g. Smedslund, 1995).

A further consideration is worth adding. The corollary of immanent formal causation leads beyond both teleological causality and the reification of levels of explanation. As to teleological causality, the recognition of the immanency of the dynamics implies that the reproduction of the organization is not the purpose motivating and orienting the process. Rather, the organization is the condition of the selection of the structure. Thus, the process reproduces itself not as the way of pursuing a purpose, but just because the organization is the constraint that "determines the dynamics of interaction and transformation." The organization simply works and in working the observer is enabled to describe it as being reproduced over time. To make an analogy, the reproduction of the process looks like the reproduction of a language over time – people do not use the language *in order* to keep it alive. Rather, people speak within the constraint of the language organization (the semantic and syntactic relations which make that language just that language and not another) and in so doing language works and can be recognized by the observer as reproducing itself over time.

A similar vein can be adopted for highlighting how the immanent formal causation enables the multiplication of levels of explanation to be avoided. On the one hand, as we said above, since it is the immanent form of the process, the organization may not be seen as a super-ordered frame working in terms of downward causation. On the other hand, the organization is a set of constraints, rather than a propositional rule – it determines the structural changes – but it does so not in the sense that it *prescribes* them, but it "determines" in the sense that it establishes which structural changes are compatible with the identity of the process. Accordingly, this kind of formal causation can be defined as *neg-form*.

2.2.5 Assumption 2 – Mind is the Psychological Object

This assumption is not self-evident, especially in the context of the contemporary psychology that tends to consider the behavior as its object.

However, while behavior can be defined in accordance to a modelistic, metatheoretical perspective (see Uher, Addessi, & Visalberghi, 2013; see also Uher, 2014), it needs to be included in a more comprehensive framework. The first reason is because the behavior has to be explained, both for theoretical and practical purposes; and second, and above all, because the definition of behavior cannot but entail a reference to more primitive categories. This is evident in the theoretical definition of behavior by Uher, Addessi, and Visalberghi (2013) – one of the few that have been elaborated within the realm of current psychology. According to these authors, behavior is defined as "external activities or externalization of living organisms that are functionally mediated by environment in the present" (pp. 427–428). A few lines on, Uher and colleagues underline that "externality differentiates behavioral phenomena from psychological phenomena, which ... are entirely internal phenomena" (p. 428). Thus, the definition of behavior shows that it requires the reference to the more primitive internal–external dichotomy, in turn entailing (though implicitly) the idea of an inner world, namely, the idea of a mind. And this is the same as saying that, in the final analysis, the very concept of behavior is part of one more general definition that encompasses the idea of mind, that is, what is neither behavior nor environment.

2.2.6 Assumption 3 – Mind Is the Process of Decoupling from Environment

Mind is here intended as the process through which a living organism treats its structural change as the local substitutive version of the environment with which to relate. Accordingly, the mind is the way the living organism decouples from the immanency of the current environmental states.

This metatheoretical definition has several implications and aspects that are worth highlighting. First, it reflects the intensional approach discussed above – the mind is not intended here as a concept referring to something that is there in the world, but as a theoretical category grounding the definition and the modeling of psychological phenomena. Second, and consistently with it, the mind is here intended as a process, rather than an entity, and this makes the category somewhat far from the commonsensical idea of what mind is (if one reviews the definition provided by the main dictionaries, "mind" is intended in a tautological and reified way: as an entity endowed with certain properties – faculties – that produce as their effect what, according to common sense, are considered mental phenomena, that is, feelings, thoughts, and so forth). Third, the abstract definition of mind puts it logically before the important distinctions of inner–outer and mind–body because it does not concern the content and the form of the instantiation of the substitutive version of the environment. Fourth, it is worth noting that the substitution is not absolute, but concerns the ongoing current interplay between environment and living organism – for this reason I have called it "local." Fifth, even if abstract and very generalized, the definition has its boundaries, and this allows psychological phenomena to be differentiated from other kinds of phenomena. Indeed, any living organism enters relations with the environment not only through the instantiation of a substitutive local version of the latter – e.g., in the case of a physiological reaction, the living organism selects a structural change that directly modifies the bond with the environment, rather than instantiating a substitutive, decoupling version of it.

2.2.7 Assumption 4 – Mind Is Sensemaking

The metatheoretical definition of the mind grounds the chance of modeling it in terms of *sensemaking* – namely, as an infinite recursive dynamics of semiosis consisting of the infinite flow of signs through time. A sign is something that stands for something else, with such a relation having to be interpreted by a further sign (Peirce, 1897/1932). Thus, a sign does not have an inherent content; rather it acquires its value owing to the transition of which it is a part, that is, the capacity to refer to "something else" as *defined by another sign* – and so on, in an infinite chain. As I have said elsewhere (Salvatore, 2016), the *meaning is the sign that follows*.

In the framework of assumption 3, the sign can be modeled as a living organism's structural change that works as the ongoing interpretation of the previous chain of signs and in so doing instantiates a version of the environment, namely, an interpretation defining – and constraining – the domain of the possibilities of life. For instance, consider a person who shouts "Fire!" A structural change has taken place – the body modification of which the shout consists – that produces an environmental modification (the sound emitted). In so doing a sign has been enacted and through it a potential local version of the environment has been instantiated. Once a following sign will interpret the previous one – e.g., another person hearing the former and thinking "we have to escape from here!," or just starting to run – then the previous sign acquires the semiotic status of the (semiotic) substitutive version of the environment – substitutive because the person will select his/her adaptive structural changes in accordance to it, rather than in accordance to the previous environmental state.

2.2.8 Assumption 5 – Sensemaking Is Inherently Dialogical

As intended here, the notion of dialogicality concerns the constitutive role of otherness in sensemaking (Linell, 2009; Salvatore & Gennaro, 2012). Dialogicality, therefore, is something more and something different from the intersubjective standpoint. The interpreting function of the sign that follows entails the fact that the following sign is, however, the Other's sign, even when this otherness is enacted by the same person that has enacted the previous sign. This is so because interpretation is not a way of stating something that is already contained in the sign (in that case the interpretation would be a task of recognition, namely, a repetition of what is already given). Needless to say, in many cases the interpretation consolidates/validates the previous local state of the meaning; yet the validation is possible precisely because it is expressed by a potential otherness – it consists of the local neutralization of such inherent otherness.

In short, sensemaking is an infinite recursive chain of interpretations that is fostered by the inherent potentiality of any interpreting sign to introduce something new, namely, to move in the other's direction. Without such a potentiality, no sensemaking would be possible.

2.3 The Dynamics of Sensemaking

In this section, I draw nine tenets from the assumptions outlined above. Such tenets are intended as a theoretical and methodological apparatus for building a comprehensive model of the dynamics of sensemaking, intended as the core purpose of the general theory of psychology.

2.3.1 Tenet 1 – Sensemaking Is a Field Dynamics

Since the meaning is the sign that follows, signs have no fixed content – they acquire meaning via the infinite game of referring to something else. And this is the same as saying that the value of a sign is a function of the field, that is, of the position the sign has within the semiotic chain of which it is part. The same sign can express very different meanings depending on which other signs it is linked to. This is the contingency of human affairs: actions and events are acts of meaning whose value and significance lie in the position they have in the dynamics of sensemaking for which they work (Salvatore et al., 2009).

2.3.2 Tenet 2 – Meaning Emerges from Sensemaking

This is a different formulation of the previous tenet. Indeed, the claim that signs do not have content and that their meaning is a function of the transitions they establish with each other means that sensemaking generates the meaning, rather than the reverse, as common sense dictates. Accordingly, elsewhere (Salvatore, 2016) I have proposed to consider the meaning as the local instant state of the sensemaking, like a still frame that captures the instant of a movement, stopping it in a picture.

This view is consistent with the pragmatist conception of meaning as consisting of the effect it produces. Moreover, it leads to a revival of interest in the process of *presentification* that was at the center of early twentieth-century psychology (Salvatore, 2012, 2016). Such a process concerns the micro-genetic constitution of experience – the emergence of meaning from the ongoing flow of engagement with the world. Representing comes later: only when the experience is presentified in terms of discrete elements can it be the target of further mental operations (i.e., it can be represented). Thus, the sensemaking is part of the constitution of the experience – namely, one does not perceive the object as if it were out there and then categorize/interpret it; rather, perceiving is already a process that creates meaning, in the very fact of foregrounding certain relations among occurrences as opposed to the many potential others. For instance, one does not perceive a piece of paper first and then categorize it as a banknote – rather, one sees the potentially infinite possibility that that piece of the world provides (the dynamic object, to use Peirce's term) through and in terms of the fact of seeing a banknote. The emergence of the meaning "banknote" is part and parcel of the perception.

2.3.3 Tenet 3 – The Transition among Signs Is the Unit of Analysis of Sensemaking

The fact that the value of signs is contingent to the semiotic chain makes us consider the transitions – rather than the single sign – as the unit of the psychological analysis of mind: in order to model the dynamics of sensemaking one has to understand how signs combine with each other through time.

This methodological tenet is widely adopted both in psychoanalysis (Salvatore & Zittoun, 2011) and in the psychosocial analysis of local cultures as well as psychological analysis of textual data and discourse (Salvatore et al., 2015; Salvatore & Venuleo, 2013)

2.3.4 Tenet 4 – Transition among Signs Is a Habit Function

The focus on transition raises the issue of how a sign is selected as the following sign. Consider sign s1. According to assumption 5, it may be potentially followed by (or, which is the same thing, it may trigger) any other sign: the set of following signs is infinite. However, the fact that a sign follows means that a sort of hierarchy within the infinite set of potentially following signs is active.

The model of transition cannot depend on the reference to higher functions – namely, one cannot treat the combination among signs as a matter of choice – evaluation, search, and so forth – carried out by an intentional agent. This kind of explanation would lead to the homunculus paradox – one would have to explain how the homunculus' combination of signs (i.e., the combination of signs making up the sensemaking process allowing the homunculus to carry out the selection of the sign) works, and so forth ad infinitum. Therefore, I propose to consider this hierarchy as a habit function, that is, a function of the history of the previous transitions that signs have been part of – the higher the relative frequency with which a certain sign (say A) has been followed by a certain further sign (say B) in the past, the greater the probability that when A is enacted, then B will follow (for an analysis of a process of sensemaking within the clinical context based on such an approach, see Salvatore et al., 2015).

In the final analysis, this way of seeing the combination highlights the embodied roots of sensemaking – the association among signs are instances of procedural knowledge, reflecting dynamic forms of the body, the ones that correspond to the preference to respond to a certain pattern of body modifications (the modifications comprising the perception/production of sign A) with a certain pattern of modifications of this pattern of modifications (the modification of the previous pattern comprising sign B).

2.3.5 Tenet 5 – Culture as the Field Distribution of Probabilities

The previous tenets lead to an abstract, computational definition of the culture – it is the *field distribution of probabilities of transition among signs*.

In other words, the culture is the matrix of asymmetrical preferences that each sign has of combining with other signs. Such matrix does not reflect any general meaning or any kind of shared normative system of values and significances – as intended here it is just the immanent status of the recursive previous combination among signs; a habit – like a path through the woods that is produced by the accumulation of passages along it, so that the passages have created the path rather than vice versa.

2.3.6 Tenet 6 – Hyperdimensionality of the Distribution

The transitions among signs are often enough foreseeable, as if they were actually regulated by a certain frame of sense working as attractor. Yet they are able to cause the new to emerge.

If the transition among signs were a function of a matrix of distribution of probabilities no novelty would be possible because each sign would always be followed by the same sign (and such a combination would be increasingly stable as a result of the learning valence of the distribution, that is, the more a certain transition happens, the greater the probability that it will happen in the future).

The way to overcome such a puzzling issue is to assume that the distribution of probability among signs is not unidimensional, but multidimensional, or better, hyperdimensional. In other words, it is a distribution of distributions, the last corresponding to a given matrix of probability of transitions. Elsewhere (Salvatore, 2016), I have conceptualized such matrixes in terms of scenarios, namely, as specific units of experience corresponding and sustained by a redundant (micro)domain of life characterized by a somewhat stable dynamic network of co-occurring signs, and therefore a particular distribution of the probability. Accordingly, a scenario is an embodied generalized domain of sense, corresponding to a mode of activation of the body associated with a prototypical unit of social life.

A scenario, then, works as a *field of sense*, namely a peculiar system of preference defining the local trajectory of signs. Thus, while sign *a* has the highest probability of being followed by sign *b* in scenario *M*, it has the highest probability of being followed by sign *c* in scenario *P*.

2.3.7 Tenet 7 – Affective Grounds of Sensemaking

Scenarios have a level of generalization and can overlap and be nested within one another. Some scenarios have clear-cut boundaries and are associated to specific patterns of social action – e.g., when one is at the restaurant and raises one's hand to attract the attention of the waitress, the probable following signs are rather limited. Other scenarios are more generalized – some of them are very generalized, encompassing the person's basic modality of relating with the world. Such a generalized level of sensemaking is possible because semiosis, in its basic functioning, is inherently affective, adopting the body's state of activation as the first sign through which the whole relation with the world is interpreted as a single, generalized totality (for a discussion of affective semiosis and its unconscious root, see Salvatore & Freda, 2011; Salvatore & Zittoun, 2011).

2.3.8 Tenet 8 – Sensemaking Works Through Ongoing Pertinentization

Given the hyperdimensionality of the probability of transition, sensemaking requires a mechanism of pertinentization, that is, of reducing the dimensionality of the distribution of probability that backgrounds the non-pertinent dimensions – and thus foregrounding a limited set of pertinent scenarios. It is only on this condition that the transition to the following sign can be carried out. In the final analysis, the pertinentization of scenario puts a local boundary on the infinite potential associability – interpretability – of the sign, enabling it to be interpreted.

It is worth noting that this view of sensemaking as a dynamics of reducing variability and placing constraints is consistent with several models concerned with learning (Landauer & Dumais, 1997), communication (Salvatore, Tebaldi, & Potì, 2006/2009), text comprehension (Kintsch, 1988), and emergence of symbolic thought (Bucci, 1997).

According to this general view, one could conclude by recalling a classic Freudian image – sensemaking works like the sculptor who makes the form emerge as the result of taking off what is not pertinent, rather than like the painter that produces the form by adding what was not there before.

2.3.9 Tenet 9 – Bivalence of Meaning: SIA and SIP

The centrality of the mechanism of pertinentization in sensemaking leads us to see meaning as composed inherently by two components. On the one hand, the meaning is in the sign that follows and interprets the previous one. On the other hand, the meaning consists of the scenario according to which the transition is made possible.

Elsewhere (Salvatore, 2016; Salvatore & Venuleo, 2013) I have called the first component *Significance in Praesentia* (SIP) and the second *Significance in Absentia* (SIA). Thus, the SIA is the pertinentized scenario according to which the trajectory of the following sign (the SIP) is enacted.

It is worth highlighting that the scenario is not a frame that exists independently from the combination of signs, working on it in top-down terms. Rather, the scenario is activated and reproduced abductively through time (on abduction, see Salvatore & Valsiner, 2010)[3] as the most efficient way of enabling the unfolding of the trajectory of signs. In other words, the SIA is not a latent meaning that pushes the trajectory of signs from the outside and in a top-down way. Rather, the pertinentization of the scenario (i.e., the SIA) and the selection of the sign working co-extensively.

2.4 Conclusion

In this chapter, I have called for the development of cultural psychology as the general theory of psychology for the twenty-first century – able to restore the unity of the discipline, nowadays fragmented in a Babylon of circumscribed and phenomena-triggered theories. I have argued that such a task requires the shift to a modelistic, theory driven approach and I have tried to make a step ahead in that direction by outlining the basic elements of a semiotic and dynamic metatheoretical framework. Such a framework assumes that psychology is the science of sense-making, the latter being modeled as a field dynamics comprising transition among signs.

In conclusion, two implications of such a pro-posal are worth highlighting. First, the frame-work implies a processual ontology that enables the reification of psychological concepts to be avoided. Thus, what are usually seen as psycho-logical primitives (individuality, self, emotion, meaning, culture) can be treated as explananda of the general theory (i.e., what has to be under-stood, rather than what is used to understand). As a result, the semiotic dynamic general the-ory may provide a new synthesis of the tradi-tional dichotomies – subject versus object; indi-vidual versus social; culture-in-the-mind versus mind-in-the-culture; micro versus macro; cogni-tion versus emotion – which hinder its current capacity for development.

Second, the model of sensemaking outlined above outlines a way of going beyond the sub-stantialist interpretation of the notion of culture – as well as others like mind, subject, environ-ment – that views it as a self-contained entity affecting the functioning of whatever interacts with it (e.g., people's way of thinking, customs, norms, and so forth). According to such a stand-point, typical of cross-cultural studies (Heine, 2011; for a criticism, Valsiner, 2007), a social group *has/shares* a culture and this culture deter-mines some of its important qualities – e.g., behavior X that is common within the group is due to the culture of the social group. Despite its closeness with common sense, this view is the-oretically untenable. In so far as the culture is defined as an entity working on other entities, this raises the issue of what the culture is made of and how this "stuff" acts, and through what kind of material linkages and vectors. As one can easily see, such issues are actually unsolvable and at the center of disputes throughout the whole history of human thought (Valsiner, 2009).

The framework outlined in this work enables such pitfalls to be avoided, providing an inten-sional and processual approach to culture. According to this conception, culture is not a meta-factor, competing with others in the con-struction of human events. Rather, it is the dynamic gestalt where human events come to life and develop. It is the immanent form of human phenomena.

Notes

1 The extension of a concept is the set of instances to which it can be applied, whereas the intension of a concept is the set of criteria defining the posi-tion within the semantic system, namely its rela-tion with the other concepts. Thus, the extensional approach is the view that the meaning of a concept consists of the set of elements of the world referred to by the category, whereas the intensional approach is the view that the meaning of a concept is given by the rules defining its position within the seman-tic system. The extensional approach therefore sees the culture as something which is in the world and, for this reason, works as the referential meaning of the corresponding scientific category. In contrast, the intensional approach considers the notion of "culture" as a concept that does not correspond to something in the world, being defined theoreti-cally, and as such used for interpreting – rather than merely indicating – a certain set of phenomena.

2 A classic example of this double level of validation is general relativity (GR), which was accepted by scientists because it was able both to provide a uni-fied mathematical description of gravity as a geo-metric property of space and time and to explain the empirical phenomenon of the perihelion precession of Mercury's orbit. On the other hand, the role of empirical validation was limited for a long time – indeed, it was only 40 years later that GR was sub-jected to a systematic program of empirical testing, once the technological devices became available.

3 According to Peirce, abduction is the inference that reconstructs an event from empirical occurrences, the latter being interpreted as the effect of the event, therefore as the indexical sign of it. Thus, abduc-tion is aimed at defining the minimal not evident (past or present) phenomenon which, by happening, makes the occurrences meaningful (i.e., makes them

a sign). In other words, the phenomenon is reconstructed due to the fact that it works as the grounds for making the co-occurrences meaningful.

References

Atmanspacher, H. & Martin, J. (2004). Reflections on process and persons. In M. Weber (Ed.), *After Whitehead: Rescher on Process Metaphysics* (pp. 161–172). Frankfurt: Ontos.

Baerveldt, C. & Verheggen, T. (2012). Enactivism. In J. Valsiner (Ed.), *Oxford Handbook of Culture and Psychology* (pp. 165–190). Oxford: Oxford University Press.

Boesch, E. (1991). *Symbolic Action Theory and Cultural Psychology*. Berlin: Springer.

Bucci, W. (1997). *Psychoanalysis and Cognitive Science*. New York: Guilford Press.

Bühler, K. (1934/1990). *Theory of Language: The Representational Function of Language*. Amsterdam: John Benjamins.

Feldman-Barrett, L. (2006). Solving the emotion paradox: Categorization and the experience of emotion. *Personality and Social Psychology Review*, 10, 20–46.

Green, C. D. (2015). Why psychology isn't unified, and probably never will be. *Review of General Psychology*, 19(3), 207–214.

Heft, H. (2013). Environment, cognition, and culture: Reconsidering the cognitive map. *Journal of Environmental Psychology*, 33, 14–25.

Heidbreder, E. (1933). *Seven Psychologies*. New York: Appleton-Century.

Heine, S. (2011). *Cultural Psychology*. San Francisco: W. W. Norton.

Henriques, G. (2011). *A New Unified Theory of Psychology*. New York: Springer.

Kimble, G. A. (1990). Mother Nature's bag of tricks is small. *Psychological Science*, 1, 36–41.

Kintsch, W. (1988). The use of knowledge in discourse processing: A construction-integration model. *Psychological Review*, 95, 163–182.

Kitayama, S. & Cohen, D. (Eds.). (2007). *Handbook of Cultural Psychology*. New York: Guilford Press.

Landauer, T. K. & Dumais, S. (1997). A solution to Plato's problem: The latent semantic analysis theory of acquisition, induction and representation of knowledge. *Psychological Review*, 104, 211–240.

Lickliter, R. & Honeycutt, H. (2013). A developmental evolutionary framework for psychology. *Review of General Psychology*, 17, 184–189. DOI: 10.1037/a0032932.

Linell, P. (2009). *Rethinking Language, Mind and World Dialogically: Interactional and Contextual Theories of Sense-making*. Charlotte, NC: Information Age Publishing.

Mandler, G. (2011). From association to organization. *Current Directions in Psychological Science*, 20, 232–235. DOI: 10.1177/0963721411414656.

Marsh, T. & Boag, S. (2014). Unifying psychology: Shared ontology and the continuum of practical assumptions. *Review of General Psychology*, 18, 49–59.

Matsumoto, D. (Ed.). (2001). *The Handbook of Culture and Psychology*. Oxford: Oxford University Press.

Maturana, M. R., & Varela, J. F. (1980). *Autopoiesis and Cognition: The Realization of the Living*. Dordrecht, Netherlands: Reidel.

Peirce, C. S. (1897/1932). *Collected Papers of Charles Sanders Peirce* (ed. by C. Hartshorne & P. Weiss, vol. 2). Cambridge, MA: Harvard University Press.

Salvatore, S. (2012). Social life of the sign: Sensemaking in society. In J. Valsiner (Eds.), *The Oxford Handbook of Culture and Psychology* (pp. 241–254). Oxford: Oxford University Press.

Salvatore, S. (2016). Cultural psychology of desire. In J. Valsiner, G. Marsico, N. Chaudhary, T. Sato, & V. Dazzani (Eds.), *Psychology as the Science of Human Being: The Yokohama Manifesto* (pp. 33–49). New York: Springer.

Salvatore, S. (2016). *Psychology in Black and White: The Project for a Theory Driven Science*. Charlotte, NC: Information Age Publishing.

Salvatore, S., Forges Davanzati, G., Potì, S., & Ruggieri, R. (2009). Mainstream economics and sensemaking. *Integrative Psychological and Behavioral Science*, 43(2), 158–177.

Salvatore, S. & Freda, M. F. (2011). Affect unconscious and sensemaking: A psychodynamic semiotic and dialogic model. *New Ideas in Psychology*, 29, 119–135.

Salvatore, S., Gelo, O. G., Gennaro, A., Metrangolo, R., Terrone, G., Pace, V., Venuleo, C., & Venezia, A. (2015). An automated method of content analysis for psychotherapy research: A further validation. *Psychotherapy Research*, 25(4), 1–13.

Salvatore, S. & Gennaro, A. (2012). The inherent dialogicality of the clinical exchange. *International Journal for Dialogical Science*, 6(1), 1–14.

Salvatore, S., Tebaldi, C., & Potì, S. (2006/2009). The discursive dynamic of sensemaking. In S. Salvatore, J. Valsiner, S. Strout, & J. Clegg (Eds.), *Yearbook of Idiographic Science* (vol. 1, pp. 39–72). Rome: Firera.

Salvatore, S. & Tschacher, W. (2012). Time dependency of psychotherapeutic exchanges: The contribution of the theory of dynamic systems in analyzing process. *Frontiers in Psychology*, 3, 253. DOI: 10.3389/fpsyg.2012.00253.

Salvatore, S. & Valsiner, J. (2010). Between the general and the unique: Overcoming the nomothetic versus idiographic opposition. *Theory & Psychology*, 20(6), 817–833.

Salvatore, S. & Venuleo, C. (2013). Field and dynamic nature of sensemaking: Theoretical and methodological implications. *Papers on Social Representation*, 22(2), 21.1–21.41.

Salvatore, S. & Zittoun, T. (2011). Outlines of a psychoanalytically informed cultural psychology. In S. Salvatore & T. Zittoun (Eds.), *Cultural Psychology and Psychoanalysis in Dialogue: Issues for Constructive Theoretical and Methodological Synergies* (pp. 3–46). Charlotte, NC: Information Age Publishing.

Smedslund, J. (1988). *Psycho-Logic*. Heidelberg: Springer.

Smedslund, J. (1995). Psychologic: Common sense and the pseudoempirical. In J. A. Smith, R. Harré, & L. van Langenhove (Eds.), *Rethinking Psychology* (pp. 196–206). London: SAGE.

Stam, H. J. (2004). Unifying psychology: Epistemological act or disciplinary maneuver? *Journal of Clinical Psychology*, 60, 1259–1262. DOI: 10.1002/jclp.20069.

Uher, J. (2014). Interpreting "personality" taxonomies: Why previous models cannot capture individual-specific experiencing, behaviour, functioning and development. Major taxonomic tasks still lay ahead. *Integrative Psychological and Behavioral Science*, 49(4), 600–655.

Uher, J., Addessi, E., & Visalberghi, E. (2013). Contextualised behavioural measurements of personality differences obtained in behavioural tests and social observations in adult capuchin monkeys (*Cebus apella*). *Journal of Research in Personality*, 47, 427–444.

Valsiner, J. (2001). Processes structure of semiotic mediaton in human development. *Human Development*, 44, 84–97.

Valsiner, J. (2007). *Culture in Minds and Societies: Foundations of Cultural Psychology*. New Delhi: SAGE.

Valsiner, J. (2009). Integrating psychology within the globalizing world: A requiem to the post-modernist experiment with *Wissenschaft*. *Integrative Psychological and Behavioral Science*, 43(1), 1–21.

Valsiner, J. (Ed.). (2012). *The Oxford Handbook of Culture and Psychology*. Oxford: Oxford University Press.

Varela, F., Thompson, F., & Rosch E. (1991). *The Embodied Mind: Cognitive Science and Human Experience*. Cambridge, MA: MIT Press.

Further Reading

Salvatore, S. & Valsiner, J. (2011). Idiographic science as a non-existing object: The importance of the reality of the dynamic system. In S. Salvatore, J. Valsiner, A. Gennaro, & J. B. Traves Simon (Eds.), *Yearbook of Idiographic Science* (vol. 3, pp. 7–26). Rome: Firera.

3 Knowledge and Experience: Interobjectivity, Subjectivity, and Social Relations

Gordon Sammut, Martin W. Bauer, and Sandra Jovchelovitch

Imagine you are approaching a bus stop on a busy morning to get a bus to work. Already standing by the bus stop is a person who is waiting to do the same. As the minutes pass, more and more passengers arrive and cluster around the pickup point waiting for the bus to arrive. Now imagine that the bus is delayed and that it becomes clear to all waiting passengers that not everyone will be able to board the next bus. Some will have to wait for the subsequent service. In these conditions, queuing helps ensure that those who arrived at the bus stop first get to board the service first, and that those who arrived later will be next in line for the following service. A queue can be defined as an organized or spontaneous arrangement of people awaiting some service. The first person in the queue is the first person in line to receive service, with later arrivals occupying subsequent spots in a spatial arrangement that ensures the provision of services in turn on a first-come-first-served basis. Economists consider queuing as one of the fair alternatives to market allocation of limited goods; however, queuing requires a moral commitment not to jump the queue (see Sandel, 2012).

So, imagine you are the second person to arrive on the spot and that as more passengers awaiting the service arrive, you spontaneously decide to take up your spot in the queue. Would you stand exactly behind the first person in a single file? Or would you stand slightly to the right or slightly to the left, such that you can perceive what the person standing in front of you is doing? And suppose now you are the third person to arrive at the scene, with a person clearly occupying the first spot and a second passenger standing loosely behind, slightly to the right. Bearing in mind that queuing at a bus stop is spontaneous, would you now take up a spot behind the first two in a single file, or would you stand adjacent to the second passenger on the left? And what if you were the fourth to arrive, and found the other three passengers occupying a triangular space in front of you forming two rows of passengers waiting to board the bus? Where would you place yourself now to respect the queue? And what if you were the fiftieth person to arrive and all you could perceive is a mass of people waiting to board the next bus with no apparent queuing arrangement other than the ones arriving before you occupy a spatial position closer to the bus stop than you in no determined order? How would you now get in line?

Instances like these occur innumerable times every day in every town or city around the globe and, most of the time, are hardly newsworthy. In these situations, human beings commonly organize themselves spontaneously toward achieving some common purpose. At other times, however, such spontaneous organization seemingly fails. When it does, it can precipitate very unpleasant consequences. How could such a seemingly simple arrangement fail? The Daboma Jack incident in Malta (Box 3.1) is illustrative in this regard.

Box 3.1 The Daboma Jack Incident

Daboma Jack was a Hungarian citizen of African descent studying for a Master's degree in Malta. On July 1, 2015, prepaid bus cards were introduced in Malta in an effort to make the service more efficient for the benefit of users. The first few days were marked by apparent chaos, as bus users and bus drivers alike familiarized themselves with the new service. This resulted in widespread delays in services and significant build-ups of queues at many bus stops around the island. Daboma Jack arrived at one of these scenes in Valletta hoping, like every other waiting passenger, to board a bus and get on his way. The queue awaiting him seemed like a disorganized mass of frustrated commuters who pushed and shoved their way to secure a place on the service each time a bus pulled up to board passengers. Not knowing exactly how to go about this business given the novelty of prepaid cards, Mr. Jack sought to help organize fellow waiting passengers in an orderly queue. To everyone else, this would appear to be a sensible and laudable act that would ensure everyone would get their fair chance of boarding a bus. His efforts, however, were met with stiff resistance on the part of other commuters. They claimed that they were already in a queue and that Mr. Jack should simply keep his place. The situation quickly degenerated and in the fracas that followed, Mr. Jack was racially abused, slapped, and spat at. Police forces from the Rapid Intervention Unit who were called to the scene proceed to physically pin Mr. Jack down to the ground and arrest him, to the claps and cheers of other passengers. He was subsequently charged with disturbing the public peace but the charges against him were dismissed in court due to lack of evidence.

Clearly, there are numerous ways by which a psychological understanding of this incident (Box 3.1) could unfold, in view of the various psychological issues that could be examined. One evident issue, however, and one that is commonly neglected in psychological inquiry, is the way the various actors perceived and interpreted the situation. Locals perceived, what to Mr. Jack was a disorganized aggregate of frustrated commuters as an everyday occurrence, that of a normal and regular queue at a bus stop (in the Mediterranean sense of queue). On this occasion, the queue was bigger in size, but no less orderly than any other bus stop queue on any other day. Mr. Jack's efforts at ordering the queue were interpreted as unwarranted interference that could only precipitate disorder, which they did. But where on the side of this debate fellow passengers fell depended on their own implicit understanding of a queue, and whether this should take a linear, triangular or circular spatial arrangement. Clearly, there is no "objective" definition of queue that passengers could appeal to in taking a side, although some understanding of queuing might get "objectified." The mass of waiting passengers was orderly or disorderly in this case depending on which cultural frames of reference apply to define the nature of the present queue. To a local, a triangular or circular queue was orderly in a way that Mr. Jack failed to perceive. On the other hand, to an outsider, such as Mr. Jack and anyone else who shares his understanding, a triangular or circular queue is in fact no queue at all, much less an orderly one.

What the Daboma Jack incident makes clear, for the purposes of the present chapter, is that interpersonal relations actuated between different subjects are inextricably tied with sociocultural frames of reference that lend meaning to particular perspectives and justify particular courses of action as opposed to others that could be taken in the circumstances. Psychology often limits itself to the investigation of the actual intersubjective exchanges which occur during these incidences to explain the turn of events. In this chapter, we argue that a focus on sociocultural frames of reference is a necessary prelude to achieve a genuine understanding of interpersonal relations and why these take the shape and form they do. Rather than arguing that one definition of a queue is necessarily right, and studying the "logic" of how some people get it wrong (we might all use this social deficit approach), we postulate, along with other scholars, that a sociocultural focus is required to understand these events as multiple realities of action and representation. This helps toward understanding how different objectifications of people, events, and objects prevalent in our contemporary surroundings go on to shape the nature of our social interactions with others. We argue that the plurality of knowledges that typifies contemporary public spheres (Jovchelovitch, 2007) brings to the fore a concern with how different systems of knowledge interrelate in the same public sphere to foster interobjectivity (Sammut & Moghaddam, 2014). This occurs among culturally diverse subjects and goes on to structure everyday social relations mediated by the use of social objects. We start by visiting the prevalent distinction between subjectivity and objectivity and proceed to outline nine theses concerning the role of interobjectivity and boundary objects in social relations. We conclude by advancing some principles for psychological research concerning interobjective architectures that help to address our propositions.

3.1 Subjectivity, Objectivity, and the In-between

The social sciences have long grappled with the duality of subjectivity and objectivity (see Coelho & Figueiredo, 2003). Broadly speaking, psychological activity is routinely placed within the domain of subjectivity, that is, phenomena that are personal and idiosyncratic that are, as it is argued, not amenable to scientific investigation because introspection is not a verifiable sci-

entific method. By contrast, material phenomena that exist independently of any perceiving subject are placed within the domain of objectivity and verifiable observation. In psychology, relations between distinct subjectivities have been framed along the lines of intersubjectivity. This refers to the human ability to adopt the perspective of the other and to relate with the other on the basis of this understanding (Daanen & Sammut, 2012). Intersubjectivity is routinely held to be the psychological answer to Cartesian reductionism that enables interaction between otherwise self-contained subjective entities (Daanen & Sammut, 2012). In an intersubjective exchange, subjects are able to communicate their mental states to one another and in this way avoid or overcome discrepancies between the two.

The issue of objectivity in psychology is generally relegated to an attribute of social cognition, such as a naïve realism bias by which individuals consider their view to be "objective" and others' differing views to be biased (Ross & Ward, 1996). In this case, an implicit social deficit approach to bias often replaces moral preference with a claim of epistemic authority. Alternatively, objectivity is an attribute of a well-executed study that is able to demonstrate a psychological property as it exists in reality without the interference of the researcher's own interpretation.

This cursory overview of the prevalent meanings of subjectivity and objectivity in psychology should suffice to highlight some of the difficulties in the conceptual tools that the discipline has relied on over the years. First, as Daanen and Sammut (2012) note, much social interaction is achieved without recourse to intersubjective exchanges that overcome different realities for distinct subjects. Second, as Asch (1987) points out, subjects' understanding of the world around them is based on objective rather than subjective criteria. Human beings do not consider the world in terms of their innate cognitive processes. They assume that the world they perceive is similarly perceived by others, and they structure their social relations in line with these premises. Even with regards to socially constructed phenomena, human subjects attribute objective criteria to these phenomena such that no space is left for subjective considerations. One cannot, for instance, subjectively dispute matters such as money, time, crime, or human rights. These and other categories are collectively treated as objective obligations by human subjects. Social relations are structured accordingly. It is therefore clear that, phenomenologically speaking, the distinction between what is subjective and what is objective is crude and leaves many relational forms unaccounted for. Recent work concerning interobjectivity, to which we now turn, has sought to shed further light on these issues (see Sammut, Daanen, & Moghaddam, 2013).

The first thesis to consider is that, as Daanen & Sammut (2012) note,

T1: routine social interaction does not rely on intersubjective exchange.

Much routine social interaction does not require the conscious interpretation of the perspective of the other, even when the same social object means different things to different people. For instance, a sandwich may be an object to buy for someone and an object to sell for someone else. This transaction, however, does not routinely require a conscious exercise of negotiating different subjective meanings of the object. Rather, this bedrock is provided by a cultural understanding that sandwiches can be bought and sold and that different individuals can position themselves accordingly in social relations. The transaction itself of buying/selling a sandwich can be undertaken with little to no interaction at all – buyer takes sandwich from fridge, places it on counter along with an amount of cash, seller spontaneously takes cash and hands over receipt, buyer walks out of shop with sandwich and receipt. No negotiation of meaning is required in this transaction that is typical of

intersubjective exchanges. Daanen and Sammut (2012) argue that

T2: intersubjectivity is better restricted to second-order derivative accounts of human understanding that instantiate in situations of rupture, that is, when a discrepancy in subjective meanings fails routine, practical interaction.

In most forms of interaction, however, the meaning of objects is immediately apparent to us without the need for conscious reflection, due to a bedrock of affordances and/or interobjective representations that grant objects the properties that actors effectively perceive from different vantage points. I do not need a subjective experience of selling sandwiches to understand that sandwiches can be sold. If I am able to buy a sandwich, I simultaneously understand that somebody is able to sell it, without any need to reconstruct the social world to accommodate diverse subjective orientations to what one can do with a sandwich. No readjustment of conduct is demanded due to the fact that this social interaction takes place within the parameters of the direct recognition of objects, as Asch (1987) noted, as well as the range of appropriate responses in their regard (Wagner, 2015; Sammut, 2015). According to Daanen and Sammut (2012), the quality of objectivity applies in routine interactions in as much as it represents knowledge of *knowing how* to act in everyday life (p. 568, italics in original).

T3: The postulation of intersubjectivity and interobjectivity refers to a class of phenomena distinguished from those that could be intrasubjective on the one hand and intraobjective on the other.

The duality subjectivity–objectivity has been expanded to include four sets (Harré & Sammut, 2013), namely those that are exclusively subjective and objective and those that lie in between. How can psychology make sense of this terminology and what are the corresponding states?

Harré and Sammut (2013) have argued that these four combinations map onto Vygotsky's cycle of zones of proximal development, which run from the "private-personal" to the "public-collective." In this cycle, idiosyncratic ways of thinking and acting emerge in the "private-personal" domain, which, displayed in the public domain constitute the class of "public-personal" phenomena. In this domain, individual ways of doing things come under public scrutiny and are used to advance public projects. Sometimes, these idiosyncratic ways of acting go on to become formally instituted in social life, allowing other individuals to take up a similar way of doing things in a formal role. At this point, the act transfers to the "public-collective" domain. Finally, individuals may adopt formal institutional practices in their personal capacity, which they exercise in some private domain. This corresponds to the "private-collective" state in Vygotsky's classification. If we replace subjectivity and objectivity with personal and collective domains, and intra- and inter- with private and personal domains, the resulting typology serves in understanding a comprehensive range of psychological phenomena that involve both an idiosyncratic class of phenomena as well as cultural practices that grant personal psychological phenomena social currency.

This classification facilitates an understanding of how personal psychological phenomena can appear in both collective and individual activities and projects (see Figure 3.1). Intersubjective phenomena transpire as personal in their location but collective in their knowability. Conversely, inter-objective phenomena are those that exist only in the joint and coordinated interaction between members of a group. These refer to coordinated activities that are public in their location and collective in their knowability (e.g., a victory parade involving the coordinated activity of particular players and supporters displayed in public and recognized as a circumscribed activity by others). In this way, we can see how a shared body of knowledge is requisite for group members to

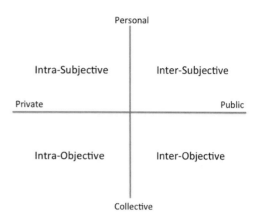

Figure 3.1 Psychological phenomena in the spaces between the personal–collective and the private–public dimensions.

be able to participate in collective episodes. We can also see how participating individuals may not have full access to the totality of such knowledge, which is available to the group as a whole. Individuals require only knowledge of how their role practices fit the general corpus to be able to participate in social life.

3.2 Object Relations, Interobjectivity, and Social Representations

The notion of interobjectivity was introduced in psychology by Moghaddam (2003, 2010) in an effort to resolve the intersubjectivity dilemma concerning the way distinct subjects can claim recourse to each other's subjective states. According to Moghaddam, this issue remains a puzzle only insofar as we adhere to an individualistic focus that locates psychological experience within the self-contained individual. Moghaddam's proposal is to postulate a normative system that preexists individuals, that is,

> T4: interobjective representations span a diversity of cultural and normative understandings.

According to Moghaddam, individual understandings arise out of collective understandings. In other words, interobjectivity is the source of intersubjectivity inasmuch as the normative system we are born into is the framework and main source of our psychological experiences; similarly the body is the scaffold of our perceptions: we need eyes and ears to see and hear.

Moghaddam's notion proposes a background of common-sense meaning that stands as a bedrock for social relations among diverse subjects and that is used as a benchmark for appraising alternative views.

T5: Interobjective understandings are those that incorporate diverse objectifications pertaining to different subjects.

Alternative views that are made to fit alongside previously enacted normative frameworks give rise to interobjective representations that are assimilated and accommodated into preexisting common sense. By extension, those that remain discrepant are perceived as nonsensical by enculturated subjects (often called metaphysical, as in the positivist demarcation of science from nonsense, see Kolakowski, 1972). As Sammut, Daanen, and Sartawi (2010) go on to note, being a fully enculturated subject effectively means that one immediately and nonconsciously knows the meaning assigned to commonplace objects, roles, and practices without the need for deliberation. While objects around us seem to take on meaning in light of a subject's intended action – for example, standing up on a chair to change a lightbulb – objects also act on us in view of what they immediately and nonconsciously represent for us. In other words, they act on us in terms of the objectification associated with the object itself in a particular group. What to one subject is a pair of wooden sticks, to another is a set of chopsticks that invite consumption of a particular cuisine.

Sammut, Daanen, and Sartawi (2010) argue that objects do not merely take on different objectifications depending on the social group who elaborates their meaning, they more specifically take on meanings for action that are triggered without the need for deliberation, that is, in an objective and direct-intentional sense. Costall (2013) argues, in the same vein, that objects reify human intentions and that reification, rather than a fallacy, is effectively a fact of life when it comes to the meaning of objects and the routine practices in which they partake. According to Costall, a chair invites sitting regardless of whether anyone happens to use it for standing on it. Costall argues that sitting is a chair's "canonical affordance" and that this is akin to an objective property for the chair. One sits on chairs, regardless of what you or I might actually be doing with it. In this way, objects are treated by subjects in terms of objective properties with which they are imbued (Asch, 1987), as detailed above. However, we might note, in many traditions there is a moral warning attached to an escalation from mere objectification to reification, which in the Western world we might recognize as the "iconoclastic impetus" (Bauer, 2015).

How action is constrained by different objectifications (objectifications can either invite or restrict action, e.g. a no-entry sign) and the role of these objectifications in structuring social relations constitutes a specific focus for Latour, whose introduction of interobjectivity in sociology predates Moghaddam's in psychology. Latour (1996) argues that objects mediate human action to the extent that objects, just as other human subjects, exercise social forces and are not only part of but also implicated in social reality. This is attested by the fact that the human–Simian transition is characterized not only by language capacity, but also by the accumulation of things, useful and useless alike, that is, material culture. Along with subjects, objects are implicated in hybrid networks constituted by an association of "actants" (i.e., humans and things) that do something to the environment in which they move and exist. In this sense, humans are fundamentally cyborgs – human-machine constructs, who have extended their social action to objects and incorporated them into their interactions. Objects thus "act" and give feedback on regulating human activity. For instance, a speed bump in the road ensures drivers slow down to the desired limit, which becomes equivalent to the moral obligation of "20 miles per hour limit." However, a traffic warden standing on the corner could achieve the same outcome. Both act on the environment by regulating the activity of human drivers. The act of "stimulating braking" is achieved by the object, rather than by the words and actions of a subject. A heavy key holder makes it more likely that you will deposit the hotel key at the reception than walk out with it in your pocket. While we might attribute intentionality only to the designer of the object; the object has at most open functionality. Consequently, Latour claims that social inquiry needs to delve into the activity that subjects and objects help to achieve in conjunction.

While Latour and Moghaddam differ in their conceptions of interobjectivity, the two might find common ground when treating interobjectivity as a social representation (Sammut & Howarth, 2014). Thus,

> T6: *social representation encompasses different objectifications in a way that permits diverse interobjective relations with the same object, according to each group's version of the object itself.*

Objects inhabit more than one single sociocultural world. This fact requires intersectional work to create interobjective representations that simultaneously meet the interobjective demands of various sociocultural projects and frames (Sammut, Daanen, & Sartawi, 2010). Interobjective representations allow diverse social groups to interrelate with the same object in different ways and without conflict, according to their particular historical project. This state of social relations is neatly captured in Bauer and Gaskell's (2008) wind-rose model of social representations. According to Bauer and Gaskell, social representations require a minimum of two interrelating subjects concerned with the same object. The objectification that is elaborated in the course of interaction serves both subjects, enabling each to acquire a particular understanding of the object in terms of the specific features that are amenable to the different projects they themselves pursue.

These objectifications can differ from another elaborated by distinct subjects who are not vested in the same social representation and who, for their own purposeful project, elaborate a different version. Consequently, different social groups elaborate a multitude of objectifications of the same object. The "real" object itself comes to stand as the linking pin between different "actual" objects, the social representations of the object that suit the object relations demands of the various groups. This social dynamic produces the real object as the sum total of all actual objects. A social representation that can accommodate diverse objectifications pertaining to different sociocultural groups in a way that satisfies the diversity of object relations required across the various groups can be termed interobjective. In these instances, particular subjects can interrelate with and through the object in meaningful ways without detracting meaning or limiting activity for others. This enables both a degree of shared reference and the functional realization of diversity. In this sense, it can be suggested that an interobjective social representation is marked by a state of cognitive polyphasia.

3.3 Boundary Objects, Borders, and Knowledge Encounters

The studies reviewed above (Box 3.2) demonstrate that interobjectivity constructs boundary objects, understood as objects that lie at the intersection of diverse objectifications. A key feature of boundary objects is to unify while separating (Marsico et al., 2013). The boundary links what is separated: it is an intrinsic characteristic of borders to distinguish distinct entities while at the

Box 3.2 Interobjectivity in Social Research

A study by Wagner et al. (2012) demonstrated such interobjective representations concerning the Muslim veil in Indonesia, a Muslim majority country, and India, a Muslim minority country. The authors found that representations of the veil in Indonesia centered around practical uses such as convenience, fashion, and modesty. There was little reference to the significance of religion in wearing this garment among Muslim women in Indonesia. By contrast, Muslim women's representations of the veil in India centered around cultural identity and religiosity. For these women, the veil was an instrument to challenge stereotypes and discrimination. This account of the veil demonstrates that the very same object has different meanings and different functional uses for different subjects depending on the sociocultural context in which they are embedded. It further demonstrates that while Muslim women are typically lumped together as a homogeneous group by outside observers – that is, Muslims – their accounts of adopting the garment differ in line with their status in society. The veil confers specific functions in both these settings that are different from one another and that contrast with prevailing Western conceptions of the garment as a religious symbol alone. These different objectifications are linked by the veil itself – an interobjective and polyphasic garment that stands at the boundary of diverse objectifications and that serves the relational demands of the different groups simultaneously.

Another study that demonstrates interobjective relational practices is the street-art study reported by Sammut, Daanen, and Sartawi (2010). The study involved an inquiry into diverse relational practices observed during the Cans Festival in London in 2008. The festival was organized by notorious graffiti artist, Banksy, in a road tunnel under London Waterloo Station, where various pieces by Banksy and other popular street artists were put up on display. The festival attracted numerous visitors over the time that the artworks were displayed. The authors report that discernible relational differences were observed by different groups visiting the street "gallery." Tourist-types flocked to the festival to see a Banksy and document the moment with a picture, mostly of themselves standing alongside the artworks. Museum-types, on the other hand, stood at some distance to admire the artworks and took their time to take the various pieces in. While there was no formal organization in the tunnel, such as ushers to direct visitors or stanchions to keep visitors at a safe distance, museum-types regulated their conduct according to norms typical of art galleries or formal museums. Street-types, on the other hand, adopted different forms of conduct that would have been in violation of typical museum norms. They interacted with the artworks, climbing on installations to pose for pictures or even adding their own amateur-graffiti to the walls.

While the conduct of some seemingly violated the prescriptions of others, no incidence of conflict was observed. Rather, visitors seemingly understood that street art allowed for relational practices that did not apply, or were purposely in contravention, to norms that regulate conduct with regards to other art forms. This, in itself, was understood by visitors to be part of the phenomenon of street art. The diversity of interactions it generated was in itself a crucial attractor. Visitors appreciated that the popularity of street art in general, and the Cans Festival in particular, was due to the fact that it appealed to a wide diversity of subjects who were all equally drawn to this art form for their own reasons. The interobjective representation of street art enabled visitors to accept that the Cans Festival had fulfilled its purpose by appealing to a diverse audience. Rather than becoming irate at others who interacted with the artworks in different ways, visitors expressed satisfaction at the fact that street art had such broad appeal and that it could draw interest from others who would typically have been expected to be unconcerned with artistic works of this or any kind. Visitors regarded the diversity of interactions as a strength of street art over other forms.

same time uniting them in some form of interrelation. Identity is gained in relation and demarcation. As noted in the Muslim veil study, distinct objectifications of the garment enable women to use it for different purposes and the justifications underpinning one objectification provide no basis for the other. To the outside observer, however, both objectifications refer to a common entity that identifies those who wear it as women of a certain kind – i.e., Muslims. The various objectifications demarcate different users – those who wear the veil as an accessory as opposed to those who wear it as an identity marker – depending on the sociocultural context in which the activity of wearing the veil is carried out, that is, majority or minority situation. The interobjective representation of the veil as a Muslim garment, constituted by the totality of meanings in both objectifications, classifies distinct users together. It serves to ascribe a distinct property to the veil that marks everyone who wears it regardless of context. The veil is a *Muslim* veil. Wearers are identifiable as Muslims when they wear the veil. The property ascribed pertains to all users and is not contingent on the perceiving subject. It is understood to be a characteristic feature of the veil itself, in other words an objective feature which serves Muslim women to structure their social relations through the veil in diverse sociocultural contexts (majority and minority). Interobjective representations, such as the one pertaining to the Muslim veil, enable the emergence of a whole out of the interplay of various parts (Marsico et al., 2013).

However, not every distinct set of objectifications is resolved interobjectively. At times,

> T7: *distinct objectifications come together in conflicting or adversarial relations. Interobjective demands imposed by one objectification may negate the possibility of meeting a different set of demands prescribed by a different version.*

In these instances, representations that coexist may go on to clash in the public sphere. Bauer's (2015) example of food production provides an illustrative case of these dynamics. Representations of food as organic and sustainable may coexist in the same public sphere alongside other representations of food as genetically modified and industrially produced. These representations compete in the same public sphere to determine the reality of food production. The food available for us to eat is the outcome of the behavior of actors who sustain and propagate different notions of what we all should eat.

This example illustrates the genesis of states of cognitive polyphasia, in which different representations of the same object coexist in the same public sphere and/or the same individual (Jovchelovitch & Priego-Hernández, 2015). Plurality of representations, however, does not mean that all representations are accepted and granted equal value. As Jovchelovitch and Priego-Hernández (2015) argue,

> T8: *some representations are more valid than others due to the fact that they resonate with, are better aligned with local customs, or because they are held by more powerful actors.*

In these encounters, proponents of different objectifications rarely meet in symmetrical terms. In clashes between representations, the objectifications proposed by less powerful others are labeled as ignorant or otherwise deficient (Sammut & Sartawi, 2012; Sammut, Bezzina, & Sartawi, 2015). The differences between competing representations can be resolved in many ways, including the use of force and violence, or by appeal to a jointly recognized authority (Bauer, 2015; Jovchelovitch & Priego-Hernández, 2015). Were different parties to meet on equal terms, a process of normalization would ensue through deliberation and compromise (Bauer, 2015). In asymmetrical conditions, the knowledge of the nondominant minority group stands at best to be accommodated into the prevailing view, shifting it slightly in its favor. At worst, it is assimilated into the mainstream requiring compliance and conformity (Sammut & Bauer, 2011).

Aside from being the subject of diverse objec tifications, artifacts themselves may be implicated in the exercise of social influence. Asch (1987) notes that social interaction produces two outcomes, that is, social facts and technical artifacts. Social influence may be achieved through artifacts by fait accompli (Sammut & Bauer, 2011; Bauer, 2015), relying on the normative power of facts that what is ought to be (Bauer, 2015). Objects are thus strong enforcers in themselves. Erecting a wall to manage community relations represents a sociotechnical solution to framing community life. Artifacts are thus components of infrastructures that require the physiological and psychological adjustment of users. They are legitimate or illegitimate forms of achieving a social purpose and require reasoned consistency with a community's aims. In this way, artifacts constrain in a double sense – they enable as well as inhibit social interactions. The construction of the Berlin Wall inhibited routine relations between Western and Eastern Germans for many years. The destruction of the wall in 1989 enabled relations to ensue. At the same time, erecting the wall enabled a separatist form of social relations that, for a time, served mutual interests. Moreover, the destruction of the wall inhibited separatist distinctions between Western and Eastern Germans. Every social construction is thus accompanied by a social destruction of an objectification that fails. Sociocultural contexts, therefore, are not independent variables for human cognition. Rather, they provide a constitutive foundation for human activity (Jovchelovitch & Priego-Hernández, 2015).

Factual norms and things both facilitate and constrain human conduct. Human subjects may be required to conform. But they also have the ability to challenge some state of affairs by creating new objectifications that suit different relational demands.

T9: The making and breaking of objectifications and reifications is as relevant in understanding the psychological life of sociocultural subjects as the making and breaking of social norms.

To return to our previous example, a wall may be an object to keep trespassers at bay, but to a graffiti artist a wall is one big blank canvas. Different people in different sociocultural contexts produce different objectifications that serve to structure social life and establish social order. As Jovchelovitch (2007) notes, mapping out these differences is a central concern to sociocultural approaches to cognition. These require both an understanding of social norms as well as human conduct in terms of restrictions imposed by material-technical artifacts that are constructed to achieve particular purposes that particular groups seek to implement (Asch 1987; Bauer, 2015).

3.4 Interobjective Architecture

Sensitivity to interobjective issues can serve sociocultural psychologists to develop a fuller understanding of the complexity of human conduct. To this end, a review of how the notion of interobjectivity has been treated in architecture to investigate its effects in everyday life can be helpful.

Kärrholm (2014) argues that theories of architecture require a focus on interobjectivity due to the fact that the subject of study requires a complex understanding in terms of human and non-human subjects, objects, and other entities that among them comprise networks of activity that are the focus of architectural designs. We argue that these various entities are also pertinent with regards to understanding the psychological life of subjects. Kärrholm goes on to argue that interobjectivity concerns enable a focus on three types of effects pertinent to architecture, that is, (i) crossroads effects, (ii) stitching effects, and (iii) radiance effects. And in a similar vein, we argue that all three are pertinent to sociocultural psychological inquiry.

According to Kärrholm (2014), interobjectivity facilitates the understanding of crossroads effects. These refer to objectifications that act at cultural crossroads and have a similar impact in different contexts. Interobjectivity guided research thus serves to investigate how different configurations can have equal effects on movement across different cultures. The use of configurations of roads, for instance, serves to understand how the same effect could be achieved across different cultures by implementing different configurations that are consistent with local practices. This highlights a further point, that the effect of a configuration may not be similarly achieved in another setting in a similar way. This is not due to the objective characteristics of the configuration alone. The outcome depends on the relations achieved by the configuration that are contingent on local practices. Sensitivity to sociocultural features in architectural designs ensures that material configurations are tailored to the environment in which these configurations are required to perform. A solution achieved for one group may be best achieved using a different configuration in another group. Alternatively, a configuration may resolve an issue for one group but compound it for another. The outcome depends on normative, sociocultural prescriptions that precipitate different forms of conduct and, therefore, different relational forms with the object itself. Sociocultural psychology, we contend, is in a position to spell out the psychological component of these various relations.

A second focus outlined by Kärrholm (2014) is in terms of a relational ontology that investigates stitching effects. According to Kärrholm, all that can be known about a thing is the totality of the activity it performs in its different relations. In other words, objects can be known in terms of their actor roles in various networks of activity. Interobjectivity facilitates an understanding of how heterogeneous networks of diverse entities are formed and linked together. Although psychology typically adopts an exclusive focus on relations among human subjects, interobjectivity guided inquiry can serve to spell out how the various entities are linked and how particular forms of conduct may be achieved through the linking up of distinct entities that include nonhuman subjects or material artifacts. In this way, sociocultural enquiry is able to furnish an account of the various positions human subjects occupy in diverse networks and provide an understanding of how that positioning is sustained through sociocultural contingencies. For instance, it is hard to understand the various uprisings in Arab countries in recent years (otherwise known as the Arab Spring) without an understanding of technological developments such as social media. In a different sociocultural setting or a different historical epoch that did not include smartphones and Internet connectivity, the various uprisings may likely not have precipitated the effects they actually did. According to Kärrholm, a focus on stitching effects implies that entities, including human subjects, can be known by tracing the relations in which they partake, that is, by investigating their actor roles in different networks.

Finally, interobjectivity guided research also enables a focus on radiance effects. These refer to aspects of the object that may be obscure at first glance but that can emerge under inquiry by distinguishing what an object does as opposed to what an object is. The identity of an object emerges in tracing its stabilization over time through the proliferation of new relations. Every new relation in which an object is implicated could generate new actor roles, but this production of roles also serves to define similarities across the various interpretations of the object. The more an object is put to the test in different situations, the more its effects are stabilized.

These three foci of interobjectivity guided research serve to highlight diverse aspects of human activity with which sociocultural psychology is fundamentally concerned. Taking the example of a wall again, a focus on crossroads effects could spell out different meanings of an object for different social groups. One can therefore understand how an object erected to prevent trespassing could also serve as a canvas for graffiti. Both circumscriptions are associated with psychological activity such as safety and well-being. Looking at stitching effects, one can gain an understanding of how the wall features in productions involving a multitude of actors. Walls may serve to put in place a barrier that keeps out motor vehicles, for instance, but enables access to human subjects through a gate or a turnstile, erected at a particular location for a particular purpose. The boundary that serves to inhibit certain relational arrangements serves, conversely, to facilitate some others, as detailed above. Lastly, looking at radiance effects, the changing nature of walls serves to identify their canonical affordance (Costall, 2013) of a boundary marker in view of the relational demands imposed by the sociocultural context in which they materialize. An agricultural rubble wall serves to mark out territory. It is designed in such a way to restrict access from one territory to another. However, by virtue of its design, a rubble wall allows water to seep through to avoid the destruction of produce by excessive water in heavy rain. It also minimizes soil erosion as soil is prevented from being carried away from the field with excessive water. On the other hand, a glass wall in a modern office serves to mark out territory as well as providing a measure of privacy while, at the same time, retaining an element of scrutiny allowed by an observing eye.

We concur with Kärrholm (2014) that the investigation of meanings produced by artifacts in real life as well as the understanding of diverse forms of human conduct that rely on social constructions that take material form requires conceptual tools that enable the comparison of different object relations and how these overlap, contradict, or complement one another (p. 76).

3.5 Conclusions

The study of the effects of artifacts and architecture is a minority concern among social scientists, who more typically focus on cognitive activity alone or on social norms and cultural prescriptions. Social psychologists are often rolled in to make things happen and advise the innovation process as "acceptance providers" after the fact. The genesis and materiality of socially constructed environments seems to be a lesser concern to psychologists seeking to explain how the mind processes information that justifies a preferred and pre-given behavioral outcome. We argued that this exercise misses a critical point – that the world we navigate is made up of material objects which meet us in the course of our everyday social relations and which impede or facilitate particular courses of action. The functioning, coming, and going of artifacts require the same psychological sensitivity as the functioning of mind and behavior. In this chapter, we have proposed nine theses for how to understand interobjectivity as central for the study of social action and social relations. We hope to have provided sufficiently adequate conceptual tools to help sociocultural psychologists come to terms with the broad diversity of human conduct in its various manifestations and in the diversified cultural settings in which it occurs worldwide.

References

Asch, S. E. (1987). *Social Psychology*. Oxford: Oxford University Press.

Bauer, M. W. (2015). On (social) representations and the iconoclastic impetus. In G. Sammut, E. Andreouli, G. Gaskell, & J. Valsiner (Eds.), *The Cambridge Handbook of Social Representations* (pp. 43–63). Cambridge: Cambridge University Press.

Bauer, M. W. & Gaskell, G. (2008). Social representations theory: A progressive research programme for social psychology. *Journal for the Theory of Social Behaviour*, 38(4), 335–353.

Coelho, N. E. & Figueiredo, L. C. (2003). Patterns of intersubjectivity in the constitution of subjectivity: Dimensions of otherness. *Culture and Psychology*, 9, 193–208.

Costall, A. (2013). Things that help make us what we are. In G. Sammut, P. Daanen, & F. M. Moghaddam (Eds.), *Understanding the Self and Others: Explorations in Intersubjectivity and Interobjectivity* (pp. 66–76). London: Routledge.

Daanen, P. & Sammut, G. (2012). G. H. Mead and knowing how to act: Practical meaning, routine interaction and the theory of interobjectivity. *Theory and Psychology*, 22(5), 556–571.

Harré, R. & Sammut, G. (2013). What lies between? In G. Sammut, P. Daanen, & F. M. Moghaddam (Eds.), *Understanding the Self and Others: Explorations in Intersubjectivity and Interobjectivity* (pp. 15–30). London: Routledge.

Jovchelovitch, S. (2007). *Knowledge in Context: Representations, Community and Culture*. Hove, UK: Routledge.

Jovchelovitch, S. & Priego-Hernández, J. (2015). Cognitive polyphasia, knowledge encounters and public spheres. In G. Sammut, E. Andreouli, G. Gaskell, & J. Valsiner (Eds.), *The Cambridge Handbook of Social Representations* (pp. 163–178). Cambridge: Cambridge University Press.

Kärrholm, M. (2014). Interobjectivity in architectural research and theory: Towards a meta-theory of materiality and the effects of architecture and everyday life. *The Journal of Architecture*, 19(1), 64–80.

Kolakowski, L. (1972). *Positivist Philosophy: From Hume to the Vienna Circle*. London: Penguin.

Latour, B. (1996). On interobjectivity. *Mind, Culture and Activity*, 3(4), 228–245.

Marsico, G., Cabell, K. R., Valsiner, J., & Kharlamov, N. A. (2013). Interobjectivity as a border: The fluid dynamics of "betweenness." In G. Sammut, P. Daanen, & F. M. Moghaddam (Eds.), *Understanding the Self and Others: Explorations in Intersubjectivity and Interobjectivity* (pp. 51–65). London: Routledge.

Moghaddam, F. M. (2003). Interobjectivity and culture. *Culture & Psychology*, 9(3), 221–232.

Moghaddam, F. M. (2010). Intersubjectivity, interobjectivity and the embryonic fallacy in developmental science. *Culture & Psychology*, 16(4), 465–475.

Ross, L. & Ward, A. (1996). Naive realism in everyday life: Implications for social conflict and misunderstanding. In T. Brown, E. S. Reed, & E. Turiel (Eds.), *Values and Knowledge* (pp. 103–135). Hillsdale, NJ: Lawrence Erlbaum.

Sammut, G. (2015). Attitudes, social representations and points of view. In G. Sammut, E. Andreouli, G. Gaskell, & J. Valsiner (Eds.), *The Cambridge Handbook of Social Representations* (pp. 96–112). Cambridge: Cambridge University Press.

Sammut, G. & Bauer, M. (2011). Social influence: Modes and modalities. In D. Hook, B. Franks, & M. Bauer (Eds.), *The Social Psychology of Communication* (pp. 87–106). New York: Palgrave Macmillan.

Sammut, G., Bezzina, F., & Sartawi, M. (2015). The spiral of conflict: Naïve realism and the black sheep effect in attributions of knowledge and ignorance. *Peace and Conflict: Journal of Peace Psychology*, 21(2), 289–294.

Sammut, G., Daanen, P., & Moghaddam, F. M. (Eds.). (2013). *Understanding the Self and Others: Explorations in Intersubjectivity and Interobjectivity*. London: Routledge.

Sammut, G., Daanen, P., & Sartawi, M. (2010). Interobjectivity: Representations and artefacts in Cultural Psychology. *Culture & Psychology*, 16(4), 451–463.

Sammut, G. & Howarth, C. (2014). Social representations. In T. Teo (Ed.), *Encyclopedia of Critical Psychology* (pp. 1799–1802). New York: Springer.

Sammut, G. & Moghaddam, F. (2014). Interobjectivity. In T. Teo (Ed.), *Encyclopedia of Critical Psychology* (pp. 991–993). New York: Springer.

Sammut, G. & Sartawi, M. (2012). Perspective-taking and the attribution of ignorance. *Journal for the Theory of Social Behavior*, 42(2), 181–200.

Sandel, M. J. (2012). *What Money Can't Buy: The Moral Limits of Markets*. London: Penguin.

Wagner, W. (2015). Representation in action. In G. Sammut, E. Andreouli, G. Gaskell, & J. Valsiner (Eds.), *The Cambridge Handbook of Social Representations* (pp. 12–28). Cambridge: Cambridge University Press.

Wagner, W., Sen, R., Permanadeli, R., & Howarth, C. (2012). The veil and Muslim women's identity: Cultural pressures and resistance to stereotyping. *Culture & Psychology*, 18(4), 79–99.

4 "Mediationism" in Cognitive and Social Theory

Alan Costall

Mediationism extends across two contrasting approaches to theory in psychology. First, the dominant tradition of individualistic, cognitive theory, and, then, the still *too* loyal "opposition" consisting of various alternative approaches seeking "to ground activity previously seen as individual, mental, and nonsocial as situated, collective, and historically specific" (Bowker & Star, 2000, p. 288). These approaches, despite their important differences, are largely agreed on one thing: we do not, and *could* not, have "direct" contact with our surroundings. Something or other is always getting in our way: internal rules and mental representations, schemas, or prototypes, in the case of standard cognitive theory, or else discourse or social representations, for example, in the case of the opposition. And once mediation in general is viewed as an all-pervasive epistemological barrier, even the well-intentioned efforts of adults in helping children discover the meanings of things and in scaffolding their actions can only seem like intrusive ways of preventing those innocent victims from finding out what things are *really* like.

Mediation in various forms is widespread, including the new representational practices based around computers which despite being *our own practices* keep being attributed, within cognitive theory, to the computers themselves. Any proper approach to human psychology will clearly have to take mediation in its various forms into account. The problem with which I am concerned is *mediationism*, making a fetish of mediation, where the various forms of mediation become abstracted from their concrete circumstances.

The considerable attraction of mediationism has long been that it *seems* to provide solutions to a whole range of problems at the heart of the Western intellectual tradition. The trouble is that we have become so enchanted by mediationism that we seldom bother to look closely at the many different problems that it claims to solve. These problems should, on reflection, no longer be so compelling as they once seemed. So the "answer," then, might not be to try to solve them, but "to get over them" (Dewey, 1910, p. 19).

4.1 Mediationism in Mainstream Cognitive Theory

Within cognitive psychology, mediationism has primarily taken the form of *representationalism:* the appeal to internal rules and representations as a necessary and sufficient basis for explanation within human psychology. Representationalism is widely regarded as the means by which modern psychology finally broke free from the yoke of behaviorism. Yet, as Fodor (1981, p. 140) has noted, "insofar as the representational theory of mind is the content of the computer metaphor, the computer metaphor predates the computer by about three hundred years."

"Cognition" has long been *defined* in terms of representation (e.g., Leeper, 1951; Tomasello & Call, 1997, p. 10). What is (relatively) new is that, since the 1980s, psychology *as a whole* has come in effect to be defined as the study of cognition:

Put plainly, psychology – including developmental psychology – has been redefined as the study of cognition. Friendship has become social cognition, affect is seen as a form of problem-solving, newborn perception is subsumed under a set of transforming rules, and psychoanalysis is reread as a variant of information processing. Cognition, the feeble infant of the late Fifties and early Sixties, has become an apparently insatiable giant. (Kessen, 1981, p. 168)

Unfortunately, there are some fundamental problems with representationalism. Most of these were identified many years before the advent of modern cognitive psychology. These problems have not gone away (see, for example, Bickhard & Terveen, 1995; Harnad, 1990; Janlert, 1987; Pecher & Zwaan, 2005; Shaw, 2003; Still & Costall, 1991a). One serious problem concerns how we can intelligently apply rules and representations to actual situations. How do we decide when these rules and representations are appropriate to the circumstances at hand? The temptation, for the inveterate representationalist, is to invoke yet another level of representations to deal with this problem of situated action, but this merely defers this particular problem. Ultimately, there has to be something beyond representation to get us out of this regress.

Another problem concerns the origins of representations, and how they come to have meaning, and "map" onto the world. In traditional perceptual theory, for example, a profound gulf is assumed to exist between perceiver and world, and internal representations are then invoked to bridge the gap. But although these representations are then claimed to derive from the "past experience" either of the individual or the species, no coherent explanation is ever provided about how this *past* experience could possibly escape the severe limitations deemed to apply to the *present*. As far as I am aware, no cognitivist theorist has ever claimed that there was once a Golden Age when we all knew exactly what was going on – not even modern day "evolutionary

psychologists" with their bizarre fixation on the Pleistocene period.

Then there is the very curious status of representationalism as a *scientific* theory. Modern representationalists are, understandably, very keen to invoke scientific evidence in their support. But, in the very process of invoking objective, scientific evidence in the cause of representationalism, they keep sawing through the branches on which they claim to be sitting. Here, for example, is Richard Gregory unwittingly engaged in such tree surgery:

it used to be thought that perceptions, by vision and touch and so on, can give direct knowledge of objective reality . . . But, largely through the physiological study of the senses over the last two hundred years, this has become ever more difficult to defend . . . ultimately we cannot know directly what is illusion, any more than truth – for we cannot step outside perception to compare experience with objective reality. (Gregory 1989, p. 94)

At one moment, we are supposed to be perfectly capable of finding out *scientifically* what things are really like (as when we engage in the physiological study of the senses), and, at the next moment, the objective evidence thus gained is then supposed to convince us that we have been trapped all along within a "worldless consciousness:"

This worldless consciousness might be compared to a room without windows which is hung with innumerable and continually changing pictures. Apparently, the self is assumed to live locked up in this room and to ponder whether "beyond" there is perhaps a "world." Is there such a consciousness, a consciousness epistemologically prior to, i.e., more immediately accessible than, the world? (Duncker, 1947, p. 530)

Until now, cognitive psychologists have mainly dealt with such problems in the following unsatisfactory ways:

1 *Handwaving:* insist that the problems will ultimately be solved, and hence are not really fundamental problems at all (e.g., Johnson-Laird, 1988, p. 34).

2 *Passing the buck:* acknowledge that the problems are indeed fundamental, but *so* fundamental that they are evidently "metaphysical" and hence a problem for the philosophers, rather than the concern of serious, no-nonsense, scientists.

3 *The Jerry Fodor option:* keep a reasonably straight face and present the very strange implications of representationalism as exciting new discoveries (as in the Gregory example, above), rather than the *reductio ad absurdum* they might otherwise be taken to be.

Representationalism is now mainly identified with mainstream cognitive psychology and even within that field there is a growing, if still very limited, recognition of its problems, and the need to move on.

Of course, mainstream cognitive psychology is not the only game in town. A wide range of alternative approaches now challenge the decontextualized, individualistic approaches of mainstream cognitive research and theory, and these have come to emphasize, instead, the importance of the social and cultural. For such approaches, the foundational problems of cognitive science can seem remote, even quaint. But just as the celebrated overthrow of behaviorism led to a remarkably long bout of complacency among the cognitive psychologists, those of us claiming to have moved safely beyond cognitivism need to reflect on what we too might have unwittingly retained.

Representationalism is deeply ingrained within the Western tradition, and linked to a wide range of long-standing and half-forgotten agendas. It is these agendas that are the real problem, and so we need to be clear what they involve if we are not to find ourselves returning to some form or other of mediationism.

4.2 Representationalism in Social Cognitive Psychology

Two of the most influential current approaches within social psychology are frank extensions of individualistic cognitive theory to the interpersonal realm, and so it is hardly surprising that representationalism figures centrally in both. This is certainly true of the "theory of mind" approach (ToMism), which has been remarkably influential over the last thirty years, and assumes an explicit dualism between what we can directly observe about other people and their feelings, beliefs, and intentions. Such mental states are supposed to exist beyond the reach of "observation," however, this is not widely regarded as a special problem for psychology, since many other more reputable sciences are also mainly concerned with inferring hidden structures (such as genes, atoms, etc.) from empirical evidence (e.g., Harré, 2002). But if psychology can claim to be in good company as a science of the hidden, then we need to be very clear about the unusual extent of the concealment of its supposedly hidden subject.

The problem of inferring mental structures is usually framed in terms of the "poverty" of the stimulus, the underspecification of mental structure by any possible observations of behavior. So, according to the dualistic premises of ToM, the stimulus is not just impoverished, it is bankrupt. There could be *no* logical relation between what we can observe about another person and their intentions and feelings. The consequences are stark for any empirical science of psychology, and, of course, for our everyday dealings with other people. As Hammond and Keat (1991) have put it, if we are really faced with a dualism of body and mind, then "no deductively valid inference can be made from statements about one such 'part' of a person to statements about the other. In particular, one cannot validly infer, on the basis of knowledge of a body, any conclusion about a mind" (p. 205).

Proponents of ToM talk coyly about "mind-reading" (see Costall, Leudar, & Reddy, 2006). And, on the assumptions of ToMism, it would be truly a *miracle* that we can ever tell what other people are thinking or feeling, or, indeed, know that they have any kind of mental life at all. As Alan Leslie (1987, p. 422), one of the main proponents of ToMism, has put it: "It is hard to see how perceptual evidence could force an adult, let alone a young child, to invent the idea of unobservable mental states." This "hard" task of reading other people's minds is claimed to be soluble, nevertheless, in a perfectly non-mysterious, naturalistic way, thanks to the existence of special representational capacities or modules which are supposed to fill the gap between the observable and the unobservable. Yet, as with similar applications of the representationalist approach in perceptual theory, the postulated gap these representations are supposed to bridge is *so* great there is absolutely no way the knowledge embodied in the representations could derive from either individual past experience or even that favorite *deus ex machina* of recent psychological theory, "evolution" (e.g., Tooby & Cosmides, 1995, p. xvii). Not even natural selection could differentiate between differences that, according to these ToMists, are deemed to make absolutely *no* difference (for an extensive criticism of theory of mind, see Leudar & Costall, 2004a; Leudar & Costall, 2009).

One of the basic problems here is that cognitive psychology, despite its rhetoric of revolution, has retained the Watsonian, objectivized conception of behavior as *antithetical*, rather than logically connected, to the mental (see Costall, 2006a; Costall, 2013; Leudar & Costall, 2004b). As Harvey Carr rightly insisted, the term "objectivism" was more appropriate than "behaviorism" to describe Watsonian psychology, since, what was really distinctive about this position was "not a distinction of subject matter (behavior) but the objective view from which it is studied" (Carr, 1915, p. 309). As many of Watson's contemporary critics were well aware, not only was the conception of psychology as the study of behavior widely accepted before Watson tried to cause a stir, but also Watson was committed to exactly the same psychophysical dualism that had led some (but not all) of the "introspectionists" to suppose that introspection could be the only proper method for the study of mind:

Embedded in the very core of the behaviorist's doctrine is the Platonic distinction between mind and matter; and behaviorism, like Plato, regards the one term as real and the other as illusory. Its very case against dualism is stated in terms of that distinction and is made by the classical metaphysical procedure of reducing the one term to the other. This metaphysical distinction, rather than empirical evidence, is the basis on which behaviorism accepts or rejects data for scientific consideration and on which it forms conceptions for dealing with them . . . Behaviorism has adopted a metaphysics to end metaphysics. (Heidbreder, 1933, pp. 267–268)

Watson, who had been a student of John Dewey, claimed he never understood what Dewey was talking about. But Dewey, in contrast, was quickly onto Watson's case:

To conceive behavior exclusively in terms of the changes going on within an organism physically separate in space from other organisms is to continue the conception of mind which Professor Perry has well termed "subcutaneous." This conception is appropriate to the theory of existence of a field or stream of consciousness that is private by its very nature; it is the essence of such a theory. (Dewey, 1914/1977, p. 445)

In addition to retaining this objectivized conception of behavior, cognitive psychology also continues to formulate its basic task of explanation in terms of the classical behaviorist formula of "stimulus and response." Much of modern cognitive theory is, therefore, not an alternative to stimulus-response psychology, but just the most recent *elaboration* of that scheme:

an attempt, as in neo-behaviorism, to fill the gap: to provide explanations of "what is going on" between stimulus and response. People are supposed to be passively stimulated by events in their surroundings, and only then to become active – *and then only subcutaneously* – in interpreting what it all might mean on the basis of stored mental representations. This commitment to the stimulus-response formula is blatant, though hardly noticed, throughout the modern cognitivist literature:

At the individual level, social cognition is the mental "filter" through which objective events and experiences are subjectively represented and remembered. It is a basic premise of the "cognitive revolution" in psychology that individuals do not respond directly to stimuli from the external environment but to their perceptions and cognitive interpretations of those stimuli. (Brewer & Hewstone, 2004, p. xi)

In fact, this commitment to stimulus-response psychology is extensive not just in mainstream cognitive psychology, but in social-cultural psychology as well. For example, Brian Schiffer, in his book on the *Material Life of Human Beings*, also insists that we should go beyond the early behaviorists by constructing models "for elucidating the knowledge and cognitive processes *that connect stimulus and response"* (Schiffer, 1999, p. 8, emphasis added). And, Rom Harré (2002, p. 104), an influential critic of mainstream psychology and exponent of discursive psychology (and who surely *does* know better), has given the following example of word recognition to explain how we should theorize more generally within psychology:

Instead of the behaviorist pattern:
Stimulus (retinal sensation) → Response (perception of word) we must have
Observable stimulus (retinal sensation) together with unobservable Cognitive process ("knowledge utilization") → Observable response (recognition of word)

However, reading is not a "response" but an intelligent activity, and the so-called "retinal sensation" is itself an *outcome* of that activity, not its starting point. Stimulus-response accounts – of either the behaviorist or cognitivist kinds – start at completely the wrong end!

Another problem for which representationalism has long seemed the obvious solution concerns our susceptibility to errors and illusions. The standard line within psychological theory has been to conclude, on the basis that we (or, more precisely, *non*-psychologists) *sometimes* get things "wrong," that "just-plain-folks" are epistemological dupes. Thus, according to the "social cognition" approach, we can only know about other people in a necessarily indirect and generally hazardous way, given the limited and ambiguous evidence:

Judgments of such internal states as emotions, personality traits, and attitudes are often *extremely difficult*. The person's internal state cannot be observed directly – *it must be inferred* from whatever cues are available. (Taylor, Peplau, & Sears, 1994, p. 51; emphasis added)

The problem of limited available information ("the poverty of the stimulus") is compounded by the existence of a host of selective biases in judging other people (Smith & MacKie, 2000, p. 85). Curiously, however, the psychologists committed to this "error paradigm" (as Funder, 1995, has characterized it) clearly regard themselves as somehow immune from these epistemological limitations, and as perfectly well placed to assess the hopeless inaccuracies of "other people" in their attempts to make sense of *other* "other people." How else could they conclude that other people, namely non-psychologists, or just-plain-folk, are *wrong?*

Representationalism has always seemed the obvious way to explain such errors, but there is a snag – and it is a big one. Although its readiness to explain illusion has always seemed one of its most conspicuous strengths, representationalism is too effective. It cannot account for our *failures* to err!

> the representative theory of knowledge . . . satisfied the craving for a real and reliable world . . . by sequestering all error and untruth in a place apart, the "subjective" world. It is remarkable that this view has been found attractive and serviceable notwithstanding the fact that at the same time it provides that all that any person can experience or know is his own subjective world – the very stronghold of error. Of course it avails nothing that there is somewhere a real and true realm if it is for ever and completely shut out from the "subjective." (Holt, 1914, p. 259; see also Gibson, 1950, p. 159; Holt et al., 1912, p. 4)

The "problem of illusion," reappears in a more general and fundamental way within the Western intellectual tradition. For, according to the ontology of modern physical science, the very world as we experience and "dwell" in it must itself be regarded as one grand illusion. Within classical physical science, "nature" came to be defined according to the limits of its methodologies (mechanism, atomism, quantification), to sustain the claim that the new science could explain *everything*. And *everything else* – the so-called secondary and tertiary qualities (sensory and aesthetic qualities and also *meaning)* – was relegated to an alternative, shadowy existence beyond nature, the realm of representation:

> In general, the connections between the experiencing individual and the things experienced – conceived in their physical reality – were reduced to a passive conditioning of states of consciousness by a mechanical nature. Into such a mind was carried . . . whatever in nature could not be stated in terms of matter in motion . . . The result of this was to force upon the mind the presentation of the world of actual experience with all its characters, except, perhaps, the so-called primary characters of things. Mind had, therefore, a representational world that was supposed to answer to the physical world, and the connection between

this world and the physical world remained a mystery. (Mead, 1938, p. 359)

The dualism of mind and matter (including the body) certainly protected the claim of the new science to explain everything, but it was also congenial to already long established patterns of thought. The assumption that *we* are not part of nature has its origins in classical Greek philosophy and Christian theology.

Now, clearly, human beings pose an increasingly dangerous threat to the continued existence of life on earth, but this is precisely because we are part of this world, even though we keep acting as if we were not. Our presence, however, is not necessarily always malign, whereas the assumption that we do not really belong in this world can be. When, for example, the Yellowstone National Park was established in 1864, in an attempt to preserve that region in a state of "nature," the Native Americans who had been living there for thousands of years were either removed or else confined in reservations. Yet the presence of those people and their sustainable practices of hunting and use of fire were an important component of the very "nature" that the authorities had been trying to conserve (Hirsch, 2000; Cronon, 1996; Stevens, 1997).

Until this point, I have been presenting the various problems behind mediationism in the form of a list, and it is already getting long. But this is what is so tricky about mediationism: there are so many underlying problems that we easily lose track of what, exactly, they are, and hence whether they are really the kinds of problems that we should still be taking seriously. So let us engage in some interim stocktaking. Long after the supposed demise of stimulus-response behaviorism, does it really make sense to be framing the problem of psychology in terms of explaining what "goes on" between the stimulus and response? Should we really be framing our theories in terms of a Watsonian, objectivized concept of "behavior"? Is it reasonable to be taking the long-rejected ontology of mechanistic physics as a serious starting point for understanding the place of mind in – or *out* – of nature? After all, physical theory went through a whole series of radical transformations throughout the late nineteenth and twentieth centuries, and no longer needs to eject mind from nature, and thereby "set up" psychology as, in effect, the science of the "unscientific." As the philosopher, Arthur Bentley, nicely put it:

Since the "mental" as we have known it in the past was a squeeze-out from Newtonian space, the physicist may be asked to ponder how it can still remain a squeeze-out when the space out of which it was squeezed is no longer there to squeeze it out. (Bentley, 1938, p. 165)

There are, however, yet further influential sources of mediationism, and they are intimately interconnected. The first of these is "the spectator theory of knowledge" which treats the knower as essentially an observer rather than an agent. This visual metaphor of knowing posits an aloof God's eye view outside the system to be known:

The theory of knowing is modeled after what was supposed to take place in the act of vision. The object refracts light and is seen; it makes a difference to the eye and to the person having an optical apparatus, but none to the thing seen. The real object is the object so fixed in its regal aloofness that it is a king to any beholding mind that may gaze upon it. A spectator theory of knowledge is the inevitable outcome. (Dewey, 1969, p. 23)

This spectator theory of knowledge, in turn, leads to a conception of knowing as representation or correspondence:

If the knower, however defined, is set over against the world to be known, knowing consists in possessing a transcript, more or less accurate but otiose, of real things . . . Knowing is viewing from the outside. (Dewey, 1917, pp. 58–59)

This approach to knowledge as "viewing from the outside" is further encouraged by the fallacy of intellectualism, the assumption that true knowing is theoretical (*episteme*) not practical (*techne*), and that it is detached not engaged (Toulmin, 1976, p. 69; see also Falmagne, 1995; Ryle, 1999). To a remarkable extent, cognitive theory continues either to *identify* knowing with highly specific and derivative practices of *abstraction*, such as classification, computation, calculation, or logical inference, or else assimilates everything else to their terms, as in the claim that perceiving is nothing but a process of unconscious inference. Here is a recent example of this commitment to the priority of abstraction that comes, remarkably enough, from a book specifically concerned with "grounding cognition":

Our ability to interact appropriately with objects depends on the capacity, fundamental for human beings, for categorizing objects and storing information about them, thus forming concepts, and on the capacity to associate concepts with names. (Borghi, 2005, p. 8)

The primacy given to abstraction is most blatant in modern psychological theory in the form of theory of mind, and related "theory" approaches, where we are *all* supposed to be living on the basis of theorizing almost *all* of the time. Yet the very experience of theorizing itself has the strange effect of seeming to remove us from the world and from other people:

When we think, we shut ourselves within the circles of our own ideas and establish, as it were, a methodological solipsism. We behave as though we were "pure subjects," observers only, unimplicated in the dynamic relatedness of real existence. (MacMurray, 1961, pp. 20–21)

The still dominant computer metaphor of cognitive theory continues to be widely regarded as a serious challenge to dualism since "brain and mind are *bound* together as computer and program," or hardware and software

(Johnson-Laird, 1988, p. 23, emphasis added). But the metaphor proves to constitute a perverse kind of reaction and a strange kind of bond. The computer metaphor is an awesome condensation (in the Freudian sense) of most of the important problems behind mediationism. First of all, knowledge and meaning are identified with representation. And then the computer metaphor, far from being anti-dualistic, implies not only the antithesis of mind and matter, since the software is separable from *any* hardware, but also the antithesis of meaning and materiality, since meaning is located solely within the software as self-enclosed symbols. This is precisely why cognitivism has been claimed – with complacent approval – as "a science of structure and function divorced from material substance" (Pylyshyn, 1986, p. 68).

Furthermore, psychologists have been so enthralled by the software or program aspect of the computer metaphor, that they have hardly bothered to spell out what precisely the *hardware* is supposed to represent, not least, whether it refers to the mind, the brain, or the body. Either way, this hardware is no more than a stimulus-response – input–output – interface. Certainly, some theorists have invoked aspects of the hardware as part of the computer metaphor, such as the central processing unit, memory stores, and buffers. Yet it is John von Neuman's *ideal* of a computer as a "general purpose machine" – a machine whose function is completely unconstrained by the hardware – that formally underpins the supposed separability of software and hardware. In fact, Neumann did not himself hold with the computer analogy (see Freeman & Nunez, 2001)!

However, according to the ideal of the computer as a general purpose machine, the hardware (as mind, brain, or body) can have no explanatory relevance at all (see Costall, 1991, 2013). The computer metaphor, as it continues to underpin modern cognitivism, does not "bind" us to the world or to our bodies. It breathtak-ingly surpasses Descartes's own inconsistent and (relatively) nuanced version of dualism (Nadler, 1997).

4.3 Déjà Vu All Over Again

Mainstream psychological theory, even in relation to so-called social psychology, has remained resolutely individualistic, not just in focusing on the individual person, but also in regarding the social as derivative, an "overlay" on our fundamental, human nature. Within the confines of such approaches, mediationism has thrived on a "double dualism" – an epistemological dualism of knower and known and a psychophysical dualism which "conceives empirical reality to fall asunder into a world of mind and a world of matter mutually exclusive and utterly antithetic" (Lovejoy, 1929, p. 3).

Many decades before the rise of modern cognitivism, there was a wide reaction against this dualistic scheme, along with the representative theory of knowledge to which it gave rise:

The supposition, so long accepted as unchallengeable, that all apprehension of objective reality is mediated through subjective existents, that "ideas" forever interpose themselves between the knower and the objects which he would know, has become repellent and incredible to many of our contemporaries; and the cleavage of the universe into two realms having almost no attributes in common, the divorce between experience and nature, the isolation of the mental from the physical order has seemed . . . to be unendurable in itself and the source of numerous artificial problems and gratuitous difficulties. (Lovejoy, 1929, pp. 3–4)

This revolt against dualism was well motivated by important developments within science itself, not just the new physics but also Darwinian theory with its emphasis on the naturalistic origins of the human mind (Dewey, 1910). Yet, as far as modern cognitive theory is concerned, all this might never have happened.

But what about those alternative non-individualist approaches that put the emphasis on the "situated, collective and historically specific" (Bowker & Star, 2000, p. 288)? Vygotsky has, of course, been an important historical influence on many of these alternative approaches, yet his own contrast between the cultural and biological lines of human development, and the way his developmental scheme prioritizes "intrapersonal" and abstract modes of thought are hardly unproblematic (Still & Costall, 1991b; Wertsch, 1996). And James Gibson, for whom the material conditions of shared experience and knowledge was an important concern (see Heft, 2001), and whose concepts such as "affordance" and "proprioception" provide important resources for a non-dualistic psychology (Costall, 2006b), unwittingly set a number of awkward traps. One of these was his failure to foreground our activity *within* and *on* the world. His approach remained largely within the schema of knowledge as *perception* (the spectator theory of knowledge). According to Edward Reed, Gibson's radical move was to shift the focus from a passive perceiver, to "the active self *observing* its surroundings" (Reed, 1988, p. 201; emphasis added). But this is not a sufficiently radical move. *Exploratory* activity does not, in itself, *change* things. Indeed, Gibson's account of affordances (i.e., the meanings of things for our possible actions) is itself framed in terms of observation, since, according to Gibson, the central claim of the theory of affordances is that "the 'values' and 'meanings' in the environment can be *directly perceived*" (Gibson, 1979, p. 127; emphasis added). Even Gibson's concept of "direct perception" is problematic because it became defined, by contrast, with so many diverse senses of "indirect or mediated," including *"socially* mediated," that it is hardly applicable to human perception at all (Costall, 1988, 1990). Despite his many profound contributions, Gibson's "direct perceptionism" is thus a counterpart, rather than a real alternative, to mediationism.

So, what about the more recent writings in the broad area of sociocultural psychology? Well, to a very large extent, we find either socialized reformulations of the traditional, individualistic dualisms, or derivative dualisms, most importantly those between nature, on the one hand, and culture, or else, history, on the other.

First of all, there is wide agreement among the "opposition" about the importance of representation, and the need to understand representation in a nonindividualistic way, and with this I have no objection. However, the general line would seem to be that we should go further, and, as in traditional theory, take representation to be *primary:*

> Where discursive and cultural psychology come together is in the recognition given to the primacy of representation (discourse, mediation, etc.), and its location in situated social practices rather than abstracted mental models. (Edwards, 1995, p. 63)

But what, then, do these representations *represent?* Just further representations? Once again, we find ourselves in "the room without windows" with just pictures on the walls. Thus, as in *some* versions of social constructivism (see Danziger, 1997), a realm of the "socially constructed" interposes itself between us and nature, and through which we cannot reach the world itself:

> It is not that constructivists deny the existence of external reality, it is just that there is no way of knowing whether what is perceived and understood is an accurate reflection of that reality. (Marshall, 1996, p. 30)

The long-standing dualism of materiality and meaning also reappears in a social guise, where meaning is not necessarily confined to individual mental representations, but to a separate domain of the symbolic:

> we must not confuse the material world, where things and people exist, and the symbolic practices and processes through which representation, meaning and language operate. Constructivists do

not deny the existence of the material world. However, it is not the material world which conveys meaning: it is the language system or whatever system we are using to represent our concepts. It is social actors who use the conceptual systems of their culture and the linguistic and other representational systems to construct meaning, to make the world meaningful and to communicate about that world meaningfully to others. (Hall, 1997b, p. 25)

Even researchers studying "*material* culture" generally take a similar line, downplaying the importance of materiality in favor of a separate realm of what is, in effect "*immaterial* culture" (cf. Costall, 1995; Hutchby, 2001; Ingold 2000; Thomas, 1999). To a remarkable extent, the concept of "culture" is now widely *identified* with representation and the symbolic. Here, for example, is Clifford Geertz's well-known definition of culture:

A historically transmitted pattern of meaning embodied in symbols, a system of inherited conceptions expressed in symbolic form by means of which men communicate, perpetuate, and develop their knowledge about attitudes towards life. (Geertz, 1975, p. 89)

But the basic point is repeated throughout the literature:

what does representation have to do with "culture": what is the connection between them? To put it simply, culture is about "shared meanings." Now, language is the privileged medium in which we "make sense" of things, in which meaning is produced and exchanged. Meanings can only be shared through our common access to language. So language is central to meaning and culture and has always been regarded as the key repository of cultural values and meanings. (Hall, 1997a, p. 1)

to explain culture is to answer the following question: why are some representations more successful in a human population, more "catching." (Sperber, 1996, p. 58)

Culture emerges from nature as the symbolic representation of the latter. (Ellen, 1996, p. 31)

How do the sociocultural avant-garde keep backing themselves into these theoretical corners? The fact that there is such a close "recapitulation" of the state of individualistic psychology suggests that we have not entirely avoided many of the problems that have always constrained and distorted traditional psychology. Indeed, much of the good rhetorical effect of social constructivism has itself depended on a traditional notion of nature – of the *natural* – as fixed, universal, and unaffected by *us*. Furthermore, much of the nuttiness of postmodernism would seem to reflect its failure, maybe refusal, to "get over" the modernist scheme it claims to have undermined (see Shalin, 1993).

These problems are compounded by others more specific to the sociocultural approaches. The first of these is a kind of methodologism where the limitation of a research method comes (as was the case in classical physical science) to define the limits of the object of study. Early anthropology was of necessity "a science of words" (Mead, 1975, p. 5) since there were no means of effectively recording gestures and actions, and indeed many of the traditional practices under study were matters only of recall, having been suppressed by the missionaries within whose train the anthropologists tended to follow. Yet, many current researchers restrict their attention to texts and transcriptions of speech, and although this, in itself, is clearly a matter of choice, they often also come close to implying that the *only* things we ever *do* are with words. And they can prove remarkably evasive when challenged on this point. Here, for example, is Michael Billig's defense of the discourse analysts' emphasis on talk, based on a deft prevarication between an inclusive and a disjunctive meaning of "action":

Discursive psychologists might be suspected of only taking words into account and not actions.

However, that is not so, for the criticism assumes that in social behavior there is a clear distinction between words and action. This is contested by "speech-act theory," which is a philosophical position underlying much work of conversation analysis . . . According to speech-act theory, making an utterance is itself an action; also many actions are performed through utterances . . . It is easy to exaggerate the difference between words and actions, as if the latter were more "real" than the former. (Billig, 1997, pp. 46–47)

A further source of trouble concerns the delicate balance between, on the one hand, demonstrating the importance of the specific sociohistorical conditions, and, on the other, *going too far*, and rendering the subjects of our studies *so alien* they no longer seem to count as "one of us." An emphasis on differences between people can appear sinister not just on the basis of "race" but also their cultural practices, as became the case for the Vygotsky-inspired expedition to study the "primitive" mentality of Uzbek peasants (see Joravsky, 1989, p. 364). Eventually, some residue is identified which is claimed to be immune from "the effects of culture," such as the lower mental functions or the irrational (see Connelly & Costall, 2000). But, as Shweder and Sullivan (1990, pp. 407–408) have pointed out, the basic cognitivist schema of structure and content has also been highly influential, where cultural influences are supposed to be restricted to the *contents* of a biologically fixed *structure*: the central processing mechanism. Although this certainly manages to draw a bottom line, and ensure some kind of ultimate unity for humankind, it is at the considerable cost of a retreat once again into the dualisms of culture *versus* nature, and culture *versus* biology.

Finally, the dualisms of matter and mind and of biology and culture are institutionalized in the very structure of modern academic disciplines. On the one hand, there are the natural and the engineering sciences and, on the other, the human or social sciences. The natural sciences have abstracted for themselves a "material world" set apart from human concerns, while the social sciences, in their turn, have constructed "a world of actors devoid of things" (Joerges, 1988, p. 220). Interdisciplinary efforts to bridge this divide, such as the "environmental sciences," have hardly thrived. They have either fractured along the old divide or else retreated to the safety of "hard science" (see Kwa, 1987).

4.4 Getting Over Mediationism

There are remarkably many different ways of talking ourselves into mediationism. Taking note of those different ways, as I have tried to do in this chapter, is just a first step toward getting over mediationism. At the beginning of the twenty-first century, the problems behind mediationism really ought no longer to appear quite so vital or urgent as they once did. Paradoxically, it might also help to set the clock back in psychological theory, to well before both modern cognitivism and postmodernism, and return to the remarkable writings of figures such as John Dewey, George Herbert Mead, and even William James, and their emphasis on the *mutuality*, rather than the duality, of mind and world (Costall, 2004):

traditional theories have separated life from nature, mind from organic life, and thereby created mysteries . . . Those who talk most of the organism, physiologists and psychologists, are often just those who display least sense of the intimate, delicate and subtle interdependence of all organic structures and processes with one another . . . To see the organism in nature . . . is the answer to the problems which haunt philosophy And when thus seen they will be seen to be in, not as marbles are in a box but as events are in history, in a moving, growing never finished process. (Dewey, 1958, pp. 278, 295)

My purpose in this chapter has emphatically *not* been to deny or minimize the importance of various kinds of mediation in human existence. I am not trying to argue for some kind of "direct" theory either of immaculate perception or even action. What I have been trying to challenge is the appeals to mediation as a way of bridging the very big gaps that we assume are supposed to separate us from the world, when, paradoxically, mediation, invoked in this way, just makes matters worse. *It always gets in the way.* It is these very gaps, opened up by dualistic thinking, that *are* the problem. Whereas mediationism, given its dualistic premises, can only regard mediation as an impenetrable barrier *between* ourselves and the world, we need to remember that our social practices of mediation are, for better or worse, taking place in the world, and actually changing it by "constitut[ing] objects not constituted before" (Mead, 1934, p. 78).

Mediationism obscures the very *conditions of possibility* for social mediation. If we are going to make sense of *mediation*, how it originates and is sustained, we will need to find a place in our theories for the existence of both meaning and mediation *before and beyond* the realm of representations and symbols, and take their materiality much more seriously. Psychological theory needs to become worldly and move beyond the antitheses of nature and history, and of materiality and meaning (Costall, 1995; Costall & Dreier, 2006). We are, in the end, *part* of what nature has become.

Acknowledgments

I am very grateful to Ivan Leudar, Patrick Renault, Ann Richards, Cintia Rodriguez, and the editors of this Handbook for their helpful comments.

References

Bentley, A. F. (1938). Physicists and fairies. *Philosophy of Science, 5,* 132–165.

Bickhard, M. H. & Terveen, L. (1995). *Foundational Issues in Artificial Intelligence and Cognitive Science: Impasse and Solution.* Amsterdam: Elsevier Scientific.

Billig, M. (1997). Discursive, rhetorical, and ideological messages. In C. McGarty & S. A. Haslam (Eds.), *The Message of Social Psychology: Perspectives on Mind in Society* (pp. 36–53). Oxford: Blackwell.

Borghi, A. M. (2005). Object concepts and action. In D. Pecher & R. A. Zwaan (Eds.), *Grounding Cognition: The Role of Perception and Action in Memory, Language, and Thinking* (pp. 8–34). Cambridge: Cambridge University Press.

Bowker, G. C., & Star, S. L. (2000). *Sorting Things Out: Classification and Its Consequences.* Cambridge, MA: MIT Press.

Brewer, M. & Hewstone, M. (2004). Introduction. In M. Brewer & M. Hewstone (Eds.), *Social Cognition* (pp. xi–xii). Oxford: Blackwell.

Carr, H. A. (1915). Review of J. B. Watson (1914). Behavior: an introduction to comparative psychology. *Psychological Bulletin, 12,* 308–312.

Connelly, J. & Costall, A. (2000). R. G. Collingwood and the idea of an historical psychology. *Theory & Psychology, 10,* 147–170.

Costall, A. (1988). A closer look at direct perception. In A. Gellatly, D. Rogers, & J. A. Sloboda (Eds.), *Cognition and Social Worlds* (pp. 10–21). Oxford: Clarendon Press.

Costall, A. (1990). Picture perception as "indirect" perception. In K. Landwehr (Ed.), *Ecological Perception Research, Visual Communication and Aesthetics* (pp. 15–22). New York: Springer.

Costall, A. (1991). Graceful degradation: Cognitivism and the metaphors of the computer. In A. Still. & A. Costall (Eds.), *Against Cognitivism* (pp. 151–170). London: Harvester-Wheatsheaf.

Costall, A. (1995). Socializing affordances. *Theory and Psychology, 5,* 467–481.

Costall, A. (2004). From Darwin to Watson (and cognitivism) and back again: The principle of animal-environment mutuality. *Behavior & Philosophy, 32,* 179–195.

Costall, A. (2006a). "Introspectionism" and the mythical origins of scientific psychology. *Consciousness and Cognition, 15,* 634–654.

Costall, A. (2006b). On being the right size: Affordances and the question of scale. In G. Lock & B. Molyneaux (Eds.), *Confronting Scale in Archaeology: Issues of Theory and Practice* (pp. 15–26). New York: Springer.

Costall, A. (2007). Bringing the body back to life: James Gibson's ecology of agency. In J. Zlatev, T. Ziemke, R. Frank, & R. Dirven (Eds.), *Body, Language and Mind. Vol. 1: Embodiment* (pp. 241–270). The Hague: Mouton de Gruyter.

Costall, A. (2012). Introspection and the myth of methodological behaviourism. In J. W. Clegg (Ed.), *Self-observation in the Social Sciences* (pp. 67–80). New Brunswick, NJ: Transaction.

Costall, A. (2013). The unconscious theory in modern cognitivism. In T. P. Racine & K. L. Slaney (Eds.), *A Wittgensteinian Perspective on the Use of Conceptual Analysis in Psychology* (pp. 312–327). London: Palgrave Macmillan.

Costall, A. & Dreier, O. (2006). *Doing Things with Things: The Design and Use of Objects*. London: Ashgate.

Costall, A., Leudar, I., & Reddy, V. (2006). Failing to see the irony in "mind-reading." *Theory & Psychology*, 16, 163–167.

Costall, A. P. & Still, A. W. (1989). James Gibson's theory of direct perception and the problem of cultural relativism. *Journal for the Theory of Social Behaviour*, 19, 433–441.

Cronon, W. (Ed.) (1996). *Uncommon ground: rethinking the human place in nature*. New York: W.W. Norton.

Danziger, K. (1997). The varieties of social construction. *Theory & Psychology*, 7, 399–416.

Dewey, J. (1910). The influence of Darwin on philosophy. In *The Influence of Darwin on Philosophy and Other Essays* (pp. 1–19). New York: Henry Holt & Co. (First published in *Popular Science Monthly*, July 1909.)

Dewey, J. (1914/1977). Psychological doctrine and philosophical teaching. In S. Morgenbesser (Ed.), *Dewey and His Critics* (pp. 439–445). New York: Journal of Philosophy. (First published in the *Journal of Philosophy Psychology and Scientific Methods*, 1914, 11(19).)

Dewey, J. (1917). The need for a recovery of philosophy. In J. Dewey (Ed.), *Essays in the Pragmatic Attitude* (pp. 3–69). New York: Holt.

Dewey, J. (1958). *Experience and Nature*. New York: Dover. (Based on the Paul Carus lectures of 1925.)

Dewey, J. (1969). *The Quest for Certainty*. New York: Putnam.

Duncker, K. (1947). Phenomenology and epistemology of consciousness of objects. *Philosophy and Phenomenological Research*, 7, 505–542.

Edwards, D. (1995). A commentary on discursive and cultural psychology. *Culture and Psychology*, 1, 55–65.

Ellen, R. (1996). Introduction. In Roy Ellen & Katsuyoshi Fukui (Eds.), *Redefining Nature: Ecology, Culture and Domestication* (pp. 1–36). Oxford: Berg.

Falmagne, R. J. (1995). The abstract and the concrete. In L. M. W. Martin, K. Nelson, & E. Tobach (Eds.), *Sociocultural Psychology: Theory and Practice of Doing and Knowing* (pp. 205–228). Cambridge: Cambridge University Press.

Fodor, J. A. (1981). *Representations*. Cambridge, MA: MIT Press.

Freeman, W. J. & Nunez, R. (2001). Restoring to cognition the forgotten primacy of action, intention and emotion. In R. Nunez & W. J. Freeman (Eds.), *Reclaiming Cognition: The Primacy of Action, Intention and Emotion* (pp. ix–xix). Thoverton, UK: Imprint Academic.

Funder, D. C. (1995). On the accuracy of personality judgment: A realistic approach. *Psychological Review*, 102, 652–670.

Geertz, C. (1975). *The Interpretation of Cultures*. New York: Basic Books.

Gibson, J. J. (1950). The implications of learning theory for social psychology. In J. G. Miller (Ed.), *Experiments in Social Process* (pp. 120–133). New York: McGraw-Hill.

Gibson, J. J. (1979). *The Ecological Approach to Visual Perception*. Boston: Houghton Mifflin.

Gregory, R. L. (1989). Dismantling reality. In H. Lawson & L. Appignanesi (Eds.), *Dismantling Truth: Reality in the Post-modern World* (pp. 93–100). London: Weidenfeld and Nicolson.

Hall, S. (1997a). Introduction. In Stuart Hall (Ed.), *Representation: Cultural Representations and Signifying Practices* (pp. 1–11). London: SAGE.

Hall, S. (1997b). The work of representation. In Stuart Hall (Ed.), *Representation: Cultural Representations and Signifying Practices* (pp. 13–64). London: SAGE.

Hammond, H. & Keat, R. (1991). *Understanding Phenomenology*. Oxford: Blackwell.

Harnad, S. (1990). The symbol grounding problem. *Physica D*, 42, 335–346.

Harré, R. (2002). *Cognitive Science: A Philosophical Introduction*. London: SAGE.

Heft, H. (2001). *Ecological Psychology in Context: James Gibson, Roger Barker, and the Legacy of William James's Radical Empiricism*. Mahwah, NJ: Lawrence Erlbaum.

Heidbreder, E. (1933). *Seven Psychologies*. New York: Century.

Hirsch, P. D. (2000). Beyond discipline: toward effective partnerships between conservation biologists and ecological anthropologists. Unpublished manuscript, Department of Ecology, University of Georgia.

Holt, E. B. (1914). *The Concept of Consciousness*. London: George Allen.

Holt, E. B., Marvin, W. T., Montague, W. P., Perry, R. B., Pitkin, W. B., & Spaulding, E. G. (1912). *The New Realism: Cooperative Studies in Philosophy*. New York: Macmillan.

Hutchby, I. (2001). Technologies, texts and affordances. *Sociology*, 35, 441–456.

Ingold, T. (2000). *The Perception of the Environment: Essays in Livelihood, Dwelling and Skill*. London: Routledge.

Janlert, L. E. (1987). Modeling change: the frame problem. In Z. W. Pylyshyn (Ed.), *The Robot's Dilemma: The Frame Problem in Artificial Intelligence*. Norwood, NJ: Ablex.

Joerges, B. (1988). Technology in everyday life: Conceptual queries. *Journal for the Theory of Social Behaviour*, 18, 219–237.

Johnson-Laird, P. (1988). *The Computer and the Mind*. Cambridge, MA: Cambridge University Press.

Joravsky, D. (1989). *Russian Psychology: A Critical History*. Oxford: Basil Blackwell.

Kessen, W. (1981). Early settlements in new cognition. *Cognition*, 10, 167–171.

Kwa, C. (1987). Representations of nature mediating between ecology and science policy: The case of the International Biological Programme. *Social Studies of Science*, 17, 413–442.

Leeper, R. (1951). Cognitive processes. In S. S. Stevens (Ed.), *Handbook of Experimental Psychology* (pp. 730–757). New York: John Wiley & Sons.

Leslie, A. (1987). Pretense and representation: The origins of "theory of mind." *Psychological Review*, 94, 412–426.

Leudar, I. & Costall, A. (Eds.). (2004a). Theory of mind. *Theory & Psychology* (special issue), 14(5), 571–752.

Leudar, I. & Costall, A. (2004b). On the persistence of the problem of other minds' in psychology: Chomsky, Grice and "theory of mind." *Theory & Psychology*, 14, 603–662.

Leudar, I. & Costall, A. (2009). *Against Theory of Mind*. London: Macmillan Palgrave.

Lovejoy, A. O. (1929). *The Revolt against Dualism: An Inquiry Concerning the Existence of Ideas*. LaSalle, IL: Open Court.

MacMurray, J. (1961). *Persons in Relation*. London: Faber & Faber.

Marshall, H. H. (1996). Clarifying and implementing contemporary psychological perspectives. *Educational Psychologist*, 31, 29–34.

Mead, G. H. (1934). *Mind, Self and Society*. Chicago: Chicago University Press.

Mead, G. H. (1938). *The Philosophy of the Act*. Chicago: University of Chicago Press.

Mead, M. (1975). Visual anthropology in a discipline of words. In P. Hoskins (Ed.), *Principles of Visual Anthropology* (pp. 3–10). The Hague: Mouton de Gruyter.

Miller, G. A., Pribram, K., & Galanter, E. (1960). *Plans and the Structure of Behavior*. New York: Holt.

Nadler, S. (1997). Descartes's dualism? *Philosophical Books*, 38(3), 157–169.

Pecher, D. & Zwaan, R. A. (Eds.). (2005). *Grounding Cognition: The Role of Perception and Action in Memory, Language, and Thinking*. Cambridge: Cambridge University Press.

Pylyshyn, Z. (1986). *Computation and Cognition*. Cambridge, MA: MIT Press.

Reed, E. S. (1988). *James J. Gibson and the Psychology of Perception*. New Haven, CT: Yale University Press.

Ryle, G. (1999). Reason. *Linacre Journal*, 3, 71–84.

Schiffer, M. B. (with A. R. Miller). (1999). *The Material Life of Human Beings: Artifacts, Behavior, and Communication*. London: Routledge.

Shalin, D. N. (1993). Modernity, postmodernism, and pragmatist inquiry: An introduction. *Symbolic Interaction*, 16, 303–332.

Shaw, R. E. (2003). The agent–environment interface: Simon's indirect or Gibson's direct coupling. *Ecological Psychology*, 15, 37–106.

Shweder, R. A. & Sullivan, M. A. (1990). The semiotic subject of cultural psychology. In L. A. Previn (Ed.), *Handbook of Personality: Theory and Research* (pp. 399–416). New York: Guilford Press.

Smith, E. R. & MacKie, D. M. (2000). *Social Psychology* (2nd edn.). London: Psychology Press.

Sperber, D. (1996). *Explaining Culture: A Naturalistic Approach*. Oxford: Blackwell.

Stevens, S. (Ed.). (1997). *Conservation through Cultural Survival: Indigenous Peoples and Protected Areas*. Washington, DC: Island Press.

Still, A. & Costall, A. (1991a). The mutual elimination of dualism in Vygotsky and Gibson. In A. Still. & A. Costall (Eds.), *Against Cognitivism* (pp. 225–236). London: Harvester-Wheatsheaf.

Still, A. & Costall, A. (Eds.). (1991b). *Against Cognitivism*. London: Harvester Press.

Taylor, S. E., Peplau, L. A., & Sears, D. O. (1994). *Social Psychology* (8th edn.). Englewood Cliffs, NJ: Prentice-Hall.

Thomas, J. (1999). Some problems with the notion of external symbolic storage, and the case of Neolithic material culture in Britain. In C. Renfrew, & C. Scarre (Eds.), *Cognition and Material Culture*. Oxford: McDonald Institute Monographs.

Tomasello, M. & Call, J. (1997). *Primate Cognition*. Oxford: Oxford University Press.

Tooby, J. & Cosmides, L. (1995). Foreword. In S. Baron-Cohen, *Mindblindness: An Essay on Autism and Theory of Mind* (pp. ix–xviii). Cambridge, MA: MIT Press.

Toulmin, S. (1976). *Knowing and Acting: An Invitation to Philosophy*. New York: Macmillan.

Wertsch, J. V. (1996). The Role of Abstract Rationality in Vygotsky's Image of Mind. In A. Tryphon & J. Voneche (Eds.), *Piaget-Vygotsky: The Social Genesis of Thought* (pp. 25–43). Hove, UK: Psychology Press.

5 Sociocultural Psychology and Interpersonal Psychoanalysis: The Semiotic Space in the Consulting Room

Philip J. Rosenbaum

5.1 Introduction: Shared Origins

There have been any number of theories aimed at understanding what transpires in the consulting room between therapist and patient. These have ranged from Freud's aspirations of making the unconscious conscious, to the more structured approaches of cognitive therapy that involve changing maladaptive belief patterns. My personal training has been in interpersonal psychoanalysis.

Historically, interpersonal psychoanalysis is a less known branch of psychoanalysis, originating during the 1930s and 1940s in the United States as a conglomeration of the works of Harry Stack Sullivan (1953a, 1953b), Eric Fromm (1941, 1951, 1956), Freda Fromm-Reichmann (1950), and Clara Thompson (1950/2003) (see also Stern et al., 1995 for a good overview of key figures and papers). Drawing heavily from the work of the American pragmatists, especially George Herbert Mead (1967) and William James (1890/1950), as well as a wide range of influences, including the linguist Edward Sapir (Sullivan, 1953a), the psychiatry of William Alanson White (Sullivan, 1953a), and the biology of Kurt Goldstein (Fromm-Reichmann, 1950), interpersonal psychoanalysis provided a needed alternative to the Freudian and ego psychoanalysis, which, especially in the United States, were the dominant forms of psychoanalysis (Rosenbaum, 2015a; Levenson, 2002). More recently, interpersonal psychoanalysis has achieved some prominence as a central contributor (along with British object relations) to the currently in vogue relational psychoanalysis (Harris, 2011; Stern, 2013).

Notably, and not surprisingly, given its overlapping influences, interpersonal psychoanalysis also shares quite a bit with cultural psychology. For example, interpersonal psychoanalysis sees the individual as a social being, always in important relationships (not just limited to the mother) that shape their growth and development. Furthermore, interpersonal psychoanalysis considers the self as multiple and thus provides an alternative to essentialist views of the self. Indeed, as early as 1950, Harry Stack Sullivan controversially declared that the self is an illusion, by which he meant that there is no aspect of the self, which is untouched by relationships (Rosenbaum, 2015a). In other words, there is no essential self that exists outside of relationships. While, at the time, this was a source of criticism and derision – interpersonal psychoanalysis has often been accused of being a "social science" and a branch of social psychology – recent developments have touted the multiplicity of self (Bromberg, 1996, 1998; Stern, 2009, 2015; Hermans, 2001; Hermans & Kempen, 1993) and the constitutive role of culture in shaping and guiding individual experiences.

These similarities are perhaps why I felt most comfortable studying interpersonal psychoanalysis given my early education as a cultural psychologist. Indeed, I have often been surprised at the lack of dialogue between cultural psychology and interpersonal psychoanalysis, as, to me, they make sense as complementary partners in thought (Stern, 2009). Not only do they share similar forefathers, as it is likely that Sullivan was not just influenced by Mead, but also the works of Charles S. Peirce (Rosenbaum, 2015b), but also philosophical and theoretical traditions. For instance, as I will elaborate below, interpersonal psychoanalysis reflects a decidedly pragmatic mindset, particularly as it relates to the importance of semiotic mediation (Rosenbaum, 2015a, 2016). Moreover, I would argue that both interpersonal psychoanalysis and sociocultural psychology are interested in understanding similar phenomena, namely, how people make meaning and construct experience. Finally, they are also both field theories.

Where they differ is in the lens they take to explore this and the goals or targets of exploration. Interpersonal psychoanalysis focuses primarily on the individual and therapeutic dyad and then occasionally extracts to the broader social context, with an aim on helping one (though sometimes both) party live their lives differently. In contrast, sociocultural psychology often starts at the level of the social and moves downward to the individual, with an interest in explicating a wider array of day-to-day processes. Moreover, as interpersonal psychoanalysis has an interest in psychopathology, or what goes wrong in individual relationships and meaning making, and in alleviating suffering from psychopathology, its emphasis is often on clinical technique and intervention. Alternatively, as sociocultural psychology is more broadly interested in the impact of culture on daily living and not a psychotherapy, there is greater room for the study of novelty, creativity, and a wider range of study. However, I view these differences as potentially

constructive areas of dialogue, which will help each field develop in new and productive ways. This is in part because of their similarities that can be seen in their methodological approaches as both are interested in the micro-genetic or moment-to-moment study of psychological processes as a method toward understanding what happens in real time.

With this in mind, my goal in this chapter is to bring these schools of thinking into greater dialogue with each other. I will begin by describing interpersonal psychoanalysis, particularly focusing on the works of important historical and contemporary clinicians. I will then shift my focus to discussing the ways in which sociocultural psychology may understand similar phenomena and how using the broader top down lens can benefit practitioners in the consulting room. In order to allow for the fullest sense of dialogue, I will pay particular attention to meaning making as understood by each school, including areas of agreement, disagreement, and needing more discussion.

5.2 The Interpersonal School

While, as stated above, interpersonal psychoanalysis began with a convergence of thinkers, the work of Harry Stack Sullivan stands out as the most systematic and comprehensive study of interpersonal conduct. For Sullivan (1938/1995, 1953a, 1953b) our proficiency as sign users, particularly our ability to make meaning of and to understand the sign usage of others while also making ourselves clear and proficient communicators, was of central importance.

He was, notably, an early adopter of field theory. Sullivan acknowledged Kurt Lewin's work (Sullivan, 1953b; Stern, 2013) and while he did not explicitly work with Lewin's language, the ideas of field theory are implicit throughout his writing. Thus, Sullivan discussed the interpersonal field considering it to be the range of thoughts and interpretations available to the patient and therapist at any given point in time. The field supports the quality of meanings that are available to be made by an individual.

5.2.1 Sullivan's Three Different Modes of Meaning Making

Sullivan considered the interpersonal field as "a continuous, inevitable social aspect of human living . . . an omnipresent, concrete, empirical reality, a sociological and psychological fact that permeates and helps to constitute every moment of every human being's life" (cited in Stern, 2013, p. 489). Individuals cannot exist outside of the field, which for Sullivan was patterned and shaped by our earliest interpersonal interactions and cultural experiences and leads to recurrent ways of thinking, feeling, and relating. Thus, Sullivan (1953a) states, "The human being requires the world of culture, cannot live *and be human* except in communal existence with it. The world of culture, is however, clearly manifest only in human behavior and thought. Other people are, therefore an indispensable part of the environment of the human organism" (p. 38).

Human development requires mediating cultures, environments, and other people, and for Sullivan leads to three types or modes of thinking (1953a, 1953b). These progress from the most disordered to normative and range in terms of clarity, organization, degree of privacy, how communicable they are, and so forth. While all individuals retain and engage in these different styles of thinking throughout their lives (i.e., they move in and out of them at different times and contexts) they can also loosely map onto different developmental periods (Rosenbaum, 2015b).

Prototaxic experiencing: The first level of thinking Sullivan termed "prototaxic." Here, thinking is not goal directed or in many senses even comprised of thoughts at all, but is more chaotic, unlinked, and unclear. It is almost like private unorganized impressions, feelings, impulses, and so forth. Diagnostically, prototaxic

thoughts are most often found in schizophrenics who are unable to communicate; though developmentally, they may also map onto very young babies and children for whom the world is felt more as impression than organized experience.

Parataxic experiencing: Prototaxic thinking gives way to what Sullivan termed parataxic thinking; which while also private, is a more organized and social way of thinking. In parataxic thinking, the individual has often begun to order the world and their experiences, but does so in overly simplistic terms (black and white), without attention to detail, or necessarily facts (data). Thus, like prototaxic thinking, parataxic thought has not been "consensually validated," but unlike prototaxic thinking can potentially become the subject of dialogue and discussion.

Syntaxic experiencing: Thinking subjected to "consensual validation," the acknowledgment of others, leads to the development of the most advanced way of thinking and being, known as "syntaxic." Consensually validated ideas are largely symbolic, having become known through relating to someone else. Thinking in a "syntaxic" fashion allows for the self to make more appropriate meanings of situations and experience and thus clears up the distorted thinking and behavior that Sullivan felt was at the heart of most pathology. Interestingly, while seeing things more clearly may alleviate distress and discomfort it often involves dealing with the source of anxiety, though hopefully with a greater range of freedom and choice.

5.2.2 Systems of Defense

Notably, Sullivan considered the use of both prototaxic and parataxic thought as a defense, which arose from our need to protect ourselves from negative appraisals of others, which would hurt our self-esteem (1950, 1953b). He described the "self-system" as the part of the self, which is always reaching out from our experience (consciously or not) to keep anxiety at a minimum and our self-esteem as high as possible.

This means that the relationships we have as children impacts our later ability to relate through shaping the field of possible interactions between those that raise anxiety and those that lower anxiety. Since individuals are comfortable (less anxious) with what they know and find predictable, they may act in ways that prevent them from achieving happiness and satisfaction; but instead help them feel secure. For instance, Sullivan (1953a) writes: "And so the unhappy child who grows up without love will have a self dynamism, which shows great capacity for finding fault with others and by the same token, with himself" (p. 22).

While finding fault with others and oneself may not lead to satisfaction, it does (re)create a sense of security through predictable relationships. The extent to which we as individuals are able to recognize patterns and then think and feel about them will shape the fields of our potential experience. For Sullivan, there is a double mechanism of action here. First, we may "selectively inattend" to the aspects of others that cause us anxiety. Thus, the unhappy child would likely not pay attention to the behaviors of others that they do not find fault with, as these could threaten their sense of security. Simultaneously, we may also inattend to the parts of ourselves that arouse anxiety in others and so the critical child may not necessarily even realize how they are affecting others. In this form of "parataxic thinking" the individual's thoughts have not been consensually validated and so are generalized, private, and distorted (Rosenbaum, 2015b; Sullivan, 1953b). In this regard, the field of meanings narrows considerably as other areas of possible meaning making are strongly blocked off.

Thus, we might say that Sullivan developed a theory of how individuals unconsciously protect themselves from constructing meaning out of their experiences if they anticipate that it will cause them anxiety. The degree to which

they anticipate anxiety relates to the strength of the distortion, with prototaxic distortions being stronger than parataxic. Notably, this is a different type of unconscious than the Freudian drive-based model of the unconscious, acting on the very selection of details from which to base meaning and experience.

For example, Lauren, a young female patient is convinced that she is not good at anything and believes no one likes her. Despite plenty of evidence to the contrary, including being a 4.0 student and involved with a number of successful clubs and activities, she feels insecure, and has low self-esteem. In this case, Sullivan, would through the use of what he termed the detailed inquiry (1953c), a way of interviewing patients, attempt to both determine the historical and current veracity of her claims (i.e., what are the facts as it were) and also open up the parts of her story that she is not attending too, presumably because they cause too much anxiety.

Thus, while the facts may be that Lauren is quite an excellent student with a number of friends, it is also true that she does not feel or see it this way. Why not? Here, there are any number of possible scenarios that we can imagine. For instance, Lauren's parents may have seen her success as a way of her separating from them, an idea which they found threatening, preventing them from validating her accomplishments. Alternatively, perhaps her parents only valued her success when she did a perfect job, implying that anything less than perfect is not good enough. Or, finally, maybe Lauren's parents secretly felt threatened by Lauren's success and so competed with her.

In all of these instances, her relationships to her parents and their relationship to her (and her success) are important and help constitute her own experience. They structure the field of available meanings – especially when Lauren is a young child and may lack other fields to draw from (such as friends, or alternative cultural scripts). Without access to a wider array of symbolic resources (see Chapter 10, this volume) Lauren may struggle to bridge the gaps between her own experiences and her parents responses, thus shaping the meaning she attaches to them.

Consider the first example where success is a form of separation. This may be very threatening to her parents who, although wanting her to succeed, also want her to remain close to them. As such, they may unintentionally communicate that while being successful is good, separating is bad. In eliciting negative reactions from her parents, when positive ones are expected, Lauren may come to feel confused about being successful and feel that she is not good enough at making her parents happy. She may develop an idea of being successful and liked as "bad," with this part of herself becoming labeled the "bad me" (Sullivan, 1953a, 1953b). Indeed, she may even think that her success is bad because it causes distance and a negative reaction. For Sullivan, until she can develop a more accurate idea about what being successful means (and have new experiences around this as well) it may be hard for her to feel good about herself.

Notably, Lauren herself may not be aware that she attaches this value judgment to success. The anxiety around exploring this "bad me" keeps her experience confused and distorted (parataxic as it were) and prevents Lauren from formulating other possible meanings or even interpreting the situation more accurately – that is, my parents appreciate my success but are also upset by it.

Even more problematic may be the second or third scenarios. Here, we can imagine that Lauren's parents in only validating and acknowledging Lauren when she has been perfect, or in not acknowledging their own competition with her, may create a type of experience where Lauren has not felt that her good self has been seen. In Sullivan's thinking (1953a, 1953b), this creates a type of "not-me" experience, where the patient dissociates themselves from any recognition of their accomplishments.

Unlike in the first example, where meaning is made of experience and generalized into the organizer of "bad"; in these two examples defensive processes prevent the construction of meaning at all. Lauren, for instance, might not be able to articulate much about her experience, resorting to saying "I don't know" and in fact meaning it. The prospective anxiety associated with not being perfect is so great that Lauren cannot recognize herself in the experience to create meaning.

Whatever the case, for Sullivan, Lauren, like all of us, suffers from a distorted view of herself and the important people in her life. Further complicating the picture is that Sullivan was sensitive to the adaptive aspect of these defensive postures. For Lauren, feeling not good enough may also have been a source of motivation, a futile attempt at proving her worth that was doomed to defeat.

5.2.3 In the Consulting Room

We might say that Sullivan felt that patients were not fully semiotically competent. They failed to either adequately interpret the world or communicate about their inner experiences within the world, or some combination of both. In the consulting room, he would work to demonstrate to the patient their patterns of conduct. Working in what has been termed the "here and now" by focusing on the way they relate to others in their lives (or himself) he would connect to the "there and then." Doing so demonstrates to patients the ways their conduct is meant to protect their self-esteem. As people become less bent on protecting themselves from the aspects of their personalities they've learned are bad or even not to be considered, they develop greater semiotic capacities to more accurately interpret reality, and thus resolve pathology.

Working to establish data points was essential for Sullivan (1938/1995). Like his pragmatic forefathers he was wary of too much metatheory. He would try to avoid conjecture, instead sticking with the data, which could include the patient's history, collaborative history, and also how they interacted with him (Sullivan, 1953c). Clarity into their situation through the use of data was thus an important goal of the consulting room. The therapist was a "participant observer," both involved in the patient's life and also outside it. Through their participation they would become aware of the areas of distortion and through their distance, they could offer expert commentary on the patient's "problems in living."

In this regard, Sullivan was very much a thinker of his times, believing in an objective reality and that it was knowable, even while acknowledging the inevitability of participation (Rosenbaum, 2015a). The therapist (or generally psychiatrist, in his terms) was expert in both aspects of participating and observing. In this regard, Sullivan, while describing different modes of experience, was not a constructionist interested in how meaning was made. Thus, while his thinking is decidedly oriented toward the field the patient inhabits, it was with the bent of resolving distorted thinking.

While distortions problematically limit the field of possibilities they are also inevitable. In emphasizing how distortions result from anxiety about the way we are seen, Sullivan provides an important contribution to the way individuals make meaning. Notably, meaning making processes are always shaped by our past experiences which we are bringing into our current context. We are motivated by the unconscious desire to appear in ways we find favorable to ourselves (whatever those might be) and others. The meanings we make about ourselves may then shape and influence future meanings in a feed forward system (Valsiner, 2007).

Of course, having said this, Sullivan was not interested in elaborating theory, but instead helping patients. Thus, he saw himself in the role of expert asserting which meanings were right and wrong (or at the very least, better and worse). In this regard, his theory of meaning making is

not particularly interested in dreams, fantasy, and imagination, but is overly constrained to interpreting situations in particularly normative fashions. It does not emphasize novelty, multiplicity, or creativity. Luckily, some of the more recent interpersonal psychoanalysts have further developed Sullivan's theory.

5.3 Recent Contributors

5.3.1 Edgar Levenson

Since Sullivan's somewhat premature death in 1949 the field of interpersonal psychoanalysis has continued to develop. One of the most prominent interpersonal thinkers is Edgar Levenson who further elaborated Sullivan's semiotic ideas. In his early and seminal work, Levenson (1979/2005, 1983/2005) utilized structuralism to make a series of important contributions to Sullivan's work.

First, for Levenson, since language itself is structured semiotically, to speak with someone is also to act with them. As a result, he does not think the therapist could be an objective observer, but is always a subjective participant with the patient (1989). This idea has certain important ramifications. It minimizes the importance of the analyst focusing on "acting out" or the ways patients may act out feelings about the therapy and therapist outside of the room while enhancing the importance of what happens within the room. Given the nature of the consulting room, where the patient does most of the talking, the relationship is slanted. As the patient's language is given priority, Levenson feels that the analyst is constantly being impinged on by the possibilities of transformation (1979/2005, 1991). In other words, the patient's language structures the analytic space in an attempt to transform the therapist, pulling them to act in certain familiar ways similar to how others act with them. The therapist then enacts certain roles that other people may have played with the patient or currently play with the patient. This continues the shift of focus to their "here and now" in order to, in Levenson's words, figure out "what is going on around here" (Levenson, 2003).

In considering language as semiotic, Levenson (1983/2005) is aware that the patient's language always carries with it all of its past associations and relations, which are brought to bear on the therapist who is in fact a new person. For Levenson (2003) this semiotic component enables the therapist to visualize what they are being told almost as if watching a movie or play unfold (Levenson, 1982). One role of the therapist is to then try and spot what is missing; the holes in the Swiss cheese of the narrative and inquire into these areas. Levenson postulates that this is where the patient's anxiety about their bad and not-me selves resides and so they have glanced over important aspects of the story. Inquiry in turn creates a vector, if you will, within the therapeutic field where the therapist becomes pulled into acting in ways familiar to the patient. While the interactions with the patient could be understood as historical, for Levenson this would remove the power from them, as they are also transpiring within the therapeutic room (Levenson, 1989).

Returning to Lauren who was discussed earlier, Levenson might argue that she would unconsciously, but inevitably, attempt to draw the therapist into acting in a number of important roles. For instance, she may cast the therapist as someone to whom she is looking for approval and then dismiss the therapist when they offer support. Similarly, Lauren may act like she wants the therapist to solve her problems and then in turn reject their attempts at doing so. For Levenson, working with the patient to understand what this form of interpersonal conduct is about is an important part of treatment. Perhaps, Lauren does not trust the therapist but is afraid of saying this. In this way she could possibly communicate her distrust of the therapist, suspecting them of hidden motives (i.e., not really wanting her to be successful since that would mean separation

and even the end of treatment) and in fact being rejecting of her. Although the therapist could resist this transformation, the patient's unconscious interpersonal dynamics would inevitably win out, until the therapist found themselves in some way rejecting the patient.

Notably, this could not necessarily be predicted. While the therapist may be aware of these qualities of Lauren's parents, until they themselves enact it with the patient, they do not quite know it in a consensually validated way. In other words, since the therapist and patient have not experienced these qualities together they are in many respects unknown to each other. These enactments, as they have been labeled, are not only ways of intimately understanding known past dynamics, but also a way of experiencing with the patient how they are in current relationships as well (Levenson, 1991).

Levenson considers enactments as ubiquitous and unavoidable. We are always in some ways enacting something with our patients. This is because we share similar language at the cultural and structural level, or, as he observes, to talk with someone is also to act with them. Thus, our actions always reverberate and are echoes of previous interactions – the source of enactments. These occur at varying levels of awareness. Just to be aware of a particular enactment, even to work around it, does not resolve the potential for enactments, but means that something else is already being enacted. For Levenson then, these occur at higher levels of abstraction (1982, 1991). In this regard, Levenson does not consider enactments to result solely from distortions on the part of the patient, but instead involve real aspects of the therapist and the therapeutic dyad (Levenson, 1991).

For example, a patient and I are talking about his relationship to dominant women. He prefers to be submissive, often giving himself over to their will and needs. We postulate in one particularly meaningful session that his submission is a way of maintaining a relationship, but also creating important space from his intrusive and controlling mother. As the session ends, I instruct him to set reminders for future sessions as he has a tendency to forget, thus reenacting the very dynamic we had been discussing!

In this regard, unlike for Sullivan whose goal was to clear up distorted thinking in all its forms, Levenson considers the therapeutic task as becoming more aware of the process of enactments, from which we can never step outside of, but hopefully instill a greater range of freedom and choice in our daily lives.

5.3.2 Donnel Stern

Levenson's work on enactments has been expanded by more contemporary interpersonal analysts, most notably Donnel Stern and Philip Bromberg. Stern (2003, 2009, 2015) has focused his attention on what he calls unformulated experiences. He considers these to be similar to Sullivan's parataxic distortions thinking of them as parts of the patient's experiences that are dissociated. Influenced by hermeneutic philosophy, especially that of Hans-Georg Gadamer, Stern argues that patients are unable to construct or formulate their experience in order to know it and learn from it (2003).

For Stern (2003), dissociation differs from repression in that when something is repressed it is metaphorically pushed outside, down, and away from consciousness, but when something is dissociated it never existed in consciousness to be repressed. Interestingly, Stern's theory is notably and explicitly a field theory (2009, 2015). The patient cannot formulate experience because the necessary conditions within the field to construct meaning are not present.

Dissociation comes in both a weak and strong sense (Stern, 2003). In weak dissociation the patient may have never considered a certain possibility; whereas in strong dissociation, something, often trauma, interferes with the patient's ability to formulate experience. In the former

case the therapist may be able to comment on aspects of the experience that the patient had not thought of or considered; whereas in the latter they are not able to at first.

For instance, a patient talking about his experiences could not understand why his friends seemed happy at a difficulty he was having. I wondered whether they had been envious of the patient's earlier successes. When I asked this the patient responded that he had not considered this, but it made sense to him. In this case, I was able to see something that he had not. We talked about why this may have been and noted that competition was a part of the patient's life with which he was uncomfortable. An older sibling, the patient said that he often felt like he had to be supportive of his younger siblings and there was not much room in his family for the times that he felt angry or annoyed with them.

In strong dissociation, both the therapist and the patient are unable to formulate experience. Note that this has considerable overlap with Levenson's idea of enactment. For Stern, the only way to realize that something has been dissociated from the therapeutic field is for an enactment to occur (2004). Here, the therapist has a sense of what Stern calls chaffing, a feeling that something is not right. This hard to pin down and identify feeling may occur at any time, but especially when something does not quite make sense or add up. In these cases, both parties have dissociated something important. Moreover, he argues that the therapeutic field does not have the required qualities of relatedness (more on this in a moment) to allow either party to venture into the space required to understand what is occurring.

For example, in a recent case presentation where I talked about a patient who was in an abusive and unsatisfactory relationship, it was pointed out to me that I did not ask what possible benefit or satisfaction the patient could have been receiving as a result of being in that relationship. The discussant postulated that we were involved in an enactment where both she and I were dissociating as a result of the roles we felt forced to play (Mark, 2016, personal communication). For me, the pressure of the field was to provide advice and I entered into the role of "rescuer," wanting to get the patient out of a bad situation. For her, it was important to present herself as in need of help (expert advice), keeping the more vulnerable and angry parts of herself outside of the room.

In another case, a patient had been talking about a relationship that was frustrating her for some time. In discussing it with me I did not quite understand what was causing her distress and to be as upset with her partner as she was. It was only after they broke up that I had the feeling of chaffing that Stern alludes to and realized that we had not been talking about sex. As it turns out, the patient was unfulfilled by her partner. However, the shame of talking about sex meant that she did not bring it up with me. So strong was her feeling of shame that I did not even think of inquiring until months later. Learning about their problematic sex life shed a whole new light on the content of what we had been talking about allowing us to understand better what had transpired.

In this respect we could say that the dissociation occurred between us as a result of the fact that our field of relatedness did not allow us to even imagine or be curious about what was happening in the bedroom. Stern notes that shame can often have this effect. It essentially creates taboo zones within the field where the patient cannot go. These can be so strong as to prevent the therapist from going there as well.

Stern (2015) considers the quality of relatedness between patient and therapist as the essential aspect of the field. Both parties contribute to the field and so neither can stand outside of it. In this manner, Stern's work further extends the work of Levenson by more explicitly considering how the mutually created field between patient and therapist (referred to by others as the "third") involves contributions from both the patient's past and present and also their therapist's past and present. Thus, the ability of both parties to formulate is constantly being brought into existence and also threatened by the presence of the other and the way they are relating. This quality ebbs and flows not only between sessions but also during sessions as well. In some cases, the field may be overly constricted, such as when the therapist is being forced to play a particular role (and also of course can identify with that role). For the therapist, one of the important goals of therapy is allowing for greater relational freedom, whereby both patient and therapist can adopt different roles and perspectives. What makes exploring this possible is the collaboration between patient and therapist.

5.3.3 Phillip Bromberg

Greater freedom allows both parties to adopt and explore their different selves and self-states. When discussing self-states, the work of Phillip Bromberg is particularly important. Bromberg (1998, 2006, 2011) details both clinically and theoretically how people are composed of different self-states. These can be thought of as different forms of consciousness or self-organization to which we have greater or lesser access. Drawing heavily from trauma theory (2003) and object relations theory (1998), Bromberg postulates that people become stuck when they are unable to "stand in-between the spaces" of these self-states. Thus, someone whose experience is that of a victim, aggressor, eating disordered individual, overachiever, and so forth may struggle to adopt and inhabit other possible selves. For Bromberg (1998), our different self-states can also achieve a type of "self-truth," which is a narrative that establishes boundaries around the characteristics each state contains (i.e., cognitive, affective, physiological, self, self-other, and so forth).

For example, a young man I work with talks about his identity as a survivor of sexual assault. At the time of the assault, however, he reports freezing and being unable to defend himself from the stronger older male aggressor. This was a traumatic and destabilizing experience for him. In response, later in life he has become an advocate for other survivors of assault, constantly looking to stand up for them in ways that he felt unable to stand up for himself. However, in situations where he feels even slightly anxious or threatened his traumatized self emerges and takes over, preventing him from acting to protect himself through common-sense actions that are readily available to him. We both marvel at the presence of these two separate selves that he cannot seem to integrate.

We can again see the overlap with Sullivan's crucial idea of distortion. For Bromberg, other selves are not only inaccessible, but in more extreme cases, we can say in Donnel Sterns language, strongly dissociated. Notably, this is often the result of some form of interpersonal trauma that makes identifying with different aspects of self and other impossible (Bromberg, 2003, 2006). As a result, the person is stuck within a particular mode and pattern of relating. They bring this mode of being into the consulting room. Since other selves have been dissociated the therapist though alert to these possibilities cannot access them and stumbles along with the patient the best they can (Bromberg, 2000). Similar to Stern, in order for the patient to begin to learn to find a new place to stand or even recognize themselves in different contexts, the therapist has to be able to imagine the patient differently (Bromberg, 2003, 2011). However, this is tricky, since if the therapist does not acknowledge and recognize the patient's current self-state they are unable to help them find new ones.

Whereas Stern pays particular attention to the quality of relatedness between therapist and patient from moment to moment, Bromberg is more interested in the affective feel of the patient (though there is a lot of overlap between the two). He has elaborated Sullivan's detailed inquiry from a focus on establishing what actually transpired in the patient's history to tracking the affective states of the patient (Bromberg, 2011). Bromberg seeks to help the patient expand and elaborate on their feeling states in order to help them expand their field of awareness. In the detailed inquiry of affective states Bromberg looks for dissociation, particularly around painful feelings not tolerable within one given self-state (2006, 2011). In lessening the dissociative pull, he hopes that patients can learn to effectively hold more than one self-state, moving them from the realm of having to act in a particular way to having a choice or range of possible actions.

Notably, certain self-states cannot be held because they are seen as intolerable or threatening to the dominant self. Much like Stern, Bromberg (1998) does not consider selves as repressed due to conflict, but rather not brought into existence in order for conflict and repression to ensue. As patient's become better able to tolerate and express different selves, conflict between the ideas, wishes, goals, motivations, and so forth of these selves may in fact emerge and become repressed. These could then be the target of interpretative efforts and pointing out the defensive forces that may be at work to keep them repressed.

5.4 Some Important Considerations

These recent contributors have signaled a shift from focusing primarily on the content of the patient's experience, what they say, to the study of ongoing psychic process. Today's therapists are more interested in how the patient goes about being themselves, which includes making meaning out of experience, regulating their emotional world and interpersonal reactions (Beebe & Lachmann, 1998, 2003). Therapists are especially attuned to how these processes play out in the consulting room. Here, the therapist shifts from becoming solely the interpreter of the patient's experience to a co-participant and co-constructor of meaning (Aron,

1991, 2001; Beebe & Lachmann, 1998, 2003; Benjamin, 1988, 1998; Boston Change Group, 2007; Bromberg, 2011; Stern 2009, 2015; Butler, 1990; Cushman, 1995; Greenberg & Mitchell, 1983; Hoffman, 1991; Mitchell, 1988, 1997). The therapist also invites the patient to participate in constructing their own experience, recognizing that the subjectivity of the therapist plays a crucial role in shaping the interpersonal field (Hoffman, 1983; Ehrenberg, 1992). Mind and selves are seen as emerging from within the interpersonal process, rather than existing independently waiting to be discovered and understood from outside of the field (Stern, 2015).

There are two important questions of interpersonal psychoanalysis ideas to briefly respond to before moving forward. First, what happens to the patient's internal world, the intrapsychic of phantasy, dream, unconscious motivation, and so forth? While critics (Mills, 2011; Eagle, 2003) have argued that the patient's mind becomes obscured from an interpersonal and relational perspective, this is not the case at all. Indeed, if anything, the internal world of the patient becomes richer and more elaborate. Although it may seemingly lack the drama of the Freudian or Kleinian landscape (to mention a few), the intrapsychic can instead be more fruitfully considered as reflecting the ongoing relationships between self-other.

The therapist still remains primarily interested in the patient's hopes and dreads, fears and wishes (Mitchell, 1995), but acknowledges that these can only be known and experienced within an interpersonal context. To speak of an aspect of a patient's internal world already requires an acknowledgment of the external world. In this respect, they are mutually constitutive, much like Valsiner (2007) has described with personal culture always being constituted within the broader societal context. This adds an important dimension to understanding these domains, which may be better thought of as private and public, respectively. From my perspective, considering the intrapsychic as standing in relation to interpsychic phenomena only adds richness and complexity through considering the ways that motivations, defenses, desires, and so forth may exist in multiple, paradoxical, and contentious ways.

The second set of questions to consider concerns the idea that anything goes for interpersonal psychoanalysts (Greenberg, 2001). Since most interpersonal therapists consider realities like selves as plural and multiple they are often accused of being relativists. However, this is not the case. Stern (2004, 2015) and Bromberg (2011), for instance, both makes it clear that reality is always constrained by a host of social and personal factors and considerations. Context and normative standards determine the extent to which meanings can be made (Bruner, 1990). Straying outside of these, while often a place of creative expressions, may also, if gone too far, represent psychotic processes or at the very least prevent one's meaning and intention from being known and appreciated (Marková, 2003a). So while there are many possible realities and areas of exploration and meaning, they also exist within the range of what can be consensually validated.

It may be that the complaint of anything goes has more to do with clinical technique, how the therapist or analyst do therapy and analysis. By now, it should be clear that the techniques in interpersonal and relational psychoanalysis differ considerably from what has historically been considered the techniques of "classical," "Freudian," or "Ego" psychoanalysis. Much as the move from classical to contemporary theory and practice has been seen as going from "one person to two persons"; technique has followed (Hoffman, 1983). However, again, changes in technique do not mean that anything goes. Boundaries, discipline, and common sense still are quite important as are typical ways of working, as well as the focus being on the patient's life as opposed to the therapists (Tublin, 2011). In fact, it is the discipline on the part of the therapist, whether this revolves around the detailed inquiry (Sullivan, 1953a), listening for "holes in the narrative" (Levenson, 1982), or establishing an intimate quality of relatedness (Stern, 2015) that creates and ensures the potential for therapy to take and for patients to get better. Thus, as we return our attention to the consulting room it should be clear that while there are many ways of working, it would be misleading to say that any of them go.

5.5 Sociocultural Psychology and the Semiotic Space in the Therapeutic Field

From the contemporary viewpoint of therapy, the actual relationship between therapist and patient is mutative (Levenson, 1979/2005, 1982). It is a laboratory for understanding and experiencing – often in real time – the ongoing psychological processes used by the patient to relate to themselves and others in the world. It is, I think, fair to say that these ongoing psychological processes of relating to self and other are decidedly semiotic as are the ways of talking about them (Levenson, 1979/2005, 1983/2005; Sullivan, 1953a, 1953b; Stern, 2003, 2009, 2015; Cushman, 1995). They are thus also cultural (Valsiner, 2007), playing an important role in constituting the individual self (Heft, 2012), and developmental. Talking, interacting, feeling, exploring all have in common the ongoing usage and interpretation of signs to inform how experience is understood and meaning is made. Furthermore, they occur within interpersonal and intrapersonal fields (Valsiner, 2007). While this is of course the case for all talk therapies, as is hopefully clear from the section above, interpersonal psychoanalysis is unique in its *conceptualization* and *realization* of the field as a semiotic and therapeutic space.[1]

Notably, as stated earlier, whereas interpersonal psychoanalysis focuses on the individual and expands upwards, sociocultural psychology, instead, focuses on the cultural and social and works downwards toward the individual

(Lehman, 2014). Considering some of the ways that individual conduct is always grounded and constituted by larger sociocultural factors provides an important complement to what transpires within the consulting room. In other words, locating therapy within broader social contexts is important for understanding what transpires within the consulting room and how it may be mutative.

In this regard, from a sociocultural perspective, therapy shares similarities and differences with other socially informed locale and experiences, such as places of prayer, doctor's offices, restaurants, shopping malls, sporting events, and so forth, where public and private selves meet (Bruner, 1990; Valsiner, 2009). The consulting space does not offer just any type of relationship, but, more specifically, a highly regulated one replete with unique constructions, ideas, goals, processes, boundaries, and so forth (Baranger & Baranger, 1961/2008; Abbey, 2007; Rosenbaum, 2016). Indeed, like with other – perhaps all – regulated social experiences, how individuals navigate, or get through them, in order to make meaning, is an important component for their own well-being.

The similarities and differences between these social situations and therapy are in fact important for the therapeutic process to take hold. Patients often come into therapy as a result of problems in navigating these other environments, such as work or family life, and struggle to see the ways that they may in fact trap themselves. And as stated above, that these processes often inevitably play out between therapist and patient speaks to the structural and semiotic components of meaning making.

In considering meaning-making processes as field phenomena, sociocultural psychology extends field theory to all domains of psychological phenomena (Salvatore, 2016; see also Chapter 2, this volume). In this regard, the psychopathology of distorted meaning making and interpersonal relationships described in the previous section are but one psychological phenomenon among many that sociocultural psychology studies. Indeed, through paying attention to culture and context, sociocultural psychology may not necessarily see the processes above as distorted or pathological, but may instead see them as reflections of different aspects of culture. Moreover, while interpersonal psychoanalysis has its writing on other phenomena (creativity, group process, and so forth), its history is one that is decidedly practical and focused on helping alleviate individual suffering. For sure, this is a noble cause, but a cultural perspective is needed to help more fully understand how mind and psychology work as it pertains to both pathological and nonpathological processes.

Cultural psychology, while not necessarily a unified field, has identified a number of important aspects of intentional meaning-making processes. These include the importance of cultural boundaries, both physical and psychological, a host of regulating processes, the centrality of language, and the importance of context.

5.5.1 Field Theories: Boundaries and Regulatory Processes

Culturally informed boundaries delineate the spaces within fields where an individual (or therapeutic dyad in our case) can travel. Boundaries can be physical, including the objects and tools in the material world, but also psychological or some combination of the two. Boundaries guide meaning-making processes, they both facilitate the construction of meanings in certain directions while also limiting them in others. This dual action of directing both through guidance and constraint delineates psychic and physical space where individuals are able to travel.

Most of the time, these processes operate seamlessly in the background, a product of cultural assimilation and internalization, but much like the sound of a phone going off in the movie theatre pulls us out of watching the movie, there are a number of experiences that may make us

more aware of the boundaries guiding our conduct. Moreover, we may become aware of how permeable or not a boundary is. A phone ringing during a movie may be a distraction, but is easily navigated by walking out of the theatre to take it. In contrast, talking on the phone during the movie quickly draws the ire of other movie watchers and becomes highly discouraged.

Within the therapeutic setting, boundaries may come in a number of forms and have a variety of effects. The physical layout and structure of the room, i.e., who sits where, what the space looks like, the gender, race, ethnicity of patient and therapist, and so forth may from the beginning of a treatment create the sense of shared culture or difference that can facilitate particular types of relationships. Indeed, cultural boundaries are already at play even before therapist and patient meet in person or talk on the phone. How the patient understands therapy, or how the practitioner advertises about therapy, may create atmospheres of openness and curiosity, a more medical and sterile environment, and a host of options in between.

How boundaries are understood and interpreted then in turn create areas where patients and therapists can travel to easily or with more difficulty. For instance, certain topics, such as sex, self-harm, negative feelings, and so forth, may be seen as taboo (Arcoverde, Amazonas, & de Lima, 2016) and thus have strong boundaries around them that are not particularly permeable. Other topics, such as marriage, job satisfaction, and friendships, may be more accepted and open to exploration. Much like Sullivan differentiated different aspects of one's self (good, bad, not-me), society canalizes experiencing and meaning making into particular zones that are more or less free (Valsiner, 2007).

The common difficulty of a patient "going there," i.e., to a vulnerable or sensitive topic, may have less to do with intrapsychic resistance and defense mechanisms and instead reflect an internalized sense that one simply does not talk about certain topics. This may result from defenses and forces at the societal level. For instance, the recent crisis of Flint Michigan, where officials failed to properly apply corrosive inhibitors to a new water source (the Flint River) leading to demonstrable levels of lead in the drinking water, but did not act on it for some time (despite being told it was a serious problem), demonstrates how societal conflict around blame, expectation, and responsibility interfere with what was and is needed to be done to effectively deal with devastating problems. While this might reflect the "darker" or more "destructive" impulses, instincts, and aspects of the self found in the writings of Sigmund Freud and Melanie Klein, it also highlights the impact of very real social factors.

Defensive structures may also have been learned and internalized from the more local cultures of an individual's home life. A patient who has seen their parent deal with adverse situations, such as working multiple jobs just to get by, and not heard them complain (even if they do so with other adults), may quickly internalize the value of struggling through silence without complaint. For some, this even becomes transformed into (and often is) a source of pride and strength. However, the rigidity of the boundary may then in turn prevent the individual from reaching out when it is appropriate (and needed) to ask for help.

This also speaks to how boundaries regulate individuals' experience by guiding their meaning-making process. Asking for help becomes a sign of weakness and not being able to handle one's business, even perhaps a sense of letting someone else down. This in turn guides how the individual interacts and structures their own interpersonal experiences. An individual who sees asking for help as a weakness may surround themselves by people who need their help, so as to be strong for others. Or, they may construct their own boundaries about not wanting to "burden" or "upset" others with their own needs as they are "strong" and can take on the problems of others.

5.5.2 The Role of Language

Notably, while interpersonal psychoanalysis has become increasingly sensitive to these mutually regulative processes, sociocultural psychology offers the possibility for an even closer look at how these meanings and interpretations develop and serve to guide future meaning making (Valsiner, 2007; see also Chapter 2, this volume). Through the micro-genetic method of breaking meaning-making processes down moment-by-moment, sociocultural psychology helps elaborate the way that fields are organized, elaborated, and deconstructed.

Not surprisingly, language plays an important role as signifiers that help organize and encode experiences as well as create and modify them (Valsiner, 2006; Brinkmann, 2014, 2016). As we move from lower levels of abstraction to higher ones (Salvatore, 2016) language itself moves from being vague and ambiguous, possibly capturing multiple meanings, to being more specific. This narrowing may serve a communicative and useful function of helping to encapsulate experience in such a way that can be useful. Interestingly, patients often express appreciation at having their ideas summarized or reflected back to them. While this may be due to a feeling of having been heard and understood, I think it is also because the therapist does more than reflect as a mirror, but instead reorganizes the thoughts in a more cohesive fashion than initially said. In hearing a different and often more organized version of what they have already said, patients (and therapists) begin to focus on certain signifiers at the exclusion of others. Notably, it is not uncommon for this to become abstract again requiring this process to continue on as the field expands.

The movement here in some ways echoes Levenson's (1983/2005) thinking on what transpires in therapy. For Levenson, experience moves from the immediate context to the past and then returns to the present. This almost involves a washing of signifiers, by which current language takes us back and then returns in new and different ways.

While psychoanalysts have paid attention to language since Freud talked about screen memories, slips, jokes, and so forth and Lacan opined that the unconscious is structured like language, cultural psychology helps answer Levenson's (1979) quip that "It's all very well to claim (from the structuralist viewpoint, correctly) that the unconscious is structured like a language. But how does one talk with it" (p. 273). Specifically, sociocultural psychology pays attention to the structuring of experience, which includes what is culturally available to the individual.

Here, the work on intersubjectivity within sociocultural psychology (Marková, 2003b) helps to articulate how language and dialogue guides the ways we construct experience. In particular, the focus on how individuals relate, not only through respectful speech, but maybe even more so at moments of difference and tension, sharpen our attention to the struggle in interpersonal relationships. Indeed, this resonates nicely within the psychoanalytic discourse on intersubjectivity. For instance, Jessica Benjamin (1988, 1998) has written about the difference between complementarity and mutuality. During complementarity periods of relationships things have an either/or quality and there is a distinction between self and other that cannot be resolved. This is similar to how Marková (2003b), following Bahktin, suggests that pure empathy leads to erasure of subjectivity as one's self becomes fully submerged (enmeshed as it were) within the subjective experience of the other, thus losing themselves. Alternatively, in mutuality the self can hold the experience of self and other, moving into a space that psychoanalytic writers have termed the "third"[2] (Benjamin, 2004). The ability to hold a both/and space requires dealing with tension, similar to Marková's discussion on active empathizing.

It is worth noting that ideas of thirdness were also discussed by Charles S. Peirce (1878/1982)

as a way of categorizing experience. While what Peirce has in mind differs from the intersubjectivity theorists, it does speak to the importance of being able to move within the field as the quality and felt nature of our experience change. Moreover, it reiterates the semiotic aspect of relating. It is through language and our interpretation of language that self–other negotiate their relationship around power, authority, responsibility, agency, and so forth – the very topics of therapy and living.

This means that in the consulting room, the deconstruction and micro-analyses of the therapeutic process and the ongoing semiotic communication between therapist and patient is not only a personal therapy or analysis, but also a social one. As a space of potential understanding, interpersonal psychoanalysis often occupies a space of challenging conventional social narratives about success, happiness, health, and so forth (Cushman, 2015). This speaks to the reification of certain ideas into cultural at large, or their social representations (Moscovici, 1961/2008; Duveen, 2007) and the processes by which they are assimilated into individual narratives. For example, for many the idea that symptoms may have alternative or symbolic meanings can be understood as a form of communication about oneself and should thus be treated as experiences to be curious about rather than to get rid of is a novel and even threatening idea. This goes against more conventional notions of health as living without symptoms (Rosenbaum & Liebert, 2015).

5.5.3 The Importance of Context

Implicitly then, the various contexts we inhabit are a large part of what makes experience understandable and interpretable. Cultural mediation – as the name implies – always occurs within a particular time and space and cultural milieu. While psychological processes may be generalizable they are not necessarily universal (beyond the tendency toward generalization) (Wagner et al., 2000, 2012). Paying attention to the context, not only of the psychological relationship, i.e., its physicality and location; but the broader context in which disease and experience are talked about and understood is crucial to making meaning (Horwitz & Wakefield, 2007).

Notably, it may also lead to very different understandings about pathology and disease than traditionally endorsed by psychoanalysis. In this regard, a cultural perspective pushes psychoanalytic reasoning to consider different phenomena through more appropriate contextual lenses than necessarily psychoanalytic ones. For instance, psychoanalysis can grapple with more "occult" or "spiritual" explanations of illness in a way that honors where they come from instead of seeking to replace it with more "dynamic" interpretations.

It is then important to ensure that the appropriate research methods are used to study phenomena (Valsiner 2009, 2014). Paying attention to the fit between phenomena and method helps to prevent a one size fits all approach to study. It further recognizes that psychological phenomena present themselves at various degrees and levels of complexity and organization and that these need to be taken into account when designing research studies and doing therapy.

Recognizing different levels of abstraction and complexity speaks to developmental processes by which certain phenomena become more or less abstract and complex. Moreover, a sociocultural perspective values the study of how one state will lead to another. Or in other words, how individuals are working to preadapt to an unknowable future (Valsiner, 2007). Here, sociocultural psychologies focus on development that offers an important corrective to interpersonal psychoanalysis, which, while maintaining a developmental theory (i.e., Sullivan, 1953a), has left it (for lack of a better word) undeveloped.

A focus on the feed-forward mechanisms by which experience is constrained helps psychologists understand why and how a particular developmental accomplishment may have occurred out of a whole host of other possibilities. Indeed, sociocultural psychology's emphasis on development as nonlinear and holistic helps ensure that interpersonal psychoanalysis does not fall into the trap of metatheoretical speculation about what *should* have occurred during childhood or certain "critical periods" during development. Notably, this reflects a greater interest in both fields in the ongoing interactive and mutually regulating developmental patterns (Harris, 2005; Thelen, 2005), which provides important abilities to consider development from a less normative way.

This is important as working with patients involves implicitly recognizing where a person is from a developmental perspective at any given point in time. The ability to tolerate increased psychic complexity and to recognize causality may be more or less available, much as the ability to formulate experience (Stern, 2003) or to stand within spaces (Bromberg, 1998). A developmental perspective recognizes the movement required to at times hold more complexity and that it may be a challenge to do so at other times. Moreover, it speaks to a model of growth and change that is not necessarily causal. Instead, of thinking of psychological change as reflecting linear causality, sociocultural psychology suggests that development may occur from seemingly nonrelated factors and does not have to be linear at all. This challenges traditional ideas about psychic causality and forces therapists to hold their ideas lightly (Orange, 2003).

5.5.4 Goals and Growth

Paying attention to culture is an important commitment for psychoanalytic practitioners. Notably, this does not mean doing so in a way of trying to become "culturally competent" to the various cultures, but instead applying an ethic of curiosity and openness (Hart, 2017). As part of this, practitioners can learn from a sociocultural perspective where meaning does not exist a priori (Salvatore, 2015) waiting to be discovered or uncovered, but rather is always in the process of being constructed and created after the fact (a posteriori). This means that the meaning-making process always involves an act of negotiation (Bruner, 1990) and looking backwards at what has transpired, rather than following more prescribed roles of the therapist as knower and authority.

Alternatively, from a sociocultural perspective paying attention to context and how different meanings may emerge, be blocked, transformed, and so forth shifts the focus to a process of continual learning. This shift seems to reflect shifts in society at large (and now perhaps also possible counter shifts as well). As Western culture has moved from a more authoritarian and patriarchal society toward one where people are more comfortable challenging authority and value democracy and transparency, being able to accommodate change has become increasingly important. Simultaneously, this speaks to an insecurity within society as well and a decentering of traditional structures and perhaps even values (though whether this has always been the case is a valid question).

This has also become noticeable within the therapeutic space. The analyst is no longer seen as the authority and knower, but, instead, a collaborator working with the patient to make sense of their experience. This in turn has shifted the emphasis away from resolving particular complexes and agreeing to particular interpretations toward processes of freeing up the field of relating so individuals can move more freely (Stern, 2015). Moreover, growth happens less as a result of insight into a problem, and more from the ability to take a different perspective and observe other aspects of the problem. The therapeutic space becomes less about interpreting experience and more about navigating existing boundaries and barriers.

Implicitly then, how people construct and label their experience as healthy or not healthy (note how this takes over the field of non-healthy, which could be interpreted in a variety of ways) reflects prevailing societal ideas of normativity and health (Horwitz & Wakefield, 2007; Brinkmann, 2014; 2016; Rosenbaum & Liebert, 2015). It is perhaps not surprising as society becomes less authoritarian and more decentered that the process of navigating instability and a capacity to deal with not knowing are becoming more relevant (Mitchell, 1997). Further, it is interesting to consider the ways that these may themselves become coopted into areas of authority or the "way to be." Holding the tension and the space to not know requires an active stance, ultimately more anxiety provoking and significantly harder than at any previous point in time. While therapy still involves a pursuit at "the good life" as society's ideas of this change it makes sense that its patients and thus goals for therapy shift as well (Levenson, 1983/2005).

5.6 Conclusion: The Value of Not Knowing

Thinking about the ability to deal with the unknown speaks, I think, to the importance of further and more explicit dialogue between sociocultural psychology and interpersonal psychoanalysis. As I hope has been made clear, both fields strive to deal with individual and social phenomena at the level of complexity that they are presented at, without reducing it to particulars or essentials. This is obviously challenging and requires working at different levels of theoretical and clinical abstraction in order to theorize both about what is transpiring at the moment and, more abstractly, about what may be going on. Further dialogue between these two fields may be an important source of understanding and growth for each, helping to shed light on particularly hard-to-reach phenomena. Moreover, dialogue ensures an openness of ideas and helps expand fields and creativity.

The need for dialogue mirrors, I think, much of where we are in the world. The consulting room has become less a place to provide answers to individuals by way of insight and interpretation and more a space that strives to help individuals deal with uncertainty by creating the space for them to be better and more creative sign users. Unlike Sullivan who thought that psychoanalysis helps individuals become semiotically competent, by which he meant able to conform with a singular reality of which he knew interpersonal psychoanalysis works to help individuals become more curious about their experience and so able to journey differently.

This occurs not necessarily by interpreting and observing their experience in more normative ways, but by being able to expand on and flexibly construct meanings from experience while living with paradox, not knowing, and ambiguity. Here, what is important is not necessarily accurately interpreting reality as a singular construct, but rather being able to move into the fields where reality can be multiple. Further complicating matters is the corresponding need of accepting that there are always numerous understandings and possibilities outside of our ability to know and understand.

Sociocultural psychology expands the therapist's thinking of how these fields are structured at the cultural level and brought into individual experience. Moreover, the focus on development ensures a process approach that focuses on becoming. In considering how one becomes, sociocultural psychology further reminds us of the value of non-normative and nonlinear models of thinking and the mind, and draws our attention to the larger context in which we live.

Notes

1 Contrast this perspective with, say, a Freudian perspective that considers conflict arising from drives,

Kleinian from destructive objects, Lacanian from the alienated self, and so forth.

2 Notably, there are many different versions of the analytic third, see, for instance, volume 73 of *Psychoanalytic Quarterly* (2004), devoted to different ideas of the third.

References

Abbey, E. A. (2007). Perpetual uncertainty of cultural life: Becoming reality. In J. Valsiner & A. Rosa (Eds.), *The Cambridge Handbook of Sociocultural Psychology* (pp. 362–372). Cambridge: Cambridge University Press.

Arcoverde, R., Amazonas, M. C., & De Lima, R. (2016). Descriptions and interpretations on self-harming. *Culture & Psychology*, 22(1), 110–127.

Aron, L. (1991). The patient's experience of the analyst's subjectivity. *Psychoanalytic Dialogues*, 1, 29–51.

Aron, L. (2001). *A Meeting of Minds: Mutuality in Psychoanalysis*. New York: Routledge.

Baranger, M. & Baranger, W. (1961/2008). The analytic situation as a dynamic field. *International Journal of Psychoanalysis*, 89(4), 795–826.

Beebe, B. & Lachmann, F. (1998). Co-constructing inner and relational process: Self and mutual regulation in infant research and adult treatment. *Psychoanalytic Psychology*, 15(4), 480–516.

Beebe, B. & Lachmann, F. (2003). The relational turn in psychoanalysis: A dyadic systems view from infant research. *Contemporary Psychoanalysis*, 39(3), 379–409.

Benjamin, J. (1988). *The Bonds of Love: Psychoanalysis, Feminism, and the Problem of Domination*. New York: Pantheon Books.

Benjamin, J. (1998). *Like Subjects Love Objects: Essays on Recognition and Sexual Difference*. New Haven, CT: Yale University Press.

Benjamin, J. (2004). Beyond doer and done to: An intersubjective view of Thirdness. *The Psychoanalytic Quarterly*, 73, 5–46.

Boston Change Process Study Group (BCPSG). (2007). The foundational level of psychodynamic meaning: Implicit process in relation to conflict, defense, and the dynamic unconscious. *International Journal of Psychoanalysis*, 88, 843–860.

Brinkmann, S. (2014). Psychiatric diagnoses as semiotic mediators: The case of ADHD. *Nordic Psychology*, 66, 121–134.

Brinkmann, S. (2016). Toward a cultural psychology of mental disorder: The case of attention deficit hyperactivity disorder. *Culture & Psychology*, 22, 80–93.

Bromberg, P. M. (1996). Standing in the spaces: The multiplicity of self and the psychoanalytic relationship. *Contemporary Psychoanalysis*, 32, 509–535.

Bromberg, P. M. (1998). *Standing in the Spaces*. Hillsdale, NJ: Analytic Press.

Bromberg, P. M. (2000). Potholes on the royal road: Or is it an abyss. *Contemporary Psychoanalysis*, 36, 5–28.

Bromberg, P. M. (2003). Something this way comes – Trauma, dissociation, and conflict: The space where psychoanalysis, cognitive science, and neuroscience overlap. *Psychoanalytic Psychology*, 20, 558–574.

Bromberg, P. M. (2006). *Awakening the Dreamer: Clinical Journeys*. New York: Routledge.

Bromberg, P. M. (2011). *Shadow of the Tsunami and the Growth of the Relational Mind*. New York: Routledge.

Bruner, J. (1990). *Acts of Meaning: Four Lectures on Mind and Culture*. Cambridge, MA: Harvard University Press.

Butler, J. (1990). *Gender Trouble: Feminism and the Subversion of Identity*. New York: Routledge.

Cushman, P. (1995). *Constructing the Self, Constructing America: A Cultural History of Psychotherapy*. Boston, MA: Addison-Wesley.

Cushman, P. (2015). Relational psychoanalysis as political resistance. *Contemporary Psychoanalysis*, 51, 423–459.

Duveen, G. (2007). Culture and social representations. In J. Valsiner & A. Rosa (Eds.), *The Cambridge Handbook of Sociocultural Psychology* (pp. 543–559). Cambridge: Cambridge University Press.

Eagle, M. N. (2003). The postmodern turn in psychoanalysis: A critique. *Psychoanalytic Psychology*, 20, 411–424.

Ehrenberg, D. (1992). *The Intimate Edge: Extending the Reach of Psychoanalytic Interaction*. New York: W. W. Norton.

Fromm, E. (1941). *Escape from Freedom*. New York: Holt, Rinehart and Winston.

Fromm, E. (1951). *The Forgotten Language: An Introduction to the Understanding of Dreams, Fairy Tales and Myths*. New York: Grove Press.

Fromm, E. (1956). *The Art of Loving*. New York: Harper & Row.

Fromm-Reichmann, F. (1950). *Principles of Intensive Psychotherapy*. Chicago: University of Chicago Press.

Greenberg, J. R. (2001). The analyst's participation: A new look. *Journal of the American Psychoanalytic Association*, 49, 359–381.

Greenberg, J. R. & Mitchell, S. A. (1983). *Object Relations in Psychoanalytic Theory*. Cambridge, MA: Harvard University Press.

Harris, A. E. (2005). *Gender as Soft Assembly* (Relational Perspectives series). New York: Routledge.

Harris, A. E. (2011). The relational tradition: Landscape and cannon. *Journal of the American Psychoanalytic Association*, 59, 701–735.

Hart, A. (2017). From multicultural competence to radical openness: A psychoanalytic engagement of otherness. *The American Psychoanalyst*, 51, 12–27.

Heft, H. (2012). Environment, cognition and culture: Reconsidering the cognitive map. *Journal of Environmental Psychology*, 33, 14–25.

Hermans, H. J. M. (2001). The dialogical self: Towards a theory of personal and cultural positioning. *Culture & Psychology*, 7, 243–281. DOI: 10.1177/1354067X0173001.

Hermans, H. J. M. & Kempen, H. J. G. (1993). *The Dialogical Self: Meaning as Movement*. San Diego: Academic Press.

Hoffman, I. Z. (1983). The patient as interpreter of the analyst's experience. *Contemporary Psychoanalysis*, 19, 389–322.

Hoffman, I. Z. (1991). Discussion: Towards a social-constructionist view of the psychoanalytic situation. *Psychoanalytic Dialogues*, 1, 74–105.

Horwitz, A. V. & Wakefield, J. C. (2007). *The Loss of Sadness: How Psychiatry Transformed Normal*

Sorrow into Depressive Disorder. Oxford: Oxford University Press.

James, W. (1890/1950). *Principles of Psychology* (vols. I and II). New York: Dover Publications.

Lehman, O. V. (2014). Towards dialogues with and within silent psychotherapy sessions: Why the person of the therapist and the client matters. *Culture & Psychology*, 20, 537–546.

Levenson, E. A. (1979). Language and healing. *The Journal of the American Academy of Psychoanalysis and Dynamic Psychiatry*, 7, 271–282.

Levenson, E. A. (1979/2005). *The Fallacy of Understanding*. Hillsdale, NJ: Analytic Press.

Levenson, E. A. (1982). Follow the fox: An inquiry into the vicissitudes of psychoanalytic supervision. *Contemporary Psychoanalysis*, 18, 1–15.

Levenson, E. A. (1983/2005). *The Ambiguity of Change*. Hillsdale, NJ: Analytic Press.

Levenson, E. A. (1989). Whatever happened to the cat? Interpersonal perspectives on the self. *Contemporary Psychoanalysis*, 25, 537–553.

Levenson, E. A. (1991). *The Purloined Self: Interpersonal Perspectives in Psychoanalysis*. New York: Contemporary Psychoanalysis Books.

Levenson, E. A. (2002). And the last shall be the first: Some observations on the evolution of interpersonal psychoanalysis. *Contemporary Psychoanalysis*, 38, 277–285.

Levenson, E. A. (2003). On seeing what is said: Visual aids to the psychoanalytic process. *Contemporary Psychoanalysis*, 39, 233–249.

Marková, I. (2003a). *Dialogicality and Social Representations*. Cambridge: Cambridge University Press.

Marková, I. (2003b). Constitution of the self: Intersubjectivity and dialogicality. *Culture & Psychology*, 9, 249–259.

Mead, G. H. (1967). *Mind, Self and Society: From the Standpoint of a Social Behaviorist* (Works of George Herbert Mead, vol. 1). Chicago: University of Chicago Press.

Mills, J. (2011). *Conundrums: A Critique of Relational Psychoanalysis*. New York: Routledge.

Mitchell, S. A. (1988). *Relational Concepts in Psychoanalysis*. Cambridge, MA: Harvard University Press.

Mitchell, S. A. (1995). *Hope and Dread in Psychoanalysis*. New York: Basic Books.

Mitchell, S. A. (1997). *Influence and Autonomy in Psychoanalysis*. Hillside, NJ: Analytic Press.

Moscovici, S. (1961/2008). *Psychoanalysis: Its Image and Its Public*. Cambridge: Polity Press.

Orange, D. M. (2003). Why language matters to psychoanalysis. *Psychoanalytic dialogues*, 13, 77–103.

Peirce, C. S. (1878/1982). How to make our ideas clear. In Thayer, H. S. (Ed.), *Pragmatism: The Classic Writings* (pp. 79–100). Indianapolis: Hackett.

Rosenbaum, P. J. (2015a). Introduction: The postmodern turn in relational psychoanalysis. In P. Rosenbaum (Ed.). *Making Our Ideas Clear: Pragmatism and Psychoanalysis*, Charlotte, NC: Information Age Publishing.

Rosenbaum, P. J. (2015b). Harry Stack Sullivan and Charles Sanders Peirce: The impact of early pragmatism on interpersonal psychoanalysis. In. P. Rosenbaum (Ed.), *Making Our Ideas Clear: Pragmatism and Psychoanalysis*. Charlotte, NC: Information Age Publishing.

Rosenbaum, P. J. (2016). Roger Bibace: An interpersonal thinker. In J. Valsiner, M. Watzlawik, & A. Kriebel (Eds.), *Particulars and Universals in Clinical and Developmental Psychology: Critical Reflections*. Charlotte, NC: Information Age Publishing.

Rosenbaum, P. J. & Liebert, H. (2015). Reframing the conversation on college student mental health. *Journal of College Student Psychotherapy*, 29, 179–196.

Salvatore, S. (2015). From meaning to sensemaking: Implications of a semiotic and dynamic model of mind for psychoanalysis. In. P. Rosenbaum (Ed.), *Making Our Ideas Clear: Pragmatism and Psychoanalysis*. Charlotte, NC: Information Age Publishing.

Salvatore, S. (2016). *Psychology in Black and White: The Project of a Theory-Driven Science*. Charlotte, NC: Information Age Publishing.

Stern, D. B. (2004). The eye sees itself: Dissociation enactment and the achievement of conflict. *Contemporary Psychoanalysis*, 40, 197–237.

Stern, D. B. (2003). *Unformulated Experience: From Dissociation to Imagination in Psychoanalysis*. Hillside, NJ: Analytic Press.

Stern, D. B. (2009). *Partners in Thought: Working with Unformulated Experience, Dissociation and Enactment* (Psychoanalysis in a New Key Book Series). New York: Routledge.

Stern, D. B. (2013). Field theory in psychoanalysis, Part I: Harry Stack Sullivan and Madeleine and Willy Baranger. *Psychoanalytic Dialogues*, 23(5), 487–501.

Stern, D. B. (2015). *Relational Freedom: Emergent Properties of the Interpersonal Fields* (Psychoanalysis in a New Key Book Series). New York: Routledge.

Stern, D. B., Mann, C. H., Kantor, S., & Schlesinger, G. (Eds.). (1995). *Pioneers of Interpersonal Psychoanalysis*. London: Analytic Press.

Sullivan, H. S. S. (1938/1995). Data of psychiatry. In D. B. Stern, C. H. Mann, S. Kantor, & G. Schlesinger (Eds.), *Pioneers of Interpersonal Psychoanalysis* (pp. 1–26). London: Analytic Press.

Sullivan, H. S. S. (1950). The illusion of individual personality. *Psychiatry*, 13, 317–332.

Sullivan, H. S. S. (1953a). *Conceptions of Modern Psychiatry*. New York: W. W. Norton.

Sullivan, H. S. S. (1953b). *The Interpersonal Theory of Psychiatry*. New York: W. W. Norton.

Sullivan, H. S. S. (1953c). *The Psychiatric Interview*. New York: W. W. Norton.

Thelen, E. (2005). Dynamic systems theory and the complexity of change. *Psychoanalytic Dialogues*, 15, 255–283.

Thompson, C. (1950/2003). *Psychoanalysis: Evolution and Development*. New Brunswick, NJ: Transaction Publishers.

Tublin, S. (2011). Discipline and freedom in relational technique. *Contemporary Psychoanalysis*, 47, 519–546.

Valsiner, J. (2006). The semiotic construction of solitude. *Sign Systems Studies*, 34, 9–34.

Valsiner, J. (2007). *Culture in Minds and Societies: Foundations of Cultural Psychology*. New York: SAGE.

Valsiner, J. (2009). Cultural psychology today: Innovations and oversights. *Culture & Psychology*, 15, 5–39.

Valsiner, J. (2014). *An Invitation to Cultural Psychology*. London: SAGE.

Wagner, W., Duveen, G., Verma, J., & Themel, M. (2000). "I have some faith and at the same time I don't believe in it" – Cognitive polyphasia and culture change in India. *Journal of Community and Applied Social Psychology*, 10, 301–314.

Wagner, W., Sen, R., Permanadeli, R., & Howarth, C. S. (2012). The veil and Muslim women's identity: Cultural pressures and resistances to stereotyping. *Culture & Psychology*, 18, 521–541.

Further Reading

Blechner, M. J. (2005). The gay Harry Stack Sullivan: Interactions between his life, clinical work and theory. *Contemporary Psychoanalysis*, 41(1), 1–19.

Cole, M. (1995). Culture and cognitive development: From cross-cultural research to creating systems of cultural mediation. *Culture & Psychology*, 1, 25–54.

Harre, R. (2015). The persons as the nexus of patterns of discursive practices. *Culture & Psychology*, 21, 492–504.

Marsico, G. (2015). Striving for the new: Cultural psychology as a developmental science. *Culture & Psychology*, 21, 445–454.

Molenaar, P. C. M. (2004). A manifesto on psychology as idiographic science: Bringing the person back into scientific psychology, this time forever. *Measurement*, 2, 201–218.

Rosenbaum, P. J. (2013). The role of projective identification in constructing the "Other": Why do Westerners want to "liberate" Muslim women? *Culture & Psychology* 19(2), 213–224. DOI: 10.1177/1354067X12456719.

Shewder, R. (1990). *Thinking Through Cultures: Expeditions in Cultural Psychology*. Cambridge, MA: Harvard University Press.

Valsiner, J. (2015). Where are you, *Culture & Psychology*? Making of an interdisciplinary field. *Culture & Psychology*, 21, 419–428.

Valsiner, J. & Rosa, A. (2007). Contemporary socio-cultural research: Uniting culture, society and psychology. In J. Valsiner & A. Rosa (Eds.),

The Cambridge Handbook of Sociocultural Psychology (pp. 1–22). Cambridge: Cambridge University Press.

Zittoun, T., Duveen, G., Gillespie, A., Ivinson, G., & Psaltis, C. (2003). The use of symbolic resources in developmental transitions. *Culture & Psychology*, 9, 415–448.

Zittoun, T. & Gillespie, A. (2015). Internalization: How culture becomes mind. *Culture & Psychology*, 21, 477–491.

Part II
Action, Objects, Artifacts, and Meaning

6 Spirited Psyche Creates Artifacts: Semiotic Dynamics of Experience in the Shaping of Objects, Agency, and Intentional Worlds

Alberto Rosa

Art denotes a process of doing or making. This is as true of fine as of technological art. Art involves molding of clay, chipping of marble, casting of bronze, laying on of pigments, construction of buildings, singing of songs, playing of instruments, enacting roles on the stage, going through rhythmic movements in the dance. Every art do is something with some physical material, the body or something outside the body, with or without the use of intervening tools, and with a view to production of something visible, audible, or tangible.

John Dewey (1994, p. 207)

This chapter is about how psyche produces artifacts of different kinds – tools to operate on material structures, symbols, rules and representations for social interaction, concepts for thinking, and symbolic resources for the regulation of behavior. These artifacts, together with the elements populating our environment, produce the experiences we feel, shape our abilities, and make us able to conceive the world and ourselves.

6.1 Psyche, Culture, and Things

Psyche and culture are peculiar creatures. Neither psyche nor culture can be seen, heard, touched, or smelled. More than entities with substance, they are creatures of speech referring to the intangible dynamics among changing things. Without arguments and symbolic tools they could not be conceived, communicated, or turned into objects of knowledge. But this does not seem to be an obstacle to our understanding of whether an experienced phenomenon belongs to the psychological or to the sociocultural realm, to both, or to none of them. It is as if the evanescent character of these two entities only gets some flesh when some kind of thing or event causes them to appear as "real" to our senses.

Psyche is what bodily structures do when keeping themselves alive (Chapter 1, this volume). That is why the study of psyche focuses on behavior, on what living organisms do when in contact with objects. Sociocultural psychology pays particular attention to how these contacts change those things and the environment and, also, how these changes affect the agents' capabilities for action. It is the iterative operation of these kinds of changes that transforms action and opens the way for the development of mental abilities, social structures, and culture.

Culture is a historical product of human action and also a set of resources and constraints for situated human action, both social and individual. Culture is a result of cultivation, of putting effort into the transformation of nature. It is made of material elements and ways of acting that frame human behavior (practices, institutions, norms, values). The latter would not exist without the former, which makes it inexcusable to refer to the material elements of which culture is made. Without things, without matter with which to pair, there can be no spirit, even if the spirit cannot be reduced to the materiality of the things to which one relates.

6.1.1 Material Culture: Artifacts, Machines, and Machinations

Material culture comprises the material traces human efforts left in the landscape – from a potsherd to a castle, a city, a park, or a levelled field – and also the tools that made those transformations possible: hoes, plows, pencils, books. Human action has crafted tools and transformed the landscape to respond to the needs of social life. The use of natural objects to serve new purposes led to the transformation of their structure when searching for a more efficient performance of the function they were given. An angled stone to tear a skin led to carving pebbles to produce sharper edges for that purpose, which, in turn, called for a new use of other stones for supporting and pounding. In short, the creation of tools is a recursive process: some tools lead to the production of other tools, and the use of one and the other transforms the capacities for action of the operator – the agent. So when archaeologists study the physical characteristics of objects coming from the past, their data are useful for guessing the lifestyle and skills as well as the symbolic, cognitive, and emotional capacities of their producers and users, because without them, those cultural products could never have been produced and put into use.

Sociocultural psychology claims the centrality of artifacts for the construction of higher psychological functions in three different time scales: cultural–historical, ontogenesis, and microgenesis. The concept of a "zone of proximal development" has frequently been understood as a way of accounting for the intersection between

the ontogenetic and micro-genetic time scales when acquiring new skills (e.g., Cole, 1998), with research often focusing on the organization of the social environments for learning or on the intricacies of the processes being developed in those interactions (e.g., Rodriguez, 2007). Most typically, ready-made cultural artifacts have been used as materials for the study of the mastery of abilities pre-identified as milestones in the course of development. In contrast, less attention has been paid to the transformation or production of new artifacts and to the processes leading to these creations – what is usually called "creativity" (see Chapter 9, this volume). The consideration of how the historical development of cultural devices may affect psychological abilities (or vice versa) has been left mainly as a matter of concern for cross-cultural studies. Other disciplines, such as archaeology, paleontology, and history, also provide data and interpretations worthy of consideration.

The concept of the *artifact* refers to many different kinds of meditational means for action. It starts with the change of use of a natural object for some purpose (a rock to crack a nut) and moves to the manufacturing of tools, the production of symbols for communication (conventional gestures, words), the development of rules for the regulation of social interaction (norms), and the shaping of social groups. All these elements get linked in a chain of operations that shapes the behavior of the operator to produce an outcome – the efficient crafting of a product. The production of artifacts is, then, closely linked to the development of agency, the capacity for planning, and the ability to set a goal and keep a steady course to reach a preset objective.

Artifacts are developed to increase the efficiency of human action, but they also canalize and constrain what humans can do when using them. Artifacts can also interact with other artifacts. Hammers, anvils, bellows, and a hearth make up a forge where a blacksmith can produce iron utensils. But tools can also work together without the participation of humans. A carburetor together with a set of combustion chambers, pistons, connecting rods, spark plugs, and electrical distributors constitute an internal combustion engine, where each of these elements coordinates with the others so that once the engine is turned on, it can keep functioning as long as its fuel lasts. These associations of tools, what we call machines, have the capacity to act autonomously, to the extent that we may forget what they are made of and they may appear to us as a kind of "black box," where the inner workings are a mystery and all that matters is that it keeps going when needed – in the same way as many people think of the engine of a car, always concealed inside a hood that is never opened.

Nowadays, neither tools nor machines are isolated; they are associated in complex networks. A factory is a large association of machines that complement each other to produce a product from a raw material. But the factory cannot be understood as confined within its walls; it also needs a logistics system for supplying raw materials and distributing their products through a road and railway system, advertising for marketing, banks that provide funding, rules governing trade relations, and also money to establish the value of all such transactions. Machines are now able to interact with each other at a distance in a kind of gigantic "machination" (Latour, 1987). Currently almost 60 percent of Internet traffic controls machines – in what has been called the "Internet of things." For example, home automation sensors are able to readjust the light or temperature in our houses to regulate our household electricity consumption. But it does not end there. The costs of these services are directly charged to the bank accounts into which our salaries are paid, which also automatically charge commissions and taxes and transmit all these data to the computers of the taxing authority. All these data get stored and processed in "calculation centers" (Latour, 1987) that, through the use of algorithms, refine indicators that produce feedback

loops for keeping the system working. If the user of any public service is dissatisfied with its workings and attempts to interact with the machination by contacting customer service – which always demands the mediation of a computer, a tablet, or a phone to establish contact – he or she will quickly find that humans have little place in these systems. The interlocutor (often a robot) will tell you what "application" should be used, how, and when, always within the limits of what "the system" allows. In short, things, tools, machines, symbols, and algorithms have come to constitute a gigantic machination in which humans appear as another piece in the intricate web of objects, as just another element for keeping the system working, whether as operators or as consumers.

Some anthropologists and sociologists of technology and science, proponents of the actor-network theory (ANT) (Latour, 1991; Law 1999), choose to treat all constituent elements of these systems equally, ignoring who or what is an agent or an instrument and whether it is human or nonhuman. They try to avoid an anthropocentric stand by choosing to talk of "actants" when referring to the elements connected in networks as a way of emphasizing that agency is distributed throughout the network. Actants are conceived as elements of the network whose structural features force one another to shape their operations so that they work according to a structural logic. So viewed, actants within a network can act as a material equivalent to a sign, a rule, or a norm – such as a sleeping policeman (a road bump) that regulates the speed of the traffic more efficiently than traffic signals or the rules of the road. When that happens, the means is literally the message (Malafouris, 2013). The consequence is that the system appears materialized, naturalized, and de-semiotized. As Callon and Latour (1981, p. 286) state, actants show "their will into a language of its own," which is not that different from a command expressed by a holder of power.

Avoiding anthropocentrism is a healthy intellectual habit, but *anthropocentrism* should not be confused with *anthropomorphism*. Malafouris (2013) claims that anthropomorphism is a biological necessity of the human condition that cannot be ignored, unless one seeks to remove humans from the world and place them above events in the position of a god who acts as an external observer. According to his argument, "being human, we are the embodied measure of all things, yet certainly not the center of all things" (p. 132). For Malafouris, anthropomorphism is essential for understanding our way of being in the world, and it also helps to explain some phenomena in evolutionary terms. There are notions that could not exist without self-referentiality, such as inside–outside, up–down, right–left, and front–back, which are hard to justify without resorting to the way in which we are in the world. This also shows in the behavioral domain: consider, for example, the asymmetry of the consequences of an error if, while hiking in the mountains, we see a silhouette and hesitate, not sure whether it is a bear or a rock. There is little doubt that in evolutionary terms, it is always safer to attribute the highest level of organization and act as if it were a bear, just in case (Gell, 1998, quoted by Malafouris, 2013, p. 131). Certainly man is not the center of all things, but when we look at how humans behave in the world, it seems that subjectivity cannot simply be regarded as an annoying inconvenience to overcome. Another thing is that when producing natural explanations, subjectivity should be approached in conditions of symmetry with natural objects, avoiding anthropocentrism and reductionism.

This is the approach that this chapter follows. Its purpose is exploring how cultural artifacts arise as the result of iterative processes going on in different time scales (cultural–historical, ontogenetic, and micro-genetic). The thesis to be presented here is that "sense" – the tendency to adapt to the environment – is an immanent feature of behavior and that sense cannot exist without a subject of experience who can feel the conse-

quences of behavior and environmental change. It is by acting that one's body and the things of the environment can turn into objects of knowledge so that both become means for expanding the capabilities for acting, transforming natural objects into tools and thus increasing the agency and the awareness of the agent. Sense and meaning (both social and individual) do not start with symbols and language; rather, these are outcomes of the varieties of behavior of organisms. That is why semiotics can be instrumental for the production of formal models suitable for describing and explaining the simultaneous development of knowledge, technology, abilities, and self-awareness. The central part of the argument to be presented below will apply a theory of semiotic action (Rosa, 2007a, 2007b) to examining how objects, artifacts (both material and symbolic), and the self arise out of sense making – a process that cannot be limited to the cognitive or the pragmatic domains but also includes emotion and aesthetic experience, play and art.

6.2 Psyche Turns Things into Objects

Psyche is a way of referring to the acts of a living body when relating to its surroundings. Psyche is inherently relational. Acts of psyche engender the mind, and the two together, when in society, dwell in culture – the realm of the spirit – where the person develops and also participates in the shaping of cultural change (Chapter 1, this volume). This view makes clear that any comprehensive account of what human beings do, and are able to do, has to begin by considering how the structural couplings between the human body and the things in its environment produce such developments (Maturana & Varela, 1992).

6.2.1 Body, Things, and Movement

James Gibson's ecological theory of perception is based on the assumption of a complementarity between the perceiver and the environment. He describes "the environment as the surfaces that separate substances from the medium in which the animals live" (Gibson, 2015, p. 119) and conceives perception as resulting from encounters between the body of the perceiver and things in the environment, in that "exteroception is accompanied by proprioception – that to perceive the world is to co-perceive oneself... The awareness of the world and one's complementary relations to the world are not separable" (p. 140). This position took him to develop his theory of affordances, since "the composition and layout of surfaces constitute what they afford. If so, to perceive them is to perceive what they afford. The affordances of the environment are what it offers the animal, what it provides or furnishes, either for good or ill" (p. 119).

Gibson took good care in developing a theory of perception grounded on this assumption and went on to study how encountering the surfaces of things – the perceptual actions of the perceiver – causes the affordances, the "values" and "meanings," of things in the environment to be directly perceived, because they are "properties of things *taken with reference to an observer* but not properties of the *experiences of the observer*. They are not subjective values; they are not feelings of pleasure or pain added to neutral perceptions" (p. 138; emphasis original). Perception, then, is an effect of action – the coupling allowed by the morphological structures of the body and the elements in the environment. The consequence is that if the perceiver's body changes, so does its motor-perceptual capabilities, with the effect that some elements of the environment may appear as changing their affordances. This is the case with a ladder, which, for a toddler, is a barrier but turns into an entrance when he or she grows up and could turn again into a barrier if his or her legs are paralyzed. As Valsiner (1998) puts it, the affordances of environmental elements and the agent's *effectivities* for action are always in balance;

together they set the *zone of free movement* of the individual.

But does this mean that movement can be reduced to the dynamic properties of the morphological structure of the body? Español (Chapter 11, this volume) claims that the study of movement cannot ignore the consideration of how the different parts of the body relate among themselves (coordinating the movements of the body's different parts) nor the patterns of body postures and motor movements developed through early infancy while in social interactions with caregivers. She emphasizes the importance of how these early bearings and forms of movement are combined and developed into a kind of improvised dance that does not refer to anything different than the changes in the body itself nor searches for a goal besides paying attention to the very dynamics of movement, which she terms "thinking in movement." This is a form of play that is both motor and social, in addition to emotional and communicative, and also has aesthetic purposes when evolving into improvised dance. The consequence is that proprioception and feelings develop together as a basis for the development of the awareness of one's self. Thus the development of posture and movement affects the concrete ways in which the operations of perceptual action are performed.

6.2.2 Perception, Action, and Affection Add Value to Things

Action is what makes the surfaces of the body and the things in the environment combine. Thus, what "we perceive when we look at objects are their affordances, not their qualities... Phenomenal objects are not built up of qualities; it is the other way around. The affordance of an object is what the infant begins by noticing. The meaning is observed before the substance and surface, the colour and form, are seen as such" (Gibson, 2015, p. 134). In other terms, the way action is applied on the environmental element being explored causes it to turn into a "phenomenal object" whose meaning is what it affords to action, its affordances – an invariant unit that does not need to be analyzed in its different features to have meaning.

Environmental elements are not completely detached; they are related among themselves by offering affordances to each other. This includes living organisms and their relation with things and among themselves. The affordance that this structured landscape offers is the ecological niche of the species – the *Umwelt* – which also has a social character. This makes the actions of others relevant for making apparent the affordances of the landscape, the values of things, and so makes them able to (vicariously) add meaning to phenomenal objects beyond the results of one's action on the thing.

Phenomenal objects are, then, a result of the awareness of the meanings arising from the encounters between bodies and things. As Valsiner (2014, p. 4) puts it, "things exist independently of actors, while objects imply particular relation with an actor. *Objects 'object' to human actions* – as they are a part of the established relation Actor–Object" (emphasis original). This makes phenomenal objects the primary elements of the human *Umwelt*. But this does not imply that the meaning of objects gets exhausted in the awareness of their affordances (the subject matter of psychology of perception). This is just the beginning. Further psychological operations are able to develop the meaning of objects by adding new values to them.

When coupling with things, some qualities can be directly felt – if tasted, salt is bitter and sugar sweet; a rock feels heavy and a flower light when lifted. These sensed qualities add formal value to the meaning of the phenomenal object.

Phenomenal objects can be grouped together in categories. Barsalou (1999, 2003) offers a convincing explanation of how perception takes to abstraction, opening the way for the construction of categories that now can also not only take into account what phenomenal objects afford but also notice their features – their qualities – even before language is used, as a result of embodied cognition. When this happens, the phenomenal object is not just some kind of awareness of what that thing affords but also something that regularly appears in the environment – a natural category (Rosch & Mervis, 1975). As Gibson suggests, affordances are the first meaning of phenomenal objects, but this does not imply that qualities and categories do not add some more meaning to the objects perceived.

Objects afford some actions and prevent others, which is what causes them to be better or more poorly suited for different uses. This permits them to obtain a particular value – that is, a functional value – in relation to the ongoing behavior of organisms. The affordances of objects do not change, but they may be attended to and perceived in ways that depend on the transient demands of the situation and the needs or desires of the agent. Phenomenal objects are not just "geographical" objects; they can also turn into "behavioral" objects and have some new values emerging from previous experiences attached to them. This is what causes us to feel the urge of, for example, "eat me" when looking at fruit or "drink me" when looking at water. It therefore acquires a kind of "demand character" that operates in different ways whether the agent is thirsty or hungry – or not (Koffka, 1935, quoted by Gibson, 2015). Objects can then become useful for changing how one feels; they can have a function in satisfying our needs. Functional value adds extra meaning to objects. It is a type of value that could not exist independently of the affordances of the object, nor without taking into account states and processes occurring within the skin of the agent when orienting its behavior and assessing its outcome. It is only through these kinds of processes that functional meaning can be added to objects.

The English word *object* is an umbrella term referring to something objective – that is, "out there" – as opposed to subjective. That is why some authors resort to the German word

Gegenstand to differentiate objects from things (*Ding* in German) and take the former as resulting from a process in which the actor (and social activities) adds value to the latter (see Chapter 8, this volume; Valsiner, 2014). That is why the term *thing* has been profusely employed above, while the term *object* has been reserved to refer to things when they have acquired values and expanded their meanings when in relation with humans. Thus the meaning of an object develops as recursive actions are applied to the thing: it starts when awareness of affordances causes a "phenomenal object" to emerge when a thing is encountered; it continues when formal and functional values are added, depending on the circumstances of the situation and the state of the agent; and it eventually can become a goal to be searched, only if the agent has a mind that, in addition to taking it as belonging to a category, can imagine it when absent.

It should not be left unsaid that objects are not only to be perceived; they can impact on other things and transform them and can also be transformed. When it is said that things afford some kinds of actions but not others, what is implied is that they keep their morphology when the perceiver's body couples with them; however, if these couplings are more rough than gentle, and some brute force is applied to them, the structure of the object may change and, with that, its affordances, its values, and its meaning, that is, its identity. The capacity for transforming the structure of objects and the landscape, together with the subsequent change of their functional values, opens the way for the production of artifacts.

6.3 Playing with Objects Produces Artifacts and Transforms Agency and the Agent

Tools and artifacts are objects transformed by human action. When we encounter something that we know in advance is an artifact, we tend to assume that its current shape had always been as it now appears and thus take for granted that its structure and affordances were tailored for the purpose it was made to serve. When we ask ourselves, "what is this?" we are also asking "what is this for?," and therefore take function to be the meaning we are searching for – and form as a hint of what that thing may be for. But what if, rather than focusing on the shape of the finished result, we pay attention to how it was first created and try to put ourselves in the place of the craftsman struggling to make it? If we do, we would find that when artisans start working on materials, they often do not have a clear idea of what the final outcome of their efforts will be like, and they try out different movements using the object without first forming a definite awareness of their goal, nor do they know the consequences these moves may have on further movements – a way of behaving very similar to the thinking-in-action mentioned above when referring to children's motor play. The consequence is that these movements, while executed, could not be taken as a means to an end, because this would have required knowing the outcome in advance. The artisan's actions, rather than purposively searching for a final result, take every change in the structure of the object as an inscription that records the outcome of previous actions and also sets possibilities and constraints for actions to come.

Lambros Malafouris (2013), working in the field of cognitive archaeology, holds that the production of the first human tools in the Paleolithic most probably started through a play of circular reactions of the kind just referred. According to his view, the repetition of actions with objects (vegetable fibers, sticks, stones, etc.) creatively explored consecutive outcomes, developing new forms until a result considered interesting or useful appears. If the modified object, resulting from these circular reactions spanning through time, turns out to be useful for something, it may get to be used as an instrument for some purpose. When this happens, movements can become progressively refined while searching for the improvement of the desired functionality. Eventually, when the product gets a more or less settled form, it could definitely turn into a permanent cultural artifact. It is only then that the movements leading to its production are ritualized.

The implications of this achievement are important. When a new object is made, a technique has been developed and a form – with a particular "style" that sets it apart from others coming from other times or places – has been established. But something even more important emerges: a goal to be achieved. It is only then that we can properly speak of instrumental movements and thus recognize the emergence of the ability to use means for ends. When this happens, we are already facing a major transformation of the forms of action, which require particular forms of social organization to enable and facilitate the development of these new individual capacities. We shall return to this later.

Malafouris recognizes this process as the development of intentionality from the "aboutness" (Haye, 2008) of Brentano's notion of intentionality (awareness is always the awareness of something) to what Searle (1983) termed "intention-in-action" – which he interprets as an ongoing adjustment between the changing structure of the object and the movements performed on it. It is only afterward that "prior intention" – the formation of a deliberate intention to act before movement starts – can appear, which would require a prior mental representation and would involve mental control over motor activity (Searle, 1983).

6.3.1 Art, Artifacts, and the Mind

When studying the development of Paleolithic art, Malafouris (2013) took a similar stand. According to his hypothesis, early inscriptions did not result from any kind of attempt to produce a finished product, much less did they arise from the intention of representing something (as a sign

does); rather, they were the result of "intention-in-action" applied on new mediators (natural pigments, twigs, pointed stones, etc.). So viewed, early inscriptions should be interpreted more as traces of motor movements and less as attempts to produce a form with meaning. Over time, and with the accumulation of random forms, the repetition of such movements would gradually become ritualized at the same time that some kind of repertoire of forms and variants of these forms is generated. The consequence, throughout the millennia of the Paleolithic, was the mutual development of motor skills and crafting technologies – which included engraving and painting – that gradually produced different types of lines, closed shapes, colors, and textures in a long process of expanding mutual scaffoldings. It was only afterward that a figure could come to be referred to as an environmental object (a sketch of human figures; a profile of a deer, horse, or bison).

If, again, we look at Paleolithic paintings not as finished products but as searching for the sequential ordering of production of the strokes that ended up making the forms, we could guess the dynamics of the artists' movements when producing the formal patterns that we can now contemplate. The evidence collected from the studies that Malafouris (2013) reviewed led him to interpret the lines that make up a final figure not as the boundaries of a closed and finished figure but as resulting from a set of consecutive inscriptions (traces of the execution of a motor action), offering support for conceiving the development of Paleolithic art as a process going through different steps: (1) movements turning into strokes, (2) strokes becoming forms, and, eventually, (3) these forms coming to refer to some element of the artist's *Umwelt*. The consequence is that a kind of material figurative inscription (image) is made to appear anew. Such an interpretation, in addition to offering an account of the mutual constitution of material culture and cognition, also shows how the development of technology makes it possible to achieve new ways of becoming aware of the physical world, to act on it and think about it.

The consequences are far from trivial. Perceiving – including visual perception – is not independent of the agent's actions on objects. It is made of skills that develop when acting within the environment and on the things populating it, rather than resulting from innate abilities of representation. The slow evolution of form in Paleolithic paintings can be interpreted as traces left from the cumulative development of material prosthesis for the exercise of sensorimotor skills that, when coupled with biological evolution, made possible the emergence of new psychological processes. As Malafouris (2013, p. 203) says, "we have to understand the Paleolithic image as a perceptual device. This means that we have to account for how lines of pigment depict anything, rather than taking for granted that they do so." Or, put another way, if the builder of lytic tools develops new ways of motor thinking, the builder of images offers a tool for developing new forms of visual thinking.

We should also not forget one of the most crucial effects of graphic images. Graphic images, once produced, are not only figures on a background; they are also signs pointing toward elements of the world. They are devices that individualize those objects and also the features that characterize the objects represented. When, in addition, the image becomes itself an object of contemplation – as a part of the *Umwelt* – and gets used as a means for social communication, it also becomes an iconic symbol able to represent something absent. In short, inscriptions can be considered as "epistemic actions" (Kirsh & Maglio, 1994, cited in Malafouris, 2013, p. 194) that not only physically transform mundane things but create technical prostheses which help new psychological skills develop. Graphic images are simultaneously scaffolding and bricks for the construction of the human mind.

6.3.2 Play and Art

The previous argument presents technology and art as evolving from movements that could be considered a form of play. Play is a type of activity that can be found in nonhuman species, predominantly in mammals and birds, as well as in humans (Pellegrini, Dupuis & Smith, 2007) and which many theorists consider to have a functional role in ontogenetic development (e.g., Groos, 1901; Piaget, 1951; Vygotsky, 1967) and also phylogenetic evolution (e.g., Bateson, 1981, 2005; Bruner, 1972; Bekoff, 1995; Carruthers, 2002). Such evolutionary and developmental relevance contrasts with some of the features often taken as typical of play behavior. As Pellegrini, Dupuis, and Smith (2007, p. 264) say, "play is a seemingly 'non-serious' variant of functional behavior. Playful behaviors resemble serious behaviors but participants are typically more concerned with the behaviors themselves (i.e., 'means') rather than the function (i.e., 'ends') of the behavior." In addition, play allows for trying new behaviors and strategies, and so provides opportunities for behavioral and cognitive innovation.

There are different kinds of playing behaviors. Human and nonhuman animals show locomotor forms of play – both with and without objects, alone or in social interaction with others – which typically start with an exploration of the possibilities of the object or the situation. Playing is also more frequent in early stages of development and, in humans, also evolves from motor play into other varieties – pretended play and rule games, which require the use of social symbols.

Dissanayake (1974) argues that art, if taken as a kind of behavior, shares many of the characteristics of play: (1) artistic behavior comes about after primary needs are fulfilled, making it seem useless; (2) when practiced or contemplated, it is self-rewarding; (3) art seems to take one outside of oneself and relate one to something else – the material and social others, or both – even if acting alone; (4) it produces excitement (tensions and releases, surprise and adventure); (5) it is pleasure oriented; and (6) it causes something to be perceived as something else, with a kind of metaphorical quality – as in imitation or pretense. These similarities take Dissanayake to argue that art originates from play: locomotor play evolves into dance, vocal play into singing, and both together into music; playing with objects evolves into graphic arts, and so on. The consequence is the mutual development of motor and cognitive abilities as well as the transformation of the objects and the situations in which one plays.

Play and art also seem to be types of behavior that are first governed by "intention-in-action," which later can evolve into "prior intention" when rule games set goals to reach, as art can also turn into crafting. What does not change, however, is that they seem to have no functional purpose: they are not "serious." For the player, the artist, or the spectator, they are means for enjoyment, for sharing enjoyment with others, and also a way of saying, doing, and producing things that would be inappropriate in more serious activities. But this does not make play and art useless. They are means of innovation and transformation, for social sharing and for the production of cultural materials, new forms of behavior, and social institutions. Gadamer (2011) comments that play, art, festival, and ritual do not only develop from each other but also are interrelated, making the beautiful relevant in the developmental processes of meaning making and in the development of culture and society (Grondin, 2001).

Play and art are activities that develop motor and cognitive skills, but they are also for the exercise of affection and excitement, for expanding knowledge and imagination, for the exploration of enjoyment, for the development of experiences of pleasure and beauty; and, with them, they contribute to the development of the agent's self-awareness, the ability for steering behavior, and the capacity for exercising agency. Play and art are not only cradles for the development of experiences but also nurse the growth of aesthetic experiences.

6.3.3 Artifacts Turn into Tools for Communication

Graphic images are *iconic* material signs, but they are not the only kind of material signs. Other inscriptions and objects are useful for pointing to something beyond their own materiality: colors painted on the skin, tattoos, feathers, garments, or batons carved on wood or ivory can all be used as signs *indexing* somebody's rank or belonging to a group. Symbols go beyond that; they do not only present or represent a phenomenal object or some of their features but they also have the capability to create new kinds of entities – virtual objects arising from operations of the mind, which can also turn into instrumental means for the direction and explanation of experience and behavior, both objective and subjective.

Symbols are born when indexicality and iconicity merge into a new kind of sign. But, again, for the new entities and concepts so produced to be conceived and communicated, this new kind of sign has to be embodied into some material substance, so that their users could play with them and acquire the necessary abilities for using them proficiently. It is only then that they can be incorporated into the reservoir of resources of a group. The invention of numbers is one of these cases – a concept that arises as a result of the production of symbols through the transformation of tokens and graphical inscriptions.

Nonverbal children, and some animal species, seem to be able to distinguish between groups of objects with more or fewer components, and even to identify the difference between small amounts of objects (up to three or four elements), as well as discriminate between operations of addition and subtraction. However, as the number of items increases, this task seems impossible to be solved without developing first the concept of cardinal number – an ability that adults belonging to some cultural groups seem not to have acquired. One can guess that such a concept would not develop unless needed for some practical purpose, which is unlikely to happen when primary needs get solved by others or by foraging within or in the surroundings of one's dwellings – as happens with children or adults living in societies of hunter-gatherers. However, if there is a surplus of some kind of goods and a deficit of others and this imbalance is corrected through commerce and bartering, accounting becomes a necessity. This is what happened following the Neolithic revolution.

Malafouris (2013) reports archaeological evidence from Mesopotamian sites that shows how accounting records evolved in the period between the years 7000 and 3000 BCE. Accounting started by people using baked beads of clay to represent units of cattle or agricultural products. These tokens were molded into different shapes according to the kind of product that they represented (cones and spheres for large or small grain baskets, ovoid with an incision for an amphora of oil, or a tetrahedron for a day of work), and their small size made them easy to handle and transport. Accounting, however, was still a matter of motor manipulation of these tokens instead of their referents, with which they were in a one-to-one correspondence. Later on, these tokens were enclosed in "envelopes" (a hollow clay ball) that kept them together for convenient transportation. As time went on, these envelopes were marked with incisions made by pressing the beads on their fresh surface before putting them in the oven. These inscriptions mark the evolution from objects for handling (tokens for motor manipulation) to bi-dimensional notation, which had the effect that accounting operations moved from the hands to the eyes. The new notation conserved the iconicity (similarity of form) and indexical signification (the number of items engraved)

coming from the beads enclosed in the container. Around 3200 BCE, clay tablets, bearing the same types of inscriptions on their surface, replaced envelopes with the advantage of being smaller, lighter, and easier to transport.

Shortly afterward, around 3100 BCE, when city-states first appeared, incisions on tablets started to be replaced by pictograms (iconic signs) of two kinds: one referring to the kinds of goods recorded and another to the number of items. This is the first record of an abstract number detached from the types of elements counted. The transition from one kind of notation to another suggests that the development from ordinal to cardinal numbers required the recording of a sign representing the name given to the position in the sequential ordering of motor operations – an ordinal number. When this new sign was employed in further operations of addition and subtraction, cardinality emerged and, with it, the path for the development of metric measure, arithmetic, and mathematics.

Soon afterward (around 3000 BCE), tablets began to include the name of the owner, sender, or addressee of the goods recorded. This was done by changing the use of some of the earlier pictograms, which now, rather than representing a type of product, came to represent the sound of the first syllable of the word designating the object represented as it sounded in the oral language of the group. This allowed the name of the person to be recorded by combining pictographs representing the sounds that when put together made a name. The resulting inscription made it possible, when read, to pronounce a word referring to an absent phenomenal object and therefore to make it present here and now, even if far removed in space and in time from the scribe or the reader.

The final step, which took two more millennia to happen, was to abandon the representation of sounds and change it to inscriptions representing phonemes. When this happened, alphabetic writing was born. This resulted in a drastic decrease in the number of signs necessary for recording speech, opening the way for the expansion of literacy.

The long process just sketched retraced not only the change from one system of recording to another but also the transition from indexical and iconic signs, which signal presence and form, to conventional symbols, which gather them together into a unity. Now an object, even if not accessible to the senses – as abstract numbers are – is presented and can be recalled and operated on through utterances or through material operations in writing.

Thus, material signs, whatever it is that gives them substance, are objects carrying a new kind of value – a semiotic value. Beyond their material affordances or qualities, they also get new social affordances and qualities: they become able to point to something present or absent, embodied or disembodied, or even imagined, as abstract numbers are. Signs are always relational, but symbols also have ontopotentiality (Valsiner, 2002) – they have the capacity of producing new objects even if these objects are devoid of matter.

Material signs are objects crafted in such a way that their affordances and qualities enhance their semiotic functionality. Symbols are literally tools for communication, artifacts devised to serve as semiotic functions, for making present the absent in communication, for constraining or opening new venues for action, for working or for enjoyment, for thinking and imagining.

Semiotic value, again, is not an immanent property of a thing or an object but a consequence of how it is used and of the abilities of the user. Semiotic tools are elements to play or work with; they are the means for experimenting with new possibilities, for producing new experiences, enjoyable or not. They open the way for new forms of action and thus for new social practices and forms of art, for ritual and religion, for literature and philosophy, for technology and science, and therefore for expanding experiences, both epistemic and aesthetic.

6.4 Experiencing the World and Oneself

Experience is a continuous flow in which objects, situations, and events appear in unity. It includes very simple phenomena, such as sensing a quality (whiteness or warmth) or an affection (pain or joy); states of mind, such as finding something comforting, desirable, moving, or dreadful; and sensing oneself to be comfortable, unsettled, or eager. Whatever the case, experiences are ways of knowing and feeling; they always refer to something else and to the self in relation to the world. The experiencer therefore takes them as indispensable for the guidance of conduct (for a discussion, see Rosa, 2015).

Experience appears to the experiencer as a unifier that gathers together the operations of different psychological processes. These processes result from perception, emotion, thought, imagination, and memory, but none of these processes are immediately experienced; they are conceptual abstractions useful to account for the psyche's actions, for the explanation of experiences and the elaboration of psychological empirical knowledge.

Experience occurs continuously, because the interaction of live creature and environing conditions is involved in the very process of living. Under conditions of resistance and conflict, aspects and elements of the self and the world that are implicated in this interaction qualify experience with emotions and ideas so that conscious intent emerges. (Dewey, 1994, p. 205)

So viewed, experience is also an abstraction. What we empirically feel are actual concrete experiences taken one by one. As Dewey (1994, p. 205) puts it,

in contrast with such experience, we have *an* experience when the material experienced runs its course to fulfillment. Then and then only is it integrated within and demarcated in the general stream of experience from other experiences. A piece of work is finished in a way that is satisfactory; a problem receives its solution; a game is played through; a situation, whether that of eating a meal, playing a game of chess, carrying on a conversation, writing a book, or taking part in a political campaign, is so rounded out that its close is a consummation and not a cessation. Such an experience is a whole and carries with it its own individualizing quality and self-sufficiency. It is *an* experience. (emphasis in original)

Experiences, then, are singular, each having its own particularity:

An experience has a unity that gives it its name, that meal, that storm, that rupture of friendship. The existence of this unity is constituted by a single quality that pervades the entire experience in spite of the variation of its constituent parts . . . In going over an experience in mind after its occurrence, we may find that one property rather than another was sufficiently dominant so that it characterizes the experience as a whole. (p. 206)

Particular experiences are at once general and individual. On one hand, all experiences can be described and explained by referring to the operation of a set of psychological processes; and, on the other hand, they are particular, because they are about an individual object or event that receives a name:

In final import they are intellectual. But in their actual occurrence they were emotional as well; they were purposive and volitional. Yet the experience was not a sum of these different characters; they were lost in it as distinctive traits. (p. 206)

6.4.1 Aesthetic Experience

What makes an experience "aesthetic" is its appreciative character, its orientation toward enjoyment. "It denotes the consumer's rather than the producer's standpoint. It is Gusto, taste" (Dewey, 1994, p. 207). But this does not mean that the aesthetic attitude is merely contempla-

tive. It is in operation whenever something is being created:

The act of producing that is directed by intent to produce something that is enjoyed in the immediate experience of perceiving has qualities that a spontaneous or uncontrolled activity does not have. The artist embodies in himself the attitude of the perceiver while he works. (p. 208)

Such a view makes the aesthetic experience a distinctive feature not only of the practice of art but also of crafting and action at large, so long as their practitioners look for perfection in their execution and "perceive and enjoy the product that is executed" (Dewey, 1994, p. 207). Aesthetics, then, is not about a property of an object but about a way of relating to objects and action. It has more to do with the perceiver's and crafter's capabilities for enjoying – with taste. Aesthetics is made of emotional and motivational abilities that can be trained. It is a matter for "sentimental education" that is not foreign to ethics, to the cultivation of virtue – the search for excellence (Rosa & González, 2013). And, as such, it has a relational character; it refers to the products to be crafted but also to others, to social life.

Aesthetic experiences, and experience at large, belong to the experiencer and result from an exercise of abilities, of psychological processes governing behavior. Their effect shows when in relation with objects and with others – in perception, in action, and in communication – and also when experiencing one's own actions and oneself. They are means for self-direction and also operate in the construction of the concept of oneself and others.

Aesthetic experiences therefore perform another function. They add aesthetic value to meaning. Objects, actions, situations, and people can thus get an extra quality that expands beyond what their shape, utility, or functionality afford, but also because they themselves are a means of searching for excellence – enjoyment, beauty, virtue. To say that something or somebody is "nice" results from an aesthetic judgment that gathers together feelings "of grace and proportion in right conduct, a perception of fusion of means and ends" (Dewey, 1994, p. 215).

So viewed, aesthetic experiences are not useless side effects of the workings of psyche; they influence the direction of action for improving its products and also the development of awareness, agency, and self-awareness. They have a role in the processes of development, in giving value to objects, actions, one's own abilities, and one's own self as an object. This leads us into the examination of the fabric of experience and how it develops.

6.5 The Formal Fabric of Experience: Semiotics of Behavior and Experience

Experience is what makes us feel alive in the world. Experiences are informative but also deceptive; they present real objects but also fictional entities (angels, demons, leprechauns, phlogiston), even entities with no extension (pain, sentiments, duration, or succession). Experiences make it possible to profit from learning but also lead to mistakes; they can be enjoyable but also dreadful; they also make me feel myself – they are always *my* experiences. They are useful for the direction of behavior, for volition.

What are experiences made of? How is it that the structural coupling between material structures seems able to make such ethereal entities such as numbers, rationality, beauty, joy, or virtue to arise? The argument so far developed took material things and movement as key elements in this process. Body movements cause couplings to happen. These movements respond to the needs of living material entities whose structure allows those movements when searching for the negative entropy that supports their own structure. This gives them the impulse for moving and their surroundings the materials with which to couple and the energy needed for it. These processes go on

as long as the entity and its surroundings keep in a dynamic equilibrium. When they do not, the structure degrades and dies.

The structural flexibility of living bodies is what makes movements possible and also to discern the varied effects it produces in the environment and on its own inner equilibrium. So viewed, the changes of the body, while connecting with things, are informative about what things are like (sensation) and about their value for the maintenance of the inner equilibrium of the body (affection). Emotions are responses to sensations that appraise how the body feels affected and are then aroused for action. Thus the structure of the iterative movements (volition) informs as to what the elements of the environment afford (perception), while affection and emotions add value to the outcomes of those movements and also to the things with which those movements connect. In sum, movements (volition) and the affordances of things (sensation and perception) inform about the environment, and affections add value to the elements of the environment so that the three act together to create sense for things to turn into objects; and, in so doing, they also attribute meaning to objects, situations, and events. But neither sense nor meanings are material things: they are produced from what living bodies do and feel when relating to their environment. And as the shape of movements evolves through their iterative coupling with things, so do the meanings of objects, actions, situations, and the agent itself; the consequence is that new forms of meaning appear.

Experience, so viewed, is the informative capability that movements have when producing value. In other words, movements (volition), sensation, and affection are basic psychological processes that together turn things into objects to be perceived, liked or disliked, desired, or despised. So viewed, experience is able to orient behavior within an environment where different values are attributed to elements, in other words, experiences act as signs. This makes semiotics – the

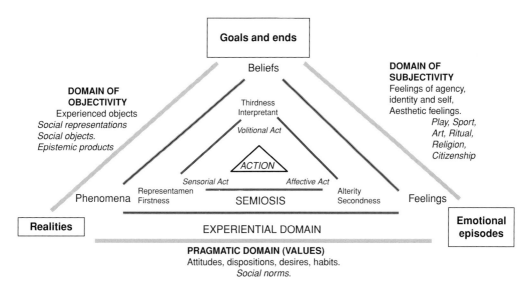

Figure 6.1 Triadic formalisms accounting for action, semiosis, experience, and realities.

science of supplying formal devices to explain the shaping and evolution of signs – a valuable instrument for the study of how experiences unfold.

6.5.1 Semiotics of Action

The semiotic approach of C. S. Peirce holds that anything can be used as a sign of something else, as long as there is some respect or capacity relating the sign and the thing it refers to (its *object*) for some particular purpose. In this way, meaning is not a fixed entity but the result of a process of *semiosis*.

Semiosis is a triadic process: it includes a *representamen* (first); something that has the capacity of acting as a sign that refers to something else – the *object* – (second) because both (the representamen and the referent) have something in common (form for *icons*, presence for *indexes*, or some conventional value for *symbols*); and a new sign – *interpretant* (third) – that interprets the relation between sign and object as a possibility (*rhema*), a fact (*dicent*), or a regularity or reason (*argument*). Semioses are recursive, which means that the *interpretant* – the situated interpretation

that somebody will form of the way the first sign refers to its object – can become a sign (a new representamen) for a next semiosis, in effect producing a new interpretant, and so on ad infinitum. *Interpretants* can take many shapes. They can manifest as behavior (a body reaction, a gesture); as some kind of performance (a habit, a dance, or a stroke); as a scream, a word, or an utterance; or as some cognitive operation. This causes semiosis to be not only a meaning-making device but also a logical device for the explanation of thinking in action.

The triadic structure of semiosis is isomorphic to the structure of action, when the action is conceived as a composition of three kinds of acts (sensorial, volitional, and affective) (see Figure 6.1). This isomorphism opens the way for developing a theory of semiotic actuations in which experience results from the semiotic properties of body movements when in contact with the things of the environment (for a lengthier explanation, see Rosa, 2007a, 2007b).

This isomorphism allows experiences, behavior, and their material outcomes (drawings, pictures, crafted artifacts, or written utterances) to be conceived as resulting from semiotic processes.

In this way, semiosis does not only provide sense to action and behavior; it also offers formalisms for explaining the way objects are manipulated and transformed, making objects and artifacts both means and results of semiotic processes.

The above reviewed "theory of material engagement" (Malafouris, 2013) offers a convincing argument of how the semiotic properties of the manipulation of objects are instrumental for the explanation of the development of higher psychological processes. Malafouris's approach argues that action with objects is a form of thinking-in-action – which he terms "enactive semiosis" – in which the signifier and the signified generate each other. His argument is that as an action transforms an object, the resulting artifact can become a sign signaling to a new entity, even if the latter never existed before within experience – as is the case with figures and numbers. The consequence is that artifacts are materialized interpretants of enactive semioses and concepts an effect of the use of signs.

Objects, as presented in our experience, are the result of a series of recursive semioses, which go on until the interpreter gets satisfied with the interpreted result or gives up. Semiotized objects result from chains of particular semioses. We can think of objects only because signs present them. They may have a transcendental *ontic* nature or not (e.g., stones, birds, hobbits, Madame Bovary, phlogiston, obscure matter, the *pi* number), but their *ontology* is provided by semioses (Rosa & Pievi, 2013).

6.5.2 From Action to Intentional Schemas, Habits, and Dramatic Actuations

Action (a triad of sensorial, volitional, and affective acts; see Figure 6.1) is the basic mechanism of body couplings. However, its structure is very rigid and can only account for basic reactions in which the organism simply reacts to changes of the environment. To explain the flexibility of behavior for adapting to changing circumstances and profiting from accumulated experience, something else is needed – a formalism that also could take into account the changes in the inner state of the organism while coupling with the environment so that a different volition act could emerge. The iteration of actions in circular reactions, and their composition in novel structures in the shape of recursive semiosis, is able to produce such emergent properties.

The *intentional schema* combines three consecutive actions within a novel triadic structure. This new structure is the basis on which more complex psychological processes, such as perception, emotion, learning, and new forms of intentionality, can start to develop. These are effects of the semiotic processes that this structure allows, which makes it possible to combine simultaneously the reference to things of the environment to the inner state of the organism (affections) and so open the way to the attribution of values to two kind of objects: things of the environment and the organism itself.

The intentional scheme (Figure 6.2) has some properties worth mentioning. It combines three semioses, but with the peculiarity that while the first and second semioses (OBA and ABC) (see Figure 6.2) have as a referent[1] the inner affect that the encountered thing produced in the organism of the interpreter (B), the third semiosis (CBD) (see Figure 6.2) takes the reiteration of the inner organismic state (C) (see Figure 6.2) as representative of the affection felt (B) (the referent again) in the last encounter with the thing, producing in turn an interpretant that is a volitive act (D) addressed to the environment – a *desire*. Thus affect (B) plays a key role in this process, because it is the permanent (inner) outcome of the encounter between the organism and the thing. The consequence is that affect and its reiteration and transformation throughout time (mood: C) (see Figure 6.2) become key elements for the development of mental representations.

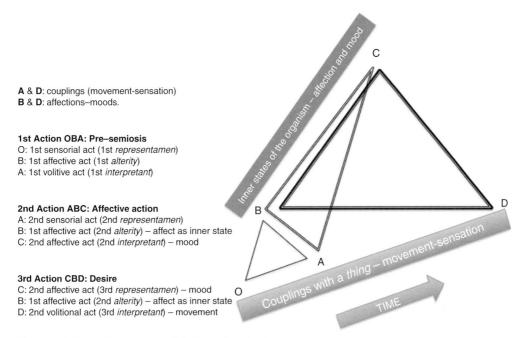

A & D: couplings (movement-sensation)
B & D: affections–moods.

1st Action OBA: Pre–semiosis
O: 1st sensorial act (1st *representamen*)
B: 1st affective act (1st *alterity*)
A: 1st volitive act (1st *interpretant*)

2nd Action ABC: Affective action
A: 2nd sensorial act (2nd *representamen*)
B: 1st affective act (2nd *alterity*) – affect as inner state
C: 2nd affective act (2nd *interpretant*) – mood

3rd Action CBD: Desire
C: 2nd affective act (3rd *representamen*) – mood
B: 1st affective act (2nd *alterity*) – affect as inner state
D: 2nd volitional act (3rd *interpretant*) – movement

Figure 6.2 Semiotic structure of the *intentional scheme*.

Without the dynamics of affect, no sense could appear.

The intentional scheme is a structure capable of accounting for the directionality of behavior as an effect of affect and mood. It is a chain of three recursive semioses sharing the same referent (B) – the inner affect produced by repeated encounters with the *thing*. The resulting semiotic structure is that of a *legisign* – an interpretant able to signal to regularity (D) – a volitive act addressed to the thing, the intent to reproduce the result of the encounter with the thing (B): a desire. Legisigns are the semiotic basis for the production of permanent objects.

Actuations are structures resulting from the semiotic structure of the intentional scheme. As Figure 6.3 shows, (1) intentional (volitive) action (ABD) and (2) the formal properties of semiotized objects (perception) (ACD) develop as processes as interpretative actions unfold throughout time.

Volitive action (intentional behavior) is a direct outcome of the intentional scheme. It is represented in Figure 6.3 by the ABD action semiosis. Thus sensorial act A acts as signal to inner state B, producing a volitive act D, addressed to again produce B (the affect). This is the beginning of intentional action and also the basis for the development of habits.

Perceptual action (ACD) takes a sensed property of the object (A) as a sign of the repetition of moods felt (C), producing a new act toward the thing (D). In this way, volitive and perceptual actions are simultaneous effects of the intentional scheme and signal the emergence of intentional behavior and the stabilization of experience. Both movements and sensorial qualities can now signal objects, and behavior can be driven by sensations that can perform as signals as a result of previous experiences.

The reiteration of actuations on the same thing will enrich the meaning of the object by adding further formal, functional, and aesthetic values as emerging from the semiotic structures of actuations when encountering the thing.

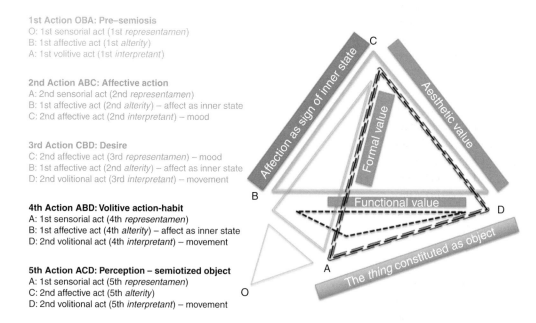

1st Action OBA: Pre–semiosis
O: 1st sensorial act (1st *representamen*)
B: 1st affective act (1st *alterity*)
A: 1st volitive act (1st *interpretant*)

2nd Action ABC: Affective action
A: 2nd sensorial act (2nd *representamen*)
B: 1st affective act (2nd *alterity*) – affect as inner state
C: 2nd affective act (2nd *interpretant*) – mood

3rd Action CBD: Desire
C: 2nd affective act (3rd *representamen*) – mood
B: 1st affective act (2nd *alterity*) – affect as inner state
D: 2nd volitional act (3rd *interpretant*) – movement

4th Action ABD: Volitive action-habit
A: 1st sensorial act (4th *representamen*)
B: 1st affective act (4th *alterity*) – affect as inner state
D: 2nd volitional act (4th *interpretant*) – movement

5th Action ACD: Perception – semiotized object
A: 1st sensorial act (5th *representamen*)
C: 2nd affective act (5th *alterity*)
D: 2nd volitional act (5th *interpretant*) – movement

Figure 6.3 *Actuation*: Semiotic development of *intentional action* and *objects*.

Several consequences follow: (1) sensorial qualities can trigger intentional volitive actions, (2) things turn into objects as their affordances are grasped through action, (3) objects acquire values through successive active encounters, (4) affect turns into moods and feelings (Russell, 2003) as semioses actions iterate, and (5) the interpretative construction of objects through semioses (actions) comes together with an increasing sense of one's own agency, as volitive actions get progressively tuned in successive couplings.

Actuations, as so far described, are enactive semioses, i.e., semioses in which resulting interpretants are motor actions. They produce legisigns that stabilize the experience of the world through the development of habits and intentionality; they have indexical (sense of presence) and iconic (formal) properties (Peirce's signs types 5, 6, and 7; see Rosa 2007a).

This opens the way for identifying whether the encountered thing is a novelty or a known object, making the development of habits possible and enhancing the capability for adjusting behavior to environmental conditions, that is, learning and early forms of intelligence.

The repetition and variation of actuations on the same environmental element end up producing a conceptualization of the object – a reiteration of the same semiotic structure, which makes the resulting successive volitive actions (interpretants) possible, which could then act as signs referring to the object being constituted, so that its meaning grows as new values are added. Once the thing gets constituted as a permanent object, it becomes an otherness able to be presented by signs referring to their presence (indexes) and form (icons), e.g., a pain felt (B) can signal a harmful quality (A) of an object, which causes me to scream and move away (D). The withdrawal movement and the scream are a consequence of what the object is – a bush of nettles – but they are also signals that may warn others about the qualities of the encountered thing, so they are informed of how to behave in relation to it.

Affects (B), moods (C), and emotional reactions (BCD, Figure 6.3) play an important role in communicative processes. On one hand, they are able to act as intra-organismic signs of the encountered thing, and on the other hand, they produce behavioral reactions that can act as signs of both the internal state of the reacting organism and the aesthetic values of the encountered thing. This has the effect of giving a semiotic capability to affects, moods, and feelings – they can act as signs of the thing in addition to adding affective value to other values that give meaning to the semiotic object in constitution.

The communicative and informative nature of the volitive action adds a dramatic nature to actuations – they can be interpreted as signals by others, who may take it as information about an object of the environment or about an intention of the actor. This also makes actuations *dramatic actuations*, which then are not only a result of encounters with things of the environment but also a means for communicating with others. Thus motor volitive acts (the final interpretant of actuations – D) can be shaped for communication purposes and can get progressively ritualized. This eventually results in the production of gestures and words (new ritualized enactive objects) tailored for efficient communication. The consequence is that a new kind of sign arises – the symbol.

6.5.3 Symbols and Arguments to Experience Objects beyond Material Encounters

Symbols are conventional signs. They are objects able to represent other objects, resulting from habit, social communication, and conventionalization. This is the case for ritualized movements (gestures) or their material outcomes, such as artifacts resulting from human action (tokens, figures made with traces on a surface, pronounced or written words, etc.). Symbols are artifacts for efficient communication – saying "nettles" when walking in the fields is a way of preventing harm to others, if the speaker and the listeners know what this word means. Symbols make present here and now something still not noticed or absent (a harpsichord, a deceased friend, or the amount of my mortgage) just by uttering a word or by seeing some figures on a piece of paper.

Symbols not only represent objects resulting from couplings with environmental things; they also inform the values and qualities making up the meaning of the object. These values are a result of the previously mentioned semiotic processes, which include elements such as affects, moods, feelings, desires, sensorial qualities, and patterns of behavior, which are also signs able to refer to an alterity. This opens the way for identification mistakes and also for the production of other bizarre objects never physically encountered – fictitious creatures (angels, elves, fairies) or abstract entities such as phlogiston, energy, or intelligence. But if such entities come to exist as creatures of experience, it is not because they have a material structure with which our bodies can couple; they result from a new mental ability that symbols allow – imagination – which is an ability that can only appear as an outcome of recursive interpretative semioses, which combine symbols to produce a new kind of sign: arguments.

Arguments (Peirce's type 10 signs) are able to produce new meaning by combining sets of symbols following some rules (a grammar of some type). These rules start to develop from the constraints and possibilities that actuations in the environment provide, but they can evolve and be transformed into many varieties in different

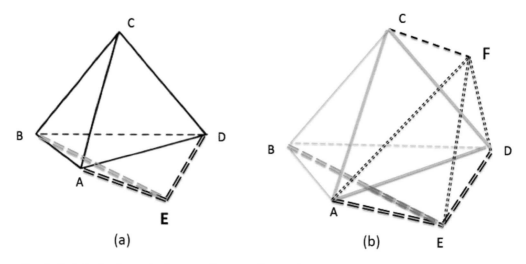

(a)   (b)

Semiotic tetrahedrons in the constitution of experience
ABCD: Actuations
ABDE: Dramatic actuations produce symbols (E)
DEAF: Symbols (E) produce arguments (F)
FCAD: Arguments became able to raise (aesthetic) emotions and behavior

Figure 6.4 Fractal structure of experience and behavior: Development of *symbols* and *arguments*.

environments for different purposes – such as ethnic natural languages. They can also be artificially devised for particular purposes – such as mathematics, logic, or computer programming. This causes different symbolic codes to appear adapted to the purposes and conditions of their use – e.g., alphabetic notation, flag codes, sign language, traffic signals, musical notation, numbers, algebraic notation. Such codes reciprocally adapt the structure of symbols and the rules for their combination, searching to enhance their functionality.

Whatever the case, arguments are logical machines for creating new symbols and meanings and therefore for producing new objects one can think of, irrespective of the ontological status they may have. Witches, angels, unicorns, justice, the *pi* number, and the gravitational constant are creatures arising from these processes. They could never exist without previous arguments that provide them with a structure, if not a substance.

Whether the ontological status attributed to entities of these kinds is to be taken as true or false, real or imaginary, is a matter of judgment not independent of the kind of code and grammar applied, the way they were applied, and the social norms and beliefs of the communities and individuals making those judgments for some purpose (juridical, epistemic, artistic, religious, etc.).

Arguments are therefore the semiotic structure behind higher psychological processes like imagination, memory, and symbolic thinking. Figure 6.4 sketches how symbols (E) develop from actuations, and arguments (F) from actuations, with the mediation of symbols. As these appear, both symbols and arguments are able to signal to affects (B) or emotions (C), to sensorial qualities (A), and are also able to steer behavior (D). This is what makes angels appear radiant and attractive and witches ugly and repulsive; it is what attributes aesthetic value to artistic compositions or elegance to mathematical equations –

and the reverse: how sensorial qualities, feelings, or body movements can be taken as signs relating some object to another, such as in the production of metaphors.

As Figure 6.4 shows, the semiotic structure of actuations can be represented by a tetrahedron, a structure that is replicated as new semiosis actions appear in the flow of experience. The consequence is that the semiotic structure of the flow of experience and behavior resembles a dynamic system with a fractal structure of which the basic unit is the actuation (see Figure 6.4b).

6.5.4 The Semiotic Constitution of Social Objects and Intentional Worlds

Actuations are the basic units of intentional behavior; they produce legisigns (symbols and arguments) capable of stabilizing experience and thus shape *semiotic objects* of different kinds. Whatever nature they may have, *semiotic objects* appear instantiated in some kind of material artifact resulting from previous actuations (gestures, uttered or written words, tools, crafted or industrial products). This causes material symbols, concepts, and semiotic objects to be historically contingent sociocultural products, making up the cultural stock of each particular group.

Social (semiotised) *objects* (Wagner et al., 1999) can get to exist and be shared within a group only if at some moment they were instantiated in some material element for a conventionalized use. This makes material artifacts indispensable tools for the kind of communication that enables a social tuning of individuals' behavior and experience. They provide the environmental elements that permit sociocultural phenomena.

A *sociocultural phenomenon* is the interpretation an observer makes of somebody else's actuation on an environmental element, so that the element could be taken as a sign of the possibility (*rhema*) of a previously semiotized object. It is because of the interpretation of such a possibility that the "reality" of a semiotic object, presented by a phenomenon, could eventually be accepted. The availability of a common tool kit of artifacts (Wertsch, 1991), icons, symbols, and arguments for their use in shared cultural practices is what makes it possible for social phenomena to act as signs of the presence of sociocultural objects within the dynamic flow of current experience.

Social phenomena do not appear chaotically, nor are social objects randomly produced in uncoordinated performances, utterances, or inscriptions. They get assembled into argumentative semioses in which interpretants are new kinds of objects – *social virtual objects* (such as boss, daughter, bartering, money) that are abstract categories that can also get embodied in individual objects, which, when invoked by a symbol, embody a network of (social) values when experienced.

Scenes and events are also creatures of this kind. They result from recursive arguments that relate objects of many kinds – semiotized natural objects (stones, trees, cows) and social objects (friends, foes, property, home) – so that the ongoing drama of social life gets stabilized and becomes understandable. The consequence is that further arguments make more objects appear, such as scripts for actuations and social rules. When the latter are also stabilized, they can become references for further argumentative semioses, making new entities appear, such as morality, justice, responsibility, authority, indignity, family, identity, or belonging.

Again, none of these new objects could come to exist without some kind of material support. If symbols are embodied in gestures, sounds, or iconic displays of many different kinds (pictures, statues, pictograms, letters, flags, mathematical signs, musical notation, rituals), arguments can only materialize when material symbols are combined within *texts* of different kinds. Texts, then, are the material support for the production of argumentative *discourses*, irrespective of the material that gives them substance or the form they take. Thus an arrangement of letters, words, and sentences on whatever surface (marble, paper, or computer screen) is a text; but a picture, a road with painted lines and traffic signs, a parade, a church, a theatre performance, or a graduation ceremony is a different kind of text too. All are made up of sets of symbols arranged according to rules able to convey significance to their users. Texts are syntactic constructions resulting from their authors' enactive semioses but not yet semanticized by an audience.

The formal features of the symbols, and the purpose and functions they serve in a particular realm of sociocultural life, set the rules for their use. The code provides the syntactic possibilities texts have for producing significance. This makes some codes better suited for some purposes than others, and then more or less familiar or foreign to members of different cultural groups.

Discourses are semanticized texts (Magariños, 2008). They are semiotic machines for creating entities and for giving them value. It is this semiogenic capacity that makes it possible for discursive semioses to create metadiscourses and, with that, to abstract objects further removed from the sensorial experience, for example, literature, grammar, musicology, algebra, logic, theology, and cosmology (but also astrology, demonology, and ufology). These are domains of knowledge (or fiction?) populated by plenty of creatures (morphemes and syntagms, characters and plots, chords and beats, integers and functions, black holes and antimatter) far removed from empirical experience, which sometimes seem to be accepted either as plausible or real, as capable of conveying or producing truth or leading to mistakes.

Many texts instated in a great variety of codes have been produced throughout time – books, tableaus, frescoes, churches, palaces, arches of triumph, and city squares are among them. Each ethnic group has a language, professional guilds have their own peculiar different codes adapted to their tasks, and institutions and groups have developed different social languages. The discourses so produced are a variegated mixture: booklets of instruction, sacred scriptures, philosophical essays, romantic novels, epic poetry, science handbooks, political speeches, news reels, celebration or mourning rituals, tragic theatre performances, or memorial monuments are all examples of different discursive genres tailored to serve different communication purposes. Even this proliferation of cultural materials allows individuals access to only a fraction of the texts, symbols, arguments, and discourses available within the sociocultural space in which they live.

The symbols, arguments, and discourses that one individual is exposed to and somehow manages to master for one's own use constitute the tool kit of *symbolic resources* (Zittoun, 2017). These are the resources that one has available to make sense of personal lived experiences; to identify objects; to think and argue; and also to judge whether one's immediate experience (as an object, an event, a cause, or a consequence) is real or fictitious, subjective or objective, or a belief resulting from social convention – even if the line dividing one experience from another is not always very clear. If the outcome resulting from such a judgment attributes some reality to what is felt, the resulting behavioral actuation restarts the process.

Figure 6.5 sketches the unfolding of the process described in this section. The structural couplings of the organism and environmental elements trigger series of recursive semiotic actions, which simultaneously produce transformations in the environment (behavior, inscriptions, texts) and lead to the experience of semiotic objects that enrich their meaning as more values (phenomena, qualities, functions) are added. The final outcome is the *intentional world* (Magariños, 2008) which one believes oneself to be living in when performing an actuation.

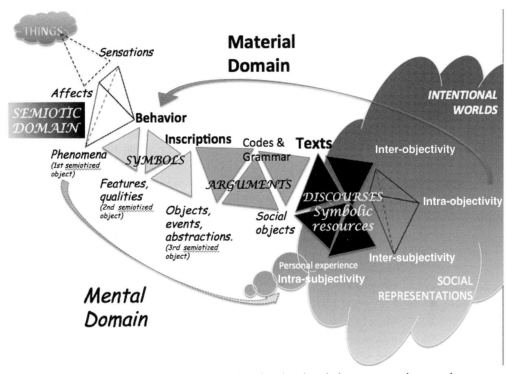

Figure 6.5 Substitutive semioses in the dynamics of sociocultural phenomena and personal experiences.

The experiences making up the objects, events, norms, and beliefs that compose an *intentional world* are simultaneously objective and subjective. They could not exist without the mediation of environmental materials, nor without carrying out successive coupling actions on the material tools developed throughout this process. In this view, the mental domain is made of signs (which material support cannot be but body changes) whose presentative or representative capability is provided by the semiotic structure of recursive actions. These accumulative structures make up the dynamic system that supports the development of new abilities and higher psychological processes. This does not make body structures or the nervous system a repository of stored ideas, meanings, or beliefs. Experiences and beliefs are fleeting semiotic outcomes of a dynamic system of successive encounters of body structures with environmental elements. As Brentano (1874) said, experience is immanently objective, it is always intentional, and it invariably refers to something else.

6.6 Conclusions: Action Turns Things into Objects and Artifacts When Valuing Experience for the Direction of Behavior

This chapter explains how innovation is produced; how perception turns things into objects; and how action changes the use of objects, their shapes, and their values. Innovation is exploration and the trying out of new possibilities; it is more playing and enjoying than mere trial and error and only turns into labor once a new use is given to the product crafted, so that what before was experimentation is now ritualized, disciplined operations.

The main points that were developed in the argument above can be summarized as follows:

1 Phenomenal objects result from couplings between bodies and things. It is through action that values are attached to environmental elements. Objects are semiotized entities.

2 Perception and production of artifacts are related processes: both are consequences of how adaptive behavior adds values to the encountered environmental elements and to their changes.

3 Value is a relational concept; it is how something is related to something else. Meaning is the set of values attributed to objects.

4 Affective processes are crucial for the production of value, sense, and meaning: they not only arouse action and appraise the elements encountered and the results of actions but also signal the agent's agency and so add value to the agent, causing a new object to appear – the self. Human agents cannot act, gauge their actions, and value their outcomes and themselves without feelings.

5 The objects that populate our world and the artifacts we produce result from human action and knowledge that are instantiated in material inscriptions accumulated throughout time to embody value and meaning, so to direct our behavior. Action and cognition, objects and perception, knowledge and crafts are like the two sides of a coin minted for presenting the values that things have for life.

6 Material culture is made of the accumulation of artifacts, inscriptions, texts, and landscape transformations, resulting from the labor of previous generations. It is the semiotization of these artifacts that turns them into the tool kit of discourses that together constitute the set of intersecting semiospheres (Lotman,

2005) giving meaning to the shared *Umwelt* of the group.

7 To participate in the social life of a group, a newcomer must share its cultural values. This requires becoming familiar with the use of artifacts and inscriptions when participating in social activities, developing the skills for doing so, and also taming emotions so they become tuned to the values and norms of the group. Sociocultural scripts regulate not only what to do but also how to feel.

8 Experience is the subjective outcome of the semiotic value of these meditational means (signs, symbols, and arguments belonging to a variety of codes) for guiding action when participating in sociocultural activities. Experience is somehow co-extensive to consciousness (which also includes unconscious processes) and therefore related to a family of psychological constructs like controlled cognitive processes, executive functions, or the will.

9 The structural isomorphism of action and semiosis, and their recursive capabilities, opens the door for a semiotic analysis of behavior addressing how experience (conscious or unconscious) provides sense to behavior and operates in personal governance.

10 Semiotics offers formalisms for explaining how things turn into objects and are manipulated and transformed: artifacts are materialized interpretants of enactive semioses.

It is only when novelty is produced that new values are made to appear. Play and art are sociocultural activities for producing enjoyment in their participants; they leave room for originality and also frequently praise innovation. They are like sociocultural greenhouses for the production of new artifacts, values, and meanings, such as social laboratories for the experimentation of new emotions (Vygotsky, 1974), and also a school for the *éducation sentimentelle* of their participants.

In contrast, technology and labor do not create new values but expand the circulation of those that already existed. They are sociocultural activities that conserve the legacies of past innovation and serve the needs and interests of their practitioners and of those who profit from the manufactured products.

Play and labor, art and technology, are practices developed from the sociocultural dynamics of human history. They furnish our *Umwelt* with artifacts produced by psyches spirited by the cultural values embodied in the matter with which they play, in the machines that make our lives easier, and in the machinations that constrain our liberty. The question remains whether these artifacts, while used for working or playing, can add enjoyment or suffering to our lives, whether they are a help for us living a meaningful life.

Note

1 I have chosen to speak of referent (*thing* or alterity) rather than object, as Peirce did, when describing the three elements of a semiosis, in order to leave the term *object* to refer to the semiotized object, once it has acquired values and thus is conceptualized as an entity.

References

Barsalou. L. W. (1999). Perceptual symbol systems. *Behavioral and Brain Sciences*, 22, 577–660.

Barsalou, L. W. (2003). Abstraction in perceptual symbol systems. *Philosophical Transactions of the Royal Society*, 358, 1177–1187. DOI: 10.1098/rstb.2003.1319.

Bateson, P. P. G. (1981). Discontinuities in development and changes in the organization of play in cats. In K. Immelmann, G. Barlow, L. Petrinovich, & M. Main (Eds.), *Behavioral Development* (pp. 281–295). New York: Cambridge University Press.

Bateson, P. P. G. (2005). Play and its role in the development of great apes and humans. In A. D. Pellegrini & P. K. Smith (Eds.), *The Nature of Play: Great Apes and Humans* (pp. 13–26). New York: Guilford.

Bekoff, M. (1995). Playing with play: What can we learn about cognition, negotiation, and evolution. In D. Cummins & C. Allen (Eds.), *The Evolution of Mind* (pp. 162–182). New York: Oxford University Press.

Brentano, F. (1874). *Psychologie von Empirische Standpunkte*. Leipzig: Dunker und Humbolt.

Bruner, J. S. (1972). The nature and uses of immaturity. *American Psychologist*, 27, 687–708.

Callon, M. & Latour, B. (1981). Unscrewing the big Leviathan. In K. Knorr-Cetina & A. Cicourel (Eds.), *Advances in Social Theory and Methodology: Towards an Integration of Micro- and Macro-Sociology* (pp. 277–303). London: Routledge & Kegan Paul.

Carruthers, P. (2002). Human creativity: Its cognitive basis, its evolution, and its connection with childhood pretence. *British Journal of the Philosophy of Science*, 53, 225–249.

Cole, M. (1998). *Cultural Psychology: A Once and Future Discipline*. Cambridge, MA: Harvard University Press.

Dewey, J. (1994). Art as Experience. In S. D. Ross (Ed.), *An Anthology of Aesthetic Theory* (pp. 204–220). Albany: State University Of New York Press.

Dissanayake, E. (1974). A hypothesis of the evolution of art from play. *Leonardo*, 7, 211–217.

Gadamer, H. G. (2011). *Truth and Method*. Gloucester, UK: Continuum.

Gell, A. (1998). *Art and Agency: An Anthropological Theory*. Oxford: Oxford University Press.

Gibson, J. (2015). *The Ecological Approach to Visual Perception*. New York: Psychology Press.

Grondin, J. (2001). Play, festival and ritual in Gadamer: On the theme of the immemorial in his later works. In L. K. Schmidt (Ed.), *Language and Linguisticality in Gadamer's Hermeneutics* (pp. 51–58). Lanham, MD: Lexington Books.

Groos, K. (1901). *The Play of Man*. London: Heinemann.

Haye, A. (2008). Living being and speaking being: Toward a dialogical approach to intentionality. *Integrative Psychological and Behavioral Science*, 42, 157–163. DOI: 10.1007/s12124-007-9051-6.

Kirsh, D. & Maglio, P. (1994). On distinguishing epistemic from pragmatic action. *Cognitive Science*, 18, 513–549.

Koffka, K. (1935). *Principles of Gestalt Psychology.* London: Routledge.

Latour, B. (1987). *Science in Action.* Cambridge, MA: Harvard University Press.

Latour, B. (1991). Technology is society made durable. In J. Law (Ed.), *A Sociology of Monsters: Essays on Power, Technology and Domination* (pp. 103–131). London: Routledge.

Law, J. (1999). After ANT: Complexity, naming and topology. In J. Law & J. Hassard (Eds.), *Actor Network Theory and After* (pp. 1–14). Oxford: Blackwell.

Lotman, J. (2005). On the Semiosphere. *Sign Systems Studies*, 33(1), 206–229 (trans. by Wilma Clark). Retrieved from www.ut.ee/SOSE/sss/Lotman331.pdf.

Malafouris, L. (2013). *How Things Shape the Mind. A Theory of Material Engagement.* Cambridge, MA: Massachusetts Institute of Technology Press.

Magariños de Morentín, J. (2008). *La semiótica de los bordes.* Retrieved from www.magarinos.com.ar/Impresion.html.

Maturana, H. & Varela, F. (1992). *The Tree of Knowledge: The Biological Roots of Human Understanding.* Boston: Shambhala.

Pellegrini, A. D., Dupuis, D., & Smith, P. K. (2007). Play in evolution and development. *Developmental Review*, 27, 261–276. DOI: 10.1016/j.dr.2006.09.001.

Piaget, J. (1951). *Play, Dreams, and Imitation in Childhood.* London: Routledge and Kegan Paul.

Rodriguez, C. (2007). Object use, communication, and signs: The triadic basis of early cognitive development. In J. Valsiner & A. Rosa (Eds.), *Cambridge Handbook of Sociocultural Psychology* (pp. 257–276). New York: Cambridge University Press.

Rosa, A. (2007a). Acts of psyche: Actuations as synthesis of semiosis and action. In J. Valsiner & A. Rosa (Eds.), *Cambridge Handbook of Sociocultural Psychology* (pp. 205–237). New York: Cambridge University Press.

Rosa, A. (2007b). Dramaturgical actuations and symbolic communication: Or how beliefs make up reality. In J. Valsiner & A. Rosa (Eds.), *Cambridge Handbook of Sociocultural Psychology* (pp. 293–317). New York: Cambridge University Press.

Rosa, A. (2015). The reflective mind and reflexivity in psychology: Description and explanation within a psychology of experience. In G. Marsico, R. Ruggieri, & S. Salvatore (Eds.), *Reflexivity and Psychology* (Yearbook of Idiographic Science, vol. 6, pp. 17–44). Charlotte, NC: Information Age Publishing.

Rosa, A. & González, F. (2013). Trajectories of experience of real life events: A semiotic approach to the dynamics of positioning. *Integrative Psychological and Behavioral Science*, 47: 395–430. DOI: 10.1007/s12124-013-9240-4.

Rosa, A. & Pievi, N. (2013). Semiotic methodology for the analysis of the cultural and individual dynamics of social representations: A view from cultural psychology. *Papers on Social Representations*, 22, 19.1–19.29.

Rosch, E. & Mervis, C. B. (1975). Family resemblances: Studies in the internal structure of categories. *Cognitive Psychology*, 7, 573–605.

Russell, J. A. (2003). Core affect and the psychological construction of emotion. *Psychological Review*, 110(1), 145–172. DOI: 10.1037/0033-295X.110.1.145.

Searle, J. (1983). *Intentionality: An Essay in the Philosophy of Mind.* Cambridge: Cambridge University Press.

Valsiner, J. (1998). *The Guided Mind: A Sociogenetic Approach to Personality.* Cambridge, MA: Harvard University Press.

Valsiner, J. (2002). Irreversibility of time and ontopotentiality of signs. *Estudios de Psicología*, 23(1), 49–59.

Valsiner, J. (2014). The *Raumaesthetik* of Theodor Lipps as a dialogical research programme. Invited Lecture at the 8th International Conference on Dialogical Self. Den Haag, August 21, 2014. Retrieved from www.academia.edu/11513380/Raumaesthetik_of_Theodor_Lipps.

Vygotsky, L. (1967). Play and its role in the mental development of the child. *Soviet Psychology*, 12, 62–76.

Vygotsky, L. (1974). *Psychology of Art*. Cambridge, MA: MIT Press.

Wagner, W., Farr, R., Jovchelovitch, S., Lorenzi-Cioldi, F., Marková, I., Duveen, G., & Rose, D. (1999). Theory and method of social representations. *Theory and Method of Social Representations* [online]. London: LSE Research Online. Retrieved from: http://eprints.lse.ac.uk/2640.

Wertsch, J. (1991). *Voices of the Mind*. Cambridge, MA: Harvard University Press.

Further Reading

Harré, R. (2012). Positioning theory: Moral dimensions of social-cultural psychology. In J. Valsiner (Ed.), *The Oxford Handbook of Culture and Psychology* (pp. 191–206). Oxford: Oxford University Press.

Vygotsky, L. (1934/1987). Thinking and speech. In Robert W. Rieber & Aaron S. Carton (Eds.), *The Collected Works of L. S. Vygotsky. Volume 1: Problems of General Psychology* (pp. 37–285). New York: Plenum Press.

7 Making Social Objects: The Theory of Social Representation

Wolfgang Wagner, Katrin Kello, and Andu Rämmer

7.1 Veneration and Violence

Whenever Muslim believers assemble in a mosque for Friday's prayer, they jointly pray to a supernatural entity that comes into existence in these moments: a being called "Allah" that is the target of the activities of the assembled people. If you asked one of the attendees, they would say that Allah is the all-merciful and all-mighty god and responsible for everything on earth and in heaven. This particular phenomenon can be observed with any religion where people assemble and ritually worship their gods according to their beliefs. As different as their beliefs may be, the result will always be the same, that is, the creation of the target of worship that makes its presence felt by the participants.

There has recently been abundant evidence attesting to the power of this process in the ways that some radical exemplars of the faithful of different religions face adherents of other religions and, in particular, atheists. In several interpretations, their god's existence demands elimination of the faithless, a process that state powers in most countries call terrorism. Thus, the mental being that manifests its existence in collective rituals has earthly consequences for the victims of the believers' rage. Let's not be myopic: this violent phenomenon is not limited to Muslim "extremists," but was, and is, an unavoidable potential side effect – or "collateral damage" – of all religions in history, whether Christian (Pratt, 2010), Jewish (Aran & Hassner, 2013; Gubler & Kalmoe, 2015), Muslim (Ginges et al., 2016; Putra & Sukabdi, 2014), or Hindu (Sen & Wagner, 2009).

In the course of such behaviors, be it venerating one's god in a mosque, temple, synagogue, or church, or violently confronting nonbelievers – for example, in Paris 2016 – and "non-chosen" others – for example, Palestinians in the case of Israel – (e.g., Hirsch-Hoefler, Canetti, & Eiran, 2016), people establish and give reality to the object of "god." In the end, the reality of these social objects extends even to outsiders, countries, and governments as far as they feel a need to respond to a threat.

In this chapter, we present and discuss three social objects that range from the concrete and material such as a wheelchair to institutionalized discursive objects such as "global warming" as well as national identity and nation state. The construction and the dynamics of social objects can be explored within the framework of social representation theory. Originally, the theory was conceived as a means to understand ways of representing new scientific insights and theories that became popularized in a society (Moscovici, 1961, 2008). It was part of the French tradition of "*vulgarisation scientifique*," a movement dedicated to science education (Bauer, 1993; Jacobi, 1977). Over the last few decades, this "narrow" view of social representation theory has developed into a much broader theoretical framework that can be applied to a wide variety of social processes and social as well as cultural objects as can be seen in a recent handbook (Sammut et al., 2015) and in the examples that we provide in the rest of the chapter.

Note that the use of the term "representation" is ambiguous. In the title we use the term to express the activity of representing. In the following we distinguish its use in the sense of activity from the other meaning, representations as products of the activity of representing: substantial and imaginary constructs observable in behavior and speech.

7.2 Social Representation Theory

7.2.1 Belief and Communicating

Communities can be characterized by the fact that their members maintain a web of communication by sharing in a meaning system and the associated language. This system of meanings describes and, indeed, defines their local world and the objects populating it. The basic part of the shared meaning system comprises cultural items that derive from traditions and long-term historical processes. Such collective representations (Durkheim, 1920) are relatively stable and comprise core ideas about the world. They give the religious and moral justification for what is right or wrong, and comprise the rules of the community's social structure.

In modern times, mass media, and now the so-called social media have amended the repertoire of communication tools. These tools have given rise to a more dynamic and fleeting construction of meanings that may appear and fade like fashions, but also add more dynamic "entries" in the "book of cultures."

Communication, beliefs, and knowledge frequently refer to images and metaphorical thinking when it comes to talking about novel things. Such metaphorical images allow an initial framing of the new in terms of the old and well known, a process that Moscovici (2008) called anchoring. He refers to metaphorical images as "figurative schemata" that capture the gist of an issue. Even if people engage in talk and use a propositional language when communicating about an object or issue, the majority of scholars in the field maintain that a representation can best be conceptualized as iconic and metaphorical and not propositional. The metaphorical structure shows the relationship between the source and target domains. In this situation the understanding of the novel is linked – or anchored – to the familiar, and the unfamiliar target domain is rendered intelligible by projecting the basic structure of the source onto the target item (Wagner, Elejabarrieta, & Lahnsteiner, 1995). The image incorporates the meaning of the novel and is tinted by the affects and connotations that derive – at least in part – from the source domain (Wagner & Hayes, 2005).

This has been vividly demonstrated in a study about intergroup relations in conflict. In interview studies, the researchers used newspaper pictures of recent events to stimulate responses of Muslim and Hindu focus group participants during the political tensions around the year 2000 in India. The pictures reliably triggered emotional reactions from members of both groups and made them express their mutual representations of each other's stereotypes and actions (Sen & Wagner, 2009).

While it is true that social representations comprise cognitive and affective elements that can be located both at individual and social levels, another and equally important part comprises behavior and action, directed toward the material surroundings as well as other people. This makes social representation theory an approach that covers the crossroads and intersection between individual psychology and collective behavior and discourse. In the end it is the overt behavior which allows us to construct and define social objects.

7.2.2 Behaving and Acting

Social representations emerge, are transformed, and elaborated in societal discourse. They are a form of knowledge that allows discursive communities to engage in debates about socially relevant issues. If the issue of the debate retains a lasting importance the representation will eventually become "emancipated" or even "hegemonic" in the sense that large sectors of the community unthinkingly subscribe to it. In communication theory this process is called "cultivation" of an issue (Morgan & Signorelli, 1990; Moscovici, 1988, 2008).

Knowledge, discourse, and talk, however, are not enough for social objects to emerge. The critical interface between minds and talk on one hand and objects on the other is behavior and action. As a consequence, social representations must be conceptualized as simultaneously comprising mental and overt behavioral aspects.

The dominant view in psychology follows everyday psychology in maintaining that attitudes, beliefs, norms, and intentions are independent from, and causally producing, behavior, as illustrated by numerous models where behavior stands at the end of a series of arrows connecting mental states with behavior and action (Ajzen, 1991; Bandura, 1977; Fishbein & Ajzen, 1975). This understanding of how the mental relates to behavior is also deeply ingrained in our everyday understanding and a crucial part of vernacular psycho-logic (Smedslund, 1988).

In contrast, social representation theory does not conceptualize the mental as being independent from and informing or even causing behavior (Moscovici, 2008). The mental and overt behaviors are just different expressions of one and the same representation on the individual and on the collective level. It is in this space spanned by the mental and behavior of actors that social objects are situated (Wagner, 2015, 2016).

Social objects emerge as a pattern of correlated behaviors across actors and situations because "individuals or collectives to some extent see [them] as an extension of their behaviour and because, for them, it exists only because of the means and methods that allow them to understand the object." Just as the objects are an extension and part of behaviors, the behaviors are an extension and indeed part of the representation. The representation endows the behaviors with meaning, because "there is no definite break between the outside world and the world of the individual" (Moscovici, 2008, p. 8). Actors with their reasons and agenda do what they do, not because they want to realize some implicit representation, but because they want to achieve something concrete; people represent social objects in and through goal-directed action.

Consider the example of the hosts of mentally handicapped patients in Jodelet's (1991) study who took pains to keep their own crockery and clothing separate from their guests' when washing and storing. This behavior corresponded to a deep-seated belief in contagion and sympathetic magic that things in contact will spread impurity and transmit mental illness. These people represented mental illness in a comprehensive way where their verbal responses to the researcher's inquiry and their everyday behaviors were just divergent expressions of the same thing: the fear of "madness" of their guests.

Note that behavior, that is any voluntary overt movement, would be just an arbitrary movement if the representation's meaning were not attached to it. It is the representation's situated meaning that allows justifying and accounting for behaviors, making them actions in a social context. Voluntary *behavior* becomes an *action* whenever it is part of a social representation and therefore endowed with meaning.

7.2.3 Interaction and Cooperation

The diversity of activities by many different actors that unfold in a group's daily life can be bewildering for an outside observer. On one hand there are behaviors related to agriculture and gardening, building and construction, production and commerce, and many others serving a reproductive purpose in all walks of daily life.

Such activities involve largely similar purposes and aims across cultures and observers with some knowledge of similar activities in their own culture will be able to get a feeling of the purpose and aims of these activities, even in foreign cultures. They will understand these behaviors, their aims, and, perhaps, the technology involved. On the other hand there are behaviors of which the purpose and details are puzzling to an uninitiated observer. Most often these are related to ritual and religion, be it celebrating birth, coming of age, marriage, death, or worship. Although these also consist of overt behaviors, they do not easily disclose their aims and details except as a gross hunch. Observers may guess the reasons and occasions for them, but their concrete meaning escapes superficial observation. In contrast to the former group of activities, the latter carries a significant symbolic burden.

The symbolic burden that camouflages the sense in a pattern of interactions for the outsider is the cultural meaning carried and conveyed by the representation that a group has elaborated in their local world. The production of social facts in collective interaction endows the facts and "representations in interaction" with validity as the mere existence of the facts are the circular evidence for their own "truth." Representation and action "remodel . . . and reconstitute . . . the elements of the environment in which the behavior takes place" (Moscovici, 2008, p. 9). Representations must be seen as the meaning in concerted behaviors by integrating them into a network of relations in which it is bound up with its object (Moscovici, 2008). Hence, representations are objectified when the actors recognize the objects as evident and true. Our acting – the very way we do things – co-constructs our world and simultaneously is the evidence for its "truth."

Social objects that are collectively enacted in their social representation can be very concrete, such as planting a tree as a step toward combat-ting the "green-house effect" or as abstract as the idea of god enacted by elaborate rituals in all religions the world over. The central tenet of social representation theory is that individual actors and social objects are mutually implied within their shared field (Moscovici, 2008). In other words, through their actions, actors define meaning and social characteristics of the objects with which they are interacting and vice versa, the objects of their actions define particular characteristics of people: your home decoration, for instance, interacts with your social standing and personality.

There is a precondition to interaction and cooperation that is sometimes neglected. Actors naturally have their own representation at their disposal and enact it in an interactive situation. But they also need to have an idea of how their interactants represent the situation and the objects therein. An actor's mental image and related behaviors therefore will comprise aspects of their own and inferred aspects of the other's ideas and intentions. The actor's representation of a social situation takes a *holomorphic*, that is, a comprehensive form by including meta-knowledge about the other (Wagner & Hayes, 2005, p. 276). It is this inclusive character of social representations that allows concerted interaction to occur, be it constructive as in the "dance of the sexes" in courtship or destructive as in violent conflict (Sen, 2012; see also Elcheroth, Doise, & Reicher, 2011, p. 739).

Before we look at concrete examples of social objects, let's look at the meaning of historical events for ethnic groups. In January 2013, a group of historians presented their new book on the Estonian medieval era. The book was a tome in a semi-popular series on Estonian history, attempting an up-to-date overview based on academic research. It came as a surprise to the authors that journalists picked up a nuance in their book as "revolutionary": the book used the term "North-East European Crusade" instead of "Ancient Freedom Fight." The authors were harshly criticized by parts of the general public, being even called "traitors" in some discussions. What had happened was that the authors had not paid their dues to the symbolic value of the "Ancient Freedom Fight" as the designation for local resistance against German and Danish crusaders from 1208 to 1227. According to a popular core narrative, the heroic, though lost struggle was followed by centuries of oppression by various foreign powers, but finally freedom achieved in the similarly heroic "Freedom War" from 1918 to 1920 (Tamm, 2008).

When a crucial element of national identity was perceived as endangered by a fresh historical account, the public discourse defended the imaginary object. This shows two things of relevance in the present context. First, evoking social objects may have a strong organizing force when they are constituents of ethnic identity. Second, social objects can attain a surprisingly explicit reality in discourse and collective action even after having remained dormant and implicit for a long time. On one hand, people who were outraged by historians' "denial" of the "Ancient Freedom Fight" expected "historical truth" of historians. On the other hand they already "knew" what the "truth" was, and wanted the historians to participate in its enactment (see Chapter 22, this volume).

7.2.4 Social Objects

Finally, how do things become social objects? Without intending to enter a philosophical discussion it is useful to assume that what we call the world is the ensemble of an infinite set of matter, energy, phenomena, relationships, events, you name it. Organisms and humans, being part of this set, are endowed with the capacity to cut reality's pulp into entities that are necessary to sense the world in a way that allows them to secure their survival and procreation. Modern times' scientific methods and insights do the same by showing and explaining to us the composition, structure, and dynamics of some regions in the fabric of the world. By doing their scientific work and publishing their results, scientists contribute to the "zoo" of social objects that have a name, are being talked about, and acted on in every society and culture.

One can say that the part of the world – the things, relationships, and events therein, which have a name, are being talked about and acted on – constitutes the domesticated world of everyday life. Whenever persons express an opinion, attitude, or belief with regard to an object, we must assume that they already have a representation that relates to it, because the object and the belief "take shape together." The belief is not a response to the object, "it is, to a certain extent, its origin" (Moscovici, 2008, pp. 8–9). Hence, if behavior, being part of the representation, links the person and the object, it does not make sense to juxtapose a representation to its object as alluded in the expression "representation *of* object X." It is only through the behavior that is part and parcel of the representation, that the object becomes *socialized* in the first place; the representation is the origin of the social object (Wagner, 1996).

Using the word "object" with its "material" connotation in the present context might unduly restrict our understanding of the things populating our local world. Due to their materiality, objects like stones, tree roots, as well as unnamed "somethings" can hurt us when we trip over them independently of whether the object is socially represented or not. Once represented, the thereby socialized material objects constitute a significant part of our local world. There are, however, a host of objects that we cannot literally trip over, but which are as relevant as the former. This class of objects should better be called "social facts" or even "issues," because they are not physical in the original sense. They owe their existence to patterns of concerted collective behaviors.[1]

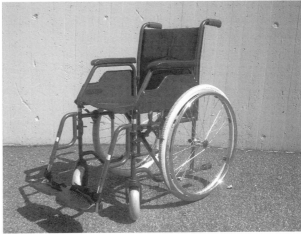

(a)   (b)

Figure 7.1 An antique (a) and a modern (b) wheelchair. The antique chair has been used by Margarete Steiff (1847–1909), a victim of polio and the inventor of the teddy bear. Source: Wikimedia, public domain: (a) https://commons.wikimedia.org/wiki/File:Steiffmargarete.jpg (b) https://commons.wikimedia.org/wiki/File:Standard_rollstuhl.jpg.

Let us remind you of the aforementioned example of the term "Ancient Freedom Fight" having been omitted in a recent textbook on Estonian history. The people's behavior, in fact, their commotion about this omission, marks the social fact of an historical issue, given importance by the people's beliefs and behaviors.

Let's look at a clear-cut example of a social object that we all have experience with and that is also embodied in a technical artifact: disability and wheelchairs. In many countries, the discourse surrounding disability and people with disabilities has undergone a transformation in recent decades. In Sweden, for example, Gustavsson (1996, 1997) describes different discourses about intellectual disability in the context of an advanced welfare system. The oldest and most basic level refers to intellectually disabled people as "slow," "weak," "disabled," and "disadvantaged." This level is complemented by the speech about "the right to special education, subsidized work," "the right to an ordinary life, among others," and "the right to equality," which has become more dominant when the state welfare system introduced an integration policy during the last decades. In the social reconstruction of the object "disability," considering equality and integration mark a fundamental change in the speech, in the ways of interaction between people on the street and the "objects" construed by the representation, that is, the handicapped persons. Consequently, disabled people change their behavior and self-image and the social "object" of handicap is fundamentally different from understanding handicap hundred years ago. Here again, we can observe an example of a *holomorphic* representation integrating the "average" and the handicapped person's ideas and behaviors – the latter assertively defending autonomy and the former respecting the autonomy of the other but being ready to help if necessary. This example illustrates how social representations give rise to historically variable objects, notwithstanding the differences between mental and physical disablement (Anastasiou & Kauffman, 2013).

Figure 7.1 shows the technical equivalent to the change in the representation of the physically disabled during the last hundred years. The construction of antique chairs reflects the formerly widespread view of disabled persons as dependent on others, indicated by the prominent push handle in the back. Chairs with large front wheels are difficult to handle even with hand rims. In addition, three wheels as shown in Figure 7.1(a) give little stability. Today, the chair is constructed differently, supporting the modern image of the disabled as self-determined, affirmative, and independent people (e.g., Swain & French, 2000). Large rear wheels with a hand rim greatly facilitate self-propelling, which gives the users relative independence and reduces the need for assistance. Wheelchairs are social objects that illustrate well the overarching role of representations and their materialization in technical devices. Their details are a direct consequence of the changed ways in which able-bodied people interact with handicapped individuals and how they collectively enact a "material social object."

To summarize, social objects are constituted by social representations in a threefold way: by individual behavior, by collective interaction, and by belief. First, behavior links people with the objects of the outside world and substantiates their existence. In fact, social representations always imply a relationship of the person to the object. Second, the relationship between people holding a representation and the social object is also expressed by collective interaction; and it is the cooperation of many subscribers to a representation that gives rise to the multitude of nonmaterial constructions in a culture and society, such as gods, justice, and the myriad of ideas that populate modern minds and can be talked about. Third, social objects, their names, and the ways we imagine and talk about them, can be called mental entities; these provide the framework of meanings that a representation implies and that are attached to its object. In the following sections

we will present two examples of more complex objects.

7.3 The Paradigmatic Emergence of a Representation: "Climate Change"

7.3.1 From Science to Communal Discourse

There are not many recent social processes that offer themselves as a paradigmatic example and illustration of the principal components of social representation theory as pointedly as the discourse about "global warming" or "climate change" during the last three decades. The emergence of this social object is characterized by at least three periods that we will describe step by step (see also Castro, 2012): first, a scientific development and insight that carries relevance for daily life; second, a media process, agenda setting, and the associated public discourse; and third, the uptake of the issue by politics, the ensuing institutionalization, and its reifying effect on public discourse.

At the beginning there was a series of observations by climate scientists across the world, showing that after the medieval warm period and the subsequent "little ice age" until the nineteenth century the average global temperature appeared to rise in an unprecedented way since the 1950s due to mankind's burning of fossil hydrocarbons. This fact alone might not have ignited the imagination of journalists was it not for a potentially bleak outlook on our daily quality of life in the decades to come. Once a useful catchphrase was found, such as "global warming," "greenhouse effect" or "climate change" (Whitmarsh, 2009), the media set the agenda, and nongovernmental organizations (NGOs) and the general public engaged in an extended discourse about the causes and conceivable remedies for this development (e.g., Caillaud & Flick, 2013; Castro, 2015; Grundmann & Scott, 2014; Uzelgun & Castro, 2014; Liu, Vedlitz, & Alston, 2008).

This second phase in the development of a social representation is characterized by a communal discourse in the public sphere where people may dispute the existence and human-made character of the phenomenon and where they are free to express their support or doubt. Both believers and skeptics of global warming may engage in debate and accept each other's arguments as justified and noteworthy.

During this period the media engage in suggesting a variety of different images and metaphors in an attempt to capture the essential characteristics of the issue. Given the fact that sections of society have also local media, the imagery may vary widely within a society (Höijer, 2010; Luke, 2015; Moloney et al., 2014; Nerlich, 2015; Uzelgun & Castro, 2014; Weingart, Engels, & Pansegrau, 2000).

7.3.2 Political Institutionalization and Reified Discourse

An issue as important and threatening as global warming must rather sooner than later be taken up by politics and its national actors. As a global phenomenon, the issue was deemed relevant enough to set up international meetings and negotiate agreements (Jaspal & Nerlich, 2014). This phase of institutionalization by governance, international treaties, and the setup of the Intergovernmental Panel on Climate Change (IPCC) marks the time when the discourse about the issue of global warming also changed its tone.

While in the earlier communal form of discourse people were unrestricted in expressing their opinion, a step toward institutionalization marks the beginning of a reified discourse. In this period, the representation and its associated discourse were increasingly molded according to the institutional definitions negotiated

by the involved institutions, the United Nations (UN) and IPCC, the European Union (EU), NGOs, national politics, and the media. The phenomenon, its human causes, the meteorological consequences, and anything that these things imply for humankind's future became represented in discourse in a narrowing way, restricting diversity. This goes hand in hand with increasing hegemony of the dominant and "politically correct" representation (e.g., Callaghan & Augoustinos, 2013; Jaspal, Nerlich, & Koteyko, 2012; Uzelgun & Castro, 2015). The social ideas "global warming" and "climate change" finally became objectified as an institution.

In this phase the majority of actors accepted the available evidence of climate change as convincing and sufficient. It was characteristic for this stage of the process that the communal multiplicity of opinions and attitudes that is so significant for daily communication and conversation became eroded and replaced by a narrow social representation. It became increasingly difficult to express doubt in the phenomenon itself and in its human-made character in conversations without facing stiff resistance, such as "shit storms" in social media that any outspoken skeptic risks (see Jaspal & Nerlich, 2014; Jaspal, Nerlich, & Van Vuuren, 2015). This funneling is a typical characteristic of reified discourse in the context of institutionalization processes (Wagner, Mecha, & Carvalho, 2008) and has been theorized as "semantic barriers" in disputes (Gillespie, 2008).

In theoretical terms, the social object becomes a discursive truth and a fully objectified representation. It becomes an element of a group's local world, a dominant fiduciary truth that is beyond doubt. In this situation, actors are no longer free to assert whatever they wish because even without any vested interests expressing ignorance or doubt is no longer warranted within one's group and may be socially sanctioned (Habermas, 1985, p. 44; Wagner & Hayes, 2005). Often such institutionalized objects play an important role for a group's identity as we showed above with the example of the Estonian myth of the "Ancient Freedom Fight."

7.3.3 Mass Media

It is the mass media in modern societies that play a significant role in constructing a social object by taking up scientific and technological advances. The media process accompanies and drives to a certain extent the public discourse about global warming, genetic engineering, and, more recently, synthetic biology as well as other social objects in the making. Genetic engineering, for example, gained prominence by years long media reporting and setting the agenda in Europe, where this technology met widespread resistance.

Initially, during the stage of communal discourse, media experimented with metaphors and pictures that were able to anchor the basic idea of genetic engineering to varying degrees. Later, the media discourse converged to a few images and metaphors that often had to do with tomatoes as the quintessence of healthy looking natural food being "violated" by genetic manipulation (Wagner, Kronberger, & Seifert, 2002). This was when public opinion and attitudes converged on an objectified representation of genetic engineering and synthetic biology that typically differed between social sectors and professions as is the case with global warming (see Grundmann & Scott, 2014). Additionally, information derived from media reporting led to polarization between groups with different levels of involvement in the issue, and increased opinion certainty (Kronberger, Holtz, & Wagner, 2012; Uzelgun & Castro, 2015).

Hence, the two-stage process of collective symbolic coping with a new and potentially threatening phenomenon, that is, from the change of open-minded and communal to a narrow and reified discourse, has its counterpart in the two stages of mass media reporting: the change from divergent images to converging on a few dominant images in media reports and pictorial illustrations that depict the objectified social object of "biotechnology." In this representation, "genes" are seen as foreign to natural organisms and as potentially dangerous justifying rejection of the technology (Wagner, Kronberger, & Seifert, 2002). A similar parallelism between media depictions and subjective ideas and images was found for the issue of climate change (Smith & Joffe, 2012), illustrating the importance of the "short-circuit" between media reporting and the general public's discourse.

7.4 National Identity as an Emerging Social Object in History

7.4.1 Building a Nation: Estonia

Nations and national identities are excellent examples of social construction processes in that they exemplify how "objective" conditions such as the existence of an ethnic group in a certain cultural, economic, and political situation are interwoven with "subjective" interpretations, self-awareness, and discourses. A "nation-building" process exemplifies how a social representation is linked to consensual groups that engage in concerted interaction. This consensus will never be complete, but needs to reach a functionally necessary number of people for collective phenomena to emerge (Wagner & Hayes, 2005, p. 221).

There are different disciplinary traditions to define "nation" and "nationalism": a state-based Anglophone tradition opposes a culture- and heritage-focused definition within the German-speaking tradition. The latter offers a better understanding of the cultural and national formation characteristics of dominated ethnic groups in nineteenh-century Europe (Hroch, 2015). In the

Estonian case, language, culture, and a myth of common descent were the most important elements in the process, prevailing over history, religion, and state (Raun, 2003, p. 140) as defining elements of a nation (see Chapter 23, this volume).

A distinct language is the most important attribute to distinguish oneself from other groups in a "naturalizing" way that reifies group boundaries. In Estonia up until the nineteenth century, Estonian was the dominant language among peasants, whereas German dominated among non-peasant classes. The German-speaking elites favored neither social mobility of peasants nor the learning of German, as German was considered the language of higher status and education. Instead, the Bible and later secular literature were published in Estonian. For the few Estonian peasants who climbed the social ladder, their advancement meant becoming "German" as being "Estonian" meant being a peasant, and vice versa (e.g., Siimets-Gross & Kello, 2018). Only in the wake of the nineteenth-century "romanticism" an ever growing number of individuals decided to "remain Estonian" despite advancing socially. They were, in fact, the first Estonian nation builders.

Thus, before the nineteenth century ethnic self-awareness existed as distinction from other social and language groups such as Germans, Russians, and Swedes. As words and concepts denoting ethnicity and status overlapped, it is difficult to distinguish "ethnic" identity from "class" consciousness in early modern Estonia. Nevertheless, Estonian-speaking peasantry was the main and rather homogeneous population group which was represented as a clear-cut historical entity in an oeuvre as authoritative as the Bible itself. Since 1739, the Estonian-language Bible started with an "historical introduction" that constructed the Estonians as an entity and an historical subject (Viires, 2001, pp. 23–24): "it is known about the old times that your

ancestors had lived here in this country for over 2.5 thousand years as pagans...as God sent some people of German origin to this country six hundred years ago...who through God's guidance heralded the holy Christian teaching to your ancestors" (Viires, 2001, p. 23). Later, since the second half of the nineteenth century, this pre-Christian time was reframed as a golden era of "ancient freedom" in nationalist history writing. From then on, the "Ancient Freedom Fight" (i.e., they finally lost wars against Danish and German invaders from 1206 to 1227) took the position of one of the central events in Estonian history, both in history books and in historical fiction (Viires, 2001, pp. 31–36). It has since offered a resource of national pride for generations.

In a Herderian vision of culture, the first generations of nineteenth-century national ideologues promoted the idea that Estonians should first and foremost pursue modern education and economic advancement combined with valuing the heritage of previous generations. Such aims could rely on the already high literacy rates among peasants and their high esteem for education. This Estonian national "awakening" went along with a broad movement of voluntary associations (Figure 7.2) that united groups of people engaging in music, theatre, sports, education, and public welfare (Raun, 2003; Jansen, 2007). Together with an increasing upward social mobility, the association culture became the basis of a modern Estonian culture by the first decades of the twentieth century (Karjahärm, 2009). Among other things, since 1869 the association culture brought forth the all-Estonian song festival tradition as an anchor of unity, which continued in the post-World War I Estonian Republic and during the Soviet era.

First attempts to politicize the national movement were made in the 1870s with the demand for legal equality between Estonians and Baltic Germans (Jansen, 2007, p. 501). The voluntary associations "began to be seen as the

Figure 7.2 Choir from Tõstamaa 1865. Source: Estonian National Museum, ERM Fk 355:90; http://muis.ee/museaalview/665317.

basis...for future political activity," enhanced by the Estonian-language press that expanded rapidly. In the 1880s and 1890s, the national movement acquired a mass basis with an annual average of Estonian book titles increasing from 148 in the 1880s to 254 in the 1890s and with an Estonian-speaking population of just under one million (Raun, 2003, pp. 136, 144).

Many dominated ethnic groups in Europe developed a "cultural nationalism" (Hroch, 2015) and the Estonian national movement was no exception with an emancipation movement that gradually turned into a full-blown mass movement by the end of the nineteenth century. The idea of political autonomy gained considerable ground during the revolution of 1905 and was realized in 1918 after the fall of the tsarist regime (Raun, 2003).

7.4.2 Collective Memory Work

History-based identities are a powerful social "object" in nearly all countries and they are an unavoidable part of international policy making and conflict. This is particularly visible at times where there are changes in social dominance and subordination. It is during such periods of change that people engage in collective memory work, reinterpretations of the past and present, and it is here that new narratives are constructed to support one's self-image and identity.

In the Estonian case, historical consciousness and written scholarly history were not the first and foremost factors in the national movement, but their importance grew in the course of the nineteenth century (Raun, 2003). By the time of establishing the Estonian state in 1918, the framing of Estonian history as consisting of an age-old struggle against Germans had been accepted by the masses and became an important driving force in the Independence War of 1918–1920 (Tamm, 2008).

A military coup in 1934 brought about a change from a multiparty system to an authoritarian government, which was a fertile ground for some proponents of academe and army to project Estonia's statehood far into the past: "Estonians had been a state-based nation even under the rule of the Teutonic Order" and the "Estonian state is not young, it is . . . a societal-political construction spanning from a primeval age to the present time" (Tamm, 2008, p. 504). Irrespective of the scientific veridicality of the claim, projecting one's statehood into the deep past was obviously considered necessary to engage the people as followers of the present state and to collectively secure its enduring existence.

During the period of the independent Estonian state in the 1920s and 1930s, Estonians maintained their interest in forming associations. Societies and clubs became widespread and most people were members of at least one of them. It was still as if the Estonians had participated in a collective enactment of their nation. Later, many remembered this period as rather non-hierarchical and communal (Bennich-Björkman, 2006; Kõresaar, 2004). It was a broadly peasant and middle-class society considering visible social distinction as inappropriate. At the same time, such egalitarianism did not necessarily indicate a collectivist mindset because peasants need to behave and think quite individualistic, careful, and responsible in guarding land and property (Bennich-Björkman, 2006). Throughout the Soviet era and into the 1990s, this pre-World War II period would figure as the "golden age" of free Estonia and would become a template for reconstructing the state half a century later.

The abrupt rupture from a newly gained independent state to a nation among many in the Soviet Union lasted from 1940 until about 1990 and was only punctuated by a to and fro during World War II when first the Germans occupied the Baltic region and the Soviets reoccupied it in 1944. Being part of the USSR, Estonians had to accept the dominant representation that located them in the "friendly Soviet family of nations" under the leadership of the Russians.

The Soviet rule worked by maintaining control over public discourse and stifling open discussions (see Marková, 1997). Soviet media did not offer a venue for debates in the public sphere. Reminders of earlier political events, for example, the names of streets, statues of past politicians, or the books of authors who did not fit the regime's current ideology, were removed or destroyed. These restrictions aimed at eliminating memory of the previous era, called "the bourgeois republic" in Soviet historiography.

This situation provoked concerns about how to preserve Estonian language, culture, and historical memory particularly when the demographic composition of Estonia changed because of officially encouraged immigration from other parts of the USSR. One way of preserving the endangered identity was the conscious preservation of former narratives and ways of life, that is, creating a counter culture in families and among small friendship circles. First, the past was an important symbolic resource for distinction and identity maintenance on an everyday level (Gillespie & Zittoun, 2010). Specific cultural taste and material environment, such as home decoration and clothing, maintaining continuity with prewar (1930s) ideals, and creating new distinctions by accommodating modern "non-Soviet" Western styles, was a widespread identity strategy of Estonian-ness (Kannike, 2006; Rakfeldt, 2015). It is noteworthy that, while the idea of an Estonian nation had been inspired by German culture and the Finnish model in the nineteenth century, it was created in opposition to the German ruling elites. Later, mainly since World War II, Germans were replaced by Russians and Russia in their role as the "main negative other" (Petersoo, 2007). Second, a considerable number of Estonians did not accept the Marxist "newspeak" (Ahonen, 1997) that was used to talk about Estonian past and to retouch unwelcome facts such as the forceful annexation and large-scale deportations. Instead, "grassroots" counter-memories of officially "forgotten" or reinterpreted events were cultivated. Many people quite clearly differentiated between the official history taught at schools and the "true one" that was passed on in the family. This allowed for a rather broad and coherent body of communicative memory to be maintained "from the Estonian perspective" for over half a century.

As the gradual liberalization in the Soviet Union since 1985 gave space for public debates, a public history was reconstructed in part exactly based on such grassroots memories. Reconstructing the "true" history was a work to which historians – some of whom became politicians later – as well as writers and ordinary people contributed (Kivimäe, 1999; Wulf & Grönholm, 2010).

7.4.3 Reifying National Identity as a State

By the end of the Soviet Union there were several important resources available that the new nation builders could use: a vision of the nation's history shared by a big part of the population as well as strong personal networks from which various new associations could spring (Bennich-Björkman, 2007). Environmental and heritage protection movements (including the so-called "Phosphorite War" that opposed planned mining and new immigration of Russian-speaking workers) were the first since 1987, and the movement of the "Popular Front" followed in 1988. Different social movements mobilized approximately 70 percent of the Estonian population during this period (Lauristin & Vihalemm 2009).

During the Soviet era, the song festival tradition, established in 1869 (see Figure 7.2), had continued as an accommodated field for national feelings, a space where national pride and unity could be experienced briefly while singing some nationalist songs in between Soviet ones. Starting in the spring of 1988, at first spontaneous and later organized singing events with up to 300,000 participants became pivotal for expressing discontent with the Soviet regime and consolidating popular demands (Brüggemann, 2015). As no social representation would be complete without enacting its symbolic side, as early as 1988 the freshly established Estonian Heritage Society promoted restoration of the monuments of the Estonian War of Independence that were built during the 1920s and 1930s, but were destroyed by the Soviets in the 1940s.

Consequently, the years from 1987 onwards became a period of collective public shows of cultural uniqueness. All this became known as the "Singing Revolution," was highly visible to everyone, and contributed to strengthening ethnic feelings. Like in many post-communist countries, individual members of the local elite played a role in organizing the politics that finally led to independence of the Estonian nation. Unlike some other formerly socialist countries this elite had already been active as a "counter elite" during Soviet times (Bennich-Björkman, 2007). The shared visions elaborated during the Soviet era made "real politics" easier in the late 1980s and 1990s. This fact may explain the relative success of post-Soviet Estonia compared to other post-Soviet and post-socialist countries in implementing political and economic reforms (Bennich-Björkman & Likić-Brborić, 2012). The intentions of the new elites, however, would have been much more difficult to realize if they could not build on the collective memory work and the widespread feeling of identity as a delimited ethnic group with a well-remembered history.

The social object that emerges when an ethnic identity is being enacted necessarily also involves setting boundaries and excluding others. In the reestablished Estonian state there were ample numbers of Russian-speaking people (about 30 percent), Russian workers and administrators, who had immigrated during the 50 years of Soviet rule. This immigration was seen as a threat by the Estonian "silent majority." Although the value structures of the two communities were similar on a macro level (Titma & Rämmer, 2006), they were not perceived as such by the "silent majority" and a symbolic distinction from Russians was an important part of everyday life. After their dominant position during Soviet times, Russian-speakers suddenly became an unwelcome sector of the country's population. Always an uneasy relationship, this became a burning issue in the decades to come (Raudsepp, 2009).

The existence of a Russian-speaking community was constructed by many as a potential trigger for Russian interference. This constellation resembles a kind of "siege mentality" (Bar-Tal & Antebi, 1992), which resulted in automatically granting citizenship only to those whose ancestors had lived in the Estonian Republic before 1940. The principal reason was that politicians had no interest in allowing a large number of Russian-speakers to attain citizenship and thus parliamentary representation. This would have implied an unwelcome "Russian-speaking" influence on lawmaking. Second, of course, the simple psychological desire to collectively "pay back" for past oppression also played a role.

In the end, the Estonian case illustrates how an ethnic identity becomes institutionalized in a national state. Like other such social objects, this "macro"-object is maintained by beliefs conveyed in communication, collectively informed individual action, and cooperation. It has a name, a history, a foundation myth, and possesses a discriminating attribute such as a language; the members act concertedly in the creation and confirmation of collective events such as collective singing and established symbols, all underpinned by a strong affective component.

The development of the Estonian nation provides an example of the psychological components and collective large-scale processes involved in constructing a social object by social representation. Additionally, it appears that Estonians could cling to their ethnic self-image, preserve it in collective memory, and use it to reconstruct their statehood because no other overarching institution provided an identification target. In countries like Poland and Lithuania, Catholic religion merged with nationalism in a highly effective amalgam while Estonian nationalism became a similarly emotional, but secular, feeling of attachment to the new state. And, yes, like any religion, a national identification also harbors the potential for violence and hatred against the Other (Raudsepp & Wagner, 2012).

7.5 Conclusion

Social representation theory provides a framework that allows us to look at small- and large-scale social processes in an integrative way. The theory takes into account the social psychology of individuals – how they represent social issues, that is, what are their ideas, memories, perceptions, and feelings related to the issues, and how ideas correlate with behaviors in a larger social context. Hence, if we conceive of individual behaviors as part of a representation, the behaviors are fundamentally social and will, on a larger scale, translate into a behavioral pattern that is the collective mirror image of the individual's ideas. In providing a link between the individual and the collective level of analysis, the theory embraces the individuals' minds, their actions in an intrinsically social world, societal discourses, and the forming of collective events and social objects.

The example of handicap and its changing representation over time reveals the close link between discourse and material objects as exemplified in the wheelchair. The unfolding discourse on global warming illustrates the process of the stages from a scientific insight through a period of relaxed conversations and disputes about a potential climate threat to a reified and institutionalized representation that meets deviating opinions with suspicion.

The object of an ethnic identity, finally, marks a reflexive social group that is aware of its groupness. How the group represents and reflects itself has consequences for how outsiders are pictured. The outsiders' characteristics will be represented alongside the ingroup's self-image as a kind of meta-knowledge. As shown before, knowing about another group's identity is a prerequisite for interaction and characterizes a representation that encompasses one's own as well as the other's image (Wagner & Hayes, 2005, p. 276). One can say that in its identity-related discourse is the organizing principle that allows a group to reflexively create itself as an object of reference in relation to others.

The reemergence of a national state objectifies a long history of ethnic consciousness and feelings of identity that did not proceed smoothly, unlike the story of global warming, but overcame a series of historical obstacles. Hence, social objects can be imagined as attractor points where mental, discursive, and behavioral expressions of a social representation converge in a system that is probably less chaotic and more resilient than it appears at first sight.

Acknowledgments

The authors gratefully acknowledge the helpful comments and editorial remarks by Maaris Raudsepp, University of Tallinn, and Paula Castro, ISCTE, Lisbon. Katrin Kello and Andu Rämmer received funding from the Estonian Ministry of Education and Research (grant number IUT 20–38).

Note

1 In Meinong's (1904) *Gegenstandstheorie* (theory of objects) this sort of objects has been called "subsistent" in contrast to "existent" objects: the latter having a material and temporal existence, the former not.

References

Ahonen, S. (1997). A transformation of history: The official representations of history in East Germany and Estonia, 1986–1991. *Culture & Psychology*, 3, 41–62.

Anastasiou, D. & Kauffman, J. M. (2013). The social model of disability: Dichotomy between impairment and disability. *Journal of Medicine and Philosophy*, 38(4), 441–459.

Ajzen, I. (1991). The theory of planned behavior. *Organizational Behavior and Human Decision Processes*, 50, 179–211.

Aran, G. & Hassner, R. E. (2013). Religious violence in Judaism: Past and present. *Terrorism and Political Violence*, 25(3), 355–405.

Bandura, A. (1977). Self-efficacy: Toward a unifying theory of behavioral change. *Psychological Review*, 84(2), 191–215.

Bar-Tal, D. & Antebi, D. (1992). Siege mentality in Israel. *Papers on Social Representations*, 1, 49–68.

Bauer, M. (1993). Francophone research on popular(izing) science: A commented bibliography, 1960–1992. Unpublished manuscript, Science Museum, London.

Bennich-Björkman, L. (2006). A political culture in exile: The Estonian inter-war generation in Canada and Sweden. *Journal of Baltic Studies*, 73(1), 68–93.

Bennich-Björkman, L. (2007). The cultural roots of Estonia's successful transition: How historical legacies shaped the 1990s. *East European Politics and Societies*, 21, 316–347.

Bennich-Björkman, L. & Likić-Brborić, B. (2012). Successful but different: Deliberative identity and the consensus-driven transition to capitalism in Estonia and Slovenia. *Journal of Baltic Studies*, 43(1), 47–73.

Brüggemann, K. (2015). "One day we will win anyway": The "Singing Revolution" in the Soviet Baltic republics. In W. Mueller, M. Gehler, & A. Suppan (Eds.), *The Revolutions of 1989: A Handbook* (pp. 221–246). Vienna: Verlag der Österreichischen Akademie der Wissenschaften.

Caillaud, S. & Flick, U. (2013). New meanings for old habits? Representations of climate change in

France and Germany. *Revue internationale de psychologie sociale*, 26(3), 39–72.

Callaghan, P. & Augoustinos, M. (2013). Reified versus consensual knowledge as rhetorical resources for debating climate change. *Revue internationale de psychologie sociale*, 26(3), 11–38.

Castro, P. (2012). Legal innovation for social change: Exploring change and resistance to different types of sustainability laws. *Political Psychology*, 33(1), 105–121.

Castro, P. (2015). Social representations of sustainability: Researching time, institution, conflict and communication. In G. Sammut, I. Andreouli, G. Gaskell, & J. Valsiner (Eds.), *The Cambridge Handbook of Social Representations* (pp. 295–308). Cambridge: Cambridge University Press.

Durkheim, É. (1920). *Sociologie et philosophie: Représentations individuelles et représentations collectives, détermination du fait moral, jugements de valeur et jugements de realité.* Paris: Félix Alcan.

Elcheroth, G., Doise, W., & Reicher, S. (2011). On the knowledge of politics and the politics of knowledge: How a social representations approach helps us rethink the subject of political psychology. *Political Psychology*, 32(5), 729–758.

Fishbein, M. & Ajzen, I. (1975). *Belief, Attitude, Intention, and Behavior*. Reading, MA: Addison-Wesley.

Gillespie, A. (2008). Social representations, alternative representations and semantic barriers. *Journal for the Theory of Social Behaviour*, 38(4), 375–391.

Gillespie, A. & Zittoun, T. (2010). Using resources: Conceptualizing the mediation and reflective use of tools and signs. *Culture & Psychology*, 16(1), 37–62.

Ginges, J., Sheikh, H., Atran, S., & Argo, N. (2016). Thinking from God's perspective decreases biased valuation of the life of a nonbeliever. *Proceedings of the National Academy of Sciences*, 113(2), 316–319.

Grundmann, R. & Scott, M. (2014). Disputed climate science in the media: Do countries matter. *Public Understanding of Science*, 23(2), 220–235.

Gubler, J. R. & Kalmoe, N. P. (2015). Violent rhetoric in protracted group conflicts: Experimental evidence from Israel and India. *Political Research Quarterly*, 68(4), 651–664.

Gustavsson, A. (1996). Reforms and everyday meanings of intellectual disability. In J. Tøssebro, A. Gustavsson, & G. Dyrendahl (Eds.), *Intellectual Disabilities in the Nordic Welfare States* (pp. 214–236). Kristiansand: Høyskole Forlaget.

Gustavsson, A. (1997). Integration, stigma and autonomy: Bright and dark sides of the subculture of integration. In A. Gustavsson & E. Zakrzewska-Manterys (Eds.), *Social Definitions of Disability* (pp. 190–208). Warsaw: Zak.

Habermas, J. (1985). *Theorie des kommunikativen Handelns. Band 1: Handlungsrationalität und gesellschaftliche Rationalisierung.* Frankfurt: Suhrkamp.

Hirsch-Hoefler, S., Canetti, D., & Eiran, E. (2016). Radicalizing religion? Religious identity and settlers' behavior. *Studies in Conflict & Terrorism*, 39(6), 500–518.

Höijer, B. (2010). Emotional anchoring and objectification in the media reporting on climate change. *Public Understanding of Science*, 19(6), 717–731.

Hroch, M. (2015). *European Nations: Explaining Their Formation* (trans. by Karolina Graham). London: Verso.

Jacobi, D. (1977). La vulgarisation scientifique: Un outil pour les formateurs? *Education Permanente*, 39–40.

Jansen, E. (2007). Summary. In T. Tannberg, J. Arukaevu, & H. Tamman (Eds.), *Eestlane muutuvas ajas: seisuseühiskonnast kodanikuühiskonda* [Estonians in a changing world: From estate society to civil society]. Tartu: Eesti Ajalooarhiiv.

Jaspal, R. & Nerlich, B. (2014). When climate science became climate politics: British media representations of climate change in 1988. *Public Understanding of Science*, 23(2), 122–141.

Jaspal, R., Nerlich, B., & Koteyko, N. (2012). Contesting science by appealing to its norms: Readers discuss climate science in the Daily Mail. *Science Communication*, 35(3), 383–410.

Jaspal, R., Nerlich, B., & Van Vuuren, K. (2015). Embracing and resisting climate identities in the Australian press: Sceptics, scientists and politics. *Public Understanding of Science*, 25(7), 807–824. DOI: 10.1177/0963662515584287.

Jodelet, D. (1991). *Madness and Social Representations*. London: Harvester Wheatsheaf.

Kannike, A. (2006). Creating cultural continuity in the domestic realm: The case of Soviet Estonia. *Acta Historica Tallinnensia*, 10, 212–229.

Karjahärm, T. (2009). Eesti rahvusliku liikumise mudelid uusimas historiograafias [Models of the Estonian national movement in recent historiography]. *Acta Historica Tallinnensia*, 14, 146–171.

Kivimäe, J. (1999). Re–writing Estonian history? In M. Branch (Ed.), *National History and Identity: Approaches to the Writing of National History in the North–East Baltic Region Nineteenth and Twentieth Centuries* (pp. 205–211). Helsinki: Finnish Literature Society.

Kõresaar, E. (2004). *Memory and History in Estonian Post-Soviet Life Stories: Private and Public, Individual and Collective from the Perspective of Biographical Syncretism*. Tartu, Estonia: University of Tartu Press.

Kronberger, N., Holtz, P., & Wagner, W. (2012). Consequences of media information uptake and deliberation: Focus groups' symbolic coping with synthetic biology. *Public Understanding of Science*, 21(2), 174–187.

Lauristin, M. & Vihalemm, P. (2009). The political agenda during different periods of Estonian transformation: External and internal factors. *Journal of Baltic Studies*, 40(1), 1–28.

Liu, X. S., Vedlitz, A., & Alston, L. (2008). Regional news portrayals of global warming and climate change. *Environmental Science & Policy*, 11(5), 379–393.

Luke, T. W. (2015). The climate change imaginary. *Current Sociology Monograph*, 63(2), 280–296.

Marková, I. (1997). The individual and the community: A post-communist perspective. *Journal of Community & Applied Social Psychology*, 7, 3–17.

Meinong, A. (1904). Über Gegenstandstheorie. In *Untersuchungen zur Gegenstandstheorie und Psychologie* (pp. 1–50). Leipzig: Barth Verlag.

Moloney, G., Leviston, Z., Lynam, T., Price, J., Stone-Jovicich, S., & Blair, D. (2014). Using social representations theory to make sense of climate change: What scientists and nonscientists in Australia think. *Ecology and Society*, 19(3), 1–9.

Morgan, M. & Signorelli, N. (1990). *Cultivation Analysis*. Newbury Park, CA: SAGE.

Moscovici, S. (1961). *La psychanalyse son image et son public*. Paris: Presses Universitaires de France.

Moscovici, S. (1988). Notes toward a description of social representations. *European Journal of Social Psychology*, 18, 211–250.

Moscovici, S. (2008). *Psychoanalysis – Its Image and Its Public*. Cambridge: Polity Press.

Nerlich, B. (2015). Metaphors in science and society: The case of climate science and climate scientists. *Language and Semiotic Studies*, 1(2), 1–15.

Petersoo, P. (2007). Reconsidering otherness: Constructing Estonian identity. *Nations and Nationalism*, 13(1), 117–133.

Pratt, D. (2010). Religion and terrorism: Christian fundamentalism and extremism. *Terrorism and Political Violence*, 22(3), 438–456.

Putra, I. E. & Sukabdi, Z. A. (2014). Can Islamic fundamentalism relate to non-violent support? The role of certain conditions in moderating the effect of Islamic fundamentalism on supporting acts of terrorism. *Peace and Conflict: Journal of Peace Psychology*, 20, 583–589.

Rakfeldt, J. (2015). Home environments, memories, and life stories: Preservation of Estonian national identity. *Journal of Baltic Studies*, 46(4), 511–542.

Raudsepp, M. (2009). Ethnic self-esteem and intergroup attitudes among the Estonian majority and the non-Estonian minority. *Studies of Transition States and Societies*, 1(1), 36–51.

Raudsepp, M. & Wagner, W. (2012). The essentially Other: Representational processes that divide groups. In I. Marková & A. Gillespie (Eds.), *Trust and Conflict: Representation, Culture and Dialogue* (pp. 105–122). London: Routledge.

Raun, T. U. (2003). Nineteenth- and early twentieth-century Estonian nationalism revisited. *Nations & Nationalism*, 9(1), 129–147.

Sammut, G., Andreouli, E., Gaskell, G., & Valsiner, J. (Eds.). (2015). *The Cambridge Handbook of Social Representations*. Cambridge: Cambridge University Press.

Sen, R. (2012). Hetero-referentiality and divided societies. In D. J. Christie (Ed.), *The Encyclopedia of Peace Psychology* (vol. 2, pp. 506–510). Chichester: Wiley-Blackwell.

Sen, R. & Wagner, W. (2009). Cultural mechanics of fundamentalism: Religion as ideology, divided identities and violence in post-Gandhi India. *Culture & Psychology*, 15(3), 299–326.

Siimets-Gross, H. & Kello, K. (2018). Plurality of legal sources in trials concerning a person's status at the end of the 18th century – cui bono? In M. Luts, I. Kull, & K. Sein (eds.) *Legal Plurality – cui bono*? Tartu, Estonia: University of Tartu Press.

Smedslund, J. (1988). *Psycho-logic*. Berlin: Springer.

Smith, N. & Joffe, H. (2012). How the public engages with global warming: A social representations approach. *Public Understanding of Science*, 22(1), 16–32.

Swain, J. & French, S. (2000). Towards an affirmation model of disability. *Disability & Society*, 15(4), 569–582.

Tamm, M. (2008). History as cultural memory: Mnemohistory and the construction of the Estonian nation. *Journal of Baltic Studies*, 39(4), 499–516.

Titma, M. & Rämmer, A. (2006). Estonia: Changing value patterns in a divided society. In. H.-D. Klingemann, D. Fuchs & J. Zielonka. (Eds.), *Democracy and Political Culture in Eastern Europe* (pp. 277–307). London: Routledge.

Uzelgun, M. A. & Castro, P. (2014). The voice of science on climate change in the mainstream Turkish press. *Environmental Communication*, 8(3), 326–344.

Uzelgun, M. A. & Castro, P. (2015). Climate change in the mainstream Turkish press: Coverage trends and meaning dimensions in the first attention

cycle. *Mass Communication and Society*, 18(6), 730–752.

Viires, A. (2001). Eestlaste ajalooteadvus 18.-19. sajandil [Historical consciousness of Estonians in the 18th and 19th centuries]. *Tuna*, 3, 20–36.

Wagner, W. (2015). Representation in action. In G. Sammut, E. Andreouli, G. Gaskell, & J. Valsiner (Eds.), *The Cambridge Handbook of Social Representations* (pp. 12–28). Cambridge: Cambridge University Press.

Wagner, W. (2016). Embodied social representation. *Journal for the Theory of Social Behaviour*, 47(1), 25–31. DOI: 10.1111/jtsb.12113.

Wagner, W. & Hayes, N. (2005). *Everyday Discourse and Common Sense: The Theory of Social Representations*. Basingstoke, UK: Palgrave-Macmillan.

Wagner, W., Elejabarrieta, F., & Lahnsteiner, I. (1995). How the sperm dominates the ovum: Objectification by metaphor in the social representation of conception. *European Journal of Social Psychology*, 25(6), 671–688.

Wagner, W., Kronberger, N., & Seifert, F. (2002). Collective symbolic coping with new technology: Knowledge, images and public discourse. *British Journal of Social Psychology*, 41(3), 323–343.

Wagner, W., Mecha, A., & Carvalho, M. R. (2008). Discourse and representation in the construction of witchcraft. In T. Sugiman, K. Gergen, W. Wagner, & Y. Yamada (Eds.), *Meaning in Action: Constructions, Narratives and Representations* (pp. 37–48). Tokyo: Springer.

Weingart, P., Engels, A., & Pansegrau, P. (2000). Risks of communication: Discourses on climate change in science, politics, and the mass media. *Public Understanding of Science*, 9(3), 261–283.

Whitmarsh, L. (2009). What's in a name? Commonalities and differences in public understanding of "climate change" and "global warming." *Public Understanding of Science*, 18(4), 401–420.

Wulf, M. & Grönholm, P. (2010). Generating meaning across generations: The role of historians in the codification of history in Soviet and post-Soviet Estonia. *Journal of Baltic Studies*, 41(3), 351–382.

8 Beyond the Distinction between Tool and Sign: Objects and Artifacts in Human Activity

Reijo Miettinen and Sami Paavola

8.1 Introduction

This chapter addresses the significance of objects and artifacts in human activity. Vygotsky discussed object and objectification in his theory of creativity and imagination as well as in his discussion of the significance of object substitutes in the development of play and symbolic thought. It is, however, A. N. Leontiev's concept of object of activity (1978) that has extensively been discussed and debated in the cultural-historical tradition (e.g., *Mind, Culture and Activity*, 2005) if not so much in the sociocultural tradition.

Vygotsky distinguished between internally oriented signs and externally oriented tools. He also, however, found that the integration and unity of sign mediation and tool use is "the essence of complex human behaviour" in human adults (Vygotsky, 1978, p. 24). We suggest that a much richer and versatile language than the one based on the distinction between sign and tool is needed to understand mediation in human activity in a changing society with increasingly complex objects and social challenges. Mediational means tend to form complex constellations of artifacts or instrumentalities in which semiotic and practical functions are fused and intertwined in many ways. We also suggest that an analysis and redesign of these instrumentalities are essential for the transformation of human activities.

It has been customary to draw a distinction between two research programs within activity theory and the Vygotskian legacy (e.g., Martin

& Peim, 2009). The first, sociocultural theory, has focused on mediation by signs and the use of language as a foundation of thought, communication, and meaning making – often characterized as semiotic mediation. It is based on Vygotsky's seminal view of mediation by signs and the internalization of language as a foundation of higher psychological functions. This research program has studied the dialogic nature of thought and self as well as communication, cultural mediation, and human discourses.

The other research program, that is, cultural-historical activity theory (CHAT) is based on the concept of object-oriented activity introduced by Leontiev. He adopted concepts of practice and work from Marx, in particular, as well as from Hegel. In his *Economic and Philosophic Manuscripts of 1844*, Marx (1964, p. 177) stated that "the outstanding achievement of Hegel's *Phenomenology* is that it grasps the essence of labour . . . and comprehends objective man . . . as an outcome of man's own labour." Work is here understood as a prototype of practice, a creative transformation of the environment resulting in the development of new human capabilities. In this process, the objectification of human thought and activity into cultural artifacts plays a central role (Ilyenkov, 1977a; Lektorsky, 1980; Bakhurst, 1991). It creates "humanized nature," an environment composed of human-made and therefore meaningful objects, norms, and institutions. The interaction between an individual and humanized nature has been analyzed as co-evolution in terms of cycles of internalization and externalization. An individual not only internalizes or appropriates cultural resources and ways of acting but also participates in their transformation in creative work, where the results of an activity are objectified into new cultural artifacts and resources.

Vygotsky indicated the importance of analyzing the intertwining of tool use and mediation by signs (1978, p. 24): "Although practical intelligence and sign use can operate independently in young children, the dialectical unity of these systems in the human adult is the very essence of complex human behaviour." The challenge, however, lies in determining whether and in which ways a symbolic activity's organizing function "penetrates the process of tool use" (1978, p. 24). For our own studies, this is a "natural" question to analyze since we have studied the development and implementation of new technologies in which materiality is constantly present and the repeated failures of experiments are a reminder of the objectivity of activity. In order to understand better the object–means relationship, we will shortly discuss some concepts of objects developed in social sciences – among them, epistemic object (Knorr-Cetina, 2001), boundary object (Star & Griesemer, 1989), and intermediary object (Vinck, 2011). To elaborate the integration of different types of means we utilize Wartofsky's (1979) idea of functionally different kinds of artifacts and the concept of "instrumentality," that is, a constellation of different artifacts as suggested by Engeström (2007). In this chapter, we will analyze constellations of artifacts and instrumentalities in two activities: oral health care and construction design.

We will proceed as follows: first, we analyze how the concept of an object of activity introduced by Leontiev has been used in activity theoretical studies. We think that without an object of activity it is hard to understand the mediating artifacts and social forms of collaborative activity. We will discuss how the concept of the object of activity is related to certain object concepts introduced by the social sciences. Second, we discuss the relation between the concepts of sign, tool, and artifact. We will discuss the function theories of artifacts and their relationship to the objectification. We analyze two examples of such instrumentalities. These instrumentalities comprise concepts, symbolic resources, standard procedures, and different kinds of tools. In the first case, a new care model was not realized because the use of other artifacts in the instrumentality (manuals, care plan, diagnostic imaging) were not redesigned. In the second case, we analyze how a specific digital technology, building information modeling (BIM), is implemented and used in construction design. It has multiple shifting functions during a design process. It functions as a tool of individual designers, as an object of joint attention and problem solving, as well as an evolving intermediary outcome of the design work.

8.2 The Object of Activity and Its Uses in Studying Human Activities

In his theory of imagination and creativity Vygotsky discussed external objects in two senses. First, Vygotsky (2004, p. 20) postulated a cycle of imagination which is completed in external embodiment: "once it has been externally embodied, that is, has been given material form this crystallized imagination that has become an object begins to actually exist in the real world, to affect other things." Vygotsky says that "the imagination's drive to be embodied...is the real basis and motive force of creation" (2004, p. 41). He cites and agrees with Ribot's statement according to which "creative imagination in its full form attempts to affirm itself by taking some objective form that exists not only for the creator himself but for everyone else as well" (Ribot cited in Vygotsky, 2004, p. 41). This concept is an early formulation of the theory of objectification and externalization of thought that was subsequently developed by E. V. Ilyenkov in his theory of the ideal (1977b).

Second, Vygotsky analyzed the role of objects in his theory of the development of play and symbolic thought. In this development the use of object substitutes help children to separate their thoughts from perceived objects and events (Karpov, 2005, p. 122). As an example Vygotsky (1978, p. 98) provided a stick used as a horse by a child: "He cannot detach meaning from the object, or a word from an object, except by finding a pivot in something else. Transfer of meaning is facilitated by the fact that the child accepts a word as the property of a thing . . . For a child, the word 'horse' applied to the stick means 'there is a horse,' because mentally he sees the object standing behind the word." The followers of Vygotsky developed further the idea of the role of object substitutes in the development of symbolic thought (e.g., Elkonin, 2005).

Leontiev introduced the concept of the object of activity and object-orientedness in activity theory. Russian and German languages have separate words for an object (*objekt* in both languages) that is an existing material thing and an object of activity (*predmet*, *Gegenstand*), that is an object of conscious transformation by humans able of resisting the projections of the humans (Kaptelinin, 2005). In the English language, the term object is used for both meanings, which is a cause for confusion. Leontiev (1978, p. 52) gave two basic meanings to the concept of "object of activity." First, it has a dual nature as something given and as something imagined and projected.

Thus the object of activity is twofold: first, in its independent existence as subordinating to itself and transforming the activity of the subject; second, as an image of the object, as a product of its property of psychological reflection that is realized as an activity of the subject and cannot exist otherwise. (Leontiev, 1978, p. 52)

This definition aims at surpassing the Cartesian dualism between the objective (given) and the subjective (imagined). It underlines that human thought needs to be studied as a part of practical activity, that is, as bodily transformative interaction with the environment which can be characterized as objective activity.

Second, Leontiev stated that the "object is a real motive of activity" and that an activity is recognized based on its object:

The main thing that distinguishes one activity from another lies in the difference between their objects. It is the object of activity that endows it with a certain orientation. In the terminology I have been using the object of activity is its *motive*. (Leontiev, 1977, p. 52)

This statement was related to Leontiev's distinction between the goal-oriented actions of individuals and groups, and collective activity based on a division of labor. When Engeström (1987) further developed Leontiev's ideas into a theory of expansive learning, he located these concepts in the context of the political economy, that is, in the context of the production and consumption of commodities in a capitalist society (e.g., Engeström & Blackler, 2005). In this way the concepts developed in psychological theory became a means of analyzing the transformation of work activities in society and were applied in the study of various types of work such as health care, teaching, scientific research, and the design of ICT systems (Engeström, 1990; Miettinen, 1998; Kaptelinin & Nardi, 2006).

In the context of the development of work, the term "object of activity" assumed a double meaning. On the one hand, it referred to the "purpose" or aim, in other words the motivating background rationale of an activity: it is a horizon for actions that constantly need to be reinterpreted in a changing society (Engeström, 1990). The joint reflection on the changing historical circumstances of an activity, defining its contradictions, and the formulation of "a new model of activity" (or a model of a zone of proximal development) in interventionist studies serve such a historical reinterpretation. The second meaning of object of activity was a concrete object of activity, something that is designed and produced in the form of a product, a service, or a commodity. The relation between these two was sometimes characterized by saying that a concrete object to be constructed is an "instantiation" of the motive of the activity (Nardi, 2005) or a separate type of a "project object" (Hyysalo, 2005). The expression "construction of an object" (a product, service, IT system, building) was partly formulated because of the influence of the constructivist science and technology studies that theorized and analyzed the production of facts and technological artifacts.[1]

In the 1990s and 2000s, new dimensions and meanings of an "object" of activity were introduced. These include its complex and contradictory, open-ended, multifaceted, and expanding nature. This complex and contradictory nature (referring to the functional complexity of the objects to be constructed) was discussed in product development literature and in science and technology studies (Hobday, 1998; Miettinen, 1999). Complex products are composed of subsystems whose design and construction call for the contribution of a different kind of expertise. Correspondingly, different actors have different interpretations of the object. The contradictory nature of objects refers to the tension between use and exchange value in them, as well as to the differing interests of the participants that need to be negotiated as a part of the object construction (Miettinen & Virkkunen, 2005).

In science and technology studies, Karin Knorr-Cetina introduced the concept of an epistemic object analogous to an object of inquiry in science, in which "the lack in completeness of being is crucial" (Knorr-Cetina, 2001, p. 182). Knorr-Cetina argues (2001) that in a contemporary knowledge society, the objects of professional work are rapidly changing. Compared with mass products or services, these objects are ever more complex, dispersed, and

in constant need of being redefined. This is why they can be characterized in terms of open, constantly unfolding epistemic objects. The theme of the open and expansive nature of objects has been further developed by introducing the term "runaway object," ambiguous large-scale global phenomena which are not in anyone's control and which have far-reaching consequences that are difficult to anticipate (Engeström, 2008). Completely new forms of transnational distributed agency are needed in order to tackle such objects and problems. The increased complexity of objects is evident both in the construction industry and the ICT industry. The sheer size of buildings and the complicated devices and technology embedded in them has increased the number of contributors and correspondingly the need for coordination and collaboration.

The increased number of relevant stakeholders has created the need for understanding how they are able to collaborate and coordinate their actions. The concept of boundary object originally introduced by Star and Griesemer (1989) has been used to make sense of this problem (Gal, Lyytinen, & Yoo, 2008; Whyte & Lobo, 2010). In terms of activity theory, this concept mostly refers to the means or infrastructure of activities, not to the object of an activity. A lesson from the discussion of the object of activity is evident. The increasing complexity of the object of activity requires increasingly versatile constellations of means and artifacts and new forms of collaboration.

8.3 The Relationship between Language and Tool Use in Vygotsky and in Studies of Work

Vygotsky (1978) made a basic distinction between two types of mediational means: tools and signs. Tools and signs are both cultural means; they differ in the way that they orientate an activity. Tools are externally orientated and are used to transform objects (mastering their nature). Signs are used to coordinate the actions of individuals in a collaborative activity. Signs are also used as psychological tools, that is, to direct and control an individual's behaviors and actions (mastering oneself). In addition, Vygotsky says (1978, p. 55) that these two activities are mutually linked "just as man's alteration of nature alters man's own nature." He analyzes this in terms of the integration of practical intelligence and sign use (speech) in child development where "the creation of these uniquely human forms of behaviour later produce the intellect and become the basis of productive work: the specifically human form of the use of tools" (Vygotsky, 1978, p. 26).

In their essay "Tool and Symbol in Child Development" (1994), Vygotsky and Luria criticize the prevailing "zoologist" approach to the study of child development, in which the preverbal forms of child development are compared to those of apes. They conclude that "[t]he child's use of tools is comparable to that of ape's only during the former's pre-speech period" (1994, p. 108). The planning and self-regulation function that speech brings to problem solving is missing from the apes. The main thesis is to show that (1994, p. 116) "the transition from the biological to the social way of development constitutes the central link in this process of development, the cardinal turning point in the history of child behaviour." The transition becomes visible in the uses of egocentric speech in problem solving by the young children. This is used for arguing for the emergence of the specifically human higher psychological functions that constitute a foundation for a psychological science.

Many authors have pointed out (Wertsch, 1985; Leiman, 1999; Arievich & Stetsenko, 2014) that Vygotsky and Luria do not analyze the preverbal intelligence of children in depth. Vygotsky and Luria (1994) use various terms for it: practical intelligence or thinking (p. 102), instrumental thinking (p. 102), tool use (p. 109), elementary process or function (p. 144), primi-

tive processes of problem solving (p. 131), and, finally, in their conclusions, a *biological line of development* (p. 148), which then is integrated with a "social or cultural" line of development based on the use of signs. We think that this rhetorical distinction does not give justice to the social and cultural nature of preverbal behavior of the children, to which Vygotsky himself refers (1978, p. 30).[2] A one-year-old child imitating the voice of an engine when playing with a toy car is evidently a cultural phenomenon. The child's operations with objects are mediated by interaction with the mother and other significant people and with the cultural environment, and they acquire a cultural meaning and emotional coloring through these interactions.[3] This acquisition of the meanings of objects might well be characterized as an early form of semiotic mediation (Leiman, 1999). Also Lektorsky (1999, p. 111) suggests, based on studies on the education of deaf and blind children, that a baby can only appropriate genuine speech after appropriating meaningful social modes of dealing practically with human-made objects.

We find a sign- and language-bound conception of semiosis to be limited. First, it seems that the concept of an object is underdeveloped in semiotic approaches to cultural mediation. Semiotic relationships are often seen from the point of view of symbols and language, which themselves, however, include indexical and practical relationships. Peirce's seminal works on semiotics define a sign as mediating between its object and interpretant, or, roughly, its meaning (Peirce, 1998, pp. 477–491). He defines semiotic relationships not just with symbols but also with indices, which have a physical connection to objects and with icons that represent objects with their characters. Human beings use not only talk, but gestures, bodily dispositions, and affordances or semiotic features of the environment in their activities (Goodwin, 2000).

The excessive focus on speech, narrative, and discourses also makes activity theory vulnerable to the critique of pragmatism, phenomenology, and ethnomethodology that underlines the significance or primacy of habits, skills, and embodied forms of intelligence. These approaches argue that human practice is composed of bodily ways of acting or of habits. Reflection and the use of language are needed primarily when a habit breaks or to legitimate the ways of acting. According to these approaches, learning skills and tool use may take place by imitation and by trial and error without systematic instruction and the use of language.

A recurrent observation of studies of practitioners and professionals in work is that they are unable to formulate verbally why they do as they do (e.g., Engeström & Engeström, 1986). A key statement of the pragmatism-inspired theory of professional knowledge by Argyris and Schön (1978) is that professional practitioners present verbally an "espoused theory" which deviates from the real way of acting, a "use theory" that can be uncovered by studying the actual work process. These findings question the idea that a speech or a verbally formulated plan in itself is able to guide the uses of tools. They rather suggest that there may be incompatibilities or loss of interaction between future-oriented "where-to" models (Engeström, 2007) and meanings embodied in different types of artifacts already used in work. If cultural means – as we will suggest – comprise complexes of various means having different origins, it is likely that there are tensions and contradictions between them. This leads us to the analysis of different kinds of means and their interaction activity.

8.4 Artifacts and the Concept of Instrumentality

In sociocultural psychology and activity theory, it has become customary to refer to both signs and tools with terms such as mediational or cultural means, instrument (e.g., Engeström, 1987) and artifacts (Cole, 1996).[4] The concept

of artifact refers to a human-made object that has a meaning and constitutes a part of our culture.[5] Engeström adopted (1987) the concept of an artifact from the historical epistemology of Marx Wartofsky (1979). Wartofsky draws a distinction between primary, secondary, and tertiary artifacts. Tools and related bodily skills are primary artifacts. Secondary artifacts, typically models, are "distinctive artifacts created for the purpose of *preserving* and *transmitting* skills, in the production and use of 'primary' artefacts" (Wartofsky, 1979, p. 201). Tertiary artifacts are alternative imaginative perceptual models, "a representation of possibilities which go beyond present actualities" (p. 209). Although Wartofsky's levels have not been extensively used in empirical research and provide only a rough classification, they are important in suggesting that artifacts have different functions in an activity beyond the distinction between sign and tool.

Engeström (2007) has used Wartofsky's term "tertiary artifact" characterizing it as a where-to type of cognitive artifact that is used to orient to the future and to imagine and define alternative forms of activity. Engeström (2007, p. 34) has also made a distinction between epistemologically different levels of orienting models used in work and in teaching. For example, procedural models included in guidelines and instruction books mainly express the order in which actions and operations are to be done. They do not provide knowledge of why the defined order is selected nor of the nature of the object of the work. Answers to these issues require systems models or theoretical models. For the development of activities, it is a major challenge to study empirically the functions of various artifacts and their interdependencies.

The prevailing theory of artifacts both in philosophy and in design studies, is a theory of the functions of artifacts. In design theories, designers deliberately create the functions of an artifact or organize material affordances in order to satisfy the needs of the users (e.g., Norman, 2002).

The function theory in analytic philosophy also analyzes the functions or capabilities and dispositions of cultural artifacts (Preston, 1998; Houkes & Vermaas, 2004). A multiplicity of functions of artifacts emerges when users invent uses that depart from the focal use planned by the designer. The function theories are compatible with the theories that regard the objectification of human activity into artifacts as a central mechanism of cultural development. Ilyenkov (1977a, p. 277) suggests that "all forms of activity (active faculties) are passed on only in the form of objects created by man for man." Actor-network theory has studied the agency of material artifacts and the delegation of human functions and norms to objects (Latour, 1992). According to Latour (1994, p. 31), technical artifacts have a script, an affordance, a function or a program of action and goals.

Dewey (1938/1991, p. 52) finds that: "A tool or a machine, for example, is not simply a simple or complex physical object having its own physical properties and effects, but is also a mode of language. For it *says* something, to those who understand it, about operations of use and their consequences." Dewey underlines that the utilization of embodied norms of and understanding the consequences require the learning of embodied skills. Lektorsky's characterization includes three objectified elements (1980, p. 137): "The instrumental man-made objects function as objective forms of expression of cognitive norms, standards and object-hypotheses existing outside the individual." However, these general definitions do not uncover how specific functions are embodied in different artifacts and how these different artifacts together constitute what is needed in a mediated collaborative activity. Engeström has introduced the concept of instrumentality (2007). The concepts, models, and tools in work "are not separate meditational entities, but form integrated toolkits...tool constellations or instrumentalities" (p. 33). They "include multiple cognitive artefacts and semiotic means

used for analysis and design, but also straightforward primary tools used in the daily practice and made visible for examination, reshaping and experimentation" (Engeström 2005, p. 188). The term instru-*mentality* reminds us that intellectual and practical embodied functions are inseparably and in various ways interconnected in an instrumentality and even in single artifacts within it.

The concept of instrumentality has an analogy in Elinor Ostrom's (2007) concept of a *rule constellation* or *rule configuration* which is used in the analysis of institutional change in self-organizing resource governance systems. Ostrom underlines the configurational nature of rules (2007, p. 18): "One needs to know the basic contents of a *full* rule configuration, rather than a single rule, to infer both the structure of the resulting situation and the likely outcome of any particular rule change." For the examination of the transformation of rules, she has made a distinction between seven clusters of rules according to the element of action and the decision-making situation they directly affect (2007, p. 11).

After the emergence of the Internet, ICT researchers have likewise pointed out that digital objects cannot be studied as separate, standalone, or single artifacts or tools (Henfridsson & Bygstad, 2014). Digital artifacts are relational and modular and tend to form complex systems, mediate activities of several organizations and knowledge domains, and create connections between distant data sources through the Internet. Information systems research suggests that information or digital infrastructures constitute a new type of information artifact (Henfridsson & Bygstad, 2014). These views agree on the "expansive potential" of the systems: because of their inherent digitally enabled scalability and flexibility, they are generative: they grow and evolve. To enable the integration of new modules into the evolving systems, gateways and standards are core elements of the infrastructures (Hanseth & Lyytinen, 2010, p. 4).

8.5 A New Vision does not Suffice: A Failed Remediation in Oral Health Care

A conscious change in an instrumentality as a part of developing an activity has been characterized as remediation. Remediation includes the formulation of a vision or a model of an alternative way of approaching an activity (a where-to model or a working hypothesis) as well as a change in the whole constellation of artifacts and social forms of collaboration (Miettinen & Virkkunen, 2005). To clarify this, we will shortly analyze an example of an attempt to develop dental care for adults with periodontal diseases in Finland.

As a result of demographic change and a more inclusive level of dental care, periodontal and gum diseases have become the most frequently encountered oral health problem among the adult population in Finland. In a study of adults over 30 years, 64 percent of the studied adults had periodontitis to some degree of difficulty (Teräs & Nuutinen, 2010, p. 56). Periodontitis is a serious gum infection that damages the soft tissue and destroys the bone that supports the teeth. Periodontal and gum diseases call collaboration between dentists and oral hygienists as well as active preventive self-care by patients. A new model, called a health-centered teamwork model, was outlined for dental care in two projects in the years 2007–2010 by representatives of a university dental clinic, an oral hygiene clinic of a university of applied sciences, and a city dental-care clinic. The model was defined in a graphic form in the thesis of one of the participants in 2009. It envisioned three kinds of transformations in the care: first, a transition from individual care to teamwork; second, from a pathogenesis-based orientation to a health and preventive orientation; and third, from expert-centered to patient-centered and activating care. The key elements in the graphic model were "Preventive advancement of the health of the mouth" and

"An environment that supports health behaviour" (Teräs & Nuutinen, 2010, p. 55).

The model was planned to be experimented on and put into practice in an interim period in a dental clinic in the city of Helsinki. In the interim period, dental students and oral hygienist students together cared for adult patients under the supervision of their teachers. Two patient care trajectories of nine sessions were recorded and analyzed in a study (Teräs, 2015) to find what kind of changes took place in the collaboration and in the division of labor between the professionals and in the interaction between the professional and the patient. The study provided an opportunity to study whether and in which ways the new model, to use Vygotsky's expression, "penetrated the process of tool use." For that, the instrumentality used in the collaborative care activity needed to be characterized. A distinction can be drawn between seven types of means.

1 The model of health-centered teamwork.
2 Instructions and manuals defining good practice – one for the dental students (PARO Manual) and one for the oral hygienist students (instruction for the care of adult patients).
3 Diagnostic means: (a) X-ray images, (b) digitized pictures, and (c) an instrument for measuring the depth of the gum pockets.
4 A care plan: the patient's diagnosis (see Figure 8.1) and a plan of care measures.
5 The means of evaluation.
6 The instruments for caring for the teeth and gums.
7 The instruments used by the patients in self-care.

The researchers (Teräs & Nuutinen, 2010, p. 58) used the concept of a "script" to characterize the tools of the second category (instructions and manuals). They provided a description of the phases of the care process and characterized the actions and operations included in each of the phases. A decisive means in this system is without doubt the care plan. The details of the

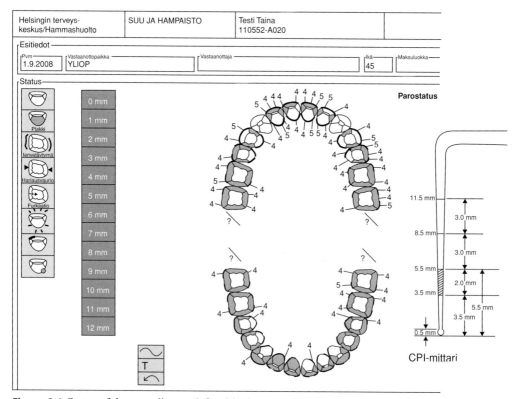

Figure 8.1 Status of the gum disease defined in the care plan.

diagnosis are assembled in it (see Figure 8.1), which provide a basis for the plan of care measures, most important of which are removing the dental plague and cleaning the gum pockets. The care plan combines an object hypothesis (analysis of the state of the disease) and an operational plan for care.

The results of the analysis of the communication and tool use during the care trajectories show that the new ideal model of the collaborative patient-centered model tended to remain an "espoused theory." An important reason for this is that the ideas presented in it were not included in the manuals that regulate the care activity. For example, although consultation and dialogue with the patients to stimulate self-care was a central goal in the model, no space was reserved for this in the care process defined in the manuals. Nor were the diagnostic pictures

of the patient's teeth used in the consultation to clarify the status of the disease for the patients. The care plan was not shown to the patient, who, according to the new model, was supposed to take increasing responsibility for the care. The care plan remained a means of the professionals. The short discussions with the adult patient focused on very elementary measures of caring for the teeth and questions covered topics such as smoking, the use of an electric toothbrush, or flossing. As mentioned before, no information of the state of the disease whether illustrated in pictures or defined in the care plan was shown to the patients. The ideals presented in the new model and the traditional ways of professional work embodied in the instruction manuals were in gross contradiction. The exclusive use of diagnostic tools and the care plan by the professionals also contradicted the model.

8.6 Shifting Multiple Functions of Building Information Modeling

We have been involved in studying the implementation of building information modeling (BIM) in the construction industry in Finland (Miettinen & Paavola, 2014). BIM is a new technology that combines 3-D digital representations of a building with parametric data of the objects (parts) of the building. BIM tools allow new levels of spatial visualization and – as a result of the parametric data of the objects – simulations of the behavior of the building such as energy consumption and lighting. BIM was developed from standards that allow interoperability of information between "native" design models and data sharing (at least potentially) between various partners in the construction process, that is, between architects, structural engineers, HVAC (heating, ventilation, air conditioning, electricity) engineers, customers, contractors, and site engineers. The most important of the BIM standards is the IFC (Industry Foundation Classes) data format, published in 1997. The standard enables the creation of a unified model or data repository shared by all stakeholders during the planning process and the lifecycle of a building (Miettinen & Paavola, 2014). According to the proponents of BIM, this possibility will revolutionize the collaboration both between designers and between designers and other stakeholders in the construction industry, but it requires the development of new ways of working with BIM. It is expected to lead to an integrated way of working and to the increased productivity of the industry.

Like most digital artifacts, BIM is not a separate entity. It is composed of a number of different software programs, most of which may be used interactively thanks to the standards. In the Finnish construction project that we studied, the designers used nine different software programs from seven different providers (Table 8.1).

Each program has specific pre-planned functions, such as allowing architectural design, calculating energy consumption, and viewing the clashes between the models. BIM is not an established infrastructure or a system. New special purpose software is continually emerging and different firms configure their own unique systems of them to meet their needs and develop their own particular expertise and organizational forms to utilize these programs. The process resembles the creation of enterprise information systems, which have been characterized as architectural or configurational technologies (Fleck, 1994). Typically, parts and modules developed by several vendors are combined and adjusted to meet the local needs of the users. In addition, in each construction project, the key partners must agree on which software will be used in the project and how. That is why we characterize BIM as an evolving, configurational, and constantly re-negotiated instrumentality.

The disciplinary software programs are used to produce native models (plans of the building) that play a central role in its design. These models work as intermediary artifacts or objects in the design work and collaboration. The term "intermediary object" has been used to refer to the open and evolving nature of the design process instead of the traditional model of design as a linear and sequential process (Boujut & Blanco, 2003; Ewenstein & Whyte, 2009; Vinck, 2011). The term intermediary object depicts the nature of the design process as composed of cycles of collaborative design during which the disciplinary native models (architectural, structural, HVAC) produced by different design disciplines using special-purpose software (see Table 8.1) are fused into combined models. The models are simultaneously a partial outcome of joined work and a means of joined reflection and problem solving concerning the following cycles of design. The function of BIM changes during the design cycles from a tool used by the designers to an intermediary object and back to a tool again.

Table 8.1 *BIM-related software used in a Finnish construction project in 2011–2012.*

Software	Main users	Main uses and outcomes
1 ArchiCAD	Architects	Architect model
2 Tekla Structures	Structural engineers	Structural model
3 Tekla BIM Sight	Structural engineers Architects	Creating a combined model and checking the compatibility of the native models (1 and 2)
4 MagiCAD	HVAC engineers	HVAC-models (electricity, plumbing, ventilation)
5 Dialux	HVAC engineers	Lighting
6 NavisWorks	HVAC engineers	Combining HVAC models and checking the compatibility of the native models (4)
7 Solibri Model Checker	BIM expert	Creating combined models of all native models and clash detection lists
8 Solibri Model Viewer	All designers	Viewing the clashes (7)
9 Riuska	HVAC engineers	Energy simulations

The BIM software and models are used in the design process in the following ways.

1 *As tools for design work within each design discipline:* The designers of different fields, individually and as a group, construct native models using BIM software (software 1, 2, 4, and 5 in Table 8.1).

2 *As tools of constructing combined models* (software 3, 6, and 7 in Table 8.1).

3 *The combined models function as tangible and indexical objects of joint problem solving* and reflection, and as intermediary outcomes of joint work.

4 *The combined models function as means of coordination* of the further work of the designers.[6]

5 *The models function as a data source* for (a) simulations of the behavior of the building (energy, lighting), (b) for cost calculations, (c) for project planning, and (d) for completing the orders from the suppliers.

A simple distinction between sign and tool can hardly be used to characterize BIM. The designers use BIM software as the main operative tool to produce the native models. The software is packed with symbolic and operative knowledge. Energy simulation software, for example, embodies theoretical knowledge of the physical properties of construction materials and is used as a tool to provide calculations of the energy consumption of the building alternatives to the clients. In the area of engineering design, the uses of sketches, paper drawings, and plans have been seen as tools of collaboration and communication as the designers engage with these artifacts in design meetings in indexical and even tactile ways (Ewenstein & Whyte, 2009; Henderson, 1999). The use of BIM models does not change these basic functions and uses of design plans. The combined models are not only symbols but modifiable intermediary artifacts, or "special objects" (Ilyenkov, 1977a, p. 280) that are revised collaboratively during the design process. Ilyenkov characterizes a special object using the example of the drawings in an architect's work: "In changing it he potentially alters the real house, i.e. changes it ideally, potentially, which means that he alters *one sensuously perceived object instead of another*" (Ilyenkov, 1977a, p. 280).

We consider one novel feature of BIM models as intermediary artifacts to be their capacity to provide new means for collaboration and to play several functions in the course of a design process: a tool of disciplinary design work, a tool of collaborative problem solving as well as an immediate object of reflection, and an evolving intermediary object to which the outcomes of the cycles of design are objectified. The modifiable, updatable, modular, and variable nature of digital artifacts allow this flexibility (Kallinikos, Aaltonen, & Marton, 2010). This changing status is compatible with the activity theoretical view, according to which any entity may gain different functions depending on its position in the structure and course of an activity. In the temporal process of an activity an object can become a tool and a tool can become an object. The most evident transformation takes place when an outcome of the design phase, an as-designed model, is handed over to the constructors and becomes a tool of the construction work. Because of the modifiability of digital artifacts, the transitions between functions seem to be much more flexible than when using traditional tools.

8.7 Conclusions

In the activity-theoretical tradition, the distinction between sign and tool drawn by Vygotsky has been a central starting point. Vygotsky, however, found the intertwining and unity of sign mediation and tool use at the center of complex human behavior. Our cases indicate the increasing significance of preparatory work and planning in professional activities. In preparatory work, models and plans are typically worked on as "special objects" instead of a final object. These tend to be hybrids fusing intellectual and practical-operational functions, as in case of a care plan or a building information model. In addition, artifacts of different types and levels within an instrumentality complement each other.

Since the artifacts within the constellation have, however, been adopted at different times and have different origins, different meanings and operational logics have been embodied in them. Our example of the instrumentality of the oral care of adults showed that different artifacts

can be incompatible. The old artifacts in use, relations of power, and traditional ways of professional thinking and acting resisted the implementation of a new model or an idea of activity. It is therefore essential for the transformation of an activity to achieve a sufficient fit and coordination between the artifacts. If this is not done, the "tertiary," or where-to artifacts, or the verbalized visions of alternative practices, risk remaining utopias unable to become the practical transformation of an activity. It seems to us that analyses of instrumentalities, that is, the different levels and types of artifacts, their specific functions, and their interdependencies characteristic of different activities, are needed to enlarge our understanding of semiotic, practical, and cultural mediation. Such analyses are also important for well-informed remediation in interventionist studies.

The study of BIM revealed that the constellation of artifacts not only constitutes complex constellations, but the artifacts also constantly evolve, are locally configured and call for constant negotiations between partners in collaborative projects. The building information modeling also showed that during the cycles of design BIM software functioned as a basic tool of design disciplines, an immediate object of collaborative problem solving, and an intermediary outcome of joint work as well as a means of collaboration. BIM models as intermediary artifacts play several functions in the course of a design process. The modifiable, updatable, modular, and variable nature of digital artifacts contributes to the flexibility of their functions.

Notes

1 Nardi (2005, p. 40) argued that "the notion of *constructing* an object is ambiguous in much of the activity theory literature." According to her, "we speak of constructing an object when we mean *formulating* it, that is, figuring out what it should be. *Instantiating* an object then refers to the work that goes into realizing a particular object, to achieving an outcome."

2 "This complex human structure is the product of a developmental process deeply rooted in the links between individual and social history" (Vygotsky, 1978, p. 30).

3 Evidence of the beginning of the social and cultural development of human fetuses and newborns is accumulating. During the last trimester of pregnancy human fetuses develop sensitivity to melody contour in both music and language. A newborn prefers his or her mother's voice over other voices and distinguishes prosodically different languages based primarily on melody (e.g., Mampe et al., 2009).

4 The root of the term instrument may be found in Vygotsky, who speaks about instrumental as synonymous with "artificial" and in opposition to natural. He also uses the term "artificial device" (1981, p. 137).

5 Miller (2011) warns about the danger of using the concept of artifact, because it hides the distinction between sign and tool. This interpretation seems dichotomic in studying such modern mediational means discussed in this chapter as a care plan or a digital model of a building.

6 The definition of the functions of the combined models depends on the temporal perspective. In a joint meeting of designers, they are immediate objects of attention, from the point of view of the following cycle of design they are means of coordination, and from the point of view of the entire design process they are intermediate objects or outcomes.

References

Argyris, C. & Schön, D. A. (1978). *Organizational Learning: A Theory of Action Perspective*. Reading, MA: Addison-Wesley.

Arievich, I. & Stetsenko, A. (2014). The "magic of signs": Developmental trajectory of cultural mediation. In A. Yasnitsky, R. van der Veer, & M. Ferrari (Eds.), *The Cambridge Handbook of Cultural-Historical Psychology* (pp. 217–244). Cambridge: Cambridge University Press.

Bakhurst, D. (1991). *Consciousness and Revolution in Soviet Philosophy: From Bolsheviks to Evald Ilyenkov*. Cambridge: Cambridge University Press.

Boujut, J.-F. & Blanco, E. (2003). Intermediary objects as a means to foster co-operation in engineering design. *Computer Supported Cooperative Work*, 12: 205–219.

Cole, M. (1996). *Cultural Psychology: A Once and Future Discipline*. Cambridge, MA: Belknap/ Harvard University Press.

Dewey, J. (1938/1991). *The Later Works of John Dewey, 1925–1953. Volume 12: Logic: The Theory of Inquiry* (ed. by Jo Ann Boydston). Carbondale: Southern Illinois University Press.

Elkonin, D. B. (2005). Theories of play. *Journal of Russian and East European Psychology*, 43(2), 3–89.

Engeström, Y. (1987). *Learning by Expanding: An Activity Theoretical Approach to Developmental Research*. Helsinki: Orienta Konsultit.

Engeström, Y. (1990). Constructing the object in the work activity of primary care physicians. In Y. Engeström (Ed.), *Learning, Working and Imagining* (pp. 107–129). Helsinki: Orienta Konsultit.

Engeström, Y. (2005). From individual action to collective activity and back: Developmental work research as an interventionist methodology. In Y. Engeström, *Developmental Work Research: Expanding Activity Theory in Practice* (pp. 171–199). Berlin, Lehmanns Media.

Engeström, Y. (2007). Enriching the theory of expansive learning: Lessons from the journeys toward coconfiguration. *Mind, Culture and Activity*, 14(1–2), 23–39.

Engeström, Y. (2008). *From Teams to Knots: Activity-theoretical Studies of Collaboration and Learning at Work*. Cambridge: Cambridge University Press.

Engeström, Y. & Blackler, F. (2005). On the Life of the Object. *Organization*, 12(3), 307–330.

Engeström, Y. & Engeström, R. (1986). Developmental work research: The approach and an application in cleaning work. *Nordisk Pedagogik*, 6(1), 2–15.

Ewenstein, B. & Whyte, J. (2009). Knowledge practices in design: The role of visual

representations as "epistemic objects."
Organization Studies, 30(1), 7–30.

Fleck, J. (1994). Learning by trying: The
implementation of configurational technology.
Research Policy, 23, 637–652.

Gal, U., Lyytinen, K., & Yoo, Y. (2008). The
dynamics of IT boundary objects, information
infrastructures, and organizational identities: The
introduction of 3D modelling technologies into
architecture, engineering, and construction
industry. *European Journal of Information
Systems*, 17, 290–304.

Goodwin, C. (2000). Action and embodiment within
situated human interaction. *Journal of
Pragmatics*, 32, 1489–1522.

Hanseth, O. & Lyytinen, K. (2010). Design theory
for dynamic complexity in information
infrastructures: The case of building Internet.
Journal of Information Technology, 25(1), 1–19.

Henderson, K. (1999). *On Line and on Paper: Visual
Representations, Visual Culture, and Computer
Graphics in Design Engineering*. Cambridge,
MA: MIT Press.

Henfridsson, O. & Bygstad, B. (2014). The generative
mechanisms of digital infrastructure evolution.
MIS Quarterly, 37(3), 907–931.

Hobday, M. (1998). Product complexity, innovation
and industrial organization. *Research Policy*,
26(6), 689–710.

Houkes, W. & Vermaas, P. E. (2004). Actions versus
functions: A plea for an alternative metaphysics
of artefacts. *The Monist*, 87(1), 52–71.

Hyysalo, S. (2005). Objects and motives in a product
design process. *Mind, Culture, and Activity*,
12(1), 19–36.

Ilyenkov, E. V. (1977a). *Dialectical Logic: Essays on
Its History and Theory*. Moscow: Progress
Publishers.

Ilyenkov, E. V. (1977b). The concept of the ideal. In
*Philosophy in the USSR: Problems of Dialectical
Materialism* (pp. 71–99). Moscow: Progress
Publishers.

Kallinikos, J., Aaltonen, A., & Marton, A. (2010). A
theory of digital objects. *First Monday*, 15(6).

Kaptelinin, V. (2005). The object of activity: Making
sense of the sense-maker. *Mind, Culture, and
Activity*, 12(1), 4–18.

Kaptelinin, V. & Nardi, B. A. (2006). *Acting with
Technology: Activity Theory and Interaction
Design*. Cambridge, MA: MIT Press.

Karpov, Y. V. (2005). *The Neo-Vygotskian Approach
to Child Development*. Cambridge: Cambridge
University Press.

Knorr-Cetina, K. (2001) Objectual practice. In
T. Schatzki, K. Knorr-Cetina, & E. von Savigny
(Eds.), *The Practice Turn in Contemporary
Theory* (pp. 175–188). New York: Routledge.

Latour, B. (1992). One turn after the social turn. In
E. McMullin (Ed.), *The Social Dimensions of
Science* (pp. 272–294). Notre Dame, IN:
University of Note Dame Press.

Latour, B. (1994). On technical mediation:
Philosophy, sociology, genealogy. *Common
Knowledge*, 3(2), 29–64.

Leiman, M. (1999). The concept of sign in the work
of Vygotsky, Winnicot and Bakhtin: Further
integration of object relations theory and activity
theory. In Y. Engeström, R. Miettinen, & R-L.
Punamäki (Eds.), *Perspectives of Activity Theory*
(pp. 419–443). Cambridge: Cambridge
University Press.

Lektorsky, V. A. (1980). *Subject Object Cognition*.
Moscow: Progress Publishers.

Lektorsky, V. A. (1999). Historical change of the
notion of activity. In S. Chaiklin, M. Hedegaard,
& U. Juul-Jensen (Eds.), *Activity Theory and
Social Practice: Cultural-historical Approaches*
(pp. 104–113). Aarhus, Denmark: Aarhus
University Press.

Leontiev, A. N. (1977) Activity and consciousness. In
*Philosophy in the USSR: Problems of Dialectical
Materialism*. Moscow: Progress Publishers.

Leontiev, A. N. (1978). *Activity, Consciousness and
Personality*. Englewood Cliffs, NJ: Prentice Hall.

Mampe, B., Friederici, A., Chistophe, A., & Wermke,
K. (2009). Newborns' cry melody is shaped by
their native language. *Current Biology*, 19(23),
1994–1997.

Martin, D. & Peim, N. (2009). Editorial: Critical
perspectives on activity theory. *Educational
Review*, 61(2), 131–138.

Marx, K. (1964). *The Economic and Philosophic
Manuscripts of 1844* (ed. by K. J. Struik). New
York: International Publishers.

Miettinen, R. (1998). Object construction and networks in research work: The case of research on cellulose-degrading enzymes. *Social Studies of Science*, 28(3), 423–463.

Miettinen, R. (1999). The riddle of things: Activity theory and actor network theory as approaches of studying innovations. *Mind, Culture, and Activity*, 6(3), 170–195.

Miettinen, R. & Paavola, S. (2014). Beyond the BIM utopia: Approaches to the development and implementation of building information modeling. *Automation in Construction*, 43, 84–91.

Miettinen, R. & Virkkunen, J. (2005). Epistemic objects, artefacts and organizational change. *Organization*, 12(3), 437–456.

Miller, R. (2011). *Vygotsky in Perspective*. Cambridge: Cambridge University Press.

Mind, Culture and Activity (2005). 12(1). Perspectives on the object of activity (special issue).

Nardi, B. A. (2005). Objects of desire: Power and passion in collaborative activity. *Mind, Culture, and Activity*, 12(1), 37–51.

Norman, D. A. (2002). *The Design of Everyday Things*. New York: Basic Books. (Originally published in 1988 as *The Psychology of Everyday Things*.)

Ostrom, E. (2007). Developing a method for analyzing institutional change. Working Papers 07–1. Workshop in Political Theory and Policy Analysis, Indiana University.

Peirce, C. S. (1998). *The Essential Peirce: Selected Philosophical Writings. Volume 2 (1893–1913)*. Bloomington: Indiana University Press.

Preston, B. (1998). Why is a wing like a spoon? A pluralist theory of function. *The Journal of Philosophy*, 95(5), 215–254.

Star, S. L. & Griesemer, J. R. (1989). Institutional ecology, "translations" and boundary objects: Amateurs and professionals in Berkeley's Museum of Vertebrate Zoology, 1907–39. *Social Studies of Science*, 19(3), 387–420.

Teräs, M. (2015). Inter-professional working and learning: Instructional actions and boundary crossing or boundary making in oral healthcare. *Journal of Education and Work*, 29(5), 614–636.

Teräs, M. & Nuutinen, E. (2010). Ammattikorkeakoulu-ja yliopisto-opiskelijat oppimassa työtä yhdessä [Polytechnic and university students are learning to work together]. *Ammattikasvatuksen aikakauskirja* [The Finnish journal of vocational and professional education], 12(2), 55–67.

Vinck, D. (2011). Taking intermediary objects and equipping work into account in the study of engineering practices. *Engineering Studies*, 3(1), 25–44.

Vygotsky, L. S. (1978). *Mind in Society: The Development of Higher Mental Functions* (ed. by Michael Cole, Vera John-Steiner, Sylvia Scribner and Ellen Soberman). Cambridge, MA: Harvard University Press.

Vygotsky, L. S. (1981). Instrumental method in psychology. In J. V. Wersch (Ed.), *The Concept of Activity in Soviet Psychology* (pp. 134–143). Armonko, NY: Sharp.

Vygotsky, L. S. (2004). Imagination and creativity in childhood. *Journal of Russian and East European Psychology*, 42(1), 7–97.

Vygotsky, L. S. & Luria, A. (1994). Tool and symbol in child development. In R. van der Veer, & J. Valsiner (Eds.), *The Vygotsky Reader* (pp. 99–174). Oxford: Blackwell.

Wartofsky, M. (1979). *Models: Representation and Scientific Understanding*. Dordrecht, Netherlands: Reidel.

Wertsch, J. V. (1985). Introduction. In J. V. Wertsch (Ed.), *Culture, Communication and Cognition* (pp. 1–20). Cambridge: Cambridge University Press.

Whyte, J. & Lobo, S. (2010). Coordination and control in project-based work: Digital objects and infrastructures for delivery. *Construction Management and Economics*, 28(6), 557–567.

9 The Sociocultural Study of Creative Action

Vlad Petre Glăveanu

It is undeniable that creativity is currently one of the "hot" topics in both science and society, from economy and management to education and politics (Dubina, Carayannis, & Campbell, 2012). In a world marked by connectivity, globalization, and rapid changes, creativity is often considered essential for adapting to new circumstances and as the driving force of progress in a variety of applied areas. We are constantly told we need creative leaders and creative followers, creative teachers as well as creative students, creative marketing campaigns and consumers ready to understand and express creativity, and so on. What exactly each one of these slogans implies by "creativity" is not exactly clear and, when forced to clarify their choices, teachers, for example, often end up preferring "good" (meaning obedient) rather than "creative" students (see Karwowski, 2010). Meanwhile, psychologists more or less consistently endorse a product-based definition of creativity as the psychological process leading to the generation of new, original and valuable, or meaningful outcomes (Stein, 1953). The question remains of how we can account for processes when considering outcomes alone, for instance, number and quality of ideas in divergent thinking tests. More than this, what can a focus on ideas tell us about real-life processes of creating, about the embodied nature of making new objects, crafting new practices, and renewing cultural traditions?

While today's psychology of creativity perfected its study of cognitive and even neurological mechanisms involved in creative ideation, it is still struggling to account for material and socio-cultural factors within creative action. Despite a growing interest in the role of the social since the 1980s (e.g., Simonton, 1975; Amabile, 1983; Amabile, Hennessey, & Grossman, 1986; Csikszentmihalyi, 1988), the main concern has been to demonstrate how social dimensions *shape* (from the outside) the creative processes of individuals. In contrast, sociocultural psychology starts from the premise of the social and cultural as *intrinsic* components of the human mind as it creatively acts within and on the world (Glăveanu, 2010a, 2014; Moran & John-Steiner, 2003). The general lack of more sociocultural thinking in the psychology of creativity is both a consequence and an outcome of the long history of individualizing this notion and making it the – sometimes exclusive – quality of isolated individuals or, rather, isolated individual minds. Recently, significant efforts have been made to rethink creativity from a sociocultural perspective (Glăveanu, Gillespie, & Valsiner, 2015) and these efforts need to be consolidated and connected to other current developments in the sociocultural study of the imagination (Zittoun & Gillespie, 2015) and human agency (Gruber et al., 2015). This chapter hopes to contribute to this general direction.

The sociocultural study of creativity starts from the basic idea that creativity is not a purely mental process but a quality of human action (see also Joas, 1996; Sawyer, 1995; Glăveanu, 2013a, 2014). In other words, creativity is not a constellation of personality traits, cognitive styles, or neural associations, for as much as these features contribute to the creative process. A sociocultural, thus holistic, way of understanding creativity starts from its expression in activity or action. As such, it is the process of *creating* rather than a reified, unitary, and universal notion of "creativity" that interests sociocultural psychologists. However, in order to develop a holistic and developmental approach to the study of creating or creative action, specific for sociocultural psychology, we need to go beyond "elements" and investigate the dynamic relations between them (Glăveanu, 2015a). These relations, as I argue here, are represented by various forms of (*inter*)*action*. In this chapter, I use several sociocultural theories to shed new light on the nature of self – other – culture interactions within creativity and, toward the end, consider the broader conceptual and methodological consequences of this exercise. But, before developing these ideas further, it is worth considering a more fundamental question: why exactly do we need a sociocultural theory (or theories) of creativity?

9.1 Theoretical Roots

Change, emergence, development, transformation, imagination, agency, appropriation – all these topics have been extensively studied by sociocultural psychologists belonging to different orientations, from cultural-historical and activity theory (Leontiev, 1978; Cole, 1996), pragmatism (James, 1981; Dewey, 1934), and semiotics (Peirce, 1977; Valsiner, 2007) to social representations (Moscovici, 2000; Jovchelovitch, 2007) and dialogicality (Bakhtin, 1981; Marková, 2003). These diverse schools of thought are ultimately all reunited by an interest in the dynamic between the new and the old, stability and change, the internalization and transformation of culture and mind. One would rightfully expect, under these circumstances, for creativity to be firmly placed on the agenda of sociocultural researchers. Surprisingly, however, except for some attention paid to Vygotsky's work on creativity and imagination (Vygotsky,

2004; Moran & John-Steiner, 2003), there is little collaboration between creativity and culture specialists. As mentioned in the introduction, this state of affairs relates first and foremost to prioritizing individuals over groups, ideas over actions, and cognition over culture in the study of creativity. Moreover, the notion of creativity is often bound in public debates with ideals specific for neoliberal economies, capitalism, and consumption societies (creating new goods and constantly trying to persuade others of their value). The mixture of individualism, cognitivism, and capitalism shaping contemporary discourses of creativity contributed to its lack of appeal for sociocultural thinkers.

And yet, as I argue here, more sustained exchanges between researchers focused on creativity and researchers interested in culture would be highly beneficial for both. Let's consider, in order to exemplify this, two essential problems faced by experts in both areas: the nature of the creative process and the relation between mind and culture.

Models of the creative process have been proposed for more than a century in psychology. Some of the first ones, inspired by the accounts of celebrated creators such as the mathematician Henri Poincaré (1924), postulated a succession of different stages within creating, from preparation to incubation, illumination, and, finally, verification (Wallas, 1926). These stages are descriptive and leave open the issue of what exactly people do when they create – the question of creative processes (Lubart, 2000). In order to address this question, creativity researchers turned first and foremost to cognitive psychology and, to date, there are a variety of thinking processes supposed to underpin creative production (e.g., divergent thinking, Guilford, 1968; conceptual combination, Ward, 2001; bisociation, Koestler, 1964; Janusian thinking; Rothenberg, 1971; lateral thinking, de Bono, 1970). Creative cognition, as the dominant paradigm in the field, systematized its findings with the help of both autobiographic and experimental research (Finke, Ward, & Smith, 1992) while rarely questioning its basic assumptions. Key among them is that the creative process is reduced to the production of ideas (idea generation) and thus located within the mind (with its cognitive structures, personality traits, motivation, neurological processes, and so on). Where are the body and the material world within this dynamic? What about other people and the symbolic resources made available by culture? When operationalized in research, these often appear as external "constraints" on the creative process, factors that come to influence what takes place before or after the creative act of ideation (see Runco, 2015). For as useful as this paradigm might be for experimental studies – as it greatly simplifies the number of variables one should focus on and try to control – it visibly falls short of explaining real-life acts of creativity outside of the laboratory. And this is because, when people create in their daily lives, at home, at work, at school, and so on, they do so as members of society and culture and not as independent brains or isolated minds. While cognition is crucially important for understanding creative ideation, it can never fully account for creativity as a psycho-sociocultural and material process (Glăveanu, 2011). It is toward a deeper understanding of this complexity that sociocultural theory can make a significant contribution.

On the other hand, sociocultural researchers would benefit from insights drawn from the psychology of creativity. In their efforts to theorize mind and culture as interdependent phenomena (Shweder, 1990; Cole, 1996; Valsiner, 2007), the emphasis often falls on how the mind appropriates, understands, and is transformed by culture. The developmental roots of sociocultural psychology become evident in questions related to the internalization and use of cultural elements; what about their production? In other words, what about the transformation of culture through the creative work of minds, people, and communities? While a purely cognitive theory

of creating does not suffice, the concept of creativity itself should not be thrown out with the proverbial bath water. Moreover, cognitive and even neurological studies of creativity can inspire new efforts to understand creative action systemically – from the brain to society across the developmental lines of phylo-, socio-, onto-, and micro-genesis. If culture is both the premise and outcome of human action, then creativity occupies a key role in understanding the continuous cycle between contributing to and renewing our shared legacy (Festinger, 1983). If the relation between mind and culture stands at the core of sociocultural interests, then this relation cannot be separated from the notion of creativity, even if it is often expressed in other terms such as imagination, transformation, or co-evolution. Indeed, many (I would dare say most) sociocultural psychologists are studying, one way or another, creative processes under the guise of other conceptual labels. What would it mean to actually consider these processes as forms of creativity, among other things? The implications of this conceptual move, for both creativity and sociocultural researchers, are explored in more detail below.

9.2 A Sociocultural Proposal for the Study of Creativity

Creative action is *distributed* across people, people and objects, and time (Glăveanu, 2014). This means that, in order to study creativity, one cannot stop at the level of the creative product or at scores of divergent thinking. Questions related to sociality, materiality, and temporality need to be raised for a comprehensive, sociocultural exploration of creative action. And these questions do not address exclusively "eminent" creators and revolutionary creations. On the contrary, they point us toward the everyday, habitual basis of creativity as it unfolds in human relations, interactions, and communication. A deeper understanding of creativity can only be *systemic*

(Csikszentmihalyi, 1988; Gruber, 2005) and rely on the articulation of different levels of analysis from the intrapersonal and interpersonal to society and culture. Even those types of creative expression that seemingly do not leave a visible mark – for example, children's creative expression – reflect the complexity of creativity as a system. They bring together different social roles (e.g., the creator and the audience), make use of material and symbolic resources (at minimum the use of language, to externalize thoughts and images), and draw on a variety of existing cultural traditions (in the case of children's play, the rich basis of norms, values, and tools mobilized to construct a play situation). For a long time, the study of creativity focused on celebrated creators and creations at the expense of more mundane forms of creative production (Glăveanu, 2010b). Sociocultural psychology reverses this hierarchy: Big-C creativity cannot be understood outside of its microsocial, cultural, and developmental roots.

We can take as an example the focus on everyday or mundane forms of creativity embedded within cultural traditions such as the decoration of eggs for Easter. This is a cultural practice specific for several societies around the world and prominent in eastern European countries such as Romania, where artisans, usually in rural communities, decorate eggs all year long using wax and different color pigments (see Figure 9.1). The marker of creative action in folk art is represented by the potential to combine and recombine existing cultural elements (in this case, decoration motifs and tools) in the making of artifacts that are never perfectly identical with one another (Glăveanu, 2013b). This example also points us to the systemic nature of creativity – the decoration of eggs is not an activity learned and practiced in isolation and based exclusively on mental abilities. It involves mind and body, decorator and community, personal habits and tradition in order to exist, as well as a variety of material, tools (from eggs, wax, and color pigments to

Figure 9.1 Decorated eggs at different stages. Source: Eggs decorated by Maria Ciocan; photograph taken by the author.

instruments used to "write" on the egg, to warm up the wax, etc.), and other people (those who decorate eggs, those who buy them, and so on). Moreover, studying this kind of mundane creativity in a systemic and longitudinal manner – by considering how the practice developed, how it is acquired and performed, how it is transmitted, and so on – can inspire the study of Big-C forms of creativity in the same area of decorative art (one can think here about the famous Fabergé egg, pieces of jewelry praised for their design and the craftsmanship that contributed to their making).

9.2.1 The Five A's of (Distributed) Creativity

In this regard, sociocultural psychology operates with a distinct framework from the traditional four P's of creativity: person, process, product,

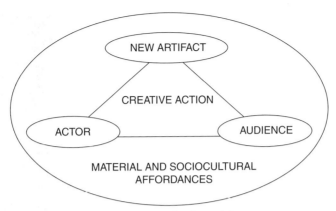

Figure 9.2 The five A's framework of creativity.
Source: Glăveanu, 2013a, p. 72

and press (Rhodes, 1961). While outlining these various "components" of the creativity complex can be a useful analytical step, it is undoubtedly insufficient. This is because the different facets of creativity remain largely disconnected from each other. In theory, persons create products through a process that takes place within a certain environment (press). In practice, each one of these can and has been studied independently of the rest. In contrast, a sociocultural framework for the study of creativity replaces the four P's with the five A's of actor, audience, action, artifact, and affordance (Glăveanu, 2013a). This rewriting goes beyond a simple change of names; it actively stresses the interdependence of each component within the system: actors create in relation to multiple audiences, their actions exploit material and cultural affordances and lead to the generation of new and useful artifacts. Most of all, this framework places action at the center, organizing the rest of the A's around this central notion (see Figure 9.2).

What Figure 9.2 depicts is the centrality of action within a *mediational model* of creativity. Drawing on the legacy of numerous mediational schemas in sociocultural psychology (see Zittoun et al., 2007), the present theoretical proposal uses a basic actor–audience–artifact triad in order to study creative action. Within this triad, creative

artifacts mediate (shape, facilitate, make possible) the relation between actors and audiences, that is, between creators and the different other people, groups, and communities they address. In this sense, the newly produced artifact – it can be a concrete product, an idea, a performance, and so on – connects creators and others through collaborative processes of making and sensemaking (i.e., understanding the novelty being produced). In turn, creative actors mediate the relation between the new artifact and audiences who get to use and transform it. Creators, in this regard, present their work to others and persuade them of its qualities. Last but not least, audiences also mediate the relation between actors and their own productions. It is only by seeing one's work "through" the eyes of others that we get to understand it and its creative potential better. All these action-based processes are grounded in the use of material and sociocultural affordances.

In summary, a sociocultural approach to creativity starts from considering it in terms of *relations* – between self and other; self and objects; present self, past self, and future self, and so on – rather than as a stable property of people or outcomes. And these relations are quintessentially expressed in actions (or, rather, interactions). As such, the study of action in creativity is not restricted to the activity of making something (the artifact). On the contrary, various actions bind together actors, audiences, and artifacts thus resulting in particular *ecologies of creating*, a *creativity complex* that goes beyond isolated people and products or even specific moments in time (for example, getting the creative idea). In what follows, I will unpack further these types of actions with the conceptual means of sociocultural psychology/psychologies. In particular, I will focus on understanding what kind of creative actions define the relations between actors and audiences, audiences and artifacts, actors and audiences, and how these actions make use of environmental affordances. In doing so, I am not trying to offer an exhaustive list of authors or texts useful for exploring creativity – the space of one chapter would not suffice; rather, I aim to give a brief overview of some concepts and theories from outside the "mainstream" psychology of creativity that can meaningfully inform current debates about how we create.

9.2.2 Creative Action in Actor–Artifact Relations

The most studied relation within the creativity complex is that between the actor (creator) and artifact (creation). Mainstream approaches understand this relation primarily in terms of the mental processes of the creator – for example, conceptual combination, bi-association, divergent thinking, and so on – thus, in effect, reducing the relation to only one "pole": the mind. Yet, in sociocultural terms, the very essence of creative production is represented by forms of "doing" or "making," the visible externalization of thought into action (Moran & John-Steiner, 2003). This externalization is bi-directional, pointing both toward the person and the materiality of the artifact being created (more details about the latter can be found in Section 9.2.5). In this section I will focus mostly on what sociocultural theories tell us about the making of new and useful (thus at least potentially creative) artifacts.

It is worth noting again that the term "artifact" does not designate exclusively material objects but also includes symbolic and processual outcomes (e.g., the production of speech, of dance, and of music).

What is the essence of creative action in bringing about such artifacts? A close dialogue between *material-making* and *meaning-making* is intrinsic to this facet of creativity. This is because creative actors are producing a materialized (in a broad sense) product as well as its meaning. The notion of artifact itself, as described in sociocultural psychology (see Cole, 1996), points to its double – material and symbolic – nature. Creative artifacts are, from the initial process of making, products of culture because they are not only crafted but also made sense of. In other words, they are represented, evaluated, and symbolically placed within a cultural universe well before being shown to other people or used by them. The creative actor is, recurrently, the creator and the first receiving audience for his or her own nascent creations (Dewey, 1934). The meaning(s) given to what is made can be later negotiated with others (as we will see in the following section), but they are also dialogical from the start. In order to understand what is being made, why it is novel and potentially creative, what its uses might be, and so on, the creative actor needs to see it from multiple (other) perspectives, oftentimes contradictory. This tension between potential meanings is shaping material forms of making and guides creative action; at the same time, the state of what is being created in the material world impacts and constrains the possible meanings assigned to it.

The alternation between immersion and detachment, between doing and observing – from a symbolic and/or physical distance – the effect of what has been done, is placed by different strands of sociocultural theory at the core of creative action. John Dewey (1934), for example, offered a classic account of creativity in art that articulates "doing" and "undergoing," acting in the world and being acted on by the world. This account not only emphasizes the importance of perception in creativity but also postulates a bi-directional relation between actor and artifact, between creator and emergent creation. In Dewey's words:

A painter must consciously undergo the effect of his every brush stroke or he will not be aware of what he is doing and where his work is going. Moreover, he has to see each particular connection of doing and undergoing in relation to the whole that he desires to produce. (Dewey, 1934, p. 47)

Although Dewey referred specifically to the work of artists, his cyclical relation between doing and undergoing is the marker of creative action in a multitude of other domains (for an example see Glăveanu et al., 2013). It also resonates with current theorizing in the psychology of creativity, including the branch of creative cognition. The geneplore model (Finke, Ward, & Smith, 1992), for instance, describes creativity as an interplay between the generation and evaluation of ideas. Despite a clear lack of materiality, including the materiality of the creative artifact, this model alludes nonetheless to an element of "undergoing" in the form of evaluation – deciding which ideas are indeed novel and useful and should be developed further. This is a central part of what sociocultural psychologists, particularly drawing on semiotics, would define as meaning-making. Indeed, as argued above, the creative actions that connect actors and artifacts coordinate both material and symbolic forms of "making." In the process of creating, what is being physically made or expressed is only part of the process. The other part, often less visible, has to do with the hierarchy of signs constructed by the creator to make sense of the new artifact (see also Valsiner, 2014). A sociocultural study of these processes would focus on when and how the sign "creative" emerges within the process, what other meanings are associated with it, and how it comes to regulate ongoing action.

9.2.3 Creative Action in Audience–Artifact Relations

It is common to assume that creativity concerns primarily, if not solely, the relation between actor (creator) and artifact (creation), a relation defined, as explained above, by different forms of making or producing. However, from a sociocultural standpoint, the creative act is never "complete" in the absence of a second position – that of the audience (see Figure 9.2, also Glăveanu, 2015b). While the actor or creator him/herself is the first audience of the artifact being produced, this kind of distantiation can only be achieved by internalizing the perspective of others on one's work. This means that, in order to be an audience to your own creation, a history of interaction with others is needed. From the young child showing her parents colorful drawings, excited to get their praises, to the student fearfully awaiting exam grades and the employee reading a feedback report, we exist in a social world that constantly confronts us with the "view of the other," a view we come to incorporate into our own activity, including creative activity (for more details see Section 9.2.4). This outside perspective is essential for creativity because it infuses the creative act and its product with new meaning and value. Essentially, the relation between audience and artifact is one of evaluation and meaning-making, appropriation (often through use) and, ultimately, transformation. In this section I use the notion of audience both to designate specific others (e.g., family members, collaborators, critics) and "generalized" others (society, the public, etc.; see also Mead, 1964).

In the study of creativity as action, the relations between actor–artifact and audience–artifact operate as two sides of the same coin. In Vygotsky's terms, these relations are defined by externalization and internalization, respectively (see Moran & John-Steiner, 2003), by expression and reception. However, the audience never occupies simply a "receptor" position in the creativity triad. On the contrary, *audiences are creative actors in their own right*. This is because they never passively "receive" the creations of others – audiences have to appropriate them. In what follows, I will focus on three types of actions included in this process of appropriation: interpretation, evaluation, and use. Each of these actions leads to a more or less marked transformation of what is being created, from new meaning to physical or embodied aspects. In this sense, all audiences of a creative artifact ultimately become co-creators of its value (Taillard et al., 2014), contributing to its "creativity."

Audiences of new artifacts necessarily begin by interpreting, in their own terms, what has been made. In the previous section, we noticed how actors both make and give meaning to their creations (often by becoming their first audience and adopting an evaluative position in relation to them). This original meaning is often already inscribed within the physical properties of the artifact, metaphorically defining its "intentionality" (for an account of human existence within an intentional world, see Shweder, 1990). This intentionality, however, almost always has to be negotiated with audience members who might very well interpret the artifact differently, subverting its original meaning. This kind of process is at the basis of many contemporary art installations in which common objects like urinals or bicycles become something they were not meant to be, including art objects. The creative process at play here, on the side of the audience, is that of interpretation. Interpretation itself ranges from perception to re-presentation. The former was defined by Dewey as a constructive process of engaging with existing work. He notes in relation to art:

For to perceive, a beholder must *create* his own experience. And his creation must include relations comparable to those which the original producer underwent. They are not the same in any literal sense. But with the perceiver, as with the artist, there must be an ordering of the elements of the

whole that is in form, although not in details, the same as the process of organization the creator of the work consciously experienced . . . There is work done on the part of the percipient as there is on the part of the artist. (Dewey, 1934, p. 56)

Perception as a creative, constructive way of relating to the world and its new artifacts forms the basis of creative action for audiences and creators alike, whenever the former adopt an audience position to their own work. But beyond perception there is also a need to represent the new artifact, to anchor it within existing structures of meaning and signification, in other words to "domesticate" its unfamiliarity and turn it into something that is known and thus usable (for interesting parallels see the theory of social representation; Moscovici, 2000; Marková, 2003). Important to note, representing here is not used in the cognitive sense of creating a mental image of external objects, although this might be part of the process. What I am referring to here are literally processes of re-presentation, of appropriating artifacts in ways that make them seem "new" to others, including their creators. Consider, for example, classic creations such as the *Mona Lisa*. If we apply our current definition of creativity to it – novelty plus value – we can immediately notice the fact that, while immensely valuable (particularly if we consider its worth estimates), it certainly is no longer a "new" artifact by any standards. And yet, what makes it continuously new is its reception and re-presentation by diverse audiences (if you want to convince yourself of this, just type "Mona Lisa funny" in an image search engine and you will discover various forms of irreverent appropriation of this image by users).

At the same time, there is another fundamental role audiences have in relation to the creativity status of artifacts such as the *Mona Lisa*. They evaluate it and, when in a position of gatekeepers (which includes critics, museum curators, collectors, etc.), they validate it as a product of creativity or even genius. This kind of action/relation is what Csikszentmihalyi (1988) argues for in his systemic model bringing together creators, field, and domain. In order for something to be integrated within a cultural domain as a creative addition, formal recognition by the field (of experts) is needed. From this position, the audience emerges as a judge of what is creative and what is not, what is worth keeping and transmitting and what can be neglected or forgotten. Of course all these judgments are contingent on history and group membership but they reveal yet another necessary contribution made by audiences to the creative act – its evaluation.

Last but not least, beyond interpretation and evaluation very often audiences are faced with the possibility of using new artifacts in their own activity. From this position they are asked to imitate the creator(s) and others in their use of what was created and, often enough, to transform the creation for their own purposes. For the former we can think about a parallel with basic processes of socialization through which children become competent users of the objects surrounding them. Baldwin's (1894) theory of imitation is useful to understand this dynamic by postulating a creative underlining dimension even for the most basic acts of imitation and particularly what he calls "persistent imitation" – the act of repeatedly trying to appropriate a new artifact. For the latter we can be reminded of the active involvement today of users in the production of innovation. User-generated content and objects (see Van Dijck, 2009; Potts et al., 2008) are increasingly recognized as engines of creativity for both business and society. Examples ranging from Wikipedia to fan-made novels and games illustrate the increasingly blurry line that separates actors and audiences in the process of creating, a topic I discussed in more detail below.

9.2.4 Creative Action in Actor – Audience Relations

As suggested in the previous sections, from a sociocultural standpoint, all creative artifacts are,

ultimately, *co-created* and creative action itself is collaborative in nature (see also Barron, 1999, for a similar argument). As such, actor–audience relations not only constitute the basis of creativity as distributed action (see also Figure 9.2) but they also ground it in the interaction and communication processes that bring together creators and their multiple audiences. These interactions are, first and foremost, bidirectional, which means they are not restricted to creative actors persuading audiences nor to audiences imposing their views on creators. The essence of self–other relations in creative expression is *dialogue*, the exchange and negotiation of perspectives leading to the acceptance, transformation, or rejection of the new artifact.

Often in the psychology of creativity the creator's relations and interaction with other people (e.g., collaborators, observers, evaluators) is considered separately from the creative process as an external factor coming in to influence its dynamic (through peer pressure, surveillance, rewards, etc.). This led to a growing literature in the past decades on "the social psychology of creativity" (Amabile, 1983; Amabile, Hennessey, & Grossman, 1986) and, in a more narrow sense, prompted group creativity research (for a review, see Paulus & Nijstad, 2003). While informative in their own right, experimental research findings about the impact of other people on the creator's mental states and actions constitute only one aspect of actor–audience relations. This aspect relates to forms of direct, face-to-face or mediated, online communication between people as they generate ideas (together or in the presence of others). Are the same processes these studies uncover supposed to characterize real-life, long-term forms of collaboration as well? Another field of study, typically drawing on sociocultural theory such as the writings of Lev Vygotsky, focuses on creative collaboration in science, art, and society (e.g., John-Steiner, 1992). The main benefit of adopting a creative collaboration rather than a group creativity perspective in research is that the former considers social relations as an integral part of creative action. Creators not only create with others but also for and because of others, based on their inputs and knowledge.

However, the question for many researchers remains whether we are better off creating together or alone? Here group creativity research pointed for a long time to the necessity of generating ideas alone, at least at times (Lamm & Trommsdorff, 1973). While it is undeniable that, across domains of activity, combining stages of individual and group work is probably the best solution, the question itself of whether people are more "creative" alone or together is misleading. This is so because it starts from the premise that the social aspects of creativity can be disentangled from its processes by simply removing the physical presence of other people. A dialogical analysis (see Bakhtin, 1981; Marková, 2003) of creative action problematizes such an easy assumption. Most of all, it challenges the presupposition that being alone is an asocial state. On the contrary, by considering the mind as dialogical, sociocultural psychology focuses on dialogues with the internalized voices of others even in those moments in which creative actors work in perfect solitude (Barrett, 1999). In other words, creators do not require direct exchanges with other people while producing their artifacts (although other people are never completely absent since, for example, most creativity requires "invisible" forms of division of labor; see Becker, 2008); these exchanges are internalized as creators themselves regularly adopt the perspective of different audiences while working. We can once more return to Dewey's (1934, pp. 110–111) thoughtful analysis of artists' activity to highlight this issue:

The external object, the product of art, is the connecting link between artist and audience. Even when the artist works in solitude all three terms are present. The work is there in progress, and the artist has to become vicariously the receiving audience. He can speak only as his work appeals to him as one spoken to through what he perceived. He observes and understands as a third person might note and interpret.

The possibility to understand the creative artifact as other people would is founded on our capacity for perspective-taking. Seeing oneself – and, by extension, one's action and its outcomes – as another would is fundamental for the development of the self (Mead, 1964) and agency (Martin & Gillespie, 2010). It is also one of the key psychological processes underpinning creative action (Glăveanu, 2015b). In previous work, I suggested understanding the generation of creative ideas, objects, or performances as an interplay between perspective-taking and the reflexive turn, in other words, the process of relating one's "first person" perspective with "third person" ones. Once more, dialogue – this time between perspectives – is postulated as a condition for creative action. This theoretical position not only manages to integrate the social aspect within creativity but also gives it a privileged role when it comes to creative action. The essence of creativity, it is argued, rests precisely in being able to decenter from one's position and, in a collaborative, dialogical act of relating to others and their views, to gain a new understanding of what is being made and how other people might perceive it. This evaluative aspect is intrinsic to creative cognition (Finke, Ward, & Smith, 1992) and both its origin and dynamic are, at once, cognitive and sociocultural. The direct consequence of alternating between perspectives is that our creative action becomes adaptive and flexible, a flexibility that allows us to exploit existing affordances and even discover new ones.

9.2.5 Creative Action in Using Material and Cultural Affordances

Up to this point, I have discussed at length the role of both actor and audience in relation to the creative artifact and in relation to each other.

It is important to notice, however, that creative action and its intricate system of social relations does not take place in a material vacuum. For as much as existing models of the creative process, including the geneplore, emphasize the mental or cognitive dynamic of creativity, the fact that creativity is, ultimately, materialized action should not be forgotten. Similarly, we need to account for the fact that creative action not only leads to the emergence of (new and meaningful) artifacts but also uses existing artifacts as tools in this very process. How can we include this material dimension within creativity theory and, most of all, how can we relate it to the actor–audience–artifact triad explored until now?

One option, drawing again on sociocultural sources, is to use the notion of *affordance*. This concept was first introduced by Gibson (1986) to denote the action-based nature of our perception of the environment. What he rightfully observed is that when we perceive the things that surround us we "see" much more than their color, texture, or consistency – we grasp also what can be done with them or how they can be used. This observation is highly relevant for understanding creative action since, in essence, such action generates new artifacts by exploiting, in a new and original manner, the affordances of already existing artifacts. Importantly, these affordances do not derive solely from the material properties of things, accessible directly to our perception, as Gibson suggested at some point (see Gibson, 1986, p. 140) but they are culturally organized (see Costall, 1995). While Gibson himself was not sensitive to how affordances can be transformed – as he considered them to either exist or not – the first task of sociocultural researchers is precisely to reformulate this notion in ways that emphasize (re)construction and learning. This is because the things we make use of in order to create reveal their action potential only to a mind shaped by culture and interaction with other people. How else would we become aware, for instance, of what a computer affords? Almost

nothing of what can be done with a computer is obvious from perceiving it, closed, in front of us. It is our personal history of socialization and acculturation that guides the use of objects within the intentional world of culture (Shweder, 1990). And these uses are represented by exploiting existing affordances in a new way, perceiving new affordances that we were not aware of before, or using affordances in ways that are initially sanctioned by culture (for more details, see Glăveanu, 2012).

The use of objects within creativity represents a wide and yet largely unexplored area of research, at least within psychology. While the material world is usually accounted for in terms of constraints or mental representations (Finke, Ward, & Smith, 1992), this conceptualization is insufficient as it sidesteps questions related to materiality and embodiment. All the creative processes outlined in this chapter – making and meaning-making, appropriation and use, perspective-taking and reflexivity – have a materialized dynamic that brings together minds, bodies, objects, and institutions. In order to understand the kinds of affordances used in each case we need to operate with a sociocultural rather than purely cognitive framework. Figure 9.2 points to the fact that actors, audiences, and creative affordances, as well as the system of actions and interactions that unite them, exist within a material and cultural environment. This environment should not be understood only as a "place" or an "influence," but the very locus of creativity – the *encounter* between person and world (see also May, 1974). Affordances are not only used but constrain creative action and guide it. While many things can be done with one and the same object, not everything is possible or "afforded" by it, even as a prop for imagination and creativity. The meanings we invest into objects and the forms of doing we engage in when relating to them are "responded" to by the material properties of these objects; this response is one we have to undergo in order to continue creating (Dewey, 1934). Many authors talk in this regard about the continuous dialogue between creator and creation (e.g., Mace & Ward, 2002), mediated by material tools and social relations. This dialogue is not based on rudimentary forms of anthropomorphism although, phenomenologically, many creators might in fact experience objects as agents in their own right (see Glăveanu et al., 2013; Gell, 1998). It is rather a sign of *co-agency* (Glăveanu, 2015c), of interdependence between self and object, action and context, that marks creativity at each stage of its unfolding.

9.3 Concluding Thoughts on How to Study Creative Action

In this chapter, I argued that the sociocultural study of creativity considers this phenomenon in ecological, systemic, and distributed terms. The ecology of creative action expands far beyond creators and their creations and includes other people, objects, and the relations between them. These relations, expressed in action, not only contribute to the creation of new artifacts but represent its different facets. As such, it is not only (and sometimes not even primarily) the relation between actor and artifact that defines "creativity," but different audiences and the action/relations they establish with both creator and creation. Moreover, *time* has a crucial role to play in sociocultural studies of creativity. The processual nature of creative action engages various registers of temporality, from the historical to the personal (life course) and the microgenetic (moment-to-moment). In this sense, the system of actions and interactions that brings together the actor–artifact–audience triad (see Figure 9.2), evolves in time and should be studied, whenever possible, longitudinally. Last but not least, this ecology of relations is also *domain dependent* (for a review, see Kaufman & Baer, 2005). Since creative action is largely domain-specific, the five A's and the relations between them can only be specified in a domain-based

manner. Sociocultural psychology offers a useful framework for this study but does not postulate relations in advance.

The study of creative action, within the sociocultural tradition, needs to be context dependent, developmental, ecological, and emic (Glăveanu, 2010b). This of course poses great challenges to a traditional methodological apparatus built around the use of tests and experiments. Without claiming these tools are useless, it is important to understand them as insufficient, encouraging a kind of methodological reductionism described by Montuori and Purser (1997). This is because the methods above often take individuals and their psychological states as a unit of analysis. In contrast, for sociocultural psychology, the unit of analysis in creativity research is a complex that articulates actors, audiences, artifacts, actions, and affordances (Glăveanu, 2013a). In order to investigate the creativity complex we need to develop more process-oriented methods, methods capable of studying creativity forward, as it unfolds, and not only backward, based on finished products or the number of new ideas (Ingold & Hallam, 2007). Qualitative methods are well equipped to deal with such complexity and they should more often inform and complement the dominant use today of psychometric tools. The call for more qualitative investigations of creativity comes at a time when key journals within the field (e.g., *Creativity Research Journal*; *Psychology of Aesthetics, Creativity, and the Arts*) actively deter authors from submitting this type of studies. The shortsightedness of such editorial decisions has consequences for the current development (or lack thereof) of creativity theory.

Sociocultural psychology is but one of the many approaches to creativity, alongside the cognitive, biological, evolutionary, and sociological, to name just a few. In consequence, its position needs to be articulated with that of other disciplines and more interdisciplinary dialogue is needed to elaborate comprehensive and inclusive theories and methods in this area. However, the sociocultural approach has an advantage that many other orientations lack: its view is, from the start, systemic and integrative. Enriching this conceptual framework is therefore a task that transcends the boundaries of isolated domains and exclusive methodologies. Just as creative action itself is distributed and collaborative, so should theory-building be in order to achieve a wider synthesis and a more clear sense of its practical applications. This chapter stands as an open invitation for culture and creativity researchers to engage in a more sustained dialogue; the promise of such dialogue far exceeds creativity or psychology itself as it can shed new light on the nature of emergence in the mind and that of change and transformation in society and in culture.

References

Amabile, T. M. (1983). The social psychology of creativity: A componential conceptualization. *Journal of Personality and Social Psychology*, 45, 357–377.

Amabile, T. M., Hennessey, B. A., & Grossman, B. S. (1986). Social influences on creativity: The effects of contracted-for reward. *Journal of Personality and Social Psychology*, 50, 14–23.

Bakhtin, M. M. (1981). *The Dialogic Imagination: Four Essays* (ed. by M. Holquist, trans. by C. Emerson & M. Holquist). Austin: University of Texas Press.

Baldwin, J. M. (1894). Imitation: A chapter in the natural history of consciousness. *Mind*, 3(9), 26–55.

Barrett, F. (1999). Knowledge creating as dialogical accomplishment: A constructivist perspective. In A. Montuori & R. Purser (Eds.), *Social Creativity* (vol. 1, pp. 133–151). Cresskill, NJ: Hampton Press.

Barron, F. (1999). All creation is a collaboration. In A. Montuori & R. Purser (Eds.), *Social Creativity* (vol. I, pp. 49–59). Cresskill, NJ: Hampton Press.

Becker, H. S. (2008). *Art Worlds: Updated and Expended*. Berkeley: University of California Press.

Cole, M. (1996). *Cultural Psychology: A Once and Future Discipline*. Cambridge, MA: Belknap Press.

Costall, A. (1995). Socializing affordances. *Theory & Psychology*, 5, 467–481.

Csikszentmihalyi, M. (1988). Society, culture, and person: A systems view of creativity. In R. Sternberg (Ed.), *The Nature of Creativity: Contemporary Psychological Perspectives* (pp. 325–339). Cambridge: Cambridge University Press.

de Bono, E. (1970). *Lateral Thinking: Creativity Step-by-Step*. New York: Harper & Row.

Dewey, J. (1934). *Art as Experience*. New York: Penguin Books.

Dubina, I. N., Carayannis, E. G., & Campbell, D. F. (2012). Creativity economy and a crisis of the economy? Coevolution of knowledge, innovation, and creativity, and of the knowledge economy and knowledge society. *Journal of the Knowledge Economy*, 3(1), 1–24.

Festinger, L. (1983). *The Human Legacy*. New York: Columbia University Press.

Finke, R. A., Ward, T. B., & Smith, S. S. (1992). *Creative Cognition: Theory, Research, and Applications*. Cambridge, MA: MIT Press.

Gell, A. (1998). *Art and Agency: An Anthropological Theory*. Oxford: Clarendon Press.

Gibson, J. J. (1986). *The Ecological Approach to Visual Perception*. Hillsdale, NJ: Lawrence Erlbaum.

Glăveanu, V. P. (2010a). Paradigms in the study of creativity: Introducing the perspective of cultural psychology. *New Ideas in Psychology*, 28(1), 79–93.

Glăveanu, V. P. (2010b). Principles for a cultural psychology of creativity. *Culture & Psychology*, 16(2), 147–163.

Glăveanu, V. P. (2011). Creativity as cultural participation. *Journal for the Theory of Social Behaviour*, 41(1), 48–67.

Glăveanu, V. P. (2012). What can be done with an egg? Creativity, material objects and the theory of affordances. *Journal of Creative Behavior*, 46(3), 192–208.

Glăveanu, V. P. (2013a). Rewriting the language of creativity: The five A's framework. *Review of General Psychology*, 17(1), 69–81.

Glăveanu, V. P. (2013b). Creativity and folk art: A study of creative action in traditional craft. *Psychology of Aesthetics, Creativity, and the Arts*, 7(2), 140–154.

Glăveanu, V. P. (2014). *Distributed Creativity: Thinking Outside the Box of the Creative Individual*. Cham, Switzerland: Springer.

Glăveanu, V. P. (2015a). On units of analysis and creativity theory: Towards a "molecular" perspective. *Journal for the Theory of Social Behaviour*, 45(3), 311–330.

Glăveanu, V. P. (2015b). Creativity as a sociocultural act. *Journal of Creative Behavior*, 49(3), 165–180.

Glăveanu, V. P. (2015c). From individual to co-agency. In C. W. Gruber, M. G. Clark, S. H. Klempe, & J. Valsiner, J. (Eds.), *Constraints of Agency: Explorations of Theory in Everyday Life* (pp. 245–266). London: Springer.

Glăveanu, V. P., Gillespie, A., & Valsiner, J. (Eds.). (2015). *Rethinking Creativity: Perspectives from Cultural Psychology*. London: Routledge.

Glăveanu, V. P., Lubart, T., Bonnardel, N., Botella, M., de Biaisi, M.-P., Desainte-Catherine, M., Georgsdottir, A., Guillou, K., Kurtag, G., Mouchiroud, C., Storme, M., Wojtczuk, A., & Zenasni, F. (2013). Creativity as action: Findings from five creative domains. *Frontiers in Educational Psychology*, 4, 1–14.

Gruber, H. (2005). The creative person as a whole: The evolving systems approach to the study of creative work. In E. Gruber & K. Bödeker (Eds.), *Creativity, Psychology and the History of Science* (pp. 35–104). Dordrecht, Netherlands: Springer.

Gruber, C. W., Clark, M. G., Klempe, S. H., & Valsiner, J. (Eds.). (2015). *Constraints of Agency: Explorations of Theory in Everyday Life*. London: Springer.

Guilford, J. P. (1968). *Creativity, Intelligence and Their Educational Implications*. San Diego, CA: EDITS/Knapp.

Ingold, T. & Hallam, E. (2007). Creativity and cultural improvisation: An introduction. In E. Hallam & T. Ingold (Eds.), *Creativity and Cultural Improvisation* (pp. 1–24). Oxford: Berg.

James, W. (1981). *Pragmatism* (ed. by B. Kuklick). Indianapolis: Hackett.

Joas, H. (1996). *The Creativity of Action*. Cambridge: Polity Press.

John-Steiner, V. (1992). Creative lives, creative tensions. *Creativity Research Journal*, 5(1), 99–108.

Jovchelovitch, S. (2007). *Knowledge in Context: Representations, Community and Culture*. London: Routledge.

Karwowski, M. (2010). Are creative students really welcome in the classrooms? Implicit theories of "good" and "creative" students' personality among Polish teachers. *Procedia – Social and Behavioral Sciences*, 2(2), 1233–1237.

Kaufman, J. C., & Baer, J. (Eds.). (2005). *Creativity Across Domains: Faces of the Muse*. Hillsdale, NJ: Lawrence Erlbaum.

Koestler, A. (1964). *The Act of Creation*. New York: Penguin Books.

Lamm, H. & Trommsdorff, G. (1973). Group versus individual performance on tasks requiring ideational proficiency (brainstorming): A review. *European Journal of Social Psychology*, 3(4), 361–388.

Leontiev, A. N. (1978). *Activity, Consciousness, and Personality*. Englewood Cliffs, NJ: Prentice-Hall.

Lubart, T. I. (2000). Models of the creative process: Past, present and future. *Creativity Research Journal*, 13, 295–308.

Mace, M. A., & Ward, T. (2002). Modeling the creative process: A grounded theory analysis of creativity in the domain of art making. *Creativity Research Journal*, 14(2), 179–192.

Marková, I. (2003). *Dialogicality and Social Representations: The Dynamics of Mind*. Cambridge: Cambridge University Press.

Martin, J., & Gillespie, A. (2010). A neo-Meadian approach to human agency: Relating the social and the psychological in the ontogenesis of perspective-coordinating persons. *Integrative Psychological and Behavioral Science*, 44, 252–272.

May, R. (1974). *The Courage to Create*. New York: Dell.

Mead, G. H. (1964). *Selected Writings: George Herbert Mead* (ed. by A. J. Reck). Chicago: University of Chicago Press.

Montuori, A. & Purser, R. (1997). Le dimensioni sociali della creatività [Social creativity: The challenge of complexity. *Pluriverso*, 1(2), 78–88.

Moran, S. & John-Steiner, V. (2003). Creativity in the making: Vygotsky's contemporary contribution to the dialectic of development and creativity. In R. K. Sawyer, V. John-Steiner, S. Moran, R. J. Sternberg, D. H. Feldman, J. Nakamura, & M. Csikszentmihalyi (Eds.), *Creativity and Development* (pp. 61–90). Oxford: Oxford University Press.

Moscovici, S. (2000). *Social Representations: Explorations in Social Psychology* (ed. by G. Duveen). Cambridge: Polity Press.

Paulus, P. & Nijstad, B. (Eds.). (2003). *Group Creativity: Innovation Through Collaboration*. New York: Oxford University Press.

Peirce, C. S. (1977). *Semiotics and Significs* (ed. by C. Hardwick. Bloomington: Indiana University Press.

Poincaré, H. (1924). *The Foundations of Science* (trans. by G. B. Halstead). New York: Science Press.

Potts, J. D., Hartley, J., Banks, J. A., Burgess, J. E., Cobcroft, R. S., Cunningham, S. D., & Montgomery, L. (2008). Consumer co-creation and situated creativity. *Industry and Innovation*, 15(5), 459–474.

Rhodes, M. (1961). An analysis of creativity. *Phi Delta Kappan*, 42, 305–311.

Rothenberg, A. (1971). The process of Janusian thinking in creativity. *Archives of General Psychiatry*, 24, 195–205.

Runco, M. A. (2015). A commentary on the social perspective on creativity. *Creativity. Theories – Research – Applications*, 2(1), 21–31.

Sawyer, R. K. (1995). Creativity as mediated action: A comparison of improvisional performance and product creativity. *Mind, Culture, and Activity*, 2(3), 172–191.

Shweder, R. (1990). Cultural psychology – What is it? In J. Stigler, R. Shweder, & G. Herdt (Eds.), *Cultural Psychology: Essays on Comparative Human Development* (pp. 1–43). Cambridge: Cambridge University Press.

Simonton, D. K. (1975). Sociocultural context of individual creativity: A transhistorical time-series analysis. *Journal of Personality and Social Psychology*, 32(6), 1119–1133.

Stein, M. (1953). Creativity and culture. *Journal of Psychology*, 36, 311–322.

Taillard, M., Voyer, B., Glăveanu, V. P., & Gritzali, A. (2014). Value creation and consumption: When consumer creativity generates value in online forums. *Advances in Consumer Research*, 42, 381–385.

Valsiner, J. (2007). *Culture in Minds and Societies*. New Delhi: SAGE.

Valsiner, J. (2014). *An Invitation to Cultural Psychology*. London: SAGE.

Van Dijck, J. (2009). Users like you? Theorizing agency in user-generated content. *Media Culture Society*, 31, 41–58.

Vygotsky, L. S. (2004). Imagination and creativity in childhood. *Journal of Russian and East European Psychology*, 42(1), 7–97.

Wallas, G. (1926). *The Art of Thought*. London: Jonathan Cape.

Ward, T. B. (2001). Creative cognition, conceptual combination, and the creative writing of Stephen R. Donaldson. *American Psychologist*, 56(4), 350–354.

Zittoun, T. & Gillespie, A. (2015). *Imagination in Human and Cultural Development*. London: Routledge.

Zittoun, T., Gillespie, A., Cornish, F., & Psaltis, C. (2007). The metaphor of the triangle in theories of human development. *Human Development*, 50(4), pp. 208–229.

Further Reading

Vygotsky, L. S. (1978). *Mind in Society: The Development of Higher Psychological Processes* (ed. by M. Cole, V. John-Steiner, S. Scribner & E. Souberman. Cambridge, MA: Harvard University Press.

10 Symbolic Resources and Imagination in the Dynamics of Life

Tania Zittoun

The notion of "symbolic resources" was proposed out of the need to account for the fact that when people internalize specific artifacts, these maintain their power of semiotic guidance (Zittoun, 2001). Although the term had been used before in the social sciences, a first attempt to systematically explore the semiotic functions, consequences and conditions of use of symbolic resources was then started. Over the past fifteen years the heuristic power of that notion has become clear through many studies. Uses of symbolic resources have been studied in youth transitions (Märtsin, Chang, & Obst, 2016; Zittoun, 2006b), in the access to the army (Hale, 2008), in young parenthood (Zittoun, 2004b), in migration (de Abreu & Hale, 2011; Greco Morasso & Zittoun, 2014; Kadianaki, 2010; Mehmeti, 2013), at war (Zittoun et al., 2008), or more generally in the life course (Martin & Gillespie, 2010; Perret-Clermont, 2015; Zittoun, 2003, 2012a; Zittoun et al., 2013). Interpersonal social dynamics involved in uses of symbolic resources have been explored at school (Hale & de Abreu, 2010; Zittoun, 2014b; Zittoun & Grossen, 2012), in experimental situations (Breux, Miserez Caperos, & Perret-Clermont, 2013; Cerchia, 2009; Psaltis, 2011), within musical practice (Diep, 2011), in religious settings (Baucal & Zittoun, 2013; Dahinden & Zittoun, 2013; Zittoun, 2006a), or in parliamentary debates (de Saint-Laurent, 2014). Also, theoretical clarification and expansion have also been brought in (Zittoun & Gillespie, 2013, 2015b), notably to highlight the emotional and semiotic aspects of the processes involved (Zittoun, 2004a, 2004b, 2008, 2011a); and attempts have been made to confirm the model quantitatively (Grossen, Baucal, & Zittoun, 2010; Märtsin, Chang, & Obst, 2016; Stankovic, Baucal, & Zittoun, 2009). Finally the theorization of symbolic resources has joined a more general theory of imagination, as shown here (Zittoun & Gillespie, 2015a, 2016). Hence, today, "symbolic resources" appears as a concept, located within a broader sociocultural theory of the life course which underlies the role of imagination in development.

This chapter is therefore constructed as follows: first, it sketches a sociocultural psychology of life course and its challenges. Second, it presents imagination as concept for sociocultural psychology, and third, symbolic resources. For these two sections, a short historical exploration is proposed and then a model is outlined. The fourth section puts these two concepts at work and shows how they participate to the definition of the life course and societal change, but also that these can be constrained. The last section of the chapter puts forward further theoretical and methodological questions.

10.1 Sociocultural Psychology of the Life Course

As this volume shows, the sociocultural perspective on human development has been in full development since the 1990s. Although a relatively marginal domain within psychology, it has been fortunate enough to be carried on persistently by scholars and their groups in institutions that could preserve such approaches and allow its authors to explore it further, both theoretically and empirically, in dialogue with the history of sciences and other disciplines in the social sciences and beyond. In very broad lines (but see this volume), sociocultural psychology has the project to describe and understand the processes whereby humans develop in and through their worlds of culture, and how in doing so, they become unique and participate in the transformation of culture. Sociocultural psychology can thus be understood as a project for a general psychology that starts with a core assumption – the cultural nature of human life as we know it (Valsiner, 2014; Vygotsky, 1971).

A sociocultural approach to the life course in addition focuses on the trajectories of living, on how people develop as the move through historico-culturally defined time-spaces. It pays special attention to the fact that how people *experience* time spaces does not strictly correspond to "objective," physical, or, more simply, to a third-person perspective view. Hence, if time can be physically described as irreversible and as people have to be seen as located in one and only one sociocultural, time-space location, human experience is different. People can imagine the future and the past, feel the layers of present and past experiences in any specific situations, or be located somewhere while hoping to be somewhere else (Brinkmann, 2014; Hviid, 2015; Zittoun et al., 2013; Zittoun & Gillespie, 2015a, 2016). The richness of cultural life courses has been described in terms of people's engagements, sensemaking, experiences, or interests. Also, explorations over the past fifteen years (and to be honest, the past two thousand years) have invited researchers to examine people's lives when these seem to be engaged in the usual – routines, behavioral settings, etc. – as well as in unusual situations. Studies of disruption,

crises, and ruptures have been the locus of many scholars interested in the life course (Bühler, 1973; Erikson, 1959; Konopásek, 2000; Levy et al., 2005; Schuetz, 1945a, 1945b; Sherif & Sherif, 1965; Zittoun, 2006b; Zittoun & Gillespie, 2015c). It is precisely looking at these studies that it progressively became clear that, from a sociocultural perspective, people's cultural and imaginary lives play a core role. It is often through imagining how life could be that we initiate change and decide to transform our lives, and it is usually when our ordinary lives are disrupted that we have to find new ways of handling things, explore alternatives, remind us of the past, or explore what could be (Zittoun & Valsiner, 2016). In effect, within the permanent movability of our lives, people also need some sense of sameness – what Erikson used to call integrity and continuity – in which imagination plays a core role to allow change and maintain sameness, to feed forward and live backward, to anchor and to explore. And, as we will see, symbolic resources are precisely culturally cultivated techniques for guiding imagination.

10.2 Imagination as Sociocultural Concept

In the history of humanities and social sciences (*Geisteswissenschaften*) and psychology, one recurrent distinction is between the real and the non-real, the actual and the possible, what is immanent or transcendent, what is and what could be, what belongs to human and what belongs to deities, spirits, or angels. In psychology, this articulation has been regularly addressed under the notion of *imagination* as opposed to reality. This exclusive opposition creates more problems than it solves, and it prevents the apprehension of the role and function of imagination in real life. In contrast, imagination and the real are seen as mutually related opposites within a whole (Valsiner, 2015; Valsiner & Lawrence, 1997; Zittoun et al., 2013).

10.2.1 Imagination as Forgotten Concept

Interestingly, since the beginning of the study of the relation between human psyche and culture, one recurrent theme appears: that of the role of arts, fiction, and, more generally, imagination in human life (Kant, Vico, James, Freud, Vygotsky, etc.). In philosophy, the question has for a long time been about the status of these things we "see" when they are not there, that is to say, in the "mind's eye." The debates, from the Greek to the seventeenth and eighteenth-century philosophers, organized the field in a series of oppositions: is imagination reproductive (only things we know appear in mind) or can it be genuinely creative? Is it based only on a visual experience or can it be based on other aspects of our experience? And after all, is the fact that we imagine (which is often full of emotions and different from reality) a primitive or childish form of thinking that should be replaced by reason, or is there something that is specific to our humanity in it (Jørgensen, 2018; Marková, 2016; Zittoun & Gillespie, 2016)? In that realm, Giambattisto Vico was one of the few to consider imagination as fundamental in the ways in which humans constructed their environment and created culture as we know it (Marková, 2016; Zittoun, 2015b; see also Chapter 22, this volume).

The same division could be found in psychology. If imagination, or as it was long called, fantasy, interested some fields of psychology in the eighteenth century, this was soon forgotten with the development of so-called scientific psychology (Cornejo, 2015). Only psychoanalysis took the time to consider seriously what people do when they do not reason or are not engaged with what their community considers as reality – in daydream, night dreams, artistic activities, and creation. Looking at extreme cases where fantasies impeded human action – as in neurosis – Freud actually built a theory of fantasy, or imagination. His model, accounting both for individual imagination and collective culture, was based on the assumption of a continuum of human experience, from its more intimate and unrealistic to those responding to the demands of the socially shared reality, in its embodied and emotional aspects. He developed a semiotic understanding of psyche. Finally, his approach to theories and facts could be seen as pragmatist or, at least, empiricist (Zittoun, 2011b, 2015a). In his view, imagination is a dynamic reassembling traces of experiences of different modalities – sounds, images, tastes – from different layers of our experience – recent past, marking situation from the past, myths we know or arts we experience, or social representation we met – and recombining these in a unique way, according to some emotional-experiential configuration. Freud devised a "grammar" of such a recombination, known as the "dream work," and included the processes of displacement, condensation, figuration, and synthesis. Finally, Freud rightly identified that imagination allows us to live some experiences on a plane that have emotional consequences, yet none in the socially shared reality: one can imagine punching one's manager, feel the relief it may bring, yet while not touching the actual manager (Freud, 1940, 1957, 2001a, 2001b).

Well versed in Freud's work and also very interested in the arts, Lev Vygotsky proposed an unequalled conceptualization of imagination at the articulation of human psyche and the social – this time emphasizing not only the cultural nature of the material with which we imagine, but also the cultural outcomes of imagining. Vygotsky thus proposed:

When, in my imagination, I draw myself a mental picture of, let us say, the future life of humanity under socialism or a picture of life in the distant past and the struggle of prehistoric man, in both cases I am doing more than reproducing the impressions I once happened to experience. I am not merely recovering the traces of stimulation that reached my brain in the past. I never actually saw this remote past, or this future; however, I still have my own idea, image, or picture of what they were or will be like. All human activity of this type, activity that results not in the reproduction of previously experienced impressions or actions but in the creation of new images or actions is an example of this second type of creative or combinatorial behavior. (Vygotsky, 2004, p. 9)

He elaborates further that imagination is the ability to combine elements in a new way and that this ability "is an important component of absolutely all aspects of cultural life, enabling artistic, scientific, and technical creation alike" (Vygotsky, 2004, p. 9). Although Vygotsky inspired studies on children's play as well as creativity, his proposition – to see imagination as the process allowing to conceive the future of human life under socialism or our prehistoric past – has received little attention (for an overview, see Singer & Singer, 2005). Contemporary psychology has mainly reduced imagination to a process eventually leading to cognition or as one of its variations as, for instance, in hypothetical reasoning (Bogdan, 2013; Byrne, 2005; Harris, 2000).

Only social sciences and anthropology have conceived imagination in their social and collective dimensions – as in the sociological or the geographical imagination (Harvey, 2006; Mills, 1959/2000). For these approaches, imagination enables either social scientists or groups of people to see beyond the limit of their direct apprehension. This is also the case in theoretical imagination, or when laypeople develop new imaginations for themselves or their communities thanks to new media and transnational movement (Appadurai, 1996). Hence, for these approaches, imagination is a process or product of collective activity.

From a sociocultural perspective, imagination can be considered as a type of psychological process, with origins, guidance, and outcomes in the social and cultural world. Our claim is that it actually designates the very process by which humans actively participate to the transforma-

tion of the cultural world that allows their very existence (Zittoun & Gillespie, 2016; Zittoun & Glăveanu, 2018).

10.2.2 Imagination as an Integrative, Sociocultural Concept

In order to reconceptualzse imagination as a sociocultural process, we need to redefine the old distinction between real and non-real. We thus establish a theoretical distinction between experiences that occur in a given socially "shared reality," from those that are in a given historico-cultural space, socially acknowledged as "non-real." The "socially shared reality" in a given societal context groups the material and social construction of certain settings by following a certain number of physical and social rules. In most occidental societies, basic rules about reality include temporal succession, causalities, and certain setting-specific rules (what some have called scripts, e.g., Strauss & Quinn, 1998, such as a dinner at a restaurant, watching a film, or a classroom discussion). Within it, each person can individually engage in different *spheres of experience*: being mainly engaged with what is actually going on and respecting these rules (e.g., ordering food, thanking the waitress, unfolding one's napkin while waiting), which we have called a *proximal sphere of experience*; or being engaged in any other, distant experience in which one or many of these rules can be suspended (thinking about yesterday's discussion, imagining the taste of the food to come, wondering how it is to eat in another country), which we have called *distal experiences* (Zittoun & Gillespie, 2015a, 2016). Based on these distinctions, imagination can be defined as *the process of temporarily disengaging from the here and now of a proximal sphere of experience* (Zittoun & Gillespie, 2015a).

This temporary disengagement can be further described as a sequence of imagining: first, something triggers this disengagement (boredom, surprise, cultural guidance); second, the

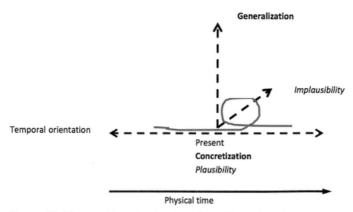

Figure 10.1 Loop of imagination in a three-dimensional space.

person "loops" into a distal experience; and finally, he or she reengages in a proximal sphere of experience, now slightly changed by this experience, which may have different outcomes – what Vygotsky called "altering the present."

The "loop of imagination" (Figure 10.1) can be described along three different dimensions, or three vectors: its time orientation, its degree of generalization, and its degree of plausibility in a given social and cultural setting (Zittoun & Gillespie, 2016). Imagining going to the moon was thus until the 1950s a future oriented, relatively abstract, and still relatively implausible idea. Since the 2000s, imagining going to the moon is an alternative present, quite likely and quite concrete – it is a matter of having the money or the skills to gain a seat in a rocket.

The model thus allows grouping many instances of imagination or, rather, many sociocultural activities as variations of imagination. First, for example, a person remembering their childhood is remembering about the *past*; remembering one specific occurrence – the summer when we lost the cat – or a generalized set of events – when we had family meetings – makes it either a concrete, or more general, loop. If the lost cat episode is narrated in a family meeting and nobody confirms its veracity, it makes it an implausible imagination within that family. So perhaps one has only fantasized having lost

the cat? The question then becomes, in either case, what are the resources used for imagining: personal traces of experiences, pictures, stories heard about another family's cat, dream, or novels – all material which is known to enter in the work of remembering (Brown & Reavy, 2015)? If it is recurrent enough, and it finds a form of crystallization – one writes down the story, or it is narrated at every family meeting – the cat loop (whether "true" or not) becomes a distal experience for each involved person. There is, so to say, a sphere of experience that can be reactivated by the person who revisits the story about the afternoon when the cat went missing. Of course, the distal experience is always dynamically recreated, yet it has some stability in time.

A second example could be that of thinking about the future. Anticipating, desiring something, planning, daydreaming about who we could become are loops of imagination oriented toward the future. Again, these require the uses of different resources: one's own experience, other people's recognition of what we can do or examples of what they do, films seen, stories heard of read, images of magazines and arts, and so on. These can be very labile or have some stability and thus become distal experiences that become projects or plans. Their plausibility is again given by the limits and demands of the setting in which the person's sphere of experience takes place.

A third line of examples comes from our various fictional experiences. Playing online games, role playing, getting lost in a movie, but also enjoying a symphony, a theater play, or a contemporary art installation, all demand loops of imagination. Their temporal orientation might be less relevant and their generality might vary. In a given social setting, their plausibility varies and is partly a matter of genre conventions. Hence, a documentary film is meant to be plausible, yet a "fantasy" story not. In terms of resources used, all demands to draw on one's own embodied emotions, past art experiences, and personal events. Yet the specificity of this type of imagining is the very strong cultural guidance: having a cultural experience is to have a semiotically guided experience of imagining. This point will be specifically addressed in the next section.

Two other variations of imagination need to be considered. One is collective imagination: instances where resources are brought collectively and the "loop" is co-created or shared among people. Typically, children playing together all add material that can become resources for the general play ("say, I was the father," "say, the cat got lost," etc.) (Gillespie, 2006b; Hviid & Villadsen, 2018). It is also the case in collective situations of task solving, to such an extent that one cannot say who is doing the imagining – it is a shared experience and a collective emergence (Hilppö et al., 2016). The other question is that of who has the authority in determining the criterion of plausibility in a given sociocultural setting. To come back to our previous point, imagination demands the suspension of the rules organizing a given sociocultural setting. Accordingly, in many cases these are consensual, given a state of socially shared knowledge. Hence, most nineteenth-century European citizens probably did not imagine the mobile phone. Yet some individual, typically artists or visionary, could, within the same environment, imagine ways to communicate beyond walls and material limitation (e.g., de

l'Isle-Adam, 1886/2000). In some cases, some groups confer themselves or are given the role of authorities who control the degree of plausibility of others' imaginings. Hence, visionary scientist or philosopher's imagining can be considered as implausible by censors, scientific or political authorities – usually because these contest the rules taken for granted by a given society.[1] Let us now go back to the quite banal cases of imagination guided by cultural elements in our everyday life.

10.3 Symbolic Resources as Sociocultural Concept

Human culture has devised many artifacts to expand people's capacities and power in time and space. One range of artifacts are *cultural elements* which allow guided imagination, that is, experiences of fiction (e.g., when watching a film) or alternatively belonging to a different, non-mundane reality (e.g., in a ritual) or liminal experiences (Stenner, 2018). Hence we can distinguish two main types of cultural elements. Books, movies, pieces of art and pictures, are made out of semiotic configurations of various codes (musical, graphic, verbal, etc.), bounded by a material support (Diep, 2011; Zittoun, 2012c, 2013a, 2013b; Zittoun & Gillespie, 2014). *Symbolic systems* such as religion, political, or ethnic systems are also organizations of signs, including texts or rules of reference, objects and places for rituals, and "wardens" or authorities that fix the system's boundaries (Geertz, 1972; Grossen & Perret-Clermont, 1992; Zittoun, 2006a).

Cultural elements allow people to have cultural experiences: guided experiences where they see, feel, hear, embody, through different modalities (touch, view, sound, etc.), and that are not given by proximal spheres of experiences. Common cultural experiences include listening to music, watching a film, enjoying a theatre play, playing an online game, or participating in a religious ritual.

People do not only have cultural experiences. These semiotically guided experiences can be internalized to some extent; people can then "go back" to such experiences, even in the absence of the actual cultural element. People can remember the feeling of a film scene, have a bit of song coming to mind, or recall some lines of poetry. They can also feel the urge to read again a specific scene in a novel, or to pray. In other words, people can partly guide their experience from within, having internalized the path of their imagination through actual cultural experiences. In other words, "what has been internalized, is the pattern of experience guided by a semiotic configuration; only then, a similar experience can be guided from within" (Zittoun & Gillespie, 2015b). Why would they do so? Because these guided experiences allow them to do something. These can be used as symbolic resources.

Although the terms of "symbolic resources" designate a familiar phenomenon, it has only recently been the object of a systematic theoretical enquiry (Zittoun et al., 2003, 2008; Zittoun & Gillespie, 2013; Zittoun & Grossen, 2012). As concept, "symbolic resources" aim at offering a theoretical understanding of people's uses of cultural artifacts, or semiotic tools, as developmental resources, especially when they face new, unpredictable situations.

10.3.1 A Very Short History of the Concept of Symbolic Resources

The concept of symbolic resources is, first of all, rooted in cultural psychology as it has developed over the past thirty years, mostly in the Anglo-Saxon world (Bruner, 1990, 2003; Cole, 1996; Valsiner, 1987, 1998; Wertsch, 1998), where it is an offspring of the idea of psychological mediation promoted by Vygotsky (Toomela, 2015; Vygotsky, 1971, 1975, 1986). It follows the distinction between tools – mediation that acts on the world – and signs – cultural mediation that act on minds (Zittoun & Gillespie, 2013). In

that sense, indeed, symbolic resources are semiotic mediations grouped in specific culturally defined configurations. Second, the concept was inspired by French anthropology and sociology. Lévi-Strauss (1966) observed people engaging in symbolic *bricolage*, using bits and pieces of the symbolic and material means available to them to confer sense to events. Sociologists also emphasize the logics of users of cultural goods: people often use new manufactured objects in a very unpredictable way according to their needs and the context (Lévi-Strauss, 1966; Perriault, 1989). Third, the concept of use has a psychoanalytical origin in the work of Winnicott (Winnicott, 1968, 2001; Zittoun, 2013a), who observed the emergence of the children's capacity to "use" their mother, then transitional objects, and then the potential space of cultural experiences. "Use," here, is an emotional investment in an object, which can then acquire some psychic function: it externally supports and transforms feeling and thinking. The concept of symbolic resource carries echoes from these various anchorages.

10.3.2 Defining Symbolic Resources

A person using a symbolic resource is a person using a novel, a film, a picture, a song, or a ritual, to address another situation in her everyday life. This person is thus not simply *having* the cultural experience of watching the film or hearing the music, or even of only remembering it: she has that experience, or remembers it, *in relationship to something else*, located in her social world or in her inner life. This *aboutness* is an intention in the most elementary way (Brentano, 1995) and does not need to be a conscious goal orientation. For example, when Paul comes back from work feeling tense and irascible, and immediately listens to his preferred band, he is using the music as a symbolic resource to modify his mood and, possibly, to prepare himself for a nice evening with Julie. After having been told that she would have to spend three months in Spain, Julie entertains herself by reading Spanish novels, watching Spanish films, and developing an interest for Spanish music. Julie is using these various cultural elements as symbolic resources to develop some representations about the Spain awaiting her, and to envisage possible futures. Hence, using a symbolic resource is something we all do, at times in a very unaware way – when we start to hum "I'm singing in the rain" because some pleasant idea popped in our mind while we were walking through a spring shower, or sometimes, in a more explicit way, when we discuss romantic films that we have seen with friends and relate them to personal events. There are three important conditions for a cultural element to be considered a *symbolic resource*.

1 A person must be *using* such a cultural element (e.g., a picture, a song, a film) or part of such a symbolic system (e.g., a religious metaphor) with some intention, that is, in relationship to something that is at least partially exterior to that cultural element (its "aboutness").

2 The notion is restrained to uses of symbolic resources in situations normally not contained by the cultural element, that is, beyond the immediate cultural value or meaning of that cultural element (e.g., Julie does not listen to the song for its melody, but to feel closer to Paul).

3 Additionally, the notion of symbolic resource refers only to the cultural elements that require an imaginary experience – the creation of a sphere of experience beyond the here and now of the socially shared reality (the "musical space" of a song; the sacred space of a ritual; the vicarious experience enabled by fiction).

First, a symbolic resource is not just a cultural object that can potentially be used as resource; it is the fact of being used that turns a cultural device into a symbolic resource (Zittoun & Gillespie, 2013). A symbolic resource is to an artifact or symbolic system what an utterance

is to language (Bakhtin, 1996; Wertsch, 1998), or what an used "instrument," is to a potential "tool" (Rabardel, 2001). Second, the notion has also to be distinguished from that of a cultural scheme, or model, as these are meant to organize canonical situations in a smooth an automatic way (see, for example, Strauss & Quinn, 1998, on marriage), whereas symbolic resources are by definition used "out of place." Third, we propose to limit the concept "symbolic resources" to designate the use of semiotic constructs that have a clear delimitation and demand an imaginary experience; in contrast, we thus propose to say that fragments of social representations or media discourse are used as semiotic resources, not symbolic resources (contrary to an earlier definition; Zittoun et al., 2003). Finally, a perspective focused on the persons' unique use of artifacts radically different from cultural, social, or cognitive approaches to films, the mass media, or television; it does not refer to analyses in terms of "gratifications," "effects," or "influences" of media (e.g., Blumer, 1933; Young, 2000).

10.3.3 A Model for Analyzing uses of Symbolic Resources

Studying people's uses of symbolic resources offers an interesting access for investigating processes of change in their lives. People are indeed most likely to use cultural elements as symbolic resources when they face situations that question the taken for granted or one of many of their spheres of experience. What are the semiotic dynamics through which symbolic resources will help the person to explore alternatives, reduce uncertainty, and to open new possibilities? Different uses of symbolic resources can be described along three dimensions, related to the modalities of the guided imagination they allow. Mainly, uses of symbolic resources can orient imagination along time, it can become more or less generalized, and it can allow more or less plausible imagination. In addition, it can have different intentions, that is, aim at different types of outcomes and because of this become more or less generative. This also implies that, although cultural elements have stable forms, symbolic resources are dynamic and transformed by their (often repeated) uses.

10.3.4 Time Orientation of Symbolic Resources

Although cultural elements' duration unfolds in an extended present, symbolic resources guide imagination which escapes the irreducibility of time. As with all semiotic dynamics, uses of symbolic resources have a location within the flux of time (Valsiner, 2001). For one part, cultural experiences always require some knitting of past and future in the present. In order to "understand" the cultural experience, one has to draw on memories of past impressions and feeling to nourish images, words, and melodies; one also has to use cultural knowledge (about narrative, musical, or cinematographic genres) to create some expectations about what will come next. For the other part, the *aboutness* of the use, which is also located in time, can be detached from these temporalities. One can see a film set in Paris, and remember one's own past trip to Paris. Before travelling to Ladakh, tourists watch films such as *Little Buddha* that enable them to shape a representation of their future (Gillespie, 2006a). Finally, symbolic resources can be used to support a current, enduring experience. The movie *The Dreamers* (Bertolucci, 2004) follows a love triangle over a couple of weeks in the Paris of the 1960s during the glorious years of the French cinema. The young people are continuously watching films together, quoting these, and playing out some of their scenes. Films – and especially *Jules et Jim* (1962), a classical love triangle – are here symbolic resources through which the young people are creating what is shown to be the enduring presence of that love affair. Of course, these time orientations are mutually dependent. While traveling, the tourist may also have "their" past version of *Little Buddha* probably transformed by the trip and opening other futures; and young people quoting films as they live go back and forth between reality and imaginary, in the past and what is about to come; their enduring present is a dense fabric bound between past and immediate future.

10.3.5 Level of Mediation of Symbolic Resources

Psychic life is possible through semiotic mediation, or symbolic elaboration, that turns perceptions, impressions, affects, intuition, actions, and desires into thinkable thoughts or sharable experiences. It is through semiotic elaboration that these experiences can then be linked to one's memories and understanding, that is, become part of semiotic dynamics and thinking. Semiotic elaboration is partly done through the mediation of our knowledge and memories, but can also be supported by the semiotic environments; as, for example, when one realizes being sad while listening to sad music. The music, not memories, provides a semiotic configuration that enables distancing from sadness. One of the dimensions on which loops of imagination vary is that of their generality: for example, the imagining of eating strawberries is quite concrete, while imagining *Sehnsucht* – this rather abstract nostalgic feeling coined in German language – is more abstract or general because it is based on a multiplicity of other experiences. It is because cultural experiences provide us with the external means to support such an elaboration of experience that symbolic resources can be "used" at all. Symbolic resources can thus enable one to take a more or less distant position toward one's immediate and embodied experience. They can thus bring various "levels" of distancing, each progressively less dependent on the specific experienced situation or of a more general situation (Gillespie & Zittoun, 2013; Valsiner, 1998,

2007; Werner & Kaplan, 1963; Zittoun, 2006b). Following Valsiner's propositions, four levels of distancing can be proposed.

A person can be in a state of diffuse feelings and impressions – what Valsiner (2007) calls a field. At a first level of mediation, the symbolic resource can group those immediate, embodied experiences, reflect them, and enable a person to identify them. Hence, Emma Bovary and her lover are watching the sky on the boat back home after a romantic escape:

The moon rose, and they greeted it with no lack of phrases, finding the planet melancholy and full of poetry. She even began to sing: *"Un soir, t'en souviens-t-il? Nous voguions,"*[2] etc. (Flaubert, 1857/2007, p. 279)

Here, Emma uses this song as symbolic resource to contain, reflect, and fix the diffuse melancholy, sadness, and anxiety she shares with her lover and which is diffracted onto the landscape. It mediates a first level of reflection that enables the acknowledgment of a state of experience.

At a second level, semiotic mediations offered by a symbolic resource can help to identify and label a specific current state of mind or situation – a point-like mediation (Valsiner, 2007). Hence, Emma Bovary finds herself in an incomprehensible state of exaltation after her first intimate meeting with a man; she then recalls romantic novels she used to read, which make her realize: *she has a lover!* She thus articulates in a symbolic manner her experience, which makes it thinkable and communicable.

At a third level, symbolic resources can be used to define class or categories of conduct or events, or attributes of self. Again, Flaubert makes a point at showing us that Emma Bovary has used all her religious and romantic readings to build a distinction between "friendly, but boring marital relationships," and "fascinating, exciting, adulterous passions." On the basis of these two categories, Emma aims at defining herself as belonging to the second type ("passionate

lover"). At this third level, the world and herself become classifiable and organized.

At a fourth level, symbolic resources can be used to define and clarify higher-level rules and principles or commitments. Such commitments have the power to organize categories (level 3), or to sustain specific actions (level 2). Hence, Emma Bovary seems to have used her romantic reading to develop the overarching principle that "life is not worth living without passion," which leads her to see herself as a martyr (a category to define self at level 3) and to commit suicide (a specific conduct at level 2).

At each level, thus, the semiotic mediators offered by symbolic resources meet some aspect of Emma's experience, and re-present it in a transformed, more distant way: from an embodied state to contained and fixed emotional patterns; from these patterns to a labeled situation; from the labeled situation to categories grouping various experiences of self and the world; and from categories to orienting values. Symbolic resources provide such distancing possibilities because they create a distal, imaginary sphere where personal, unique experiences meet culturally elaborated versions of other people's comparable experiences as signs can, more generally, integrate first person and third person perspectives (Chapter 13, this volume). Again, using different levels of distancing of symbolic resources transforms one's relationship to cultural elements and thus one's symbolic resources: these may gain more depths, or progressively use their power, leading to other ones (Zittoun, 2007b) (see also Section 10.3.8).

10.3.6 Plausibility

Because uses of symbolic resources are instances of imagination guided by cultural elements, there degree of plausibility depends on the acceptance and status of that very cultural element in a given community or sociocultural setting. If one uses one James Bond film – say, *Skyfall*

(2012) – as symbolic resource to imagine that one could recover a former physical condition, the imagination is both shareable (many people know about it) and plausible. In effect, although most people are unlikely to become MI6 agents, the very status of the cultural element as shared fiction makes it available to be used as a partly ready-made metaphor for physical recovery.

10.3.7 Aboutness of Symbolic Resources

Finally, if imagination is often gratuitous, it can also have outcomes in a given situated activity in one's life trajectory or at a more collective level – yet this outcome is not necessary planned ahead. In contrast, most uses of symbolic resources have a conscious or unconscious intention or direction of use or *aboutness*. In effect, a cultural element that a person uses as a symbolic resource is always put in relationship with something that exceeds the cultural experience it offers and is related to the experience of the person in her world.

As with other cultural tools, when a symbolic resource is used, it can produce meaning or action about self, about others, and/or about the socially shared reality. A novel can be used "about" *self* when it is used to deepen one's understanding of oneself or experience new aspects of self or change oneself. Jack London narrates the story of Martin Eden who aimed at educating himself and becoming a writer through patient and systematic readings; fiction becomes here a means to change his own identity and his social position (London, 1909/1994). A novel can be used as a way to connect, to cooperate, or to share some experience with *others* – such as when two friends discuss their readings, which will then become part of their relationship. Famous literary or philosophical friendships, such as the one between Jean-Paul Sartre and Simone De Beauvoir exemplify such uses of symbolic resources. A symbolic resource can be

used to understand a contemporary historical or political *world* situation. Watching *South Park* (1997) can be used as resource to develop a new perspective on current politics. Hence, symbolic resources are cultural elements which, when used intentionally, become *about* something else (Zittoun et al., 2003). During uses, these about-ness, level of mediation, and time orientation can of course change; these changes of modalities of use are likely to be actual transformation of the symbolic resources for the person (that is, the internalized version of a cultural element or the sense it has for him or her) (see also Chapter 24 and Chapter 30, this volume). This can also lead to further resources, as we will now see.

10.3.8 Generativity of Symbolic Resources

The tridimensional model artificially separates various modalities of uses of symbolic resources. In fact, people using symbolic resources usually combine dimensions and modalities of uses. The outcomes of such combinations can be extremely diverse. Emma Bovary's uses of symbolic resources are particularly dramatic: although they first open alternative lives (the young countryside woman lives new adventures), they quickly bring her to a point where she has no other option but to kill herself (at the end of the novel, she has lost her lover and ruined her husband; inspired by her readings, she drinks poison). Yet uses of resources can also be highly generative. A generative use of resources usually moves across a wide range of modality of uses. For example, Julia, a fan of a British pop band, the *Manic Sreet Preachers*, uses their songs as resources to soothe her in a mourning period (*about* self); she then uses this music as a means to meet other fans (*about* others). Also, she realizes that the lyrics of that band have some political meaning; trying to understand them, she starts to see the world in a new way (*about* the social world). The uses also vary on the time perspective: Julia first uses the songs, that speak about poor English regions, to think about the place where she grew up (*past orientation*), before using them for making plans for her *future* (which professional position might bring her to improve this region). The songs finally enable here to progressively distance herself from her experience. The sad melodies first contain and reflect her sad and fuzzy feelings (level 1); she then realizes that the lyrics seem to name her feelings and re-present them to her (level 2); the lyrics also give her a position in the world: she is a revolted person, the world contains injustices (level 3); finally, they bring her to define political values that will guide her actions (level 4). At each of these changes of modality of uses, Julia picks up new symbolic resources (novels or poems mentioned in the lyrics) to support her moves. These uses of resources are highly generative: they bring her to new transitions and open up new possible situations of choices and uses of resources (Zittoun, 2006b, 2007b).

10.4 The Study of Symbolic Resources and Imagination in the Life of People and Societies

In this section, I now put at work the sociocultural concepts of symbolic resource and imagination to show their participation to the life course, but also to social and cultural transformation. I finally explore some constraints on these as well as one way to see the emancipatory power of imagination.

10.4.1 Symbolic Resources and Imagination in the Life Course

The capacity to imagine *and* to use symbolic resources both develop early on in people's lives. They are linked to the mastery of the symbolic capacity, but demand specific type of interactions. As shown elsewhere, imagination grows in very elementary interactions in which infants and then children are able, through specific semi-

otic guidance, to detach from the here and now and anticipate others' moves (Trevarthen, 2012; Zittoun & Gillespie, 2016); similarly, infant and very young children's humor can be seen as the capacity to circle out and expect, if not explore, things to come (Reddy, 2008). The emergence of the capacity of using symbolic resources also develops in early interactions through regular patterns of shared and culturally defined actions with adults, progressively internalized by the child, that allow qualitative changes in her possible thinking and actions in the world (Lyra & Valsiner, 1998; Moro & Rodriguez, 1998; Nelson, 1996, 2007). To summarize these dynamics, a *semiotic prism* was proposed (Figure 10.2; see also Zittoun, 2006b; Zittoun et al., 2007). The prism expresses a topological configuration: the fact that symbolic resources demand the establishment by a person, of a relation between a given cultural element and its socially shared meaning, and the personal sense it has for him or her – this double relation always taking place in relation to social others. It is a topological configuration because none of its poles (e.g., sense, self) are fixed points. Especially, personal sense is dynamic and evolves from a vague emotional field to life philosophies; similarly, the other can be one person associated to a first vision of a film, but replaced by others with time. Hence, the general topology of the prism is preserved although it can be transformed and evolve (Brown & Reavey, 2015; Lewin, 1936).

Ontogenetically, this prism includes the infant, a state of the world, a reflecting parent, and a symbol with which the parent will reflect the child's recognition of the state of the world (Fonagy et al., 2005; Green, 2005). Basic symbolic abilities are fundamental for later uses of symbolic resources. It is also quite likely that later uses of symbolic resources will emerge within similar interactive pattern. In short, the transformation of cultural experiences into usable symbolic resources is likely to occur *when two persons interact on a regular basis about a*

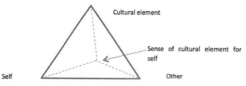

Figure 10.2 Semiotic prism.

*symbolic object and come to an acknowledg-
ment of the shared meaning it designates (the
shared and/or objective referent) and a mutual
acknowledgment of its personal sense, that is,
what it means/feels for each of them personally (within each person's internal, embodied
representational and emotional world).*

When parents read a bedtime story to their
child or sing her a lullaby when she is anxious,
they create such a temporary configuration of the
semiotic prism (see Figure 10.2) encompassing
them, the child, the story or the lullaby, and the
emotional state of the child (reflected by the
parents, perceived by the child, adjusting in a
feedback loop). The child who then asks for her
preferred lullaby or bedtime story is already a
user of a symbolic resource: she uses that element as a way to regulate her emotions and open
an imaginary space in the comforting and mediating presence of her parents. The parents might,
or might not, acknowledge the function of that
use. The child might then be confronted with a
multitude of such semiotic experiences in which
the parents might be replaced by other adults
or peers; hence the pole "other" of the semiotic
prism is changing, until it might become a generalized Other pole; the mediating position of these
others or the generalized others will eventually
be internalized by the child. Mothers singing
rhymes to their babies or telling them traditional
tales, fathers supporting their child's reading
taste, parents commenting on their children's
television watching, teachers accompanying
children in their discovery of stories, pictures, or
the Bible, can support such semiotic dynamics.
Eventually, these mediations and the presence
of others will be internalized, and the child will
take a progressive distancing from cultural expe-

riences (for a child's use of a story as symbolic
resource, see Miller et al., 1993). The developmental hypothesis proposed here is thus that
the internalization of such interpersonal semiotic dynamics, or semiotic prisms, will enable
further uses of cultural elements as symbolic
resources (Zittoun, 2010; Zittoun & Gillespie,
2015b).

It is likely that in good enough conditions,
and independently of socioeconomic factors,
people develop a way to relate to stories, images,
and symbolic objects, and to link these with
their experiences in the world. Social or cultural
differences can affect *what* will become a symbolic resource – a traditional tale, one's preferred
videotape, a painting in a museum – but not *how*
these will be used. It is interesting to observe
that, although children or people might be
exposed to the same available cultural elements
in a given social and cultural environment, the
fact that these might become symbolic resource,
and how these might be used, is highly variable
and personal. People might use the same element
for different uses or might use different elements
comparably. Some highly socially promoted
cultural elements might not be used at all as
symbolic resource by some, and some unlikely
cultural element might be life turning for others
(Zittoun, 2004a, 2006b, 2013a). As a whole,
trajectories of uses of symbolic resources are
highly personal and unique, and constitute also
the person's unique melodies of living (Zittoun,
2007a, 2010, 2016b; Zittoun & Grossen, 2012;
Zittoun et al., 2013).

In the life course, the outcome of symbolic
resources can have short or long-standing consequences. Any daily situation might be enriched
by using symbolic resources: looking at a landscape and recalling a particular painting which
infuses our contemplation and quoting a film
character in a conversation to underline some
exchange are such examples. Similarly, in many
situations we loop back and forth from the ongoing action to some distal experiences to solve
a task, bake a cake, or write a letter. Similarly,

loops of imagination can enrich a given activity, such as when children imagine various scenarios to solve a problem in the classroom or when a sportsman imagines complex movements to guide his or her action. Imagination and patterns of guided imagination, as in symbolic resources, enrich our daily life, add thickness to our exchange, and create the cultural and personal semiotic harmonics that resonate with our daily conduct and that constitute the fabric of our lives. Yet, imagination and symbolic resources are useful to question such easy-going, flowing, and taken for granted moments.

In the longer term, uses of symbolic resources can thus play an important role in the orientation of life trajectories, first because these are often used in periods of transitions (Fuhrer, 2003; Habermas, 2012; Young, 2000; Zagórska & Tarnowski, 2004; Zittoun, 2007b, 2014a) and, second, because their use might create ruptures that lead into their following transitions (Rosenberg, 1993; Zittoun & Gillespie, 2016). In addition, imagination plays an important role in exploring possible present and future alternatives to our living and thus guide its course both in real and imaginary ways (Zittoun & Valsiner, 2016). This is the case as much in children's and young people's lives as in adult and elderly persons' lives (Hviid & Villadsen, 2018; Zittoun & de Saint-Laurent, 2015; Zittoun & Sato, 2018).

A final issue is how uses of symbolic resources and imagination develop along the life course. Our hypothesis is that, as with any other competencies and abilities, these can develop over time – or immediately. Eventually, as people develop other skills and fields of expertise and engage in various imagination and cultural experiences, they can draw on more resources and these can also be used more or less intentionally or reflectively (Gillespie & Zittoun, 2010b; Zittoun, 2004b, 2010; Zittoun et al., 2008). Uses can become more differentiated, especially if it goes with formal mastery of specific semiotic systems; they can be more generalized, at times

more reflective, or, also, more diffused. At times these can develop into personal life philosophies – but, again, some may be more generative than others. Some longitudinal analyses indicate these developments (de Saint-Laurent & Zittoun, 2017; Gillespie et al., 2008; Gillespie & Zittoun, 2013, 2015; Zittoun, 2007a, 2014a, 2016a, 2016b; Zittoun & de Saint-Laurent, 2015; Zittoun & Gillespie, 2015a), but many more have to be done to show the diversity of developmental trajectories and the role of imagination and uses of symbolic resources.

10.4.2 Symbolic Resources and Imagination in Sociocultural Change

People use symbolic resources and imagination in specific situations, and this has consequences in the short term and for their life trajectories; yet these uses also take place within the texture of social relationships, institutions, and, more generally, cultural and social environments. Thus, imagining and uses of symbolic resources can participate not only in psychological development, but also in social and cultural change.

First, as people internalize symbolic resources and imagination, drawing on a variety of resources, they might end up externalizing various semiotic forms – from the informal evaluation of a film to the more expert production of a new cultural element. Hence, writing a theater play, composing a piece of music, or painting an Easter egg can be seen as the creation of a new cultural element on the basis of their creators' imagining and uses of symbolic resources (Glăveanu, 2014; Klempe, 2018; Tanggaard, 2015; Zittoun, 2016d; Zittoun & Rosenstein, 2018), elements that then can become resources to others.

Second, these new externalizations can thus create collective trajectories of imagination, from individual creation to shared utopia, until new social realities are formed. Hence, the story of the moon conquest can be seen as a trajectory going from the first Greek or Roman representations of Selene, the goddess of the moon, into representations of Selenites; the invention of the telescope in the sixteenth century allowed authors to develop new stories, depicting the moon as a place similar to earth, inhabited by the type of creatures imagined at that time; at the end of the nineteenth century, Jules Verne drew on these stories and his knowledge of cannons developed at that time to imagine and share his stories of visits to the moon; these inspired further shared imagination; among others, Hergé's *Tintin* trips to the moon in the 1950s, this time propelled by a V-20 shape rocket. Only ten years later, scientists fed by these stories could use the techniques finally available to them to enable the first trip to the moon, with men in costumes looking just like those of Tintin's (Zittoun & Gillespie, 2016, pp. 114–118). In such cases, then, the imagination of some people, nourished and guided by the cultural elements available used as symbolic resources, allowed the creation of new cultural elements available to others. Over time, these cultural elements continue to be internalized, feed the imagination of many who, eventually, given their other resources and expertise, externalize and create new cultural and material realities. In this sense, the trip to the moon can be seen as resulting from a distributed, or collective, imagination whose outcome affected the lives of many as well as the history of a society.

A further example of collective imagination based on the uses of similar cultural elements by many who contribute themselves to new cultural elements and which are resources for further imagining that eventually lead to major social changes is that of any collective movement. It is the case for revolutions, especially when these appear as "people led" – for example, the Russian Revolution, the end of apartheid (Engeström, 1999), the Velvet Revolution in the Czech Republic (Zittoun, 2018), and the Arab Spring (Wagoner, Jensen, & Oldmeadow, 2012). Globalization has also been said to allow new imaginings:

having access to TV series or images representing life on the other side of the planet allow billions of people to use these as symbolic resources to imagine new possible futures for themselves or their children, leading to major societal transformations and movements of population (Appadurai, 1996). Finally, the same dynamics are at the heart of any local or collective utopia (or dystopias). Reversely, however, social, economic, or political powers that aim at preventing change have always controlled the production and diffusion of cultural elements, mainly in an attempt to channel individual and collective imagination in a specific direction only – the one reinforcing their power (Marková, 2018).

10.4.3 Constraints in the use of Symbolic Resources and Imagination

Because uses of symbolic resources and imagination are always culturally, institutionally, and socially located practices, these can also be constrained socially and culturally.

For economical, geographical, political, or social reasons, a person's access to cultural elements might be reduced. Yet it seems that socioeconomic factors do not predict how symbolic resources are used (Livingstone, 2005). Rather, it is important to question the settings *in which* the person's sphere of experience is embedded. These might indeed support legitimate or prohibit uses of cultural elements as symbolic resources.

Hence, we have observed that certain classroom dynamic allow pupils to explore the personal sense of books they read in class, and not only their relevance to a school task. Using the prism model, we have shown that their possible uses as resources depend on the teachers' work of acknowledging that the teacher as well as the students can engage personal sense-making and imagining guided by a book, even though the teachers have more expertise and knowledge (Zittoun, 2014b, 2015c). Therefore, learning to

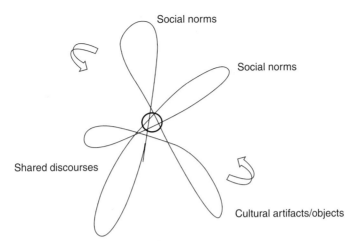

Figure 10.3 A star-like model.

use symbolic resources occur in interpersonal situations, located in institutional settings, which thus can support or hinder students' engagement in more personal, imaginary experiences, and hence, in imagination (Marková, 2016; Zittoun, 2014b, 2015c).

Also, wider social and cultural dynamics – such as gender dynamics, socioeconomic forces, and religious belongings – can orient and guide what elements are available to whom, how they can be used, and for what result (Lawrence, Benedikt, & Valsiner, 1992; Zittoun et al., 2003). Societal forces (political, economic, or ideological) can impinge on these spheres of activities: they can impose or prohibit access to cultural elements (through cultural monopole or censorship, or through control of their circulation); they can control the uses made out of these resources (controlling interpretations and critics); they can endanger the social and psychological spaces in which these resources are used (by controlling interpersonal or group communication about symbolic resources; by imposing forms of life that prevent people to become absorbed in worlds of imagination; and by condemning symbolic thinking) (Marková, 2016; Zittoun & Gillespie, 2016; Zittoun & Perret-Clermont, 2009).

We have also tried to sketch more generally how, in any situations, a person is taken at the heart of multiple streams of determination: social norms, shared discourses, and social representations; others with whom one has emotional, social, or power relations; available cultural elements, and so on. Very often, people can "use" one of the elements to resist another tensed situation: for example, a rich family life may allow resisting unpleasant professional conditions, literature may allow resisting political coercion, and so on. Each time the resistance to the threat of alienation – losing one's self – is partly supported by other elements used as resources for what is experienced, such as thinking, feeling, acting, and imagining, in other spheres of experiences. Imagination thus depends on the possibility to draw on and beyond these social and cultural elements to constitute a new and personal sphere of experience (Zittoun, 2016a). The star-like model (Figure 10.3) was thus proposed to represent the field of possibilities and constraints that shape or constitute the semiotic streams and social forces in some zone of the field of a person's experience; the center designates the emergence, away from yet through these forces of a new, unique experience – a subjective one, or an imagination (Zittoun, 2012b).

In other words, society and culture at large constrain, guide, and enable human experience, both at the scale of the life course and of collective history – but these are also the very conditions of the emergence of newness: imagination is the emancipating force that draws to, yet away from, them, or to lead elsewhere, into the yet-unknown.

10.5 Openings

The concept of symbolic resources gives an entrance to the study of imagination in the dynamics of life. The past 15 years have confirmed the heuristic power of the concept. They have allowed sketching three-dimensional models by which both symbolic resources and imagination could be described in their variation, along three vectors. Such analysis has participated to the construction of integrative models of life trajectories, for instance, showing the layering of human experience, proximal and distal, as people move through time and space (Gillespie & Zittoun, 2015; Zittoun & Gillespie, 2015a). More longitudinal studies as well as situated analysis in a variety of settings might help to pursue such theorization in dialogue with current developments in the sociocultural analysis of lives, as in this volume. In this last section, theoretical and methodological advances and points still to be explored are finally suggested.

10.5.1 Theoretical Problems

One of the constant challenges of sociocultural psychology is to understand the ways in which societies participate in the shaping of the human mind and the definition of unique personal lives, and how individual people participate to the transformation of settings and societies. On a theoretical level, the three core concepts of this section in the Handbook's offer entries in: actions, of the human in the world, yet guided; signs, which are the means by which we make sense of the world and render psyche possible; and meaning, both personal and cultural. In this chapter, we propose to consider cultural elements as cultural productions that need to be invested by a person's experience to start to be meaningful – individually and collectively – as one locus for the meeting of the person and the sociocultural environment. The study of symbolic resources suggests that, behind these, it is imagination that plays a core role in the development of people and societies. Additionally, we also recently suggested that the conceptual analysis that can be done of semiotic work at stake in uses of symbolic resources and imagining, opens a new route to understand the processes of internalization at the heart of the sociocultural psychological project (Zittoun & Gillespie, 2015b). This route is, however, still open, and old problems surface, such as how to fully articulate emotional and embodied and more distanced experiences (Gfeller, 2017), or the boundary between imagining and other forms of thinking allowed by such internalization.

In more general terms, as a concept, imagination and symbolic resources demand to reopen many taken-for-granted oppositions and notions, and calls for reconceptualization of basic concepts related to change, time, or experience. At a metatheoretical level, the elements sketched here also show the need to develop general, flexible, nonlinear models to conceive human development and emergence.

10.5.2 Methodological Implications

How to study people's uses of symbolic resources, as well as imagination in the life course, has of course been a constant interrogation over the past fifteen years. It has progressively become clear that there are three main routes for accessing these, and that it probably needs a combination of these to apprehend phenomena at its best.

The first route is the dominant in psychological research: identify a person or a group of persons or a situated activity, and define ways to produce, document, or collect their externalization. For studying people's uses of symbolic resources, the most common technique has been to interview people retrospectively, usually about one or a series of transitions (among others, Gyger Gaspoz, 2014; Gillespie, 2005a; Greco Morasso & Zittoun, 2014; Hale, 2008; Märtsin, 2010; Zittoun, 2004b, 2006b, 2011a). The analytical model presented above was also the basis of some questionnaires to document uses of symbolic resources (Grossen, Baucal, & Zittoun, 2010; Märtsin, Chang, & Obst, 2016; Stankovic, Baucal, & Zittoun, 2009). Finally, observation was used to document uses of symbolic resources or collaborative imagination in interactions (Cerchia, 2009; Grossen, Zittoun, & Ros, 2012; Hilppö et al., 2016; Zittoun & Grossen, 2012).

The second route is the oldest one in psychology, yet also the one that was the most ignored over the last century – it is that of introspection or self-reflection of the researcher. These methods can be done directly or through various mediational techniques, and bring important insights based on the researcher's own experience of phenomena (Binder, Hirokawa, & Windhorst, 2009; Clegg, 2013; Danziger, 1980; Lyons, 1986; Vermersch, 2009; Zittoun, 2015d). The recent exploratory turn in qualitative methods has brought these techniques again to the fore (Brinkmann, 2013; Corti et al., 2015; Dauphinee, 2010; Ellis, Adams, & Bochner, 2010; Fox et al., 2013; Rosenbaum & Valsiner, 2011; Valsiner, 2013).

The third route is that of observing everyday situations in the sociocultural world as well as other people's externalization based on that world – that is, turning non-data into data (Brinkmann, 2012; Valsiner, 2014). Again, this can be done by producing secondary analysis of existing data, or analyzing media or cultural elements. A specific and most fruitful example of this route consists in using longitudinal data, such as in long-term letter exchanges, longitudinal documentaries, and diaries, or even the public media (Gillespie, 2005b, 2013; Gillespie & Zittoun, 2016; Zittoun, 2014a, 2016b; Zittoun & de Saint-Laurent, 2015; Zittoun & Gillespie, 2016). Although such data are not usually produced for research purposes, it informs rich developmental case studies in which variations of imagining and uses of symbolic resources clearly come to the fore (Gillespie & Zittoun, 2010a; Zittoun & Gillespie, 2012, 2016).

Altogether, it is, however, through a confrontation of perspectives that these complex phenomena can be best investigated, as well as in dialogue with theory through abduction (Tanggaard & Brinkman, 2018; Zittoun, 2015d). Yet, how to fully accede to these dynamics, partly psychological, partly embodied, needs still to be refined when it escapes verbalization.

10.5.3 And Future

Sciences sometimes grow from the margins. The study of symbolic resources started as an exploration of often overlooked informal learning, and eventually it was brought to reconceptualize imagination (Zittoun, 2016c). Part of the problems that were not studied in a psychological science because they were thought to be too complicated – such as people's relation to arts and imagination – were revealed to be simple and essential (Valsiner, 2015). Pragmatically, indeed, these concepts invite reconceptualizing many aspects of our theories; and they also enable a fresh look at many old empirical problems or identifying new ones, thus indicating possible modes of actions. There is a future for imagination.

Notes

1 A variation of this question is that of the meeting between groups that have adopted very different

sets of assumptions: don't we risk considering as implausible any sets of beliefs different from ours? What is the status of entities considered as real by various religious or cultural groups? Some groups of people participate to cultural systems in which it is clear that gods or spirits are part of everyday life (Nathan, 2007). In such cultural system, if it is part of the rules of the shared social and material settings that Beings can be either visible or non-visible, then spirits are part of people's proximal spheres of experiences. In contrast, if spirits are met only through specific rituals, with a clear frame, and techniques to leave the here and now (e.g., drug or ritual induced trances, possessions, etc.) then these spirits are met in a distal sphere of experience where certain of the daily rules are suspended (e.g., where it is possible to talk to non-visible beings). In such cases, these culturally guided imaginings usually allow people to return enriched with new knowledge from another world. Our model describes the looping dynamic and its pragmatic outcomes: it does not evaluate the real/unreal status of the beings. (I thank Dieter Haller for bringing this point to my attention.)

2   French in the original English version. A translation of the verse would be: "One evening, do you remember? We were sailing."

References

Appadurai, A. (1996). *Modernity at Large: Cultural Dimensions of Globalization*. Minneapolis: University of Minnesota press.

Bakhtin, M. M. (1996). *Speech Genres and Other Late Essays*. Austin: University of Texas Press.

Baucal, A. & Zittoun, T. (2013). Religion as dialogical resource: A socio-cultural approach. *Integrative Psychological and Behavioral Science*, 47(2), 207–219.

Binder, M. D., Hirokawa, N., & Windhorst, U. (Eds.). (2009). *Introspection*. In *Encyclopedia of Neuroscience* (p. 2034). Berlin: Springer. Retrieved from http://link.springer.com/referenceworkentry/10.1007/978-3-540-29678-2_2573.

Blumer, H. (1933). *Movies and Conduct*. New York: Macmillan.

Bogdan, R. J. (2013). *Mindvaults: Sociocultural Grounds for Pretending and Imagining*. Cambridge, MA: MIT Press.

Brentano, F. (1995). *Psychology from an Empirical Standpoint* (2nd edn.). New York: Routledge.

Breux, S., Miserez Caperos, C., & Perret-Clermont, A.-N. (2013). Les jeunes enfants en interaction autour d'une activité cognitive: Quand le genre s'en mêle. *Cahiers de Psychologie et Éducation*, 49, 13–22.

Brinkmann, S. (2012). *Qualitative Inquiry in Everyday Life: Working with Everyday Life Materials*. London: SAGE.

Brinkmann, S. (2013). Practice of self-observation in the phenomenological traditions. In J. W. Clegg (Ed.), *Self-observation in the Social Sciences* (pp. 195–222). New Brunswick, NJ: Transaction Publishers.

Brinkmann, S. (2014). Getting in touch with the world: Meaning and presence in social science. In M. H. Jacobsen, M. S. Drake, K. Keohane, & A. Petersen (Eds.), *Imaginative Methodologies in the Social Sciences: Creativity, Poetics and Rhetoric in Social Research* (pp. 133–154). Burlington, VT: Ashgate.

Brown, S. & Reavey, P. (2015). *Vital Memory and Affect: Living with a Difficult Past*. London: Routledge.

Bruner, J. S. (1990). *Acts of Meaning*. Cambridge, MA: Harvard University Press.

Bruner, J. S. (2003). *Making Stories: Law, Literature, Life*. Cambridge, MA: Harvard University Press.

Bühler, C. (1973). Humanistic psychology as a personal experience. *Interpersonal Development*, 4(4), 197–214.

Byrne, R. M. J. (2005). *The Rational Imagination: How People Create Alternatives to Reality*. Cambridge, MA: MIT Press.

Cerchia, F. (2009). Young children's use of symbolic resources in an experimental setting testing metaphor comprehension. *Psychology & Society*, 2(2), 200–211.

Clegg, J. W. (Ed.). (2013). *Self-observation in the Social Sciences*. New Brunswick, NJ: Transaction Publishers.

Cole, M. (1996). *Cultural Psychology: A Once and Future Discipline*. Cambridge, MA: Belknap Press.

Cornejo, C. (2015). From fantasy to imagination: A cultural history and a moral for cultural psychology. Niels Bohr Lecture presented at Aalborg, Denmark. Retrieved from www.ccp.aau.dk/digitalAssets/98/98719_from-20fantasy-20to-20imagination.pdf.

Corti, K., Reddy, G., Choi, E., & Gillespie, A. (2015). The researcher as experimental subject: Using self-experimentation to access experiences, understand social phenomena, and stimulate reflexivity. *Integrative Psychological and Behavioral Science*, 49(2) 1–21.

Dahinden, J. & Zittoun, T. (2013). Religion in meaning making and boundary work: Theoretical explorations. *Integrative Psychological and Behavioral Science*, 47(2), 185–206.

Danziger, K. (1980). The history of introspection reconsidered. *Journal of the History of the Behavioral Sciences*, 16(3), 241–262.

Dauphinee, E. (2010). The ethics of autoethnography. *Review of International Studies*, 36(3), 799–818.

de Abreu, G. & Hale, H. (2011). Trajectories of cultural identity development of young immigrant people: The impact of family practices. *Psychological Studies*, 56(1), 53–61.

de l'Isle-Adam, V. L. (1886/2000). *Tomorrow's Eve* (trans. from French by M. Adams). Urbana: University of Illinois Press.

de Saint-Laurent, C. (2014). "I would rather be hanged than agree with you!": Collective memory and the definition of the nation in parliamentary debates on immigration. *Outlines. Critical Practice Studies*, 15(3), 22–53.

de Saint-Laurent, C. & Zittoun, T. (2017). Memory in life transitions. In B. Wagoner (Ed.), *Oxford Handbook of Culture and Memory*. Oxford: Oxford University Press.

Diep, A. (2011). "On connaît la musique?" Un regard socioculturel sur le travail des musiciens. Master's thesis, University of Neuchâtel. Retrieved from http://doc.rero.ch/record/28829?ln=fr.

Ellis, C., Adams, T. E., & Bochner, A. P. (2010). Autoethnography: An overview. *Forum Qualitative Sozialforschung/Forum: Qualitative Social Research*, 12(1). Retrieved from www.qualitative-research.net/index.php/fqs/article/view/1589.

Engeström, Y. (1999). Activity theory and individual and social transformation. In Y. Engeström, R. Miettinen, & R.-L. Punamaki (Eds.), *Perspectives on Activity Theory* (pp. 19–38). Cambridge: Cambridge University Press.

Erikson, E. H. (1959). *Identity and the Life Cycle: Selected Papers*. New York: International Universities Press.

Flaubert, G. (1857/2007). *Madame Bovary* (trans. from French by G. Wall). London: Penguin Books.

Fonagy, P., Gergely, G., Jurist, E., & Target, M. (2005). *Affect Regulation, Mentalization, and the Development of Self* (1st edn.). New York: Other Press.

Fox, K. C. R., Nijeboer, S., Solomonova, E., Domhoff, G. W., & Christoff, K. (2013). Dreaming as mind wandering: Evidence from functional neuroimaging and first-person content reports. *Frontiers in Human Neuroscience*, 7, 412. Retrieved from https://doi.org/10.3389/fnhum.2013.00412.

Freud, S. (1940). *An Outline of Psychoanalysis*. London: Penguin Classics.

Freud, S. (1957). Five lectures on psycho-analysis. In J. Strachey & A. Freud (Eds.), *The Standard Edition of the Complete Psychological Works of Sigmund Freud. Volume XI (1910): Five Lectures on Psycho-Analysis, Leonardo da Vinci and Other Works* (pp. 1–56). London: Hogarth Press.

Freud, S. (2001a). On dreams (1901). In *The Complete Psychological Works of Sigmund Freud* (new edn., vol. 5, pp. 631–714). London: Vintage Classics.

Freud, S. (2001b). *The Interpretation of Dreams* (original 1900, vol. 4–5). London: Vintage.

Fuhrer, U. (2003). *Cultivating Minds: Identity as Meaning-making Practice*. New York: Routledge.

Geertz, C. (1972). La religion comme système culturel. In R. Bradbury, C. Geertz, M. E. Spiro, V. W. Turner, & E. H. Winter (Eds.), *Essais d'anthropologie religieuse* (pp. 19–66). Paris: Gallimard.

Gfeller, F. (2017). Imagination as embodied activity? Combining Zittoun's "imaginary loop model" with Schuetz' "provinces of meaning." In G. Sullivan, J. Cresswell, B. D. Ellis, M. Morgan, &

E. Schraube (Eds.), *Resistance and Renewal in Theoretical Psychology* (pp. 136–144). Ontario: Captus University Publications.

Gillespie, A. (2005a). Giving the future form: Non-reflective and reflective uses of symbolic resources. In A. Gülerce, A. Hofmeister, & I. Staeuble (Eds.), *Contemporary Theorizing in Psychology: Global Perspectives*. Toronto: Captus University Publications.

Gillespie, A. (2005b). Malcolm X and his autobiography: Identity development and self-narration. *Culture & Psychology*, 11(1), 77–88.

Gillespie, A. (2006a). *Becoming Other: From Social Interaction to Self-reflection*. Greenwich, CT: Information Age Publishing.

Gillespie, A. (2006b). Games and the development of perspective taking. *Human Development*, 49(2), 87–92.

Gillespie, A. (2013). Nuclear brinkmanship: A study in non-linguistic communication. *Integrative Psychological and Behavioral Science*, 47(4), 492–508.

Gillespie, A., Cornish, F., Aveling, E.-L., & Zittoun, T. (2008). Living with war: Community resources, self-dialogues and psychological adaptation to World War II. *Journal of Community Psychology*, 36(1), 35–52.

Gillespie, A. & Zittoun, T. (2010a). Studying the movement of thought. In A. Toomela & J. Valsiner (Eds.), *Methodological Thinking in Psychology: 60 Years Gone Astray?* (pp. 69–88). Charlotte, NC: Information Age Publishing.

Gillespie, A. & Zittoun, T. (2010b). Using resources: Conceptualizing the mediation and reflective use of tools and signs. *Culture & Psychology*, 16(1), 37–62.

Gillespie, A. & Zittoun, T. (2013). Meaning making in motion: Bodies and minds moving through institutional and semiotic structures. *Culture & Psychology*, 19(4), 518–532.

Gillespie, A. & Zittoun, T. (2015). Social and psychological movement: Weaving individual experience into society. In B. Wagoner, N. Chaudhary, & P. Hviid (Eds.), *Integrating Experiences: Body and Mind Moving between Contexts* (pp. 279–294). Charlotte, NC: Information Age Publishing.

Gillespie, A. & Zittoun, T. (2016). The gift of a rock: A case study in the emergence and dissolution of meaning. In J. Bang & D. Winther-Lindqvist (Eds.), *Nothingness: Philosophical Insights to Psychology* (pp. 89–106). New Brunswick, NJ: Transaction Publishers.

Glăveanu, V. P. (2014). *Thinking Through Creativity and Culture. Toward an Integrated Model*. New Brunswick, NJ: Transaction Publishers.

Greco Morasso, S. & Zittoun, T. (2014). The trajectory of food as a symbolic resource for international migrants. *Outlines. Critical Practice Studies*, 15(1), 28–48.

Green, A. (2005). *Key Ideas for a Contemporary Psychoanalysis Misrecognition and Recognition of the Unconscious* (1st edn.). New York: Routledge.

Grossen, M., Baucal, A., & Zittoun, T. (2010). Using cultural elements as symbolic resources in and out school: Results of a questionnaire submitted to young persons in three upper secondary schools. Research report SYRES no. 5 (Funding FNS no. 100013-116040/1), Universités de Neuchâtel & Lausanne, Switzerland.

Grossen, M. & Perret-Clermont, A.-N. (Eds.). (1992). *L'Espace thérapeutique: Cadres et contextes*. Lausanne, Switzerland: Delachaux & Niestle.

Grossen, M., Zittoun, T., & Ros, J. (2012). Boundary crossing events and potential appropriation space in philosophy, literature and general knowledge. In E. Hjörne, G. van der Aalsvoort, & G. de Abreu (Eds.), *Learning, Social Interaction and Diversity – Exploring Identities in School Practices* (pp. 15–33). Rotterdam: Sense Publishers.

Gyger Gaspoz, D. (2014). Donner voix à l'espace physique: Lorsque la chambre perpétue et écrit l'histoire de l'adolescent au travers d'objets significatifs. Le cas des jeunes en itinérance géographique. *Strenæ. Recherches sur les livres et objets culturels de l'enfance*, 7. Retrieved from http://strenae.revues.org/1265.

Habermas, T. (2012). Identity, emotion, and the social matrix of autobiographical memory: A psychoanalytic narrative view. In D. Berntsen &

D. C. Rubin (Eds.), *Understanding Autobiographical Memory: Theories and Approaches* (pp. 33–53). Cambridge: Cambridge University Press.

Hale, H. C. (2008). The development of British military masculinities through symbolic resources. *Culture & Psychology*, 14(3), 305–332.

Hale, H. C. & de Abreu, G. (2010). Drawing on the notion of symbolic resources in exploring the development of cultural identities in immigrant transitions. *Culture & Psychology*, 16(3), 395–415.

Harris, P. L. (2000). *The Work of the Imagination* (1st edn.). Oxford: Wiley-Blackwell.

Harvey, D. (2006). The sociological and geographical imaginations. *International Journal of Politics, Culture, and Society*, 18(3–4), 211–255.

Hilppö, J. A., Rajala, A., Zittoun, T., Kumpulainen, K., & Lipponen, L. (2016). Interactive dynamics of imagination in a science classroom. *Frontline Learning Research*, 4(4), 20–29.

Hviid, P. (2015). Borders in education and living – a case of trench warfare. *Integrative Psychological and Behavioral Science*, 50(1), 44–61.

Hviid, P. & Villadsen, J. W. (2018). Playing and being: Imagination in the life course. In T. Zittoun & V. P. Glăveanu (Eds.), *Handbook of Culture and Imagination* (pp. 137–166). Oxford: Oxford University Press.

Jørgensen, D. (2018). The philosophy of imagination. In T. Zittoun & V. P. Glăveanu (Eds.), *Handbook of Culture and Imagination* (pp. 19–46). Oxford: Oxford University Press.

Jules et Jim. (1962). [Film] Directed by F. Truffaut. France: SEDIF.

Kadianaki, I. (2010). Negotiating immigration through symbolic resources: The case of immigrants living in Greece. PhD dissertation. University of Cambridge.

Klempe, H. (2018). Music and imagination. In T. Zittoun & V. P. Glăveanu (Eds.), *Handbook of Culture and Imagination* (pp. 243–270). Oxford: Oxford University Press.

Konopásek, Z. (Ed.). (2000). *Our Lives as Database. Doing a Sociology of Ourselves: Czech National Transitions in Autobiographical Research Dialogues*. Prague: Univerzita Karlova v Praze, Nakladatelství Karolinum.

Lawrence, J. A., Benedikt, R., & Valsiner, J. (1992). Homeless in the mind: A case-history of personal life in and out of a close orthodox community. *Journal of Social Distress and the Homeless*, 1(2), 157–176.

Lévi-Strauss, C. (1966). *The Savage Mind* (original French publication 1962). Chicago/London: University of Chicago Press/Weidenfeld and Nicolson.

Levy, R., Ghisletta, P., Le Goff, J.-M., Spini, D., & Widmer, E. (Eds.). (2005). *Towards an Interdisciplinary Perspective on the Life Course*. Amsterdam: Elsevier.

Lewin, K. (1936). *Principles of Topological Psychology* (trans. by F. Heider & G. M. Heider). New York: McGraw-Hill.

Livingstone, S. (2005). Internet literacy among children and young people. Findings from the UK children go online project. Research report, London School of Economics.

London, J. (1909/1994). *Martin Eden* (ed. by A. Sinclair). London: Penguin Classics.

Lyons, W. E. (1986). *The Disappearance of Introspection*. Cambridge, MA: MIT Press.

Lyra, M. C. D. P. & Valsiner, J. (1998). *Construction of Psychological Processes in Interpersonal Communication*. Stamford, CT: Ablex.

Marková, I. (2016). *The Dialogical Mind: Common Sense and Ethics*. Cambridge: Cambridge University Press.

Marková, I. (2018). From imagination to well-controlled images: Challenge for the dialogical mind. In T. Zittoun & V. P. Glăveanu (Eds.), *Handbook of Imagination and Culture* (pp. 319–344). Oxford: Oxford University Press.

Martin, J., & Gillespie, A. (2010). A neo-Meadian approach to human agency: Relating the social and the psychological in the ontogenesis of perspective-coordinating persons. *Integrative Psychological and Behavioral Science*, 44(3), 252–272.

Märtsin, M. (2010). Rupturing otherness: Becoming Estonian in the context of contemporary Britain. *Integrative Psychological and Behavioral Science*, 44(1), 65–81.

Märtsin, M., Chang, I., & Obst, P. L. (2016). Using culture to manage the transition into university: Conceptualising the dynamics of withdrawal and engagement. *Culture & Psychology*, 22(2), 276–295.

Mehmeti, T. (2013). Réussite scolaire de jeunes femmes kosovares: Quels processus psycho-sociaux? *Dossiers de Psychologie et Éducation*, 70, 1–133.

Miller, P. J., Hoogstra, L., Mintz, J., Fung, H., & Williams, K. (1993). Troubles in the garden and how they get resolved: A young child's transformation of his favorite story. In C. A. Nelson (Ed.), *Memory and Affect in Development* (vol. 26, pp. 87–114). Hillsdale, NJ: Lawrence Erlbaum.

Mills, C. W. (1959/2000). *The Sociological Imagination*. Oxford: Oxford University Press.

Moro, C. & Rodriguez, C. (1998). Toward a pragmatical conception of the object: The construction of the uses of the object by the baby in the prelinguistic period. In M. C. D. P. Lyra & J. Valsiner (Eds.), *Construction of Psychological Processes In Interpersonal Communication* (pp. 53–72). Stamford, CT: Ablex.

Nathan, T. (2007). *Nous ne sommes pas seuls au monde: Les enjeux de l'ethnopsychiatrie*. Paris: Points.

Nelson, K. (1996). *Language in Cognitive Development: Emergence of the Mediated Mind*. Cambridge: Cambridge University Press.

Nelson, K. (2007). *Young Minds in Social Worlds. Experience, Meaning, and Memory*. Cambridge, MA: Harvard University Press.

Perret-Clermont, A.-N. (2015). The architecture of social relationships and thinking spaces for growth. In C. Psaltis, A. Gillespie, & A.-N. Perret-Clermont (Eds.), *Social Relations in Human and Societal Development* (pp. 51–70). New York: Palgrave Macmillan.

Perriault, J. (1989). *La logique de l'usage: Essai sur les machines à communiquer*. Paris: Flammarion.

Psaltis, C. (2011). The constructive role of gender asymmetry in social interaction: Further evidence. *British Journal of Developmental Psychology*, 29(2), 305–312.

Rabardel, P. (2001). Instrument mediated activity in situations. In A. Blandford, J. Vanderdonckt, & P. Gray (Eds.), *People and Computers XV – Interactions Without Frontiers* (pp. 17–30). Berlin: Springer.

Reddy, V. (2008). *How Infants Know Minds*. Cambridge, MA: Harvard University Press.

Rosenbaum, P. J. & Valsiner, J. (2011). The un-making of a method: From rating scales to the study of psychological processes. *Theory & Psychology*, 21(1), 47–65.

Rosenberg, D. (Ed.). (1993). *The Movie that Changed My Life* (1st edn.). New York: Penguin Books.

Schuetz, A. (1945a). On multiple realities. *Philosophy and Phenomenological Research*, 5(4), 533–576.

Schuetz, A. (1945b). The homecomer. *American Journal of Sociology*, 50(5), 369–376.

Sherif, M. & Sherif, C. W. (1965). *Problems of Youth: Transition to Adulthood in a Changing World*. Chicago: Aldine.

Singer, D. G. & Singer, J. L. (2005). *Imagination and Play in the Electronic Age*. Cambridge, MA: Harvard University Press.

Skyfall. (2012). [Film] Directed by S. Mendes. USA: Sony Pictures.

South Park. (1997). [Animated TV program] Created by T. Parker & M. Stone. USA: Celluloid Studios.

Stankovic, B., Baucal, A., & Zittoun, T. (2009). Uses of symbolic resources in youth: Moving from qualitative to quantitative approach. *Psihologija*, 42(4), 437–457.

Stenner, P. (2018). *Liminality and Experience: A transdisciplinary Approach to the Psychosocial*. London: Palgrave Macmillan.

Strauss, C. & Quinn, N. (1998). *A Cognitive Theory of Cultural Meaning*. Cambridge: Cambridge University Press.

Tanggaard, L. (2015). The socio-materiality of creativity: A case study of the creative processes in design work. In V. P. Glăveanu, A. Gillespie, & J. Valsiner (Eds.), *Rethinking Creativity: Contributions from Cultural Psychology* (pp. 110–124). New York: Routledge.

Tanggaard, L. & Brinkman, S. (2018). Methodological implications of Imagination. In T. Zittoun & V. P. Glăveanu (Eds.), *Handbook of Imagination and*

Culture (pp. 87–108). Oxford: Oxford University Press.

The Dreamers. (2004). [Film] Directed by B. Bertolucci. UK: Recorded Picture Company.

Toomela, A. (2015). What are higher psychological functions? *Integrative Psychological and Behavioral Science*, 50(1) 91–121.

Trevarthen, C. (2012). Embodied human intersubjectivity: Imaginative agency, to share meaning. *Cognitive Semiotics*, 4(1), 6–56.

Valsiner, J. (1987). *Culture and the Development of the Children's Action: A Cultural-Historical Theory of Developmental Psychology*. New York: John Wiley & Sons.

Valsiner, J. (1998). *The Guided Mind: A Sociogenetic Approach to Personality*. Cambridge, MA: Harvard University Press.

Valsiner, J. (2001). Process structure of semiotic mediation in human development. *Human Development*, 44, 84–97.

Valsiner, J. (2007). *Culture in Minds and Societies: Foundations of Cultural Psychology*. New Delhi: SAGE.

Valsiner, J. (2013). Foreword: Breaking a Social Taboo: Introspection Restored. In J. W. Clegg (Ed.), *Self-Observation in the Social Sciences* (pp. vii–xi). New Brunswick, NJ: Transaction Publishers.

Valsiner, J. (2014). *An Invitation to Cultural Psychology*. London: SAGE.

Valsiner, J. (2015). Preface. In J. Valsiner, G. Marsico, N. Chaudhary, T. Sato, & V. Dazzani (Eds.), *Psychology as a Science of Human Being: The Yokohama Manifesto* (vol. 13, pp. v–vii). Dordrecht, Netherlands: Springer.

Valsiner, J., & Lawrence, J. A. (1997). Human development in culture across the life span. In J. W. Berry, P. R. Daseb, & T. S. Saraswathi (Eds.), *Handbook of Cross-Cultural Psychology* (vol. 2, pp. 69–106). Needham Heights, MA: Allyn & Bacon.

Vermersch, P. (2009). Describing the practice of introspection. *Journal of Consciousness Studies*, 16(10/12), 20–57.

Vygotsky, L. S. (1971). *The Psychology of Art*. Cambridge, MA: MIT Press.

Vygotsky, L. S. (1975). Internalization of higher psychological functions. In M. Cole (Ed.), *Mind in Society* (pp. 52–57). Cambridge, MA: Harvard University Press.

Vygotsky, L. S. (1986). *Thought and Language* (ed. by A. Kozulin, rev. edn.). Cambridge, MA: MIT Press.

Vygotsky, L. S. (2004). Imagination and creativity in childhood. *Journal of Russian and East European Psychology*, 42(1), 7–97.

Wagoner, B., Jensen, E., & Oldmeadow, J. A. (2012). Changing times, changing science. In B. Wagoner, E. Jensen, & J. A. Oldmeadow (Eds.), *Culture and Social Change: Transforming Society Through the Power of Ideas* (pp. 1–15). Charlotte, NC: Information Age Publishing.

Werner, H. & Kaplan, B. (1963). *Symbol formation: An organismic-developmental approach to language and the expression of thought*. New York: John Wiley & Son.

Wertsch, J. V. (1998). *Mind as Action*. /Oxford: Oxford University Press.

Winnicott, D. W. (1968). On "the use of an object." In C. Winnicott, R. Shepherd, & M. Davis (Eds.), *Psycho-Analytic Explorations* (pp. 217–246). Cambridge, MA: Harvard University Press.

Winnicott, D. W. (2001). *Playing and Reality*. Philadelphia, PA: Routledge.

Young, S. D. (2000). Movies as equipment for living: A developmental analysis of the importance of film in everyday life. *Critical Studies in Media Communication*, 17(4), 447–468.

Zagórska, W., & Tarnowski, A. (2004, July). Historical re-enactment in young adulthood: Experiences and psychological functions. Poster presented at the 18th Biennial ISSBD meeting, Ghent, Belgium.

Zittoun, T. (2001, December). *Engendrements symboliques. Devenir parent: Le choix du prénom*. PhD thesis, University of Neuchâtel, Switzerland.

Zittoun, T. (2003). The hidden work of symbolic resources in emotions. *Culture & Psychology*, 9(3), 313–329.

Zittoun, T. (2004a). *Donner la vie, choisir un nom: Engendrements symboliques*. Paris: L'Harmattan.

Zittoun, T. (2004b). Symbolic competencies for developmental transitions: The case of the choice of first names. *Culture and Psychology*, 10(2), 131–161.

Zittoun, T. (2006a). Difficult secularity: Talmud as symbolic resource. *Outlines. Critical Social Studies*, 8(2), 59–75.

Zittoun, T. (2006b). *Transitions: Development Through Symbolic Resources*. Greenwich, CT: Information Age Publishing.

Zittoun, T. (2007a). Dynamics of interiority: Ruptures and transitions in the self development. In L. Simão & J. Valsiner (Eds.), *Otherness in Question: Development of the Self* (pp. 187–214). Greenwich, CT: Information Age Publishing.

Zittoun, T. (2007b). Symbolic resources and responsibility in transitions. *Young. Nordic Journal of Youth Research*, 15(2), 193–211.

Zittoun, T. (2008). Janet's emotions in the whole of human conduct. In R. Diriwaechter & J. Valsiner (Eds.), *Striving for the Whole: Creating Theoretical Synthesis* (pp. 111–129). Piscataway, NJ. Transaction Publishers.

Zittoun, T. (2010). How does an object become symbolic? Rooting semiotic artefacts in dynamic shared experiences. In B. Wagoner (Ed.), *Symbolic Transformations: The Mind in Movement through Culture and Society* (pp. 173–192). London: Routledge.

Zittoun, T. (2011a). A girl like a will-o'-the whisp: Listening to reports of cultural experiences as a methodological mean of accessing the preconscious dynamics of sense making. In S. Salvatore & T. Zittoun (Eds.), *Cultural Psychology and Psychoanalysis: Pathways to Synthesis* (pp. 151–179). Charlotte, NC: Information Age Publishing.

Zittoun, T. (2011b). Freud and cultural psychology. In S. Salvatore & T. Zittoun (Eds.), *Cultural Psychology and Psychoanalysis: Pathways to Synthesis* (pp. 67–86). Charlotte, NC: Information Age Publishing.

Zittoun, T. (2012a). Lifecourse. In J. Valsiner (Ed.), *Handbook of Culture and Psychology* (pp. 513–535). Oxford: Oxford University Press.

Zittoun, T. (2012b). On the emergence of the subject. *Integrative Psychological and Behavioral Science*, 46(3), 259–273.

Zittoun, T. (2012c). The art of noise: Comment on the sound of silence. *Culture & Psychology*, 18(4), 30–41.

Zittoun, T. (2013a). On the use of a film: Cultural experiences as symbolic resources. In A. Kuhn (Ed.), *Little Madnesses: Winnicott, Transitional Phenomena and Cultural Experience* (pp. 135–147). London: Tauris.

Zittoun, T. (2013b). Religious traditions as means of innovation: The use of symbolic resources in the life course. In H. Zock & M. Buitelaar (Eds.), *Religious Voices in Self-Narratives Making Sense of Life in Times of Transitions* (pp. 129–148). Berlin: Walter de Gruyter.

Zittoun, T. (2014a). Three dimensions of dialogical movement. *New Ideas in Psychology*, 32, 99–106.

Zittoun, T. (2014b). Trusting for learning. In P. Linell & I. Marková (Eds.), *Trust and Language* (pp. 125–151). Charlotte, NC: Information Age Publishing.

Zittoun, T. (2015a). Compatibility between early psychoanalysis and pragmatism. In P. J. Rosenbaum (Ed.), *Making Our Ideas Clear: Pragmatism in Psychoanalysis* (pp. 23–42). Charlotte, NC: Information Age Publishing.

Zittoun, T. (2015b). From Vico to the sociocultural imagination. *Culture & Psychology*, 21(2), 251–258.

Zittoun, T. (2015c). Social relations and the use of symbolic resources in learning and development. In C. Psaltis, A. Gillespie, & A.-N. Perret-Clermont (Eds.), *Social Relations in Human and Societal Development Social Relations in Human and Societal Development* (pp. 134–146). New York: Palgrave Macmillan.

Zittoun, T. (2015d). Studying "higher mental functions": The example of imagination. In J. Valsiner, G. Marsico, N. Chaudhary, T. Sato, & V. Dazzani (Eds.), *Psychology as a Science of Human Being: The Yokohama Manifesto* (vol. 13, pp. 129–147). Dordrecht, Netherlands: Springer.

Zittoun, T. (2016a). Imagining self in a changing world: An exploration of "Studies of Marriage." In M. Han & C. Cunha (Eds.), *The Subjectified and Subjectifying Mind* (pp. 85–116). Charlotte, NC: Information Age Publishing.

Zittoun, T. (2016b). Reflexivity, or learning from living. In G. Marsico, R. A. Ruggieri, & S. Salvatore (Eds.), *Reflexivity and Psychology* (vol. 6, pp. 143–167). Charlotte, NC: Information Age Publishing.

Zittoun, T. (2016c). Symbolic resources and sense-making in learning and instruction. *European Journal of Psychology of Education*, 32(1), 1–20.

Zittoun, T. (2016d). The sound of music. In H. Klempe (Ed.), *Cultural Psychology of Musical Experience* (pp. 21–39). Charlotte, NC: Information Age Publishing.

Zittoun, T. (2018). The Velvet Revolution of land and minds. In B. Wagoner, F. M. Moghaddam, & J. Valsiner (Eds.), *The Psychology of Radical Social Change: From Rage to Revolution* (pp. 140–158). Cambridge: Cambridge University Press.

Zittoun, T., Cornish, F., Gillespie, A., & Aveling, E.-L. (2008). Using social knowledge: A case study of a diarist's meaning making during World War II. In W. Wagner, T. Sugiman, & K. Gergen (Eds.), *Meaning in Action: Constructions, Narratives and Representations* (pp. 163–179). New York: Springer.

Zittoun, T. & de Saint-Laurent, C. (2015). Life-creativity: Imagining one's life. In V. P. Glăveanu, A. Gillespie, & J. Valsiner (Eds.), *Rethinking Creativity: Contributions from Cultural Psychology* (pp. 58–75). New York: Routledge.

Zittoun, T., Duveen, G., Gillespie, A., Ivinson, G., & Psaltis, C. (2003). The uses of symbolic resources in transitions. *Culture & Psychology*, 9(4), 415–448.

Zittoun, T. & Gillespie, A. (2012). Using diaries and self-writings as data in psychological research. In E. Abbey & S. E. Surgan (Eds.), *Emerging Methods in Psychology* (pp. 1–26). New Brunswick, NJ: Transaction Publishers.

Zittoun, T. & Gillespie, A. (2013). Symbolic resources. In K. Keith (Ed.), *The Encyclopedia of Cross-Cultural Psychology* (pp. 1259–1262). Malden, MA: John Wiley & Sons.

Zittoun, T. & Gillespie, A. (2014). Sculpture and art installations: Towards a cultural psychological analysis. In B. Wagoner, N. Chaudhary, & P. Hviid (Eds.), *Cultural Psychology and Its Future: Complementarity in a New Key* (pp. 167–177). Charlotte, NC: Information Age Publishing.

Zittoun, T. & Gillespie, A. (2015a). Integrating experiences: Body and mind moving between contexts. In B. Wagoner, N. Chaudhary, & P. Hviid (Eds.), *Integrating Experiences: Body and Mind Moving Between Contexts* (pp. 3–49). Charlotte, NC: Information Age Publishing.

Zittoun, T., & Gillespie, A. (2015b). Internalization: How culture becomes mind. *Culture & Psychology*, 21(4), 477–491.

Zittoun, T. & Gillespie, A. (2015c). Transitions in the lifecourse: Learning from Alfred Schütz. In A. C. Joerchel & G. Benetka (Eds.), *Biographical Ruptures and Their Repairs: Cultural Transitions in Development* (pp. 147–157). Charlotte, NC: Information Age Publishing.

Zittoun, T. & Gillespie, A. (2016). *Imagination in Human and Cultural Development*. London: Routledge.

Zittoun, T., Gillespie, A., Cornish, F., & Psaltis, C. (2007). The metaphor of the triangle in theories of human development. *Human Development*, 50, 208–229.

Zittoun, T. & Glăveanu, V. P. (2018). Imagination at the frontiers of psychology. In T. Zittoun & V. P. Glăveanu (Eds.), *Handbook of Imagination and Culture* (pp. 1–16). Oxford: Oxford University Press.

Zittoun, T. & Grossen, M. (2012). Cultural elements as means of constructing the continuity of the self across various spheres of experience. In M. César & B. Ligorio (Eds.), *The Interplays between Dialogical Learning and Dialogical Self* (pp. 99–126). Charlotte, NC: Information Age Publishing.

Zittoun, T. & Perret-Clermont, A.-N. (2009). Four social psychological lenses for developmental psychology. *European Journal for Psychology of Education*, 24(2), 387–403.

Zittoun, T. & Rosenstein, A. (2018). Theatre and imagination to (re)discover reality. In T. Zittoun & V. P. Glăveanu (Eds.), *Handbook of*

Imagination and Culture (pp. 223–242). Oxford: Oxford University Press.

Zittoun, T. & Sato, T. (2018). Imagination in adults and the aging person: Possible futures and actual past. In T. Zittoun & V. P. Glăveanu (Eds.), *Handbook of Imagination and Culture* (pp. 187–208). Oxford: Oxford University Press.

Zittoun, T. & Valsiner, J. (2016). Imagining the past and remembering the future: How the unreal defines the real. In T. Sato, N. Mori, & J. Valsiner (Eds.), *Making of the Future: The Trajectory Equifinality Approach in Cultural Psychology* (pp. 3–19). Charlotte, NC: Information Age Publishing.

Zittoun, T., Valsiner, J., Vedeler, D., Salgado, J., Gonçalves, M., & Ferring, D. (2013). *Human Development in the Lifecourse: Melodies of Living*. Cambridge: Cambridge University Press.

Part III

The Agent Rises a Reflective Self: Education and Development

11 Early Infancy – a Moving World: Embodied Experience and the Emergence of Thinking

Silvia Español

11.1 Introduction

The linguistic turn that occurred in human sciences in the twentieth century produced extraordinary conceptual reorganizations. It especially gave us the chance to see the implications of language and hence the symbolism in almost every human issue: in the construction of reality and subjectivity, in our criteria of truth, and in our interpersonal relationships. From it, a second turn seems to have been born and is now bearing its first fruits. That which Maxine Sheets-Johnstone (2009) calls the corporeal turn. It proposes that we open the door to ways of thinking outside any system of symbols able to mediate a reference to something else. It assumes paying attention to what is and what is presented (not what is represented). It is also expected that we see our dynamic body in resonance with others as an indivisible unity with our mind (see Chapter 1, this volume, for a clear argument in favor of this indivisible unit). Concomitantly, the corporeal turn leads to a shift toward the study of the body in movement. For example, in the twentieth century cave art was seen as the first manifestations of the human symbolic world, its possible nature of symbolic representation monopolized attention. Currently, however, Lambros Malafouris (2013, cited in Chapter 6, this volume) analyzes cave art from the movement that produced it: the stroke. He thinks those strokes did not begin as an attempt to produce a finished product, or a representative intention of something, they are the result of intentions into

action. Alberto Rosa (Chapter 6, this volume) suggests that, with repetition in time, strokes would become ritualized gestures intended to produce forms; and in the very long term, these first "graphic babblings" would derive in progressively more complex ways.

As shown, the foregrounding of corporeal perceptual/kinesthetic present experience does not deny our symbolic nature, but does limit its domain. In relation to early development, it leads us to notice the self's and the other's non-symbolic, essentially kinetic perception and organization (Stern, 1985, 2010; Español, 2010, 2014). It evidences the biological, psychological, and cultural weaving of the first "strokes" in ontogenesis. These are strokes in the air or on the ground: the marks of playful movement and movement toward the standing position. The singularity of our prolonged immaturity is probably human ontogeny's most impressive biological fact (Bruner, 1972). This fact is linked to several features that make us who we are. Among others, the emergence of adult–infant social play forms, between a baby's second and fifth months (Fagen, 2011), and with our slow (compared to other species) motor development (Feldenkrais & Beringer, 2010).

Social play requires an organization of sensitivity toward the other's behavior to act as part of a coordinated system (Raczaszek-Leonardi, Nomikou, & Rohlfing, 2013). When adults play, they color the baby with their personal movement style. In the heart of their social play they make the baby's first strokes appear. His first kicks, arm movements, head turns, and spine column snaking will have roughly the timing, scope, and intensity of the movements of their culture. In the Afro-Colombian community of Guapi in Colombia, it is possible to see a six-month-old baby girl resting on her sit bones on her mother's lap, letting a pulsing and striking rebound of her mother's legs pass through her own body. And later one can see her incorporating the rebound to generate a strong and broad flexion and extension movement involving her whole body resembling the snaking column of the *mapalé*, a typical dance of their region. Her movement is only possible because support in her seat bones leaves her pelvis free to move back and forth. Such freedom and vitality of body movement is characteristic of adults in her culture who transmit it to their babies through early social play (Ospina & Español, 2014). The spirit, as lived in each culture reaches the baby through movement. As noted by Jaan Valsiner and Alberto Rosa (Chapter 1, this volume) a living body can be encouraged by the spirit of a culture.

Our long immaturity period also affects our motor development. The road to bipedalism is not phylogenetically programmed. We learn to move, turn, sit, and stand up and we need time to do so. Moshe Feldenkrais showed that this – never error-free – organic learning provides experiences of freedom and self-control every time a reversible movement is reached (Feldenkrais & Beringer, 2010). Each culture's raising patterns affect the baby's organic learning, building his corporeality. Some tie or wrap their babies tightly around their bodies so that they can barely move (as Hopi tribes, Bolivians, the Turks), in turn, others encourage movement, as in the Colombian Choco where it is thought that if not allowed to move their little baby bones become stuck, impeding normal movement later on (Arango, 2014).

When a catastrophe occurs early in life, such as anaclitic depression in socially deprived babies (Spitz, 1963), motor development breaks down.

In the short film, *Emotional Deprivation in Infancy: Study by Rene A. Spitz* (1952; www.youtube.com/watch?v=VvdOe10vrs4 – specifically from 2:22 to 4:30 minutes) it is possible to see how psychological pain is expressed by Lam, a 9-month-old baby, unsuccessfully trying to join hands (something usually achieved by three–four months), it can also be seen how after each attempt, with stiff fingers and palms, the baby goes back to a tense undifferentiated side-to-side balancing movement of his entire body. Pain is seen in his movement's form and quality. Movement fully expresses our being in all stages of life's cycle.

In developmental psychology, the increasing shift toward the study of movement is grounded in theoretical, gradual, and profound changes. In the first place, it is given by psychology's deepening in embodiment theory, and in social cognition's second-person approach; and second, by the relationship established with the somatic discipline. This work is the product of the second change, which is even more recent than the first. In Section 11.2, I discuss fundamental aspects of these theoretical bodies: the role of experience in motor development, the enactive program's quality of mindfulness, the emergence of the field of somatics, and the qualities of body awareness. In Section 11.3, I attempt to outline a developmental trajectory of the first months of the baby's life that does not have the emergence of the symbolic capability as an ethos (ending point of the most acknowledged developmental theories). By rather paying attention to the baby's experiences with gravity, of being held, of breathing, I intend to show our initial ways of being in the world and of organizing our experience. This is a status that, although with changes and transformations, subsists in adult life. To outline this psychological path, I use a progression of corporeal patterns proposed in the somatic discipline. In Section 11.4, I briefly present the kind of thinking that the corporeal turn allows to recognize and name, and give some examples of how they operate. Finally, I point out the main conclusions of this work.

11.2 Motor Development, Experience, and Body Awareness

11.2.1 Motor Development and Iterative Experience

Esther Thelen (2000a) discusses Piaget's founding assumption that the goal of human development is increasing abstract thinking and estranging from its predecessors, perception, and action. Like all those defending embodiment theory, she believes that the endeavor of mental activity is to continually perceive and act in the world not only in the initial state, but throughout life. The mind is embodied: it emerges from corporeal interactions and is continually influenced by it. It is not just a matter of seeing the sensorimotor origins of cognition, but the intimate and inextricable linkage between thinking and action throughout life. Thinking starts with perceiving and acting, retaining its sign of origin forever. From day one, in the embodied experience, motor and nervous systems relate with the environment. The nervous system is dynamic and embedded in and with the body. Nervous system and body are inserted into and coupled with the environment; at no point in development are they not paired. What changes is the nature of the coupling. In development, it is not about describing how purely abstract cognition structures arise but to understand the emergence of a flexible and dynamic merge between direct online cognition and one less closely connected to the immediacy of the senses. Adopting Edelman's theory of neuronal group selection, Thelen (2000a) points out that the brain's functional mapping depends on experience, especially on experience coming from perception and motor examination. When babies are awake they continuously move and search for things. Every acquired experience adds to a network where some paths are strengthened. We are talking about experiential selection: the weakening and strengthening of synapses populations in virtue of experience. The neural map is based on lived experience. Experience shapes the brain.

Thelen's view of development implies understanding children as online problem solvers and emphasizing goal-oriented actions. This is her theory's great directive line. In earlier work she noticed that rhythmic movements of the baby's body parts (such as rhythmic kicks) where repeated at least three times in intervals of a second or less. She described around 47 types of rhythmic stereotypes, thought of as transitional behavior when preceding more complex activities or appearing while the baby gained control over new positions. She stated that development proceeds from non-goal-oriented stereotyped behaviors toward more variable and goal-oriented ones (Thelen 1979).

In Thelen, Corbetta, and Spencer (1996), the infant's reaching is a natural solution to get a distal object and bring it to the mouth. It has one goal: to orally examine the object. Dynamical systems theory emphasizes that new skills must arise from the interplay of new demanding tasks with already existing movements. In line with this, they describe movements involved in reaching and non-reaching (like bringing hands to the face, a pattern established before the baby can grasp an object). They point out that some non-reaching movements, like certain rhythmic arm movements, are spontaneous and act in conjunction with goal-oriented ones (reaching an object). Sooner or later, each baby in its own unique manner makes contact with the object – through padding, touching, or sliding its hand over it. These moments of contact select certain moves, carving patterns that are repeated more frequently. The cycle   arousal activation by the sight of an object, action, and occasional contact – will be repeated for weeks. Finally at about the fourth month, the efficient, successful action of object reaching emerges. The movements involved in the whole cycle are described in the same way: direct or indirect, soft or abrupt, fast or slow, or with sudden or tortuous sections. Regardless of the action being performed, movement has inherent traits that define it. However, the description is subsumed to the action's crucial feature: its goal-oriented nature essentially defines it in terms of success or failure. The authors note that babies have different initial conditions, such as body size and energy level, thus face different postural and biomechanical problems so that each child finds a solution following individual developmental paths. Some have hectic movements of arms and legs, like a working windmill. From the beginning, they have to learn to control their arms' agitation in order to grab the object and bring it to their mouths. Others are quieter and spend much time with hands close to the face: they must learn to expand and extend their arms enough to reach the toy. As we can see, biomechanic and postural descriptions focus on the limbs' distal movements unattached to the center. It is proper of academic psychology to pay attention to hands, mouth, and eyes forgetting the center, the navel area, the *tantien* zone of Eastern tradition, thinking it is possible to describe baby movement evolution without considering it.

While far from proposing phylogenetically prefigured complex behaviors, Thelen does not militate in favor of a *tabula rasa* either. In Thelen (2005) she says that in order to be formed through self-organization, patterns must be minimally organized in their initial state. Development cascades and is organized around a small node or disturbance in the homogeneous field. Opposing to Colwin Trevarthen's patterns of visually elicited pre-reaching in newborns explained in terms of maturity (the reaching pattern is there waiting to be refined), Thelen wonders if this apparent visually elicited pre-reaching is not simply a tightening of the extremities, accompanied by a flexor tone, that activates at object sight. She wonders about the minimum that needs to be built

to trigger the developmental cascade leading to reaching.

In an exercise of admirable parsimony she suggests that reaching may arise from a few perception/action biases, some basic processes, and the infant's active problem-solving skills. By bias she means that certain neuronal connections are intrinsically favored and their activation strengthens and increases. Biases considered are: (i) looking at contrasting patterns and moderately complex stimuli (babies like to look at interesting visual stimuli); (ii) suction – having something in your mouth feels good; and (iii) grasping or hand closing when hand receptors are stimulated (although some believe it is a remnant reflex from climbing trees, she believes it is only a reflection of the newborn's flexor muscle tone, not a remnant reflex from climbing). These biases, together with (i) basic processes of interest and habituation (that ensure the baby fills his visual world with changing scenarios); (ii) the tight coupling between vision, hand, and mouth touch (the tendency to put your hand on the mouth, to respond with mouth movements to interesting visual stimuli); and (iii) the ability to repeat a pleasant result or circular reaction is sufficient to start a cascade culminating in the emergence of distal object reaching to the mouth. Initial biases and basic processes establish the substrate for motivation. The action of reaching is not prefigured.

As Thelen (2000b) notes, descriptive studies on motor development flourished around 1920 with the work of Arnold Gessel, Myrtle McGraw, and others. The notion that motor development was due to universal principles ended this line of research in the 1950s. Thelen's findings show that motor development is an interesting field of study that can be reopened. If maturation is not decisive, there are interesting psychological processes to be explained. Thelen was intensively trained in the Feldenkrais method of somatic education – which she referred to in one of her articles (Thelen, 2005). It probably enhanced her clear awareness on experience as a fundamental category of analysis in development and on the relevance of *iterative movement experience*. She focused on a fraction of the experience of baby movement: one voluntarily self-made, goal-oriented in relation to objects out in the physical world. In Section 11.3, I will show that self-oriented or oriented-to-others baby movements can also be interesting. Apparently the brain's functional mapping depends on repeated experience through perceptual-motor examination. If, as actually occurs, the baby's perceptual-motor examination is not limited to the physical environment but encompasses the exploration of his own and the other's body, the brain is shaped by corporeal experiences lived by the baby on his own and in early reciprocity patterns.

11.2.2 Experience and Awareness

In a sense, Thelen seems to adhere to the cognitive school's tacit and arguable assumption that cognition is all about solving problems. Also, her concept of embodied experience seems limited. It is not enough to indicate that in embodied experience the motor system is related to the nervous system and the environment. The embodied experience supposes a body consciousness and a sensemaking of our world.

The enactive program proposed by Francisco Varela, Evan Thompson and Eleanor Rosch (1991) is probably the intellectual initiative that more openly addressed the experiential dimension of human life in cognitive science. This program's basic intuition is that our understanding is rooted in the structure of our biological embodiment but is lived and experienced within consensual action and cultural history.[1] Cognition is not understood as problem solving (from representations) but as a world enactment – bringing about a world – through a viable history of structural coupling. Cognitive skills are linked together as vivid stories. Thus, intelligence is not the ability to solve problems but the ability to enter into a

shared world of significance, allowing us to make sense of our world or to "have a world." They suggest embodiment has a double meaning: the body as (i) a lived experiential structure and (ii) a field of cognitive processes. Our bodies are lived and experiential structures, biological and phenomenological events. Cognition depends on the experiences originated in possessing a body with many sensorimotor skills embedded in a biological, psychological, and cultural context. Cognition rises from repeated sensorimotor patterns that allow action to be perceptually guided. Motor and sensory processes cannot be separated from lived cognition.

The enactive program is constructed on the concept of experience. Although Varela, Thompson, and Rosch recognized phenomenology as a Western philosophical perspective dealing with human experience and emphasizing its pragmatic corporeal context, they noted that it was put together in a purely theoretical way. Merleau-Ponty – they argue – tried to learn the immediacy of our nonreflective experience and to give it a voice in conscious reflection. But because it is a *post factum* theoretical activity, he failed to capture the wealth of experience. Thus his work could only be a discourse on experience. Searching for a tradition that examines human experience in the aspects of reflective and immediate life, and allows cognitive science to include immediate experience, they turned to Eastern philosophy, particularly to the Buddhist tradition of mindfulness/awareness.[2] I always thought this program puts experience in its rightful place since it does not limit or destroy it (as do other versions of enactivism). But my ignorance on Buddhism and meditation practices, and my belief that they are essentially first person activities, prevented me from following them.

Recently, Schmalzl, Crane-Godreau, and Payne (2014) distinguished the "movement-based embodied contemplative practices." They include Eastern meditation practices, such as yoga, and modern approaches to somatic education, such as the Feldenkrais method and the Alexander technique. The cultivation of interoceptive, proprioceptive, and kinesthetic awareness combines these Eastern and Western practices entwined with the enactive program proposal opened by Varela, Thompson, and Rosch. Schmalzl, Crane-Godreau and Payne make the interconnection clear. In embodiment theory, it is understood that one's experience in the world as a cognizant being portrays a complex interplay between brain, body, and environment, and the seamless integration of interoceptive, proprioceptive (including vestibular), kinesthetic, tactile, and spatial information. In consonance, movement-based embodied contemplative practices all emphasize on paying attention to the interoceptive, proprioceptive, and kinesthetic qualities of experience. They also use expressions like "being in one's body," to promote an embodied experience of the self. Likewise, they stress that movement is a fundamental characteristic of the embodied state, and the enactive approaches propose that one's ability for self-movement is a constitutive part of all cognitive processes. Movement-based embodied contemplative practices are based on internally generated self-willed movement that, opposed to externally evoked or purely passively imposed ones, is intrinsic to the sense of agency, thus central to self sense development. Every contemplative practice involves some sort of movement. Even in the most static forms of seated meditation the whole body is constantly in subtle motion with the breath's rhythm. The principal focus of movement-based practice is on the intentional induction or the disinhibition of overt movement or subtle internal sensations of movement. In a similar way, in movement-based practices, redirecting attention entails cultivating awareness of bodily sensations and proprioceptive feedback related to the specifically used movement and breathing techniques. Regarding the neural mechanisms under contemplative states, studies in neurophenomenology show that practices based on meditation engage selective brain areas and neural networks involved in attention, body awareness, emotion regulation, and the sense of self. Finally, they say they are also forms of movement-based embodied contemplative practices (as many Eastern movement-based systems) that involve two people (master and disciple, teacher and student, therapist and client, or co-practitioners). Together, they enter a state of enhanced connectivity referred to as "resonance." In this state, affective and somatosensory experiences are largely automatically shared; apparently they involve a simultaneous activation of affective and sensory brain structures in both individuals.

Although now included in the enactive program, these practices have been a subject of reflection for some time in the nonacademic world. Thomas Hanna (1986, 1988) identified a broad field called "somatics" which he defined as the art and science of processes or concurrent synergistic interaction between awareness, biological functioning, and environment. Somatics refers to practices in the field of movement studies emphasizing internal physical perception. Used in movement therapy the term signifies an approach based on internal body perception, and in dance is an antonym for techniques such as ballet that care about the audience's observation of movement. The field encompasses Eastern practices and various methods of somatic education, among others, the Feldenkrais method, body-mind centering, Laban-Bartenieff fundamentals – that is, contemplative embodied movement-based practices – but also extends to certain dance techniques like contact improvisation. In all cases, there is an appreciation and a validation of the living body experience closely linked to how we organize ourselves as we move into our coupling with the world. And the body of proprioception and interoception is addressed, the one perceived from within. It is about interactive practices affecting two or more people. Some involve hand-on practices or listening to the other's body through one's whole body; the latter have, as a distinctive feature, the corporeal contact or touch with the other. They all intend to refine the kinesthetic and proprioceptive senses and assume that consciousness can be expanded. They look for the expansion of awareness of the vital moving body in its physical and social environment.

In the field of somatics, body awareness is at the center. As Alan Fogel (2013) points out, formal education emphasizes awareness of our thinking processes and the ability to regulate them toward specific goals, such as planning or problem solving. However, self-consciousness – in the sense of thinking about oneself – is not the same as feeling yourself in a corporeal consciousness. Embodied self-awareness involves interoception (sensing our breathing, arousal, emotion) and the body outline (movement awareness and coordination between different parts of the body or between the body and the environment). Embodied self-awareness begins before birth, during the last months of life in utero and continues to grow throughout life as we learn more complex living and acting in the world forms. It is fundamentally linked to the conscience of others. Interoception begins with ergoreceptors, receptors placed in different body tissues that sense internal states. Exteroception includes receptors for sound, light, taste, and smell. Interoception and exteroception rely on different sets of receptors and different neural pathways to and through the brain. The afferent nerve cell fibers that originate in the ergoreceptors are small and unmyelinated. Myelin is a protective coating around nerve cell fibers that speeds transmission. Therefore, unmyelinated fibers are slow conductors. This partially explains why it often takes several minutes to feel particular embodied sensations and sense their source within the body. Expanding embodied self-awareness is slow and deliberate when compared to the rapid and instantaneous generation of ideas and thoughts in conceptual self-awareness. The faculty of conceptual reasoning is so powerful and rapid in humans, it can

hinder the growth of embodied self-awareness which requires our conceptual mind to slow down and take a break from its continual stream of ideas. According to Fogel, there's an indirect transition between embodied and conceptual self-awareness. We cannot be in conceptual and embodied states of self-awareness at the same time, but under certain circumstances we can regulate the switch. Taking on Fogel's assumption, Silvia Mamana (2016) says that keeping the perception of sensations active requires a deliberate and systematic training that implicates learning to quiet our minds among other things. She prefers the term "open awareness," closer to Varela, Thomson, and Rosh's proposal (instead of embodied self-awareness), more consistent with the goals of somatic education: opening to internal perceptions consciousness, but also to environmental stimuli.

Many methods of somatic education have a direct link with motor development knowledge. Feldenkrais's (1972) awareness through movement classes are based on accurate observation of baby movements. Bonnie Bainbridge Cohen (2012) – creator of body-mind centering – describes in detail the patterns of movement from life in uterus to bipedalism. Peggy Hackney (2002) reinterprets Bainbridge Cohen's post-birth patterns linking them to Bartenieff fundamentals (where Rudolph Laban's imprint, father of modern dance, is obvious). Years ago, Fogel explicitly proposed linking the science of movement to developmental psychology (Fogel, 1992). I want align with his proposal and extend that link to other ways of movement knowledge. In the next point I will concentrate on the baby's development process following Hackney's synthesis on afterbirth patterns, and I will attempt to cross it with some of the ideas presented above.

In terms of movement, birth involves a dramatic change: the baby faces gravity and the experience of being supported by some kind of surface. He also transitions from being in the womb, fully in contact, to, especially in our culture, be dispossessed of full contact, be released in the air, and experience partial contact (the back, the stomach) depending on how he is supported. He goes through the birth canal and breathes on his own for the first time. Gravity, support, breathing will be constant throughout our life history (except under singular conditions) and are key to the formation of our psyche or our way of being in the world. I will try to demonstrate this in the next point.

11.3 The Fundamental Patterns of Total Body Connectivity

The essence of movement is change. As we move we are constantly changing. In the process of movement change we go on creating our embodied existence. Change is not random or pre-established. It is relational. As we move we are always making connections, building relationships within and among us and the world. Connections created by the use of our body become patterned as we grow. Some patterns, like primitive reflexes, righting reactions, and equilibrium responses, are built in our neuromuscular system. But every human being is physiologically compelled to perform certain bodily developmental tasks to become fully functional and expressive. We all go through a similar progression of movement patterns from lying down to standing up. This progression is largely made possible by the display of fundamental patterns of total body connectivity. They represent a primary level of development and experience. Each one of them organizes a way of relating with oneself and with the world. As development patterns are being established, each individual is forming its experience of interaction with the world, and, consequently, this interaction is included within the body pattern. Although there is a sequence, development is not linear and patterns overlap. There is not a single path for all people; each engaging story is unique and culturally defined. This is Hackney's (2002) idea in a nutshell. Her

work, as a proposal for somatic education is focused on the process of re-patterning (returning to basic patterns to facilitate skill development or technical virtuosity or personal creativity and artistry). My interest, however, is in her description about patterning; I think it opens the door to a dimension of the baby's bodily experience that psychology has not incorporated until now. In this, my first approach, I will consider only some aspects of the first three fundamental patterns (out of six described) and combine them with some concepts mentioned above to draft a comprehensive description of the baby's kinetic experience during the first months. All I present below on fundamental patterns of total body connectivity is taken from Hackney's text.

11.3.1 Breath Pattern

Birth is the entrance to the world of breathing air. The baby fills and empties his body, expands and contracts his whole being on his own, tuning in with his internal body impulse, being an undifferentiated whole. It is the breathing pattern. Breathing is our first experience with internal space. The space in our world is displayed in three dimensions – vertical (up and down), sagittal (forward-backward), and horizontal (side to side). With each breath you may experience changes in all three dimensions. In inhalation, the diaphragm expands the thorax area's three dimensions (the vertical by pushing down the tendon, the horizontal by raising the lower ribs, the sagittal by raising the higher ribs using the spine). During exhalation, the diaphragm movement contracts the three dimensions of the thorax area. Though breathing is involuntarily, it is influenced and is a reflection of changes in consciousness, feelings, and thoughts as these are developed. Therefore it is considered a pattern. In the baby we can assume it is a reflex influenced by arousal changes in performed activities and the stimuli received.

Breathing is a rhythmic movement that contains the phrase's key. Movements happen in phrases. Each individual organizes and sequences their movements within meaningful units. Breathing's round phrasing "inhale-exhale-pause" is the base of voluntary movement phrasing; it organizes all subsequent fundamental patterns. The breathing pattern is the foundation and support base of those coming next. All movements emerging later will organize and find support in the breathing pattern. Breathing also allows a primary experience of being with others. In Bartenieff's fundamentals, in body-mind centering and in the Feldenkrais method (and other methods of somatic education), there are many exercises promoting participation in the "Mind of Breathing" (in the words of Bainbridge Cohen taken up by Hackney). Using breathing as the central organizer of consciousness, moving in such a way that reality's nature is experienced as the pace of the birth pattern organization, and providing bodily knowledge of what it is to be empathically attuned with another person through a breath pattern (walking, dancing, running, quiet). The conscious cultivation of breathing is also recognized in several Eastern disciplines – like t'ai chi – as an important element for attuning individual and universe in a spiritual connection.

We can then imagine a newborn baby in arms, participating in the "mind of breathing" attuned to the other's body breath pattern, living one of his first mutuality experiences where each other's phrased breaths fall into place. The baby is there almost an undifferentiated totality with the other. We can also imagine him awake and alone, leaning against a nonliving surface (which does not provide reciprocal information about his own vitality and experience), tuning in with his inner space and respiratory phrasing. Breathing is a dynamic way of being with himself and with others as an undifferentiated unit. The baby experiences vitality forms in the movement of filling and emptying his body, or in the inhale-exhale-pause original phrasing. When in arms, adult and baby live the same form of vitality in the respira-tory phrase's unity (see next point for an explanation of the concept of vitality forms). Since the baby is unaware of any disturbing consciousness (such as adult conceptual consciousness, the quick and almost permanent flowing of ideas, images, memories), he fully and deeply lives his breathing in open awareness.

11.3.2 Core–Distal Connectivity Pattern

The fundamental pattern of core–distal connectivity or umbilical radiation is one of radial symmetry, with the center of control in the middle of the body. Patterns of flexion and full extension develop in the uterus during the last trimester of intrauterine life and both contribute to the basic postural tone. Being born is experiencing gravity, when the baby is prone there is an increased flexor tone throughout his body, when lying supine there is an increased extensor tone. Both lead the baby to the ground and provide a sense of grounding. The baby feels the connection with the earth. The center's value becomes apparent when holding a newborn: you have to continually hold his head because at any moment he will pull it backwards. But if you pay attention you will see that the movement does not start in the neck but in the navel. And when the baby cuddles in arms one can see that the total bending of the body occurs from the navel. The core–distal pattern holds the basic rhythmic relationship to go inward, toward oneself, and out into the world in an organism with limbs connecting to the center. The baby radiates outward, away from his center, and returns to it. The organized pattern of flexion and extension emerges.

This movement pattern establishes the "twoness" of the "inward-outward" experience as opposed to the "oneness" of the breathing pattern. In the basic patterns of entering and leaving the center, and of breathing, the rate of "input and output" is essential. But there is a difference: breathing organizes our entire body in a fluid form, while the pattern connecting center with limbs is less circular. It resembles a star that presses and releases energy from the center toward the ends. The pattern of becoming concave or convex can be seen as a primary experience of phrase contrast, this means a phrase built in two differentiated parts. In microanalysis of adult movement in contexts of social play, particularly in infant directed performances, adults often build multimodal phrases on movement phrases resembling flowing backgrounds of going to and fro in the sagittal plane (Español & Shifres, 2015). Apparently, when the baby enters into the primordial experience of phrase contrast through this fundamental pattern, adults show and illuminate (by using temporal arts' resources) the same kind of phrase contrast in social interactions.

From the theoretical framework of communicative musicality – very close to this work – Gratier and Trevarthen (2008) describe adult–infant early vocalization exchanges as a nonverbal, musical narrative or a narrative with communicative musicality. They recognize that narratives are typically about something worth telling, about events involving other people that a person feels impelled to recount. But suggest that although baby and mother do not relate events or talk about other people's actions, they construct a nonverbal narrative with contents in the form of "aboutness." In the same way that Jazz musicians describe the feeling of telling something through music, or telling a story when jamming, mother and infant tell something in their vocalization exchanges. "Phrases" – they say – might constitute the events that build narrative. I'm not sure adult–infant exchanges are a narrative. I think that perceiving, creating, and exercising units of meaning is a basic mode of organizing the world and ourselves. And although subsumed to the creation of linguistic, gestural, or musical narratives, it also forms non-narrative non-referring ways of organizing the world. The phrases' value must not be reduced to narrative or reference, both

linked to language and symbol. When thinking in movement, phrasing organizes our corporeal coupling with the world, this means with the earth and those that inhabit it. And that is relevant. Phrase sequence does not necessarily generate narratives; it could result in dance improvisation, scaling a mountain, simple repeated baby movements, or simple vowel exchange sequences. This might make sense in the next section, when I talk about thinking in movement.

11.3.3 Head–Tail Connectivity Pattern

Returning to fundamental patterns, the following is linked to the spinal level. Head and tailbone are the spine's ends; they are in a constant and ever-changing interactive relationship. The spinal movement is organized by differentiating *yield and push* and *reach and pull* patterning. Development is never linear, it occurs in overlapping waves, first the baby learns to yield and push and later to reach and pull in an effective phrasing. During life in the uterus, especially in the last weeks before birth, the spine is primarily flexed. Both, head and tailbone, have chances of being in contact with the uterine wall. The fetus gains proprioceptive knowledge when yielding and pushing against this container, sending messages through the spinal cord from the head to the tailbone and vice versa. When holding or watching a newborn in the cradle one can notice he continues to push the head or the tailbone by elongating and shortening. Some seem to like pushing against the end of the crib. Others seem to climb upwards when resting on their caregiver's chest.

Yielding provides a supporting bond, before pushing for separation. Reaching provides space goal-orientation before pulling. The yield and push pattern relates to grounding and to a sense of self. When resting on our belly and actively yielding the body weight on the ground, passing the weight through the forearms, we feel an immediate confirmation of our embodied existence. When ground and yielding meet, yielding turns into pushing and raising up from the floor is possible. Yielding before pushing connects us with gravity and earth and creates a link behind the eventual separation brought by the push. By pushing, the baby momentarily compresses his body (bones, muscles, and organs), stimulating proprioceptive knowledge about the strength or structure of being. Pushing also empowers getting away, separating the self from the ground or a supporting other; establishing one's own kinesphere, becoming an individual. The yield and push pattern at the spinal level usually develops during the first six months and relates to strength development. It promotes internal attention to heavy and grounded movement. The reach and pull pattern gives us the ability to move in the world, in a space beyond the individual. Attention is focused outwards enabling the baby to move toward the environment. This expands attention and limbs into a space beyond personal. It is the beginning of intended-to-space movement (key to movement in dance), an open door to the possibility of going somewhere or toward someone. The reach and pull pattern involves more outside attention and lighter movements. Yielding and pushing has to do with establishing the kinesphere, reaching and pulling with going through it. Both are linked to the molding of the baby's spine. The spinal curves are different in newborns and adults. Newborn's vigorous kicking and crying during the first months of life develop the muscles needed to produce and stabilize the lumbar curve in its convex direction toward the front. This curve needs to be established for the baby to lift his head up. When the baby throws his arms and legs, turns his head side to side, or lifts it up when he lies down, he is gradually developing the muscles and ligaments that control the secondary curves. From here on, the cervical and lumbar curves, and therefore the ability to support himself, come in response to his desire to see the world, to develop in interaction with the world.

Discriminating between yielding and pushing and reaching and pulling – with their unitary phrasing stated at the spinal level – will continue in all the following fundamental patterns. Reaching (the action of reaching an object) is linked to yielding and pushing and reaching and pulling patterns, and immersed in other fundamental patterns that I will not describe here. But their beginnings are here. Reaching's developmental history – which called much attention in developmental psychology – is bounded by the grasping bias, the desire to mouth a distal object, and other processes described by Thelen summarized in the previous section. But the evolutionary history leading to the motivational cascade starts here. Reaching is not a natural solution to obtain a distal object and bring it to the mouth, or is not only or essentially that. Reaching is a manifestation of the baby's vitality and complex history of blending with the ground and the world. It allows him to rise from the floor and stand on his own, roll, and change positions. It moves him into a direction he finds attractive due to light, temperature, company, or an eye-catching object.

11.4 Thinking in Movement

Developmental psychology has recognized the existence of two modes of thought: the mathematical logical thinking and narrative thinking. Undoubtedly, the second is one of the major reformulations of the linguistic turn. Jerome Bruner (1990) contrasted the narrative to the logical thinking and drew attention to the child's ease or readiness to organize experience narratively. He suggested that the narrative structure is present in social interaction before acquiring its linguistic expression and provides a certain prelinguistic predisposition for meaning. Narrative thinking has referential palatability (Español, 2012), its analysis showed everything there is to language before the child acquires language (protoconversations, protodeclaratives, deictic and symbolic gestures, pretend play).

Sheets-Johnstone (2009) proposes there is a way of thinking that is not "about something," that does not represent something different than itself. This is thinking in movement. She takes improvised dance, particularly contact improvisation, as a paradigmatic example of thinking in movement. She describes it as a continuous flow of movement from an ever-changing kinetic world of possibilities where goal-reaching is not required, where nothing is achieved or fails to be so. And suggests that ways of thinking in movement may differ considerably: it has exploratory-organizational purposes in infancy and aesthetic ones in dance. In both cases it is not necessary to refer to, or to have a verbal level to create meaning. Thinking in movement in infancy creates (does not refer to), among other things, a sense of self as separate and bonded to others, largely thanks to movement's double mode of presence. This means the bimodal nature of self-produced movement – visual and proprioceptive – that allows us to perceive movement from within and from outside.

Sheets-Johnstone links thinking in movement with processes described in current developmental psychology, especially in social cognition's second-person approach. Reciprocity characterizes all of our interpersonal encounters. In these moments of meeting, behavior is influenced by each other's presence. Locating reciprocity in the center of our interpersonal world arises from the adoption of a comprehensive second-person approach on it. The second-person approach is part of the embodiment framework in which the emotional world, the perceptual processes, movement, and action take center stage for the understanding of psychological processes. In this framework, our interpersonal world is mainly based on perceiving others directly, the experience of "making together," and dynamic and reciprocal exchanges. According to Reddy (2008), being in contact with another person presupposes an assembling between exteroception and proprioception:

perceiving someone directing their attention and action to oneself inescapably involves the proprioception of our response to them. Many exteroception/proprioception phenomena reflect movement's dual mode of presence. For example, a baby bringing hands together collects proprioceptive information that allows him to organize his own movements (where to stop moving one hand in order to touch the other) and also receives exteroceptive information (sees his hand passing in front of his eyes). The baby feels and sees how his hands move at exactly the same time and apportioned. On countless occasions he experiences the perfect exteroception/proprioception contingency. It will become a self's invariant that will last a lifetime. It will be faced against the different and repeated noncontingent experience between the exteroception of the other's hand and the proprioception of his own moving hand (or lack of proprioception if not moving) that specifies others (Reddy, 2008, Sheets-Johnstone, 2009). Other cases of thinking in movement that relate to the sense of authorship or agency have been described (a synthesis can be found in Español, 2010, 2012).

I believe that thinking in movement is paying attention to the experience of forms of vitality. Daniel Stern (2010) had set movement at the forefront by saying that the dynamic experience of movement is the original source of psychological life. Movement and its consequent proprioception are the earliest manifestations of being animate, providing a primary sense of aliveness. He proposed a "dynamic pentad" that creates the experience of vitality composed by movement, time, force, space, and direction/intention. A form of vitality is a gestalt, the spontaneous integration of these five elements emerging from holistic experiences. Our minds grasp dynamic events through this pentad. Vitality forms are perceived as felt experiences of temporally contoured moving forces, and a sense of being alive. Forms of vitality outcome form experiences and can be directly observed in another's behavior.

They involve the style in which we make things, the "how." Di Cesare et al. (2013) used functional magnetic resonance imaging (fMRI) finding that the somatosensory-insular-limbic circuit could be under the observers' capacity to understand the vitality forms conveyed by the observed action.

Stern (2010) found in early social play a ground where forms of vitality become evident. Sometimes early social play is almost purely a play on vitality forms (e.g., sudden almost explosive movements when a mother tickles her child). Adults usually play with forms of vitality to avoid the child's habituation and boredom. The result is a theme-and-variation format of vitality forms. The form of repetition-variation helps adults to level, modulate, and play off the baby's arousal as much as themselves. Stern also defends the idea that forms of vitality are a meeting point between early social play and time-based arts: the feelings that run from excitement to quietness, tension to relaxation, characteristic of early social play, are the same feelings that time-based arts such as dance and music express with mastery; and together with early social play they share the same backbone: the repetition-variation form. In early social play, adults manipulate forms of vitality through the repetition-variation form, while the baby participates primarily as a receptor. Recent microanalysis of early social play using analytical categories and analysis methodologies of music performance and movement analysis in contemporary dance (Español & Shifres, 2015) empirically confirm this hypothesis.

Finesse in manipulating or elaborating vitality forms is most likely to be acquired along development, and interactive play is certainly a privileged context for a safe rehearsal. At some point in infancy, early social play turns into forms of vitality play when the child actively wields these vitality forms with repetition and variation. Now child and adult play together with forms of vitality. Forms of vitality play is a pleasant and joy-

ful play frame, where adult and infant elaborate units (or motifs) of movement and/or sound (like moving a spring forward, stretching and shaking it) according to a repetition-variation form. These units are repeated at least twice with variations in the rhythm of sound and movement patterns, in the form, the dynamic or the quality of movement, in melodic contours, sound sonority, dynamics, and timbre. The whole activity unfolds around the varied repetition of sound and movement, making it the core of this activity (Español et al., 2014, 2015).

Original and improvised adult–infant social play are ways of thinking in movement, as are forms of vitality play, proper to the third year of life. Their improvised character and the unattachment to the achieved unity, liken them to contact improvisation. The fundamental patterns of total body connectivity described in the previous point are also ways of thinking in movement. In fact, Bainbridge Cohen (2012) suggests that contact improvisation – the paradigmatic example of thinking in movement – is a recapitulation of early experiences of the baby's movements, which makes it a very enticing form of dance. However, with all these, descriptions happens as with the most recognized embodiment approaches in early development (see Needham and Libertus's [2011] state of the art description on embodiment in early development): they treat specific issues, isolated, without tracing a path or a developmental becoming.

11.5 Conclusion

This work's pledge has been linking developmental psychology to scientific, practice, and experiential understanding of human movement. I think it opens the door to a dimension of the infant's bodily experience that psychology has not incorporated until now. By paying attention to interoceptive, proprioceptive, and kinesthetic qualities of infant's experiences and his states of enhanced connectivity or resonance with others,

I tried to imagine and describe how the mapping of infant embodied awareness develops. According to somatic understanding, the fundamental patterns represent a primary level of development and experience. Each one of them organizes a way of relating with oneself and with the world. I think each one of them can also relate to ways of making contact and having experiences with others. It is what I tried to show in the patterns I described – breathing pattern, core–distal connectivity pattern, and head–tail connectivity pattern.

Each infant movement fundamental pattern is an occasion for learning, expressing feelings, and developing cognition. This is this work's first conclusion. The second one is that shared movements, even the most basic, such as breathing, are an occasion for intersubjective encounter. The third one is that the spirit, as lived in each culture, reaches the baby through movement's vitality forms perceived, received, and shared with others. This is the complex process that molders in socially deprived babies. They are the ontogenetic strokes, the sensible levels of development and experience, which are affected when motor development breaks down in socially deprived babies.

What we have today in psychology is a fragmented, incomplete, and disconnected picture of infant movement development. I think if we incorporate the vision on motor development provided in the field of somatic education (interlaced with the field of dance), if we allow the fundamental patterns to guide our look on infant development, we could have a temporal order where to place particular findings. Those coming from embodiment in early development studies, as well as those coming from cognitive developmental psychology, that are compatible. We could thus be gaining understanding of the baby's experience and his developmental changes, of his full awareness states.

In this chapter, I have only presented a few aspects of some fundamental patterns as described by Hackney. The patterns that follow them could be incorporated and open the proposal to prenatal patterns exposed by Bainbridge Cohen and the complexity of his description of postnatal patterns, which render more explicit its obvious link with vitality forms and the second person approach. If done, I think we would be continuing the enactive program's original proposal. I think we could then expand and transform assembled intuitions we have about thinking in movement in a more precise idea. And maybe aim in that way toward the elaboration of a theory of development.

Acknowledgment

I am grateful to Alberto Rosa who encouraged me to think and write about these issues, and his trust in how it would turn out.

Notes

1 Some current versions retain this trait of origin and point to that experience, far from being an epiphenomenon, it intertwines with being alive and immersed in a world of meaning (Di Paolo, Rohde, & De Jaegher, 2010).
2 It is worth mentioning they distinguish the sense they give to the term "mindfulness" from the non-Buddhist meditative sense used by Ellen Langer to refer to certain widespread practices in today's Western world.

References

Arango, A. M. (2014). *Velo que bonito: Prácticas y saberes sonoro-corporales de la primera infancia en la población afrochocoana* [Look how nice: Sound–body practices and knowledge of early infancy in Afro-Chocoana population]. Bogotá, Colombia: Ministerio de Cultura.

Bainbridge Cohen, B. (2012). *Sensing, Feeling, and Action: The Experiential Anatomy of Body–Mind Centering*. Northampton, MA: Contact Editions.

Bruner, J. S. (1972). Nature and uses of immaturity. *American Psychologist*, 27(8), 687–708.

Bruner, J. S. (1990). *Acts of Meaning*. Cambridge, MA: Harvard University Press.

Di Cesare, G., Di Dio, C., Rochat, M. J., Sinigaglia, C., Brushweiler-Stern, N., Stern, D. N., & Rizzolatti, G. (2013). The neural correlates of "vitality form" recognition: An fMRI study. *Social Cognitive & Affective Neuroscience*, 51(10), 1918–1924.

Di Paolo, E. A., Rohde, M., & De Jaegher, H. (2010). Horizons for the enactive mind: Values, social interaction, and play. In J. Stewart, O. Gapenne, & E. Di Paolo (Eds.), *Enaction: Towards a New Paradigm for Cognitive Science* (pp. 33–87). Cambridge, MA: MIT Press.

Español, S. (2010). Los primeros pasos hacia los conceptos de yo y del otro: La experiencia solitaria y el contacto "entre nosotros" durante el primer semestre de vida [The first steps towards the concepts of self and other: Lonely experience and "between us" contact during the first half of life]. In D. Pérez, S. Español, L. Skidelsky, & R. Minervino (Eds.), *Conceptos: Debates contemporáneos en filosofía y psicología* (pp. 308–334). Buenos Aires: Catálogos.

Español, S. (2012). El desarrollo semiótico [Semiotic development]. In M. Carretero & J. A. Castorina (Eds.), *Desarrollo Cognitivo y Educación: Los inicios del conocimiento* (vol. I, pp. 219–240). Buenos Aires: Paidós.

Español, S. (2014). La forma repetición variación: Una estrategia para la reciprocidad [The repetition-variation form: A strategy for reciprocity]. In S. Español (Ed.), *Psicología de la música y del desarrollo: Una exploración interdisciplinaria sobre la musicalidad humana* (pp. 157–192). Buenos Aires: Paidós.

Español, S., Bordoni, M., Martínez, M., Camarasa, R., & Carretero, S. (2015). Forms of vitality play and symbolic play during the third year of life. *Infant Behavior and Development*, 40, 242–251.

Español, S., Martínez, M., Bordoni, M., Camarasa, R., & Carretero, S. (2014). Forms of vitality play in infancy. *Integrative Psychological and Behavioral Science*, 48(4), 479–502.

Español, S. & Shifres, F. (2015). The artistic infant directed performance: A mycroanalysis of the adult's movements and sounds. *Integrative*

Psychological and Behavioral Science, 49(3), 371–397.

Fagen, R. M. (2011). Play and development. In A. D. Pellegrini (Ed.), *The Oxford Handbook of the Development of Play* (pp. 83–100). Oxford: Oxford University Press.

Feldenkrais, M. (1972). *Awareness Through Movement*. New York: Harper & Row.

Feldenkrais, M. & Beringer, E. (2010). *Embodied Wisdom: The Collected Papers of Moshé Feldenkrais*. Berkeley, CA: North Atlantic Books.

Fogel, A. (1992). Movement and communication in human infancy. *Human Movement Science*, 11(4), 387–423.

Fogel, A. (2013). *Body Sense: The Science and Practice of Embodied Self-Awareness* (Norton Series on Interpersonal Neurobiology). New York: W. W. Norton.

Gratier, M. & Trevarthen, C. (2008). Musical narrative and motives for culture in mother–infant vocal interaction. *Journal of Consciousness Studies*, 15(10), 122–158.

Hackney, P. (2002). *Making Connections: Total Body Integration Through Bartenieff Fundamentals*. New York: Routledge.

Hanna, T. (1986). What is somatics? *Somatics: Magazine-Journal of the Bodily Arts and Sciences*, 5(4). Retrieved from http://somatics.org/library/htl-wis1.

Hanna, T. (1988). *Somatics: Reawakening the Mind's Control of Movement, Flexibility, and Health*. Cambridge, MA: Da Capo Press.

Mamana, S. (2016). Educación somática: Más allá de la propia piel [Somatic education: Beyond one's skin]. *Kiné*, 120, 21.

Needham, A. & Libertus, K. (2011). Embodiment in early development. *Wiley Interdisciplinary Reviews: Cognitive Science*, 2(1), 117–123.

Ospina, V. & Español, S. (2014). El movimiento y el sí mismo [Movement and self]. In S. Español (Ed.), *Psicología de la música y del desarrollo: Una exploración interdisciplinaria sobre la musicalidad humana* (pp. 111–155). Buenos Aires: Paidós.

Rączaszek-Leonardi, J., Nomikou, I., & Rohlfing, K. J. (2013). Young children's dialogical actions: The beginnings of purposeful intersubjectivity. *IEEE Transactions on Autonomous Mental Development*, 5, 210–221.

Reddy, V. (2008). *How Infants Know Minds*. Cambridge, MA: Harvard University Press.

Schmalzl, L., Crane-Godreau, M. A., & Payne, P. (2014). Movement-based embodied contemplative practices: Definitions and paradigms. *Frontiers in Human Neuroscience*, 8, art. 205.

Sheets-Johnstone, M. (2009). *The Corporeal Turn: An Interdisciplinary Reader*. Exeter, UK: Imprint Academic.

Spitz, R. A. (1963). *La première année de la vie de l'enfant* [The first year of the child's life]. Paris: Presses universitaires de France.

Stern, D. N. (1985). *The Interpersonal World of the Infant: A View from Psychoanalysis and Developmental Psychology*. New York: Basic Books.

Stern, D. N. (2010). *Forms of Vitality: Exploring Dynamic Experience in Psychology, the Arts, Psychotherapy and Development*. New York: Oxford University Press.

Thelen, E. (1979). Rhythmical stereotypes in normal humans infant. *Animal Behavior*, 27, 699–715.

Thelen, E. (2000a). Grounded in the world: Developmental origins of the embodied mind. *Infancy*, 1 (1), 3–28.

Thelen, E. (2000b). Motor development as foundation and future of developmental psychology. *International Journal of Behavioral Development*, 24, 385–397.

Thelen, E. (2005). Dynamic systems theory and the complexity of change. *Psychoanalytic Dialogues*, 15 (2), 225–283.

Thelen, E., Corbetta, D., & Spencer, J. P. (1996). The development of reaching during the first year: The role of movement speed. *Journal of Experimental Psychology: Human Perception and Performance*, 22, 1059–1076.

Varela, F. J., Thompson, E., & Rosch, E. (1991). *The Embodied Mind: Cognitive Science and Human Experience*. Cambridge, MA: MIT Press.

12 Object Pragmatics: Culture and Communication – the Bases for Early Cognitive Development

Cintia Rodríguez, Marisol Basilio, Karina Cárdenas, Sílvia Cavalcante, Ana Moreno-Núñez, Pedro Palacios, and Noemí Yuste

In *Doctor Brodie's Report*, the Argentinian writer and literature Nobel Prize winner, Jorge Luis Borges, talks about the Yahoos, a very remote tribe situated in a faraway place. He says that only a very few individuals have names, and that to address one another they fling mud. Because "they lack the capacity to fashion the simplest object," they believe ornaments like gold pins are natural.

To the tribe my hut was a tree, despite the fact that many of them saw me construct it and even lent me their aid. Among a number of other items, I had in my possession a watch, a cork helmet, a mariner's compass, and a Bible. The Yahoos stared at them, weighed them in their hands, and wanted to know where I had found them. They customary reached for my cutlass not by the hilt but by the blade, seeing it, undoubtedly, in their own way, which causes me to wonder to what degree they would be able to perceive a chair. (Borges, 1970/1972, p. 114, translated by Norman Thomas di Giovanni in collaboration with the author)

Beyond the beautiful fiction by Borges, it would be chaotic for humans to relate to one another disregarding the *functional* attributes of objects. Objects are defined by *what they are for* in everyday life. Communicating in a meaningful and functional way implies a regard for their pragmatic aspects, that is, their practical purposes (Groupe μ, 1992). The functional attributes of

objects, obvious to adults, are not so to children in their first months of life. For them, things have no names. They do not see chairs, or everyday objects, for what they are. This has evident consequences for psychological development. Observing children shows that the *same* object can be *used* to do very *different* things. The first thing children usually do with objects is sucking, banging, or throwing them, irrespective of the object. Only gradually do they abandon these undifferentiated noncanonical uses to acquire the cultural uses of the community. *Object* and *use* do not coincide. One thing is the object and another is the use of it.

Because children are not born knowing the functions of objects (as evidenced by how they use them), these functions have to be learned. Here, the *adult guide* the *educational action* – done by parents and teachers, for instance – intervenes through different semiotic systems (language, gestures, intonation, rhythm, uses of objects, and so on). This idea is in tune with one of the most deeply rooted sociocultural maxims: the child does not discover meaning or signifies the world on his/her own. It is evident that to "learn to write, add or use a map, help is needed from other more competent persons who know how to interpret writing, numbers and maps" (Martí, 2003, p. 21). Schooling and educational intervention provide the necessary guidance (Vergnaud, 2013; Saada-Robert, 2012).

There is no reason not to apply these maxims to babies, who are in greatest need of the presence of others. The observation unit to understand the emergence of meaning-making is *adult–child–object triadic (educational) interaction*, which occurs right from the beginning of life. The popular idea that triadic interaction begins at the end of the first year, when children can communicate intentionally with others (Tomasello, 2014), is therefore subject to question. Before then, someone has communicated intentionally with children, providing them significant clues to functionally understand the world. Adults *offer their intentions* by involving children in their own action (Rodríguez, 2006) while cleaning, caring, feeding or interacting freely (Rodríguez, Benassi, et al., 2017). Indeed, adults promote the first triadic interactions in the most diverse scenarios and children take part in them long before they know it. During these early triadic interactions, adults communicate *with* and *about* objects. Language alone does not suffice to generate shared meaning because it is too complex. Objects are not mere external referents, but instruments for communication (see Figure 12.1) that children understand and use before they can speak.

In the first edition of this Handbook, Rodríguez (2007) referred to Bruner's (1975) pragmatics of speech position, opposing Chomsky's formalism and claiming that children learn to speak by *using* language in everyday life. Our objection back then was that applying this pragmatic approach to language alone does not suffice and that objects, too, should be analysed regarding their range of uses in everyday communicative situations. When objects are used, they "come to life" (see with adults in Clark, 2003).

Fortunately the sociocultural paradigm no longer banishes objects from culture or relegates them to "physical reality." The idea of objects having social status is gaining momentum (Kontopodis & Perret-Clermont, 2016; Moro, 2016; Sinha, 2014; Valsiner, 2016; Zittoun, 2010; see also Chapter 6, this volume), resembling, thus, to semiotic systems traditionally considered *cultural*, whether language (Nelson, 2015), images (Sonesson & Lenninger, 2015), calendars for understanding social time (Tartas, 2008), maps (Brizuela & Cayton-Hodges, 2013), or graphic representations of number (Martí, Scheuer, & de la Cruz, 2013).

To assert that children "explore" or "play with" objects during their first years of life is imprecise and absolutely banal. It is necessary to analyze what they do in everyday life with objects and instruments, how and what for they use them, and with what degree of semiotic complexity. In this chapter we will deal with the diversity and development of first uses of objects (and instruments) from a pragmatic perspective. The role of the adult is also addressed.

We will begin with *functional, canonical uses*. If objects and instruments are used with specific functions (the bottle to drink, the spoon to eat, the cradle to sleep, etc.), we must ask: How do children appropriate them? How do they get to canonical uses of objects? Using objects by their function means they become permanent. This permanence is *functional*, pragmatic, and shared with others. This does not coincide with the "physical" object permanence proposed by Piaget, and the competent baby paradigm (see discussion in Rodríguez, 2012). We will conclude this section by suggesting a possible relation between the functional permanence and the origin of concepts.

Rhythmic-sonorous uses occur when children produce sound with objects. They are the most basic uses along with undifferentiated *noncanonical uses* (such as sucking or throwing any object). Even though developmental psychology has reserved an important place for rhythm in studies on early dyadic intersubjective interactions, few studies have investigated the rhythmic-sonorous characteristics of adult–baby–object triadic interactions.

When children know social uses of objects, they share with the adult a common ground that becomes a base for more complex uses (linked to new forms of communication). That is the case of *symbolic uses*. They are "traveling uses" referring to momentarily absent situations performed out of context that are neither effective nor efficient. There is a debate about the origin of symbols. Here, we argue that the root of symbolic uses is found in the functional uses of objects. Without that socially shared base, it would be impossible to comprehend children (and adults!) when they use an object as another, or when they change their attributes.

We will also mention *metacanonical uses*. They are uses that, as symbols, are rooted in functional or canonical uses. Here, the object is momentarily used in an efficiency way to do something functional for which it was not conceived. Thus, the object "breaks in" a function that does not belong to it. For example, using a chair, instead of a stair, to reach a book on a very high shelf. They are very creative uses. They corroborate that *object* and *use* do not coincide. *Metacanonical uses* confirm that it would be very strange that every specific use could only be realized with a unique object.

Another consequence of knowing functional uses is that children become able to *self-regulate* and correct themselves when they have difficulties with *these uses*. This fact has important consequences. The first is that language cannot continue to be considered the first nor the unique instrument of self-regulation. Although within the "semiotic approach" of sociocultural psychology, language is *the* privileged semiotic system (Vygotski, 1934/1985; Rivière, 1985; Bronckart, 2002), while gestures and uses are now recognized for their self-regulation utility. This confirms that executive functions are functional from the end of the first year of life, before language occupies the hegemonic place.

We will end with *numerical uses*. There is an important debate between advocators of the competent baby paradigm, which consider that children are born with the concept of number (core knowledge), and who defend more constructivist and sociocultural approaches that state number is the result of a complex process of construction. In this process, the communicative and educative influence of the adult cannot be ignored.

12.1 How do Children Learn to Use Objects According to their Function?

This is the first question that needs to be answered.

To do that it is important to distinguish between *object* and *uses* of the object. Adults, who no longer remember how they learned to relate functionally to objects, consider both things equivalent. Adults automatically see objects according to their practical purposes. Upon seeing a chair they think: "I can sit on it"; a cup: "I can drink from it"; a spoon: "I can eat with it." If they sit on chairs or drink from cups, it is not because they make an individual decision, or randomly discover their function, but because it is what their ancestors have done for ages. These are ancient objects, manufactured with a clear purpose (Tilley et al., 2006), they are part of the cultural practices that transcend individual decisions, that is, socially conveyed knowledge. During ontogenesis, children have to acquire this knowledge, internalize the objects' social rules of use. Our first step was to study this process.

In the first edition (Rodríguez, 2007), we described the longitudinal study in which six Spanish children (Rodríguez & Moro, 1999) and six Swiss children (Moro & Rodríguez, 2005) were observed in their homes at 7, 10, and 13 months of age, interacting with their mothers, a replica telephone and a shape sorter truck.[1]

Children performed three types of uses: (1) *non canonical*, (2) *protocanonical*, and (3) *functional* or *canonical*. Despite the various efforts by their mothers, children at seven months never used *those* objects according to their function, that is, canonically. They did not interpret their mothers' intentions when pointed at and touched the hole through which the blocks were meant to fit in the shape sorter. The children also performed *protocanonical* uses when "riding" on the adult's functional action as a consequence of the *magnet effect*: the adult's action on the object was like a "powerful magnet" to the child, who stretched his/her hands toward it. Some *canonical*, or functional, uses were performed at 10 months and increased at 13 months, by which time the children also understood the mothers' intentions when they used gestures (see Dimitrova & Moro, 2013 on the relationship between understanding adult gestures and object function).

Adults did not behave as though children learned by "direct" imitation (if they had done so, they would have repeated the canonical use over and over). Their actions were diverse and adjusted to the children's actions, first stressing ostensive interventions[2] (with gestures or uses in which the objects were always *part of the communicative act*) and subsequently, invitations. Adults also performed many gestures of varying degrees of semiotic complexity, of which the most efficacious were *ostensive gestures* (*sign* and *referent* coincide) such as *showing, giving*, or *placing* objects to children (Rodríguez et al., 2015). Adults also realized pointing gestures, either touching or keeping a distance to the referent.

An important insight derived from these studies is that when children use objects canonically, it is because they have acquired a type of *functional permanence*, shared with the community. This permanence is not the same as Piaget's (physical) permanence of the object, or as the permanence recently proposed by supporters of the "competent baby" (Rochat, 2012; Karmiloff-Smith, 2012). Functional permanence allows objects to be considered not as unique specimens, but as members of classes. Know-

ing the canonical use of cups and telephones implies using *any* cup as a cup, *any* telephone as a telephone (see discussion in Rodríguez, 2012). This does not seem farfetched if we consider that objects in daily life are functionally permanent to adults, who relate to children on the basis of this assumption.

Functional permanence may be a pragmatic link in the origin of concepts.[3] If first concepts, relative to the function of objects, are rooted in socially shared everyday meanings, they may arise as a product of educative interactions, and functional uses may play a major role in their development.

12.2 Rhythmic-Sonorous Uses of Objects

Rhythm is ubiquitous in children's lives from the moment of birth. Piaget (1936/1977) referred to rhythm in the movements of his newborn children. Rhythm is such an essential feature of baby–adult interaction (Papoušek, 1996; Trevarthen, 2003; Reddy, 2008, 2012; Trehub, 2003) that if it was stripped away not much would be left (Perinat, 1993; see also Chapter 11, this volume). A classic example is the way mothers rock their children making use of babies' pauses while nursing (Kaye, 1982/1986). Considering biological rhythms, such as breathing tempo, heart rate, or intensity of body movements, and consistently acting according to them, improves adult–child interaction (Foster & Kreitzman, 2004). All that is very helpful with hospitalized infants in music therapy sessions (Del Olmo, Rodríguez, & Ruza, 2010).

However, "triadic rhythms", when there is an object between the adult and the child, have gone unnoticed. Adults do not present objects to children "anyhow", but in an organized, rhythmic manner, often adding sonority (Rodríguez & Moro, 2008).[4] The rhythmic-sonorous components facilitate making the objects shared referents. Triadic rhythmic interactions start very

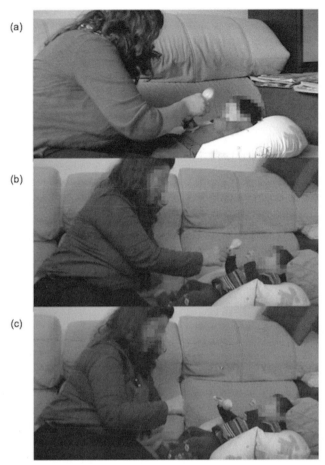

Figure 12.1 Triadic interaction. L. (age two months) pays
attention to her mother's rhythmic-sonorous use of the rattle
and begins to use it herself according to function (Moreno-
Núñez, Rodríguez, & del Olmo, 2017). (a) At two months,
L. pays attention to the ostensive gesture of the rattle when
presented by her mother. The rattle is both sign and referent at
the same time. (b) At four months, L. holds the rattle offered by
her mother. (c) L. shakes it slightly while watching her mother.

early (sometimes even as early as at age one
or two months[5]), when the adult communicates
intentionally by presenting and using objects *for*
the child, sharing the same referent (see Figure
12.1), and introducing the child in "his own finalized action". These joint actions clearly illustrate
how the adult introduces the child to the functional use of the object long before the child takes

any initiative him/herself. Before knowing it, the
child is already a "user according to function"
when the adult "lends his/her intentions".

Rhythmic-sonorous uses (along with noncanonical uses) are the first uses of objects that
children perform without the help of others. As
shown in Figure 12.1, by four months, children
start using rattles according to its function, by

shaking them and producing sound. These are the first instances, however rudimentary, of an instrument being used according to its social function. By six months, children are active agents, seeking and producing sounds with any object. And 7-month-olds produce sounds by banging objects together. At 10 months children are "skillful percussionists" (Rodríguez & Moro, 1999).

Rhythmic-sonorous uses deserve special attention for two other reasons: (1) because very little is known about musical development during the first years of life, and (2) because rhythm may be a basic ingredient for cultural (canonical, symbolic, self-regulatory, metacanonical or numerical) uses of objects in general.

12.3 Symbolic Uses of Objects: What is Their Relationship to Functional Uses?

Another milestone in early development is when children produce symbols, representing absent objects or situations with differentiated signifiers (Bronckart, 2012; Español, 2004; Martí, 2012; Rivière, 1990). There is plenty of literature on symbols, nevertheless, several questions remain, such as in what previous meanings are they rooted. For instance, according to Leslie (1987) and Baron-Cohen and Swettenham (1996) previous meanings are literal. Piaget claims that there is no need for previous conventions. Symbols are solitary products, although he does not explain how he managed to understand his children (Piaget, 1945/1976; Belsky & Most, 1981; McCune, 1995). Another position that is gaining ground is that the child requires meanings agreed on with others regarding objects as the basis for symbolic uses (Barthélémy-Musso, Tartas & Guidetti, 2013; Rodríguez, 2006; Vygotski, 1931/1995a; Wallon, 1942/1970; Zittoun, 2010).

Another unresolved issue is that of similarity between symbol and referent. The dominant position (explicit or implicit) is Piaget's (1945/1976), which claims that similarity exists

between objects (signifier and signified). However, according to Vygotski (1931/1995b) similarity is not perceptual (related to how objects look) but *functional* (related to *how objects are used*). This is a key point because canonical – functional – uses of objects may be the root of symbolic uses.[6] Similarity should be found between *uses* (canonical and symbolic), not between objects (Rodríguez et al., 2014).

Developmental psychology is not conclusive regarding the emergence of first symbols. What are the minimum requirements for a given behavior to be considered symbolic? According to the prevailing position, there needs to be substitution of one object by another (El'konin, 1966; Leslie, 1987; Lillard et al., 2013; Piaget, 1945/1976; Tomasello, 1999), for instance, when pretending to "eat with a pencil" (where the pencil represents the spoon). However, it seems difficult to claim that "eating" with an empty spoon is not symbolic because it is the same spoon with which eating is effectively performed.

Following Vygotski, the functional uses of objects seem good candidates as anchor points for symbols. To pretend one is eating with an empty spoon, or one is talking on a replica mobile telephone, one needs to know that spoons are used for eating and mobile telephones for talking. The conventional rules of use arise from "genuine" objects, from where they "transfer" and are applied to (1) situations different from the everyday, such as "eating" with an empty spoon out of context (level 1); (2) to different objects, by substitution, such as "eating" with a pencil (level 2); (3) without an object, with the empty hand representing the spoon (level 3); and (4) narratives of symbols in action, when several symbols are linked (level 4) (Palacios et al., 2016).

Symbolic and canonical uses differ in that canonical uses must be *efficacious* (if one eats with a spoon, the contents must reach the mouth without spilling), and *efficient* (if possible, without dirtying oneself), whereas symbolic uses need not be – no one gets dirty while *pretending* to eat. How does this "functional knowledge" affects the origin of symbols? The adult as a guide plays an important role in this process. But we do not know of any studies on how children construct their first symbols in triadic interaction with adults, even though the need to study this topic has been widely recognized (Adamson, Bakeman, & Deckner, 2004; Carpendale & Lewis, 2004, Göncü & Gaskins, 2011).

In various triadic interaction studies with children with typical[7] and atypical development, adults communicate using objects symbolically long before children do. And that works! Children pay attention and include themselves in the adults' symbolic scenarios. The first symbols (the more frequent ones) occur with the same object with which canonical use is made (level 1). Although they are "very close" to canonical uses, they are still symbols because they are abbreviated and lack the efficacy of the missing elements. Nevertheless, symbols by substitution (level 2) or without material support (level 3) are not usual. Sometimes adults correct "inadequate" children symbols, such as "drinking" from a plastic replica horse (see observations in Palacios et al., 2016).

Children also perform the first and most frequent symbolic uses with the same object of the canonical use (level 1). A very interesting example happens with the instrument spoon. The symbolic use (Palacios et al., 2016) is very different from the functional one when they effectively eat with it (Ishiguro, 2016; Rodríguez, Estrada, et al., 2017).

The low percentage of symbols by substitution and *in absentia* shows the complexity of transferring the rule of use to other objects or without material support, suggesting that rules for canonical uses disengage gradually from the niche where they first arose, in order to be "transferred" (to other objects or to no object).

Knowing whether or not a child produces symbols (their first manifestations should be identified) is important in typical development, and even more so in children with *different developmental paths*, for example, autism or Down syndrome. This information may help to guide the actions of child educators and early childcare professionals. Since children with Down syndrome tend to have delayed language development, nonverbal communication works as a strategy to compensate their linguistic deficits (Jackson-Maldonado, Badillo, & Aguilar, 2010). It is thus highly relevant to understand prelinguistic semiotic systems, including symbols.

In general, more variability was observed in the symbolic uses of children with Down syndrome[8] than in typically developing children. In triadic situations with their mothers, they performed their first symbolic uses between 12 and 21 months' chronological age (Cárdenas, Rodríguez, & Palacios, 2014), much earlier than usually mentioned in the literature (mental age is considered to enable comparison with typically developing children).

The diversity and complexity of symbols performed may be influenced by the greater or lesser complexity of the proposals from adults. It is important for the adult to know what the child is able to do, to promote increasingly complex uses (see Figure 12.2). Knowledge of each individual should prevail over any stereotypical belief about "what children with Down syndrome can or cannot do" at early ages (Cárdenas, 2012, p. 232).

It is well known that peer interaction provides an important source of learning at nursery school (Amorim, dos Anjos, & Rossetti-Ferreira, 2012; Li, 2012). It could be thought that the specific object is irrelevant in the production of symbols, however, this is not true. In a study carried out at the nursery school about peer interaction,[9] it became apparent that with replica objects, children aged 11 months already produced symbols with the same object of the functional use (level 1). What is noteworthy here is that the observed symbolic level remained simple. Children aged 15–24 months did not perform more complex symbols by substitution or

(a)   (b)   (c)

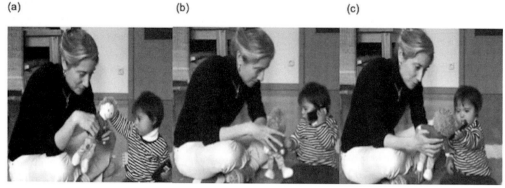

Figure 12.2. V. interacting with her mother performing symbolic uses of objects (Cárdenas, Rodríguez, Miranda-Zapata and Palacios, forthcoming). (a) At 21 months old, V. with DS offering the doll to her mother. (b) V. "talking" on the telephone. (c) V. positioning the mobile phone near the doll for it to "talk."

without material! Replica objects did not reflect children's more advanced symbolic ability. One possible explanation is that replica objects facilitate the first symbols at 11 or 12 months, but may limit higher symbolic levels later on. These objects are "strongly marked" and it is difficult to turn them into something else.

In an ongoing study on 20 children, aged 11 to 21 months, everyday artifacts were added (Yuste, Rodríguez & de los Reyes, forthcoming). Preliminary results show that 11-month-olds with an expert peer perform symbolic uses (level 1) with replica objects. At 13, 15, 17, 18, and 21 months, they produce more complex symbols (level 2 by substitution and level 3 *in absentia*), but *only with artifacts*. These first results seem to confirm the "ceiling effect" of replica objects. The type of object seems to influence the symbolic level achieved by children who do not yet talk. This important finding needs to be explored further on.

We will finish the section by referring to *metacanonical uses*. Halfway between canonical and symbolic uses are the *metacanonical uses*, which are efficacious and efficient, like canonical uses, but performed with objects or instruments which were not designed for that purpose. They are "creative uses" very frequent in everyday life. Children begin to perform them during the sec-

ond year of life when they apply, through generalization, the rule of canonical use to any object which enables an efficacious result. One example was observed with a 13-month-old child (Rodríguez & Moro, 1999). During the recording session he used the shape sorter effectively and a few minutes later went to the kitchen and showed the hollow plastic block to the mother, asking her to fill it with water, thus *doubling the use* of the plastic block as a *cup*. This was not a symbol since the child was not pretending to drink from the shape, but rather wanted to use it as a functional cup to hold real water.

12.4 Functional Uses of Objects and Executive Functions before Language

In the sociocultural tradition, language is *the* instrument of self-regulation (see Winsler, 2009, for a review). Vygotski dedicated much attention to private speech due to its "transitional" status between *communication* with others, and self-regulation or *communication* with *oneself*. Katherine Nelson (2015) recently studied the "crib speech" of children alone in their cot before sleeping. She considers it "private in a double sense (1) being addressed to the self (2) with no one else present" (p. 172). Self-regulation comes from the internalization of semiotic tools employed previously with others (Wertsch, 1979; Wood, Bruner, & Ross, 1976; Tartas, Perret-Clermont, & Baucal, 2016). Luria (1979) develops this tradition in neuropsychology: the prefrontal cortex and other neurological systems form interactive – not modular – functional systems, which enables conscious regulation of one's own behavior.

Now, is language the first and unique instrument for cognitive self-regulation? Can other previous semiotic systems serve that purpose? If the answer to the second question is "yes," we must say *which* and *from when* they are functional.

There is increasing support within the sociocultural paradigm for the idea that private gestures are used for self-regulation and may be precursors for self-regulation through language (Delgado, Gómez & Sarriá, 2009, 2011). Children direct pointing gestures toward themselves with a private, contemplative function (Bates, Camaioni & Volterra, 1975) before pointing to others (Carpendale & Carpendale, 2010). Symbolic and aesthetic self-directed gestures (Español, 2006), such as shaking the head to forbid and signs taught in nurseries as part of the Baby Signs Program (Vallotton, 2008), may also serve for self-regulation.

Besides, if children already know the functional uses of some objects of their everyday life, we should ask what place do this knowledge has within the first forms of cognitive self-regulation when, for instance, they have difficulties with the functional use to which they hope to arrive. The timing of the first manifestations of executive functions (end of the first year of live) (Zelazo & Müller, 2004) fits very well with the idea that gestures and objects can serve a function for self-regulation before language.

In a longitudinal case study with N., a child with Down syndrome, on the last day of recording, when N. was 18 months old, an interesting situation took place. As N. could not insert a ring on a vertical pivot, she began producing self-directed gestures *before* attempting the complex use, without asking her parents for help. We published a paper dealing exclusively with this observation session (Rodríguez & Palacios, 2007). In a detailed analysis we identified these behaviors as *private gestures* (ostensive gestures and immediate pointing gestures) with a self-regulatory purpose. As she was unable to achieve her aim – placing ring on the stick – she corrected again and again. And although she did not say anything during the session, there was no doubt that she was attempting to use the object according to its function. There was also no doubt that she *knew what the function* was, but had difficulties regarding *how* to do it. It had become a cognitive challenge, which is why she sought various solutions with private gestures *before* attempting it repeated times.[10] Language, therefore, is neither the first nor the only instrument for cognitive self-regulation.

Instruments can also be used for self-regulation. Two recent studies on children 11 to 18 months old (Basilio & Rodríguez, 2011; 2016) showed once again that triadic interactions with complex objects and instruments[11] provide scenarios that are highly appropriate for triggering self-regulatory behavior with preverbal signs. In both studies, we observed children's use of *private gestures* (ostensive, indexical, and symbolic gestures), supporting previous preliminary evidence suggesting that these gestures may be the early precursors of private speech.

Moreover, the conventional uses of these objects allow researcher to interpret children's semiotic productions reliably in relation to the regulation of their actions when using the objects conventionally. For example, if a child is attempting to put a ball through a hole with a hammer, tries several times but fails, and at that moment the child extends her arm to *show* the hammer to her father, one can interpret such *ostensive gesture* as a *request for help* (Basilio & Rodríguez, 2011; see also Moreno-Núñez, Rodríguez, &

(a)   (b)

(c)   (d)

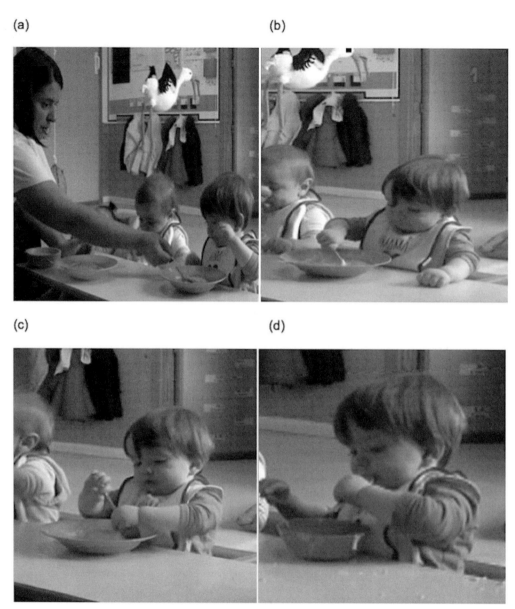

Figure 12.3 Self-regulation with private gestures and protocanonical uses. At 11-month-old, I. self-regulates with *private gestures* and *protocanonical uses* until he is able to use the spoon according to function. His teacher presents a challenge, which the child accepts. (a) The teacher *places* the spoon in the plate: "How about it?" She confronts him with a new challenge. (b) After grasping the spoon, I. performs *protocanonical uses*, sliding the spoon left to right and right to left as he seeks the right position to fill it. (c) I. seeks the position through *private ostensive* gestures with the spoon. He alternates *protocanonical uses* and *private gestures*. (d) He finally manages to eat with the spoon – *functional use* – with the dessert. He achieves the aim set for him with the puree. Source: Rodríguez, Estrada, et al., 2017.

Miranda-Zapata, forthcoming). It is the precise circumstance of the performance of the gesture in relation to the use of the object (Rodríguez, 2009) which gives an observer the grounds for interpreting the cognitive function of this communicative behavior. Asking for help is a widely accepted behavior interpreted as a self-regulatory control strategy. It implies knowledge of how (a) the goal has not been achieved, (b) the current strategy is not working therefore a different one is needed, (c) that someone knows how to achieve the goal, and (d) how to communicate this request. Not only did children self-regulate with private gestures, but they could also do so in communicative situations such as this.

We shall conclude this section with a case study of a child (I.) aged 11 months and 9 days, regarding the first manifestations of executive functions at mealtime at the nursery school[12] (Rodríguez, Estrada, et al., 2017). Child I. manages to eat with the spoon after a laborious process of self-regulation. He knows that spoons are for eating, but at the beginning of the session, he does not know *how* to do it himself. After asking his teacher with gestures (symbolic, pointing, emotional) to feed him (as usual) and faced by her refusal (she challenges him by *placing* the plate of puree and the spoon within his reach, "How about it?"), I. begins a series of increasingly successful approaches to the goal he is given: to eat alone, without help, using the spoon (see Figure 12.3). The first obstacle is how to hold the spoon *to* eat, anticipating its future use (11-month-olds do not have problems with holding objects), and he performs successive *attempts* at *holding*. He tells himself that "he is hungry" with private symbolic gestures of "eating." After much hesitation and attempts at holding, he manages to pick up the spoon. The next obstacle is how to fill it with puree. He self-regulates with *private ostensive gestures* (changes the hand holding the spoon repeatedly, looking at it carefully, in order to find the best position), with *private pointing gestures* and *protocanonical* uses

with the spoon – dragging it horizontally left to right, right to left, inside and outside the dish, constantly approaching the goal. Finally, and without seeking any help (rejecting it when the teacher tries to guide his hand to his mouth), he manages to eat dessert with the spoon.

This case illustrates that executive functions begin at the end of the first year of life (Zelazo & Müller, 2004), and material objects (here, an instrument) are protagonists in this process through self-directed gestures and uses. We join the voices claiming the need to study self-regulation and executive functions in their sociocultural contexts (Moro, 2012; Müller & Kerns, 2015).

12.5 From the Uses of Objects in Interaction with an Adult to Numerical Uses

There is an open debate since the 1980s regarding whether babies possess or not early numerical abilities. According to the advocators of the competent baby paradigm (Spelke, 2000), the baby would come equipped with the concept of number as a core knowledge. However, children aged 3 or 4 have many difficulties to functionally use numbers (Martí, Scheuer, & de la Cruz, 2013). There is, therefore, the following paradox. If children are so competent at birth and already have the concept of numbers: Why are they such slow learners and such clumsy users of numbers (even with small quantities) in everyday life situations, between two and four years of age? (see discussion in Rodríguez & Scheuer, 2015).

Part of the debate on the use of numbers is related to the fact that only what is segmented can be counted (what is continuous cannot be counted). It also relates to *what to* count and *for what* to count. This seems trivial, but without practical and pragmatic aims, why would children want to use numbers?

It is very striking what we found in a study. At 24 months, the children could not have

(a)

(b)

Figure 12.4 Numerical uses of objects. P. interacting with his mother, performing the pony task at ages 27 and 33 months. (a) The mother points at/touches the dots to quantify them rhythmically (ooone, twooo, . . .), while the child, at 27 months, watches his mother's demonstration. (b) Six months later, the mother guides P.'s hand to point at/touch each dot, while P., aged 33 months, accompanies the action rhythmically with numerical words (ooone, twooo, . . .). Source: Cavalcante & Rodríguez, 2015.

comprehended the aim of the game – a "pony" (replica) was "hungry" (see Figure 12.4) and had to reach "food" (represented by a bottle top) at the end of a "road" (represented by a strip of rubber) – without some conventional-symbolic understanding enabling them to accept all that (Cavalcante & Rodríguez, 2015).[13]

The aim was to "feed" the "hungry" pony by (1) rolling the die, (2) counting the dots, and (3) moving the pony forward along the road by the number of squares indicated by the die, until it

reached the "food." At 24 months of age, children had serious difficulties *with* the *numerical part* of the task, despite the enormous help of their mothers. Children used the die as a "projectile" to knock the pony down, as a "seat" for the pony, or took the pony directly to the "food," without ever resorting to numbers either to count the dots on the die or the squares on the road.

They also had difficulties counting the dots of the die. And when they achieved that, they had problems in *using* the numerical information to count the squares of the road where the pony was meant to advance. There was a misalignment between both things.

Nevertheless, in the last session, at 36 months of age, they used the die conventionally, or counted the dots, to regulate the pony's progress along the squares. Between the first and last sessions, the children gradually understood the rules of the game and the conventional – numerical – uses of the objects.

In most studies on this subject, children resolve tasks alone (Martí, Scheuer, & de la Cruz, 2013). In our study,[14] children received help from their mothers. We analyzed the use of objects and gestures performed by the children at ages 24, 27, 30, 33, and 36 months and their mothers. We do not know of any other longitudinal studies on numbers in triadic interaction (Cavalcante, 2016; Cavalcante & Rodríguez, 2015).

Particularly interesting was the *new function of pointing gestures*[15] as a support for counting (Graham, 1999; Schaeffer, Eggleston, & Scott, 1974). The mothers and children pointed at (usually by touching) and accompanied by a numerical word, the dots on the dice and the squares on the road *to* count (see Figure 12.4). This new use of the pointing gesture highlights the fact that any entity, which is counted, must be treated as a *single*, segmented, item (Fuson, 1988), with one-to-one correspondence (Gelman & Gallistel, 1978).

Another striking observation was that mothers pointed at and touched the dots on the die while *rhythmically* saying, "ooone, twooo, three, and fooour," for example (see Figure 12.4). *Rhythmic-sonorous* aspects were key to ensuring correspondence between numerical words, dots, and the pony's progress along the squares. Some children did it at 30 months. Sometimes children and mothers performed joint actions, for example, one pointing and the other counting (Cavalcante & Rodríguez, 2015). Adults' multimodal interventions (language, gestures, uses of objects) were essential for "anchor-ing" the numerical system in prior semiotic systems (that children could understand and employ).

In short, success in children's play with the die suggests that the numerical uses of objects are based on semiotic systems previously constructed with adults. These results question seriously the nativist approach to numbers.

12.6 Conclusions

As everybody knows, in their first years of life children do not communicate as adults do. It is also obvious that children and adults differ in the way they use objects.

There is a great amount of research devoted to communicative and linguistic development; the same does not apply with objects. One important reason is that psychology often has *naturalized* the material world, considering objects as the "physical reality," with only physical properties. Often psychology has ignored that humans use objects in the everyday life according to their function, to their pragmatic properties. Fortunately, this reasoning is changing. Voices are gaining ground within the sociocultural psychology field reclaiming a social status of objects as part of the material culture (Moro & Muller Mirza, 2012; Sinha, 2014, see also Chapter 1, this volume).

The same happens within the ecological perspectives. Alan Costall (2012) for instance, refers to *canonical* or *cultural affordances*. They differ from *affordances* (Gibson, 1979/2014) in that cultural factors influence canonical affordances. Culture in chimpanzees gain further ground, for example, when they use or make instruments or convey techniques to new generations (Goodall, 1990).

To say children "explore" objects is absolute banal. Children only "explore" objects when they realize noncanonical uses. When they do not know the rules of use and do with objects what they physically allow.

In this chapter, we have examined the following *cultural* uses: *rhythmic-sonorous, protocanonical, canonical or functional, symbolic, metacanonical, uses with a self-regulatory function, and numerical uses*. These uses are linked between them. Their development during the firsts years of life is spectacular. Their presence, as a cascade, follows a developmental "ordered" path.

Canonical or functional uses have a pivotal status. Once children use objects by their function, according to specific rules, in the everyday life, they become permanent by their function. This means they are not unique exemplars, as they become *members of classes*. And the community of users shares classes (any spoon belongs to the class of the spoons, any telephone, any house, any car belong to a class and we know it as users). If first concepts are related to this "everyday doing things in an user's community," functional permanence may be a pragmatic link in the origin of concepts (Rodríguez, 2015). Once an object has functional permanence and becomes a member of a class, the door is open to *new* and *more complex uses*. If children and adults understand symbolic uses, it is because there is similarity between uses (symbolic and canonical), not between objects. The same happens with metacanonical uses. Symbolic uses, metacanonical uses, numerical uses, and self-regulation are based in a way or on another in this functional knowledge.

More complex forms of communication arise with *symbolic, metacanonical, self-regulating*, and *numerical uses*. We have stressed several things about the cultural uses.

(1) Infants produce rhythmic-sonorous uses (the most basic cultural ones) owing to adults' interventions. As we have shown, they might appear as early as two months of age. They are users before knowing it, in joint action scenarios, when the other offers her/his intentions and introduces him/her into a functional material universe. They know it later in development. First triadic interactions start at the beginning. And little by little children take the initiative through their first year of life.

(2) Adults also realize cultural uses – *rhythmic-sonorous, canonical or functional, symbolic, metacanonical, numerical uses*, and so on – *for* children. When children can do them, both adults and children take part in a *common ground* of meanings in the everyday life.

(3) This common ground affects *how they communicate*. Everybody knows that. Once children use spoons to eat, adults adapt their tools of communication to this functional shared knowledge. The communicative scenario is very explicit when adults present the spoon for the first time to children: gestures, diverse demonstrations of use, invitations, suggestions, challenges, and so on, will be part of it. Shared knowledge between adults and children about the function of objects and instruments impacts communicative intention.

(4) When an adult uses an object *for* the child, the *object used* (regardless of the use) is part of the communicative act. This use is a referent and a sign at the same time. This means that objects can be part of the communicative act. The same happens with children. When adults and children use objects, they communicate with each other. This is essential when objects have no names yet for children. All that is part of the "life of objects."

In conclusion, objects are social in a double sense, because (a) they are part of the material culture, and (b) often they are part of the communicative act. This implies that objects need to be included as protagonists in a pragmatic turn that considers seriously what happens in the everyday life with them.

Acknowledgments

This chapter has been written with the support of the Ministry of Economy of Spain (EDU2015–64129-P MINECO: FEDER). We would like to thank Alberto Rosa for very valuable comments on previous drafts of the chapter.

Notes

1 Other common denominators among the studies addressed in this chapter are: (1) longitudinal design, (2) naturalistic settings (participants' homes or room at nursery school), (3) all interactions observed were triadic: adult–child–object (or sometimes child–object–child); the instructions were "play with your child as you usually do," and (4) they all used micro-genetic analyses.

2 Adults performed distant demonstrations (i.e., using the object itself to communicate about the object), immediate demonstrations (involving children directly in the uses), and preparations and adjustments (to facilitate use). This resulted in episodes of *joint action* as from seven months of age.

3 Rosch, known for her theory of prototypes, recently proposed an "ecological" theory for the ordinary use of concepts: "concepts, categories and other conceptualisations are participating parts in life games" (Rosch 2009, p. 202, cited in Duque & Packer, 2014).

4 In a longitudinal study on three parents and their children at ages two, four, and six months, at home, parents and children were given three rings containing beads (which rattled when shaken) and three hollow rings (which did not rattle). Adults preferred the rattling rings and performed many *rhythmic-sonorous uses* which helped segment and organize their own action *for* the child. At four and six months, children paid close attention both to the adult and to their own actions. The *magnet effect* occurred when children stretched their arms out towards the adult's action, triggering episodes of *joint action*. By six months, children were active agents, seeking and producing sounds themselves (Moreno-Núñez, Rodríguez & del Olmo, 2015).

5 In another study (Moreno-Núñez, Rodríguez & del Olmo, 2017), children at two, three, and four months old were offered a very light rattle (see Figure 12.1) of which the functional use is sonorous. Mothers *showed* the rattle (ostensive gestures are the simplest, as sign and referent are the same) often at all three ages. They *gave* it to their children more often as age increased from two to four months, inviting the children to be agents. Adult rhythmic-sonorous structured uses (with pauses) were more frequent than nonstructured (without pauses). Structured uses enabled children to become involved and pay more attention. Nonstructured uses occurred more frequently at two months, when children have greater difficulty in becoming involved in the adult's action. At two months, parents tapped the rattle directly on the child's body (immediate demonstrations). They did less often at three and four months. However, they placed the rattle in the child's hand and performed *joint* rhythmic-sonorous *uses* at two months, increasing at three and four months. The children were very active and nearly all of them held the rattle given to them by the adult as from two months. Some of them did so on their own initiative at three months.

6 At another level, according to Alessandroni (2016), the emergence of metaphorical though does not proceed from a transparent world, but it is an emergent result from prelinguistic cultural semiotic systems.

7 In two longitudinal studies on Spanish children at ages 9, 12, and 15 months (Palacios & Rodríguez, 2015) and Mexican children at ages 9, 12, 15, and 18 months (Palacios et al., 2016), dyads were allowed to interact freely with 10 everyday objects: *replica objects* – rag doll, plastic horse and mobile telephone; *artifacts* (human-made objects) – empty pot of skin cream, lighter, toothbrush, rag, empty cardboard box with a string attached to one end, and wooden spoon; and a *natural object* – a rock. Adults performed symbols to communicate with 9-month-olds. They created scenarios, delimiting structure, content, and objects involved. Most of the symbols were level 1: using the *same* object involved in functional use.

8 In two longitudinal studies using the same objects, a similar pattern was observed in children with Down syndrome – chronological ages 12 to 21 months (Cárdenas, 2012; Cárdenas, Rodríguez & Palacios, 2014; Cárdenas et al., forthcoming). The first symbolic uses were performed with the referent object, e.g., "eating" with an empty spoon or

"talking" on the telephone (see Figure 12.2). It is confirmed that similarity exists between uses – a symbolic use present to the observer and another conventional use which is absent, represented by the symbol. Object substitution and symbolic narratives in action were also observed, as occurred in 18-month-old, typically developing children.

9 In a study on symbols in peer interaction, ages 9 months to 24 months, at nursery school (Yuste, 2012), we used replica objects included in the supplies received at nursery schools, with which the children were familiar. These replicas were (1) set of dishes and cutlery, including plates, forks, spoons, cups, and glasses; (2) hair styling set, including dolls with hair, brushes, combs, and dryers; and (3) telephone set, including complete telephones, mobile telephone, and headset. It was confirmed that the production of symbols is a gradual process. Nine-month-olds did not produce symbols, but 12-month-olds did, even when interacting with young peers rather than adults. Symbols were level 1: they "eat," "drink," or "push the food around the plate"; they "comb" their own or companion's hair. They "talk" on the telephone. At 15, 18, 21, and 24 months, children produced symbols during longer times and symbolic narratives in action (Palacios et al., 2016), always at level 1, with the object of functional use. At 24 months they set plates on the mat (on the ground) to "set the table", "eat", and "clear the table".

10 These findings are consistent with what happened with a 13-month-old Swiss child (Moro & Rodríguez, 2005; see also Moro et al., 2015) who, on being unable to insert a block through a hole, instead of persevering, performed an ostensive gesture by showing himself the block *before* attempting to perform the conventional use again.

11 We chose objects with a clear but challenging goal: a shape sorter and a hammer toy to push balls into a box, and a set of houses with keys. They all involve different objects and instruments that need to be coordinated in unified conventional uses. The children received guidance by their parents through gestures and demonstrations. Children older than 12 months all understood the aim or function of the objects, but had difficulties regarding *how* to do it. The conventional uses of the aforementioned

complex objects impose cognitive challenges once children understand and internalise their goals: putting shapes through the right holes, hammering balls until they fall into the box, positioning and turning keys to unlock doors. These challenges present the need for self-regulation. This is of paramount importance when eliciting children's self-regulatory behaviours, because without a cognitive challenge, self-regulation is not necessary (think of the difficulties of a rattle compared to these complex objects).

12 La Cigüeña María in Madrid.

13 At age 12 months, children made a replica pony "gallop," or "galloped" themselves, or the parents made a doll gallop on the pony (see Palacios & Rodríguez, 2015; Palacios et al., 2016).

14 Mothers were to play with their children, following the rules as far as possible. Two boys and one girl, at ages 24, 27, 30, 33, and 36 months, were filmed at home with their mothers. They had never played with dice before.

15 In contrast, there is a vast literature about younger children pointing to objects (Butterworth, 2003; Liszkowski, Carpenter, & Tomasello, 2007). See also the section about self-regulation with private gestures.

References

Adamson, L. B., Bakeman, R., & Deckner, D. F. (2004). The development of symbol-infused joint engagement. *Child Development*, 75(4), 1171–1187.

Alessandroni, N. (2016). Development of metaphorical thought before language: The pragmatic construction of metaphors in action. *Integrative Psychological and Behavioral Science*. DOI: 10.1007/s12124-016-9373-3.

Amorim, K. S, dos Anjos, A. M., & Rossetti-Ferreira, M. C. (2012). Processos interativos de bebês em creche. *Psicologia: Reflexão e Crítica*, 25(2), 378–389.

Baron-Cohen, S. & Swettenham, J. (1996). The relationship between SAM and ToMM. In P. Carruthers & P. Smith (Eds.), *Theories of Theories of Mind* (pp. 158–168). Cambridge, MA: Cambridge University Press.

Barthélémy-Musso, A., Tartas, V., & Guidetti, M. (2013). Prendre les objets et leurs usages au sérieux: Aproche développementale de la co-construction de conventions sémiotiques entre enfants. *Psychologie Française*, 58, 67–88.

Basilio, M. & Rodríguez, C. (2011). Usos, gestos y vocalizaciones privadas: De la interacción social a la autorregulación. *Infancia y Aprendizaje*, 34, 181–194. DOI: 10.1174/021037011795377593.

Basilio, M. & Rodríguez, C. (2016). How toddlers think with their hands. social and private gestures as evidence of cognitive self-regulation in guided play with objects. *Early Child Development and Care*, 1–16. DOI: 10.1080/03004430.2016.1202944.

Bates, E., Camaioni, L., & Volterra, V. (1975). The acquisition of performatives prior to speech. *Merril-Palmer Quarterly*, 21(3), 205–226.

Belsky, J. & Most, R. K. (1981). From exploration to play: A cross-sectional study of infant free play behavior. *Developmental Psychology*, 17(5), 630–639.

Borges, J. & Di Giovanni, N. (1970/1972). *Doctor Brodie's Report* (trans. N. di Giovanni). London: Allen Lane.

Brizuela, B. & Cayton-Hodges, G. (2013). Young children's self-constructed maps. In B. Brizuela & B. Gravel (Eds.), *"Show Me What You Know": Exploring Student Representations across STEM Disciplines* (pp. 22–42). New York: Teachers College Press.

Bronckart, J. P. (2002). La explicación en psicología ante el desafío del significado. *Estudios de Psicología*, 23(3), 387–416.

Bronckart, J. P. (2012). Contributions of Piagetian constructivism to social interactionism. In E. Martí & C. Rodríguez (Eds.), *After Piaget* (pp. 43–58). New Brunswick, NJ: Transaction Publishers.

Bruner, J. (1975). From communication to language: A psychological perspective. *Cognition*, 3(1), 255–287.

Butterworth, G. (2003). Pointing is the royal road to language for babies. In S. Kita (Ed.), *Pointing. Where Language, Culture and Cognition Meet* (pp. 9–33). Mahwah, NJ: Lawrence Erlbaum.

Cárdenas, K. (2012). *Primeros usos simbólicos de niños con síndrome de Down en contextos de interacción triádica: Un estudio longitudinal entre los 12 y 21 meses de edad*. Unpublished doctoral dissertation, Facultad de Psicología, Universidad Autónoma de Madrid, Madrid, Spain.

Cárdenas, K., Rodríguez, C., Miranda-Zapata, E., & Palacios, P. (forthcoming). Usos simbólicos de los objetos de niño/as con síndrome de Down de 12 a 21 meses: Un estudio longitudinal en interacción niño/a-adulto-objeto.

Cárdenas, K., Rodríguez, C., & Palacios, P. (2014). First symbols in a girl with Down syndrome: A longitudinal study from 12 to 18 months. *Infant Behavior and Development*, 37, 416–427. DOI: 10.1016/j.infbeh.2014.06.003.

Carpendale, J. I. M. & Carpendale, A. B. (2010). The development of pointing: From personal directedness to interpersonal direction. *Human Development*, 53, 110–126.

Carpendale, J. I. M. & Lewis, C. (2004). Constructing an understanding of mind: The development of children's social understanding within social interaction. *Behavioral and Brain Sciences*, 27, 79–151.

Cavalcante, S. (2016). *Desarrollo del número de dos a cuatro años: De los usos de objetos en interacción con un adulto a los usos numéricos*. Unpublished doctoral dissertation, Facultad de Psicologia, Universitat de Barcelona, Barcelona, Spain.

Cavalcante, S. & Rodríguez, C. (2015). The understanding of die as an object that has numerical functions: A longitudinal study using two children from the ages of 24 to 36 months interacting with an adult / La comprensión del dado como objeto con funciones numéricas: Un estudio longitudinal con dos niños desde los 24 a los 36 meses en interacción con un adulto. *Estudios de Psicología*, 36, 48–70. DOI: 10.1080/02109395.2014.1000028.

Clark, H. (2003). Pointing and placing. In S. Kita (Ed.), *Pointing: Where Language, Culture and Cognition Meet* (pp. 243–268). Mahwah, NJ: Lawrence Erlbaum.

Costall, A. (2012). Canonical affordances in context. *AVANT*, 3(2), 85–93.

Delgado, B., Gómez, J. C., & Sarriá, E. (2009). Private pointing and private speech: Developing parallelisms. In A. Winsler, C. Fernyhough & I. Montero (Eds.), *Private Speech, Executive Functioning, and the Development of Verbal Self-regulation*. Cambridge, MA: Cambridge University Press.

Delgado, B., Gómez, J. C., & Sarriá, E. (2011). Pointing gestures as a cognitive tool in young children: Experimental evidence. *Journal of Experimental Child Psychology*, 110(3), 299–312.

Del Olmo, M. J., Rodríguez, C., & Ruza, F. (2010). Music therapy in the PICU: 0 to 6 month-old babies. *Music and Medicine*, 2(3) 158–166.

Dimitrova, N. & Moro, C. (2013). Common ground on object use associates with caregivers' gestures. *Infant Behavior and Development*, 36, 618–626.

Duque, M. P. & Packer, M. J. (2014). Pensamiento y lenguaje: El proyecto de Vygotski para resolver la crisis de la Psicología. *Tesis Psicológica*, 9(2), 30–57.

El'konin, D. B. (1966). Symbolics and its functions in the play of children. *Soviet Education*, 8(3), 35–41.

Español, S. (2004). *Cómo hacer cosas sin palabras: Gesto y ficción en la infancia temprana*. Madrid: Antonio Machado.

Español, S. (2006). Possible precursors of private speech: Deictic, symbolic and aesthetic self-directed gestures. In I. Montero (Ed.), *Current Research Trends in Private Speech: Proceedings of the First International Symposium on Self-regulatory Functions of Language* (pp. 120–124). Madrid: Ediciones UAM.

Foster, R. & Kreitzman, L. (2004). *Rhythms of Life: The Biological Clocks that Control the Daily Lives of Every Living Thing*. London: Profile Books.

Fuson, K. (1988). *Children's Counting and Concept of Nnumber*. New York: Springer.

Gelman, R. & Gallistel, C. R. (1978). *The Child's Understanding of Number*. Cambridge, MA: Harvard University Press.

Gibson, J. (1979/2014). *The Ecological Approach to Visual Perception* (classical edn. New York: Psychology Press/Taylor and Francis Group.

Göncü, A. & Gaskins, S. (2011). Comparing and extending Piaget's and Vygotsky's understanding of play: Symbolic play as individual, sociocultural, and educational interpretation. In A. D. Pellegrini (Ed.), *The Oxford Handbook of the Development of Play* (pp. 48–57). Oxford: Oxford University Press.

Goodall, J. (1990). *Through a Window: My Thirty Years with the Chimpanzees of Gombe*. Boston: Houghton Mifflin Company.

Graham, T. (1999). The role of gesture in children's learning to count. *Journal of Experimental Child Psychology*, 74, 333–355.

Groupe μ (1992). *Traité du signe visuel: Pour une rhétorique de l'image*. Paris: Seuil.

Ishiguro, H. (2016). How a young child learns how to take part in mealtimes in a Japanese day-care center: A longitudinal case study. *European Journal of Psychology of Education*, 31(1), 13–27.

Jackson-Maldonado, D., Badillo, B., & Aguilar, N. (2010). Verbal and non-verbal requests in Spanish-speaking children with Down syndrome. *Down Syndrome Research and Practice*, 12(2), 98–102.

Karmiloff-Smith, A. (2012). From constructivism to neuroconstructivism: The activity-dependent structuring of the human brain. In E. Martí & C. Rodríguez (Eds.), *After Piaget* (pp. 1–14). New Brunswick, NJ: Transaction Publishers.

Kaye, K. (1982/1986). *La vida mental y social del bebé. Cómo los padres crean personas*. Barcelona: Paidós.

Kontopodis, M. & Perret-Clermont, A.-N. (2016). Educational settings as interwoven socio-material orderings: An introduction. *European Journal of Psychology of Education*, 31, 1–12. DOI: 10.1007/s10212-015-0269-2.

Leslie, A. (1987). Pretense and representation: The origins of "theory of mind." *Psychological Review*, 94(4), 412–426.

Li, X. (2012). Peer relations. In J. Valsiner (Ed.). *Oxford Handbook of Culture and Psychology* (pp. 1–22). Oxford: Oxford University Press.

DOI: 10.1093/oxfordhb/9780195396430.013.0045.

Lillard, A., Lerner, M. D., Hopkins, E. J., Dore, R. A., Smith, E. D., & Palmquist, C. M. (2013). The impact of pretend play on children's development: A review of the evidence. *Psychological Bulletin*, 139(1), 1–34. DOI: 10.1037/A0029321.

Liszkowski, U., Carpenter, M., & Tomasello, M. (2007). Reference and attitude in infant pointing. *Journal Child Language*, 34, 1–20.

Luria, A. (1979). *The Making of Mind: A Personal Account of Soviet Psychology* (ed. by M. Cole & S. Cole). Cambridge, MA: Harvard University Press.

Martí, E. (2003). *Representar el mundo externamente: La adquisición infantil de los sistemas externos de representación*. Madrid: Antonio Machado.

Martí, E. (2012). Thinking with signs: From symbolic actions to external systems of representation. In E. Martí & C. Rodríguez (Eds.), *After Piaget* (pp. 151–170). New Brunswick, NJ: Transaction Publishers.

Martí, E., Scheuer, N., & de la Cruz, M. (2013). Symbolic use of quantitative representations in young children. In B. Brizuela & B. Gravel (Eds.), *"Show Me What You Know": Exploring Student Representations across STEM Disciplines* (pp. 7–21). New York: Teachers College Press.

McCune, L. (1995). A normative study of representational play at the transition to language. *Developmental Psychology*, 31(2), 198–206.

Moreno-Núñez, A., Rodríguez, C., & Del Olmo, M. J. (2015). The rhythmic, sonorous and melodic components of adult–child–object interactions between 2 and 6 months old. *Integrative Psychological and Behavioral Science*, 49(4), 737–756. DOI: 10.1007/s12124-015-9298-2.

Moreno-Núñez, A., Rodríguez, C., & Del Olmo, M. J. (2017). Rhythmic ostensive gestures: How adults facilitate infants' entrance into early triadic interactions. *Infant Behavior and Development*, 49, 168–181.

Moreno-Núñez, A., Rodríguez, C. & Miranda-Zapata, E. (forthcoming). Getting away from the point: The emergence and functions of ostensive gestures. *Gesture*.

Moro, C. (2012). Heuristique des thèses sémiotiques vygotskiennes pour l'approche du développement des fonctions exécutives chez le jeune enfant. *Rivista Italiana di Filosofia del Linguaggio, Vygotskij and language/Vygotskij e illinguaggio*, 6(2) 210–224.

Moro, C. (2016). To encounter, to build the world and to become a human being: Advocating for a material-cultural turn in developmental psychology. *Integrative Psychological and Behavioral Sciences*, 50, 586–602. DOI: 10.1007/s12124-016-9356-4.

Moro, C., Dupertuis, V., Fardel, S., & Piguet, O. (2015). Investigating the development of consciousness through ostensions toward oneself from the onset of the use-of-object to first words. *Cognitive Development*, 36, 150–160.

Moro, C. & Muller Mirza, N. (Eds.). (2012). *Sémiotique, culture et développement psychologique*. Villeneuve d'Ascq, France: Presses Universitaires du Septentrion.

Moro, C. & Rodríguez, C. (2005). *L'objet et la construction de son usage chez le bébé: Une approche sémiotique du développement préverbal*. New York: Peter Lang.

Müller, U. & Kerns, K. (2015). The development of executive function. In R. Lerner, L. S. Liben, & U. Müller (Eds.), *Handbook of Child Psychology and Developmental Science. Volume 2: Cognitive Processes* (pp. 1058–1160). Hoboken, NJ: John Wiley.

Nelson, K. (2015). Making sense with private speech. *Cognitive Development*, 36, 171–179.

Palacios, P. & Rodríguez, C. (2015). The development of symbolic uses of objects in infants in a triadic context: A pragmatic and semiotic perspective. *Infant and Child Development*, 24, 23–43. DOI: 10.1002/icd.1873.

Palacios, P., Rodríguez, C., Méndez-Sánchez, C., Hermosillo, A. E., Sahagún, M. A., & Cárdenas, K. (2016). The development of the first symbolic uses in Mexican children from the pragmatics of object/ Desarrollo de los primeros usos simbólicos en niños mexicanos desde la Pragmática del Objeto. *Estudios de Psicología*, 37, 59–89. DOI: 10.1080/02109395.2015.1122437.

Papoušek, H. (1996). Musicality in infancy research: Biological and cultural origins of early musicality. In I. Deliegé & J. A. Sloboda (Eds.), *Musical Beginnings: Origins and Development of Musical Competence* (pp. 37–55). New York: Oxford University Press.

Perinat, A. (1993). *Comunicación animal, comunicación humana*. Madrid: Siglo XXI.

Piaget, J. (1936/1977). *La naissance de l'intelligence chez l'enfant*. Paris: Delachaux et Niestlé.

Piaget, J. (1945/1976). *La formation du symbole chez l'enfant*. Paris: Delachaux et Niestlé.

Reddy, V. (2008). *How Infants Know Minds*. Cambridge, MA: Harvard University Press.

Reddy, V. (2012). Moving others matters. In A. Foolen, U. M. Lüdtke, T. P. Racine, & J. Zlatev (Eds.), *Moving Ourselves, Moving Others: Motion and Emotion in Intersubjectivity, Consciousness and Language* (pp. 139–163). Philadelphia: John Benjamins.

Rivière. A. (1985). *La psicología de Vygotski*. Madrid: Antonio Machado.

Rivière, A. (1990). Origen y desarrollo de la función simbólica en el niño. In J. Palacios, A. Marchesi, & C. Coll (Eds.), *Desarrollo psicológico y educación, I Psicología Evolutiva* (pp. 113–130). Madrid: Alianza.

Rochat, P. (2012). Baby assault on Piaget. In E. Martí & C. Rodríguez (Eds.), *After Piaget* (pp. 71–82). New Brunswick, NJ: Transaction Publishers.

Rodríguez, C. (2006). *Del ritmo al símbolo: Los signos en el nacimiento de la inteligencia*. Barcelona: Horsori.

Rodríguez, C. (2007). Object use, communication and signs: The triadic basis of early cognitive development. In J. Valsiner & A. Rosa (Eds.), *The Cambridge Handbook of Socio-Cultural Psychology* (pp. 257–276). New York: Cambridge University Press.

Rodríguez, C. (2009). The "circumstances" of gestures: Proto-interrogatives and private gestures. *New Ideas in Psychology*, 27, 288–303.

Rodriguez, C. (2012). The functional permanence of the object: A product of consensus. In E. Martí & C. Rodríguez (Eds.), *After Piaget* (123–150). New Brunswick, NJ: Transaction Publishers.

Rodríguez, C. (2015). The connection between language and the world: A paradox of the linguistic turn? *Integrative Psychological & Behavioral Science*, 49, 89–103. DOI 10.1007/s12124-014-9274-2.

Rodríguez, C., Benassi, J., Estrada, L., & Alessandroni, N. (2017). Early social interactions with people and objects. In A. Slater & G. Bremner (Eds.), *An Introduction to Developmental Psychology* (3rd edn., pp. 211–257). New York: John Wiley & Sons.

Rodríguez, C., Estrada, L., Moreno-Llanos, I., & de los Reyes, J. L. (2017). Executive functions and educational actions in an infant school: Private uses and gestures at the end of the first year / Funciones Ejecutivas y acción educativa en la Escuela Infantil: Usos y gestos privados al final del primer año. *Estudios de Psicología* (special issue on Executive Functions / Funciones ejecutivas), 38(2), 385–423.

Rodríguez, C., Moreno-Núñez, A., Basilio, M., & Sosa, N. (2015). Ostensive gestures come first: Their role in the beginning of shared reference. *Cognitive Development*, 36, 142–149.

Rodríguez, C. & Moro, C. (1999). *El mágico número tres: Cuando los niños aún no hablan*. Barcelona: Paidós.

Rodríguez, C. & Moro, C. (2008). Coming to agreement: Object use by infants and adults. In J. Zlatev, T. Racine, C. Sinha, & E. Itkonen (Eds.), *The Shared Mind: Perspectives on Intersubjectivity* (pp. 89–114). Amsterdam: John Benjamins.

Rodríguez, C. & Palacios, P. (2007). Do private gestures have a self-regulatory function? A case study. *Infant Behavior and Development*, 30(2), 180–194. DOI: 10.1016/j.infbeh.2007.02.010.

Rodríguez, C., Palacios, P., Cárdenas, K., & Yuste, N. (2014). Les symboles: Des formes de second ou de troisième sens? In C. Moro & N. Muller Mirza (Eds.), *Sémiotique, culture et développement Psychologique* (pp. 99–116). Villeneuve d'Ascq, France: Presses Universitaires du Septentrion.

Rodríguez, C. & Scheuer, N. (2015). The paradox between the numerically competent baby and the slow learning of two- to four-year-old children / La paradoja entre el bebé numéricamente competente y el lento aprendizaje de los niños de dos a cuatro años de edad. *Estudios de Psicología*, 36, 18–47.

Rosa, A. (chapter 6 this volume).

Rosa, A. & Valsiner, J. (chapter 1 this volume).

Saada-Robert, M. (2012). From individual to didactic microgenesis: Studies on situated knowledge transformations. In E. Martí & C. Rodríguez (Eds.), *After Piaget* (pp. 187–205). New Brunswick, NJ: Transaction Publishers.

Schaeffer, B., Eggleston, V. H., & Scott, J. L. (1974). Number development in young children. *Cognitive Psychology*, 6, 357–379.

Sinha, C. (2014). Signification et matérialité: Le langage au fondement des artefacts symboliques. In C. Moro & N. Muller Mirza (Eds.), *Sémiotique, culture et développement psychologique* (pp. 117–138). Villeneuve d'Ascq, France: Presses Universitaires du Septentrion.

Sonesson, G. & Lenninger, S. (2015). The psychological development of semiotic competence: From the window to the movie by way of the mirror. *Cognitive Development*, 36, 191–201.

Spelke, E. S. (2000, November). Core knowledge. *American Psychologist*, 55, 1233–1243.

Tartas, V. (2008). *La construction du temps social par l'enfant*. New York: Peter Lang.

Tartas, V., Perret-Clermont, A.-N., & Baucal, A. (2016). Experimental micro-histories, private speech and a study of children's learning and cognitive development. *Infancia y Aprendizaje*, 39(4), 772–811. DOI: 10.1080/02103702.2016.1221055.

Tilley, C., Keane, W., Küchler, S., Rowlands, M., & Spyer, P. (Eds.). (2006). *Handbook of Material Culture*. London: SAGE.

Tomasello, M. (1999). *The Cultural Origins of Human Cognition*. Cambridge, MA: Harvard University Press.

Tomasello, M. (2014). *A Natural History of Human Thinking*. Cambridge, MA: Harvard University Press.

Trehub, S. (2003). The developmental origins of musicality. *Nature Neuroscience*, 7(6), 669–673.

Trevarthen, C. (2003). *Conversations with a two-month-old*. Philadelphia, PA: Whurr Publishers.

Vallotton, C. (2008). Infants take self-regulation into their own hands. *Zero to Three*, September, 29–34.

Valsiner, J. (2016, July). The human psyche on the border of irreversible time: Forward-oriented semiosis. Invited address at the 31st International Congress of Psychology, Yokohama, Japan.

Vergnaud, G. (2013). Pourquoi la théorie des champs conceptuels? *Infancia y Aprendizaje*, 36(2), 131–161.

Vygotski, L. S. (1931/1995a). El problema del desarrollo de las funciones psíquicas superiores. In L. S. Vygotski, *Obras escogidas* (vol. III, pp. 11–46). Madrid: Visor.

Vygotski, L. S. (1931/1995b). La prehistoria del desarrollo del lenguaje escrito. In L.S. Vygotski, *Obras Escogidas* (vol. III, pp. 183–206).Madrid: Visor.

Vygotski, L. S. (1934/1985). *Pensée et langage*. Paris: Terrains/Editions Sociales.

Wallon, H. (1942/1970). *De l'acte à la pensée*. Paris: Flammarion.

Wertsch, J. V. (1979). From social interaction to higher psychological processes. *Human Development*, 51(1), 66–79.

Winsler, A. (2009). Still talking to ourselves after all these years: A review of current research on private speech. In A. Winsler, C. Fernyhough, & I. Montero (Eds.), *Private Speech, Executive Functioning, and the Development of Verbal Self-regulation* (pp. 3–41). Cambridge, MA: Cambridge University Press.

Wood, D., Bruner, J. S., & Ross, G. (1976). The role of tutoring in problem solving. *Journal of Child Psychology and Psychiatry, and Allied Disciplines*, 17(2), 89–100.

Yuste, N. (2012). Desarrollo simbólico e interacción entre iguales en la escuela infantil. Unpublished DEA dissertation, Facultad de Psicología, Universidad Autónoma de Madrid, Madrid, Spain.

Yuste, N., Rodríguez, C., & de los Reyes, J. L. (forthcoming). Interacción entre iguales y el estatus de los objetos en la producción de usos simbólicos.

Zelazo, P. D. & Müller, U. (2004). Executive function in typical and atypical development. In U. Goswami (Ed.), *Blackwell Handbook of Childhood Cognitive Development* (pp. 445–469).Oxford: Blackwell.

Zittoun, T. (2010). How does an object become symbolic? Rooting semiotic artifacts in dynamic shared experiences. In B. Wagoner (Ed.), *Symbolic Transformation: The Mind in Movement through Culture and Society* (pp. 173–192). New York: Routledge.

Zulauf, M. (2002). Limites et promesses de quelques théories du développement musical. In M. Wirthner & M. Zulauf (Eds.), *À la recherche du développement musical* (pp. 19–51). Paris: L'Harmattan.

13 Distinguishing Two Processes of Self-reflection

Alex Gillespie

Self-reflection can be defined as a temporary phenomenological experience in which self becomes an object to oneself. According to theorists like Mead and Vygotsky, self-reflection is a defining feature of humans and fundamental to the higher mental processes such as self-regulation. Central to a sociocultural approach to self-reflection is the idea that it entails using semiotic mediators to distantiate from self and the immediate situation (Valsiner, 1998).

Naming (i.e., using a semiotic mediator to pick out) an affective experience or a situation distances the individual from that experience or situation. Furthermore, such naming turns self and the situation into objects among other objects in the social world (i.e., capable of being the object of action). For example, in order to conceptualize obtaining dinner one must first name either one's hunger or the object to be eaten. This naming, which is a moment of self-reflection, is the first step in beginning to construct, semiotically, a path of action that will lead to dinner.

What triggers this process of semiotic mediation? Exactly how do semiotic mediators enable distancing in general and self-reflection in particular? What is it in the structure of semiotic mediators, or signs, that enables this "stepping out" from immediate experience? And how are these signs combined into complex semiotic systems (representations, discourses, cultural artifacts, or symbolic resources) that provide even greater liberation from the immediate situation?

The present chapter will address these questions by beginning with a review of sociocultural theories of the origins of self-reflection.

Four types of theory can be distinguished: rupture theories, mirror theories, conflict theories, and internalization theories. In order to address the limitations of these theories, Mead's theory of the social act is advanced. These theories are then evaluated against an empirical instance of self-reflection and a novel conception of complex semiotic systems is proposed.

13.1 Rupture Theories

Rupture theories of self-reflection posit that self-reflection arises when one's path of action becomes blocked or when one faces a decision of some sort. Peirce provides an early articulation of this idea:

If for instance, in a horse-car, I pull out my purse and find a five-cent nickel and five coppers, I decide, while my hand is going to the purse, in which way I will pay my fare.... To speak of such a doubt as causing an irritation which needs to be appeased, suggests a temper which is uncomfortable to the verge of insanity. Yet looking at the matter minutely, it must be admitted that, if there is the least hesitation as to whether I shall pay the five coppers or the nickel (as there will sure to be, unless I act from some previously contracted habit in the matter), though irritation is too strong a word, yet I am excited to such small mental activities as may be necessary in deciding how I shall act.... Images pass rapidly through consciousness, one incessantly melting into another, until at last, when all is over – it may be in a fraction of a second, in an hour, or after long years – we find ourselves decided as to how we should act. (Peirce, 1878/1998, pp. 141–142)

According to Peirce, the problematic situation stimulates reflective thought. Even a small irritation, or rupture, can stimulate a stream of thought. This is a phenomenological experience that many people would be inclined to agree with. But why should a rupture spontaneously generate the semiotic system necessary for distancing?

Dewey (1896), developing Peirce's ideas, argued that in the ruptured situation the object ceases, from the perspective of the actor, to be objective and becomes, so to speak, subjective. Specifically, the object becomes subjective because the actor has two or more responses toward the object. Dewey gives the example of a child reaching for a flame. The child is attracted to the flame because it looks like something to play with; but the child is also afraid of the flame because of a previous burn. Thus there are two contradictory responses in the child: to reach toward the flame *and* to withdraw from the flame. It is due to the disjunction between these two responses, Dewey argues, that self-reflection arises.

Mead (1910; see also Gillespie, 2005) criticized this theory arguing that there is nothing in having two contradictory responses which necessarily leads to self-reflection. In nonhuman animals there are conflicting responses, yet there is no self-consciousness. Pavlov (1951), for example, trained dogs to salivate on seeing a circle, and not to salivate on seeing an ellipse. In successive trials he reduced the difference between the two contradictory stimuli, until the ellipse was almost a circle. When the stimuli became difficult to differentiate, thus evoking two contradictory responses, the dogs, usually placid, became frantic and remained disturbed for weeks afterward. Pavlov called this "experimental neurosis." Assuming that these dogs did not become self-reflective (and there is no evidence to suggest they did), then these experiments show that contradictory responses can coexist without leading to self-reflection. Indeed, rather than contradictions leading to self-reflection, it is self-reflection

and semiotic mediation that enables us to become aware of such contradictions.

Piaget (1970) offers a more contemporary variant of the rupture theory. According to Piaget the child is forced to abstract and reorganize his/her developing schemas when those schemas lead to unfulfilled expectations. For example, the child expects the consequence of action X to be Y, but instead the consequence of action X is Z. Like the other rupture theorists, Piaget points to a proximal cause of self-reflection, namely a problematic situation, but he does not give us much purchase on the semiotic processes through which self-reflection arises. Again, one can ask, why should a rupture stimulate the emergence of semiotic mediators? In order to address this question we need to move beyond the subject-object relation that Dewey and Piaget were working with, and examine the self–other social relation.

13.2 Mirror Theories

The defining feature of mirror theories of self-reflection, compared to the rupture theories, is the presence of a significant social other. These theories assume that the other perceives more about self than self can perceive. The reflective distance from self which self-reflection entails first exists in the mind of other. This "surplus" (Bakhtin, 1923/1990; Gillespie, 2003) can be fed back to self by other, such that self can learn to see self from the perspective of other. In this sense, mirror theories assume that the other provides feedback to self in the same way that a mirror provides feedback about appearance that we cannot perceive unaided. An early variant of this theory can be found in the writings of Adam Smith:

Were it possible that a human creature could grow up to manhood in some solitary place, without any communication with his own species, he could no more think of his own character, of the propriety or demerit of his own sentiments and conduct, of the beauty or deformity of his own mind, than the beauty or deformity of his own face. All of these are objects which he cannot easily see, which naturally he does not look at, and with regard to which he is provided with no mirror which can present them to his view. Bring him into society, and he is immediately provided with the mirror which he wanted before. It is placed in the countenance and behavior of those he lives with. (Smith, 1759/1982, p. 110)

For Adam Smith it is "fellow man" who teaches self the value of self's actions, who is a "mirror" redirecting self's attention to the meaning of self's own actions. Growing up alone, without such a mirror, Smith writes, there is nothing to make a person reflect on him/herself. The "mirror" is the "countenance and behaviour" of other.

The metaphor of society as a mirror, leading to self-reflection, was elaborated in Cooley's (1902, p. 184) concept of the "looking-glass self." According to Cooley, the self is a social product formed out of three elements: "the imagination of our appearance to the other person; the imagination of his judgment of that appearance, and some sort of self-feeling, such as pride or mortification." Interestingly, self-reflection for Cooley is always entwined with judgments, leading to emotions such as pride, shame, guilt, or gloating. Unfortunately, much of the literature which has taken up Cooley's ideas has become mired in examining the extent to which self is "actually" able to take the perspective of the other (Shrauger & Schoeneman, 1979; Lundgren, 2004).

Psychoanalysts, on the other hand, have bypassed this trivial question, and have developed a sophisticated theory based on the mirror metaphor. According to Lacan (1949), before the mirror stage the child is fragmented: feelings, desires, and actions are unconnected. Within this scheme the mirror reveals the child to him/herself as a bounded totality, a gestalt. The self, by perceiving itself as bounded, and thus isolated, becomes alienated through self-reflection. This idea of mirroring, and especially reflecting emo-

tions back to the child, is still current in theories that draw on the psychoanalytic tradition (e.g., Hobson, 2002; Gergely & Watson, 1996; Winnicott, 1971).

The social feedback theories, despite articulating a proximal cause of self-reflection in social interaction, encounter three problems if extended into a theory of the origin (i.e., ontogenesis) of self-reflection. First, many nonhuman animals live in complex societies and are constantly exposed to feedback from others, yet they do not demonstrate the same level of elaborate consciousness of self as evident in humans. Presumably the difference between humans and other animals is that humans take the perspective of the other in the mirroring process, such that they have dialogic representations (Tomasello et al., 2005). However, this only raises the second problem, namely, how does self take the perspective of the other? This seems to be assumed in mirror theories rather than explained (Whiten, 2005). The third problem is the apparently neutral nature of the other in mirror theories. The idea that the other is a passive mirror, neutrally reflecting emotions, actions, and facial expressions, is problematized by the third group of theories dealing with self-reflection, namely, the conflict theories.

13.3 Conflict Theories

According to the conflict theories, self-reflection arises through a social struggle. Hegel's theory of self-consciousness as exemplified in the master–slave allegory is a paradigmatic example (Marková, 1982). Self-consciousness, Hegel argues, arises through gaining recognition from an other who is not inferior to self. According to the master–slave allegory, initially, self and other treat each other as physical objects, and thus deny any recognition to each other. Due to this mutual denial, self and other enter into a struggle, the outcome of which is a relation of domination and subordination, that is, the master–slave relation. The master dominates the slave and in that sense is free, while the slave, having lost the struggle, is in bondage to the master and is, thus, not free. The slave is in the service of the master and sees the master as superior, while the master sees the slave as inferior. According to Hegel's logic of recognition, the paradoxical outcome of this situation is that the slave can get recognition from the master, but the master cannot get recognition from the slave. The slave struggles for recognition from the master and thus works toward increased self-consciousness and eventually equality with the master. The master, on the other hand, cannot satisfy the need for recognition because recognition by the slave is worthless. The interesting dynamic that Hegel describes is that self-consciousness, and thus self-reflection, arise through *struggling* for recognition from the other. In sociocultural psychology one can find variations on this basic idea at the levels of interaction, institution, and representation.

At the interactional level, for example, the tradition of research on socio-cognitive conflict has clearly established that conflict between self and other over how to proceed in a joint task can lead to cognitive development (Doise & Mugny, 1984). Moreover, recent research has shown that a key component of durable cognitive development results from social interaction that takes the form of "explicit recognition" (Psaltis & Duveen, 2006), which is defined as the interaction or conversation where new acquired knowledge for self is recognized by other and self. Sigel's psychological distancing theory expresses a similar dynamic. Sigel (2002, pp. 197–198) asserts that discrepancies introduced by the utterances of others can put a cognitive demand on the child which can in turn lead to representational work and thus distancing.

Moving to the institutional level, activity theorists posit that contradictions between different components of an activity system lead to reflection. Activity theory has much in common with Dewey's ideas (Tolman & Piekkola, 1989), but it differs from Dewey by extending the definition of the problematic situation to include problems introduced by the perspective of others. This is quite clear in Engeström's (1987) concept of "expansive learning," which refers to participants within an activity system prompting each other to reflect on the conditions and rules of their ongoing interaction. The roots of expansive learning are to be found in "disturbances, ruptures and expansions" which arise in communication within an activity system (Engeström et al., 1997 p. 373).

Finally, at the level of representation, recent work in social representations theory emphasizes the contradictions between different bodies of knowledge circulating in modern societies (Moscovici, 1984). Bauer and Gaskell (1999) argue that people become aware of representations at the points at which they overlap or contradict each other. "It is through the contrast of divergent perspectives that we become aware of representations, particularly when the contrast challenges our presumed reality" (Bauer & Gaskell, 1999, p. 169). Divergent representations, sustained by different groups in different domains of practice, can come together and clash in the public sphere (Jovchelovitch, 1995). When this occurs, individuals and groups may come to participate in conflicting representations. According to Bauer and Gaskell, it is this conflict which produces awareness of representations. This coexistence of multiple forms of knowledge in society, and consequently, in the individual minds of members of society engenders a state of "cognitive polyphasia" (e.g., Wagner et al., 1999), which can, but does not necessarily, lead to self-reflection.

By critically examining the conflict theories, one could say that they have the same basic structure as the rupture theories. In the rupture theories, tension is introduced through a problematic self–object relation, while in the conflict theories tension is introduced through a problematic self–other relation. This similarity exposes the conflict theories to similar critiques, namely, while a social conflict may be a proximal cause of self-reflection it does not necessarily explain how self-reflection can arise in the first place; again, social conflict occurs throughout the animal kingdom without leading to the evolution of mechanisms for self-reflection. The question to ask is: what is it about the social situation (self–other relation) that is not present in the practical situation (self–object relation) and which can account for the emergence of self reflection at both ontogenetic and phylogenetic levels? One possible answer to this question is provided by the internalization theories.

13.4 Internalization Theories

The idea that thought is a self-reflective internal dialogue with absent others goes back, at least, to Plato (e.g., *Sophist*, 263e; *Theaetetus*, 190). Forms of internalization are evident in the theories of Freud (in the formation of the superego), Bakhtin (the super-addressee), and Vygotsky. Today this line of theory is carried forward by Hermans (2001), and Josephs (2002). Within this tradition of theorizing, one can conceptualize self-reflection as arising through internalizing the perspective that the other has on self, followed by self taking the perspective of other on self. Or more simply: self-reflection arises through an intra-psychological dialogue between internalized perspectives.

There are, however, problems over how the metaphor of "internalization" should be understood (Matusov, 1998). Wertsch (1985, p. 163) has called the idea that social relations are simply "transmitted" into psychological structure "uninteresting and trivial." While some theorists make this mistake, Vygotsky (1997, p. 106) emphasized that the process of internalization is a process of "transformation," rather than simple "transmission" (see also Lawrence & Valsiner, 1993). The process of transformation is clearly

evident Vygotsky's analysis of the emergence of pointing (1997, pp. 104–105).

According to Vygotsky, the child becomes able to point only when he/she is able to reflect on the meaning of the pointing from the standpoint of others. How does this come about? "Initially," Vygotsky (1997, p. 104) writes, "the pointing gesture represents a simply unsuccessful grasping movement directed toward an object and denoting a future action." At first the child is not self-conscious of pointing, and thus is not trying to communicate anything. Rather, the child is simply reaching for something out of reach. However, from the perspective of the mother, the child's reaching is meaningful, it indicates that the child desires the reached-for object. Vygotsky (p. 105) states: "In response to the unsuccessful grasping movement of the child, there arises a reaction not on the part of the object, but on the part of an other person." The grasping first has the meaning of pointing for the mother, and only later has meaning for the child. It is only when the grasping becomes a meaningful gesture for the child that we can say the child is pointing, for it is only then that the child knows the meaning of his/her gesture for others. The child, Vygotsky (p. 105) writes, "becomes for himself what he is in himself through what he manifests for others." That is to say, the child becomes self-aware of his/her own being through how he/she appears to others.

Summarizing the emergence of self-reflective meaning through internalization, Vygotsky (1997, p. 105) writes: "Every higher mental function was external because it was social before it became an internal, strictly mental function; it was formerly a social relation of two people." Social relations, like conversations, become internalized and constitute the higher mental functions. Self-reflection, for example, can be understood as a change of perspective within the individual (analogous to the change of perspective between people taking turns in a conversation). "I relate to myself as people related to me. Reflection is a dispute" (Vygotsky, 1989, pp. 56–57).

The tale that turns grasping into pointing can also be used to articulate Vygotsky's concept of the sign. According to Vygotsky (1997), signs are first used to mediate the behavior of others, and are later used to talk about self, reflect on self and mediate the behavior of self. The child learns to point, first in order to direct the attention of others, and later to direct his own attention (for example, using his/her finger to keep his/her eyes focused on the text). Equally, the child learns to ask questions of others before he/she asks questions of him/herself. But what is it in the structure of the sign that enables humans, on the one hand, to communicate and, on the other hand, to self-reflect?

The difference between grasping and pointing is that grasping is a response (to the stimulus of the desired object), while pointing is a response that is also a stimulus to both self and other. While grasping may be a stimulus to other, it is not a stimulus to self. Pointing becomes a sign when it is *not just a response but also a stimulus to self in the same way that it is a stimulus to other*. Thus, signs differ from other stimuli because "they have a reverse action," that is, signs are responses which can also be stimuli (Vygotsky & Luria, 1930/1994, p. 143). The classic example of "reverse action" is tying a knot in a handkerchief as a mnemonic aid. Self ties a knot in a handkerchief (a response), so that later, the knot will function as a stimulus, reminding self that something must be remembered. The idea of "reverse action" is fundamental to Vygotsky's concept of the sign, which he initially theorized as a "reversible reflex" (Vygotsky, 1925/1999).

Only human actions and their products possess the key property of "reverse action." A naturally occurring tree might be a stimulus, but it is not a response. A dog might bare its teeth in response to the stimulus of a wolf. The baring of teeth may be a stimulus to the wolf, but it will never become a stimulus to the dog itself. A human's angry ges-

ture is a response which may become a stimulus to the other. But crucially, the angry gesture may also become a stimulus to self, in the same way that it is a stimulus to other. To the other person the angry gesture may be evidence of an impulsive personality, and self may also become aware of this possible meaning of his/her angry gesture. If the gesture becomes a stimulus with the same meaning for self as it has for other, then it is a sign.

Vygotsky's conception of the sign is astonishingly close to Mead's concept of the significant symbol. Mead (1922) defines the significant symbol as a gesture which self experiences both from the perspective of self and from the perspective of other. As Mead (1922, p. 161) writes: "It is through the ability to be the other at the same time that he is himself that the symbol becomes significant." The key point of similarity is that both Mead and Vygotsky conceive of the sign (or significant symbol) as comprising two perspectives. On the one hand, there is the embodied actor perspective (the response) toward some object (e.g., the reaching child desires the object). On the other hand, there is the distance introduced by the observer perspective of the other on the action (e.g., the mother sees the child's grasping as indicating desire). When the child takes both his/her own grasping perspective and the mother's perspective toward that grasping, then the grasping becomes pointing. Thus there is an equivalence between Vygotsky's concept of "reverse action" and Mead's concept of taking the perspective of the other.

Vygotsky's theory of the sign, and Mead's theory of the significant symbol, are fundamentally different from the theories of Peirce, Saussure, Bühler, and Morris (Gillespie, 2010). The last all have monological theories of the sign. Simply put, they conceive of the sign as representing something or some relation to the world. However, according to the present reading of Vygotsky and Mead, the sign (or significant symbol) is a composite of two different perspectives, namely, an actor perspective and an observer perspective. Thus the sign (or significant symbol) is fundamentally intersubjective: *it evokes both actor and observer perspectives in both self and other*.

The fruitful consequences of the present conception of the sign are immediately evident when one tries to explain the role of the sign in either empathizing or self-reflection. In empathy, the sign carries the empathizer from an observer perspective (on, for example, the suffering of the other) to an actor perspective (participating in that suffering). In self-reflection, or distantiation, the sign carries the person from an actor perspective (a fully absorbed action orientation toward something) to an observer perspective (reacting to the absorbed action orientation).

In the context of the present review of theories of self-reflection, Vygotsky's theory of the sign and Mead's concept of the significant symbol are landmark contributions, because both theories specify precisely the semiotic structure that can account for self-reflection. However, a gap remains. How does the child come to react to his/her own grasping in the same way that the mother responds? How do the perspectives of self and other, actor and observer, become fused into semiotic structures such as signs? How are these two perspectives brought together? In order to address this question we turn to Mead's theory of the social act.

13.5 The Social Act

Mead's theory of the social act is a theory of institutional structures (Gillespie, 2005) and people moving in time (Gillespie & Martin, 2013; Gillespie & Zittoun, 2013). The first defining feature of humans for Mead is that they move among positions within a relatively stable social, or institutional, structure. Of course social structure is not unique to humans. Within an ant colony one will find the queen, workers, foragers, nurses, and soldiers. But it is not simply the existence

of social structure that is fundamental for Mead. Rather, it is *position exchange within the institutional structure*. In nonhuman societies there is a division of labor, but there is never frequent position exchange. However, humans frequently exchange positions within institutional structures. For example, people sometimes host parties and at other times attend parties. The perspectives of host and guest are quite divergent. If these social positions were never exchanged, or reversed, then it is unlikely that either would be able to take the perspective of the other. However, because people are sometimes hosts and sometimes guests this means that most adults have experience of both perspectives, and thus are able to take the perspective of the other when they are in either social position.

Additional social acts in which frequent position exchange occurs include: buying/selling, giving/receiving, suffering/helping, grieving/consoling, teaching/learning, ordering/obeying, winning/losing, and stealing/punishing. Each of these social acts entails reciprocal actor and observer positions and, importantly, because most people have enacted both social positions, they have both the actor and observer perspectives for each social act and thus are able to take the perspective of each other within a social act. Returning to the example of pointing, the child cannot learn the meaning of his/her own pointing without first having been in the social position of responding to the pointing of others.

However, having previously been in the social position of the other, within a social act, does not mean that self will necessarily take the perspective of the other. Why should the perspective of the other be evoked in self when self is not in the social position of the other? The problem is that most of the stimuli for self and other are quite divergent. The child, who desires the object and is grasping toward it, is in a completely different situation to the mother, who is attentive to the child's grasping. Even if the child had previously responded to the grasping of others, why should the child now respond to his/her own grasping? The feeling of grasping is quite different to the sight of someone else grasping. What is common in these two situations that could serve to unite these two perspectives in the mind of the child? Mead (Mead, 1912; see also Farr, 1997) points to the peculiar significance of the vocal gesture. Stimuli in the auditory modality (like vocal gestures) sound the same for self as they do for other. Accordingly, the vocal gesture is ideally poised to integrate both actor and observer perspectives. Because self hears self speak in the same way that self hears other speak, so self can react to self's utterances in the same way that self reacts to other.

It is often asserted that self and other co-emerge in ontogenesis. For example, Baldwin (1906, p. 321) famously wrote that: "The Ego and the Alter are thus born together." However, Mead would disagree with this, arguing that the other exists for self (and self exists for other) before self exists for self. First self reacts to other, then self changes social position with the other, and finally self is able to react to self (in the same way that self previously reacted to other). Empirical evidence for rejecting the co-emergence thesis, in favor of Mead's theory, is found in studies of children's use of words denoting self and other, which have shown that children talk about other before talking about self (e.g., Cooley, 1908; Bain, 1936).

Mead's theory of the social act fits closely with his theory of the significant symbol. The structure of the significant symbol (or sign) is a pairing of an actor perspective engaged in some action with an observer perspective reacting to that action. The social act is the institution that, first, provides individuals with roughly equivalent actor and observer experiences and, second, integrates these perspectives within the minds of individuals.

When both actor and observer perspectives within the significant symbol (or sign) are evoked, then there is self-reflection, because self is both self and other simultaneously. The question then is: what can trigger this double evocation? Simply, there are two ways in which self can arrive at an observer perspective on self (i.e., self-reflection). The process can begin with either an actor perspective engaged in some action, or an observer perspective on someone else's action. Either of these perspectives can evoke, *via* the structure of the significant symbol (or sign), the complementary actor and observer perspectives, thus resulting in self-reflection. Specifically, with this model we can distinguish two conceptually distinct pathways to self-reflection. First, there can be distantiation from self (moving from an actor to an observer perspective) and, second, there can be identification with other (moving from an observer to an actor perspective). The next section illustrates these two forms of self-reflection.

13.6 Two Processes of Self-Reflection: An Illustration

The following analysis is taken from a study on the interactions between tourists and Ladakhis, in northern India (Gillespie, 2006a). Ladakh, on the border of Tibet, is a popular backpacker destination. Tourists are led to Ladakh by representations of the Himalayan mountains, spirituality and traditional culture. Usually the tourists in Ladakh reject the idea of package tourism, and claim to be searching for something more authentic. In the following exchange, an English university student is explaining, to me and another tourist, how she wants to have an authentic experience of Ladakh:

LAURA: I wanted to come up here for longer, to do voluntary work, to be more part of it, rather than just a tourist passing through, taking photos and buying things, eh, eh, I am quite disappointed I haven't, I don't know, eh, in eight days you can't, em, . . . it's just, having been with a family in the first place, I now want everything to be personal, to see proper India rather than just the India that everyone – that sounds rather clichéd – but that tourists see (pause) – (sigh) so I am a tourist really.

The actor perspective that Laura is initially embedded in is that of wanting "to be more part of" Indian life, and wanting "to see proper India." This desire for an authentic experience is positioned against the other tourists who are merely "passing through" and touring "the India that everyone ... sees." Before traveling to Ladakh, Laura had spent two months in south India, living with an Indian family, and thus having seen the "proper India." Although she had planned to stay in Ladakh for longer, and even do voluntary work, she is now planning to leave Ladakh after just eight days. Accordingly, it is difficult for her to claim the position of someone who has experienced the "proper" Ladakh. The reality is that she, like many other tourists, is merely "passing through." The contradiction becomes apparent and leads to two interrelated, but theoretically distinct, processes of self-reflection.

13.6.1 Self-Reflection via Distantiation from Self

The first movement of self-reflection, which culminates in the utterance "that sounds rather clichéd," is quite straightforward. Laura begins in the actor perspective of wanting an authentic experience of India and Ladakh, and then, in the self-reflective utterance ("that sounds rather clichéd") switches to an observer perspective on her previous actor perspective. She ends up reflecting on herself, suggesting that such a search for the "proper" Ladakh is in fact a tourist cliché. How can this self-mediation be explained?

The rupture theories are obviously inadequate, because there is no pragmatic subject–object rupture. The mirror theories have more to contribute, because this self-reflection is embedded in a social situation. Laura is speaking to me and another tourist, and her self-reflection may have been stimulated by social feedback. For example,

she may have perceived skeptical looks concerning her search for authenticity, thus triggering this self-reflection (Gillespie, 2006b). But the feedback she received was not neutral. Her utterance ("that sounds rather clichéd") is pejorative. Such a cliché is an embarrassment. Thus we could describe Laura as struggling for recognition from her audience. However, such an analysis, while insightful, does not explain the semiotic process underlying Laura's self-reflection. The internalization theories, on the other hand, do provide a model. According to these theories one could argue that Laura became self-aware by taking the perspective of her audience. But how does she take the perspective of her audience? The answer is to be found in Mead's concept of the vocal gesture.

Laura's phrase, "that sounds rather clichéd," is particularly revealing because according to Mead it is precisely the sound of her previous utterances that trigger self-reflection. The peculiar significance of vocal gestures is that they sound the same to self as they do to other. Laura hears her own utterances (expressing a desire to see the "proper India") in the same way as her audience. Accordingly, she is able to react to her own utterance as if it were the utterance of an other. Presumably, if Laura heard another tourist talking about finding the "proper India" she would think that it sounded clichéd. Using Vygotsky's terminology, one could say that Laura's initial utterance is not only a response to my question, it is also a stimulus to herself. In short, she becomes self-aware because she reacts to herself in the same way that she reacts to others. The key process underling this instance of self-reflection is a movement from an actor perspective to an observer perspective on her previous actor perspective. The vocal gesture is the semiotic means that carries Laura from being embedded in an actor perspective (searching for the "proper" India), to an observer perspective on herself (that what she says sounds clichéd).

13.6.2 Self-Reflection via Identification with Other

The second movement of self-reflection culminates in the utterance, "so I am a tourist really." This movement begins with the contradiction between Laura's criticism of tourists "passing through, taking photos and buying things" and the fact that she only spent eight days in Ladakh (and, as she mentioned elsewhere, that she took many photos and bought many souvenirs). This movement is analytically distinct from the first instance of self-reflection, because here, the movement is from an observer perspective on other tourists (criticizing them for having a shallow experience) to an observer perspective on self (specifically, seeing herself in the other, as opposed to seeing, or hearing, the other in herself).

The rupture theories again are of little use in this analysis because there is no subject–object rupture. Both the mirror and conflict theories can contribute an understanding of the proximal cause of Laura's self-reflection. One could speculate that the gaze of the audience made the contradiction salient, thus leading to a collapse of the self–other distinction (Gillespie, 2007). But again, this does not explain the semiotic process through which this might occur. Interestingly, the internalization theories also have little to contribute. Laura is not taking the perspective of the other, *rather she is taking her own perspective on the other tourists and turning this on herself.*

Vygotsky's theory of the sign and Mead's theory of the significant symbol, however, can begin to unpack this movement of self-reflection. When Laura is criticizing the other tourists, she is using signs (or significant symbols) to describe the other. She says that other tourists are just "passing through, taking photos and buying things." In the moment of speaking, Laura is blind to the fact that this is exactly what she has done. However, because signs are pairings of actor and observer perspectives, describing the other always evokes

an empathetic actor response in self. In Laura's case, this empathetic response "resonates" with her own experiences. She hesitates ("eh, eh") and begins to speak ("I am quite disappointed I haven't") and then hesitates again ("I don't know, eh") and finally we discover what it is that is welling up in her mind, namely, that she has only spent eight days in Ladakh (and was leaving the next day). The significance of this takes time to manifest explicitly and, when it does, Laura can only say that, despite her wishes, she is a tourist just like any other tourist in Ladakh ("so I am a tourist really"). This is self-reflection via identification with the other (i.e., other tourists) because it begins with an emphasis on the difference between self and other, and then this difference collapses and self becomes equivalent to other.

Mead's theory of the social act takes the analysis even further. *Laura's self-reflection via identification can only occur because of frequent exchange of social positions within the social act.* If Laura had not been in the actual social position of the other tourists, if she had not been merely "passing through," taking photos and buying souvenirs, then the self-reflection could not have occurred. Stating the case even more forcefully, position exchange is a necessary precondition for this type of self-reflection. In this type of self-reflection, one can see clearly that self and other do not co-emerge, as argued by Baldwin, but rather that the characteristics first associated with "they" become subsequently recognized as characteristics of "me." First there is action, second, there is observing the other doing the same action, and finally, in the integration of these perspectives, there is self-reflection.

13.7 Complex Semiotic Systems

The analysis of Laura's self-reflection, as outlined so far, could be criticized on two fronts: first it is too individualistic (isn't Laura's self-reflection part of a larger cultural pattern?) and, second, it is overly concerned with individual signs (what about more complex semiotic systems?). Both of these criticisms are well placed. Laura is not the first tourist to hypocritically criticize other tourists (Prebensen, Larsen, & Abelsen, 2003). Moreover, Laura's description of other tourists as just "passing through, taking photos and buying things" is a complex collective and historical product. Neither Vygotsky nor Mead provides an adequate theory of the more complex transindividual semiotic systems that circulate in society. One of the significant advances of sociocultural psychology, since the work of Mead and Vygotsky, has been the theorization of these complex semiotic systems in a variety of ways: as social representations (Moscovici, 1984), cultural artifacts (Cole, 1996), symbolic resources (Zittoun et al., 2003; see also Chapter 10, this volume), narratives (Bruner, 1986), interpretive repertoires (Potter & Wetherell, 1987), and discourses with subject positions (Harré & Van Langenhove, 1991).

Laura participates in a collective and historical discourse that contains several subject positions. First, there is the subject position of the tourist dupe. This is the tourist who just passes through, takes photos, and buys souvenirs. Most tourists willingly ascribe this subject position to other tourists, yet few ascribe this position to themselves. Instead, tourists try to occupy one of the more favorable subject positions, like that of adventurer, spiritual searcher, or reflexive post-tourist. Laura, for example, tries to occupy the position of having authentic encounters with the local population, as evidenced by her aspirations to do voluntary work and live with a local family.

The question is: How can these complex semiotic systems be used to help explain the semiotics of self-reflection? The interesting thing about the discourse is not simply that it has several subject positions, but that Laura claims, in discourse, one position, while enacting, in action, a different position. On the one hand, Laura's actions conform to typical tourist practices. She has been led,

by various representations, to a tourist destination where the only obvious paths of action are to sightsee, take photos, and buy souvenirs. Laura thus participates in a discourse that conceives of these typical tourist actions as shallow and instead aspires to less attainable subject positions (i.e., having authentic encounters). Thus Laura is caught in a contradictory stream of cultural meanings. This collectively produced, and historically sustained, fault-line makes self-reflection via distantiation and identification immanent.

The fault-line in the cultural stream corresponds to the structure of the sign. The contradiction is between the semiotic guidance of tourist action (actor perspective) and the criticism of other tourists (observer perspective). There is, at the level of discourses and representations, then, a lack of integration between actor and observer perspectives. It must be emphasized that this is not simply a contradiction between two semiotic systems (i.e., a conflict theory of self-reflection), rather it concerns a very specific contradiction, namely between actor and observer perspectives. The position that self claims and the position that self enacts are disjunctive. This is what Ichheiser (1949) called a mote-beam divergence and what in common sense is called hypocrisy. The prevalence of this divergence reveals that the lack of integration between actor and observer perspectives is not simply something that occurs at the level of individual signs, but something that is played out in much more macro-semiotic dynamics. The point, then, is that the structure of the sign (or significant symbol), is not only evident at the level of individual words or gestures, but is evident in the macrostructure of whole complex semiotic systems.

13.8 Concluding Discussion

Returning to the questions raised at the outset of this chapter, it is now possible to offer some concise answers. The proximal reasons for self-reflection are diverse. Humans can be led to self-reflection by ruptures (problems with the subject–object relation), social feedback (where the other acts as a mirror), social conflict (in the struggle for recognition), and internal dialogues (through internalizing the perspective of the other on self). Moreover, there is a cultural level to the analysis; the complex semiotic systems in which people are embedded contain contradictions that can make self-reflection immanent. However, fundamental to all these proximal causes of self-reflection is the logic of the sign.

Before the formation of the sign (or significant symbol) there is undifferentiated experience (level 0 experience in Valsiner's [2001] terminology). But this experience is structured by social acts: it contains experience belonging to both actor and observer perspectives. The magic of the social act is that it integrates these actor and observer experiences, or perspectives, into the formation of signs. Conceiving of the sign as this integration of perspectives elucidates the logic of self-reflection. Whenever one uses a sign to describe self's own actor experience, the sign may carry self from an actor perspective to an observer perspective on that experience (as illustrated by Laura's self-reflection via distantiation). Equally, whenever one uses a sign to describe, or observe, the actions of others, the sign may carry self from this observer perspective to an empathetic actor participation in the actions of the other (which in Laura's case leads to self-reflection via identification).

Introducing the concept of the sign (or significant symbol) into our conception of complex semiotic systems entails abandoning the assumption that the complex semiotic systems "mirror" the world, and instead conceptualizing these semiotic systems as architectures of intersubjectivity (Rommetveit, 1974) which enable the translation between actor and observer perspectives within a social act.

Consider, for example, narratives. It has been argued by Nelson (2000) that the key to self-consciousness is awareness of self in time, and that this implies narratives. According to Nelson, the developing child is offered self-narratives, and by appropriating these, the child is able to conceptualize him/herself in time. Combining this with the present theoretical approach, we can say that before appropriating a narrative a child will have certain fields of undifferentiated experience. For example, the child may have experienced the loss of a loved one, but have not any reflective articulation of this experience (i.e., they have not put it into words). The narrative offered to the child provides an observer's perspective on their actor experience of loss – giving raw experience a name and thus externality. And it is the integration of actor and observer perspectives, that enables the child to distantiate from the experience (while simultaneously being connected to it), thus enabling them to talk about the loss.

A similar dynamic is evident in Zittoun's (Chapter 10, Section 10.2.3, this volume) analysis of Emma Bovary's use of novels as a symbolic resource. Initially, Emma is embedded in the actor perspective of being in love. She feels exalted and has no self-reflective awareness of this experience. Then she thinks of some romance novels that she's read. These provide her with an observer's perspective on an other's love. Combining the actor perspective (elation) with the observer perspective (on the love of others) results in the self-reflective awareness of herself being in love. Thus the narrative is not just a narrative that is analogical to self's own experience, it is an intersubjective structure that enables translations between actor and observer perspectives.

Partially integrated actor and observer perspectives are the precondition for self-reflection. Rupture, feedback, and social conflict can cause self-reflection because of a preexisting, and only partially integrated, architecture of intersubjectivity. These social dynamics can provide the impetus for self-reflection, and thus have a part to play in constructing the architecture of intersubjectivity. However, these social dynamics, in themselves, cannot explain the semiotic process underlying self-reflection. The origin of self-reflection is not just in social interaction, but in social acts, or institutions, which provide structured actor and observer perspectives, and a mechanism for integrating these perspectives in the minds of individuals.

References

Bain, R. (1936). The self-and-other words of a child. *The American Journal of Sociology*, 41(6), 767–775.

Bakhtin, M. (1923/1990). Author and hero in aesthetic activity (trans. by V. Liapunov). In M. Holquist & V. Liapunov (Eds.), *Art and Answerability: Early Philosophical Essays by M. M. Bakhtin* (vol. 9, pp. 4–256). Austin: University of Texas Press.

Baldwin, J. M. (1906). *Mental Development in the Child and the Race*. New York: Macmillan.

Bauer, M. W. & Gaskell, G. (1999). Towards a paradigm for research on social representations. *Journal for the Theory of Social Behaviour*, 29, 163–186.

Bruner, J. (1986). *Actual Minds, Possible Worlds*. Cambridge, MA: Harvard University Press.

Cole, M. (1996). *Cultural Psychology: A Once and Future Discipline*. Cambridge, MA: Harvard University Press.

Cooley, C. H. (1902). *Human Nature and the Social Order*. New York: Charles Scribner's Sons.

Cooley, C. H. (1908). A study of the early use of the self words by a child. *Psychological Review*, 15, 339–357.

Dewey, J. (1896). The reflex arc concept in psychology. *Psychological Review*, 3(July), 357–370.

Doise, W. & Mugny, G. (1984). *The Social Development of the Intellect*. Oxford: Pergammon.

Engeström, Y. (1987). *Learning by Expanding: An Activity-Theoretical Approach to Developmental Research*. Helsinki: Orienta Konsultit.

Engeström, Y., Brown, K., Christopher, L. C., & Gregory, J. (1997). Coordination, cooperation and communication in the courts: Expansive transitions in legal work. In M. Cole, Y. Engestrom, & O. Vasquez (Eds.), *Mind, Culture and Activity: Seminal Papers from the Laboratory of Comparative Human Cognition* (pp. 369–385). Cambridge: Cambridge University Press.

Farr, R. M. (1997). The significance of the skin as a natural boundary in the sub-division of psychology. *Journal for the Theory of Social Behaviour*, 27, 305–323.

Gergely, G. & Watson, J. S. (1996). The social biofeedback theory of parental affect-mirroring: The development of emotional self-awareness and self-control in infancy. *International Journal of Psychoanalysis*, 77, 1181–1212.

Gillespie, A. (2003). Surplus & supplementarity: Moving between the dimensions of otherness. *Culture & Psychology*, 9, 209–220.

Gillespie, A. (2005). G. H. Mead: Theorist of the social act. *Journal for the Theory of Social Behaviour*, 35, 19–39.

Gillespie, A. (2006a). *Becoming Other to Oneself: A Meadian Study of Culture Tourism in Ladakh*. Greenwich, CT: Information Age Publishing.

Gillespie, A. (2006b). Tourist photography and the reverse gaze. *Ethos*, 34, 343–366.

Gillespie, A. (2007). Collapsing self/other positions: Identification through differentiation. *British Journal of Social Psychology*, 46, 579–595.

Gillespie, A. (2010). The intersubjective nature of symbols. In B. Wagoner (Ed.), *Symbolic Transformations: The Mind in Movement through Culture and Society* (pp. 23–37). London: Routledge.

Gillespie, A., & Martin, J. (2013). Position exchange theory: A socio-material basis for discursive and psychological positioning. *New Ideas in Psychology*, 32, 73–79.

Gillespie, A. & Zittoun, T. (2013). Meaning making in motion: Bodies and minds moving through institutional and semiotic structures. *Culture & Psychology*, 19, 518–532.

Harré, R., & Van Langenhove, L. (1991). Varieties of positioning. *Journal for the Theory of Social Behaviour*, 21(4).

Hermans, H. J. M. (2001). The dialogical self: Toward a theory of personal and cultural positioning. *Culture & Psychology*, 7, 243–281.

Hobson, P. (2002). *The Cradle of Thought*. London: Macmillan.

Ichheiser, G. (1949). Misunderstandings in human relations: A study in false social perception. *American Journal of Sociology*, 55, 1–72.

Josephs, I. E. (2002). "The Hopi in me": The construction of a voice in the dialogical self from a cultural psychological perspective. *Theory & Psychology*, 12, 161–173.

Jovchelovitch, S. (1995). Social representations in and of the public sphere: Towards a theoretical articulation. *Journal for the Theory of Social Behaviour*, 25, 81–102.

Lacan, J. (1949/1977). The mirror stage as formative of the function of the I as revealed in psychoanalytic theory. In *Écrits: A Selection* (pp. 1–9). London: Tavistock.

Lawrence, J. A. & Valsiner, J. (1993). Conceptual roots of internalization: From transmission to transformation. *Human Development*, 36, 150–167.

Lundgren, D. C. (2004). Social feedback and self-appraisals: Current status of the Mead–Cooley hypothesis. *Symbolic Interaction*, 27, 267–286.

Marková, I. (1982). *Paradigms, Thought and Language*. Chichester, UK: John Wiley & Sons.

Matusov, E. (1998). When solo activity is not privileged: Participation and internalization models of development. *Human Development*, 41, 326–354.

Mead, G. H. (1910). Social consciousness and the consciousness of meaning. *Psychological Bulletin*, 6, 401–408.

Mead, G. H. (1912). The mechanism of social consciousness. *The Journal of Philosophy, Psychology and Scientific Methods*, 9, 401–406.

Mead, G. H. (1922). A behavioristic account of the significant symbol. *Journal of Philosophy*, 19, 157–163.

Moscovici, S. (1984). The phenomenon of social representations. In R. Farr & S. Moscovici (Eds.), *Social Representations*. Cambridge: Cambridge University Press.

Nelson, K. (2000). Narrative, time and the emergence of the encultured self. *Culture & Psychology*, 6, 183–196.

Pavlov, I. P. (1951). *Psychopathology and Psychiatry: Selected Works* (trans. by D. Myshne & S. Belsky). Moscow: Foreign Languages Publishing House.

Peirce, C. S. (1878/1998). *Charles S. Peirce: The Essential Writings* (ed. by Edward C. Moore). New York: Prometheus Books.

Piaget, J. (1970). Piaget's theory. In P. H. Mussen (Ed.), *Carmichael's Manual of Child Psychology* (3rd edn., pp. 703–732). New York: John Wiley & Sons.

Potter, J. & Wetherell, M. (1987). *Discourse and Social Psychology*. London: SAGE.

Prebensen, N. K., Larsen, S., & Abelsen, B. (2003). I'm not a typical tourist: German tourists' self-perception, activities and motivations. *Journal of Travel Research*, 41, 416–420.

Psaltis, C. & Duveen, G. (2006). Social relations and cognitive development: The influence of conversation type and representations of gender. *European Journal of Social Psychology*, 36, 407–430.

Rommetveit, R. (1974). *On Message Structure: A Framework for the Study of Language and Communication*. London: John Wiley & Sons.

Shrauger, J. S. & Schoeneman, T. J. (1979). Symbolic interactionist view of self-concept. *Psychological Bulletin*, 86, 549–573.

Sigel, I. E. (2002). The psychological distancing model: A study of the socialization of cognition. *Culture & Psychology*, 8, 189–214.

Smith, A. (1759/1982). *The Theory of Moral Sentiments* (ed. by D. D. Raphael & A. L. Macfie). Indianapolis, IN: Liberty Fund.

Tolman, C. W. & Piekkola, B. (1989). John Dewey and dialectical materialism: Anticipations of activity theory in the critique of the reflex arc concept. *Activity Theory*, 1, 43–46.

Tomasello, M., Carpenter, M., Call, J., Behne, T., & Moll, H. (2005). Understanding and sharing intentions: The origins of cultural cognition. *Behavioral and Brain Sciences*, 28, 675–691.

Valsiner, J. (1998). *The Guided Mind*. Cambridge, MA: Harvard University Press.

Valsiner, J. (2001). Process structure of semiotic mediation in human development. *Human Development*, 44, 84–97.

Vygotsky, L. S. (1925/1999). Consciousness as a problem in the psychology of behavior. In N. N. Veresov (Ed.), *Undiscovered Vygotsky: Etudes on the Pre-History of Cultural-Historical Psychology*. Bern: Peter Lang.

Vygotsky, L. S. (1989). Concrete human psychology. *Soviet Psychology*, 27, 53–77.

Vygotsky, L. S. (1997). *The Collected Works of L. S. Vygotsky* (vol. 4, ed. by R. W. Rieber, trans. by M. J. Hall). New York: Plenum Press.

Vygotsky, L. S. & Luria, A. (1930/1994). Tool and symbol in child development. In R. Van de Veer & J. Valsiner (Eds.), *The Vygotsky Reader* (pp. 99–174). Oxford: Blackwell.

Wagner, W., Duveen, G., Themel, M., & Verma, J. (1999). The modernization of tradition: Thinking about madness in Patna, India. *Culture & Psychology*, 5, 413–445.

Wertsch, J. V. & Stone, A. (1985). The concept of internalization in Vygotsky's account of the genesis of higher mental functions. In J. V. Wertsch (Ed.), *Culture, Communication and Cognition: Vygotskian Perspectives* (pp. 162–179). Cambridge: Cambridge University Press.

Whiten, A. (2005). The imitative correspondence problem: Solved or sidestepped? In S. Hurley & N. Chater (Eds.), *Perspectives on Imitation: Mechanisms of Imitation and Imitation in Animals* (vol. 1, pp. 220–222). Cambridge, MA: MIT Press.

Winnicott, D. W. (1971). *Playing and Reality*. London: Tavistock.

Zittoun, T., Duveen, G., Gillespie, A., Ivinson, G., & Psaltis, C. (2003). The use of symbolic resources in developmental transitions. *Culture & Psychology*, 9, 415–448.

Further Reading

Perret-Clermont, A. N. (1980). *Social Interaction and Cognitive Development in Children*. London: Academic Press.

14 Making Memory: Meaning in Development of the Autobiographical Self

Katherine Nelson

The construct of an "autobiographical self" (in the title of this chapter) is the self that emerges from one's accumulation of memories from the past. There is of course no single "self" that emerges from this source: one's adolescent self, for example, may seem alien to the present self. Nonetheless, the self in the past is recognized as an earlier version of "me." The account here considers the emergence of autobiographical memory and the concept of "self" in early childhood, while recognizing that significant further development of both self and memory takes place after that point. The central implication is that the continuity of memories over one's lifetime is meaningful – and may even be necessary – for self conception. This claim relies on two other parts of the title above: "making memory" and "meaning" as the source of memory contents. The "autobiographical self" overall is viewed as one perspective on the many versions of self available to the adult introspector (Neisser, 1988).

Of major interest here is how memory changes over human infancy and early childhood, with implications for understanding the almost universal accumulation of long-lasting memories derived from past experiences and their recollection in adulthood. In what sense do we "make memory" and why? How does this change over time, especially in the early years of life? In what ways does the social and cultural world frame the self that emerges from this source? If – as Merlin Donald (2012) claims – autobiographical memory is unique to humans and

ultimately arises from cultural experience, what ensures that it appears in individual lives? I begin with an overview of early development in which both meaning and memory play a major role. I then consider the emergence of autobiographical memory within this framework, emphasizing its reliance on social and cultural models. Finally, I will discuss the tangled issues of self and self-understanding as they relate to this process.

14.1 Experience, Meaning, and Memory in Development[1]

The development of memory in the social-cultural environments of infancy and childhood is considered here from an ontological framework that views development of humans within an evolutionary historical cultural ground. This frame has roots in Vygotsky's (1962) work and thus relates as well to many others working within that and related perspectives, perhaps most specifically that of Michael Cole (1996) and his colleagues. It derives also from the evolutionary framework of Merlin Donald (1991, 2001). The specific developmental approach based on Donald's work was elaborated in *Language in Cognitive Development* (Nelson, 1996). As Donald's analysis makes clear, the complexity and enlargement of the modern human brain, and its cognitive operations, can only be understood in terms of its evolutionary and cultural history. It can also only be understood in terms of its development in human infancy and childhood. In a sense this is a proposal of extended epigenesis, where the process involves not only extended biological development but development within and dependent on social and cultural environments.

Donald's model envisions three major cultural eras, each defined in terms of its communicative and cognitive potentials. The first (among pre-*Homo sapiens* primates) is termed *mimetic* and relied on the use of mimesis for communication between individuals and within cultural groups. The emergence in *Homo sapiens* of oral language between persons and within groups enabled the beginnings of both narrative and argument – group exchanges inconceivable without language. This mode, termed *mythic*, is most distinguished by group participation in the telling of oral narratives, the cultural mode that young children enter from infancy as they develop language competence. Such narratives include not only fictional stories but accounts of events in the past and anticipated future. This mode is so dominant in humans that the neurologist, Damasio (1999) views it as the natural mode of human memory. Jerome Bruner (1986) proposed that it is one of two dominant modes of human thought (the other being logical or rational thinking). A major cultural change (termed *theoretic* by Donald) emerged much later in human history, about four millennia ago, following the invention of alphabetically based written scripts and their preservation in documents on paper and other media. It was intensified with the invention of printing and subsequent widespread literacy and scholarship in the sixteenth through nineteenth centuries. These later changes are associated with the emergence of modern science and technology and literary works – including biography and novels – accessible to all who can read.

Overall these culturally based language evolutions have meant radical revisions in people's brains, cognitive processes, and ways of life. "Living in a linguistic community is largely a question of mastering and performing conceptually complex representational skills in a social context . . . human social life has become dominated by a public theater of language acts, and *narrative accounts of experience are constructed essentially as real or latent public performances"* (Donald, forthcoming; italics in original). To fully enter the literate world children must be tutored in the skills of reading alphabetical scripts and the uses of these resources, requiring lengthy formal schooling. Most very young children worldwide do not participate in this written part of the culture, but are embedded in the still vibrant oral culture of childhood. This gradual introduction to the complexities of the language-using world may be appropriate for the kinds of biocultural development that naturally takes place in the first five years of life, as well as providing the practices that enable moving into the more complex literate world.

The influence of language on memory and mind, of human knowledge, and representation is incontestable. Considering the impact of language on the development of individual minds is essential to our understanding of how mature minds emerge. The course in development is obviously not the same as that experienced through evolution or history. Just as the onset of shared language that supported group narratives such as myth was a critical point in human evolution, so experiences in early childhood with conversations and stories may be viewed as analogous critical points of development. All human behavior takes place in social and cultural context, but that context is only relevant to an individual to the extent that it is discernible, through action, perception, language, or memory. Although lacking language, the infant develops in an intensely social world and begins to understand its contours in interactive activities, developing scripts or scenarios for them (Bruner, 1983; Nelson, 1986, 2007). All aspects of the environment that are not personally engaged, however, remain outside the child's memory and knowledge base. In late infancy the child slowly becomes a user of the local language, thus entering into the language-based cultural surround that was previously hidden. Fortunately, the social environments of most young children include older persons who support them in the adventure into this new "mythic" context.

It is important to recognize that what changes for the child in the early childhood years is access to the vast areas of the social and cultural world that are inaccessible to anyone – including babies – without language. The cultural milieu that slowly emerges with language challenges the child's previously established personal knowledge base derived from nonlinguistic experience as an infant and very young child. It is reasonable to assume that even the physical world is perceived differently by those who have a shared communicative system for interpreting it. Previously hidden aspects of the cultural world include basic frameworks such as temporal and spatial categories and terms, family relationships, and the life spaces and activities of people beyond the bounds of one's personal experience.

14.2 Experience Space and Its Constraints

An abstraction of the bounds of experiential space is sketched in Figure 14.1, designed to represent the range of constraints on personal experience in any environmental event or encounter (Nelson, 2007). How these constraints operate

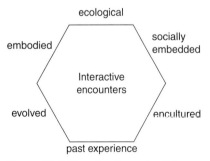

Figure 14.1 Bounds of experiential space in an environmental event or encounter.

through developmental time is of particular interest in this account. I refer here to "events" because that is what people experience. (We rarely experience simple "scenes" except in photographs or paintings.) In Figure 14.1 the center of the hexagon is the person's (constrained) experience within any given context or time. Each segment of the hexagonal boundary indicates individualized boundaries on such experience, regardless of the "objective" space as viewed from outside. As depicted, the person's experience is constrained by variable conditions in both the individual person and the environment.

The left segments of the hexagon are the physical or biological constraints through evolution (lower segment) and current individual conditions of body and mind, such as health, state of growth, and current stature (upper left). These are continuously modified by the specific conditions of the body and mind, including health as well as learning and skills, and by all specific individual characteristics of these. The top segment represents the constraints of the particular physical and material environment within which the individual experiences ongoing events, including its familiarity or novelty. The top right segment is the space of social conditions and interactions (including the use of language) that surround the child from the beginning, which may include various known and unknown figures, familiar or not. The bottom right refers to the ongoing cultural background whether apparent to the experiencer or not. It consists of the cultural store of language and social interactions, and of any relevant cultural organizations or practices in the given situation (e.g., home, school, or church). Whether or not the language, knowledge, or practices are known or familiar to the experiencer is one of the possible parameters of these constraints on experience.

The bottom segment of the diagram is memory for prior experience. The main point here is that all of these conditions or constraints work simultaneously in determining what aspect of any present experiential encounter the individual will observe and perhaps interact. Given differences among the participants in a given event, on any of these dimensions, it is clear that different persons will vary in their experience of the same event. There is in fact a great deal of experimental research verifying this. The point, of course, is that each participant derives different meaning and therefore different memory from any given event.

That Figure 14.1 absorbs language into the cultural and social components of experience is not to downplay the significance of language in human experience; rather, it assumes that language is a cultural endowment that is realized through social interactions and grows with experience. Although the figure is static, an important assumption of this model is its constantly changing components: mental and physical growth, temporal and seasonal change of physical environment, expanding social and cultural worlds, developing and expanding memory. All change at different rates, and what was "in sync" for a child at one point may easily be "out of sync" within days, weeks, or months. The basic biology of the lower left segment is no different in this regard: physical and mental growth proceeds inescapably regardless of other conditions, even though many such developments depend on social and cultural as well as nutritional and physical conditions for their success. In the present context, what enters memory from any experience may change over time as these different constraints change.

What determines whether an aspect of any encounter enters memory, and thus becomes available for future informative purposes, is *meaning*. Meaning lies at the center of all cognitive activity, not only or primarily in language. Meaning emerges initially from the operation of sensorimotor, affective, and cognitive systems relevant to "interests" based on needs, wants, emotions, and prior experiences. Memory has a central role in recognizing meaning in experiential encounters. Memory is involved in two ways:

in partially determining what is attended to and how it is interpreted; and in filtering meaningful parts of the experience for memory and future reference. This applies to all kinds of experience at all ages and for all types of memory, short-term, long-term, semantic, or episodic. From this meaning perspective we can better understand the development, operation, and significance of autobiographical memory.

A major point of this model is that engagement with the environment (physical, social, cultural) through perception, action, or language is conditioned by meaning, arising from present or past (remembered) encounters and from any of the sources delineated on the hexagon. What is noticed, as contemporary theories of perception recognize, is not what is "there" but what is individually meaningful in the present context. The major implication of this point for the present purposes is that what the infant, the young child, the older child, and the adult may "see" in a scene or a narrative may each be different, depending on the meaningful context they each expect and partially provide for interpretation. This is true for the language that the child hears and learns as well as for the physical scene before his or her eyes. For example, the scene may demand attention through rapid continuous changes or through bright colors, while the child may experience pain, sleepiness, or indigestion interfering with a response, and social-cultural interactions pose demands, questions, situations, and practices.

The model implies that meaning is interior to the participant, guiding the interaction as well as memory related to it. Meaning may emerge from biological sources such as hunger or thirst, and may be biased by other genetic or ontogenetic conditions, shared across species or individuals. For example, a given child may be especially drawn to shapes, another to colors within a scene. Much of what is meaningful to the individual child or adult resides in what is in memory, shaping the future. This sense of memory is generic, applicable to all memory, not just recallable information or narrative. It may reside in one's physical experiences and be far from consciousness. However, much is present in the immediate encounter, evoking knowledge or past experience. In this sense meaning is similar to relevance, where relevance is individually determined. It is essential to understanding how words, narratives, poetry, and politics work, through shared symbolic and sometimes implicit meanings evoked in the individuals who experience them. Meaning is essential to understanding the development of children's language, knowledge and behavior over years reaching from no experience in the world to the accumulation of vast quantities of cultural knowledge (Nelson, 2017). In short, both meaning and memory are vital conditions of all sentient creatures: necessary for engaging in environmental encounters (Millikan, 2006).

14.3 Memory

As just argued, memory – including autobiographical memory – is intimately related to meaning, indeed dependent on it. From this perspective the construction of a self-construct also emerges naturally. As possible meanings change over developmental time and new meanings emerge, so memory develops from infancy to early childhood, enabling the accumulation of experience and derived knowledge in infants and children from birth. That very young infants remember aspects of the experienced world is well established (although prior to the mid-twentieth century infant memory was doubted by many experts). Retention of memory increases over the first two years (Bauer, 2007). A scene watched by a 9- or 12-month old infant may be recalled one or even two months later. By 18 months a child's memory may be extended to a full year. The child's use of relevant language at the time of initial viewing aids later recall: children with little or no productive language at presentation recall less (indicated through speech,

action, or gesture) at the later test. Recallable memory by two- to three-year-olds is, however, still limited in length of retention time and in content. For example, Peterson and Rideout (1998) reported a study of 18- to 20-month-old toddlers who had each suffered illness or injuries requiring emergency room treatment. When interviewed about the experience six months later, most remembered little or nothing of the presumably traumatic and memorable event. Greater use of language by the child at the time of the injury was associated with greater likelihood of recalling some parts of it. Two-year-olds were much more likely to recall some of the incident at six months, and some retained the memory for another six months to a year.

It may be inferred that memory in the first and second year of life greatly expands the infant's familiarity with people, places, objects, and activities, accumulating much personal learning and cultural knowledge, but its recall time span is much more limited than in older children and adults. About one year is generally found to be the longest retention for two-year-olds. What kind of memory is this? One view is that early memory is based in the sensorimotor system, which is referred to as *procedural*. Such memory is context-dependent, not declarative, or recallable out of the context of its use (that is, it is not accessible to consciousness). Procedural memory is clearly evident in other primates (as well as other mammalian species such as cats and dogs). Procedural memory continues as part of the general human system relevant in activities such as sports, dance, or bicycling.[2] Karmiloff-Smith (1991) proposed that procedural memory underlay the later more complex knowledge systems developed through analytic processes.

Two types of declarative or recallable memory recognized by most memory theorists are termed *episodic* and *semantic*, as distinguished by Tulving (1983). Episodic memory is memory for a *specific happening* from *the past* encoded from *self experience*, not one that emerged from others' accounts or general history. In Tulving's view, episodic memory is uniquely human, allowing us to travel back into time to reexperience an event (Tulving, 2005). From this position, the memory is necessarily self-oriented or *anoetic*.[3] The second major characteristic of episodic memory in Tulving's account is the sense of "pastness" that enables reference to experience in a specific past time. It may appear that all memory is "about" the past, but as Tulving (1993) has argued (see also Nelson, 1993), basic memory is oriented to the present and future; its basis on past experience is incidental to its value in the present. Location in the past is clearly part of autobiographical memory: it is an account of what happened in one's personal past life. But it may not be relevant to all memories of specific events in short or long term memory that have little relevance to one's ongoing life experience. For example, one may remember experiencing a song or a novel or movie without being able to place it in a specific person-relevant time slot.

The second and complementary type of declarative memory – semantic memory – is not about either the past or the self but is constituted of general knowledge about the world, whether assembled from direct experience or conveyed through other sources such as stories, books, school, or interpersonal communication, including gossip. Often, this kind of memory does not retain information about its source, when and where one learned a fact; the fact may simply be encoded for future use.

That memory is basically oriented to future use has important theoretical implications. It may be relevant to questions about why some memories drop out or are nullified and others continue. It sheds light on the beginnings of memory in all species, as well as our own, in infants and young children. Very young children have no specific concept or interest in the past. The present is where they live and in which they are interested, as well as limited interest in what will happen

next. In addition, compared with older children and adults, the life spaces of infants and young children change with great rapidity as they grow both physically and mentally, giving rise to different daily routines and possibilities for action. Familiarity is a product of memory but it is not the same as "past." Retaining what was remembered about a specific past event would be only confusing in the rapidly changing conditions of infancy. With no motivated interest in the past it is not surprising that young children do not begin acquiring a self history or autobiographical memory until nearly school age.

14.4 Emergence of Autobiographical Memory

Autobiographical memory is distinguished by its focus on the self in experiences from one's past life. For many people these memories appear to make up a "life story," a super-narrative of the self over time. It may then be considered a meta-narrative while each episode within it contributes a narrative to the whole. This self-involved memory has been of continuing interest in psychology since the late nineteenth century, but remained on the sidelines of serious research for most of the next century. One issue of continuing interest over that period was "childhood (or infantile) amnesia," that is, the absence for most adults of any memories from one's life before the age of three years, and the relative paucity of these before the school years (age 7 to 10). This initial gap for all memory from the first years of life was highlighted by William James in his 1890 *Principles of Psychology* as the cause of the lack of any genuine "warm" feeling of "self" with regard to the person's first years. Freud (1905/1953) famously attributed the absence of such early memories to repression associated with sexual anxiety during these years.

Studies of adults' earliest memories, using written or interview questionnaires, accumulated over decades before and during the twentieth century and established that their onset (among European-Americans) appeared on average at about 3.5 years of age. Little more was studied with regard to this absence (or to the later persistence of memories over the long term) until the late twentieth century[4] when identification of episodic memory as a special kind also brought attention to its long-term persistence (Tulving, 1983). More specifically, Tulving's criteria for episodic memory, focused on self and about the past, appear most clearly characteristic of memories of the long-term autobiographical kind.

Whereas episodic memory is the kind of personal experience memory that constitutes the typically vast accumulation of autobiographical memories, not all episodic memories are retained for the very long term. Rather they may exist as a kind of record of currently relevant aspects of our daily lives, subject to extinction or forgetting, just as infant memory is. Most episodic memories will turn out to be repetitions of prior experiences – nothing very new or meaningful there. Bauer (2007), whose account of autobiographical memory is a greatly valued resource in this area, views autobiographical memory as a subset of episodic memory. In my view, however, the relation is more complex, in that autobiographical memory is assembled from a subset of episodic memories, specifically those that contribute to the *self story* of a continuous life in the past. Specification of time in the past is expected in the narrative of "what happened" that characterizes episodic memory and much but not all of what is included in autobiographical memory. The selection of episodic memories that are retained over long periods of time requires some discrimination among the great number of possible candidates. How such discrimination is made – by what process and what criteria – is not at present known. It is clear from the study of trauma and unwanted but lasting memories that not all that are retained are consciously valued.

Bauer and many others emphasize that both episodic and autobiographical memories involve conscious awareness of "re-experiencing" something that happened in the past. Episodic memories may or may not include such conscious awareness of reexperiencing, but rather the weaker "bringing to mind" some of the continuing meaningful aspects of a previous event and in most cases letting go of the vast majority of both details and whole events. Those retained in autobiographical memory are rightly considered a special kind, constructed from the basic episodic kind, and they may (but not necessarily) be worthy of the conscious awareness of "reexperience." Reexperience appears to involve experiencing the event from the conscious perspective of the past self. An alternative is viewing the memory as a story or movie from the observer's perspective about the prior self's actions and feelings. Another alternative is viewing the event from the experiencer's perspective but with the interpretive sense of the older self.

Blurring the distinction between episodic and autobiographical memory is a barrier to any account of the fact that very few episodic memories from the preschool years (3 to 5) are retained even into the school years much less over the longer term. The evidence seems clear that during these years children are recounting memories of specific episodes. Very few of these specific memories continue on from that age in autobiographical memory, some for decades, some for a lifetime.[5] What determines their continuous availability is not easily explained, nor is the determination of the reasons for either loss or retention, despite decades of study of memory in this period.

The most detailed and long-term study in adults of retention and loss of memory for significant events that were recorded daily over a one-year period was documented by White (2002, reported in Bauer, 2007). This study revealed an 83 percent loss of memories after a one year delay (no memory at all of the recorded event remained). Other studies have shown that we remember more memories from some of the years of our lives than of others (Rubin, Rahhal, & Poon, 1998). Bauer (2007) provides a full accounting of the work on forgetting and retention from infancy to adulthood, emphasizing that the same processes operate through the lifespan, but that the motivations for retention of memories may differ from childhood to later life.

The point here is that the initial (unconscious) decision (in the hippocampus) to record and consolidate a memory does not explain its retention over time. As argued earlier, that initial decision depends on meaning, and it seems probable that retention does as well. However, as previously noted, meaning cuts a broad swath and varies depending on all the conscious and unconscious circumstances of the person's life. There is unlikely to be a singular cause of the deletion of a memory in part or whole over the lifespan. It is important in this connection to also emphasize the great variability, among individuals and within individuals, across cultures, and at varying ages, of both the extent and the content of autobiographical memory. This variability is to a large extent reflective of the dependence of the system on meaning, individual and momentary, or social and cultural, sustained over many years or decades.[6]

The ability to reconstruct the personal past and to imagine a personal future, in addition to the construction of the cultural and historical past and visualized future, is essential to social and cultural cognition and communication. Narratives of episodic memory, reporting on specific events in personal experience build on the experiential memory of infancy and early childhood. Autobiographical memory then builds on these episodic memories of everyday life. These moves require experience with other rememberers and the construction of a specific kind of self that changes over time but has continuity from birth to death.

14.5 The Self in Autobiographical Memory

The claim that autobiographical memory is uniquely human has been met with little contradiction. Moreover, its typically late and patchy start implies developmental reliance on social and cultural experiences. Development of narrative appropriate language, enabling memory exchange with others, is important, analogous to the mythic culture in Donald's model, providing accounts of both the personal and cultural past. In brief, both self and autobiographical memory emerge from social-cultural experiences in relevant contexts (Nelson, 2003b, 2014, 2012; Nelson & Fivush, 2004).

The self in memory is central to the conception of autobiographical memory as a record of past experience. This raises a relevant question: Is a clear concept of self necessary to the retention of long-term memories of personal episodes? Or do memories in effect construct a specifically human version of self? Both – self and story – develop in concert, typically in the late preschool years of childhood. In a broad sense, all memory is derived from self experience – including that from infancy – but the memory may retain neither the self or the experience (in the sense of the occurrence of a specific event) but only the perceived sight, sound, meaning, learning, facts, language, information, or speculation related to it. What is unique to autobiographical memory is its prototypical form as a coherent scene or event involving people and self in different settings and happenings. Any part of this may be eroded in time so that the rememberer is left with a vague sense of knowing or remembering but with few or no details to report. As a whole, autobiographical memory is essentially a life story, requiring the capability of forming an extended causal–temporal sequence. Such abilities have not yet cohered in infancy or early childhood.

Furthermore, specific awareness of the past must be dependent on the establishment of a personal past and future time line, which is then readily extendable to the group or cultural past. Prior to this development memory without consciousness of the specific past (e.g., "it happened" but not "it happened one time") certainly exists for facts about the world or the way events can be expected to unfold (e.g., script knowledge, see Nelson, 1986). Talk among adults and with small children frequently refers to past and future events, and children acquire past tense markers relatively early, thus setting favorable conditions for entering the realm of "pastness." At the same time, the child's semantic memory may contain information about past happenings or the existence of unexperienced things (e.g., dinosaurs) without invoking a personal past. Viewing the past self as the same as but different from the present self may require considerable experience with both adult and peer talk about what happened, as well as introspection on self in time (Moore & Lemon, 2001; Nelson, 2001, 2008).[7]

An extensive body of research on talk between parents and children about their experience in past events (Fivush, 2014; Nelson & Fivush, 2004; Reese, Haden, and Fivush, 1993) has shown that many children have ample opportunities to learn the cultural modes of talking about the personal past and become more capable of doing so themselves by the age of four to five years. Some of this talk refers directly to the child's perspective on an event (e.g., "how did you feel?" "Were you scared?"). Such experience (which varies among parents and children in both content and in elaborating on the child's contribution) may well support the child's ability to conceive the personal past as interesting and valuable, and to perceive the self in the past as of interest to the self in the present. In short, the past self becomes meaningful within the social-cultural exchange in a way that was inaccessible earlier.

The social-cultural view of "self" in social exchange can have an important impact on the child's concept of self. Cultural expectations about children's memory accounts have been found in adult–child talk to vary in different societies (Wang, 2014). Specifically, Chinese parents are more likely to emphasize children's learning from speech rather than American parents' typical emphasis on the child's personal experience. Both Japanese and Chinese adults include more social relationships in their accounts, especially those among relatives, than do American children and adults. In some rural Indian settings memories of the long-ago personal past are considered irrelevant to present life and not worth remembering (Leichtman, Wang, & Pillemer, 2003). The conclusion from studies from different cultures is that children learn *how* to remember their personal past self and the position of self in society through conversational exchange with both adults and peers. The result is a social-cultural construction of what is in fact an inevitably very private self.

From the child's and, later, the adult's view (rather than the observer's), however, the discovery of the past self and continuing accumulation of episodes involving it may have the effect of projecting a new version of self altogether. Prior to its appearance in autobiographical memory the self in infancy is intricately connected to the social relations within which it exists. There is no doubt that there is awareness of the physical reality of the individual being, but beyond that the relationship of self with others dominates. In general in infancy there is conscious awareness of the outside world but not of the internal world. The independent physical and social self begins to emerge during the second year as an awareness of individuality apparent in the ability to recognize the self in a mirror (Lewis & Brooks-Gunn, 1979), and to use personal pronouns (e.g., "I" and "you") to refer to self and other. This is a present self, not one in time with a past and future. Some experts assume a self concept in the two-year-old, seeing it reflected in the bits and pieces of young children's memories. These fragments, however, lack the sense of a self in time, a narrative self.

The recalled memories of the two-year-old are reports on aspects of a situation or a scene, a part of an event, rather than a narrative of the event (Hudson, 1991).

Early experiences with narrative reminiscing may "trigger" the onset in the young child of narrative thinking, a basic mode of human thought (Bruner, 1986). As hearing language spoken around the child triggers the urge to learn the language, so hearing events narrated may trigger the disposition to narrate one's own stories of things experienced. During the third and fourth year children typically hear many accounts of narratives, in the form of stories or personal experience, providing a route into the intricacies of temporal relations and the narrative frames that make talking and thinking about sequences, causes, beliefs, and motives possible, as well as the characters that are presented as protagonists or participants in different narratives. Thus a framework is provided for memory to interiorize a self story from past to present.

The narrative frame sets the self in particular roles, such as recipient or protagonist, or simply observer. It enables as well the possibility of reflection on the actions of the past self and on the reactions of the social others in the scene or event. The self that emerges from these experiences then is a self in a social-cultural framework; or, in different language, a self in a community of minds, a self like other selves, with minds to share (Nelson, 2005). Henceforth, it depends in part on the accumulation of self experiences in autobiographical memory. With the realization of the past self the possibility of comparison with the present self may become possible together with the realization that the self is changeable over time. The self in the remembered past is quintessentially an earlier version of the present self; but the subject reflecting on the memory may also recognize that the self in the remembered event was a younger, less knowledgeable, more naïve version of the present, yet still recognizably "me." The origin of this interiorized "me self" arises within the development of memory, concepts of the physical world and self, understanding of past and future reference, and reflective processes. These cohere during the later preschool years, in conjunction with social-cultural interactions and narratives. The interiorized self in autobiographical memory is not simply the agent in action but is part of an ongoing realization of a "continuing me" (Nelson, 2008).

Psychologists have in fact long recognized that a change in children's interior self-awareness is evident toward the end of the preschool period (e.g., Harter, 1999). Recently, the philosophers Hutto (2010) and Bogdan (2010) have each pointed to aspects of children's growing insight into their own minds and selves in response to their experience with social and cultural models by way of conversation and stories. Consistent with the present emphasis, in both accounts this emerging sense of self depends to a large extent on language use in narrative and interchange with others, especially adults. Through these experiences, a child may come to recognize the interiority of beliefs and motives that are involved in the intentionality of others and their actions.

Two points here are important: one, as Hutto has emphasized, is the child's recognition of other people's interior experience as different from one's own, highlighted in works such as the classic Aesop's fables. Second, as Bogdan has claimed, the child is exposed to others' interiority – their thinking and feeling – through specific uses of language in natural contexts, in narrative, or direct conversational exchange, inducing thereby an emerging consciousness of one's own self and mind. These effects take place during the later preschool years (age four to five), which is consistent with the onset of autobiographical memory. Not so incidentally, this is also the age range of achievement on the classic measure of "theory of mind," the "false belief" task (Hutto, 2010). For the present purposes, what is important is that a new *interior sense of self* emerges together with the sense of one's own and others' minds (Bogdan, 2010). This interior self has both a past, accessible through memory, and a future, accessible through the imagination. Henceforth, the standard idea of the self that is continuous over time (Sani, 2008), and distinctive in terms of experience, perspective, and emotional reactions from those of others, takes hold.

How such self-awareness affects memory to support a self history of experiences, retaining times and places as well as people and events, is beyond the scope of this inquiry. It is clear that some major change takes place in the period between four and eight years revealed in studies of the beginnings and accumulations of early childhood memories by adults. There are wide individual differences in all measures related to these developments, as well as cultural differences in both the nature of the self that is established and the degree to which a personal record of the past is valued and thus fostered by a particular community, as discussed earlier. These differences in memory and self understanding within contemporary cultures have been well documented.[8]

In summary, the self in autobiographical memory is historical in nature, existing in a record of more or less meaningful events of the personal past, connecting the adult to the child who was, and also to the older person who can be foreseen. I have focused on the emergence in the early years of this self as it relates to autobiographical memory, but this self continues to change over time while maintaining its identity as a present self. Each version of self may be viewed in terms of the meanings that led to its retention of memories over time. The self at a younger age has different wants and values recognized by the more mature self as immature but understandable in the context of the past age. Because the memories that are retained over long periods of time were initially formed on the basis of then relevant meanings these may no longer resonate with the older self, with the possible result of selective forgetting.

This is one possible determiner of which old memories are retained for the future and which are left behind. Retention, not forgetting, is the critical issue here; the vast majority of even "outstanding" daily episodic memories are forgotten over a year's time (Bauer, 2007). Both meaning and self must be involved in "decisions" of retention, but the formula is unlikely to be a straightforward one. Of course, autobiographical memory is but one part of the entire memory system, which also retains a vast quantity of social-cultural information without personal reference, some of it over very long periods of time. Forgetting occurs within that part of memory as well; thus how remembering and forgetting are balanced within the system is a question that applies to memory in general and not only to autobiographical memory. Referring back to Figure 14.1, meaning emerges from memory as well as from the physical, social, and cultural surroundings of the bodily self. We can hope to understand the parameters of such a system but not its individual outcomes for retaining long-term memory over a lifetime.

Finally, addressing the implicit question of the title of this chapter: what is meaning in the development of the autobiographical self? I have discussed the role of meaning in memory at length here, as well as the characteristics of autobiographical memory and the role of self therein. However, the very notion of "the self" in that context is misleading, as both the remembered self and the remembering self are continuously being updated over time. The self of 20 years ago lacks the experiences of the present-day self; the meanings that led to its retention over time may not be the same as the meanings that bring it back to consciousness in the present. The current self may struggle to make sense of this old/younger self, even as that self has played a role (however minor) in the revised sense of self in the present. In brief, development never ends. "The" autobiographical self exists only as an abstract construct, not as a psychological reality. Nonetheless, there is typically a sense of continuity over time and the younger self is generally recognizable as the "same me." Autobiographical memory is a major reason for this feeling of continuity.

Notes

1 The heading of section 14.1 is the same as the title I initially proposed for my 2007 book, published as *Young Minds in Social Worlds*. I am content with the final book title (which I later submitted at the urging of my editor who was no doubt correct that it would win more readers than the original one). The final subtitle retained the first four words of the section heading used here and much of what this section includes is condensed from the book's first chapter.

2 Donald (1991) in fact implies that the first major breakthrough to conscious thought appeared in *Homo erectus* as the ability to *recall* memory of physical action patterns out of the context of their origin for the purpose of practicing skills. He claims that this is the foundation for the emergence of signs and eventually symbols.

3 Neither its uniqueness to humans or its self-knowing (anoesis) is universally accepted by other theorists or by researchers of animal memory.

4 But see Neisser (1982) and Rubin (1982) for accounts of emerging interest and early research.

5 As one who clearly remembers an episode from the age of 3 (although the "episode" appears to be a merging of two separate events), I rely to some extent on my own memory facts in this account, but the overall data do not counter it, only providing more content from a broader sample. By the age of three-and-a-half years I have very clear memories of a number of episodes, although each is fragmentary. Only one could be considered a narrative, a traumatic one of an accident and subsequent trip to a hospital. By four years I had begun accumulating episodic memories that still seem meaningful, involving family moves, medical treatment, and neighborhood play.

6 Most researchers of autobiographical memory, like myself, probably have rich long-lasting self memory themselves and assume that others do too; unless they have frequent contact with those who remember very little self-oriented information from their life history. My husband, for example, has extensive, detailed, and reliable memory for professional and historical materials, but very sketchy and few reliable autobiographical memories at any age.

7 See Nelson (1989) for analyses of one child's ventures in this domain.

8 See also Nelson (2003b) for speculation about historical influences on some of this change within European-American cultures.

References

Bauer, P. J. (2007). *Remembering the Times of Our Lives: Memory in Infancy and Beyond*. New York: Psychology Press.

Bogdan, R. J. (2010). *Our Own Minds*. Cambridge, MA: MIT Press.

Bruner, J. S. (1983). *Child's Talk: Learning to Use Language*. New York: W. W. Norton.

Bruner, J. S. (1986). *Actual Minds Possible Worlds*. Cambridge, MA: Harvard University Press.

Cole, M. (1996). *Cultural Psychology: A Once and Future Discipline*. Cambridge, MA: Harvard University Press.

Damasio, A. R. (1999). *The Feeling of What Happens: Body and Emotion in the Making of Consciousness*. New York: Harcourt.

Donald, M. (1991). *Origins of the Modern Mind*. Cambridge, MA: Harvard University Press.

Donald, M. (2001). *A Mind so Rare: The Evolution of Human Consciousness*. New York: W. W. Norton.

Donald, M. (2012). Evolutionary origins of autobiographical memory: A retrieval hypothesis. In D. Bentsen & D. C. Ruben (Eds.), *Understanding Autobiographical Memory: Themes and Approaches* (pp. 269–288). New York: Cambridge University Press.

Fivush, R. (2014). Maternal reminiscing style: The sociocultural construction of autobiographical memory across childhood and adolescence. In P. J. Bauer & R. Fivush (Eds.), *The Wiley Handbook on the Development of Children's Memory* (vol. 2, pp. 568–585). New York: Wiley Blackwell.

Fivush, R. & Nelson, K. (2006). Parent–child reminiscing locates the self in the past. *British*

Journal of Developmental Psychology, 24, 235–251.

Freud, S. (1905/1953). Childhood and concealing memories. In A. A. Brill (Ed., trans.), *The Basic Writings of Sigmund Freud* (pp. 30–37). New York: Modern Library.

Harter, S. (1999). *The Construction of the Self*. New York: Guilford Press.

Hudson, J. A. (1991). Learning to reminisce: A case study. *Journal of Narrative and Life History*, 1, 295–324.

Hutto, D. (2010). *Folk Psychological Narratives: The Socio-cultural Basis of Understanding Reasons*. Cambridge, MA: MIT Press.

James, W. (1890). *Principles of Psychology*. Cambridge, MA: Harvard University Press.

Karmiloff-Smith, A. (1991). Beyond modularity: Innate constraints and developmental change. In S. Carey & R. Gelman (Eds.), *The Epigenesis of Mind: Essays on Biology and Cognition* (pp. 171–197). New York: Lawrence Erlbaum.

Leichtman, M. D., Wang, Q., & Pillemer, D. B. (2003). Cultural variations in interdependence and autobiographical memory: Lessons from Korea, China, India, and the United States. In R. Fivush & C. A. Haden (Eds.), *Autobiographical Memory and the Construction of a Narrative Self: Developmental and Cultural Perspectives* (pp. 73–98). Mahwah, NJ: Lawrence Erlbaum.

Lewis, M. & Brooks-Gunn, J. (1979). *Social Cognition and the Acquisition of Self*. New York: Plenum.

Millikan, R. G. (2006). *Varieties of Meaning*. Cambridge, MA: MIT Press.

Moore, C. & Lemon, K. (2001). *The Self in Time: Developmental Perspectives*. Mahwah, NJ: Lawrence Erlbaum.

Neisser, U. (1982). *Memory Observed: Remembering in Natural Contexts*. San Francisco: W. H. Freeman.

Neisser, U. (1988). Five kinds of self knowledge. *Philosophical Psychology*, 1, 35–59.

Nelson, K. (1986). *Event Knowledge: Structure and Function in Development*. Hillsdale, NJ: Lawrence Erlbaum.

Nelson, K. (1989). *Narratives from the Crib*. Cambridge, MA: Harvard University Press.

Nelson, K. (1993). The psychological and social origins of autobiographical memory. *Psychological Science*, 4, 1–8.

Nelson, K. (1996). *Language in Cognitive Development: The Emergence of the Mediated Mind*. New York: Cambridge University Press.

Nelson, K. (2001). Language and the self: From the "Experiencing I" to the "Continuing Me." In C. Moore & K. Lemmon (Eds.), *The Self in Time: Developmental Perspectives* (pp. 15–34) Mahwah, NJ: Lawrence Erlbaum.

Nelson, K. (2003a). Narrative and self, myth and memory: Emergence of the cultural self. In R. Fivush & C. A. Haden (Eds.), *Autobiographical Memory and the Construction of a Narrative Self: Developmental and Cultural Perspectives* (pp. 3–28). Mahwah, NJ: Lawrence Erlbaum.

Nelson, K. (2003b). Self and social functions: Individual autobiographical memory and collective narrative. *Memory* (special issue on Functions of Autobiographical Memory), 11, 125–136.

Nelson, K. (2005). Language pathways into the community of minds. In J. W. Astington & J. Baird (Eds.), *Why Language Matters to Theory of Mind* (pp. 26–49). Cambridge: Cambridge University Press.

Nelson, K. (2007). *Young Minds in Social Worlds: Experience, Meaning, and Memory*. Cambridge, MA: Harvard University Press.

Nelson, K. (2008). Self in time: Emergence within a community of minds. In F. Sani (Ed.), *Self Continuity: Individual and Collective Perspectives* (pp. 13–26) New York: Psychology Press.

Nelson, K. (2014). Sociocultural theories of memory development. In P. J. Bauer & R. Fivush (Eds.), *The Wiley Handbook on the Development of Children's Memory*. New York: Wiley Blackwell.

Nelson, K. (2017). The cultural basis of language and thought in development. In N. Budwig, E. Turiel, & P. Zelazo (Eds.), *New Perspectives on Human Development* (pp. 402–424). Cambridge: Cambridge University Press.

Nelson, K. (forthcoming). The cultural construction of memory in early childhood. In B. Wagoner (Ed.), *Handbook Of Culture And Memory*. New York: Oxford University Press.

Nelson, K. & Fivush, R. (2004). The emergence of autobiographical memory: A social cultural developmental theory. *Psychological Review*, 111, 486–511.

Peterson, C. & Rideout, R. (1998). Memory for medical experiences by 1- and 2-year-olds. *Developmental Psychology*, 34, 1059–1072.

Reese, E., Haden, C. A. & Fivush, R. (1993). Mother–child conversations about the past: Relationships of style and memory over time. *Cognitive Development*, 8, 403–430.

Rubin, D. C. (1982). On the retention function for autobiographical memory. *Journal of Verbal Learning and Verbal Behavior*, 21, 21–38.

Rubin, E. C., Rahhal, T. A. & Poon, L. W. (1998). Things learned in early adulthood are remembered best. *Memory and Cognition*, 26, 3–19.

Sani, F. (2008). *Self Continuity: Individual and Collective Perspectives*. New York: Psychology Press.

Tulving, E. (1983). *Elements of Episodic Memory*. New York: Oxford University Press.

Tulving, E. (1993). What is episodic memory? *Current Directions in Psychological Science*, 2(3), 67–70.

Tulving, E. (2005). Episodic memory and autonoesis: Uniquely human? In H. S. Terrace & J. Metcalfe (Eds.), *The Missing Link in Cognition: Origins of Self-reflective Consciousness* (pp. 3–54). New York: Oxford University Press.

Vygotsky, L. (1962). *Thought and Language* (trans. by E. Hanfmann & G. Vakar). Cambridge, MA: MIT Press.

Wang, Q. (2014). The cultured self and remembering. In P. J. Bauer & R. Fivush (Eds.), *The Wiley Handbook on The Development of Children's Memory* (pp. 605–625). New York: Wiley Blackwell.

White, R. (2002). Memory for events after twenty years. *Applied Cognitive Psychology*, 16, 603–612.

Further Reading

Bruner. J. (1997). A narrative model of self construction. In J. G. Snodgrass &. R. L. Thompson (Eds.), *The Self Across Psychology* (pp. 145–162). New York: New York Academy of Sciences.

Fivush, R. & Nelson, K. (2006). Parent–child reminiscing locates the self in the past. *British Journal of Developmental Psychology*, 24, 235–251.

Linton, M. (1975). Memory for real-world events. In D. A. Norman & D. E. Rumelhart (Eds.), *Exploration in Cognition* (pp. 37–64). San Francisco: W. H. Freeman.

15 Mapping Dialogic Pedagogy: Instrumental and Non-instrumental Education

Eugene Matusov

The concept of dialogue has become increasingly popular in diverse areas of social sciences. In the field of psychology, a dialogic framework has been introduced from studies of emotions (Garvey & Fogel, 2007) to the studies of memory (Fernyhough, 1996). Interest in the concept of dialogue can be found in many classical psychologists who have influenced modern sociocultural psychology: Vygotsky, Piaget, Mead, and so on. There has also been affinity between sociocultural psychology and dialogic framework (Wertsch, 1991). One of the major issues that dialogic approaches have faced in diverse social science fields is to conceptualize dialogue itself (e.g., O'Connor & Michaels, 2007). What is dialogue? What is a good dialogue? In this chapter, I want to discuss diverse approaches to dialogic framework in education as an independent sociocultural practice that sociocultural psychology investigates and consider how the field of dialogic pedagogy tries to address this issue of conceptualizing dialogue. I introduce non-instrumental dialogic pedagogies where dialogue is viewed as the medium, in which and through which meaning making and truth live. This view is contrasted with instrumental approaches to dialogic pedagogy that view dialogue as a tool for more effective education. Although being particular to the field of education, these conceptual and even political tensions in education may affect important debates in sociocultural psychology.

15.1 The Growth of Interest in Dialogic Approaches

An interest in the concept of "dialogic pedagogy" (aka "dialogic teaching," "dialogic education," "dialogic learning") has also been growing in education in the last twenty years. On November 24, 2015, Google Search showed 50,300 combined entries on these terms. Google Ngrm Viewer (https://books.google.com/ngrams) shows that the use of these terms in academic books in English emerged in 1965 and has grown since. Although modern interest in dialogic pedagogy seems to emerge only in the 1960s, it was a very old and probably widespread educational practice. Perhaps, one of the best known examples of dialogic pedagogy in the ancient times is Socrates's dialogic pedagogy practice described by his student Plato (1997). However, dialogic practices and dialogic pedagogy existed in ancient Greece, before, during, and after Socrates's time, although possibly in some other forms than those depicted by Plato (Apatow, 1998). There has been a long tradition of dialogic pedagogy, called *chavruta*, *chavrusa*, or *havruta*, in Jewish Yeshivas, involving dialogic studies of Talmudic texts, that goes back to the eras of the *tannaim* (rabbis of the Mishnaic period, 10–220 CE) (Hezser, 1997). A famous economist, Nobel prize winner, Amartya Sen argues that dialogic pedagogy has been well situated within the Indian religious and civic traditions and spread across

Asia with the rise of Buddhism (Sen, 2005), however, I think that this claim has to be tested and studied systematically. Historic research of dialogic pedagogy practices and ideology in the ancient time is needed.

15.1.1 What Is Dialogic Pedagogy?

So, what is dialogic pedagogy? For the purpose of this chapter of mapping dialogic pedagogy, I define this term as a self-reference – whenever an educator claims that he or she desires or engages in "dialogue" in his/her teaching or learning or education, he or she is involved in "dialogic pedagogy" as opposition to "monologic pedagogy." Of course, what educators may mean by "dialogue," by "pedagogy/education/learning/teaching," and the relationship between these two concepts may vary from educational participant to educational participant. My goal here is to try to map these differences.

I argue that the modern emergence of "dialogic pedagogy" has been rooted in the three main common related trends. The first common trend among probably all dialogic pedagogy approaches is *dissatisfaction with the conventional education*, based on diverse forms of transmission of knowledge. In this conventional form of education, teachers cover/transmit the curricular material, selected by the teachers and/or other authorities, while students remain passive and silent receptacles (Rogoff, Matusov, & White, 1996). Dialogic critique of a conventional institutionalized pedagogy is its disinterest in and insensitivity to students' subjectivity often leading to teachers' insensitive guidance and students' alienation (Matusov & Marjanovic-Shane, 2012). The second trend is educators' *attraction to and interest in the concept of dialogue itself as the foundation of education*. Some dialogic pedagogy educators see the concept of dialogue as one of the main possible remedies (if not *the* remedy) to address the problems of a conventional edu-

cation (although non-dialogic approaches alternative to conventional education are also available). However, for some other dialogic education, the opposition to conventional education is less important. Dialogism triggers students' activity to make learning active, meaningful, and deep. The third common trend involves the nature of *a relationship between "monologic pedagogy" and "dialogic pedagogy."* This relationship can vary from a dichotomy to a juxtaposition in or even mutual complementing of diverse types of dialogic pedagogy. Sometimes, but not always, this trend relates to the first trend of dissatisfaction with a conventional education that is often considered and criticized as being "monologic."

At the same time, ironically, these three common trends in dialogic pedagogy also distinguish and at times polarize the diverse dialogic pedagogy approaches themselves. Although all dialogic pedagogy frameworks may be dissatisfied with a conventional institutional pedagogy, their dissatisfaction differs in degree and quality. They may answer differently to what is wrong with a conventional education and why dialogism is necessary for education. Similarly, although they all are attracted to the notion of dialogue, they may understand this notion differently as I will discuss below. Finally, the monologue–dialogue opposition may have diverse forms in diverse dialogic pedagogy frameworks and can be viewed as a dichotomy, a dialectical contradiction, complementary aspects, or even a stylistic juxtaposition. Thus, these three trends of similarities and differences provide me with lenses on my analysis of the similarities and differences among the existing diverse dialogic pedagogy approaches.

Of course, non-dialogic pedagogies – pedagogies that are not interested in the notion of dialogue – have their own great diversity as well. They involve both conventional transmission of knowledge/skills/attitudes/values approaches and non-dialogic innovative approaches, such as discovery learning, scaffolding, apprenticeship, problem-based learning, and so on. Innovative non-dialogic pedagogies may also criticize conventional institutionalized education but they do not evoke the concept of dialogue to address its problems. Some non-dialogic pedagogies may involve dialogue but they may not emphasize its pedagogical importance and/or dialogue that may exist on the periphery of the pedagogical and learning efforts. Incidentally, sociocultural educational approaches may or may not involve a dialogic framework either. The non-dialogic pedagogies will remain in the background of my analysis here as they remain "dialogic opponents" for diverse dialogic pedagogy.

15.1.2 Diverse Dialogic Pedagogies: Instrumental and Non-Instrumental Education

My analysis of diverse approaches to dialogic pedagogy has been limited to analyzing diverse *conceptual* dialogic frameworks, focusing on their declarative nature – i.e., the espoused theory of practice – rather than on how educational practitioners enact their espoused dialogic pedagogy in their particular pedagogical practice – i.e., the theory-in-action (Argyris & Schön, 1978). In other words, the "data material" for my analysis were pedagogical texts articulating their particular concepts of dialogic pedagogy – theoretical work, educational manifesto, and even empirical studies that involved conceptualization but not analysis of educational practices directly. The last can be an important and necessary study on its own. Thus, my finding claims can be warranted only for espoused dialogic pedagogy framework.

The main finding of my investigation is that the literature on dialogic pedagogy presents a vast terrain of diverse conceptual families and approaches; and within this vast terrain two big strains of dialogic approaches that I call "instrumental dialogic pedagogies" and "non-instrumental dialogic pedagogies" that vary in how they see the major purpose and function of education (see Figure 15.1).

By "instrumental dialogic pedagogies," I define a family of diverse dialogic pedagogies that treat dialogue as *a tool or a means* for achieving otherwise non-dialogic goals that exist outside of dialogue. These non-dialogic goals usually involve varied curricular endpoints, such as particular philosophical truths (Plato & Bluck, 1961), state defined educational standards (Lefstein & Snell, 2013), or preset social justice and equity values (Freire, 1978; Paley, 1992; Rule, 2015). Dialogue is often viewed as a better or the best (more/most effective) way to achieve these preset curricular endpoints so the students deeper understand, accept, and socialize in them. The biggest issue for instrumental pedagogies – dialogic or not – is how to make students arrive at the preset curricular endpoints in the most effective and deepest way for each student. The instrumental dialogic pedagogies see dialogue as the answer to this question.

By "non-instrumental dialogic pedagogies," I define a family of diverse dialogic pedagogies that views the meaning making process as inherently dialogic (Bakhtin, 1986, 1999; Matusov, 2009a; Sidorkin, 1999; Wegerif, 2007). Meaning making, on which arguably genuine education is based, emerges and lives in dialogue. Outside of dialogue meaning does not exist. From this point of view, dialogue cannot be a tool for achieving non-dialogic goals. It cannot be a tool or a means – period. Also, dialogue as meaning making transcends any particular activity and practice. Dialogue cannot be exited or avoided, but dialogue can be distorted by excessive monologism or by excessive dialogism (Bakhtin, 1999; Matusov, 2009a). Non-instrumental dialogic pedagogy approaches to open dialogic investigations focus on how to promote the power of dialogue, as a meaning-making process, cleaning it from distortions of excessive monologism (and, to a lesser degree, of excessive dialogism). The difference among these non-instrumental approaches is in emphasis. Some non-instrumental dialogic pedagogies

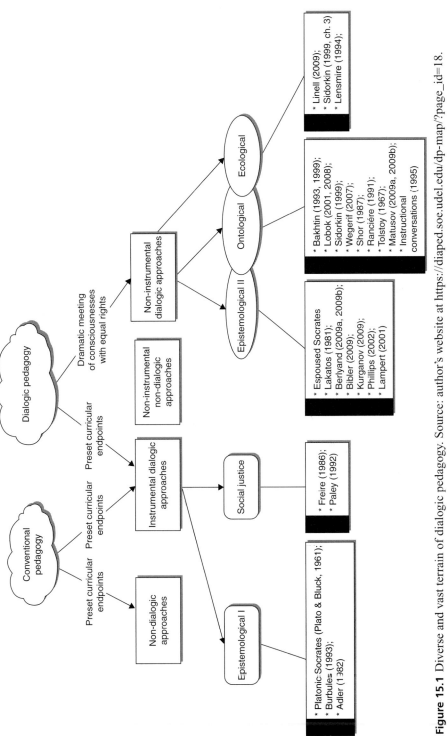

Figure 15.1 Diverse and vast terrain of dialogic pedagogy. Source: author's website at https://diaped.soe.udel.edu/dp-map/?page_id=18.

emphasize dialogic production of knowledge (Lakatos, 1981), some emphasize ontology of the participants (Sidorkin, 1999), and yet some may emphasize ecological well-being of the participants (Linell, 2009).

Previous discussions of my terminology with my dialogic pedagogy colleagues have revealed several possible confusions that I want to clarify from the beginning of the presentation of my findings. By labeling "instrumental" versus "non-instrumental" families of dialogic pedagogy approaches, I want to emphasize that for the first family instrumentality is what defines the role of dialogue in dialogic pedagogy. Of course, instrumentality also plays a role in the non-instrumental dialogic pedagogy family of approaches. Thus, certain instrumentality can promote good dialogue – e.g., instrumental organization of the pedagogical time–space (i.e., "chronotope" Bakhtin, 1991; Matusov, 2009a, 2015a; Renshaw, 2013) of the educational process (i.e., pedagogical design). However, this instrumentality does not define the role of dialogue in these dialogic pedagogies. In contrast, instrumentality does define the role of dialogue in the instrumental dialogic pedagogies.

Thinking deeper about my main 2010 finding of the division of the terrain of dialogic pedagogy approaches on "instrumental" and "non-instrumental," I have come to a conclusion that it probably reflects a bigger divide in the entire field of education (and probably beyond, in social sciences). Instrumental education views education as a servant for other spheres of human activity, necessities, survivals, and needs. Non-instrumental (or intrinsic) education views education as a goal in itself, as a fundamental existential human need, not reducible to other needs (i.e., as "the final cause" in Aristotelian terms) (Matusov et al., 2017). Public debates on education often reveal its instrumental role (Labaree, 1997). Education is often viewed as a means for achieving upward social mobility, leadership in global economic competition, morality,

social cohesion, health, economic reproduction, social justice, citizenship, economic and political equity, patriotism, nationalism, ethnic and racial tolerance, and so on. Educational sociologist David Labaree (1997) conceptualizes these instrumental public goals of education as follows: (1) democratic participation, (2) social efficiency, and (3) social mobility. When I presented Labaree's research to my education research graduate students by coding their own goals of education, we often found the forth common goal that we called "education for education's sake" or "education for growth" or "education as self-actualization." When on request of my graduate students I contacted David Labaree about this fourth goal of education, he replied that he would not count it as "a *public* goal of education." In my view, David is both right and wrong. He is right that "education for education's sake" is an inherently and fundamentally personal need, and thus a fundamental human right, that cannot be imposed or demanded by society, in contrast to the three instrumental goals that he listed. But, I respectfully disagree that society does not have interest in promoting the inherent, non-instrumental, sphere of education rooted in the fundamental private need or that the public does not engage in debates on the non-instrumental education, although it is true that these public debates are more quiet and less recognized.

The fact that the intrinsic, non-instrumental, sphere of education is not publicly well recognized may have deep historical and sociocultural roots. The notion of education expressed by the Greek word "school" means "leisure" and was understood as a leisurely pursuit of critical examination of the self, life, world, and society (Arendt, 1958; Plato, 1984). This type of leisurely pursuit of critical examination, freed from labor and work, became available for free male citizens of a Greek democratic polis and was based on exploitation of slaves and women (Arendt, 1958). Until people again become free from labor and work – free from survival and necessities – non-instrumental education for self-actualization cannot be mass education. Currently most of economic and institutional practices require people to act as smart machines: to predictably arrive at preset goals and to be mutually replaceable (Mitra, 2013). But it is true that humans can never act as perfect smart machines even when they engage in the most routine work (Wenger, 1998), the so-called "human factor."

It is also true that the instrumentalized modern economic and institutional practices require their own architects and designers – an intellectual elite – who do not act as smart machines but are engaged in the creative imagining of new goals, new values, new practices, new art, new theories, and so on. Besides, the fundamental need of people for self-actualization and personal growth, remaining mostly unrealized for the majority of modern humanity (Maslow, 1943), also pushes for non-instrumental education. These pressures apparently create oases and safe havens of non-instrumental education (e.g., Greenberg, 1992; Neill, 1960) in the vast ocean of instrumental education.

However, we may come increasingly closer to the point when a need for human instrumentality will diminish through robotization, automatization, and telecommunication, when economic and institutional practices may not need mass human employment in general (so-called "technological unemployment") and smart machine-like employment in specific (Ford, 2015; Markoff, 2015; Rifkin, 2014). These growing changes in technology, economy, and institutional practices may create a new demand for mass non-instrumental education. Thus, the tension in the field of dialogic pedagogy may reflect bigger historic sociocultural tectonic tensions in our society, if not in modern civilization.

Finally, I want to warn my readers about my biases. I subscribe to a particular non-instrumental ontological dialogic pedagogy that, like the ancient Greeks, views education as a leisurely pursuit of critical examination of the self, life, world, and society embedded in a critical dialogue (i.e., "internally persuasive discourse"; Bakhtin, 1991). I present the terrain of dialogic pedagogy not from the objective bird's eye view, which I view as impossible and undesirable, but from my own interested – read "biased" – perspective.

15.2 Instrumental Dialogic Pedagogies

The instrumental dialogic pedagogies criticize the conventional institutionalized education for its inefficiency to engage students into deep understanding of the preset curricular academic material. They argue that this is especially true for students from disadvantaged communities, whose learning is mainly based on memorization and drills (Adler, 1982). Freire (1986) criticized conventional pedagogy as "the banking model," in which teachers deposit knowledge and skills in the heads of the students without this knowledge and skills being critically examined by the students.

Dialogue is supposed to address this main problem of conventional education, "Dialogue is an activity directed toward discovery and new understanding, which stands to improve the knowledge, insight, or sensitivity of its participants" (Burbules, 1993, p. 9). There are various way of defining understanding of what dialogue is in the instrumental dialogic pedagogies. In some instrumental pedagogies, dialogue is understood as an interactive genre of guidance, where the teacher–student talk ratio is low (O'Connor & Michaels, 2007). Thus, describing pedagogical dialogue, Burbules (1993) focuses on behavioral interactivity: increasing students' talk, asking open-ended questions, setting interactional turns, avoiding lecturing, and so on what he calls "dialogue game." In another instrumental dialogic pedagogy, dialogue is understood as "heteroglossia" – juxtaposition of diverse voices of the students (and the teacher), referring to

Bakhtin's (1986) notion (e.g., Lefstein & Snell, 2013). Some other instrumental dialogic educators define dialogue as a Socratic method of questioning students about their own beliefs and knowledge to lead them to the correct knowledge (Adler, 1982). Yet, other instrumental dialogic educators argue for engaging the students in the analysis of dialectical, mutually constituting, contradictions in the studied material (Freire, 1986). I am sure that this list of definitions of instrumental pedagogical dialogue is not complete.

The relationship between dialogue and monologue can also vary in diverse instrumental dialogic pedagogy approaches. It is complementary in writings of Adler and some others (e.g., Lefstein & Snell, 2013). Thus, Adler argued that new material, unfamiliar for the students, has to be known monologically via a lecture and/or demonstration (and drills of new skills) and then the new knowledge and skills, experienced by the students, can be deepened through a Socratic method of (instrumental) pedagogical dialogue of carefully defined leading questions. Elsewhere, I characterized this relationship between dialogue and monologue in the following way,

Dialogic method can be done once a week or one hour a day or not at all – it can be dosed, scheduled, and well located in the classroom.[1] This claim [of instructional dialogue's efficiency – EM] can be tested empirically by comparing students' learning stemming from dialogic and non-dialogic instructions. This prescriptive approach focuses on consideration when dialogic instruction is needed for better learning of new material or for reconceptualization of already known material, for learning factual information or for learning conceptual understanding, for younger students or for older students, for math or social studies, and so on (see for proponents of the weak dialogism in education: Adler, 1982; Burbules, 1993; C. Phillips, 2002; Renshaw, 2004). (Matusov, 2009a, p. 75)

However, the dialogue–monologue is dichotomous in the writings by Freire. For Freire, dialogue is a part of human nature and social relationship rather than a pedagogical method or technique,

first of all we should understand liberating dialogue not as a technique, a mere technique, which we can use to help us get some results. We also cannot, must not, understand dialogue as a kind of tactic we use to make students our friends. This would make dialogue a technique for manipulation instead of illumination.

On the contrary, dialogue must be understood as something taking part in the very historical nature of human beings. It is part of our historical progress in becoming human beings. That is, dialogue is a kind of necessary posture to the extent that humans have become more and more critically communicative beings. Dialogue is a moment where humans meet to reflect on their reality as they make and remake it. (Shor & Freire, 1987, p. 13)

In my view, the difference between Freire's instrumental dialogic pedagogy approach and many other instrumental approaches is that his approach is focused on social justice rooted in the oppression–liberation dichotomy, while others' approaches are focused on epistemology of acquiring and producing knowledge. I will consider this issue further.

Finally, all instrumental dialogic pedagogy approaches are aimed at making students arrive at the preset curricular endpoints at its minimum. Of course, arrival at the preset curricular points have to be personal – via a student's own unique learning trajectory rooted in the student's own biography and subjectivity – and deep. By deep, it means a student has to be able to prove and defend these endpoints through a dialogic argumentation. Also, through pedagogical dialogue, students may come to additional endpoints beyond ones that were preset by the teacher, school, or state (although the legitimacy of the student's emerging endpoints is often established by the authority). At times, instrumental dialogic educators can be critical of state preset curricular endpoints (i.e., educational standards), when they disagree with them. However, they are usually not opposed to the educational standards and their assessment through testing per se. Often they show effectiveness of instrumental dialogic pedagogy by citing test scores (Brown & Campione, 1994; Burbules, 1993; Lefstein & Snell, 2013). At the same time, instrumental dialogic pedagogy educators often argue that testing is not enough to assess depth of students' understanding and other types of assessments are needed (e.g., portfolios, observations, dialogic assessment). In many (but probably not all) instrumental dialogic pedagogy approaches, educational standards seem to define and ensure the minimum quality of education. Thus, the instrumental dialogic pedagogy can be characterized as *standards/testing plus dialogue*. It is compatible with the progressive pedagogical movement seeking for individualized subjective pathways for achieving curricular endpoints preset by the society. Thus, Dewey (1956) argued for "double psychologizing" the societal preset curriculum by analyzing the historic psychological needs for the society to arrive at this curriculum and by grounding this preset societal curriculum in the psychology of the student. It can be concluded that the instrumental dialogic pedagogy sees dialogue as a means for such double psychologizing, insisted on by progressivist educators.

The nature of the preset curricular endpoints is different for different instrumental dialogic pedagogy approaches. For epistemological instrumental dialogic pedagogy approaches, these preset endpoints are knowledge- and skills-based. For social justice instrumental approaches, these preset endpoints are involved social justice and equity. Thus, Adler's "paideia proposal" endorses the recent Common Core educational standards In the United States,

Paideia supports the shift of emphasis from content to skills – preparing students to learn independently and throughout life. Paideia especially supports the improvement in student assessments, so they

measure students' skills, not just their ability to recall facts. Paideia offers resources aligned with the Common Core, integrating all four language arts skills. We believe the Paideia approach to Socratic Seminar is the best way to teach students the essential, lifelong skills of reading, speaking and listening, and writing. (http://www.paideia.org/about-paideia/common-core-standards/)

Similarly, Freire (1978) was not apologetic to accept and actively promote the preset socialist state curricular goals in Guinea-Bissau and Sao Tome because these preset curricular goals were socially just, from his point of view, regardless how dogmatic, authoritarian, and problematic these preset socialist views on social justice actually were (Matusov, 2009a). Suddenly, Freire's passion for a critical discourse disappeared. Not all alternative ideas are allowed in instrumental dialogic pedagogy with focus on social justice. Certain endpoints, at which students may arrive in a critical dialogue, are not legitimate and have to be silenced by the authority (including a critical meta point that education may not or should not serve social justice at all or not only). Similarly in Paley's instrumental dialogic pedagogy, children could deeply discuss issues of social justice, they had experienced in the classroom, until their impasse to address the injustice. After the impasse was detected, Paley (1992) simply imposed her vision of social justice on the children and powerfully shut down the dialogue (see my analysis, Matusov, 2009a, chs. 7, 8).

Before, considering epistemological and social justice instrumental dialogic pedagogies, I want again to warn the readers that when I make a distinction between these two instrumental approaches I focus on their priorities of the preset curricular endpoints: epistemological versus social justice. Of course, epistemological instrumental approaches may involve issues of social justice but these approaches treat these social justice issues as particular knowledge along with other knowledge. Similarly, social justice instrumental approaches may involve many epistemological issues but these pedagogies treat them through the prism of social justice issues contributing to people's "liberation" (Shor & Freire, 1987).

15.2.1 Epistemological Instrumental Dialogic Pedagogies (Epistemological I)

The epistemological instrumental dialogic pedagogy is characterized by the use of dialogue between the teacher and the students and among the students to achieve some *intellectual, epistemological* curricular endpoints, preset by the teacher. Dialogue here is a pedagogical method (e.g., Socratic Method) or an instructional strategy along with other pedagogical methods and instructional strategies which can be switched on and off. Thus, both Adler (1982, 1983) and Burbules (1993) argue that presentation of unfamiliar material or new information should be done by the teacher in a straightforward lecturing or in general direct instruction ways, while deepening understanding has to be done in a form of (Socratic) dialogue. Since the students do not have any prior knowledge of unfamiliar material, it does not make sense to dialogue about it, from this instrumental perspective. This approach to dialogue as a method can be traced in Plato's Socrates when Socrates gives an example of giving directions to a certain place to someone as a task of not worthy and not appropriate of dialogic investigation (Plato & Bluck, 1961). Thus, the epistemological instrumental dialogic pedagogy is primary concerned with deepening students' intellectual understanding about something but this deepening has some curricular endpoints like, for example, in case of the *Meno* dialogue, that the virtue is problematic and inherited, or that, in mathematics, by increasing the sides of a square twice, the area of the square will increase four times.

The dialogic method of the epistemological instrumental pedagogy is organized in a series of questions and answers usually initiated by the teacher (but not always) and often goes through four phases.

1 Engaging the students into the teacher-defined material – as the *Meno* dialogue shows, it can be quite a struggle because the students might have their own agendas and/or might not be immediately interested in the teacher-defined issues.

2 Searching for and revealing misconceptions in the students' subjectivity on the teacher-defined issues – this revelation is firstly done for the teacher him or herself as the students often are not aware that they have misconceptions and contradictions in their thinking and perception of the reality. Here is where a genuine dialogue is more permitted and tolerable by the teacher.

3 Leading the students into numbing contradictions about their misconceptions (so-called "torpedo touch") – it is important to develop in the students a sense of paralysis from the revealed contradiction between two strong alternatives rooted in the students' own subjectivity; all ways out suggested by the students should be convincingly blocked by the teacher.

4 Leading the students into the preset curricular endpoint as the only possible and logical solution of the contradiction – the teacher usually blocks any alternatives in themes and in solutions. Here is where usually genuine dialogue is less permitted and tolerant by the teacher.

As in the case of Plato's Socrates, I suspect that the teacher's manipulation of the students' subjectivities often involves self-manipulation of the teacher's own consciousness to truly believe that the preset curricular endpoint is the only one possible and logical. Indeed, it is a mathematical fact that the area of a square is equal the square of its sides. What can be problematic there? But, as I showed with the example of $2 + 2 = 4$, it is never the case – anything and everything is questionable and problematic if there is desire to look deeper (Matusov, 2009a). As Bakhtin (1986) argued, understanding is always unfinalized and, thus, bottomless.

Elsewhere I argued (Matusov, 2009a, ch. 2), that Plato's Socratic Dialogic method is a bizarre combination of radical pedagogical constructivism, based on dialogic investigation of truth though revealing contradictions in people's thinking, and radical philosophical positivism, based on the preset curricular endpoints reflecting the eternal, universal ideas. Now, I wonder if this combination of radical pedagogical constructivism and radical philosophical positivism is a birthmark of the epistemological instrumental dialogic pedagogy in general. Since Socrates, this position has been reinforced by the rationalism of the Enlightenment (the modernism), according to which reasonable, well-intended people with access to the same information will come to the same conclusion (Rawls, 1993). The modernist rational mind has to subordinate itself to the iron logic of the universal necessity and purify itself from any other irrational and corrupting influences like emotions, values, beliefs, responsibility, traditions, social justice, loyalties, and judgments (Matusov, 2015b). In this approach, consensus and agreement are prioritized – because by achieving a rational consensus among rational people through the free marketplace of ideas becomes a proxy for reaching the truth (Habermas, 1984). When the rational consensus is reached, it sets a curricular endpoint for education. In my view, necessity is only an aspect of discourse and by itself it is shaped by other aspects (e.g., values, emotions) and penetrates them as well (Matusov & Marjanovic-Shane, 2015). People's logic does not need to follow the necessity and does not need to slavishly submit it but also define it. The logic and necessity do not provide "alibi-in-being" using Bakhtin's metaphor (Bakhtin, 1993).

Finally, I want to comment on the inherently elitist nature of the epistemological instru-

mental dialogic pedagogy. Since the truth and power associated with it is rooted in the dialogic method of investigation, people who profess in the method have to be on the top of the society – this is a rather logical conclusion from the epistemological instrumental dialogic pedagogy. According to Plato's *Republic*, the world has to be ruled by philosophers.

15.2.2 Social Justice Instrumental Dialogic Pedagogies

Sufferings generated by social injustice, unfairness, and oppression are symptoms of social untruth. In my view, uncovering, naming, revealing, analyzing, and addressing this social untruth is a very legitimate goal of dialogue and dialogic pedagogy. Some dialogic pedagogies prioritize social justice (e.g., Ferrer Guardia, 1913; Freire, 1986; McLaren & Lankshear, 1994; Shor, 1987) and try to consider all other human phenomena through the prism of social (in)justice. This by itself does not necessarily make these dialogic pedagogies instrumental (especially, if nonsocial justice approaches are also permitted). However, in my contested analysis, some of them (Freire, 1978, 1986; Paley, 1992) indeed become instrumental (Facundo, 1984; Matusov, 2009a). The basic premise of social justice is that at some point social action, social engineering, promoting the correct social justice is more important and more responsible than a dialogue.

In my analysis, a social justice instrumental dialogic pedagogy goes through three phases.

1 Critical dialogic pedagogy revealing evidence of social injustice, its naming, analysis of its contemporary structure and its historical causes, and ways to undermine and eliminate it. Here is where a genuine dialogue is more permitted and tolerable and even promoted by the teacher.

2 Coup/revolution forcefully imposing the right social conditions on the students by the teacher that must promote social justice in time. Dialogue is not allowed anymore.

3 Regime of social engineering focusing on the enforcement of the right social conditions, collecting proofs of the successes, promoting propaganda. Free and genuine dialogue is actively suppressed through manipulation and violence.

For example, Freire's (1986) famous and influential book describing dialogic principles of his critical pedagogy work with Brazilian peasants seems to fit the first phase of a social justice instrumental pedagogy – critical dialogic pedagogy in which Freire helps his students reveal and analyze instances and conditions of social oppression they experience and through that they learn "to read and write the world." Freire's (1978; Freire & Macedo, 1987) less known and less influential books are about his pedagogical work in Africa in socialist Guinea-Bissau and Sao Tome where social coup/revolution already occurred. Freire saw his educational role in promoting the party efforts in socially engineering social justice in these socialist countries. No genuine dialogue was allowed but totalitarian monologic discourse with "tertium non datum" (Bakhtin, 1999) is imposed on the students. Here is an example of Freire's brainwashing of peasants with the party's dogmatic ideology taken from Freire's own account:

The next theme dealt with in the Second Popular Culture Notebook is:

National Reconstruction: II

We saw, in the previous text, that to produce more on the farms, in the factories, and to work more in the public services is to struggle for national reconstruction. We also saw that, for us, national reconstruction means the creation of a new society, without exploited or exploiters. A society of workers. For this reason, the national reconstruction demands of us:

- *Unity*
- *Discipline*
- *Work*
- *Vigilance*
- *Unity* of all, having the same objective in sight: *the creation of a new society*.
- *Discipline* in action, in work, in study, in daily life. Conscious discipline, without which nothing is done, nothing created. Discipline in unity, without which work is lost.
- *Work*. Work on the farms. Work in the factories. Work in public service. Work in schools.
- *Vigilance*, much vigilance, against the internal and external enemies, who will do anything they can to deter our struggle for the creation of the new society.

This text, as simple as it was, posed the problem of the national reconstruction and played with the words *unity*, *discipline*, *work*, and *vigilance*. Obviously, the theme of the national reconstruction or the reinvention of the society of Sao Tome **is imposed by its present state**. The game played with the words *unity*, *discipline*, *work*, and *vigilance*, which appear in a great number of slogans, was introduced to present them **in a dynamic text preserving or recovering their most profound meaning (threatened by the uncritical character of clichés)**. (Freire & Macedo, 1987, pp. 79–80; italics in original; bold added)

While analyzing the Marxist totalitarian regimes of the twentieth century, Laclau and Mouffe (2001) came to a conclusion that ontological privilege of unquestioned power (i.e., the party dictatorship) in association with the extreme epistemological certainty of the political leadership leads to totalitarianism. It does not help that Freire and Paley provide some critical comments about their own pedagogy (e.g., see bolded text above) because they constitute the phenomenon of "awareness without responsibility," probably, aiming on self-manipulation to co-opt the educators' own consciousness (Matusov, 2009a, chs. 4, 8).

The logic of a social justice instrumental dialogic pedagogy seems to be rather persuasive on the first glance. Indeed, if we, educators, understand and explore with our students the harmful consequences of social injustice – economic and political oppression, in the case of Freire, and systematic social exclusion of some children by other children, in the case of Paley – is it morally and pedagogically irresponsible for the teacher to continue the status quo? For how long can we dialogue with our students while some of them keep suffering? Isn't it legitimate to stop dialoguing and start to act? Isn't it the legitimate and most important professional responsibility by the teacher to ensure social well-being of the students? Dialogue without action becomes irresponsible blah-blah-blah (verbalism in terms of Freire).

My response to that very powerful and legitimate call for the teacher's responsibility is that: (1) truth does not live in statements produced by dialogue, it does not have internal territory (using Bakhtin's metaphor), but lives only in dialogue of many truths and (2) any action is a part of discourse and it has a discursive aspect, which makes it meaningful. When the teacher stops and suppresses a free dialogue in the classroom, he or she does not stop discourse but rather makes it oppressive. Totalitarianism does not solve previous oppressions but rather transforms and intensifies them by total assault on the participants' freedom, in which imposed systematic social inclusion arguably becomes more oppressive than systematic social exclusion (in the case of Paley) and imposed total equality arguably becomes more oppressive than systematic inequality (in the case of Freire), leading to totalitarianism, concentration camps, and mass murders in their historical extremes of the twentieth century.

In my book (Matusov, 2009a, ch. 8), my colleague Mark Smith and I discussed possibilities for the teachers' dialogic impositions on students, which we called "dialogic objectivizations," and their contrast with social engineering promoted by a social justice instrumental dialogic pedagogy. In the proposed dialogic impositions, the teacher's unilateral actions are viewed as tests of ideas that are evaluated by the entire community. Dialogic impositions can be in space (i.e., in some part of the communal space the participants experience new and in some old social regime) or in time (i.e., in the past there was the old social regime but starting from some time there will be a new social regime defined by the teacher). In contrast to social engineering, the participants through experience of the consequences of this action and democratic decision-making can decide to return to the status quo, to remain in a new regime, or to keep changing it. In our view, the issue with a social justice instrumental dialogic pedagogy leading to totalitarianism is not only in the teacher's unilateralism or imposition themselves but more importantly in the suppression of dialogue.

15.3 Non-Instrumental Dialogic Pedagogies

In contrast to the instrumental approaches to dialogic pedagogy, the non-instrumental approaches to dialogic pedagogy view dialogue not as an effective means or a powerful pathway or a strategy for achieving meaning, truth, knowledge, justice, and so on, but the medium in which meaning, truth, knowledge, justice, and so on, live (Bakhtin, 1986, 1999; Matusov, 2009a; Morson & Emerson, 1990; Sidorkin, 1999). As Bakhtin (1986) pointed out, meaning lives in the relationship between a genuine question seeking for information and a sincere answer aiming at honest addressing this question. Any statement by itself makes sense only because it is embedded in dialogic relationships of the address and the response. This dialogic relationship is often invisible and taken for granted, which creates an illusion in people that statements make sense by themselves rather than being tokens and knots of the dialogic relationships. This illusion often leads to the conventional, monologic goal of education as promoting preset curricular endpoints – self-contained statements, skills, values, and dispositions – to the students. Thus, educational standards are not only a bad idea for good education, hindering meaning making, but also a misleading and unreal concept. And this is the main critique of a conventional institutionalized education based on preset curricular endpoints. In a genuine dialogue, any truth can be tested and is forever testable (Morson, 2004) and emerging endpoints are always provisional, transcending, and never fully predictable for any participant or observer. Meaning making is never given (preset, finalized, positive) but always emergent, unfolding, unfinalized, and relational, in the eye of the beholder.

What is considered "genuine dialogue" beyond meaning making varies in diverse non-instrumental dialogic pedagogy approaches. Thus, the epistemological II and the ontological non-instrumental dialogic pedagogy approaches define "genuine dialogue" as critical and puzzlement-based, while this is not necessary in the ecological non-instrumental dialogic pedagogy. These two approaches view the overall pedagogical goal as in helping students to develop their own strong voices through making authorial judgments informed by other in a critical dialogue. The epistemological II approach puts its emphasis on intellectual self-growth often rooted in the intellectual achievements of the high culture[2] (e.g., "dialogue of high cultures" – elitism), which would define "genuine dialogue." In contrast, the ontological approaches prioritize people's being-in-the-world (Packer & Goicoechea, 2000) in defining "genuine dialogue." Finally, the ecological approaches are more interested in the ecology of human beings free of pedagogical coercion. In contrast to the epistemological II approaches, the ontological and the ecological dialogic pedagogy are concerned with both the mundane low and high cultures (Matusov, 2009b) in their defining the concept "genuine dialogue."

Since meaning making has the inherently dialogic nature, according to the non-instrumental dialogic pedagogy approaches, dialogue is ubiquitous and omnipresent. There is nothing but dialogue. Dialogue is inescapable. Anything meaningful is dialogic. Monologue as a negative and even ethically evil force is still a form of this ubiquitous dialogue – a distorted dialogue. For example, Hegel (Hegel & Baillie, 1967) convincingly showed in his analysis of slave–owner's dream for "the ideal slave" that beneath such inhumane, oppressive, and abusive relationship of slavery, there is a human desire for genuinely human care and dialogism, however, the slavery relationship distorts this dialogism. Thus, excessive monologism of dogmatism, silencing, or radical relativism (Bakhtin, 1999) is a fallen angel of the genuine dialogism (Matusov, 2009a). The "genuine dialogue" is dialogue, constantly experienced by all of us, cleaned from the distortions of excessive monologism (and excessive dialogism). A part of this distortion is caused by scarcity of and competition for resources and by the fact that the majority of people still need to spend a huge part of their time on providing for their living rather than on self-actualization, envisioning good life, and self-growth. From this point of view, any pedagogy is dialogic, although the dialogism of any pedagogy can be very distorted by excessive monologism. Here, the dialogue and monologue are not genres of the teacher's instruction (e.g., instructional conversation vs. lecture), but degree and nature of distortion of the genuine dialogue as free, open-ended, interested, honest, and (critical) meaning-making never-ending discourse. At the same, dialogue–monologue relationship can legitimately take a form of a dichotomy[3] when dialogue and monologue become opposing, antagonistic, paradigmatically different pedagogical and human values, mobilizing people for different conflicting actions, relationships, ideologies, and practices.

15.3.1 Epistemological Non-Instrumental Dialogic Pedagogies (Epistemological II)

The epistemological non-instrumental dialogic pedagogy prioritizes the sublime intellectual critical achievement. It focuses on "the eternal intellectual damn final questions" raised by diverse high cultures. It is interested in the mundane only because it can give it the material and opportunity to move to the sublime inquiries (e.g., "what is moderation," see Phillips, 2002, as a good example). The non-instrumental "epistemological dialogue" (the term has been introduced by Sidorkin, 1999) is a purified dialogue to abstract a single main theme, a development of a main concept, and unfolding the logic. Due to this purification, epistemological dialogue occurs in de-ontologized space and time. As a tool of investigation of an ontological dialogue, this purification can be legitimate. However, modeling classroom discussion after an epistemological dialogue can lead to pedagogical coercion as a way of "disciplining the students' minds" so they remain staying on the theme defined by the teacher as the most important. It brackets the complexity and interconnection of the diverse themes and makes certain "irrelevant" agendas, interests, strengths, desires, and ontological groundings as inappropriate and illegitimate (which, in its own turn, requires policing the discourse and punitive actions for violators of the epistemological regime).

In my view, one of the good representatives of the epistemological non-instrumental dialogic pedagogy is Lakatos (1981) focusing on the pedagogical development of math ideas via non-instrumental epistemological dialogue. Lakatos starts his book with a very keen and thoughtful observation on his own endeavor. He ended his introduction to the book with the following words, "The dialogue form [in his book] should reflect the dialectic of the story [i.e., history of the discoveries and developments of math ideas]; it is meant to contain a sort of *rationally reconstructed or 'distilled' history*" (Lakatos, 1981, p. 5, emphasis in original).

I want to focus on this nature of "distillation" or purification that Lakatos mentioned. Lakatos was talking about distillation, reconstruction, and purification of the history of the math practice, while I am interested in his distillation, reconstruction, and purification of ontological dialogue. History represents an ontological dialogue that occurred in certain physical time and space. But ontological dialogues can also be ahistorical and even imaginary (Dostoevsky's novels is an example, see Bakhtin, 1999).

What are the differences between epistemological and ontological non-instrumental dialogues? Let me start with making observational notes about their similarities. First, like epistemological dialogue, ontological dialogue can also involve abstractions from and reconstructions of live conversations (and it can be entirely fictional). So, it is not focused on "exactness" that produces the difference, although it is true that ontological dialogue has more of what can be called "life details." Second, ontological dialogue can also focus on epistemological issues. Thus, it is not that thematic focus makes the difference. Third, epistemological dialogues usually (or maybe even always) preserve particular voices and generate person-ideas, although in an epistemological dialogue, the person is subordinated and deduced from the idea. Hence, the strong presence and depiction of particular rich voices does not distinguish ontological and epistemological dialogues. Fourth, both types of dialogues can both promote (as well as deviate from) the regime of "internally persuasive discourse" (IPD) described by Bakhtin (1991) as open-ended honest search for truth by all the participants (but not as a sense of "appropriation" of the teacher's voice by the voices of the students, see instrumental dialogue) (Matusov & von Duyke, 2010). Fifth, they both can be carnivalistic with throning and dethroning the authority (Bakhtin, 1984; Sullivan, Smith, & Matusov, 2009). Sixth, both types of dialogue can involve dramas of ideas and people, although in an epistemological dialogue, drama of the ideas defines a life drama of the participants.

I argue that the distillation, reconstruction, and purification nature of epistemological dialogue is about creation of the comprehensive, totalized, focus of all the participants of the dialogue on some unfolding theme (what is probably called by Berlyand, 2009a; Bibler, 2009, as "a dialogic notion"; Kurganov, 2009). In contrast to ontological dialogue, epistemological dialogue is essentially mono-topic and comprehensive. Epistemological dialogues are self-contained. Let me provide ethnographic evidence for my conclusion. I will group my evidence around themes that are present in ontological dialogue and absent in epistemological dialogue.

From ontological dialogic position, intellectual positions cannot be separated from people's ontology – i.e., how one lives his/her life (see a detailed discussion of this concept below). Who is speaking can be no less important than what is spoken. The person's ontology changes the meaning of the statements. Thus, Bakhtin defined the notion of "voice" as one that "includes a person's worldview and fate. A person enters into dialogue as an integral voice. He participates in it not only with his thoughts, but with his fate and with his entire individuality" (Bakhtin, 1999, p. 293). The person's fate cannot be reduced to one dialogue, to person's position in a dialogue, to the theme, to the logic, or to the sublime. Although, people can never be reduced to their mundane life circumstances, in which the people are thrown and find themselves, the deeds that the people made in these mundane circumstances penetrate and color the sublime dialogue, which is the primary interest of the proponents

of the non-instrumental epistemological dialogic pedagogy. For example, the mundane fact that a father of the American Revolution, Thomas Jefferson, was a slave-owner to the end of his life (he had 187 slaves), who fathered black children, who became slaves (he freed all of them before or after his death), from a slave concubine Sally Hemings (Sloan, 1998), colored (or smeared) his sublime position on freedom and equality to the point that has allowed some scholars legitimately claiming that Jefferson was not only a father of modern democracy but *also* a father of modern racism as the practice of the slavery, which Jefferson was a part, and his claim that "all men are created equal" written in the Declaration of Independence required a justified exclusion of slaves from the notion of "men" – i.e., the ideology of racism (D'Souza, 1995). Jefferson's voice and fate in a dialogue on freedom has been an uneasy intertwinement of the sublime freedom loving philosopher and politician and the mundane slave owner, enslaving his own children and lover.

Let me now turn to differences between non-instrumental epistemological and ontological dialogues. First, epistemological dialogue does not involve an ontological meeting of the participants: their emergent sociocultural, historical, and political relations among each other and with and in the world (see Bakhtin's notion of "encounter"). Lakatos' dialogue starts his epistemological dialogue with the following disclaimer:

The dialogue takes place in an imaginary classroom. The class gets interested in a *PROBLEM*: is there a relation between the number of vertices V, the number of edges E and the number of faces F of polyhedra – particularly of *regular polyhedra* – analogous to the trivial relation between the number of vertices and edges of *polygons*, namely, that there are as many edges as vertices: $V = E$? This latter relation enables us to classify polygons according to the number of edges (or vertices): triangles, quadrangles, pentagons, etc.

An analogous relation would help to classify *polyhedral*. (Lakatos, 1981, p. 6, emphases in original)

What is interesting here for me is how this imaginary "class gets interested in a PROBLEM" is taken outside of the brackets of Lakatos' dialogue. We do not know how and why this interest was developed and negotiated. We do not know how this interest is grounded in the participants' lives. It is unclear of why the participants care about the problem and what makes them care. What if some of the participants had not cared about this math problem in particular or math in general – how did Lakatos made them interested or, at least, cooperate with his dialogue? Was pedagogical coercion and pedagogical violence involved in that process and if so, how? What (and how) created conditions for this classroom? Could the participants have freedom to leave it at any moment (like participants of Socrates' dialogues, for example)?

From a pedagogical point of view, an assumption or an expectation that all participants are automatically and non-problematically interested in a problem can lead to big pedagogical disasters and eventually to oppressive pedagogical violence. Yes, it is true that a common interest in a particular problem can emerge in the classroom but I argue that it usually requires a lot of work from the teacher and/or it is relatively short lived and ecologically (i.e., emotionally, intellectually, physiologically, motivationally, and relationally) unsustainable.

Second, there is no ontological diversity – i.e., diversity in the ways the participants live their lives – nor it is clear how the participants' interests and agendas intertwine in epistemological dialogue. In Lakatos's dialogue all the participants are totally committed to the problem set by the teacher. In contrast, in an ontological dialogue, the participants are involved in a problem space (not one problem) that often has the shared and collective ownership and the diverse

agendas. This problem space is often shaped by diverse, multiple, often fuzzy, simultaneous and dynamic ontological concerns by the participants. For example, in the ontological dialogue example (see below), the participants had multiple ontological concerns about fairness, grades, past interpersonal alliances and conflicts, making and maintaining friendships, explanation of percentages, academic motivation, and so on. All of these mundane concerns – the mundane noise – seem to be annoying for an educator working in the non instrumental epistemological dialogic pedagogy who wants to bracket and suppress them from the public space of the dialogue.

Third, there are no ontological concerns in participants about their reputation that emerges in and transcends the epistemological dialogue. Dialogue can change people's relationships, professional and institutional stands, careers, fates – it can open and close institutional, relational, and societal opportunities that might have little to do with the theme of the sublime dialogue at hand. All that is often bracketed in epistemological dialogues, probably, are spoilers of the purity of the arguments. Nothing outside of epistemological dialogue, outside of its world of ideas – "pulp" of the life – is a concern.

Participants of an epistemological dialogue are often involved in drama, but it is a drama of ideas. In Lakatos's dialogue, student Alpha leaves the dialogue, slapping the door in disgust, so to speak. However, his dramatic actions can be deduced from the unfolding logic of colliding ideas in the dialogue. People, their personalities, their actions, their relations are reduced to their ideas (see Bakhtin, 1999, on the notion of "person-idea"). They are puppets of the self-contained logical development. For example, some proponents of epistemological dialogue view suicide by famous German quantum physicist Paul Ehrenfest in 1933, as a logical development of his position in a debate with Einstein and Bohr (Kurganov, personal communication, July 2008) rather than as a possible tragic result of his struggle with chronic depression (Klein, 1985) (or a combination of both). In an epistemological dialogue, the participants' ontology originates and is produced by the development of ideas rather than in their lived experiences.

Fourth, there is no ontological urgency in an epistemological dialogue. The chronotope of epistemological dialogue is the world of ideas. Here-and-now ontological urgency of life is not known epistemological dialogue. Arguments can be postponed for 300 years or even more. Epistemological dialogue can occur whenever and wherever. Historical time is bracketed, physical and embedded semiotic space is bracketed. Historical time with its ontological urgency is random, shallow, and unimportant (Lakatos placed his historical comments into footnotes, probably in order not to interrupt the flow of his epistemological dialogue).

Fifth, epistemological dialogue does not know interest in the ontological ecology of the participants (e.g., what is going on with their bodies and feelings at the moment) – only in the universal logical necessity (which can be multiple, according to Bibler, another proponent of the non-instrumental epistemological dialogic pedagogy; see the Russian founder of the school of dialogue of culture pedagogical movement Berlyand, 2009b; Bibler, 2009). In contrast to the spirituality of the sublime, emphasized by the non-instrumental epistemological dialogue, the ontological ecology – the corporality of the mundane – is essentially non-dialogic but it can be pulled in a sphere of ontological dialogicity. For example, with aging, I have noticed that I become crankier, more irritable, impulsive, and even depressed in late evenings. Although, at the time of these evenings, I'm feeling that I have a reason to be like that – something or somebody bothers me and gets on my nerves – I have learned to know that it is probably a result of some biochemical imbalance in my body. In the morning, I'm fine: full of enthusiasm, optimism, patience, and sensitivity. I try to dialogize my non-dialogic ecology by my attempts to use

(not always successful) the famous Russian saying, "The morning is wiser than the evening" and not to make important relational decisions in the evening. Epistemological dialogue does not know ecological concerns, rather it mandates its regime of mono-topic total commitment and purity of the spiritual sublime.

Sixth, despite all assurance to the contrary (e.g., Phillips, 2002), the overall contempt for the mundane that the non-instrumental epistemological dialogic pedagogy expresses generates a kind of elitism with all its moral, ethical, and political consequences. If the "unexamined life is not worth living" (Socrates–Plato), the worth of life and, ultimately the person living this life, is defined by the degree of how much a person can be a dialogic epistemological philosopher, examining his or her own life and lives of others (Kukathas, 2003). The intellectual discourse on life – it is discursive examination – becomes more important than the life itself (examined or unexamined). Using Aristotle's (2000) terms, the episteme overrules the phronesis (and the *techné* and the *sophia*). The epistemological dialogue is focused not just on *any* dialogue but rather on dialogue of *the high cultures*. Thus, Bibler's idea for school as "The School of the Dialogue of Cultures" can be characterized as "The School of the Dialogue of High Cultures" (see my debate on this issue with Irina Berlyand in Matusov, 2009b). Mundane chat or mundane activities might have different and sometimes more important wisdom than philosophical discussion of the sublime.

I think that epistemological dialogue can inform, inspire, and provoke an ontological dialogue. Ontological dialogue can be legitimately studied by reducing it to an epistemological dialogue (e.g., for tracking the logic of some particular theme unfolding in a dialogue). But epistemological dialogue should not guide ontological dialogue, especially in education, because in my view, the pedagogical regime of epistemological dialogue with its insistence on the "discipline of the mind" based on the total commitment on the mono-topic development of an idea and bracketing the ontology of the participants can be supported only by pedagogical violence. People cannot simply commit totally all the time to the development of one theme, by themselves without an external coercive, if not violent, push on them.

15.3.2 Ontological Non-Instrumental Dialogic Pedagogies

As far as I know the term "ontological dialogue" was coined by educational philosopher Alexander Sidorkin (1999) in opposition to other understandings of the notion of dialogue such as "instrumental dialogue," "epistemological dialogue," "communicational dialogue," "linguistic dialogue," and so on. Sidorkin argues,

Notion of dialogue is treated [in an ontological understanding of dialogue] as central for defining human existence, not merely a form of communication. To experience what it means to be human, one needs to engage in dialogical relations. We are human in the fullest sense when we engage in dialogue. This ontological understanding of dialogue has its implications for education. I argue that schools should focus on helping children experience and learn what it means to be human. Therefore, the entire social arrangement called "school" should be designed around this purpose of introducing children to the life of dialogue. (Sidorkin, 1999, p. 4)

The word "ontological" does not refer to just any kind of particular being, neither does it deal with the existence of dialogue; it refers specifically to *human existence*. This may not be the most conventional use of the term, but from my point of view, it is the most accurate one. The ontological concept of dialogue explores the place of dialogue in *the human way of being-in-the-world*. One of the reasons for using the adjective ontological is a need to distinguish between what I propose and a number of non-ontological concepts of dialogue. The very existence of a human

being in his or her human quality is a result of dialogue. In the non-ontological conception of dialogue, this relation between dialogue and human existence is reversed: dialogue is treated as secondary to human existence, mainly as a form of communication (Sidorkin, 1999, p. 7).

Let me provide my understandings and inferences from Sidorkin's deep and dense definition:

1 I understand the polysemic notion of ontology, "human being," "human existence," as our big and small deeds and relations with others that define us in the world that we create, find ourselves, and are thrown in (Packer & Goicoechea, 2000). Ontology has priority over epistemology – i.e., what and how we know about the world. Ontology is charged with ethic, moral, judgment, politics, aesthetics, desire, will, emotions, responsibility, and so on. Epistemology is embraced by ontology, "How we breathe is how we write" (Soviet poet Bulat Okudzhava's lyrics) but not the other way around, despite the fact that ontology is often the object of investigation by epistemology.

2 Ontological dialogue penetrates all aspects of the human existence. "Buber and Bakhtin, like Copernicus, discovered the new center of the human universe, the dialogical. It is the center in a sense that the very fact of human existence is contingent on engagement in dialogical relations. An individual may exist as an organism in a physical or a biological sense. But we are truly human only when we are in a dialogical relation with another. The most important things in human lives happen between human beings, rather than within or without them" (Sidorkin, 1999, p. 11). Ontological dialogue penetrates both minute, routine, mundane, as well as big in time and the sublime. It does not have the beginning and the end. It penetrates even evil deeds, like slavery. Any teaching even, super conventional and monologic, is penetrated by ontological dialogue.

Oppressive regimes generate distorted onto-logical dialogue.

3 The concept of ontological provides two major frameworks: descriptive (i.e., how things are, see no. 2 above) and prescriptive, normative (i.e., how things should be).

Where is ontological dialogue? I do not try to mystify ontological dialogue but it is different than traditional methodology of "operationalization." Ontological dialogue is not in the text but always in dialogic, questioning and answering – addressing and responding – relationships between the beholder and other people. Let me provide an example to provoke and engage you, my reader, in what I mean.

In the mid-1980s, I, in my twenties lived in a big Moscow apartment with my wife, my very young son, my grandmother Tanya, in her mid-80s, and her older sister, my grandaunt Klara, who was almost 90 at that time. Klara used to be a technical editor but also she worked infor-mally (and illegally, according to the Soviet laws of the time) all her life as a tailor almost until her death making and adjusting dresses for our big extended family. Once at a dinner when we all met at a circle table, Klara asked us why her niece Rosa, who was in her late 60s then, had not come recently. Rosa often visited her aunts run-ning errands for them and provided them with company. I try to reconstruct our conversation that my wife and I had with Klara – I combine us as "we" because neither I nor she can remem-ber our exact utterances and who made them. I do not remember Tanya verbally participating in the conversation but she smiled showing sympa-thy with my wife and me.

KLARA: I wonder why Rosa has stopped showing up at our place.
WE: We aren't surprised at all! You called her "cow" last time. She was upset. We think she probably still feels being offended by you.
KLARA: Why would she become offended with me? She brought a new dress and asked my opinion. I told her my honest opinion that in this dress she looked like a cow. You know that I like to tell "mama-truth" ["pravda-matka" in Russian] in people's face. It's not my fault that she looked like a cow in this dress.
WE: You hurt her feelings. You didn't need to lie to Rosa but you could deliver your truth to Rosa in a more soothing and nice way. For example, you could have said something like, "It seems to me that this dress makes you look a bit chubby, no?"
KLARA: That would have been a lie. I did not "seem" but I saw with my own eyes that she looked like a cow in it. Not "a bit" and not "chubby," but as a cow! Somebody must tell that to her.
WE: Klara, she wanted to hear a word of encouragement from you, not your offending "mama-truth."
KLARA: Truth can't be offending. "Don't blame the mirror, if your face is ugly!" If Rosa had wanted to hear a complement, she should have gone to men-suitors – not to me.
WE: But admit, Klara, you don't like truth about yourself when it's unpleasant.
KLARA: I always love the truth whatever it is. I always like when people tell me the truth even when it is bitter.
WE: Do you? What about when people say that you are rude and insensitive? [we gave her a specific example when Klara did not like some truth about her said by a relative]
KLARA: I don't like it because that simply isn't true.

So, is it an example of ontological dialogue? Not, by itself, until it starts puzzling and interest you. It puzzles and interests me. I wonder if Klara's logic is based on some kind of logical fallacy that grants her the right to tell unpleasant "mama-truth" to others, while rejecting this right when she is on the receiving end of "mama-truth". Or her logic is OK – it is consistent and correct, but logic, itself, is not omnipotent in humans' affairs. I wonder if Klara would agree that truth can-not be rude and insensitive, that rudeness based on meanness, while insensitivity is based on the wrong perception. With Rosa, as with many other people, Klara was not mean-spirited but rather sincere and useful to Rosa (remember Gricean maxims of good communication: be truthful, be informative, be relevant, and be clear?) (Grice, 1975).

Arguably, Klara fulfilled all of these maxims in communication with Rosa, but we argued that it was not enough. Of course, Klara's observational judgment that Rosa looked like a cow in the new dress could have been wrong, but we did not challenge Klara's professional fashion judgment – we agreed with Klara that the new dress did not suit Rosa well. My wife and I were concerned not with the truth of whether or not the new dress really suited Rosa (not with whether or not grandma's soup is salty, using another example), but with something else altogether that may (or may not) be equally or even more important than concerns about truth. Besides truth, one can be concerned about psychological well-being of another person, as it is in the case of Klara, or about being appreciative of another labor as in a case of grandma's over-salted soup. Of course, the concern about truth can overweight these non-truth concerns. At least, this something else has to be taken into account when a person provides a response. However, it is interesting for me in this example that my wife and I chose Klara's own way of delivering "mama-truth" to communicate to her about the limitations of this way of relating with people. We were telling Klara our bitter "mama-truth" in her face about possible reasons of why Rosa stopped visiting us. Not only did Klara use her narrow selective logic in response to us, we also tried this same narrow reasoning to address her, and showed the limitations of using such narrow reasoning. The difference was that she believed in using selective logical reasoning and we did not. Was it our hypocrisy? Could we defeat Klara using her own weapon? Using Audre Lorde's (1984) famous phrase, "Can master tool be used to dismantle the master house?" Lorde thought it cannot, but Lisa Delpit (1995)

thinks it can. Could we present our objections to Klara in a different way without using her telling-mama-truth-to-your-face logical way? If so, what might it be? Should teachers tell their students mama-truth about their shortcomings to their face? Why? Why not? What are the alternatives? Finally (for now), does presentation of truth affect the truth itself? Ontological dialogue involves an inquiry puzzle that emerges in and addresses life. It involves a critical examination of life, self, world, and society to understand and envision life not only as it is but also as it is "supposed to be."

This case of ontological dialogue is outside of an educational institution but arguably it has an educational value of an inquiry and it placed us, my wife and me, in the role of educators, facilitating exploration of this inquiry. But is this pedagogical dialogue really ontological? This question cannot be addressed without taking the observers into consideration. Dear reader, if my excerpt managed to interest you to such an extent that you wish to discuss these issues further with me, Klara, my wife, silent Tanya, Grice, Lorde, Delpit, and other people that I did not mentioned above, my example of ontological dialogue has been successful, but if not, then, sorry, it was not successful. As a successful example, ontological dialogue does not exist without your, the reader's, engagement. I used my case because I thought it would be easier to engage you in a puzzle (but I could be wrong – if so, sorry). However, sociolinguists (and Bakhtin) used very mundane, almost dull, trivial examples to discuss and analyze ontological dialogue (see, for example, Linell, 1998). See the following examples from Bakhtin,

In the ordinary speech of our everyday life such a use of another's words is extremely widespread, especially in dialogue, where one speaker very often literally repeats the statement of the other speaker, investing it with new value and accenting it in his own way – with expressions of doubt, indignation, irony, mockery, ridicule, and the like. (Linell, 1998, p. 194)

The embedding of words and especially of accents from the other's rejoinder in Makar Devushkin's speech is even more marked and obvious in the second of the quoted passages. The words containing the other's polemically exaggerated accent are even enclosed here in quotation marks: "He's a copying clerk" In the preceding lines the word "copy" is repeated three times. In each of these three instances the other's potential accent is present in the word "copy," but it is suppressed by Devushkin's own accent; however, it becomes constantly stronger, until it finally breaks through and assumes the form of the other's direct speech. We are presented here, therefore, with gradations of gradual intensification in the other's accent: "I know very well, of course, that I don't do much by copying... [then follows a reservation] Why, what if I am a copying clerk, after all? What harm is there in copying, after all? 'He's a COPYING clerk!'" We have indicated by italics and underscoring the other's accent and its gradual intensification, which finally dominates utterly the line of discourse enclosed in quotation marks. But even in these final words, obviously belonging to the other, Devushkin's own voice is present too, for he polemically exaggerates the other's accent. As the other person's accent intensifies, so does Devushkin's counter-accent. (Bakhtin, 1999, pp. 208–209)

The notion of ontological dialogue reminds me of a quantum particle that is both localized and distributed. Ontological dialogue is localized in the events – it is always here-and-now (like a particle). But it is also distributed in time and space – it does not have the beginning and the end (like a wave). It does not have cause or genesis.

Another important feature of the (ontological) dialogue, according to Bakhtin, is that it knows neither genesis nor causality. Dostoevsky did not use such a fundamental German classical philosophical category as becoming or evolution. For him, the central philosophical categories were such notions as "coexistence and interaction" (Bakhtin, 1999, p. 28). Drawing from Dostoevsky, Bakhtin questioned the relevance of

dialectics when it comes to a finalizing synthesis of contradictions and differences. This was not a particularly safe thing to do in a thoroughly Marxist and therefore "dialectic" country. For Bakhtin, differences never fully merge, instead, they coexist in an engaged interaction. Dostoevsky, an embodiment of dialogical thinking for Bakhtin, saw everything as coexisting in one single moment. He could only understand the world as coexistence of different things. This does not mean that Bakhtin denied the importance of change. What he rejected was the ideas of genesis, where the past determines the present. He also rejected the reduction of difference (synthesis) as the end of development. Dialogue does not reduce plurality of human worlds and yet it connects various parts of this plurality (Sidorkin, 1999, p. 18).

Studying and revealing ontological dialogue means to engage and change it. It cannot remain the same and non-contaminated by the new understanding that the researcher brings, by the researcher addressing and replying to its participants, since a case of ontological dialogue is in the researcher's response provoked by the presented case and its participants. Interobservational consensus is not a proxy of the validity of interpretation anymore as traditional research is. An interpretation is validated through its testing and depth – i.e., through internally persuasive discourse involving agreements, disagreements, and changing topics. Ontological dialogue requires very different research than traditional social research. It is oriented toward a dialogic partner – rather than toward a silent object (Bakhtin, 1986).

15.3.3 Ecological Non-Instrumental Dialogic Pedagogies

I am not sure that the non-instrumental *ecological* dialogic pedagogy exists in the sense that I have understood it. But it may exist in practice in a way that has not been described and/or published yet, or I have not accessed or recognized yet. I have got a gist and inspiration of this approach by reading sociolinguist Per Linell's book (1998) and educational philosopher Alexander Sidorkin's book (1999). The non-instrumental ecological approach to dialogic pedagogy focuses on:

1 the dialogicity (Bakhtin, 1999; Matusov, 2009a, ch. 5) of the mundane everyday social interaction;

2 the non-constrained nature of this interactional regime in which the participants can have freedom to move in and out of the interaction, remain silent, change and modify the themes, and engage simultaneously in several activities and agendas;

3 absence or minimum of pedagogical coercion and violence.

Using the agricultural metaphor of "free-range chicken," I would define the participants in this dialogue as free-range dialogic participants.

Arguably, Sidorkin (1999, pp. 73–108) has pioneered the description of this free-range mundane dialogue in his ecological theory of three drinks. Observing restrained and unrestrained social interactions among children in school, he extracted three types of dialogue that he compared with types of dialogue one can experienceat a party involving alcohol: (a) monothematic, (b) polythematic, and (c) chaotic. In his book, Sidorkin argues that these three types of dialogue (and their dynamics) constitute the necessary fabric of overall dialogic ecology. Any attempt to temporarily extend one type of dialogue at expense of the others puts stress on the participants' psychological well-being (the participants become extremely tired), the quality of their relation, and emergence of aggression, non-cooperation, and pedagogical violence. However, many conventional and even innovative pedagogies prioritize exactly the monothematic dialogues in their classroom and put a lot of efforts on suppressing any emergence of the chaotic dialogues with multiple and highly ill-defined themes (or better to say germs of the

themes). The last mentioned can be crucial for the participants' socializing, negotiation, and goal defining processes. I see this interesting development in the literature on dialogue and dialogic pedagogy as a potential call for "free-range dialogic pedagogy."

In my view, famous avant-garde composer John Cage helped to visualize a version of the non-instrumental ecological approach in the following Buddhist legend,

We are inevitably, each minute, wherever we are, without lifting a finger, without anything being transmitted, unavoidably being educated [p. 115] . . .

I think you have to begin, quite conscientiously, with the notion that education is taking place without its being any effort, without doing anything – that would already be a step in the right direction. I give you two instances. In the 12th century there was a great man in the time of Dante and Meister Eckhart, but he lived in Tibet, and his name was Mila Repa. He studied, first Black Magic because he wanted to get even with his mother's relatives who had been cruel to her – and he was able, from a distance, to bring hailstorms down on their property, but at the same time not to have the hail destroy his mother's property. He was able to bring buildings down when they came together for dances and killed whole groups of the evil relatives. After he accomplished all this revenge and Black Magic activity, he then went to a teacher of White Magic, to study White Magic in a spirit of repenting, you know. Well, that teacher taught him absolutely nothing for years – just let him live in the house and eventually Mila Repa became very impatient, because he was of the opinion that he wasn't learning anything – nothing was being taught to him. At one point he became so alarmed that he secretly left the teacher and went to another teacher, but the first teacher was clairvoyant and knew where he was going and what he was doing and everything and sent a message, mentally, to the second teacher telling him to refuse to take Mila. So Mila Repa was obliged to come back to his teacher who looked as though he were teaching him nothing and by this process of not teaching, he ultimately educated him: and he became one of the greatest leaders of Tibetan spiritual life. This story occurs over and over again in the annals of Zen Buddhism – the student who comes to the teacher and begs him for instruction. The teacher says nothing – he's just sweeping up leaves. The student goes off into another part of the forest and builds his own house and when he is finally educated what does he do? He doesn't thank himself: he goes back to the teacher who said nothing and thanks him. It's this spirit of not teaching which has been completely lost in our educational system. We had a great man in the United States, Thorsten Veblen, who wrote a book called "Higher Learning in America." The original subtitle was "A Study in Total Depravity." Why? Because the educational system in the United States is under the control of all the things to do with politics and economics. All of these things which are transmitted as though they were the things we had to learn are, in truth, means to force us into the accepted social structure. Therefore, the educational system as it is at present distorts and enslaves the mind. You want to know the basic thing I am interested in? The basic thing, I would say, is to do nothing. The second thing would be to do, so to speak, what enters our heads. It should not be fixed in advance what that would be. (Filliou & Cage, 1970, p. 116)

There can be several objections of the non-instrumental ecological approach to dialogic pedagogy:

1 reduction of the notion of dialogue to any social interaction;
2 "mundanization" of dialogue and learning (i.e., no education, no the sublime, no high culture);
3 no critical view on the free-range dialogue that might have very violent overtone even in the absence of pedagogical violence (i.e., vertical, authority-based) but the emergence of mob-type horizontal violence of peers (see Lens-mire, 1994, for his wonderful ethnography and analysis of this possibility);
4 ecological formalism – focus on the intersubjective forms of dialogue and psychological

dynamics at expense of the dialogic meanings and dialogic events.

Although I agree with this critic of this extreme (pure) ecologic approach to dialogic pedagogy, I appreciate its concerns with human ecology of dialogue and with vertical authority-based pedagogical coercion and even violence. Both concerns are not typical and rare for our educational community.

15.4 Anti-Conclusion

In this final section, I want to raise several unresolved issues with the instrumental versus non-instrumental education in general and with the (ontological) dialogic pedagogy in specific. My first issue is the relationship between non-educational and educational *goals* in educational practices, regardless of how education is defined. Educators are often faced with non-educational goals such as babysitting, ensuring personal and social safety, providing health, policing students/ children, and so on. Of course, all these non-educational goals and concerns have educational aspects but I am talking here about necessity of non-educational actions that go beyond and even against educational goals. Although, I argue that on average educational goals have to be prioritized in educational practices, there can be moments when non-educational goals must take priority. The drawing of legitimate boundaries between educational and non-educational goals and concerns are very important in educational practices, as arguably non-educational goals often illegitimately invade the sphere of education (e.g., "the zero tolerance" policies in the USA) (Matusov & Marjanovic-Shane, 2011).

My second issue is about the relationship between *educational* instrumental and non-instrumental spheres. When one of these spheres are prioritize by educators the relationship between these espoused pedagogical approaches become adversarial. However, when these spheres are seen as aspects of the educational practice and not as priorities, their relations can be complementary, although not symmetrical. Thus, even in non-instrumental ontological dialogic pedagogy, the issue of instrumental aspect of this pedagogy is there on different levels. One level is instrumentalism of pedagogical design, which generates the issue of the pedagogical design of ontological dialogic pedagogy and its spirit.

The third issue is about the relationship among instrumental, creative, and critical *aspects* of any education, which involve learning the existing practice as it is, transcending the given practice, and critical examination of the existing and imaginative practices. Even though, critical ontological dialogic pedagogy prioritizes critical examination, it stills involves the other two aspects. One hypothesis is that the other two aspects are by-productive but it requires a more systematic investigation. This issue may also relate to the issue of the relationship between pattern recognition, creative meaning making, and critical meaning making (Matusov & Marjanovic-Shane, 2017) – what are differences among all of these processes from a critical ontologic (i.e., critique of the current life) dialogic pedagogy point of view?

The fourth issue is about the *relationship* between the critical ontologic dialogic pedagogy and all other educational approaches: dialogic or not, instrumental or not. On the one hand, the critical ontological pedagogy provides a vision of "the best" pedagogy for the proponents of this approach. However, on the other hand, it argues for a dialogic relationship with, rather than annihilation of, others. From a Bakhtin-inspired ontological dialogic pedagogy's point of view, this approach has inherent internal dialogism: even adversarial approaches contribute to the meaning defining ontological dialogic pedagogy. Paraphrasing Bakhtin's famous statement about culture, ontological dialogic pedagogy does not have its internal territory but lives on boundaries with other, alternative, pedagogical approaches (including non-dialogical, instrumental, and adversarial). Also, from the critical ontologic dialogic pedagogy, the issue of what constitutes good education has to be included in education as a part of itself (Matusov & Marjanovic-Shane, 2012, call this principle "praxis of praxis"). The principle of internal dialogism and the principle of praxis of praxis push the critical ontological dialogic pedagogy for pluralism that can be expressed by paraphrasing the famous motto about pluralism of speech, "I may disagree with your pedagogical approach but I'm ready to give my life for your freedom to practice it." This tension between the visionary aspect and the pluralist aspect of the critical ontological pedagogy may constitute important dualism in the critical ontological dialogic pedagogy (Matusov & Marjanovic-Shane, 2011, 2016).

Finally, the fifth issue about the instrumental-non-instrumental opposition in education I want to bring here is sociocultural. As I argue above, non-instrumental education, as a fundamental human desire for education for education sake, requires freedom from survival and necessities, from labor and work (Arendt, 1958). This freedom is always relative, both for the individual and for society. Thus, within the individual there will always be pressure and a need for instrumental education along the line with a desire for non-instrumental education. As to the society, there may still be division of the society with those who may primarily (or entirely) engage in labor/work and those who may primarily (or entirely) engage in leisure that can afford non-instrumental education (Gorz, 1989). Resolving this non-universality, i.e., hybridity, of a leisure-based society will be probably based on advances of technology of smart machines, political will and struggle, economic and environmental pressures, and contended cultural definitions of justice and "good life." Until then, critical ontological dialogic pedagogy may remain on the periphery and in oases of the formal educational institutional sphere, even perceived by some as elitist, suitable only for those who are not very pressed by survival or necessities.

I wonder if these tensions between instrumental and non-instrumental education in general and in dialogic pedagogy in specific penetrates other field of social sciences in general and psychology in specific by being important, relevant, or at least interesting.

Acknowledgments

I want to thank Dana Simone, Ana Marjanovic-Shane, and Nermine Abd Elkader for their feedback, editing, and discussions of earlier versions of the manuscript.

Notes

1   "Once in the mid-1990s, I wanted to visit an innovative school in California but the founder of the school told me that I could not come on Tuesday because they 'do community of learners' only on Mondays, Wednesdays, and Fridays" (Matusov, 2009a, p. 75; see also, Matusov, von Duyke, & Han, 2012).

2   "High culture" often refers to high esteem cultural products of arts and science of the past and present. "In more popular terms, it is the culture of an upper class such as an aristocracy or an intelligentsia, but it can also be defined as a repository of a broad cultural knowledge, a way of transcending the class system. It is contrasted with the low culture or popular culture of, variously, the less educated, barbarians, Philistines, or the masses" https://en.wikipedia.org/wiki/High_culture

3   There has been an unfortunate modern trend in social sciences to categorically and universally reject any dichotomy by often referring to complexity of social phenomena. In my view, this is an unfortunate development for two main reasons. First, social sciences do not study complexity of social phenomena per se, as positivists claim, but our human relationships with this complexity, which do not preclude us from our dichotomist judgment for particular purposes and

contexts. Second, ironically, an anti-dichotomist stand, which dividing positions on dichotomous and non-dichotomous with the former being bad and the latter being good, is self-contradictory because it is meta-dichotomist in itself. My position is that some dichotomies are good but some bad and this is not solely defined by how complex a social phenomenon is but also, and even more importantly, it depends on our relationship with the phenomenon, our purposes, and other contexts. For example, such a complex socio-politico-economic phenomenon as slavery may warrant both a dichotomous moral analysis of its oppression and a non-dichotomous historical analysis of attempts to soften slavery. Non-positivist rehabilitation of dichotomies is badly needed in social sciences.

References

Adler, M. J. (1982). *The Paideia Proposal: An Educational Manifesto*. New York: Macmillan.

Adler, M. J. (1983). *Paideia Problems and Possibilities*. New York: Collier Macmillan.

Apatow, R. (1998). *The Spiritual Art of Dialogue: Mastering Communication for Personal Growth, Relationships, and the Workplace*. Rochester, VT: Inner Traditions.

Arendt, H. (1958). *The Human Condition*. Chicago: University of Chicago Press.

Argyris, C. & Schön, D. A. (1978). *Organizational Learning: A Theory of Action Perspective*. Reading, MA: Addison-Wesley.

Aristotle. (2000). *Nicomachean Ethics* (trans. by R. Crisp). Cambridge: Cambridge University Press.

Bakhtin, M. M. (1984). *Rabelais and His World* (trans. by H. Iswolsky). Bloomington: Indiana University Press.

Bakhtin, M. M. (1986). *Speech Genres and Other Late Essays*. Austin: University of Texas Press.

Bakhtin, M. M. (1991). *Dialogic Imagination: Four Essays by M. M. Bakhtin* (trans. by C. Emerson & M. Holquist). Austin: University of Texas Press.

Bakhtin, M. M. (1993). *Toward a Philosophy of the Act* (1st edn.). Austin: University of Texas Press.

Bakhtin, M. M. (1999). *Problems of Dostoevsky's Poetics* (vol. 8). Minneapolis: University of Minnesota Press.

Berlyand, I. E. (2009a). A few words about Bibler's dialogics: The school of the dialogue of cultures conception and curriculum. *Journal of Russian & East European Psychology*, 47(1), 20–33. DOI: 10.2753/RPO1061-0405470101.

Berlyand, I. E. (2009b). Puzzles of the number: Dialogue in the early grades of the school of the dialogue of cultures. *Journal of Russian & East European Psychology*, 47(1), 61–95. DOI: 10.2753/RPO1061-0405470103.

Bibler, V. S. (2009). The foundations of the school of the dialogue of cultures program. *Journal of Russian & East European Psychology*, 47(1), 34–60. DOI: 10.2753/RPO1061-0405470102.

Brown, A. L. & Campione, J. C. (1994). Guided discovery in a community of learners. In K. McGilly (Ed.), *Classroom Lessons: Integrating Cognitive Theory and Classroom Practice.* (pp. 229–270). Cambridge, MA: MIT Press.

Burbules, N. C. (1993). *Dialogue in Teaching: Theory and Practice.* New York: Teachers College Press.

Delpit, L. D. (1995). *Other People's Children: Cultural Conflict in the Classroom.* New York: New Press.

Dewey, J. (1956). *The Child and the Curriculum and the School and Society* (combined edn.). Chicago: University of Chicago Press.

D'Souza, D. (1995). *The End of Racism: Principles for a Multiracial Society.* New York: Free Press.

Facundo, B. (1984). Freire-inspired programs in the United States and Puerto Rico: A critical evaluation. Retrieved from www.bmartin.cc/dissent/documents/Facundo/Facundo.html.

Fernyhough, C. (1996). The dialogic mind: A dialogic approach to the higher mental functions. *New Ideas in Psychology*, 14(1), 47–62.

Ferrer Guardia, F. (1913). *The Origin and Ideals of the Modern School.* New York: Putnam.

Filliou, R. & Cage, J. (1970). *Lehren und Lernen als Auffuehrungskuenste: Teaching and Learning as Performing Arts.* New York: Koenig.

Ford, M. (2015). *Rise of the Robots: Technology and the Threat of a Jobless Future.* New York: Basic Books.

Freire, P. (1978). *Pedagogy in Process: The Letters to Guinea-Bissau.* New York: Seabury Press.

Freire, P. (1986). *Pedagogy of the Oppressed.* New York: Continuum.

Freire, P. & Macedo, D. P. (1987). *Literacy: Reading the Word & the World.* South Hadley, MA: Bergin & Garvey Publishers.

Garvey, A. & Fogel, A. (2007). Dialogical change processes, emotions, and the early emergence of self. *International Journal for Dialogical Science*, 2(1), 51–76.

Gorz, A. (1989). *Critique of Economic Reason.* London: Verso.

Greenberg, D. (1992). *The Sudbury Valley School Experience.* Framingham, MA: Sudbury Valley School Press.

Grice, H. P. (1975). Logic and conversation. In P. Cole & J. L. Morgan (Eds.), *Syntax and Semantics* (vol. 3, pp. 41–58). New York: Academic Press.

Habermas, J. (1984). *The Theory of Communicative Action.* Boston: Beacon Press.

Hegel, G. W. F. & Baillie, J. B. (1967). *The Phenomenology of Mind.* New York: Harper & Row.

Hezser, C. (1997). *The Social Structure of the Rabbinic Movement in Roman Palestine.* Tübingen, Germany: Mohr Siebeck.

Klein, M. J. (1985). *Paul Ehrenfest* (3rd edn). Amsterdam: North-Holland.

Kukathas, C. (2003). *The Liberal Archipelago: A Theory of Diversity and Freedom.* Oxford: Oxford University Press.

Kurganov, S. Y. (2009). Reading and literature in the primary and middle schools of the dialogue of cultures. *Journal of Russian & East European Psychology*, 47(2), 30–58.

Labaree, D. F. (1997). *How to Succeed in School without Really Learning: The Credentials Race in American Education.* New Haven, CT: Yale University Press.

Laclau, E. & Mouffe, C. (2001). *Hegemony and Socialist Strategy: Towards a Radical Democratic Politics* (2nd edn.). London: Verso.

Lakatos, I. (1981). *Proofs and Refutations: The Logic of Mathematical Discovery* (Repr. with corrections). New York: Cambridge University Press.

Lampert, M. (2001). *Teaching Problems and the Problems of Teaching*. New Haven: Yale University Press.

Lefstein, A. & Snell, J. (2013). *Better than Best Practice: Developing Teaching and Learning through Dialogic Pedagogy*. New York: Routledge.

Lensmire, T. J. (1994). Writing workshop as carnival: Reflections on an alternative learning environment. *Harvard Educational Review*, 64(4), 371–391.

Linell, P. (1998). *Approaching Dialogue: Talk, Interaction and Contexts in Dialogical Perspectives*. Philadelphia: John Benjamins.

Linell, P. (2009). *Rethinking Language, Mind, and World Dialogically: Interactional and Contextual Theories of Human Sense-making*. Charlotte, NC: Information Age Publishing.

Lobok, A. (2001). *The Probabilistic World: The Chronicles of the Philosophical-Pedagogical Reflections of an Educational Experiment*. Yekaterinburg, Russia: Association of Small Businesses.

Lobok, A. (2008). *The Diamond-Filled Land of Olonkho Pedagogy*. Yekaterinburg, Russia: Self-press.

Lorde, A. (1984). *Sister Outsider: Essays and Speeches*. Trumansburg, NY: Crossing Press.

Markoff, J. (2015). *Machines of Loving Grace: The Quest for Common Ground between Humans and Robots*. New York: HarperCollins.

Maslow, A. H. (1943). A theory of human motivation. *Psychological Review*, 50, 370–396. DOI: 10.1037/h0054346.

Matusov, E. (2009a). *Journey into Dialogic Pedagogy*. Hauppauge, NY: Nova Science.

Matusov, E. (2009b). The school of the dialogue of cultures pedagogical movement in Ukraine and Russia. *Journal of Russian & East European Psychology*, 47(1), 3–19.

Matusov, E. (2015a). Chronotopes in education: Conventional and dialogic. *Dialogic Pedagogy: An International Online Journal*, 3, A65–A97. DOI: 10.5195/dpj.2015.107.

Matusov, E. (2015b). Four ages of our relationship with the reality: An educationalist perspective.

Educational Philosophy and Theory, 47(1), 61–83. Doi: 10.1080/00131857.2013.860369.

Matusov, E., Baker, D., Fan, Y., Choi, H. J., & Hampel, R. (2017). Magic learning pill: Ontological and instrumental learning in order to speed up education. *Integrative Psychological and Behavioral Science*, 51(3), 456–476.

Matusov, E. & Marjanovic-Shane, A. (2011). The state's educational neutrality and educational pluralism: A revolution proposal. Retrieved from https://diaped.soe.udel.edu/SEN/.

Matusov, E. & Marjanovic-Shane, A. (2012). Diverse approaches to education: Alienated learning, closed and open participatory socialization, and critical dialogue. *Human Development*, 55(3), 159–166. DOI: 10.1159/000339594.

Matusov, E. & Marjanovic-Shane, A. (2015). Rehabilitation of power in democratic dialogic education. In K. Jezierska & L. Koczanowicz (Eds.), *Democracy in Dialogue, Dialogue in Democracy* (pp. 193–209). Farnham, UK: Ashgate.

Matusov, E. & Marjanovic-Shane, A. (2016). The state's educational neutrality: Radical proposal for educational pluralism (editorial). *Dialogic Pedagogy: An International Online Journal*, 4, E1–E26. DOI: 10.5195/dpj.2016.170.

Matusov, E. & Marjanovic-Shane, A. (2017). Many faces of the concept of culture (and education). *Culture & Psychology*, 23(3), 309–336.

Matusov, E., & von Duyke, K. (2010). Bakhtin's notion of the internally persuasive discourse in education: Internal to what? (A case of discussion of issues of foul language in teacher education). In K. Junefelt & P. Nordin (Eds.), *Proceedings from the Second International Interdisciplinary Conference on Perspectives and Limits of Dialogism in Mikhail Bakhtin*, Stockholm University, Sweden June 3–5, 2009 (pp. 174–199). Stockholm: Stockholm University.

Matusov, E., von Duyke, K., & Han, S. (2012). Community of learners: Ontological and non-ontological projects. *Outlines: Critical Social Studies*, 14(1), 41–72.

McLaren, P. & Lankshear, C. (1994). *Politics of Liberation: Paths from Freire*. New York: Routledge.

Mitra, S. (2013). Build a school in the cloud. Retrieved from www.ted.com/talks/sugata_ mitra_build_a_school_in_the_cloud.

Morson, G. S. (2004). The process of ideological becoming. In A. F. Ball & S. W. Freedman (Eds.), *Bakhtinian Perspectives on Language, Literacy, and Learning* (pp. 317–331). New York: Cambridge University Press.

Morson, G. S. & Emerson, C. (1990). *Mikhail Bakhtin: Creation of a Prosaics*. Stanford, CA: Stanford University Press.

Neill, A. S. (1960). *Summerhill: A Radical Approach to Child Rearing*. New York: Hart Publishing.

O'Connor, C. & Michaels, S. (2007). When is dialogue "dialogic"? *Human Development*, 50(5), 275–285.

Packer, M. J. & Goicoechea, J. (2000). Sociocultural and constructivist theories of learning: Ontology, not just epistemology. *Educational Psychologist*, 35(4), 227–241.

Paley, V. G. (1992). *You Can't Say You Can't Play*. Cambridge, MA: Harvard University Press.

Phillips, C. (2002). *Socrates Café: A Fresh Taste of Philosophy*. New York: W. W. Norton.

Plato (1984). *Great dialogues of Plato* (trans. by W. H. D. Rouse). New York: Mentor.

Plato (1997). *Complete Works* (trans. by J. M. Cooper & D. S. Hutchinson). Indianapolis, IN: Hackett.

Plato & Bluck, R. S. (1961). *Meno*. Cambridge: University Press.

Rancière, J. (1991). *The Ignorant Schoolmaster: Five Lessons in Intellectual Emancipation* (trans. by K. Ross). Stanford, CA: Stanford University Press.

Rawls, J. (1993). *Political Liberalism*. New York: Columbia University Press.

Renshaw, P. D. (2013). Classroom chronotopes privileged by contemporary educational policy: teaching and learning in testing times. In S. Phillipson, K. Y. L. Ku & S. N. Phillipson (Eds.), *Constructing Educational Achievement: A Sociocultural Perspective* (pp. 57–69). Oxford: Routledge.

Rifkin, J. (2014). *The Zero Marginal Cost Society: The Internet of Things, the Collaborative Commons, and the Eclipse of Capitalism*. New York: Palgrave Macmillan.

Rogoff, B., Matusov, E., & White, C. (1996). Models of teaching and learning: Participation in a community of learners. In D. R. Olson & N. Torrance (Eds.), *The Handbook of Education and Human Development: New Models of Learning, Teaching and Schooling* (pp. 388–414). Malden, MA: Blackwell.

Rule, P. N. (2015). *Dialogue and Boundary Learning*. Rotterdam: Sense Publishers.

Sen, A. K. (2005). *The Argumentative Indian: Writings on Indian History, Culture, and Identity*. New York: Farrar, Straus and Giroux.

Shor, I. (1987). *Freire for the Classroom: A Sourcebook for Liberatory Teaching* (1st. edn.). Portsmouth, NH: Boynton/Cook.

Shor, I. & Freire, P. (1987). What is the "dialogical method" of teaching? *Journal of Education*, 169(3), 11–31.

Sidorkin, A. M. (1999). *Beyond Discourse: Education, the Self, and Dialogue*. Albany: State University of New York Press.

Sloan, S. (1998). *The Slave Children of Thomas Jefferson*. Santa Monica, CA: Kiseido Publications.

Sullivan, P., Smith, M. P., & Matusov, E. (2009). Bakhtin, Socrates and the carnivalesque in education. *New Ideas in Psychology*, 27(3), 326–342. DOI: 10.1016/j.newideapsych.2008.12 .001.

Tolstoy, L. (1967). *Tolstoy on Education* (trans. by L. Wiener). Chicago: University of Chicago Press.

Wegerif, R. (2007). *Dialogic, Educational and Technology: Expanding the Space of Learning*. New York: Springer.

Wenger, E. (1998). *Communities of Practice: Learning, Meaning, and Identity*. Cambridge: Cambridge University Press.

Wertsch, J. V. (1991). *Voices of the Mind: A Sociocultural Approach to Mediated Action*. Cambridge, MA: Cambridge Press.

16 Development and Education as Crossing Sociocultural Boundaries

Giuseppina Marsico

16.1 Axiomatic Premises

All human activity – if seen in the framework of time – takes place on the border.[1] The border, between what already exists in the life of a person and that which could still come into being in the next moment, is the norm – rather than the exception – of human psyche. As Simmel (1918/2010, p. 1) pointed out:

Man's position in the world is defined by the fact that in every dimension of his being and behavior he finds himself at every moment between two boundaries. This condition appears as the formal structure of our existence.

We live in between more or less, right and left, above or below, and better or worse. Borders are "means for finding direction in the infinite space of our worlds" (p. 1). Borders are created precisely for such a move toward the expected but not yet certain future. Borders help to create security for the future. In that process, they stabilize the otherwise nonstable flow of events.

According to Simmel, borders are necessary, yet every single specific border can be stepped over or crossed. Nevertheless, in such acts we find or create a new border. In crossing the borders we confirm their reality. In Simmel's words "the unified act of life includes both boundedness and the transcendence of the boundary" (p. 3). Simmel called this process the transcendental movement between more-life and more-than-life. I will point out that this perfectly fits with what research in human development has attempted to do since the pioneering efforts of James Mark Baldwin, Jean Piaget, and Lev Vygotsky. The developmental perspective implied in the notion of transcendence through the border is elegantly illuminated by Simmel's (1994, p. 7) words: "It is absolutely central for humanity that it set itself a boundary, but with freedom, that is, in such a way that it can also remove this boundary again, that it can place itself outside it."

This chapter aims to discuss the role of border conditions in the context of development and education.

16.1.1 Transcending Function of Education

As humans, we live in a multibounded world we ourselves constantly create, regulate, and cross to modulate our relationships with the environment and with others (Marsico et al., 2013; Valsiner, 1999). Hence education – with its liminal and always future-oriented nature – undoubtedly occupies a leading position because it constantly works on the border of the "beyond-area" (Boesch, 1991).

Education is the outer border of human development, but it is the only border that is never actually crossed. It is a borderland of indeterminacy; it is our unreachable horizon that moves with us. At every step, we move forward to the new, higher level of education, and the horizon is moving with us.

The idea beyond this conceptualization of the educational processes is the notion of *being on the move* within culturally organized life contexts (school, family, church, etc.) within specific spatiotemporal coordinates. Striving for uncertainty is an unavoidable characteristic of the human sociocultural locomotion, which implies crossing the borders between different social settings within the insurmountable limit of the irreversible time.

The border condition makes evident the relevance of the "space in between" (Marsico, 2011), which is a challenging issue in development and educational psychology. What discourses and practices saturate this interstitial zone and/or cross from one side to the other? How many kinds of human activities, educational processes, and social dynamics are made possible because of this "betweenness"?

The crossing borders phenomena, which entail migrating from one place to another while living in this liminal state, are themselves developmental and educational processes. Yet they have rarely been recognized as a relevant part of the individual developmental and educational enterprise.

16.2 Meanings of the Border

The term *border*, in many Indo-European languages, may be ascribed to "pull," "drag," or "plow" and describes the border as a sign or a trace left on the ground. The border is the furrow that the plow tracks in the soil. It is here where the first signs – indexical in Peirce's terms – are constructed (Peirce, 1901/1935).

This sign marks an area that, in ancient times, would be a demarcation between town and countryside. This sign, or trench, circumscribes a defined space that can be, then, bounded in a tangible way by stones, fences, or walls. Between the border and the space it bounds exists a close relationship that is expressed not only through a visible trace on the ground but also through the process of its progressive appropriation.

In fact, drawing a line on the ground is not enough to define a space, as you should also occupy it and make it "yours" if you want to be able to claim rights to it. Space is essential for establishing the "sovereignty" of a state: without a territory, a nation cannot exist. However, it is also an important starting point for the affirmation of its rights and of its "own culture," an indispensable element for groups and individuals in need of a spatial context where they can express themselves.

The mark that indicates the space for the first time takes it away from the "nothingness" and gives it existence. In addition, it allows us to take possession of it and establish a right (Brunet-Jailly, 2005; Sevastianov, Laine & Kireev, 2015). This has not merely to do with a fragmentation of the territory but deals with the human need to control what is precarious and vague. What is different and unknown anguishes human beings, who try to put a limit on the unknown and to create a sanctuary of well-known things, approved rules, and shared beliefs. It not only gives a sense of protection from the dangers "out there" but also limits the anxiety caused by the uncertain, the darkness, and the unknown.

16.2.1 Line as the Minimal Border

The line is the most immediate image that we associate with the concept of the border. The simplest way to represent a border is, indeed, to draw a line that is somehow visible. Nevertheless, a border can be represented in several other ways or even be present without taking any visible form. In both cases, it shows its effects on the social and psychological realms. Thus it is not just a matter of concreteness, because a border organizes and regulates our lives even if it is invisible or if it is a visible mark (Marsico & Varzi, 2016).

There are, for example, administrative borders, between municipalities and regions, and borders

Figure 16.1 In the elevator: regulation of sociocultural, interpersonal, and inner borders. Source: Courtesy of Dr. Graciana Azevedo, Recife, Brazil, 2016.

that demarcate private property as opposed to public spaces (fences, walls, gates, etc.). There are, of course, natural borders marked by morphological elements (rivers, mountains, etc.), but there are also borders as a result of a political agreement between states (i.e., the borders that determine where the national waters end and the international waters begin or the boundaries between two states that run through a forest or a desert).

Borders are not only in the physical world; they exist in time (the beginning and the end of life or of a football game) in the individual mind and between people (Figure 16.1).

It is difficult to confine the concept of border to a single rigid definition, unchanging and stable over time. In Euclidian terms (Euclid, 1970), a border is the edge of something; it is a place distinct from other places that has the specific property of being in relation to all the others, but in such a way as to suspend or neutralize the system of already designated relations (Foucault, 1972, p. 37). Borders limit and define at the same time. Like the contours of a figure, they attribute identity to things, events, and people.

16.3 Making Borders, Causing Ambivalence

When one identifies the differences and creates distinctions between individuals, groups, things, or events, one also automatically creates boundaries that refer to such distinctions and set the stage for human action to determine the respective belongings.

Making distinctions and creating identifications and belongings are simultaneously opposite and complementary functions in the border-construction process. The existence of differences allows us to build borders and bound our psychological and sociocultural territories within precise contours. Yet, in parallel, these same borders act in recognizing, underlining, and reinforcing these differences.

Establishing a border means an action of differentiation based on certain criteria. Hence, within the newly established entity (i.e., group, territory, category, etc.), those units (i.e., individuals, things, dimensions, etc.) that meet the selected criteria will be included and acquire a special value, while those that do not have these characteristics will be excluded. As a result, once a boundary is established, it operates to strengthen this distinction, reducing the internal differences and making possible the perception, construction, or even invention of a homogeneous unit.

The border-making process determines at the same time what might be included in the "bounded region" and what should stay out. Therefore meaning making, distinction making, and value adding are the three processes that an individual uses to construct borders in the mind and in society (Marsico et al., 2013) through which human beings try to organize, negotiate, and hierarchically integrate the surrounding world and make sense of their relationships with self and others. It is precisely in this border construction, ideal for reducing ambiguity, that ambiguity is increased. So far, three ambivalent features of the borders have been emphasized: they simultaneously differentiate and identify and divide while connecting, as well as both including and excluding. Lessening ambiguity while at the same time increasing ambiguity is the inescapable fate of any process of border construction!

16.4 Permeable Borders

In general terms, the function of a border is to define a space, to encompass the content of that space, and to exclude what is not part of it. The border is a sign of demarcation, a separation between what is inside and what is outside. However, it is not only a tool to keep two spaces divided but can also be a point of contact between two different worlds and cultures. In this case, more than a sign of separation, the border can be seen as a threshold that allows movement between the delimited spaces (Innis, 2016). In biological terms, this equals the "membrane" that facilitates the bidirectional transfer of something from inside to outside in a biological system and permits the cell movement within the larger biological environment (Beloussov, 1998). Thus, on one hand, borders are a way to keep your distance, and on the other hand, they may become an opportunity to meet and know others. The border invokes different feelings, depending on whether it is a closed space or a symbol of openness. It can provoke a feeling of fear of what is different or unfamiliar, triggering a need to defend oneself, or it can stimulate curiosity and a desire to learn, leading to overcoming the barriers and meeting the other.

A border, however, even if well built, cannot guarantee to "remove" or "enclose" all that we want, because, at any time, it could be overtaken by something or someone. A boundary does not guarantee its total impermeability, because, as with the cell membrane, it is inherently permeable (Marsico, 2011). The border is thus neither inwardly nor outwardly impermeable – we can always cross the line that separates us from the others. In the same way, others can cross the threshold and enter our space.

16.4.1 Borders Are for Crossing

Crossing a border changes the relationship between the individual, the space, and the border itself, with consequences for both those who cross the boundary and those who have to accept someone that was on the other side of the border (Marsico, 2016). This move from side to side can provoke different reactions in people: attitudes of acceptance or rejection, of inclusion or exclusion, or all at the same time. This is exactly what is happening with the massive flux of migrants that is transforming the geography of the planet. The outcome of a border-crossing phenomenon is always uncertain, because beyond a border can be recognition or marginalization.

16.5 Borders in the World and Borders in the Mind: The Theoretical Aspects of the Border in Cultural Psychology

It seems that we desperately need to draw borders, for instance, by labeling, categorizing, and making distinctions between both concrete and abstract objects and things. As Varzi (2011, 2013) pointed out, we, as human beings, must define and determine the world around us in order to understand it – or we will become lost. In other words, by defining the world and distinguishing objects from one another, we create an understanding of the world, but at the same time, we are creating partitions within the whole. As a consequence, new part–whole dynamics emerge with all the psychological implications in regulating our relationships in this new set of circumstances (Marsico & Varzi, 2016). In addition, the three processes of border construction (meaning making, distinction making, and value adding) occur on the basis of the understanding of the human condition we have at that specific moment. All these issues make border construction and border regulation very interesting psychological phenomena to investigate.

16.5.1 Epistemological Focus

Yet what is the "nature of the borders"? From a very abstract and philosophical standpoint,[2] we can adopt a realist or a constructivist perspective to decide on their nature. One of the main determinations would be whether borders are natural or artificial. At this point, we can introduce a first conceptual differentiation between bona fide borders – based on some objective discontinuity or qualitative heterogeneity – and fiat or formal borders, which are the result of conventional demarcations of political, social, and administrative agreements, defining, as in the case of geopolitical borders, where a territory starts and ends (Smith, 1997; Smith & Varzi, 2000; Varzi, 1997). In other terms, bona fide are natural borders, while formal borders are limits established by humans. Although formal borders are artificially produced by human action, their power is no less binding than that of a natural border, and they have practical effects on the management of our daily lives. You need only think of all the walls and fences we build in our ordinary lives (i.e., urban environment), which indicate the property of the individual owners, or at the geopolitical level, the invisible and imaginary lines in the sky from which derive practical consequences in the air traffic between different states.

This aspect assumes a crucial role in cultural psychology's perspective. In fact, the arbitrariness of the borders allows us to negotiate, reorganize, and, ultimately, modify them. What is imperative to investigate from a psychological point of view is, then, not only the borders per se but also the process of border crossing and the human vicissitudes that take place on those borders. Equally important from the theoretical point of view is the triadic nature of border pro-

cesses. They happen in the present time, which is the inevitable border between past and future (Marsico & Valsiner, 2016). Therefore, border construction and border regulation are definitively driven by the imagery of the future (Marsico, 2015b).

If psychology as science starts looking at borders, it has to presume inherent ambivalence of the border zone in between the world "where we are" and the world "out there." After all, psychological phenomena exist at the border of the person and the environment; for this reason, psychology is intrinsically an "in-between" science.

16.6 The Future-Oriented Nature of the Life-Course Organization

The peculiar nature of psychology as a science of human liminal constructions will become even more evident if the assumption of the future-oriented nature of our life-course organization is brought into the discourse.

I can act in a specific way because of previously existing conditions (i.e., the reactivity assumption), but I can also act in that same way, but based on my expectation of some future goal I have set up. The focus on the future introduces the relevance of phenomena that do not exist but are important in the present and of the human capability of making future plans (and their possible modification) while acting (or not acting) on the environment.

Imagination, therefore, plays a role in thinking and acting in terms of *as-is/as-if* possibilities (Tateo, 2015).

Here again, recalling Simmel (1918/2010), it is something that is more than life. Developmental issues imply the need to reconsider the role of the nonexisting objects (Meinong, 1902/1910) in the human trajectory. What is already developed is a basis for something that does not exist but is expected to come. This is the theoretical foundation of Vygotsky's notion of the "zone of proximal development" (Valsiner & Van der Veer, 2014). In both cases, the relationship between the existing and nonexisting objects, worlds, lives, and so on, is central. The world of nonexisting objects has a predominance over the existing objects. "Any assumption about what might happen in the future is the basis for emergence of the new present. Our imagination leads our further development" (Valsiner, 2014b, p. 297).

16.7 Beyond Ontology: From Mereotopology to Development

Defining two kinds of linked realities – the worlds of existing and nonexisting objects (Meinong's attempt) – has a limitation in the ontological effort to make sense of a world that is in constant movement. What we need is to move from ontological classifications to an ontogenetic perspective.

The effort to build a general developmental perspective is evident in the work of James Mark Baldwin, who elaborates a developmental logic of things (Baldwin, 1895, 1906, 1908, 1911, 1915). Baldwin brings the notion of irreversible time into developmental logic and elaborates on Meinong's ideas as they fit into developmental time sequences.

In Baldwin's perspective, things do not merely exist or not exist; rather, they develop and change. Thus, if we want to know them, we must identify the difference between what they were like before and afterward.

The same ontological limit is of that of mereotopology and its ontological analysis of formal structures of parts and whole (Smith, 1997; Smith & Varzi, 2000; Varzi, 1997, 1998). Mereotopology is interested in the existence of some static entities at a given time. Dealing with qualitative time-based changes, instead, development is antithetical to any ontological system. It is founded on the *epistemology of becoming* and is bounded into the *irreversibility of time* (Valsiner & Van der Veer, 2014).

The theoretical focus on phenomena in "becoming" implies the centrality of time and of transitional processes. The reliance of time needs to go together with the idea of directionality: any developing person moves from a previously settled – already known – state to an area of indeterminacy (a *not-yet region*), crossing a series of boundaries in the space in between (Marsico, 2011, 2015).

16.8 Borders in Time: Temporal Border Zone and Developmental Issues

The irreversibility of time comes together with the idea that the novelty is a main feature of human life, and therefore, the future – as well as the present and the past – plays a central role in the temporality of human experiences. The process of development links the past with the future in the present, making the boundary between present (including elements from the past) and the future the real space for "becoming." This view of time is of irreversible time, which entails the continuity of the change from the infinite past toward the infinite future. A living being seems to experience his or her relation with the world on the border between the immediate present – an infinite small time that links the vanishing past – and the approaching unrevealed future. Thus temporality is not only the awareness of time passing but also made up of different layers of experience that intertwine with the dimension of goal orientation. In developmental processes, indeed, the time issue is interwoven with the construction of goals (teleologic/guided development and teleogenetic/self-guided development). Through semiotic activity, steps and rhythms of development are continuously negotiated and guided within cultural frameworks. Individual development in society is marked by temporal signs that regulate the relationship between social time, temporality, and goal orientation (Marsico & Valsiner, 2016).

During development, individual everyday life is characterized by the tension between being time-liness and being displaced in time with respect to the negotiation between guided and self-regulated transitions. "You are too young for that" or "It's time to grow up" are examples of such socially guided rhythms that are negotiated at the intersubjective level with the self-guided developmental trajectory. The experience of temporality is thus situated in a temporal border zone where the negotiation between different levels of time (from the inner temporal dimension to the settled social timing) happens (Marsico, 2015a). But what exactly happens in this temporal border zone?

16.8.1 Time, Borders, and In-Betweens

The example of a situation involving a 25-year-old undergraduate student, coming late on her course of study, with her ambivalence toward others and social timing (Tateo & Marsico, 2015), would be illustrative of the negotiation that goes on in a personal developmental trajectory on the border of different time levels. One may suppose that she feels "behind" with a sense of discomfort. Where does this inner temporal experience of "feeling behind" come from? It is one of the possible outcomes of the modulation between different temporal levels in a temporal border zone. In this case, the personal experience of "coming to it late" is due to a temporary desynchronization of personal time (as a student) with the institutional time frame (provided by university) and the wider historically set sociocultural timing that values a young age as a proper life stage for learning. Only a short delay is allowed along this path. So one may term this phenomenon "institutional setting up of temporal borders" along the life's course, which strongly guides human development prescribing and, consequently, what is normal, abnormal, or deviant. The institutional setting up of tempo-

ral borders represents the way values are guiding development. Culture establishes the kind of acceptable outcomes on the basis of the set values of developmental objectives. These kinds of values are instantiated in a given institution to be put in practice and interrelate with self-regulated development. The student's process of negotiation between the academic scanning of stages and the individual temporal organization and reorganization of goal orientation represents instead self-guided development. The outcomes of this process are the result of the negotiation in the temporal border zone between guided development – constrained by societal timing – and self-guided development. The understanding of development as a process that takes place in irreversible time has come back as a central focus in developmental sciences.

This relationship is, however, extremely complex. In this respect, we can say that time puts development in question and development sometimes puts time in question. First, what we call time is a multilayered construct involving several levels. Second, a modulation takes place between different temporal levels in a temporal border zone. Third, time as context intersects with an articulated idea of development in which goal orientation exists at two different levels: teleologic (guided development) and teleogenetic (self-guided development that involves setting future goals through signs and acting toward attaining these) (Valsiner, 1999, 2014a). Borders, guidance, and time are interwoven, neither avoidable nor fixed coordinates in the navigation of the unknown river of human development (Tateo & Marsico, 2015). On the contrary, they shape the human experiences of temporality in perennial transformation and self-transformation. Development constantly deals with crossing sociocultural borders in a movement toward the unknown future, keeping with both sides between guided and self-guided development and hiding in the darkness of the night while looking for others' complicity.

As we have discussed so far, *fiat* (artificial) boundaries are artificial but not, for this reason, less binding. By analyzing the way in which the double contemporaneity (one along the axis of the mutually shaped time levels – through the temporal border zone – and the other along the axis of irreversible flow of time, past to present to future) acts over the emerging set of potentialities, it would be possible to define a conceptual framework able to explain the qualitative transformation of previous configurations into new ones. This embryonic attempt should provide the basic temporal mereotopological rules to support the understanding of the complex phenomena of dynamic borders moving through time, which is a fundamental feature of any developmental process.

16.9 Ordinary Life on the Border

If it is true that we move from one place to another every day, would it then not be beneficial to pay more attention to these phenomena crossing our paths (Marsico, 2013)? Where, for example, do such social movements take place? Are these spaces merely "empty places" that do not offer anything to the understanding of our psychological world, or are they rather spaces where life events of various kinds happen, helping to shape our developmental paths?

Yet, it seems that psychology refuses to accept emptiness. Everything has to be filled by some concept of an ending, in such a way as to exclude from scientific reflection the extraordinary heuristic significance of the places "in-between" (Marsico, 2011).

If we assume, instead, that an individual's entire existence takes place along the axis of irreversible time (Sato & Valsiner, 2010), we should admit that each transit, though short-lived, leaves a trace in the individual's life (just think of all the times you have entered an airport). And if these transits are not occasional but rather occupy a specific time slot in a person's daily life (as

in the case of a commuter who takes the same seven o'clock train), we should assume that these nonplaces are the stage of many ordinary microstories that are built and knotted together.

Furthermore, I am more and more convinced that the places to be observed are exactly those many "in-between places" where existence unfolds and the intersubjectivity is possible.

But what are these places of which these interfaces, gaps, and in–between spaces are made? And in between what? They are, basically, in between contexts, objects, events, and situations that have delimited borders. I call this place the *border zone*.

16.10 An Educational Border Zone: The Early-Morning Entrance Routine at School

The conceptual difficulties of making sense of a border zone are particularly evident in the case of specific social institutions (i.e., kindergartens, schools, churches, workplaces, family) that are set up for guiding human development in some specific social direction. While the general directionality of such frames is relatively easily specifiable, the concrete *mechanisms* through which such guidance operates still need to be clarified. In recent years, new efforts for understanding the processes of schooling (Daniels, 2010, 2015; Marsico & Iannaccone, 2012; Marsico, Komatsu, & Iannaccone, 2013) have provided examples of where the search for those mechanisms and meaning-making processes could be productive. One of these loci is the social structure of schools and the border zone between school and nonschool.

More specifically, school entrances are an example of an environment where, through a process of "bordering" the institutional place, the explicit–implicit–tacit encoding of suggested knowledge occurs (Bernstein, 1999, 2000) (Figure 16.2), producing a special school *borderscape*.

Figure 16.2 "School borderscape" (gates and fences as "bordering" devices) of a primary school entrance in the province of Naples, southern Italy. Source: Photograph by Marsico (2015).

Figure 16.3 The school border zone (lines are spatial locations of cultural suggestions). Primary school courtyard in the province of Naples, southern Italy. Source: Photograph by Marsico (2015).

According to Ogawa et al. (2008), schools "adopt formal structures that reflect their institution, which are enacted and carried out by *coercive*, *normative*, and *mimetic* mechanisms" (Ogawa et al., 2008, p. 90).

The use of border devices such as gates and fences creates a border zone between school–nonschool domains. This liminal social space simultaneously divides and connects the school territory with the public environment "on the outside." What is at stake is the *constraining of access to the school area* and the way in which the space in-between is delimited (Figure 16.3). The entrance to the institutional space is strictly framed – from beginning to end. The school border system is ambivalently set up – the visitors are both wanted (if they have legitimate activities to perform, as in the case of students and teachers) and unwanted (generic audiences, tourists, vagabonds, and other outsiders). Thus, even if the school entrance is an apparently open and accessible location, a special invisible border control takes place on the threshold.

In more general terms, discrete barriers (walls, fences, etc.) furnished with designated places for border crossing (and conditions for such crossings) set the stage for social semi-permeability of the border structures. Persons who encounter such borders will carry tacit knowledge about the sociocultural border and its crossing (Marsico & Valsiner, 2016).

The yellow lines in Figure 16.3 in an Italian primary school courtyard are not for parking cars but for grouping the students of each class before entering the school.[3] They are *fiat borders* (in mereotopological terms) that simultaneously differentiate and identify the students. They encode the institutional guidance and strongly regulate the way in which students daily cross sociocultural borders between outside and inside the educational context (Marsico et al., 2015).

The daily entrance (and exit) routine from the school, as shown in Figure 16.2 and Figure 16.3, follows specific institutional rules that make the borders very effective and the school sometimes inaccessible from the exterior. This sociocultural-borders school system makes it possible to develop a certain set of experiences while limiting others. For instance, this social structure of places promotes the horizontal relationship between students of the same age and same class, while inhibiting vertical interactions among different age levels. The vertical/horizontal and

Figure 16.4 The border zone within a school: the entrance hall of a primary school in Rome, Italy. Source: Photograph by Marsico (2015).

classification/framing devices are here set up in space (lines in Figure 16.3) and in time (the short time of the daily entrance morning routine) in the border zone between school and nonschool that students are asked to cross every day.

16.10.1 Institutional Borders as Social Membranes

So far, we have seen how the structure of educational borders (and the psychological climate produced by them) can enable some "boundary behavior" (in terms of Lewin, 1951), promoting or disabling the emergence of innovation.

In my international research program on border-crossing phenomena, I explored another border zone within the school territory: the entrance hall (Figure 16.4). It is a space in-between school and not-yet school activities, where the permeability of the border plays a crucial role and the complex dynamic of border construction and border negotiation is at stake. The main research focus was on understanding how students cross the borders of the school context, entering into a sociocultural setting different from that of the family (and of the other not-school places they eventually meet in their daily migrations from home to school) and how family and school regulate this daily encounter

by allowing or prohibiting access of the parents who accompany the children within the school territory.[4]

Figure 16.4 shows the exact moment of crossing the school threshold of the main entrance after the bell rings. Differently from the rigidity of the sociocultural bordering processes encoded in the yellow lines (see Figure 16.3), here the students have not previously been grouped according to age, and the entrance hall becomes the arena for possible social interactions between students independently from their formal belonging to a specific class. The students will be grouped within the set limits of the class when they cross the threshold of the classroom.

Thus the bordering processes will take place in different points in time and space (in the courtyard, at the main entrance, in the entrance hall, or at the classroom threshold) depending on the structural border system the institution adopts. However, the school boundary constitutes an extended border zone of selective and sequential institutional accessibility both for students and for parents.

The access of other persons to the school entrance hall, which is already part of the school territory (aside of teacher, principals, students, and staff), is theoretically limited and happens under specific circumstances, within the

Figure 16.5 School entrance hall as a social membrane between school and family. Daily routine interaction between a mother and a teacher in a primary school entrance hall in Rome, Italy. This short meeting happened regularly, each morning, over the month of the data collection and was repeatedly recorded on video. Source: Marsico (2015).

framework of an institutionally *guided partici-pation* as in school–family meetings (Marsico & Iannaccone, 2012). However, the entrance hall sometime operates like a social membrane, connecting family and school beyond the school–nonschool dichotomy.

Figure 16.5 shows a mother–teacher interaction in the entrance hall during the 15 minutes in between the ringing of the bell (8:15 a.m.) and the start of class activity (8:30 a.m.). This daily meeting, which happens in such a short time and in a specific place, illuminates the meaning-making process and the border negotiation in the school structure. In this way, a compelling prospect is to analyze the heterogeneity and the ambivalence of social suggestions *within* a school. A daily massive presence of all the parents of the entire school population during the early-morning routine entrance seems impracticable. A generalized practice like that would create an enormous number of problems for the regular school activities; thus it is strictly regulated. Yet, a little deviation from the general rules is somehow tolerated and even welcomed, because it tacitly inoculates the idea of a flexible institution authentically interested in positive cooperation with the parents,

yet within the border of a *guarded* participation (Valsiner, 2000).

The school entrance hall shows its permeability and its ambivalence of being a place where explicit "pulls" of opposite suggestions are at work. Being both school and nonschool territory, the entrance hall is the borderland (Marsico, 2016) of different crossing processes.

16.11 Concluding Remarks: Crossing Sociocultural Borders in Development and Education

So far, we have discussed how a border is not just a nonplace but a space with its own characteristics. According to our conceptualization, it is not just a thing that can be removed from our conceptualization. A border is not a fixed line but an oscillatory activity that takes place in a border zone where crossing phenomena are possible. The border's conditions are characterized by an inherent vagueness, and since they deal with what is no longer A but not-yet B, they place theoretical focus on phenomena ("becoming") and on the emergence of the novelty. Thus the epistemology of becoming and the crossing border phenomena become the core of the investigation in developmental and educational psychology.

After all, the entirety of human existence is performed on the borders, since development and change – toward which the human being is naturally oriented – happen on the boundary between inner and outer parts of the self, between one context and another, between one social setting and another. Those distinctions generate borders as a result of a sophisticated ability of humans to make distinctions in the field of meaning and then project them onto the public settings where they live. Boundary making is an effort to diminish the ambiguity between person, others, and environment while creating another ambiguous "something in-between." In the attempt to overcome this ambivalence and the tension of the boundary condition, novelty emerges (Abbey, 2012). Novelty is the key feature in all developing systems. Development, then, entails movements beyond the settled borders toward a never pre-known immediate future, while education creates borders that guide development. In fact, the whole enterprise of education is placed in a sort of peripheral area. It is the frontier of the developmental process. Education, indeed, can be fully realized only in a border zone, which implies crossing the line between "here" and the "beyond" (Boesch, 1991). In such a way, education mostly deals with the "not-yet events" and entails a crossing condition.

The inherent fluid nature of "betweenness" makes education the border zone par excellence for human development. This calls for a renewal in psychology's conceptual system in order to grasp the vagueness and heuristic richness of boundary processes (Marsico et al., 2015). By placing the crossing sociocultural borders phenomenon at the very center of our research interests, we could illuminate the dynamic part of our psychological existence, which deals more with uncertainty and ambiguity than with security and immovability.

Education serves future development. It is a complex process through which individuals become human that operates on the border between the actual and the possible (Marsico, 2015). Yet, what is actual and what is possible are culturally determined (Bruner, 1986), and what is possible for one person would not be possible for another under different sociocultural conditions. The "window of possibilities" for human development is mostly determined by the border-construction process of life experience. The actual and the possible, usually considered polar opposites, are mutually linked in what is called *bounded indeterminacy*, which simultaneously eliminates and provides a range of possible new forms in the future (Valsiner, 1997).

In the act of making a border, we both demarcate the reality and frame the space of opportunities beyond the passive acceptance of the reality itself. Borders, while structuring the human condition in the present time, also set the stage for future horizons.

Borders in mind and society are mostly constructed artifacts to culturally organize and shape human psychological functioning. They are thus the outcomes of conventional agreements. Although they give an essential structure to the otherwise chaotic flux of the events, it does not mean that they represent objective possibilities or impossibilities (Varzi, 2016). This claim, which seems to be just an epistemological stance, has instead enormous implications with respect to the developmental and educational issues. The sociocultural borders are not a given reality but a human product that could be either a potential arena for fostering human development or a set of constrains and limitations that can produce and reproduce the social inequalities. Hence, if we are aware of our agentive role (at individual and collective levels) in bounding our life experiences, we will probably also work at opening the "window of possibilities for human development" as much as we can.

Notes

1 *Border/borders and boundary/boundaries* are used as synonyms.

2 I am referring here to *mereotopology*, which is a part of contemporary philosophy that provides tools for the ontological analysis of formal structures of parts and whole (Smith, 1997; Smith & Varzi, 2000; Varzi, 1997, 1998). Mereotopology faces, from an ontological point of view, the part–whole issue and, therefore, the question of the relationship between a border and the thing it encloses. Mereotopology rises from the ambitious attempt to provide a unified framework of the way we represent space, the objects that occupy it, and the relationships between them. It consists of a combination of *topology* – the discipline that deals with the qualitative aspects of geometric structures – and the "theory of parts and the whole" (or *mereology*), whose Aristotelian roots have been systematized by Brentano (1981).

3 In the Italian school system, the class is formed by students of the same age and remains identical over the years, unless a student fails or drops out.

4 The research on the school border zone was carried out in Rome and Salerno (Italy) and in Salvador da Bahia (Brazil). It was part of a wider research project aimed at exploring the crossing boundaries phenomenon and the intersections between family and school. Over one month, students of primary schools in the selected countries and their parents were observed and video recorded in their early morning arriving and entering the school. The parents were informed of the research project and gave permission to be recorded on video. With respect to the parents: the data analysis showed three different patterns: (a) parents who accompany the child, but do not enter the school, remaining outside; (b) parents who accompany the child, enter the school entrance hall, but do not interact with the teachers; (c) parents who accompany the child, enter the school entrance hall, and interact with the teacher and the child's classmates.

References

Abbey, E. (2012). Ambivalence and its transformation. In J. Valsiner (Ed.), *The Oxford Handbook of Culture and Psychology* (pp. 989–997). New York: Oxford University Press.

Baldwin, J. M. (1895). The origin of a "thing" and its nature. *Psychological Review*, 2, 551–573.

Baldwin, J. M. (1906). *Thought and Things: A Study of the Development and Meaning of Thought, or Genetic Logic. Volume 1: Functional Logic, or Genetic Theory of Knowledge*. London: Swan Sonnenschein & Co.

Baldwin, J. M. (1908). *Thought and Things: A Study of the Development and Meaning of Thought, or Genetic Logic. Volume 2: Experimental Logic, or Genetic Theory of Thought*. London: Swan Sonnenschein & Co.

Baldwin, J. M. (1911). *Thought and Things: A Study of the Development and Meaning of Thought, or Genetic Logic. Volume 3: Interest and Art Being Real Logic*. London: Swan Sonnenschein & Co.

Baldwin, J. M. (1915). *Genetic Theory of Reality*. New York: G. P. Putnam's Sons.

Beloussov, L. V. (1998). *The Dynamic Architecture of a Developing Organism*. Dordrecht, Netherlands: Kluver Academic.

Bernstein, B. (1999). Vertical and horizontal discourse: An essay. *British Journal of Sociology of Education*, 20(2), 157–173.

Bernstein, B. (2000). *Pedagogy, Symbolic Control and Identity* (rev. edn.). Lanham, MD: Rowman & Littlefield.

Boesch, E. (1991). *Symbolic Action Theory and Cultural Psychology*. Berlin: Springer.

Brentano, F. (1981). *Philosophical Investigations on Space, Time and the Continuum*. London: Croom Helm.

Bruner, J. S. (1986). *Actual Minds, Possible Worlds*. Cambridge, MA: Harvard University Press.

Brunet-Jailly, E. (2005). Theorizing borders: An interdisciplinary Perspective. *Geopolitics*, 10, 633–649.

Daniels, H. (2010). The mutual shaping of human action and institutional settings: A study of the transformation of children's services and professional work. *British Journal of Sociology of Education*, 31(4), 377–393.

Daniels, H. (2015). Boundaries within and between contexts. In G. Marsico, V. Dazzani, M. Ristum, & A. C. Bastos (Eds.), *Educational Contexts and*

Borders through A Cultural Lens – Looking Inside. Viewing Outside (Cultural Psychology of Education, vol. 1, pp. 11–27). Geneva: Springer.

Euclid. (1970). *Gli elementi* (trans. by A. Frajese and L. Maccioni). Turin, Italy: UTET.

Foucault, M. (1972). *The Archaeology of Knowledge* (trans. by A. M. Sheridan Smith). New York: Pantheon Books.

Innis, R. E. (2016). Between philosophy and cultural psychology: Pragmatist and semiotic reflections on the thresholds of sense. *Culture & Psychology*, 22(3), 331–361.

Lewin, K. (1951). *Field Theory in Social Science*. New York: Harper & Row.

Marsico, G. (2011). The "non-cuttable" space in between: Context, boundaries and their natural fluidity. *Integrative Psychological and Behavioral Science*, 45, 185–193.

Marsico, G. (2013). Moving between the social spaces: Conditions for boundaries crossing. In G. Marsico, K. Komatsu, and A. Iannaccone (Eds.), *Crossing Boundaries: Intercontextual Dynamics between Family and School*. Charlotte, NC: Information Age Publishing.

Marsico, G. (2015a). Developing with time: Defining a temporal mereotopology. In L. M. Simão, D. S. Guimarães, and J. Valsiner (Eds.), *Temporality: Culture in the Flow of Human Experience* (pp. 1–18), Charlotte, NC: Information Age Publishing.

Marsico, G. (2015b). Cultivating possibilities for cultural psychology: Jerome Bruner in his becoming. In G. Marsico (Ed.), *Jerome S. Bruner Beyond 100: Cultivating Possibilities* (Cultural Psychology of Education, vol. 2, pp. 241–245). Cham, Switzerland: Springer.

Marsico, G. (2016). The borderland. *Culture & Psychology*, 22(2), 206–215. DOI: 10.1177/1354067X15601199.

Marsico, G., Cabell, K. R., Valsiner, J., & Kharlamov, N. A. (2013). Interobjectivity as a border: The fluid dynamics of "betweenness." In G. Sammut, P. Daanen, & F. Moghaddam (Eds.), *Understanding the Self and Others: Explorations in Intersubjectivity and Interobjectivity* (pp. 51–65). London: Routledge.

Marsico, G., Dazzani, V., Ristum, M., & Bastos, A. C. (Eds.). (2015). *Educational Contexts and Borders Through a Cultural Lens: Looking Inside, Viewing Outside* (Cultural Psychology of Education, vol. 1). Geneva: Springer.

Marsico, G. & Iannaccone, A. (2012). The work of schooling. In J. Valsiner (Ed.), *Oxford Handbook of Culture and Psychology* (pp. 830–868). New York: Oxford University Press.

Marsico, G., Komatsu, K., & Iannaccone, A. (Eds.). (2013). *Crossing Boundaries: Intercontextual Dynamics Between Family and School*. Charlotte, NC: Information Age Publishing.

Marsico, G. & Valsiner, J. (2016). Making history: Apprehending future while reconstructing the past. In R. Säljö, P. Linell, & Å. Mäkitalo (Eds.), *Memory Practices and Learning: Experiential, Institutional, and Sociocultural Perspectives* (pp. 355–372), Charlotte, NC: Information Age Publishing.

Marsico, G. & Varzi, A. (2016). *Psychological and social borders: Regulating relationships*. In J. Valsiner, G. Marsico, N. Chaudhary, T. Sato, & V. Dazzani (Eds.), *Psychology as a Science of Human Being: The Yokohama Manifesto* (Annals of Theoretical Psychology, vol. 13, pp. 327–335), Geneva: Springer.

Meinong, A. (1902/1910). Ueber Annahmen. *Zeitschrift für Psychologie und Physiologie der Sinnesorgane* (suppl.).

Ogawa, R. T., Crain, R., Loomis, M., & Ball, T. (2008). CHAT-IT: Toward conceptualizing learning in the context of formal organizations. *Educational Researcher*, 37(2), 83–95.

Peirce, C. S. (1901/1935). *Collected papers of Charles Sanders Peirce*. Cambridge, MA:Harvard University Press.

Sato, T. & Valsiner, J. (2010). Time in life and life in time: Between experiencing and accounting. *Ritsumeikan Journal of Human Sciences*, 20(1), 79–92.

Sevastianov, S. V., Laine, J. P., Kireev, A. A., Golunov, S. V., Meževič, N. M., et al. (Eds.). (2015). *Introduction to Border Studies*. Vladivostok, Russia: Dalnauka.

Simmel, G. (1918/2010). *The View of Life: Four Metaphysical Essays with Journal Aphorisms* (trans. by J. Andrews). Chicago: University of Chicago Press.

Simmel, G. (1994). Bridge and door. *Theory Culture Society*, 11(5), 5–10.

Smith, B. (1997). Boundaries: An essay in mereotopology. In L. H. Hahn (Ed.), *The Philosophy of Roderick Chisholm* (pp. 534–561). Chicago: Open Court.

Smith, B. & Varzi, A. (2000). Fiat and bona fide boundaries. *Philosophy and Phenomenological Research*, 60, 401–420.

Tateo, L. (2015). What imagination can teach us about higher mental functions. In J. Valsiner, G. Marsico, N. Chaudhary, T. Sato, and V. Dazzani (Eds.), *Psychology as the Science of Human Being* (pp. 149–164). New York: Springer.

Tateo, L. & Marsico, G. (2015). Navigating the unknown river of development. In J. Cresswell, A. Haye, A. Larrìn, M. Morgan, & G. Sullivan, *Dialogue and Debate in the Making of Theoretical Psychology* (pp. 30–39). Ontario, Canada: Captus University Publications.

Valsiner, J. (1997). *Culture and the Development of Children's Action* (2nd edn.). New York: John Wiley & Sons.

Valsiner, J. (1999). I create you to control me: A glimpse into basic processes of semiotic mediation. *Human Development*, 42, 26–30.

Valsiner, J. (2000). *Culture and Human Development*. London: SAGE.

Valsiner, J. (2014a). *An Invitation to Cultural Psychology*. London: SAGE.

Valsiner, J. (2014b). Functional reality of the quasi real: Gegenstandstheorie and cultural psychology today. *Culture & Psychology*, 20(3), 285–307.

Valsiner, J. & Van der Veer, R. (2014). Encountering the border: Vygotsky's *zona blizhaishego razvitia*

and its implications for theory of development. In A. Yasnitsky, R. van der Veer & M. Ferrari (Eds.), *The Cambridge Handbook of Cultural-Historical Psychology* (pp. 148–173). Cambridge: Cambridge University Press.

Varzi, A. (1997). Boundaries, continuity, and contact. *Noûs*, 31, 26–58.

Varzi, A. (1998). Basic problems of mereotopology. In N. Guarino (Ed.), *Formal Ontology in Information Systems* (pp. 29–38). Amsterdam: IOS Press.

Varzi, A. (2011). Boundaries, conventions, and realism. In J. K. Campbell, M. O'Rourke, & M. H. Slater (Eds.), *Carving Nature at Its Joints: Natural Kinds in Metaphysics and Science*. Cambridge, MA: MIT Press.

Varzi, A. (2013). Boundary. In E. Zalta (Ed.), *The Stanford Encyclopedia of Philosophy* (Winter 2013 Edition). Retrieved from https://plato.stanford.edu/archives/win2015/entries/boundary/.

Varzi, A. (2016). Ai Limiti del Possibile. In L. Taddio (Ed.), *In dialogo con Maurizio Ferraris* (pp. 91–107). Milan: Mimesis.

Further Reading

Augé, M. (1992). *Non-lieux: introduction à une anthropologie de la surmodernité* (vol. 20). Paris: Seuil.

Smith, B. & Brogaard, B. (2000). Quantum mereotopology. AAAI Technical Report WS-00–08, 25–31.

Valsiner, J. (2011). Constructing the vanishing present between the future and the past. *Infancia y Aprendizaje*, 34(2), 141–150.

Part IV
Institutional Artifacts for Value

17 Ownership and Exchange in Children: Implications for Social and Moral Development

Gustavo Faigenbaum

17.1 Introduction

Most readers of this *Handbook* probably share the conviction that children are born into a social world. What this social world is made of, however, is unsettled. It seems to be populated by heterogeneous entities, such as individual agents (aka "humans"), interpersonal relations, organizations, artifacts, symbols, ideologies, norms, and values. The list is incomplete and somewhat arbitrary: depending on the theoretical point of view one embraces, some element of society might be emphasized while some others might be neglected.

In this chapter, we will focus on some aspects of children's social life that have been typically overlooked in psychological research. We will begin by presenting what is currently known about the development of *ownership of objects* in children. Second, we will discuss *peer exchange* and *reciprocity*. Finally, we will make the point that both *ownership* and *exchange* belong to an unmapped domain that we call *institutional experience*, and will discuss this domain's significance for children's development.

17.2 From Possession to Ownership

When two children want to play with the same toy, they sometimes oppose each other violently by both pulling on the object, pushing or hitting the other child. In such situations, the strongest or most dominant individual usually prevails. However, the law of the jungle creates an unstable condition which, in the long run, is detrimental for all. Since possession has to be decided in each case from scratch, everybody is threatened at some point.

Alternatively, a possession conflict can reach a peaceful resolution via the introduction of a rule for sharing the scarce resource, such as taking turns. One remarkable discovery of psychological research is that very young children appear to minimize possession conflicts by observing rules. Bakeman and Brownlee (1982) hypothesized that young children are capable of spontaneously developing rules "as a consequence of a fundamental human propensity to regulate social interaction in a ruleful manner." The authors observed children between one and three years of age who engaged in possession episodes (interactions in which a child tries to take an object from another child), and analyzed the rate of success by object takers and the rate of resistance attempts by object holders. They found that *previous possession influences the outcome of possession episodes*. If a taker has had prior possession of the object, then her take attempt is more likely to succeed. In other words, already in one-year olds, the outcome of possession episodes is not simply a matter of brute force or social dominance, but can be partly explained by reference to a prior possession rule. The researchers also found that one-year-olds are as likely to resist a taker who has had prior possession as not, while three-year-olds were less likely to resist a taker who has had prior possession. This suggests that among the three-year-olds the prior possession claim is recognized by both children. Toddlers, Bakeman and Brownlee (1982) conclude, "may have a far greater capacity for ruleful regulation of their social affairs than we usually grant them, a capacity which only careful observations of young children playing with their age-mates is likely to reveal."

The pioneering work by Bakeman and Brownlee (1982) was corroborated by other studies (see examples in Ross, 1996) confirming that previous possession increases the chances of winning a possession conflict. Some of these studies conclude that 18-month-old children already recognize that previous possession entitles individuals to hold and use objects. This rule may partly derive from our evolutionary history. It has been shown that *current* possession is respected in several species, including nonhuman primates. Members of those species do not attempt to take objects from other individuals, even when the current possessor is a subordinate (Brosnan, 2011). This is a relevant evolutionary precursor of the *prior* possession rule observed by toddlers.

In addition, children between 18 and 24 months already recognize the habitual possessor of a thing even when that person is not present (Blake & Harris, 2011; Bloom, 1973; Fasig, 2000). Also, at about 18 months of age, children start using the possessives "my" and "mine," especially in the context of object requests and possession conflicts with siblings or other peers (Bates, 1990; Deutsch & Budwig, 1983; Hay, 2006; Tomasello, 1998). Possessive phrases such as "daddy's cup" appear on average at about 22 months of age (Blake & Harris, 2011). It is remarkable that children start using first-person possessive expressions well before the appearance of self-referencing words such as the personal pronoun "I" or the child's proper name. The

early appearance of such expressions is probably fostered by their frequent use in possession episodes. Second- and third-person possessive pronouns also appear later than first-person possessive pronouns. First come "my" and "mine;" later come "I," "George," and "yours."

Possession conflicts are an important aspect of children's everyday life. Ross (1996) observed children in their homes when they were between two and six years old, and found that access to personal or family property was the most frequent reason of fighting among siblings. Similarly, a study by Dunn (1988) shows that possession is "an issue at the center of many conflicts" between 24 and 36 months of age.

Rossano et al. (2011) made two- and three-year-old children participate in situations in which a puppet took stuff (such as a scarf or a hat) from another person and attempted to throw it away. They found that two- and three-year-old children protested when the puppet tried to take their stuff. However, only three-year-old children protested when a third party's item was involved. This suggests, according to these researchers, that around three years of age children begin to understand the normative dimensions of property rights. In the authors' words: "Standing up for the property rights of a third party, demonstrates . . . young children's emerging understanding of the normative dimension of property as it applies to all persons equally in an agent-neutral manner. It is not just that I do not like it when someone takes or throws away an object that doesn't belong to them; it is wrong." Three-year-olds already understand ownership rules as agent-neutral, and therefore protest transgressions against ownership when they affect a third party and not only when they affect their own interests.

Dunn (1988) claims that children at 36 months are most likely to engage in argumentation or justifications in disputes about those very issues over which children at 18 months are most angry or distressed, and that those disputes usually concern the right to use a certain object or to perform a certain activity. Disputes about compliance with conventional rules, destruction of objects, or aggression toward siblings or parents are less likely to occasion argumentation. The novelty at 36 months is, then, the explicit use of arguments to justify ownership claims.

Children's first arguments are not very sophisticated. The most common reason given by two-year-olds is "I want" (Dunn, 1988), a simple assertion of will. But, by three years of age, kids are no longer satisfied with other people simply acknowledging their temporary possession of things; they also want to be recognized as the legitimate proprietors of those things, and they can justify this aspiration: "They gave me this doll for my birthday," "My daddy said I could have this pen," "I saw it first," and so on.

One of the most extended and basic ways to claim an object is to apply the principle of first possession, which grants ownership to the party that gains control of the object before other potential claimants. Typically, children shout things like "I had it first," "I came here first," or "I got dibs." We've already seen that children at 18 months of age seem to recognize prior possession in their *behavior*; but at three years of age they can use prior possession as an *argument* against a competitor. This type of argument stays with us throughout our life and is still common sense for most adults (Friedman & Neary, 2009): we ardently demand a parking spot based on the fact that we arrived there first or even that we saw it first; we consider ourselves as owners of an idea simply because we "had it" (meaning "it occurred to us") first. Even nations claim sovereignty over territories on the grounds that their explorers were first to set foot in them. And most legal systems tend to prioritize possession when dealing with property disputes (Holmes, 1991, p. 245). The view that ownership begins with taking possession is a basic tenet of property law around the world (Lueck, 2008), and has a philosophical justification in John Locke's (Locke, 1690) labor theory of property, according to which an individual can gain ownership of previously unowned natural resources (such as land or game) by mixing her labor with the resource before anybody else. Thus, Locke's labor theory of property rests on a right established by first possession (see Rose, 1985, especially note 4).

A number of studies have shown that the principle of first possession plays a crucial role in both children's (Friedman et al., 2013; Kanngiesser, Rossano, & Tomasello, 2015; Rochat et al., 2014) and adults' (Friedman & Neary, 2009) reasoning about ownership. Friedman and Neary (2008) studied children's abilities to infer who owns what from contextual cues and found that three- and four-year-olds assume that the first person to possess an object is its owner, an assumption shared by adults (Friedman & Neary, 2009). Verkuyten, Sierksma, and Thijs (2015) studied the use of the "first arrival" principle in disputes about land ownership in children between 9 and 12 years of age. Their study concluded that "children believe that a person owns a particular land relatively more when that person arrived first." Furthermore, the first arriver is considered to own the land relatively more even when she did not work the land, compared to the later arriver who did work it; first arrival outweighs the laboring of the land of the later arriver. Children connect first possession with entitlement.

Developmental psychology, legal theory, anthropology, and philosophy all agree on the ubiquity of the principle of first possession. However, children sometimes use other arguments to justify ownership. Here are some common examples:

Creation: "I built this chair myself."
Discovery: "I found this cave."
Transaction: "My brother gave this pen to me."
Adverse possession: "Nobody was using this bike, so I started using it and taking care of it."

Sometimes these principles clash. For example, one person asserts that a table belongs to her because she built it, while another argues that she had previously discovered the wood the table was built with. Some types of ownership claim might be more decisive, fundamental or relevant than others. Consequently, some scholars have wondered whether it would be possible to establish a hierarchy of ownership principles according to which, for example, "creation" trumps "discovery" (or the other way around).

Rochat et al. (2014) studied how children from different cultures apply ownership principles. three- and five-year-olds were presented with a series of scripts involving two identical dolls fighting over an object. Participants had to decide which of the two dolls should own the object. Each script enacted a potential reason for attributing ownership: creation, familiarity, first contact, or equity. For example, in one of the scripts, a doll claims to have created the object, while the other one only asserts that the object is hers without providing a competing reason. Results show that, across cultures, children are significantly more consistent in attributing ownership when one of the protagonists created the object, as compared with other kinds of reasons such as first contact, familiarity with the object, or equity considerations. "Creation" appears to be more stable across cultures than the other criteria.

Levene, Starmans, and Friedman (2015), in a study with adults, conclude that "creation trumps first possession as a means of acquiring ownership." Kanngiesser, Gjersoe, and Hood (2010) made a researcher and a participant borrow modeling-clay objects from each other to mold into new objects. Participants were more likely to transfer ownership to the second individual after she invested creative labor in the object than after other manipulations (holding the object, making small changes to it). This effect was significantly stronger in preschool children than in adults. In the context of the experiment, then, invested effort and creative labor overruled the first-possessor bias for preschool children.

An alternative interpretation of this experiment, however, is that while the original owner had prior possession of the play dough (the raw material), the person who models a new object is the first possessor of the object just created.

Faigenbaum, Sigman, and Casiraghi (forthcoming) tested children and adults in order to look for differences in the application of the principle of first possession. Participants watched videos that featured ownership conflicts. In one of the scripts, a girl climbs a mountain, discovers a cave and inscribes her name on the entrance. Later, a second girl finds the cave and starts living there. In another script, a boy discovers some pieces of wood and puts them aside; a second boy arrives and manufactures a chair with them. It was found that, while reacting to exactly the same stories, children are significantly more likely than adults to grant ownership to the character that was the first possessor of the object under dispute (84% versus 55% of cases when summarizing all stories, respectively). Children's reasoning rests on first possession significantly more than adults. There seems to be a developmental trajectory that weakens the weight of first possession on ownership reasoning as the child grows.

Most dictionaries define ownership as a *legal right of possession*. Possession and ownership are in fact synonyms and can be used interchangeably in many contexts. However, the verb "to possess" emphasizes the *physical control* of the thing, whereas "to own" highlights the fact that one *holds a right* to possess the object. For example, if I rent my car to someone else, I do not possess it for some time, yet I am still its owner (and other people should recognize this legal title). Ownership creates an abstract link between the owner and the object that does not depend on the physical traits of the object but is rooted in social norms only.

Babies, up to about 18 months of age, *use* stuff. Toddlers starting at about 18 months *possess* things, in the sense that they actively fight for exclusive access to the object, and want their possession to be recognized and respected by others. Toddlers are frequently interested in the things other people have or are paying attention to, yet they seem to observe some basic, practical version of the prior possession rule. At about 36 months of age children want to be explicitly recognized as owners. They uphold property rights even when a third party object is at stake. They can now justify why they are the legitimate owners of a certain object ("I saw it first," "my mommy gave it to me"), and infer who the owner of a certain object is in many everyday settings. The principle of first possession plays a prominent role in three-year-olds' ownership reasoning: children explicitly ground ownership in prior possession. In other words, they translate into words and arguments the practical rules that govern their relationships with their peers (i.e., one does not take stuff from someone who had it first). Yet, three-year-olds also go beyond physical possession: they treat ownership as an abstract relationship between owner and object. They can go on vacation for one month, but they still know that the toys they left behind are theirs.

The developmental progression we are proposing, then, is: (1) use, (2) possession, and (3) ownership. Insofar as we start having a more permanent bond with our "stuff," mere possession becomes property; we go from physical seizure of the object, through public recognition of possession, to *property rights*.

Children's participation in the normative, conflicting world of possession and ownership probably impacts on other domains. Levine (1983) hypothesizes that the tendency to claim and defend toys by using the possessive adjective "mine" and territorial behaviors in general establish boundaries between self and other, and are therefore relevant for self- (and other-) definition. Fasig (2000) suggests that, by controlling the toy's use and by recognizing the relationship between the toy, the self, and the other, children gain knowledge of their own self. In addition, cherished possessions facilitate temporal cognitive links among one's past, present, and future by providing biographical references. Thus Fasig (2000) argues that children's ability to link objects to owners "indicates knowledge of the self as continuous in time." Rochat (2009) provides an in-depth exploration of the role that possession and ownership conflicts play on the emergence of self-consciousness, while taking into account not only the cognitive, but also the affective aspects of development, with special focus on social emotions like shame and guilt.

17.3 Exchange and Reciprocity

At around nine months of age, children start to engage in give-and-take games with adults (Bruner & Watson, 1983; Stern, 1998). "No parent and no observer can fail to be aware of how often very young children show, offer, and give objects to others. Often such gestures appear to be social overtures, friendly actions or attempts to engage another in interaction" (Dunn, 1988, p. 99). By 18 months, children regularly give objects to (and receive objects from) their peers; they understand that a sibling wants what they have and on occasion will offer to share before they have been asked. By three years of age, children not only recognize what the other wants, but also grasp the idea that sharing is often expected (especially if it is food) and use this as a justification for their own demands (Dunn, 1988, p. 106).

In addition, at age three, children are often able to make explicit agreements (for example, in turn-taking). It is true that two-year-olds already can share (toys, food), have negotiation skills, and can give up some things in order to obtain others. But it is only at three that children start articulating rules and contracts such as "you use it for a while, then I use it for a while." Obviously, we are not saying that physical aggression has disappeared or that three-year-olds "talk things out" whenever there is a dispute. Yet, it seems to be the case that many conflicts over possession are now ended by means of verbal argumentation, sharing, turn-taking, and reconciliation, without adult intervention (see Ross & Conant, 1995; Ross, Conant, & Vickar, 2011). Three-year-olds are capable of making *explicit agreements*.

Typically, an owner can use, modify, destroy, or lend her possessions. In certain circumstances, she can also *alienate* her property; that is, she can transfer ownership to another person. Children at three years of age are able to justify their ownership claims, seal *contracts* (deals, agreements) with other persons and *transfer ownership* of their property (Faigenbaum, 2005). This opens up a new range of experiences for them: they now participate in *exchanges*. For the purpose of this discussion, we will define an exchange as an interaction in which ownership of an object is voluntarily transferred from an individual to another. For example, three-year-olds grow increasingly interested in presents. They understand that a gift is more than the friendly gesture of handing out an object: gifts bestow ownership.

Kindergarten and primary school children trade objects with their peers. A vibrant underground economy is alive in the schoolyards of the world (Faigenbaum, 2005; Webley, 1996). There, girls and boys trade cards, marbles, sweets, toys, and even intangible goods (such as favors or the right to participate in a game). Ecological observation reveals that these activities are not random: children's peer societies distinguish between legitimate and illegitimate transfers, and enforce procedural and moral rules that govern exchanges.

Things change hands. Economists, anthropologists, and sociologists agree that social exchanges involve *reciprocity*, the rule that establishes that a person has the obligation to pay back in kind what other people has provided her. Sometimes the obligation created is vague or unspecified (as in gifts); at other times it is precisely defined (as in sales). Faigenbaum (2005) studied spontaneous peer-interaction in the schoolyard with the aim of uncovering the values, rules, and conceptions of reciprocity implicit in children's exchanges.

An analysis of children's argumentative discourse supported the distinction of two kinds of reciprocity in children: *associative* and *strict*.

Associative reciprocity takes place when children exchange for the sake of establishing or re-defining personal bonds. Children often give goods to their peers while invoking favors received in the past, favors they shall receive in an undefined future, alliances, or membership in a common group. The following are spontaneous utterances recorded in the schoolyard (Faigenbaum, 2005):

"I like to make presents to my best friends . . . I give away the cards that are repeats" (7-year-old).
"He gave me a teddy bear, so I promised I was going to give him a marble" (7-year-old).
"You don't give me the swing; I will not give you my paints. I am no longer your friend. You will never come to my house again, and at my birthday party you won't blow my candles" (3-year-old).
"[You will not borrow my puppet] because you don't trade cards with me" (10-year-old).

Associative reciprocity predominates in most exchanges in kindergarten children. Although it never disappears completely, older children become increasingly interested in maximizing the value of the objects obtained in their exchanges, and accordingly do trades that involve a tit-for-tat, *strict reciprocity*. For example, when trading cards, they save the "repeats" in order to trade them for cards they lack. When assessing the precise value of each card, they consider several factors (beauty, scarcity, etc.) Strict reciprocity becomes progressively more important throughout primary school.

Developmental psychologists are ever more interested in reciprocity in children. Warneken and Tomasello (2013) designed experimental situations in which children had to share resources with a researcher. They found that it is not until 3.5 years of age that children modulate their sharing contingent on their partner's antecedent behavior. Babies and young toddlers already have prosocial tendencies; helping and sharing emerge before children begin to worry about directly reciprocating what others have provided to them. Later in development, they seem to become more sensitive to reciprocity, adjusting their behavior accordingly. In summary, children's prosocial behavior emerges spontaneously but is later mediated by reciprocity. Olson & Spelke (2008) also found that 3.5-year-old children already have a tendency to share resources with close relations, with people who have shared with them (direct reciprocity), and with people who have shared with others (indirect reciprocity).

Rochat et al. (2009) studied fairness in three- and five-year-olds. They made children distribute small collections of candies, either between the participant and an adult experimenter or between two dolls. The authors compared the responses of children growing up in seven different cultural and economic contexts. Across cultures, three-year-olds tend to optimize their own gain, not showing many signs of self-sacrifice or generosity. By five years, overall, children tend to show more fairness in sharing. What varies across cultures is only the magnitude of young children's self-interest, but the direction of development (from selfishness to fairness) seems to be universal.

Robbins and Rochat (2011) define *strong reciprocity* as the propensity to sacrifice resources to be kind or to punish in response to prior acts. They tested three- and five-year-old children in a sharing game involving the participant child, a generous puppet, and a stingy puppet. At the end of the game, the child was offered an opportunity to sacrifice some of her personal gains to punish one of the puppets. They found that only five-year-olds show some evidence of strong reciprocity by orienting their punishment systematically toward the stingy puppet (thus manifesting what the authors call an "ethical stance"). The authors suggest that strong reciprocity depends

on culture, since they were not able to replicate the results originally obtained in America with Samoan children.

The literature on economic games and bargaining offers another approximation to the development of reciprocity. For the last thirty years, there's been a surge of research on games like *ultimatum, dictator*, and *common good* in children. In *ultimatum*, the first player or "proposer" receives something valuable (money, stickers, candy) and proposes a method to divide it between herself and another player. The second player or "responder" chooses to either accept or reject the proposal. If the responder accepts, the goods are split according to the proposal. If the responder rejects, neither player receives anything. The game is typically played as a one-shot interaction, so that future reciprocation is not an issue. In the *dictator* game, the first player or "dictator," determines how to split an endowment between herself and another player. The second player or "recipient" simply receives what the dictator assigned to her; her role is entirely passive and has no input into the outcome of the game.

Harbaugh, Krause, and Liday (2003) had children aged 7 through 18 play ultimatum and dictator games. They found that bargaining behavior changes substantially with age. Children at age seven already make strategic proposals: they offer the partner a smaller amount than what they keep for themselves, but not small enough to offend the partner and lose all the money. Thus, on average, younger children make and accept smaller ultimatum proposals than older children. What improves with age is children's preference for fairness, but not their bargaining ability. Similarly, Murnighan and Saxon (1998) report on a study of bargaining attitudes in children from kindergarten through ninth grade. While they found a similar strategic behavior in elementary school children, they also discovered that kindergartners made quite "unstrategic" proposals: sometimes they told the experimenter they would give away everything they had.

Fehr, Bernhard, and Rockenbach (2008) used a modified version of the dictator game to test children between three and eight years of age. They found that, at age three–four, the overwhelming majority of children behave selfishly, whereas most children at age seven–eight prefer resource allocations that remove advantageous or disadvantageous inequality. They conclude that the force behind other-regarding choices in seven- and eight-year-old children is inequality aversion. Inequality aversion is, however, modulated by parochialism, a preference for favoring the members of one's own social group.

If we now put together the results of these different studies on peer exchange, reciprocity, and economic games, a general picture emerges:

1 Three-year-olds show self-optimizing and hoarding behaviors. Should they be labeled as selfish capitalists who optimize their own gain? Before jumping to conclusions, let us remember that, in the context of the family, children regularly receive food, toys, and other stuff from adults, and that they are not always obliged to reciprocate or share what they receive. Children acting as ultimatum proposers (and receiving candy from an adult researcher) might see themselves as fully entitled to whatever they get. Occasionally, however, children go from extreme selfishness to extreme generosity: they can give *everything* to the other player. How to explain this discrepancy? We should take into account that, in their daily life, children do give stuff to their peers (for example, when trying to make new friends). Preschool children do not frame their relationships in terms of strict-reciprocity contracts. It should be no surprise that their behavior in economic games and fairness experiments is consistent with a culture of associative reciprocity and the gift economy, which predominate in the context of familial institutions

and peer relationships at this age. Preschoolers might appear as nonstrategic from the point of view of economists who identify rationality with calculating the best means to achieve a desired end-result (individual profit, equality, etc.), but they are actually well adapted to their real social context.

2 The apparently selfish tendencies of three-year-olds moderate themselves as children mature, so that between five and seven years of age (depending on the specific study) children start demanding fairness and rejecting inequality. In certain cases, they even embrace an ethical stance and engage in costly punishment. This emerging mindset is in harmony with the strict reciprocity embedded in experiences such as bartering with peers or dealing with money and prices, which gain prominence in children's daily life as they grow up. In the culture of adults, barter and monetary transactions are considered fair when both parties receive an equivalent value. Similarly, fair distributions between partners with the same merit are expected to be 50/50. This kind of institutional context comes to dominate children's interactions and provides them with a new sense of fairness.

To sum up: preschool children can sometimes be quite shrewd and egotistic, and at other times they can be generous and prosocial, but in general they do not frame their relationships in terms of strict reciprocity contracts. By way of contrast, the strategic thinking of seven-year-olds relies on a calculation of what their partners would accept as a good deal, and in that sense it presupposes a contractual framework (see congruent evidence in Lucas, Wagner, & Chow, 2008). Three-year-olds already have a certain sense of fairness that they apply to the distribution and exchange of objects (Rochat et al., 2009); however, this sense evolves as children engage in different exchange practices, framed by age-specific cultures and institutions.

17.4 Institutions and Institutional Experience

There are people, out there in the social world, who acquire, use, and sell property. Some researchers take it for granted that children obtain information about those ownership-related events by witnessing them directly and by complementary sources such as verbal input provided by adults or the mass media. They consider children as embarked in the "cold" enterprise of conceptualizing ownership, which is supposed to be "an interesting cognitive problem" (Kalish & Anderson, 2011) involving distant adult institutions. Consistently, these scholars use individual interviews with children to present third person, hypothetical situations to participants so as to uncover their concepts and reasoning about social institutions, which are treated as *external phenomena.*

In order to navigate the social world, children need to master norms regulating ownership. Picture a child entering a room full of toys: she will need to apply some kind of heuristics to identify the owner of each object; she will need to follow specific procedures to ask for permission to use a given object. An example of heuristic reasoning is provided by Friedman et al. (2011), who show that both adults and children usually expect human-made objects (artifacts) to belong to someone, since making an object typically establishes ownership over it. Natural kinds (a bird, a tree in a forest) are commonly assumed not to belong to anybody. Children also infer that the person who gives permission to use an object is its owner (Neary, Friedman, & Burnstein, 2009).

This progressive mastery of social norms, however, may not happen as a cold exercise in social cognition, but as a hot engagement with a world of conflicting claims. Children do not merely witness social phenomena; they are deeply immersed in a first-person experience. They navigate social institutions (family, school, peer societies) from dusk till dawn. Successfully dealing with ownership-related rules and

practices is crucial in such an environment, and ownership experiences can become emotionally charged. Conflicts always pop up, because "the intent to appropriate or deal with a thing as owner can hardly exist without an intent to exclude others" (Holmes, 1991, p. 221). As Rochat (2009, 2014) argues, these experiences shape children's identities, their place in the social world, their sense of justice. Think only about the feelings of jealousy that arise when a sibling gets the best presents for Christmas; or about how showing off expensive stuff brings about prestige for an owner, envy and humiliation for her friends.

Our environment is both natural and social. The social dimension of our environment is itself complex and includes diverse types of entities such as persons, cultural artifacts, rituals, and institutions. We consider Searle's (1995) theory as the most illuminating characterization of the institutional milieu in which humans live. Searle's account is based on the insight that human beings, in their everyday life, create *institutional facts* by means of a particular type of rules that he calls "constitutive." Constitutive rules can be expressed by the formula *X counts as Y* (Searle, 1995, 2005). For example, a certain move in a football game *counts as* scoring a touchdown; a given set of voting procedures *counts as* the election of the president of the United States. In all constitutive rules, the *X* term identifies certain features of an object and the *Y* term assigns a special status to that object.

Ownership is clearly an institution, since it is constituted by rules of the type *X count as Y*, such as "taking possession of something in such and such circumstances counts as becoming its owner." Gift, barter and sale are also institutions according to this criterion. For example, giving something to someone in a given context, while saying certain words, counts as "making a present."

Searle emphasizes that institutions populate and shape our everyday world. His list of examples of institutions include money, rule games, property, promises, schools, marriage, birthday parties, presents, friendships, tenure, summer vacations, and industrial strikes, among many others. Searle explains that institutions have deontological consequences, that is, they create rights and obligations. For instance, when a child owns certain toys she has concurrent rights such as playing with them without asking for permission, but also duties such as picking them up when she's done playing. And all these rights and duties interlock with other social institutions (Searle, 2005), such as borrowing or sharing. Searle claims that the capacity to collectively assign social functions to objects, thus creating institutions, rights and duties, is specifically human.

Children inhabit an institutional environment since early in their life. If it is the case that institutions shape children's actions, values, beliefs, and forms of thinking, then they should be studied by developmental psychologists. What are the consequences for human beings of living in an environment that is saturated with institutions such as ownership?

"Ownership is both invisible and abstract" (Noles & Keil, 2011) and yet, as research shows, its fundamentals are grasped by young children. The fact that ownership pervades our everyday life may favor specific, abstract forms of thinking as a matter of adaptation to a world saturated with abstract, "invisible" constitutive rules. This adaptation may also impact in the development of other domains, such as morality. "The development of a moral sense in children finds a particularly rich soil in the early inclination to possess and appropriate things to the self . . . [the development of a sense of ownership] correlates with *and possibly causes* the emergence of a moral sense" (Rochat, 2011; emphasis added). Similarly, Ross, Conant, and Vickar (2011) argue that children's observance of property rights might contribute to the development of morality: "Children's understanding of ownership rights may provide the

clearest and most compelling example of reciprocal moral principles originating in the society of children rather than that of adults" (Ross, Conant, & Vickar, 2011). Morality might be primarily framed by our "hot," rich experiences with institutions such as ownership, which create a fertile ground for the development of mutual respect.

In the previous section we suggested that institutional experience impacts on children's conceptions of fairness. This hypothesis receives indirect support from intercultural research on economic games with adults, as it was summarized and integrated in Henrich et al. (2005). The authors of this ambitious paper emphasize the importance of local institutions in shaping individuals' responses to economic games. They mention the case of the whale hunting people on the island of Lamalera (Indonesia), where performance at the ultimatum game mirrors the fishers' behavior when distributing a large prey. Henrich and colleagues also note that the Tsimane of Bolivia and the Machiguenga of Peru, who live in societies with little cooperation or exchange beyond the family unit, tend to make low ultimatum offers. Lamalera proposers in the ultimatum game think of the money as owned in common with the recipient, whereas Tsimane and Machigenga proposers see the money as their own and feel entitled to keep it (see also Gowdy, Iorgulescu, & Onyeiwu, 2003; Henrich, 2000).

In the same vein, J. Ensminger (another contributor to Henrich et al., 2005) studied the Orma, a tribe living in East Africa, and concluded that the presence or absence of wage or trade income in a community is a highly significant predictor of offer size in ultimatum games. People with more exposure to a free market (those engaged in wage labor and trade) have a greater tendency to propose ultimatum fair offers than those habitually engaged in subsistence production. This is coherent with the teachings of anthropologists such as Mauss (1967) or Godelier (1999), who show how reciprocity is embedded in local practices.

Markets are institutions that teach people how to coordinate their actions equitably with other, anonymous individuals. It might be counterintuitive to think about markets and money as promoting fairness (rather than selfishness), but the interpretation makes sense: it is only in the context of market institutions and commercial transactions that fairness comes to be identified with the equitable (either equal or proportional) distribution of benefits. Again: institutions and social practices impact on individual's conception of what is fair.

Henrich et al. (2005), after a thorough review of the evidence, conclude that economic organization and the structure of social interactions explain a substantial portion of the behavioral variation across societies: the higher the degree of market integration and the higher the payoffs to cooperation in everyday life, the greater the level of prosociality expressed in experimental games. By way of contrast, economic and demographic variables do not explain game behavior, either within or across groups. As Baumard, André, and Sperber (2013) sum it up, respondents interpret the experimenters' instructions in terms of their everyday practices.

Intercultural research, then, has shown that there are broad differences in the way people act in economic games, and that the reasons for this divergence are mostly found in local practices, shaped by markets and other institutions that regulate the exchange and distribution of objects. This account is basically the same that we proposed in the previous section to explain children's performance at economic games. In the context of the family, preschool children regularly receive food, toys, and other stuff from adults, without an obligation to reciprocate. In the context of peer societies, preschool children use presents in order to establish alliances, define social relationships, and make new friends. This is a plausible explanation for the apparently irrational, non-strategic performance of children younger than five in economic games. They do not yet under-stand fairness in terms of tit-for-tat reciprocity. The apparent altruism of some children (or the altruism of adults that is reported by intercultural researchers) should not be seen as resulting from a lack of rationality, but as expressing the predominance of the institutions of associative reciprocity.

In spite of the evidence showing that reciprocity is to some extent shaped by institutionalized practices, Baumard, André, and Sperber (2013) suggest that there is an innate, core representation of fairness "inside the head" of each individual. This core is postulated to be identical (or very similar) across cultures. This nativist conception of fairness assumes that cultural specificities cause participants in economic games to misunderstand the researchers' instructions. An alternative view (that we endorse) is that institutions model basic conceptions of reciprocity from the very beginning of development, and that culture in general interacts with humans' innate capacities such as empathy all along (see Castorina & Faigenbaum, 2002, for a discussion of how social constrains can be treated as an integral part of epistemological processes, rather than as an external limitation). There is no misunderstanding of the experimenters' instructions; rather, people have no option but to use institutional frameworks to make sense of their interactions.

17.5 Conclusion

In this chapter, we described certain aspects of children's social development in the domains of ownership and exchange. We highlighted some important cognitive milestones in the development of ownership, such as the acquisition of possessives, the use of heuristics to attribute objects to persons, and the understanding of property rights. We postulated a transition from mere use of objects (since birth), to possession (at about 18 months), and to ownership (at about three years of age).

Children defend their possessions by argumentation and trade them with their peers. Gifts, associative reciprocity, and apparently selfish behaviors predominate in kindergarten children. Primary school children engage in strict reciprocity exchanges (barter and monetary transactions) which promote fairness-oriented and inequality-averse thinking. Everyday social practices influence children's conceptions of fairness.

Fairness, reciprocity, and other moral notions are partly shaped by institutions present in children's everyday life. According to Searle (1995, 2005) ownership and exchange are institutions, since they are constituted by rules of the type *X count as Y*. Beyond the innate pro-social tendencies shared by all humans, individuals are also required to master institutional reality in order to function in their social world. They need to deal with ownership, gifts, barter, trade, and money on a daily basis. Development can be seen as a progressive appropriation of such institutional reality, a process which seems to impact back on the agent's reasoning processes. For example, since ownership relations are not self-evident and are not displayed as physical traits of objects or owners, they demand a kind of abstract reasoning that appears at a very early age. Similarly, exchange practices might play a role in the development of the understanding of quantities. Institutions provide a framework for thinking. We hope that future research will offer a more detailed picture of children's social development, their institutional life and the interactions between ownership, exchange, and other domains of knowledge and experience.

References

Bakeman, R. & Brownlee, J. R. (1982). Social rules governing object conflicts in toddlers and preschoolers. In *Peer Relationships and Social Skills in Childhood* (pp. 99–111). New York: Springer.

Bates, E. (1990). Language about me and you: Pronominal reference and the emerging concept of self. In D. Cicchetti & M. Beeghly (Eds.), *The Self in Transition Infancy to Childhood* (pp. 165–182). Chicago: University of Chicago Press.

Baumard, N., André, J. B., & Sperber, D. (2013). A mutualistic approach to morality. *Behavioral and Brain Sciences*, 36(1), 59–78.

Blake, P. R. & Harris, P. L. (2011). Early representations of ownership. *New Directions for Child and Adolescent Development*, 132, 39–51. DOI: 10.1002/cd.295.

Bloom, L. (1973). *One Word at a Time: The Use of Single Word Utterances before Syntax*. The Hague: Mouton De Gruyter.

Brosnan, S. F. (2011). Property in nonhuman primates. *New Directions for Child and Adolescent Development*, 132, 9–22. DOI: 10.1002/cd.293.

Bruner, J. & Watson, R. (1983). *Child's Talk: Learning to Use Language*. New York: W. W. Norton.

Castorina, J. A., & Faigenbaum, G. (2002). The epistemological meaning of constraints in the development of domain knowledge. *Theory & Psychology*, 12(3), 315–334. DOI: 10.1177/0959354302012003013.

Deutsch, W. & Budwig, N. (1983). Form and function in the development of possessives. *Papers and Reports on Child Language Development*, 22, 36–42.

Dunn, J. (1988). *The Beginnings of Social Understanding*. Cambridge, MA: Harvard University Press.

Faigenbaum, G. (2005). *Children's Economic Experience: Exchange*. Buenos Aires: LibrosEnRed.

Faigenbaum, G., Sigman, M., & Casiraghi, L. (forthcoming). Young children use first possession significantly more than adults for deciding ownership.

Fasig, L. G. (2000). Toddlers' understanding of ownership: Implications for self-concept development. *Social Development*, 9, 370–382.

Fehr, E., Bernhard, H., & Rockenbach, B. (2008). Egalitarianism in young children. *Nature*, 454(7208), 1079–1083. DOI: 10.1038/nature07155.

Friedman, O. & Neary, K. R. (2008). Determining who owns what: Do children infer ownership from first possession? *Cognition*, 107(3), 829–849.

Friedman, O. & Neary, K. (2009). First possession beyond the law: Adults' and young children's intuitions about ownership. *Tulane Law Review*, 83, 1–12.

Friedman, O., Neary, K. R., Defeyter, M. A., & Malcolm, S. L. (2011). Ownership and object history. *New Directions for Child and Adolescent Development*, 132, 79–89. DOI: 10.1002/cd.298.

Friedman, O., Van de Vondervoort, J. W., Defeyter, M. A., & Neary, K. R. (2013). First possession, history, and young children's ownership judgments. *Child Development*, 84(5), 1519–1525. DOI: 10.1111/cdev.12080.

Godelier, M. (1999). *The Enigma of the Gift*. Chicago: University of Chicago Press.

Gowdy, J., Iorgulescu, R., & Onyeiwu, S. (2003). Fairness and retaliation in a rural Nigerian village. *Journal of Economic Behavior & Organization*, 52, 469–479. DOI: 10.1016/S0167-2681(03)00026-X.

Harbaugh, W. T., Krause, K. S., & Liday, S. J. (2003). Bargaining by children. University of Oregon Economics Working Paper No. 2002.4. DOI: 10.2139/ssrn.436504.

Hay, D. (2006). Yours and mine: Toddlers' talk about possessions with familiar peers. *British Journal of Developmental Psychology*, 24, 39–52. DOI: 10.1348/026151005X68880.

Henrich, J. (2000). Does culture matter in economic behavior? Ultimatum game bargaining among the Machiguenga of the Peruvian Amazon. *The American Economic Review*, 90(4), 973–979.

Henrich, J., Boyd, R., Bowles, S., Camerer, C., Fehr, E., Gintis, H., McElreath, R., Alvard, M., Barr, A., Ensminger, J., Henrich, N. S., Hill, K., Gil-White, F., Gurven, M., Marlowe, F. W., Patton, J. Q., & Tracer, D. (2005). "Economic man" in cross-cultural perspective. Behavioral experiments in 15 small-scale societies. *Behavioral and Brain Sciences*, 28(6), 795–815.

Holmes, O. W. (1991). *The Common Law*. New York: Dover Publications.

Kalish, C. W. & Anderson, C. D. (2011). Ownership as a social status. *New Directions for Child and Adolescent Development*, 132, 65–77. DOI: 10.1002/cd.297.

Kanngiesser, P., Gjersoe, N., & Hood, B. M. (2010). The effect of creative labor on property-ownership transfer by preschool children and adults. *Psychological Science*, 21(9), 1236–1241.

Kanngiesser, P., Rossano, F., & Tomasello, M. (2015). Late emergence of the first possession heuristic: Evidence from a small-scale culture. *Child Development*, 86(4), 1282–1289. DOI: 10.1111/cdev.12365.

Levene, M., Starmans, C., & Friedman, O. (2015). Creation in judgments about the establishment of ownership. *Journal of Experimental Social Psychology*, 60, 103–109. DOI: 10.1016/j.jesp.2015.04.011.

Levine, L. E. (1983). Mine: Self-definition in 2-year-old boys. *Developmental Psychology*, 19(4), 544–549. DOI: 10.1037/0012-1649.19.4.544.

Locke, J. (1690). *Second Treatise of Government* (pp. 267–302). London: Whitmore and Fenn.

Lucas, M., Wagner, L., & Chow, C. (2008). Fair game: The intuitive economics of resource exchange in four-year olds. *Journal of Social, Evolutionary, and Cultural Psychology*, 2(3), 74–88.

Lueck, D. (2008). Property law, economics and. In S. N. Durlauf & L. E. Blume (Eds.), *The New Palgrave Dictionary of Economics Online* (2nd edn.). Basingstoke: Palgrave Macmillan. doi: 10.1057/9780230226203.1352.

Mauss, M. (1967). *The Gift: Forms and Functions of Exchange in Archaic Societies* (vol. 21). London: Cohen & West.

Murnighan, J. K. & Saxon, M. S. (1998). Ultimatum bargaining by children and adults. *Journal of Economic Psychology*, 19(4), 415–445. DOI: 10.1016/S0167-4870(98)00017-8.

Neary, K. R., Friedman, O., & Burnstein, C. L. (2009). Preschoolers infer ownership from "control of permission." *Developmental Psychology*, 45(3), 873–876. DOI: 10.1037/a0014088.

Noles, N. S. & Keil, F. C. (2011). Exploring ownership in a developmental context. *New Directions for*

Child and Adolescent Development, 132, 91–103. DOI: 10.1002/cd.299.

Olson, K. R. & Spelke, E. S. (2008). Foundations of cooperation in young children. *Cognition*, 108(1), 222–231. DOI: 10.1016/j.cognition.2007.12.003.

Robbins, E. & Rochat, P. (2011). Emerging signs of strong reciprocity in human ontogeny. *Frontiers in Psychology*, 2(December), 1–16. DOI: 10.3389/fpsyg.2011.00353.

Rochat, P. (2009). *Others in Mind: Social Origins of Self-Consciousness*. New York: Cambridge University Press.

Rochat, P. (2011). Possession and morality in early development. *New Directions for Child and Adolescent Development*, 132 23–38. DOI: 10.1002/cd.294.

Rochat, P. (2014). *Origins of Possession: Owning and Sharing in Development* [Kindle edn.]. Cambridge: Cambridge University Press.

Rochat, P., Dias, M. D. G., Broesch, T., Passos-Ferreira, C., Winning, A., & Berg, B. (2009). Fairness in distributive justice by 3- and 5-year-olds across seven cultures. *Journal of Cross-Cultural Psychology*, 40(3), 416–442. DOI: 10.1177/0022022109332844.

Rochat, P., Robbins, E., Passos-Ferreira, C., Donato Oliva, A., Dias, M. D. G., & Guo, L. (2014). Ownership reasoning in children across cultures. *Cognition*, 132(3), 471–484. DOI: 10.1016/j.cognition.2014.04.014.

Rose, C. M. (1985). Possession as the origin of property. Faculty Scholarship Series, Paper 1830.

Ross, H. (1996). Negotiating principles of entitlement in sibling property disputes. *Developmental Psychology*, 32(1), 90–101. DOI: 10.1037/0012-1649.32.1.90.

Ross, H. & Conant, C. L. (1995). The social structure of early conflict: Interaction, relationships and alliances. In C. U. Shantz & W. W. Hartup (Eds.), *Conflict in Child and Adolescent Development* (pp. 153–184). New York: Cambridge University Press.

Ross, H., Conant, C., & Vickar, M. (2011). Property rights and the resolution of social conflict. *New Directions for Child and Adolescent Development*, 132, 53–64. DOI: 10.1002/cd.296.

Rossano, F., Rakoczy, H., & Tomasello, M. (2011). Young children's understanding of violations of property rights. *Cognition*, 121(2), 219–227.

Searle, J. R. (1995). *The Construction of Social Reality*. New York: Free Press.

Searle, J. R. (2005). What is an institution? *Journal of Institutional Economics*, 1(1), 1–22. DOI: 10.1017/S1744137405000020.

Stern, D. N. (1998). *The Interpersonal World of the Infant: A View from Psychoanalysis and Developmental Psychology*. London: Karnac Books.

Tomasello, M. (1998). One child early talk about possession. In J. Newman (Ed.), *The Linguistics of Giving*. (pp. 349–373). Amsterdam: John Benjamins.

Verkuyten, M., Sierksma, J., & Thijs, J. (2015). First arrival and owning the land: How children reason about ownership of territory. *Journal of Environmental Psychology*, 41, 58–64. DOI: 10.1016/j.jenvp.2014.11.007.

Warneken, F. & Tomasello, M. (2013). The emergence of contingent reciprocity in young children. *Journal of Experimental Child Psychology*, 116(2), 338–350.

Webley, P. (1996). Playing the market: The autonomous economic world of children. In P. Lunt & A. Furnham (Eds.), *Economic Socialization: The Economic Beliefs and Behaviours of Young Children* (pp. 149–161). Cheltenham, UK: Edward Elgar.

18 Possessions and Money beyond Market Economy

Toshiya Yamamoto and Noboru Takahashi

18.1 Basic Viewpoint for Analyzing Possessions and Money

18.1.1 Money as a Cultural Tool

A human is a creature who uses tools. Such tools could be physical instruments or psychosocial ones, such as signs, which Vygotsky (1997) advocates – concept, thought, and social system. Humans have sociohistorically inherited and developed these tools into the creation of personal inner life, interpersonal communication, and, moreover, a social system. Here we follow the usage extended by Cole (1996) – we use the concept of tools with such expansiveness. Money is one of the basic tools generating human economic activity. Money is, however, not just an economic tool. An economic tool is merely one type of cultural tool. This is our basic standpoint in our discussion on the economy and the cultural nature of money.

Generally, money is regarded as a simple economic tool that represents exchange value and thus mediates exchange, becomes a unit of price, and stores' value. Its only use value is that money can represent exchange value. Money can be exchanged for any kinds of goods. For that reason, the value of money is universal – anyone who has money can use it – and neutral. It does not depend on any specific personal relationship.

Money as an economic tool has been created through the development of barter exchange. However, barter exchange hinges on the practical use value of goods to be exchanged and, in many cases, depends on the specific personal relationship between those who exchange. In this context, the value neutrality of money is not absolute.

Gift exchange is the most basic pattern of social exchange and completely depends on specific personal or intercommunity relationships. Those who exchange gifts do so based on their personal relationships, and such exchange cannot be established when a relationship does not exist.

Humans are the only species to interact with others through social exchange using various kinds of media, including materialistic objects, such as money, goods, and gifts, and spiritual objects, such as words, concepts, and thoughts. All of these interactions are based on human symbolic function or a psychological system of signs.

18.1.2 Two Types of Exchange and EMS

Here we can schematize the structure of such human-specific interaction using the concept of expanded mediational structure (EMS), as shown in Figure 18.1. The figure shows how subject 1 approaches subject 2 using some sort of object as a medium (object 1); then, subject 2 responds to subject 1 using an object (object 2), and all of these interactions are mediated or guided by a normative element of some kind (normative mediator).

The media can be money or goods in an economic interaction, gifts in a gift exchange, or words in a conversation. The normative mediator can be common practice in social interaction, including economic exchange or logic or

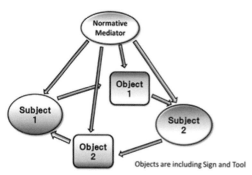

Figure 18.1 Expanded mediational structure (EMS).

rules in discussion. Subjects act out appropriate roles in respective interactions, which means they become sellers and buyers in a market exchange or listeners and speakers in a conversation.

Using this schema, the different nature that money has in market exchange and that a gift has in gift exchange can be explained as follows. In a market economy, neutral subjects that do not have individual personalities exchange money for goods as objects, and those objects are regarded simply as representing a neutral exchange value. These interactions are mediated by a highly abstract and universal law (normative mediator). On the other hand, in gift exchange, subjects exchange gifts based on their personal relationships, maintaining mutual credibility and following certain customs or ethics.

Nevertheless, when analyzing a specific economic phenomenon in daily life, gift exchange and market exchange cannot always be differentiated in such an absolute manner. This is particularly true when trying to understand cultural difference and cultural conflicts in a global economy or the process of children learning about money through their daily exchange practices.

For example, when children buy certain goods, they often talk with their friends about appealing points of a product. Through their conversation, the product develops its subjective value, which is shared by the children. In this way, value becomes an intersubjective substance. The shared intersubjective value functions as a medium that accommodates the children's interactions over the product.

Meaning is also given to a subject who uses money. Just like the rich are expected to return their money to society, every adult uses money mediated by his or her role according to the socialized meaning of the subject. In the case of a company officer, he or she is anticipated to use money to benefit the company. But the same person as a father or mother in the home is expected to use money for the family and his or her own personal use.

Money as an object functions as a special exchange tool in such multiple mediational structures comprising subjects having a social role, objects a given social or intersubjective meaning, and some norms accommodating their interactions. A person plays the role of a subject with given cultural meaning and exchanges an object with value while following social normative constraints and being mediated by money, and thus the socioeconomic system functions. Understanding money from a psychological perspective means analyzing the multiple mediational structures and understanding the generating and changing processes of the structure with given meaning (see also the discussion about the relationship between objects that people possess and use to extend the self; Simmel 1950, 322).

18.1.3 Polysemic Nature of Money

Although money is regarded as neutral from a market economy viewpoint, as mentioned above, money and possessions bear polysemy, which cannot be described only by a one-dimensional value structure; in our lives, we find that many things hold subjective values and that those values differ from their market values (Belk, 1988, 1991). Memory-laden objects, including gifts, family photographs, souvenirs and mementos, heirlooms, antiques, and monuments, are typical examples (e.g., Belk, 1991; Dittmar, 1992). We can find numerous examples that indicate that possessions carry subjectively important meaning for individuals. For the aged, roles are given to possessions in providing control and mastery – moderating emotions, cultivating the self, symbolizing ties with others, constituting a concrete history of one's past (Kemptner, 1989). On the other hand, loss of possessions due to theft or disaster accompanies a strong sense of loss and depressing feelings (Belk, 1988). Following James (1890), we see that those possessions have a "Material Me" nature, or an "expanded self," in our terms, which is seen as representing the possessor's intention or will.

Although people have the strong notion that money is free from specific human relationships and that it is abstract, they refrain from using it in some cases. A typical example is money as a gift (Webley, Lea, & Portalska, 1983). In the case of a gift, a sender gives an item that the sender made an effort to make or select, and a receiver accepts it. In the specific relationship between a sender and a receiver, a gift exists as a symbol representing a specific effort (or goodwill) of a specific person (Csikszentmihalyi & Rochberg-Halton, 1981). Because money transposes the value built on a specific individual relationship and/or experience onto the criteria used for all other items and grade such values, it is shied from. In addition to its use as a gift, money is avoided for use as a return for the goods or help given by neighbors (Webley & Lea, 1993b). In Korean farm villages, when help is given by a neighbor to a resident, it is common to give help to the neighbor in return. But if the resident is a part-time farmer, giving help by labor becomes difficult. In that case, some start to pay for the labor in return. This also means such a family losing its role as a full member of the community of mutual collaboration. This kind of exchange is not carried out based on market economy principles but rather based on communal exchange rules (Mills & Clark, 1982).

Although money is avoided in some cases owing to its neutrality, it is not always neutral (versatile in its use). According to excerpts from Webley, Lea, and Portalska (1983), European currencies were usually used to purchase ordinary goods and native money was used for purchasing wives in West Africa. From the end of the nineteenth century through the beginning of the twentieth century in America, income earned by labor of a household wife in a lower economic stratum was regarded as an extension of her housekeeping, and the income was appropriated for the purchase of daily necessities, while her husband's income was used as the money that circulated in a market economy, such as in investments (Zelizer, 1989). Two important points here are that (1) money does not hold the neutrality that allows it to be exchanged for anything but has specific applications and specific meanings in some cases and (2) such meaning is not fixed but varies historically and culturally. Therefore money and possessions are not issues that can be grasped within and explained by a neutral money-goods exchange system in a market economy. Rather, they should be understood in the context of the cultures and histories of the societies in which people are living.

18.1.4 Dialectical Study of Culture

Money is a cultural tool which has a specific meaning in each culture. While the universal meaning of money is its function as medium for market exchange, its cultural meaning appears through the way people acquire, share, and use the money and through their evaluation of those behaviors. We can elicit patterns of meaning-giving to money through interviews, observations, or questionnaires and interpret their cultural meanings.

How should we interpret these meanings? When considering this question, one of the biggest theoretical and methodological difficulties that cultural studies have faced becomes important, that is, what is the best way for researchers to overcome ethnocentrism and obtain somewhat common meaning?

Herein, two strategic poles can be considered to relativize a researcher's cultural perspective. One, as presented by Lévi-Strauss's structuralism, is to extract a formal structure for overcoming the limit of "subjective interpretation" (Lévi-Strauss, 1950, 1964). In this case, mathematics as a tool is considered as a universal form of thinking independent from any particular culture and thus required to serve as the basis for objectivity. However, what we question is the world of meanings itself, and this method does not give an answer.

The other extreme is, conversely, to become deeply involved in a specific world of meanings and to describe the other party's world of meanings, which is different from one's own world of meanings, following the other party's world of meanings as much as possible. Participant observation embodies such an ideal. We find the cultural nature of money in such a world of meanings.

However, the ideal of these meanings encounters the following difficulty: studying the world of meanings of a different culture requires a researcher to get inside, to share the same world of meanings, and, as a researcher, to record and analyze the acquired world of meanings using his own words. It is a textual construct process called "writing culture" (Clifford, & Marcus, 1986), and the work cannot avoid being an ethnographer's translation/representation of a particular culture (Asad, 1986, p. 163).

In this case, the following issue arises between two different cultural worlds of meanings, which means between the culture to be described and the culture to which a describer, researcher, or researcher group belongs: "the anthropological enterprise of cultural translation may be vitiated by the fact that there are asymmetrical tendencies and pressures in the languages of dominated and dominant societies" (Asad, 1986, p. 164).

Research is primarily intended to create the world of meanings communally among researchers, and a member of the culture to be described is usually placed outside this world of communal meanings. As long as a researcher tries to introduce his or her acquired world of meanings of the target culture unilaterally by translating it into his or her own world of meanings, the world of meanings of the researcher dominates, and consequently, the issue of ethnocentrism arises again.

Therefore, the real issue is how to avoid ethnocentrism brought about by a researcher's world of meanings, aiming to understand the target world of meanings. One such effort is our dialectical research. Therein, researchers with their own cultural backgrounds interpret the meaning of a different culture, explain the meaning in their own culture, relativize their own culture by referring to other researchers' cultural interpretations as a mirror, and then try to interpret the meaning at a higher level, which enables both parties to understand the cultural meanings of the other party. We regard the process itself as research.

Understanding culture here is not unilateral work where a researcher regards the culture as a static substance and translates it into the words of his or her own culture. Rather, it is an interactive creation process where researchers mutually adjust their different interpretation schemes of culture. For example, as discussed later, we have found that there are considerable differences in the reciprocated giving between Japanese and Korean children. Researchers observed a negative attitude in Japanese children toward gifting, while researchers noticed a more positive attitude toward gifting in Korean children. Through the reciprocating process, the meaning of treating is understood that "both treating and bill-splitting are intended to respect others and maintain good relationship, but their approaches are different." Here the higher-level world of meanings is shared while maintaining worlds of meanings for both parties without indicating which is superior.

Important for us is not a descriptive taxonomy of culture viewing the culture from an external standpoint but creating a new recognition of culture dialogically, and for researchers to interact and mutually adjust recognition of culture starting from their own cultural viewpoints, so that culture is analyzed as an intersubjective and dynamic product in the ongoing adjustment process.

Using the concept of EMS, we can describe the process as follows. It started when a researcher who has certain cultural nature encountered and was surprised by "the different ways of living" (different EMS). Encounters with the people with whom a researcher tries to create EMS but fails to share it lead to the discovery of difference in mutual communality, reflectively giving shape to their own worlds of meanings and those of others. Researchers living in different cultural worlds of meanings serve as cultural mirrors. This means culture does not exist statically within each individual researcher but emerges, taking specific shape whenever different communalities are encountered and researchers become aware of differences. This is the fundamental perspective of our "cultural psychology of differences" (Takahashi, 2016; Yamamoto, 2015, 2017).

This effort is the creation process of new EMS between research subjects who have different cultural backgrounds. What proceeds thereafter is a kind of communication practice which integrates meaning giving to an object, transformation of a subject, and readjustment of normative relationships. The study of the cultural nature of money viewed from such a perspective shows us a new aspect of the meanings in the real-life, daily practices of people. Research itself is one of these cultural practices.

The cultural meaning of money can be elicited and interpreted in the same way. Children's allowances are one of the significant phenomena paving the way to new semantic generative and dialectical practical research.

18.2 Children and Money: An Overview

18.2.1 Children and Economics

People have different desires. These desires vary and, seemingly, have no end. Meanwhile, the means of satisfying those desires – especially material needs – involve the use of goods and services that are the objects of such desires. Bargaining between people, who try to create balance between their desires and scarce resources, is the basis of economic behavior at a micro level. Experimental studies about children's economic activities have been carried out from economics and economic psychology viewpoints. These studies were conducted to find out if children would behave as the logic of economics assumes – in other words, how rationally children would behave in economic decision-making (see the examples of Harbaugh, Krause, & Liday, 2003; Murnighan & Saxon, 1998). The research demonstrates that children behave rationally even when they are young, and their knowledge becomes more consistent with age, improving the level of rationality in economic decision-making.

However, children's economic activities in daily life are not always based on rationality. They sometimes choose behaviors that deviate from economic rationality to build and maintain peer relationships. An ethnographic study of children in England playing with marbles (Webley & Lea, 1993a) indicates that the children exchange marbles, following a rational scarcity-based principle of exchange, while intentionally carrying out disproportionate exchanges, such as giving marbles as a pledge of friendship to a new classmate. In a similar study, various phenomena of "treats" are observed among children in Korea (see the following section). These studies imply that the social function of establishing and maintaining interpersonal relationships and economic activities are closely tied. Therefore, the valid research strategy is not to trace the development of economically rational behavior. Instead, we inquire how children become independent from parents and develop interpersonal relationships through money in their ecological environments – all united by the economic nature of human activities. Therefore, developmental psychology for money is not predicated on *Homo economicus*. Rather, it inquires into the foundation of human relationship structures that make exchange and possession possible.

18.2.2 Beyond Children as Individuals

While much research has systematically approached children's understanding of money and economic concepts and has grouped it into several stages based on the Piagetian framework, and, therefore, universal developmental stages of their understandings (e.g., Berti & Bombi, 1988; Strauss, 1952), there were also wide cultural differences among them (Jahoda, 1983; Leiser, Sevón, & Lévy, 1990; Ng, 1983). Jahoda (1983) demonstrates that Zimbabwean children (who do not have direct experience of selling and buying commodities but see their parents make and sell commodities) understand the relationship between selling and buying and a shop clerk's wage as well as its system more quickly than European children do. Likewise, children in Hong Kong, where economic activities are bustling, understand banking systems more quickly than Western children do (Ng, 1983). Children do not build up their knowledge about economic systems independently or separately from their lifeworlds.

Children's attitudes toward economic inequality, such as poverty and wealth, is another theme in which understanding of economic events cannot be separated from real life (Dittmar, 1996; Emler & Dickinson, 1985, 2004; Furnham, 1982; Leahy, 1981; Leiser & Ganin, 1996).

According to Bourdieu (1979), social strata reproduce themselves through categorization of consumption-style differences and social worlds as well as internalization of value systems. Cultural assets that comprise children's lifeworlds differ within the social stratum or culture, and children build up their thinking about the social world under such circumstances. Additionally, understanding about the causes of being rich and poor and the attitudes toward them are neither the knowledge which exists within individuals nor the substance which exists externally; rather, they are socially constructed and shared as predominant knowledge (see Moscovici, 2001).

Research on children's understanding about the causes of poverty and wealth found differences among the different classes, on one hand, and the potency of predominant knowledge in the culture beyond classes, on the other. According to Furnham (1982), in which interviews about the causes of economic inequalities were held in England, the relatively rich public school students tend to attach weight to individualistic explanation about the causes of poverty, while state school students, who are financially below the middle class, attach weight to a society-conscious explanation. Alternatively, according to a study of American junior and senior high school students, children in any economic status give reasons such as competence of and efforts by individuals instead of social factors, while children who belong to a lower economic status tend to be more positive about the possibility of eliminating poverty through social change (Leahy, 1981). According to comparative research conducted in 15 countries, which mainly consist of European countries, children who belong to the middle class accept present situations as a whole more readily than children in a more individualistic country (Leiser & Ganin, 1996). Therefore developmental psychology for money does not focus on the process of a child acquiring internal knowledge as an individual. Rather, it discusses that such knowledge is built up in association with the societies and cultures in which children grow.

18.2.3 The Sociocultural Use of Children's Allowances

Here we specifically discuss the cultural nature of money and focus on phenomena involving children's allowances. With adults, the normative nature of money remains almost unconscious and difficult to find. Observing the process where children learn how to use the special tool called an allowance helps researchers uncover the norms usually not recognized among adults in parents' disciplinary actions with money and conflicts between parents and children concerning money. Additionally, comparison of these recognized norms among different societies makes the cultural nature of these norms clearer.

Children's allowances especially demonstrate the cultural nature of money in the following way. When considering acquisition, allowances are resources given as a gift. Whereas adults typically acquire money through market exchange, children acquire allowances as a gift unilaterally given by adults. In gift giving, the personal relationship between subjects has greater significance than in market exchange. Therefore processes where children acquire or use allowances firmly incorporate the characteristics of personal relationships with adults and thus reflect cultural nature in an easy-to-understand manner (cultural difference in parent–child relationships involving money).

Next, when considering the use of allowances, allowances are special resources that can be exchanged for a variety of commodities. But because of this special power, children's misuse may lead to unrestrained, runaway desires. That's why children are strongly constrained

by parents in their use of money. The manner of such parental constraint provides clear guidance to children on the use of money from implicit knowledge that adults possess as well as cultural logic concerning its control (cultural differences in constraints on use of allowances).

Furthermore, when considering its use in human relationships, in addition to personal consumption, money is used as a resource to adjust interpersonal relationships. Children are in the process of learning ways to establish cultural interpersonal relationships where the appropriate use of money with friends is directed by adults. In this process, the characteristics of cultural interpersonal relationships can easily be observed (cultural differences in uses of money in human relationships).

In the following section, we will focus on the cross-cultural developmental research involving allowances that we conducted with researchers from Japan, China, Korea, and Vietnam and then we identify cultural characteristics of parent–child relationships and peer relationships observed in the learning process of using money and describe how children create cultural worlds of meanings using money as a tool.

18.3 East Asian Children and Money as a Cultural Tool

In our project, we call money a "tool" rather than a "symbol": money is a tool to realize our desires and serves to link relationships between people. Our project aims to disclose how human relationships, including parent–child and peer relationships, develop in different cultures through the use of money and how individual children culturally sophisticate themselves. Our project, named straightforwardly the "Pocket Money Project," intends to show the following three points. First, money is not only a tool of exchange in the market economy but also a tool that mediates human relationships in each culture and is actually used while mediated by norms about the usage. Second, the norm structures are different across cultures, and even the same behavior has different meanings in different cultures – once the norm structure in a culture is identified, the meaning of behavior in that culture also becomes clear. Nevertheless, third and most important, it should be indicated that such a norm structure and meaning of behavior in a culture do not exist as substances in a cultural group in the manner of stable preferences.

These points emerge dynamically in the research process, although we can recognize crystallized, static forms of them. Researchers can study a culture only from their own perspective. Studying and understanding cultures takes dialogical effort for both parties, wherein researcher A (who is concurrently a member of culture A) tries to understand cultural practices of a member of a different culture B, and simultaneously, a researcher B (who is concurrently a member of culture B) continuously tries to understand cultural practices of a member of a different culture A. "Cultural psychology of differences" aims not to extract such a crystallized "culture" as substance but rather to show the possibility of understanding a different culture with a prescription to handle and analyze the process by which it is being crystalized and, through this, ultimately to show a practical way to "understand different cultures."

18.3.1 Outline of the Project

In this project, researchers from the four East Asian countries of Japan, Korea, China, and Vietnam jointly conducted research in various combinations on the relationship between money and children in each country. While countries in East Asia, which have a mixed history of peaceful and/or antagonistic relationships, have many differences in their lifestyles and cultures, research

on comparative studies between East and West has emphasized their homogeneity (e.g., Hofstede, 1991; Triandis, 1995). Even if a few studies have indicated their diversity, it merely concerned subcultures in what was considered a dichotomous world (Kashima et al., 1995; Kim et al., 1994). It is, then, both theoretically and practically important to understand different cultures within East Asian countries.

Three main methods were used: first, researchers visited the other three countries for home visits, during which they interviewed children and parents. Second, researchers visited the other three countries to directly observe children shopping at various places, such as candy stores, stationery shops, bookstores, and supermarkets. Third, researchers handed out a questionnaire about pocket money to fifth-, eighth-, and eleventh-grade students as well as to their parents in the four countries. The questionnaire was made up of questions regarding ways of receiving and using pocket money, right and wrong judgments and allowable level judgments on use, and parent–child and peer relationships revolving around money.

In this section, we will outline the results of the project. We will summarize the three main findings: life in a consumer society, the structure of parent–child relationships, and that of peer relationships for children in the four countries of Japan, Korea, China, and Vietnam. The differences between the four countries are visualized through the practice of cultural psychology of differences, in which the researchers from the four countries continuously discussed these based on the data and tentatively reached a mutual understanding of their cultural meaning. Therefore, these are not stable entities but have been dynamically taking on their forms. The main results of the project have already been reported elsewhere (Oh et al., 2012; Takeo et al., 2009; Yamamoto, & Takahashi, 2007; Yamamoto et al., 2012).[1]

18.3.2 Children's Lives in a Consumer Society

Undeniably, our lives have become more affluent and convenient with the development of the commodity economy; the changes are also apparent in children's allowances. Children participate in their social lives as single consumers and build relationships with others.

The following is a simplified summary of children's lifestyles in the four countries as part of consumer societies. In Japan, children tend to use their money entirely for the fulfillment of their own desires. Namely, children's allowances are in principle separated from their households; therefore, they have their own place in the consumer society, in which they need to learn how to use the money and control their desire for possession. Their rights are basically limited to their personal activities, and children are negative about borrowing from or lending money to friends. Similar to Japanese children, children in Korea use the money mainly for fun. However, contrary to Japanese children, they are positive about borrowing from or lending money to friends. In addition, the interchange of money is generally more active in Korea; children have more chances to acquire and, therefore, use money. In China, while the situation has been gradually changing due to the quick economic growth, children's allowances are mainly regarded as being within the framework of the household, where children's free use of money tends to be suppressed. Consequently, the range of their money use is limited compared with children in Japan and Korea; however, it steadily extends with age. Children in China are not particularly negative about borrowing or lending money. In Vietnam, children have fewer chances to get monetary allowances, and the amount of money is small. Moreover, children are not positive about using money for themselves. Vietnamese children seemingly have a sense of unity with the family and depend on their parents in regard to how they use the money because it is not completely separated from their households. The children's world around money is limited predominantly within their family lives; their personal activities are not very important to them. The present study about children's allowances among these four countries illustrates the diversity of their lives in consumer societies.

While the development of a consuming economy reflects the type of affluence in a country, the development indicates that our relations with things converge into a simple picture, namely, the relations are mediated entirely through money. This may imply that relations between people and things have become significantly poorer (Hamada & Itō, 2010). In exchange for the affluence and convenience of a consuming society, we may impair the symbiotic feelings between parents and children. While children grow principally within their relationships with their parents and other adults, the involvement of parents and the household in children's allowances in China and Vietnam particularly makes us recall the origin of parent–children symbiosis.

The cultural diversity in the children's lifestyles involving allowances can be comprehensively interpreted only by characterizing them within both parent–children relationships and children's individuality. Since concluding these surveys, the Chinese economy has grown rapidly, and the economy in Vietnam has shown marked development. As we can see from the differences between Japan and Korea, the situations in China and Vietnam must be different from those in Japan and Korea. In general, both the marketization and growth of the market economy strongly affect the lives of children; however, these never led to changes in their lifestyles in a single manner. With such high diversity, we must find a way to portray the children's lifestyles in detail.

18.3.3 Parent–Child Relationships Mediated by Allowances

Most Japanese children in elementary and junior high schools are given fixed allowances at regular intervals. The children at those ages agree that parents should keep their promises to their children about allowances, while they disagree that an allowance belongs to parents because it is provided by them. Japanese children secure their territory, such as their own money and their desires, while the parents respect the children's territory.

In contrast in Korea, how much allowance is provided and when are determined through direct communications between parents and children. Such characteristic relationships involving allowances are found to be extended outside of the family, for example, to the parents' brothers and sisters and to friends of the parents and the children. The results from the Korean children illuminate their distinct way of creating trusting relationships with others, which is developed through direct communications with familiar persons and the flexible exchange of money based on these.

In China, many children have experienced that "parents use the children's allowances without asking" for daily food, groceries, and school expenses; however, they feel that this cannot be avoided, since "the allowances do not necessarily belong to the children." As Chinese children grow older, they develop through experiencing such conflicts with parents while accepting them. Through the process of accepting direct demands from their parents, Chinese children, even though they sometimes feel frustrated, may build trusting relationships with their parents.

The results of the questionnaire show that children in Vietnam are positive about paying living and education costs, such as "the family food expenses" and "the school expenses including the food service fees," from their allowances, whereas they are mostly negative about using allowances for personal fun. In addition, the inter-view survey shows that Vietnamese children are usually negative about "getting their allowances in compensation for their assistance with the housework," and many children think that children should help around the house as members of the family. It is seemingly not surprising for Vietnamese children to place the family's demands ahead of personal fun. For the children, "the family's demands and personal fun" may not be alternatives; they may think that working for the family leads to satisfying their desires. The circumstances involving children's allowances reflect the value of "doing good for the family" in Vietnam.

Money circulates through the global market economy and exchanges with anything as a universal tool. However, when money is used as an allowance circulating from parents to children, the circulation is very individual and varies depending on specific relationships. Although relationships between oneself and others in East Asian countries have been described as collectivistic, the relationships are mediated by various cultural tools, including allowances, and show diverse cultural characteristics that cannot be explained by cultural dichotomy.

18.3.4 Friendship and Money

Without doubt, it is common in all countries for both parents and children to wish that children form good relationships with friends at school; furthermore, children are expected to spend their money wisely and not waste it. What, then, is the best way for children to spend money within their relationships with friends, and how should children use their own money to form good friendships? In this section, we uncover friendships mediated through money, with a particular focus on children's feelings and actions regarding treats, bill splitting, and borrowing and lending money between friends.

In the questionnaires, we asked children questions about treats, bill splitting, and borrowing and lending money between friends, such as "Children should not treat or get treated by their friends" and "Can you lend money to your friends without hesitation, if they are strapped for money?" In the interview surveys, we asked them, for example, "Which do you more often do, treating your friends or splitting the bill with them?" "When do you treat your friends?" and "What do you think about treats and bill splitting?" We summarize the characteristics of friendships mediated through money in the four countries as follows.

Japanese think bill splitting is better than treats among friends. For Koreans and Vietnamese, treating friends is common; they think splitting the bill with friends at all times should be avoided for good friendships. In China, children both treat friends and split the bill with friends, depending on the situation. Importantly and interestingly, people's feelings and actions in regard to treating and bill splitting are different for Japan, Korea, and Vietnam. In addition, for Japanese, "treat" corresponds to "money" with a negative image, while in Korea and Vietnam, "bill splitting" is connected negatively with "money," although the underlying purpose of "forming a good relationship with friends" is the same for these countries.

We define a relationship that allows for treating or borrowing and lending money between friends as a reciprocal friendship, while a relationship where treating or borrowing and lending money is relatively unfavorable is defined as a self-limiting friendship. Japanese prefer a self-limiting way of thinking and action, while Koreans and Vietnamese prefer a reciprocal way. We aim not to impose our personal value judgments when defining the relationships as reciprocal and self-limiting friendships. However, with the normative view in each country considered, the "self-limiting" friendship could be redefined negatively as a "selfish and isolating" friendship or positively as an "independent and self-responsible" friendship. Similarly, "reciprocal" could be redefined negatively as a "dependent and self-irresponsible" friendship or positively as a "mutually supporting and harmonious" friendship.

One could expect that the normative view about friendship and money will be related to growing consumption along with the development of the economy in each country. The four countries can be arranged in decreasing order of GDP per capita as follows: Japan, Korea, China, and Vietnam. However, contrary to expectations, this GDP difference does not necessarily directly reflect feelings and normative views about friendship mediated through money in these countries. Instead, as the section on "children's lives in a consuming society" illustrates, children's lives in terms of "individualism" and "relationships with others," or as the section on "parent–children relationships" discusses them from the perspective of allowance, the normative view about friendship is also likely to be determined in association with parent–children relationships and the children's positions in a society.

18.4 Beyond the Dualism of Collectivism versus Individualism

Next, among findings about the cultural nature of the meaning given to allowances, we focus on cultural differences found in good or bad judgment of treating, refer to the collectivism versus individualism argument that cross-cultural psychology has emphasized (e.g., Hofstede, 1984; Triandis, 1995), and propose our new dialectical methodology to compare cultures and read out cultural meanings.

The East Asia region covered by our Pocket Money Project has been regarded as adhering to collectivism (e.g., Triandis, 1995, among others). The "treating" of the others on which we focus in this chapter is not a market exchange but rather a gift exchange involving a formation of a personal connection and an important activity which represents social characteristics of the interpersonal relationship. If the way in which gifts are exchanged is regarded as inappropriate between subjects, it easily leads to serious problems where both parties negatively perceive a personal connection or personality. Actually, it is one of the culture shocks that Chinese and Korean students encounter in Japan, where they interpret the Japanese habit of bill splitting to indicate a "cool relationship" (Oh, 2016).

Based on the theoretical viewpoint of the collectivism versus individualism argument, we can interpret "treating" as collectivist behavior that emphasizes relationships over self and bill splitting as individualist behavior that puts an individual ahead of a relationship. However, as mentioned before, positivity toward "treating" cannot be explained by the simple "marketization = individualism" scheme when considering marketization level and GDP per capita.

Meanwhile, in our research, the phenomenon that can be interpreted as individualism enhanced through marketization is the expansion of one's personal realm through the purchase of goods to "create his own world," such as a hobby (Pian, 2016). Money is the tool that allows an individual to acquire goods as he or she desires without considering another's will. But when the individual wants to "deepen the relationship with the other through treating," he or she can also use money for "the world with the other" in a collectivist manner.

In fact, the increase in disposable income along with market economy penetration is used for treating in Korea, but the same is not true in Japan. Behind this, completely opposite logics of cultural interpersonal relationships are observed: treating each other is to value friendship in Korea, while being self-responsible without putting a burden on others is valued for maintaining good friendships in Japan (Oh, 2016). This results not from the difference in marketization level but from the difference in the cultural logic of interpersonal relationships.

Hereby the limits and potential of the collectivism versus individualism perspective toward understanding culture and how marketization changes people and culture become visible. Concerning the former, the collectivism versus individualism argument relativizes ethnocentrism, a psychological theory based on the modern Western perspective of humanity, with collectivism, which is considered as a nonmodern and non-Western (and rather more equal to an Eastern) principle, in cross-cultural psychology. But, with the rise of the Chinese economy, two of the world's top three GDP countries are in East Asia, and the economic size of Japan, China, and Korea exceeds the GDP of the European Union's top ten countries (IMF, 2015). Thus, in the drastically multipolarized present world, analyzing cultural conflicts with theories of collectivism and individualism as a key perspective has already become difficult. This is exactly what we observe in cultural differences in "treating" within East Asia.

Every human society has the issue of relationship adjustment between the individual and a group, wherein conflict between individualism and collectivism universally arises in every culture. This is why a collectivism versus individualism comparison is persuasive. Nevertheless, the theoretical and practical tasks that we face now would be to discuss "in which aspect Japan and Korea are collective or individualistic," by exploring their internal structures. For the aforementioned reason, the same issue arises whenever any society is compared to another.

Next, concerning the last point above, it is obvious that a market economy system brings significant cultural transformation to a society. As one aspect, there is no doubt that it universally enhances the individualization of the economic unit from a community embedded in a village or household to a "*Homo economicus* or economic man" based on the free economic activities of individuals. On the other hand, market exchanges are conducted for individuals to create their own worlds of meaning given through the acquisition of goods, whereby how to create a world of meanings becomes an issue: What is worth acquiring? How should an individual compete for or share with others such valuable things? How should an individual form a self, and what kinds of human relationships should be constructed? As repeatedly described, a market economy system is often considered as a culturally neutral and universal system. But it is established and maintained by participants in economic activities who create their own worlds of meaning and involve others. People constitute a group, such as an enterprise, a nation, or a regional community, and steer the economy while carrying their histories and mutually adjusting their senses of values.

The market economy system and money as its tool are integrated uniquely into people's lives in their respective cultural worlds of meaning, and thus marketization cannot unify cultures in the world. As observed in our Pocket Money Project, this is the reason that market exchange behaviors have cultural differences and are reproduced. In such a context, the cultural conflicts seen in the present economic activities are conflicts between worlds of meaning. Cultural barriers in the economy also arise as an extension of this. Thus the core issue is not to interpret the abstract identity of a formal social system but to understand the specific diversity of the worlds of meaning in which people live.

18.5 Conclusion

Human beings are unique because they create their environments using tools. Tools are not just physical objects but objects that function as signs. A sign is cultural in its nature, and a tool is inevitably a cultural tool. By sharing the meaning of a sign, humans create an intersubjective world of meaning, and in such a world of meaning, subjects' social roles are created. In a shared world of meaning, subjects interact and develop certain norms to accommodate their conflicts. Societies of all kinds are created in such a manner and become intersubjective.[2]

These social interactions are created through individual, specific interactions by the use of a tool, where various patterns of interaction emerge depending on subjects, their environments, and combinations of subjects and environments. However, through this adjustment process, choices are made on various patterns, and the chosen patterns are elaborated by people and become steadily shared among some people.

When a subject who uses the pattern (EMS 1) shared by some people encounters people who share a different pattern (EMS 2) with other people, the subject may find that the subject's own pattern and the pattern of the other are respectively unique to the group to which each belongs. In this context, the subject's own group is differentiated from the group of the other, and such groups emerge as cultural groups.

Money is one of the tools that creates the economic intersubjective interaction called market exchange, and it is a cultural tool. Thus interaction through money shows cultural properties. The abstract pattern of market exchange, that is, the exchange of equivalence between objects each of which represents an equivalent amount of neutral exchange value, is universal, although its practical meaning varies.

In fact, we find that pocket money has diverse meanings among children in Asian countries. Such diversity in the meaning of money corresponds with various relationships between children and parents or friends, and such cultural meanings of money create a culturally unique pattern of interaction or human relationships.

These findings cannot be explained simply by the concept of marketization or the dichotomy of collectivism versus individualism. Moreover, such cultural difference often leads to serious economic conflicts that do not disappear through a process of marketization or individualism. For that reason, to ease conflicts created in the marketization process and promote mutual understanding among cultural groups, we should explore a different type of study and theory on the cultural nature of human beings. The socio-cultural psychology that this *Handbook* helps develop takes one new direction in theory and research. Our cultural psychology of differences views culture dynamically through dialogical interactions among researchers who have different cultural backgrounds and is one of the afore-mentioned efforts in psychology.

Notes

1   This section is a summary of Takahashi et al. (2016). Respective findings were the result of the efforts of project members from four countries to understand meanings in a mutual and reflective manner through the practice of cultural psychology of differences. The part for "Lives in a Consumer Society" was summarized by Pian, the part for "Parent–Child Relationships" was by Takeo, and the part about "Friendship and Money" was by Oh. The author discusses each section comprehensively in Takahashi and Yamamoto (forthcoming).

2   To be exact, we should differentiate intersubjectivity at two different levels. The first level is composed of two parties who share their present world of meaning. The second level of intersubjectivity is composed of three parties, and such a triadic configuration gives a certain objectivity to the first-level intersubjectivity. The normative mediator in EMS is the third party and stabilizes interactions between two parties. Thus such an interactional system emerges as a kind of stable substantial object. The intersubjectivity that may generate social interaction is the second-level or collective-intersubjective one (Yamamoto, 2015, 2017, n.1).

References

Asad, T. (1986). The concept of cultural translation in British social anthropology. In J. Clifford & J. E. Marcus (Eds.), *Writing Culture: The Poetics and Politics of Ethnography* (pp. 141–164). Berkeley: California University Press.

Belk, R. W. (1988). Possessions and the extended self. *Journal of Consumer Research*, 15, 139–168.

Belk, R. W. (1991). The ineluctable mysteries of possessions. *Journal of Social Behavior & Personality*, 6(6), 17–55.

Berti, A. E. & Bombi, A. S. (1988). *The Child's Construction of Economics*. Cambridge: Cambridge University Press.

Bourdieu, P. (1979). *La distinction: Critique sociale du jugement*. Paris: Editions de Minuit.

Clifford, J. & Marcus, G. E. (1986). *Writing Culture: The Poetics and Politics of Ethnography*. Berkeley: University of California Press.

Cole, M. (1996). *Cultural Psychology: A Once and Future Discipline*. Cambridge, MA: Harvard University Press.

Csikszentmihalyi, M. & Rochberg-Halton, Y. (1981). *The Meaning of Things: Domestic Symbols and the Self*. Cambridge: Cambridge University Press.

Dittmar, H. (1992). *The Social Psychology of Material Possessions: To Have is To Be*. Hemel Hempstead, UK: Harvester Wheatsheaf.

Dittmar, H. (1996). Adolescents' economic beliefs and social class. In P. Lunt & A. Furnham (Eds.), *Economic Socialization: The Economic Beliefs and Behaviours of Young People* (pp. 69–92). Cheltenham, UK: Edward Elgar.

Emler, N. & Dickinson, J. (1985). Children's representations of economic inequalities: The effect of social class. *British Journal of Developmental Psychology*, 3, 191–198.

Emler, N. & Dickinson, J. (2004). Children's understanding of social class and occupational groupings. In M. Barrett, & E. Buchanan-Barrow (Eds.), *Children's Understanding of Society* (pp. 169–198). Hove, UK: Psychology Press.

Furnham, A. (1982). The perception of poverty among adolescents. *Journal of Adolescence*, 5, 135–147.

Hamada, S. & Itō, T. (2010). *"Kachu" no shinrigaku he* [Toward a psychology of "involvement"]. Tokyo: Shin-Yo-Sha. (In Japanese, translated by the author of this article.)

Harbaugh, W. T., Krause, K., & Liday, S. G. (2003). Bargaining by children. University of Oregon Economics Department Working Papers.

Hofstede, G. (1984). *Culture's Consequences: International Differences in Work-related Values*

(Cross-Cultural Research and Methodology Series). London: SAGE.

Hofstede, G. (1991). *Cultures and Organizations: Software of the Mind*. New York: McGraw-Hill.

IMF (International Monetary Fund). (2015). World Economic Outlook Databases. Retrieved from www.imf.org/external/pubs/ft/weo/2015/02/weodata/index.aspx.

James, W. (1890). *The Principles of Psychology*. New York: Henry Holt.

Jahoda, G. (1983). European "lag" in the development of an economic concept: A study In Zimbabwe. *British Journal of Developmental Psychology*, 1, 113–120.

Kashima, Y., Yamaguchi, S., Kim, U., Choi, S.-C., Gelfand, M. J., & Yuki, M. (1995). Culture, gender, and self: A perspective from individualism–collectivism research. *Journal of Personality and Social Psychology*, 69, 925–937.

Kemptner, N. L. (1989). Personal possessions and their meanings in old age. In S. Spacapan & S. Oskamp (Eds.), *The Social Psychology of Aging* (pp. 165–196). Thousand Oaks, CA: SAGE.

Kim, U., Triandis, H. C., Kâğitçibaşi, Ç., Choi, S.-C., & Yoon, G. (1994). *Individualism and Collectivism: Theory, Method, and Applications*. Thousand Oaks, CA: SAGE.

Leahy, R. J. (1981). Development of the conception of economic inequality: II. Explanations, justifications and concepts of social mobility and change. *Child Development*, 19, 111–125.

Leiser, D. & Ganin, M. (1996). Economic participation and economic socialization. In Lunt, P. & Furnham, A. (Eds.), *Economic Socialization of Children* (pp. 93–129). Cheltenham, UK: Edward Elgar.

Leiser, D., Sevón, G., & Lévy, D. (1990). Children's economic socialization: Summarizing the cross-cultural comparison of ten countries. *Journal of Economic Psychology*, 11(4), 591–614.

Lévi-Strauss, C. (1950). *Introduction a l'œuvre de Marcel Mauss*. Paris: Presses Universitaires de France.

Lévi-Strauss, C. (1964). *Mythologiques: Le cru et le cuit*. Paris: Plon.

Mills, J. & Clark, M. S. (1982). Exchange and communal relationships. In L. Wheeler (Ed.), *Review of Personality and Social Psychology* (vol. 3, pp. 121–144). Beverley Hills: SAGE.

Moscovici, S. (2001). *Social Representations: Explorations in Social Psychology*. New York: New York University Press.

Murnighan, J. K. & Saxon, M. S. (1998). Ultimatum bargaining by children and adults. *Journal of Economic Psychology*, 19, 415–445.

Ng, S. H. (1983). Children's ideas about the bank and shop profit: Developmental stages and the influence of cognitive contrasts and conflict. *Journal of Economic Psychology*, 4, 209–221.

Oh, S.-A. (2016). Bunkasa ga tachiarawareru toki, sore o norikoeru toki [When cultural difference appears and when we transcend it]. In N. Takahashi & T. Yamamoto (Eds.), *Kodomo to Okane* [Child and money]. Tokyo: University of Tokyo Press.

Oh, S.-A., Takeo, K., Pian, C., Takahashi, N., Yamamoto, T., & Sato, T. (2012). Pocket money and children's sense about money matters in Japan, Korea, China, and Vietnam: Children's affluence and structure of human relations. *Japanese Journal of Developmental Psychology*, 23, 415–427. (In Japanese with English abstract.)

Pian, C. (2016). Shohi shakai o ikiru kodomotachi [Children living in a consuming society]. In N. Takahashi, & T. Yamamoto (Eds.), *Kodomo to Okane* [Child and money]. Tokyo: University of Tokyo Press.

Simmel, G. (1950). *The Sociology of Georg Simmel* (ed. and trans. by K. H. Wolff). New York: Free Press.

Strauss, A. L. (1952). The development and transformation of monetary meanings in the child. *American Sociological Review*, 53, 275–286.

Takahashi, N. (2016). Nihon no kodomotachi ni totte no okane: Hattatsu no setaigaku teki bunseki kara [Money for Japanese children: An ecological analysis of child development of money]. In N. Takahashi, & T. Yamamoto (Eds.), *Kodomo to Okane* [Child and money]. Tokyo: University of Tokyo Press.

Takahashi, N. & Yamamoto, T. (Eds.). (2016). *Kodomo to Okane* [Child and money]. Tokyo: University of Tokyo Press.

Takahashi, N. & Yamamoto, T. (forthcoming). *Children and Money: Cultural Developmental Psychology of "Pocket Money."* Charlotte, NC: Information Age Publishing.

Takahashi, N., Yamamoto, T., Takeo, K., Oh, S. A., Pian, C., & Sato, T. (2016). East Asian children and money as a cultural tool: Dialectically understanding different cultures. *Japanese Psychological Research*, 58, 14–27.

Takeo, K., Takahashi, N., Yamamoto, T., Sato, T., Pian, C., & Oh, S.-A. (2009). Developmental changes in parent–child relationships, as mediated by money as a cultural tool. *Japanese Journal of Developmental Psychology*, 20, 406–418. (In Japanese with English abstract.)

Triandis, H. C. (1995). *Individualism & Collectivism*. Boulder, CO: Westview Press.

Vygotsky, L. S. (1997). The instrumental method in psychology: Problems of the theory and history of psychology. In R. W. Rieber & J. Wollock (Eds.), *The Collected Works of L. S. Vygotsky* (trans. by R. van der Veer, vol. 3). New York: Plenum Press.

Webley, P. & Lea, S. E. (1993a). Towards a more realistic psychology of economic socialization. *Journal of Economic Psychology*, 14(3), 461–472.

Webley, P. & Lea, S. E. (1993b). The partial unacceptability of money in repayment for neighborly help. *Human Relations*, 46, 65–76.

Webley, P., Lea, S. E., & Portalska, R. (1983). The unacceptability of money as a gift. *Journal of Economic Psychology*, 4, 223–228.

Yamamoto, T. (2015). *Bunka toha nani ka? Doko ni aru noka?* [What is culture? Where is it? Psychology about conflict and coexistence.] Tokyo: Shinyosha.

Yamamoto, T. (2017). Cultural psychology of differences and EMS: A new theoretical framework for understanding and reconstructing culture. *Integrative Psychological and Behavioral Science*, 51(3), 345–358. DOI: 10.1007/s12124-017-9388-4.

Yamamoto, T. & Takahashi, N. (2007). Money as a cultural tool mediating personal relationships: Child development of exchange and possession. In J. Valsiner & A. Rosa (Eds.), *The Cambridge Handbook of Sociocultural Psychology* (pp. 508–523). New York: Cambridge University Press.

Yamamoto, T., Takahashi, N., Sato, T., Takeo, K., Oh, S.-A., & Pian, C. (2012). How can we study interactions mediated by money as a cultural tool: From the perspectives of "cultural psychology of differences" as a dialogical method. In J. Valsiner (Ed.), *The Oxford Handbook of Culture and Psychology* (pp. 1056–1077). New York: Oxford University Press.

Zelizer, V. A. (1989). The social meaning of money: "Special monies." *American Journal of Sociology*, 95, 343–377.

Further Reading

Bakhtin, M. M. (1981). *The Dialogic Imagination: Four Essays by M. M. Bakhtin* (ed. by M. Holquist, trans. by C. Emerson & M. Holquist, pp. 259–422). Austin: University of Texas Press.

Freud, S. (1916). *Vorlesungen zur Einführung in die Psychoanalyse*. Leipzig, Germany: H. Heller.

Mead, G. H. (1934). *Mind, Self and Society*. Chicago: University of Chicago Press.

Valsiner, J. (2007). *Culture in Minds and Societies: Foundations of Cultural Psychology*. New Delhi: SAGE.

Yamamoto, T. (1992). Shogakusei to Okozukai [Elementary school children and pocket money]. *Hattatsu*, 51, 68–76.

Part V
Aesthetic and Religious Experiences

19 The Sociocultural Constitution of Aesthetic Transcendence

Mark Freeman

For some, the very title of this chapter may seem contradictory. Generally speaking, the idea of transcendence, in the aesthetic sphere and beyond, connotes a realm *beyond* culture – indeed, perhaps, beyond the material world. As I put the matter some time ago (Freeman, 2004), in speaking of transcendence, "I refer not simply to a feeling (akin, for instance, to the oceanic feeling about which Freud speaks) but to an experience of that which is assumed to exist in a realm beyond the earthly, material one that houses most of everyday life" (p. 214). As I quickly added, the word "assumed" was key: "Whether in fact there *is* such a realm cannot, of course, be decided." Nevertheless, the idea of transcendence would seem to bear within it this dimension of beyondness, the most basic premise being that the experience in question somehow surpasses the more ordinary realm we usually inhabit and thus cannot be contained by the kinds of sociocultural frameworks privileged in volumes like this one. In what follows, I hope to show that the idea of aesthetic transcendence and the idea of the sociocultural constitution of experience are not only compatible but require one another, the requisite condition of the transcendent being our very belongingness in and to culture. The task is a difficult one, entailing nothing less than showing how the everyday world we inhabit becomes ecstatic. I also believe it to be an important one, that serves to clear a space for thinking anew about some significant features of the human condition.

19.1 Wagering on Transcendence

According to George Steiner (1989), perhaps the preeminent spokesperson on behalf of the idea of aesthetic transcendence, the very experience of meaning presupposes a transcendent dimension. Contra Nietzsche and company, for whom God is (in Steiner's view) essentially understood as "a phantom of grammar, a fossil embedded in the childhood of rational speech," Steiner wants to argue that "any coherent understanding of what language is and how language performs, that any coherent account of the capacity of human speech to communicate meaning and feeling is, in the final analysis, underwritten by the assumption of God's presence" and that "the experience of aesthetic meaning in particular, that of literature, of the arts, of musical form, infers the necessary possibility of this 'real presence'" (p. 3). Developing this line of argumentation further, Steiner goes on to state that

the wager on the meaning of meaning, on the potential of insight and response when one human voice addresses another, when we come face to face with the text and work of art or music, which is to say when we encounter the other in its condition of freedom, is a wager on transcendence. This wager – it is that of Descartes, of Kant, and of every poet, artist, and composer of whom we have explicit record – predicates the presence of a realness, of a "substantiation" (the theological reach of this word is obvious) within language and form. It supposes a passage, beyond the fictive or the purely pragmatic, from meaning to meaningfulness. The conjecture is that "God" is, not because our grammar is outworn; but that grammar lives and generates worlds because there is the wager on God (Steiner, 1989, p. 4).

Music looms especially large for Steiner. In encountering the music of composers such as Bach, Haydn, Mozart, and Beethoven, there are "felt intimations of open horizons, of well-springs of recuperation and self-surpassing for a constricted and worn humanity" (p. 63). Later in his essay, Steiner returns to this theme by asking whether, in the end, "a hermeneutics . . . of valuation – the encounter with meaning in the verbal sign, in the painting, in the musical composition, and the assessment of the quality of such meaning in respect of form – can be made intelligible, can be made answerable to the existential facts, if they do not imply, if they do not contain, a postulate of transcendence" (1989, p. 134). Steiner speaks also of "enchantment" and

the inviolate enigma of the otherness in things and in animate presences. Serious painting, music, literature or sculpture make palpable to us, as do no other means of communication, the unassuaged, unhoused instability and estrangement of our condition. We are, at key instants, strangers to ourselves, errant at the gates of our own psyche. (p. 139)

A "radical flinching" is involved in such encounters, even a kind of "embarrassment." And this embarrassment, which we may feel "in bearing witness to the poetic, to the entrance into our lives of the mystery of otherness in art and in music, is of a metaphysical-religious kind." So it is that Steiner offers a "wager" on the idea of transcendence. There is, and can be, no proof for it. All there is, is experience; and for him, it is quite enough to put forth the wager at hand.

At the heart of Steiner's "postulate" of transcendence is the experience of "otherness."

Music and dance, he suggests, "are of themselves primordial motions and figurations of the human spirit which declare an order of being nearer than is language to the unknown of creation" (1997, p. 74). Certain music, in particular, seems "closer to the border-crossing into 'otherness,' into the *terra incognita* of a humanity beyond itself than, perhaps, any experience else. Song leads us home to where we have not yet been" (p. 75). As for the challenge of coming to terms with such experience, "I know of no deeper, more neglected conundrum in epistemology, in semiotics and the cognitive *sciences de l'hommes*" (p. 78). Indeed, "The more captive our delight, the more insistent our need of 'answering to' a piece of music, the more inaccessible are the reasons why" (p. 83). Whatever these reasons may be – or, for that matter, if they even exist – there remains "the reality of a presence, of a factual 'thereness'" (p. 84), as palpable as the things of the material world.

Admittedly, it is not entirely clear what Steiner means by "transcendence." Moreover, assuming he wishes to speak about it in "objective" terms, as above – that is, in terms that posit the "real presence" of some sacred realm outside the perimeter of the self – there is no getting around the fact that his own affirmation of the ostensibly objective nature of transcendence derives in large measure from his own subjective experience. Finally, it is open to question whether a wager on transcendence is the same as a wager on *God*. These qualifications notwithstanding, Steiner makes a claim in his work that is surely worthy of attention: there is no deep and abiding aesthetic experience that does not bring us an intimation of transcendence. Indeed, what he seems to suggest is that aesthetic experience – at least of the deep, ecstatic sort being considered – is in a certain sense transcendentally constituted. As such, not only is it difficult to avoid raising the question of whether such experience makes *some* sort of contact with an other-than-human realm; it is difficult to avoid the abiding conviction that it *does* make such contact.

For a somewhat more measured perspective on the idea of transcendence, we might also turn to some of the work of Iris Murdoch (1970). First, a question: "Are you speaking of a transcendent authority or a psychological device?" The question is an important one. "As with so many of these large elusive ideas," she notes, "it readily takes on forms which are false ones." People latch onto these false forms with alarming frequency, seeking just that sort of comfort and consolation that illusions so readily provide. She therefore asks again: "Is there ... any true transcendence, or is this idea always a consoling dream projected by human need onto an empty sky?" (p. 57)

Whether transcendence is to be considered "true" or not – and we will have occasion shortly to question this very question – it is clear that, for Murdoch, it is only to be associated with great works. She writes:

The chief enemy of excellence in morality (and also in art) is personal fantasy: the tissue of self-aggrandizing and consoling wishes and dreams which prevents one from seeing what is there outside one ... We cease to be in order to attend to the existence of something else, a natural object, a person in need. We can see in mediocre art, where perhaps it is even more clearly seen than in mediocre conduct, the intrusion of fantasy, the assertion of self, the dimming of any reflection of the real world. (Murdoch, 1970, pp. 57–58)

The fact is, she continues, "Art presents the most comprehensible examples of the almost irresistible human tendency to seek consolation in fantasy and also of the effort to resist this and the vision of reality which comes with success. Success is in fact rare. Almost all art is a form of fantasy consolation and few artists achieve the vision of the real" (pp. 62–63). Even these few, she notes, are "'personalities' and have special styles ... But the greatest art is 'imper-

sonal' because it shows us the world, our world and not another one, with a clarity which startles and delights us simply because we are not used to looking at the real world at all" (p. 63). As Murdoch goes on to suggest,

Consider what we learn from contemplating the characters of Shakespeare or Tolstoy or the paintings of Velasquez or Titian. What is learnt here is something about the real quality of human nature, when it is envisaged, in the artist's just and compassionate vision, with a clarity which does not belong to the self-centred rush of ordinary life. It is important too that great art teaches us how real things can be looked at and loved without being seized and used, without being appropriate into the greedy organism of the self. (1970, pp. 63–64)

Here, then, is Murdoch's answer to the questions posed earlier:

There is ... something in the serious attempt to look compassionately at human things which automatically suggests that "there is more than this." The "there is more than this," if it is not to be corrupted by some sort of quasi-theological finality, must remain a very tiny spark of insight, something with, as it were, a metaphysical position but not metaphysical form. But it seems to me that the spark is real, and that great art is evidence of its reality. Art indeed, so far from being a playful diversion of the human race, is the place of its most fundamental insight, and the centre to which the more uncertain steps of metaphysics must constantly return. (pp. 71–72)

It may be helpful to know that Murdoch was not a believer – if by "believer" we mean someone who subscribes to some specific god or set of religious principles. In this respect, she would almost certainly consider Steiner's proclamations to be excessive given their theological tinge. This, in my view, makes her perspective that much more compelling. For, the primary evidence has nothing whatsoever to do with faith commitments. Rather, it has to do with experience itself.

As Murdoch states in a subsequent work (1993),

A hymn of praise in gratitude for the joys and consolations and general usefulness of art might run as follows. Art is informative and entertaining, it condenses and clarifies the world, directing attention upon particular things. This intense showing, this bearing witness, of which it is capable is detested by tyrants who always persecute or demoralise their artists. Art illuminates accident and contingency and the general muddle of life, the limitations of time and the discursive intellect, so as to enable us to survey complex or horrible things which would otherwise appal us . . . It calms and invigorates, it gives us energy by unifying, possibly by purifying, our feelings. In enjoying great art we experience a clarification and concentration and perfection of our own consciousness. Emotion and intellect are unified into a limited whole. In this sense art also *creates* its client; it inspires intuitions of ideal formal and symbolic unity which enable us to co-operate with the artist and to be, as we enjoy the work, artists ourselves. The art object conveys, in the most accessible and for many the only available form, the idea of a transcendent perfection. Great art inspires because it is separate, it is for nothing, it is for itself. It is an image of virtue. Its condensed, clarified, presentation enables us to look without sin upon a sinful world. It renders innocent and transforms into truthful vision our baser energies connected with power, curiosity, envy and sex. (Murdoch, 1993, p. 8)

More simply put, "It is the height of art to be able to show what is nearest, what is deeply and obviously true but usually invisible" (p. 90).

Why invoke the language of transcendence to describe all this? On Murdoch's (1993) account, the key, again, is *experience*. In encountering the good, in art and elsewhere,

We *experience* both the reality of perfection and its distance away, and this leads us to place our idea of it outside the world of existent being as something of a different unique and special sort. Such experience of the reality of the good is not like an arbitrary and assertive resort to our own will; it is a

discovery of something independent of us, where that independence is essential. If we read these images aright they are not only enlightening and profound but amount to a statement of a belief which most people unreflectively hold. Non-philosophical people do not think that they invent good. They may invent their own activities, but good is somewhere else as an independent judge of these. Good is also something clearly seen and indubitably discovered in our ordinary unmysterious experience of transcendence, the progressive illuminating and inspiring discovery of *other*, the positive *experience* of truth, which comes to us all the time in a weak form and comes to most of us sometimes in a strong form (in art or love or work or looking at nature) and which remains with us as a standard or vision, an *orientation*, a *proof*, of what is possible and a vista of what might be. (p. 508)

Again, this is not theology; Murdoch is talking about ordinary experience, and what is revealed in it, to anyone able to truly see, hear, and feel.

19.2 The Priority of the Other in Aesthetic Transcendence

Following Steiner and Murdoch in broad outline, it is clear that the kind of rapturous, ostensibly transcendent experience they are considering entails an encounter with an "Other" or "otherness" of some sort, one that takes hold of the experiencing person. In addition, I would suggest that such experience entails what I have referred to as the *priority* of the Other (Freeman, 2004, 2014a) – which, in the present context, refers to the felt conviction that this Other or otherness is larger than me and that it bespeaks a dimension of reality that is somehow *prior* to ordinary experience.

Let me try to bring these issues closer to psychology by bringing William James into the picture. As James notes in *The Varieties of Religious Experience* (1902/1982), "It is as if there were in the human consciousness *a sense of reality, a feeling of objective presence, a perception* of what we may call '*something there*,' more deep and more general than any of the special and particular 'senses' by which the current psychology supposes existent realities to be originally revealed" (p. 58). The strongest evidence for the existence of this sense is to be found in hallucinations. For instance, "The person affected will feel a 'presence' in the room, definitely localized, facing in one particular way, real in the most emphatic sense of the word, often coming suddenly, and as suddenly gone; and yet neither seen, heard, touched, nor cognized in any of the usual 'sensible' ways" (p. 59). In calling attention to this, James is thus acknowledging that what may *feel* like the priority of the Other – the "wholly Other," as Rudolph Otto (1923/1958) has put it – may actually refer to nothing more than the hallucinatory imagination – which is to say, a product or projection of the psyche. This does not rule out the possibility that the "something there" about which he speaks is, at times, actually there. It simply means that we ought not jump too quickly to transcendental conclusions.

Two points warrant emphasis at this juncture. Phenomenologically speaking, James, not unlike Steiner, is referring here to "a feeling of objective" – that is, *real* – "presence." It is something "there," outside the self, *Other*. Moreover, this Other, insofar as it appears "more deep and general than any of the special and particular 'senses,'" is felt to be primary, primordial, *prior*. Bearing these two points in mind, I want to offer a working definition of transcendence drawn from some of my own previous work. At a most basic level, transcendence involves "an experience of *that which is assumed to exist outside ourselves, in a realm that is beyond the more ordinary one that houses most of everyday life*" (Freeman, 2014a, p. 153; emphasis in original). The word "assumed" is tricky; "felt" would be easier. But the (phenomenological) fact is, experiences of the

sort being described here generally bear within them the conviction that this realm is real. The word "beyond" is tricky too, especially if it connotes a realm metaphysically separate from the one we ordinarily inhabit. As shall become clear shortly, however, one need not posit such a realm when invoking the idea of transcendence. On the contrary, it may well be that being in contact with the ordinary, the quotidian, is the very condition of possibility for transcendent experience to emerge. For now, in any case, I wish to supplement the aforementioned definition of transcendence by suggesting that the "Other" or "otherness" to which it refers may be understood as "*an extra-ordinary object of attention that, for the experiencing person, carries within it the magnetic force of a realm that is felt and assumed to be transcendent*" (Freeman, 2014a, p. 154; emphasis in original).

In view of this working conception, I shall be using the language of the priority of the Other in advancing my own views about the sociocultural constitution of aesthetic transcendence. In doing so, I shall abide by the customary epistemological "rules" of academic psychology by remaining within the sphere of phenomenology. Unlike Steiner, in other words, who, as we saw, seemed comfortable extrapolating a theological dimension from his phenomenological considerations, I will be more restrained about such extrapolating. The fact is, bringing the divine into the picture entails an "over-belief," as James (1902/1982) might put it, a going-beyond the data given; and as even Steiner himself would likely acknowledge, there is no way of knowing, for certain, whether what is *felt* to be so, when it comes to transcendental otherness, really *is* so. The issue at hand is thornier than it may appear. This is clearest in the case of religious experience. As Louis Dupré has argued in his book *Religious Mystery and Rational Reflection* (1998), "All living religion centers around a nucleus that its believers consider to be transcendentally *given*. To exclude that nucleus from phenomenological reflection means to abandon what determines the religious attitude" (p. 6). Not unlike what was just said about Steiner, Dupré also realizes that there is no way of knowing, for sure, whether what believers consider to be transcendentally given really *is* so given. This too is an over-belief – or, to use the more common parlance, a matter of *faith*. But it is emphatically not a matter of "blind" faith, in the sense of an a priori conviction that one brings to the table of experience. For, whatever one's convictions may be, "the religious act ... displays a distinct quality in the passive attitude that the subject of this act adopts with respect to its object. That object," Dupré tells us, "appears as providing its own meaning rather than receiving it from the meaning-giving subject" and thus "resists all attempts to define its meaning exclusively as actively projected" (p. 7).

Dupré also employs the language of "disclosure" in this context:

Religious insight enriches all facets of the real with a new ontological destiny ... This insight appears as given gratuitously, an unearned disclosure of truth. However much the religious mind is aware of its own creative part in concretizing this all-comprehensive vision in rituals, myths, and institutions to express its new symbolic richness, the Source is experienced as surpassing the mind. They serve as privileged symbols allowing the transcendent meaning to penetrate all of reality. (Dupré, 1998, p. 18)

The upshot of this formulation is that is that some intimation of the divine – "the Source" – is, in a sense, *built-in* to the very idea of religious experience, which in turn implies that there is no getting away from transcendental claims that extend beyond the sphere of the phenomenological.

Returning to the question of aesthetic transcendence, it may be that Steiner and company would adhere to much the same sort of conception as Dupré: the proposed "postulate," for him too, seemed to be built-in to the very fabric of aesthetic experience. It should be noted, of course, that plenty of people have addressed comparably intense aesthetic experiences *without* such a postulate. Turning to the baldest, most theologically grounded, formulation of aesthetic transcendence, however, does well to underscore what is ultimately at stake in thinking the issue through. You will recall that Steiner swooned over Bach, Beethoven, and others. Murdoch, in her own more measured way, did much the same over the likes of Velasquez and Titian. I have my own artistic idols, as do the rest of us. In music, mine tend to be hard rockers. In painting, I am especially drawn to some of the abstract expressionists. Now, it is possible that Bach, Beethoven, Velasquez, Titian, and other such renowned heroes have in fact tapped into aspects of reality that are of universal significance. This is, of course, debatable; and I would venture that there are some who read Steiner or Murdoch and see them as aesthetic imperialists, advancing their own decidedly Western aesthetic predilections as universal. This criticism is a familiar one; for now, we will have to let it go. When it comes to my own predilections, in any case, the claim for universality would be harder to make. Not only is much of the music I find ecstatically transporting relatively unknown to people in faraway lands, it would likely be alien to many of these same people.

This brings us to a fact about aesthetic transcendence that will serve as a takeoff point for much of what is to follow – namely that, however powerful the objects inciting aesthetic transcendence may be, and however much their power may be felt to issue from from the objects themselves, in their otherness, these same objects are frequently *local* in nature – which is also to say that the magnitude of their power is likely to vary, considerably, as a function of persons and, perhaps most important for present purposes, *culture*. As is the case with mystical experience, the objects in question embody meanings that are, in part, a function of prevailing beliefs, values, ideals, and, of course, knowledge (see, e.g., Belzen,

1997; Hollenback, 1996; Katz, 1978; Proudfoot, 1986). This is surely one reason why many of the objects that incite aesthetic transcendence in one person or culture would not, and could not, do so in another. By all indications, however, there is more at work than beliefs, values, ideals, and knowledge. These sound very cognitive in nature. In considering aesthetic transcendence, there is frequently a much more sensuous, visceral connection, one that feels wholly unmediated and that cannot readily be traced back to this or that form of cognitive preparation. In any case, it seems safe to say that the power aesthetic objects possess has somehow been "acquired" in and through the culture in question. This in turn suggests that, even though the experiences in question may feel wholly and utterly unmediated, they are not. Now, it could be that our responses to aesthetic objects are simply learned, conditioned in some way. There is little doubt that basic principles of conditioning may in fact be operative in these experiences. But such principles cannot possibly account for the sheer intensity of such experiences. Something else is clearly going on. What? How do certain aesthetic objects, local though they may be, come to possess the transcendent power they have?

Let me try to sharpen the problem before us. On the one hand, through Steiner, Murdoch, and, in the context of religious experience, Dupré, we have essentially been told that the ecstatic power of certain objects is "transcendentally given," and that, as such, this power is a function not of the self but of the *Other*, whatever it may be. On the other hand, the cultural specificity of many of these objects would seem to suggest that, appearances notwithstanding, there has to have been a process whereby they acquired, or became infused by, culture-specific meaning and value. Knowing that this process is a function of extant beliefs, values, ideals, and knowledge, though surely important to acknowledge, does not account sufficiently for the sheer ecstatic power such objects may have.

We therefore need to explore the process further and to see whether there are some other "factors" that might be brought to bear on the dynamic at hand. How does the world become ecstatic? And how is it that the specific world of aesthetic objects becomes a primary site for gathering this ecstatic power? More to the point still: how might one preserve the idea of aesthetic transcendence while also recognizing its deep sources in the life of culture?

19.3 Transcendence Within Immanence

By way of translating the above questions into more explicitly philosophical terms, the challenge at hand is to articulate a view that entails *transcendence within immanence* – that is, transcendence, as we have defined it via the idea of the priority of the Other, emerging in and through the immanent fabric of culture. Let us see if we can make some headway in working through this difficult challenge.

Returning to Steiner (1989, 1997) for a moment, I acknowledged that some would reject his theologically oriented point of view out of hand for the simple reason that there is too much cultural variability in the arts for so "absolutist" a perspective. As Storr (1992) puts the matter, referring to music, "I don't believe that musical reality exists apart from the minds that create it ... It's too dependent on widely differing cultural traditions to be regarded as an absolute" (pp. 182–183). But there is a conflation of two quite distinct issues here: the reality of music, whether it is an "autonomous" one or somehow a part of the mind, and its alleged universality. For Storr, in other words, the only way to posit the transcendent is to posit universality; and because there is so much cultural variability in music, and all the other arts as well, the notion of its tapping into some realm of transcendental otherness has to be rejected.

A similar conflation may be found in Hollenback's (1996) contextualist critique of the essentialist view of mystical experience referred to earlier. According to Hollenback, "The contextualist thesis implies that mystical experience in its 'pure' state (free from all context-dependent influences) simply does not exist...There is never a moment, from the time that a mystical experience begins to form until the time that it is over, when it is not being shaped by context-dependent elements" (p. 10; see also Katz, 1978; Proudfoot, 1986). Hollenback goes on to speak of the capacity of mystical experience "to exhibit an almost infinite plasticity in reifying and rendering concretely present the beings, objects, and spiritual locales posited by the mythology of any given religious tradition" (1996, p. 77). He also speaks of "the amazing sensitivity of the mystical experience to the subject's religious and philosophical assumptions" (p. 79). According to Hollenback, this experience is therefore "anything but spontaneous" (p. 78). But this last assertion does not follow. The contextuality of mystical experience, Hollenback has told us, is necessarily correlative with its lack of spontaneity. But there is no reason whatsoever why there cannot be true spontaneity within the discursive confines of culture and history. As has been suggested already, we are often moved by objects that are local in nature, objects whose very meanings are mediated by and enmeshed within culture. But this says nothing about the spontaneity of our response. Contra Hollenback, I maintain that there is ample room for true spontaneity within a perspective that recognizes the contextuality of mystical experience. People do not need to "leave" culture in order to experience transcendence; oftentimes, I have suggested, the experience of transcendence emerges in and through the fabric of culture itself. What this implies is that we are somehow hermeneutically "readied" for such experience, that its very condition of possibility is our own existence in tradition (e.g., Gadamer 1975).

As Clifford Geertz (1983) has noted, "The chief problem presented by the sheer phenomenon of aesthetic force, in whatever form and as a result of whatever skill it may come, is how to place it within other modes of social activity, how to incorporate it into the texture of a particular pattern of life" (p. 136). Central to this view is the idea that "art and the equipment to grasp it are made in the same shop" (p. 118). On this account, it may be that art objects acquire their transcendent power by virtue of their ability to embody and explicate a particular cultural lifeworld. "Embody" and "explicate": these may not be the right words. For what has to happen, for this power to emerge, is that there has to be some sort of *standing-forth*, such that the hidden potential of the lifeworld is, as Heidegger (1971) has put it, "unconcealed." Taking this idea one step further, such standing-forth may be seen as correlative with the kind of ecstasy – *ekstasis*, following the ancient Greek – found in aesthetic transcendence.

Consider once more the experience of music. "People take such satisfaction in music," Stephen Crites (1971) has written,

because it answers to a powerful if seldom noticed aspect of everything they do, of every gesture, every footstep, every utterance; answers to it and gives it purified expression. Courtship, worship, even violent conflict, call forth musical expressions in order to give these activities a certain ideality, a specific ideality rooted in the activities themselves. That is why the music of a culture or subculture has such a vital connection, so revealing yet so hard to define, with its whole style of life. The music of a people, or even a cohesive group, is peculiarly its own. It is the particular musical style that permits a group's life style, its incipient musicality, to express itself in full dance and song. (pp. 293–294)

Crites goes on to highlight the fact that "There is a beautiful paradox in the peculiar intensity with which a person responds to music which is 'his own': Even if he has not heard it before it is familiar, as though something is sounding in it that he has always felt in his bones; and yet it is really new. It is his own style, revealed to him at an otherwise unimaginable level of clarity and intensity" (p. 294). What we see in Crites' way of framing the issues, once again, is that cultural context, far from precluding transcendence, may be understood as its very condition of possibility; it is precisely what allows for revelation, of the new within the old and the old within the new.

But what is it that allows for this revelation? How might we understand the process? Seen from one angle, we are considering "the famil-iar's sacramental transformation into the alien" (Edwards, 1997, p. 212). "The setting-into-work of truth," Heidegger (1971) adds, "thrusts up the unfamiliar and extraordinary and at the same time thrusts down the ordinary and what we believe to be such" (p. 75). Seen from another angle, how-ever, we are considering a kind of *recognition*, "knowing something as that with which we are already acquainted," which "always implies that we have come to know something more authen-tically than we were able to do when caught up in our first encounter with it" (Gadamer, 1986, p. 47). The heretofore alien thus becomes recog-nizable, familiar, seen anew, in fuller measure.

With this putative paradox, we have in hand a potential key to deepening our understanding of the sociocultural constitution of aesthetic tran-scendence. But there is another paradox, that may serve to bring us still closer to addressing ade-quately the challenge at hand. The poet and critic Yves Bonnefoy (1989), reflecting on the power of poetry, speaks of "the moment when the young reader opens passionately a great book and finds words, of course, but also things and people, and the horizon, and the sky: in short, a whole world given at once to his thirst" (p. 162). For the author of these words, the experience may be more intense still; for, "this world which cuts itself off from the world seems to the person who creates it not only more satisfying than the first but also more real" (p. 164). Bonnefoy goes on to speak of the "impression of a reality at last fully incar-

nate, which comes to us, paradoxically, through words which have turned away from incarnation" (p. 164). As for the result, it is the opportunity "to bear witness to an existence beyond, to a being, to a plenitude they don't even know how to name" (p. 167). The situation is a quite remark-able one: words, language, products of discrete cultural worlds, sometimes become imbued with such power and passion as to awaken an "exis-tence beyond," a magnetic "plenitude" that bears within it intimations of a truly extraordinary reality.

One may also be reminded here of the won-derful passage from *The Varieties of Religious Experience* (James, 1902/1982) that articulates the "deeper significance" we sometimes experi-ence in encountering works of art.

This sense of deeper significance is not confined to rational propositions. Single words, and conjunctions of words, effects of light on land and sea, odors and musical sounds, all bring it when the mind is tuned aright. Most of us can remember the strangely moving power of passages in certain poems read when we were young, irrational doorways as they were through which the mystery of fact, the wildness and the pang of life, stole into our hearts and thrilled them. The words have now perhaps become mere polished surfaces for us; but lyric poetry and music are alive and significant only in proportion as they fetch these vague vistas of a life continuous with our own, beckoning and inviting, yet ever eluding our pursuit. We are alive or dead to the eternal inner message of the arts according as we have lost this mystical susceptibility. (pp. 382–383)

But where exactly is the "existence beyond" that Bonnefoy identifies, unnamable yet supremely real? How *far* beyond is it? And what exactly are we to make of these "vague vistas of a life contin-uous with our own" about which James speaks? As Marcel (1973) adds, "I think that each of us is invited, as it were, apart from any appeal to faith, which does not concern us here, to restore the traces of a world which is not superimposed from without ours, but is rather this very world grasped in a richness of dimensions which ordinarily we are simply unaware of" (p. 212). The artist is no "superman," Merleau-Ponty (1964a) insists, no direct path to the divine – if, by divine, we are referring to some wholly Other realm. "One admires as one should," he writes,

only after having understood that there are not any supermen, there is no man who does not have a man's life to live, and that the secret of the woman loved, of the writer, or of the painter, does not lie in some realm beyond his empirical life, but is so mixed with his mediocre experiences, so modestly confused with his perception of the world, that there can be no question of meeting it face to face apart from his life . . . The painter himself is a man at work who each morning finds in the shape of things the same questioning and the same call he never stops responding to. (1964a, p. 58)

Each painting, in turn, is "a response to what the world, the past, and the completed works demanded" (p. 59). "To live in painting," therefore, "is still to breathe the air of this world – above all for the man who sees something in the world to paint. And there is a little of him in every man" (p. 64). For Merleau-Ponty, then,

The difficult and essential point here is to understand that in positing a field distinct from the empirical order of events, we are not positing a Spirit of Painting which is already in possession of itself on the other side of the world it is gradually manifested in. There is not, above and beyond the causality of events, a second causality which makes the world of painting a "suprasensible world" with its own laws. Cultural creation is ineffectual if it does not find a vehicle in external circumstances. (Merleau-Ponty, 1964b, p. 68)

So far so good: for Bonnefoy and James, and now Marcel and Merleau-Ponty, there is no need – or no immediate need – to invoke some wholly Other world. The Other, such as it is, is found right here, in this one, woven into its very fabric. Speaking for myself, I would not be one

to preclude the possibility that aesthetic transcendence *also* makes contact with some wholly Other realm; indeed, I think it is well worth our entertaining this possibility, if only to cast into question the thoroughgoing naturalism that pervades academic psychology (see Freeman, 2014b, 2015; also Slife & Richardson, 2014). For present purposes, however, it will be quite enough to acknowledge that we can plausibly speak about aesthetic transcendence within the confines of the earthly, culturally saturated world. Generally speaking, in fact, it would seem that the ability of art and artist to make contact with this world is a precondition for this very transcendence. The question remains: How does this work?

19.4 Metaphor and the Standing-Forth of the World

There are numerous accounts of the process by which aesthetic transcendence comes about, most of them essentially "ego-centric" and individual-centered, in nature. In Ernst Schachtel's (1959) seminal piece on memory and childhood amnesia, for instance, there is the classical notion that art is fundamentally recollective, that it seeks to restore and recover those more pure and unsullied modes of experiencing, exemplified especially in the spontaneity of childhood, that predate the sort of conventionalized, highly schematized modes of experiencing that characterize adult life. The power of art, from this perspective – which is a sort of amalgam of Plato and Freud – thus derives from its capacity to reawaken those modes of experiencing, some of which may be preverbal in nature, that have largely been superseded by the demands of adult life but not entirely forgotten. The ineffability of aesthetic experience may thus have as much to do with the preverbal nature of early experience as it does with some alleged transcendent realm. The otherworldly thus refers precisely to that sort of otherness that consists of the unspoken vestiges of the distant past.

Another version of psychoanalytic thinking about aesthetic experience may be found in Anton Ehrenzweig's *The Hidden Order of Art* (1967), which, to risk oversimplification, explores the undifferentiated "inner fabric" of art, particularly modern art, in relation to the undifferentiated structure of unconscious perception. For Ehrenzweig, the primary interest is not to locate hidden psychic contents, à la Freud. Nor is it to establish a deep link, via memory, between the child's mode of experiencing the world and the adult's, à la Schachtel. Rather, it is to try to show how it is that the heterogeneous, fragmented, even manifestly chaotic, structure of much of modern art can resonate with us – if we can endure the anxiety – by virtue of our own inner heterogeneity and fragmentation. As for the depth and possible profundity of the resultant aesthetic experience, it owes itself precisely to what is occurring in the deepest, most obscure, strata of the psyche.

A similar idea may be found in the context of religious experience. According to Jones (1991), for instance, the experience of the sacred has a transcendental quality "not because the sacred is a wholly other object but because such experiences resonate with the primal originating depths of selfhood" (p. 125). As he explains in a later (Jones, 1998) work, those defenses that function as barriers to connection to ourselves and to others can also prevent access to the sacred. "When these barriers are broken through and the real self emerges," Jones writes, "a sense of connection with or concern about the transcendent often surfaces" (pp. 183–184). This is a variant of the same idea: "transcendence," such as it is, is a function of release, of defenses being broken down, revealing the "real self" in its primal givenness; it is the "sense" one may get on realizing the full depth and measure of one's inner life.

Important though these sorts of accounts are, they do not take sufficient account of culture. More specifically, they do not take sufficient account of the way in which the aforementioned

"standing-forth" of the world occurs. Let us therefore return to the idea of "transcendence within immanence" to see if we can make some additional headway.

"As a rule," James (1902/1982) notes, "mystical states merely add a supersensuous meaning to the ordinary outward data of consciousness. They are excitements like the emotions of love or ambition, gifts to our spirit by means of which facts already objectively before us fall into a new expressiveness and make a new connection with our active life" (1902/1982, p. 427). There is, again, a standing-forth, and in this standing-forth, the making of a "new connection": a bridge has been built between the "facts already before us" and some sort of new rendering of them.

This is precisely where the idea of metaphor enters the picture. According to Paul Ricoeur (1981), the task of metaphor is to fashion a new "resemblance." "Things or ideas which were remote appear now as close. Resemblance," therefore, "ultimately is nothing else than this rapprochement which reveals a generic kinship between heterogeneous ideas" (p. 233). In offering this perspective, Ricoeur draws on Kant's concept of productive imagination by referring to "predicative assimilation." This process "consists . . . in *making* similar, that is, semantically proximate, the terms that the metaphorical utterance brings together" (p. 234). As he explains,

In order that a metaphor obtains, one must continue to identify the previous incompatibility *through* the new compatibility . . . . The insight into likeness is the perception of the conflict between the previous incompatibility and the new compatibility. "Remoteness" is preserved within "proximity." To see *the like* is to see the same in spite of, and through, the different. (p. 234)

Translated into the terms we encountered earlier, the familiar – the "old" – becomes revivified, as it were, via the act of predicative assimilation; it becomes transformed into something other than what it was, gaining new energy, new life, through its new "kinship" with what had heretofore been different. Speaking of poetic language, in particular, Ricoeur goes on to suggest that it is

no less about reality than any other use of language but refers to it by the means of a complex strategy which implies, as an essential component, a suspension and seemingly an abolition of the ordinary reference attached to descriptive language. This suspension, however, is only the negative condition of a second-order reference, of an indirect reference built on the ruins of the direct reference. This reference is called second-order reference only with respect to the primacy of the reference of ordinary language. For, in another respect, it constitutes the primordial reference to the extent that it suggests, reveals, unconceals . . . the deep structures of reality to which we are related as mortals who are born into this world and who *dwell* in it for a while. (p. 240)

In sum: "In the same way as the metaphorical sense not only abolishes but preserves the literal sense, the metaphorical reference maintains the ordinary vision in tension with the new one it suggests" (pp. 240–241).

None of what Ricoeur has told us about the metaphorical process necessarily leads to aesthetic transcendence. The fact is, some metaphors are "dead," and may thus yield little in the way of the "deep structures of reality" to which he refers. Others, however, are quite alive, and may serve just the sort of "unconcealing" function Ricoeur is positing. In trying to unpack this set of ideas, I want to turn to some of my own thoughts from *The Priority of the Other* (Freeman, 2014a). "The experience of encountering the familiar-made-alien," I have suggested, "is another way of speaking about and encountering the *Other*": the world stands forth, becomes visible, in its otherness. At the same time, there is also a reference "backward," as it were, to the heretofore concealed, such that in this very newness there is, in addition, a dimension of familiarity and recognition. "The simultaneous experience of familiarity and recognition," therefore, "may in turn be understood in terms of the Other's *priority*," which in turn may carry with it an intimation that there is *more* to the world than meets the eye. "This world that comes before me is infinitely larger than me, the mystic" – or the poet – "might say, but it is also one to which I belong." I have framed this experience as "a kind of *homecoming*, wherein one's very belongingness in and to the world is revealed in and through its otherness." It is perhaps this quality of belongingness that calls for the transcendent dimension we have been exploring throughout this chapter: "Insofar as the world is revealed as home, as the place where I belong, I am 'at one' with it, able, if only momentarily, to move beyond the condition of ordinary oblivion against which the experience is juxtaposed" (p. 171). Such experience

may thus be understood to embody a kind of dialectical tension between the ordinary and the extraordinary. The notion of the extraordinary itself reflects this tension; there is reference to a world or a sphere of reality that is *other* than the one ordinarily inhabited. However otherworldly mystical [or aesthetic] experience may feel, therefore, the condition of this otherworldliness is its relation to, and difference from, the "this-worldly" experience that surrounds it. In this respect, there is a *metaphorical* dimension to [such] experience: the "old" world and the "new" one that supersedes it are somehow held together, resulting in the aforementioned co-presence of the familiar and the alien. The world is *refigured* and, through this refiguring, *remade*, such that it appears *realer* and *truer*. The sudden irruption of [this] experience may thus be tied to the rapture of discovery, wherein the hidden potentiality of ordinary life is disclosed. (Freeman, 2014a, p. 171)

I will not pretend to have solved the problem at hand. Indeed, in view of what I suggested earlier when I raised the possibility that aesthetic transcendence may in fact bespeak the existence of the *wholly* Other, in Steiner's more explicitly theological sense, I do not know that the idea of problem-solving even applies here. It may be that there *is* no "problem" nor a "solution" but only *mystery* (Marcel, 1950) – the mystery that the world *is* and that, by degrees, it can come to light. And it may be that this is enough to set the wheels of transcendence in motion and to thereby "restore the traces of a world which is not superimposed from without ours," as Marcel (1973) had put it, "but is rather this very world grasped in a richness of dimensions which ordinarily we are simply unaware of" (p. 212). The main point, in any case, is, again, that our belonging in and to this world – to tradition (Gadamer, 1975) – is the very condition of possibility for the "rapture of discovery" we may experience when seeing it anew, through art. In this respect, we might speak of *historically* or *culturally prepared* transcendence (Freeman, 2004, 2014a).

On some level, Forman (e.g., 1990, 1998) and others who reject contextualism (at least in its constructivist forms) in their conceptualization of mystical and religious experience are quite right when they suggest that such experience is not *created* from culture, in the sense of being a "construction." "Not created by culture, this structure ... comes with the machinery of being human" (1998, p. 27). It does not follow, however, that transcendent experience is wholly unmediated or that "we must all be able to temporarily let go of the contents of our own minds" (p. 27) so as to let the putative "pure consciousness experience" emerge. As Gass (1999) puts the matter, "We should not imagine that such moments involve the cancellation the self. A union is not a cancellation. What has to be left out of the self is its selfishness, but not its particular quality of mind" (p. 144). And not, I would reiterate, the *world* in which this mind has taken shape.

19.5 Re-Imagining Transcendence

Oftentimes, the issue of transcendence is posed in either/or terms: either there is some sort of projection or "construction" involved in its genesis or there is something otherworldly going on, something that leaps beyond the confines of history and culture.

I will say it again: it is possible that there *is* such a leap, and, following James (1902/1982) especially, we ought not to be too hasty in ruling it out. But there is no need to posit it either. As he told us earlier, mystical states and the like "merely add a supersensuous meaning to the ordinary outward data of consciousness" and are thus best regarded as "gifts to our spirit by means of which facts already objectively before us fall into a new expressiveness and make a new connection with our active life" (1902/1982, p. 427).

Whether or not there is a giver of such gifts, the gifts themselves remain. In receiving them, we should certainly take measure of the mysterious way in which the everyday, culturally-saturated world stands forth. In the end, it may not matter what the "ultimate" source of aesthetic transcendence is, for the result remains the same. Elaine Scarry puts the matter well in her discussion of the frequently made claim for the "immortality" of beauty, in art and beyond. "Even when the claim on behalf of immortality is gone, many of the same qualities – plenitude, inclusion – are the outcome" (Scarry, 1999, p. 47). Experientially speaking, Scarry continues, "beautiful things ... always carry greetings from other worlds within them." We can be grateful for that. And we can also be grateful for their impact on our lives. "What happens when there is no immortal realm behind the beautiful person or thing is just what happens when there *is* an immortal realm behind the beautiful person or thing: the perceiver is led to a more capacious regard for the world" (pp. 47–48). This is the pragmatic dimension of aesthetic transcendence, and it is mysterious in its own right. For, in being led to this more capacious regard for the world, we are also led to an appreciation of its very existence and our great good fortune in being a part of it.

References

Belzen, J. A. (1997). Cultural psychology of religion: Synchronic and diachronic. In J. A. Belzen (Ed.), *Hermeneutical Approaches in Psychology of Religion* (pp. 109–128). Amsterdam: Rodopi.

Bonnefoy, Y. (1989). *The Act and Place of Poetry*. Chicago: University of Chicago Press.

Crites, S. (1971). The narrative quality of experience. *Journal of the American Academy of Religion*, 39(3), 291–311.

Dupré, L. (1998). *Religious Mystery and Rational Reflection*. Grand Rapids, MI: William Eerdmans.

Edwards, J. C. (1997). *The Plain Sense of Things: The Fate of Religion in an Age of Normal Nihilism*. University Park: Pennsylvania State University Press.

Ehrenzweig, A. (1967). *The Hidden Order of Art*. Berkeley: University of California Press.

Forman, R. C. (1990). Introduction: Mysticism, constructivism, and forgetting. In R. C. Forman (Ed.), *The Problem of Pure Consciousness: Mysticism and Philosophy* (pp. 3–49). New York: Oxford University Press.

Forman, R. C. (1998). Introduction: Mystical consciousness, the innate capacity, and the perennial psychology. In R. C. Forman (Ed.), *The Innate Capacity: Mysticism, Psychology, and Philosophy* (pp. 3–41). New York: Oxford University Press.

Freeman, M. (2004). The priority of the Other: Mysticism's challenge to the legacy of the self. In J. A. Belzen & A. Geels (Eds.), *Mysticism: A Variety of Psychological Perspectives* (pp. 213–234). Amsterdam: Rodopi.

Freeman, M. (2014a). *The Priority of the Other: Thinking and Living Beyond the Self*. New York: Oxford University Press.

Freeman, M. (2014b). Listening to the claims of experience: Psychology and the question of transcendence. *Pastoral Psychology*, 63, 323–337.

Freeman, M. (2015). Can there be a science of the whole person? Form psychology, in search of a soul. *New Ideas in Psychology*, 38, 37–43.

Gadamer, H.-G. (1975). *Truth and Method*. New York: Crossroad.

Gadamer, H.-G. (1986). *The Relevance of the Beautiful and Other Essays*. Cambridge: Cambridge University Press.

Gass, W. H. (1999). *Reading Rilke: Reflections on the Problem of Translation*. New York: Alfred A. Knopf.

Geertz, C. (1983). *Local Knowledge*. New York: Basic Books.

Heidegger, M. (1971). *Poetry, Language, Thought*. New York: Harper Colophon.

Hollenback, J. (1996). *Mysticism: Experience, Response, and Empowerment*. University Park: Pennsylvania State University Press.

James, W. (1902/1982). *The Varieties of Religious Experience: A Study in Human Nature*. New York: Penguin Books.

Jones, J. W. (1991). *Contemporary Psychoanalysis and Religion*. New Haven, CT: Yale University Press.

Jones, J. W. (1998). *In the Middle of This Road We Call Our Life*. San Francisco: HarperCollins.

Katz, S. T. (1978). Language, Epistemology, and Mysticism. In S. T. Katz (Ed.), *Mysticism and Philosophical Analysis* (pp. 22–74). New York: Oxford University Press.

Marcel, G. (1950). *The Mystery of Being. Volume 1: Reflection and Mystery*. Chicago: Henry Regnery Company.

Marcel, G. (1973). *Tragic Wisdom and Beyond*. Evanston, IL: Northwestern University Press.

Merleau-Ponty, M. (1964a). *Sense and Non-Sense*. Evanston, IL: Northwestern University Press.

Merleau-Ponty, M. (1964b). *Signs*. Evanston, IL: Northwestern University Press.

Murdoch, I. (1970). *The Sovereignty of Good*. London: Routledge.

Murdoch, I. (1993). *Metaphysics as a Guide to Morals*. London: Penguin Books.

Otto, R. (1923/1958). *The Idea of the Holy*. Oxford: Oxford University Press.

Proudfoot, W. (1986). *Religious Experience*. Berkeley: University of California Press.

Ricoeur, P. (1981). The metaphorical process as imagination, cognition, and feeling. In M. Johnson (Ed.), *Philosophical Perspectives on Metaphor* (pp. 228–247). Minneapolis: University of Minnesota Press.

Scarry, E. (1999). *On Beauty and Being Just*. Princeton, NJ: Princeton University Press.

Schachtel, E. (1959). *Metamorphosis: On the Conflict of Human Development and the Problem of Creativity*. New York: Basic Books.

Slife, B. D. & Richardson, F. C. (2014). Naturalism, psychology, and religious experience: An introduction to the special section on psychology and transcendence. *Pastoral Psychology*, 63, 319–322.

Steiner, G. (1989). *Real Presences*. Chicago: University of Chicago Press.

Steiner, G. (1997). *Errata: An Examined Life*. New Haven, CT: Yale University Press.

Storr, A. (1992). *Music and the Mind*. New York: Ballantine Books.

20 Sociocultural Science of Religion and Natural Belief

James Cresswell

20.1 Introduction

The purpose of this chapter is to outline an approach to the study of religion by challenging reliance on self-contained mechanistic approaches to cognition. I will realize this purpose by discussing the cognitive science of religion (CSR; see Barrett, 2007). CSR researchers write about religion as "natural" in the sense of what I will call *phenomenological naturalism*. This phrase refers to the way that people's seemingly immediate experience manifests to them (for discussion of using the notion of natural in this way see Corcoran, 2009).[1] Believers live beliefs in a way that simply seems natural because they are taken-for-granted as truisms. Researchers, such as those inspired by CSR, outline how such taken-for-granted beliefs intuitively emerge as epiphenomena of cognitive mechanisms cumulatively working together (see Barrett, 2007). Hence, researchers in CSR address how religious beliefs seem to come naturally to religious believers as intuitive presuppositions that are manifestations of unseen laws of human nature (e.g. Barrett, 2008; McCauley, 2011; Slone, 2004). I will discuss how this approach to phenomenological naturalism misses the richness of the socioculturally constituted religious beliefs and so ignores the very thing that is most pragmatically valuable to religious believers: how religious beliefs are experienced as phenomenologically natural in a way that includes specific content (see Cresswell, 2017; McLean, Cresswell, & Ashley, 2016). I seek to outline a socioculturally informed science of religion by outlining an approach that can address the givenness of religious belief without predicating itself on socioculturally decontextualized mechanisms.

To address this challenge I must first discuss how CSR researchers also use "natural" to also refer to their scientific enterprise (e.g., Bering, 2011; McCauley, 2011; Slone, 2004; for discussion see Jong, Kavanagh, & Visala, 2015). They use the notion of natural to refer to an approach that seeks to use the methods of science to understand the general laws of the physical universe (see Chirkov, 2016; Polkinghorne, 1983). CSR rests on a presumption of cognitive mechanisms that function universally similar regardless of sociocultural particularities. A challenge is that this amounts to a metaphysical naturalism that is too narrow because, as I will show, it actually does not include materiality as well as sociality. Drawing on William James, I will outline how a fixation on universal laws of human cognition cannot account for the sociocultural constitution of religious beliefs and actually ignores an organism's physical embeddedness in its milieu. To do justice to phenomenological naturalism one must also take an approach that incorporates the material embedded functioning of humans that entwines sociocultural phenomena with the physicality of organic systems. As such, I draw on Humberto Maturana and Evan Thompson's *enactive* approach to cognition to propose how researchers can rework their understanding of cognition in a way that allows for a broader approach to scientific naturalism. The chapter concludes by cycling back to sociocultural theory and a discussion of Mikhail Bakhtin.

20.2 Religious Belief

Researchers in CSR note that there is an ostensive giveness to religious belief and write comments such as: "humans are often generally unaware of the reasons for their thoughts and actions in the first place . . . our thoughts and actions simply make sense at the time" (Slone, 2004, p. 9). They are trying to get at how religious belief tends to come to most people as an immediate given such that the *naturalness* of cognition" refers to how "the more transparent a thought's (presumed) soundness, the more elaborated the judgment, and the faster it dawns, the more natural is the cognition involved" (McCauley, 2011, p. 13). The naturalness of religious cognition pertains to how a thought comes without any effort and this approach is a claim about how people phenomenologically experience religious cognition in the flow of life.

The explication for why such cognition is so immediately available is predicated on a particular understanding of what is meant by natural. Slone (2004),[2] for example, reviews theories about religion to show how it is important to turn to cognitive science as a way of providing a naturalist explanation of religious belief. One particular group that is subject to near-vitriolic aspersion are what he dubs "sociocultural" theorists and writes that "we know that cultural theories of religion are impoverished by a lack of understanding of how the mind works and thus of why humans think what they think and do what they do" (p. 121). This discussion of how "the mind works" hearkens to the well-worn notion that humans operate per two cognitive systems: one that is intuitive and fast and another that is slow and analytical (Kahneman, 2011; Gervais & Norenzayan, 2012). There is a pervasive theme

that humans operate according to unseen mechanisms that facilitate beliefs in things like super-agents.

Natural, in this sense, pertains to the idea that religious beliefs are experienced as phenomenologically natural because they are taken fundamentally to be epiphenomena of the natural world (see Barrett, 2012; Sperber, 1996). Per theorists in CSR "the study of religion must be informed by an updated epistemology and philosophy of science" (Slone, 2004, p. 124; see also Barrett, 2012). What is meant by an updated form of science is one that resonates with a search for natural laws of human functioning (see Jong, Kavanagh, & Visala, 2015). It entails an approach that searches for the underlying mechanistic laws of behavior captured as the "nature of things" (Crotty, 2004, p. 20; for discussion see Nola & Sankey, 2007, pp. 312–336). Religious beliefs are experienced as phenomenologically natural because they are operations of mechanistic principles underlying the laws of nature.

Researchers in CSR turn to such scientific naturalism because they take the position that an insider's view of religion and/or folk psychology cannot help understand the cognitive underpinnings of religious belief. In CSR, development of religious cognition is treated as maturing along a predetermined path as environmental input facilitates it. Much of this work involves examining children with the hopes of assessing them at a young enough age to preclude the meaningful influence of enculturation and so get at the intuitive beliefs (e.g., Barrett, 2012; Keleman, 2004; Spelke & Kinzler, 2007). A central presupposition entailed in this work is that children have such capacities as a function of hard wired mechanisms. While such mechanisms are taken to have been developed over evolutionary time, language as an immediate influence on such cognitive architectures is relegated to the status of input stimuli (e.g., Slone, 2004; Sperber, 1996). Doing so allows scholars to "reduce the complexity [of religion] one layer at a time" (Slone, 2004, p. 43) to explain the underlying cognitive unity of all religions. When researchers in CSR seek to embody scientific naturalism, what they mean is discovering natural laws and predictors that supposedly underlie behavioral outcomes associated with religiosity.

An effective place to critically consider the forgoing position in CSR is William James because he wrote a substantial amount on the topic of religious belief (e.g., James, 1982). He highlighted how the phenomena of belief works in a way that leads to reconsidering CSR and how scientific naturalism is approached. It is first necessary to discuss James and then return to CSR's form of scientific naturalism.

20.2.1 William James and Religious Belief

James (1981, 1996) wrote about psychology in a way that contradicts approaches that are disembodied and abstract. To refer to belief as abstract involves conceiving of it unnecessarily tied to the actual happenings of life because it belongs to the realm of mind. He highlighted how belief is about relationships in the sense that one can have knowledge about another thought or another thing but it always involves a relation to another thing. All things that fall under the banner of religious belief involve relationships so that we do not have any element of belief that is isolated and on its own. That is, every belief is related to something else and it simply does not make sense to talk about a belief that stands as an isomorphic proposition.

To say that belief is disembodied refers to Descartes' famous mind–body split where the mind is considered abstract in its ethereal nature and this abstractness meant that it is not necessarily tied to the body or anything physical. James contrastingly argues that belief is best characterized in terms of a collection of "sensible natures" (1996, p. 27). Experience, at its most basic level,

includes how our senses entwine with happenings in life. We move through life with our body responding in relation to things and so one experience passes into another in a constant flow. The constant flow of experience involves more complexity than merely being stimulated by an environment. Previous flows of experience bleed into the current flow to give sensory stimulation shape. James (1996) pointed out that experience includes a constant flow of stimuli in-relation-to one another and in-relation-to psychological phenomena like concepts and emotions. Experience involves an inseparable relation among psychological phenomena and physiological ones. The flow of human experience includes continual relations among a range of elements and so it does not make sense to abstract conscious phenomena like religious belief from the concrete materiality of the world and one's action in it. Religious beliefs are thereby entwined with materiality so that they involve a complete way of relating to the world that shapes reality that feels objective. When someone is faced with a situation, religious beliefs come to bear in their experiential sense and entail immediate bodily dispositions.

It is in this way that James wrote about belief being both objective and subjective (e.g., 1996, p. 10; for a sophisticated discussion on the fallacy of the subjective–objective fallacy see Chapter 3, this volume). A belief in another belief can be subjective but the web of relations involved in belief never stops in self-contained subjectivity. All belief eventually comes into necessary relation with something in the world we share with others. To paraphrase James (1981), if one dies and stops believing in something, belief rarely disappears and it continues on without dependence on any single individual: "I could perfectly well define [belief], what the knowing actually and practically amounts to – leading towards, namely, and terminating in percepts, through a series of transitional experiences *which the world supplies*" (James, 1996, p. 25). He therein opens the possibility of considering psychological phenomena like religious belief as sociocultural phenomena and principally not self-contained subjective phenomena. An implication is that considering religious belief requires recognition of it social-relational quality that is entwined with concrete acts of life.

Returning to James reveals a challenge to the practice of reducing phenomenological naturalism to cognitive mechanisms. One challenge to CSR researchers is that they take an approach that treats religious belief as, what James would consider, abstract and disembodied. James (1996) would be critical of the notion that focusing on cognitions gets at religious belief because he was against idea that religious belief can be disentangled from the world in the way that an abstract approach implies. CSR does not intend to explain religion away, but just the *cognitive level* of analysis and so focuses on intuitive cognitions that are taken to be universal laws. Consider how, in CSR, the "key to understanding religion – especially 'lived' religion – is to identify aspects of cognition that constrain religious behavior" (Slone, 2004, p. 122). This approach to cognition is about abstract mental modules that are not easily seen without a set of guiding disciplinary presuppositions (for discussion see Cresswell, 2017). This approach amounts to metaphysical naturalism that presumes unseen laws underlying the observable happenings in the word (see Nola & Sankey, 2007, p. 313). The mechanisms are not really treated as natural phenomena in the world as they are locked within the mind as self-contained processing mechanisms. If we plan to get at the way belief is lived, then it cannot be done by examining it as presumed metaphysical cognitive mechanisms. Despite attempts to provide a natural account, CSR takes an approach that is largely disembodied.

James, in contrast, drew attention to the importance of understanding belief from the embodied perspective of the people who live it and so from a wider consideration of what is entailed in the phenomenologically natural experience of religious belief. In his seminal *The Varieties of Religious Experience* (1982), he pointed out how religious beliefs are often relegated to a "nothing but -" and the forgoing addressed how CSR could result in treating belief as nothing but a-relational mechanisms (see Slone, 2004, pp. 9, 47). In contrast, "what you want is a philosophy that will . . . make some positive connection with this actual world of finite lives" (James, 1981, p. 9). A concrete and embodied approach is one that does not dismiss folk psychology or materiality. James shows us how we ought not to take the study of religious belief out of the hands of religions people or the materiality in which they are embedded. We need to grasp their perspective from within if we seek to understand religious beliefs and, to outline how this would be so, I will turn to a view of mind that is not disembodied and abstract. That is, I propose a scientific naturalism non-reductively inclusive of both materiality and sociocultural context is needed.

20.3 Non-Reductive Scientific Naturalism

Researchers interested in CSR may note that the addressing of the complex culturally embedded content of religious belief comes at a sacrifice, which is the seeming loss of a naturalist science. Slone, for example, ironically accuses socioculturally oriented theorists of "biophobia" in this vein (2004, p. 43). I propose that grasping religious belief in a broader way that includes sociocultural content is more robust insofar as it need not exclude biology in the way readers like Slone suggest. My position is that including folk psychology is to give a rich account of phenomenologically natural religious belief. What is possible is an approach to religious belief without preconceptions such as abstract and disembodied cognitive mechanisms, which miss the phenomena. I will outline this proposal by first articulating how cognition is socioculturally constituted as an enacted phenomenon and then how we could retheorize religious cognition.

20.3.1 Sociocultural Cognition: Enacting Psychology

An ontological split among mind, body, and folk psychology is misguided and this claim can be understood by first discussing what we can observe in caregivers and their children. Consider Thelen and Smith's (1996) discussion of learning to walk and what it tells us about cognition. What they noted is that walking is not a case of a complex function emerging along genetically hard-wired maturational paths from digit-grade to heel-strike gait. That is, what they address is how constraints and enablements on development need not be by blueprint or design. A heel-strike gate is not possible at an early stage as multiple systems work in concert to resist gravity. Such systems include coordinating balance with a caregiver, dynamically stabilizing the legs, coordinating the forgoing with other movement and proprioceptive faculties, and so forth. The heel-strike in walking comes much later after a massive systematic integration has taken place. In fact, Thelen and Smith point out that "everytime someone speaks or touches an infant . . . the infant receives time-locked multimodal sensations" (Thelen & Smith, 1996, p. 193). It is the development in a dynamic adjustment among multiple systems where organisms manage to function effectively in their contexts. A crucial point is that *autonomous* walking activity is not an a-social behavior. That is, researchers who tend to look at one aspect of development and isolate it from its interdependence with other systems actually create an abstraction from real life. In the case of learning to walk, the eventual emergence of load-bearing heel-strike gait depends on the interaction among infants' own systems and those present in the environment. Rather than treating walking as an unfolding maturing capacity stored as mechanistic know-how, they point

out that it is the emergence of competent performance among many interrelated systems. Rich interconnectivity among many mutually interdependent biological and social systems is needed for any kind of activity to develop (see Thelen & Smith, 1996, p. 189).

Walking is a comparatively simple illustration that can be used as a bridge to understanding higher mental functions. Like walking, psychology does not need to come from an initial blueprint or design because it can be understood as *enacted*. A well-known developmental theorist in sociocultural psychology, Barbara Rogoff (2003), discusses such interdependent systems in terms of human interaction and the development of the skill to perform higher mental functions. She shows how every community has its repertoire of concepts and categories by which the world of its participants' experience is structured. They enact such categories and concepts in their language-use of terms like "God" and "Kharma" because the practiced use of the terms constitutes the perceptual categories. Infants should learn how words are meant and in what contexts such meanings are used so that, when they enact them, they do so in a way that is appropriate according to the normative standards of a community. Just like walking entail multiple social and material systems, language involves many different components working in concert to be acquired and developed.

An implication is that cognition is about enacting language to shape the same world as others and so participate in the same phenomenological nature of the world. We can see from observing human interactions that competently experiencing phenomenologically natural life like others means participating in the community by virtue of how our perceptual activities fall into rhythm with others. It means to enact what is phenomenologically natural in ways that others in a community recognize as legitimate and sensible. Religious believers become legitimate participants in communities through dynamic co-regulation that shapes our capacity to perform normatively appropriate cognition, which in turn entails what is phenomenologically natural.

This view of human development is very different from CSR because the latter treats sociocultural phenomena very differently. The characterization of sociocultural approaches to religious cognition can, at times, be framed in terms of cultural rules being imposed on a *tabula rasa*. For example, Slone (2004) accuses socio-culturally oriented theorists of treating religion as a symbolic system governed by group-specific rules or codes. The codes supposedly ought to be impressed on people's minds and so religious cognition is formed. This characterization leads to concerns that a socioculturally oriented approach cannot explain diversity because all members of a culture should be carbon copies of each other. After all, if his challenge of a sociocultural position is correct, people's tacit assumptions that are not in line with official doctrines should not happen.

Such a characterization misses that culture is not codified and static (see Baerveldt & Voester-mans, 2005). Figures such as Thelen and Smith (1996) and Rogoff (2003) point out that a care-giver's response is not unidirectional in its effect. Rogoff, for example, is interested in showing how caregivers and children are mutually inter-dependent as co-regulators in the performance of cognition. Their interactions are dynamic inso-far as people depend on the flow of interaction together to accomplish normativity that is con-textually appropriate. That is, infants are respon-sive as they are learning to enact a phenomeno-logically natural world and they do not repeat a caregiver's cognition with exact mimicry. Infants also take action in the sense that they enact cogni-tion in ways that are generically similar enough to be recognizable, otherwise a caregiver would not respond or would respond with corrections. They are nevertheless inexact replications – always cre-ating novelty – because infants grow into active-

responsive agents. This give-and-take is dynamic in terms of the interdependent give-and-take in relationships that enables participation and point out the need for a view of cognition that diverges from the metaphysical naturalism like we see in CSR.

20.3.2 Enactivism and the Socio-Material Embeddedness of Cognition

Humberto Maturana and Evan Thompson are central figures who propose an enactive approach to cognition. Enactivism provides an approach to cognition that fits well with the foregoing and it is predicated on a view that gets away from dis-embodied and asocial representations and cogni-tive mechanisms (Maturana, 1978; Maturana & Varela, 1980; Thompson, 2007; Varela, Thomp-son, & Rosch, 1993). It moves us toward a view that addresses the enactment of cognition by pre-senting a phenomenon called *autopoiesis*. This phenomenon refers to how a living organism can be an autonomous agent that actively generates and maintains itself. In particular reference to humans and cognition, a person develops over time to bring forth its own cognitive domain in the sense that it performs psychological phenom-ena in an appropriate manner. It learns to do so insofar as it adequately organizes itself to effec-tively function in a given environment. As such, neuro and physiological components of a human system dynamically organize in order to perform in a generically similar manner to conspecifics. This organization includes abstract qualities of human interaction such as language and so orga-nizing oneself autopoietically is to dynamically form a relation among components that define and specify a system as an individual (see Mat-urana, 1978). A human is demarcated by being able to self-organize in such a way that there is generically consistent performance of cognition and it is this organization that defines a human system as a composite unity.

Neurophysiology entwines with symbolic systems like language and concomitant emotions to enable a person to perform religious cognition. Physical sensation, memory, auditory capacity, sight (as caregivers point to things), and emotions are all entwined in the cultivation of language performance. That is, human perceptual capacities enabling a sensible environment do not form in a vacuum because an infant is born into a community of people who experience a world as ordered and sensible through their language and interactions. Instead of relying on cognitive mechanisms and self-contained representations, an autopoietic system is a network of productions of components that recursively interact to realize the network of productions as a unity (see Varela, Thompson, & Rosch, 1993). This approach means to come to a point where one organizes one's experience to experience phenomenologically natural religious experiences.

It is important to realize that an autopoictic system is conceived of as being very different from a self-contained system detailed in most CSR theory. Evan Thompson (2007) argues that an autopoietic system involves enacting cognition through a network of relations within its boundary and that this network of relations generates components of the system. That is, cognition involves a human experiencing the phenomenologically natural world as a personal experience and can generate such experience for itself. This idea does not lead to a self-contained view of cognition because such a system has a semi-permeable boundary. Maturana (1978) argues that systems interact recurrently to realize the autopoiesis of each other and he describes the process as follows:

The outcome of continued interactions of structurally plastic systems in a medium with redundant or recurrent structure, therefore, may be the continued selection in the system of its structure that determines in it a domain of states and a domain of perturbations that allow it to operate recurrently in its medium without disintegration. I call this process "structural coupling." If the medium is also a structurally plastic system, then the two plastic systems may be reciprocally structurally coupled through their reciprocal selection of plastic structural changes during their history of interactions. (pp. 35–36)

Structural coupling is when autopoietic systems impact each other and, in a sense, perturb each other into mutually shaping each other. It is for this reason that Thompson (2007) proposes that self-organizing dynamic systems are constitutionally integrated with the world. In the words of enactivists, "the activities performed by the perceiver/actor with basic level objects are part of the cultural, consensually validated forms of life of the community in which the human and the object are situated, they are basic-level activities" (Varela, Thompson, & Rosch, 1993, p. 177). They present themselves to us in its culturally constituted experiential richness because experience does not have an object standing over against us as a distinct subject. As such, as opposed to merely computational mechanics, cognition can be understood in terms of contextually bound embodied action.

20.3.3 Rethinking Religious Cognition

Rather than taking a fundamentally sociocultural activity and projecting it into the heads of individuals like we see in CSR's approach to scientific naturalism, this approach avoids mystifying cognition as properties of self-contained individuals that cannot be observed. Thinking, feeling, and religious believing are understood in terms of dynamic self-organization in relation to a milieu. In contrast to the idea of domain-specific processing mechanisms where the authors "do not intend a reading of domain as content domain, in the folk sense of domains individuated by the meaning of their constituents" (Barrett & Kurzban,

2006, p. 630), folk meaning is central in an enactive view. Where the paradigm generally presented by CSR rests on the presumption that cognition pertains to happenings rooted in naturalist laws, enactivism treats it as belonging to the whole sensorimotor activity of an embedded and contextually located person. Cognition extends beyond the brain into the whole body "such as the sensory organs, the musculoskeletal system, and relevant parts of the peripheral nervous system" (Robbins & Aydede, 2009, p. 4; Varela, Thompson, & Rosch, 1993). At the neurological level, for instance, "individual neurons do not detect objectively defined features. Rather, assemblies of neurons make sense of stimulation by constructing meaning, and this meaning arises as a function of how the brain's endogenous and nonlinear activity compensates for sensory perturbations" (Thompson, 2007, p. 530). What looks like self-contained religious cognition could be reinterpreted as an autopoietic system coupled to a milieu.

Thompson (2007) also points out that human cognition, as such, should not be separated from the environment in terms of stimuli and domain-specific processing mechanisms because it is always coupled with something beyond itself. It is for this reason that he wrote "'inner' and 'outer' are not pre-existing separate spheres, but mutually specifying domains enacted or brought forth by the structural coupling of the system and its environment" (Thompson, 2007, p. 26). In accordance with William James, stimuli would not be considered triggering conditions because, with the dismantling of the dichotomy between "inner" and "outer," there is a blurring of the boundary between world and cognition. Instead of treating it as an environment with stimuli, it is treated as phenomenologically natural as per communal constitution realities. As such "(1) perception consists in perceptually guided action and (2) cognitive structures emerge from recurrent sensorimotor patterns that enable actions to be perceptually guided" (Thompson,

2007, p. 173). Religious realities, insofar as they can possibly be experienced, are constituted by such dynamic mutuality. Realities present themselves to us in ways that compel us because they are integral to us and our embodied engagement in life. A generative implication is that cognition is shaped in its coupling with others in a way that intrinsically includes sociolinguistic practices. The vision for this updated version is one that considers socioculturally constituted folk psychologies to include the content-specific religious meanings seen in communities.

Treating cognition as enacted adds a deeper view that explicitly integrates materiality (see Baerveldt & Verheggen, 2012). Language is coupled to the sensorimotor engagement with life, making language deeply embodied. There never is a natural reality over which experience is laid because it is experienced as laden with sociolinguistically constituted value and meaning: it presents itself to us in it experiential richness. Simply put, enactivists further show how cognition can also be understood as experientially bound to realities constituted by sociolinguistic practices in which we are embodied participants. This view opens up an approach to cognition that can handle a phenomenological naturalism within which people, including religious practitioners, live. It makes sociocultural theorists naturalists in a very strong sense that explicitly includes material systems in addition to folk psychology.

It entails consideration of how cognition is something that people naturally do and so move scientific efforts toward observation and participation in cognitive systems. Where CSR can characterize sociocultural approaches to presume consistent religious cognition and static doctrine, the enactive approach to cognition presumes dynamic and flexible normativity that is generic, yet not determinist. Such an approach matches well with what we see in everyday religious believing: inconsistent beliefs that are generically recognizable. A sociocultural approach that I will outline below leaves room for dynamics and captures the way religious belief is performed in everyday life.

As such, I have sought to provide a background on which I can briefly transition to sociocultural theory. My aim is to further show how sociocultural theory offers substantial insight into the working of mind in terms of offering a comparatively broader account of phenomenological naturalism. In what follows, I will turn to sociocultural theory to outline an account of the working of mind to contradict Slone and similar minded researchers in CSR.

20.4 Sociocultural Theory and Phenomenological Naturalism

The previous sections orient readers to my challenge that CSR's approach to scientific naturalism impoverishes what people experience as phenomenologically natural because it runs the risk of coming at the expense of everyday sociality and materiality. Other authors in this volume highlight how specific religious beliefs are central to the constitution of mind. Guerro (Chapter 28, this volume) shows how specific religious concepts are sociocultural phenomena that show our mind. Others, such as Zittoun (Chapter 10, this volume), show how sociocultural symbolic resources provide guides that constitute imagination. Such sociocultural phenomena shape everyday life and we cannot understand human minds without them. It is important to tie the forgoing into broader sociocultural theory.

20.4.1 Mikhail Bakhtin, Sociocultural Theory, and Embodying Language

A proponent of CSR would say that such an endeavor is irrelevant because what matters is what happens underneath in the realm of naturalist mechanisms (e.g., Boyer, 2001; Guthrie, 2002; Sperber, 1996; Slone, 2004). This position

is fine for cognitive scientists who believe in naturalist laws of cognitive functioning. I and others in the volume, however, have shown that a specific religious belief involves particular content that is integrated with emotional entanglement with the world and wider aspects of belief. People may indeed have simplistic basic cognitions, but they are fractionally relevant to religious belief as it shows up in life because of how complex culturally embedded folk psychologies are just as crucial in phenomenological naturalism. To study natural laws, CSR must reduce the phenomena and this reduction impoverishes the research. The attention to abstract mechanisms bypasses this integration and loses what it means to have the experience of religious belief.

Sociocultural psychology is ideal for considering religious belief in a manner that compliments James and enactivists because it highlights how interpreting belief as an abstract and disembodied phenomenon is misguided. Hampson (2005), for example, points out the insiders' views and folk psychology cannot be dismissed because our understanding of the phenomenon becomes impoverished. As such, he promotes a turn to religious belief that takes sociocultural phenomena very seriously. A socioculturally informed approach is ideal because it has been explicitly concerned with meanings entailed in insiders' views and folk psychologies (see also Belzin 2010, p. 25). Hampson (2005) specifically argues for the necessity of enfolding theology into the study of religious belief and so takes the opposite stance to CSR. Such an approach is one that does not treat what people themselves say about their religious beliefs as secondary. To understand our research participants, CSR researchers ought to turn to folk psychology about metaphysical agents to address how people actively make sense of the world in sociocultural practices.

Mikhail Bakhtin is a philosopher who has inspired work in sociocultural theory and he offers a view of language that can help us understand folk psychologies as they relate to experience. Bakhtin's early work described how people are caught up in just living life and so offers insight into the phenomenological quality of religious belief. That is, he described how people act in a flow of experience: "all that which is given, present-on-hand, already realized and available – recedes, as such, into the background of the action-performing consciousness" (Bakhtin, 1990, p. 43; see also p. 85). Consider Bakhtin's comment that "the act performed proceeds in an objectively valid context: in the world of narrowly practical ends (ends relative to living one's daily life), in the world of social and political values, the world of cognitive validities (the act of cognition)" (1990, pp. 138–139). When he writes about an act proceeding in an objectively valid context he is talking first about how we are caught up in life. When Bakhtin writes about notions like "an objectively valid context" and "the validity of the object," he was addressing how the world is immediately experienced as seemingly natural. The "objectively valid context" also involves "social and political values" and "cognitive validities" and these constitute the insiders' folk psychology that is just as real as anything else.

What makes Bakhtin's claims sociocultural is that he writes about folk psychologies in term of language and speech genres (Bakhtin, 1986, pp. 76–78). A community of religious people, for example, would have a speech genre that includes a particular repertoire of terms that involve sociocultural shaping of the world (see Cresswell, 2011). That is, the folk psychology expressed in insiders' speech genre shapes the way that people understand the world; they shape meaning by way of shaping how people apprehend the world around and within them. Such understanding is meant in a deeply pervasive sense to Bakhtin as speech genres are embodied and so include experience. Consider how Bakhtin argued for in intimate relationship between language to embodied notions such as

an emotional-volitional tone (1990, p. 31). In childhood, humans are socialized into how to feel about the world (Bakhtin 1990, pp. 50–52, 153–154; see also McLean, Cresswell, & Ashley, 2016). A significant part of language is the experiential insofar as generic terms used to describe an experience are not separate from the experience. A repercussion is that language is bound to experiences socialized in a community through language and researchers ought to learn insiders' folk psychology to apprehend the concomitant experience.

I have argued elsewhere that an implication of the foregoing is that there is an ideological ought entwined with the language that shapes the world people take to be phenomenologically natural (Cresswell & Teucher, 2011; McLean, Cresswell, & Ashley, 2016). As a child develops thinking and emotion through interpersonal interaction, she is developing as caregivers feel she ought to develop, which implies a morally performative quality to participation in community. Authentic participation in a community is to competently perform the communal categories and feel them in the appropriate way when speaking them. It is for this reason that to be competent is to perform in a manner that resonates with one's milieu in a deeply pervasive sense that includes caregivers' cognitions. A child does not develop to *have* emotions because she, rather, enacts them as per an appropriate fit with the world. Just like knowing how to walk is a matter of being able to perform in concert with the dynamic demands of one's own self-propelled locomotion in tandem with environmental contingencies, knowing how to think or feel is being able to perform such activities authentically in an contextually appropriate way. According to the normativity of a community, one is competent when one speaks using categories that are performed and felt as they ought to be.

Bakhtin leaves us with an understanding of religious belief that complements the foregoing. Religious belief manifests in the world with seemingly concrete reality because "non-incarnated thought, non-incarnated action, non-incarnated fortuitous life is an empty possibility" (Bakhtin, 1993, p. 43). It is in this way that religious belief involves an experience of the world that it shows up in life as ostensibly natural. James's pragmatism and Hampson's (2005) advocacy for sociocultural psychology is a radical turn to "what is." It offers a science looking at facts as they show up in the experience of religious beliefs rather than dismissing them. We must address the deeply experiential feature of religious belief if we want to get at the socioculturally constituted givenness of religious belief. Bakhtin inspires an inductive approach that can potentially address the deeply meaningful *and* phenomenologically natural experiences that people live as part of their participation in religious communities. This approach broadens the study of religious belief to include the meanings people enact in their religious believing. Researchers are no longer restricted to looking at simple intuitive beliefs and can consider the more ecologically valid religious experiences. This approach differs from the approach that we usually see in CSR because it deals with what beliefs are about.

A sociocultural approach takes on a fallacious claim sometimes seen in CSR: that all knowledge is local if one takes a sociocultural view (e.g., Slone, 2004, p. 37). I'm taking a position that helps grasp local knowledge but does not preclude comparative discussion as we are not only concerned with subjective perspectives. It is one of epistemic humility that attempts to grasp religious belief from the inside of a community by taking a richer approach to phenomenologically natural experience. It looks to lived religion as it is constituted in language and so grasps local experiences but this understanding is not merely subjective. A sociocultural approach treats cognition as constituted in language practices that are not reducible to individual subjectivities or, as I discuss above, static religious codes.

20.5 Moving Forward

I have advocated a turn to sociocultural theory that is predicated on a broader conception scientific naturalism. This move means to consider the phenomenological realities religious believers live instead of realities that researchers determine a priori. When we take an approach inspired by James, we turn to the shared realities that are not entirely objective. Such realities, however, are not just subjective because they are constituted in sociocultural contexts. The forgoing departure from abstract and disembodied mechanisms does not mean a collapse into studying the subjective fancies of religious believers. As such, it is possible to study religious experience while staying grounded in sociocultural realities. Importantly, such facts include a rich approach to phenomenologically natural religious belief.

There is an important ethical implication bound up with this proposal. Teo (2008) discusses "epistemic violence" that emerges in much of psychologically oriented research. I showed how the concern for cognitive mechanisms means that much of what we write about in CSR from a metaphysically naturalist perspective is speculative because the subject matter in cognitive science cannot literally be seen. The speculative quality of CSR is not a problem so long as researchers are not intending to say anything to religious believers. A challenge is that researchers cannot remain cloistered among like-minded academics and researchers are commonly branching out to speak to practical concerns. It is in this context that Teo (2008) notes how speculation has serious practical, behavioral, or existential consequences and I argue that such consequences are rooted in the manner that speculation is a communally situated practice. One community can relegate another's purview as inferior and

as soon as these speculations construct the "Other" as problematic or as inferior, with possible negative consequences for the "Other," one should speak of a form of violence that is produced in "knowledge." In these cases, interpretative speculations (and not data!) turn into *epistemological violence*. (Teo, 2008, p. 57)

The danger in CSR is that it is possible to commit a form of ethical violence when we claim to know someone else. That is, a bypass or reduction of phenomenologically natural religious belief to a "nothing-but . . . " is an articulation of how ethical violence can be perpetrated on others.

Addressing phenomenological naturalism in the broader way that I propose allows us to develop a more sophisticated approach to such competing moral ontologies and things like God's existence. A challenge is that we cannot just collect information about various groups. When a dispute over the facts of experience becomes serious the facts themselves can be questioned and ultimately one side of a dispute must show a more practical difference over another, but this is not enough. Such an approach raises a challenge against the individualist presuppositions and subtle epistemological violence that can potentially emerge in CSR. This means that, to practically understand others, one needs to think in terms of a deeply pervasive form of context dependency. It means to apprehend what is phenomenologically natural to others and move into dialogue from there.

Notes

1 I am using this term to describe how people experience the world as natural and not in technical reference to phenomenology.

2 One challenge to discussing a large body of work is that there are many variants and this challenge holds true in the case of CSR. I will largely draw on Slone (2004) as a disciplinary representative because he specifically engage sociocultural approaches. He is an apt author to hold in focus for the purposes of this *Handbook* and readers interested in some of the varieties of CSR are referred to Cresswell & Farias (2016).

References

Baerveldt, C. & Verheggen, T. (2012). *Enactivism*. In J. Valsiner (Ed.), *The Oxford Handbook of Culture and Psychology* (pp. 165–190). New York: Oxford University Press.

Baerveldt, C. & Voestermans, P. (2005). Cultural psychology and the normative structure of reality. *Theory and Psychology*, 15, 449–473.

Bakhtin, M. (1986). *Speech Genres and Other Late Essays* (trans. by V. McGhee). Austin: University of Texas Press. (Original Russian publication 1970–1979.)

Bakhtin, M. (1990). Author and Hero in Aesthetic Activity (trans. by V. Liapunov & K. Brostrom). In M. Holquist & V. Liapunov (Eds.), *Art and Answerability: Early Philosophical Essays*. Austin: University of Texas Press. (Original Russian Publication 1979.)

Bakhtin, M. (1993). *Toward a Philosophy of the Act* (trans. by V. Liapunov). Austin: University of Texas Press. (Original Russian publication 1986.)

Barrett, J. (2007). Cognitive science of religion: What is it and why is it? *Religion Compass*, 1(6), 768–786.

Barrett, J. (2008). Coding and quantifying counterintuitiveness in religious concepts: Theoretical and methodological reflections. *Method and Theory in the Study of Religion*, 20, 308–328.

Barrett, J. (2012). *Born Believers: The Science of Children's Religious Belief*. Toronto: Free Press.

Barrett, H. & Kurzban, R. (2006). Modularity in cognition: Framing the debate. *Psychological Review*, 113(3), 628–647.

Belzin, J. (2010). *Towards Cultural Psychology of Religion: Principles, Approaches, Applications*. New York: Springer.

Bering, J. (2011). *The Belief Instinct: The Psychology of Souls, Destiny, and the Meaning of Life*. New York: W. W. Norton.

Boyer, P. (2001). *Religion Explained*. New York: Basic Books.

Chirkov, V. (2016). *Fundamentals of Research on Culture and Psychology*. New York: Routledge.

Corcoran, T. (2009). Second nature. *British Journal of Psychology*, 48(2), 375–388.

Cresswell, J. (2011). Being faithful to ourselves: Bakhtin and a potential postmodern psychology of self. *Culture & Psychology*, 17, 462–479.

Cresswell, J. (2017). *Culture and the Cognitive Science of Religion*. New York: Routledge.

Cresswell, J. & Farias, R. (2016). Cognition, culture and religion: The ontogenetic role of culture and its consequences in the study of religious experiences. *Open Theology*, 2(1). DOI: 10.1515/opth-2016-0009.

Cresswell, J. & Teucher, U. (2011). Embodiment and language: M. M. Bakhtin on ontogenetic development. *New Ideas in Psychology*, 29, 106–118.

Crotty. M. (2004). *The Foundations of Social Research*. Thousand Oaks, CA: SAGE.

Gervais W. & Norenzayan, A. (2012). Analytic thinking promotes religious disbelief. *Science*, 336, 493–496. DOI: 10.1126/science.1215647.

Guthrie, S. (2002). Animal animism: Evolutionary roots of religious cognition. In I. Pyysiäinen & V. Anttonen (Eds.), *Current Approaches in the Cognitive Science of Religion* (pp. 38–67). New York: Continuum.

Hampson, P. (2005). Cultural psychology and theology: Partners in dialogue. *Theology and Science*, 3(4), 259–274.

James, W. (1981). *Pragmatism*. Indianapolis: Hackett.

James, W. (1982). *The Varieties of Religious Experience*. New York: Penguin Books.

James, W. (1996). *Essays in Radical Empiricism*. Lincoln: University of Nebraska Press.

Jong, J., Kavanagh, C., & Visala, A. (2015). Born idolaters: The limits of the philosophical implications of the cognitive science of religion. *Neue Zeitschrift für Systematische Theologie und Religionsphilosophie*, 57(2), 244–266.

Kahneman, D. (2011). *Thinking, Fast and Slow*. New York: Farrar, Straus and Giroux.

Keleman, D. (2004). Are children "intuitive theists"? Reasoning about purpose and design

in nature. *Psychological Science*, 15(5), 296–301.

Maturana, H. (1978). Biology of language: The epistemology of reality. In G. Miller, E. Lenneberg, & E. H. Lenneberg (Eds.), *Psychology and Biology of Language and Thought: Essays in Honor of Eric Lenneberg* (pp. 27–63). New York: Academic Press.

Maturana, H. & Varela, F. (1980). *Autopoiesis and Cognition*. Hingham, MA: Reidel Publishing.

McCauley, R. (2011). *Why Religion Is Natural and Science Is Not*. New York: Oxford University Press.

McLean, M., Cresswell, J., & Ashley, C. (2016). Psychologists finding religion: Enhancing cognitive science of religion with cultural psychology. *Culture & Psychology*, 22(1), 44–64. DOI: 10.1177/1354067X15621482.

Nola, R. & Sankey, H. (2007). *Theories of Scientific Method*. Montreal: McGill-Queen's University Press.

Polkinghorne, D. (1983). *Methodology in the Human Sciences: Systems of Inquiry*. Albany, NY: SUNY Press.

Robbins, P. & Aydede, M. (2009). A short primer on situated cognition. In P. Robbins & M. Aydede (Eds.), *The Cambridge Handbook of Situated Cognition* (pp. 3–10). New York: Cambridge University Press.

Rogoff, B. (2003). *The Cultural Nature of Human Development*. New York: Oxford University Press.

Slone, D. (2004). *Theological Correctness: Why Religious People Believe What They Shouldn't*. New York: Oxford University Press.

Spelke, E. & Kinzler, K. (2007). Core knowledge. *Developmental Science*, 10(1), 89–96.

Sperber, D. (1996). *Explaining Culture: A Naturalistic Approach*. Malden, MA: Blackwell.

Teo, T. (2008). From speculation to epistemological violence in psychology: A critical-hermeneutic reconstruction. *Theory & Psychology*, 18(1), 47–67.

Thelen, E. & Smith, L. (1996). *A Dynamic Systems Approach to the Development of Cognition and Action*. Cambridge, MA: MIT Press.

Thompson, E. (2007). *Mind in Life: Biology, Phenomenology, and the Sciences of Mind*. Cambridge, MA: Harvard University.

Varela, F., Thompson, E., & Rosch, E. (1993). *The Embodied Mind: Cognitive Science and Human Experience*. Cambridge, MA: MIT Press.

21 *Psyche* and *Religio* Face to Face: Religion, Psychology, and Modern Subjectivity in the Mirror

Luis Martínez Guerrero

Within the realm of activities that constitute the human experience, religion is one of the most outstanding. This is because, over time, religion has produced a heavy cultural engineering of guidance and control of individuals' built-upon stories, rites, symbols, images, chants, prayers, and so on, which have been employed day and night, at different times of the year, at decisive moments in life, on certain sexual customs, on food, on clothing, and so on. The application of this entire symbolic universe has resulted in a psychologically problematic arena to respond to with respect to the formation of the personal and collective identity (Rosa, Bellelli & Bakhurst, 2000), the development of habits for action (Bellah, 1985; Giner, 1996), or the introduction of ethical, aesthetical, and moral values (Luckmann, 1971).

Due to the sociocultural role that psychology has been given in the study and interpretation of *psyche*, it is not strange that it takes charge of creating an understanding of how the phenomenological context of the individual is organized based on religious practices and ideas by considering them as tools guiding their actions in the world.

The aim of this chapter is to invert that premise. What happens if we put psychology in front of a mirror? What if the physiognomy of *psyche* as we currently think about it – a virtual set of functions and skills culturally stabilized for action – has been forged on environments such

as religion? Doesn't psychology, a producer of official images of what an individual should be,[1] owe its own identity largely to religion? Are these questions we ask ourselves not an effect of the conditions of possibility generated deep down by religious thought?

If we agree on the fact that the formal cause of both *psyche* and psychology – which is a cultural artifact that informs us about the properties attributed to a *psyche* at a given moment – lies in the cultural regimes of meaning, religion must be considered one of the main highways of meaning through which both have traveled. In this regard, certain sociology schools of thought and critical thought have studied religious practices as techniques that culturally and historically create specific ways of being an individual (see, for example, Bourdieu, 1999; Elias, 2000; Foucault, 1990; Sombart, 2005; Weber, 2001).

The logic of our work is then located within the historiographical tradition with genealogical traits, seeking to explore this cultural decantation process of modern subjectivity (see, for example, Danziger, 1997; Rose, 1996) and attempts to account for some of those processes which have taken part in shaping such a contemporary statute of the self. Our chapter will therefore attempt to propose an explanation for these matters by trying to respond to (1) how *psyche* is conceived of by modern thought and how it can be studied; (2) what image of religion allows it to be considered a source of cultural resources for the configuration of *psyche* and psychology; and (3) what role genealogical methodology can play in this matter. Finally, we will exemplify all these aspects through the case of the *Spiritual Exercises* of Ignatius of Loyola and his Christian conception of subjectivity and the government of emotions.

21.1 Modern Subjectivity in Times of Liquid Identities: *Psyche* as an Historical Object

We remain unknown to ourselves, we seekers after knowledge, even to ourselves: and with good reason. We have never sought after ourselves, so how should we one day find ourselves? (Nietzsche, 1988, p. 3)

A constructivist perspective that denaturalizes the unitary and ahistorical notion of *psyche*, from a long tradition in Western philosophy, must be born from an estrangement forged in modern times: the idea of the compositional and heterogeneous nature of the individual and his consciousness. According to Taylor (1992), such an idea would be an inescapable effect of any society based on a liberal economy that places the individual at its core as an autonomous and responsible being (Osborne & Gaebler, 1993). This psychological *ethos*, perfectly grasped by Illouz (2008) as the summit of the Delphic maxim ("know thyself"), has resulted in the discursive exaggeration of the realm of subjectivity, placing the individual itself as one of many objects of knowledge in epistemic projects such as psychology.

Indeed, the effect of such a state of affairs would have been that subjectivity itself – explanatory hypertrophied – is conceived of as a problem to be studied, largely signing the death certificate of the self when understood as an innate and universal entity, taking instead consciousness of its composition from certain theoretical sensitivities within and without psychology (Bourdieu, 1999; Danziger, 1997).

Therefore, in contrast to any intrapsychic conception of subjectivity, new formulations arise from it, conceived of as a liquid and unstable fiction (Bauman, 2004), an historical object (Rosa & Blanco, 2007) resulting from the fabric of values, concepts, beliefs, moral guidelines, ethical and aesthetical criteria, and so on, in a set of specific historical and cultural situations (Arruda-Leal, 2011).

Subjectivity, understood then as the frame of semiotic mediations each person has at a given moment to interpret and assign a meaning and significance to reality, is thereby understood as a virtual object segregated through the practices and contingent devices of history, which have conformed their own historical methods of subjectivation (Foucault, 1982/2005; Rose, 1999). Subjectivity is then generated through its concomitant relationship with cultural artifacts, specifically through those which have the purpose of managing the conscience that Foucault calls "technologies of the self" (*techniques de soi*) (1991).

Foucault defines these technologies as the cultural devices that allow individuals to carry out certain types of operations on their bodies, thoughts or behavior, thereby obtaining a transformation of themselves with the purpose of attaining a certain state of happiness, purity, wisdom, or immortality by shaping desires, aspirations, and dissatisfactions through the inculcation of certain practices of introspection and self-awareness. From this perspective, the individual has an active involvement in the formation of his own self.

The fact that the individual and the technologies of the self are developed in parallel to each other gives us a hint into how a simple exploration of these technologies, which are present at each moment in history, can reflect the process of transit, retreat, change, and so on, from some conceptions of subjectivity to others. Of the several anthropological projects, and, therefore, of the historical development of the successive theories of the individual that grow at the same point of the social objects through which they crystallize, human history can then be considered a chronicle of this process of self-construction (Blanco, 2002).

The effort to understand the constitution of the modern subject, which can result only from an analysis through time of the processes of stabilization or change which have set their orientation in the present, is devoid of purpose without the support of genealogy (Nietzsche, 1988). Thus, genealogical thought (Foucault, 1991) focuses on technologies of the self that place human beings within specific regimes of the person from the logic of governance, while the shape taken by that technical relationship of the individual with himself has been the subject of all manner of levels of rationality which have intended to shape the way in which we comprehend and lead our existence as human beings in the name of certain moral, aesthetic, political, religious, and epistemological objectives.

One of the objectives of such a genealogical project, about which we commented above, is the dismantling of the individual as a sort of "ideal" object, underscoring instead his contingent nature that stems from the conveyance of a highly heterogeneous amalgam of trails of thought, regulation techniques, organizational problems, and so on, understanding "interiority" as a type of bend or fold of exteriority that does not imply the existence of a background structured a priori inside him (Deleuze, 1992).

Thus, genealogy represents the instrument that allows for the exploration of the precursors of modern subjectivity, which seeks its own formation process through the analysis of proper subjectivation technologies of diverse areas of knowledge within the culture which several theories about human nature have disseminated, which have arrived at the present time and which fields such as psychology have picked up.

21.2 Christianity as an Outstanding Source of Technologies of the Self

The Western body is Christian. Two thousand years of Christian discourse – anatomy, medicine, physiology, of course, but also philosophy, theology, and aesthetics – have fashioned the body we inhabit. And along with that discourse we have inherited Platonic-Christian models that mediate our perception of the body, the symbolic value of the body's organs, and their hierarchically ordered functions . . . All have contributed to Christianity's sculpting of the flesh . . . our image of ourselves . . . None of this could exist in the absence of the above-mentioned discourse. (Onfray, 2011, p. 47)

Religion can be understood as one of the realms of rationality in which the technologies of the self have been used and promulgated with greater emphasis through time. Specifically, Christianity – due to its historical relevance in the West – saturates with its meanings the natural world and its phenomena (death, pain, suffering) through the personal psychological realm (experience, habits, conscience) and the community environment (values, guidelines, beliefs), teleologically intertwining the destinations of man, the group, and the universe itself into a common fabric of values.

This is because the shadow that Christianity has cast over Western civilization is immeasurable to the point that, without using it as a reference, the culture of European roots would be completely incomprehensible.[2] Therefore, it seems unquestionable that, at least in the West, most of the human cultural capital for managing and developing directive functions has been concentrated within religious devices from Christianity (del Río & Álvarez, 2007) and from other equally influential religions, such as Judaism (Speltini & Passini, 2014; Loewenthal, 1992) and Islamism (Tiliouine, Cummins, & Davern, 2009; Haque, 2004).

Nonetheless, identifying the nature of the religious as a cultural occurrence in addition to its theological connotations was neither a spontaneous nor an evident assumption for the social sciences (Smith, 1991). Just like with *psyche*, *religio* has a long history as a supernatural entity. After a long historical process, *religio* gradually split off into two identities: one of them considered a system of transcendental ideas in hand with theology, philosophy, and the phenomenology of religion, and the other a practice that shapes cultural devices such as myths, rites, and institutions, which were embodied in the work of anthropologists, sociologists, and historians.

The cultural analysis of the religion is, then, only possible by the late nineteenth century with this constructivist and conventional understanding of it in lieu of the naturalist interpretations of the religious experience.[3] A movement would develop in parallel – not by chance, we believe – with the progressive psychologization of Western culture and along with constructivist approaches to subjectivity.

Thus, from just a modern standpoint, we can state that, independently from our opinion on religious beliefs (i.e., whether we identify ourselves as believers, atheists, or secular), Westerners are culturally religious (Christians) because such meanings and values can be found, metaphorically speaking, at the very heart of our cultural constitution as persons.

Hence, even if the content of religious attitudes – whether the sacred, divinity, mystery, the absolute, or the supernatural – is subjected to belief or lack thereof, but not to science, religious standpoints themselves constitute instead an unquestionable anthropological reality ruled by the same principles of those of any social phenomenon and are therefore susceptible to a possible scientific expression. This is because, in the words of Fierro (1979), "the existence of gods is uncertain...But religions, those do exist and they are from this world" (p. 17).

Consequently, religious action is deeply ingrained in the cultural dimension, in the symbolic system of meanings through which each society finds a meaning for reality. If culture is that frame of reference common to a whole populace, which provides ideas, values, and explanations about society, man, and the world, which guides, motivates, and gives a sense to actions both individual and collective, religion is undoubtedly a very significant part of such a frame.

Excluding, henceforth, metaphysical considerations reserved for personal beliefs, anthroposocial sciences – those fields that cultivate cultural phenomena to a highly epistemological degree – should engage in its study without delay. Such study should undoubtedly encompass cultural psychology and the genealogical project it comprises to comprehend the current statute of subjectivity.

21.3 *Psyche* and *Religio* Face to Face: A Genealogical Approach From Cultural Psychology

If we agree, then, on the fact that culture is an immense driving force in the shaping of the individual and his experience, it will therefore be unquestionable for the psychological explanation that the context be at the core of its workings. One of the theoretical schools of thought that has the greatest compromise with this premise is cultural psychology, since its research field would concentrate on the space formed by the crossroads of cultural artifacts and psychological processes, placing the meaning and the mediated action at the core of its concerns (Valsiner & Rosa, 2007).

The task of cultural psychology is to account for how culture and mind configure each other through chronotopic dispositions[4] which are always personal; this calls for constant support of the historical explanation, since it absolutely cannot comprehend psychism without considering the specific developmental conditions that shaped it. Thus, cultural psychology has understood the religious universe as one of its main fields of study, as a spontaneous "laboratory" where the ways in which cultural artifacts and the mind are affected in parallel can be generally understood (Belzen, 2010).

Hence, from this idea, we can infer two lines of constantly overlapping work within cultural psychology in regards to religion.

One approach is to emphasize a synchronic analysis of the instruments and psychological effects that the usage of religious technologies implies in the management of the conscious experience. It would thus involve considering the mental mechanisms though which religion becomes psychologically relevant, requiring, to that effect (a) the analysis of the operational structures of religious practices and (b) the type of conscience phenomena they produce for the management of the everyday experience nowadays.

This is particularly relevant in a time when zealotry leads to harsh wars, when the strength of creeds can mobilize populations and when moral and ethical crises transform societies. In summary, an understanding of the life of the individual of the twenty-first century is affected by religion.

This approach, therefore, researches prayer and its properties for the affectionate-cognitive regulation under certain circumstances of particular vulnerability for the individual (Pargament, 1997; Martínez Guerrero, 2010), also studying the role of religious discourse in the development of the identity and *habitus* (Jesús, 2011; Belzen, 2011), conversion processes and discourse shifts of the individual from a narrative standpoint (Popp-Baier, 2008; 2012), the analysis of religious beliefs when making moral decisions (Day, 2007), and so on.[5]

Furthermore, it is not only that trying to understand our experience without contemplating religion is set to fail given the complexity and intensity of its anthropological and social implications, and that the contribution of psychological insight becomes irreplaceable when trying to comprehend the impact such a phenomenon has had – and still has – over human patterns of activity. Our point goes beyond that; if we agree that psychology does not describe natural categories it "encountered" during its epistemic activity, but that they are rather a product of history (Smith, 1991), psychology itself should also reorient its focus toward how the anthropological conception it accommodates, the tools of analysis it employs and, overall, its own endeavors which largely prescribe what a person "should be like" today are the result of a long process of historical segregation, among other realms of activity, of the same religious practices (see, for example, Loredo & Blanco, 2011; Cohen, 2011; Balltondre, 2011; Loredo, 2005).

In a manner of speaking, the "genetic code" of psychology is imbued with technologies employed by religion, which have set historical conditions of possibility for psychology as a field to be a viable project. Although psychology has progressively dislodged the theological sense from Christian practices, the anthropological model they generate is still unsuspectingly in effect, which proves that, after all, they are still cultural architectures which are very much alive. Consider the redefinition that psychology has made in regards to figures such as that of the spiritual director or the confessor, the examination of conscience, self-observation, and visualization techniques, and so on. Psychology should also be part, then, of a historical project in itself that makes aware the fact that it is also the product of time that informs the genealogy of the progressive psychologization of Western culture (see, for example, Danziger, 1997; Rose, 1996; Elias, 2000).

This is why in a set of recursions that should never stop, cultural psychology must operate an endless circular motion between present and past times that researches and acknowledges the process of development of its technologies and analysis categories from religious practices of other times but also be aware of the fact that they have set the conditions of possibility for such a questioning to be carried out in current times.

To sum up, psychology can only find the genesis of its own rationale – the one that seeks to explain itself from the past and in the present – in the frame of a genealogical model that tracks those areas, especially the religious ones, from which it may have surfaced. Thus, we can establish a contemplation loop in which religion is psychologically relevant as much as psychology itself has been religiously fundamental in the past. While this line of research is still in its early stages, we will demonstrate the potential it has for better understanding modern subjectivity from realms of activity as relevant as religions by means of a case we have developed in other places (Martínez Guerrero, 2015).

21.4 Emotions, Self-Governance, and Religious Development of the Inner Life

Emotions constitute one of the main areas of subjectivity which have been developed in the West with the greatest force through their overlapping with the fabric of religious practices. The importance that affectivity has had in the conformation of the model of the Western person seems to be free from questioning (Corrigan, 2007). One of the reasons for it can be found in the persistent support that anthropologies offered by Christianity have given it with respect to such an endeavor, constructing through it the leitmotif of knowledge of the self as a guardian of the moral constitution of the individual.

At the heart of Christian theology, emotions have been a constantly problematized phenomenon within ethical discussion in the aspect of its influence over action. They appear, then, as forces that can obstruct the progress of an organized life around faith (under ideas such as temptation), or as a means of celestial contemplation (the heart as a *via regia* toward God). In any case, these must be subjected to proper regulation through a set of rules, precepts, and technologies of the self as devices for action, identity, and deliberation.

Given that Christianity would have understood action itself as the direct consequence – among other aspects – of the ways of feeling, its role with respect to this aspect would have been to conform the way in which people experienced their emotions under the light of an axiology that saturated the representational environment of affective life by cultivating among its followers those emotions it considered relevant (love, compassion), while at the same time inhibiting others considered undesirable (envy, pride), imbuing with its significance the secular aspects of life (family, work), creating the situations, both external (temples, liturgical calendars) and internal (difficulties, anxiety, guilt) where emotions "should have" been felt, as well as the specific activities that would have stimulated or inhibited them (prayer, confession) (Emmons, 2005).

Christian subjectivity, built around morals, finds in the education of affections and will the pillars on which self-governance supports itself. The Christian, therefore, is turned into a philologist of his own spirit, which should be explored to find God concealed within his own emotions. In this sense, it would not be very hard for us to identify the history of theology as a discussion of the subject of the functions of feelings in the management of the conscience, life in a society and knowledge of the afterlife.

If the progressive control and acknowledgment of affections has managed to identify itself in the Western way of thinking with the development of subjectivity itself – supported by the prescribed manners (largely religious) of organizing, understanding, and expressing the repertoire of emotions sponsored by a series of socially structured mechanisms for private and collective introspection (Foucault, 1990) – Christianity represents an inexhaustible source for examining and understanding how psychological categories of affections were built. Consequently, this development affected the construction of a more complex agency which bestowed on the individual a constantly growing inner space for deliberation when acting.

21.4.1 The *Spiritual Exercises* at the Dawn of Modern Subjectivity

Some of those sets of Christian technologies of the self for the regulation of affection which reach their summit during the sixteenth century are the *Spiritual Exercises* of Ignatius of Loyola (1491–1556).

Ignatius of Loyola, founder of the Society of Jesus, represents one of the decisive milestones in the history of spirituality and thought that merges with the appearance of the modern subject in the sixteenth century. In this regard, the *Spiritual Exercises* were the founding text over which most of this process balanced from the viewpoint of its religious school of thought.

What are the *Spiritual Exercises* and what is their purpose? The origin of the Ignatian exercises lies in his personal experience as a man searching for growing in union with God and to discern God's will. During this process, he kept a journal as he gained spiritual insight and deepened his spiritual experience. He added to these notes as he directed other people and discovered what "worked." Eventually, Ignatius compiled a set of meditations, prayers, reflections, and contemplative practices into a carefully designed framework of a retreat, which he called "spiritual exercises," to help people deepen their relationship with God. Ignatius wrote that the exercises "have as their purpose the conquest of self and the regulation of one's life in such a way that no decision is made under the influence of any inordinate attachment" (Loyola, 1548/2010, para. 21).[6] In this process, the individuals must undertake these exercises with the assistance of an experienced spiritual director who will help them shape the retreat and understand what they are experiencing.[7]

In any case, Ignatian exercises did not emerge *ex nihilo*. Many of their elements can easily be found in previous sources. Paul Rabbow (1954) demonstrated that the exercises of Loyola were nothing more than the result of the Christian understanding of a certain philosophical tradition with a Graeco-Roman origin – Stoicism – applied, through Neoplatonism, based on a different ascesis linked to the moral environment that gradually developed from the fourth to the sixteenth century led by the Desert Fathers and Philocalia, through the Augustinian doctrine, the scholastic conception, the Franciscan criticisms to Nominalism and, finally, through Erasmus' Humanism and its psychological anthropology. (For a detailed walkthrough of this process, see Martínez Guerrero, 2015.)

From the standpoint of the development of subjectivity, the relevance given to the exercises gained significance in the context of a change in the *locus* of mind control, shifting from an external consideration linked to certain collective solidarities (masses, fief), to another one which was fully internal and individualist, which we could agree to consider modern (Verger, 1999). This transition was particularly intense within the realm of religious life where, not by coincidence, ethics and mysticism were the practices on which the subjectivist shift was forged faster, shifting faith from the medieval research mostly concerned with God toward a theological idea of man which sought to reveal the mysteries of metaphysics based on human nature through self-development and self-cultivation. This direction resulted in a concern for the nursing of the soul as a manifestation of that new religious trend of the interior as a means to achieve community piety.

Either way, this process gravitated over the *Spiritual Exercises* of Loyola, a perfect synthesis of Renaissance humanism and Christianity, which were simultaneously an incentive for and an expression of that shift in the anthropological paradigm that enriched the soil for modernity with the advent of autonomy and self-consciousness and, consequently, the realm of freedom and individual responsibility with it.

21.4.2 On the Notion of Exercise: A Book for Building Yourself

In this regard, within the psychological realm, the pedagogy of the *Spiritual Exercises* is based precisely on this development of the will (willingness) and, consequently, the development of character (habits of willingness) and the encouragement of self-governance. To that effect, its whole system focuses on the control of emotions, considering that they have the key to the will and, therefore, to moral action.

The *Spiritual Exercises* are therefore a complex psychological methodology concentrated on correcting the flawed physiognomy of the soul to achieve the proper and normal development of its spiritual functions and on educating affection so that it results in a pedagogy of the will that is naturally ambivalent until it is turned into an affection oriented toward God (Arzubialde, 2009). That is how Ignatius himself puts it when he defines the exercises as "every way of preparing and disposing the soul to rid itself of all the disordered tendencies, and, after it is rid, to seek and find the Divine Will as to the management of one's life for the salvation of the soul" (Loyola, 1548/2010, para. 1).

An objective by which the exercitant is taken through an exhaustive program of activities that includes exercises both general and particular for testing the conscience, a written objectiva-

tion of the processes week by week and day by day, different types of prayers required depending on the weekday, processes of scrutiny of the concealed meaning that emotional reactions may hold, imagination training that results in an increased exercise efficacy, exercises of summaries and repetitions through which the exercitant has had the most intense affectionate experiences, regulation of the daily space and time with prayers, aesthetic configuration of appropriate internal scenarios for each weekday that include elements relating to the body, food, climate, and so on, recommended reading, attendance of liturgical services, and so on – all of this under the supervision of a director who verifies that each exercise is properly performed.

This complex structure of exercises is set up with the sole goal of enabling the exercitant to learn to find, study and discern the origin and cause of the subtle internal movements of his spirit, which may originate from both God and the disarray of their affection itself, according to Ignatius, thereby setting up the discernment that precedes any choice aligned with the divine will or against it (Loyola, 1548/2010).

The exercises can then be interpreted as knowledge that stems from the praxis, a development and learning of the dynamism of the internal space that grows from the continuous motion the exercitant is subjected to during its many exercises, with the end purpose of generating a repertory of experience over the mental life that allows him to achieve an increasing autonomy (Peeters, 1926). In spite of its brevity, the book of the exercises contains up to 118 different verbs of activity referring as much to external actions as to those which are mainly internal (García de Castro, 2002).

This is the reason why, besides being considered a dialectic of the spirit, they are mainly a dialectic of will that provides an entire psychological tactic of transformation of the person who, through his own efforts, allows himself to conquer himself (Codina, 1931).

21.4.3 Realizing and Relishing Things Interiorly: Knowledge of the Self

As we can see, the *Spiritual Exercises* are a time for training the functions that prepare the exercitant to chart, comprehend, and study the meaning and tendency that each affection he feels leads him to make decisions. From this item, we can infer that the main exercise present across the Ignatian exercises is the examination of consciousness, which will constitute the realms of the mind as a formally psychological space in which the possible consequences of each intention and action can be unraveled through their continuous practice. For Ignatius, consciousness is therefore positioned at the core of human reality, which is why both piety and metaphysics would adopt an unmistakably psychological direction based on his work (Aldea, 1993).

Thus, ruling yourself (that is, conquering yourself) unfailingly implies knowing yourself, specifically, according to Ignatius, conversing with our feelings or knowing the tendencies toward which they lead us in both thought and deed. Therefore, the main objective of Loyola's method for the exercitant is that he learns as soon as possible to delve inside himself, learning to interpret the language of God through the emotions and affections rooted in his experience (Hormaza, 2010). This is the reason why Loyola could then be fairly seen as a "logo-technician," in other words, as founder of a language of interiority (Barthes, 2000).

The Ignatian method is, therefore, a practice that produces a profound psychological density among exercitants, since it involves them carrying out a fine observation and scrutiny on themselves with respect to their internal states to deal with psychological subtleties which are enormously complex. It is a work that involves the spiritual reading of the complex inner life, which, for man, is a permanent endeavor of seeking self-control and an increasingly lucid, penetrating, and subtle discernment of that world of emotions and thoughts that often cross paths, collide in the realm of freedom, and move in opposite directions.

Therefore, we can consider the exercises as a psychological technology for the creation of a self that helps in distancing the individual from his soul. This is because the effect of continuous reflection on the self that Loyola proposes ultimately causes an internal diffraction that turns the exercitant into a subject and an object at the same time: one part of him appears in the third person as an analyst and judge, while the other – the one who acts in the first person – goes through the experiences. Whether a participle or a noun, the subject is an object possessed by the exercitant (according to Gillespie's taxonomy – Chapter 13, this volume – this process of self-reflection would be found within the rupture theories of reflexivity).

That is why the method of Loyola is based fundamentally on introspection and dialogue, on a deep reflective character over the experience. The growing importance of the subject in the realm of knowledge, which has left its mark across the whole of modern epistemology, can already be noticed in Loyola's proposal.

21.4.4 Disciplining Experience – On Giving Someone "The Way and Order": The Development of Subjectivity Through the Rhetoric and Fractal Structure of the Exercises

The Ignatian praxis by which the exercitant shapes his inner world is far from an arbitrary or confusing process. It involves a regulated procedure that carries a specific conception, a logic on the development of the inner life. Due to their condition as a method, the *Spiritual Exercises* require a structure more than do other types of texts (García Mateo, 2000), so much so that we can even state that its meaning can be discovered only by and through form.

For these reasons, we can consider the Ignatian working model as less mystical than rhetorical (Fessard, 2010) because, just as in classic oratory, Loyola seeks to set rules to locate, pick up and lay out the most proper arguments that allow the exercitant to establish a relationship with his "speaker" – and with himself as a third party – to obtain an answer from him. Loyola dubbed this capability of the exercises to regulate experience as giving someone "the way and order" (*dar modo y orden*) (Loyola, 1548/2010, para. 2).

By order, Ignatius refers to a set of elements of content (reflective and affective) as well as to psychological and material resources (moments during the day, places, climatological elements, body positions, etc.) set in accordance with the principle and foundation (para. 23)[8] and with it as a basis (Iglesias, 1989). The order would then involve the logical concatenation of the materials and meditations present within the exercises (Loyola, 1548/2010, para. 2). In this regard, for Ignatius, the order of the exercises would reveal the order and logic of the spiritual life itself, the grammar of interiority directed at the prosecution of "the End" (Salvation). The way refers to the method itself, the technique that sets off the order (para. 3) (Iglesias, 1989).

As evidenced above, the basis of Ignatian spirituality is the language, the grammar of the thought (Barthes, 2000). Therefore, it is not just that Loyola's text is the result of a conscious application of the humanistic rhetoric of the sixteenth century over the world of Christian practices, as proposed by Rogelio García Mateo (2000), but rather that they constitute an elaborate theory of the *bene dicendi scientia*. To sum up: the *Spiritual Exercises* do not apply a rhetoric, but are rather a rhetoric themselves.[9]

From this standpoint, any spiritual exercise is dialogic because it involves a true exercise of presence before oneself as a third party, forcing the subject to divide and allowing him to change his point of view, attitude and conviction (submitting to reason). It is for this reason that communicating with oneself implies, at the same time, fighting oneself with eyes set on this transformation of the characterization of the world (Hadot, Davidson, & Palacio 2006).

However, to prevail in this struggle, exposing the truth will not suffice; it is necessary to persuade. Therefore, the purpose of the dialogue is not as important as is the manner in which it takes place, the mediums seized to generate the solution (Kennedy, 1999; Billig, 1999). Herein lies the importance of the rhetoric, seen in a sophistic light, that Plato confronted, as a *logography*; in other words, that its object is the plausible, the illusion and worship rather than the truth.

As a result, attempting to reconstruct the orientation of those exercises through a method set forth by rhetoric – especially the deliberative genre, which focuses on advocating for that which is useful and persuading against that which is detrimental – would be the way to learn how the self-persuasion that will constitute the "voice of the conscience," that the *Spiritual Exercises* posit, is formally oriented.

Loyola rhetorically organized his *Spiritual Exercises* around three formal units that delved into the densification of the conscience of the exercitant (exercise, day, and week). These three units are prone to be seen, not by chance, as part of a single fractal structure. This is a structure that delves into the idea of a dynamic evolution of the agency mediatized by certain technologies of the self that, due to their recursive nature within the processes of meaning, allow for progressively increased levels of self-governance of the action.

Thus, as discussed above, the exercitant progressively adopts certain reflective guidelines dealing with psychological states – emotions, thoughts – which regulate their actions, delving into the mediational structure of the relationship with himself, appearing, then, as a sort of "multitude" of viewpoints from which he should distance himself and handle to face his reality through his choices. It is then that the dialogue-related aspect of the conscience of the exercitant takes hold as part of a dramatic action that involves him performing on himself continuous excisions that enable him to simultaneously consider several viewpoints when acting and knowing what to do (Hermans, 2001; see also Chapter 13 and Chapter 15, this volume).

The exercises thereby favor the creation of criteria, methods, and guidelines for self-evaluation that individuals should apply to their experiences. The whole life becomes a continued spiritual exercise, a continuous reflection about the self in which everything in the life of the exercitant is a mirror that constantly forces him to look at himself.

Therefore, the main contribution of the exercises is, as mentioned, enabling a system, providing a method that allows the exercitant to give "the way and order" to his inner experience. They can thus be considered a metalanguage of regulation that reveals (or recreates) the base syntax on which experience and the reflective process of self-control that – with the influence of the company of Jesus starting in the sixteenth century in conformation with most intellectual realms – will cause such a grammar to support varied scientific and artistic projects and ends up becoming secularized with the passage of time into fields such as psychology (Martínez Guerrero, 2015).

21.5 Conclusions: Toward a Genealogy of Psychological Rationality

The question that gave rise to our work was related to the role that religion – and more specifically, Christianity – may have played in the way and form in which individuals, at least in the West, were capable of thinking about themselves. This is a phenomenon we broadly dub "subjectivity" and it influences the way psychology pictures *psyche* and the development of the way to

set the working of *psyche* and the shaping of conscious experience. The suspicion of the relevance of this influx stemmed from the historical attestation that the development of the main forms of organization and comprehension of public and private life in Europe had grown under Christian practices as a set of cultural artifacts useful when providing the collective of the human experience with a moral sense.

We said that the emergence of such a stance over the religious found its justification in the heart of a new anthropological concept that questioned the innate character of human psyche, placing it within the domain of cultural objects and inside the historiography arena as a phenomenon embedded in a set of specific social relationships that shape it. In this regard, subjectivity would be conceived of as a process that emerges at the concomitance of individuals with cultural artifacts through which they operate within a socially informed reality. Specifically, the Foucaultian hypothesis held that subjectivity would be more closely related to the use of those artifacts for which the main function was the management of interiority, of the conscience, which the French philosopher dubbed "technologies of the self."

Thus, once the ontological symmetry was established between the culturalist representation of religion and subjectivity, the conditions were open for the possibility that the psychology of constructivist sensitivity would question the realm of religiosity and the technologies of the self related to it as a psychologically fertile ground for the harvest of subjectivity in which a good measure of the image of the contemporary Western subject has been constructed.

It is for this reason that, besides the psychological relevance we may give religion nowadays in guiding the behavior of people, in our opinion psychology should aspire to a more ambitious project, such as the genealogical one, which seeks the foundations of its own rationale. In other words, there was a "psychology" before

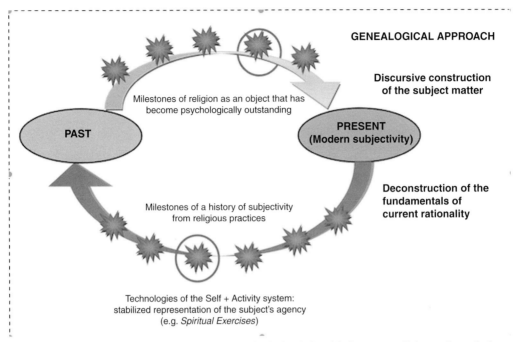

GENEALOGICAL APPROACH

**Discursive construction
of the subject matter**

Milestones of religion as an object that has
become psychologically outstanding

PAST

PRESENT
(Modern subjectivity)

**Deconstruction of the
fundamentals of
current rationality**

Milestones of a history of subjectivity
from religious practices

Technologies of the Self + Activity system:
stabilized representation of the subject's agency
(e.g. *Spiritual Exercises*)

Figure 21.1 An eternal obsessive loop. The genealogical relationship between religion and psychology.

"*psychology*" that imprinted its form, allowing us to ponder the importance and relevance that certain religious practices acquired in the historical process of the present constitution of subjectivity, specifically in the development of reflexive forms of self-control by employing technologies of the self which have enabled the cultural construction of inner life, of the "spiritual life." Such is the case we have seen in relation to emotions and the *Spiritual Exercises* of Ignatius of Loyola. The Christian individual is therefore a fundamental precursor of the modern individual on whom he is based.

Psyche, vested as soul by *religio*, abandoned that old garment but still holds many of its elements in current times. This is the reason why many philosophical and religious practices would turn, after their Christian transformation, into introspective techniques such as confession or the *Spiritual Exercises* which, at the origins of modern subjectivity, would enable techniques, already secularized, of an institutionally psycho-

logical nature (psychotherapy, coaching, etc.), even though they were not devoid of a moral frame (see Note 1).

This is why the historical overview carried out between Christianity and Western rationality, isomorphic in their foundations, is so intense that it may lead us to wonder whether an epistemological and disciplinary project such as psychology would possibly be separated from the culture forged in the West. As demonstrated by many studies in light of this revelation, the conceptual and anthropological dependency that the social sciences – all of them with European roots – have in regards to Christian rationality is so intense (structure of the inner world, causes of the action, formation of agency, explanatory dualisms, time irreversibility, causality of the action) that any attempt to study the human action separated from its conceptual frame could result in its meaning getting lost. If religion such as Christianity was the only valid discourse for over 1000 years for explaining itself and reality in the European continent, belief in this hypothesis is not so far-fetched.

Therefore, we can infer that a close relationship exists between *religio* and *psyche* as cultural objects which have developed in parallel. As seen in Figure 21.1, exercising this metaconscience implies simultaneously considering that religion is revealed in the socio–historical–cultural perspectives as a discursive process that is progressively self-conscious of its dimension or psychological relevance (arrow that goes from the past toward the present). On the other hand, psychology, stemming from the contemporary configuration of that same subjectivity, at the same time delves into the importance and relevance that certain religious practices and technologies of the self-obtained during the historical process of its current constitution (arrow that goes from the present toward the past).

The study of religion therefore allows for an understanding of the conditions of feasibility through which psychology developed, while this last one, at the same time, allows for the comprehension of the psychological functioning of religious practices. *Religio* shows as a manifestation of the working of *psyche* at the same time that *psyche* is the result of the shape conferred to it by religious practices.

For all this, the work scheme proposed by cultural psychology involves a new manner in which to understand religion and psychology itself, which can be of great help when attempting to understand phenomena as complex and elusive as these – where *psyche* and *religio* stand face to face and understand each other through their mutual reflection.

Notes

1 Far from any axiological objectivity, the moral and biopolitical dimension of psychology cannot be overlooked because each of its theoretical orientations provides a legalistic anthropological conception of what a human being is and what he "should be."

2 While the significance of other confessions is also relevant, the fact remains that the concept of religion itself was based on the Christian faith taken as a conceptual and historical model for its definition during the nineteenth century. This thesis, which does not hide its ethnocentrical nature, cannot be defended from any other religion (on this matter see, for example, Fierro, 1979; Smith, 1991; Hick & Knitter, 2005).

3 In fact, its link to culture today is such that several authors have considered them perfectly symmetrical notions (Tillich, 1974; Smith, 1991).

4 The chronotope concept, from the Greek *kronos* (time) and *topos* (space), references the insoluble intertwining of the temporal and spatial dimensions that comprise the organizational core of narrative events. These have the role of shaping the meaning of the cultural discourse. Bakhtin, who took the concept from physics, employed it as a methodological instrument with a double function: bringing to light the interior and the exterior of the discourse and, at the same time, attesting to how, within the discourse of the agents, such "historical-geographical" knowledge is evidenced by the way it is expressed in its psychological, aesthetical, moral, religious, and other notions (Bakhtin, 1981).

5 For a more detailed overview of this psychological approach to religion, visit division 36 of the APA: www.apadivisions.org/division-36/

6 This quote and subsequent quotes correspond to the classic division of the text into paragraphs.

7 The book of *Spiritual Exercises* is a text to be used by the director, not by the person doing the exercises.

8 The principle and foundation focuses on the anthropologic framework (what is man?) of the entire Ignatian spirituality. It is thereby the guide that comprises the backbone of the purposes set forth by the exercises which are continually repeated throughout the whole experience. For this reason, it contains (1) a teleological – and theological – description of man as a nature spontaneously oriented towards divine transcendence; (2) the practical principle of this orientation across all the environments of the individual (psychological, social, etc.) and, consequently, its Nemesis, the criteria of disarray; and (3) the

fundamental attitude that will must have to achieve such an orientation. As is evident based on its religious context of rationale, Ignatian anthropology is still a theomorphic anthropology because human matters find in transcendence a model that is not accidental, but constitutive.

9 The parts of the discourse present since antiquity in asceticism are likewise found within the internal organization of the exercises, zealously abiding with the parts of the Ciceronian *orations – exordium, narratio, argumentatio*, and *peroratio* – present within the different units of formalization of the training (exercise, day, week, month).

References

Aldea, Q. (Ed.). (1993). *Ignacio de Loyola en la gran crisis del siglo XVI* [Ignatius of Loyola in the great crisis of the sixteenth century]. Santander, Spain: Sal Terrae.

Arruda-Leal, A. (2011). La experiencia de subjetividad como condición y efecto de los saberes y las prácticas psicológicas: producción de subjetividad y psicología [The subjectivity experience as condition and effect of psychological knowledge and practices: Subjectivity production and psychology]. *Estudios de Psicología*, 32(3), 359–374.

Arzubialde, S. (2009). *Ejercicios espirituales de san Ignacio. Historia y análisis* [Spiritual exercises of St. Ignatius. History and analysis]. Santander, Spain: Sal Terrae.

Bakhtin, M. (1981). *The Dialogical Imagination: Four Essays by M. M. Bakhtin* (ed. by M. Holquist). Austin: University of Texas Press.

Balltondre, M. (2011). La oración como técnica de subjetivación en la espiritualidad Cristiana del siglo XVI [The prayer as technology of the self in sixteenth-century Spanish Christian spirituality]. *Estudios de Psicología*, 32(3), 375–388.

Barthes, R. (2000). *Sade, Fourier, Loyola*. Cambridge: Farrar, Straus and Giroux.

Bauman, Z. (2004). *Identity: Conversations with Benedetto Vecchi*. Cambridge: Polity Press.

Bellah, R. N. (1985). *Habits of the Heart: Individualism and Commitment in American Life*. Berkeley: University of California Press.

Belzen, J. A. (2010). *Towards Cultural Psychology of Religion: Principles, Approaches, Applications*. New York: Springer.

Belzen, J. A. (2011). La perspectiva cultural en la psicología de la religion: estudio sobre la espiritualidad "bevindelijke" a modo de ejemplo [The cultural psychological perspective in Psychology of religion: Research on "enlightened" spirituality by way of example]. *Estudios de Psicología*, 32(1), 103–130.

Billig, M. (1999). *Arguing and Thinking: A Rhetorical Approach to Social Psychology*. New York: Cambridge University Press.

Blanco, F. (2002). *El cultivo de la mente. Un ensayo histórico-crítico sobre la cultura psicológica* [The cultivation of the mind: A historical-critical essay on the psychological culture]. Madrid: Antonio Machado.

Bourdieu, P. (1999). *Language and Symbolic Power*. Cambridge, MA: Harvard University Press.

Codina, A. (1931). Entendimiento y voluntad en los Ejercicios de San Ignacio [Understanding and will in the exercises of St. Ignatius]. *Manresa*, 7(27), 229–235.

Cohen, M. A. (2011). Erwin Rohde y la genealogía del dualismo alma/cuerpo [Erwin Rohde and the genealogy of soul/body dualism]. *Estudios de Psicología*, 32(1), 69–83.

Corrigan, J. (Ed.). (2007). *The Oxford Handbook of Religion and Emotion*. Oxford: Oxford University Press.

Danziger, K. (1997). *Naming the Mind. How Psychology Found Its Language*. London: SAGE.

Day, J. (2007). Moral reasoning, religious reasoning, and their supposed relationships: Paradigms, problems, and prospects. *Adult Developments*, 10(1), 6–10.

Deleuze, G. (1992). *Expressionism in Philosophy: Spinoza*. New York: Zone Books.

del Río, P. & Álvarez, A. (2007). Prayer and the kingdom of Heaven: Psychological tools for directivity. In J. Valsiner, & A. Rosa (Eds.). *The Cambridge Handbook of Sociocultural Psychology* (pp. 373–403). Cambridge, MA: Cambridge University Press.

Elias, N. (2000). *The Civilizing Process: Sociogenetic and Psychogenetic Investigations*. Oxford: Blackwell.

Emmons, R. (2005). Emotion and religion. In R. F. Paloutzian & C. L. Park (Eds.), *Handbook of Psychology of Religion and Spirituality* (pp. 235–252). New York: Guilford Press.

Fessard, G. (2010). *La dialéctica de los Ejercicios Espirituales de san Ignacio de Loyola* [The dialectic of the *Spiritual Exercises of St. Ignatius of Loyola*]. Santander, Spain: Sal Terrae.

Fierro, A. (1979). *Sobre la Religión: Descripción y teoría* [On religion: Description and theory]. Madrid: Taurus.

Foucault, M. (1982/2005). *The Hermeneutics of the Subject: Lectures at the Collège de France 1981–1982*. London: Picador.

Foucault, M. (1990). *The History of Sexuality, Volume 2: The Use of Pleasure*. New York: Vintage Books.

Foucault, M. (1991). *Tecnologías del Yo* [Technologies of the Self]. Madrid: Paidós.

García de Castro, J. (2002). ¿Qué hacemos cuando hacemos Ejercicios? [What do we do when we do Exercises?]. *Manresa*, 74(290), 11–40.

García Mateo, R. (2000). *Ignacio de Loyola: Su espiritualidad y su mundo cultural* [Ignatius of Loyola: His spirituality and cultural world]. Santander, Spain: Sal Terrae.

Giner, S. (1996). La religión civil [Civil religion]. In R. Diaz-Salazar, S. Giner, & F. Velasco (Eds.), *Formas modernas de religión* [Modern ways of religion]. Madrid: Alianza Universidad.

Hadot, P., Davidson, A., & Palacio, J. (2006). *Ejercicios espirituales y filosofía antigua* [Philosophy as a way of life: Spiritual Exercises from Socrates to Foucault]. Barcelona: Siruela.

Haque, A.(2004). Psychology from Islamic perspective: Contributions of early Muslim scholars and challenges to contemporary Muslim psychologists. *Journal of Religion and Health*, 43(4): 357–377.

Hermans, H. J. (2001). The construction of a personal position repertoire: Method and practice. *Culture & Psychology*, 7, 323–365.

Hick, J. & Knitter, P. F. (Eds.). (2005). *The Myth of Christian Uniqueness: Toward a Pluralistic Theology of Religions*. Eugene, OR: Wipf & Stock.

Hormaza, M. L. de la (2010). No el mucho saber harta y satisface al anima, mas el sentir y gustar de las cosas internamente [For it is not much knowledge that fills and satisfies the soul, but the intimate understanding and relish of the truth]. *Manresa*, 82(324), 221–226.

Iglesias, I. (1989). Dar "a otro modo y orden," Part 2 [On giving someone "the way and order"]. *Manresa*, 61(241), 355–366.

Illouz, E. (2008). *Saving the Modern Soul: Therapy, Emotions, and the Culture of Self-Help*. Berkeley: University of California Press.

Jesús, P. (2011). Meaning-creation, selfhood, and religion: From religious metanarratives to spiritual self-narratives. *Estudios de Psicología*, 32(1), 131–145.

Kennedy, G. A. (1999). *Classical Rhetoric and its Christian and Secular Tradition from Ancient to Modern Times*. Chapel Hill: The University of North Carolina Press.

Loewenthal, K. M. (1992). Depression, melancholy and Judaism. *International Journal for the Psychology of Religion*, 2, 101–108.

Loredo, J. C. (2005). La confesión en la prehistoria de la psicología [Confession in the prehistory of psychology]. *Anuario de Psicología*, 36(1), 99–116.

Loredo, J. C. & Blanco, F. (2011). La práctica de la confesión y su génesis como tecnología psicológica [The practice of confession and its genesis as psychological technology]. *Estudios de Psicología*, 32(1), 85–101.

Loyola, I. de (1548/2010). *Ejercicios Espirituales*. [Spiritual Exercises]. Santander, Spain: Sal Terrae.

Luckmann, T. (1971). *The Invisible Religion: The Problem of Religion in Modern Society*. London: MacMillan.

Martínez Guerrero, L. (2010). Dominus illuminatio mea: Una aproximación al estudio del rezo como artefacto psicológico para la regulación emocional en situaciones de afrontamiento [God is my light: An approach to the study of prayer as a psychological artefact for emotion regulation in coping situations]. Unpublished MA dissertation, Universidad Autónoma de Madrid.

Martínez Guerrero, L. (2015). Tecnologías del yo, afectividad y gramáticas del autogobierno en los Ejercicios Espirituales de Ignacio de Loyola (1491–1556): Un hito en la genealogía de la subjetividad moderna [Technologies of the self, emotions and grammars of self-government in the Spiritual Exercises of Ignatius of Loyola (1491–1556): A milestone in the genealogy of modern subjectivity]. Unpublished doctoral dissertation. Universidad Autónoma de Madrid.

Nietzsche, F. (1988). *Zur Genealogie der Moral* [On the genealogy of morals]. Stuttgart, Germany: Reclam.

Onfray, M. (2011). *Atheist Manifesto: The Case Against Christianity, Judaism, and Islam*. New York: Arcade Books.

Osborne, D. & Gaebler, T. (1993). *Reinventing Government*. Boston: Addison-Wesley.

Pargament, K. I. (1997). *The Psychology of Religion and Coping: Theory, Research, Practice*. New York: Guilford Press.

Peeters, L. (1926). ¿Cuál es el fin principal de los Ejercicios? [What is the main purpose of the Spiritual Exercises?]. *Manresa*, 2(8), 306–321.

Popp-Baier, U. (2008). Life stories and philosophies of life: A perspective for research in psychology of religion. In J. A. Belzen & A. Geels (Eds.), *Autobiography and the Psychological Study of Religious Lives* (pp. 39–74). Amsterdam: Rodopi.

Popp-Baier, U. (2012). Religious experience as narrative: Reflections on the advantages of a narrative approach. In A. Budriūnaitė (Ed.), *Proceedings of* Religious Experience & Tradition.International Interdisciplinary Scientific Conference (pp. 13–17), May 11–12, Kaunas, Lithuania.

Rabbow, P. (1954). *Seelenführung: Methodik der Exerzitien in der Antike* [Spiritual direction. Methodology of the Exercises in ancient times]. Munich: Kösel Verlag.

Rosa, A., Bellelli, G., & Bakhurst, D. (Eds.). (2000). *Memoria colectiva e identidad nacional* [Collective memory and national identity]. Madrid: Biblioteca Nueva.

Rosa, A. & Blanco, F. (2007). Actuations of identification in the games of identity: Social practice/psychological theorizing. Retrieved from www.sppt-gulerce.boun.edu.tr/article7.aspx.

Rose, N. (1996). *Inventing Ourselves: Psychology, Power and Personhood*. Cambridge: Cambridge University Press.

Rose, N. (1999). *Governing the Soul*. London: Free Associations Books.

Smith, W. C. (1991). *The Meaning and End of Religion*. Minneapolis, MN: Fortress Press.

Sombart, W. (2005). *El burgués: Contribución a la historia espiritual del hombre económico moderno* [The quintessence of capitalism: A study of the history and psychology of the modern business man]. Madrid: Alianza.

Speltini, G. & Passini, S. (2014). Cleanliness/dirtiness, purity/impurity as social and psychological issues. *Culture & Psychology*, 20(2), 203–219.

Taylor, C. (1992). *Sources of the Self: The Making of the Modern Identity*. Cambridge, MA: Harvard University Press.

Tiliouine, H., Cummins, R., & Davern, M. (2009). Islamic religiosity, subjective well-being, and health. *Mental Health, Religion & Culture* 12 (1), 55–74.

Tillich, P. (1974). *Filosofía de la religión* [Philosophy of religion]. Buenos Aires: Megápolis.

Valsiner, J. & Rosa, A. (2007). *The Cambridge Handbook of Sociocultural Psychology*. Cambridge, MA: Cambridge University Press.

Verger, J. (1999). *Gentes del saber en la Europa de finales de la Edad Media* [Men of learning in Europe at the end of the Middle Ages]. Madrid: Editorial Complutense.

Weber, M. (2001). *La ética protestante y el espíritu del capitalismo* [The Protestant ethic and the spirit of capitalism]. Madrid: Alianza.

Part VI
Practices and Artifacts for Imagining Identity

22 Imaginative Processes and the Making of Collective Realities in National Allegories

Luca Tateo

22.1 Introduction

In our contemporary troubled times (but what times in human history haven't been troubled?), some striking events are questioning psychological knowledge about the way intangible concepts affect people's actions. I always wonder how it is possible that human beings can kill thousands of their fellow humans or devastate the environment in the name of intangible concepts such as "faith," "progress," "free market," "homeland," "freedom," "democracy," "truth," "protection of life," "security," "stability," or even "world peace." Sometimes, one looks for the "false consciousness" beyond these motives, attributing these evil behaviors to more mundane goals such as profit, power, money, and so on. When, instead, those intangible concepts drive people to altruist, idealistic, or artistic actions, then we tend to praise the inherent nobility of human spirit. On the other hand, prototypical figures – like the "hero" who kills to right a wrong, the "martyr" who dies for the good, the "pop star" who does art for money, or the "self-made man" who is the hero of the free market – look like counterfactuals to the common sense idea of idealistic versus opportunistic motives. Human cultures are very good at producing extremely inspiring stories of "conversion" from one condition to the other. The self-made man turns into a philanthropist, the pop star turns into a religious activist, the hero turns into a politician. From Moses to Siddhartha, from Mary Magdalene to Jeanne D'Arc, from Ronald Reagan to Donald Trump, religions and ideologies have built on these profoundly ambivalent narratives of conversion. Actually, they are exactly the process of conversion and the ambivalence of motives that make possible any kind of moral system in a given culture. Doing wrong actions for the sake of "noble motives," "merry-gone-wrongs," "sacrifice," and "redemption" are all specific signs that regulate individual and collective conducts with respect to the ambivalences of power relationships. Without the availability of these kinds of signs, the person and the group would not have the possibility of constructing, maintaining and demolishing meanings. Indeed:

> the complex social activities in the field of communication are commonly based on the inherent tension and ambivalence of the complex systems of meaning that constantly develop new elements in the fuzzy field of quasi-truth, that can feed either into "lie" or "truth." (Tateo, 2016a, p. 445)

The point is that, despite the fundamental philosophical and existential questions about the origin of good and evil in human life, we still do not have a complete understanding of the way these highly ambivalent and evasive concepts and ideals, that we cannot touch, smell, or see, that we cannot throw, eat, steal, or give to our offspring to survive, have, however, the capability to affect our lives as if they were concrete objects, provided with their own reality outside the realm of thinking.

Extended killing, social exclusion, and suicidal behaviors under the flag of "faith" or "nation" are still waiting to be fully understood, both at the individual and collective level, by social sciences in general and by psychology in particular.

These deaths bring us abruptly face to face with the central problem posed by nationalism: what makes the shrunken imaginings of recent history (scarcely more than two centuries) generate such colossal sacrifices? I believe that the beginnings of an answer lie in the cultural roots of nationalism. (Anderson, 2006, p. 7)

Exactly one century ago, Sigmund Freud, confronted with an explosion of violence and death never seen before World War I, wrote:

It is, to be sure, a mystery why the collective individuals should in fact despise, hate and detest one another – every nation against every other – and even in times of peace. (Freud, 2001, p. 302)

A few decades later and after a second world bloodbath, some of the most innovative works in social psychology emerged from the need to account for the motives and processes related to human violence (Becker, 1968; Lewin, 1948), including a "more general concern about authority" (Milgram, 1977, p. 92).

My purpose in this chapter is to develop a theoretical reflection about some psychological processes involved in human actions related to and led by abstract and intangible concepts, such as "nation," "love," "faith," or "freedom." On the other hand, I would like to reflect on the process through which very concrete objects and people that we meet in everyday experience become allegorical representations of those abstract concepts. My argument will be that in these psychological phenomena, imaginative processes play a major role, understanding imagination as a higher mental function that enable us to treat concrete objects as if they were abstract concepts and vice versa (Tateo, 2016b). The biggest part of individual life in the context of the collective is populated by these kinds of objects: "The cultural *umwelt* is a collective act of imagination, regulated by reason but not composed of reason" (White, 1976, p. 668).

I will support my argument by examples related to the phenomena of "nation," "nationalism," and "national identity" and how these concepts, basically imaginary abstractions (Anderson, 2006), are elaborated in psychic life through imaginative processes. I will refer to basic processes of abstraction from experience and creation of metonymical representations of abstract concepts, exemplified by the very common allegorical personifications of "nation-states" that emerged in the mid-nineteenth century. These processes have been, for instance, scrutinized from the perspectives of discursive practices (Billig, 1995), of social representations (see Chapter 7, this volume), and of collective memory construction (Jovchelovitch, 2012). Besides, the relationship between verbal and iconic dimensions of the discursive productions have been jointly analyzed through different methods of semiotic analysis (Liu & O'Halloran, 2009; Lonchuk & Rosa, 2011; Ma, 2014).

Though these works address a number of complex phenomena and processes, they have in common a persisting separation between the representational and the semiotic dimensions. On the one hand, social representation theory, as a theory about knowledge and communication, is still lacking a theory of meaning and semiosis. Signs are not "out there" (Tateo, 2016a) ready to be used, but are produced by the directionality of the interpretant. Something becomes a sign when something else moves toward it, be it a footprint in the wood for hunting an animal or a complex political message for a citizen (Lonchuk & Rosa, 2011). The question of directionality, reads "intentionality," of the interpretant is crucial in understanding the semiosis: "the sign-interpretant relationship is characteristic of intersubjective action" (Ma, 2014, p. 379). A sign is what denotes something for someone, it is "connected with its object by virtue of the idea of the symbol-using mind, without which no such connection would exist" (Peirce, 1998, p. 9).

On the other hand, the studies on the multimodality or complementarity between verbal and iconic language are still considering the two channels as separate, though mutually reinforcing and being the vehicle of mainly conceptual (the verbal) and affective (the iconic) contents. The understanding of collective knowledge, identity, memory, and movements would benefit, in my opinion of a more integrated contribution from the study of semiosis (Rosa, 2007). In particular, I will explore the relationship between the multiple modalities *within* a sign, that is, the intertwining of linguistic, iconic, echoic, and so on, dimensions of the sign. Though I will mainly focus on allegorical representations, this process is not limited to the images but can involve any kind of sign. As Wagner, Rämmer, and Kello (Chapter 7, this volume) show, the religious experience is a good example of how the directionality of the interpretant can be a sort of impalpable, collective, and affective atmosphere for which the religious setting of the temple is purposefully built. But let me begin with a 270-years "jump back" in history.

22.2 Vico's Axioms

In the seventeenth century, the Italian philosopher Giambattista Vico first tried to systematically outline a theory of the historical development of human epistemology through culture (Tateo, 2015a). He stated the general laws of development of the different forms of knowledge and civilization and how they are connected with the *psyche*. His intuition was that the historically situated cultural forms are, fundamentally, solutions that human beings collectively developed to solve, for account, and cope with the phenomena of existence (natural powers, birth, death, regu-

lation of instincts, etc.). Vico claimed that there is a relationship between the phylogenetic development of the human mind and the historical development of culture. That is, mind and culture develop together through the mediation of artifacts (e.g., language, tools, ideas, images, and social institutions). Human existence is mediated by signs and, by general agreement, verbal language is the most powerful and flexible sign system:

a man is properly only mind, body and speech, and *speech stands as it were midway between mind and body*. Hence the certitude of law began in mute times with the body. Then when the so-called articulate languages were invented, it passed to certain ideas or verbal formulae. (Vico, 1744/1948, p. 353; emphasis added)

He also maintained that if we look at prehistoric men, the origin of the historical development of mind and culture must necessarily start from the human being's self, from the own body:

Because the human mind was at first unable to form abstractions, it used metaphors involving the body and the senses. Because of this, Vico held that the first perceptions of all cultures were structurally consistent, a means of thinking through things (*bricolage*, as the anthropologist Claude Lévi-Strauss would call it). (Kunze, 2012, p. viii)

The idea that the relationship between mind and culture is basically egocentric and embodied was clearly expressed in some of the axioms that Vico placed as principles of his "new science," namely the science of human civilization. I will refer here to three among these axioms that represent an insightful starting point for the discussion of the process of formation and use of abstractions and personification in the human experience of "nation." The very first axiom of Vico's "new science" states: "Because of the indefinite nature of the human mind, wherever it is lost in ignorance, man makes himself the measure of all things" (Vico, 1744/1948, p. 54).

Vico's idea was that the leap of primitive human beings to the condition of cultural beings happened through an act of imaginative anthropomorphism of natural phenomena (Granatella, 2015). In other words, they imagined the cause of overwhelming natural events (thunder, storm, light, and darkness, etc.) in the form of an enormously powerful anthropomorphic being: the imaginative universal form of *divinity*. This incredibly original invention allowed the spring of cultural phenomena and the human capability to use these "imaginatively abstract" concepts to regulate individual and collective behavior.

They make possible a model of concept formation where imagining is not simply an alteration of ordinary thought, but it is a different process of thinking in which the reference to concrete human experience is brought together with the need to find concepts both universal and shareable. (Granatella, 2015, p. 191)

A set of distinctions and relationships of "otherness" appeared for the first time together with human history. For instance, the distinction between "human" and "nonhuman" arouse from the first imaginative act of divinity, and it was a distinction as well as a relationship between the realm of egocentric experience and the realm of allocentric phenomena, that could include a wide field of experience and meaning. What is not-human can be either "divine," "natural," but also "quasi-human," "quasi-divine," and "quasi-natural." This field of productivity for human sensemaking was, according to Vico, fundamental for the development of human civilizations. At the same time, this complementary process of distinction and relation led to a progressive differentiation of local solutions to the existential problems. Thus, the different communities of humans, who were spreading around different environments, developed diverse "traditions." This led to further domains of distinctions and relationships, as Vico states in two other axioms:

Every nation, according to him, whether Greek or barbarian, has had the same conceit that it before all other nations invented the comforts of human life and that its remembered history goes back to the very beginning of the world. (Vico, 1744/1948, p. 55)

and

To this conceit of the nations there may be added that of the scholars, who will have it that whatever they know is as old as the world. (Vico, 1744/1948, p. 55)

At the collective level, the historical differentiation of local cultures, distinctions, and relationships take the form of cultural continuity and discontinuity: "as enculturated human beings we indeed can and commonly do interpret the words and conduct of the others 'by our own lights'" (Norton, 1996, p. 44–45).

The more a collective of people builds a system of ideas, institutions, and artifacts, working for the continuity of the cultural transmission, the more distinctions are co-generated (Tateo, 2016a). At the same time, distinctions call for relationships, so that human collectives cannot help to establish "otherness" without relating to it, whether in the form of communication, marriage, war, killing, or superstition. Besides, the co-generative movement of psychological development and cultural development leads to a well-known process in which the development of cultural artifacts allows for richer social interactions and possibilities of exploring the world, thus having more possibilities of establishing new distinctions, based on praxis and technology, and richer relationships in a complementary form. Vico's initial intuition of a co-development of imaginative processes and artifacts in the relationship between mind and culture has later on been developed in different forms by Cattaneo (Tateo, 2015b), Wundt and Moscovici (Tateo & Iannaccone, 2012), and developed in the concept of crystallized imagination (Vygotsky, 2004).

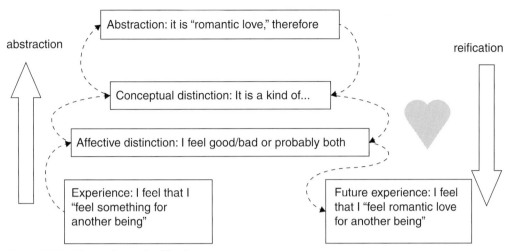

Figure 22.1: Abstraction and reification.

From the collective action, some objects of individual experience are elaborated in the form of more abstract concepts. They then become available to the community once detached from the contingent conditions of their creation (Tateo, 2015c). These "externalized" or "crystallized" forms are then used as frameworks to make sense of the future experiences. Following the semiotic principle that all human psychological life is mediated by signs – that are constructed, maintained, and demolished as they form dynamic hierarchies (Valsiner, 2014) – one can see how this process of abstraction/reification occurs through specific signs, that are both linguistic and iconic (Tateo, 2015c). For instance, once that the concept of "romantic love" is created out of experience, it becomes collectively available to guide the sensemaking of I–Other relationships and self-regulating the future course of action (Figure 22.1).

What is crucial here is the fact that "romantic love" (as well as "fatherland" and "holiness") is a specific sign which is produced as abstract generalization of a specific experience, later acquiring its own ontological status of "reality." We can historically trace back the moment in which this sign has been created[1] and has become a collec-tive resource. But we treat things as if they were abstract concepts and concepts as if they were real things (Tateo, 2015c). So, "romantic love" *is* something and can *cause* events in the real world. People can regulate their own conducts by inhibiting or promoting specific actions and by attaching specific meanings to those conducts. The constant renovation of the social world is made possible through the complementary movement of abstraction and reification that are features of language. So, the concept of "romantic love" is not only used to frame and guide future experience (it is "romantic love," *therefore . . .*), but it is also provided of a "body," so it is reified in a range of artifacts and practices (cupids, chocolates, valentines, songs, rings, movies, honey moons – you name it). To observe the dramatic power of this complementary movement of abstraction and reification one can easily visit any public place (shops, restaurants, ballrooms, cruise boats) on Valentine's Day to see what a huge range of very mundane and concrete economic activities flourish around this abstract concept and how quite ordinary objects (like chocolate and flowers) become the reification of this concept so I can actually *give* and *receive* romantic love.

I argue that the psychological process allowing the creation of the concept of "romantic love" (initially probably by an anonymous bard of the high Middle Ages and today by the massive industry of chocolate!) and the reification of it (so that a normal chocolate becomes a "Bacio Perugina"), is of the same nature of Vico's imaginative universals (Granatella, 2015; Tateo, 2015c). This is a process regulated by a particular form of imaginative and affective logic that:

> primarily uses metaphor "conveyed by analogy of physical properties to designate *abstract mental operations*." Metaphor therefore is the original form of raising the particular to the universal by means of pictorial representation to achieve an immediate revelation of the whole . . . In the logic of imagination, the "example" acts as the first form of the coordination of ideas, and this "example" which, as Vico puts it, "contents itself with a *single similar thing*" and belongs to the domain of the logic of imagination assumes the same function as induction does in rational logic. Vico explicitly distinguishes rational induction, "which needs *several similar things*" from the "example," which requires only *one* similarity in order to convince. (Grassi, 1976, p. 568; emphases in original)

In this sense, the imaginative and affective logic I am outlining here, on the basis of Vico's insight, works as a process of *inductive abduction*, that leads to the creation of abstract signs (e.g., love, homeland, etc.) working as affective universal concepts (Valsiner's hypergeneralized signs, 2014). Several questions now arise from this first argument. Who (and how) has the power to create these abstractions? Who (and how) has the power to create these symbolic resources (Zittoun, 2007)? How do these imaginative processes work in collective life? How the complementary processes of distinction/relation, continuity/discontinuity, and abstraction/reification can be used to understand the kind of individual and collective phenomena related to intangible concepts? I will try to provide some initial answers in the next section by considering a concept slightly more trivial than "romantic love": the concept of "nation."

22.3 National Identity and the Imagined Communities

One of the most "vichians" among contemporary scholars is probably Benedict Anderson. In his seminal work he adopts an original perspective to account for the origin, development, and historical meaning of "nationalism." He clearly echoes Vico's idea of the study of civilizations when he states:

> nationness, as well as nationalism, are cultural artifacts of a particular kind. To understand them properly we need to consider carefully how they have come into historical being, in what ways their meanings have changed over time, and why, today, they command such profound emotional legitimacy. (Anderson, 2006, p. 4)

Anderson's main claim is that the concept of "nation" is the historical product of a collective construction, namely an imaginative production, that emerged at the edge of nineteenth century and developed in contemporary word, going through several transformations while keeping its nature of cultural artifact. A very important element in the historical process leading to the construction of this cultural artifact is the progressive detachment from the individual characters of kings and heroes. Rancière (1994) shows how the conception of history slowly moved from the "chronicles" and "genealogies" of royal families to a more collective and abstract conception:

> a new history of things is possible only on the condition that we hold fast to the reality of names and particularly to those names that succeed the name of the king – France, the native land, the nation, those "personified abstractions" denounced by the empiricist routine of the chronicles. (Rancière, 1994)

Figure 22.2 *The Triumph of Henry IV*, Peter Paul Rubens, oil on wood (ca. 1630), Metropolitan Museum Online Collection, New York. http://images.metmuseum.org/CRDImages/ep/web-large/DT5154.jpg.

Both Rancière (1994) and Anderson (2006) point to the affective relationships established by people with their rulers and their collective subjects. The ideal of the collectivity was literally personified and embodied by the "body" of the king. This was a sacred body that was kept apart from public exposure, from the corroding gaze of the mob. It was carefully exposed in very few and solemn events, that confirmed the sacredness of that personification exactly through their rarity (Figure 22.2).

In this oil sketch Rubens depicts king Henry IV (1553–1610) entering Paris in an ancient Roman triumph style. It is a preliminary sketch of a painting that is located on the end wall of the east gallery of the *Palais de Luxembourg* in Paris, among a cycle of twenty-four canvases illustrating the life of Henry IV. In this powerful drawing, it is very evident how the "body of the king" is depicted as a sacred object. Several elements concur to establish this kind of affective imme-diate feeling into the observer. First, the body is put in a higher position on a golden coach, on the model of ancient Romans. Then, the king is holding an olive branch, reminding the common depictions of the triumphal entrance of the Christ in Jerusalem. The crowd is depicted like a tide which is lifting the coach toward the shore, emphasizing even more the figure of the king, who is meanwhile crowned with laurel by the allegory of lofty Victory.

During the eighteenth century, things started to change, until they culminated in the sacrilegious act through which that very same tide, who had previously raised the king's body, ended up beheading the very same body. Yet, what can replace the body of the king? How can people establish a different affective relationship with a collective of fellows? Anderson (2006) claims that a different imaginative product started to emerge at that moment: the concept of nation.

It is imagined as sovereign because the concept was born in an age in which Enlightenment and Revolution were destroying the legitimacy of the divinely ordained, hierarchical dynastic realm. Coming to maturity at a stage of human history when even the most devout adherents of any universal religion were inescapably confronted with the living pluralism of such religions, and the allomorphism between each faith's ontological claims and territorial stretch, nations dream of being free, and, if under God, directly so. The gage and emblem of this freedom is the sovereign state. (Anderson, 2006, p. 7)

The collective life was changing as fast as the technological and economical innovations were establishing new forms of social distinctions and relationships. Namely, Anderson (2006) argues that the modern idea of nation began to spread in the colonies overseas among an indigenous middle class in the English colonies on the east coast of North America and in the Spanish and Portuguese dominions in Central and South America that was gaining influence. The reason for that primacy was originated by the distinction between European-born, Creoles, and indigenous, that the ruling class of Continental origin had established in those societies. These distinctions (Figure 22.3) implicd that European-born ruling class could have access to the higher functions in connection with the Continental governments (for instance becoming viceroy), while relying on the Creoles (born in the colonies from European families) to become the lower administrative functionaries, traveling the country and aspiring to finally land in the capital city. The *indios* were instead the lower or slave workforces, at the margin of the state but fundamental as number.

The distinction between European and non-European born, in which the former is a closed set, while the latter is a potentially infinite set, was instrumental for the colonizers to mark a power structure, and to naturalize a dominance relationship. But this very same distinc-

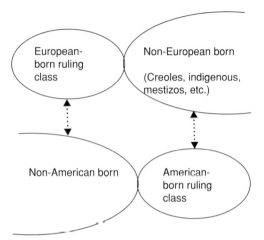

Figure 22.3 Changing configurations of distinctions and relationships.

tion was also establishing a relationship of communality between all those American-born that were indeed provided with a different form of mutual relationship. For a certain period at the beginning of nationalist movements in South America, indeed, also the *indios* were somehow to be included as citizens of the national state, though with a subaltern position. According to Anderson (2006), there were three main factors that determined this reversal of distinction/relationship structures in favor of the emergence of national states: (a) the fact that a common national language was accidental, derived from the colonizers; (b) the development toward capitalistic colonial economy, so that a centralized state administration required a large number of local functionaries traveling the country; and (c) the diffusion of print media, that became a form of imaginative relation between people. Literate middle-class citizens were imaginarily united every morning by the same gesture of opening a newspaper and feeling a sense of abstract and affective familiarity with anonymous thousands that were supposed to do the same.

These elements led to the transformation of the national versions of the colonizers' language (an administrative tool for large and diverse territories) to language as a *prius*, an element of distinction and a feature of originality. This also led to a progressive reification of the latter, and a praxis becomes naturalized as a feature of the national identity. Speaking the local version of Spanish, Portuguese, or English, and reading newspapers run in the same languages became a sign of national identity, at the same time a relationship with thousands of anonymous fellow citizens and a distinction from the non-Americans (Anderson, 2006).

One can believe the distinction/relation complementarity to be a historically situated phenomenon in the development of nationalism. It is instead a very current issue, for instance, in the present debate in the United States. Goldstein (2015) shows how the same cultural artifact (the American Constitution) can be at the same time the grounding principle for establishing the relationship of mutual belonging for all American citizens and the basis for discrimination and advocacy of the use of political violence.

If the Constitution defines who we are, it equally defines who we are not. Constitutional nationalism has long provided a neutral, patriotic language for expressing restrictive ideas about who is and who is not a real American. (Goldstein, 2015, p. 5)

In his study on the development of constitutional movements and militias in the United States, the very same struggle for the definition of what is "American" immediately evokes the complementary distinction of what is "non-American." Thus, the very core of "American creed" becomes the starting point either for social inclusion of minorities or for violent action of deliberate killing (like in the Oklahoma City bombing in 1995) and "martyrdom" (the death of 76 in the Branch Davidian compound in Waco, Texas).

The concept of nation, is thus an abstract naturalization of a set of distinctions and relationships, it is:

an imagined political community – and imagined as both inherently limited and sovereign. It is imagined because the members of even the smallest nation will never know most of their fellow-members, meet them, or even hear of them, yet in the minds of each lives the image of their communion . . . In fact, all communities larger than primordial villages of face-to-face contact (and perhaps even these) are imagined. Communities are to be distinguished, not by their falsity/genuineness, but by the style in which they are imagined. (Anderson, 2006, p. 6)

Once the abstract concept of nation has been created and collectively adopted, as we argued in the first section, it starts to guide the sensemaking process and the orientation of future experiences. So, no difference, in psychological terms, between the two statements "I do X, *therefore* I am Italian" and "I am Italian *therefore*, I do X." Nevertheless, for the abstraction of "nation" to be effective, it must go from the people experience back to the realm of objects, becoming reified in order to "cause" something in the world. When this model of nation became an active political movement that led to the emergence of national-states – in America first and later in Europe – the concept of "nation" required a body. This kind of imaginative and affective logic is surprisingly similar to the conduct of schizophrenic patients:

Another characteristic that I described in the schizophrenic is the concretization of the concept. What in a normal person is conceived of in an abstract way assumes a concrete, perceptual, or quasi-perceptual representation in schizophrenic thinking. Vico described similar processes in ancient people . . . Thus concepts become personified, anthropomorphized. In some mentally ill patients, particularly the schizophrenic, the abstract idea is translated in to a perception, in the form of a hallucination, fantasy, or delusion which is mediated by images (Arieti, 1976, p. 748)

Although in this kind of patients the process that links abstract and concrete levels seems to short-circuit, it still gives us a hint into the process itself. Some kind of hallucinatory nuance seems to characterize the individual experience in the context of collective phenomena such as those described by Wagner, Rämmer, and Kello (Chapter 7, this volume) or any form of collective ritual (political gatherings, musical events, football matches) that aim at promoting the performance of the individual into the collective context (externalization) as well as the performance of the collective into the individual (internalization) (Valsiner, 2014).

22.4 In Search of a New Body

The new abstract concept of "nation" needs a new concrete body. It needs to be reified in images and metaphors that allow the establishment of affective relationships. A repertoire of these images, or *topoi* (Rosa, 2007), was somehow already available since the Renaissance. For instance, the Italian poet Dante Alighieri in the fourteenth century had already provided in his "Divine Comedy" the first vivid personalization of the concept of "nation." In the sixth *canto* of the *Inferno*, he meets the soul of a country-fellowman and throws one of his famous poetic invectives:

Ah, slavish Italy! thou inn of grief!
Vessel without a pilot in loud storm!
Lady no longer of fair provinces,
But brothel-house impure! this gentle spirit,
Even from the pleasant sound of his dear land
Was prompt to greet a fellow citizen
With such glad cheer: while now thy living ones
In thee abide not without war; and one
Malicious gnaws another; ay, of those
Whom the same wall and the same moat contains.
(Dante Alighieri, 1909–1914:
Canto VI, verses 76–85).

In these *tercets*, Dante creates the personification of Italy as a lady, creating at once the first collective image of Italy as a nation and its first personified allegory.

Yet, allegorical personifications were already available (Whitman, 2003) and used in the construction of political discourses long before the birth of the modern concept of nation, drawing on the infinite repertoire of classical mythology (Figure 22.4).

Rubens's canvas *Consequences of War* was painted during the Thirty Years War between Catholics and Protestants in Europe. It is an allegorical representation of the devastation provoked by the long conflict on a global scale. Its message was so powerful that Pablo Picasso draw directly from it his inspiration in the conception of Guernica 300 years later. Europe is represented in the left part of the painting as a woman in a black dress to show grief and suffering. The small angel to her immediate bottom left carries a cross-topped globe that represents the Christian world. She is running from the Janus temple with the open doors, that represents the war time according to the ancient Roman tradition. Rubens was also a diplomat, and through this painting, he tried to deliver his passionate message supporting the end of the war, which involved Spain, France, Sweden, Denmark, the Netherlands, Austria, Poland, the Ottoman Empire, and the Holy Roman Empire. What is relevant in this picture is the fact that even a more abstract concept at that time, namely Europe, could be represented through allegorical personification, in order to raise an affective relationship with the observer more powerful and expressive than any conceptual form.

Personification and anthropomorphism of concepts was a very common feature of human civilization, as we learn from Vico. They were a fundamental cultural artifact to create abstract generalizations from concrete experience, and then to build stable systems of sensemaking for the future events (Granatella, 2015). At the time in which Anderson (2006) places the emergence and raise of the modern concept of nation, early personifications in the Western world praised the majestic nature and the unity of national

Figure 22.4 Peter Paul Rubens, *Consequences of War*, 1638–1639, Galleria Palatina, Florence.

communities, including Britannia, Germania, Hibernia, Helvetia, Polonia, Italia, and Mother Russia (Figure 22.5 and 22.6).

The poster in Figure 22.6 represents the "Triple Entente" allies in World War I, with a Cyrillic

Figure 22.5 *Italia and Germania* by Friedrich Overbeck, 1811–1828, Neue Pinakothek, Munich, Germany. https://commons.wikimedia .org/wiki/File:Friedrich_Overbeck_008.jpg.

inscription on top that reads "concord." There are the female personifications of France (Marianne on the left with a heart, [*sic*]), Russia (Mother Russia holding an Orthodox Cross), and England (Lady Britannia on the right with an anchor). Other personifications of abstract concepts, indirectly related to the concept of nations are, for instance, the Statue of Liberty, Columbia, or the Lady of Justice. The most parts of these images where related to the original model of the goddess Athena, as representation of the most important democratic state of the antiquity. Besides, it did not lack representations of collectivity in the form of the every man or citizenry like Deutscher Michel, Monsieur Dupont, Uncle Sam, and John Bull (Hobsbawm & Ranger, 2012; Lonchuk & Rosa, 2011). Nevertheless, if we consider that the active citizenship was attributed only to men, it is not surprising that the personification took the form of beautiful, curvy, and somehow ambiguous women, reserving to the female audience the privilege of striving for this ideal model of patriotic femininity (Figure 22.7).

Figure 22.6 Female personifications of France, Russia, and Britain in a 1914 Russian poster. https://en
.wikipedia.org/wiki/File:Triple_Entente.jpg.

Figure 22.7 Demonstration against same-sex marriage in Paris on January 13, 2013, photo by © Marie-Lan Nguyen/Wikimedia Commons, CC BY 2.5. https://commons.wikimedia.org/w/index .php?curid=23849328.

Although the process of personification can also take place through the use of metaphorical language in political discourse (Leith & Soule, 2011), at least since the recurring metaphor of the body-state from classical antiquity, there is a specific power in the construction of a "body" of the nation. I argue that this special affective relationship is based on an imaginative process that links the abstract concept to its reification. Yet, before moving ahead to further theoretical elaborations, I have to mention another kind of reification and embodiment of the concept of nation. The body of a national state is also its territory with its affective correlate: the landscape.

If politics is the art of possible, then possibilities for legitimacy include appeal to the earth itself, to the aesthetics of landscape, the native (in the sense "one born in"), and to autochthony. Failing nations, then, the land is sacred. (Thornton, 1996, p. 153)

The administrative national territory becomes an abstraction of the real land, through census and cartography is build a representation that become malleable matter in the hand of the creators of nations (Anderson, 2006). We are still suffering today from this lack of consistency between the imagined territory and the lived one. A very famous example is that of the so-called

Sykes–Picot Agreement in 1916, in which two almost anonymous functionaries of the British and France foreign affairs designed the new status quo of the Middle East simply drawing a straight line (Figure 22.8) on a map (Barr, 2011).

This historical document is the map, showing Eastern Turkey in Asia, Syria, and western Persia, that was used to define the areas of control and influence agreed between the British and the French after the fall of the Ottoman Empire. The map is signed in the bottom right corner by Mark Sykes and François Georges-Picot and dated May 8, 1916. It clearly shows that we are in the presence of a different kind of imagined territory, the abstract representation of the map on which one of the most long-lasting wars of the last century was created by drawing "a line from the 'e' in Acre to the last 'k' in Kirkuk" (Barr, 2011, p. 18).

The affective landscape and the conceptual territory are both equally imagined, suggests Anderson (2006). Usually they do not overlap, suggests history. Nevertheless, they co-define, together with the fuzzy linguistic communality, another set of distinctions and relationships.

The nation is imagined as limited because even the largest of them, encompassing perhaps a billion living human beings, has finite, if elastic, boundaries, beyond which lie other nations. No nation imagines itself coterminous with mankind. (Anderson, 2006, p. 7)

The interplay of territory and landscape creates, and is created by, the construction of imagined boundaries. Rivers, planes, straits, and high grounds are existential and practical points of reference that at the same time establish the discontinuity and the continuity of the experience – both unite and divide (Marsico, 2016). While only colonial functionaries can be passionate for a map in 1916, it is a matter of fact that a hundred thousand people felt so passionately for a landscape to be able to kill or die for it.

Two very interesting examples of the affective embodiment established in landscape come

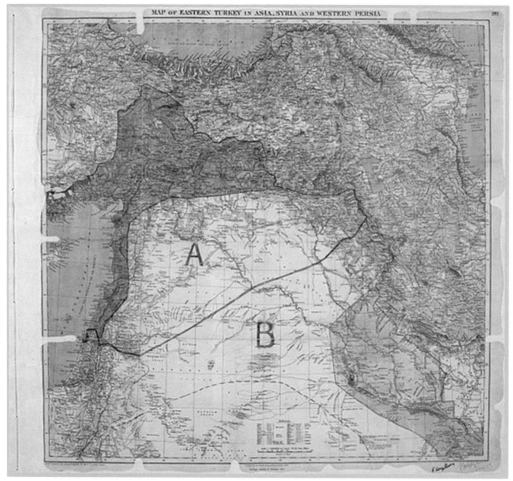

Figure 22.8 Map of Sykes–Picot Agreement. Source: Royal Geographical Society, The National Archives (UK). https://en.wikipedia.org/wiki/Sykes%E2%80%93Picot_Agreement#/media/File: MPK1¶426_Sykes_Picot_Agreement_Map_signed_8_May_1916.jpg.

from a recovered and a lost land. The former is accounted by Thornton (1996) as follows:

On 9 May 1994, Nelson Mandela addressed the people of South Africa on the occasion of the opening of the new Parliament. He did not speak of "the people" or "the nation." As he stood on the balcony of the Cape Town City Hall with the majestic Table Mountain as his backdrop, he pointed to the landscape on which the "beginning of the fateful convergence" of Black and White had begun. If nations are, as Benedict Anderson as argued, "imagined communities," then countries

are imagined geometries of landscape. South Africa, the country, is a geometry for conflict and accommodation, but above all it is a landscape. Looking out over the bay to Robben Island on the horizon, he spoke of his own imprisonment and subsequent freedom. With a few gestures to the landscape, he thus summed up over 350 years of history as one might sum up the shape of jelly by pointing to its container. (Thornton, 1996, p. 153)

In Mandela's discourse, it is the landscape that "imagines" the nation, as it fills with his affective consistency the abstract conceptualization of

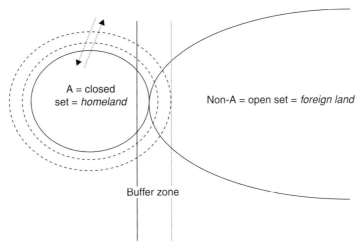

Figure 22.9 The imagined land.

a new and somehow nonexisting community, like the scattered and multiform South African population. But there is another possibility, while in one case the landscape can define the collectivity (e.g., the highlanders in Scotland), in another case is the collectivity (understood as a network of affective relationships) that defines the landscape. This latter case is exemplified by Michael Jackson's account of the experience of refugees:

Second, just as ego and alter are implicated in any conception or sense of who one is, so there are seldom fixed or impermeable boundaries between the worlds of persons, words, ideas, animals, and things. Accordingly, ancestral homelands, family graves, family dwellings, spoken words, personal names, material possessions, spirit entities, and significant others may figure severally, equally, and actively in the field of the intersubjective. Experientially, all these elements merge with and become indispensable parts of one's own being; one cannot live without them. As such, subjectivity is not really a fixed attribute of persons, but the product of any purposeful and committed activity we enter into with those we love and the things we value. This view is poignantly captured in the words of a Greek Cypriot refugee, pining for home. "You ask me, what is the essence of the village, if it's the fields and the houses, which we've lost, or

the people, our fellow . . . villagers. My answer is that it's the people and the houses and fields – all together" (cited in Loizos 1981:131). (Jackson, 2002, p. 66)

The two examples define a complementary relationship between the landscape as a lived by experience, an intersubjective context for meaningful event to happen, and at the same time an abstract concept that guides the affective relationship of the dwellers. Any landscape is anthropized, both in the sense that can be shaped by the human activity (e.g., the unmistakable atmosphere of the hills of Tuscany or the fields of Ireland is the outcome of millenary dwelling), and in the sense that it a cultural construction of the observer. Once the specific identity of the landscape is abstracted (it becomes the English, French, or Italian landscape), then it constitutes the frame for the imagined dweller (the John Bull or the indigenous). The map and the landscape are the two ways in which the concrete affective experience of the place can be turned into the abstract concept of the "homeland," which, once created, frames the future experience of the "homelander" in return. The kind of distinction/relationship it establishes is depicted in Figure 22.9.

The creation of the imagined land begins with a very simple act of drawing an affective border that immediately evokes an affective distinction and requires a new form of affective relationship. The generally received version of the myth of the foundation of Rome is a very nice example of this process. The very simple act of digging a trench around the Palatine to define the city boundary, turned Romolus and Remus into a citizen and a foreigner. The imagined homeland immediately evoke the foreign land and its dwellers. Even the kinship must succumb to the powerful distinction of imagined boundaries (Marsico, 2016) and must be replaced by a new form of relationship. But the myth of Romulus and Remus does not tell us the whole story. It tells us that our relationship with the other is inevitably both egocentric and ethnocentric. We are self-centered in exploring the world and our embodied perspective goes toward the inner-outer direction, while the complementary perspective of the world is oriented according to the outer-inner opposite direction. So, our boundary making, the sign of the homeland, must necessarily create a closed set (Figure 22.9).

The most messianic nationalists do not dream of a day when all the members of the human race will join their nation in the way that it was possible, in certain epochs, for, say, Christians to dream of a wholly Christian planet. (Anderson, 2006, p. 7)

The complementary region that coexist with the bounded region is instead an open set of infinite possibilities, as we saw above. This is apparently only a binary opposition. The three elements (A; non-A; and their boundary zone), indeed, coexist and codefine each other (Marsico, 2016). Besides, the bounded region (A), though remaining a closed set, can dynamically expand or constrict over time in the relationship with the open set (non-A) in the buffer region, corresponding to the marginal instances of a given collectivity. Without this ternary system, no development is possible(Tateo, 2016a): when there is only in and

out, the situation is stuck and Remus can only perish.

Cultural psychology is just the discipline interested to the forms of tension, hybridization, and marginality that dwell in the buffer zones, and whose symbolic and material potential can lead to development over time (Tateo, 2016a). The contemporary world is full of these kinds of buffer zones (e.g., Crimea; Golan Heights; Malvinas/Falklands Islands; Senkaku/Diaoyutai Islands; Guarani Indios demarcated lands on the Brazilian territory; Alsace/Lorrain), in which all the different categories of homelander, foreigners, immigrants, refugees, nomads, and so on, are dynamically set as A–non-A in the different conditions over time, probably always dwelling the buffer zone, but changing as soon as the bounded region is expanding or constricting (dotted circles in Figure 22.9). The example of the American Constitution is extremely clear (Goldstein, 2015). The co-definition between the closed set "legitimate American citizens" and the open set "non-Americans" (potentially the rest of the world) has been sensibly changing over time in relation to the directionality of the interpretant: who establishes the view point and is also locating herself in the "A" position. It is exactly in the buffer zone where potentialities for social inclusion and civil rights movements can be express. But every definition of a new form of inclusion is at the same time the definition of an exclusion, so that the same buffer zone can be a space for the development of racist and segregationist movements.

The special virtues, as well as particular values and qualities, of the nation are established alongside the rejection and denial of those who do not share these attributes – who are seen as outsiders, excluded from the national community of values. While such "others" may well be foreigners, they may also be conationals and as much a physical part of the nation as anyone else. The process of construction of national identity is therefore inherently divisive, a process based as much on inclusion as on exclusion. (Lambert, 2006, p. 30)

Figure 22.10 Exotic at home and homeness in the exotic. Source: Photo by Luca Tateo (2013).

This complementary distinction is not geographical but symbolic. We can establish and maintain the complementarity between homeland and foreign-land almost everywhere, even in a "typical" Thai restaurant in a small Danish town (Figure 22.10).

People can go to an exotic restaurant in which a small fraction of a foreign land is reconstructed and find it perfectly normal to have national flags everywhere. On the other hand, it is exactly the meaning of being "at home," signaled by the Danish flags, that makes the restaurant "authentically" exotic. They co-define a comfortable buffer zone, in which it is possible to be "at home" and "exotic" at the same time.

Thus, the homeland and the foreign land, the body of the nation and its counterpart, dynamically co-define each other in the same way that the "body" of the national personification and the "foreign" body co-define each other (Figure 22.11).

So far, I have tried to show how the imaginative processes work in concrete to construct

the abstract concept of "nation," that denotes an imagined and somehow nonexisting cultural object, out of an affective distinction/relationship. The same imaginative processes, I have argued, allow to reify the concept again into an embodied image to which an affective relationship can be established (Tateo, 2017). The next question is then: how is it possible that such imaginative processes are internalized and externalized in everyday life, leading to actions like killing or dying for that intangible concept? How is it possible that:

regardless of the actual inequality and exploitation that may prevail in each, the nation is always conceived as a deep, horizontal comradeship. Ultimately it is this fraternity that makes it possible, over the past two centuries, for so many millions of people, not so much to kill, as willingly to die for such limited imaginings. (Anderson, 2006, p. 7)

There is a last type of "body" that is related to the reification of the nation. It is in a certain sense the "absent" or "anonymous" body of the average

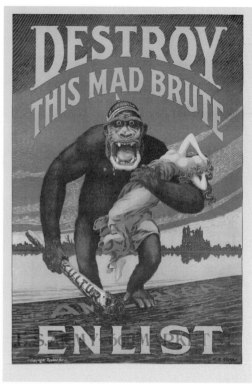

(a)   (b)

Figure 22.11 World War I propaganda posters advocating intervention. https://commons.wikimedia
.org/wiki/File:Danza_trieste_italia.jpg and https://commons.wikimedia.org/wiki/File:Harry_R._
Hopps,_Destroy_this_mad_brute_Enlist_-_U.S._Army,_03216u_edit.jpg.

citizen, the one who can be anyone of us exactly because is not really none of us, a product of the modern mass warfare: the unknown soldier. The psychoanalyst Richard Koenigsberg writes:

In war, the body and the blood of the sacrificed soldier give rise to the reality of the nation. Killing and dying substantiate the idea that nations exist. The sound and fury of the battle function to convince everyone that something profound and real is occurring. Warfare testifies to the existence of nations. Battle – the bodies of dead and wounded soldiers – anchors belief in material reality – persuading us that countries are more than social constructions. Surely, we reflect, human beings would not – could not – kill and die in the name of nothing. (Koenigsberg, 2009, p. 66)

We are asked to keep the memory of the unknown soldier's sacrifice for the nation in the very same moment in which we can only "imagine" him. According to Anderson (2006), what is buried in these cenotaphs are not the unidentifiable remains of unfortunate soldiers, yet rather the ghostly images of a nation. By a lack of knowledge (many of the actual identities of the buried, scattered bones) a certainty is created (what else they can be if not heroes, what identity they can have if not Italian, French, Argentinean, American, etc.?) (Anderson, 2006). The unknown soldier memorials (but also the collective memorials that read thousands of names, losing the individuality of the name in the anonymous crowd of the slaughter) show how the abstraction of the concept of "nation" is built on the concrete bones of the war victims, and the victims themselves become "heroes" only in function of the existence of the abstract concept of the nation. Besides, the abstract concept of the "unknown soldier" (a nonexisting object, to the extent that every soldier was formerly known at least by some of his kin) is originated by framing the war casualties into the concept of nation.

Needless to say that the function of this aid to collective memory is not made for remembering, but to guide the future actions of citizens toward the repetition of that "heroic" behavior. In this sense, the "unknown soldier" is a sign analogous to the "newspaper" (Anderson, 2006) in the construction of the intangible concept of "nation": it links anonymous and distant people exactly because of its impersonality. We imagine a collective gesture without knowing who actually is performing it, without possibility of refutation.

22.5 How Abstraction and Reification are Constructed in Collective Action

In classical rhetoric, there are different figures of substitution: metaphor, allegory, and metonymy. The role of metaphor in the construction of experience has been widely discussed (Lakoff & Johnson, 1980). Allegory is considered as a form of extended metaphor, in which the relationship established between two fields of meaning is unfolded through storytelling, like in the case of Plato's allegory of the cave. Metonymy is the rhetorical trope in which one name is replaced by another. Differently from metaphor, in which the replacement is made by creating a short circuit of meaning and in analogy in which two different objects are put together by similarity, in metonymy the two ideas arbitrarily stand for each other. In Hayden White's interpretation of Vico (H. V. White, 1976), the tropological transformations of speech figures, from metaphor, to metonymy, to synecdoche to irony, play a role in

the construction of the collective historical narratives, corresponding to the transformations of the society. But, as Vico himself claimed, not all the rhetorical figures have the same affective power and emotional involvement.

The theory of social representations, in so far as theory of collective knowledge, has focused on the figurative core of the metaphor (Wagner, Elejabarrieta & Lahnsteiner, 1995). So far I have described several examples of allegorical personifications that fall under the mechanism of metonymical substitution. Allegorical visualizations (e.g., Rubens' Europe, the Marianne, the Statue of Justice, etc.) personify abstract ideas by relating the concrete image and the intangible concept in an *affectively* loaded relationship. All iconoclastic movements were, and still are, aware and afraid of the immense epistemological and communicative *power* of metonymy (Kibbey, 1986). The human reception of the shift from text to figure, and from figure to text, is affective. For instance, in Islamic culture (which is icono-phobic) calligraphic art is the sense of the infinite potential within the word that gives rise to something else in the iconic representation (Marks, 2010, 270). Verbal meaning and patterns are interchangeable!

The existence (or destruction) of the image – as well as of the "word," like in the case of *damnatio memoriae* – is an immediate affectively loaded action on the idea itself. But the metonymical substitution is at the same time a relationship of identity and distinction. The concrete object is not the idea itself, allowing the use of metonymy to avoid the direct censorship to block the representation of the idea in explicit form. As both distinction and relationship, metonymy could be a considered general form of which metaphor and analogy represent special cases.[2] In the imaginative processes that I have outlined above, the things that establish a metonymic relationships are the concrete and the abstract, as shown in the example of the so-called "umbrella revolution" in Hong Kong, September 2014 (Figure 22.12).

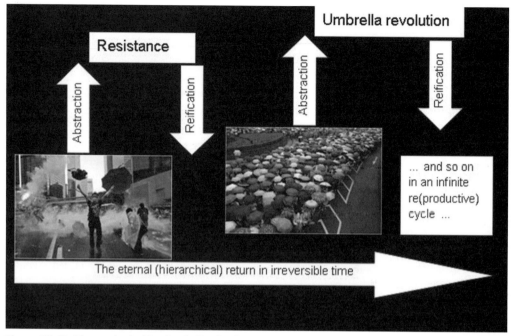

Figure 22.12 Abstraction/reification in "umbrella revolution."

During the fall of 2014, an "Occupy Central" movement started in Hong Kong to protest against the attempt of the Chinese central government to exert a stronger control over the local elections. Protestors used symbolic artifacts, including the yellow umbrella, to produce aesthetics experience that compressed messages about complex ideologies or reform initiatives into pictorial symbols and performative sessions (Lim, 2015). The individual action of using umbrellas as shields from police's tear gas is repeated and spread until, once detached from immediate experience, becomes a symbol of resistance. The human activity creates a generalizable abstract representation of life, starting from very situated individual acts. Such institutionalized representation, which is at the same time epistemological, ethical, and aesthetical, becomes a tradition, within which the meaning of the experiences to be make sense in return. The "umbrella" becomes then the image of the concept of "revolution." This abstract concept is reified in return into a creative collective action detached from the original cause (using an umbrella as a way of manifesting and writing slogans on top of them), and it is again abstracted in a symbol of the "umbrella revolution" at a higher hierarchical level (Figure 22.12 from left to right). At this step, a "life-form" (Simmel, 1918/2010) of the "umbrella revolution" has been collectively established, and any new individual action of protest and resistance will be framed into it. Once imagination has created a symbol that represents the cause of an event or a plan of future action, detaching it from the immediate experience of its presence, it can be used to self-regulate the behavior in different conditions and can be communicated to other people in different situations (Valsiner, 2014). This process has been at work in several moments of history. The aesthetic experience by metonymical substitution, once established as collective abstraction, framed in return the following events (e.g., Tea Parties, Prague Spring, Carnation Revolution, Jasmine Revolution, etc.) up to the most recent "Arab Spring" (Awad & Wagoner, 2015).

22.6 Conclusion

In this chapter, I have outlined a theoretical argument about the relationship between abstraction/reification and distinction/relationship in imaginative processes. I have shown how they can help us to understand the psychosocial dynamics through which collective experience, artifacts, and intangible concepts can establish affective, aesthetic, and ethic totalities that can lead to even extreme collective actions. The case of "nation" is an example of this process through which an abstract concept is created and used to frame in return the future oriented meaning-making. The realms of ideals and everyday life situation are put in relationship through several practices of ritual collective action (Mendonsa, 1982, p. 12). Michael Billig (1995) analyzes, for instance, the construction of "banal nationalism" in the everyday discursive practices. I suggest that there are more arenas in which the imaginative processes are at stake in the creation, elaboration, maintenance, and destruction of the affective relationships regulated by the kind of symbols that I have described above.

The intangible concepts, like "nation," are not only internalized and externalized through discursive practices. They are rather "enacted" in several public and private everyday ritual actions. Goldstein provides us with some hints:

From an early age, in picture books, the daily recitation of the Pledge of Allegiance, history textbooks, and countless other ways, Americans are taught that what unites us is a shared devotion to ideals found in the Constitution. We are also taught that these ideals are worth fighting for and worth dying for. (Goldstein, 2015, p. 5)

We are often the audience of the enactment and embodiment of abstract concepts like "nation," "patriotism," etc. We attend to public demonstrations, parades, theatrical performances that build powerful affective reifications of the ideals (Kruger, 1992).

But we often forget that we are also "actors" rather than mere "spectators." In her study on the Ghana school system, Cati Coe brilliantly shows how the public enactment of traditions in schools can be used to build a collective sense of belonging (Coe, 2005). She writes:

in Ghana schoolchildren have been turned into *performers* in national events. Through their performances, culture as drumming and dancing has become part of their bodily, habitual experience. Those performances have helped the schoolchildren to internalize a new set of assumptions about themselves and their world, to gain a new subjectivity that makes sense within a world they see as natural and real. (Coe, 2005, p. 54)

Of course, Coe (2005) demonstrates how concepts like "traditional" and "national" are themselves artifacts, imaginative abstractions, that are used by the different powers of Ghanaian society (government, churches, tribal chefs, etc.) to distinguish and gathering people according to their conception of the society to be. But what is crucial here is that the process of abstraction and reification takes place through active conducts. People internalize abstract concepts by acting them, typically in the school context. Surprisingly, this is an overlooked research topic. Despite the fact that these kind of activities are widespread (e.g., school plays for Christmas, Thanksgiving, celebration of national historical events, etc.), their role in the internalization and externalization of social values has not been stressed enough (Figure 22.13).

Yet according to the imaginative processes I have sketched above, this is one of the most

Figure 22.13 Schoolchildren rehearse for the Empire Games in New South Wales, 1938. State Library of New South Wales. https://commons.wikimedia .org/wiki/File:Empire_Games_rehearsal,_c._1938,_by_Sam_Hood_ (5423632955).jpg.

interesting forms of reification through personification: we "become" the abstract concept ourselves. We internalize the concept by enacting it, and reify it by personifying it through our body.

In the first part of this chapter, I have tried to outline the basic imaginative process through which, according to Vico, we create abstract universalistic concepts starting from concrete experience. In the second section, I have described the complementary process of reification, through which we give a body to abstractions, and I have applied it to Anderson's (2006) concept of "imagined community." Though I have used mainly examples based on iconic representations, the same analysis can be conducted on different symbol complexes, such as national anthems (Lauenstein et al., 2015). My main point is that the relationship between linguistic and iconic dimensions is constitutive of every type of symbol. In the case of allegorical personification, it is easier to show the work of the imaginative and affective logic that leads to the creation of abstraction through inductive abduction, and the metonymical substitution of the abstract concept with the concrete object in return.

Finally, I have proposed that the next step should be the study of those everyday ritual events in which we enact this process, for instance, in the schoolchildren school rehearsals. We still need a better understanding of the processes through which we create abstract concepts from everyday collective experience and then use those cultural artifacts to guide our future conduct. Only in this way can we come to account for those sometimes astonishing phenomena through which nonexisting and intangible ideals (like "nation," "tradition," "love," "freedom," "gods," etc.) can become so "real" to exert an effect on people's real life. I have tried to outline a theory of imaginative processes that could play a small part in this process of discovery by hopefully fostering more research idea(l)s, in which the complex forms of human activity return to be the focus of the psychological sciences (Tateo, 2017).

Notes

1 This is the sense for instance of the use of the etymological and philological methods in Vico's *New Science* (Vico, 1744/1948).
2 Interestingly, also Jacques Lacan identified metaphor and metonymy as the two fundamental mechanisms through which the unconscious tries to foil the censorship constituted by the symbolic order's established categories of language and avoid the payment of the symbolic debt (Bracher, 1999).

References

Alighieri, Dante (1909–1914). *The Divine Comedy* (trans. by Henry F. Cary, The Harvard Classics, vol. 20). New York: P. F. Collier & Son.

Anderson, B. (2006). *Imagined Communities: Reflections on the Origin and Spread of Nationalism*. New York: Verso.

Arieti, S. (1976). Vico and modern psychiatry. *Social Research*, 43(4), 739–752.

Awad, S. H. & Wagoner, B. (2015). Agency and creativity in the midst of social change. In C. W. Gruber, M. G. Clark, S. H. Klempe & J. Valsiner (Eds.), *Constraints of Agency: Explorations of Theory in Everyday Life* (pp. 229–243). New York: Springer.

Barr, J. (2011). *A Line in the Sand: Britain, France and the Struggle that Shaped the Middle East*. London: Simon & Schuster.

Becker, E. (1968). *The Structure of Evil: An Essay on the Unification of the Science of Man*. New York: Free Press.

Billig, M. (1995). *Banal Nationalism*. London: SAGE.

Bracher, M. (1999). *The Writing Cure: Psychoanalysis, Composition, and the Aims of Education*. Carbondale: Southern Illinois University Press.

Coe, C. (2005). *Dilemmas of Culture in African Schools: Youth, Nationalism, and the Transformation of Knowledge*. Chicago: University of Chicago Press.

Freud, S. (2001). Thoughts for the times on war and death. *Standard Edition of the Complete Psychological Works of Sigmund Freud* (vol. 14, pp. 273–302). London: Vintage.

Goldstein, J. A. (2015). To kill and die for the constitution: How devotion to the constitution leads to violence. Roger Williams University Legal Studies Paper no. 158. Retrieved from http://ssrn.com/abstract=2570893.

Granatella, M. (2015). Imaginative universals and human cognition in *The New Science* of Giambattista Vico. *Culture & Psychology*, 21(2), 185–206. DOI: 10.1177/1354067X15575795.

Grassi, E. (1976). The priority of common sense and imagination: Vico's philosophical relevance today. *Social Research*, 43(3), 553–580.

Hobsbawm, E. & Ranger, T. (Eds.). (2012). *The Invention of Tradition*. Cambridge: Cambridge University Press.

Jackson, M. (2002). *The Politics of Storytelling: Violence, Transgression, and Intersubjectivity*. Copenhagen: Museum Tusculanum Press.

Kibbey, A. (1986). *The Interpretation of Material Shapes in Puritanism: A Study of Rhetoric, Prejudice, and Violence*. Cambridge: Cambridge University Press.

Koenigsberg, R. A. (2009). *Nations Have the Right to Kill: Hitler, the Holocaust, and War*. New York: Library of Social Science.

Kruger, L. (1992). *The National Stage: Theatre and Cultural Legitimation in England, France, and America*. Chicago: University of Chicago Press.

Kunze, D. (2012). *Thought and Place: The Architecture of Imagination in the Philosophy of Giambattista Vico*. Boalsburg, PA: Cyrano.

Jovchelovitch, S. (2012). Narrative, memory and social representations: A conversation between history and social psychology. *Integrative Psychological and Behavioural Science*, 46(4), 440–456. DOI: 10.1007/s12124-012-9217-8.

Lakoff, G. & Johnson, M. (1980). *Metaphors We Live By*. Chicago: University of Chicago Press.

Lambert, P. (2006). Myth, manipulation, and violence: Relationships between national identity and political violence. In W. Fowler & P. Lambert (Eds.), *Political Violence and the Construction* of National Identity in Latin America (pp. 19–36). Basingstoke, UK: Palgrave Macmillan.

Lauenstein, O., Murer, J. S., Boos, M., & Reicher, S. (2015). "Oh motherland I pledge to thee … ": A study into nationalism, gender and the representation of an imagined family within national anthems. Nations and Nationalism, 21(2), 309–329.

Leith, M. S. & Soule, D. P. (2011). Political Discourse and National Identity in Scotland. Edinburgh: Edinburgh University Press.

Lewin, K. (1948). Resolving Social Conflicts. Washington, DC: American Psychological Association.

Lim, T. W. (2015). The aesthetics of Hong Kong's "Umbrella Revolution" in the first ten days: A historical anatomy of the first phase (27 Oct 2014 to 6 October 2014) of Hong Kong's Umbrella Revolution. East Asia, 32(1), 83–98.

Liu, Y. & O'Halloran, K. L. (2009). Intersemiotic texture: Analyzing cohesive devices between language and images. Social Semiotics, 19(4), 367–388. DOI: 10.1080/10350330903361059.

Lonchuk, M. & Rosa, A. (2011). Voices of graphic art images. In M. Märtsin, B. Wagoner, E.-L. Aveling, I. Kadianaki, & L. Whittaker (Eds.), Dialogicality in Focus (pp. 129–144). New York: Nova Science.

Ma, J. (2014). The synergy of Peirce and Vygotsky as an analytical approach to the multimodality of semiotic mediation. Mind, Culture, and Activity, 21(4), 374–389. DOI: 10.1080/10749039.2014.913294.

Marks, L. U. (2010). Words dream of being flowers, birds dream of language. In S. Zielinski & E. Fürlus (Eds.), Variantology 4: On Deep Time Relations of Arts, Sciences and Technologies in the Arabic-Islamic World and Beyond (pp. 267–288). Cologne, Germany: Walther König.

Marsico, G. (2016). Borderland. Culture & Psychology, 22(2), 206–215.

Mendonsa, E. L. (1982). The Politics of Divination: A Processual View of Reactions to Illness and Deviance among the Sisala of Northern Ghana. Berkeley: University of California Press.

Milgram, S. (1977). The Individual in a Social World: Essays and Experiments. Reading, MA: Addison-Wesley.

Norton, D. L. (1996). Imagination, Understanding, and the Virtue of Liberality. Lanham, MD: Rowman & Littlefield.

Peirce, C. S. (1998). What is a sign? In Peirce Edition Project (Ed.), The Essential Peirce: Selected Philosophical Writings (pp. 4–10). Bloomington: Indiana University Press.

Rancière, J. (1994). The Names of History on the Poetics of Knowledge. Minneapolis: University of Minnesota Press.

Rosa, A. (2007). Acts of psyche: Actuations as synthesis of semiosis and action. In J. Valsiner & A. Rosa (Eds.), Cambridge Handbook of Sociocultural Psychology (pp. 205–237). New York: Cambridge University Press.

Simmel, G. (1918/2010). The View of Life: Four Metaphysical Essays with Journal Aphorisms (trans. by J. A. Y. Andrews & D. N. Levine). Chicago: University of Chicago Press.

Tateo, L. (2015a). Giambattista Vico and the principles of cultural psychology: A programmatic retrospective. History of the Human Sciences, 28(1), 44–65. DOI: 10.1177/0952695114564628.

Tateo, L. (2015b). The providence of associated minds: Agency in the thought of Giambattista Vico and the origins of social and cultural psychology. In C. W. Gruber, M. G. Clark, S. H. Klempe, & J. Valsiner (Eds.), Constraints of Agency: Explorations of Theory in Everyday Life (pp. 31–43). New York: Springer.

Tateo, L. (2015c). Giambattista Vico and the psychological imagination. Culture & Psychology, 21(2), 145–161. DOI: 10.1177/1354067X15575695.

Tateo, L. (2016a). Toward a cogenetic cultural psychology. Culture & Psychology, 22(3), 433–447. DOI: 10.1177/1354067X16645297.

Tateo, L. (2016b). What imagination can teach us about higher mental functions. In J. Valsiner, G. Marsico, N. Chaudhary, T. Sato, & V. Dazzani (Eds.), Psychology as the Science of Human

Being: The Yokohama Manifesto (pp. 149–164). New York: Springer.

Tateo, L. (Ed.). (2017). *Giambattista Vico and the New Psychological Science*. New Brunswick, NJ: Transaction Publishers.

Tateo, L. & Iannaccone, A. (2012). Social representations, individual and collective mind: A study of Wundt, Cattaneo and Moscovici. *Integrative Psychological and Behavioral Science*, 46(1), 57–69. DOI 10.1007/s12124-011-9162-y.

Thornton, R. (1996). The potentials of boundaries in South Africa: Steps towards a theory of the social edge. In R. P. Werbner, & T. O. Ranger (Eds.), *Postcolonial Identities in Africa* (pp. 136–161). London: Zed books.

Valsiner, J. (2014). *An Invitation to Cultural Psychology*. London: SAGE.

Vico, G. (1744/1948). *The New Science of Giambattista Vico* (trans. T. Goddard Bergin & M. H. Fisch). Ithaca, NY: Cornell University Press.

Vygotsky, L. S. (2004). Imagination and creativity in childhood. *Journal of Russian & East European Psychology*, 42(1), 7–97. DOI: 10.1080/10610405.2004.11059210.

Wagner, W., Elejabarrieta, F., & Lahnsteiner, I. (1995). How the sperm dominates the ovum: Objectification by metaphor in the social representation of conception. *European Journal of Social Psychology*, 25(6), 671–688.

White, H. V. (1976). The tropics of history: The deep structure of the new science. In G. Tagliacozzo & D. P. Verene (Eds.), *Giambattista Vico's Science of Humanity* (pp. 65–85). Baltimore, MD: Johns Hopkins University Press.

White, S. H. (1976). Developmental psychology and Vico's concept of universal history. *Social Research*, 43(4), 659–671.

Whitman, J. (Ed.). (2003). *Interpretation and Allegory: Antiquity to the Modern Period*. Boston: Brill Academic.

Zittoun, T. (2007). The role of symbolic resources in human lives. In J. Valsiner & A. Rosa (Eds.), *The Cambridge Handbook of Sociocultural Psychology* (pp. 343–361). New York: Cambridge University Press.

23 National Identities in the Making and Alternative Pathways of History Education

Mario Carretero, Floor van Alphen, and Cristian Parellada

History education strongly influences the construction of national identities through so-called myths of origin. Taught and subsequently appropriated by students these myths play an important role in most educational systems and practices. This chapter is concerned with how this happens. For this purpose a number of studies will be analyzed focusing on the interdisciplinary relation between a sociocultural framework and research in learning and representing history. Most of the latter has been carried out in the field of history education, analyzing textbooks and curricula, and in a cognitive, developmental, and instructional psychological vein. However, more recently social and cultural psychological studies have made significant contributions. This chapter aims at developing a reflective view on what history education could offer as an area of interest for sociocultural research, particularly through the analysis of two cultural tools employed in constituting national identities in terms of their historical contents. Both master narratives and historical maps are symbolic supporters of the national identity construction process, enabling the appropriation of particular representations of history by students from a very young age in formal and informal learning environments. Even though there are various studies about the master narrative tool (Alridge, 2006; Straub, 2005), work on historical maps is still very scarce. The current chapter on the one hand reflects on this pathway of history education, mainly concerned

with fostering national identities. On the other hand, it proposes that alternative pathways can be developed aimed at historical contents other than national histories and territories. Such pathways consider the student as more than just a national subject. They form a new and dynamic field of research open to sociocultural investigation.

23.1 Historiography and History Education Fabricating National Identities

The dramatic changes in academic thought on nation toward the end of the twentieth century have much influenced current ideas about national identities. Anderson (1983) and Hobsbawm and Ranger (1983/2004) had a decisive role in the debates about nations as either essential or constructed political entities. In historiography the concept of nation is generally approached in two ways: from a romantic and a modernist point of view. The former, also known as perennialist, characterized historiography during the eighteenth and nineteenth centuries. From this viewpoint the nation is understood as a natural reality and the national sentiment is seen as spontaneous and innate. National identities are considered to be permanent and rooted in the remote past. Modern nations are placed on a continuum with earlier communities established within the same territory or even viewed as the same timeless object, unaffected by the changes taking place through the centuries (Smith, 2002). In the second half of the twentieth century the modernist approach to national phenomena was developed confronting this romantic approach. National identities came to be seen as artificial inventions, directed by political interests (Gellner, 1978). The national sentiment is thus supposed to be developed by schooling, and through other cultural and political artifacts such as military service, in contrast with the natural character that was presupposed in the romantic view.[1]

The essential role of state education in the process of the social, cultural, and political construction of nations has been investigated and acknowledged by many historians (Hobsbawm, 1997). Most educational systems around the world were initiated about 200 years ago, including history as an important subject matter. The appearance of history as a professional and academic activity and of history as a school subject are almost synchronical: at the middle of the nineteenth century (Berger, 2012). The main and almost exclusive objective of history education has been the indoctrination of students via the transmission of an invented national past. Another coincidence between history writing and history education is therefore their shared goal of fabricating national identities among the citizenry. History education was severely criticized in the decades between World War I and World War II, because of its saturation with nationalism and stereotypical views of other nations, nationals, and their pasts, particularly of neighboring countries (Carretero, 2011). The enormous human and political catastrophe of World War II demonstrated that blind nationalism was real and unfortunate. Since the 1970s and 1980s the field of history education has increased its interest in providing students with a critical view of the social and political issues of different societies in the past. One important factor contributing to this improvement has been the gradual

inclusion of social sciences contents in history curricula, as early twentieth century educational thinkers already foresaw (Dewey, 1915; Piaget, 1933). Nevertheless, this explicit goal of providing a critical view on past and present social issues through history education is very recent. In many Western countries it did not appear before the 1980s and in a number of countries it is considered to be very innovative.

Researchers today generally agree that the history curricula from diverse countries are still full of nationalist contents, which do not coincide with contemporary historiographical research on nations and their origins (Foster, 2012; Rosa & Brescó, 2017). It is acknowledged that national frameworks strongly determine school history contents. We think that the persistence of such contents is not merely an educational anomaly. Rather, it clearly reflects the prevalence of two parallel objectives of history education (Carretero & Bermudez, 2012). On the one hand, the aim to provide students with the means to achieve a disciplinary and critical understanding of past and present social and political realities. On the other, the implicit and explicit aim to contribute to the construction of national identities through intellectual and emotional experiences and representations related to the national past. To some extent this distinction can also be applied to history as an academic discipline, as seen in the opposition between perennialist or nationalist historiography and contemporary modernist or transnational historiography (Berger, Eriksonas, & Mycock, 2008). Current discussions about the complex relation between historiography and collective memory studies can also be interpreted in these terms (Carretero & Van Alphen, 2017). In the history education context, these two different kinds of educational aims related to different ways of accessing the past developed over time – are not always acknowledged as such (Carretero, Castorina & Levinas, 2013; Lee, 2012). This is probably because history education research has focused mainly on the development of historical thinking skills, that is, a progression toward a disciplinary understanding of the past. However, we think that national identity formation and maintenance has continued to influence how young students and future citizens represent history in and out of the school, as it will be further elaborated below.

23.2 Sociocultural Views on Imagining History

The distinction between the production and consumption of cultural tools (see Wertsch, 1998) is useful for indicating historical contents aiming at cultivating national identities on the one hand and the process of appropriation among students and citizens on the other. Such production and consumption processes have mostly been studied separately. The extensive research related to textbook and curricula production (Foster & Crawford, 2006) has not been related to the studies about students' learning and representation processes. To some extent, the innovative approaches to history education that are currently influential (Seixas & Morton, 2013; Wineburg, Martin & Montesano, 2011) were developed taking the cognitive and instructional studies about *how* to teach and learn history into account (consumption). Yet, they do not necessarily bear on *what* to teach (production). The critical analysis of how school historical contents are consumed by students and citizens in general and the implications this has for the construction of national identities – that is, the typical production process – has not been initiated until very recently (Van Alphen & Carretero, 2015; Epstein, 2009; Freedman, 2015). Furthermore, the theoretical debates on whether national contents should or should not be the focus of history curricula in globalized, reflective and democratic societies are quite recent (Grever & Stuurman, 2007; Seixas, 2012). This is an important issue, related to production and consequently consumption, because in most countries half of the history curriculum contents

concern national history and the other half relates to world history.

Applying the distinction of "official" versus "unofficial" histories, related to the nation and the history told from its perspective, the work by Wertsch (1998, 2002) has been important for developing sociocultural research into the realms of history education. This distinction already appeared in one of the first critical comparative studies about the "use and abuse" of school history contents in different countries (Ferro, 1984). The contributions by Wertsch and his collaborators have played a central role in introducing a sociocultural point of view on history learning. This work has been inspired by both Anderson (1983) and Hobsbawm (1997), clearly demonstrating how historiography and sociocultural research and theorizing can fertilize each other. Wertsch and Rozin (2000, pp. 41–42) recognized

"three basic functions of an official history . . . first . . . a kind of cognitive function having to do with cultural and psychological tools required to create what Anderson (1983) has termed "imagined communities," especially nation-states . . . without instruments such as print media, maps, and texts about history, it may be impossible to imagine communities or to "think" the nation . . . a second function of official histories is to provide citizens of nation-states with some sense of group identity . . . the third related function of official histories is to create loyalty on the part of citizens to the nation state."

In other words, a sociocultural framework provides empirical and theoretical support for the historiographical argument that history education as a cultural artifact basically develops "imagi-nations" (Carretero, 2017).

Adopting the term used by Wertsch (2004), national narratives become a kind of *schematic narrative template* – more abstract and generic narratives that are socially shared – which is fundamental when building specific historical narratives. For example, in the case of the United

States, there are two *schematic narrative templates* present in the vast majority of national narratives, based on the concept of progress and that of liberty. Students use these *schematic narrative templates* to explain past events (Barton & Levstik, 2008). Consequently, the resistance of Native Americans when facing waves of European colonists is seen as an obstacle in achieving progress and the Vietnam War is justified by the need to bring freedom to that country. Sociocultural analyses of school history contents have shown how closely these are related to *official narratives* that purposefully seek to determine subjects' representations of the past. A nation's past, present, and future are organized in official versions of the so-called "nation's history" distributed at school. These official accounts display an argumentative continuity in which the identitary "us" is constituted, and the nineteenth century conception of the "nation" as a community of destiny (Berger, Eriksonas, & Mycock, 2008; Smith, 1991) is transmuted into imagined communities. Hobsbawm (1997) defined this as the nation's programmatic mythology.

Indeed, school history accounts unite stories with different degrees of importance and a clear hierarchy in a long narrative chain, thus linked by virtue of the role they play in the construction of what we might call the nation's "saga." According to these sagas, designed by a teleological historiography, destiny is already contained in the origins, and knowledge of the "roots" of a nation is indispensable for knowing how to act in the future. This is not surprising if we take into account that the teaching of history emerged at the end of the nineteenth century with marked identity purposes, connected to nation building, and therefore with the purpose of decisively contributing to reaching the aforementioned goals (Boyd, 1997). This type of narrative substantially influences the way in which students understand and analyze information about the past (VanSledright, 2008). In short, we think that the sociocultural contribution to

investigating the understanding and representation of history is basically a meaningful psychological effort to analyze in detail how human beings imagine the past of national communities, as was postulated by Anderson (1983) and other theorists of nationalism.

23.3 Approaching National Identity in History Education

The historiographical work instigating a change from an essentialist to a socially constructed conceptualization of nation also propels a changing view on national identity. If the nation has been imagined or invented then the same goes for its corresponding identity. Nevertheless, in the field of history education it seems that historicizing national identity is even harder than de-essentializing the concept of nation. In the following, we reflect on how national identity has been approached in history education by educators, researchers and ultimately students. First the changing educational aims and means are scrutinized. Then ongoing research on students' identities in relation to their representations of history is discussed. And recent sociocultural research on how students appropriate national historical narratives is presented before we move on to consider other means for national historical representation. In the changing approach of national identity, the coincidence between critical historiography and sociocultural studies again plays an important role, this time in conducing from a rigid and singular to a dynamic and multiple national identity conception. This is greatly enabled by distinguishing students as agents from the national historical cultural tools they appropriate in different degrees. A sociocultural move that, as we will argue later on, also opens up alternative pathways of history education and their investigation.

As we have seen, incorporating history as a school subject was not meant to make students understand the problems of historiography but rather to awaken love for their country through knowledge of their nations great historical events. History education was considered indispensable for the development of a national identity (Berger, 2012; Carretero, Asensio, & Rodríguez-Moneo, 2012). Nowadays this educational objective is disputed and the strong relation between history education and developing a sense of national belonging has been called into question (Barton & Levstik, 2008; Barton, 2012; Epstein, 2009). Not only critical reflections on nationalism and its devastating consequences have contributed to this but also the development of other disciplinary aims, as discussed above, and the extensive research on textbooks, curricula, teaching and learning over the last decades. Specifically, history education researchers have drawn attention to the fact that significant parts of the population tend not to be represented in the official histories focusing on an exclusive and naturalized or ethnic national identity. It has been argued that history teaching needs to take the existing diversity of identities into account, for example, through teaching a more global or universalist history (Grever & Stuurman, 2007; Grever, 2012; Tutiaux-Guillon, 2012). In this ongoing debate, also known as the "history wars" on what history to teach and for whom, not that much attention is paid to the challenge for history education that comes with changing approaches toward national identity. Because middle and late twentieth-century historiography enabled the development of a critical and historicized concept of national identity, the latter can now be understood as a complex, multifaceted phenomenon that is constantly changing and never permanent nor exclusive (Barton, 2001; Terzian & Yeager, 2007). The change from an essentialist, rigid, and naturalized national identity to its socially constructed, dynamic, and contextualized conception seems to have influenced history education to some extent, as its focus has been redirected in some countries from constructing an exclusive and passive national identity toward fostering an inclusive and active *civic* identity (e.g., Tutiaux-Guillon, 2012), however, this is not unproblematic (Tutiaux-Guillon, 2017). A more historicized or dynamic notion of collective identity could still bear more heavily on the issue of what history to teach (see also Rosa, 2012), as will be developed further on. As we will see, in much research carried out with students a traditional and essentialist notion of collective identity, whether it be national, social, ethnic or cultural, is still quite common and only gradually changing.

23.4 Continuities and Changes in History Education Studies

When looking at the empirical research done among students, focused on how the different aims and means of history education affect them or on how they encounter and understand history, two tendencies immediately draw our attention. First, the historical contents used for different studies, even those assessing the students' historical thinking, reading or reasoning ability, are still in line with traditional history education objectives in terms of their contents. They are typically part of the national history of the countries in which these studies are carried out. The research that has been done in the United Kingdom by Peter Lee and colleagues uses material on the ebb and flow of the Roman Empire in Britain (e.g., Lee, Dickinson & Ashby, 1997). The research done in the United States by Sam Wineburg and colleagues uses specific parts of US history (e.g., Wineburg, 1991, Wineburg, Martin & Montesano, 2011). This informs us about how curricula still mainly include national history, but also about how researchers may take for granted that learning history is learning national history at least in comparison with other possible historical contents. Second, students' identities (not only national identities, but also gender identities and ethnic identities) have often been independent variables and (implicitly) conceived as essential and time-transcending characteristics that includes them in some group and excludes them from others. Thus, how students relate to historical contents, represent or learn them, has been found to vary according to their collective identities. Often without considering how these identities and a sense of belonging develop and change, and that they might be the explanandum instead of the explanans.[2] The investigations among students in the field of history education are, however, diverse and some development in the approach of collective identity can be observed on reviewing them.

Studies over the last decade have indicated that students' national, ethnic, political, and religious backgrounds all play a role in their interpretation of the meaning and significance of history (Barton, 2012). In relation to students' various identities, it has been primarily investigated what histories or parts of history they find important, that is, which historical events they judge as significant. Various studies emphasize that both national and ethnic identities are explicitly or implicitly related to what history students consider important (Epstein, 2000; Grever, Pelzer, & Haydn, 2011; Levstik & Groth, 2005; Liu et al., 2012). Their cultural and ethnic identities particularly relate to the representation of history (Epstein & Schiller, 2005; Goldberg, 2013, Peck, 2010). A study in Northern Ireland indicated that young adolescents were most likely to identify with parts of history, presented to them in pictures, that related to their national, religious, and cultural backgrounds (Barton & McCully, 2005). This study does not merely approach identity as a categorical entity but rather looks at students' active identifications and also explicitly entertains a sociocultural approach. Research looking at how students relate to history in the United States found that while Caucasian high school students identify with the nation's history and situate family experiences within a national framework, African American high school students are critical toward US history. Their accounts do not exactly align

with the national narrative of freedom, progress, and glory. They tend to reject this national history, arguing that it does not sufficiently represent the contributions and experiences of people of color (Epstein, 2000, 2009). Similar research in the United Kingdom on how adolescent students from ethnic minority backgrounds approach history found that some prefer the narratives they hear at home or in their ethnic group over the national narratives learned at school (Hawkey & Prior, 2011). These studies on students' (lack of) identification have given much support to a more inclusive framing of history education beyond national confines. In studies carried out with Canadian students, their ethnic identifications were found to play a central role in determining both the narrative template(s) they employ and the criteria they use to select events to build a specific historical narrative of the Canadian past (Peck, 2010). Also, students' narratives indicated different affective connections to the Canadian nation (Lévesque, Létourneau, & Gani, 2013) and the stronger students feel they belong to a particular (sub)national community, the more their specific narratives presented militant orientations (Lévesque, 2014). Ongoing investigations in different countries therefore suggest that students' cultural and ethnic identities and the form and content of their historical narratives are strongly related. Particularly regarding the relation between history representation and national identity, it has been found that Spanish students represent Spanish national history in a different way than Greek national history, even though the national historical narratives of those two countries are very similar (López, Carretero, & Rodríguez-Moneo, 2015). In the case of the Spanish Reconquest, their narratives make a clear territorial claim and demonstrate moral justification: the Spaniards were taking back what was rightfully theirs. This was not the case when they reflected on the end of the Ottoman Empire and Greek independence: they rather described a process of historical change. This raises the question whether national identification affects historical understanding, because lacking this identification with the Greek national history the students were able to construct a more critical historical account.

Apart from the relation between student' identities and what they find historically significant as well as how they represent history, the relation with historical understanding has been an important research subject. In this vein, students' identities and moral values have been considered both a resource for history learning and an impediment for developing disciplinary historical understanding (Bellino & Selman, 2012; Goldberg, 2013; Kolikant & Pollack, 2009; Straub, 2005). Typically, learning is easier when the historical content is (made) meaningful or significant to the students, hence the studies on historical significance. If historical contents are not meaningful or positively connected to students' collective identities teachers can encounter resistance in transmitting them. In a general sense, collective identity has been recognized as both a burden and a benefit in history education (Hammack, 2010). It is a burden "particularly with regard to social processes of reproduction. In this frame, youth are conceived as relatively blind appropriators of a status quo of narrative stalemate, thus unwittingly participating in the essentialism and reification of identity" (Hammack, 2010, p. 174). On the other hand, collective identity provides individual meaning and collective benefit "particularly for youth who are members of low-status groups. In this frame, emphasis is placed on collective identity as a tool for social change and liberation from oppression" (p. 175). Indeed, in terms of benefit, history learning studies indicate that students can resist historical narratives that they do not consider to be their own, that is, when they consider them as oppressive and rivaling accounts of other social groups. They also contribute perspectives to the history classroom, particularly when their collective voice is excluded from the official historical contents and accounts

(Barton, 2008; Epstein, 2000). And, in terms of a burden, recent studies have shown that even university students understand national identity as a timeless essence, rather than a constructed sense of belonging or as related to citizenship (López, Carretero, & Rodríguez-Moneo, 2015). In this particular study, national identity becomes something that students implicitly construct in their narratives instead of an independent variable. As their narratives reproduce the great stories of the nation it is not surprising that students develop naturalized or essentialist understandings of national identity. To account for both resistance and reproduction of historical narratives and at the same time study national identity in action Wertsch's sociocultural approach is particularly well suited.

23.5 Master Narrative Dimensions and Their Persistence

Through adapting a sociocultural approach national identity can be conceptualized and investigated differently in relation to history learning and representation, that is, both as a narrative construction and as a matter of degree of narrative appropriation. In line with Wertsch, national histories and *myths of origin* have been conceptualized as *master narratives*, produced and disseminated by nationalist historiography and history education as to construct national identities, and mastered or appropriated by students and citizens (Alridge, 2006; Carretero & Van Alphen, 2014; Van Alphen & Carretero, 2015). Based on an extensive theoretical and empirical review, Carretero and Bermudez (2012) proposed that the master narrative is characterized by (a) a homogeneous unified historical protagonist, (b) simplified teleological or monocausal historical events, (c) an essentialist concept of nation and timeless national identity, (d) an implicit identification with the national protagonists and their goals, (e) a moral justification or positive evaluation of the events, and (f) a heroic exemplary status of the people involved. These master narrative characteristics have been found in the narratives that Argentine high school students construct about the historical event that symbolizes the origin of the Argentine nation (Carretero & Van Alphen, 2014). Historical research draws another picture about events such as the Boston Tea Party in the United States and the *Cabildo Abierto* in Argentina, but through years of politically using these histories they have assumed the form of a national *myth of origin* or master narrative (see Chiaramonte, 2013). Most students, instead of considering the specific people involved in the events on May 25, 1810, in Buenos Aires, that is, the political and economical colonial elite with different ideas about the future of the Viceroyalty of River Plate, narrate about a homogeneous and timeless "people" that they even identify with as they talk about "us" or "we." These people did not quarrel about what to do with the political vacuum existing at the time, but, in the majority of the students' narratives strove together for Argentine independence from Spain (referred to as "them"; "they"). The narrative protagonists either were or wanted to be Argentine, according to the majority of 13-year-olds that were interviewed. Sixteen-year-old students mostly admitted that Argentina nor the Argentines could have existed at that time, yet their narratives are predominantly about a homogeneous group looking for a common goal, similar to the master narrative characterizing the events as a revolution toward independence. Appropriation of such a master narrative suggests that the students have, or rather feel, something of a national identity, even though differences in identification or feelings of belonging exist and the master narrative can also be resisted (Van Alphen & Carretero, 2015). The relation between the national past and the present, constructed in the narratives by the students, is typically that of the master narrative: idealizing the past, teleologically relating it to the present or

even assuming a time transcending national bond between the people then and now. This gives an idea of how they conceptualize national identity: as a historical example, as a (future) goal, and as a continuous entity or belonging. Overall, the historical understanding of May 25th seems to be constrained by the master narrative even in 16-year-olds that have received more detailed history education on the matter.

23.6 Representations of Nations and Their Historical Borders as Cultural Tools

Master narratives were traditionally meant to foment national identity in people and at the same time they construct a particular kind of national identity that is time transcending and exclusive toward others. As recent studies have started to analyze, not only the appropriation of master narratives but also other essentialist tools contribute to (re)presenting national identity as timeless and unique vis-á-vis other nations, specifically the borders of a national territory drawn on maps. Throughout different societies, history textbooks include maps, which often do not properly indicate the historical changes of the territory. On the contrary, they represent the national territory as if it has always been just so. Anderson (1983) specifically counted maps among the cultural tools producing the imagination of communities, even though he was probably referring to geographical maps representing the territory in a specific moment of history. It is no coincidence that every public school setting typically includes a national map. It seems that the way current geographical maps are presented, separating countries or territories, constitutes the territorial boundaries of a nation as an image of its own, deep in people's minds (Lois, 2014). National identity is therefore more likely to be understood as an inclusive and collective "we," sharing a common national history. This "us" in opposition to "them" is observed in the students'

Figure 23.1 Map of the Iberian Peninsula around 710.

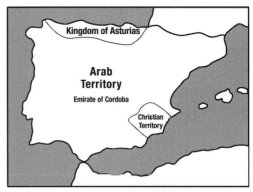

Figure 23.2 Map of the Iberian Peninsula around 721, about ten years after the arrival of the Arabs.

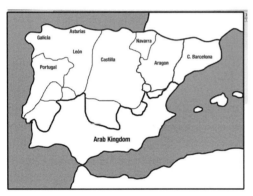

Figure 23.3 Map of the Iberian Peninsula around 1212.

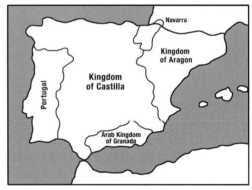

Figure 23.4 Map of the Iberian Peninsula around 1491, about one year before the expulsion of the Arabs by the Catholic Kings.

Source: Adapted from García de Cortazar, *Atlas de Historia de España*. Barcelona: Planeta, 2005.

narrations on the nation's past in Argentina as well (Carretero & Van Alphen, 2014). Their narratives echo the national master narrative, which emphasizes the shared past of those inhabiting the territory, situating them as members of a nation and presenting a national continuity from past to present to future.

We are referring to historical maps, usually compiled by historians in historical atlases, rather than to geographical maps when considering that just a few researchers have discussed how and why the former type of maps is usually absent from history textbooks (Kamusella, 2010;

Kosonen, 2008). In some cases they are included, however, not in a very precise way. This particular way of producing historical imagery might be responsible for essentialist representations of the nation.

Focusing on what can be further investigated as part of a process of appropriating national imagery, a study among Spanish university students demonstrates that they represent or imagine the territory to be essentially national and are typically unaware of the historical changes of the territorial boundaries (López, Carretero, & Rodríguez-Moneo, 2015). The Iberian

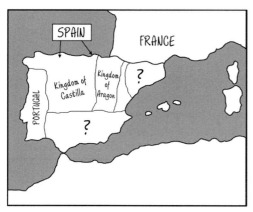

Figure 23.5 Map of the Iberian Peninsula around 710, completed by a university student.

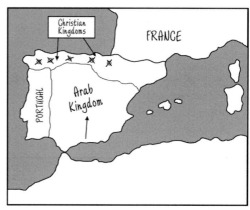

Figure 23.6 Map of the Iberian Peninsula around 721, about ten years after the arrival of the Arabs, completed by a university student.

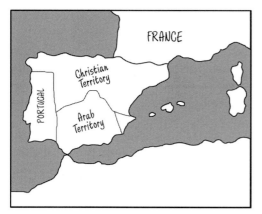

Figure 23.7 Map of the Iberian Peninsula around 1212, completed by a university student.

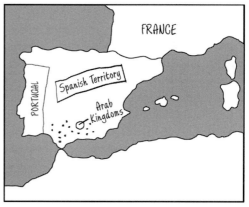

Figure 23.8 Map of the Iberian Peninsula around 1491, about one year before the expulsion of the Arabs by the Catholic Kings, completed by a university student.

Source: Adapted from López, Carretero, & Rodríguez-Moneo (2015).

Peninsula had been invaded by Arab forces by the year 711. They took complete control over the whole territory in less than 10 years. Their presence in this territory lasted until 1492. During these eight centuries a number of both Christian and Arab kingdoms competed for the same territory. These fights implied dramatic border changes over the centuries. In Figures 23.1, 23.2, 23.3, and 23.4 borders of 700, 721, 1212, and 1491 can be seen, as established by historical research. In the investigation, university students were asked to draw the borders corresponding to these dates on a map of the Iberian Peninsula. As can be seen in Figures 23.5, 23.6, 23.7, and 23.8 the maps fill out by the students tend to plot the current borders of Spain, Portugal, and France as permanent since as early as the eighth century. They tend to represent present borders as if they were always there. For example, the border between what today is Portugal and the Castilian territories suffered a number of changes from the seventh century to the fifteenth century (see Figures 23.1, 23.2, 23.3, and 23.4) but students represented in an ontological way as if those territories were the same as they are nowadays (see Figures 23.5, 23.6, 23.7, and 23.8). This can also be observed in relation to the borders of the different Iberian kingdoms such as Castile and Aragon. In the same study, the students expressed their idea that the medieval "Spaniards" – even though at that time they considered themselves Castilians, Aragonese, or something else – had the right to expel the Arabs from "their territory," as if it had always been a national property. This study demonstrated that most of the university students have an essentialist view of this historical process and they labeled it "The Spanish Reconquest." This view agrees with the traditional Spanish nationalist point of view, even though it is not taught at school anymore. Most of the current Spanish textbooks present this historical period in terms of feudal times instead of Spanish Reconquest. Nevertheless, their are other cultural influences, for example, the material and symbolic heritage presented in terms of Christian as opposed to Arab culture. Summer festivities based on rituals fights of "Moors against Christians" are very common in southern and eastern Spanish towns.

23.6.1 Alternative Pathways of History Education as Matters of Sociocultural Investigation

The research thus far raises various questions for further investigation in a sociocultural vein, particularly along pathways of history education that remain under-explored. First and foremost, how is the construction of the students' collective identities related to different types of history education with different purposes? As we have seen, in history education national identity construction is no longer an exclusive aim. Civic identity or more inclusive and dynamic notions of national identity have been introduced. Do master narratives also lead the way to civic identities, civic identification, or civic agency? In the sense of civic education replacing national education, the way is already being paved theoretically (Haste & Bermudez, 2017; Carretero, Haste, & Bermudez, 2016) and the challenge is to figure out whether and how master narratives might enable civic identities, that is, dispositions toward certain actions as group members or in favor of the group, and what other cultural means might be involved here. Even though the concept of agency has been drawing attention in history education research, both as a characteristic of historical narratives (Peck, Poyntz, & Seixas, 2011) and as something that can be fostered in students (Barton, 2012), how this might happen and how both are connected is a matter still open for investigation. So is the question whether master narratives and other symbolic and instructive tools such as maps have a constitutive role in the student's national identity. Do they actually contribute to the student feeling that she/he belongs to the national group? Students' previous identities and identifications, or viewpoints developed in the passage through collective frameworks, might have a more active role in the appropriation of master narratives or other kinds of tools provided by history education by the time they reach high school. Polman (2006) investigates the students' identity development and history learning as parallel processes, based on the work by Erikson (1968) on the one hand and by Wertsch on the other. Before or instead of assuming a constitutive relation between the two processes they are rather supposed to be intermediated by narrative cultural tools or other national symbolic means. Other means of access to the past that are not strictly national might very well intervene.

Furthermore, master narratives and a disciplinary understanding of national history are often opposed to each other. However, do representations based on these different outlooks on history contradict each other or do they coexist in the minds of students? From the point of view of social representations theory, it has been suggested that different and even contradicting representations or narratives about particularly polemic past events cognitively coexist, or that hegemonic representations agreeing with the dominant or victorious social group's viewpoint make alternative interpretations of the past disappear into nothingness (Barreiro, Castorina, & Van Alphen, 2017). Does this also mean that different ideas about national identity coexist or engage in semantic struggles for power?

As we have seen, sociocultural psychology has given much insight into formal and informal history education processes through focusing on cultural devices such as master narratives. One other important theoretical as well as empirical development in the research field is changing the focus from static "identity" to complex, active, intersecting, or layered identification processes. Theoretically various suggestions have already been made (Bamberg, 2011; Barton, 2012; De Fina, 2003; Grever & Ribbens, 2007; Valsiner, 2012; Van Alphen, 2012): identification is a fluctuating process in which students have an active role, they can change identity niches from time to time, navigate their identity constellations, or this constellation is in itself dynamic in engaging with the environment. Students' layered or intersecting identification processes, in which local, ethnic, cultural, social, national, religious, and global identities are combined, might play an important role in their interpretation of the meaning and significance of history and construction of historical narratives. In the existing research among students a tendency toward considering their dynamic identifications can be observed (e.g., Barton & McCully, 2005). However, the

students' active and dynamic role can be much further explored in relation to the idea of an individual agent as an irreducible feature of the mediated action of appropriation (see Wertsch, 1998) or to the idea of the active construction or navigation of identity (see Bamberg, 2011) or, indeed, the passage through different collective frameworks (see Halbwachs, 1992).

An alternative pathway of history education worth further consideration has been developed by Rüsen (2004). He has greatly inspired the field of history education with his notion of students' narrative competence and call for a "comprehensive psychology of historical learning" (p. 81) to study the development of historical consciousness in students, which is related to how they construct historical narratives. Rüsen subdivides this "competence concerned with making sense of the past" in terms of form, content, and function, that is: (a) a competence of historical experience, involving "the capacity of learning how to look at the past and grasp its specific temporal quality, differentiating it from the present"; (b) a competence of historical interpretation, involving "the ability to bridge time differences between past, present, and future through a conception of a meaningful temporal whole comprising all time dimensions"; (c) a competence of historical orientation, involving "guiding action by means of notions of temporal change, articulating human identity with historical knowledge, and interweaving one's own identity into the concrete warp and woof of historical knowledge" (Rüsen, 2004, pp. 69–70). He theorizes a progression through different types of historical consciousness that offer different temporal orientations: from a *traditional* type of historical consciousness emphasizing the origins and the repetition of social obligations, through an *exemplary* type emphasizing general timeless rules or principles of conduct, and a *critical* type providing "counter-narratives" and deconstructions of pre-given temporal orientations, to a *genetic* type emphasizing that change gives sense to history and that transformation or development of life patterns allows for maintaining their (dynamic not static) permanence. Investigating how these temporal orientations develop or might coexist in students is of great interest for both sociocultural analyses of how people represent the past and for history education. Both Rüsen (2004) and Wertsch (2002) entertain an idea of progression in temporal orientation or outlook on history, toward a genetic historical consciousness and away from an official history with no irony at all. As it is further detailed below, theoretical and empirical elaboration in this vein would not only enrich the research on the students' notions of nation and national identity but could also contribute to a change of these notions.

23.7 Toward an Ironical and Dialogical Understanding of Nation and National Identity in History Education

In this chapter, we have argued that a sociocultural paradigm stands in close dialogue with findings from historiographical research. This dialogue further enables analyzing and historicizing the national frames of reference that are operating in history education. In this context, we think that alternative pathways of history education are enabled by the de-essentialization of nation and national identity and openly discussing their constructed and historical character. This involves making the actual institutional – culturally mediated – construction of identities more explicit, and recognizing as well as analyzing the social dimension of constructing knowledge about the past. In this vein, developing an ironical understanding of nation and national identity provides a future perspective for (re)thinking educational interventions as well as investigations in the interdisciplinary framework presented. The notion of *ironic understanding* has been developed by sociocultural and narrativist approaches

(Egan, 1997; Wertsch, 2002). Perhaps Umberto Eco was (1980) one of the first to realize how crucial an ironic orientation on the past is for the development of citizenship in present globalized societies, even though he developed his ideas in a medieval setting in *Il nome della rosa*. Perhaps Maurice Halbwachs (1992), asserting that the passage through or communication between collective frameworks of memory enriches the outlook on the past, already made an early step in this direction, even though this outlook is shared rather than individual. The educational and psychological theorist Kieran Egan describes ironic understanding in terms of a high degree of metacognition about the conceptual resources that we have at our disposition to understand the world. For our purposes, we can maintain that this capacity involves developing a critical reflection on the explanations of past events, and the narrative tools relied on. Ironic understanding can thus be understood as a reflexive capacity involving sufficient cognitive flexibility to recognize that certain mechanisms of vigilance and self-regulation operate in knowledge in daily life. Thinking and narrating about a past event depends on how particular knowledge and memories are combined with others and how the individual negotiates this. In ironic comprehension different stories about the past become alternative perspectives. These are not necessarily in opposition to each other. Some may be valued more than others. Yet, what characterizes ironic comprehension is suspending one singular narrative or vision of the past as the "true account." This suspension of the "truth" does not lead to naïve relativism, but rather enables the recognition of the multifaceted world and political character of knowledge and, moreover, narrative. It would demonstrate that the construction of historical knowledge and narrative already *is* political, through its intrinsic connection to the nation-state, as has been revealed by late twentieth century historiography (Lorenz, 2008; Rüsen, 2004).

Thinking about educational interventions based on research is a complex matter, because history education is a practice where many educational objectives and even more identities of students, understood as values or shared orientations, are at play. Nevertheless, apart from generating research that actively de-essentializes nation and national identity, sociocultural studies can help analyze history education practices that aim at overcoming these static notions and singular outlooks on the past. The irreducible tension between individual agency and the historical, social, and cultural dimension materialized in mediational means such as national historical narratives (Wertsch, 1998), allows for thinking more profoundly about developing ironic understanding in students. Carretero and López (2012) suggest both to consider students' identities and to foster their historical thinking in the educational process by addressing national identity and the narratives of nation explicitly as cultural tools. The awareness of these historical constructions and their functions might increase the student's agency in handling them. Emphasizing the complex social and dynamic character of national identity is crucial for overcoming essentialist conceptions as well as augmenting the student's critical agentic role, which is not only an idealized aim of history education. One possible way to do this would be critically reflecting on the collective narrative and the national identity it constitutes together with students, implementing insights from sociocultural analyses.

For example, Van Boxtel and Van Drie (2017) have developed a fruitful instructional initiative through a dialogical framework, relevant to developing ironic understanding in educational environments. They consider learning as entering into a community of practice (Lave & Wenger, 1991) and achieving specific concepts and procedures. From this point of view the historians' practice is also based on a dialogical activity. The work by Van Boxtel and Van Drie stems

from the contributions made in a cognitive psychological vein, well consolidated in the history education field, aimed at developing historical thinking (Wineburg, 1991). However, based on Bakhtin's ideas (1981) about the nature and importance of dialogue, they think that historical expertise is not only based on individual cognitive operations, such as the sourcing, corroboration, and documentation related to historical text inquiry. For them it is also essential to consider dialogical activity, mostly in relation to multiple views on both historical narratives and concepts. They therefore confront students in the classrooms with a number of dialogical activities in which they have to compare and evaluate different views on the same historical issue. This issue is considered not just a topic but a problem asking for diverse answers and discussions of the related concepts and justifications. Ultimately, developing ironic understanding in history learning implies not only recognizing alternative takes on history, but also critically reflecting on and comparing this knowledge (see also Carretero & Van Alphen, 2017). As an alternative pathway of history education the ironic understanding of nation and national identity means recognizing that there is always a perspective, or a cultural tool being employed, to be aware of rather than to never be reflected on. Thus, we may suggest directing the interdisciplinary exchange between critical historiographical work and sociocultural studies on history learning at genetic historical consciousness, from a rigid and singular to a dynamic and multiple national identity and a perpetually reimagined nation. In an attempt to answer the question what history to learn, in terms of irony and change we could say that history learning can be about the nation when it is reflected on in comparison to other possible perspectives on the past and treated as inherently historical, that is, changing. This way, "what" and "how" to learn when facing the past may eventually become intertwined. An alternative pathway of history education is thus both enabled by sociocultural studies and constitutes a most interesting field for further – applied – research.

Notes

1 Ichijo and Uzelac (2005) indicated that intermediate views, between romantic and modernist, should be considered, such as the ethno-symbolic paradigm. This view considers that although nationalism is a modern ideology, nations are built on premodern heritage and it is indeed possible to recognize a nation before the onset of modernity.
2 Halbwachs (1992), who has famously coined "collective memory," has also considered that collective frameworks are dynamically intersecting and that individuals while passing through various frameworks import and export ideas about history (see Middleton & Brown, 2005).

References

Alridge, D. P. (2006). The limits of master narratives in history textbooks: An analysis of representations of Martin Luther King, Jr. *Teachers College Record*, 108(4), 662–686.

Anderson, B. (1983). *Imagined Communities. Reflections on the Origin and Spread of Nationalism*. London: Verso. (New edition, 1991.)

Bakhtin, M. M. (1981). *The Dialogic Imagination: Four Essays* (ed. by M. Holquist, trans. by C. Emerson & M. Holquist). Austin: University of Texas Press.

Bamberg, M. (2011). Narrative discourse. In C. A. Chapelle (Ed.), *The Encyclopedia of Applied Linguistics*. Oxford: Wiley-Blackwell.

Barreiro, A., Castorina, J. A. & van Alphen, F. (2017). Conflicting narratives about the Argentine "Conquest of the Desert": Social representations, cognitive polyphasia, and nothingness. In M. Carretero, S. Berger, & M. Grever (Eds.), *Palgrave Handbook of Research in Historical Culture and Education* (pp. 373–390). London: Palgrave.

Barton, K. (2001). You'd be wanting to know about the past: Social context of children's historical understanding in Northern Ireland and the United States. *American Educational Research Journal*, 38, 881–913.

Barton, K. (2008). Research on students' ideas about history. In L. Levstik & C. A. Thyson (Eds.), *Handbook of Research on Social Studies Education* (pp. 239–258). New York: Routledge.

Barton, K. (2012). School history as a resource for constructing identities: Implications of research from the United States, Northern Ireland, and New Zealand. In M. Carretero, M. Asensio, & M. Rodríguez-Moneo (Eds.), *History Education and the Construction of National Identities* (pp. 93–107). Charlotte, NC: Information Age Publishing.

Barton, K. & Levstik, L. (2008). History. In J. Arthur, I. Davies, & C. Hahn (Eds.), *Handbook of Education for Citizenship and Democracy* (pp. 355–366). London: SAGE.

Barton, K. & McCully, A. W. (2005). History, identity, and the school curriculum in Northern Ireland: An empirical study of secondary students' ideas and perspectives. *Journal of Curriculum Studies*, 37, 85–116.

Bellino, M. J. & Selman, B. L. (2012). The intersection of historical understanding and ethical reflection during early adolescence: A place where time is squared. In M. Carretero, M. Asensio, & M. Rodríguez-Moneo (Eds.), *History Education and the Construction of National Identities* (pp. 189–202). Charlotte, NC: Information Age Publishing.

Berger, S. (2012). De-nationalizing history teaching and nationalizing it differently! Some reflections on how to defuse the negative potential of national(ist) history teaching. In M. Carretero, M. Asensio, & M. Rodríguez-Moneo (Eds.), *History Education and the Construction of National Identities* (pp. 33–48). Charlotte, NC: Information Age Publishing.

Berger, S., Eriksonas, L., & Mycock, A. (Eds.). (2008). *Narrating the Nation: Representations in History, Media and the Arts*. New York: Berghahn Books.

Boyd, C. P. (1997). *Historia Patria: Politics, History and National Identity in Spain 1875–1975*. Princeton, NJ: Princeton University Press.

Carretero, M. (2011). *Constructing Patriotism: Teaching of History and Historical Memory in Globalized World*. Charlotte, NC: Information Age Publishing.

Carretero, M. (2017). Teaching history master narratives: Fostering *imagi-nations*. In M. Carretero, S. Berger, & M. Grever (Eds.), *Palgrave Handbook of Research in Historical Culture and Education* (pp. 511–528). London: Palgrave.

Carretero, M., Asensio, M., & Rodríguez-Moneo, M. (Eds.). (2012). *History Education and the Construction of National Identities*. Charlotte, NC: Information Age Publishing.

Carretero, M. & Bermudez, A. (2012). Constructing histories. In J. Valsiner (Ed.), *Oxford Handbook of Culture and Psychology* (pp. 625–646). Oxford: Oxford University Press.

Carretero, M., Castorina, J. A., & Levinas, M. L. (2013). Conceptual change and historical narratives about the nation: A theoretical and empirical approach. In S. Vosniadou (Ed.), *International Handbook of Research on Conceptual Change* (2nd edn., pp. 269–287). New York: Routledge.

Carretero, M., Haste, H., & Bermudez, A. (2016). Civic learning. In L. Corno & E. M. Anderman (Eds.), *Handbook of Educational Psychology*. (3rd edn., pp. 295–308). London: Routledge.

Carretero, M. & López, C. (2012). Commentary: Identity construction and the goals of history education. In M. Carretero, M. Asensio, & M. Rodríguez-Moneo (Eds.), *History Education and the Construction of National Identities* (pp. 139–152). Charlotte, NC: Information Age Publishing.

Carretero, M. & Van Alphen, F. (2014). Do master narratives change among high school students? A characterization of how national history is represented. *Cognition and Instruction*, 32(3), 290–312. DOI: 10.1080/07370008.2014.919298.

Carretero, M. & Van Alphen, F. (2017). History, collective memories or national memories? How the representation of the past is framed by master narratives. In B. Wagoner (Ed.), *Oxford Handbook of Culture and Memory* (pp. 283–303). Oxford: Oxford University Press.

Chiaramonte, J. C. (2013). *Usos políticos de la historia: Lenguaje de clases y revisionismo histórico* [The political use of history: Language of classes and revisionism]. Buenos Aires: Sudamericana.

De Fina, A. (2003). *Identity in Narrative: A Study of Immigrant Discourse*. Amsterdam: John Benjamins.

Dewey, J. (1915). The aim of history in elementary education. In *The School and Society* (pp. 155–164). Chicago: University of Chicago Press.

Eco, U. (1980). *Il nome della rosa*. Milan: Bompiani.

Egan, K. (1997). *The Educated Mind*. Chicago: University of Chicago Press.

Epstein, T. (2000). Adolescent perspectives on racial diversity in US history: Case studies from urban classrooms. *American Educational Research Journal*, 37(1), 185–214.

Epstein, T. (2009). *Interpreting National History: Race, Identity, and Pedagogy in Classrooms and Communities*. New York: Routledge.

Epstein, T. & Schiller, J. (2005). Perspective matters: Social identity and the teaching and learning of national history. *Social Education*, 69(4), 201–204.

Erikson, E. H. (1968). *Identity: Youth and Crisis*. New York: W. W. Norton.

Ferro, M. (1984). *The Use and Abuse of History; or, How the Past is Taught after Great Fire*. London: Routledge. (Original version in French, 1981. Revised edition, 2002.)

Foster, S. (2012). Re-thinking historical textbooks in a globalised world. In M. Carretero, M. Asensio, & M. Rodríguez-Moneo (Eds.), *History Education and the Construction of National Identities* (pp. 49–62). Charlotte, NC: Information Age Publishing.

Foster, S. J. & Crawford, K. A. (Eds.). (2006). *What Shall We Tell the Children? International Perspectives on School History Textbooks*. Greenwich, CT: Information Age Publishing.

Freedman, E. B. (2015). "What happened needs to be told": Fostering critical historical reasoning in the classroom. *Cognition and Instruction*, 33(4), 357–398.

Gellner, E. (1978). *Thought and Change*. Chicago: University of Chicago Press.

Goldberg, T. (2013). "It's in my veins": Identity and disciplinary practice in students' discussions of a historical issue. *Theory & Research in Social Education*, 41(1), 33–64.

Grever, M. (2012). Dilemmas of common and plural history: Reflection on history education and heritage in a globalizing world. In M. Carretero, M. Asensio, & M. Rodríguez-Moneo (Eds.), *History Education and the Construction of National Identities* (pp. 75–92). Charlotte, NC: Information Age Publishing.

Grever, M., Pelzer, B., & Haydn, T. (2011). High school students' views on history. *Journal of Curriculum Studies*, 43, 207–229. DOI: 10.1080/00220272.2010.542832.

Grever, M. & Ribbens, K. (2007). *Nationale identiteit en meervoudig verleden* [National identity and the plurality of the past]. Amsterdam: Amsterdam University Press.

Grever, M. & Stuurman, S. (2007). *Beyond the Canon: History for the 21st Century*. Basingstoke, UK: Palgrave.

Halbwachs, M. (1992). *On Collective Memory*. Chicago: University of Chicago Press. (Edited and translated from Les cadres sociaux de la mémoire, published 1952, and *La topographie légendaire des évangiles en terre sainte: Etude de mémoire collective*, published in 1941. Paris: France: Presses Universitaires de France.)

Hammack, P. (2010). Identity as burden or benefit? Youth, historical narrative, and the legacy of political conflict. *Human Development*, 53, 173–201.

Haste, H. & Bermudez, A. (2017). The power of story: Historical narratives and the construction of civic identity. In M. Carretero, S. Berger & M. Grever (Eds.), *Palgrave Handbook of Research in Historical Culture and Education* (pp. 527–548). London: Palgrave.

Hawkey, K. & Prior, J. (2011). History, memory cultures and meaning in the classroom. *Journal of Curriculum Studies*, 43(2), 231–247.

Hobsbawm, E. (1997). *Nations and Nationalism since 1780: Programme, Myth, Reality*. Cambridge: Cambridge University Press.

Hobsbawm, E. & Ranger, T. (1983/2004). *The invention of tradition*. Cambridge: Cambridge University Press.

Ichijo, A. & Uzelac, G. (2005). *When Is the Nation?* New York: Routledge.

Kamusella, T. (2010). School history atlases as instruments of nation-state making and maintenance: A Remark on the invisibility of ideology in popular education. *Journal of Educational Media, Memory, and Society*, 2(1), 113–138.

Kolikant, B. & Pollack, S. (2009). The asymmetrical influence of identity: A triadic interaction among Israeli Jews, Israeli Arabs, and historical texts. *Journal of Curriculum Studies*, 41, 651–677.

Kosonen, K. (2008). Making maps and mental images: Finnish press cartography in nation-building, 1899–1942. *National Identities*, 10(1), 21–47.

Lave, J. & Wenger, E. (1991). *Situated Learning: Legitimate Peripheral Participation*. Cambridge: Cambridge University Press.

Lee, P. (2012). *Series introduction*. In M. Carretero, M. Asensio, & M. Rodríguez-Moneo (Eds.), *History Education and the Construction of National Identities* (pp. ix–xiv). Charlotte, NC: Information Age Publishing.

Lee, P., Dickinson, A. K., & Ashby, R. (1997). "Just another emperor": Understanding action in the past. *International Journal of Educational Research, Teaching and Research*, 27, 233–244.

Lévesque, S. (2014). French-Canadians, national identity and historical consciousness: Learning from the views of Franco-Ontarians. Presentation at the School and Memory Conference, Prague. Retrieved from www.schoolxmemory.eu/files/BOOK_Eng.pdf.

Lévesque, S., Létourneau, J., & Gani, R. (2013). "A giant with clay feet." Quebec students and their historical consciousness of the nation. *International Journal of Historical Learning, Teaching and Research*, 11(2), 156–172.

Levstik, L. S. & Groth, J. (2005). "Ruled by our own people": Ghanaian adolescents' conceptions of citizenship. *Teachers College Record*, 107, 563–586.

Liu, J. H., Paez, D., Hanke, K., Rosa, A., Hilton, D., Sibley, C., Cabecinhas, R., Zaromb, F., Garber, I.,

Leong, C., et al. (2012). Cross-cultural dimensions of meaning in the evaluation of events in world history? Perceptions of historical calamities and progress in cross-cultural data from thirty societies. *Journal of Cross-Cultural Psychology*, 43(2), 251–272. DOI: 10.1177/0022022110390926.

Lois, C. (2014). *Mapas para la Nación: Episodios en la Historia de la Cartografía Argentina* [Maps for the nation: Episodes in the history of argentine cartography]. Buenos Aires: Biblos.

López, C., Carretero, M., & Rodríguez-Moneo, M. (2015). Conquest or reconquest? Students' conceptions of nation embedded in a historical narrative. *Journal of the Learning Sciences*, 24(2), 252–285. DOI: 10.1080/10508406.2014.919863.

Lorenz, C. (2008). Double trouble: A Comparison of the politics of national history in Germany and Quebec. In S. Berger & C. Lorenz (Eds.), *Nationalizing the Past: Historians as Nation Builders in Modern Europe* (pp. 49–70). Basingstoke, UK: Palgrave Macmillan.

Middleton, D. & Brown, S. (2005). *The Social Psychology of Experience Studies in Remembering and Forgetting*. London: SAGE.

Peck, C. (2010). "It's not like [I'm] Chinese and Canadian. I am in between": Ethnicity and students' conceptions of historical significance. *Theory and Research in Social Education*, 38(4), 574–617.

Peck, C. L., Poyntz, S., & Seixas, P. (2011). "Agency" in students' narratives of Canadian history. In D. Shemilt & L. Periklous (Eds.), *The Future of the Past: Why History Education Matters* (pp. 253–280). Nicosia, Cyprus: Association for Historical Dialogue and Research.

Piaget, J. (1933). Psychologie de l'enfant et enseignement de l'histoire [Child psychology and history teaching]. *Bulletin trimestriel de la Conférence internationale pour l'enseignement de l'histoire, 2*, 8–13.

Polman, J. (2006). Mastery and appropriation as means to understand the interplay of history learning and identity trajectories. *Journal of the Learning Sciences*, 15(2), 221–259.

Rosa, A. (2012). What history to teach? Whose history? In M. Carretero, M. Asensio, & M. Rodríguez-Moneo (Eds.), *History Education and the Construction of National Identities* (pp. 63–74). Charlotte, NC: Information Age Publishing.

Rosa, A. & Brescó, I. (2017). What to teach in history education when the social pact shakes? In M. Carretero, S. Berger, & M. Grever (Eds.), *Palgrave Handbook of Research in Historical Culture and Education* (pp. 513–526). London: Palgrave.

Rüsen, J. (2004). Historical consciousness: Narrative structure, moral function, and ontogenetic development. In P. Seixas (Ed.), *Theorizing Historical Consciousness* (pp. 63–85). Toronto: University of Toronto Press.

Seixas, P. (2012). Indigenous historical consciousness: An oxymoron or a dialogue? In M. Carretero, M. Asensio, & M. Rodríguez-Moneo (Eds.), *History Education and the Construction of National Identities* (pp. 125–138). Charlotte, NC: Information Age Publishing.

Seixas, P. & Morton, T. (2013). *The Big Six: Historical Thinking Concepts*. Toronto: Nelson Education.

Smith, A. D. (1991). *National Identity*. London: Penguin Books.

Smith, A. D. (2002). Dating the nation. In D. Conversi (Ed.), *Ethnonationalism and the Contemporary World: Walker Connor and the Study of Nationalism* (pp. 53–71). London: Routledge.

Straub, J. (Ed.). (2005). *Narration, Identity and Historical Consciousness*. New York: Berghahn Books.

Terzian, S. & Yeager, E. (2007). That's when we became a nation: Urban Latino adolescents and the designation of historical significance. *Urban Education*, 42(1), 52–81.

Tutiaux-Guillon, N. (2012). A traditional frame for global history: The narrative of modernity in French secondary school. In M. Carretero, M. Asensio, & M. Rodríguez-Moneo (Eds.), *History Education and the Construction of National Identities* (pp. 109–124). Charlotte, NC: Information Age Publishing.

Tutiaux-Guillon, N. (2017). History in French secondary school: A tale of progress and universalism or a narrative of present society? In M. Carretero, S. Berger, & M. Grever (Eds.), *Palgrave Handbook of Research in Historical Culture and Education* (pp. 275–294). London: Palgrave.

Valsiner, J. (2012). Monuments in our minds: Historical symbols as cultural tools. In M. Carretero, M. Asensio, & M. Rodríguez-Moneo (Eds.), *History Education and the Construction of National Identities* (pp. 327–345). Charlotte, NC: Information Age Publishing.

Van Alphen, F. (2012). Identities: Never the same again? *Integrative Psychological and Behavioral Science*, 46, 296–302. DOI: 10.1007/s12124-012-9201-3.

Van Alphen, F. & Carretero, M. (2015). The construction of the relation between national past and present in the appropriation of historical master narratives. *Integrative Psychological and Behavioral Science*, 49, 512–530. DOI: 10.1007/s12124-015-9302-x.

Van Boxtel, C & Van Drie, J. (2017). Engaging students in historical reasoning: The need for dialogic history education. In M. Carretero, S. Berger, & M. Grever (Eds.), *Palgrave Handbook of Research in Historical Culture and Education* (pp. 573–590). London: Palgrave.

VanSledright, B. (2008). Narratives of nation-state, historical knowledge, and school history. *Review of Research in Education*, 32, 109–146.

Wertsch, J. (1998). *Mind as Action*. Oxford: Oxford University Press.

Wertsch, J. (2002). *Voices of Collective Remembering*. Cambridge: Cambridge University Press.

Wertsch, J. (2004). Specific narratives and schematic narrative templates. In P. Seixas (Ed.), *Theorizing Historical Consciousness* (pp. 49–62). Toronto: University of Toronto Press.

Wertsch, J. & Rozin, M. (2000). The Russian Revolution: Official and unofficial accounts. In J. F. Voss & M. Carretero (Eds.), *Learning and Reasoning in History* (pp. 39–60). New York: Routledge.

Wineburg, S. (1991). Historical problem solving: A study of the cognitive processes used in the evaluation of documentary and pictorial evidence. *Journal of Educational Psychology*, 83, 73–87.

Wineburg, S., Martin, D., & Montesano, C. (2011). *Reading Like a Historian*. New York: Teachers College Press.

24 The Politics of Representing the Past: Symbolic Spaces of Positioning and Irony

Brady Wagoner, Sarah H. Awad, and Ignacio Brescó de Luna

> Who controls the past controls the future; who controls the present controls the past.
>
> George Orwell, *1984*

In *1984* Orwell depicted an extreme totalitarian society in which all information was in the hands of the regime and citizens had few degrees of freedom in how they were to behave. A central component of information control concerned how the past was to be remembered. The famous quotation above describes in no uncertain terms how the past is used to move toward a particular future by the ruling regime. Moreover, it highlights that this is an issue of power: those at the top control the resources for imagining the past in the present. In this chapter, we will follow Orwell in exploring the political uses of memory and their past–present–future dynamics. However, we will argue that in any society – regardless of how strong the presence is of official and/or partisan discourses about the past – there are always free spaces for alternative ideas and interpretations to develop. Even in totalitarian regimes most people do not simply believe the official story told by the authorities but learn to keep their opinion private to avoid standing out (Moghaddam, 2013; Wertsch, 2002). When those in power suppress ideas they simply go underground and later resurface in public through unconventional channels. In this way, social movements are often creative in finding new means of expressing their vision of social reality. This is frequently done through irony, in which the words of the authority are appropriated and mocked. Irony is a highly illustrative example of how propaganda does not reach a passive audience but can even be actively transformed into its opposite. Orwell's other famous work *Animal Farm* – where farm animals overthrow the farmer only to be later ruled by the pigs – is itself a wonderful illustration of irony as a tool of critique.

To elaborate on these politics of representing the past we present two case studies: the Basque conflict and the conflict between groups in the aftermath of the 2011 Egyptian revolution.[1] In addition to the direct use of violence and protest, both cases involve the development and use of symbolic weaponry, in the form of narratives and images, that function to construct a past and present social reality in which it is not only acceptable, but also a duty, to undertake actions to defend the rights of one's group. In these examples, we see how the use of symbolic tools also *positions* a person within the landscape of a conflict. The analysis of the Basque conflict foregrounds the interplay between different narratives constructed from particular political position, while the Egyptian case focuses on positioning vis-à-vis images in public space (namely, the graffiti of social movements and government billboards). Images can be understood as condensed expressions of a particular position and work to trigger various narratives circulated by the groups to which one is a member. In both cases we point out the importance of positioning and irony as a symbolic means of reflection and distancing on a situation. But before jumping into the two cases, we will first theoretically elaborate our main concepts of symbolic tools, positioning, and irony.

24.1 Theoretical Framework: Symbolic Tools, Positioning, and Agency

As already mentioned, narratives and images of the past are approached in this chapter as symbolic tools through which people position themselves in conflicts. These tools create a symbolic space for representing reality that develops together with the space of action and events but is not reducible to it. An act of representation involves symbolic mediation using these tools, which in turn shapes what is being represented into a given cultural form, rather than as operating as a faithful copy of reality. Mitchell (1990) aphoristically describes the process as "no representation without taxation." Moreover, these symbolic tools are social rather than individual in origin (Vygotsky & Luria, 1994). Different groups within a society provide their members with varied symbolic tools, such as narratives, which necessarily select particular events, omit others, provide valuations of them and fit them into a broader context of interpretation. As Burke (1969) puts it, "any selection of reality must, in certain circumstances, function as a *deflection* of reality" (p. 59). This is not to say there cannot be better or worse accounts of the past. But how to understand the meaning of an event, its place in history, and its use is open to different interpretations. Whether a person is a professional historian (with disciplinary standards of scholarship) or a member of the lay public, an interpretation of the past is achieved through the use of varied narrative resources.

Thus, people remember both *from* a certain position and *with* the use of a group's shared cultural resources. This creates a dynamic in which conflicts and memory are often two sides of the same coin, seamlessly feeding into each other (Wagoner & Brescó, 2016). It is not uncommon to hear statements like "*they* wronged *us*," "*we* have not been respected by *them*," "*we* have acted in good faith, while *they* have responded with violence," and so on. Warring factions typically deploy a wide range of symbolic weaponry in order to define the conflict's origin and thus legitimize their respective positions in light of a set of supposed rights and duties (Harré & Van Langenhove, 1999). In this way, narratives – as symbolic tools for interpreting the past, present, and future – simultaneously underpin and are underpinned by the position held by each actor. Conflicts then unfold within a symbolic and argumentative context (Brescó & Wagoner, 2016) saturated by different partisan narratives. These narratives are in turn the symbolic tools or meditational means (Wertsch, 1991) through which people come to give sense to conflicts and build a position accordingly. In such divided and multivoiced contexts, the possible standpoints on the conflict are constrained by warring factions' discourses and voices, which people tend to appropriate and make their own. Even in those situations in which a window for peace seems to emerge, alternative approaches tend to be overshadowed by partisan ways of interpreting reality.

In the differentiated modern societies, where different positions and narratives are at play, remembering becomes a *dialogical process* (Märtsin et al., 2011), where multiple versions of the past compete and respond to each other in giving an account. In this way, individuals take an active role within the collectives that provide them with symbolic tools of remembering, in order to manage different perspectives. Collective memory can thus not be treated as a unitary process, where all members of the group remember in unison. As Bartlett (1932) famously put it, remembering is done *in* a group not *by* a group. Although the symbolic tools borrowed from a group are essential to remembering, they are actively appropriated, transformed, and put into dialogue with other groups' tools. It is in these spaces of dialogue that new ways of representing a situation can be constructed and human agency comes to the fore. Agency can be found in both the production and reception of symbolic material. It is not so much about freeing oneself from social influences, but playing them off one another. As such, agency becomes a situated process of distancing and reflecting on action with the symbolic tools available at hand, under the definite constraints of a given sociocultural milieu.

24.2 Narratives About the Past: The Case of the Basque Conflict

The Basque Country conflict in Spain – now on the way to being resolved – is a clear example of this.[2] After fifty years of violence, the armed group ETA (acronym for *Euzkadi ta Azcatasuna* or *Basque Country and Freedom* in English) announced a permanent ceasefire in March 2006, an announcement surrounded by controversy since the very beginning. On the one hand, ETA regarded the ceasefire as the first step to negotiate the independence of the Basque Country from the Spanish State. On the other hand, the Spanish government (headed at that time by the Socialist President José Luís Rodríguez Zapatero) considered the ceasefire as an opportunity to initiate a peace process and to eventually reach a solution to the conflict. By its part, the main opposition party (the right wing People's Party) deemed the ceasefire as a "truce-trap" and accused the government of having secret deals with the terrorists and surrendering the country to ETA. In December that year, ETA planted a bomb in a car park at Madrid airport, causing two deaths. That attack – justified as a response to the supposed government's passivity – was the culmination of nine months of tension during which the main political actors devised different accounts to justify their own positions vis-à-vis a process understood as the "democratic process," "peace process," or a "trick process."

Thus, following the attack, different ways of understanding that process were consolidated by means of various opposing accounts; accounts that also acted as tools by which people could interpret, recall, and draw conclusions from the ceasefire depending on the extent to which they identified with the main figures involved. This is not to say that agency vanishes amid warring factions' narratives and voices. That is, people do not simply *reproduce* those discourses provided by warring factions in a completely passive way. However, they do not *produce* new discourses out of the blue either. Rather, people's accounts are mediated by those previous discourses available in a particular social setting. Agency is, in this sense, distributed between those cultural tools or mediational means people have at hand – in this particular case, the public narratives about the ceasefire period provided by warring factions – and the specific way in which these resources are used in each particular occasion – namely, the way they are used by individuals as a tool for reconstructing the past. Action is thus irremediably mediated and therefore shaped by "the inherent tension between mediational means and their unique instantiation" (Wertsch, 1994, p. 206). In Bakhtinian terms this implies different forms of multivoiced authoring (Bakhtin, 1981; see also Wertsch & O'Connor, 1994) in that different voices (in this case, those pertaining to the main figures involved in the conflict[3]) would be appropriated and adapted to individuals' own intentions in different specific contexts. Such a personal appropriation of social discourses on the part of lay individuals may take different degrees of agency and authorship, ranging from reproduction and acceptance, on the one hand, to entire rejection on the other (Brescó, 2016; Wertsch & O'Connor, 1994). However, in polarized contexts saturated with partisan discourses, it is often the case that the rejection of one implies embracing some other. It is in these particular contexts – such as the Basque conflict – where, in the absence of alternative resources, personal appropriation of these discourses in the form of irony or satire becomes a way of resisting – and even mocking – the warring factions' militant discourses saturating the public sphere.

24.2.1 Three Case Studies

Drawing on previous works (e.g., Brescó, 2016), this section aims to compare different versions of the abovementioned ceasefire period stemming from three subjects identified to varying extents with the main political actors involved in that Basque conflict: (1) the Spanish Socialist government, (2) ETA and its political arm Batasuna, and (3) the right-wing People's Party (see Note 2). These three cases form part of a broader study in which a total of 16 participants – from the Autonomous University of Madrid and the University of the Basque Country – were asked to define the Basque conflict and to provide an account of the 2006 ceasefire period by using 23 short documents extracted from different Spanish newspapers.[4] Of particular interest here is showing how these three subjects appropriate and use different narratives of the truce period in light of their respective identification with the main figures involved. Along these lines, results include, on the one hand, two versions reproducing the story line provided by two of these figures, and on the other hand, a version characterized by a more personal, critical, and ironic appropriation of these narratives.

Participant 1: Green[5] is an 18-year-old male who studies psychology at the University of the Basque Country and who identifies with Batasuna's position. The following is Green's definition of the Basque conflict and his account of the ceasefire period:

Definition of the Basque conflict: "It is a conflict between an oppressed nation and two oppressor states (Spain and France) which refuse to recognize the right all democratic states have: the right to self-determination. This situation has led to an armed conflict."

Account of the ceasefire period: "ETA declares a truce and ceases all its actions. The government says that it is willing to meet with ETA. Batasuna expresses its willingness to negotiate the future of the Basque Country. The Spanish state keeps imprisoning, torturing, and oppressing the Basque people, especially Batasuna and its supporters. Given the course of events and the government's inability to move forward, ETA decides to send out a warning to the government by planting a bomb at Madrid airport. The government doesn't react and the truce comes to an end. Then, ETA returns to its armed struggle."

Green clearly takes Batasuna's position and makes it his own, thus defining the conflict as one caused by the oppression of the Basque People by both the Spanish and French state. In light of this standpoint, this participant justifies and delegitimizes the actions of the main figures involved in the ceasefire period. According to his version, despite ETA's good intentions, the Spanish government failed in its democratic duty by not listening to the Basque people, thereby causing ETA to exercise its right to resume the armed struggle. It is also worth noting that in order to support his version of events, this participant omitted all documents (included among the material handed out to the subjects) referring to ETA's violent activities during the ceasefire, and instead used the news article from *Gara* (see Note 4) which spoke of arrests and torture concerning Batasuna and its supporters. Here, it is the government that is responsible for the truce's failure by not responding to ETA's warning in the form of a bomb attack. This is a peculiar way of constructing the peace-making process; one in which violence is seen as a form of dialogue.

Participant 2: Blue is an 18-year-old female who studies psychology in Madrid and sympathizes with the right-wing People's Party. She sees the conflict and the ceasefire period as follows:

Definition of the Basque conflict: "There is a group of people from that region who don't feel Spanish so they use violence."

Account of the ceasefire period: "Thanks to a series of secret agreements between ETA and the Socialist Party, with many concessions made by the latter, a truce was achieved. During the supposed truce period, the government was completely willing to hold talks with the terrorists while they kept on committing terrorist acts. Thousands of Spaniards marched, demanding that Zapatero stop yielding to ETA's claims. In turn, the People's Party split with the government due to Zapatero's erroneous strategy. This event ended with the terrorist attack on Madrid Airport, which caused two casualties (this is, in fact, the only way ETA understands dialogue). After this attack, we are still supposed to believe that the government has dropped negotiations with ETA."

Blue identifies the violence exerted by a supposed anti-Spanish faction as the origin of the conflict, thus somehow assuming a connection between not feeling Spanish and resorting to violence; a standpoint that precludes dialogue as a way out of the conflict. In examining Blue's version of the events, we can see how this participant takes the People's Party's stance on the ceasefire period, and in accordance to that, tends to use those newspapers closer to that party (see Note 4). Thus, unlike Green's version, she assesses the truce in quite a negative light, even going so far as to describe it as a "plot" between the Socialist government and ETA, pretty much in line with those newspapers and politicians who supported the conspiracy theory along the truce process. For instance, Blue makes use of one of the pictures provided which features numerous people "*demanding that Zapatero stop yield-ing to ETA's claims*" and also some of the news referred to ETA's terrorist activities during the truce period included in the material. Blue's words also echo a People's Party member statement, included in the material provided, through which ETA's ceasefire announcement was linked to Zapatero's previous set of concessions to that group. From Blue's perspective, the position taken by the People Party's throughout the ceasefire period is not regarded as failure, but as a patriotic duty against a prior immoral agreement. Additionally, Blue explicitly mentions the terrorist attack and the two resulting casualties – an attacked depicted in one of the pictures provided. Interestingly, her comment on this tragic outcome, which she referred to as ETA's only way of understanding dialogue, echoes Green's version in which the attack was a mere warning. This would further prove the uselessness of dialogue with the terrorists in line with the People Party's position against the government's attempt to reach a peace agreement with ETA.

Participant 3: Gray is a 23-year-old male who studies psychology in Madrid. He sympathizes with the Socialist Party and *Izquierda Unida* (United Left), a party to the left of the former which also supported the peace-making process. Gray's view on both the conflict and the truce period is as follows:

Definition of the Basque conflict: "This is a somewhat fictitious conflict. I don't think that it's about the Basque people's claim for independence, or at least, it's not just about that. I believe that both sides feed off each other's positions and live off keeping the conflict alive to some extent."

Account of the ceasefire period: "On the 22nd of March three gentlemen wearing hoods and fancy dress appear on TV announcing a truce. They pledge not to kill for a certain period of time whereas the government undertakes nobody knows what. Everybody is very happy about what is deemed the beginning of a peace process and because the end of violence is thought to be near.

Immediately afterwards, all the political and media machinery is set in motion. The politicians start to calculate every move in terms of electioneering benefits. On the one hand, the People's Party, in order to discredit the Socialists, insinuates that ETA's and the government's interests are basically the same. On the other hand, the Socialist Party does everything in its power to prevent the process from getting out of hand, trying to please everybody with promises. As for the Basque extreme nationalists, they try to appear as the champions of peace in order to obtain greater support among the people and thus reinforce their presence in the institutions. The constant attacks and innuendos launched by the People's Party end up undermining Zapatero's popularity, thus leading the government to adopt a tougher line against ETA. At the same time, the members of ETA who are not interested in giving up the struggle manage to impose their strategy which finally results in the bomb attack at Madrid airport. With this tragic episode, both the peace process and the cheap farce set up around it come to an end."

Gray's stance is removed from the position of the actors in the conflict as he sees the conflict as something fictitious, fueled by the actors themselves. From this standpoint, the claims deriving from each position become meaningless insofar as they constitute a resource for nourishing a conflict that all sides wish to keep alight. Such a critical distance is reflected in the way the truce period is narrated. Thus, from the very first sentence ("*On the 22nd of March three gentlemen wearing hoods and fancy dress appear on TV announcing a truce*"), this participant makes clear his resistance to take seriously what the actors involved in this episode claim to be doing – in this case, the content of the picture provided in the material in which three hooded ETA members are announcing the ceasefire. This ironic stance on what is considered a fictitious conflict is further reinforced by his explicitly likening the peace process to a "*cheap farce*." Along these lines, the whole episode is narrated as if it were a play, one that starts off with the appearance

on the stage (in this case, on television) of the three members of ETA announcing the ceasefire and the activation of all the political and media machinery, which continues to operate until the attack on Madrid airport. This way of reconstructing the peace process moreover underscores the fictitious nature of the position of the actors involved, actors whose "performance" is aimed more at making their respective audiences happy, that is, not losing popularity among their voters and supporters, than at having their claims satisfied – be it achieving independence, reaching an agreement through dialogue, or defending the unity of the Spanish state.

24.2.2 Militant Discourses and Militant Irony in the Basque Conflict

As we can see, participants Green and Blue identify themselves with the position of certain political actors (ETA and the People's Party, respectively), thus assuming and to some extent reproducing their corresponding versions of the truce period, including the claims, criticisms, and justifications contained in such versions. As a result, we have two militant accounts in which each participant seems to accept and adopt the voice of one of those actors and make it their own. From a Bakhtinian perspective, we could say that the actors' voices speak through the participants' accounts, or stated another way, that participants have been to some degree talked – or ventriloquized – by those actors' voices.

Contrary to Green's and Blue's acceptance of such voices, Gray's critical stance on both ETA and People's Party positions is reflected through a clearly ironic, even satirical, narrative style by which this participant criticizes the absurd logic that characterizes these actors' conduct. This is carried out by means of a certain way of using the voices of the actors themselves – those associated with the Socialist government, the People's Party, and ETA – in order to highlight their absurdity during the peace process. This resource, linked to irony, is close to the Bakhtinian concept of "double-voicedness," "refer[ring] to the use of someone else's words in order to express one's own intentions and meanings that are hostile to others' words" (Marková, 2003, p. 63). We can see examples of this at the beginning of Gray's account, when he speaks ironically about both ETA's ceasefire (*"they pledge not to kill for a certain period of time whereas the government undertakes nobody knows what"*) and the general optimism and faith in relation to the truce and the end of the conflict (*"everybody is very happy about what is deemed the beginning of a peace process and because the end of violence is thought to be near"*).

Here we find a greater degree of agency in reconstructing the truce period compared to the cases of Green and Blue. Thus, whereas in the last two cases the participants' words expressed the view of the main political actors on the truce period – as they were transmitted through the media – in Gray's case the words of those political actors are used to express the participant's more personal view of it. In this regard, Gray's satirical and distant stance is not incompatible with the adoption of his own positioning on the episode in question. As Frye (1957) points out in his work, *Tropics of Discourse*, "satire is militant irony: its moral norms are relatively clear, and it assumes standards against which the grotesque and absurd are measured" (p. 223). This moral dimension related to the use of tropes and genres is further developed by the philosopher of history Hayden White who argues that the narrative forms used in reconstructing the past inevitably convey a moral content (White, 1986). In the particular case of irony, this author considers this genre as a meta-trope, a trope related to self-consciousness in the use of language when talking about the past. In White's own words, "[irony] represents a stage of consciousness in which the problematical nature of language itself has become recognized" (White, 1973, p. 37).

24.3 Images About the Past: The Case of the Egyptian Revolution

In parallel to the analysis of how the different discourses in the public sphere, where appropriated by participants according to their social positions of the Basque conflict, we look here at the appropriation of the narratives of the past through images in Egypt after the 2011 revolution.

Similar to Mr. Jones in Orwell's *Animal Farm*, the Egyptian former president Mubarak was successfully uprooted by the Egyptian revolution in 2011 only to be followed by similar autocratic system setup with other leaders taking power. In the short interval of time between 2011 and 2014, the Muslim Brotherhood president was elected in 2012 followed by a coup, then a military backed regime in 2014, both of which claimed to act in the name of the very Egyptian revolution but ended up repeating the same authoritarian strategies as the old regime. The high expectations of an idealized democratic future of "bread, freedom, and social justice" were quickly put down by the reality of the subsequent governments. This left the revolutionaries with a rupture, seeing their newly found agency being forcefully repressed by military and police forces.

Since the beginning of the revolution in 2011, many activists resorted to proclaiming and utilizing public space to communicate their ideas to the wider public as well as to authority. This resulted in the blooming of revolution street art and graffiti, which became effective tools for expressing opposition to the government, mobilizing people for the revolutionary goals, documenting the memory of the revolution, and honoring those who lost their lives in protests (Awad & Wagoner, 2015; Awad, Wagoner, & Glăveanu, 2017). This form of expression, however, paralleled the progression of the revolution; after its peak in 2011, it slowly declined as despair spread among activists and as the security measures over freedom of expression tightened with every succeeding government. On the other hand, authority also utilized its power over public space by erasing the revolution street art and graffiti, and adding its own images through billboards advocating its own official narrative.

Following certain images in the public space informs us about the different narratives at play; in this context, the image becomes a sign in a specific narrative, a communicative device that poses a certain argument in opposition to another (Lonchuk & Rosa, 2011). As will be seen in the examples below, not only is the production of an image of interest, but also its social life: that is, its transformation, interpretation, reconstruction, and possible destruction. The understanding of the social life of images helps analyze the dialogue and tension happening in the society at large between the different narratives of the past and the power relations between those narratives. For example, what images get to stay in public space and how are they perceived versus what images communicate a narrative that is not tolerated by authority or general public and how is it refuted or erased (Awad, 2017).

Drawing from previous research (Awad, Wagoner, & Glăveanu, 2017; Awad, 2017), we look here at the production, interpretation, and reconstruction of images in the public sphere as dependent on different social actors in the society, these social actors include the producers as well as the consumers of those images. The examples below will show different social actors as they position themselves through images of the past: revolution graffiti artists as they produce certain representations of the past, authority campaigns as they respond to the graffiti images with opposing narratives, and citizens as they interpret and appropriate the images in their city space. The images used for this research are those related to two specific narratives about the recent past events since 2011. First, the narrative represented in many of the revolution graffiti: the revolution shortly succeeded in overthrowing Mubarak's 30 year regime, but that was followed by military and Muslim Brotherhood dominance, progressing to a current counterrevolution authoritarian

regime. Second, images produced by authority in the form of billboards, posters, and wall paintings of government buildings and public schools, communicating the official narrative; advocating for the military as the main protector of the people in two revolutions: the 2011 one overthrowing Mubarak, the 2013 coup overthrowing the Muslim Brotherhood, and calling for people to unite with the military to fight terrorism and economic struggles. In the following, we will focus on two examples: the first tackles one graffiti artist's representation of the events from 2011 to 2015. Our analysis here concerns how the image was continually reconstructed to reflect the progression of events. The second example draws out the different interpretations that citizens have of an image, produced by the military, according to their social position.

24.3.1 Irony in Images: Representing Authority Figures

Many of the graffiti murals that started with the revolution have been reproduced in different places and reconstructed to parallel the progression of the events as they unfolded. Figure 24.1 depicts an example of this: the authority faces in this mural have been changing in every reconstruction of it, reflecting how they are all different faces of the same problem (See Awad & Wagoner, 2015; Hamdy & Karl, 2014). The first version of this mural was painted by an Egyptian graffiti artist known as "Picasso" in Mohamed Mahmoud street in the Tahrir Square area, revolutionary graffiti's central location. The initial version was of a face that is half Mubarak (the ousted president) and half Tantawy (the chairman of the Supreme Council of Armed Forces, who was in charge after Mubarak), expressing that the first was removed, only for a similar authority to replace him. Then other faces were added to the painting triggered by the local authority erasing it. During the first election after the revolution it included two candidates who were considered part of the old regime. Later as the

Figure 24.1 Street art on the presidential palace wall in Cairo, June 2013.
Source: Street art by Omar Fathy (Picasso); photo credit: Walls of Freedom.

Muslim Brotherhood took power, the faces of Morsi (the elected Muslim Brotherhood president) and Badei (the supreme guide of the Muslim Brotherhood) were added.

Figure 24.1 is a reproduction of the mural painted by the same artist two years after the first version, but this time by the presidential palace where protests were growing against Morsi in July 2013. The painting reflects a critical time when El Sisi (back then chief of Armed Forces) announced the removal of Morsi and assigned an interim government. The text underneath reads "He who delegates authority has not died," transforming an Egyptian proverb that expresses how children resemble their parents so in a way parents never die. Similarly the graffiti puts the faces of Mubarak, Tantawy, and Morsi, but this time adds the expected new ruler of Egypt, as an unknown silhouette with the beret of the military. The heading of the painting reads "Down with all those who betrayed, Mubarak, Military, and Brotherhood."

The transformation of this image expresses the irony of the many new faces rising to power after the revolution only to be copies of the same kind of authority that the revolution has aspired to remove. The latest version adds yet another anticipation regarding who is next, after the military has gone to the front line again by removing the elected president. The confusion between the artist's feelings of relief and hopefulness that the Muslim Brotherhood are removed accompanied by fearful and cautious feelings of a "coup" unfolding is expressed in how the artist modified the painting the following day by removing the beret from the image. This was a response to the celebrations taking place by the presidential palace after the removal of Morsi and an optimism for a future with a leader that is not identified as betraying the people, namely, Mubarak, military, and Brotherhood (Hamdy & Karl, 2014, pp. 234–235). The visual simplicity and clearness of the series of images of this mural tell the story of this revolution (as well as many others) and predicts a future yet to come.

24.3.2 Citizen Interpretations of Images Produced by the Military

The artist's feared future scenario came true: El-Sisi resigned from his military post and ran as a presidential candidate. Since El-Sisi was sworn into office in June 2014, there has been an unprecedented crackdown on freedom of expression, while the state utilized media channels, public space, and school curriculum to advocate for the official narrative mentioned earlier. In a previous study (Awad, 2017), 25 participants who

Figure 24.2 Government poster in Cairo, February 2016. Text reads: "The army and the people are one hand." Source: Photo taken by author.

reside in Cairo were shown different state sponsored images including the image in Figure 24.2 and asked about their interpretation of them. Below are three examples of different interpretations of the image by citizens from different political positions and how they appropriated the recent past as presented by the image.[6]

Nour, a 34-year-old entrepreneur, was critical of the naivety of the poster, even though he supports the government and its campaigns:

The poster is a portrayal of reality. Army protected people not once but twice, that's what an army should be to Egyptians . . . they did mistakes but they had to, we're not in an easy time and priority now is security.

When asked if he sees the image as an effective promotion of the government, he said:

Not for me or you, this is naive advertisement, but it works with the general public, they need to feel attached to and protected by the army now.

Sherin, a 38-year-old who works in social development and is a mother of two, communicated her position against the government through an ironic interpretation of the image:

See . . . like why are the people in diapers? When I first saw this poster I joked with a friend that the army and their supporters had an affair and this child is the outcome . . . He doesn't even look Egyptian . . . But it is a true portrayal of how they see the public: immature and incapable infants that need parenting, it goes along with the patriarchal presidential speeches we get . . . This as well as their other posters are everywhere in the city, they want to make it clear that they own and rule every inch of the city. And if I don't agree with them, then I don't love my country and I am a terrorist.

For Lobna, a 34-year-old who identifies herself as apolitical, the image was of interest as she recalled her reinterpretation of it as she saw it in the city at different times in the past years:

You know this photo reminds me of how things are changing so fast. When this photo was first spread in 2011 it was very true. Army did stand by the people against Mubarak and the appearance of tanks in Tahrir Square was a relief, it meant protestors are finally safe. And families would go to Tahrir square with their children and give their child to the soldier on the tank to take a picture with him and that is exactly what is portrayed in the picture. When I first saw it in 2011, I was very touched by it. But later when those same tanks started killing protestors, I felt the photo is not as idealistic as I had thought. Seeing the photo again made me feel disappointed, it was a painful reminder of those who died.

24.3.3 Irony as a Mode of Resistance

The above data presented examples of the agency of each actor as they positioned themselves in relation to the past: the graffiti artist through the serial reproduction of his painting, the government through its poster, and the citizens through their interpretation of that poster. The three citizens' quotes, similar to the case of the Basque conflict, took different degrees of authorship over the image: from reproduction and acceptance to rejection and sarcasm. The appropriation varied by their political position, stance on the past events, and emotions toward the visual representation of the soldier and the child. The interpretation process here is an argumentative one where the viewer enters a dialogue with the meanings suggested by the image and produced through the image's counterarguments as well (Lonchuk & Rosa, 2011).

While power plays a role in controlling the resources for representing certain narratives of the past that orients toward a particular future, the examples emphasize the diverse ways through which people appropriate that past based on their political positioning and personal memories of the revolution. Even within repressive atmospheres where only the official discourses or "public transcripts" gets exposure in the public sphere, individuals do create social spaces where they communicate their "hidden transcripts" challenging the authority's power over discourses (Scott, 1990).

The use of irony has been one of the main themes in the opposition narrative (as seen in the graffiti image and in Sherin's comment on the authority's image), being often used to ridicule the dramatic contrast between what the revolution has called for versus the current reality. Irony was used by the participant, Sherin, as a means of reflection and distancing from the situation, in a way resisting the dominant discourses. As mentioned earlier, the use of irony shows how governments' propaganda is not received passively, but can even be actively transformed into its opposite. The silencing of opposition from traditional media outlets has triggered wider use of social media for opposition. Expression in those alternative outlets utilize irony in a way that reaffirms the activists' denied freedom and the sanction on any kind of opposition to the president, by flipping this power relationship temporarily using humor. This is seen in caricatured images of authority figures, who in other media outlets would be untouchable, as well as using the president's official speeches as material for countering their messages. While these symbolic tools may provide relief for the actor putting their voice out in public and symbolically challenging the powerful by positioning them in a funny and demeaning manner, it also reaffirms the helplessness of the actor having only symbolic power through these tools for resistance.

In the city space, images are perceived and remembered according to perceivers' own current opinions and orientations, so it is doubtful that a graffiti image would make a government supporter change his mind, or an image promoting the government would make activists reconsider their opinions. It has been argued that propaganda in dictatorships functions not so much to gain believers but mark off what can be publicly said (Moghaddam, 2013; Wertsch, 2002) and produce a city space atmosphere of power and domination (Awad, 2017). Getting alternative versions of reality into this public space is an act of resistance that challenges that conformity. This presence reflects the dynamics between the powerful narratives versus the alternative narratives, with the alternative narratives reaffirming for the activists that their voice is still there and promoting a sense of solidarity.

24.4 Concluding Thoughts: Symbolic Action and Reaction

This chapter has presented narratives and images as symbolic tools that both position their audience as actors in political conflicts and provide possible means of reflection and agency. Using examples from narratives in the context of the Basque country conflict as well as images created in the public space after the 2011 Egyptian revolution, we illustrated how these symbolic tools prescribe certain orientations and actions to be conducted according to a particular group's goals. Narratives are objectified in images and provide the interpretive background to understanding them. Both images and narratives remind us of what happened, what the current situation is, and thus point to what people are expected to do, as a function of their placement in the plot of the narrative for a depicted scenario. Taking Schank and Abelson's (1977) terminology, we can say that these cultural tools provide individuals with a kind of script; a script that once internalized might be formulated as follows: "we know this story, and we know its awful outcome, and we also know what must be done in response to it" (Tölölyan, 1989, p. 112). However, people are also active in interpreting and appropriating these messages based on their own social and personal background; in other words, we cannot read the reception of some material from an analysis of its content or its intended use. Thus, people have agency in making use of the material as a function of their own background and motivations.

The metaphor as a cultural tool is appropriate here in that narratives and images can be used in different ways by different people for different purposes. Narratives and images have typically been employed to establish loyalty to a particular group (e.g., historical accounts of the nation as good, or flags as symbols of national unity), but they can also provide a means of reflecting on one's position and constructing it anew (e.g., being confronted with an alternative version of events through a different story or an ironic take on the existing one). The same material that is used to construct social reality and one's place in it can also function to distance oneself from that very construction when it is put in dialogue with another perspective. As Wertsch (2017) points out, "narrative tools do not mechanistically determine human discourse and thinking. Instead, the very notion of a tool implies an active user and

suggests an element of variability and freedom." This leads us to the question of agency raised above and to highlight the fact that human beings are not only influenced by the symbolic materials they encounter but are also constructive in reshaping them as they continue to live, creating new orientations to the future (Wagoner, 2017). If this were not the case, no new visions of society would emerge and social change would be impossible. The meeting and conflict of perspectives and material can be a great stimulus to social change (Bartlett, 1923).

In highlighting the active nature of audiences, we do not wish to downplay the importance of power. Clearly certain groups have more influence over which messages get communicated and can create an environment in which alternative voices are not tolerated. As already mentioned, this tends to create general public conformity, in which people learn to keep their perceptions of social reality private (Moghaddam, 2013). Social movements, however, may find ways of navigating prohibitions to advocate an alternative stance, putting new voices into the public sphere. For this reason protests are not tolerated by dictatorships – they demonstrate that many others share a perspective on social reality, and thus overcome a society's pluralistic ignorance (i.e., the belief that "others do not share my alternative belief"), as well as challenge the dominance of the authority over visual representation in the public space. The interplay of perspectives can be highly generative for reflecting on the current situation and material circulating about it, giving people tools for neutralizing or countering the argument of certain narratives of images. This was particularly clear in the examples of people's uses of irony.

We need to, however, be careful not to overly praise irony as a symbolic weapon of less powerful groups for two reasons. First, irony can function to tame and familiarize images and discourses that nonetheless go against the project of one's group. This was pointed out during

Trump's presidential campaign statements (often racist) and scandals, which were widely satirized in memes and by comedians. Yet, their ironic repetition may have been a key factor in normalizing them. Second, whether irony alone can lead to social action is questionable. More often than not it functions more as a displacement of action. Those involved in a conflict of extreme violence would rarely display irony toward it. By contrast, irony tends to encourage a distanced rather than engaged stance toward social reality, as can be seen in Gray's narrative on the Basque Country issue above. Distancing implies establishing one's own individuality from others' symbolic tools and what they represent (Werner & Kaplan, 1963). In so doing it might not only detach us from action but also from collective solidarity under a common cause. With distancing we become more aware of the arbitrariness of representation, that narratives and images are attached to positions in society and are not neutral or natural.

In this way, irony can be used as a resource aimed at preventing individuals from *naturalizing* certain versions of the past. Taking Kieran Egan's (1997) concept of *ironic understanding* when consuming historical narratives, we would agree with Blanco and Rosa (1997) in stating that "perhaps it would not be a bad goal to look for an ironic citizenship, but an irony based on reflection and informed dialogue, not cynicism" (p. 15). From this perspective, the ideal scenario would consist of guiding actors to become reflexive authors endowed with agency to co-construct their own versions of the past in internal debate with themselves and in open dialogue with others. Of course, power asymmetries between different social actors mitigate the possibilities of achieving this. It is rare that different groups' narratives are given equal space. In such a situation irony may function more as a means of mocking the words of partisan and powerful actors, and symbolically pull them down as authorities, as can be seen in some of the Egyptian revolu-

tionary graffiti (such as Figure 24.1). The social power-based dialogue becomes one of selective censorship on the one side and ironic mockery on the other.

Notes

1 Some have argued we would do better to speak of a "potential revolution," because the fundamental changes to society were never achieved.

2 The Basque Country is a region situated in the northern part of Spain endowed with specific cultural characteristics (e.g., the Basque language) and a high level of political autonomy. Due to the strong sense of identity of this region, a significant number of people in the Basque Country do not feel part of the Spanish nation and would like this region to be an independent country. This scenario is strongly marked by the presence of the Basque terrorist group ETA which, since its first action in 1969 (at the end of Franco's dictatorship), has caused nearly 900 casualties, including civilians, politicians, and military men. For the last ten years, ETA has been losing strength in terms of both its operational capacity and social support. In October 2011, ETA announced the definitive cessation of its armed activity. However, the conflict has still not been definitively resolved as the Spanish government is waiting for ETA to relinquish its arms.

3 There are several actors involved in the Basque Country issue: political parties of different ideological orientation and positioning regarding the independence of this region, institutions such as the Spanish government and the Basque Autonomic region, and different associations, including, on the one hand, the so-called Association of Victims of Terrorism (mostly formed by those injured by ETA, as well as their families), and on the other hand, the association of relatives of prisoners of ETA (Etxerat). In this study we will focus on those actors that had a major role during the ceasefire period: (1) the Spanish socialist government, who defended the legitimacy of the peace-making process; (2) ETA and its political arm Batasuna, who advocates for the independence of the Basque Country and legitimizes the armed struggle; and (3) the right-wing People's Party – the main group of the opposition at

that time – who delegitimized the peace-process by accusing the government of making political concessions in exchange for keeping the peace.

4 Participants were allowed to use the documents in any way they wished (e.g., only using those already supporting their views, omitting those others they found irrelevant or conflicted with their views, and adding whatever extra information they reckoned appropriate). The documents – all of them dated and arranged chronologically – were composed of five pictures, ten broadsheet headings and eight brief extracts of statements delivered by some political actors. The selected sources were: *El Mundo* and *ABC* (centre-right wing newspapers, close to the People's Party), *El País* (centre-left wing newspaper, close to Zapatero's Socialist Party), *Gara* (newspaper close to Batasuna – ETA's political arm), and *La Vanguardia* (a Catalan centre-right newspaper). All sources were balanced in order to obtain an evenly distributed view regarding the Basque issue.

5 Participants' names have been changed.

6 For anonymity, names used do not correspond to real names of participants.

References

Awad, S. H. (2017). Documenting a contested memory: Symbols in the changing city space of Cairo. *Culture & Psychology*, 23(2), 234–254.

Awad, S. H. & Wagoner, B. (2015). Agency and creativity in the midst of social change. In C. W. Gruber, M. G. Clark, S. H. Klempe, & J. Valsiner, (Eds.), *Constraints of Agency: Explorations of Theory in Everyday Life* (pp. 229–244). New York: Springer.

Awad, S. H., Wagoner, B., & Glăveanu, V. (2017). The street art of resistance. In N. Chaudhary, P. Hviid, G. Marsico, & J. Villadsen (Eds.), *Resistance in Everyday Life: Constructing Cultural Experiences* (pp. 161–180). New York: Springer.

Bakhtin, M. M. (1981). *The Dialogic Imagination*. Austin: University of Texas Press.

Bartlett, F. C. (1923). *Psychology and Primitive Culture*. Cambridge: Cambridge University Press.

Bartlett, F. C. (1932). *Remembering: A Study in Experimental and Social Psychology*. Cambridge: Cambridge University Press.

Blanco, F. & Rosa, A. (1997). Dilthey's dream: Teaching history to understand the future. *International Journal for Educational Research*, 27(3), 189–200.

Brescó, I. (2016). Conflict, memory and positioning: Studying the dialogical and multivoiced dimension of the Basque conflict. *Peace & Conflict: Journal of Peace Psychology*, 22(1), 36–43.

Brescó, I. & Wagoner, B. (2016). Context in the cultural psychology of remembering. In C. Stone & L. Bietti (Eds.), *Contextualizing Human Memory* (pp. 69–85). London: Routledge.

Burke, K. (1969). *A Grammar of Motives*. Oakland: University of California Press.

Egan, K. (1997). *The Educated Mind*. Chicago: University of Chicago Press.

Frye, N. (1957). *The Anatomy of Criticism: Four Essays*. Princeton, NJ: Princeton University Press.

Hamdy, B. & Karl, D. (2014). *Walls of Freedom: Street Art of the Egyptian Revolution*. Berlin: From Here to Fame Publishing.

Harré, R. & Van Langenhove, L. (Eds.). (1999). *Positioning Theory*. Malden, MA: Blackwell.

Lonchuk, M. & Rosa, A. (2011). Voices of graphic art images. In M. Märtsin, B. Wagoner, E. L. Aveling, I. Kadianaki, & L. Whittaker (Eds.), *Dialogicality in Focus: Challenges to Theory, Method and Application* (pp. 129–146). New York: Nova Science Publishers.

Marková, I. (2003). *Dialogicality and Social Representations: The Dynamics of Mind*. Cambridge: Cambridge University Press.

Märtsin, M., Wagoner, B., Aveling, E. L., Kadianaki, I., & Whittaker, L. (2011). *Dialogicality in Focus: Challenges to Theory, Method and Application*. New York: Nova Science Publishers.

Mitchell, W. J. T. (1990). Representation. In F. Lentricchia & T. McLaughlin (Eds.), *Critical Terms for Literary Study* (pp. 11–22). Chicago: University of Chicago Press.

Moghaddam, F. (2013). *The Psychology of Dictatorship*. Washington, DC: American Psychological Association.

Schank, R. C. & Abelson, R. P. (1977). *Scripts, Plans, Goals, and Understanding*. Hillsdale, NJ: Lawrence Erlbaum.

Scott, J. C. (1990). *Domination and the Arts of Resistance: Hidden Transcripts*. London: Yale University Press.

Tölölyan, K. (1989). Narrative culture and the motivation of the terrorist. In J. Shotter & K. J. Gergen (Eds.), *Texts of Identity* (pp. 99–118). London: SAGE.

Vygotsky, L. & Luria, A. (1994). Tool and symbol in child development. In J. Valsiner & R. van der Veer (Eds.), *The Vygotsky Reader* (pp. 99–172). Oxford: Blackwell.

Wagoner, B. (2017). *The Constructive Mind: Bartlett's Psychology in Reconstruction*. Cambridge: Cambridge University Press.

Wagoner, B. & Brescó, I. (2016). Conflict and memory: The past in the present. *Peace & Conflict: Journal of Peace Psychology*, 22(1), 3–4.

Werner, H. & Kaplan, B. (1963). *Symbol Formation: An Organismic Developmental Approach to Language and the Expression of Thought*. New York: John Wiley & Sons.

Wertsch, J. V. (1991). *Voices of Mind: A Sociocultural Approach to Mediated Action*. Cambridge, MA: Harvard University Press.

Wertsch, J. V. (1994). The primacy of mediated action in sociocultural studies. *Mind, Culture, and Activity*, 1(4), 202–208.

Wertsch, J. V. (2002). *Voices of Collective Remembering*. Cambridge: Cambridge University Press.

Wertsch, J. V. (2017). National memory and where to find it. In B. Wagoner (Ed.), *Handbook of Culture and Memory* (pp. 259–282). Oxford: Oxford University Press.

Wertsch, J. V. & O'Connor, K. (1994). Multivoicedness in historical representation: American college students' accounts of the origins of the U.S. *Journal of Narrative and Life History*, 4(4), 295–310.

White, H. (1973). *Metahistory: The Historical Imagination in 19th-century Europe*. Baltimore, MD: Johns Hopkins University Press.

White, H. (1986). Historical pluralism. *Critical Inquiry*, 12(3), 480–493.

Further Reading

Bartlett, F. C. (1940). *Political Propaganda*. Cambridge: Cambridge University Press.

Tripp, C. (2013). *The Power and the People: Paths of Resistance in the Middle East*. Cambridge: Cambridge University Press.

25 Beyond Historical Guilt: Intergenerational Narratives of Violence and Reconciliation

Giovanna Leone

The aim of this chapter is to discuss social and psychological theories exploring the role played by intergenerational narratives in the processes of intergroup reconciliation. Apart from their differences, all theories reviewed deal with the issue of if and how the old generation presents young members of a community, born after the end of extreme violent episodes or wars, with this controversial past of their group. The core idea of this chapter is that intergenerational narratives of historical pasts play a crucial role in the complex web of social and psychological processes involved in slowly building new intergroup relations after the ends of conflicts. Many empirical works show how biased narratives of past violence are crucial for the social production of contemporary intergroup hatred (see, e.g., Das, 1998). However, while they sometimes fuel old hatred toward past enemies, making these hatreds feel real and present again, at other times, intergenerational narratives about past history may enhance reconciliation. This chapter focuses on these last kinds of communication.

We cannot address the discussion of reasons why intergenerational narratives can cause such opposing reactions if we do not consider, as a starting point, the very basic issue that social conversations about the past support individual memories.

25.1 Intergenerational Narratives Support Individual Recollections and Positive Family Identities

While observing real-world situations, we may notice that, starting from infancy, new members of a community are exposed to "an avalanche" (Brescó de Luna & Rosa, 2012, p. 300) of intergenerational narratives that insert their own lives into the lives of groups in which they happen to be born. These narratives – which will later develop to include recollections of the past of "imagined communities," such as the national memory (Anderson, 2006) – *begin very early in life*, when adults recollect small episodes of their children's lives involving the lives of their family and friends (e.g., remembering when they visited the grandparents' home or when they received birthday presents). Owing to contemporary advances in videotaping technologies, recent real-world research has observed this kind of communicative interaction between children and adults. Moreover, a longitudinal perspective has often been taken, comparing these conversations at different points in children's lives and taking the development of their speaking and cognitive abilities into account.

Among these studies is an important one by Reese, Haden, and Fivush (1993; see also Fivush,

2008), which compared four repeated observations of mother–child conversations about past episodes, taken from when children were 40 months old, i.e., when they were just beginning to participate fully in conversations about the past (Eisenberg, 1985), to when they were 70 months old, i.e., when they were becoming competent in narrating autonomously (Hudson & Shapiro, 1991; Peterson & McCabe, 1983). Such a comparison showed that first conversations played a fundamental role in shaping the *basic format of the episodic autobiographical memories* of children. When they become able to give their own spontaneous autobiographical recalls, children of highly articulate parents assume their parents' rich narrative format, while children of less articulate parents produce simple, practical memories (Reese, Haden, & Fivush, 1993; see also Fivush, 2008). These data suggest that intergenerational narratives of the family past lend scaffolding support to the first formation of children's personal reminiscing.

Many years before videotaping technologies could support observational research, and when sophisticated distinctions between different facets of human memory (semantic, episodic, procedural, etc.; for a description of all memories that can be observed in experimental and ecological contexts, see Neisser & Winograd, 1995) were not yet assessed, the French sociologist Maurice Halbwachs had already focused scholars' attention on the importance of family narratives of the past. In his pioneering studies, however, he highlighted a very specific aspect of this phenomenon linked to his original theoretical claim that individual memories were impossible if not inserted in the frame of concrete social practices (Halbwachs, 1925/1992). Halbwachs noted that, in the more intimate setting of their face-to-face conversations, families showed a social practice of remembering used only when interacting with the family's members. In these kinds of conversations, specific episodes were repeatedly narrated, chosen from among several that had occurred

in the family's past. Although knowing them by heart, members of the family always listened to this repeated social sharing of overnarrated memories with evident pleasure and cherished them as a kind of family treasure. Interestingly, these same episodes, so often rehearsed in family conversations, were not shared with strangers (Halbwachs, 1925/1992).

According to Halbwachs, these family memories were chosen to be repeatedly shared in daily conversations because they conveyed to all members of this little social community a *basic positive impression* of the nucleus in which they were born. In his seminal books, Halbwachs (1925/1992, 1950/1980) proposed, therefore, that repeated family memories *supported the personal positive identity of young generations*. By repeatedly sharing family memories that were not told to strangers, families were giving to their younger members a positive image of the nucleus from which they originated and therefore of the fabric of which all of the family members were made: an "emotional armor" aimed at protecting them in the future, when they needed to cope with life's difficulties.

25.2 From Autobiographical and Family Memories to Historical and Cultural Knowledge

Halbwachs noted that contents of these family recollections sometimes referred to *memories of historical events* as well as to *memories of past ways of living* as experienced by the older generations but subsequently gone. Quoting the example of narratives related to grandchildren when staying in their grandparents' home, Halbwachs defined these special periods spent living with grandparents as the first trip of children not only in space but also in time. The rich and affectively loaded interactions with grandparents made an earlier period of the community's past understandable to children living in a completely different historical situation.

These nuances of the phenomenon of repeated family memories, first highlighted in Halbwachs's books (1925/1992, 1950/1980), are easy to observe in everyday life interactions. For instance, European baby boomers have usually been exposed to grandparents' memories of major events from World War II as well as narratives of the way their grandparents had to live in order to cope with all threats, difficulties, and shortages during times of war. Using Halbwachs's very words, we could say that the function of this specific kind of family memory is to present young people with a *"living" image of history*.

In a similar vein, many years later, Assmann (1992, cited in László, 2003) proposed to call *communication memory* the collective memories of a community that appeared in a vivid and "lived" way to young generations, since they received them through interpersonal communication from older generations. These kinds of collective memories extend back for about a century of the community's history, that is, over three generational changes. Collective memories about the in-group past that took place before this time span instead reach the young generations only as a semantic knowledge. Therefore, Assmann (1992) proposed to call them *cultural memories*, in order to distinguish them from communication memories received through the intergenerational narratives of those who witnessed consequential events of the collective past or lived in historical situations subsequently gone.

Interestingly, communication and cultural memories can sometimes overlap when semantic contents conveyed through cultural artifacts (statues, names of streets and squares, movies and books, museums, commemorations, public speeches, etc.) referred to episodes that happened in the time span of three generations and were also presented in interpersonal witnessing or family remembering. A concrete example of how family narratives can be linked to social ones may be seen in the Russian case of the so-called Bessmertnyi Polk. On May 9, 2015, impressive parades of the Russian "Immortal Regiment" (Bessmertnyi Polk) that fought in World War II were organized, in which purportedly millions of Russian citizens marched with pictures of their relatives who had served in World War II.

But social narratives and family narratives do not always tell the same story. To give another example, two focus group discussions of young Italian people were confronted with four other focus group discussions: two involving young Italian participants who in their youth lived during World War II and two involving baby boomers born immediately after the end of the war. Focus groups were invited to recall personal memories of moments in which they happened to think about the historical framing of their lives. All focus groups spontaneously recalled Italian Fascism as an issue that they thought about. However, older participants evoked mostly their *autobiographical memories* (fear when their cities were bombed, food shortages, but also solidarity and courage). In contrast, young participants evoked *narratives* received both in history classes and during family conversations (László & Ehmann, 2012; Jovchelovitch, 2012; see also Hammack & Pilecki, 2012). Interestingly, when these narratives conveyed a conflicting meaning of these times (for instance, when grandparents claimed that Fascism did something good for Italy, providing, for instance, social assistance for poor children or new infrastructures), young people actively avoiding taking a clear stance between the different points of view received from school and family narratives, trying not to negatively judge their grandparents' witnessing of the historical past (Leone & Curigliano, 2009).

We cannot discuss at length in these pages the fascinating problem of how different historical narratives, coming from different sources, could be integrated into a tentative cognitive polyphasia (Jovchelovitch, 2012). We limit ourselves to signaling how, referring to cultural memories and their possible clash with communicative ones, a crucial set of intergenerational narratives is offered to students through *history books*. Scholars' opinions on these issues appear somehow controversial.

On one hand, when narratives included in history books concern the past of "imagined communities" (Anderson, 2006), first of all national ones, they support a *positive image of the nation-state* where students are born (Liu, Onar, & Woodward, 2014). Narratives with a similar aim are also received during family conversations or through literature, media, and fiction (László, 2003). On the other hand, however, sometimes history books are sharply different from these other kinds of intergenerational narratives, since they are meant to convey *knowledge* about the past, linked to scientific research. When historical events happened that challenge the positive image of the group, either morally or socially, history books cannot avoid also teaching these aspects of the past to students. Moreover, owing to globalization, classrooms are increasingly multicultural, and using history teaching as a technology of the nation-state (Liu, Onar, & Woodward, 2014) often seems inadequate. Currently more than ever, history teaching stands apart from other kinds of intergenerational narratives, since – at least in democratic regimes – its specific role is to seriously support *both historical knowledge and cultural memory*. When considering their social aims and psychological effects, therefore, a dividing line has to be drawn between studies in history books and studies on other kinds of historical narratives about cultural memory (Leone, 2017).

Summing up all these studies and empirical observations, we may conclude that intergenerational narratives support individual recollections, from the more intimate and concrete set of autobiographical and family memories to the more collective and abstract set of historical and cultural heritages.

For the aims of this chapter, we focus only on this last set of intergenerational narratives. Before discussing the complex role of these kinds of narratives in reconciliation processes, however, we must first consider what may drive youths to get acquainted with their historical past and to listen to older generations narrating it. It is common to think that young people are indifferent to history and somehow embedded only in the present. In the following section, we review important theoretical proposals claiming the opposite: that youths *want and need* to be acquainted with their historical past.

25.3 "What Is the Use of History?" Why Youths Need to Understand Their Historical Past

A first valuable insight into the meaningfulness of historical narratives for young people could be taken from the classic little book by Bloch, *The Historian's Craft or Apology of History* (1954). Bloch (1886–1944), perhaps the most important European historian medievalist of his time and cofounder with Lucien Febvre of *Annales* (1929), wrote this unfinished meditation on the writing of history shortly before being executed in 1944 as a leader of the French resistance. In the very first pages of this posthumously published book, Bloch remembered that, as Paris was taken by the Nazi troops and French culture knew all of a sudden its *étrange défaite*, his 12-year-old son asked him, "What is the use of history?" The whole of this classic book is an answer to this question, and it is touching that Bloch, one of the most prominent historians of his time, introduced this issue by recalling a question that had occurred during a family conversation instead of referring to his teaching or academic activities.

As if replying to his son, Bloch explained historical accounts not as a matter of advice or strategic counseling but as a basic law of the human mind and of its "instinctive need of understanding." From his original point of view, historical facts were inextricably merged with psychological processes. Certainly, Bloch accepted that historical facts, either sublime or brutal, are linked to situational forces, but he stressed that their action "is weakened or intensified by man and his mind." By repeatedly narrating the history of their group, conversations between generations take part in this never-ending collective effort to give meaning to past events and, because of this activity of human mind, contribute toward shaping their impact on present days (Sweeny, 1993).

By discussing the function of history as a fulfilment of a *basic psychological need of understanding*, Bloch claimed that it is impossible to disentangle historical facts from the way in which they are "weakened or intensified" by their human understanding. Therefore, when listening to older generations sharing their knowledge and experiences with them, young people are also exposed to older generations' interpretation of historical facts and more generally to their viewpoints of the world, to their *Weltanschauung* (Kansteiner, 2014). However, this close intertwining between facts and interpretations, between past narratives and *Weltanschauung* of the historical period narrated, raises a crucial point concerning a basic ambivalence of intergenerational narratives. On one hand, they assure a continuity among generations, making new ones aware of the history that preexisted their birth. On the other hand, each generation opens up to new viewpoints, to a renewal of *Weltanschauung* orienting the social life of the group.

Both these points were strongly addressed during the past century, when European scholars struggled to understand the dramatic social situations in which they were living – situations eventually leading to the traumatic collapse of European democratic governments, to totalitarian regimes, and finally to the world wars. Although very different from each other, all these scholars conducted seminal studies on the importance of narratives of in-group history to young individu-

als. In these works, the need for both continuity and discontinuity between generations became apparent.

25.4 Continuity and Discontinuity: Natality and Human Historical Preexistence

Referring to the issue of *continuity*, in his classic book on the revolt of the masses, Ortega y Gasset (1930/1957) pointed out that the "strange condition of human person" is *"his essential preexistence,"* that is, the fact that lives of humans do not begin with their birth but are pre-shaped by the history of their community. However, at the very moment in which he described our lives as historically founded, Ortega y Gasset argued that the past of the community in which a person happens to be born "instead of imposing on us one trajectory . . . imposes several, and consequently *forces us to choose*" (Ortega y Gasset, 1930/1957, p. 31; emphasis added). Refusing any positivistic attitude, in his theoretical frame, Ortega y Gasset described intergenerational historical narratives as basic tools for young adults, enabling them to grasp their starting points in life. Therefore, his theoretical stance considers past in-group history not in a deterministic way but as a cultural instrument allowing young people – made aware of their historical past – to make wiser decisions about their own futures.

On the other hand, referring to the issue of *discontinuity*, Arendt proposed intergenerational narratives to be a source of knowledge but not a prearranged inheritance, forcing descendants to assume the same historical destiny as their ancestors. The opening sentence of the preface to her book *Between Past and Future* (Arendt, 1977) is a quote from French poet and resistance fighter René Char: *"notre héritage n'est précédé d'aucun testament,"* which she translated as "our inheritance was left to us by no testament." In fact, although she described the intergenerational narratives as a bridge over the inescapable gap between generations, in her book, Arendt also stressed how young people were not passive receivers of previous generations' narratives but elaborated these contents according to their own original points of view. Assuming this theoretical stance on discontinuity, Arendt incorporated in her thoughts Walter Benjamin's lesson on one of the most awful consequences of the violence of World War I: "It is as if something that seemed inalienable to us, the securest among our possessions, were taken from us: the ability to exchange experiences" (Benjamin & Zohn, 1963, p. 81).

Arendt wholeheartedly agreed with Benjamin's idea that the unbelievable violence of World War I – not to mention the atrocities of World War II – disempowered any possibility of direct communication of traumatic experiences between generations. In her essay on Benjamin, Arendt fully recognized his concept of the *experience of war endlessly losing its value.* However, Arendt added to the work of Benjamin a further step. Although she accepted his insight of a profound change of intergenerational storytelling, she conceived it not as an end of this kind of communication but as a transformation of it.

To make this shift clear, she commented on Benjamin's work by quoting some lines from Ariel's famous song in Shakespeare's *The Tempest*, in which Ariel describes how the sea turns relics or drowned bodies into "something rich or strange," as corals or pearls. Arendt used this same image to describe the intellectual work of Benjamin. According to her, he was not only the scholar who described how intergenerational communication came to an end because of literal incommunicability of war violence after the world wars. According to her, Benjamin was also the thinker who revealed how storytelling may use any fragmented experience as a pearl, thus showing how the human mind can operate surprising transformations on hopeless miseries. Quoting the great Danish writer Isak Dinesen, Arendt reminded us that "all sorrows can be borne if you put them into a story or tell a story about them." Therefore, in Arendt's essay, Benjamin is presented "like a pearl diver who descends to the bottom of the sea, not to excavate the bottom and bring it to light but to pry loose the rich and the strange, the pearls and the coral in the depths and to carry them to the surface" (Arendt, 2001, p. 203).

Commenting in such a way on Benjamin's work, Arendt turned his sad awareness of the end of intergenerational storytelling about experiences of war violence into a new possibility for social advance and change. This inspired interpretation was linked to two innovative insights produced by Arendt's theoretical stance: her deep understanding of *transformative effects of storytelling* and her new concept of *natality* (Arendt, 1958). Introducing the new idea of *natality* at the very core of the description of intergenerational narratives, Arendt argued that the real source of novelty in social life is linked to the fact that each birth represents a new beginning for the community – since, once born, each human being may start something unexpected and new. By the notion that she called natality, Arendt recovered for our understanding of social changes the lesson she learned from Augustine, to whom she devoted her doctoral dissertation at the University of Heidelberg under Karl Jaspers's supervision in 1929: "*Initium ergo ut esset, creatus est homo*" (Augustine, *De civitate Dei*, XII, 21).

Both theoretical proposals of Ortega y Gasset (1930/1957) and of Arendt (1958, 1977) give us important insights into the dual role of intergenerational narratives about the community past, jointly developing both continuity and discontinuity between generations. This intrinsic ambivalence performs a crucial function, especially when narratives deal with traumatic or controversial historical experiences.

The first insight refers to the idea of *historical preexistence* of the human mind (Ortega y Gasset, 1930/1957). According to this theoretical perspective, intergenerational narratives on past historical crimes are offered to descendants of perpetrators because these stories are, in spite of all, cultural tools needed by young generations to understand their current social positions. By these narratives, in fact, older generations enhance the historical awareness of the younger ones about their in-group past, enabling them to act better in the social arena.

The second insight refers to the notion of *natality*. In this other theoretical perspective, intergenerational communication is described as a never-ending process of coping with the inescapable gap between generations – being aware that this gap is the essential driver for social change (Arendt, 1958, 1977).

Taken together, both ideas allow us to better grasp the reasons why narratives about the in-group historical past must be explored not only from the perspective of older generations but also from the intrinsic novelty introduced by the ways in which younger generations can receive and elaborate these difficult contents. In this sense, the gap between generations requires a narrative bridge, but it will never be totally reduced by narratives. On the contrary, it is precisely the inescapable difference between older generations and new ones that may open up real opportunities for intergroup reconciliation as well as the surprising renewal of old hates fueled by memories of an apparently remote past, suddenly switched on again in the social discourse. One of the main reasons why intergenerational narratives on past violence are sometimes tools for reconciliation, while at other times they renew old hatreds, may be because of the influence of a *societal ethos of conflict* (Bar-Tal et al., 2012) on these accounts of the past.

25.5 Intergenerational Narratives of Violence: Building Up and Marginalizing the Ethos of Conflict

Intergroup violence cannot be explained or understood without taking into account what

Daniel Bar-Tal and colleagues call the societal *ethos of conflict*. The start of intergroup violence is announced and promoted by a shift to a *conflict ethos*, that is, a change in societal normative assumptions, based on the emergence of the idea that the other group is an enemy, and therefore intergroup relations have to be conceived as a threatening zero-sum game that can come to an end only when one of the players is completely defeated (Bar-Tal et al., 2012). Only according to this new societal ethos is it possible to perceive violence not as a behavior to be refused, sanctioned, or barely accepted but as a heroic way to protect the in-group from being defeated and destroyed by its enemies.

Bloch's idea that historical facts cannot be severed from their perception and understanding explains perfectly the practical consequences of this societal shift to a conflict ethos. *The shift to a conflict ethos triggers the perceiving of the other group as an enemy*, consequently implying that violence against the enemy is the right way to stay loyal to one's own in-group, a terrible yet valiant choice. Violence against and the death of out-group members are suddenly perceived not as shameful actions but as heroic ones, and narratives vary accordingly.

However, when conflict settlement is finally achieved and agreements are negotiated between leaders through peace treaties, a new intergroup situation arises where social and psychological processes turn completely. In this new intergroup balance, the perception of the other group as an enemy has no room anymore, since reconciliation instead of violence is becoming socially expected. Reconciliation processes, therefore, may be essentially seen as a slow *marginalization of the idea of the enemy* from the way in which ordinary people think in relation to their own social identities (Kelman, 2008). It means that removing the idea of an enemy from the core of one's own social identity rules out violence from the set of plausible strategies to use when facing the other group. Evidently, it changes both representations and narratives concerning inter-group relations. However, the idea of an enemy, once accepted, is hard to put aside, and it thus remains hidden as a potential collective memory (Halbwachs, 1950/1980), ready to be used again as a prearranged way of perceiving the other group if new opportunities for violence arise in intergroup contacts.

Again, if we take seriously the theoretical point made by Bloch (1954), changes of social situations, on one hand, and of social perceptions, on the other hand, cannot be neatly disentangled, nor reduced to a simple deterministic explanation, since narratives vary according to the external situation of intergroup relations (conflict vs. conflict settlement), but intergroup relations are also legitimated or challenged by the way in which they are narrated and understood. Intergenerational narratives could therefore be seen both as a consequence and as an enhancement of ongoing intergroup processes.

However, this tension between narratives revolving around the threats of enemies and narratives marginalizing this idea may be observed from two different temporal perspectives. On one hand, *longitudinal changes* can be appreciated, showing either progress toward marginalization of the image of an enemy when reconciliation advances or regressions to a conflict ethos when intergroup violence arises anew. On the other hand, a set of *simultaneous processes* may be observed, where one group is ready for a conflict ethos while at the same time another group is refusing it. As Serge Moscovici (1976) convincingly argued in his classic work on social influence, social representations and social discourse observed at any given point in time – either during wartime or after peace treaties – cannot be reduced to the dominant point of view of majorities.

This means that when the dominant social discourse on intergroup relations fuels a conflict ethos, there are still some *active minorities* refusing to see the other group as the enemy

and also refusing to see killings as heroic acts. When peace treaties are set up and new cooperation with former enemies emerges, the point of view of these active minorities suddenly becomes functional to the new state of affairs, and those who privately appreciated that uncommon attitude toward the out-group, but kept it silent because of social conformity, can finally openly change their minds.

Observing, after a long period of intergroup reconciliation, how heroism can no longer be used to account for past violence against former enemies makes it evident how active minorities deeply influenced and eventually changed the general orientation of historical narratives. In fact, after the turning point of conflict settlement (Kelman, 2008), the innovative point of view of active minorities refusing to adhere to the dominant ethos of conflict is suddenly able not only to grasp another viewpoint on social life but also to transform the way in which majorities look at this violent past. Similarly to all social representations that describe the current state of affairs between groups, the ethos of conflict is not "a quiet thing": it changes inasmuch as society changes its grasp on reality (Howarth, 2006).

However, marginalizing the *ethos of conflict* (Bar-Tal et al., 2012), although crucial, is only a first step toward intergroup reconciliation. The image of an enemy, in fact, is essential to *justify* violence – either before or after enacting it. But the image of an enemy is not enough to *explain* violence. The search for the meaning of past violence requires simultaneously taking into account the roles of perpetrators, of victims, and of apathetic bystanders. A triadic structure, seen in any experience of direct violence, becomes particularly important for scholars to describe massive violence and killings (Staub, 2001), although, of course, it has to be seen as a research tool describing experiences that are much more fluid and that cannot be completely captured in dangerous entitative terms (Vollhardt & Bilewicz, 2013).

Having marginalized the enemy image is not enough to narrate past violence in a way that could sound bearable for all protagonists, and their descendants, of these dramatic events. These elaborate narratives are told down the generations to protect the need for an acceptable social and moral image of the in-group (Allpress et al., 2014), so that when violence is justified, it reinforces the historical understanding of violence, acknowledging the loss of moral and social virtues (Vollhardt, Mazur, & Lemahieu, 2014). Social denials have shaped narratives for a long time to fit the image of the in-group rather than supporting the true facts.

25.6 Biases in Historical Narratives: Violence as Seen from the Point of View of Victims, Perpetrators, and Bystanders

Immediately after the end of violence, perpetrators, as well as victims and bystanders, use silence when among former foes as a first implicit communication concerning past events. This first silence helps to restore a sense of "normality" to everyday life and enhances initial viable local life, allowing perpetrators, apathetic bystanders, and victims to live side by side and to continue their unavoidable social exchanges (Eastmond & Selimovic, 2012).

However, after this first, protective silence, and because of the need to adapt quickly to the joyful but also startling declaration that war is finally over, a new struggle will break out between old protagonists to safeguard the image of each other's own group.

On very rare occasions, this symbolic competition between former enemies is quickly solved through an overt and clear acknowledgment of atrocities committed. If successfully managed, this risky communicative move is used as a key element for consolidating the end of direct violence, as it was in the case of the Truth and Rec-

onciliation Commission in South Africa. Here, in the presence of the local community and its authorities, the narratives of violence were overtly negotiated between those who experienced the violent times, including victims, perpetrators, and bystanders. Leaders who suggested this very dangerous move agreed that the highly possible reenactment of violence after the signing of the first settlement of this bloody conflict had been avoided mainly thanks to these social activities (Meiring & Tutu, 1999). However, it is very hard to understand what made the difference here from many other situations, when silence and denials immediately took place after the settlement of the conflict. Many suggestions have been advanced, although only as a matter of speculation. For instance, Nadler and Shnabel (2008) proposed distinguishing between reconciliation meant to re-create harmony between former enemies, to enable them to live together in the same community, and reconciliation meant to enable former enemies to set apart old conflicts to live in two distinct communities that, having settled their conflict, have no further reason to interact. Many times, these two kinds of reconciliation are needed at the end of a conflict internal to a group, for reconciliation meant to reinstate harmony, or at the end of an intergroup conflict, for reconciliation meant to establish a complete separation between former enemies. In the case of South Africa, a relevant case of a conflict dividing a national group, the search for harmony was reached through a risky yet successful rise of internal communication of members of the same community in front of their own authorities.

Another speculative reason that is often quoted to explain the success of truth and reconciliation committees in South Africa is linked to the particular culture of these communities, based on the idea of *ubuntu*, that is, of the importance of saving and recovering social unity as a paramount value that orients everyday life and that has been invoked to support this reconciliation strategy. It would suggest that truth and reconciliation committees could not be used as a sort of successful recipe to solve the conflict in the aftermath of violence in all cultural contexts if they do not refer to this same cultural expectancy of evaluating unity and social support of the community as intrinsically important aims for public actions (Murithi, 2009).

We do not have enough room in these few pages to discuss such an interesting and challenging research question. We simply want to stress that the choice of clear and straightforward communication between perpetrators and victims regarding violent facts is extremely rare. Quite often, many years have to elapse and several generations are needed before trust and open communication between groups can be established. In these situations, before reaching the difficult goal of trust – that is, a goal and a process of reconciliation at the same time (Bar-Tal & Bennink, 2004) – intergenerational narratives on past violence keep showing subtle signs of social denial at work for many years after peace treaties. During this long period, the need for narratives to protect a good social or moral image of the older generations is greater than the need to take into account the different perspectives of all groups involved in the violence, which would have enabled young generations to understand what really happened in the in-group's past.

According to some scholars (see Kelman, 2008), when narrating violence that threatens the in-group image, a biased perspective is always to be expected, although building trust between groups requires the construction of narratives that sound acceptable to all descendants of violence actors – perpetrators, victims, and bystanders. However, to consider this controversial issue in more depth, two aspects have to be taken into account. The first refers to the very notion of social denial, which could affect narratives about the historical past in different ways. The second refers to the different perspectives of victims, perpetrators, and apathetic bystanders.

Referring to the first point, Cohen (2001) proposes that denial may occur at different degrees in the social discourse as an active refusal: to admit the historical reality of violent facts (*literal denial*), to recognize the moral responsibility of the in-group for these facts (*interpretive denial*), or to assume the practical consequences of acknowledging one's own responsibility for past violence (*implicatory denial*) (Cohen, 2001).

Referring to the second point, until now, scholars' attention has focused mainly on the perspective of perpetrators and victims, while the social and psychological aftermath of the apathy of bystanders has somehow been neglected. Referring to the perspectives of victims and perpetrators, a well-consolidated theory foresees different social and psychological needs for these two groups. In particular, according to this theory, perpetrators need to avoid social exclusion due to their cruel misdeeds, while victims need to regain control over their own lives and destinies (Nadler & Shnabel, 2008, 2015). Narratives could be biased to ameliorate the impaired dimensions of the identities of both groups: the agency dimension of identity of the victims' group and the moral and social image of the perpetrators' group (Nadler & Shnabel, 2015).

However, other biases could be traced in narratives about past violence involving the in-group. For instance, even many years after violent incidents, narratives may allow interpretations based on a conflict ethos (Bar-Tal et al., 2012). These narratives do not deny facts but present descendants of former enemies with a story stressing how both groups were engaged in a struggle for survival, thus justifying the violence used by the in-group as legitimate self-defense. An interpretive denial may in this case allow descendants of perpetrators to avoid the full acknowledgment of moral responsibilities of their group. Similar interpretive shortcuts are offered by narratives based on competitive victimhood, when interpretation of past crimes is based on the idea that perpetrators reacted because they too were victimized (Noor et al., 2012). There are also mixed situations in which groups were at once victims and perpetrators; we may say that this is actually the case in many conflicts (SimanTov-Nachlieli & Shnabel, 2014). Moreover, while accepting the need to acknowledge moral responsibility for violence that took place in the past, perpetrators' descendants may listen to narratives that try to diminish the moral responsibilities of the in-group, for example, by presenting the past behavior of the group as legitimate (Baumeister, 1997) or minimizing the severity of the inflicted harm (Bandura, 1999).

This huge corpus of scholars' observations takes into account the cognitive and affective functions of narratives, which allows linking of different pieces of information into a well-organized schema, leading to meaningful sense (Bruner, 1990). Using the definition of social denial provided by Cohen (2001), all these biased narratives could therefore be enlisted as *interpretive denials*, or as *implicatory denials* if they imply also a refusal to accept consequences stemming from old violence.

But all these biases, and their practical consequences in present-day situations, where social representations of the past could act as historical charters (Liu & Hilton, 2005) for promoting future intergroup relations (either fueling new aggressions or opening up to a new trust), are very different from *literal social denial*, when knowledge itself of historical facts is not made available to descendants.

25.7 Down the Collective Black Hole: The Literal Social Denial

There is no need to invoke some obscure manipulation, or even conspiracy, to recognize the banality of the phenomenon of literal social denials, as we may see them today in many examples: the prohibition to speak about the Armenian genocide (Hovannisian, 1998; Bilali, 2013); the covering up of French collaboration with Nazi occupa-

tion (Campbell, 2006); the social amnesia about the Italian colonial crimes perpetrated during the occupation of Ethiopia (Leone & Sarrica, 2014); the rhetoric of official discourses on Thanksgiving Day, when US presidents neglect to mention the role of Native Americans in episodes commemorated by this special day (Kurtiş, Adams, & Yellow Bird, 2010), to name only a few. Instead of well-organized manipulation, historical denials are often simply the result of "a gradual seepage of knowledge down some collective black hole" (Cohen, 2001, p. 13). In these social situations, reconciliation is therefore linked to every intelligent effort performed to oppose such an easygoing and generalized seepage, choosing to narrate violence to younger generations instead of letting it disappear down those overwhelming "black holes" – especially when direct witnesses are about to disappear and communication memories are close to being substituted by cultural ones.

Despite the efforts of active minorities struggling to reinstate the historical truth about violence – especially when victims are too weak or socially isolated and cannot make their voices heard – literal denial of violence often take places in the social arena and goes on for a long time across the subsequent generations.

The present-day European collective memories of colonialism give us insightful examples of current consequences of the different kinds of social denial Cohen (2001) described. Sometimes it is possible to observe implicatory denials related, for instance, to the difficulty of adopting political decisions that take into account the economic consequences of long-lasting exploitation of resources of colonized countries; at other times, an interpretive denial may be observed among descendants of colonizers, still representing the colonial past of their countries not only as a systematic exploitation but also as a kind of civilization; and finally, when victims have not gained enough power to impose on the research agenda the study of the history of violence they have suffered, a denial of facts could also be seen, as in the case of collective amnesia of war crimes committed by the Italian Army during its colonial invasions, or in the case of the long-lasting silence concerning Belgian atrocities in Congo (for a review of these different kinds of sociopsychological aftermaths of colonialism in the collective memories of descendants of colonizers, see Volpato & Licata, 2010).

Denials of in-group crimes affecting narratives meant for descendants of former colonizers until recent times show how it has taken years for atrocities to be overtly recognized and officially narrated to descendants of perpetrators' groups (Leone & Mastrovito, 2010; Cajani, 2013; Leach, Zeineddine, & Čehajić-Clancy, 2013). Moreover, when literal social denial lasts from one generation to the next, sometimes *historical myths* can replace factual knowledge, fulfilling somehow the young people's need to learn about their group's historical past (Ortega y Gasset, 1930/1957).

This was the case in the myth of Italians as soldiers full of humanity and incapable of any war crimes. This myth – well known in the historical and sociopsychological literature as the myth of *Italiani, brava gente* (Italians, good fellows) – has only recently been proven to be widespread in the social discourse of the Italian community (Mari et al., 2010). Opposing this myth, a few Italian historians (e.g., Labanca, 2002) arrived at this conclusion after in-depth studies into the evidence of serious war crimes committed by the Italian Army during its colonial invasion of Africa. Despite these important advances in historical research, the public debate has continued to express doubts concerning these facts, and until now, the historical myth of Italians as good fellows is difficult to challenge in the Italian social discourse (see Del Boca, 2005).

Along the same lines, a frank narrative of these facts has only recently been found in Italian history books, that is, more than seventy years after the crimes took place (Cajani, 2013; Leone & Mastrovito, 2010). Nevertheless, when exposed to narratives of these crimes, extracted from currently used historical textbooks, young Italian university students use facial expressions (Ekman, Friesen, & Ellsworth, 2013) that clearly show their initial reactions of surprise or doubt (Leone et al., 2018).

In fact, intergenerational narratives shared and received in this situation of literal social denial – if not of hegemonic historical myths fully contradicting past historical facts – have to face serious interpersonal and social obstacles to reinstate the truth. Referring to the specific case of historical narratives addressed to a young generation that break a long-lasting literal social denial and/or challenge a widespread historical myth, we agree with the theoretical proposal of Foucault (1983) that a clear distinction has to be drawn, distinguishing these demanding historical narratives from other kinds of truth-speaking ones. In fact, when intergenerational narratives are biased by social denials, as is often the case, narrative shift restoring factual information about the past may ameliorate the impaired dimensions of the identities of groups involved in past violence. However, as we have already seen, social denials may be literal (i.e., avoid stating facts), interpretive, or implicatory (Cohen, 2001). We think that literal social denials, which make the knowledge of historical facts unavailable, are the more dangerous among all states of social denials. Therefore we have proposed (Leone, 2017) to set apart the study of the intergenerational narratives *breaking a literal denial*, because we assume that knowing historical facts is the first step toward meeting the different needs of descendants of both perpetrators and victims, that is, the agency dimension of identity of the victims' group and the moral and social image of the perpetrators' group (Nadler & Shnabel, 2015). We proposed to call these specific kinds of intergenerational narratives about the in-group's past *parrhesia* (Leone & Sarrica, 2014; Leone, 2017).

25.8 Breaking Down Literal Social Denials: The Dangerous Game of *Parrhesia*

According to Foucault's original taxonomy of various forms of truth speaking (Foucault, 1983), we propose to define *parrhesia* as the intergenerational narratives that dangerously expose those who clearly and fearlessly speak to young people about an inconvenient historical truth formerly denied in the social discourse about an in-group's past (Leone & Sarrica, 2014; Leone, 2017). *Parrhesia* is a classic Greek notion, which Foucault brought to our attention, proposing that this old idea could help us to distinguish a specific kind of truth speaking that at the same time holds considerable risks for speakers, but also empowerment for receivers. Uncertainty of the trade-off between risks for speakers and empowerment for receivers disentangles this specific way of communication from other kinds of truth speaking, conveying, for instance, a technical truth or an existential wisdom. On the other hand, during parrhesiastic communication about a collective past, speakers are guided by empowering intentions, since presenting receivers with a hurtful truth enables them to better understand their current situation. These intentions distinguish *parrhesia* from aggression. When using *parrhesia* to convey inconvenient information about past in-group crimes, it is not to damage or humiliate receivers but to give them a realistic understanding of their own historical preexistence (Ortega y Gasset, 1930/1957).

Furthermore, by confronting receivers with a truth that was denied before, but that could enable them to better understand historical debts inherited by previous generations, *parrhestiases* (i.e., those who speak about dangerous topics without fear of the negative consequences they could encounter because of their words) choose "frankness instead of persuasion, truth instead of falsehood or silence . . . the moral duty instead of self-interest and moral apathy" (Foucault, 2001,

p. 19). It means that, apart from the reaction of receivers, which cannot be fully predicted in advance, *parrhesiastes* are able to express of their own accord their will to act in a decent way, protecting at least their own moral integrity. Therefore, their frankness may also be seen as a kind of self-enhancement or, to use Foucault's very words, an act of *cura sui* (Foucault, 1983).

Finally, those who speak with *parrhesia* are implicitly showing their confidence in their receivers' strength and moral judgment (Foucault, 1983). By choosing to tell them an uneasy truth, they are declaring an implicit trust in their receivers' capacity to cope with this difficult knowledge. Speakers will not be completely clear on past atrocities of an in-group if they suspect that descendants of the social groups that were involved will react negatively to their message (Gross, 1998) and will regulate and evaluate the usefulness of information before passing it on. But of course, this is only an intention based on hope, since speakers obviously cannot fully predict the effect of their communication on receivers. Therefore its risky features single *parrhesia* out from all other kinds of truth speaking about historical in-group crimes, making it not only a narrative but a real "*communication game*" (Foucault, 1983) between generations.

A parrhestiastic communication will be successful depending on how both older speakers and younger receivers play this game. To play it, the older generation's move is to choose what and how to narrate, and the younger generation's move is to acknowledge their ancestors' negative behaviors and to adopt a stance to them. By frankly speaking about the role of ancestors during past violence, *parrhesia* opens up new communication strategies, once the avoiding strategy has been discharged. On one hand, the decision to speak frankly enables young descendants of the social groups involved in past violence to better evaluate the impairment of the social and moral image that has characterized their historical preexistence, thus allowing them to better judge current intergroup relations. On the other hand, this historical knowledge threatens their basic need for a positive social identity. To explore how frank intergenerational narratives contribute to the general unfolding of intergroup reconciliation processes, therefore, it is essential to observe how young people cope with the unsettling truths they are told by previous generations.

25.9 Pragmatic Consequences of Historical Truth: The Crucial Role of Group-Based Moral Emotions

For understanding if and how intergenerational narratives ease reconciliation processes, especially in the case of *parrhesia*, we have to observe them first of all by referring to basic characteristics of the narrative format (László, 2008), but we must also consider the pragmatic consequences. In fact, intergenerational narratives contribute to reconciliation processes not only in the way in which they are told by the older generations but also in the way they are received by the younger ones. This implies that our attention has to focus not only *downward*, on the information old generations choose to share with younger ones or to hide from them (Leone & Sarrica, 2014), but also *upward*, on emotional reactions and subsequent judgments expressed by young adults about the past inherited from their ancestors (Leone, 2000; Leone et al., 2018).

According to this point of view, the role of *group-based moral emotions* of young receivers of historical narratives becomes crucial.

Certainly it is not possible to fully review in a few pages all empirical works that contributed to this new field of research. Nevertheless, it is interesting to note how these kinds of contributions shifted their research's focus in the last decade.

From the point of view of descendants of *perpetrators*, after focusing for a long time on the classic issue of biases protecting the need for a positive social identity (Tajfel & Turner,

1986; Turner et al., 1987), research on group-based emotions of perpetrators' descendants has recently shifted attention to the sociopsychological need of young generations so that the social group, where they happen to be born, may reach some basic levels of moral decency (Allpress et al., 2014). This shift has made our theoretical models concerning moral group-based emotions more complex. We are in fact passing from the fascinating yet somehow elusive notion of "collective guilt" (Branscombe & Doosje, 2004), expected in descendants of perpetrators because of past in-group wrongdoings, to more precise observations of the wider emotional set enacted by young generations when facing a narrative of past historical crimes: not only guilt but, prior to it and sometimes instead of it, also anger, contempt, surprise, doubt, social shame, moral shame, and so on. According to recent developments in this burgeoning field of research, it has been proposed that focusing mainly on the reactions of *historical guilt* of young descendants of perpetrators is not enough to understand how they are able to turn the page on the historical crimes of their ancestors. On the contrary, it has been suggested that we have to pay attention to the more general set of group-based emotions due to the acknowledgment of historical evidence of in-group violations and crimes (Shepherd, Spears, & Manstead, 2013).

Interestingly, a similar focus on multiple emotions and their change in time could be observed also from the point of view of descendants of *victims*. As we have already stressed in previous pages, the main emotion attributed to victims and their descendants has been shame for past helplessness. Therefore empowerment is supposed to be the main social and psychological need of victims, since it allows them to regain a sense of control over their lives as opposed to the shame of having been unable to defend themselves (Nadler & Shnabel, 2008, 2015). However, in an intriguing article about the changing themes in psychological theory with regard to post-traumatic effects of the Holocaust on its survivors, Nadler (2001) points out that in the first place, clinicians focused mainly on the question of who survived. In the second place, the main question was if survivors were psychologically healthy or sick. Finally, the main question concerning clinical studies has shifted again to a focus on understanding whether the post-traumatic effects have extended beyond the survivors (e.g., to their families). It is clear that these different research questions imply that different sets of moral emotions are to be expected from survivors and their families, contributing to different semantic nuances of the concept of shame. Another important research line, referring to moral emotions of victims and their relatives, refers also to the issue of resentment – starting from the pivotal work of Jean Améry – which could not too easily be reduced to a "negative" emotional reaction (Klein, 2011).

Finally, rare but interesting research has concentrated on the moral emotions of *bystanders* and their descendants. In this somehow underdeveloped field of study, a recent work of Wojcik, Bilewicz, and Lewicka (2010) has shown that descendants of bystanders born in communities where massive violence occurred were eager to learn the history of their town. Classic theoretical perspectives expressed by Bloch (1954) and Ortega y Gasset (1930/1957) could greatly contribute toward explaining these data.

Taken together, these developments allow us to move from group-based moral emotions to a *self-awareness*, which allows for more detailed moral emotions expressing a *judgment* of the older generation's behavior. In this sense, the centrality of the notion of historical guilt is now challenged by more comprehensive approaches also taking into account emotions brought on by other condemning processes (Haidt, 2003).

According to the communicative strategies used by older generations – to narrate past in-group crimes more openly or to avoid the more difficult aspects of the past by using elusive narratives or even covering it all up by meaningful social silences – descendants of social groups involved in past violence are faced with different emotional challenges. Our studies could greatly profit from the theoretical choice to pay attention to both directions of intergenerational narratives about the historical past: *downward*, to see if older generations kept silent or told a never-ending story of conflicting self-victimization and retaliation or eventually tried to evolve toward more inclusive and complex points of view, but also *upward*, to see if younger generations are expected to carry the weight of responsibility that this difficult historical preexistence put on their shoulders or if they can express their historical uniqueness, judging the actions of their ancestors from the perspective of those born after the crimes and therefore assuming their historical responsibility as new citizens, free at last from any direct moral charge.

Research and studies reviewed in these pages suggest that for intergenerational narratives addressed to descendants of all protagonists of violence – perpetrators, victims, bystanders – knowledge is necessary, but it is not enough. To finally turn the page and prevent past violence from arising again, younger generations have to be allowed not only to know but also to *judge* the history inherited from previous generations.

Emotions of self-awareness based on narratives about the in-group past, such as guilt and shame, meaningfully signal a sense of *continuity* between generations, because of the need for a historical entitativity of the group (Sani, Bowe, & Herrera, 2008). According to this theoretical perspective, group-based emotions of self-awareness, shown by young people born long after crimes perpetrated or suffered by their ancestors, powerfully demonstrate how social representations of the past literally weigh on the present day (Liu & Hilton, 2005).

However, sometimes younger generations, when presented with narratives of historical violence lived by previous generations, show not only emotions as a result of self-awareness, such as guilt, moral, or social shame, but also emotions as a result of other condemning processes, such as those contained in the triad of contempt–anger–disgust – especially contempt (Bartels et al., 2015). When historical narratives break down literal social denials, emotions linked to the loss of a positive self-image, such as sadness, as well as immediate reactions of disgust could be observed (Leone and Sarrica, 2014; Leone et al., 2018). These different group-based emotions signal how natality (Arendt, 1977) opens the way for the judgment on previous generations' choices, as natality allows for the *discontinuity* of the group.

25.10 General Conclusions

Before concluding this chapter, I would like to sum up its main points. First of all, the basic role of intergenerational narratives for supporting personal reminiscing as well as the protective aim of presenting young people with a positive image of the community in which they happen to be born have been stressed. These supporting functions and the conveying of a positive image of one's own group are so important that all socializing agencies, starting with the family, offer self-serving and group-serving narratives to young people. However, the tendency to relate a positive bias of the past competes with the need of youths to know the history of their group to become able to act in the social and political forums as self-aware citizens. There is a very strict link between the knowledge of one's own "historical preexistence" (Ortega y Gasset, 1930/1957) and the adult civic participation that is expected in democratic societies. Therefore, for the study of intergenerational narratives of violence, we are sometimes confronted with the processes that we are observing to "foster the development of the intelligent, autonomous, reflective, active characteristics of mature adults, whereas others encourage the development of immature, passive, dependent

uncritical cognitive capabilities resembling those of a submissive child" (Deutsch & Kinnvall, 2002, p. 17). Social denials meant to present an idealized narrative of the in-group past could be more useful for political regimes that treat their citizens as submissive children than for democracies where citizens are expected to know their in-group past, not only to judge it, but also to understand current in-group and intergroup situations.

In reconciliation processes, which are the main focus of the chapter, the first illusion about the past that mature adults have to get rid of is the conflict ethos (Bar-Tal et al., 2012) that justifies violence against enemies. Similarly, after peace treaties, when leadership has forbidden the use of violence against the other group, the image of the enemy – along with states of social denial (Cohen, 2001) that serve the image of the in-group and, indirectly, the self-image – remains for a long time. Very often these denials are passed down through the generations and can be traced in the way that violence is narrated, either by failing to confront the moral responsibilities of the in-group or refusing to acknowledge "the psychological, political, or moral implications that conventionally follow" (Cohen, 2001, p. 8). But, even before these interpretive or implicatory denials, the literal denial of violent facts that happened in the past history of the in-group is a predictable process, especially when victims are weak, socially marginalized, and despised.

Nevertheless, when all intergenerational narratives about the in-group choose to ignore a violent past, historians and history teachers have to deal with these facts. That is the reason why – since the seminal work of Halbwachs (1950/1980) on collective memory – a theoretical proposal has been advanced to draw a dividing line between narratives aimed at improving our historical knowledge and narratives aimed at constructing a social representation of it. When history teaching breaks down a widespread social denial in all other intergenerational narratives of the past, a dangerous communication game is exposed between generations – a communication that we propose to call *parrhesia* (Leone, 2017; Leone & Sarrica, 2014), according to the theoretical distinction of Foucault (2001) regarding different kinds of truth speaking.

Directly observing the reactions of young Italian participants when presented with a frank narrative of in-group colonial crimes, denied in the social discourse, as well as their self-assessment of a list of emotions, showed not only the presence of group-based emotions of self-awareness usually expected for perpetrators' descendants, such as shame or guilt, but also other condemning emotions, such as contempt, emotions linked to the loss of a positive self-image, such as sadness, and immediate reactions of disgust (Leone and Sarrica, 2014; Leone et al., 2018). Taken together, these emotions and reactions may be seen as signals that the new generations are distancing themselves from older ones and are finally judging them.

According to these data, a frank narrative of moral shortcomings of the in-group may cause uneasiness and even sadness to young people receiving it. At the same time, however, these reactions to the dangerous communication that unveils difficult truths on past in-group responsibilities could also allow young people to express at last their own *third-part morality* (Rozin et al., 1999), which steps back from any confusing overtones sometimes hidden in the very concept of collective guilt (Arendt, 1945).

We may conclude that all intergenerational narratives of past violence that break down self-serving illusions and convenient social denials are exposed to the danger of provoking negative group-based emotions for young people discovering difficult truths. Similarly, in the field of study of intergenerational narratives the issue of truth is better discussed not from an epistemological but from a pragmatic point of view, that is, by paying attention to the effect of communication on the recipients (Foucault, 2001). Nevertheless, when speaking about emotions (especially group-based

emotions), the label of "negative" should not be taken at face value. Despite possible backlashes, well-regulated (Frijda, 1986) negative reactions to the collapse of biases and social denials may enable young descendants of perpetrators to disentangle past historical facts from any egocentric need to assert one's own positive social identity.

Looked at from a pragmatic point of view, studies of narratives of the historical past focusing only on threats to the moral and social image of the group could hide the crucial point that young people are protected only when they are told the historical truth. The awareness that knowledge of history cannot be severed from its interpretation, however, cannot be extended to the idea that all interpretations have the same impact. Ignoring relevant facts of one's own history makes it impossible, for a young person, to judge both on decisions taken by previous generations and on decisions her own generation will take in the future. It means that, also in intergenerational narratives of intergroup violence, the risky choice to convey frankly a difficult truth may be fruitful, being "not a matter of exposure which destroys the secret, but a revelation that does justice to it" (Benjamin, 1977, p. 31).

Acknowledgment

The writing of this chapter was facilitated by the research opportunities offered to the author by her participation in the ISCH COST Action IS1205 Social Psychological Dynamics of Historical Representations in the Enlarged European Union.

References

Allpress, J. A., Brown, R., Giner-Sorolla, R., Deonna, J. A., & Teroni, F. (2014). Two faces of group-based shame: Moral shame and image shame differentially predict positive and negative orientations to in-group wrongdoing. *Personality and Social Psychology Bulletin*, 40(10), 1270–1284.

Améry, J. (1966/1999). *At the Mind's Limits: Contemplations by a Survivor on Auschwitz and its Realities* (trans. by S. Rosenfeld and S. P. Rosenfeld). London: Granta Books.

Anderson, B. (2006). *Imagined Communities: Reflections on the Origin and Spread of Nationalism*. London: Verso.

Arendt, H. (1945). Organized guilt and universal responsibility. *Jewish Frontier*, 12(1), 19–23.

Arendt, H. (1958). *The Human Condition*. Chicago: University of Chicago Press.

Arendt, H. (1977). *Between Past and Future: Eight Exercises in Political Thought*. London: Penguin Books.

Arendt, H. (2001). *Men in Dark Times*, New York: Penguin Books.

Assmann, J. (1992). *Das kulturelle Gedächtnis: Schrift, Erinnerung und politische Identität in frühen Hochkulturen*. Munich: Beck.

Bandura, A. (1999). Moral disengagement in the perpetration of inhumanities. *Personality and Social Psychology Review*, 3, 193–209.

Bar-Tal, D. & Bennink, G. H. (2004). The nature of reconciliation as an outcome and as a process. In Y. Bar-Siman-Tov (Ed.), *From Conflict Resolution to Reconciliation* (pp. 11–38). Oxford: Oxford University Press.

Bar-Tal, D., Sharvit, K., Halperin, E., & Zafran, A. (2012). Ethos of conflict: The concept and its measurement. *Peace and Conflict: Journal of Peace Psychology*, 18(1), 40–61.

Bartels, D. M., Bauman, C. W., Cushman, F. A., Pizarro, D. A., & McGraw, A. P. (2015). Moral judgment and decision making. In G. Keren & G. Wu (Eds.), *The Wiley Blackwell Handbook of Judgment and Decision Making*. Chichester, UK: John Wiley & Sons.

Baumeister, R. F. (1997). *Evil: Inside Human Violence and Cruelty*. New York: Henry Holt.

Benjamin, W. (1977). *The Origin of German Tragic Drama*. London: New Left Books.

Benjamin, W. & Zohn, H. (1963). The story-teller: Reflections on the works of Nicolai Leskov. *Chicago Review*, 80–101.

Bilali, R. (2013). National narrative and social psychological influences in Turks' denial of the mass killings of Armenians as genocide. *Journal of Social Issues*, 69(1), 16–33.

Bloch, M. (1954). *The Historian's Craft* (trans. by Peter Putnam). Manchester: Manchester University Press.

Branscombe, N. R. & Doosje, B. (2004). *Collective Guilt: International Perspectives*. Cambridge: Cambridge University Press.

Brescó de Luna, I. & Rosa, A. (2012). Memory, history and narrative: Shifts of meaning when (re)constructing the past. *Europe's Journal of Psychology*, 8(2), 300–310.

Bruner, J. S. (1990). *Acts of Meaning* (vol. 3). Cambridge, MA: Harvard University Press.

Cajani, L. (2013). The image of Italian colonialism in Italian history textbooks for secondary schools. *Journal of Educational Media, Memory, and Society*, 5(1), 72–89.

Campbell, J. (2006). Vichy, vichy, and a plaque to remember. *French Studies Bulletin*, 27(98), 2–5.

Cohen, S. (2001). *States of Denial: Knowing about Atrocities and Suffering*. Cambridge: Polity Press.

Das, V. (1998). Specificities: Official narratives, rumour, and the social production of hate. *Social Identities*, 4(1), 109–130.

Del Boca, A. (2005). *Italiani, brava gente? Un mito duro a morire* [Italians, good fellows? A myth that dies hard]. Vicenza, Italy: Neri Pozza.

Deutsch, M. & Kinnvall, C. (2002). What is political psychology. In K. R. Monroe (Ed.), *Political Psychology* (pp. 15–42). Mahwah, NJ: Lawrence Erlbaum.

Eastmond, M. & Selimovic, J. M. (2012). Silence as possibility in postwar everyday life. *International Journal of Transitional Justice*, 6(3): 502–524. DOI: 10.1093/ijtj/ijs026.

Eisenberg, A. (1985). Learning to describe past experiences in conversation. *Discourse Processes*, 8, 177–204.

Ekman, P., Friesen, W. V., & Ellsworth, P. (2013). *Emotion in the Human Face: Guidelines for Research and an Integration of Findings*. Burlington, NJ: Elsevier.

Fivush, R. (2008). Remembering and reminiscing: How individual lives are constructed in family narratives. *Memory Studies*, 1(1), 49–58.

Foucault, M. (1983). Discourse and truth: the Problematization of parrhesia. Six lectures given by Michel Foucault at the University of California at Berkeley, October–November.

Foucault, M. (2001). *Fearless Speech*. Los Angeles. Semiotext(e).

Frijda, N. H. (1986). *The Emotions*. Cambridge: Cambridge University Press.

Gross, J. J. (1998). The emerging field of emotion regulation: An integrative review. *Review of General Psychology*, 2(3), 271–299.

Haidt, J. (2003). The moral emotions, in R. J. Davidson, K. R. Scherer, & H. H. Goldsmith (Eds.), *Handbook of Affective Sciences* (pp. 852–870). Oxford: Oxford University Press.

Halbwachs, M. (1925/1992). *On Collective Memory* (ed. by L. A. Coser) Chicago: University of Chicago Press. (Translated abstracts from: *Les cadres sociaux de la mémoire*, Paris, Librairie Alcan.)

Halbwachs, M. (1950/1980). *The Collective Memory* (trans. by F. J. Ditter and V. Y. Ditter). New York: Harper & Row.

Hammack, P. L. & Pilecki, A. (2012). Narrative as a root metaphor for political psychology. *Political Psychology*, 33, 75–103.

Hovannisian, R. G. (1998). *Remembrance and Denial: The Case of the Armenian Genocide*. Detroit: Wayne State University Press.

Howarth, C. (2006). A social representation is not a quiet thing: Exploring the critical potential of social representations theory. *British Journal of Social Psychology*, 45(1), 65–86.

Hudson, J. A. & Shapiro, L. (1991). Effects of task and topic on children's narratives. In A. McCabe & C. Peterson (Eds.), *New Directions in Developing Narrative Structure* (pp. 89–136). Hillsdale, NJ: Lawrence Erlbaum.

Jovchelovitch, S. (2012). Narrative, memory and social representations: A conversation between history and social psychology. *Integrative Psychological and Behavioral Science*, 46(4), 440–456.

Kansteiner, W. (2014). Generation and memory: A critique of the ethical and ideological implications of generational narration. In S. Berger & B. Niven (Eds.), *Writing the History of Memory* (pp. 111–134). London: Bloomsbury.

Kelman, H. C. (2008). Reconciliation from a social-psychological perspective. In A. Nadler, T. Malloy, & J. D. Fisher (Eds.), *Social Psychology of Intergroup Reconciliation* (pp. 15–32). Oxford: Oxford University Press.

Klein, D. B. (2011). Resentment and recognition: Toward a new conception of humanity in Améry's At the Mind's Limits. In M. Zolkos (Ed.), *On Jean Améry: Philosophy of Catastrophe* (pp. 87–108). New York: Lexington Books.

Kurtiş, T., Adams, G., & Yellow Bird, M. (2010). Generosity or genocide? Identity implications of silence in American Thanksgiving commemorations. *Memory*, 18(2), 208–224.

Labanca, N. (2002). *Oltremare: Storia dell'espansione coloniale italiana* (vol. 31). Bologna, Italy: Il Mulino.

László, J. (2003). History, identity and narratives. In: J. László and W. Wagner (Eds.), *Theories and Controversies in Societal Psychology* (pp. 180–192). Budapest: New Mandate.

László, J. (2008). *The Science of Stories: An Introduction in Narrative Psychology*. New York: Routledge.

Leach, C. W., Zeineddine, F. B., & Čchajić-Clancy, S. (2013). Moral immemorial: The rarity of self-criticism for previous generations' genocide or mass violence. *Journal of Social Issues*, 69(1), 34–53.

Leone, G. (2000). ¿ Qué hay de "social" en la memoria. In A. Rosa, G. Bellelli, & D. Bakhurst (Eds.), *Memoria colectiva e identidad nacional* (pp. 135–155).Madrid: Biblioteca Nueva.

Leone, G. (2017). When history teaching turns into parrhesia: The case of Italian colonial crimes. In C. Psaltis, M. Carretero, & S. Čehajić-Clancy (Eds.), *History Education and Conflict Transformation: Dealing with the Past and Facing the Future* (pp. 147–167). Cham, Switzerland: Palgrave Macmillan.

Leone, G. & Curigliano, G. (2009).Coping with collective responsibilities: An explorative study on Italian historical identity across three generations. *Journal of Language and Politics*, 8(2), 305–326.

Leone, G., D'Ambrosio, M., Migliorisi, S., & Sessa, I. (2018). Facing the unknown crimes of older generations: Emotional and cognitive reactions of young Italian students reading an historical text on the colonial invasion of Ethiopia. *International Journal of Intercultural Relations*, 62, 55–67.

Leone, G. & Mastrovito, T. (2010). Learning about our shameful past: A socio-psychological analysis of present-day historical narratives of Italian colonial wars. *International Journal of Conflict and Violence*, 4(1), 11–27.

Leone, G. & Sarrica, M. (2014). Making room for negative emotions about the national past: An explorative study of effects of parrhesia on Italian colonial crimes. *International Journal of Intercultural Relations*, 43, 126–138.

Liu, J. H. & Hilton, D. J. (2005). How the past weighs on the present: Social representations of history and their role in identity politics. *British Journal of Social Psychology*, 44(4), 537–556.

Liu, J. H., Onar, N. F., & Woodward, M. W. (2014). Symbologies, technologies, and identities: Critical junctures theory and the multi-layered nation–state. *International Journal of Intercultural Relations*, 43, 2–12.

Mari, S., Andrighetto, L., Gabbiadini, A., Durante, F., & Volpato, C. (2010). The shadow of the Italian colonial experience: The impact of collective emotions on intentions to help the victims' descendants. *International Journal of Conflict and Violence*, 4(1), 58–74.

Meiring, P. & Tutu, D. (1999). *Chronicle of the Truth and Reconciliation Commission: A Journey through the Past and Present into the Future of South Africa*. Vanderbijlpark, South Africa: Carpe Diem Books.

Moscovici, S. (1976). *Social Influence and Social Change*. London: Academic Press.

Murithi, T. (2009). An African perspective on peace education: Ubuntu lessons in reconciliation. *International Review of Education*, 55(2–3), 221–233.

Nadler, A. (2001). The victim and the psychologist: Changing perceptions of Israeli holocaust survivors by the mental health community in the past 50 years. *History of Psychology*, 4(2), 159–181.

Nadler, A. & Shnabel, N. (2008). Instrumental and socioemotional paths to intergroup reconciliation and the needs-based model of socioemotional reconciliation. In A. Nadler, T. E. Malloy, & J. D. Fisher (Eds.), *The Social Psychology of Intergroup Reconciliation* (pp. 37–56). New York: Oxford University Press.

Nadler, A. & Shnabel, N. (2015). Intergroup reconciliation: Instrumental and socio-emotional processes and the needs-based model. *European Review of Social Psychology*, 26(1), 93–125.

Neisser, U. & Winograd, E. (1995). *Remembering Reconsidered: Ecological and Traditional Approaches to the Study of Memory*. Cambridge: Cambridge University Press.

Noor, M., Shnabel, N., Halabi, S., & Nadler, A. (2012). When suffering begets suffering the psychology of competitive victimhood between adversarial groups in violent conflicts. *Personality and Social Psychology Review*, 16(4), 351–374.

Ortega y Gasset, J. (1930/1957). *The Revolt of the Masses*. New York: W. W. Norton. (Originally published as *La rebelión de las masas*.)

Peterson, C. & McCabe, A. (1983). *Developmental Psycholinguistics: Three Ways of Looking at a Child's Narrative*. New York: Plenum.

Reese, E., Haden, C. A., & Fivush, R. (1993). Mother–child conversations about the past: Relationships of style and memory over time. *Cognitive Development*, 8(4), 403–430.

Rozin, P., Lowery, L., Imada, S., & Haidt, J. (1999). The CAD triad hypothesis: A mapping between three moral emotions (contempt, anger, disgust) and three moral codes (community, authonomy, divinity). *Journal of Personality and Social Psychology*, 76, 574–586.

Sani, F., Bowe, M., & Herrera, M. (2008). Perceived collective continuity: Seeing groups as temporally enduring entities. In F. Sani (Ed.), *Self Continuity: Individual and Collective*

Perspectives (pp. 159–172). Hove, UK: Psychology Press.

Shepherd, L., Spears, R., & Manstead, A. S. (2013). "This will bring shame on our nation": The role of anticipated group-based emotions on collective action. *Journal of Experimental Social Psychology*, 49(1), 42–57.

SimanTov-Nachlieli, I. & Shnabel, N. (2014). Feeling both victim and perpetrator: Investigating duality within the needs-based model. *Personality and Social Psychology Bulletin*, 40, 301–314.

Staub, E. (2001). Genocide and mass killing: Their roots and prevention. In D. J. Christie, R. V. Wagner, & D. Winter (Eds.), *Peace, Conflict, and Violence: Peace Psychology for the 21st Century* (pp. 76–86). Englewood Cliffs, NJ: Prentice-Hall.

Sweeny, R. C. (1993). Time and human agency: A re-assessment of the Annales legacy. *Left History*, 1(2).

Tajfel, H. & Turner, J. C. (1986). The social identity theory of intergroup behavior. In S. Worchel & W. G. Austin (Eds.), *Psychology of Intergroup Relations* (pp. 7–24). Chicago: Nelson Hall.

Turner, J. C., Hogg, M. A., Oakes, P. J., Reicher, S. D., & Wetherell, M. S. (1987). *Rediscovering the Social Group: A Self-categorization Theory*. Oxford: Oxford University Press.

Vollhardt, J. R. & Bilewicz, M. (2013). After the genocide: Psychological perspectives on victim, bystander, and perpetrator groups. *Journal of Social Issues*, 69(1), 1–15.

Vollhardt, J. R., Mazur, L. B., & Lemahieu, M. (2014). Acknowledgment after mass violence: Effects on psychological well-being and intergroup relations. *Group Processes & Intergroup Relations*, 17(3), 306–323.

Volpato, C. & Licata, L. (2010). Collective memories of colonial violence. *International Journal of Conflict and Violence* (special issue), 4(1), 4–10.

Wojcik, A., Bilewicz, M., & Lewicka, M. (2010). Living on the ashes: Collective representations of Polish–Jewish history among people living in the former Warsaw Ghetto area. *Cities*, 27, 195–203.

Further Reading

Absolon, K. E. & Absolon-Winchester, A. E. (2016). Exploring pathways to reconciliation. *Consensus*, 37(1), art. 2.

Erikson, E. H. & Senn, M. J. E. (1950). Growth and crises of the "healthy personality." In E. H. Erikson & M. J. E. Senn (Eds.), *Symposium on the Healthy Personality* (pp. 91–146). New York: Josiah Macy Jr. Foundation.

Gibson, J. L. (2006). The contributions of truth to reconciliation: Lessons from South Africa. *Journal of Conflict Resolution*, 50(3), 409–432.

Lickel, B., Hamilton, D., Wieczorkowska, G., Lewis, A., Sherman, S. J., & Uhles, A. N. (2000). Varieties of groups and the perception of group entitativity. *Journal of Personality and Social Psychology*, 78, 223–246.

Liu, J. H. & László, J. (2007). A narrative theory of history and identity: Social identity, social representations, society and the individual. In G. Moloney & I. Walker (Eds.), *Social Representations and Identity: Content, Process and Power* (pp. 85–107). London: Palgrave Macmillan.

Nadler, A., Malloy, T., & Fisher, J. D. (Eds.). (2008). *Social Psychology of Intergroup Reconciliation: From Violent Conflict to Peaceful Co-existence*. Oxford: Oxford University Press.

Sen, R. & Wagner, W. (2005). History, emotions and hetero-referential representations in inter-group conflict: The example of Hindu–Muslim relations in India. *Papers on Social Representations*, 14, 2.1–2.23.

26 Psytizenship: Sociocultural Mediations in the Historical Shaping of the Western Citizen

Jorge Castro-Tejerina and José Carlos Loredo-Narciandi

It is eminently clear that there is no psychology that is not connected to a more or less explicit conception of what a human subject is and what that subject should be. In the Western world, we can trace anthropological arguments about what it is and what should be at least as far back as the texts of Plato and Aristotle. However, it was not until a much later period, between the mid-nineteenth and early twentieth centuries, that an alliance of deep psychological and political consequences was established around that connection. At that time, psychology was "founded" as a scientific discipline and, at the same time, its functions were closely tied to the design and construction of political subjects or, to put it more precisely, citizens in the modern sense. As Bruno Latour (1999) pointed out, the modern pact established the agreement that political agendas were separate from natural realities, which nevertheless ensured that the former could be justified through the latter.

The idea that is central for our chapter is that the alliance between the psychological subject and the political subject led to the emergence of an intricate and diffuse theoretical and practical domain. In this sphere, psychological, philosophical, biological, ethical, anthropological, and social ideas converge to justify normative projects of a political and moral nature. It is thus difficult to distinguish a "scientific" program for psychology from a "political" program for the West: modern citizenship does not seem conceivable without dimensions relating to the design of

the subject and psychological expertise, and psychology as an institutionalized discipline cannot be understood if its connection with the governability exercised by modern states and the consequent need to produce good citizens are forgotten (Rose, 1998).

In recent writings, we have used the neologism "psytizenship" to refer to this intricate connection that has been constitutive for both psychology and for the Western political agenda up to the present (Castro-Tejerina, 2014, 2015; Cabanas, 2016). Of course, its vicissitudes have been many and diverse, and they arrive on the current scene interwoven with global, multicultural logics that incorporate highly complex, accelerated and "liquid" individual and social transformations (Kymlicka, 1995; Bauman, 2005; Ong, 2006). We will analyze this scenario from the standpoint of a sensibility located halfway between the genealogical and the historiographical arenas of knowledge. It is a sensibility that aspires to outline the historico-cultural conditions on which the modern age configured the relationship between psychology and citizenship through the idea of self-government. Following that, we will resort to a cultural perspective to analyze the current construction of a political subject that would vary between the psychological heritage received from the modern age and the sociocultural conditions that typify postmodernity. Finally, we will offer a possible outlook to understand the technological agenda of today's psychology, bearing in mind that current psychology is already handled in many parts of the world as a privileged medium for solving the current subject's problems and crises. Whatever its theoretical or applied orientation may be, psychology explicitly or implicitly becomes an inevitable mediating device when extracting the sense of the subject's experience in the world. Let it be said before proceeding that, when we speak here of the "citizen subject" – and its premodern, modern, and postmodern avatars – we are speaking of ideal types in the Weberian manner. We have no doubt that the contrast between these ideal models and what specific individuals do and say in their daily lives will impugn the more generalist aspects of our proposal. Be that as it may, our proposal should be understood as a mere outline of historico-genealogical paths that will make it possible to profile general trends. They would serve as a framework for the discursive and practical play of the relations between psychology and citizenship up to the present.

26.1 Historico-genealogical Approach to the Self-Governed Psytizen

Psychological discourse invaded the interpretation of social reality long before the role of the professional psychologist as we understand it today emerged. From the middle of the nineteenth century, the psychologization of culture – and, as a consequence, of groups and individuals – advanced in the Western world with the aid of doctors, teachers, journalists, politicians, and all sorts of reformist intellectuals. Most of them thought of their populations in organic, malleable terms, as a kind of social mass awaiting the right agents and social technologies to set the machinery of order and progress characteristic of the modern nation-state in motion. With this in mind, what interests us as we continue is simply to outline two historico-genealogical paths that we consider indispensable for understanding the relationship between psychology and the ideal of

modern citizenship (a more ample and precise discussion of this historico-genealogical framework can be consulted in Castro-Tejerina, 2015). These two paths have to do, on one hand, with the project for constructing the self-governed subject in the West, and, on the other hand, with the complementary domain of its possible alteritics.

26.1.1 Psychogenesis and Modernity

The first of the two paths aims, from the early modern age, at the ideal configuration of a self-governed subject that we may identify with the modern "citizen." This would be a political subject able to interiorize the normative codes that characterize the Western liberal, democratic nation-state, thus distanced from the normative codes typifying the premodern formulas of the *ancien régime*.[1] Through historic episodes such as the independence of the United States and the French Revolution, the concept of citizenship gradually acquired density, extending itself throughout the populational mass and taking on a growing importance. Also fundamental in the process were the devices for producing *the notion of the social* administered by the elites of the nation-states, particularly through the universalization and homogenization of education and government intervention in subjectivizing and socializing practices characteristic of the family nucleus (Anderson, 1983; Rose, 1996; Castel, 1997; Donzelot, 1997).[2] Among other purposes, the function of these devices would be to promote the subject's ability to handle coexistence (life with others), social responsibility, and his or her own self-government. In contrast to the premodern scenario, the technical objective for that self-government is to operate beyond the classic devices of control and punishment, whether they are internalized – religious morality, guilty conscience, sin-based guilt, fear of punishment after death, and so on – or external – repression by public authorities, torture, the death penalty, and so on (Rose, 1998; Foucault, 1991, 2007). Finally, the values and normative codes that characterized the "imagined community," shaped by the new-fangled nation-state, came to replace or overlay[3] the type of community link sustained by values and normative codes of a religious nature, typical of the *ancien régime*.

Although this process was not exhausted in them, all the great psychological agendas through which modernity was deployed, from Wundt's original work and its immediate corollaries (the Würzburg school, the psychology of the act and phenomenological psychology, gestalt, functionalist psychology, etc.), accomplished the naturalization of this new type of citizen subject. The scientific enterprise aimed at revealing the "true nature" of the human being, a project that finally assumed that it was possible to show how the good citizen's psychological gears worked (Loredo-Narciandi, 2012a).

In fact, at the beginning of the twentieth century, some of the great psychological theories were expressly linked to social engineering proposals that included reflections on the subject's adaptation to the supposed social normality, when not to the very concept of citizenship (Castro-Tejerina, 2015). A paradigmatic case is that of John Dewey (1922), whose functionalist conception of human nature was inseparable from the justification of liberal democracy. All in all, beyond specific cases, the crucial aspect of practically the entire psychological project had to do with a generalized agreement centered on a basic supposition: the psychogenesis of the personality and the psychological functions, or at least the idea that the psychological architecture of the human being is composed of an assembly of strata that include virtually everything from the most basic mental and behavioral operations or processes – physiological, automatic, instinctive, unconscious, immediate, contingent, and so on – to the most sophisticated and complex operations and processes – tied to thinking, self-controlled, cognitive, conscious, exter-

nally influenced, stabilized by learning, and so on. Beyond their politico-ideological motivation and independently of their theoretical diversity, most of the important psychologies of the twentieth century would undoubtedly assume this supposition. Based on that supposition, it will be obvious that, at the end of the psychogenetic passage, the good citizen emerges – that is, the adult who is master of himself/herself when assuming responsibilities with his or her fellow citizens or is, at least, fully adjusted to them. However, the assumption of an ability to self-govern in the individual in a full political sense – the sense of the highest degree of direct participation of each and every citizen in sociopolitical decisions – was not immediate, not even a desirable thing in the origin of the liberal democracies of the West.[4] Perhaps the most appropriate approach would be to speak of a sort of self-government that was configured with variable degrees of restriction from the end of the nineteenth century and, of course, distributed in multiple and different ways according to the diverse nation-state projects. The arc of self-government would thus extend from a pole where individuality is synonymous with freedom of action and personal decision – full self-government, as awareness of the ability to participate actively in the design of the social project – to a pole where individuality is synonymous with singularity and the ability to submit or adjust oneself to the appropriate place in the social fabric – restricted self-government, as conscious assumption of one's own aptitudes and limitations.

In this way, self-government was progressively implemented as the technology of the subject, and enabled most of the population to take its "natural" place in the social design; "nature" that nuanced the very right to vote given to the citizen, or rather, "proto" or "pseudo-citizen" (Castro-Tejerina, 2015). Thus, if under the *ancien régime* there was a tension between disciplinary power and free will, the purpose of the latter being to ensure the subject's submission to Church and monarch, in the modern age of the nineteenth century the tension arose between the citizen's freedom and the need for a certain degree of personal sacrifice (normally expressed in terms of responsibility) for the benefit of the national community.

With the progressive growth of the consuming middle classes throughout the twentieth century, self-government gained more and more terrain for autonomy, personal decision, and the rationalization of life – including emotional life (Illouz, 2007) – which characterizes today's Western democracies. Psychology accompanied this transition and persevered in its intention of constantly supporting and protecting the design of the subject demanded by modernity. It accomplished this, moreover, not only through psychotherapies centered on the client and his or her individual demands or motives. Even principles such as "democratic rationality" could be scientifically legitimized by subsuming them in a human nature that had to precede the political agenda. Along these lines, Jürgen Habermas' recourse (1976) to the work of Jean Piaget to prop up his defense of ideal communication situations as a guarantee of democracy based on universal rationality (López, 1998) is well known. In a similar sensibility, we can also point to the invocation made by Martyn Griffin (2011) of Lev Vygotski's thesis to justify deliberative democracy. Another example comes from Richard Sennett (2012), who founds his communal conception of human relations on supposed facts discovered by scientific psychology, thus naturalizing his political commitment to cooperation.[5]

Parallel to the democratic and liberal models, especially restricted versions of self-government also had their own deployment in the West under the totalitarian regimes represented by the fascisms or the Soviet bloc. Of course, psychology also contributed to the design of these social projects and the model of the ideal subject they demanded. Psychology went so far as to dream of its own utopias of restricted self-government, occasionally impugned by literary dystopias such

as *1984* or *Brave New World*. The paradigmatic case is surely depicted in B. F. Skinner's *Walden Two*, where the logic of the aims and the communal – not state – functioning are superimposed on the supposed freedom and happiness of the particular individual, or at least are made to coincide with it. In general, since Watson's time, behaviorism also contributed to the trends toward restricted self-government by taking each individual as a particular, unique subject and attempting to guarantee his/her adjustment in the social fabric. Even in the absence of a concern for or acceptance of the upper processes of consciousness, associative and learning programs demanded the involvement and development of expertise or specialization by the subject – even in his or her supposed natural tendencies, all in line with some specific social objectives.[6]

What interests us here with respect to the horizon of development of this first historico-genealogical path is the possible convergence of *psytizenship* with a "Western subject" mode who is aware of his/her self-regulating potential. In any case, it is a question of a subject that has also progressively become disconnected from the social contract which, with greater or lesser concessions and personal sacrifices, had been established between the subject and his or her nation-state. As Nikolas Rose (1996, 1999) and Richard Sennett (2000) have demonstrated, approximately during the years following the Cold War, the nation-state began to withdraw from the performance of individual life in the West. The Western liberal democracies are no longer directly and actively accompanying, protecting, or guaranteeing the structure and basic milestones of its citizens' life cycle. To some extent, this has brought about a situation in which all those born within the logic of government characteristic of the last two-thirds of the past century, based on psychogenetic conceptions of life and centered on the power of the nation-state, have been condemned to uncertainty. However, this does not mean that psychology has renounced its classic functions of promoting the "adjustment" between the citizen subject and the new ways of life. We will return to this matter later.

26.1.2 Alterities in Modern Citizenship

The second historico-genealogical path that we announced above would be related to the figures of otherness that are defined with respect to the idealized or normalized citizen presented in the first path. Such figures must be understood both in a temporal sense, as previous images of the subject that are set against each other but which can also be mounted, hybridized, or assembled on the new function of self-government – which is the case of figures characteristic of the *ancien régime*, such as the subject, the serf, the parishioner, and so on – and in a topological sense, as images that concur within the same territory and living space occupied by the typical national citizen – migrants from other latitudes, social minorities, and individuals who are excluded for all sorts of reasons, and so on. The naturalization of the human essence and, with it, of the good citizen, accomplished from the Western ethnocentric standpoint, scarcely left a chink for an interpretation of those alterities apart from their "infantilism" or "immaturity," in the best cases, or their "maladjustment" and "dangerousness," in the worst cases.

It is here where the role of psychology has called for within the social engineering domains of the modern age is best detected, as well as its pretension of scientifically backing the psychogenetic nature of the citizen. The task of psychology would then be to give impetus to, and to rechannel the citizen's development and adjustment through technologies such as psychopedagogy, clinical psychology, criminology, professional orientation, or, in acknowledgment of today's usage, coaching. What is more, the psychogenetic imperative affects not only the model citizen of the Western democracies. Since it was based on a universalist conception of human nature, it was capable of being extended to all

the cultural and national collectives. As Glenda Sluga (2006) has clearly shown, after World War I and the Paris Peace Conference of 1919, the psychological identification that welded maturity to self-government justified Western domination of the countries of the so-called Third World. Further, the apparently just and cordial slogan "the self-determination of peoples," a representation of self-government understood in the psychogenetic sense, was the perfect alibi for neocolonialism. It legitimized the virtual control by the new Western powers (France, England, and the United States, above all) of extensive regions of Asia and Africa as long as, supposedly, these regions did not reach the state of maturity to be able to govern themselves.

Entering the postmodern age, and having surpassed even the relevant criticisms of the postcolonial studies of the acceleration of globalization and delocalization, the progression along this path shows us a doubly "altered" alterity. Apart from its geopolitical and economic motives, the neocolonial determination to "civilize" the Third World generated collectives that were reflective with respect to their supposed cultural "identities." It empowered – symbolically and materially – subjects who were capable of claiming the "right" to their "singularity," subjects who became aware of the concepts of independence and self-determination before being introduced to the principle of individual self-government understood in the Western manner. And this was not limited to the international sphere: the alterities of standardized citizenship that existed within the very borders of the Western nation-state – the excluded groups, minorities, or marginalized people – had also been in the process of recognizing themselves for some time as legitimate figures and ways of life. From the end of the nineteenth century, for example, workers and anarchist movements had taken charge of their voices and education as political subjects. In short, self-government promoted the appearance of alternative ways of being in the world that competed with the ones ideally envisioned by the

Western social elites. They showed that the model advocated by those elites was not the only possible one, nor was it the standard or reference from which to establish the supposed politico-social normality.

Strictly speaking, even the "standardized" and reflective Western citizens – whom we can associate with the middle and bourgeois classes – became progressively aware of the point to which their right to administer their freedom and directly negotiate the model of coexistence and government with the state powers was arriving. Indeed, the difference between that group of citizens and their alterities – international or intranational – is that, for the latter, the empowerment produced by reflecting on identity was not necessarily accompanied by an interest in readjusting the model of ideal self-government and perhaps not even to the model of liberal government in the broad sense. That accounts for the fact that identities and ways of life can conflict with the agreements of the liberal Western social pact (Rose, 1999; Ong, 2006). With the twenty-first century well under way, with the strengthening of the migratory flows and communication technologies, the citizenship scenario proves to be even more complex. The classic cultural alterities of the traditional Western citizen enter into an especially close contact with the liberal democracies of the so-called First World. Thus, they confront cultural codes of government, coexistence, and social responsibility that, as we have already remarked, are themselves subject to a profound transformative process.

26.2 Post-modern Transitions of Psytizenship

What the historico-genealogical drift that we have just outlined delivers to the current scenario are *psytizen* formulas that must be readapted to new sociocultural conditions. These are hybrid transition formulas in which, logically, functions and conceptions characteristic of modernity persist. In fact, it is surely premature to assert that the

symbiosis between the functions of psychology and the liberal nation-state project is exhausted. Beyond the psychologist's important facet as a liberal professional, many of the most important official organizations in Western countries – in such areas as health care, security, education, and so on – contemplate the figure of the psychologist on their staff. However, in recent years the social functions of psychology have undergone a reconfiguration as the modern idea of the nation-state entered in crisis. We can summarize in three points the most important aspects of the transformation and the appearance of *psytizenship* on the postmodern horizon.

The first of these points would have to do with making invisible the close relationship between the design of the self-governed subject of the modern age and the project of psychology as a discipline. In a sense, this project, explicit in the work of the reformists of late nineteenth century and the beginning of the twenty-first century, "died of success" at the point at which the self-governed subjects began to see themselves as consubstantial with the West, and even with the human species itself, apart from specific cultural engineering efforts. At the same time, the psychological domain, which the same reformist intellectuals of the late nineteenth and early twentieth centuries had interwoven with the sociopolitical agenda of the liberal nation-state, was standardized in the form of a technico-scientific discipline with an explicit health care and regulating mission. Psychology became specialized and attained recognition as a profession – requestable on demand – and even as a discipline aspiring to be the foremost in the "hard sciences" (see Castro-Tejerina & Rosa, 2007; Castro-Tejerina, 2016). Perhaps as a consequence of this, such concepts as citizenship, so completely assimilated by that technico-health care device, almost completely disappeared from the explicit agenda of contemporary psychology, although in recent years they seem to have returned, hand-in-hand with critical stances (see, for example, Condor, 2011). However, these stances are distant from the systematic, comprehensive ambition of foundational psychologies such as those of John Dewey, for example, inextricably bound to a social reform agenda based on principles of political philosophy.

The second point has to do with a more technical, applied, or interventional aspect: the preservation of the objective of adjustment between the subject and the ideal model of coexistence, government, and responsibility. The historical loyalty to this objective observed by the great majority of the schools of psychology – with few exceptions, such as some tendencies of antipsychiatry, critical psychology, or the postcolonial approaches – has been perfectly compatible with the promotion of a strong disciplinary and professional identity. Indeed, both things have operated as conditions of mutual possibility: the technical ends demand disciplines with experts who understand them and the disciplines provide "objectivity" to those same ends. It is not surprising that currently, in the terrain of basic research, the aim of the thriving neuroscience field remains the forging of relations between psychological functions and cerebral processes, where it seems that the researchers continue to pursue the ultimate secret of the supposed adjustment between organisms and their environment, which, the more biological it is, the more natural it is considered to be (see Rose & Abi-Rached, 2013). Similarly, in the realm of applied psychology, it would be difficult to justify the social need for a psychology that, in line with the adjustment imperative, would renounce constituting a technical and specialized application. A different matter is the current conception of that adjustment, which is more attentive to the demands of private individuals and the managerial functioning of clinical, pedagogical, and occupational devices than to directly serving the needs of a nation-state.[7]

The third point has to do with the shifting of the classic responsibility imperative – and even the imperative of personal sacrifice – in the interest of collective prosperity aiming toward the imperative of individual happiness. To a great extent, this was already happening in parallel with the logic of the development of the economic model of the liberal democracies progressing for decades, above all at the point where "progress" began to depend as much on the productivity of the population as on its capacity for consumption. What we see here are the two sides of the same coin, which have become obvious in the so-called European welfare state. However, the equivalence between personal happiness and social welfare also begins to weaken with the changes in the economic structure of the late modern nation-state. In the postmodern scenario, companies move their production outside their national borders – affecting the intranational economic circuit that linked productivity and consumption, and governments begin privatizing public services – affecting citizens' guarantees in basic aspects such as health care and education. According to some analysts (see, for example, Balibar, 2013), in this scenario democratic rationality itself, based on equality and participation, suffers for the benefit of a mercantile exchange system. This would revolve solely around individual happiness and in detriment to any idea of common good. In fact, if this logic is taken to its limit, it gives rise to the paradox that this happiness is both a sort of natural condition of the subject, as proclaimed by so-called positive psychology, and an objective that the individual himself or herself is obligated to achieve and administrate independently. In view of this outlook, psychology continues to capillarize society and diversify itself into a movement that wavers between loyalty to its traditional technico-health care mission linked with nation-states and the production of self-realized subjects who are simultaneously the cause and consequence of that is commonly defined as neoliberalism. Above all, within the latter possibility we could understand the emergency affecting such psychological variants as coaching, organizational citizen behavior, or the previously mentioned positive psychology (see Cabanas & Sánchez, 2012; Castro-Tejerina, 2015; Cabanas, 2016).

All things considered, in the same way that the uncoupling of self-awareness from self-government took place, in the postmodern period the disconnection affects the relations between self-government and the model of coexistence, government, and responsibility originally designed by the nation-state. In the next section, we will attempt to delineate some psycho-cultural keys that will help understand this process.

26.3 Postmodern Citizenship from a Psycho-cultural Perspective

Understanding the relationship between the multifaceted postmodern subject and the concept of the typical modern citizen involves rethinking the idea of psychogenesis and the nature of the supposed higher and lower psychological processes. To this end, in the following paragraphs, and assuming a reader with a predominately psychological education, we will establish a series of distinctions regarding (1) the conception of the reflective capacity and modern self-government as a cultural artifact, (2) the surpassing of the idea of adjustment according to a given theory of activity, (3) the reconceptualization of the psychological subject within the idea of an influenced life project, and (4) the understanding of citizen alterity as an experimental space for identity play.

26.3.1 Modern Reflective Capacity as a Cultural Artifact

In contrast with the ethnocentric association between psychogenesis and the self-governed subject that we have presented in our historico-genealogical outline, we believe that it is essential not to lose sight of the fact that the emergence of any process or content of those called psychological is interwoven, constitutively and indistinguishably, with sociocultural processes or contents that can be symbolic or material – contents and processes that frame the subject's activities in the world. As Michel Cole (1996) stated some time ago, speaking of the limitations of Vygotskian thought, it is not possible to establish where a basic or psychophysiological process ends and a historico-cultural process begins. Both converge contextually and idiosyncratically in the activity through which the subject enculturates in his community – or communities – of reference throughout his life. For this reason, a type of self-governed consciousness like the one required by the modern Western agenda should not be considered as a natural outcome of psychogenesis. Rather, it should be understood as a sophisticated tool or mediating artifact that emerges and is reconfigured with new functions in a certain sociohistorical scenario. In fact, according to this viewpoint, any individual or social behavior is intrinsically mediated by historico-cultural artifacts, to the point that, without them, it would be meaningless even to discuss activity (Blanco & Sánchez-Criado, 2009; Sánchez-Criado, 2008; Cole, 1996; Engeström, 1987, 1990).

It can be considered that the self-governed subject, as we understand him/her in the West, is not a consequence of preexisting psychological universals. It is, rather, a product or historical result of the work of psychology itself in convergence with other artifacts and technologies of the subject – the massive spread of literacy, exposure to new communication media, official articulation of group or class identity discourses, and so on. It is not, therefore, a "discovery" or an abstract or ahistorical object captured by science. Modern reflective capacity is an artifact that appeared relatively late and was concocted according to certain cultural demands which it helps transform in turn: the demands that typified the modern Western nation-state. However, as we will see under the next heading, the design of an artifact does not guarantee the control of all its performative possibilities and, consequently, its potential for construction of types of subject.

26.3.2 A Theory of Activity as a Means of Surpassing Adjustment

We have already suggested that an unforeseen effect of the sociopolitical undertaking of the modern age was that the potentiation of the reflective capacity did not automatically entail its interlocking with the self-government ideally demanded by the agenda of the Western nation-state. According to the logic of the *reflective modernity* that Ulrich Beck pointed to (1994; see also Beck & Beck-Gernsheim, 2002), the very development of modernity transformed and even destroyed, at times, the conditions of its existence. In this regard, it is evident that the very aim of self-government was surpassed because, among other things, of the same type of reflective consciousness that it helped to promote. Thanks to it, there were changes in the possibilities of the experience lived by the subjects who, in one way or another, had made contact with the modern project. In a certain sense, the symbiosis between that reflective consciousness and the complexity and acceleration of the modern world multiplied or at least transformed the conditions of experience (Connerton, 2009). It revolutionized the alternatives between those that the subject had to or could decide on, beyond the imperative of the sociocultural adjustment demanded and legitimized by the psychogenetic perspective.

Actually, that effect is nothing more than an awareness of the manner in which the human being configures activity and the meaning of his or her life, always under the opening of possibilities to surpass the standardized practices and systems designed and stabilized by the culture. From this standpoint, one can question an idea of psychogenetic development that predicates the subordination of supposed higher stages of development to lower stages. The mediating circumstances and artifacts that burst into ontogenetic courses are fully substantive and constitutive of the emergence of new situations. In no case can these configurations be explained by or reduced to precursory components occurring earlier in time, as, for example, would occur with the germinal psychological or cultural structures assumed by authors such as Freud or Lévi-Strauss. Artifactual mediations do not have to be considered as something that functions according to an intrinsic logic or a previous meaning underlying the system; rather, they may be understood as arising contingently and with constant surpassing instances in the manner of *agencements* (Deleuze & Guattari, 1975; Castro-Tejerina & Loredo-Narciandi, 2015).

Apart from that, it is not a question of denying in absolute terms a certain organicity or continuity in the course of an activity or in the development of an action; that is, certain borderline tendencies or structures that impede any artifactual mediation at any time. Obviously, the spectrum of predictable results of activity is never infinite, although it is indefinite or indeterminate, with diverse ranges of predictability according to the contexts and situations – what can be expected of the daily activities of a cloistered nun is not the same as what can be anticipated of those of a *bon vivant* given to adventure. Nor is it a question of denying the specific effects derived from the baggage of experiences and a specific human being's ability to make sense of his or her activity – a matter we will return to further on. The question is that what one can and cannot do, including the degree of complexity or expertise entailed, is not exclusively determined by the level of sophistication attained by the subject's internal operations; above all, insofar as these operations are supposedly the result of a progressive deployment of human nature. In line with the neopragmatism of Richard Rorty (1989), for example, one could conceive activity from a more experimental or trial-and-error viewpoint, considering its assembly and reconfiguration in the development of the activity itself.

The main psychologies (humanistic, psychoanalytical, cognitive-behavioral, positive, etc.), on the contrary, have worked more to guarantee and control the stabilizations and their logical, progressive deployment than to wonder about and try to understand the mechanisms of surpassing and contextually reconfiguring them. Hence, probably, their historical fidelity to the cliché of adjustment and self-government. It is not banal that psychology has generally tended to see novelty and creativity through the prism of exceptionality or genius. And that in most cases, since it is well known that it has also constantly had recourse to the concepts of anomaly, or at least neurophysiological peculiarity, as a way of explaining the surpassing of adjustment. Nevertheless, from our perspective, the possibility of invention or novelty appears whenever, to a greater or lesser degree, the openness and versatility of the courses of the culturally possible activity and signification mesh with the specific subject's singular experience (Blanco & Castro, 2005; Glăveanu & Gillespie, 2015, Castro-Tejerina & Loredo-Narciandi, 2015).

In line with the above, it is clear that what we define as historic moments of crisis, acceleration, or radical change of the meaning systems, practices, mediating artifacts, and sociocultural structures that frame subjects' lives are especially sensitive for the dynamics of resignification, surpassing, and personal and cultural recomposition. The process of transforming the subject of the *ancien régime* into the subject of today's nation-state was surely an example of that, in the same way as the tension and mutation being imposed on the modern subject by the current logics of globalization, multiculturalism, neoliberalism, or cyberspace is.

26.3.3 Experience Beyond Decision and Fragmentation

The possibility of reflective and identity empowerment enjoyed by many of the faces of the postmodern subject, unforeseen in the agenda of the citizenry of the modern age, is a sociohistorical result of the dynamics of surpassing adjustment.

This situation has developed in parallel with the multiplication of alternatives to give meaning to life itself, something that would seem to have opened a sort of identity market where the subject can choose, in a more or less structural or strategic way, among different possibilities, even in correlation with specific situations. Indeed, relational (Gergen, 1991), dialogical (Hermans, 2001), positional (Harré & Moghaddam, 2003), and liquid psychosociological theories (Bauman, 2005) have addressed the multiplicity of alternatives or positions that the same subject can take in his or her daily life, proceeding as far as to induce the crisis of the very concept of the self as the resort that guarantees the purposiveness and continuity of experience. Thus, it could be said that, where the most popular psychology has remained bound to the idea of adjustment, other perspectives have addressed its crisis and the postmodern polyphony, observing how the subject's experience exploded in a thousand scattered, nearly autonomous pieces.[8]

However, those pieces, which cannot be reassembled by themselves within a supposed universal psychogenetic architecture, and are not exactly options among which the subject simply chooses freely, nor are they mere structural affiliations determined by the situation. The postmodern subject is not only the yuppie who becomes saturated and fragmented by dealing with a thousand tasks at once (Gergen, 1991): he or she is also the immigrant who is torn or falls to pieces as the result of having to leave his or her entire world behind to cross a border on the other side of which another world awaits that is not always understanding and welcoming (Bathia & Ram, 2001; Bathia 2002). Sometimes the subject must take charge of his or her life or, worse, has to suffer from seeing how something takes it apart, truncates it and dramatically transforms it into something else. In a more or less reflective way, according to the mediating instruments available, he or she is, in a sense, always the same being – or the same organism if we prefer – the one that is the leading actor, if only in a biographical sense. The subject accomplishes this, moreover, through a previously accumulated life baggage that constantly questions him or her and necessarily meshes with the subject's manner of confronting experience and making sense of it (Boesch, 2007a, 2007b; Valsiner, 2013). The subject, therefore, is not detached from constructing the meaning of his or her life, but fully participates in the signification process, although material artifacts and the culturally available meanings mediate in that process in a decisive way (Rosa, 2007a, 2007b; Salvatore, 2013). In these terms, there are plans to make a life from a life plan, to subject life to a discipline, passionately or impotently.

The consequences of taking charge of life are not exhausted in the supposed intentional use of artifacts by humans. Artifactual realities do not passively aspire to see the agent take charge of them. They function as specific conditions for activity that are enormously versatile, variable, and dynamic. Further, it is not sufficient to think of them in terms of broad cycles or historico-cultural contexts, although we ourselves are assuming that perspective to some extent in this text. The specific progression of activity, the micro-genesis and morphogenesis of practices, are constantly establishing realities to which the human being submits himself or herself. To express it in an almost aphoristic manner, *what we do makes us do and be*. For that reason, on most occasions the generic act of signification – the fact of doing something that is difficult to specify exactly or contextualize a priori – precedes the act that we could consider characteristically a citizen's act, one coherent with the established model of citizenship. That act only becomes a citizen's act once it is contextualized and acquires meaning in a given situation (Isin, 2008). As in what happened to Rosa Louise Park when, in 1955, she refused to get up from her seat on the bus at the request of a white American citizen, we sometimes unexpectedly find ourselves entangled in citizens' acts without premeditation, almost out of pure dramatic performance. In the section below we will see to what extent we can identify this with respect to citizen dynamics and grammars characteristic of the postmodern scenario.

26.3.4 Empowered and Dissolved Psytizens

As regards the possibilities of the postmodern subject or subjects, the opening of alternatives of action and signification, together with the progressive dissolution of the classic functions of the nation-state, may mean a great variability in the ways of resolving the misalignments between reflective self-awareness and self-government. Now, the self-governed, responsible citizen, who had internalized the norms and guarantees of democratic coexistence imposed by the nation-state, must become an entrepreneur, a manager of himself or herself; a subject who would seek to maximize his or her symbolic (Bourdieu, 1998) and emotional capital (Illouz, 2007). Thus the game of affiliations to the nation-state loses strength in the benefit of other games that are faithful only to the self – in the full sense of neoliberal individualism – or to the links of solidarity established voluntarily with the community that the individual recognizes as truly close or immediate (Rose, 1999; Vázquez, 2006).

Far from implying an aberration from a supposed anthropological standard or from human nature,[9] these new mediations and ways of life are a sample of recomposition of the self-government artifact bequeathed by the nation-state of the modern age, because the nation-state abandons its commitment to look after the life cycle of its citizens. This is the case, for example, of the practices of community solidarity and the forms of charity and mutual aid that Andrea Muehlebach (2012) has ethnographically recorded in northern Italy. There the traditional – or premodern – practices of charity linked to the

Roman Catholic culture have been assembled in a model of virtuous citizenship that, in the absence of the public authorities of the state, puts disinterested help and volunteering in the foreground. In those two activities, paths are defined to happiness and personal fulfilment that are inseparable from the commitment to the community. Actually, the state has not disappeared, but has transformed its classic function of meeting "social" needs. In accordance with an impeccable neoliberal logic, its objective is now the promotion and administration of virtues of empowerment that take as their objective the private individual or small communities. Explicitly governmental initiatives, such as the *Big Society* promoted by conservative British Prime Minister David Cameron, with an explicit psychological base in the theories of Robert Kegan, constitute another clear example of this (Rowson, Mezey, & Dellot, 2012).

As we remarked at the beginning, the classic alterities of citizenship have also reconfigured the reflective consciousness of the modern age. Among other things, they have *become conscious* of the fact that their identity agenda is culturally legitimate and can be carried out. Such alterities are thus positioned before the alternatives of assuming or resisting the standardized norms of coexistence, government, and responsibility assumed by the Western self-government model. But we are not speaking of a mere structural, passive, or "maladjusted" resistance, typical of the "expectable" in an alterity of modernity. The awareness of the contrast between normative systems can be perfectly clear; it can strengthen the identification and contra-identification of the subject with respect to different systems and can permit a strategic use of the situation. Our reflective capacity would thus enable us to abstract the experience of the original culture or the group to which we belong, or to put it between quotation marks, and promote planned uses of identity self-recognition. At the most, distancing ourselves from our own culture would enable us, for example, to handle its referents in a more

competent way and to articulate, manipulate, and make explicit our requests for legitimacy, exceptional status, or the singularity of our identity within the supposed system of general normative citizenship. But not only that. The hybrids through which we resolve dilemmas opposing identity – as a priority of group or cultural affiliation (and citizenship) as a set of rights and duties self-assumed by all legal inhabitants of a territory – are multiple and unpredictable. For example, far from the resistance offered by certain cultural minorities to being marginalized, there are processes afoot in some countries classified as emerging (for example, in Southeast Asia) where certain migrant groups are beginning to surpass native citizens in social and even national rights (Ong, 2006). The reason is their professional expertise and their optimum adjustment to the logics of economic and productive development demanded by the governments of such countries. Finally, such a circumstance is used by these governments to warn their own native citizens of the change in the nature of the condition of citizen and its subjection to global logics (Ong, 1999, 2006; Ong & Collier, 2005). Once again, these are examples that transcend the idea of the nation-state to begin to revolve around globalized entrepreneurship.

Postmodern *psytizenship* invites us to think of the very dissolution of what, originally, the Western project referred to with the term "citizenship." In fact, since the 1990s authors such as John Shotter (1993) have avoided defining beforehand what citizenship is (or should be), preferring to subordinate its study to the construction of people's specific acts of identification in daily life. Shotter, moreover, emphasizes the possibility that, in view of the absence of an ultimate (psychological) foundation for identity of the citizen or of whatever type, the very subject who exercises acts of identification acquires a sort of meta-reflective awareness of his or her identity commitments. However, as we have attempted to argue, not even that sophisticated reflective act can be thought of beyond the socio-historical conditions generated and provided for a very specific cultural space: the liberal Western space.

Be that as it may, that reflective act not only enables acts of "hybrid" affiliation or withdrawal like the ones to which we have referred. At least in theory, we could also leave the door open to suspending all the well-defined identity policies in order to pursue a paradoxical activity that would consist of a constant exercise or game of identity deconstruction. It would be a sort of forward flight – perhaps an extenuating one – bound to a permanent creation of ourselves as works of art (Foucault, 1984), a narcissistic recreation of the self that would remotely evoke the recreation performed by the dandies of the late nineteenth and early twentieth centuries (Loredo-Narciandi, 2012b). In any case, with this effort we would not be escaping from reflection, but rather, in the best case, taking it to its extreme and entering a new sort of properly postmodern hyper-reflective state (Pérez, 2003). What we would indeed seem to be discarding along this path is any ontological or substantive conception of both "citizenship" and "cultural identity," although surely the analysis of these matters as signifying activities and acts of identification would remain an indispensable task to understanding the transitions and sociohistorical crises of today's subject.

26.4 Psytizen Carnivalization

After everything that has been discussed here, it seems difficult to think of a mother rock inside the subject from which progress could be made until a model of citizenship could be founded. And there is no question of thinking of that mother rock that guarantees the citizen's virtues, when it is not even very clear what it is that we should understand today by the term *citizen*, to say nothing of *good citizen*. With respect to the project of modernity, postmodernity has certified the surpassing of that ideal model. It has offered

new forms of personal construction around the domain of the citizen that shows its irreducibility to natural psychogenetic structures – that is, a psyche predisposed to citizen virtue or to deliberative democracy – and the impossibility of subjecting it with any guarantee to social engineering procedures. Since this is the norm, is the alternative then to accept the critical and relatively widespread idea according to which psychology is a mere device for oppression and depoliticization, perchance an accomplice of late modern gentrification and neoliberal individualism (Rendueles, 2004)? We believe that the question is much more complex. Beyond power conspiracies and asymmetries, what the *psytizenship* project has bequeathed us is an antecedent and much more problematic urgency: the conflict between identity self-awareness and citizen self-government.

This conflict has had many and very diverse forms of resolution, some of which are terribly dramatic. For that reason, without losing sight of its vanishing points, excesses and surpassing of practices and meanings, it would seem that Western culture – or, more precisely, Westernized culture – cannot renounce mediating instruments that ease adjustment or readjustment between the subject and the different available models of coexistence, government, and responsibility. In this regard, the technologies of the subject characteristic of the modern and postmodern world are inevitable, in the same way that other historical periods and other cultures also needed theirs. For better or for worse, psychology has contributed and continues to contribute to shaping our ways of understanding ourselves and of understanding the world in the West or in the Westernized countries. Actually, to refer to "types of subjects" in the plural is by no means trivial, since it is a matter that affects psychology itself or, more accurately, psychologies. The plurality of psychological approaches and practices, far from representing a transitory or paradigmatic stage awaiting a future scientific unification that would finally put true human nature under examination, probably responds to the very multiplicity of ways of life, although obviously not in a biunivocal way (Blanco, 2002; Ferreira, 2001; Ferreira et al., 2012, 2013). As in the modern age, ways of life affect and are affected by psychology and many other techniques that increasingly share the same culture medium, although this often takes the form of relations of rivalry or competition, as could be the case of philosophical consulting or therapy with Tibetan bowls. The interaction between the psychological artifact and the subject falls within the domain of a heterogeneous set of practices applied to produce certain types of subject or, if the reader prefers, subjectivities (Bradley, 1989; Ferreira, 2011; Latour, 2012).

Strictly speaking, from its founding, scientific psychology was always interwoven with other techniques involving the subject, many of which, such as religion, are premodern (Castro-Tejerina, 2016). Perhaps the differential historic aspect is the fact that the function of psychology is surpassing the commitments of the Latourian modern pact as a tool for the construction of good citizens. From the disciplinary standpoint, it would seem that, in recent years, the longing for an alleviating theoretical unification has been dwindling, since we seem to have succeeded in protecting a disciplinary terrain of our own with professionalizing and expertise-backed fences. Without question, being recognized in engineering and scientific expertise continues to provide psychology with great benefits in the form of sociotechnical influence. But if these last institutional walls were to fall or be displaced, psychology could probably be comfortably recognized in the tradition of the spiritual exercises and classic technologies of the construction of the subject (Foucault, 2005, 2010, 2011, 2016; Hadot, 1998, 2010). In this regard, authors such as Bruno Latour (2012) have pointed out that practices such as those used in psychotherapy make it possible to appreciate, with relative independence of the general theories on human nature, what psychology offers in experimental terms and in the opening of possibilities, in the production and performance of types of subject and ways of life.

Further, if it seems impossible today to conceive the eradication of psychological techniques as pertinent tools when administrating the transition between the modern and postmodern subject, it also seems difficult to imagine a postmodernity without reflective capacity and plurality of identities. Where self-government or citizen government stands in this entire scenario is an important problem that will have to be solved, perhaps as the result of a new pact that, through globalization, might induce a crisis in the very idea of multiculturalism. In all this, the reflective capacity that modernity bequeathed us will inevitably play a crucial role. However, after the postmodern period, there seems to be no space left for a scientific revelation of the true, necessary, or just social reality, nor for a psychological engineering that would cooperate in its exhumation with exquisite neutrality. Being a *psytizen* is a condition or a way of being in the world, not a perfect meshing of gears supervised by watchmakers who are experts in the human soul.

26.5 Concluding Remarks

From an eminently historico-genealogical and sociocultural sensitivity, in this chapter we have asserted that Western citizenship is the product of a series of sociocultural mediations articulated through specific practices and devices. Among these, psychology and related disciplines have had a crucial function, very particularly for Western culture. Specifically, we have suggested that:

1 It is difficult to conceive of a psychology that is not explicitly or implicitly linked to a given model of what a human being is and should be, to include ethical and political dimensions. Considering the context of the modern age, as this term is understood in the Western and Westernized world, we could call that

connection the psytizen condition, a condition that is substantivized particularly through the alliance between psychology as a discipline and an ideal model of the self-governed, responsible citizen.

2 However, that very inextricable union joining subjects' activity and the sociocultural frameworks in which that activity goes forward generates overflows of that ideal model. The cultural discourses and practices through which the subject configures his or her life continually impugn the suppositions of "adequate adjustment" and human "true nature" that are sorely missed by foundational psychology and its ethical and political implications.

3 Particularly, the shift toward what in recent decades has been called postmodern life and reflection includes, as a dislocation of modern psytizenship, many unforeseen effects. They are courses of activity that intertwine with cultural diversity, identity politics, and even the very psychologization of society derived from the scientific-institutional standardization of psychology and the knowledge and practices associated with it. Strictly speaking, with the advent of postmodernity psychology has been fully incorporated into the heritage of available tools enabling each subject to think of himself or herself as such today.

4 All in all, psychology is not what it was during the modern age. Postmodernity is forging a re-psychologization of the subject that is necessarily conflictive and plural. Conflictive because there is an evident competition with practices and discourses that concern subjectivity but are not institutionally recognized as psychological. And plural because, in fact, from the same modern origins until today, different institutionalized psychologies coexist. Our thesis is that this disciplinary plurality is constitutive, structural, not conjunctural, and has to do precisely with the relationship between the different models of the human being (or citizen) and the attempts at

psychological fundamentation of those models. The postmodern fragmentation of ways of life reveals this psychological diversity even more clearly.

5 In conclusion, psychology could be understood as a device for producing subjectivity that necessarily includes ethical and political aspects. But this does not exhaust the citizen condition characteristic of Western or Westernized countries. Citizenship reflects a space for the permanent negotiation of what we are and what we can be in common (Stengers, 2008); a space for practices that, necessarily, already surpasses the objectives of any social engineering and rationalization project.

Acknowledgment

This work was done with the financial support of the European project titled "Between the Representation of the Crisis and the Crisis of the Representation." This project has received funding from the European Union's Horizon 2020 research and innovation program under grant agreement no. 649436.

Notes

1 As Gilles Deleuze (1984) emphasizes, following Foucault, it could be considered that the first connection between citizenship and subjectivity occurred in classical Greece. The circumstance that the best had to govern by virtue of the principle of isonomy – and therefore those who knew, above all, how to govern themselves – gave rise to the emergence of the very experience of subjectivity. Thus, an idea of "interior" would be configured that acquired ontological autonomy with respect to the domains of knowledge and power, although it derived from and was defined on the basis of knowledge and power. An important difference established by modernity is that that interior or subjective domain is no longer understood as derived and facultative, but as primary and obligatory. Being a subject is foundational, and modern citizenship, the concept that is linked to the

nation-state, and the rationalization of society then must directly address that type of subjectivity. As we will see, it is a matter of subjectivity or interiority considered natural and, above all, universal, consubstantial to the entire population.

2   It should be noted that we are speaking of constructing the notion of the social because we do not assume that society constitutes an ahistoric or perennial reality existing before the cited devices or apart from them. The ways in which some humans relate with others and with other nonhuman entities are innumerable and, contrary to what some psychosocial theories seem to assume, they do not necessarily pass through the archetypical model of Western society. In any case, the last's specific ways are the ones we take as a reference here.

3   The citizenship associated with the nation-state assumes subjects that internalize normative codes and apply them of their own volition and conviction. As internalized principles that guide behavior, they can have a moral sense similar to the sense that the observance of a religious principle would have. But a fundamental difference lies in the fact that the religious principle depends on an immovable truth revealed by the divinity, while the codification of citizens' behavior is subject to the possibility of variation, consistent with the idea of progress and historical change that characterizes the social project of the modern nation-state. This introduces a certain distance with respect to what must be respected or not at each historic moment, and even from one culture to another. Modern self-government is consubstantial with this relativization of the norm, in such a way that the subject's decision to avail himself or herself of the norm assumes respect for the social covenant or the community agreement more than submission to a transcendental truth. For the Western case, this is something that is clearly reflected in the constant revision and reinterpretation of judicial, legislative, professional, or ethical codes, in contrast to the immobility of the revealed word in the religions of the book. In any case, the fact that both types of principles, the religious and the civic, are guides to behavior, evokes the appearance of dialectics and hybrids in the determination of what the subject "must and must not do" and "why." Although not only these normative hybridizations become perfectly evident in the moral and personal codes that

the modern individual embraces in his or her daily life.

4   In the purest sense, it is not either of those things today: even the most progressive viewpoints do not assume the democratic logic of suffrage and representation, a mechanism based on the delegation of decision making and political responsibility. The parliamentary formulas and so-called direct democracy – as a concept of full political participation by the citizen – only appears in some forms of local government and in a very restricted manner. On the other hand, the conflicts that arise when intentionally and extensionally defining citizenry are still tied to exclusions of sectors of the population whose rights are not recognized, or are recognized conditionally (Ong, 2006).

5   "Cooperation becomes a conscious activity in the fourth and fifth months of life, as babies begin to work with their mothers in breast-feeding; the infant starts to respond to verbal cues about how it should behave, even if it does not understand the words, for instance responding to certain tones of voice by snuggling into position to help. Thanks to verbal cueing, anticipation enters the repertoire of the infant's behaviour. By the second year of life infants become responsive to each other in a kindred way, anticipating each other's movements. We now know that such cued behaviour – the stimulations of anticipating and responding – helps the brain activate previously dormant neural pathways, so that collaboration enables the human infant's mental development" (Sennett, 2012, p. 9). Significantly, however, the psychological theming of the mother–child relationship in didactic terms (by such authors as H. Rudolph Schaffer, 1984) dates back not much more than three decades.

6   In *Walden Two* Skinner writes:

"But as the child grows older," I said, "doesn't he naturally single out particular individuals as objects of interest and affection? // That's exactly what we Intend," said Frazier. "It may happen because of common interests: the artistically inclined will naturally be attracted to artists, the potential farmer will like to hang around the dairy. Or it may arise from a similarity of character or personality. In the family, identification is usually confined to one parent or the other, but neither one may have characteristics suitable to the child's developing personality. It's a sort of coerced identification, which we are glad to avoid" (Skinner, 1948/2005, pp. 134–135).

7 It is advisable to bear in mind here the distinction between the classic liberal nation-state and the current idea of neoliberalism. By contrast with the ancien régime, the liberal nation-state, in its nineteenth century conception, would be associated with the free circulation of ideas and beliefs (or freethinking), of people between social classes or countries, of economic capital beyond its concentration in oligarchies, and so on. But all of these considerations would remain under the strict vigilance or observation of customarily protectionist national governments, in the economic, cultural, social, and so on, sense, still distant from the global free market theses and the capitalism that today's neoliberals wield. Nor does this mean, of course, that today's state will stop being interventionist, but it is in another sense. Now it would actively promote the withdrawal of the public authorities from certain services, in the same way that it would enact laws to ensure certain ways of economic performance, of the exercise of citizenship, of hybridization between public and private institutions, and so on.

8 Francisco Vázquez (2005) makes quite a good summary of the abundant panorama of theories regarding the subject, or rather, regarding the subjectivities produced in the realm of philosophy and the human sciences. In consonance with our distinctions on the modern and postmodern approaches, Vázquez distinguishes between two perspectives. On one hand, those perspectives that seek an ultimate foundation of subjectivity, or at least a general explanatory key to the transformations of modern individuality, often including a certain sensibility half way between nostalgia and a critique formulated on the political scale. On the other hand, those other perspectives would appear which, using Michel Foucault's well known metaphor, are limited to recording the disappearance or transformation of subjectivity like "a face drawn in the sand on the seashore," or consider it a product of mere mediational processes with nothing underlying them. Among the first perspectives are those of Richard Sennett, Christopher Lasch, Charles Taylor, and Paul Ricoeur, who, in different ways, tend to elaborate metanarratives about

the development of modern subjectivity and/or make assumptions about it that we could call universalist or abstract. Among the second set of perspectives are those of Gilles Lipovetsky and the genealogical approaches of Michel Foucault, Nikolas Rose, and Mitchell Dean. Vázquez also emphasizes the contributions to the sociology of individualization made by Anthony Giddens, Ulrich Beck, and Pierre Bourdieu, who highlighted the way in which different subjectivities are intrinsically bound to social practices. These are authors who also underline the reflective (and self-reflective) nature of certain variants of modern subjectivity.

9 In consonance, for example, with the conception of neoliberalism that David Harvey seems to suggest (2005).

References

Anderson, B. (1983). *Imagined Communities: Reflections on the Origin and Spread of Nationalism*. New York: Verso.

Balibar, E. (2013). Neoliberalismo y desdemocratización [Neoliberalism and de-democratization]. In *Ciudadanía* [Citizenship] (pp. 167–194). Buenos Aires: Adriana Hidalgo.

Bathia, S. (2002). Acculturation, dialogical voices and the construction of diasporic self. *Theory and Psychology*, 12(1), 55–77.

Bathia, S. & Ram, A. (2001). Locating the dialogical self in the age of transnational migration, border crossings and diasporas. *Culture and Psychology*, 7(3), 297–309.

Bauman, Z. (2005). *Liquid Life*. Cambridge: Polity Press.

Beck, U. (1994). The reinvention of politics: Towards a theory of reflexive modernization. In U. Beck, A. Giddens, & S. Lash, *Reflexive Modernization: Politics, Tradition and Aesthetics in the Modern Social Order* (pp. 1–55). Cambridge: Polity Press.

Beck, U. & Beck-Gernsheim, E. (2002). *Individualization. Institutionalized Individualism and its Social and Political Consequences*, London: SAGE.

Blanco, F. (2002). *El cultivo de la mente: Un ensayo histórico-crítico sobre la cutura psicológica.* [The cultivation of the mind: A historical-critical essay on the psychological culture]. Madrid: A. Machado Libros.

Blanco, F. & Castro, J. (2005). Psicología, arte y experiencia estética: Manual para náufragos [Psychology, art and aesthetic experience: Handbook for the castaway]. *Estudios de Psicología*, 26(2), 131–137.

Blanco, F. & Sánchez-Criado, T. (2009). Speaking of anorexia: A brief meditation on the notion of mediation. In I. Montero & A. Winsler (Ed.), *Self-regulatory Functions of Language* (pp. 213–222). Madrid: UAM.

Boesch, E. (2007a). The sound of the violin. In W. J. Lonner & S. A. Hayes (Eds.), *Discovering Cultural Psychology. A Profile and Selected Readings of Ernest E. Boesch* (pp. 177–196). Charlotte, NC: Information Age Publishing.

Boesch, E. (2007b). Culture-individual-culture: The cycle of knowledge. In W. J. Lonner & S. A. Hayes (Eds.), *Discovering Cultural Psychology: A Profile and Selected Readings of Ernest E. Boesch* (pp. 201–212). Charlotte, NC: Information Age Publishing.

Bourdieu, P. (1998). *Practical Reason: On the Theory of Action*. Palo Alto, CA: Stanford University Press.

Bradley, B. S. (1989). *Visions of Infancy: A Critical Introduction to Child Psychology*. Oxford: Basil Blackwell.

Cabanas, E. (2016). Rekindling individualism, consuming emotions: Constructing "psytizens" in the age of happiness. *Culture & Psychology*, 22(3), 467–480.

Cabanas, E. & Sánchez, J. C. (2012). Las raíces de la psicología positiva [The roots of positive psychology]. *Papeles del Psicólogo*, 33(3), 172–182.

Castel, R. (1997). *Las metamorfosis de la cuestión social: Una crónica del salariado* [The metamorphosis of the social question: A chronicle of wage labor]. Barcelona: Paidós.

Castro-Tejerina, J. (2014). "Psytizens": The Co-construction of the professional identity of psychology students in the postmodern world. *Integrative Psychological & Behavioral Science*, 48(4), 393–417.

Castro-Tejerina, J. (2015). Psiudadanos: Ciudadanía y autogobierno en el horizonte postmoderno [*Psytizenships*: Citizenship and self-government in the postmodern horizon]. In M. F. González & A. Rosa (Eds.), *Hacer(se) ciudadan@s: Una psicología para la democracia* [Becoming citizens: A psychology for democracy] (pp. 363–367). Buenos Aires: Miño y Dávila.

Castro-Tejerina, J. (2016). Psicología y ciudadanía: El gobierno psicológico de la subjetividad en el mundo latino (1880–1930) [Psychology and citizenship: The psychological government of subjectivity in the Latin world (1880–1930)]. *Revista de Historia de la Psicología*, 37(1), 3–7.

Castro-Tejerina, J. & Rosa, A. (2007). Psychology within time: Theorizing about the making of sociocultural psychology. In J. Valsiner & A. Rosa (Eds.), *The Cambridge Handbook of Sociocultural Psychology* (pp. 62–81). Cambridge: Cambridge University Press.

Castro-Tejerina, J. & Loredo-Narciandi, J. C. (2015). Evolution, activity and assembled mediation: A neo-Balwinian response to the universalism of evolutionary psychology. *Culture & Psychology*, 21(1), 111–123.

Cole, M. (1996). *Cultural Psychology*. Cambridge, MA: Harvard University Press.

Condor, S. (2011). Towards a social psychology of citizenship: Introduction to the special issue. *Journal of Community & Applied Social Psychology*, 21, 193–201.

Connerton, P. (2009). *How Modernity Forgets*. Cambridge: Cambridge University Press.

Deleuze, G. & Guattari, F. (1975). *Kafka: Pour une littérature mineure*. Paris: Les Éditions du Minuit.

Deleuze, G. (1984). *Foucault*. Paris: Minuit.

Dewey, J. (1922). *Human Nature and Conduct: An Introduction to Social Psychology*. New York: Henry Holt.

Donzelot, J. (1997). *The Policing of Families*. Baltimore, MD: Johns Hopkins University Press.

Engeström, Y. (1987). *Learning by Expanding*. Helsinki: Orienta-Konsultit.

Engeström, Y. (1990). *Learning, Working, and Imagining: Twelve Studies in Activity Theory*. Helsinki: Orienta-Konsultit.

Ferreira, A. A. L. (2001). Por que existem tantas psicologias? [Why so many psychologies?] *Revista do Departamento de Psicologia da UFF*, 13, 9–16.

Ferreira, A. A. L. (2011). La experiencia de subjetividad como condición y efecto de los saberes y las prácticas psicológicas: Producción de subjetividad y psicología [The experience of subjectivity as condition and effect of psychological knowledges and practices: Production of subjectivity and psychology]. *Estudios de Psicología*, 32(3), 359–374.

Ferreira, A. A. L., Gomes, E. B., Moura, J. de, Zornoff, P., Azevedo, G. de, Barbosa, N., Viola, P. S., & Pires, R. J. (2012). A Psicologia para além das epistemologias: Um espaço plural de produçao de subjetividades [Psychology beyond epistemology: A plural space of production of subjectivities]. *Redes*, 18(34), 59–84.

Ferreira, A. A. L., Pereira, N. B., Miguel, M. V., Brandao, J. T., Ruthes, K., & Foureaux, B. (2013). Tecendo subjetividades em rede: Tanteando as primeiras pistas em uma divisão de Psicologia aplicada [Weaving subjectivities in a network: Trying the first clues in a division of applied psychology]. *Revista Ator-Rede*, 1, 1–14.

Foucault, M. (1984). Qu'est-ce que les Lumières? [What is Enlightenment?]. *Magazine Littéraire*, 207, 35–39.

Foucault, M. (1991). Governmentality. In G. Burchell, C. Gordon, & P. Millet (Eds.), *The Foucault Effect: Studies in Governmental Rationality* (pp. 87–104). Hemel Hempstead, UK: Harvester Wheatsheaf.

Foucault, M. (2005). *The Hermeneutics of the Subject*. New York: Picador.

Foucault, M. (2007). *Security, Territory, Population*. London: Palgrave Macmillan.

Foucault, M. (2010). *The Government of Self and Others*. London: Palgrave Macmillan.

Foucault, M. (2011). *The Courage of Truth*. New York: Picador.

Foucault, M. (2016). *On the Government of the Living*. New York: Picador.

Gergen, K. (1991). *The Saturated Self: Dilemmas of Identity in Contemporary Life*. New York: Basic Books.

Glăveanu, V. P. & Gillespie, A. (2015). Creativity out of the difference: Theorizing the semiotic, social and temporal origin of creativity acts. In V. P. Glăveanu, A. Gillespie, & J. Valsiner (Eds.), *Rethinking Creativity: Contributions from social and cultural psychology* (pp. 1–15). New York: Routledge.

Griffin, M. (2011). Developing deliberative minds: Piaget, Vygotsky and the deliberative democratic citizen. *Journal of Public Deliberation*, 7(1), 1–27.

Habermas, J. (1976). *Communication and the evolution of society*. Boston: Beacon Press.

Hadot, P. (1998). *¿Qué es la filosofía antigua* [What is ancient philosophy]? Mexico: FCE.

Hadot, P. (2010). *No te olvides de vivir: Goethe y la tradición de los ejercicios espirituales* [Do not forget to live: Goethe and the tradition of spiritual exercises]. Madrid: Siruela.

Harré, R. & Moghaddam. F. (Eds.). (2003). *The Self and Others: Positioning Individuals and Groups in Personal, Political, and Cultural Contexts*. London: Praeger.

Harvey, D. (2005). *A Brief History of Neoliberalism*. Oxford: Oxford University Press.

Hermans, J. M. (2001). The dialogical self: Toward a theory of personal and cultural positioning. *Culture Psychology*, 7(3), 243–281.

Illouz, E. (2007). *Cold Intimacies: The Making of the Emotional Capitalism*. Cambridge: Polity Press.

Isin, E. F. (2008). Theorizing acts of citizenship. In E. F. Isin & G. M. Nielsen (Eds.), *Acts of Citizenship* (pp. 15–43). London: Palgrave Macmillan.

Kymlicka, W. (1995). *Multicultural Citizenship: A liberal Theory of Minority Rights*. Oxford: Clarendon.

Latour, B. (1999). *Pandora's Hope: Essays on the Reality of Science Studies*. Cambridge, MA: Harvard University Press.

Latour, B. (2012). *Enquête sur les modes d'existence* [Investigation about the modes of existence]. Paris: La Découverte.

López, O. (1998). El influjo de Jean Piaget en la teoría de la acción comunicativa de Habermas [The influence of Jean Piaget on the Habermas's theory of communicative action]. *Revista Novum*, 18, 42–49.

Loredo-Narciandi, J. C. (2012a). "Como un pájaro en el cable": Tanteos sobre psicología y política. ["Like a bird on the wire": Trials on psychology and politics]. In S. Trujillo & H. C. Pulido-Martínez (Eds.), *Libertad y psicología: Tensiones y perspectivas desde Iberoamérica* (pp. 77–95). Bogotá: Pontificia Universidad Javeriana.

Loredo-Narciandi, J. C. (2012b). El yo como obra de arte en el dandismo: Una primera aproximación. [The self as a work of art in dandyism: A first approach] *Revista de Historia de la Psicología*, 33(1), 29–50.

Muehlebach, A. (2012). *The Moral Neoliberal: Welfare and Citizenship in Italy*. London: University of Chicago Press.

Ong, A. (1999). *Flexible Citizenship: The Cultural Logics of Transnationality*. Durham, NC: Duke University Press.

Ong, A. (2006). *Neoliberalism as Exception: Mutations in Citizenship*. Durham, NC: Duke University Press.

Ong, A. & Collier, S. J. (Eds.). (2005). *Global Assemblages: Technology, Politics, and Ethics as Anthropological Problems*. Malden, MA: Blackwell.

Pérez, M. (2003). *Las cuatro causas de los trastornos psicológicos* [The four causes of psychological disorders]. Madrid: Universitas.

Rendueles, G. (2004). *Egolatría* [Egotism]. Oviedo: KRK.

Rorty, R. (1989). *Contingency, Irony, and Solidarity*. Cambridge: Cambridge University Press.

Rosa, A. (2007a). Acts of psyche: Actuations as synthesis of semiosis and action. In J. Valsiner & A. Rosa (Eds.), *The Cambridge Handbook of Sociocultural Psychology* (pp. 205–237). Cambridge: Cambridge University Press.

Rosa, A. (2007b). Dramaturgical actuations and symbolic communication, or how beliefs make up reality. In J. Valsiner & A. Rosa (Eds.), *The Cambridge Handbook of Sociocultural Psychology* (pp. 293–317). Cambridge: Cambridge University Press.

Rose, N. (1996). The Death of the Social? Re-figuring the territory of government. *Economy and Society*, 25(3), 327–356.

Rose, N. (1998). *Inventing Ourselves: Psychology, Power and Personhood*. Cambridge: Cambridge University Press.

Rose, N. (1999). *Powers of Freedom: Reframing Political Thought*. Cambridge: Cambridge University Press.

Rose, N. & Abi-Rached, J. M. (2013). *Neuro: The New Brain Sciences and the Management of the Mind*. Princeton, NJ: Princeton University Press.

Rowson, J., Mezey, M. K., & Dellot, B. (2012). *Beyond the Big Society: Psychological Foundations of Active Citizenship*. London: RSA.

Salvatore, S. (2013). The reciprocal inherency of self and context: Outline for a semiotic model of constitution of experience. *Interacçioes*, 24(9), 20–50.

Sánchez-Criado, T. (2008). Introducción: En torno a la génesis de las ecologías humanas [Introduction: On the genesis of human ecologies]. In: T. Sánchez-Criado (Ed.), *Tecnogénesis. La construcción técnica de las ecologías humanas* [Technogenesis: The technical construction of human ecologies] (vol. 1, pp. 1–40). Madrid: AIBR.

Schaffer, H. R. (1984). *The Child's Entry into a Social World*. London: Academic Press.

Sennett, R. (2000). *The Corrosion of Character*. New York: W.W. Norton.

Sennett, R. (2012). *Together: The Rituals, Pleasures and Politics of Cooperation*. New Haven, CT: Yale University Press.

Shotter, J. (1993). Psychology and citizenship: Identity and belonging. In B. S. Turner (ed.), *Citizenship and Social Theory* (pp. 115–138). London: SAGE.

Skinner, B. F. (1948/2005). *Walden Two*. Cambridge: Hackett.

Sluga, G. (2006). *The Nation, Psychology, and International Politics, 1870–1919*. New York: Palgrave Macmillan.

Stengers, I. (2008). Experimenting with refrains: Subjectivity and the challenge of escaping modern dualism. *Subjectivity*, 22, 38–59.

Valsiner, J. (2013). *An Invitation to Cultural Psychology*. London: SAGE.

Vázquez, F. (2005). *Tras la autoestima: Variaciones sobre el yo expresivo en la modernidad tardía*

[After self-esteem: Variations on the expressive self in late modernity]. San Sebastián: Tercera Prensa.

Vázquez, F. (2006). "Empresarios de nosotros mismos": Biopolítica, mercado y soberanía en la gubernamentalidad liberal ["Entrepreneurs of ourselves": Biopolitics, market and sovereignty in liberal governmentality]. In S. Arribas, G. Cano, & J. Ugarte (Eds.), *Hacer vivir, dejar morir: Biopolítica y capitalismo* [Making life, letting die: Biopolitics and capitalism] (pp. 39–61). Madrid: CSIC/La Catarata.

Part VII
Experiences Make the Person

27 The Human Experience: A Dialogical Account of Self and Feelings

João Salgado and Carla Cunha

The basic claim of a dialogical perspective is that, in order to better understand human activities, we need to assume that the basic foundation of human life is social relatedness. Every human agent, every *ego*, is always in relation and responding to an *alter* (a virtual and/or material audience) about a certain object (Marková, 2003) by using semiotic means.

There is no consensual definition of what constitutes a dialogical perspective, but six basic common principles have been outlined (Salgado, Cunha, & Bento, 2013; Salgado & Gonçalves, 2007; Salgado & Valsiner, 2010). It starts by assuming the primacy of relations over entities (*relationality*). Therefore, life in general, and human life in particular, calls for a look that focus on human-life-in-relations; these relations are dynamic (*dynamism*), mediated by signs (*semiotic mediation*), implying an Other (*alterity*), with whom each and every one establish dialogical relationships (*dialogicality*) within a socio-cultural context (*contextuality*). It is assumed that psychological actions entail all these features simultaneously.

The dialogical perspective has been successfully applied in several fields of psychology and in varied ways. For example, it originated the dialogical self-theory, developed by Hubert Hermans (Hermans & Kempen, 1993; Hermans & Hermans-Konopka, 2010), which still stands as the most popular branch of the dialogical-Bakhtinian approach to psychology. There are also some other important developments, such

as dialogical perspectives on psychotherapy (see Leiman, 2011, 2012; Martinez, Tomicic, & Medina, 2014; Seikkula, Laitila, & Rober, 2012), the use of dialogical influences on the socio-cultural approach to psychology (see Salvatore, 2016; Valsiner, 2007, 2012a, 2012b, 2014; Zittoun et al., 2013), the articulation between the theory of social representations and the dialogical perspective by Marková (2003), and so many other examples.

In this chapter, we will take those important developments as the general background to explore a specific question: How can we describe the human experiential mind within a dialogical perspective? In our view, a dialogical perspective may help psychology in better explaining one of its core elements: the constitution of human experience and the consequent human subjective sense of having a mind. Dialogically informed perspectives replace the overarching ego of its foundational position. However, this does not eliminate consciousness and self-awareness of this inquiry. As Jacques (1982/1991) claimed, "consciousness is no longer the architect of the communication relation, but its inhabitant. It realizes and accomplishes itself during the semic building blocks available for communication within an organized community" (p. 216). Thus, the human and self-aware mind needs to be framed within a dialogical perspective.

In previous works, in collaboration with several colleagues, we have developed different aspects of a dialogical model of our subjective processes (Salgado & Ferreira, 2005; Salgado, Ferreira, & Fraccascia, 2005; Bento, Cunha, & Salgado, 2012). This chapter is another step in that direction by exploring the role of feelings in the constitution of a dialogical perspective of the mind.

27.1 Taking Some Lessons from James

This endeavor revolves around the very basic ground of psychology. To look for a dialogical description of the human mind touches some of the foundational questions of this science. What is the object of psychology? What are the phenomena involved? In what phenomenological grounds we come to agree that there is such a thing we call "psychology"? We are not oblivious to the sociohistorical background of our apparent intuitions, but none of us doubts that what we coin as "psychological" refers to *specific* aspects of our life, and these are highly dependent on our constant subjective experiencing. Thus, we will start by stating that psyche or the human mind has in its phenomenological awareness of human experience one of its key distinctive features. As Brentano (1874/1995) argued long ago, mental phenomena need to be distinguished from physical phenomena. Following Brentano's seminal work, in which he reintroduces notions from scholastic medieval philosophy, this distinction is based on the "intentionality" of the mind: mental acts are always "about" something, they always have an object beyond itself, something that does not apply to physical phenomena, at least without the intervention of beings capable of original intentionality. Thus, the intentional mind is capable of "experience" and the definition of this feature lies at the very core of the birth of psychology as a scientific discipline (see Valsiner, 2012a, for a more detailed historical account).

But how to describe this mind?

Our point of departure here will be William James. We believe he gives a very accurate description of what can count as the "human experiencing mind." Actually, it may be argued that he was far from original, since his description was previously set by the German look of the nineteenth century at "experience." Nevertheless, it has become a very popular point of departure for Western psychology and it is coherent with our following arguments.

His point of departure is the following: the main subject of psychology is our "consciousness of thought." In his words: "*The first fact for us, then, as psychologists, is that thinking of some sort goes on. I use the word thinking . . . for every form of consciousness indiscriminately*" (James, 1890, p. 225).

His option is to take the whole field of consciousness as the main point of interest, instead of those supposedly more basic elements, such as sensations. Thus, he is clearly escaping the atomistic perspective, adopting a holistic position:

Most books start with sensations, as the simplest mental facts, and proceed synthetically, constructing each higher stage from those below it. But this is abandoning the empirical method of investigation. No one ever had a simple sensation by itself. Consciousness, from our natal day, is of a teeming multiplicity of objects and relations, and what we call simple sensations are results of discriminative attention, pushed often to a very high degree. (James, 1890, p. 225)

In this last excerpt, it is important to clarify that in the context of James's nineteenth century German background, "empirical" is synonym of "experiential," and therefore he is clearly denying the atomistic orientation of the positivistic philosophy. To him, to be empirical meant to be close to the phenomena as these are actually experienced by the person. We do not have perceptions in an isolated way: our experience comes in the form of integrated totalities or gestalts.

Up to this point, he is clarifying what should be the matter of primary concern to us, psychologists. Psychology studies human conscious minds that we all are aware of having and our mind is experienced as a totality.

Then, he goes on to ascertain some other features:

How does it go on? We notice immediately five important characters in the process . . .

1 Every thought tends to be part of a personal consciousness.
2 Within each personal consciousness thought is always changing.
3 Within each personal consciousness thought is sensibly continuous.
4 It always appears to deal with objects independent of itself.
5 It is interested in some parts of these objects to the exclusion of others, and welcomes or rejects – *chooses* from among them, in a word – all the while. (James, 1890, p. 226)

James continues his chapter explaining these five features. From his explanations, we will retain the following:

- Human normal consciousness is a *personal* consciousness, meaning that it implies a first-person state, and some kind of property. In other words, psyche always involves a feeling of subjectivity and selfhood.
- Our consciousness is always changing and its main feature is its operation as an irreducible stream.
- It has a sensible basis that establishes the feeling of continuity.
- Consciousness always involve some intentionality or aboutness, i.e. toward an object of consciousness.
- It is selective, and therefore, active about its momentary focus.

In this way, James takes the terms "stream of thought, consciousness, or subjective life" as synonymous (p. 240). At the same time, James is paving the way to admit that consciousness has a sensuous base, as it becomes even clearer in the following passage:

When we read such phrases as "naught but," "either one or the other," "a is b, but," "although it is, nevertheless," "it is an excluded middle, there is no tertium quid," and a host of other verbal skeletons of logical relation, is it true that there is nothing more in our minds than the words themselves as they pass? What then is the meaning of the words which we think we understand as we read? What makes that meaning different in one phrase from what it is in the other? "Who?" "When?" "Where?" Is the difference of felt meaning in these interrogatives nothing more than their difference of sound? And is it not (just like the difference of sound itself) known and understood in an affection of consciousness correlative to it, though so impalpable to direct examination? Is not the same true of such negatives as "no," "never," "not yet"? The truth is that large tracts of human speech are nothing but signs of direction in thought, of which direction we nevertheless have an acutely discriminate sense, though no definite sensorial image plays any part in it whatsoever. Sensorial images are stable psychic facts; we can hold them still and look at them as long as we like. These bare images of logical movement, on the contrary, are psychic transitions, always on the wing, so to speak, and not to be glimpsed except in flight. Their function is to lead from one set of images to another. As they pass, we feel both the waxing and the waning images in a way altogether peculiar and a way quite different from the way of their full presence. If we try to hold fast the feeling of direction, the full presence comes and the feeling of direction is lost. The blank verbal scheme of the logical movement gives us the fleeting sense of the movement as we read it, quite as well as does a rational sentence awakening definite imaginations by its words. (pp. 253–254)

Thus, James introduces a distinction between perceptions (sensorial images) and these "signs of direction" embedded in our stream of consciousness. We are unable to hold on to these feelings, since their transformation in sensorial images would kill their movement. They are distinctive states of mind, felt elements, but not fully articulated thoughts. James goes on in other directions throughout that essay, but he was opening the door to the notion that there is a strong connection between our psychic life and our embodied felt sense. More than clear elements in our mind, we feel them as vague; they seem to be almost pure dynamism, movement in itself, or the feeling of the movement:

Some will interpret these facts by calling them all cases in which certain images, by laws of association, awaken others so very rapidly that we think afterwards we felt the very *tendencies* of the nascent images to arise, before they were actually there. For this school the only possible materials of consciousness are images of a perfectly definite nature. Tendencies exist, but they are facts for the outside psychologist rather than for the subject of the observation. The tendency is thus a *psychical* zero; only its *results* are felt.

Now what I contend for, and accumulate examples to show, is that "tendencies" are not only descriptions from without, but that they are among the *objects* of the stream, which is thus aware of them from within, and must be described as in very large measure constituted of *feelings* of *tendency*, often so vague that we are unable to name them at all. It is in short, the re-instatement of the vague to its proper place in our mental life which I am so anxious to press on the attention. (p. 255)

This rich description tells us something quite different from the modernist conception of the mind: each person feels one's mind. Thus, in our opinion, James is not only pointing to the ambiguous features of our lives (that can be at the very core of our being; see Abbey, 2012; Ferreira, Salgado, & Cunha, 2006; Valsiner, 2007), but to the felt sense as a fundamental piece of our consciousness. He did not claim that as clearly as we are doing now, since he places these feelings in the middle of some other mental constituents and not necessarily as a fundamental one. How-

ever, it makes all the sense to claim that these feelings of tendency, the feeling of our movement from the present state to the anticipated future may be understood as a vital element of the self-organization of our phenomenal field (see also Smallwood & Schooler, 2015). We are conscious because we are constantly feeling what is happening to us and centering it in ourselves (Damásio, 1994, 2010; Salgado & Hermans, 2005). As Valsiner (2007, 2014) has stated: our psyche is a felt mind. Thus, to have a conscious mind and to feel are intertwined in the creation of our subjective life: the phenomenological field created moment-by-moment always comes with a self-referential bodily felt sense.

27.2 A Dialogical and Sociocultural Look at the Human Experiencing Mind

Taking James's view as the source of inspiration, as well as the Bakhtin heritage (see Salgado & Clegg, 2011), and some suggestions from neurosciences (Damásio, 2010), our proposal is that human mind refers to the ability of having experiences about something else simultaneously in a self-referential mode and in an other-referential mode.

By "experience" we are referring to the mindful or subjective constitution of an image of something else. Beforehand, it implies a relationship between an agent and an object. This latter may be an ache in a stomach, or one's arm, or a something in the past, and so on. Within this relationship, the agent is sensing and representing (in a broad notion of representation) something (in the environment, in oneself) – therefore, an experience is always something I am feeling "about" something else. If I am having an experience of listening to music, it means that I am, as an agent, in a relationship with this particular piece of music, which I am sensing. The scenario is even more complex, since human beings not only sense those "objects," but they also sense them in a self-referential way (what also may be termed as self-awareness): if someone "experiences," let's say, the sound of music, it implies that this person is feeling music as "something happening to me." Finally, and adding even more complexity to the puzzle of the human mind, all this interaction we have with the world is socially regulated. Every particular object is socially rooted. Taking music again as an example: in a song, the specific "materiality of the sounds" gets organized, performed, and shared in socially meaningful ways. Thus, even if privately felt, any particular human experience is rooted in social practices, and its subjectivity is always dependable on social codes.

In synthesis, we will claim that the phenomenological or experiential the human mind can be described in the following way:

- The mind operates by the creation of gestalt or experiential fields.
- These states of mind are always in a process of dynamic change, but in its regular normal processing, they are felt as continuous.
- This embodied sense of continuity, regardless the sense of discontinuity on the contents of consciousness, implies self-referential processes.
- We claim that the most basic level of explanation to such a process is the constant bodily felt sense, by which, under normal circumstances, the experiential fields are felt in an embodied way.
- These felt self-referential processes will also be key elements to the emergent sense of subjectivity, centeredness, and agency.
- Feelings, in themselves, involve some form of embodied response to some actual or potential situation.

The remainder of this chapter will explore in more detail this general picture.

27.3 First, Second, and Third-Person Perspectives Within the Human Mind

Before us, we have a world that is felt as an "object," a kind of external entity that impinges itself in our lives. However, every one of us feels these interactions with the segments of the world as private experiences. Finally, between these two poles, the interaction between the human agent and the object is rendered intelligible only within a socially organized world. Thus, and according to these distinctions, the person is not only interacting with an object: by using social means in that interaction, the person is also in a social relationship with others – what we may call a dialogical relationship. Moreover, since social and cultural life is embedded in the object itself, the materiality of those objects is impregnated with socially charged meanings, making the object always a social and symbolic entity. Therefore, within a single human experience, we will always have an I interacting with an object (an "it," which may be a "him," "her," but also a "you," a "me," "us," "we," or "them"), and this takes place within a socially embedded situation. In other words, there are three conflating perspectives within each single mindful experience: a first-person (an I), a second-person (the social audience), and a third-person (the object) perspective.

27.3.1 The First-Person Perspective

This is the inward felt experience of the focal object and its surroundings, the perspective from within. This may be understood as the "phenomenal self-awareness." It is the "feeling of what happens" (Damásio, 1999) and what gives a full subjective sense to any experience it is the felt origin of the "self." It may be useful to distinguish within this first-person perspective two layers: on the one hand, we have the phenomenological awareness with a referential function, by which the person is representing an "external" segment of the world – for example, I may be hearing a piece of music, while looking through a window to this forest; on the other hand, all this process is also self-referential, and the person becomes self-aware. The referential function comes with the ability of sensing and representing something "outside" – the intentionality of the mind. The mind needs a content and the content is always about something. However, this representation comes also with one of the most extraordinary capacities of the human mind: the self-referential feeling. The person knows that "this" event is happening to me and that it is affecting me. Without this kind of implicit and embodied knowledge, there would be no subjective feeling of the experience: the mind would be only a matter of representation and automatic action. With this feeling, mental contents become subjected to self-awareness and to a feeling quality that will be vital to human affairs. As we will argue later, these feelings will be the most basic grounds of human motives for action.

It may be argued that there are moments in which the person is deprived of this self-awareness – like in sleep or during crisis of epilepsy. However, these are exceptions to the basic functioning that only show the dramatic dependence we have on self-awareness for our usual daily functioning.

27.3.2 The Second-Person Perspective

This is the social dimension of the human mind and the one that dialogical perspectives have been highlighting. There is, simultaneously, an external and an internal dimension to this social quality of the mind. Our world is materially and symbolically socially organized, and therefore, our mental contents are also socially organized and addressed. Thus, we develop our mind within that external social world that is given to us. At the same time, by this necessary social articulation, the mind appropriates this external world, making it part of the mind itself. Thus, everything that happens in the mind has a social nature. For example, if you are talking with someone else, you are coordinating with that someone; if you are alone, writing a letter, the addressee of your message is invoked; if you are just thinking about something, you are still using socially acquired means (semiotic tools) in order to develop your thoughts and, more importantly, you are addressing at least one or more virtual others that somehow shape the course of your thoughts. Meaning, in terms of human affairs, has always these social roots, since it always involves the coordination between at least two agents.

Social organization starts from the very beginning of life, in the relationship between caretakers and the baby: their mutual coordination is crucial for the global safety, well-being, and development of the infant. We live in a social world that organizes itself in different ways: conventions, routines, habits, activities, each one involving coordination between social actors and between different settings. Sleeping and feeding are socially marked, but also the pattern of proto-dialogues by which the infant is brought to the world of human communication. Thus, newborns are right there introduced to a social world that constrains the possible pathways of development. Moreover, from a certain point on, human beings are socialized into symbolic forms of communication, by which they become able to coordinate with others (and, consequently, in a self-referential way, with themselves) in more complex forms. In other words, the mind becomes semiotic, since it starts using semiotic means to represent "objects" and also to coordinate with the social world in subtler and more complex ways.

From a dialogical point of view, as part of the family of sociocultural psychological theories represented in this volume (see also Salvatore, 2016; Valsiner & Rosa, 2007; Valsiner, 2012b, 2014; Zittoun et al., 2013), this sociogenesis of the mind will always be a core dimension. The human mind is always a matter of meaningful social coordination with others. Such social coordination involves communication with others and, therefore, creates meaning. At the same time, social coordination is dependent on the use of semiotic tools: two coordinated agents need to use signs and a semiotic shared system. Verbal language is the clearest case of the use of signs, but there are also some possible others: for example, you may see tears in someone's else eyes as a sign of sadness, or a smile as a sign of happiness.

Thus, the relational nature of the mind, previously highlighted in the description of the first-person perspective, has a socio-relational layer. Most of the theories in this volume share this view, but it is still frequently forgotten in psychological theories.

27.3.3 The Third-Person Perspective

The third-person perspective refers to the more "externalized" properties of the mind. What happens in the mind, happens to me (first-person), and convokes a social background in which it is embedded (second-person); yet, it is also "about something else" (third-person). The "aboutness" or "intentionality" of the mind (in the philosophical sense of intentionality, meaning that the mind is referring to something beyond itself), previously described, is the core element for this third-person perspective.

This is rendered possible through, first, by the perceptual abilities of the mind, but in the case of human beings, it is much further developed by the symbolic semiotic ability of the mind. In our stream of experiences, we not only have perceptions or images that map the world – we also have complex forms of thought that involve manipulation of symbolic signs. "Sign" can be defined as some sort of "sensorial object" (visual, auditory, olfactory, taste, and tactile) that stands for something else. The smell of a rose announces its existence, the perfume of a loved one reveals her presence, footsteps in the snow denounces the solitary walk of a human being. Likewise, the vision of these printed words before your eyes also create sentences in your mind that enables you to read and follow this reasoning. Human beings have developed highly complex semiotic systems based on verbal signs in which the meaning of a sign is dependent on the relation it establishes with other signs within socially created semiotic systems. These interconnected networks are vital to the most complex activities of the human beings.

Signs are socially articulated and addressed, but they also allow to refer to something else (see Rosa, 2007 or Salvatore, 2016 for more elaborated accounts on semiosis). By representing and substituting the referred objects, signs and sign-mediated activities, in some sense, become impersonal or supra-personal – thus, they may be shared with third parties socialized in the specific semiotic code in use. Of course, when brought to life in the mind of someone else, signs also become lived experiences and, therefore, become personal and social. But semiotic productions may gain some material independence, such as happens in books, DVDs, or chess boards. At the same time, they are vital elements for the human world of meaning, since meaning is always rooted in these semiotic elements and activities.

The contents of our mind refer to "it," and this semiotically mediated "it" becomes part of the mind. These objects are always represented objects, and representation that initially is only sensorial and motoric becomes later symbolic. Thus, the "semiotic objects" of our mind become analyzed, fragmented, compared, put in logical and dialectical relations with other signs. Thus, the inner feeling of, let's say, a melody may become an explicit (and not only implicit) object of our awareness. We are not only aware of our experience, we also create verbal descriptions of our life. We build narratives, for instance, in which we describe personal experiences within a time frame. We formulate plans for the future. And we engage in self-reflection. This involves not only a felt experience and a succession of events; it also implies the possibility of codifying those moments into a symbolic system that treats all these experiences as "objects" or "things." Moreover, it also implies the development of abstract notions (e.g., causality, laws, etc.) and the possibility of situating personal episodes within a specific time frame (e.g., "This happened yesterday"; "The game is about to end"; "Tomorrow I will go to the zoo").

We must highlight that these three perspectives co-occur simultaneously and feed each other. Starting with the third-person perspective, its connection with the second-person perspective is clear in the social rootedness of our language: we are only able to develop a language through the social guidance of others and the semiotic systems are introduced by a given sociocultural background. The other way around is also true: it is only by referencing to the world through signs that we dialogically coordinate and communicate with others – that is, signs enable our communication with others. The same applies to the relation between feelings (first-person) and the semiotic accounts (third-person). We can only refer to something that somehow is experienced – even if we are talking about fictional objects, such as dragons or Lilliput, we have some sort of "experience" of that fiction (imaginary, in that case). At the same time, every feeling is a potential event for semiotic description. Finally, as we will be elaborating later, every felt experience is actually also socially rooted and addressed, something that demonstrates the connection between the first- and second-person perspectives.

It is important to notice that in this view, what has been frequently treated as pure cognitive operations or cognitive contents become connected with an embodied feeling. The connection between the cognitive and the felt experience gives a phenomenological background to abstract ideas. Notions, concepts, ideas, they have meaning through this connection (rather unstable, sometimes) between those three poles (personal, social, and abstract). Take, for instance, the notion of "past": this notion is not only a matter of taking the logical or "purely" cognitive properties of the past; it carries a "way of feeling things" – largely developed in a social medium. In this case, we are discussing time, but the same may be applicable to any kind of concept. That is why, we propose, that concepts are far beyond the "words" – paradoxically, concepts involve the preconceptual embodied feeling in themselves!

Within this framework, the human mind may be described as composed by these three distinct but highly interdependent layers or perspectives. We have a layer of subjective self-centered experiences (first-person), which are socially organized, developed, and addressed (second-person), referencing something else through signs embedded in specific semiotic systems (third-person perspective). Figure 27.1 aims to describe these three interconnected perspectives of the mind. A person looks to the clock (a socially organized event) and realizes that it is later than expected, creating a feeling of alarm and the verbal account "Gee, I'm late!." All these three layers make this a meaningful experience to the person, but also to potential audiences: if we were witnessing this in an airport and watched the person immediately starting to run right after hearing her say "Gee, I'm late!," we will guess that the person is late for a flight.

In a certain way, psyche is this social and embodied world of "ideas" or "concepts." We also believe that this picture may bridge some of the long quarrels between idealists and empiricists traditions of thought. But this also may explain why pure sign-operating machines, such as computers, do not have a mind – and therefore,

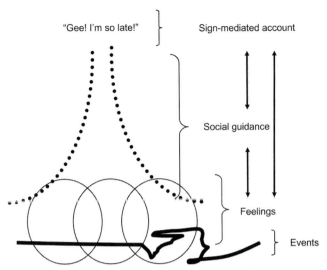

Figure 27.1 The three layers of the human mind: first-, second-, and third-person perspectives.

why pure cognitive sciences are only touching a part of the elephant, even if a very significant one.

27.4 Putting the Mind in Motion: The Notion of Position

Taking this perspective as the general background, our inner subjectivity may be described as an experiential field in which our feeling of being in the world (a first-person experience, composed by our general felt and perceptual organization of the lived moment) is semiotically articulated within a dialogical and communication relation with others (present or absent). For example, I see a tree at this moment while feeling a sense of beauty in the movements of its branches and leaves. The tree, then, becomes my focal object, that fills my awareness as the main matter of my present moment. This sense of the tree and the accompanying thought constitutes a general field of experience; the position assumed toward this focal object also socially situates the person. Nobody is here to listen to my thoughts, nobody but a virtual other. Beyond this virtual other, I also have other internal audiences that

are implicitly invoked by this position – the previous relations that now enable this experience and position at this moment. Thus, I have a felt experience, but this experience is already socialized, it is guided by previous dialogical articulations. The virtual other is the addressee of my thought (thinking is generally conceived here as an inner-directed chain of utterances). Those inner audiences are not "objects" in themselves, but "patterns of relating with" that are relevant to the situations (e.g., all my social experiences around observing nature). Thus, we have the responsive and purposeful action of the person (the position assumed) toward the object (a relation that is mediated by signs); through this position toward the object, that has an experiential side (the felt quality of the experience), the person assumes a position toward others (present or absent). Then, we may distinguish between the addressed others (virtual or real); and internal audiences, somehow involved in the meaning-making of the situation.

Then, one person comes in, and I can share this moment and feeling. A new addressee, a real person comes to the scene and the utterance is externally expressed. She understands the

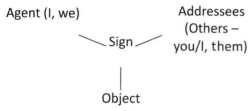

Figure 27.2 The triadic structure of a dialogical position.

situation and validates it – "yes, it is really a beautiful movement." A dialogical dance between I and Other starts, in which her agreement means more than a mere identification. In this case, her agreement may mean that a feeling of mutual and reciprocal understanding arises; a sense of excitement may be brought to the situation by this sudden mutual contact; and so on. Her response calls for a response from me. In sum, we may say that at each moment, a person is always assuming a position toward the world and toward others.

In order to depict this notion of position we may use the following diagram (Figure 27.2), largely borrowed from Karl Bühler (1934/1990; see also Salgado & Valsiner, 2010), which shows its triadic nature. At the same time, this diagram implies the three layers of perspectives previously presented.

In other works, we have developed this notion of self-position, since we believe that this notion can represent an excellent unit of analysis for our dialogical studies (see Salgado, Cunha, & Bento, 2013). Here, we will only briefly describe this notion. It is argued that the agent is always assuming a personal position (which may be also representative of a group, community, etc.) toward specific addresses about an object. Thus, a position involved what may be called, in a Bakhtinian perspective (Bakhtin, 1929/1984), "double-directedness": the position is simultaneously directed to the object and to an audience. Every position has also a responsive and evaluative nature based on affective processes. We propose that the energetic quality of human life is embedded in and fed by our affective life.

27.5 A Dialogical Account of Feelings

To establish this sort of perspective places feelings as vital elements of a subjective life. For some, this may seem a retreat to egological models, and contradictory to the dialogical foundations of our proposal. That would be true if we would be unable of rendering a dialogical account of feelings and affectivity. However, we believe that feelings are not only vital elements to unite body and mind, but a promising door to the dialogical conceptions of subjectivity. Thus, if we want to better develop our notion of a subjective mind we need to have a better hold on good theories about feelings and emotions.

Feelings have several dimensions that should be carefully decomposed, even if they take place simultaneously. As several researchers in this area have been claiming for a long time (Greenberg & Safran, 1987) each feeling has:

- an inner and bodily sensuous quality;
- an aboutness – it is always about something, that is, it has a referent;
- a responsive directionality – it assigns value to different courses of action and consequences; in other words, it involves some evaluation of the past, present and future referent, and therefore, it presents itself as a tendency of action or response to it (e.g., avoidance/approach);
- An expressive and communicational value, since we do not only feel in our body, but we also express it to others.

In our view, the conjugation of these features allows us to establish a dialogical account of feelings as shown in Figure 27.3.

Thus, feelings (and emotions, as their counterpart) have three simultaneous dimensions, which correspond largely to the three

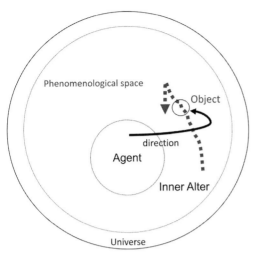

Phenomenological space

Object

direction

Agent

Inner Alter

Universe

Figure 27.3 A dialogical conception of feelings.

aforementioned dimensions of the experiential mind (first-, second-, and third-person).

- An inner dimension: This includes the sensuous flux of changes taking place here-and-now in the body-in-action. The obtained feeling creates a sense of subjectivity, a first-person or personal consciousness.
- A responsive dimension: The feeling is integral part of the response to the lived situation. As James argued, we feel the movement of our consciousness and these feelings are *signs of direction*. They carry a tendency of action, they move the person in certain ways toward that *something* – the current task. Through feelings, the person is moving to a specific positioning toward her or his experience. Usually, this feeds an *instrumental action* toward the world (e.g., feeling something like "I want more of this" while holding an apple and biting it). Meanwhile, since this positioning is also felt as a first-person experience, this positioning is a personal positioning.
- An expressive and communicational dimension: Feelings and emotions are expressive and embodied responses. Thus, they link a communicational agent to a real or potential addressee. Through emotions, we express or

"say" something, even if not with words. It is not contrary to our purposes to claim that some of these emotions seem to be clearly biological prewired, since this does not exclude communicational and dialogical properties. It only means that our own biological features, such as our emotional abilities, are also dialogically based: they were selected, at least, partially, because of their communicational value. Evolutionary perspectives seem to endorse the vital importance of the expressive and communicative value of emotions in the process of natural selection (see Damásio, 2010). Thus, emotions involve also a *communicational action toward a social world*.

The final picture portrays feelings and emotions as involved in several simultaneous processes: in the instrumental actions toward the world, in the communicational actions toward social others, and in the personal feeling of being a subjective agent.

Our claim is that the expressive communicational dimension associated with feelings is essential to make the bridge between I and others, but also between I and oneself. Let's say that one person feels sad. On the one hand, this person is feeling sadness, and this is inwardly communicated, allowing the person to become aware of her or his present state; on the other hand, this sadness may be expressed through the body, which may call for a response from others – compassion, for instance. Indeed, the constant background feelings that go with every moment of our consciousness are communicated from oneself to oneself. In fact, emotional expression is not only something to call attention from others, but also contains some crude or general reciprocal expectation (crying expects help, expression of rage expects fear, and so on). Throughout our infancy, the kind of social regulation that these situations ignite is vital to what will happen next. For example, what is the child supposed to control autonomously and what are the situations in which the child will be appeased by others? The kind of dialogical articulation started by each felt moment socializes that very feeling, instituting new expected answers; and from the moment that a feeling originates those expectations, it allows a new form of answer to the felt situation.

Overall, we are arguing that feelings come to acquire meaning in this dialogical engagement with others. They operate as signs, directed inwardly and outwardly. However, it is in the articulation between expression of the agent and answer of the addressee that they will acquire their full life. Feelings expect something from others. And therefore, even in their inward orientation, they also are marked by this distinction between agent (the one who expresses) and addressee (the one who interprets and reacts to the expression).

The following passage from the novel *The Shadow of the Wind* may illustrate this complex dialogical dance of feelings. The narrator, Daniel, tells us that he lost his mother when he was four years old and how that affected his daily life throughout his childhood:

Six years later my mother's absence remained in the air around us, a deafening silence that I had not learned to stifle with words ... As a child I learned to fall asleep talking to my mother in the darkness of my bedroom, telling her about the day's events, my adventures at school, and the things I had been taught. I couldn't hear her voice or feel her touch, but her radiance and her warmth haunted every corner of our home, and I believed, with the innocence of those who can still count their age on their ten fingers, that if I closed my eyes and speak to her, she would be able to hear wherever she was. Sometimes my father would listen to me from the dining room, crying in silence.

On that June morning, I woke up screaming at first light. My heart was pounding in my chest as if my very soul was trying to escape. My father hurried into my room and held me in his arms, trying to calm me.

"I can't remember her face. I can't remember Mummy's face," I muttered, breathless.

My father held me tight.

"Don't worry, Daniel. I'll remember for both of us." (Ruiz Zafon, 2001/2004, pp. 1–2)

First, we have the absence of his mother, revealed by the feeling quality of the silence – not yet stifle with words. He longs for her, she is not there for him, and this contact between the agent and the physically absent addressee creates a need to be fulfilled. Thus, Daniel, driven by this need, seeks for contact (the action tendency) and, as a child, freely uses his imagination to talk with her, letting him feel "her radiance and warmth." Thus, his feeling of sad "absence" leads him toward an imaginative world where he recreates her presence and contact, letting him feel her response that comes in the form of maternal love. Thus, the need for real contact and the response of absence feeds an imaginative form of connection, which is reciprocated. Daniel's complex subjective felt mind takes the form of a complex play between him and her mother. In parallel, his father witnesses all this interplay and Daniel's feelings, which are also externally directed, make him feel deeply sad, crying alone. This in turn makes Daniel aware of the real absence of his mother. However, in that day of June, when Daniel becomes unable to recall her face, his cry for help is immediately responded to by his father, who holds him and appeases him with those beautiful words – "I'll remember for both of us." They are united in their dramatic loss. Thus, there is simultaneously an internal and external drama driven by strong feelings and needs, which leads the agent toward specific positions and forms of living through the current situation.

As such, feelings share the Janus qualities of signs, since they are deeply involved in the relation between *ego* and *alter* (Marková, 2003), they differentiate an agent and an addressee. Initially, these feelings act as basic tools of social communication (Trevarthen & Aitken, 2001): in fact, in the early phases of life, the very possibility of starting joint action is dependent on these emotional expressions. These relational patterns, with emotions as their basic currency, seem deeply important to establish a kind of sensuous knowing-how of being in the world – borrowing from Ruiz Zafon, not yet stifle with words. From then on, progressively, complexity will be increasingly higher: the child will learn to name feelings, to coordinate feelings with specific contextual demands, and later to articulate the felt quality of abstract thought with fuzzy systems of values and ideals. At that point, we will have a full dialogically engaged agent in a sociocultural world. But the heart, even when solitary, will remain in-between.

27.6 Conclusion: Where Is the Self Then?

In this chapter, our aim was to contribute to the clarification of what we mean by "human sense of experience" when following a dialogical perspective. That started a travel throughout some basic questions in search for a description of our phenomenological sense of being in the world. We ended up with a proposal that distinguishes three basic interconnected layers for the human mind: a basic felt sense, a social and dialogical field in which the person assumes positions toward the world, and a semiotic component that allows symbolic actions and reflections. We then explored a little further the affective side of the mind, since the subjective basis of our minds calls for more attention to this basic layer.

We also believe that this may help us to better configure an answer to the following somewhat intriguing question: "Where" is the self within a dialogical perspective? Based on our proposal, we may argue that "self" refers to a multilayered process, in which the first-, second-, and third person perspectives conflate. First, the basic sense of self involves an embodied felt sense, from which self-awareness and self-centeredness are derived. This is the subjective feeling, the level where the agent feels that "this is happening to me." At this first-person level, embod-

ied feelings play a core role (first-person). The phenomenological perception of what happens is always mapped against that simultaneous embodied felt sense. Thus, the perception of the world and the perception of oneself are two faces of the ongoing conscious interchange with the world. This creates a basic self-feeling, which is the basic ground for what we usually name as the "self." These feelings, and the corresponding basic sense of self, also assign explicit value to the current lived situation, which is highly important to determine future courses of actions or to future eventual introspective reflections. We also believe that this corresponds globally to the notion of I-as-subject from James.

In what sense, then, is the self "dialogical"? All this takes place within a social background, which regulates the events taking place and their meaning. In other words, that basic self is largely regulated by this social and dialogical dimension (second-person). As we have argued, the person is always assuming a position toward social audiences, which are constitutive of the position in itself. Thus, the position of the self is always social and dialogical. Finally, the self has also a third-person dimension, related with the semiotic abilities of the mind. All that happens is not only felt, but also has content and becomes explicit, and by being explicit it becomes possible to create narratives about oneself. We believe that this last layer corresponds to the "Me" from James. Taking together these three layers, the self becomes then a matter of creating meaningful narratives and other forms of semiotic accounts that may guide the person through life's endeavors, rooted in specific patterns of dialogical self-positions and pursuing basic values and needs related with one's well-being.

Acknowledgment

This article was supported by the Portuguese Foundation for Science and Technology (FCT) Grant PTDC/MHC-PCL/1991/2014, POCI-01-0145-FEDER-016840.

References

Abbey, E. (2012). Ambivalence and its transformations. In J. Valsiner (Ed.), *Oxford Handbook of Culture and Psychology* (pp. 989–997). New York: Oxford University Press.

Bakhtin, M. (1929/1984). *Problems of Dostoevsky's Poetics* (trans. by C. Emerson) Minneapolis: University of Minnesota Press.

Bento, T., Cunha, C. C., & Salgado, J. (2012). Dialogical theory of selfhood. In J. Valsiner (Ed.), *The Oxford Handbook of Culture and Psychology* (pp. 421–438). Oxford: Oxford University Press.

Brentano, F. (1874/1995). *Psychology from an Empirical Standpoint* (trans. by A. C. Rancurello, D. B. Terrell, & L. L. McAlister). London: Routledge.

Bühler, K. (1934/1990). *Theory of Language: The Representational Function of Language* (trans. by D. F. Goodwin). Philadelphia, PA: John Benjamins.

Damásio, A. (1994). *Descartes' Error: Emotion, Reason, and the Human Brain*. New York: Avon Books.

Damásio, A. (1999). *The Feeling of What Happens: Body and Emotion in the Making of Consciousness*. New York: Houghton Mifflin Harcourt.

Damásio, A. (2010). *The Self Comes to Mind: Constructing the Conscious Brain*. New York: Pantheon.

Ferreira, T., Salgado, J., & Cunha, C. (2006). Ambiguity and the dialogical self: In search for a dialogical psychology. *Estudios de Psicologia, 27*, 19–32.

Greenberg, L. S. & Safran, J. D. (1987). *Emotions in Psychotherapy: Affect, Cognition, and the Process of Change*. New York: Guilford Press.

Hermans, H. J. & Hermans-Konopka, A. (2010). *Dialogical Self Theory: Positioning and Counter-Positioning in a Globalizing Society*. Cambridge: Cambridge University Press.

Hermans, H. J. M. & Kempen, H. J. G. (1993). *The Dialogical Self: Meaning as Movement*. San Diego: Academic Press.

Jacques, F. (1982/1991). *Difference and Subjectivity: Dialogue and Personal Identity* (trans. by A. Rothwell) New Haven, CT: Yale University Press.

James, W. (1890). *Principles of Psychology* (vol). 1. Retrieved from

Leiman, M. (2011). Mikhail Bakhtin's contribution to psychotherapy research. *Culture & Psychology, 17*, 441–461.

Leiman, M. (2012). Dialogical sequence analysis in studying psychotherapeutic discourse. *International Journal for Dialogical Science, 6*, 123–147.

Marková, I. (2003). *Dialogicality and Social Representations*. Cambridge: Cambridge University Press.

Martinez, C., Tomicic, A., & Medina, L. (2014). Psychotherapy as a discursive genre: A dialogic approach. *Culture & Psychology, 20*, 501–524.

Rosa, A. (2007). Acts of psyche: Actuations as synthesis of semiosis and action. In J. Valsiner & A. Rosa (Eds.), *The Cambridge Handbook of Sociocultural Psychology*. Cambridge: Cambridge University Press.

Ruiz Zafon, C. (2001/2004). *The shadow of the wind* (L. Graves, Trans.). London: Phoenix.

Salgado, J. & Clegg, J. W. (2011). Dialogism and the psyche: Bakhtin and contemporary psychology. *Culture & Psychology, 17*, 421–440.

Salgado, J., Cunha, C., & Bento, T. (2013). Positioning microanalysis: Studying the self through the exploration of dialogical processes. *Integrative Psychological and Behavioral Sciences, 47*, 325–353.

Salgado, J. & Ferreira, T. (2005). Dialogical relationships as triads: Implications for the dialogical self theory. In P. Olés & H. Hermans (Eds.), *The Dialogical Self: Theory and Research* (pp. 141–152). Lublin, Poland: Wydawnictwo KUL.

Salgado, J. Ferreira, T., & Fraccascia, F. (2005). Il sè dialogico come un sistema triadico: L'Io come una parte del Noi [The dialogical self as a triadic system: The I as part of the We]. *Ricerche di Psicologia, 28*, 13–38.

Salgado, J. & Gonçalves, M. (2007). The dialogical self: Social, personal, and (un)conscious. In A. Rosa & J. Valsiner (Eds.), *The Cambridge Handbook of Sociocultural Psychology* (pp. 608–621). Cambridge: Cambridge University Press.

Salgado, J. & Hermans, H. J. M. (2005). The return of subjectivity: From a multiplicity of selves to the dialogical self. *E-Journal of Applied Psychology: Clinical Section*, 1, 3–13.

Salgado, J. & Valsiner, J. (2010). Dialogism and the eternal movement within communication. In C. B. Grant (Ed.), *Beyond Universal Pragmatics: Studies in the Philosophy of Communication* (pp. 101–121). New York: Peter Lang.

Salvatore, S. (2016). *Psychology in Black and White: The Project of a Theory-Driven Science*. Charlotte, NC: Information Age Publishing.

Seikkula, J., Laitila, A., & Rober, P. (2012). Making sense of multi-actor dialogues in family therapy and network meetings. *Journal of Marital and Family Therapy*, 38, 667–687.

Smallwood, J. & Schooler, J. W. (2015). The science of mind wandering: Empirically navigating the stream of consciousness. *Annual Review of Psychology*, 66, 487–518.

Trevarthen, C. & Aitken, K. J. (2001). Infant intersubjectivity: Research, theory, and clinical applications. *Journal of Child Psychological Psychiatry*, 42, 3–48.

Valsiner, J. (2007). *Culture in Minds and Societies: Foundations of Cultural Psychology*. New Delhi: SAGE.

Valsiner, J. (Ed.). (2012a). *A Guided Science: History of Psychology in the Mirror of Its Making*. New Brunswick, NJ: Transaction Publishers.

Valsiner, J. (Ed.). (2012b). *Oxford Handbook of Culture and Psychology* (pp. 989–997). New York: Oxford University Press.

Valsiner, J. (2014). *An Invitation to Cultural Psychology*. London: SAGE.

Valsiner, J. & Rosa, A. (Eds.). (2007). *The Cambridge Handbook of Sociocultural Psychology*. Cambridge: Cambridge University Press.

Zittoun, T., Valsiner, J., Vedeler, D., Salgado, J., Gonçalves, M., & Ferring, D. (2013). *Human Development in the Lifecourse: Melodies of Living*. Cambridge: Cambridge University Press.

28 Knowing Ourselves: Dances of Social Guidance, Imagination, and Development by Overcoming Ambivalence

Seth Surgan, Aurora Pfefferkorn, and Emily Abbey

All development is a future-oriented process based on overcoming the ambivalence between what is known now, and what might be the case in the next moment. As people stand in the present they are always looking toward the future providing themselves with imaginations for what could be the case in the immediate or not so immediate next moment (Josephs, Valsiner, & Surgan, 1999). Imaginations guide us as we go throughout our day, week, or any period of time. For instance, as one wakes up, the mind immediately fills with speculations of the day ahead. These are vague but provide a guiding framework as we rise from bed and begin the day. Not so different from this, the jazz musician plays and improvises while moving through a series of chord progressions knowing something about the present with the idea where he is going that will only be determined as the music actually emerges from his fingers. The reader of a paper or journal knows something about the writer's message or has some ideas of its connection to other scholarship but does not know where the paper will end or the fruitfulness of those scholarly connections. Humans can know quite a bit about the present but only have vague ideas of the unknown future. These two aspects of meaning are simultaneously present at every moment, given there is no sameness in human lived experience (Bergson, 1913). There is an ambivalence between what we know

of the present and what we imagine would be the case in the future (Abbey, 2007, 2012). As outlined in those papers, all development is based on our continued attempts to overcome this ambivalence between what we know of the present and what we imagine would be the case in the future.

This chapter aims to extend beyond those papers, and the first edition of this volume by closely linking the person and his or her process of meaning construction with the environment in which that meaning making takes place. The human–environment relationship is one of inclusive separation (Valsiner, 2000). In accordance with co-genetic logic (Herbst, 1995), people and the environment are distinguishable from one another but each comes into being on the basis of the other and exists in relation to each other. From the clothing we wear to the things we can talk about and the things we can never mention, the romances that are allowed and the ones that are forbidden, and so on; society structures our daily lives, reaching deeply – sometimes too deeply – into our lived experience. Given how intimately humans are tied to their social worlds, it's important to extend the analysis in the first edition of this *Handbook* (Abbey, 2007) to include a focus on society, broadly conceived. This chapter first explores how society and the individual interrelate in the processes of overcoming ambivalence through McGinty's *Becoming*

Muslim (2006) and then by looking at Germany before, during, and after World War II, as analyzed through Günter Grass's memoir, *Peeling the Onion* (2007), where he expresses deep regret about his participation in activities surrounding the holocaust. Through Grass's words it is possible to see how an individual can experience sometimes very strong levels of ambivalence, while at other times suppress it altogether through the use of circumvention strategies. It will conclude with some remarks that try to link what is learned in this analysis with the previous ones.

28.1 Ambivalence

Human thought, feeling, and emotion are organized by shifting fields of meaning that link the individual to the collective cultural sphere as well as his or her past and future. As we make meaning, we use tools (signs) that have been created historically within particular interpretive communities, transformed as they are shuttled across social and historical contexts, and inflected through their use and transformation within an individual's life history. The flexible relationship between a sign and its meaning allows for both the soaring freedom of the human mind (e.g., through aesthetic creations and experience) and the opposite (e.g., through social guidance of what is thinkable and unthinkable). As human beings, we have been blessed with the ability to come to terms with the past, make sense of the present, and imagine the future. We have also been cursed with the struggle to do exactly that.

One of the fundamental characteristics of the human struggle for meaning is the ambivalent relationship between what we know of the present, and what we know could be the case in the next moment (Abbey, 2007, 2012). As people make meaning, they are situated on the boundary between the barely known immediate moment and the unknown future.

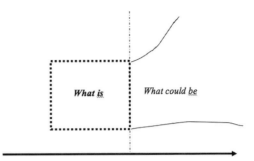

Figure 28.1 The openness of the sign to future meaning.

As such, the sign speaks to both a *re*presentational sense of the world as it *is*, and pre-presentational starts to guide the person to what might emerge in the unknown future. The representational sense of the sign is somewhat known, and this is depicted as "what is" in Figure 28.1. That said, the pre-presentational sense of the sign is always vague and diffuse and more a sense of "what could be." Described in Lewinian terms (Lewin, 1936) then, the person who is making meaning is doing so from within some ambivalence. Ambivalence is in this sense characterized by at least two vectors pulling the meaning maker in different directions and/or intensities (Abbey, 2012). A *vector* is simply a psychological force that promotes a change from the current state toward or away from possible future states. In order to understand how the notion of vector can be helpful for our understanding of meaning making, meaning itself (and the process of meaning construction) must be conceptualized in such a way that it revolves around the relationship between current and possible future states.

People make meaning to come to terms with events and manage one's own feelings and actions (or those of others), participate in the perilous process of communication, and so on. Meaning seems to be the tool of choice for our species (along with violence, which itself is regulated by meaning; see, for example, Capezza & Valsiner, 2008). Our success in these endeavors hinges on the ability to create meanings that meet the demands of the present circumstances and allow us to prepare for the possibilities of the coming and uncertain future. We do this by using signs of different kinds. In the moment before a sign is used, there is only a need or a perceived lack of understanding, control, communication, and so on. This feeling or awareness provides an implicit direction for thought and further meaning making. Simply put, this is a vector promoting the move from a condition of non-meaning (the "null condition") to the first attempt at meaning construction.

The driving force of lack (e.g., lack of satisfaction, lack of understanding, lack of resolution, etc.) was an important factor in the psychology of thinking (*Denkpsychologie*) at the turn of the twentieth century. Consider this example from Karl Bühler's (1908/1951) study of thinking, where participants were given the task of understanding complex sayings:

(Do you understand?) "We despise everything that can be explained." – Yes (6 seconds) – "The slogan 'The charm of the mysterious' (internally spoken), came immediately. *I know that this can eliminate the paradox. Yet a residue of dissatisfaction remained*. Then I remembered the period of Enlightenment and my attitude toward it (I find it bad taste to want to explain everything). *But there still remained a discomfort. Then suddenly came the shift*: to explain means to master, what is explained is mastered and thereby settled. *Only this game me a satisfying comprehension*." (Bühler, 1908/1951, p. 56; emphasis added)

Here, the participant (at the researcher's request) actively strives for understanding (i.e., "to eliminate the paradox") and he explicitly states how his (largely unarticulated) process of thinking was driven by a lingering lack of satisfaction. Although the realities of thought – including the volitional aspects of thinking – have fallen out of the spotlight in contemporary psychology (Surgan, 2012), we take this felt need – a vector promoting movement from the null state toward the stipulation of an initial attempt at meaning making – as the starting point (and motivation for) the meaning-making process.

The person moved beyond the null state by introducing a sign, which is intended to serve as an anchor for the developing meaning. However, inserting this sign into the current context (i.e., contextualizing the sign) brings with it more than its lexical or dictionary meaning. In Vygostky's famous (and often quoted) words:

A word's sense is the aggregate of all the psychological facts that arise in our consciousness as a result of a word. Sense is a dynamic, fluid, and complex formation which has several zones that vary in their stability. Meaning is only one of these zones of the sense that the word acquires in the context of speech. In different contexts, a word's sense changes. In contrast, meaning is a comparatively fixed and stable point . . . The actual meaning of the word is inconstant. In one operation, the word emerges with one meaning in another, another is acquired . . . Isolated in the lexicon, the word has only one meaning. However, this meaning is nothing more than a potential that can only be realized in living speech, as in living speech, meaning is only a cornerstone in the edifice of sense. (Vygotsky, 1934/1987, pp. 275–276)

Vygotsky paints a complex picture of the psychological life of the words that we use so fluently every day. At any moment in time, the full sense of a word entails a wide variety of "psychological facts" that may exist at different levels of awareness. Stretching this complex structural account across the arrow of time, we might claim that the sensemaking process (begun with the use of the first sign) continues with the working-through of a potentially wide range of "psychological facts" that arise with each attempt to use a sign to further specify the developing sense-in-the-making. This process is a potentially complex one, as each zone of sense will reveal its own set of "psychological facts" once it is brought under the focus of attention. For example, take Bühler's participant, who only found satisfaction after traversing both "*the charm of the mysterious*" and its opposite, "*the tiresomeness of over-explanation*." Although this process was productive over a short span of time in this example, it can just as easily go on ad infinitum – unless stopped somehow (e.g., through circumvention strategies; Josephs & Valsiner, 1998).

After the initial sign (A) is used, a field of associated "psychological facts" is immediately created. We call this field non-A. Driven by the feeling of incompleteness, the thinker may attempt to clarify or elaborate by exploring aspects of non-A. These may include typical associations, such as synonyms, antonyms, or phrase completions as well as more idiosyncratic associations rooted in memories, one's narrative framing of events, emotional state, or imagination. By bringing the original sign (A) into a dialogical relationship with one or another specific feature of non-A, the full significance of the sign may be clarified or transformed.

In this stage of the meaning-making process, where the meaning of the initial sign (A) is being transformed through its dynamic interactions with various features of the non-A field, we can see how multiple vectors can be established within the sphere of meaning within which the individual is operating, which provides the basis for ambivalence and further attempts at meaning construction. As an example, consider this excerpt from an interview study on immigration and identity. The participant is in his twenties and came to the United States for his doctoral work. He is discussing why he tends to present himself as Transylvanian (as opposed to Romanian) and why, as a political science student, thinking of himself as Romanian is "very strange":

PARTICIPANT: It's more difficult for me to associate myself to what Romanianness means, like Bucharest and a certain sense of lifestyle than what a Transylvanian life means.

INTERVIEWER: You gotta unpack that for me. What is Bucharest and that lifestyle?
P: Oh God, that's the speedy, uh, capital, kind of rather superficial, lifestyle. To make it all, I don't know, it's it's a bit, uh, yes, it's Bucharest is yeah, very, very, um . . . uhhh, trying to think of how to describe it. It's very dynamic, but still quite superficial sometimes, and it's a different world because um um people talk differently, people behave differently than in Transylvania, usually.

In this excerpt, the participant makes quite an effort to try to find a "satisfying comprehension" and eventually accomplishes this by systematically relating different zones of sense, each of which emerged under shifts of attention. Each shift of attention, in turn, was motivated by a feeling of incompleteness – a vector promoting a move from one zone of the non-A field to another. Being Transylvanian, for the participant, is primarily understandable by contrasting it with Romanianness. In this first step, the field of non-A is specified and the identity talk proceeds within this Transylvanian–Romanian complex (and the artificially enhanced ambivalence brought about by the researcher's probing). It is from within the space "in between" those two concepts that a satisfying comprehension will eventually emerge. Almost immediately, the participant focuses on one aspect of Romanianness: "Bucharest." With this elaboration of the non-A field, the participant begins in earnest to explicate the gist of what makes Romanianness difficult for him to identify with: "capital," "superficial," "dynamic." All of these specifics not only give us a sense of the participant's impressions of life in Bucharest but, by extension, his persistent feelings toward Romanianness in general. Perhaps most importantly, all of these elaborations allow everyone involved in the interaction (both the participant and the interviewer) to understand what is valuable and desirable about Transylvanianness through its "contrapuntal" specification vis-à-vis Romanianness. Once this has been established, the speaker returns in a more satisfying way to his position as Transylvanian and establishes Romania, once and for all, as "a different world," thereby bringing to an end the potentially infinite process of meaning construction.

We can see the initial denial of ambivalence: the participant portrays himself as Transylvanian, while thinking of himself as Romanian would be "very strange." In Abbey's framework, this "very strange" would be considered a *strong sign*. Strong signs set out a particular relation that is rigid and is not open to modification (i.e., dichotomized, Frenkel-Brunswik, 1949). The function of strong signs is to reduce a dynamic and dialogical interaction to one which is monological. The process of this reduction is quite straightforward: first there is an attempt to split that which is ambiguous into two "pure" opposites. Then, there is an act of dichotomizing, during which those "opposites" are separated from one another, and where only one is accepted into the meaning-making process.

Prompted by the researcher, the participant leaves behind the strong sign (and the simple dichotomization/ambiguity denial strategy that was being offered) and moves into a more delicate attempt to meaningfully distinguish what it means to be Transylvanian from what it might mean to be Romanian. In this context, the participant introduces several *fragile signs* – ones that partially and insufficiently reflect the speaker's goals of representing both himself and others in particular ways. In this context, new meanings emerge and new oppositions form the basis for continued meaning making. The erratic attempts to wrangle a fully satisfying idea are characteristic of fragile signs and a mild to moderate level of ambivalence (as the participant struggles to validate the previously absolute and clear distinction between being Transylvanian and being Romanian). In the end, another *strong sign* ("a whole different world") is brought in to eliminate the ambiguity and allow the participant to return to the null state.

28.1.1 Extending the Model of Development Through Overcoming Ambivalence

As it exists, the model of development through overcoming ambivalence (Abbey, 2007, 2012) provides useful insights into the driving role of ambivalence within the meaning-making process. It orients attention toward how people use signs to modulate their own experienced levels of ambivalence and how different patterns of meaning making (e.g., ambiguity-denying strong signs and the erratic flow of weak or fragile signs) tend to appear under different circumstances.

The model, however, is missing one component that may make it an even more useful addition to contemporary cultural psychologies. Although the model helps us conceptualize the dynamics of ambiguity and meaning-making on the personal (psychological) level, there is no clear connection between the individual-level meaning construction process and social or historical aspects of meaning making. This is important to highlight because the meanings that we use in personal, idiosyncratic ways, even in our most secret thoughts, are inherently social – saturated with a social history and first encountered in social contexts. Consider Bakhtin's well-cited reminder:

The word of language is half alien. It becomes "one's own" when the speaker inhabits it with his intention, his accent, masters the word, brings it to bear upon his meaningful and expressive strivings. Until that moment of appropriation the word is not existing in neutral and faceless language (the speaker does not take the word from a dictionary!), but [it exists] on the lips of others, in alien contexts, in service of others' intentions: from here it has to be taken and made into one's own. (Bakhtin, 1981, pp. 293–294)

The signs that we use in the process of making meaning exist within a social history beyond the lives and minds of any individuals that might find them useful. They exist as parts of widely accessible social representations, popular discourses, and so on – all of which form part of a densely polyphonic collective culture in which the individual is constantly immersed and from which one may "appropriate" messages and meanings for one's own purposes.

As the individual is attempting to master words that have been appropriated from the lips of others, those lips are simultaneously forced on us, like the lips of an overeager grandmother. Although Bakhtin's famous quote is often used to highlight the social nature of human subjectivity and the creative potential of individual mind, we can also see in it a reminder of the power of "the lips of others." Existing meanings, identity categories, and other kinds of representations (as those are circulated through various means and within various relationships, institutions, and so on) form the social field within which the individual may attempt to create one's own personal identity. This creates a range of possible matches and mismatches between personal and collective representations, which can set the scene for tension and ambiguity within the meaning-making process.

Consider, for example, a professor at a local university. One day, a passer-by wanders past a class in session and catches a glimpse of the activities. Perhaps the passer-by leaves with a desire to return to school and complete the degree they never finished: *Education is a process of self-improvement, an education will help you get ahead in your own life and help you live with others in a kinder, more intelligent, humane way. Education is our attempt to make the world a better place, one person at a time.* This is a popular vision of what a formal education is – and one that is promoted by educational institutions in various ways (and on many occasions).

Even though this is a popular portrayal of what an education and educators are, it is far from the only representation that is available. Another passer-by might look into the classroom and wonder at how such an act of violence can be permitted. *Existing sociocultural patterns are violated by formal education. Individual "students" are discouraged from continuing the traditions of their local communities in favor of required modes of thought and belief. Schools like this tear communities apart across generational lines. Formal education is a tool of cultural extermination/colonization. Professors are cultural agents of the state and no better than any other agents of state-mandated extermination.*

Yet another passer-by might see the classroom in action and be inspired by the revolution in the air. *Education, after all, is a revolutionary act – one that tears down previous knowledge systems in order to build new and progressive ones that make it possible for all learners to become prosperous, employed, reproductively successful, and contribute to the creation of a better tomorrow.*

These three representations of formal education (self-improvement, cultural extermination, and revolutionary act) are all easily available within the collective cultural sphere. One does not need to seek out a small, secretive, isolated interpretive community in order to hear these kinds of talk. At any moment, any of these representations (or others, or a combination) may be attributed by a passer-by to a professor leading a class. Such ideas may be propagated through the popular media, organizations promoting particular types of education reform, parent–teacher associations, labor unions, and so on. This is the complex cultural and institutional landscape within which individual professors may work to create their personal identities as professors (e.g., by accepting and personalizing certain ideas, rejecting others, and/or creating new ones).

In the case of the professor, the identity construction process most likely reaches a relatively stable state quickly and without much turmoil or ambivalence. The most self-serving notion of what it means to be a professor (i.e., a benevolent educator) is also the most popular representation – it is the dominant discourse in this domain, where both formal education and those who provide it are highly valued. There is an easy match between the individual's self-image and the (hypothetical) society's dominant way of representing people in that particular position.

In some cases, however, the social positions that individuals move into for their own personal reasons may not be highly valued within a particular society. This can set the scene for considerable tension and ambiguity within the individual's efforts to make sense of oneself, as he or she may be constantly confronted by the gaze of others who powerfully attribute meanings and motives that do not correspond to the individual's sense of him or herself. In these situations, the individual's self-understanding happens through nondominant representations, leaving him or her to constantly struggle against pervasive and privileged meanings in an effort to define himself/herself both publicly and privately.

Consider, for example, the situation of a Swedish woman who converts to Islam (McGinty, 2006). In the Swedish context, negative stereotypes regarding Muslims are prevalent and the environment can be generally hostile (p. 183). Moving into such a social position is not as easy – or as supported on the collective cultural level – as taking a teaching job at the local university. One woman, Marianne, chose to make this difficult move within the context of her relationship with a Muslim man and on the basis of her desire for self-development (p. 180). Although Marianne's conversion to Islam was of great personal significance, she quickly became aware of the popular gaze through which she would be understood within everyday life (the "Generalized Other" in Mead's [1934] terms) and the fact that her new position would look different from the outside than it does from the inside. She recalls an encounter with the *generalized other* that came when first practicing with the veil at home:

I remember standing in front of the mirror trying the towel [like a veil] after I had showered. And I looked at myself in the mirror and thought, "What the hell do I look like! Is it possible to look that silly?" I looked at myself and thought that I really didn't look quite right in the head . . . For many days I sat home and finally I went outside [with the veil on]. I was very nervous looking at everybody. (McGinty, 2006, p. 128)

Here we can see Marianne's initial shock at her own veiled appearance being articulated into suspicion of her own sanity, and finally generalizing into a nervousness within which she encountered others on the street. This conflict – between Marianne's own core values-based identity as a Muslim and the popular gaze – is here happening in private, based solely on internalized versions of public representations of Muslim women. Although Marianne's devotion to Islam is not shaken, her identity as a Muslim woman is shrouded in ambivalence, given the disparity in power between her personal representation and the meanings that will be ascribed to her by the interpretive community in which she lives. The representations circulating on "the lips of others" will, in a very real way, create Marianne's everyday lifeworld. Marianne's self-commentary continues later, when catching sight of her own reflection in full Muslim dress in public:

Then I can think, "is that *me* who looks like that? That looks that strange? Why have I done this?" It still strikes me how wired [*sic*] I look with the veil. I look strange [laughs a little]. It is another personality that I'm startled by. "Is that me?" I don't think of myself as a Muslim all the time. I see, ugh, how obvious it is. (McGinty, 2006, p. 129)

There are many ways to interpret Marianne's claim that she "doesn't think of [herself] as Muslim all the time." We offer the interpretation that, through the gaze of the dominant representations within Swedish society, wearing traditional Muslim dress implies a (perceived) thorough commitment to all aspects of Muslim life, which is sure to elicit not only presumptions, but also reactions from others. Marianne seems a little surprised at how "obvious" her new position as Muslim is – how vulnerable to others' preconceptions she will be.

This judgment by others quickly becomes a reality for Marianne. She recalls being teased by childhood friends when they see her for the first time after her conversion. Although Marianne's commitment is strong enough for her to assume the role of an "outsider" in relation to her childhood friends, she still values her Swedish background for allowing her to "see a lot that I think Muslims often are totally blind to." In other words, Marianne is, in some sense, both Swedish and non-Swedish – this ambivalence defines her relationship with her old friends, her childhood home, and herself.

Marianne simultaneously describes her disconnection with "very Arabic" women (who she feels are "very much meshed in their culture and who haven't taken in much of what is Swedish" and who are "so damn boring") and how she purposely maintains this disconnection by not learning to "speak their language." In this way, although Marianne strongly identifies as Muslim (e.g., stating that she believes being Muslim is "the best", and citing her "fantastic life as a Muslim" [McGinty, 2006, pp. 135, 136]), there is a reciprocal ambivalence in her identity as Muslim, especially in relation to the Arabic segment of that community in Sweden.

Through this brief glimpse into the life of Marianne, a Swedish woman who has converted to Islam, we can see how the process of meaning construction (in this case, identity construction) can be catalyzed through ambivalence created within the tension between personal representations and publicly available ones. In this situation, the person works with available representations (e.g., being "Swedish," "Muslim," etc.) in an attempt to create an understandable image of oneself. The vectorial (driving) nature of this ambivalence becomes clear when Marianne discusses the importance of finally finding an inter-pretive community within which her self-identity and other people's image of her are naturally aligned. Marianne explains:

I don't belong anywhere but among converts, among Swedish converts. That's the way it is. I can never feel totally at home with them [her husband's relatives]. But with converts I feel like I can be 100 percent myself . . . To be able to totally be yourself. I don't think it is particularly Islamic what they are doing [her husband's relatives]. I have converted to Islam and not to their strange culture. (McGinty, 2006, p. 137)

Marianne continues to describe the comfort she feels while surrounded by other Swedish converts:

we are totally flipped out when we converts meet. We laugh tremendously and are amused by ourselves. With the ones I know, we have some rather coarse banter. And that we can only have inwards, within the group; because see outwardly we are enormously pious. But together we can relax. If I had been with the Arabic women like I'm with them, they would have found me awfully immoral and doubted me being a believing Muslim. We [the converts] know who we are, what background and positions we have. We can let out so many other sides that we hold back in other contexts, since it seems too strange if you are totally . . . I mean there are many who believe that I can't joke because they perceive me, as Muslim, as so very serious. Maybe I live up to that image to give the impression of being so very serious. It is only with converts that I can relax . . . I can imagine that if I was totally flipped-out with Swedes, they may think, or maybe I think they think so, that I'm not a real Muslim if I'm like very ironic, the way I can be sometimes. Maybe I think that they think that I'm not really a believer if I act that way, being ironic about my own religion. When the converts meet, we are very ironic at our own expense, both about religion and Muslims in general. That is what we joke about since it is so charged; that we are supposed to be so goody-goody, that Islam is so nice and then we see how the reality is . . . we hate those damn Arabic old men. We can sit and talk shit and that we would never do in front of Swedes or other Arabs. (McGinty, pp. 142–143)

In these passages, we can hear Marianne describing the difficulties caused by the different kinds of mismatches caused by her "being 100% herself" in different contexts. Whether the audience is Swedes or Arabs, her performance would violate different expectations in different ways, leading to different anticipated consequences – and Marianne is aware of this (i.e., she "thinks they think so"). In front of Swedes, she would be afraid of giving the wrong impression of Islam. In front of Arabic women, she would be afraid of having her status as a believing Muslim questioned. In these situations, behaviors must be strategically deployed, in light of the assumptions and expectations within which they will be interpreted. Among the community of Swedish converts, the ambiguity – between being able to live within the vision Marianne has for herself and having to live within the vision others are presumed to have of her, between acting authentically and strategically, between being Swedish or Muslim – disappears and Marianne can return – happily and after a long journey of negotiating the tension between personal and public representations, but only temporarily – to the "null state."

The next section of the chapter further deepens the historical context of the analysis to see more clearly how social structures can work to guide the individual's modulation of ambiguity and uncertainty in the environment. It will explore Germany pre-, post-, and during World War II, noting how Adolf Hitler rose to power, focusing on how he gained popular support though a double-sided approach of strong popular support with deft use of propaganda and then last focusing on the well-known memoir, *Peeling the Onion*, by Günter Grass which outlines one person's ambivalent (at times) experience interacting with a very domineering social structure.

28.2 Weimar Germany and the Rise of Nazism

How could this happen? This is the question uttered with regard to Nazi Germany and the reign of Adolf Hitler. It is a question asked with disbelief, with condemnation, and with desperation. Though this is an incredibly complicated question, it can be partly answered by examining the relationship between the individual and society. The transformation of the democratic Weimar Republic into the Third Reich, led by Adolf Hitler, was swift and thorough. It is imperative to establish the societal context in which Nazism emerged and to tease out why individuals were willing to embrace drastic societal changes.

Nazism was born and fostered in an environment of creation and chaos. Weimar Germany was a liberal haven; expanded and comprehensive welfare programs were offered, such as old age pensions and better unemployment benefits (Evans, 2003; Weitz, 2007). Women achieved suffrage in Germany before women in Great Britain or the United States. Berlin was home to a large openly homosexual community. Metropolitan centers, like Munich, attracted writers and artists; expressionist and modern art – which was met with disdain in Great Britain – thrived. Germany also experienced the phenomenon of "consumer culture" and with it the appearance of new department stores. With advancements in technology, Germany was transforming from an agrarian society to an industrial economy (Weitz, 2007).

Yet the country was still grappling with the psychological, economic, and political consequences of their defeat in World War I (Weitz, 2007, p. 2). The defeat had been a shock to the German people due to the purposeful release of untrue information and the country struggled to find national pride and a group identity. Weimar Germany also suffered a devastating economic crisis. The poorly structured reparation payment scheme coupled with the American stock market crash and rampant unemployment ravaged the German economy. The government struggled to provide pensions to nearly 800,000 disabled soldiers, 360,000 war widows, 900,000 fatherless or orphaned children, and the elderly population. The unemployment relief system was also overtaxed with an unprecedented number of men out of work – by 1933 nearly six million people were registered as unemployed and three million had disappeared from employment statistics (Evans, 2003, p. 141). Many of those who were working had temporary jobs or received reduced wages. Taxes were raised to 17 percent in 1925 to cover the mounting cost, however, this too failed to raise enough funds. To reduce costs, more stringent means-testing was imposed for various welfare programs and staff was reduced at welfare instructions. In desperation the government began printing more money, which led to devastating levels of inflation compounding the financial crisis (Evans, 2003).

Historian Eric Weitz (2007, p. 2) writes, "Weimar Germany conjures up fears of what can happen when there is simply no societal consensus on how to move forward and every minor difference becomes a cause of existential political battles" The economic crisis combined with political instability created societal chaos. While the country had been democratized after World War I, the older order ruled by traditional elites remained largely unchanged which produced remarkable tension. This period was marked by political chaos, indecision, riots, protests, xenophobia, and anti-Semitism.

It was in this climate that Adolf Hitler began speaking at beer halls and Nazism evolved into a legitimate political movement. The Nazi party, which had first emerged in the 1920s, gained a noticeable following in the 1930s due to their economic promises (Evans, 2005). Amid the street riots and frequent Reichstag shut-downs Germans were craving economic and social stability. The Nazi party criticized the wealthy German elites and encouraged growing anti-Semitic and anti-communist sentiments. As the Third Reich rose, the Nazis did try to revive the economy and provide financial relief. In 1933 plans for the autobahn were unveiled, which was predicted to create 600,000 job opportunities. The construction project did employ 125,000 men by 1935, however, this was much lower than the initial calculation (Evans, 2005). Credits were made available for public-works programs and money was spent in developing rural and agricultural areas. Young couples were offered interest-free loans if wives would refrain from entering the work force; this loan could be reduced with each child the couple had (Evans, 2005).

In the 1932 Reichstag elections the Nazi party received 37 percent of the popular vote and that number rose to 44 percent in the 1933 election (Seidman, 2008). Although, as a party, the Nazis received the most support in the elections – the Social Democratic Party received the second most support with 22 percent of the vote – the Nazis still did not receive *majority* support from the German population. If the majority of Germans did not support the Nazi party, why were so many individuals complicit in the rise of the Third Reich and the atrocities committed by the Nazis? Though this is a complicated question, and it can be partially answered by examining how the Nazis used propaganda to transform society.

28.3 Propaganda and the Cult of Hitler

Although the Nazis did not solve the unemployment crisis, propaganda was continuously released celebrating the economy's revival, "boasting that the battle for work was being won" – and this claim was supported by falsified unemployment statistics (Evans, 2005, p. 333). Those who had previously doubted the Nazi party's financial promises were won over by this new "proof" and this sense of success "pumped new euphoria into the Third Reich's supporters" (Evans, 2005, p. 333). The Nazis transformed societal institutions and attitudes through a masterful use of propaganda.

Adolf Hitler himself became almost god-like, his birthday was celebrated as a national holiday as early as 1933. Hitler became not just the face of the party, but the face of Germany. The "cult of Hitler" was carefully constructed and cultivated by propaganda minister Joseph Goebbels. Bavarian Minister of Education, Hans Schemm, described the Führer as, "the artist and master builder whom the Lord God has given to us 'creating' a new face of Germany, which gave the people its final shape" (Evans, 2005, p. 122). While completing Reich Labor Service in 1943, sixteen-year-old Günter Grass had complete faith in Adolf Hitler as a man, a soldier, and a leader. Günter Grass (2007, p. 92) described Hitler as a powerful and imposing figure, with a "steady gaze, ready to meet every eye, his field gray uniform free of flashy medals." Günter felt as if Hitler was "impervious to attack" protected by some divine power (Grass, 2007, p. 92). This "cult of Hitler" was quite effective, Hitler always remained one step removed from the problems of the Reich or controversial actions – such as the "Night of Long Knives." Hitler was packaged and sold to the German population as the perfect soldier, a humble everyman, and also a "many-sided genius with a sense of destiny" (Evans, 2005, p. 122). Rituals like the *Heil Hitler* salute "cemented the formal solidarity of the regimes' supporters" and these societal practices reinforced support for the Führer (Evans, 2005, p. 123). Every moment of Hitler's public appearances were carefully scripted and planned. The roaring crowds, the songs and parades by Hitler Youth boys, the seemingly invincible wall of Storm Troopers, and Hitler's thundering voice left no room for doubt.

In 1938 Günter Grass (2007, p. 19) was just 11 years old, and he was in awe of what he saw in the movie theatres, writing that, "The Third Reich glittered in the newsreel spotlight." News-reels were shown prior to movies in the cinemas, and by 1939 all newsreels were produced by the Reich Ministry of Propaganda (Evans, 2005). Even films, regardless of genre, were made to conform to Reich Film Chamber standards, and had to support Nazi ideology and values. Many films glorified Nazi leaders and depicted Bolsheviks and Jews as villains in what were "otherwise apparently unpolitical dramas" (Evans, 2005, p. 132).

Newsreels in particular were extremely influential for young Günter. Before the movie would begin, Günter recalls what the newsreels would show: "Germany surrounded by enemies, valiantly fighting what had been defensive battles abroad – on Russia's endless steppes, in the burning sands of the Libyan desert, along the protective Atlantic Wall, at the bottom of the sea – and on the home front," there were "women turning out grenades, men assembling tanks a bulwark against the Red Tide. The German folk in a life-and-death struggle" (Grass, 2007 p. 70). Though Günter understood there was a violent war being fought, newsreels repeatedly showed only victorious soldiers returning home from battle, being celebrated with grand bands. This type of propaganda kept home-front morale high, encouraged young men to enlist, and reinforced the notion that Germany and the Führer were undefeatable.

The numerous newspapers in Germany were also controlled by the Reich, though at times to varying degrees. Günter recalls reading the newspaper in 1939, "I had been properly appalled by the "Bromberg Bloody Sunday" horror stories that were plastered all over the local Nazi daily, *Danziger Vorposten*, which made all Poles out to be treacherous murderers, and I perceived every German deed as justifiable retribution" (Grass, 2007, p. 35). Newspapers were trusted sources for information and Günter, like so many others, were influenced by the rising tide of nationalism to accept what was printed as fact. The insidious nature of Nazi propaganda cannot be overstated. Newspapers, newsreels, film, radio, pamphlets, posters, music, children books, children games, school curriculums, illustrations, packaging, fine art, books, and magazines all spoke with one voice, which encouraged or reinforced the same Nazi approved message.

One of the most infamous pieces of propaganda is the anti-Semitic children's book *The Poisonous Mushroom*. Not all pieces of propaganda were so strongly anti-Semitic or so clearly identifiable. It would have been virtually impossible to completely shield oneself from propaganda. Germans were constantly bombarded with Nazi ideology – some pieces of propaganda were forcefully obvious; others were far subtler. These messages supported the Nazi virtues of "blood and soil," encouraged loyalty to the Reich, demonized Jews and political dissenters, created new notions of "manhood" and "femininity," and celebrated obedience and sacrifice. All of this in turn informed feelings and actions of the general population. For example, the newspapers and newsreels Günter saw as a boy informed his conceptions of normalcy, manhood, and national pride.

The images provided by the Reich functioned as *strong signs* amid the national ambivalence about the future of Germany (as seen in the public protests and riots – erratic attempts at meaning making played out on the social level). Germany's difficulties were portrayed as being caused by enemies from all sides, including from within by specific segments of the population. Against this threat, German males fulfilled their heroic potential by defending the Fatherland, guided by an inspiring and invincible leader. Under the careful control of a centralized propaganda machine, popular media did not convey images or reports of the ordeals suffered by German soldiers (or their targets). There was no open discussion of the politics or wisdom of the nationalist agenda and no portrayal of the humanity of those who would be exterminated – nothing that could possibly spark or fuel doubt about what the ideal path for young German men (including Günter Grass) would be. The Nazi propaganda machine meticulously crafted an image of a soldier for young men to inhabit, and kept any possible sources of doubt hidden. These *strong signs* accomplished their purpose – they monologized the meaning-making process, diffused any tension, and provided a meaningful path forward (in this case, for young Germans eagerly into war).

28.4 Society and the Individual: The Third Reich and Günter Grass

Historians will often opine something along the lines of "we are all products of our historical context." This golden phrase reminds historians that individuals are influenced by society – by the social, political, and cultural environments of their lifetimes. To examine the relationship between the individual and society, we return to Günter Grass – who was mentioned in the previous section. Günter was born in 1927 in the Free State of Danzig – present day Poland – in the town of Langfuhr. In 2006, after numerous fiction publications, Günter published his memoir *Peeling the Onion*,[1] which recounts his experiences during World War II and his life just after the war's end. Günter is filled with doubt, regret, and shame as he recalls his own actions and feelings during the reign of the Third Reich. With each episode remembered, Günter questions himself: Why did he not have doubt as synagogues burned? Why did he not speak up as friends vanished? Why did he voluntarily enlist? Many of Günter's own questions can be answered by using his memoir to examine his relationship with society, and how social institutions influences or informed his decisions and feelings.

28.4.1 Uniforms and Propaganda

Many of Günter's decisions and feelings were influenced by his idealized image of war. At the age of 10 Günter voluntarily joined the Jungvolk, a youth organization for boys which fed into the

Hitler-Jugend – the boy's division of the Hitler Youth. It was the uniform that initially attracted Günter to the organization, however, the camaraderie was also a strong lure. The Hitler Youth became a feared organization. Children in the Hitler Youth experienced propaganda during a key moment in their development and were more susceptible to accept the radical messages. These children were indoctrinated early and empowered by the uniform. Historian Richard Evans (2005) notes that adults often feared being reported by children. A Hitler Youth leader threatening to report his 60-year-old school teacher for failing to remove his cap in the presence of the Nazi flag was not an uncommon occurrence (Evans, 2005, p. 281).

Günter (Grass, 2007, p. 35) writes about his participation in the Hitler Youth, "As a member of the Hitler Youth I was, in fact, a young Nazi. A believer till the end. I kept pace in the rank and file. No doubts clouded my faith; nothing subversive like the clandestine distribution of leaflets can let me off the hook; no Goring joke made me suspicious. No, I saw my fatherland threatened, surrounded by enemies." During the earliest years of the war, Günter's only criticism or disdain was aimed at the local party "bigwigs" who "had wormed their way out of active duty at the front." Günter – and his school friends – were fascinated by military action. The soundtrack to his childhood was the Führer's speeches, talk of blitzkriegs, submarine heroes, and ace pilots (Grass, 2007, p. 30). It is clear society played a major role in Günter's perception of war. As an adolescent society demonstrated to Günter that to serve in combat was a duty and an honor. Combat was something exciting, which gave ordinary young men an opportunity to become heroes. He admired the men in uniform, idolized in Nazi newsreels and newspapers.

At the age of fifteen Günter served in the Luftwaffe auxiliary. When he was a younger boy in the *Jungvolk* he admired the older boys wearing their Luftwaffe auxiliary uniforms. Although the position was compulsory, rather than voluntary, Günter recalls that he and the other boys enjoyed the freedom that came with living at the Kaiserhaften battery. In the Luftwaffe auxiliary the boys were free from school, from the constraints of the Hitler Youth, and parental supervision. Günter was glad to be out of the cramped two room flat that he shared with his parents and younger sister where there was no room for personal space or growth. Once again it was the comradery and the "spiffy" uniforms that endeared the boys to the position. Günter remarks, "The way we boys saw it, our uniforms attracted all eyes" (Grass, 2007, p. 65). Danzig was not the target of heavy bombings, so Günter did not see much action. "We got our eight-point-eight guns only two or three times, when a few enemy bombers were sighted in our air space in the beam of the searchlights. It looked very festive" (Grass, 2007, p. 65). It is telling that Günter describes his militaryesque service as freeing, and uses the word "festive" to describe the search lights. Social elements, like newsreels, Hitler's speeches, and newspapers, laid in place the groundwork that led Günter to embrace his position as a Luftwaffe auxiliary.

Here we can see clearly how successful the Nazi propaganda campaign was in directing Günter toward military service. Günter indicates no ambiguity – he was a "believer till the end" and "nothing clouded [his] faith." Although there were potential sources of ambiguity – leaflets, jokes, and so on – the framework that Günter had internalized by this point prevented those messages from penetrating beyond his surface awareness (Level 1 in Valsiner's [1997] laminal model of internalization). Günter's nonambivalence was also supported by the perceived social benefits of being a soldier. Through the dominant discourse installed by the propaganda office, service in the Nazi army was clearly associated with heroism and manhood and Günter believed that appearing in uniform "attracted all eyes." These eyes, in contrast to the ones that gazed on Marianne in her Muslim dress, presumably approved of and admired Günter's trajectory.

28.4.2 Adolescence and War

Günter (Grass, 2007, p. 65) writes, "What is lacking are the links in a process no one stopped, an irreversible process whose traces no eraser can rub out. It is clear: I volunteered for active duty. When? Why?" He makes sure to clarify for the reader, and perhaps for himself, "What I did cannot be put down to youthful folly. No pressure from above. Nor did I feel the need to assuage a sense of guilt at, say, doubting the Führer's infallibility, by my zeal to volunteer" (Grass, 2007, p. 65). While Günter's parents or teachers may not have pressured him to enlist, the "pressure" came at him "sideways" through social institutions or social elements. When Günter was home on weekend leave from the Luftwaffe auxiliary, he would picture himself as a "ship's mate during a stormy tower watch, swathed in oilskins, covered with spray, spyglass trained on the dancing horizon" (Grass, 2007, p. 69). Like the hero of a fiction book, Günter imagined himself easily "returning home from victorious campaigns" welcomed by "brass band and all" (Grass, 2007, p. 69). Günter had seen scenes like this on the newsreels which played in the cinemas. Soldiers were triumphant, soldiers were celebrated, idolized, and revered. Absent from the newsreels and newspapers were the stories of submarines who sank, killing every man aboard (Grass, 2007, p. 35). Günter finds himself sitting in a recruitment office at the age of 15, an age at which most individuals seek identity, purpose, and independence.

Günter seems confused by his decision to volunteer for submarine service and attempts to string together possible reasons, however, his decision to voluntarily enlist was a natural progression given the social environment in which he grew into a young man. He began wearing a uniform at the age of 11 after joining the *Jungvolk*. His national pride and sense of camaraderie was fostered in the Hitler Youth, as he carried flags, marched in parades, and loudly sang Reich songs with the other boys. The Luftwaffe auxiliary service kept Günter in uniform, and separated him from his family; this cemented his relationship with his male peers and gave him a false sense of maturity. His time as a Luftwaffe auxiliary also normalized military life – he lived and slept in barracks, practiced drills, and handled weapons.

Günter was rejected for service at the age of fifteen; first he had to complete the mandatory Labor Service. "Not even enlisted men could get out of Labor Service. That's where you do your rifle drills. And learn what real army discipline means" (Grass, 2007, p. 73). Günter traded in his Luftwaffe auxiliary uniform, for a Labor Service uniform. During Labor Service boys and girls (in separate units) devoted their time and talents to better the Fatherland and the Reich. Günter had previously met a young woman named Lili who fulfilled her Labor Service by teaching art at his school. Since Günter had artistic talent he was given the task of painting watercolor landscapes to decorate the mess hall.

Günter recalls the ceremony during which the boys were presented with pistols, "It goes without saying: every member of the Labor Service was to feel honored by the touch of wood and metal, the butt and barrel of the carbine in his hands. And we boys did in act inflate ourselves to men when we stood at attention with our guns by our sides" (Grass, 2007, pp. 82–83). Social institutions informed Günter's conceptions of "manhood." Günter's previous time in uniform as a boy, combined with the instruction of the Labor Service, and reinforced by propaganda, taught him that "manhood" was reached or earned with successful military service. These images were turned (by Günter) into fantasies for himself, which only further buffered him from any possible ambivalence. Günter yearned for the chance to serve aboard a submarine and escape from his home life. No matter how comfortable or loving that might have been, glory and manhood were not within reach. He saw no reason to delay – boys were drafted, while men *volunteered* to fight.

28.4.3 Doubt

During his time in the Labor Service there was one boy that caused Günter to experience a brief moment of doubt. Günter describes the boy as quiet and dedicated to his Labor Service tasks, but he refused to participate in rifle drills or even hold a pistol. Each time the gun was put into his hand the boy refused to clasp it, letting the sacred item fall to the ground. The boy was punished with chores, which he did without complaint. When he continued to be insubordinate, the entire unit was punished, which caused the boys to turn against the dissenter. When asked why he would not take the gun, the boy always replied, "We don't do that" (Grass, 2007, p. 86). Günter remembers, "He stuck to the plural . . . It was as though he had if not an army then at least a goodly battalion of imaginary insubordinates lined up behind him ready to repeat the phrase after him. Four words fusing into one: Wedontdothat . . . His behavior transformed us. From day to day what had seemed solid crumbled" (Grass, 2007, p. 86)

The other boys began to admire "Wedontdothat" and discipline began to deteriorate. Finally the boy was taken away, likely sent to a concentration camp. Günter admits, "I was if not glad, then at least relieved when the boy disappeared. The storm of doubts about everything I had had rock solid faith in died down, and the resulting calm in my head prevented any further thought from taking wing: mindlessness had filled the space" (Grass, 2007, p. 88). The boys speculated that the dissenter had been a "Bible nut" or a Jehovah's Witness (Grass, 2007, p. 87). "Wedontdothat" boy was not as susceptible to society's influence. The social elements of the Third Reich were forced to compete for influ-

ence with the boy's religious institution which predated the Reich.

"The image that had been crystal clear in the sixteen-year old Labor Serviceman's mind until then was turning fuzzy around the edges. Not that it had become alien, no. But my uniformed self seemed to be slipping away. It had given up its shadow and wanted to belong among the less guilty. There were plenty of people like that later on, people who 'were only obeying orders'" (Grass, 2007, p. 91). Günter may have begun doubting the Nazi ideology; however, these doubts did not lead him to alter his actions. After Günter was dismissed from the Labor Service, he heard stories of peers who had dodged the draft and went "underground." The Edelweiss Pirates were a group of similarly aged boys, "who were shaking people down in bombed-out Cologne" (Grass, 2007, p. 95). Günter did not go "underground," nor did he join a resistance group – he instead waited restlessly at home for two months until his induction letter arrived. Despite his mother's grief, Günter took the train to the Reich headquarters in Berlin to fulfill his position as a soldier. Günter does not remember feeling fear or doubt as he traveled to Berlin. The induction letter gave Günter purpose and direction again; he was leaving behind the home he found cramped and strange for the familiarity of barracks and the comfort of a uniform.

During this episode, Günter encounters something not described before – disobedience. The actions of the "Wedontdothat" seem to have been motivated by some set of beliefs that Günter cannot articulate, but he describes the power of the boy's behavior itself. It creates the first seed of doubt. Günter reports that "discipline began to deteriorate," while he himself had "storms of doubt about everything I had rock solid faith in," and even that his "uniformed self seemed to be slipping away." The protest by "Wedontdothat" demanded an interpretation from the group as a whole. The other boys attempted to make sense of "Wedontdothat" by speculating about his religious background – an erratic effort at meaning construction, which – if successful – could provide the boys with a way of short circuiting the influence of the protesting boy. Without a stable meaning to alleviate the ambiguity, the boys were unable to either fully stand behind "Wedontdothat" or enforce the status quo. The relatively high level of ambiguity was perceived as a threat by the Labor Service, who removed "Wedontdothat." Following the disappearance, Günter reports a decrease in ambivalence and corresponding relief: "the resulting calm in my head prevented any further thought from taking wing: mindlessness had filled the space." The disappearance of "Wedontdothat" was not simply the removal of a disruptive force. It was a strong sign – a zero signifier (Ohnuki-Tierney, 1994) from the Labor Service inserted into the space where "Wedontdothat" had been that eliminated ambivalence and restored the status quo.

When Günter arrives in Berlin his life as a soldier begins. It is here that he has his first real contact with the war. Berlin had sustained heavy bombing, and as Günter arrived an all-clear had just sounded. Even though buildings were burning all around the city the people of Berlin seemed uninterested as, "fires were considered normal by then" (Grass, 2007, p. 107). If the destruction gave Günter pause he cannot remember it, "I can picture my fellow recruits jabbering. We are curious, as if on an adventure. We're in a good mood" (Grass, 2007, p. 108). When he receives marching rations, including cigarettes, Günter trades them for marzipan potatoes, a treat reserved for Christmas. Society has taught Günter that war is an adventure, that it is the coming of age trial that will establish him as a man. He believes he is standing on the precipice of adulthood, about to achieve greatness. The propaganda has established this belief and the boys feed each other's excitement and reinforce these beliefs in this group setting.

Günter is assigned to a Waffen SS unit to be a gunner on the eastern front, and travels with his unit to the Bohemian Woods for training. Günter's only complaint about training was his assigned daily chore of bringing the troop leaders their coffee. This task took up most of his allotted breakfast time and continually made him late for morning roll. He was punished for his tardiness by being made to run up and down a hill wearing a gas mask and a heavy pack. Günter eventually decided to exact revenge each morning by peeing into the coffee. "We may assume that my repeated revenge, my regular morning gesture of futility, helped me to endure the drills, and even the worst tortures, with an inner grin. Just before one of those punishment drills, a recruit in the company next to ours hanged himself with the strap of his gas mask" (Grass, 2007, p. 114). Although we know nothing about the boy who committed suicide, the argument can be made that his relationship with society was less stable than Günter's relationship with society. Günter feels it is unfair that he has to complete the coffee chore, but he does not have complaints about the overall training experience. "Otherwise, I did everything I was ordered without a second thought. Shooting moving targets. Night marches with combat pack. Knee bends with rifle held at arm's length. It was all supposed to make a man out of me" (Grass, 2007, p. 114). This demonstrates Günter's positive relationship with society – the social institutions that have influenced his life have taught him that this experience is necessary for his growth and development so Günter is eager to complete this task.

When Günter's unit is transferred to Dresden, he witnesses an event that, in retrospect, he believes should have signaled to him the imminent defeat of the Third Reich. As the boys traveled to Dresden by train they saw, "charred bundles piled one on top of the other between the tracks and in front of torched facades. Some claimed to have seen shriveled corpses, others heave knows what. We covered up our horror then by quarreling over what had happened" (Grass, 2007, p. 119). Günter realizes now this moment is horrifying and should have caused him distress or doubt, but does not recall his younger self realizing this. Doubt, at that moment as he travels to the front lines would have been far too distressing for the 16-year-old soldier to accept. As Günter was about to face the enemy to defend Germany, with only his comrades to rely on, doubt would have been catastrophic. Günter realizes he "covered up" his horror, and did so because had he acknowledged his doubt, a distressing ambivalence would have resulted.

Günter's relationship with society begins to deteriorate with his first encounter with Russian soldiers and his first lesson in fear. When his unit is attacked by Russian tanks, Günter and a higher ranking soldier hide beneath their tank until the Russians move on. Günter recalls the other soldier who was "the very picture of a newsreel hero such as we schoolboys had been fed from the screen for years" was also terrified, teeth chattering, and looked "ridiculous" afterward when he issued orders, stepping over the broken crumbled bodies of the dead and injured (Grass, 2007, p. 125). Günter admits he is grateful to this soldier because he "completely undermined the image of the hero" that he had cherished for so long and admired (Grass, 2007, p. 125). Günter realizes for the first time that the images he has been shown are not realistic. His relationship with society becomes strained, and his is concerned now with survival more so than being heroic or earning "manhood."

At this moment, close to death and seeing a soldier of the kind he had been trained to idolize and emulate being more concerned with individual survival than with defending the Fatherland, Günter's ambivalence reaches its highest levels. The story of the heroic soldier clashes with the image of a man scared for his life. Not only does a second image appear on the scene, but it comes to dominate. When the scared man attempts to act in the role of the heroic soldier (by standing over the bodies of the less fortunate and issuing orders), he appears "ridiculous" in Günter's eyes. Heroism through warfare is no longer an option for Günter – nor is it for anybody else.

Despite Günter's fear and doubt during his first encounter with the enemy he does end the war by following his marching orders, to the letter. After being separated from numerous units, having watched comrades die violently – Günter was briefly lost in the woods and then traveled with a new companion, both boys move westward carrying their fear of being arrested for desertion (because they had no marching orders) and their fear of being killed by the Russians. While eating breakfast one morning Günter is wounded by a grenade. He endures a hellish journey by train in a dark freight car with other wounded soldiers, many of whom did not survive the journey. At the overcrowded hospital he learned he had a piece of grenade lodged in his shoulder and leg. His wounds was deemed "non-serious," "They did not deem me worthy of an operation, nor did they waste a tetanus shot on me" (Grass, 2007, p. 154). He finally received new paper, ordering him to report to Marienbad. He does not remember how he traveled over the mountains only that he became feverish and was cared for briefly by a couple whose son had perished at the front.

The couple offered Günter new clothes, and they offered to shelter him until the war was over, but Günter refused. "I didn't stay. I wanted to go where my travel papers ordered me to go, to cross the mountains in my own trousers" (Grass, 2007, p. 157). Despite his doubts, despite all the fear and chaos of war, Günter wanted to complete his orders and officially finish his service, which society had trained him to do his entire adolescence. Feverish and weak Günter made it to Karlsbad where he collapsed in the street. He was taken by a policeman to Marienbad, as instructed by his marching orders, and it was here the war ended for the 16-year-old soldier. With the defeat of the Third Reich all the social institutions – like the Hitler Youth and Nazi newsreels –

fell away, and Germans, like Günter, were forced to defend and reconcile their choices and feelings without the corresponding influential societal elements. Despite carrying a pistol, rile, and machine gun at various points, Günter (Grass 2007, p. 144) writes, "I never looked through a sight, never felt for a trigger, and thus never fired a shot" The fact that he never fired his weapon is the one thing that alleviates some of Günter's shame.

When Günter awoke from his fever he learned that Adolf Hitler was dead. "His departure was taken as only expected. He was gone as if he had never been, had never quite existed and was not to be forgotten, as if you could live perfectly well without the Führer. By the same token, his 'heroic death' was lost in the mass of individual deaths and was soon no more than a footnote" (Grass, 2007 p. 160). The Führer, whom Günter never doubted, who was "above death" and the model of a perfect soldier simply vanished from Günter's life. Günter had been socially directed to revere Hitler; social institutions like the *Jungvolk* built loyalty to the Führer, social programs endeared people to Hitler and fear of the Gestapo kept potentially conflicting voices silent. With the end of the Third Reich, without the influence of society, Hitler became an ordinary man, his death of no real consequence to Günter Grass.

Like many others in his position, Günter is left looking back on his service and questioning how he could have become part of the Nazi war machine and the implications for his understanding of himself. Was he a good person caught in terrible circumstances? Was he weak while others, like "Wedontdothat" were strong? Through his process of meaning construction, Günter finds a way to forgive himself, at least partially, for his contributions to the Nazi regime by reminding himself that he never fired a shot as a soldier. We do not know if this claim is true and, if it is, how this might have happened. If it was because of circumstances beyond Günter's control, then the fact that he never fired a shot does not vindicate

him. If it was because of his own objection to the idea of potentially killing another human being, then it calls into question important aspects of his story – he was not as brainwashed by the Nazi propaganda as he claims to have been and must accept more personal responsibility for his decision to become a Nazi soldier than he seems willing to accept. Despite the apparent strength of this sign, it is not enough to grant Günter (in contrast to Marianne) a peaceful return to the "null state."

28.5 Conclusions

The model of development through overcoming ambivalence represents not only the duality of meaning construction, but also its *temporal embeddedness*. As humans go about the process of making meaning, that process is necessarily influenced by time, and the relationship that the person has with the uncertainty that constantly lies before him or her. The aim of this chapter has been to expand the model by considering the social context of the meaning making process through McGinty's *Becoming Muslim* (2006) and by looking at Germany before, during and after World War II, as analyzed through Günter Grass' memoir *Peeling the Onion* (2007) where he expresses deep regret about his participation in activities surrounding the Holocaust. In the examples presented in this chapter, we saw that "social others" are more than ready to help the meaning maker in his or her process of meaning construction. We saw the goal of social others is often to have their meanings, rather than the person's own emerging ones, used in meaning making. We also saw that the individual – be it Günter or Marianne – can make these interventional efforts of social others functional by accepting the meanings and allowing it to organize their relationship with the world (for example, as Günter did in many instances with Nazi propaganda). The individual is equally able to reject the meanings social others present, and this is why we see the extreme redundancy of social suggestion as social institutions all try hard to avoid this outcome (e.g., the case of over-proliferation of Nazi propaganda in Günter's story.)

Judging from the over-proliferation of messages from various social institutions which all function in redundant manner to communicate the same message, we can see that rejection is the usual state of affairs when social others aim to intervene in our meaning constructive processes. While we are at times ready to let social others "help" us, it is a complicated situation because the moment we decide we do not want their help is not the moment they stop forcing their efforts on us. It is easy enough to understand why the social other should do this, but harder to see how on earth the meaning maker should be able to make sense of it all. It is no surprise that we often return to the null state – a retreat from the pressures we are put under in the process of coming to know ourselves (and others), for instance, as Günter and Marianne do at times. To be sure, we are good at blocking a lot of the incoming social suggestion that we receive, forcing the social system to work "wastefully" to try and overcome our human efforts to drown it out. Nonetheless, we cannot drown out all of it and at times it can become an overwhelming cacophony.

In sum, humans develop in a decidedly future-oriented manner by overcoming the ambivalence between what they believe to be true at the present, and what they imagine could be the cause in the uncertain next moment. Within this process, moods can wax and wane in strength and as it grows stronger, this is when social others are likely to intrude and offer prescriptive suggestions as to how to think, feel, and/or act. Humans have a broad capacity to ignore these attempts to control their minds, however they do sometimes retreat to the safety of the null condition where no meaning is made, until they are ready to reenter the ever-ambivalent space of meaning making where they continue to engage in the ongoing process of coming to know themselves.

Note

1 *Peeling the Onion* was written in German and published in 2006, the English translation which was used for this chapter was published in 2007 and translated by Michael Henry Heim.

References

Abbey, E. (2007). Perpetual uncertainty of cultural life: Becoming reality. In J. Valsiner & A. Rosa (Eds.), *Cambridge Handbook of Sociocultural Psychology*. Cambridge: Cambridge University Press.

Abbey, E. (2012). Ambivalence and its transformation. In J. Valsiner (Ed.), *Oxford Handbook of Culture and Psychology* (pp. 989–997). New York: Oxford University Press.

Bakhtin, M. (1981). *The Dialogic Imagination: Four Essays*. Austin: University of Texas Press.

Bergson, H. (1913). *Time and Free Will*. London: George Allen.

Bühler, K. (1908/1951). On thought connections. In D. Rappaport (Ed.), *Organization and Pathology of Thought: Selected Sources* (pp. 39–57). New York: Columbia University Press.

Capezza, N. M. & Valsiner, J. (2008). The making of nonviolence: Affective self-regulation in a shooting game. In E. Abbey & R. Diriwächter (Eds.), *Innovating Genesis: Microgenesis and the Constructive Mind in Action* (pp. 67–91). Charlotte, NC: Information Age Publishing.

Evans, R. (2003). *The Coming of the Third Reich*. New York: Penguin Books.

Evans, R. (2005). *The Third Reich in Power*. New York: Penguin Books.

Frenkel-Brunswik, E. (1949). Intolerance of ambiguity as an emotional and perceptual personality variable. *Journal of Personality*, 18(1), 108–143.

Grass, G. (2007). *Peeling the Onion: A Memoir* (trans. by Michael Henry Heim). New York: Harcourt.

Herbst, D. P. (1995). What happens when we make a distinction: An elementary introduction to co-genetic logic. In T. A. Kinderman &

J. Valsiner (Eds.), *Development of Person–Context Relations* (pp. 67–82). Hillsdale, NJ: Lawrence Erlbaum.

Josephs, I. & Valsiner, J. (1998). How does autodialogue work? Miracles of meaning maintenance and circumvention strategies. *Social Psychology Quarterly*, 61(1), 68–82.

Josephs, I., Valsiner, J., & Surgan, S. (1999). The process of meaning construction. In J. Brandtstädter and R. M. Lerner (Eds.), *Action & Self Development* (pp. 257–282). Thousand Oaks, CA.: SAGE.

Lewin, K. (1936). *Principles of Topological Psychology*. New York: McGraw-Hill.

McGinty, A. M. (2006). *Becoming Muslim*. New York: Palgrave Macmillan.

Mead, G. H. (1934). *Mind, Self, and Society from the Standpoint of a Social Behaviorist*. Chicago: University of Chicago Press.

Ohnuki-Tierney, E. (1994). The power of absence: Zero signifiers and their transgressions. *L'Homme*, 34(2), 59–76.

Seidman, Steven. 2008. *Posters, Propaganda, and Persuasion in Election Campaigns Around the World and Through History*. New York: Peter Lang.

Surgan, S. (2012). Rethinking word association. In E. Abbey & S. Surgan (Eds.), *Emerging Methods in Psychology* (pp. 27–64). New Brunswick, NJ: Transaction Publishers.

Valsiner, J. (1997). *Culture and the Development of Children's Action* (2nd edn.). New York: John Wiley & Sons.

Valsiner, J. (2000). *Culture and Human Development*. Thousand Oaks, CA: SAGE.

Vygotsky, L. S. (1934/1987). Thought and word. In R. W. Rieber & A. S. Carton (Eds.), *The Collected Works of L. S. Vygotsky. Vol. 1: Problems of General Psychology* (pp. 243–288). New York: Plenum Books.

Weitz, Eric. 2007. *Weimar Germany: Promise and Tragedy*. Princeton NJ: Princeton University Publishing.

29 Personal History and Historical Selfhood: The Embodied and Pre-reflective Dimension

Allan Køster and Ditte Alexandra Winther-Lindqvist

> If we succeed in understanding the subject, this will not be in its pure form, but rather by looking for the subject at the intersection of its various dimensions.
>
> Merleau-Ponty, 2012, p. 433

In the seminal first volume of this *Handbook*, the editors wrote in the preface: "Sociocultural psychology cannot leave aside anything that is human; its challenge is to address its complexity and provide tools for its explanation and understanding" (Valsiner & Rosa, 2007, p. ix). This is a grand ambition of sociocultural psychology, and we wish to contribute to that project by theorizing the phenomenon of the personal as an embodied historical process. We contend that both the personal dimension as such, and individual existence as something historical, have been significantly omitted in sociocultural theorizing (González Rey, 2008; Smolka, De Goes, & Pino, 1995; Valsiner, 1998). This tendency to neglect the personal dimension is not only characteristic of sociogenetic approaches in psychology, but has also been identified in other disciplines concerned with cultural practices and processes. For instance, Jackson and Piette (2015) recently argued that such a lack exits in the field of anthropology, where "there is a tendency to shift vitality, power, consciousness, and will from persons to the transpersonal realms of abstract ideas, global forces, historical processes, genetic patterns, social structures, and discursive formations" (p. 4). Sociocultural theories usually account for cultural practices, institutional settings, norms, values, and discourses in histori-

cal terms (Scribner, 1985). However, the same theoretical sensitivity to history is often forgotten when it comes to the person participating in these cultural settings and social practices, sometimes to the extent that the person is reduced to an empty placeholder. Although this omission holds true for the general sociocultural landscape, it should be recognized that there is an emerging body of studies of the personal dimension in sociocultural psychology and that one of the founders of the sociocultural approach, Vygotsky, did suggest terminology for the personal dimension of experience in the distinction between sense and meaning. "Meaning" denotes the conventional, general, and collective understanding of a word, whereas "sense" is reserved for the inherently personal meaning making, which is affective-volitional, fluid, and changeable (Leontiev, 1978; Valsiner, 1998).[1] Though it is impossible to provide a full account of this research here, two principal directions should be emphasized. The first explores the person as a semiotic sense-maker, and the personal dimension as a semiotic process of sensemaking (often on a sub-personal or a formal level). Valsiner's (1998) seminal work, *The Guided Mind*, is a cornerstone of this approach, and has inspired others to further explore the semiotic landscape of the personal (Salvatore, 2012). Second, alongside, and sometimes integrated with this semiotic approach, is a growing body of work on micro-genetic and life-course studies that theorize how the person develops across time through participating in various institutional settings. The study of the narrative, the (self)-reflective, active person participating in sociocultural practices through which s/he develops auto-biographical memory, goals, motives, engagements, commitments, likes/dislikes, dreams, fears, and fantasies is also a dimension of personal history currently being theorized (Hedegaard, 2011; see also Chapters 10, 14, and 30, this volume). However, where these approaches provide rich and indispensable analysis and conceptual tools for understanding personal development as it unfolds and the way in which it is embedded in sociocultural practices, they almost entirely fail to address our embodied and pre-reflective experiences. The preverbal, pre-reflective embodied landscape of experience is a blind spot in the sociocultural tradition, from its founding to the present day. This absence is unwarranted, and we suggest that the pre-reflective dimension should be considered a field open to further theorizing, rather than a denied ontology. The principal reason is that this level of embodied and pre-reflective experience is deeply saturated by sociocultural influences, and thus rightly belongs to the domain of a sociocultural psychology proper.

In order to separate the pre-reflective and the more reflective dimensions of the personal, we employ a distinction sometimes made in phenomenology between the "Self" and the "Person." Whereas the *self* designates the pre-reflective, embodied, and personal being-in-the-world, the *person* refers to the "autobiographical actualization of the self"; the person is a self "whose identity has achieved expression" (Nathanson, 1970, p. 17). Therefore, we reserve the term selfhood for the pre-reflective and embodied dimension of personal existence. Irrespective of the paramount importance of language and language acquisition in ontogeny, selfhood, as the embodied, personal being-in-the-world, remains a fundamental and continuous dimension of experience throughout life.

In the following sections, we contribute to theorizing the pre-reflective dimension in sociocultural psychology by proposing a conceptual framework of what we term "personal history" and "historical selfhood," respectively. With these concepts, we specifically target the pre-reflective and embodied level of personal existence, and therefore these terms should not be seen as replacing existing frameworks, but as supplementing the semiotic, narrative, and activity-based understandings already theorized in contemporary sociocultural theory. Whereas the term personal history specifies the broader ontogenetic and existential process through which somebody continuously becomes the person s/he is, the term historical selfhood specifically refers to a person's embodied, present style of being as a result of this.

29.1 A Turn to Phenomenology

In order to theorize this pre-reflective dimension, we propose a synthesis of sociocultural psychology and the phenomenological tradition, based on both classical (e.g., Husserl, Heidegger, Merleau-Ponty) and contemporary (e.g., Waldenfels, Zahavi, Fuchs) sources. The reasons for turning to phenomenology are many – we believe that sociocultural psychology has much to gain from a dialogue with phenomenology, since both traditions share a range of fundamental assumptions, such as prioritizing practice, studying existence as an ongoing unfolding of life, and understanding existence as essentially always being-with-others in sociocultural, historical practices, and so on. Furthermore, the phenomenological tradition is, if not the only, then the most obvious source of theorizing the pre-reflective personal dimension, since it is rooted in the first-person perspective. There is a consistent fit between the usual unit of analysis for sociocultural theorizing "person-in-context" (from a third-person perspective) and the phenomenological unit of analysis theorizing "being-in-the-world" (from a first-person perspective). Our suggested shift in perspectives is indicated by the term "personal history" as it evokes two conceptual horizons: that of the personal and the historical. First, we use the term "personal" in contrast to the concept of a "person." Whereas person usually is taken to refer to the abstract and reflective individual member of cultural and moral communities (Martin & Bickhard, 2013), the personal specifies an experiential dimension, articulated within existential phenomenology as *my* particular perspective as an individual situated in these cultural communities and practices (Waldenfels, 2000, p. 248). As we will make clear throughout our contribution, addressing the personal in this way is impossible outside of, or when devoid of, participation in historical, societal, cultural institutional, and material settings. However, participating in shared practices is also always already ontogenetically specific. No one grows up in a generic family. I grew up in *my* specific family, with *my* parents with their idiosyncrasies, strengths, shortfalls, warmth, and whims. I may live in a standard house, but it is *my home* with its particular things, smells, and atmospheres in my neighborhood, and so forth. Second, with the term history we broadly refer to the idea of historicity as it is used in the phenomenological-hermeneutical tradition of Heidegger and Gadamer. In contrast to a general tendency to equate history and narrative, the concept of history used in this tradition is considered to be much broader, a matter of facticity, or of how "the past is present in the present" (Schatzki, 2003).

29.2 Historical Selfhood as Embodied

Conceptions and models of the self are diverse, and there is little consensus in the contempo-

rary debate where positions vary greatly, defining selfhood as narrative, dialogical, postmodern, enactive, minimal, embodied, and so on (Gallagher, 2011). Within this broad palate, the pre-reflective historical selfhood we are addressing is an extended concept of embodied selfhood. In order to make this clear, a few initial distinctions need to be made. By a "pre-reflective self" we intend a dimension of selfhood that is pre-predicative or prelinguistic, in the sense that it is always already in place when we start to articulate experiences. Though richly examined in phenomenology, this embodied dimension of selfhood has so far not attracted much attention from a sociocultural psychological perspective. As we have argued, we consider this a blind spot, since the influence of sociocultural processes does not stop and start with language, but also seeps into and saturates the pre-reflective, embodied level of selfhood.

Within the phenomenological tradition, pre-reflective selfhood is sometimes characterized as an experiential self (Zahavi, 2014). This is not done to reduce experience as such to this pre-reflective level, but to accentuate the phenomenological fact that consciousness structurally implies an experiential dimension in the sense that experiences are always presented with a sense of "mine-ness" or "for-me-ness" (Zahavi & Kriegel, 2015). For instance, there is no such thing as an experience of pain that is not somebody's pain. Experiences always have their datives, and even our most primitive conscious experiences present themselves characteristically as belonging to me. There is something *it is like* to undergo conscious experience, and hence *self-awareness* is integral to the very intentionality of consciousness itself (Zahavi, 1999, 2014). Insofar as there is awareness of something, there is simultaneously *self*-awareness. Having an experience implies that there is a self that has that experience.

It is only through the body's affective capacities that something like an experiential dimension of mine-ness may arise in the first place. Therefore, the body is the basis of pre-reflective selfhood. In turn, this makes pre-reflective experience profoundly open to sociocultural shaping. In order to see this, we need to promote two rather complicated points. First, it is of paramount importance to not construe pre-reflective, embodied selfhood as a self-contained, worldless, Cartesian interiority. Rather, pre-reflective self-awareness is based on what is sometimes referred to as "hetero-affection" (Waldenfels, 2000; Zahavi, 1999). This means that though the structure of embodied experience is inherently self-affective, it is equally dependent on being affected by an otherness. In effect, self-awareness only emerges when affected and initiated by something external to the self. This notion is lucidly captured by Merleau-Ponty when he says,

Consciousness only begins to exist by determining an object, and the phantoms of an "internal experience" are only themselves possible by borrowing from external experience. Thus, consciousness has no private life. (Merleau-Ponty, 2012, p. 30)

This is not to indicate that all pre-reflective self-awareness is object intentionality, but rather that there is a reciprocity between the auto-affective capacities of embodiment and hetero-affection. In this way, the embodied self only appears to itself when it relates to something else (Zahavi, 1999, p. 123). One might therefore say that the phenomenon of a pre-reflective self is possible only when based on an initial self-differentiation in which the pre-reflective self is dependent on, and penetrated by, an alterity from which to set itself apart (Waldenfels, 2000, p. 283). This analysis is also proposed by Erwin Straus when he states,

In sensory experience I always experience myself *and* the world at the same time, not myself directly and the *Other* by inference, not myself before the *Other*, not myself without the *Other*, nor the *Other*

without myself. There is no primacy of awareness of oneself over awareness of an outside world. (Straus, 1958, p. 148)

From a phenomenological point of view, there is therefore no such thing as a closed-off self that can engage in pure introspection and worldless self-exploration; self-awareness is something that accompanies my fundamental relationship to the world.[2] Second, whereas the notion of hetero-affection motivates the basic reason that pre-reflective, embodied selfhood is radically open to enculturation, this point becomes more substantial when we consider the nature of embodiment. Within the phenomenological terminology, a distinction is traditionally drawn between the German words "Leib" and "Körper." Whereas *Körper* refers to the "body as object," or how the body is represented within the causal framework of the natural sciences (a thing among other things), *Leib* denotes the body as the pre-reflective subject, or simply embodied subjectivity, which is usually the topic of phenomenological investigations. It is important to emphasize that understood as *Leib*, I am my body in a deeply personal way, as it is my perspective and point of contact with the world. This fact is often overshadowed by a tendency in language to present the body as a vehicle for the person, as though we are merely *em*bodied or *in*corporated, and not body all the way through (Waldenfels, 2006). This emphasis on the body should not be seen as a favoring of nature over culture; rather, embodiment is inherently sociocultural. In the philosophy of Merleau-Ponty, this is expressed through a focus on the far-reaching plasticity of the human body. From what one might call our pre-intentional openness to the world, the structure of our embodied experience is characterized through establishing generality in our lives by prolonging personal acts into stable dispositions, rather than being imposed on by our instincts (Merleau-Ponty, 2012, p. 147). Merleau-Ponty famously analyzed this with examples of how we habitually *dilate* our being-in-the-world by adapting our body-schemes and incorporating instruments (p. 145), such as when a blind man integrates his cane into his basic body scheme, or an organist gradually adapting to a new organ (p. 144). These are mere examples of the more general tendency of embodiment to move beyond the body's skin by continuously dilating into its sociocultural and material setting.[3] In this way, the basic pre-reflective sense of self vitally depends on the sociocultural context into which one is born, and will always remain embedded in. Our instincts or current constitution seldom take any other form of manifestation than those of cultivated and habituated dispositions. Emphasizing this point, and drawing on Husserlian terminology, Waldenfels (2000) has recently described the body as the "point of transfer" (*Umschlagstelle*) between nature and culture, in the sense that the body is never unambiguously determined by one or the other.

The above-described level of pre-reflective embodied selfhood, constituted by hetero-affection and dilated into the sociocultural and material world is exposed to an extensive process of historical becoming, which we suggest terming historical selfhood. Historical selfhood is the result of both sociocultural practices and a deeply personal life trajectory. Hence, in an individual, embodied history, sociogenesis and ontogenesis meet. The body becomes a living display on which the history of both societal structures and individual experiences are continuously inscribed, preserved, and enacted to constitute a particular personal style of being (Køster, 2017).

29.3 Existentials of Embodied History

Drawing on Fuchs (2012) and Køster (2017) in particular and the phenomenological tradition in general, we suggest five analytical existentials that preserve personal history over

time: (1) habituation, (2) incorporation, (3) inter-corporeity, (4) hermeneutic repertoire, and (5) affective repertoire. Our use of the Heideggerian term, "existentials," emphasizes that we are addressing the very structure of our being, and that although we are able to distinguish them analytically, they are inseparable moments of experience. In describing five embodied existentials, we wish to demonstrate that these do not express any transitive hierarchical order of organization or priority (neither in importance to a sociocultural psychology of the personal, nor with regard to their origin in ontogenesis); instead, they are what Heidegger called "equi-primordial" (*gleichursprünglich*) (Heidegger, 2001). In order to unpack the particular characteristics of each existential, we provide an example of a five-year-old boy and his teddy, a case taken from everyday life, rather than from a formal empirical investigation. Each existential is illustrated with reference to this case, but when other examples illustrate the particular dimension even more clearly, we supplement with those, the purpose being solely illustrative of theoretical points that we take to be general. However, using the same case throughout emphasizes the everydayness of what we are aiming for, namely, that in every encounter and situation, the personal, embodied past plays a role in the present unfolding of experience. This past, even when it is the short one of a young child, is expressed in the present as a particular style of being-toward-the-world. Keeping in mind that there is no hierarchical order among them, we present each existential in turn.

29.4 Case Example

Peter, a five-year-old on his way home through the streets of Copenhagen cries out that he has forgotten his teddy at day-care. Knowing the importance of the teddy, his father and older sister turn their bicycles around to fetch the teddy. Upon the retrieval of the teddy at day-care, Peter fastens it to the rear rack of his bicycle, and they resume their journey home. Peter brings his teddy everywhere, carrying it around in his hands. He takes great care to never forget or misplace it, particularly when moving between his two homes and day-care. As is often the custom in Denmark, divorced parents divide the care of their children between them on alternating weeks, which means that Peter spends seven days at a time at each parent's house. As a baby, he used to a have a security blanket (a soft cloth with a teddy's head), which he found soothing and comforting. This object was his constant companion until his interest in it finally ceased (owing to an increasing demand from his surroundings to break this habit). His current habit of always having his teddy nearby developed after his parent's divorce, which created a rupture in his life.

29.4.1 Habituation

By habituation we point to the fundamental process through which we move from our pre-intentional openness to the world to inhabiting the material world in a personal way. This process involves adaptation and dilation of our basic body schemes when we interact with our surroundings – spaces, objects, artifacts, and so on. Though each case is ontogenetically specific, from the outset this process is socioculturally shaped, since our environment is culturally and historically pre-structured. Although this process starts with the establishment of basic physical habits through repetitive practices, habituation immediately and unnoticeably merges into a sense of having a *habitat* – I start to *inhabit* my world, with its familiar smells, shapes, forms, and functions. In a sense, it may be said that I am the places that I have inhabited; that my sense of self vitally depends on its distribution into place. As Jacobsen (2015), suggests: "We have a sense of self, because we build a home for ourselves" (p. 32).

In Peter's case, his habit of carrying about his teddy has become a constitutive part of his personal habitat. One might say that the teddy has become integral to his sense of self. The teddy may be seen as part of a particular way in which Peter builds a home for himself, one that he is able to bring with him across physical locations. This mobility of habitat is important, owing to the particular circumstances of his having lost his first home, and now inhabits two homes. Separation from his teddy implies a temporary loss of habitat, and to some degree, of self. Habituation is a continuous process, wherein habits and habitats are established, sustained, and reconfigured.

29.4.2 Inter-corporeity

From the perspective of inter-corporeity, first introduced by Merleau-Ponty (1964), my embodied existence is inherently social, in the sense that my own body is never isolated from others. Rather, as an embodied being, I am deeply intertwined with others – what I feel, perceive, and do is interwoven with what others feel, perceive, and do. In this way, embodiment is not only dilated into physical spaces and objects through habituation, but also into intimate others who we in a certain way inhabit and are inhabited by.[4] Integrating the idea of inter-corporeity with embodied memory, and drawing on Daniel Stern, T. Fuchs specifies inter-corporeity in the following way:

> From birth on, the infant's procedural memory incorporates an extract of repeated, prototypical experiences with significant others, thus acquiring dyadic patterns of interaction, or schemes of being-with, for example, Mamma-feeding-me, daddy-playing-with-me, etc. This results in what Stern has called implicit relational knowing – a bodily knowing of how to interact with others, how to have fun together, how to elicit attention, how to avoid rejection, etc. it is a temporally organized, musical memory for the rhythm, dynamics, and undertones inaudibly present in interactions with others. (Fuchs, 2012, pp. 14–15)

In Peter's case, the teddy may be understood as a placeholder for the physical experience of being cared for by his parents. Whereas in one sense the teddy has been a symbolic manifestation for the inter-corporeity of caring others since he was a baby, it now fills the particular role of stability. With the erosion of the original configuration of the inter-corporeity of the family, Peter must now become used to new modalities of inter-corporeity that imply the absence of one parent when he is with the other. In this configuration, we suspect that the teddy comes to serve as a form of inter-corporeal substitute for the absent parent. Therefore, if he loses his teddy, Peter loses an aspect of his persistent sense of self, insofar as the teddy connects him to the absent parent.

29.4.3 Incorporation

The term incorporation comes from Fuchs's work (2012), to make the embodied aspect of enculturation explicit. Incorporation designates the basic way in which we in-*corporate* sociocultural norms, expectations, resources, and attitudes into bodily habits. Incorporation may be broadly understood as the civilization of our bodies: how we incorporate gender, how we handle artifacts such as the appropriate use of cutlery (fork goes in the left hand), and so forth.[5] However, incorporation is also ontogenetically specific, since my personal life has its own path of enculturation: for instance, how my commitment to particular activities is preserved in embodiment (e.g., the ballet dancer as opposed to the typical academic's bodily posture) or how the mimicry of parents is taken up in the physiognomy of the children.

When Peter is sad or unsettled, and is offered a security blanket or a teddy bear, this is a cultivated, caring parental response, mediated by this particular artifact's canonical affordance. In this case, the incorporation reflects a response to typical, appropriate, gender, and age norms (only a

baby uses a security blanket and a big boy does not always carry a teddy about). However, both when complying with and transgressing these general norms, they become personally incorporated. Because he carries his teddy almost all the time, Peter's hands are largely occupied, which constrains his zone of free movement (ZFM) and participation in zones of promoted action (ZPA) (Valsiner, 1997). Sometimes, insisting on carrying the teddy is a convenient excuse allowing him to refrain from participation in ZPA/ZFM; at other times, it is just an impractical, inhibiting, and unwarranted constraint on his participation. The incorporation of the teddy as a personalized cultural artifact shapes Peter's particular mode of being-toward-the-world.

29.4.4 Hermeneutic Repertoire

By hermeneutic repertoire we refer to a historical shaping of the very structure of personal intentionality (Køster, 2017). Within a phenomenological context, the concept of intentionality broadly refers to what could be called "pre-predicative sense formation" (Tengelyi, 2004) and not as having a motive or the volition to act.[6] More specifically, it refers to the processes of sensemaking through which something reveals itself *as* something, that is, a certain mode of specificity and differentiation: this cylindrical object *as* a candle, this facial expression *as* sadness, and so on. This is not to be understood as if we first perceive the cylindrical object and then recognizing it is a candle, or seeing the pure facial expression and then interpreting it as sad, but rather, the phenomena presents themselves *directly* to perception as what one might call "gestalt units," where sense and reality cannot be set against each other. Through the various experiences of my personal history, the structure of my intentionality is gradually shaped and reshaped to constitute my particular hermeneutical repertoire. This denotes a particular experiential horizon with anticipatory features that determine how things appear to me, as a generalized and embodied tendency to perceive in a certain way. This personal structure of intentionality is fundamentally the result of my sociocultural embeddedness, practices, and semiotic sensemaking (Valsiner, 1998). However, there is also a distinct personal aspect to the hermeneutic repertoire, vitally shaped by my personal history. Drawing on Leontiev's concept of "personal sense," Mammen identifies this as the historical depth of our relations with particular objects and others (Mammen, 2002).

The above-described, dual double relation is evident in Peter's use of his teddy bear. Teddies are part of the toy industry, and a teddy is a human artifact with an impersonal or canonical affordance of collective, objective meaning (Costall et al., 2013). Many children use teddies for comfort, but not all five-year-old boys relate to their teddy in the way that Peter does. The way Peter uses *his* teddy, handles it, and keeps it with him wherever he goes, relates to his particular history with this object, and to his current situation. Peter perceives his particular teddy as comforting, which also implies homeliness and a dilation of parental caring practices (inter-corporeity). That the teddy appears *as comforting* to Peter is not determined by its canonical affordances alone, but relies on the fact that Peter, throughout his personal history, has been offered a teddy by his parents when in need of consolation. Thus, the teddy activates intentional threads that point back to his first encounters with the security blanket (also resembling a teddy). We speculate that Peter saw his security blanket as comforting and soothing, long before he could articulate it verbally, and that his prelinguistic experience of his teddy as comforting is a way the past persists in the present. Based on this, one might suggest that the reason that Peter has had a renewed interest in his teddies in his new life circumstances (living in two homes) is a heightened need for his pre-reflective repertoire of self-consolation.

29.4.5 Affective Register

Finally, we suggest an *affective register* as an integral part of pre-reflective personal existence (Køster, 2017). Drawing on Heidegger's work, we would like to emphasize that personal existence is always affectively attuned. In his existential analytics, Heidegger specifies this fundamental dimension of human existence through the concepts "Befindlichkeit" and "Stimmung" (Heidegger, 2001). Whereas *Befindlichkeit* – a neologism derived from the German reflexive verb, "sich befinden" (which both refer to "where" I am physically located and to the affective dimension of "the way I find myself to be") – refers to the phenomenological fact that my existence announces itself to me through affects, and therefore is an inescapable dimension of personal existence, *Stimmung* refers to the particular mood in which I find myself. When we take up this idea through the notion of an affective *register*, we aim to retain the musical metaphor of resonance present in the concept of attunement (*Stimmung*). Therefore, an affective register is to be understood as referring to the particular modes of embodied attunement and moods through which a person resonates or reverberates with the world affectively. Again, the existential of an affective register is not to be conceived of in isolation from sociocultural influences, such as child-rearing practices and norms of conduct (Röttger-Rössler et al., 2013). Instead, moods and affects are socialized in culturally specific ways where certain affects are connected to certain enacted virtues, values, events, and customs. Coming to know the normative practice of moods is a requirement for skillful cultural participation and social acceptance, which in turn requires comprehensive training and normative correction (Baerveldt, Verheggen, & Valsiner, 2012; Holodynski, Friedlmeier, & Valsiner, 2012).

The shaping of expressing moods is particularly visible in public (religious) rituals and at social gatherings (a funeral, at a cemetery, a wedding, a birthday party). Showing up in a grim mood at a wedding is unsuitable and expressing energetic joy and light-heartedness at a funeral is inappropriate (only toddlers are forgiven). The affective register, which one develop throughout ontogenesis, is highly dependent on the repertoire of emotions promoted and sanctioned by my important others, in the communities of practice and sociocultural settings of my everyday life. Nonetheless, there is also a fundamental personal dimension to my affective register, resulting from my particular experiences and personal history. Inseparable from the development of the other four embodied existentials, this register of affects and moods is gradually shaped and forms how I tend to find myself affectively in particular situations.

Peter's habit of using his teddy and finding it as comforting has made it part of his habitat, and thereby elicits an affective state of feeling at ease and at home. Playing on Heidegger's characterization of anxiety as a state of "Unheimlichkeit" (referring to both a state of "anxiety" and "not feeling at home" in German), one may speculate that when his teddy is missing, Peter finds himself anxiously attuned. It is important for Peter to retrieve his teddy, and until he has it with him again, he feels unsettled. However, it seems reasonable to assume, that there is a generality to this mood of *Unheimlichkeit* and anxiousness as part of Peter's personal existence at present. In the transition of adjustments into new inter-corporeal practices in his new homes, Peter finds himself more often unsettled, and *Unheimlichkeit* becomes a general way he resonates with the world during this transition. This is expressed particularly clearly in the way he approaches and responds to others (especially strangers), and how he relates to new situations in his environment. It governs his attunement as somehow reluctant, hesitant, and vigilant, which is also expressed in his incorporation of his teddy (always having it in his hand), enhancing a restricted way of partici-

pating in various activities. Owing to Peter's personal history, a particular tenor of *Unheimlichkeit* has become part of his affective register.

29.5 Sedimentation of Pre-reflective Experiential Structures

Starting from the above-mentioned considerations, we now face the question of how our embodied personal history comes into existence over time. As already stated, we are concerned with the part of our personal being that precedes narrative order, which imposes the need for a supplementing metaphor to account for processes of becoming and the preservation of our pre-reflexive, embodied personal history. We would like to propose metaphors taken from geology to account for the structuring of personal becoming as a process of sedimentation (Køster, 2017). Husserl and Merleau-Ponty have already made extensive use of metaphors such as ground, underground, and sedimentation in their attempts to describe the structures of our lifeworld and embodied subjectivity (e.g., Husserl, 1970; Merleau-Ponty, 2012). Our use of geological metaphors should be seen as a heuristic device that provides a way of accessing embodied selfhood as historical, although we are fully aware that no metaphor can ever exhaust or adequately illustrate the richness of this phenomenon.

The geological metaphor of sedimentation provides imagery for how stable, synchronic structures gradually emerge throughout a fundamentally contingent and diachronic process. It suggests how the structure of personal experience may be seen as having both depth and surface: a patent surface of susceptible and fluctuating manifestations resting on more latent depth structures less susceptible to change. Here, it is important to be aware that processes of sedimentation take many shapes, from solid, layered rock formation to the fluctuation of a seabed landscape. Although the connotation of a certain kind of *inertia* is certainly intended when using geological metaphors, our aim is not to allude to the very static imagery of unilateral and gradual build-up. Instead, by employing the metaphor of sedimentation, we wish to emphasize that we are not invented anew or "starting over" whenever we find ourselves involved in new activities, places, practices, or relationships. Our embodied subjectivity *is* historical and socioculturally shaped in ways that prevent such flux. We literally embody our past experiences in ways that are constitutive of how we encounter and respond to our immediate surroundings, the present situation as well as our immediate future.

Not all experiences have the adequate gravitas to actually deposit and sediment into personal experiential structures. Processes of sedimentation are results of responses to external forces of *adequate gravitas*: some are engraved through the gravitas of repetition (e.g., when I incorporate a piano keyboard through daily practice, or incorporate the shape of my spouse in sleeping positions), whereas others are imprinted through their significant impact (e.g., a traumatic experience). This dual emphasis on both repetitive and significant impact is supported by recent research into risk and resilience, which warns against privileging the impact of single (traumatic) events, and reminds us to emphasize the significance of repetitive exposure to routine patterns of interaction of various practices, places, relationships, and activities (Bronfenbrenner & Morris, 2006; Schoon, 2006). Those experiences that have sedimented tend to stay with me. Again, this is not a claim that a sedimented structure is static, but that in changing, new sedimented layers integrate with older ones, in much the same way that Hegel saw experience as characterized by "definite negation" (*bestimmte Negation*) (Hegel, 1970). Old or past sedimented layers do not dissipate into abstract nothingness and disappear, but become part of the designation (*Bestimmung*) of the altered structure of sedimentation. A given sedimented structure is not dictated by a previous sedimented layer, but nonetheless its particular shape is inconceivable without it. This, in turn, accounts not only for vital aspects of what we call *the depth structure of experience*, but also for the very individuality of our personal structure of experience. In this way, the process of sedimentation reflects life as lived in its particularity, and its formation is only gradual and steady to the extent that the person's experienced lifeworld is steady and stable.

In Peter's case, there has been a discontinuous yet consistent sedimentation (in all the existentials) of his relationship to his teddy throughout his life, but he will presumably not remain as integrated with his teddy as he is at present. As with the security blanket, he will soon be met with increasing demands to break his habits. This we find plausible, as the normative pressure of his surroundings will pull him toward soothing practices that are more in line with the standards of his sociocultural context (a school boy should not always carry a teddy around with him). However, since Peter's way of relating to his teddy has nevertheless sedimented with some gravitas, he will probably protest these demands on him to give it up, and the way in which this process of change play out will further sediment into his personal history. His parent's divorce caused a rupture with a profound impact on his personal existence (involving changes in all existentials, most profoundly in his habitat, and patterns of inter-corporeity with his parents), which probably explains the patience of people around him with respect to his use of the teddy. The point is that the old sedimented layers persist in the new ones, and although he may come to see his teddy as contested and conflictual, these new affects and understandings of the teddy are only comprehensible against the background of the preceding historical threads that join Peter to his teddy.

29.5.1 Sedimented Experiential Dispositions

As we have tried to illustrate, existential structures continuously undergo sedimentation of varying gravitas and in various tempi. This historical process leads to a relatively stable arrangement of dispositions, or what Aristotle called a *Hexis* (Aristotle, 2014). The ambiguous ontological status of such an existential notion of disposition, as fundamentally historical, singular, and contingent, is described clearly by Merleau-Ponty:

But in fact, here again, we must recognize a sort of sedimentation of our life: When an attitude toward the world has been confirmed often enough, it becomes privileged for us. If freedom does not tolerate being confronted by any motive, then my habitual being in the world is equally fragile at each moment, and the complexes I have for years nourished through complacency remain equally innocuous, for freedom's gesture can effortlessly shatter them at any moment. And yet, after having built my life upon an inferiority complex, continuously reinforced for twenty years, it is *not likely* that I would change … It's "unlikely" that I would in this moment destroy an inferiority complex in which I have been complacent now for twenty years. This means that I am committed to inferiority, that I have decided to dwell within it, that this past, if not a destiny, has at least a specific weight, and that it is not a sum of events over there, far away from me, but rather the atmosphere of my present. (Merleau-Ponty, 2012, pp. 465–466)

What Merleau-Ponty spells out in this passage is that sedimented dispositions are characterized by a principal contingency, which is always susceptible to being shattered. Yet it persists and retains its gravity on my reality by having become privileged to me, and therefore it is *not likely* to change. Furthermore, as Merleau-Ponty specifies in both this passage and elsewhere, sedimentation should not be thought of as a "sum of past events," or as "an inert mass at the

foundation of consciousness" (p. 131). Instead, sedimentation manifests the way the past is present in the present. The way in which experiences are preserved by sedimentation (also when deeply inscribed) emerges as an embodied readiness for participation and particular response to my immediate lifeworld. My personal history announces itself in and through my embedded, intertwined relations with my sociocultural environment. My readiness and particular openness to the world are ways in which my history is present in the present.

29.6 Agency as Responsiveness

The question we face is where this emphasis on the sedimentation of my personal history leaves the concept of agency. What kind of conceptualization of agency is consistent with a strong focus on the way in which the past is present in the present? Inspired by contemporary German phenomenologist Bernhard Waldenfels, we suggest that the notion of agency needs to be understood from an ontology of *responsiveness*. In referencing Waldenfels, we do not aspire to give a comprehensive account of his very complex philosophy, but to use elements of his responsive phenomenology to elaborate on our current question.

29.6.1 Humans as Responsive Beings

According to Waldenfels, any adequate understanding of the human condition needs to begin with the fact that, although I am always already involved in the unfolding of my life, it is neither as a privileged author nor as a self-initiating agent proper (Waldenfels, 2006, p. 73). Rather, I find myself *responding* to events that affect me, and that I did not initiate. As human beings, we always start from *elsewhere*; we are essentially responsive, and thus historical, beings. Reading from the perspective of sociocultural psychology, this strong emphasis on responsiveness may appear unsettling, since it may evoke associations of an undesired return to the mechanical-causal framework of behaviorism. However, Waldenfels's phenomenology of responsiveness is in no way to be understood along these lines. The best way to draw out this distinction may be to point out that Waldenfels's preferred term for response in German is "Antwort," literally meaning "answer" (Waldenfels, 1994). In turn, this should not be interpreted as turn-taking of giving answers and replies in a concrete dialogue. Rather, what Waldenfels is pointing to is what he calls responsiveness in a "widened sense," as an ontological structure of human existence (Waldenfels, 1994, p. 193). In order to illustrate what is meant by this, Waldenfels often refers to double binds (recognized as semiotic traps in cultural psychology), such as when somebody says: *don't listen to me!* Before actually being able to attend to the propositional content of the sentence and "not listen," we are already being demanded to listen, and hence to give a response, which may be to refuse to listen. Paraphrasing Watzlawic's famous axiom of communication, Waldenfels sums up this fundamental condition in the ontological imperative: "I cannot, not respond" (Waldenfels, 2006). I may choose to respond in this or that way, but the demand to respond is absolute. Hence, responding is not something I *choose*, but I *am a homo respondent* (Waldenfels, 2015).

The claim that human existence is a responsive existence is rooted in a phenomenological analysis of what one might cautiously call the primacy of the *pathic* dimension. According to Waldenfels, experience is characterized by the priority of passivity, of that which affects me, stings me, or even violates me, and the *deferred* (*Nachträglich*) character of that with which we respond (Waldenfels, 2002a, p. 10). In his use of the term "pathic," Waldenfels draws on the original Greek meaning of the word, which in Latin was translated to "affectus" or "emotion,"

with which we may be more familiar (Waldenfels, 2008, p. 130). The term "pathic" refers to the event that something affects me, strikes me, or demands something of me, and to which I need to respond. I am never *self-initiating* in the truest sense of the word, but as an embodied and situated individual, I am literally *initiated* by being affectively requested by a demand by my material and sociocultural worlds (Waldenfels, 2006, p. 45). These considerations lead Waldenfels to suggest a general logic of response according to which we start from the pathic, and from there respond to the demands with which we are confronted. Though it may be tempting to interpret this in causal terms, it is important to emphasize that this is not the intent. Rather, between the antecedence of the pathos and the deferment of the response, there is a characteristic time-lag (*Zeitverschiebung*), which Waldenfels refers to as "diastasis" – an originary splitting apart. However, this is only an analytical distinction between being struck by the impact of the demand, and responding, which must not be misinterpreted as a causal or even diachronic sequence. Pathos and response do not appear as two events, but as "one and the same experience shifted in relation to itself" (p. 50). Hence, it makes sense to speak of a pathos-response event, as one and the same experience, but in which each instance cannot be reduced to the other, and where the response is open, not predictable from the demand.[7]

Within the context of sociocultural psychology, this analysis should resonate with an ecological perspective, which Waldenfels also explicitly discusses with, in reference to the gestalt psychologist Kurt Lewin, among others (Waldenfels, 2000, p. 373). In ecological psychology the focus on humans as responsive beings is also implied insofar as it is emphasized that human existence always involves exposure to what we are in the midst of, materially, socially, culturally (Bang, 2008). We are affected by our situated place in the world, and called on to respond, both through our interactions with our natural environment, as presented in Gibson's (2014) relational concept of affordances, and through our interaction with artifacts and their canonical affordances (Costall et al., 2013). Our response is ontogenetically specific, as in the famous example of a child approaching a lighted candle differently after having been burned (Heft, 1989). Hence, the concept of affordance affirms an understanding of human beings as primarily pathic and always responsive.

29.6.2 Responsiveness and Personal History

How does this relate to the phenomenon of personal history and the concept of agency? In a sense, what Waldenfels refers to as the pathic dimension of human existence can be understood along the lines of what we call personal history. As Waldenfels often states, we are "born out of pathos" (Waldenfels, 2006, p. 82), and:

Everything that happens to us, right up to the limit events of birth and death which are repeated in our life in different ways, may be called pathos, which is to be understood as what in German is called Widerfahrnis. (Waldenfels, 2007a, p. 45)

The pathic dimension encompasses the entire unfolding event of what *happens to us* from birth until death. The German term "Widerfahrnis" has connotations of *friction* and *impact* (*wider*) on something that is beyond the agent's control, and the concept of experience itself (experience is *Erfahrung*). Based on this, the pathic dimension may be seen as closely related to the structuring of experience through personal history, insofar as the pathic – the dimension of being *struck* by something – bears a resemblance to what we have addressed as sedimentation through the *impact* of varied experiential gravitas. Furthermore, in this passage, Waldenfels alludes to what he calls the pre-, post- and depth-history of the self (Waldenfels, 2006, p. 54); that the self has a history, and that, from the beginning, it is more than

something to which we attribute certain definite characteristics, roles, and rights, and therefore exceeds the level of the articulated (Waldenfels, 2002b). This should not be misconstrued to suggest that my historical, pathic existence is readily accessible to me in full self-transparency. To the contrary, Waldenfels emphasizes that the embodied self is *split-self* (*gespaltenes Selbst*) that is defined by varying degrees of familiarity and alienness (*Fremdheit*) to itself, and involves several levels of self-distancing (Waldenfels, 2004).[8] In this way, personal history may have sedimented to form a historical self, but that does not imply that the intricacies of my sedimented structures are directly accessible to me. Instead, I may experience myself through increasing degrees of alienness (Waldenfels, 1997, p. 35), of being and doing something that I do not quite understand, but that is nevertheless part of my experiential reality, both pathic and responsive. These experiences may range from purely neurologically based physical twitches, to excessive nail biting, sudden surprising outbursts, or existential experiences of being increasingly anxious without quite knowing why. Through all this, the pathic dimension remains the very place from which I start to achieve an understanding, to narrate, to judge, to reject, or to affirm (Waldenfels, 2002a). I find myself in a certain way, and needing to respond. In this sense, personal history is the time-place from which we respond, and though my way of responding is not predetermined, it also does not merely grow out of the present, but is vitally determined by my personal past. As Waldenfels states, "The presence is not nothing – as a good many postmodern total dissipaters believe – but it is not satisfied with itself. Responding takes place here and now, but it begins from elsewhere" (Waldenfels, 2007b, p. 31).[9] This all-pervasive historicity of personal being is perhaps most profoundly experienced in the phenomenon Freud originally termed "Nachträglichkeit," or "afterwardsness" (Freud, 2001). Whereas in the phenomenology of Waldenfels *Nachträglichkeit* connotes a general characteristic of responsiveness, one quite different from a Freudian understanding, Waldenfels's phenomenology still allows for pathological qualities, as in the case of trauma, where the traumatizing event is only recognizable by its deferred effects. Embodied experiences of *Nachträglichkeit* reveal to us our personal being as historical, in the sense that a seemingly innocent present experience evokes sedimented structures from past personal experiences, making it present in the present once again. This is to be understood in embodied terms, as enrooted dispositions, and not as a return to a Freudian ontology of the unconscious. Furthermore, this indicates the convoluted structure of time implied by embodied personal history as not being simply chronological (like a typical narrative structure), but rather messy and highly dependent on being evoked by present contexts and events. In Peter's case, the renewed preoccupation with his teddy may be seen as such an example of *Nachträglichkeit*, insofar as past sedimented structures are evoked through the stress of his current situation.

29.6.3 Sedimented Response Registers

In order to more concretely integrate our notion of personal history with the concept of responsiveness, we suggest the term *sedimented response registers* (Køster, 2017). Sedimented response registers refer to the specific mode of experience and style of response characteristic of an individual as the result of the sedimented structures of personal history. It is "the style through which an individual engages in and resonates with the world and which, to varying degrees, persists throughout shifting contexts, practices and relations" (Køster, 2017). As already discussed in the section on sedimentation, this is not intended as a strictly static structure. Importantly, we need to distinguish between a primarily *repetitive* or *repro-*

ductive mode of response, where responses follow established, culturally patterned "answer-models," and a more productive, innovative, or creative mode of response (Waldenfels, 2006, p. 67), where the response does not follow any particular normative rhythm or rule, but breaks the established order. In any case, our contention is that responses do not emerge *ex nihilo*, but grows out of a complex intra-action between my personal history, as a register of response, and the specific demands of my particular situations.

To sum up, as responsive beings we are not endowed with spontaneous beginnings, but always find ourselves initiated from elsewhere. To be a responsive being is not to stand in a causal relation – as described by behavioristic or cognitive psychology – but to be a being that responds to the demands of the situation. In this way, the perspective of responsiveness outlines a position beyond the traditional divide between a purely *passive* notion of causal determinism, and the (Kantian) phantoms of a spontaneous, self-initiating, intentional agent. Personal history plays a vital role in this context as rooted in our pathic dimension. This implies that our understanding of agency needs to be readdressed as a matter of responsiveness. In closing, and without being able to expand on it, it may be worth remarking that this focus on responsiveness ties us vitally to the ethical dimension. The German term "Antwort" converts into "Verantwortung," and similarly, the English "response" slides into "responsibility." As responsive beings, we are able to take responsibility for our responses. As both Francois Raffoul (2010) and Judith Butler (2005) has recently argued, this perspective portends a change in focus in ethics, from an interpretation of responsibility as the *accountability* of an autonomous subject, to a much broader understanding of phenomenological responsiveness as rooted in the experience of not only having to respond, but also having to respond *in the right way*.

29.7 Concluding Remarks

In this chapter we have addressed what we identify as a blind spot in sociocultural psychology, noting that our pre-reflective and embodied dimension of selfhood is equally socially, culturally, and materially saturated, and should be considered a central field of enquiry for sociocultural psychology. We have argued that in the endeavor to study this important field, a synthesis between sociocultural psychology and phenomenology is both obvious and pertinent. More specifically, we propose a conceptual framework for addressing a rich notion of historical selfhood at the pre-reflective level, shaped throughout personal history, as embodied, historical selfhood is the *point of transfer*, not only between nature and culture, but also between sociogenesis and ontogenesis. In order to account for this process, we suggest five embodied existentials by which historical selfhood is continuously shaped, and an accompanying principle of sedimentation to account for the preservation of experiential structures. Finally, we have outlined the implications of this view with respect to the concept of agency, insofar as it has to be rearticulated within the framework of responsiveness. This we find entirely consistent with the basic insights of sociocultural psychology, emphasizing the sociocultural embeddedness of the individual. From a sociocultural perspective, there should be little conceptual space for allusions to the Kantian idea of a spontaneous beginning by a self-positing, self-initiating I. What I am, what I want, and what I do, are always responses to demands of the sociocultural facticity and the existential situation in which I am situated. This in no way dismisses the possibility of the individual's capacity to initiate *creative responses*, and to participate in processes of social change, but only emphasizing the existential fact that we always start from a historical, cultural, contextual *somewhere*, from which we are called to respond.

Lastly, we would like to point out a pending and promising line of inquiry for future research, namely, the transitional processes between pre-reflective ways of experience and how these dimensions connect with more semiotically mediated, reflected, and narrative dimensions. Understanding the intra-action between these dimensions is largely unexplored at the present, but achieving an understanding of this has great potential in both educational settings and in interventions in social work and psychotherapy. Køster (2016) has recently commenced this work by giving an account of how the pre-reflective, embodied dimension relates to personal narratives, but much work is needed in developing research strategies and methods that capture the pre-reflective dimension. Such work would be exciting to further expand our understanding of personal history, and modes of responding in enacted encounters of micro-genesis.

Notes

1 For a discussion of Leontiev's further development of Vygotsky's meaning–sense distinction of the term "personal sense," see González Rey (2008).

2 Exceptions to this position in the phenomenological tradition can, arguably, be found in the work of Michel Henry and Hermann Schmitz. For a detailed discussion on this see Zahavi (1999 ch. 7) and Waldenfels (2000).

3 That the self can dilate into the social and material surroundings is an idea well known to sociocultural psychologists, through both the legacy of William James, in his ideas of the self, and in Kurt Lewin's dynamic theory of personality.

4 Bowlby (1998) voiced a similar idea when he attempted to describe the impact of a permanent loss of attachment figures in childhood. He compared the psychology of grief with a physical wound; a cut into the flesh creating a lasting scar on the bereaved.

5 In sociology, this dimension is thoroughly theorized by Norbert Elias, Pierre Bourdieu, and Michel Foucault.

6 Though the phenomenological concept of intentionality has its roots in Brentano's work, it was immediately developed by Husserl, who understood that intentionality had a much broader philosophical significance. Since Husserl, intentionality has not only referred to the object-directedness of consciousness, implying that consciousness in not a container waiting to be filled, but also to the fact that objects always have their modality of appearance; that *something presents itself as something*. For an overview of the development of the concept of intentionality from Brentano to Heidegger's dismissal of it, see Moran (2000).

7 Waldenfels seem to draw significantly on Viktor von Weizsäcker's notion of "Der Gestaltkreis."

8 In light of a conceptualization of embodied selfhood as a split-self, Waldenfels makes it possible to understand how one's own body may be an irritant that functions as hetero-affection. This is also consistent with Vygotsky's claim that the basis of consciousness lies "in the body's capacity to be an irritant for itself" (Vygotsky, 1979).

9 This "elsewhere" that demands my response need not be rooted in my past history, although this is our concern here. The demand for a present response may also be a call from the future; that is, in the gloomy, dark, or grim moods experienced when anticipating a dreaded future. This is apparent when fearing the loss of a loved one from illness (Winther-Lindqvist, 2016).

References

Aristotle. (2014). *Nicomachean Ethics* (trans. by H. Rackham). Cambridge, MA: Harvard University Press.

Baerveldt, C. & Verheggen, T. (2012). Enactivism. In J. Valsiner (Ed.), *Oxford Handbook of Culture and Psychology* (pp. 165–190). Oxford: Oxford University Press.

Bang, J. (2008). An environmental affordance perspective on the study of development – artefacts, social others, and self. In M. Fleer, M. Hedegaard, & J. Tudge (Eds.), *Childhood Studies and the Impact of Globalization: Policies and Practices at Global and Local Levels* (World Yearbook of Education 2009, pp. 161–181): New York: Routledge.

Bowlby, J. (1998). *Loss: Sadness and Depression.* London: Pimlico.

Bronfenbrenner, U. & Morris, P. A. (2006). The bioecological model of human development. In R. Lerner (Ed.), *Handbook of Child Psychology. Volume 1: Theoretical Models of Human Development* (pp. 793–828). New York: John Wiley & Sons.

Butler, J. (2005). *Giving an Account of Oneself.* Oxford: Oxford University Press.

Costall, A. & Richards, A., (2013). Canonical affordances: The psychology of everyday things. In P. Graves-Brown, R. Harrison, & A. Piccini (Eds.), *The Oxford Handbook of the Archaeology of the Contemporary World* (pp. 82–93). Oxford: Oxford University Press.

Freud, S. (2001). Project for a scientific psychology. In J. Strachey (Ed.), *The Standard Edition of the Complete Psychological Works of Sigmund Freud* (vol. 4, pp. 283–397): London: Hogart Press.

Fuchs, T. (2012). The phenomenology of body memory. In S. Koch, T. Fuchs, M. Summa, & C. Müller (Eds.), *Body Memory, Metaphor and Movement* (pp. 9–22). Amsterdam: John Benjamins.

Gallagher, S. (2011). *The Oxford Handbook of the Self.* Oxford: Oxford University Press.

Gibson, J. J. (2014). *The Ecological Approach to Visual Perception.* New York: Psychology Press.

González Rey, F. L. (2008). Subject, subjectivity, and development in cultural-historical psychology. In B. van Oers, W. Wardekker, E. Elbers, & R. van der Veer (Eds.), *The Transformation of Learning: Advances in Cultural-Historical Activity Theory* (pp. 137–154). Cambridge: Cambridge University Press.

Hedegaard, M. (2011). The dynamic aspects in children's learning and development In M. Hedegaard, A. Edwards, & M. Fleer (Eds.), *Motives in Children's Development: Cultural-Historical Approaches* (pp. 9–27). Cambridge: Cambridge University Press.

Heft, H. (1989). Affordances and the body: An intentional analysis of Gibson's ecological approach to visual perception. *Journal for the Theory of Social Behaviour*, 19(1), 1–30.

Hegel, G. W. F. (1970). *Phanomenologie des Geistes*. Frankfurt: Suhrkamp.

Heidegger, M. (2001). *Sein und Zeit*. Tübingen, Germany: Niemeyer.

Holodynski, M., Friedlmeier, W., & Valsiner, J. (2012). Affect and culture. In J. Valsiner (Ed.), *The Oxford Handbook of Culture and Psychology* (pp. 957–986). Oxford: Oxford University Press.

Husserl, E. (1970). *The Crisis of European Sciences and Transcendental Phenomenology: An Introduction to Phenomenological Philosophy* (trans. by D. Carr). Evanston, IL: Northwestern University Press.

Jackson, M. & Piette, A. (2015). *What Is Existential Anthropology?* New York: Berghahn Books.

Jacobsen, K. (2015). The gift of memory: Sheltering the I. In D. Morris & K. Maclaren (Eds.), *Time, Memory, Institution: Merleau-Ponty's new Ontology of Self* (pp. 29–42). Athens: Ohio University Press.

Køster, A. (2016). Narrative and embodiment – a scalar approach. *Phenomenology and the Cognitive Sciences*, 16(5), 1–16. doi: 10.1007/s11097-016-9485-8.

Køster, A. (2017). Personal history, beyond narrative: an embodied perspective. *Journal of Phenomenological Psychology*, 48, pp. 163–187.

Leontiev, A. (1978). *Activity, Personality, and Consciousness*. Englewoods Cliffs, NJ: Prentice-Hall.

Mammen, J. (2002). Mapping the subject: The renewal of scientific psychology. *Journal of Anthropological Psychology*, 11, 77–89.

Martin, J. & Bickhard, M. (2013). Introducing persons and the psychology of personhood. In J. Martin & M. Bickhard (Eds.), *The Psychology of Personhood. Philosophical, Historical, Social-Developmental, and Narrative Perspectives*. Cambridge: Cambridge University Press.

Merleau-Ponty, M. (1964). *Signs*. Evanston, IL: Northwestern University Press.

Merleau-Ponty, M. (2012). *Phenomenology of Perception* (trans. by D. A. Landes). New York: Routledge.

Moran, D. (2000). Heidegger's critique of Husserl's and Brentano's accounts of intentionality. *Inquiry*, 43(1), 39–65.

Nathanson, M. (1970). *The Journeying Self: A Study in Philosophy and Social Role*. Reading, MA: Addison-Wesley.

Raffoul, F. (2010). *The Origins of Responsibility*. Bloomington: Indiana University Press.

Röttger-Rössler, B., Scheidecker, G., Jung, S., & Holodynski, M. (2013). Socializing emotions in childhood: A cross-cultural comparison between the Bara in Madagascar and the Minangkabau in Indonesia. *Mind, Culture, and Activity*, 20(3), 260–287.

Salvatore, S. (2012). Social life of the sign: Sense-making in society. In J. Valsiner (Ed.), *The Oxford Handbook of Culture and Psychology* (pp. 241–254). Oxford: Oxford University Press.

Schatzki, T. R. (2003). Living out of the past: Dilthey and Heidegger on life and history. *Inquiry*, 46(3), 301–323.

Schoon, I. (2006). *Risk and Resilience: Adaptations in Changing Times*. Cambridge: Cambridge University Press.

Scribner, S. (1985). Vygotsky's uses of history. In J. Wertsch (Ed.), *Culture, Communication, and Cognition: Vygotskian Perspectives* (pp. 119–145). Cambridge: Cambridge University Press.

Smolka, A., De Goes, M., & Pino, A. (1995). The constitution of the subject: A persistent question. In J. Wertsch, P. del Rio, & A. Alvarez (Eds.), *Sociocultural Studies of Mind* (pp. 165–184). Cambridge: Cambridge University Press.

Straus, E. (1958). Aesthesiology and hallucinations. In R. May, E. Angel, & H. Ellenberger (Ed.), *Existence: A New Dimension in Psychiatry and Psychology* (pp. 139–169). New York: Basic Books.

Tengelyi, L. (2004). *The Wild Region in Life-History*. Evanston, IL: Northwestern University Press.

Valsiner, J. (1997). *Culture and the Development of Children's Action: A Theory of Human Development*. New York: John Wiley & Sons.

Valsiner, J. (1998). *The Guided Mind: A Sociogenetic Approach to Personality*. Cambridge, MA: Harvard University Press.

Valsiner, J. & Rosa, A. (2007). *The Cambridge Handbook of Sociocultural Psychology.* Cambridge: Cambridge University Press.

Vygotsky, L. S. (1979). Consciousness as a problem in the psychology of behavior. *Soviet Psychology,* 17(4), 3–35.

Waldenfels, B. (1994). *Antwortregister.* Frankfurt: Suhrkamp.

Waldenfels, B. (1997). *Topographie des Fremden.* Frankfurt: Suhrkamp.

Waldenfels, B. (2000). *Das leibliche Selbst: Vorlesungen zur Phänomenologie des Leibes.* Frankfurt: Suhrkamp.

Waldenfels, B. (2002a). *Bruchlinien der Erfahrung: Phänomenologie, Psychoanalyse, Phänomenotechnik* (vol. 1). Frankfurt: Suhrkamp.

Waldenfels, B. (2002b). Unerzählbares. In J. Trinks (Ed.), *Möglichkeiten und Grenzen der Narration* (pp. 19–37). Vienna: Turia + Kant.

Waldenfels, B. (2004). Bodily experience between selfhood and otherness. *Phenomenology and the Cognitive Sciences,* 3(3), 235–248.

Waldenfels, B. (2006). *Grundmotive einer Phänomenologie des Fremden.* Frankfurt: Suhrkamp.

Waldenfels, B. (2007a). The power of the event. In *The Question of the Other* (pp. 37–52). Hong Kong: The Chinese University Press.

Waldenfels, B. (2007b). *The Question of the Other.* Hong Kong: The Chinese University Press.

Waldenfels, B. (2008). The role of the lived-body in feeling. *Continental Philosophy Review,* 41(2), 127–142.

Waldenfels, B. (2015). *Sozialität und Alterität: Modi sozialer Erfahrung.* Frankfurt: Suhrkamp.

Winther-Lindqvist, D. (2016). Time together – time apart: Nothingness and hope in teenagers. In J. Bang & D. Winther-Lindqvist (Eds.), *Nothingness: Philosophical Insights into Psychology* (pp. 143–168). New Brunswick, NJ: Transaction Publishers.

Zahavi, D. (1999). *Self-Awareness and Alterity: A Phenomenological Investigation.* Evanston, IL: Northwestern University Press.

Zahavi, D. (2014). *Self and Other: Exploring Subjectivity, Empathy, and Shame.* Oxford: Oxford University Press.

Zahavi, D. & Kriegel, U. (2015). For-me-ness: What it is and what it is not. In D. O. Dahlstrom, A. Elpidorou, & W. Hopp (Eds.), *Philosophy of Mind and Phenomenology: Conceptual and Empirical Approaches* (pp. 36–54). London: Routledge.

30 The Development of a Person: Children's Experience of Being and Becoming within the Cultural Life Course

Pernille Hviid and Jakob Waag Villadsen

30.1 The Development of Persons in Developmental Psychology

It is somewhat surprising that developmental psychology has existed for more than 100 years and still there is no firm theoretical and methodological grip on children's development as persons. We believe this would have surprised giants of the early developmental psychology. More than a century ago William Stern expressed great hopes for this emerging subdiscipline of psychology (Lamiell, 2009a, 2010). It would probably have disappointed James Mark Baldwin as well, who during the same period strived hard to create the foundation of a genetic psychology (Baldwin, 1930).

Stern and Baldwin both contributed greatly to the development of a genetic psychology of the developing person, but they also shared the fate of being passed by in silence by the scientific society. Some might argue that this had something to do with their personal biographies; mistakes they made that upset the scientific society (Valsiner & Van der Veer, 2000) or their bad timing in geographical transitions (Kreppner, 1992). It could also be argued that these personal facts and events came timely to a scientific society which, under the social guidance of the larger society (Danziger, 1990; Valsiner, 2012),

moved in other directions, away from a developmental perspective that included the personal level. In addition, perhaps society in general was simply not interested in or ready to accept and understand all human beings – ethnic minorities, women, and children – as persons? Would that be the case today? It makes a huge difference to understand conflicts with a child as a "passing phase" rather than as something the child resists out of a personal *concern*. How different would our relationship with children not be, if we did not interpret children in the middle of something age-appropriate or – inappropriate, but as persons pursuing and generating goals like everybody else?

In either case, the work of Stern and Baldwin is rarely made use of in the field of developmental psychology. Yet, their work is original and promising. In this chapter we will include parts of their work in a conceptualization of a cultural life-course perspective, and this will guide our analysis of children's experiences of their lives and their development as persons.

Neither Stern nor Baldwin was optimistic. In fact, they demonstrated sharp analytical eyes on what might be obstacles in the future of psychology, as it already showed in their time. We begin by pointing out some of their major critics followed by addressing some of their major contributions. In taking such an approach we intend to synthesize the perspectives laid out by Stern and Baldwin, primarily with respect to placing the person and her relationship to her sociocultural environment as an inseparable unit of analysis. Following that, we present an analysis of our empirical investigation of 13-year-old children's personal experiences with developing and growing – as persons. Our wish is to stretch the perspective of Stern and Baldwin to include a broader conceptualization of the collective level in the developmental analysis, which makes it possible to overcome the traditional dichotomy between the collective and personal dimensions of developmental processes.

30.1.1 Challenges to the Study of the Developing Person: Elementarism and Nondevelopmentalism

Stern and Baldwin unanimously articulated the concern that the particular logic of elementarism was picked up from the natural sciences and applied in psychology. Baldwin stated:

The . . . quantitative method, brought over into psychology from the exact sciences, physics and chemistry, must be discarded for its ideal consisted in reducing the more complex to the more simple, the whole to its parts, the later evolved to the earlier-existent *thus denying or eliminating just the factor which constituted or revealed what was truly genetic.* (Baldwin, 1930, p. 7; emphasis added)

Stern wrestled at that time; on the one hand with naïve personalism – a folk-psychological belief in the personality as an independently existing thing, a by-product that needed no further explications (than God maybe) – and on the other hand, psychological impersonalism, the elementaristic approach where the person is nonexisting and not needed.

A human being is not a mosaic, and therefore cannot be described as a mosaic. All attempts to represent a person simply in terms of a sequence of

test scores are fundamentally false. (W. Stern, cited in Lehmann-Muriithi, de Resende Damas Cardoso, & Lamiell, 2016, p. 216)

Elementarism is overly common in today's developmental psychology and in psychology in general. It builds on a logic in which research proceeds from the study of elements to the study of more holistic structures in a simple, additive way, implying that phenomena of higher order (personality for instance) are already existing as germs in more basic processes and functions and will appear in such an additive approach and, if it does not, is irrelevant. One could claim that the research agenda here operates at the collective level of meaning-making by investigating functions, attainments and skills that are considered to be of developmental importance within the given societal context. As such the assessment of functions is meaningful in regard to the cultural organization of human life, but this does not necessarily reflect any meaningfulness in relation to the personal life and development. By neglecting personal life as a context for the assessed functions, the only possible explanation left is either some global environmental stimuli or internal maturing factors. In this sense, Baldwin was very precise in saying that the elementaristic logic eliminates the whole idea of a developing system. Regretting this tendency Stern had a vision for psychology; " [a] *new psychology where the guiding idea will no longer be the multiplicity of psychological elements, but whose leitmotiv will instead be the concept of the unified multiplicity*" (Lamiell, 2009a, p. 114). In this perspective, the personal experience is always an experience of something, and it is this relatedness of personal being that provides the conditions for the transformative processes of the whole.

As the quotation of Baldwin marks, a consequence of elementarism is nondevelopmentalism, meaning that we are left oblivious to how the child in focus arrived at his or her particular developmental situation or what could be possible future situations for him or her. Today, the most widely applied strategy for how to arrive at a general knowledge of functions is moving from sample to population through the application of statistical procedures (Valsiner, 2015). Within this frame, an elementaristic approach strives for objectivity by studying more and more elementary "pieces" in the aim of arriving at the "true" state of a given function. Following this line of objectivity, this approach correlates particular environmental and psychological/behavioral factors in the search for predictive relationships of significant *p*-values. Yet, such correlations can only – and at their best – give hints about the dynamic nature that makes such functions meaningful (and functional) to the living person. In statistical approaches dynamics cannot be explained, since the functionality that makes the function meaningful to the person does not coincide with collective objectified appointment of the function as being important. In terms of developmental evaluation of the individual the whole statistical procedure remains a puzzle, since what is true for the mean of the sample (at different ages) is not necessarily true for any single individual (Lamiell, 2009b; Borsboom et al., 2009; Lundmann & Villadsen, 2016). What we, along with Baldwin and Stern suggest, is not to reject a collective level of meaningfulness in favor of the personal level, since this would only indicate a shift from one platonic universe to the other (Vygotsky, 1927; Hviid & Villadsen, 2014). Instead we suggest that an understanding of the personal level can only be accomplished through understanding how the person, through her active relation to this collective level of meanings, cultivates her life course in a meaningful way.

In nondevelopmental examinations it might be discovered that infants – on average – are vulnerable to maternal depression, or that teenagers – on average – are fragile to divorcing parents, but theoretical notions of the developing person that can account precisely for these vulnerabilities,

as well as what do not turn out as vulnerabilities, are not given attention. We might notice that children's responses vary on "same level" Piagetian tasks, but without looking beyond the experimental task itself and into the sociocultural life of the child, we are left to name deviations from the average performances as *decalage*; a kind of accepted categorical "instability" (Rogoff, 1990). Surprisingly, much of developmental psychology is nondevelopmental due to its preoccupation with the "true state" of a given age, thus neglecting the very processes generating the various states (Valsiner, 1997).

Baldwin and Stern set out to conceptualize the developing interdependent dynamics. Stern did so though conceptualization of a human life where experiences marked a central level, and played a crucial part in the development of the person, and Baldwin in making persistent imitation and sembling the motor of personal development. We will present selected aspects of their theoretical contributions in the following, one after the other.

30.1.2 Stern and the Experiencing Person

To Stern a *psychological* investigation of the human life must focus on experience: "*experience develops out of and into life*" (W. Stern, 1938, p. 72). A person's experience is dynamic, interdependent, and very different from a perceptive "measurement" of the objective world. Experiences evolve between the unique biographical person, impressed by the environment and teleological or teleogenetic urges by that person to act and modify tensions in his or her relations to the world. Thus, experience "ties" human beings and environment together, while at the same time cultivating this relationship, producing meaning at the personal and collective levels.

The "person" is a living whole, individual, unique, striving towards goals, self-contained and yet opens to the world around him; he is capable of having experience. (W. Stern, 1938, p. 70)

Through convergent experiencing of the socio-cultural environment and oneself, a level of intro-ceptive understanding emerges as an intuitive recognition of a personal sense of being-in-the-world. Introception is a process by which human beings strive to understand the complexity of being a person, having engagements, dedications, goals, and value orientations – either in one-self or the other (Lehmann-Muriithi, de Resende Damas Cardoso, & Lamiell, 2016). The process of introception seems close the Baldwin's notion of "sembling," to which we will soon return.

Stern's notion of experience represents a rela-tion to particular aspects of the world, but does not mirror the world in totality in any objective fashion. It is on the one side the *particular per-son's experience* but it is also always an *expe-rience of something*. Moreover "*experiences are both something of having and acting*" (W. Stern, 1938, p. 79), and thus operate as an ongoing dynamic between being and becoming. To Stern, the subjective, experienced world is fragmented (incomplete) in comparison with the objective world as such, but "*this fits perfectly into signifi-cant and purposeful connections of personal life*" (W. Stern, 1938, p. 76). Experiences point toward tensions or unevenness in the person's relation to the world. Such experienced imbalances require the person to reorganize her relationship with the world; either in shape of reorganizing her under-standing of herself in the world and vice versa, or (possibly) to act in a way to create a more mean-ingful convergence with the experienced world. In a developmental perspective, experience rep-resents a process of self-maintenance and self-development in a dialectic relationship with the world. This process endures as long as life is lived. Experience is:

an elastic envelope of many folds about the person, reflecting, with its wrinkles and hollows, tangles and variations of form, in accordance with the demands of the personal state of tension, so that the proportions are altered, the reflected light is strengthened, weakened or extinguished. (W. Stern, 1938, p. 77)

30.1.3 Baldwin and Personal Development Through Persistent Imitation

Baldwin too considered experiences of human beings central to the development of a sense of a personal living and conceptualized these in a context-inclusive fashion.

All experience as such is . . . a sembled meaning; it is not only context it is also experiencing inner life. (Baldwin, 1908, cited in Tudge, Putnam, & Valsiner, 1996, p. 198)

Building on the concept of experience as an interdependent dynamic Baldwin developed the notion of *imitation*. A distinction between *sim-ple imitation* and *persistent imitation* is impor-tant. Simple imitation appears first in ontogene-sis. Here, the copy does not move beyond what the "echo-metaphor" connotes; it does not mutate or vary.

He first imitates movements, later sounds, especially vocal sounds . . . He hears his own voice and imitates it . . . He does not improve, but goes on making the same sounds with the same mistakes again and again. (Baldwin, 1899/2007, p. 78)

Through these processes of simple imitation more persistent forms of imitation emerge. The subject creates her own conditions for develop-ment trough imitation and persistent elaborations over the imitated. In other words, the child selects volitionally what has been an impressive experi-ence (mostly pleasurable experiences or move-ments from painful to pleasurable situations), which she then imitates, thus recreating the sit-uation that caused the impressive experience in the first place (instead of waiting for it to reoc-cur). This is a feed-forward process where the child becomes co-producer of her own developmental situation. The developmental logic is thus to Baldwin that man *"is in his greatest part, also someone else"* (Baldwin, 1902, p. 96). As is shown here, the notion of persistent imitation goes far beyond the common sense "echo/mirror" understanding of the word.

Imitation to the intelligent and earnest imitator is never slavish, never mere repetition, it is, on the contrary, a means for further ends, a method of absorbing what is present in others and of making it over in forms peculiar to one's own temper and valuable to one's own genius. (Baldwin, 1911, p. 22)

Baldwin devoted special attention to what he referred to as *personality suggestions* (Baldwin, 1899/2007), which was directly related to infants' attention to and capacity for recognizing persons. Persons in the child's environment became persons in the child's life – a base from which to become a person(ality). Such persons, mothers, fathers, and siblings, behave irregularly; sometimes they comfort the child, sometimes they do not. Sometimes they play, respond, or hand over objects – and sometimes they do not. Baldwin emphasized this irregularity as the source of continued curiosity to the child. On this basis the child gets a first sense of *personal agency* (Baldwin, 1899/2007). He starts to see other human beings more as holistic entities and comes to understand that persons are more and less regular in their irregularities, and this guides his development.

He behaves differently when the father is in the room. He is quick to obey one person, slow to obey another. He cries aloud, pulls his companions, and behaves reprehensibly generally, when no adult is present who has authority or will to punish him. This stage in his "knowledge of man" leads to very marked differences of conduct on his part. (Baldwin, 1899/2007, p. 86)

Through such processes the child's self-consciousness and her social feeling or *sembling*,

a process of feeling-*into*, evolves. Baldwin gives an example of such a process in a situation where a child imitates his father's reaction to being stuck by a pointed object, for example, a nail. Upon the father's exclamation of pain ("Ouch!," withdrawing the hand, and maybe throwing the pointed object on the floor), the child imitates. Not only does he enact his father's actions, he feels the pain and experiences what "was inside the father's mind, the pain and the motive of the action... the act of his father has now become his own" (Baldwin, 1899/2007, p. 88). Knowing the feeling of pain from being stuck by a pointy object, the child "reads this back" into his father, as his psychological situation.

The child is now giving back to his parents, teachers, etc., only the material which he himself took from them. He has enriched it, to be sure; with it he now reads into the other persons the great fact of subjective agency; but still whatever he thinks of them has come by way of his thought of himself, and that in turn was made up from them. (Baldwin, 1899/2007, p. 90)

Interestingly, several aspects of Baldwin's conceptualization of the subjective and intersubjective abilities of infants are extensively validated by modern infant research (e.g., see Hviid & Villadsen, 2015; D. Stern, 1985; Beebe, 2006). Contrary to the work of Baldwin, this line of research has occupied itself with the question of which *functions* are needed in order to participate in the intersubjective processes – while neglecting what it *means* for the infant to be a subject, experiencing the world and how these experiences, as they become *meaningful* for subject, feed into the *meaning-making* of the baby's life course (Hviid & Villadsen, 2015).

Despite having only touched on a few dimensions of the extensive production of Stern and Baldwin, it seems clear that a developmental approach to the developing person requires changes or at least complements to the analytical attention to what a child *can/cannot* with the question of understanding *what it means to be a child for the person, being a child.* "The idea of *purpose* is the very key to the true understanding of personal being" (Stern in Lamiell, 2015, p. 169), and here children are no exceptions. Thus, children's *meaning-making* processes are in dialogue with the cultural arrangements they live with and through – as well as the *meaningfulness* by which they guide their lives and direct their orientation, and thus become inevitable foci to this developmental perspective.

The personal level of meaningfulness is not a pre-given or static phenomenon, nor is it just fluid and ever changing – it always operates dynamically between maintenance and the emergence of novelty. Children act in their environment – for better or for worse – to make life meaningful in accordance with their experiences. They pursue their engagements, work to sort out tensions and attempt to create what, they imagine, could be better (future) conditions. This is an interdependent and persistent constructive process that leaves traces of meaning-making acts in the very same environment that the child takes as her living conditions. Through such mutual processes of cultivation (Simmel, 1997; Fuhrer, 2004) the child projects her own life into a future on the basis of the past experiences (Hviid & Villadsen, 2015). In the section that follows, we attempt to transform these basic, theoretical notions into a methodological framework.

30.2 A Concrete Case of Investigating Children's Development as Persons

30.2.1 Design and Central Concepts

The project conducted included five 13-year-old children. They were each interviewed at their leisure time activity centre three-four times for approximately 1.5–2 hours per interview. The focus of the interviews was their experiences of living and developing as persons. As the notion: "Your development as a person" is quite abstract, we thought from the onset that the children would be in need of some kind of guidance.[1]

This was attempted by making the *spaces children live* (Muchow & Muchow, 2015) more concrete and present. By this is not meant a mathematical-geographical representation, but refers together with Muchow's elaboration of *life space* to the central places children spend and make their lives. Since the investigation dealt with their past, present, and future life, it would not be easy to re-space their lives in order to call out for experiences (e.g., by visiting places). Actually, any attempt to pre-mould their life spaces would risk producing unsuitable limitations, since each child's configuration of life space is just as unique as they are as persons. The children were offered big pieces of paper and all kinds of drawing materials and asked to select and draw their life spaces and from thereon "step inside" these (by imagination) and describe their experiences. Michael explains the first outline of his drawing, where three tenets emanate in parallel from the centre, formed as a heart (his birth):

MICHAEL POINTS TO THE INSTITUTIONAL TENET: This is my . . . what you have to go through in life; after-school centre, school and kindergarten. It is the necessary stuff, things that must happen.
INTERVIEWER: What Denmark[2] wants to happen?
MICHAEL: Precisely. Precisely. And the after-school centre became the youth club. And the school will be college. It will continue. It is not mine at all. (Michael points at his leisure time-tenet): This is what I want to happen, it's all mine . . . And the family (the tenet in the middle) . . . that is my life. It's a mixture.

The children's experiences of these places and practices were examined. In doing so the researcher cannot take convergence for granted, on what e.g. "a school," "a recess," "a lunch box" or "summer holiday" mean. The children were explicitly encouraged to correct the researcher, when sensing being misunderstood. We believe they had the courage to do so, because they were told that research would otherwise turn out bad (and they wanted to help). When the researcher was guided; efforts were praised ("I am glad that you say the Harry Potter *Universe*, because that makes me think that you have understood it.") and mistakes forgiven ("Many people get this wrong – it is complicated"). Still, keeping categories open in order to study personal engagements and tensions with the sociocultural world is, we suspect, one of the greatest challenges in this particular perspective which can be demonstrated with the following example.

Eve (13 years) explained how fond she had become of her pre-school teacher, Tutter. Tutter taught her to read, and reading was one of the most important discoveries and resources in Eve's life and in her imagination of her future. Tutter was, next to her parents, one of the most important persons in her life. But to the surprise and initial disquiet of the interviewer, Eve said that Tutter often read the book "Questioning-Jorgen" [Spørge Jørgen] to the children in the kindergarten. Now, Questioning-Jorgen is a Danish children's book written in verses. The story is about a boy, Jorgen, who asks and asks and asks and asks . . . more or less sensible questions. In the end his father has had enough; Jorgen gets spanked and is put to bed. In bed, Jorgen continues asking: "Why didn't I get pancakes? Why am I not allowed playing? Why does my bum hurt? – I will never ask silly questions again." Today, educationalists and the Danish society as a whole would consider the message of the book outdated and damaging. Admittedly, so did the interviewer. However, Eve made a different sense out of it.

INTERVIEWER: Why do you think she read that book?
EVE: It is because: There are answers to everything! I believe she read it because we asked her about everything . . . It was always her

we asked; she was somehow the "sage of the kindergarten."
INTERVIEWER: So she liked children posing questions?
EVE: She did! She said that otherwise we would not come to know anything. She loved questions where she could give really long explanations . . . in the end one felt like: "Thank you thank you, I have understood now . . . " (Laughs) She loved it when we asked.

This was a surprising interpretation indeed, which only underlines that there are infinite ways of making sense of cultural objects. Eve's way of making sense did not only promote the curiosity and curious questions of the children but also Tutter's position as a "sage of the kindergarten."

Dynamics appeared in conducting the drawings-interviews that are worth mentioning. When the children found a beginning form for their representation, they invented symbolic demarcations of personal importance like: "this line is made thicker, since starting nursery care this *is more than* the dream of going to Africa" or "this is my *motor road*" when drawing family life. Moreover, they added symbols, names, persons and events, and hereby made the representation richer – like a scrapbook in progress – and during this work, particular evaluative moments became apparent. Since a lot more was said than drawn, we were often in an evaluative situation where they were asked: "Should what you are telling me now be put on the drawing?" or when they inferred "this is for the map" or explained: "nursery-care will not be put on the map since it was just a *bump on the road*." The children thus evaluated the importance and meaningfulness of particular experiences in relation to their introceptive understanding of their being. The map-making thus promoted several processes; an *"ordering" of their lives*, a process of *sharing their experiences in life* and of *introceptive evaluations of these experiences* in relation to their *personal worlds* (W. Stern, 1938) as human beings:

the world that the person brings near to himself, because he possesses receptivity and sensitivity for it and to which he also seeks to give that form, which is appropriate to his essential nature.

(W. Stern, 1938, p. 89)

Whereas some children recommended more interviews (which is a comment to the discussion of validity) (Hviid & Beckstead, 2011) Michael's evaluation of his map was: "Yeah, this is my life." Unfortunately, only he could see it the way he saw it, as his life, although we worked on understanding his way of living. The children named their maps as "my life-map," with "life-limits," and showing "life-habits." These were their words invented along the work.

30.2.2 Analysis

The analyses are interpretative and the goal was to work as closely as possible to an understanding of the lifeworld of the (other) person, while maintaining a discussion on a theoretical level (Hviid, 2008). In this chapter, two themes are selected from the analysis: one is *timed and untimed life* and another one is *persons to copy – or being copied by*. As an analytical prerequisite to this thematic presentation, the data from each child has been analyzed separately. According to a life-space dimension questions have been: Where have they been, where are they, and where are they heading? Moreover, strong engagements (as dedication or resistance) over time have been examined, along with tensions and questions of how they maintained and changed more or less in convergence with their surroundings. In addition, we have asked for important persons in the children's lives; persons that meant something to them in sharing, supporting, needing or blocking ways. We have tried to work out what was central to their existence, maybe most clearly expressed as an insistence to maintain oneself, and not give in to changes proposed or enforced on them (Hviid, 2012). Moreover, we have examined their articulated experiences of taking part in

research and how they approached this particular context in order to make it meaningful to themselves (Hviid & Beckstead, 2011). Based on these analyses the two developmental themes are presented. We propose these to have general value in human development, although of course, the cultural and personal variations of these particular issues are varied and handled in infinite ways, and have different degrees of salient presence in each child's lifeworld. The analysis also shows their interdependence. Along with the presentation of the developmental themes we discuss the kind of knowledge such a perspective can produce, especially in comparison with traditional developmental psychology.

30.2.3 Timed and Untimed Living – A Question of Convergence

The personal life course becomes cultivated through the experience of the social world in which the cultural organization of time and space gives rise to the personal life space and life time. Life time (Stern, 1938) and life space are not considered separate entities in the experience of human living, but as ways of experiencing oneself in relation to different dimensions of the world. Baldwin's notion of persistent imitation precisely demonstrates how the child's co-construction of its own environment creates his or her future, and that space and time thus are interwoven.

In traditional developmental studies, time is an objective system of chronological units: years, months, hours, and seconds. These entities are put into use in order to investigate changes in functional capacities, as either progress or decline. Results of such analyses are often discussed in relation to normative societal standards, which promote and constrain children's activities. However, such standardized timescales do not work (alone) in a cultural life-course study, where the person's experience of him or herself in a sociocultural world is at the center of the analysis.

Chronological time is not irrelevant to human experiences, our lives are heavily structured by chronological time, and so are the children's concrete lives (Hviid, 2008). But as *personal* experiences, time is related to purposes like: "being late for school," "waiting for teachers to help," "too short recesses," "waiting an eternity for dinner," "bedtime is much too early," and so on. Time-structured childhood landscapes makes children re-experience who they are.

MICHAEL (13 YEARS): You are big and small, big and small. Last year in nursery, you are big, right? Then you get very small in kindergarten. Then you are big the last year in kindergarten. And then you are really small in school. Therefore, you are big and small, big and small, big and small . . .
INTERVIEWER: When you went from big to small, it almost sounds as if you lost something there?
MICHAEL: I did. We all did. We all came from being the biggest to being the smallest ones. We were the smallest ones in grade zero.[3]
INTERVIEWER: Yes . . . but in developmental theories. They often describe a movement that goes up, up, up. (Draws a staircase in the air)
MICHAEL: But actually, it goes up–down, up–down, up–down, up–down (draws zigzag in the air).
INTERVIEWER: Yes, that is how you move.
MICHAEL: Yes it is. All the time you get bigger – on the paper – so to speak. You grow older, but to your surroundings, you get bigger and smaller and bigger and smaller.
INTERVIEWER: It must feel somewhat . . . turbulent, to be moved around in that way?
MICHAEL: Yeah, next year we are small, right?
INTERVIEWER: Why are you small?
MICHAEL: Because we begin 7th grade. That is the smallest grade on the big level. Next year we have nothing to say.

To Michael (and the other children) movements to the next place did not make children experience themselves as bigger, but as smaller, and as small, they had "nothing to say." Eve shared her experiences transiting from nursery care to kindergarten at the age of three, which had a huge influence on her possibilities to act.

EVE: Now they were very much bigger than the biggest in the nursery care. They were six years old, right? You could see it, because they were the ones riding two-wheeled bikes. We did not ride on those bikes. We could not even get near them! They were also the ones that played football with the adults. We didn't. We only played with "My little Pony."

It is a bit of a personal change to move from being "kings of the kindergarten" to being a "grade zero – pupil," but this is nevertheless a frequent reality for most children in the world. During such cultural changes, children experience themselves anew, but not as *new* (meaning "other") persons. This is precisely the point of Stern's (1938) and Bergson's (1907/1915) conceptualizations of personal time: that personal time has duration. *Life* is not minutes, hours, and years. Bergson characterized duration as a "*continuous progress of the past which gnaws into the future and which swells as it advances*" (Bergson, 1907/1915, p. 4). In other words: present experiences can only be experienced in relation to what one has already experienced, past experiences are only meaningful in relation to present ones, and the anticipated (and pursued) future can only be anticipated on some basis of what one has already experienced; no-one can anticipate something from nothing. These continuous and simultaneous constructive-destructive-reconstructive processes stretch out and weave together "what was," "is," and "what could be." As Stern was occupied with convergence between collective and individual meanings (here: temporalities and pace), so was Bergson, who considered the process as a creative adaptation (Bergson, 1907/1915).

Sociological investigations of age-appropriateness (Neugarten, 1996) quite unanimously points to difficulties in life when not following local social norms of age appropriate behavior (see Elder & Shanahan, 2006, for an overview). Adaptations to such norms would, it seems, make life so much easier. Yet, human beings do not do so, at least not with the same social purposes as the norm possesses. Rather correspondence between social norms and personal living signifies that the person finds meaningfulness in life, living in accordance with the norms. Hence, the meaning of the social norm and personal life are never identical.

This difference between norms and the personal level of relating to the norms tends to become "naturalized" to the point that children "live" the norm. Here the personal level disappears from sight and is thus left out of the developmental explanation, only to reappear when children's behavior fall outside the norm. Hence, the personal aspect of a developing person is most often restricted to an explanation in the case of failure (Mammen, 1996) – usually articulated as a developmental disorder residing *in* the developing person. This does not mean that the personal dimension is nonexistent in norm(al) developmental processes, but it requires a closer analytical attention, and such attention could probably also inform us on the case of "un-normal" development beyond the level of disorder.

Traditional developmental psychology would investigate untimed life (development) as a question of individual *maturity*, clustering performances of different functions. However, from a *psychological* life-course perspective – how could such mismatches be understood? As presented, Michael and Eve experience tensions when following institutionalized trajectories. In the following, we take a closer look into processes that involve the issue of age-appropriateness on a local collective level in the children's lives in dialogue with family members and peers. The presentation is regrettably simplified, but we must be brief here. Michael and Eve have been introduced already; they are 13 years old.

Michael considered himself "older than I am." This meant that he primarily chose company among older children, and they chose him. In this way, he was "out of time" with societal expectations, he was "ahead of time."

I can't play with someone who is younger than I am. I have always been with those who are bigger, so it has become a life-habit to me.

A "life-habit." A life-habit seems to point to some recurring phenomenon over a lifetime that makes up the "habit," a timeless or fluid issue that nevertheless grows and becomes a pattern by which Michael knows himself as being in the world. Life-habit was his word; it does not exist in Danish language. Where did those experiences come from and why did Michael recreate this kind of experience in new contexts and relations over time? Why was that important?

It definitely pointed back to his relationships with his two older brothers. Michael admired them deeply and loved being with them. They played ice hockey, football, and computer games. He learned from them, was taught, trained, and protected. They taught him of what was to come, for example, that school would only get harder, although he could not really imagine that. He also knew of kindergarten life, long before starting, as they informed him. In addition, the three brothers shared difficult matters. When their parents recently divorced, they got closer and were Michael's greatest source of comfort. One day in their company was particularly important to him. He remembered the year and the event very clearly. It was *that* day, when they (to him) stopped paying attention to the fact that he was younger; that day when he was taken as a player of football on equal terms with them. That transformed his status from "a little brother" to a "team player" and he had dreamt of that as long as he could remember. To Michael, life with his brothers caused the "life-habit" and in his transition to kindergarten at three years old, he was already big.

It was because of my brothers. We played Dungeons and Dragons, and I knew a lot about it so I was cool, right? So I was included among the big ones, because I knew such cool things that the really big boys played, because my brothers played it.

Through the resources taught by his brothers, Michael could "get near" to what Eve could not get near when she started in kindergarten. This meant that he overcame the "becoming small-phase" rather fast. As seventh grader he still preferred spending time with older children, his friends were older than he was, and he did things older boys do. Trans-positioning his lessons from home to kindergarten, *imitating* his brothers the best he could when they were not around, and watching the positive feedback when doing so, must have supported his admiration for his brothers and his continuous need for being close to them. They were his source of future development and he recreated that outside the family. Striving to be "ahead of time" mostly made life good for Michael, but he must have put some effort into it, since judgments of his "social age" was in the hands of the others to decide, as his brothers once did.

The cultural organization frames – but does not determine – the life course of a single child. He or she will always have the possibility to construct it in a way that makes it meaningful to him or her. We assume however, that it is nevertheless more challenging to "lack behind" the age-appropriate than to strive ahead. But before turning to that, aspects of Eve's life are presented.

Eve was not only striving to become bigger, she appreciated a variety of activities regardless of their age-appropriateness. She had same-age friends with whom she talked and had fun, and she had younger friends with whom she played.

I still have a lot of imagination, I play roleplay. All my female friends have left that long time ago . . . I have always fairly well liked smaller children, I have been good at making friends with younger

children. I have friends in 4th, 5th, and 6th grade – I have no problems being with them at all. But many consider it outsider-like to be with younger ones. My friends say: "Honestly, are you going down to be with 6th and 5th graders?" It's absurd; they don't have the right to say: "Do you want to be with us or with the small ones?" This is hard, because they are my best friends with whom I can giggle and gossip. But the younger ones are those I can have fun with: play football and so on. I said: "Then I choose them, because they do not force me to choose." But it's hard . . .

Eve put herself in a difficult situation, and risked losing her relationship with close friends by doing so. What was the attraction in making such a dangerous move? The fact is, she did not "just" like to be with the small ones, she liked to do what they did. They played and Eve loved playing, imagining other worlds. And here begins a long story of Eve's imagination, which she had never shared with any adult, a story of Eve's life with Harry Potter. Long before Harry Potter was translated into Danish, her British-Danish aunt read it to her and Eve was mesmerized.

If you saw my room, you would think: "Freak, let me get out!" Harry Potter is everywhere. I am dying for the universe this figure lives in. The phenomenon "Harry Potter" is absolutely fantastic. If I am sad, I sit in my room surrounded by Harry Potter. All my posters look at me. I lock myself into it. I have a copy of Harry Potter's bed, with a red velvet curtain; I sit behind that with my necklace and my picture of my best friend. Then I become absolutely happy inside. So wonderful that Harry Potter is created (Eve looks seriously at interviewer). It can be hard to understand . . . He opened my eyes to: There is something better than the real world. I know the story is about evilness, but there is something to conquer the evil. He also taught me: Maybe you feel bad – but eventually something good happens.

"There is something better than the real world," Eve said. Eve loved to imagine being in other worlds and this is what one does when playing. Her big idol (to imitate) was of course J. K. Rowling. At 12 years old Eve started writing her own (now 300 pages) novel, and she made an arrangement with a publishing company to do her school-related obligatory trainee work with them. She imagined her future filled with such imagination. Her aim was to convince her parents to support literature studies in Oxford. In this sense she was indeed *ahead* of time, maybe even too much ahead of the timescales of a 13-year-old Danish girl.

My biggest dream is to become a writer. Like Rowling, I want to write a book that can do the same as Harry Potter once did for me.

The redundancy of imagination in Eve's life-world, seeing it "swelling as it advances into the future," as Bergson describes makes us certain that this touches on something very central to what it means "being Eve." Her search for co-imaginative players is very logical from this point of view. Yet she felt strapped in an unreasonable developmental straightjacket pushing her to converge with societal standards of age-appropriateness, requesting her to stop playing, and even though it hurt deeply, it did not make her stop. This strongly underlines a general existential premise; that personally engaged life cannot simply obey cultural standards since such life would no longer be personal – even confronted with pain, punishment, sometimes death. The tensions promoted her to think about the values she wanted to live by. Before discussing this further, we would like to bring attention to the next developmental issue of persistent imitation.

30.2.4 Someone to Copy – And Being Copied by

The phenomenon of imitation deserves to our opinion much more attention than already given in the field of developmental psychology. Nevertheless, imitation is often implied in tutorial teaching and learning (Schön, 1983) and in theories of apprenticeship (Lave & Wenger, 1991; Rogoff, 1990), but rarely examined as developmental dynamics. However, it is well known in children's worlds and personal accounts of their own development. As incidences of imitation are frequent in the data, we will build on the personal histories already presented (Eve and Michael) and only introduce little new. Maria (13 years) had experienced imitation all her life:

MARIA (13 YEARS): Every year, when the new ones start [at youth-club] you think: "Oh no, now the small ones are arriving." I also think back on when I started. My God, we were annoying. We looked so much up to the seventh graders, right?
INTERVIEWER: Yes.
MARIA: In 4th grade, you talk a lot about the big ones. Today I consider them [the small ones] quite annoying, and the big ones must have thought the same about us, right? But back then I thought: "God they are nice!," because they were the big ones.
INTERVIEWER: Is it like that everywhere?
MARIA: Yes, it is like that in school. Yes, it is like that in kindergarten. Yes, it is also like that in nursery care. In 3rd grade, I thought of the 7th graders as the really big ones. But now I consider myself very small. I think it is quite natural that people look up to each other, the smaller one is.
INTERVIEWER: I see. The next step: do you feel like that with regard to adults?
MARIA SMILES: Not the same way.
INTERVIEWER (TEASING): But being 13 years old, don't you today look up to people like me – who are beyond 50?
MARIA: To be honest, no. (Shared giggle)
INTERVIEWER: Maybe you look up to the 18-year-old ones?
MARIA: Yes, that is true, now it's like that.

As with "becoming smaller" in institutional transitions, "being bigger" has a practical side to it, which is closely linked to power to access and define contexts.

MICHAEL (13 YEARS): Mikkel and I – we were kings of the kindergarten. If there were anybody playing in the "rough-and-tumble room," we could say: "Leave! It's ours, we have reserved it." Then we took it.

INTERVIEWER: So the eldest . . .

MICHAEL: They had the power. When the small ones were sad, we comforted them, but we held power.

Moreover, small ones lack, to the elder, skills and knowledge

EVE: They enter the workshops [at the leisure-time club] and they are newcomers, but they want to sew everything! It's like [in high-pitch voice]: "Can I finish this big fashionable coat if I start today?" [normal voice] "NO, you can't, it takes three weeks **if** you work in this workshop every single day!" – They ask the strangest questions.

In the children's lifeworld we are first of all presented with what could be considered as "classical" persistent imitation, meaning imitation where the children imitate valuable others. In Michael's life, his brothers served as much inspiration for imitation in a very straightforward sense. But as all the other children interviewed, Michael had other idols, quite many in fact. There was Niklas, for instance, a young friend of the family, who inspired Michael as a professional ice hockey player, and taught him all he knew in this respect. "I will try to become just as good, and do the same, yes," Michael said.

Eve deeply respected many persons in her lifeworld: Tutter, her parents, the English teacher, the leader of the Youth Club, her godfather, a young man in the youth club who, to Eve, could handle "almost anything." However, when it came to her deepest engagement she had no one close to her, to imitate, because the community of Happy Potter readers had not bloomed in Denmark yet. Off course she had someone in the distance, so to speak.

How can she? [Rowling] It has taken her five years to write the first Harry Potter. She wrote on

everything! She has an enormous cardboard box only containing editions of the first chapter!

We do not want to underestimate the importance of this relationship, or the worshipping of her idol. But it was not entirely fulfilling, in that the process of "giving back" to the imitated was impossible, as she was absent. This process of "giving back" is, we assume, not just a "side effect" of persistent imitation, but it is foundational to a developmental relation. Eve felt alone with her engagement and it took years before her peers knew what she was talking about.

I had two good friends but we still couldn't talk about the thing that meant most of all to me – next to my parents. People thought I was crazy when I said: "This reminds me of the Snitch." "The Snitch!!? You are weird!!"

Out of her desire to share "what meant most of all to her" she introduced the story to younger children – who happened to love playing, and found it interesting. They acted out the storyline as well as they could and "little Agnes," her neighbor's daughter, was especially dedicated and willing to make herself part of this fantasy universe; and to become a little version of Eve.

EVE: She likes Harry Potter because of me. She looks for some reason very much up to me (smiles). She does the same things as I do. It's like . . . we are each other.

"We are each other," Eve said. This is not a common Danish phrase, it does not exist in Danish language – it is Eve's way of expressing something going on between her-Agnes-and-the-story. It seems important to address, since it expresses experiential dynamics of persistent imitation – but from the imitated person's point of view. Being imitated can, to our suggestion, be perceived as a *personal consolidation*, and such a "double-up" can act as a *confirmation* of, or add value to, one's being in the world, using Stern's terminology. This seems to be the case of Eve and Agnes. However, the outcome does not always follow this case when imitation is at work, and here we enter the intricate question of whom to imitate and the consequences of doing so. Opposite to Eve's accepting "we are each other," the rhyme: "*Copycat, copycat – who do you think you are looking at?*" expresses the imitated person's rejection of being imitated by that "copycat," as if these imitations damage or distort the values of the imitated.

30.3 Intermediate Summary of the Cases

The analytical framing of the analysis is built on central concepts from Stern concerning the personal level of meaning making, and Baldwin's genetic focus on the sociogenic foundation (exemplified with concept of imitation) for personal development, as well as a broader cultural perspective relating these processes to the collective organizations of cultural production. Based on this analytical frame, a pool of data has been analyzed with a special emphasis on how children's experience of living, growing, and developing can be understood as personally meaningful in relation to the sociocultural contexts in which they live. We have focused on two themes in the convergence between children and their sociocultural environment: their experience of timing within societies' temporal organization of development and their experience of persistent imitation over their life course.

30.3.1 Duration and Redundancy in the Development of the Personal Life Course

Embracing the richness of the interconnections that the engagements in children's lives generate, a dynamic and redundant picture of children's development appears which deviates markedly from the classical, linear developmental curve of child psychology. When looking at Eve's life, it could be argued that there are relations between her preschool teacher, Tutter, her ability and will to read, her joy of the English-teacher at school, her beloved British aunt, her playfulness and imagination, Harry Potter, her periodic tension with same-age female friends, her relationship with little Agnes, her novel, her trainee period at a publishing company, her imagined future studies in Oxford, and her ideas of becoming a writer. These are interconnected and redundant in the light of meaningfulness. It is as if the meaningfulness is repeated and elaborated – in many variations. These aspects have a very long duration in such a young person's short life – they stretch from her 4th or 5th year of age and into adulthood – and they are weaved together of experiences crisscrossing a broad variety of different contexts in her life-space. Taken together it generates a pattern where the redundant process, that at first leaves an impression of conservative repetition, cultivates Eve's life course and provides direction. In this process, engagements potentially transform in their meaningfulness along with the emergence of novel meanings of herself in the world, the world in her and the life course of future world–self relationships.

By incidence we know that Eve today studies literature. In that sense the cultural organization developmental time caught up with Eve's being ahead of time, and the meaningfulness at the personal and collective level converge, yet remain as personal and collective in their configuration. But even if she had not done so, we still believe that we have a fairly strong idea of what mattered being Eve, when we met her – and that this would still matter – had she chosen other directions in her educational life course.

When trying to conceptualize the importance of redundancy in the developmental experiences, Michael's notion of "life-habits" is exemplary. Here, there seems to be *repetitions-with-variations* at least in terms of: (1) directing attention to/from specific incidences; (2) specific ways of approaching/retreating from opportunities; (3) investigating something's potential/uselessness; and (4) whom to relate to/withdraw from and how. All these variations in Michael's way of relating to an ever-changing environment indicate that there is not one, two, or three functions, which, added together, ensure the developmental progress of the next "new." Where the statistical analysis of children's development most often approach this kind of variance in factorial manner, evaluating the predictive power of each factor in relation to outcome variation on its own, it becomes clear that this additive handling of elements is insufficient in ensuring the development to the concrete person. The most relevant question of how the detected functions integrate into a functional whole, which ensures sustainable and meaningful development in a constantly changing environment, is never asked (Valsiner, 2015). Within the ever-changing and unpredictable sociocultural environment that generates an infinite number of developmental possibilities, the only way to ensure developmental progress in personally meaningful ways is through simultaneous and complementary efforts, which operate as a dynamic whole – the *unitas multiplex* of the personal being. In that sense Michael is an exemplary case of a general process, yet uniquely configured within the concrete conditions that make up Michael's life and provide resources (as well as constraints) for the construction and cultivation of his future life course.

30.3.2 Multifunctional Imitation in the Life Course

Based on the analysis, we propose *self-persistent imitation* to be one of the many processes operating within such a multiplex in which the person's being in the world both constitutes and emerges as patterns of new configurations. Baldwin hit the same nerve describing this process in the flow of experience, where

pleasures and gratification be succeeded by pains of want, let impulse seek its end, finding it here and losing it there; and amid the contradictions and reiterations, the storm and stress of the accommodation of life to the world, a few great relief points begin to stand out in consciousness. They recur, they satisfy, they stand together, *they can be found when wanted.* (Baldwin, 1892, p. 406, emphasis added)

Investigating such patterning – empirically – not only in their construction but also in their reconstructing, destruction, and fading away is absolutely of great importance in a progression of knowledge of the development of persons.

With Michael's articulation of "life-habits" this was explicitly the case. But could there also be other life-habits in imitation, like life-habits of whom to be imitated by? The issue of *being imitated* as a developmental motor is implicit in Baldwin's work, but ought to have a more prominent position. Children are imitated (almost) just as early as they imitate. Selby and Bradley's (20013) empirical investigation of infants' interactions and dialogues shows an 8-month-old girl's rejection of a 6-month-old girl, when being imitated by her. Children are imitated just as much as they imitate, although "just as much" signifies an average postulate, and says nothing about specific children's specific experiences, where an enormous variation is assumed. Potentially this represents a key to understanding human beings' development as persons in that it contains a *witnessing* of the imitated child's existence, an *implicit recognition* of this living and therefore a possibility of adding value to the personal being, using the terminology of Stern. Of course, this is an empirical matter, but the data points our attention in this direction.

30.4 General Conclusion: Cultural Life Course and the Development of Children as Persons

Based on the above, the main question within the presented cultural life-course perspective is how different collective spheres of meaning-production in the person's life-space and life-time become meaningful parts of his or her life and resources for the construction of a personal cultural life course (Villadsen & Hviid, 2016a). We have in other publications examined this perspective in relationship to play (Hviid & Villadsen, 2017), education (Hviid, 2015; Hviid & Villadsen, 2014; Villadsen & Hviid, 2016a), developmental situations of uncertainty (Dalgård & Hviid, 2016; Pultz & Hviid, 2016), and in more general methodological terms (Villadsen & Hviid, 2016b; Hviid & Villadsen, 2016; Lundmann & Villadsen, 2016).

In this chapter, we have applied this perspective and developed it in relation to the question of children's becoming as persons while emphasizing the dynamic processes of children's transforming engagements. Through the investigation we have pointed out general dimensions of the process of living, which we found in concrete and uniquely configured forms at the level of each child's personal life. Therefore a standardized approach – in terms of methods and analytical tools – to the development of children as persons generate a barrier to the recognition of the dynamicity and variety of processes, which cooperate in making the (develop)mental processes meaningful to the living person. The overall conclusion of the analysis in this chapter is that knowledge on the development of persons and their construction of a personal cultural life course must be built from an idiographic methodology (Hviid & Villadsen, 2016; Salvatore & Valsiner, 2010). Hence the cultural life course perspective abandon the objective perspective of the sample average and starts its inquiry at the everyday life of the person in her sociocultural world.

The notion of *everyday life* have traditionally added to the conceptualization of children's development in terms of the child's progressive adaptations and internalization of collective meanings through participation in institutionally organized activities. In addition to this perspective, the cultural life-course perspective emphasizes that it must mean something to be a living being, taking part in the cultural (re)production and that these meanings, as they are experienced by the person, become the basis for his or her future participation in the cultural production (Villadsen & Hviid, 2016a). By emphasizing this dimension, cultural life-course studies seek to build a base from where the personal life course can be investigated and conceptualized as a general process in which the person – in the company of others – co-construct her life course, in a personal as well as collectively purposeful and meaningful manner. Hence the cultural life-course perspective aims at bringing the notion of person and purpose back in the center of psychological inquiry at the level of general theory. This telos is neither unique nor new in psychology and the works of thinkers like Stern and Baldwin have been excellent in constructing the question which psychology hundred years later still has to answer.

Notes

1 The empirical investigation was conducted by first author, Pernille Hviid. We will, however continue the chapter in a "we"-format for the sake of dissemination.

2 All societies establish childhood arrangements for their children (Cole, 1996) but I said "Denmark" trying to make my question a bit more contextual than saying "societal."

3 "Grade zero" is in Denmark the first grade in elementary school. The historical reason for the awkward name is related to the transformation of the educational practice from a pedagogically designed "institution-introductory grade," especially for children who had not previously attended preschool, to an ordinary school grade with educational aims. Children normally are not aware of this history, and properly reads "zero" as signifying their position.

References

Baldwin, J. M. (1892). Feeling, belief and judgement. *Mind*, n.s., 1(3), 403–408.

Baldwin, J. M. (1899/2007). *The Story of the Mind*. London: G. Newness.

Baldwin, J. M. (1902). *Fragments in Philosophy and Science: Being Collected Essays and Addresses*. New York: C. Scribner's Sons.

Baldwin, J. M. (1911). *The Individual and the Society*. Boston: Richard G. Badger.

Baldwin, J. M. (1930). James Mark Baldwin. In Murchison (Ed.), *A History of Psychology in Autobiography* (vol. 1, pp. 1–30). New York: Russell & Russell.

Beebe, B. (2006). Co-constructing infant–mother distress in face-to-face interactions: Contributions of microanalysis. *Infant Observation*, 9(2), 151–164.

Bergson, H. (1907/1915). *Den skabende udvikling.* [The creative development]. Copenhagen: Gads Forlag.

Borsboom, D., Kievit, R. A., Cervone, D., & Hood, S. B. (2009). The two disciplines of scientific psychology, or: The disunity of psychology as a working hypothesis In J. Valsiner (Ed.), *Dynamic Process Methodology in the Social and Developmental Sciences* (pp. 67–98). New York: Springer.

Cole, M. (1996). *Cultural Psychology: A Once and Future Discipline*. Cambridge, MA: Harvard University Press.

Danziger, K. (1990). *Constructing the Subject: Historical Origins of Psychological Research*. New York: Cambridge University Press.

Dalgård, N. & Hviid, P. (2016). Exploring the transgenerational transmission of trauma in a cultural life course perspective. In T. Sato, N. Mori, & J. Valsiner (Eds.), *Making the Future: The Trajectory Equifinality Model in Culture and Psychology* (pp. 67–86). Charlotte, NC: Information Age Publishing.

Elder, G. & Shanahan, M. J. (2006). The life course and human development. In R. Lerner & W. Damon (Eds.), *Handbook of Child Psychology* (vol. 1, pp. 668–715). Hoboken, NJ: John Wiley & Sons.

Fuhrer, U. (2004). *Cultivating Minds: Identity as Meaning-Making Processes*. London: Routledge.

Hviid, P. (2008). Interviewing using a cultural-historical approach. In M. Hedegaard & M. Fleer (with J. Bang & P. Hviid) (Eds.), *Studying Children: A Cultural-Historical Approach* (pp. 139–156). London: Open University Press.

Hviid, P. (2012). "Remaining the same" and children's experience of development. In M. Hedegaard, K. Aronsson, C. Højholt, & O. Ulvik (Eds.), *Children, Childhood and Everyday life: Children's Perspectives* (pp. 37–52). Charlotte, NC: Information Age Publishing.

Hviid, P. (2015). Borders in education and living – a case of trench warfare. *Integrative Psychological and Behavioral Science*, 50(1), 44–61.

Hviid, P. & Beckstead, Z. (2011). Dialogues about research. In M. Märtsin, B. Wagoner, E.-L. Aveling, I. Kadianaki, & L. Whittaker (Eds.), *Dialogicality in Focus: Challenges to Theory, Method and Application* (pp. 147–163). New York: Nova Science Publishers.

Hviid, P. & Villadsen, J. W. (2014). Cultural identities and their relevance to school practice. *Culture & Psychology*, 20(1), 59–69.

Hviid, P. & Villadsen, J. W. (2015). Ruptures and repairs in the cause of living – challenges to developmental psychology. In A. Joerchel & G. Benetka (Eds.), *Biographical Ruptures and Their Repair: Cultural Transitions in Development* (pp. 57–82). Charlotte, NC: Information Age Publishing.

Hviid, P. & Villadsen, J. W. (2016). Guided Intervention: Dynamics of the unique and the general. In G. Sammut, J. Foster, S. Salvatore, & R. Andrisano-Ruggieri (Eds.), *Methods of Psychological Intervention* (Yearbook of Idiographic Science, vol. 7, pp. 203–226). Charlotte, NC: Information Age Publishers.

Hviid, P. & Villadsen, J. W. (2017). Playing and being: Imagination in the life course. In T. Zittoun & V. Glăveanu (Eds.), *Handbook of Imagination and Culture* (pp. 137–166). Oxford: Oxford University Press.

Kreppner, K. (1992). William L. Stern, 1871–1938: A neglected founder of developmental psychology. *Developmental Psychology*, 28(4), 539–547.

Lamiell, J. T. (2009a). Psychology and personalism by William Stern. *New Ideas in Psychology*, 28, 110–114.

Lamiell, J. T. (2009b). Reviving person-centered inquiry in psychology: Why its erstwhile dormancy? In J. Valsiner, P. Molenaar, M. Lyra, & N. Chaudhary (Eds.), *Dynamic Process Methodology in the Social and Developmental Sciences* (pp. 31–43). New York: Springer.

Lamiell, J. T. (2010). *William Stern (1871–1938): A Brief Introduction to His Life and Works.* Lengerich, Germany: Pabst Science Publishers.

Lamiell, J. T. (2015). Personalistic undertones in *The Life Space of the Urban Child*. In G. Mey & H. Günther (Eds.) *The Life Space of the Urban Child: Perspectives on Martha Muchow's Classic Study.* (pp. 161–176) New Brunswick, NJ: Transaction Publishers.

Lave, J. & Wenger, E. (1991). *Situated Learning: Legitimate Peripheral Participation.* Cambridge: Cambridge University Press.

Lehmann-Muriithi, K., de Resende Damas Cardoso, C., & Lamiell, J. T. (2016). Understanding human being within the framework of William Stern's critical personalism: Teleology, holism, and valuation. In J. Valsiner, G. Marsico, N. Chaudhary, T. Sato, & V. Dazzani (Eds.), *Psychology as the Science of Human Being: The Yokohama Manifesto* (pp. 209–223) Switzerland: Springer.

Lundmann, L. & Villadsen, J. W. (2016). Qualitative variations in personality inventories: Subjective understandings of items in a personality inventory. *Qualitative Research in Psychology*, 13(2), 166–187.

Mammen, J. (1996). Erkendelse som genstandsmæssig virksomhed: Et svar til Jesper Döpping [Recognition as an object of business: A response to Jesper Döpping]. In M. Hedegaard, (Ed.), *Praksisformers forandring: Personlig udvikling* [Change of practices: Personal development] (pp. 255–276) Aarhus, Denmark: Aarhus University Press.

Muchow, M. & Muchow, H. H. (2015). The life space of the urban child. In G. Mey & H. Gunther (Eds.), *The Life Space of the Urban Child:*

Perspectives on Martha Muchow's Classic Study (pp. 63–146). London: Transaction Publishers.

Neugarten, D. A. (1996). *The Meanings of Age.* London: University of Chicago Press.

Pultz, S. & Hviid, P. (2016). Imagining a better future: Young unemployed people and the polyphonic choir. *Culture & Psychology*, [online]. DOI: 10.1177/1354067X16660853.

Rogoff, B. (1990). *Apprenticeship in Thinking: Cognitive Development in Social Context.* New York: Oxford University Press.

Salvatore, S. & Valsiner, J. (2010). Between the general and the unique: Overcoming the nomothetic versus idiographic opposition. *Theory & Psychology*, 20, 817–833.

Schön, D. A. (1983). *The Reflective Practitioner: How Professionals Think in Action.* New York: Basic Books.

Selby, J. M. & Bradley, B. S. (2003). Infants in groups: A paradigm for the study of early social experience. *Human Development*, 46, 197–221.

Simmel, G. (1997). On the concept of culture. In D. Frisby & M. Featherstone (Eds.), *Simmel on Culture: Selected Writings* (pp. 36–40). London: SAGE.

Stern, D. N. (1985). *The Interpersonal World of the Infant.* New York: Basic Books.

Stern, W. (1938). *General Psychology: From the Personalistic Standpoint.* New York: Macmillan.

Tudge, J., Putnam, S., & Valsiner, J. (1996). Culture and cognition in developmental perspective. In R. B. Cairns, G. H. Elder, & E. J. Costello (Eds.), *Developmental Science* (pp. 190–223). Cambridge: Cambridge University Press.

Valsiner, J. (1997). *Culture and the Development of Children's Action* (2nd ed). New York: John Wiley & Sons.

Valsiner, J. (2012). *A Guided Science.* New Brunswick, NJ: Transaction Publishers.

Valsiner, J. (2015). From person-oriented to person-centered psychology: Abstracting structures of relationships. *Journal of Person-Oriented Research*, 1(1–2), 7–14.

Valsiner, J. & Van der Veer, R. (2000). *The Social Mind: Construction of the Idea.* Cambridge: Cambridge University Press.

Villadsen, J. W. & Hviid, P. (2016a). The history of children's engagements in Danish child care. In C. Ringsmose & G. Kragh-Müller (Eds.), *The Nordic Social Pedagogical Approach to Early Years Learning* (pp. 43–62). Hamburg: Springer.

Villadsen, J. W. & Hviid, P. (2016b). From battlefield to playground: A productive position for the future of psychology. In C. A. C. Cunha & H. Min (Eds.), *The Subjectified and Subjectifying Mind* (Advances in Cultural Psychology, pp. 209–224). Charlotte, NC: Information Age Publishing.

Vygotsky, L. (1927/1997). The historical meaning of the crisis in psychology: A methodological investigation. In R. W. Rieber & J. Wollock (Eds.), *Collected Works. Vol. III: Problems of the Theory and History of Psychology* (pp. 233–344). New York: Kluwer Academic/Plenum Publishers.

Further Reading

Billmann-Mahecha, E. (2015). Martha Muchow's life space study in the context of contemporary childhood and adolescent research. In G. Mey & H. Günther (Eds.), *The Life Space of the Urban Child: Perspectives on Martha Muchow's Classic Study*. (pp. 47–59) London: Transaction Publishers.

31 The Construction of the Person in the Interethnic Situation: Dialogues with Indigenous University Students

Danilo Silva Guimarães and Marília Antunes Benedito

Because I come from the wilderness, from the *cerrado*,[1] from the country, in the woods, from the ranch in the *caatinga*,[2] I hardly go out, I have almost no friends, I can hardly bare staying in the city without being upset.

Lamento sertanejo,[3] song by Gilberto Gil and Dominguinhos

The aim of this chapter is to discuss psychological processes involved in the construction of the person in interethnic situations. The main conceptual reference discussed here is the semiotic–cultural constructivism in psychology (see Simão, 2010), a theoretical–methodological perspective concerned particularly with the investigation of personal development. The observation of relational processes involving I–other differences and the efforts they originate toward the construction of meaning are considered central to the understanding of symbolic transformations in the cultural field. From this framework, we argue in favor of the use of the notion of person in opposition to the notion of subject, because, as Cornejo (2015) stated, the notion of person addresses an empirical instance, and "inhabiting definite portions of a real space and of a real time" (James, 1890, p. 183).

The person constructs his/her self through dynamic processes of differentiation/dedifferentiation/new differentiations from others (Guimarães, 2016a). Therefore, the Amerindian construction of the person can never be fixed on a static identity, although the self's ethnic-affirmation is central in the interethnic situation:

This idea of the evidence of the I and the non-evidence of the others, that presided at the birth of our modern metaphysics, is the exact opposite of the indigenous metaphysics, according to which it is in fact the I who is at risk. One is never sure who one is, because others might have a very different idea about it, and manage to impose it on ourselves. (Viveiros de Castro, 2007)

Our research originally aimed to comprehend what the indigenous students think about being Indian today, by identifying the symbolic resources (see Chapter 10, this volume) used by them to support their ethnic self-identification in the urban context and how they evaluate the possible differences between their worldviews and those of elder people from their communities of origin. We performed semi-structured interviews with five indigenous university students. The interviews were filmed and transcribed for posterior analysis, with the free and clarified consent of all participants, in accordance to the norms required by CONEP/Brazil.

While discussing the obtained results, we established interdisciplinary articulations with information originated from anthropological, historical, and socio-demographic studies. We liaised also with discourses expressed by organized indigenous movements and other studies concerning indigenous conceptions on basic and academic education in schools and at the university. The interpretative analysis of the data was conducted according to a specific dialogical approach, combining a descendent analytic trajectory with an ascendant interpretative trajectory (Guimarães, 2016b). That is, we first organized a systematic evaluation of the focused theme-field (Spink, 2003). We then mapped some antinomies related to this theme-field, uttered in the speeches of the interviewed participants, and identified the expressive aspect associated with them. Finally, we rearticulated the selected utterances with our aim of study, creating a new, supposedly more elaborated understanding of the whole situation.

From the selected discussion presented here, we expect to make clear that the dedifferentiation/differentiation process is a cultural resource of the Amerindian academics to cope with the open-ended transformations of the environment, social relationships, and personal aspirations, allowing conviviality with the difference instead of authoritatively directing it.

31.1 Between Forest and City: The Discourse of Indigenous University Students

We selected from the answers of each participant the excerpts we considered most significant to address the tensions experienced by the students between what they understand as the way of life, the conceptions, and the ethnic-cultural values of their communities of origin and those that concern life in the urban context and academic education. All participants resided, at the time of the interview, in the urban context and were enrolled in higher education at two universities of the state of São Paulo. Their admission occurred by means of affirmative policies implemented by these universities. It is relevant to take into consideration that to participate in these affirmative policies the students needed to present substantial evidence

of their indigenousness, that is, by presenting letters from the communitarian chiefs asserting their belonging to the ethnic group and/or official documentation from the National Indian Foundation – FUNAI, Brazil.[4]

For ethical reasons, the names, ethnic group, and university of the participants were omitted, besides other information that could compromise confidentiality.

31.1.1 Participant A, Belonging to an Ethnic Group from the Brazilian Northeast

Many peoples of the Brazilian northeast, especially those who lived on the banks of the San Francisco River, intensely resisted the colonial enterprise, aimed to reduce mobility between neighboring villages and communities, assembling people in common settlements adapted to the farming culture and introduced in a rigid power structure. Since the 1950s, a great number of indigenous people from the northeast migrated to São Paulo in a process of ethnic reterritorialization:

Initially there was a flow of men only, who left the indigenous area to work for short periods in São Paulo, as a form of balancing the home budget in years of drought or in emergency situations. Without integrating themselves to the city, they always returned as soon as immediate necessities were covered or when a good winter announced itself. (Arrutti, 2005)

Participant A was born and raised in the area of traditional occupation of his people. He reported opting, after having concluded high school seven years ago, coming to São Paulo where his siblings already lived to attend university. The participant said that, once this goal is fulfilled, he intends on going back to his community. In spite of the opportunities of knowledge and employment the city offers, he states feeling "imprisoned" and that his "mind is there [in the village]." When questioned about the differences he sees between his people's traditional form of knowledge construction and the form proposed by the university, he points to the issue of work:

A: ...here either you work or you starve to death, there you don't...the first thing my father always taught me there was how to hunt, to work, not how to work as an electrician like that, to work during a part of the day. At night we went to school, but they always taught us the rituals, the *toré*.[5] ...

RESEARCHER: And when you come here how do these issues sound to you?

A: There you have those prayers, you have another view on things, you feel free as a bird. Here you don't, you feel caged, living in these apartment[s], there is no space for us to sing, to have our *toré*, our dance, it's very difficult. If you do it at one of those apartments, people start bothering, annoying us... then you have to stop. Here...we still do it, but still you have to pick a spot. Not there. There if we want to do something we do it at our own house, or instead in a yard... It has to be a big yard... there has to be a very big space, because it's a lot of people. Now here we have no means of doing that... here I feel very imprisoned. I always say I don't want to get old here, I want to finish my graduation and go back, because my goal was to come here to study, that's it. But work, I'm an electrician, I've already had some dangerous jobs... but that's that... Around here is really different from the village, because here when you step on the ground you step on what? There you walk on the land, there you have land to your heart's content. Not here, here you walk on cement and to begin with if you're going to do a dance there, you do it on dirt, and here, where would you do it?

During the interview, A reports the relevance of conviviality in the community as a form of recognition of his ethnic belonging; this includes the possibility of performing rituals which usually depend on the presence of other people and an adequate space. Therefore, for him, presence in the community allows establishing a transgener-

ational link between the person, the previous generations, and the future ones:

A: So, after you spend a long time here, the people that...when you left there you already knew, relating with them is much easier. Now, to relate, to get in touch with those that have been born and that don't remember is much harder. Because, since they don't remember even they can know that I'm not an indigenous person, isn't it? But it is very hard, that's why I want to go back there, I want to live with them, to me it is very important. Here I feel like I know nobody, it is very hard. You know people from everyday life, from work, you spend more hours at work than at home, you know them, but it's not like with people from our place.

We highlight, from the interview, some antinomies identified by participant A: the contradiction between ritualized practices of his people and the everyday practices of work in the urban context; the relation between the body and the earth, brought by the possibility of stepping on the earth versus the impossibility of doing this in the paved ground of the cities; the relation between ethnic recognition and conviviality, emphasizing the difficulty in getting to know people profoundly with the fragmented forms of conviviality and neighborhood life provided by the urban context. There is additionally a consideration about being in the open space opposed to life in small apartments, characteristic of the urban context. The last situation does not allow freedom of movement, dancing, and other ritual practices, leading the participant to differentiate himself from the citizens,[6] frequently reaffirming that in the city he feels "imprisoned."

31.1.2 Participant B, Belonging to an Ethnic Group Originally from the Brazilian Northeast

The second participant interviewed was a woman born in a county in the state of São Paulo. She reported that her grandparents came to the city where she lives, she being therefore the second generation born in the urban context. Even though she thinks her family is isolated from the rest of the relatives, she stated keeping in touch with the village by means of constant visits to the native land of her grandparents:

B: So, actually, I wasn't born in the village, my dad was born here too, in São Paulo, my grandparents were born in the village, they were raised there, and I think my grandmother came here to São Paulo when she was about fifteen, together with my grandfather basically because of work. Then they constituted a family here, even here in São Paulo, so, and I've always had contact with the village, because, as is the custom of even my grandfather, you know, of not losing the rituals, of the contact, of showing us where they came from, of giving strength to the indigenous culture. We are always visiting the village, so, like, once a year, we usually went there to visit, so, I know the village, I've been there many times, but I never lived there.

In spite of the interest and the efforts toward an ethnic self-affirmation, the family's arrival at the urban context left marks in her process of subjectivation, which made her question herself for some time as an indigenous person. According to her report, the doubt persisted until she obtained support from her relatives and felt herself valued in her indigenous ethnic belonging through the affirmative policies destined to promote admission of indigenous persons at the university:

B: I confess that to me it was very strange, thinking that for the fact of me not be . . . that I was not born in the village, you know, I . . . sometimes I found myself in the conflict: "but am I an indigenous person?" "I'm not an indigenous person, you see, because I wasn't born in the village, I don't have the customs they have." And it was something that here . . . together with other colleagues that we . . . that I recovered this in me, that I truly am an indigenous person. I have to recognize myself, you know, and reaffirm myself as an indigenous person, which was something that up until then

was very difficult, both to assume internally and transmit to others, because there is still that stereotype that the indigenous person walks around, you know, naked. You say that in school, imagine that, in high school, I would ever say I was an indigenous person. I always had contact, because . . . my cousin who graduated here, I had an aunt who was really involved as an activist, like, of the indigenous issue, so they were always taking us to the events, so . . . I remember giving an interview to a local newspaper when I was very young, so I always had a contact with the indigenous issue, but it was kind of distant because at that time I didn't recognize myself [as an indigenous person], so it was always a conflict, you know. Then, when I became older, you know, in the second, third year, I began to research university courses, and then I saw the [program of selection and follow up of indigenous university students], talked to my cousin and began to refine that idea. Still I felt apprehensive. How will I access something that I didn't see as my right? You know, because until then I didn't see myself as an indigenous person. So I didn't have the right to the program, and that was little by little, with me talking to my cousin, reading a bit about it [program of selection and follow up of indigenous university students], searching the internet, the desire, of course, of attending [a quality] university, you know? Taking a course here, so, then all this began to motivate me to go after and pursue, and really try to pass the exam . . . So, then, to me it was a conquest, even with the scholarship, even knowing my entrance may have been made easier because of it. And not in the sense that "oh, they gave me this," I now understand it is a right, even because of the access denied to my father, of him not being able to, of my grandparents not being able to. So today I, you see, can do it paying for what they . . . being compensated for what they couldn't do. So, today I have this understanding.

The ambivalence of being or not an indigenous person expressed by the participant is renewed in a singular manner in the psychological sphere. The same happens in a social dimension to her ethnic group, not only in the urban context, but in their original lands, to the extent that the colonial process introduced changes in the ways of life of the entire population. Political participation, affirmative policies, and positive discrimination have an important role in the process of elaboration of such ambivalence, allowing a novel ethnic differentiation to emerge, after a conflictive process of dedifferentiation. The efforts in the direction of articulating distinct historical-cultural trajectories happen at different levels of the experience of ethnic self-affirmation and produce cultural hybrids:

B: So, actually, it's what I said to you the last time, it's like that to me still, before it was very confusing, because at the same time the Catholic Church is very present at the village. As I said, there's a church at the center of the village, the center of the village is a catholic church, so the very name of the village is [a name with a catholic reference], isn't it? I think there's even a historical issue which I don't completely master to say why it is called that way, but I believe there's an influence, you know, in the issue of Catholicism and so you can see it's remarkable that all indigenous people worship Catholicism a lot, but they didn't lose their own rituals . . . As I said, my grandmother for example and my grandfather, they are fervent Catholics. They go to church every Sunday, my grandmother is involved in pastoral care, has always been, even in coming here to the city, but at the same time, my grandfather, he never stopped chanting the songs, when someone comes to talk about the indigenous people, he gets his *maracá*[7] and sings. And when they go there, they participate in the rituals . . . There are some rituals that are particular of this ethnic group. The *toré* itself, which is common to other ethnic groups, which is a dance, and they do it, they participate. And it's like that, to Catholicism, I think it is a point of some conflict, isn't it? If a priest for example, sees a catholic doing . . . participating in the rituals, he will say the person is not a catholic, because they are rituals of those who believe in

the Enchanted, aren't they? They don't worship only . . . one God, you know? The Holy Trinity, no. They believe there are other deities, and so, that the indigenous people . . . can make this link, of Catholicism with their own rituals, and that later on I found this very beautiful. So, because even if there was an influence that I think that, there's no way, they resisted in some way, I think maintaining the rituals is a form of resistance. Showing that, in spite they were opened and many characteristics of the ethnic group were lost, the ritual is a powerful thing. Like the language, we don't have . . . the language, but, then, in the songs some words show up, some things that are proper . . . So it is a form of resistance, you know? In spite some were lost along the way because of this influence, but I think this union of both things is important, and achieving this in the city, I think, it's still more difficult, because it is seen with . . . with eyes, you see . . . always negative, isn't it? Everything that is not from the dominant church is always very negative. The matter of the Enchanted, the matter of there being those, you know? As I told you, there are, the clothes the Enchanted use . . .

And at home we have the images of the [Enchanted]. So, if suddenly someone comes home and sees that, they will at once say it is a negative thing, they at once associate it to other religions which are also seen as negative. So, I think it is really important to show that the dominant church is not the only religion, all are and deserve respect, even if they are opposite things. If those indigenous people managed to . . . unify these two things and be well, continue worshiping . . . what they believe in, I think that is important.

Participant B brings, among other themes, the issue of conviviality as a condition for ethnic recognition and self-affirmation and indicates the existence of a process of internalization of socially experienced conflicts in this scope. On one hand, the experience of situations of prejudice and, on the other, the possibility of having one's ethnicity valued leads to a tense process that tends to reach a solution with the encounter with a descriptive narrative of the historical process of the life trajectories of their ethnic group and of their relatives – and also through an aesthetic fruition of the culture to which one belongs or aims to belong. Finally, we note the effort of integration and coexistence with two ontologies: one that pursues identity and non-contradiction, distinctly expressed in the religion of Judeo-Christian origin and the indigenous possibility of coexisting with the opposites by means of a religiosity capable of encompassing the diverse.[8]

31.1.3 Participant C, Belonging to an Ethnic Group of the Brazilian Amazon

Participant C was born and raised in the area of traditional occupation of his people, in a territory that until half of the twentieth century was little known to the Brazilian government, in terms of the ethnic groups inhabiting that specific Amazonian region. Nowadays, in the Amazon, some dozens of indigenous peoples are isolated and protected from contact with the surrounding society. This is a right secured by the Brazilian legislation, due to the pernicious consequences of the occupation of their territories, which frequently led to the almost complete decimation of some peoples.[9] Only recently, has the missionary enterprise modified itself and strived to attenuate the authoritarianism with the recognition of the right of the indigenous peoples to their own culture. The history of the colonial process leaves inevitable marks in the ways of life of these populations, that:

On the other hand, incorporate a great number of merchandise and utensils produced by the surrounding society, with which they maintain commercial relations, obtaining monetary income in the last years mainly with the production and commercialization of rubber, nuts, and handcraft (their feather art is one of the most beautiful among the tribal groups of Brazil). Of the agricultural and collecting production for the market, performed under the command of the Jesuits during the first decades of contact, they passed to self-organization of the production and commercialization of rubber in the 1980s, through an internal cooperative, organized in consonance with their form of social life. (Arruda, 1998)

Participant C aims to take back to his community some of the knowledge from his academic education after graduating, when he intends on returning to his land of origin. In the interview, he comments on the contrast he lives when circling between these two worlds:

C: Look . . . when I'm in my community, they . . . don't receive me in a university kind of way. Arriving there I say . . . "I'll be like the indigenous people who left here and came back the [same] way." Only the way we work is different, you know? In this case, you arrive with some knowledge . . . , you try to clarify for them how it is, and then they understand, you know? So, they see that we are pursuing something, and wanting, well, some help, then . . . It's like I say, it's completely [different] from living in the city, where many times you live somewhere, let's say, well locked, where you don't try . . . If you have a neighbor close by, many times you're not usually going to the house. Now, inside the community no, you're free, you know? You can go wherever you [want]. Then you go to a colleague's house, a friend's, your sister's house, your aunt's, you . . . there's no special time for this, you know? Anytime you're going: "I'm not going just to stroll around or take a walk." So . . . like, you're at the same time there around the house, but you're trying . . . seeing what's happening in the community.

In his report, ethnic belonging indicates a possibility of transit seen as more free inside community life. The borders are more permeable or less noticed in a familiar situation, allowing him to make the interethnic mediation of the "knowledge" acquired in the academic environment:

C: Maintaining them and keeping up with both, because . . . It's like, many time[s] [someone] says "oh, today the native is not like in the old days," that time is already gone, isn't it? Previously, they already know how it is. Because many time[s] . . . there are [people] that, [speak] in the interview "oh, but do natives walk around naked inside the village?" People, that's long gone!

The effort of Amerindians who come to the universities in the urban context points also to the possibility of hosting difference in the forms of knowing the world. The interethnic mediation of knowledge produces impacts on people and communitarian life. In this sense, hosting alterity becomes a necessary condition to give strength to ethnic self-affirmation and depends on a sophisticated capacity to deal with the multiplicity of perspectives present in interethnic situations:

C: So we say this: since time is, since technology is advancing and we are trying to keep up too, because if we don't keep up who will [do it] for us too, you know? It's difficult. I say this: in general, I think we'll try, to keep up, right? We see it this way. We're trying to make it happen. Like in my community, I'm . . . going, following both, right? Neither leaving the culture, nor the other side. So, I'm following my rhythm.

We highlight, from the interview with participant C, the necessity of establishing a plan of coexistence between traditional knowledge from his ethnic group and the knowledge acquired through academic scientific education. This conciliatory effort is similar to that portrayed by participant B when she affirms the capacity of her culture to conciliate the Catholic religiosity and the belief in the enchanted. The capacity to let coexist, or to "carry on both," as the interviewee says, is possible by keeping one's own rhythm of attention, allowing an autonomously regulated interchange between conviviality in the urban and communitarian context.[10] Sometimes, it ends up in a sort of syncretism and hybridization (dedifferentiation between the self and the other); other

times, it is presented as a parallelism that does not achieve any synthesis (see Guimarães, 2016a).

31.1.4 Participant D, Belonging to an Ethnic Group of the Brazilian Amazon

Participant D was born and raised in the area of traditional occupation of his people, in the Amazonian northwest, where the history of contact of certain ethnic groups with the "white man" dates back to the eighteenth century, when their lands where occupied first by religious Jesuits and later by merchants and collectors:

Long migrations were concluded by the natives due to the escapes, certainly related, among other reasons, with the super-exploration by the merchants. What seems certain is that there were population downfalls in all the groups of the Içana and Xié in this period, propagating among the natives, in a deep and lasting manner, the horror in seeing any white man approaching their villages. In this sense, these reports reinforce the hypothesis that violence in both sides of the frontier caused the downfall not only of the indigenous population, but their compulsory migration first to Brazil then to Venezuela. (Meira, 2002)

Parallel to this context of violence, some interethnic marriages caused the miscegenation of the population in this region, creating bonds of kinship and interethnic intermediation. Participant D, in his turn, affirmed that before coming to São Paulo he lived in the indigenous county of São Gabriel da Cachoeira, where about 74 percent of the population self-declares as indigenous, divided in distinct ethnic groups, according to the IBGE (2012b). He reports yet that after concluding his academic education he intends on returning to his land of origin to develop projects related to education, since he considers education to be a "strong weapon" in the indigenous plight for their rights.

When asked, D reports a significant aspect of his experience of moving to the urban context in the state of São Paulo:

RESEARCHER: And do you remember the first time you came here? How did you feel here?

D: So, actually, I had never left the state [Amazon], you know? I had been to Manaus to spend a week, just that, but there as we are used to seeing many indigenous peoples in Manaus and all, we feel normal. The difference is [because] we see a lot of buildings, a big pollution, lack of structure in the city, and other things most states have. So... and then, I came... when I was admitted at the University... When I got here, everybody said, "oh, there's a native from the Amazon, how cool, so, the Indian is coming naked." If you talk about the Amazon, especially of the frontier with Colombia, people talked to me, and when I got here I suffered prejudice for being indigenous... for being an indigenous not-indigenous person, that is, for being a native who is not naked, who doesn't know how to speak, who doesn't have... you know, autonomy. Then, I had just arrived here and I was interviewed for the TV... So, they also asked all this, everybody asks and then I explained that the original peoples, for them to be able... for us to live in the white society, we have to benefit from all possible structures, so we can learn too and afterwards take it back to our community, do you understand?

Society's expectation of a stereotyped image of the Amazonian indigenous person is lived as prejudice, as is the search for an ethnic belonging supposedly pure and unchangeable throughout time. Despite these conflictive experiences of people and their own ethnic self-affirmation, D affirms the importance of recognition of the history of the indigenous peoples and the strategies they used in order to persist existing as a distinct ethnic group and culture, despite the inevitable transformations suffered throughout time (see Chapter 23, this volume). More than any objective characteristic that could identify his ethnic belonging, to him it is relevant to know the

historical-cultural process that allows the reconstruction of the ways of life of his ancestors, the possibilities and limits lived by his contemporaries.

When questioned about the reason that led him to enroll in a course at the university, he answers:

D: Yes. What motivated me was the meetings I went to, the young natives' meeting, that one touched me a lot. Because at the meetings, in the social movements, we study history, we study who suffered, how it happened, in other cities it's like this, who died, we tell history, the stories of our grandparents, you see, it touches us and our conscience... our view on things... it changes, you see?

The participant therefore highlights some aspects already pointed by the first participants: the importance of conviviality with indigenous persons in their comprehension of the historical process that justifies the current condition of their communities of origin. He highlighted, still, the relevance of political engagement for the constitution of a meaning for the pursuit of academic knowledge, redirecting their presence in the urban context to a protection of people and the values they bring from their communities.

31.1.5 Participant E, Belonging to an Ethnic Group of the Brazilian Amazon

Participant E was born and raised in an area of traditional indigenous occupation in the Amazonian northwest, where peoples living mainly on the banks of the Uaupés river constitute an intricate hierarchical articulation between different ethnic groups (cf. Arapaso, Bará, Barasana, Desana, Karapanã, Kotiria, Kubeo, Makuna, Miriti-tapuya, Pira-tapuya, Siriano, Taiwano, Tariana, Tatuyo, Tukano, Tuyuka, and Yuruti):

The history of the contact of the peoples of the Uaupés with the non-indigenous is very old, much older than the heyday of rubber at the turn of the twentieth century. It sends back to the massive incursions of the Portuguese in search of slaves in the first half of the eighteenth century. In spite of the impact these kidnappers produced and the traumatic and lasting contact with the rubber collectors, these merchants were more interested in the bodies of the natives than in their souls; in religious terms, and maybe in social terms also, the missionaries produced the greatest transformations. (ISA, 2002)

Born and raised in his community of origin, the interviewee reported having learned Portuguese at the age of 16. Yet he pointed to some consequences of the colonial process in his family and, consequently, in his education as a person belonging to an indigenous ethnic group:

RESEARCHER: How is your relation with the elders, the people who stayed at your village . . . how is it?

E: When I was born . . . my parents and grandparents, mostly my parents were civilized . . . according to standards of the Catholic religion, you see? Because in . . . 1945, around that time, most indigenous people lived in *malocas*,[11] a big *oca*,[12] where everybody had their place, there reserved space to be with their little girl, their little boy, their family, you see? Then there was a specific place. Then . . . what happened: . . . the priest[s] went there, got there, saw that according to the religion, that was not adequate, it was not acceptable . . . by the God, I don't know, something like that. Then they said: from now on you will have to . . . you will stop using the *tanga*,[13] you will . . . stop . . . dancing, doing the *pajelança*[14] and blessings, you see? Then they began restricting. Then a bit disappeared: you get sick, the relative who is sick was not blessed anymore, it has to be according to the medicine of the non-indigenous people. Then it began . . . then there was a little . . . you see, the culture . . . It didn't continue evolving. There was a regression, let's put it this way, because it was restricted, but . . . then we lost a little . . . only that later, my dad, when I was born my dad [and] my mom . . . my dad already had a

little house apart, he didn't live in the maloca anymore. Then it began, each one of them: my uncle, my aunt, each one had their corner, with a small straw house and all . . . Then they began to live on the river banks. Then the . . . the priest[s] themselves went there, they divided: from here on, this little ranch will be called Our Lady of Fatima, the other we'll call . . . the other little ranch up there will be called Saint John, Bela Vista, Saint Luzia and there off, you see? So my relation with the elder[s], before I didn't have much . . . like, I didn't give much value to it, I was too young, so . . . you understand? Since my father was . . . is . . . educated in the standards of the Catholic religion, my father didn't give me, you see, the biggest support: "son you need to learn to bless, to dance, and so on." So there was a bit of a . . . distancing from the culture and the elders, but later I saw, that really . . . I need . . . the indigenous culture, you see? But to speak, to speak [the language of my people], I speak it fluently, I speak with the elders, you see? So they think I'm a *caboclo*[15] from the region who doesn't speak [the indigenous language]. Then I . . . I say this: "do you speak it [the indigenous language]?" "Yes." "So speak [in that language] and it will be more . . . interactive," you see? Then I speak [in my language], you see? My relation with the elders has become more interesting . . . But, since I lost my father early, I didn't have the . . . proximity with the . . . with the elders to try to learn blessings, the dance, our origin, you see? But, after I . . . I saw I was losing a lot of important things, then I began to search for, you see? Now, I have a lot of interest, more respect for . . . my ethnic group, my origins.

Despite considering the knowledge acquired in his higher education should be taken back as a contribution to his community, the interviewee realizes there is a great difficulty in expressing his culture in the urban context and at the university. Contrasting his way of life to the urban/academic way of life, he was able to reflect on the processes of dedifferentiation historically imposed by the religious missions and consider his present conflictive opportunity to construct himself as a person who reveals a novel differentiation articulated to his ethnic belonging:

RESEARCHER: How do you feel the fact that being in the city transforms your relation with your traditional culture?

E: Well, that is a bit complicated, because you don't have a place for you to . . . a proper place to do a dance, expose . . . domestic utensils, you don't have . . . you don't have space, you feel . . . your surrounding is completely different. You don't have a space to express yourself, to manifest yourself, dance, do other things, so, it's a totally separated world, you're here, your world is small, but you're there, you're a native. Only if there was space to manifest, to show the dance, then it would be an environment where you could even show where you came from, who you are, here you're in a place that is totally closed to you, you understand? You see, here, there's not one indigenous person doing presentations, saying . . . that I'm an indigenous person, I'm from that and that ethnic group, you don't have that . . . this channel to show, you see? So you stay in a closed environment, which doesn't give you any opportunity to come like, hey, I'm an indigenous person, let's dance, let's do this and that demonstration, there isn't, you see? This, in the condition of indigenous person, you see? This is lacking.

Participant E resumes central themes from the previous interviews, concerning the restrictions to perform their rituals and the contrast between two forms of spatial organization, in the community and in the city, where in the urban context the possibility of giving visibility to the indigenous way of life seems restricted due to the division/allotment of space. This same type of division has been imposed on communities in their original territories as a form of colonizing thought and the traditional ways of life, as is pointed in the disorganization of the *malocas* and the settlement in residences for each nuclear family. The process of naming communities with religious names also semiotically forced an appropriation of the territory and of the indige-

nous meanings connected to it. The movements of resistance to this process, however, persist in the singular pursuit of the Indigenous university students to reclaim the ancestral knowledge in the dialogue with those who keep the memories from the old days.

31.2 Migration to the Urban Context and the Search for Academic Education

Being an indigenous person is not a question of feather *cocar*,[16] *urucum*,[17] and bow and arrow, something apparent and evident in this stereotyping way, but a question of "state of the spirit." A way of being and not of appearing. Actually, something more (or less) than a way of being: Indianness designated to us a certain way of becoming, something essentially invisible but not less effective: an infinitesimal incessant movement of differentiation, not a massive state of "difference" anteriorized and established, that is, an identity. (It would be good if anthropologists would one day stop calling identity difference and vice versa.) Our struggle was, therefore, conceptual: our problem was getting the "still" of the common sense judgment "these guys are still indigenous people" (or "not anymore") not to signify a transitory state or a stage to be overcome. The idea was that the indigenous people had "still" not been won, and that they never would be. They never concluded nor would conclude being indigenous people, "even if still" . . . Or precisely because of it. In short, the idea was that being "indigenous" could not be seen as a stage in the ascending march to an enviable state of "white" or "civilized." (Viveiros de Castro, 2006, p. 3)

The comprehension of the processes of differentiation/dedifferentiation/new differentiations from the others emerged in our research as an alternative to face the limitations of the notion of identity articulated to the notion of property (Guimarães, 2016a). On one hand, our preliminary studies discussed the articulation between the notions of self and identity as problematic to the understanding of the construction of the person in non-Eurocentric cultural contexts (see Guimarães, 2013). On the other hand, it is relevant to say that the construction of a rigid criterion to define Amerindian identity is an aim of the Brazilian State, so as to determine the coverage of public policies (cf. Viveiros de Castro, 2006). This usually produces aberrant classifications in the fluid, processual, and impermanent Amerindian processes of self-affirmation. Considering the complexity and diversity of the notions of identity in contemporary studies, including the non-essentialist versions of the term, it is relevant to stress that a careful discussion on it is not presented in this chapter. Nevertheless, this topic is a thorn in the side of researchers that aim to collaborate with the complex contemporary political scenario, in which the demarcation of ethnic identity is a device with ideological use in the elaboration of public policies for Amerindians in Brazil.

Currently, 36 percent of the population who self-declares as indigenous in Brazil lives in urban areas (IBGE, 2012a). The indigenous presence in the cities is not recent, but as the first Brazilian urban settlements were constructed in territories traditionally occupied by the indigenous peoples, in the same place or close to where there communities were, these cities benefited from the indigenous knowledge and workforce, including slave work, for their development (Monteiro, 1994). In many cases, the reorganization of the ways of life of the indigenous people in settlements, as rural or urban workers, led to a process of concealment of their cultural bonds, objectified in the acts of religious missionaries and, later, of the Brazilian state:

The systematization of the pedagogical procedures elaborated by the Society of Jesus in the sixteenth century . . . materialized themselves . . . from the missionary experiences, from the realities experienced by the Jesuits in their work of

repression and truth speaking. Repressing the indigenous traditions, considered as examples of bad manners, signs of evil, and saying the truth about the malignity of the native customs, which should be substituted by the good customs, expression of knowledge of the true faith. Evidently, all of this process was supported in teaching, in education. (Costa, 2007)

Until the second half of the twentieth century, the political project of whitening and miscegenation of the Brazilian population aimed to promote, in a violent manner, the oblivion of some versions of history, languages, and millennial cultural practices characteristic of the diverse original peoples:

After independence, the new Brazilian imperial state faced the challenge of creating a nation and its corresponding people, until then inexistent. It was necessary to build a territorial, political, and ideological unity, producing a collective memory that could unify the populations under a single identity. The ethnical and cultural plurality, now highly valued, had no place at that time, and the ideology of the new Brazilian state was founded on European values of modernization, progress, and the superiority of the white man. (Almeida, 2012)

Education, as always, has an important role reproducing the Eurocentric ideology, but it is also a source of transformation of such ideology through the promotion of critical reflection in the population (see Moura & Guimarães, 2013). It was only with the 1988 Federal Constitution of Brazil that "the rights to their own social organization, customs, languages, beliefs, and traditions, as well as the original right to the lands they traditionally occupied, where recognized, competing to the union the duty to demarcate them, protect and guarantee respect for all their assets" (Brasil Constituição, 1988/2012, p. 130). From juridical recognition to the effectuation of the indigenous populations' rights, however, there is a great distance. In this sense, the current migration of indigenous people to the cities can only be understood as part of a colonial and postcolonial historical process, which involves the relation between the Brazilian society and the different original peoples. On the other hand, little is known of what these displacements meant from the point of view of the migrators.

A study performed with 402 indigenous people residing in five Brazilian cities (Venturi & Bokany, 2013) showed that 68 percent of them claimed the reasons for leaving their communities were economical (search for work, money, a better life, access to food, etc.). Social and familiar reasons, such as the reunion with relatives or marriages, were also significantly mentioned, as well as the search for medical treatment, the existence of internal conflicts, or conflicts surrounding the land. However, one of the strongest reasons for migration, claimed by 27 percent of the participants, was the demand for education (32% of the indigenous persons affirmed this was one of the best things offered by the city); access to the university stood out as one of the goals of this population (Venturi & Bokany, 2013).

Community leaders and indigenous movements feel it is necessary to have forms of activism that act inside the representative and operational governmental agencies. To this end, the Eurocentric origin is still upheld as being important and dominate not only the language, but also mathematics, technical-scientific knowledge, social sciences, and law, among others. The pursuit of academic education stems from a need to take control of territorial management, to strengthen the autonomy of the communities, to legitimate their own conceptions of development, and potentialize the indigenous capacity of social intervention inside and outside the community (UFRGS, 2013, pp. 129–130).

Parallel to the construction of discourses and images that contribute toward removing the Amerindian peoples as historical subjects, the communities are slowly moving from an invisibility built along the nineteenth century to a protagonist role reclaimed by political and intellectual movements with intense indigenous participation (Almeida, 2012). In this context, formal education is, although growing, still low among the indigenous population in the urban context: only 2 percent of the participants interviewed in Venturi and Bokany's research (2013) received higher education.

Among the indigenous populations there seem to be two expectations in relation to academic education: on one extreme, attending university signifies acquiring knowledge that is valued by the Eurocentric society to use it as an instrument in favor of their own communities. Other positions in the indigenous movement claim, still, a higher education guided by the intercultural dialogue:

The post-contact historical movement forced our peoples to innumerous adaptations to the "knowledge of the whites," the inverse never happened. Our knowledge is treated as cultural heritage, as if all those who have this knowledge were extinct, they talk about the contribution of the indigenous peoples to the constitution of the Brazilian culture, but limit these contributions to a few words from the native languages incorporated in the vocabulary of the Portuguese language. The universities contribute the perpetuation of this movement when they treat the indigenous issue only in the anthropology, history, linguistics, and ethnology classes. Medicine school has also much to learn with the knowledge of our peoples in the prevention, treatment, and cure of illness, engineering, agronomy, pedagogy, architecture and so many others could also learn, in a plural exchange. But it is easier to silence and ignore than to learn from the different, who is treated in Brazilian culture as the inferior. (Fernandes, 2007, p. 11)

We therefore note that the indigenous peoples also strive for a reversal from the uneven positions in the Brazilian society, by means of a redefinition of the criteria for authorizing the said scientific knowledge. Until then, this process of reversal was focused predominantly in the confrontation with the religious discourse pro-fessed by the missionaries who tried to convert the Amerindians to the Christian cosmovision, as seen in some of the excerpts from the interviews presented in this chapter. More recently, however, another issue surfaced: it is the pretentious sci-entific discourses that need to be appropriated and reversed in order not to exert a destructive colonialist role in the historic conceptions of the indigenous traditions.

Consequently, indigenous students organized in student movements are building narratives that orient the form of relating and the dialogue with the universities that they attend:

We have to highlight the importance of this meeting [1st National Meeting of Indigenous Students] as a form of giving more visibility to the indigenous students inside the schooling institutions. This allows not only non-indigenous students and professors to get to know and recognize the existence and the presence of these students in the academic space but also allows an increment in the fronts of support to the demands of the indigenous peoples. Since one of the points accorded at the end of the meeting was the need of decolonization, the occupation of the academic space (not only with the presence of indigenous students in their courses, but also with the occupation of the physical spaces of the university provided by this meeting) is a very important step toward the decolonization of an ambience that is fundamentally elitist and marked by a pretentiously superior and excluding knowledge.

The universities need to start getting in touch with the indigenous peoples of Brazil's reality and open themselves to the indigenous knowledge and wisdom, understanding them not only as "popular knowledge," but recognizing the foundations of this knowledge and its validity, even if not proven by the academic science. (ENEI, 2013, p. 21)

The scientific knowledge is, therefore, seen as knowledge that perpetuates colonization. The university is another space to be decolonized by means of a greater participation and involve-ment of the communities in the definition of goals, evaluation, and execution of academic actions, revising the pedagogical conducts and traditional theoretical contents so that they dia-logue with the indigenous knowledge without these being subjugated (Fernandes, 2007). The connection between knowledge and power is being discussed in many academic forums, espe-cially because scientists have historically appro-priated the Amerindian knowledge to develop their "findings" without acknowledging them (see Von Lewinsky, 2004; Zanirato & Ribeiro, 2007). Another issue, focused by the indige-nous academics is related to the social valua-tion of their knowledge as fiction in opposition to the supposedly reliable scientific knowledge (see Guimarães, 2011; 2012). The indigenous aca-demics present this problem as a sort of reedition of the imposition of Christianization, now with the flag of science.

It is also due to psychology, as a science and as a profession, to reflect on its role in the reproduc-tion and critical transformation of the multieth-nic spaces of our society, aiming to produce less hierarchical and more dialogical spaces among people, culture, and knowledge (see Guimarães, 2012).

31.3 Ethnic Diversity in the Urban Context: Implications to Psychology

When He made this earth, the whole world, He didn't say, this part is for the white people, this is for the black, this one is for the blue, this for the indigenous people, and this one I don't know who it is for. He didn't say this. It wasn't made only for the indigenous people, no, this land was made for everybody. For everybody to live in. But in this land we keep fighting. (Speech by indigenous leader Carlito de Oliveira, Guarani Kaiowa, in an interview in the documentary "À Sombra de um Delírio Verde"; Baccaert, Navarro & Um, 2011)

In cultural psychology, the notion of self is understood as a psychological field that covers the multiplicity of social positions singularly internalized from a person's experience in a wider sociocultural context that includes other people and the life world. The self could then be considered the place of the diverse in the person, a field of occupation and cultivation of culture, with its semi-permeable frontiers to dialogue. But how to understand the relations between the internalized positions that live within the self – which are at times conflictive – and their frontier with the others and the world?

The distinct positions in dialogue produce tension in the frontiers between distinct apprehensions of the socially represented objects, which dynamically transform at the same time as the participants in the dialogue are transformed (Marková, 2006). The culture's symbolism develops with the articulations between subjective connotations and consensual denotations, which people build about the world, theirs and others' (Boesch, 1991). The relations of the person in the world with others leave vestiges that establish themselves, in the long term, in cultural traditions with specific historical trajectories from distinct societies. These traditions guide, in a relatively stable manner, the cultivation of persons, forms of knowledge, and symbolisms (Boesch, 1991), which find resonance in diverse spheres of life, personal and collective actions, and not always ensuring the articulation of these spheres as a whole with meaning (see Guimarães, 2013).

The dialogue between psychology and Amerindian perspectivism (see Guimarães, 2011; 2016a), in its turn, has developed around the peculiar forms in which the Amerindian traditions conceive and practice the I–other–world relations, in distinction to the cultural conceptions and practices common to the traditions of naturalistic foundation and the structure of psychology as a science and profession:

Amerindian perspectivism refers to how the American Indians perceive the world and relate themselves with it: a point of view over the Indigenous point of view. Viveiros de Castro presented an innovative reading of the relationship between indigenous people and nature, founded in ancestral knowledge shared in a millennial diachronic development. According to the Amerindian perspectivism, the identities of the subjects brought into relation are deeply determined by the alterities to which they relate, as they are positioned in a vast network that unites all beings and assemblages of multiple natures (people, other animals, natural phenomena, gods, etc.) and only allow the subject to know one's own identity when contrasted to the alter with which it relates. The intersubjective asymmetry we referred to paragraphs above, if observed at the contact between an indigenous and non-indigenous, is radical: while we distinguish one nature of many cultures, for the indigenous there is a cultural form that varies little, a type of relationship with multiple natures or supernatures. (Nigro & Guimarães, 2016, p. 252)

The multinaturalistic ontology expressed in the Amerindian cultural practices and conceptions is a vector of cultural shock:

This reshuffling of our conceptual cards leads me to suggest the term multinaturalism to designate one of the contrasting features of Amerindian thought in relation to modern "multiculturalist" cosmologies. The latter notion rests on the mutual implication of the unity of nature and the multiplicity of cultures – the former guaranteed by the objective universality of bodies and substance, the latter generated by the subjective particularity of spirit and meaning. Contrary to this, the Amerindian concept would suppose the unity of spirit and the diversity of bodies. Culture or the subject would here take the form of the universal; nature or the object the form of the particular.

This inversion, perhaps too symmetrical to be more than speculative, must be developed into a phenomenologically rich interpretation of Amerindian cosmological notions, capable of determining the constitutive conditions of the contexts which might be called "nature" and "culture." Thus we must reconstitute these notions only to then desubstantiate them, since in Amerindian thought the categories of Nature and Culture are not only different in content but also do not possess the same status as their Western analogues; they do not indicate domains of being but rather relational configurations, mobile perspectives, in sum – points of view. (Viveiros de Castro, 2005, p. 37)

Therefore, from a multinaturalistic ontology, it is possible for the Christian, the scientific, and the Amerindian tradition to coexist without subsuming one into another. It is possible to have a church in the central square of a community and keep performing Amerindian rituals as much as it is possible to become a scientist carrying on the ancestral Amerindian knowledge. Such possibility of coexistence is also expressed in the words of Carlito de Oliveira introducing this subsection, about the coexistence of differences in the land. The multinaturalistic ontology of the indigenous university student guides a way of relating to knowledge production in diverse urban and academic forums, to the extent that the indigenous knowledge includes the naturalistic ontology typically found in the scientific disciplines as an instance of a broader multinaturalistic existence. It therefore allows finding a common ground for possible dialogues with the universities, in the dialogical sense of the term (Guimarães, 2014; 2016a).

In the opposite direction to the dialogue, modern sciences have historically taken further the division between myth and logos (Gadamer, 1954/2010, 1981/2010) and relegated certain myths to the condition of fables while others remain as fundamental references to scientific development (cf. Stengers, 2002). This distancing between the Amerindian ontologies and those professed at the universities produce suffering in the indigenous university students in the urban

context, who find themselves in an uncomfortable zone between distinct cosmological matrices, which at this moment are not fully possible to integrate. The university finds itself, in this sense, in a position similar to the one the Christian missionaries occupied in the past and still occupy in diverse fronts of evangelization.

31.3.1 Psychology, Multinaturalism, and the Construction of the Person

Psychology, as a field of research and reflection, is challenged to comprehend how the possibilities and limits of the interethnic dialogue are configured between antagonist cultural traditions. For this, it is necessary to focalize the historical processes linked to the psychosocial impact of the encounters between distinct peoples as well as develop consistent concepts capable of describing the personal process of elaboration of tension "in the perpetual return of the encounter" (Krenak, 1998/2000). The multinaturalistic ontology, in its turn, emerges as a mode of existence that allows and potentializes the coexistence of the diverse. The manner in which the indigenous university students encompass the dialogical multiplicity in their subjectivation processes – when they describe the articulation between the Christian religiosity and the indigenous rituals and between the traditional and the scientific knowledge – seems to us especially enriching to the comprehension of the psychosocial processes that allow hosting the diverse in oneself. The cultivation of difference in the social field unravels itself in the processes of construction of the self of the person:

Every individual self within a given society or social community reflects in its organized structure the whole relational pattern of organized social behavior which that society or community exhibits or is carrying on, and its organized structure is constituted by this pattern; but since each of these individual selves reflects a uniquely different aspect or perspective of this pattern in its structure, from its own particular and unique place or standpoint within the whole process of organized social behavior which exhibits this pattern – since, that is, each is differently or uniquely related to that whole process, and occupies its own essentially unique focus of relations therein-the structure of each is differently constituted by this pattern from the way in which the structure of any other is so constituted. (Mead, 1934, pp. 201–202)

On the one hand, Mead emphasizes an important part–whole relation in the comprehension of the multiple possibilities of developing oneself, establishing a particular focus that covers simultaneously the totality of the social field of the community in which the person develops. On the other hand, a psychological comprehension centered in the individual or one that fragments the person in terms of psychic properties without reintegrating them into their actionable whole would be limited and insufficient to comprehend the relevance of conviviality, of the forms of cultural expression and its relation with territory, songs and dances, and so on, pointed by the indigenous university students.

Reflecting on the social field depends on the person's possibility of interacting with the participants in their community, incorporating new images (i.e., terms, voices, or subjectivities) by means of the selective internalization and externalization departing from their singular position. This happens at the same time the social sphere transforms itself by means of a communicative process in the culture–person–culture relation (see Boesch, 1992). In this comprehension, the individual would not be an a priori category, but one that can emerge in societies where it is relevant to understand the person as an individual. The person always develops elaborating in a singular way the divisions that concern the fractures in the field where they were socialized.

When dealing with the socialization processes that imply the social construction of objective and subjective realities of a person, Berger and Luckmann (2003) mention at least two moments in which socialization happens, distinguishing them through the notions of primary and secondary socialization. The role of primary socialization, in its turn, would be crucial to configure a person's belonging to a determined cosmovision:

Only when he has achieved this degree of internalization is an individual a member of society. The ontogenetic process by which this is brought about is socialization, which may thus be defined as the comprehensive and consistent induction of an individual into the objective world of a society or a sector of it. Primary socialization is the first socialization an individual undergoes in childhood, through which he becomes a member of society. Secondary socialization is any subsequent process that inducts an already socialized individual into new sectors of the objective world of his society . . .

It is at once evident that primary socialization is usually the most important one for an individual, and that the basic structure of all secondary socialization has to resemble that of primary socialization. (Berger & Luckmann, 2003, pp. 150–151)

When secondary socialization does not find a continuity with the primary process of socialization, the person may live experiences of intense ruptures, understood as a cultural shock in which the stability of that which constituted itself as reality is questioned. In the expression of the indigenous university students that we interviewed, the cultural shocks brought by the displacement to the cities are evidenced, for example, in the sensations of imprisonment in the concrete and conceptual divisions of the urban context and the academic disciplines.

Roy Wagner (1981) indicates that anthropology invents the cultures it finds by means of the experience of cultural shock and the subsequent creative elaboration of meanings about the indefinable distance between the margins of each culture, surrounding what would be the other's culture and what would be our own. The constructions that emerge from this process are always misguided, when the search is for a pretense identity between the images of the other mirrored in oneself and those images mirrored in the external observer (see Viveiros de Castro, 2004); to the extent that the researchers must use themselves as an instrument in the elaboration of knowledge. The socialization of the person who produces knowledge is a condition for their possible insertion and meaning construction in a diverse cultural field, from where new reflections may be built.

The construction of the person and of the other happens in an infinite space of creativity, although this space is not completely free. We are dealing here with the notion of restricted indeterminacy (Valsiner, 1998). These considerations allow us to conceive the notion of the personal self through the metaphor of a house or as the territory of communitarian life, in opposition to a notion of the self dependent on the concept of identity and property (see Guimarães, 2013): As long as the doors or frontiers of the land/self are open, all who circulate can enter the territory and compose it. In this case, the self would then be the space for the life of "all," as was emphasized in the words of indigenous leader Carlito de Oliveira. On the other hand, many times the self becomes a territory of violent, authoritarian colonization, or of disputes between asymmetric positions, especially when the communitarian perspective internalized by the person is not capable of hosting diversity in a dialogical manner (for example, the non-acceptance by the missionaries of the traditional indigenous ways of life and conceptions, leading to an authoritarian accommodation of alterity to preconceived formats). The forms of resistance have, in these cases, taken place due to the possibility of distancing oneself, of not putting in dialogue certain aspects that are meant to be preserved.

31.3.2 Self as the Space of Circulation of Subjective Agencies

The personal self, as we are proposing here, is a result of active processes of internalization and externalization that transform in a singular way the experiences lived by a person in the social field. In the transformative intrapersonal dialogue, the person must handle a multiplicity of discourses (ideologies, master-narratives, myths) present in the social field in which they live. Many of these discourses are constituted as systems of belief, justification, and explanation of lived experiences, constructed by determined social groups (see Boesch, 1991), among which those we can consider as distinct cultures. The systems of belief, justification, and explanation of diverse ethnic groups are not always fully convergent, being many times contradictory and others not finding a plan of sharing to allow the elaboration of syntheses.

The persons who wander in the nebulous frontier of interethnic relations see themselves in the difficult task of translating, or rather, transducing (see Viveiros de Castro, 2004; Morais & Guimarães, 2015) the belief systems from one ethnic frontier to the other.[18] This process does not take place without mistakes, since the filters, assimilations, and transformations of discourses in the transit between different systems of belief always imply variation. That is, the construction that the indigenous university students make of the city and scientific knowledge demands a recreation of the academic space and elaboration of new knowledge, which points to directions still not processed by the university:

Today it is undoubtedly commonplace to say that cultural translation is our discipline's distinctive task. But the problem is knowing what precisely is, can, or should be a translation, and how to carry such an operation out. It is here that things start to become tricky, as Talal Asad demonstrated in a noteworthy article (1986). I adopt the radical position, which is I believe the same as Asad's, and that can be summarized as follows: in anthropology, comparison is in the service of translation and not the opposite. Anthropology compares so as to translate, and not to explain, justify, generalize, interpret, contextualize, reveal the unconscious, say what goes without saying, and so forth. I would add that to translate is always to betray, as the Italian saying goes. However, a good translation – and here I am paraphrasing Walter Benjamin (or rather Rudolf Pannwitz via Benjamin) – is one that betrays the destination language, not the source language. A good translation is one that allows the alien concepts to deform and subvert the translator's conceptual toolbox so that the intention of the original language can be expressed within the new one. (Viveiros de Castro, 2004, p. 5)

The translation model defended by Amerindian perspectivism supposes, as a theoretical formulation in the field of anthropology, a transduction, that is, it supposes the nonidentity between the terms of the dialogue in a creative process of signification, which presupposes equivocation and difference. The process of transduction supposes a redirecting of meaning through its being passed by the body of significance of the other culture, which establishes the basis for the cultivation of the terms it incorporates. In this sense, the notion of self, extensively developed in psychology, suffers transformations while passing the Amerindian systems or bodies of signification. We begin to understand that the construction of the person involves ritualized practices, which concern the body – singing and dancing, hunting and feeding from the forest, and so on – advancing in the comprehension of diverse specificities inherent to the relation of the indigenous people

with the urban context, the university, and the so-called scientific knowledge.

31.4 Psychology and the Construction of the Person in Interethnic Situations

Born in the heart of cultural traditions millennially affected by intense conflicts, which at the same time affirm peaceful ideologies without any perspective of truly reaching peace, psychology can benefit from and contribute to possible escapes from the blind alley in which modern societies find themselves. It seems to us promising to search outside the Eurocentric tradition, in built and highly sophisticated cultural resources directed to the production and maintenance of the diversity of the living species and ways of life.

As a science and profession, psychology needs, therefore, to be capable of opening itself theoretically and methodologically to the plurality of forms of knowledge originated from distinct ethnic matrices as foundations of sophisticated meanings and forms of knowledge, produced in forums of dialogue unknown until now. The indigenous people who reach university are those who currently also graduate as psychologists (among other professions) and are those to whom psychologists begin offering services, be it in the communities or in the urban context. Psychology, therefore, must be prepared for the inevitable transformations that these consistent fields of comprehension and ethical intervention demand.

The indigenous university students have performed the difficult task of transiting between the cosmovisions of the Western traditions at the universities and the cosmovisions from their distinct ethnic origins, without synthesizing them in a dialectic manner, which overcomes contradiction. In this circulation, they managed to organize within their self multiple possibilities of being available in interethnic situations. They have included, in a proper way, the foreign cultural practices and knowledge in their cultural frame, at the same time making visible their contemporary way of being in the urban context where they carry out their ancestral ethnic belonging. To cope with this complex, conflictive situation, they developed strategies of differentiation, dedifferentiation, and novel differentiation, available in a multinaturalistic, transductive communication.

With the violent approaches from the Eurocentric societies that have aimed for more than 500 years to impose their cosmovisions and forms of social organization over the Amerindian traditions, resistance many times happened by the denial of dialogue, by gaining distance. When that is not possible, a subjective schism takes place, along with the construction of collective and personal symbolic spaces, which maintain exclusivity of ethnic belonging. Settled on cosmovisions characteristic of their ethnic origins, the indigenous university students operate a transduction, in which the knowledge acquired in the urban context and at the university serve to feed and develop the forms of knowledge that are proper to their community, guaranteeing the maintenance and coexistence of the diverse characteristic of the multinaturalistic Amerindian ontologies.

Cities are places in the contemporary world progressively populated by people from distinct ethnic origins. In receiving people from different cultural traditions, universities may become a space of inclusion of epistemological and ethical debates that contemplate these origins. For this it is necessary to subvert the rhetorical logical proselytisms which persist in the academic world in a manner similar to the religious missionary assaults and open space for the emergence of novelty. In the academic environments open to diversity, people actively look to give visibility to the millennial knowledge and practices they inherited from their ethnic belonging, in a game of construction and reconstruction of images that concern the very genesis and transformation of ethnicities, revealing:

an entire political-cultural process of creative adaptation which generates the possibility conditions of a field of interethnic negotiation where the colonial discourse may be bypassed or subverted. The cultural intertextuality of the contact is nurtured both by this discursive ethnopolitics and by the rhetorical forms (negative or positive) by which the white people build the "Indians." However, it is not limited only to the reciprocal images of Indians and whites. The self-definition of each protagonist feeds not only on the representation built of the other, but also of the representation this other builds of him: self-representation of interethnic actors builds itself in the crossroads of the image he has of the other and their own image mirrored in the other. (Albert, 2002, p. 4)

Different from what was thought in the academic environment in the nineteenth and twentieth centuries about the supposed hermetic character of the indigenous societies (Viveiros de Castro, 2006) – just as in European medieval societies or the city-states of ancient times – currently, the perception has grown that the ontologies of the indigenous societies point to the construction of persons capable of self-affirming ethnically, at the same time as being able to live respectfully with difference (see Macena & Guimarães, 2016). These are necessary characteristics to the contemporary world, which is continuously threatened by xenophobic fundamentalisms with their technologies for constructing authoritarian personalities, whose consequences affect all peoples.

Notes

1 The *cerrado* is a biome of the central area of Brazil, with savanna-like characteristics.

2 The *caatinga* is a biome found in the northeast of Brazil. It is a shrubland and thorn forest.

3 Translated from the original in Portuguese: *Por ser de lá do sertão, lá do cerrado, lá do interior, do mato, da caatiga, do roçado, eu quase não saio, eu*

quase não tenho amigos, eu quase que não consigo ficar na cidade sem viver contrariado.

4 FUNAI, Fundação Nacional do Índio, is a Brazilian State Foundation created for the protection of the Indian interests and culture.

5 *Toré* is a ritual practice common to diverse ethnic groups in the northeast of Brazil.

6 The notion of citizen is etymologically related to the meaning of inhabiting a city. The notion of citizenship derives from that of citizen and refers to the situation in which a person is recognized under the custom or law as being a member of a nation-state. Amerindian peoples consider themselves as independent of any nation-state.

7 *Maracá* is an indigenous instrument used in a series of ritual practices.

8 On this issue we have developed the notion of dialogical multiplication as an appropriation in the field of psychology of the forms of conceiving reality from the Amerindian perspectives (see Guimarães, 2011, 2013).

9 The right to voluntary isolation of the indigenous peoples is guaranteed by article 231 of the Brazilian constitution (see Brasil Constituição, 1988/2012).

10 On the issue of the person's rhythmic regulation in culture, consult the article by Guimarães (2011).

11 Longhouse, characteristic of the peoples of the Amazon. The term is also used in Brazilian popular culture to designate a simple house.

12 Traditional collective house of the indigenous peoples.

13 Traditional indigenous clothing.

14 Series of rituals performed by a shaman, of medicinal nature.

15 A person of mixed origins, of indigenous and European ancestry.

16 Indigenous headdress.

17 Seed from which a red pigment is extracted. Many indigenous groups use it for body painting.

18 "Transduction (From the Latin transductione, 'to conduct by certain means'). The term generally refers to the reproductive process in which bacterial DNA is transferred from one bacteria to another through a virus, the bacteriophage. Here, the term refers to a speech by the poet and translator Haroldo de Campos, in which he says to be impossible translating a poem. What must be done is a process of 'transduction,' in which the 'experience' of the poem crosses one's body, providing other routes of textual comprehension so that translated words may gain meaning through feeling" (Morais & Guimarães, 2015, p. 142).

References

Albert, B. (2002). *O ouro canibal e a queda do céu: uma crítica xamânica da economia política da natureza*. Brasília: Ed. UnB.

Almeida, M. R. C. (2012). Os índios na história do Brasil no século XIX: Da invisibilidade ao protagonismo. *Revista História Hoje*, 1(2), 21–40.

Arruda, R. S. V. (1998). Rikbaktsa. In *Enciclopédia dos Povos Indígenas no Brasil*. Instituto Socioambiental. Retrieved from http://pib .socioambiental.org/pt/povo/rikbaktsa/print.

Arrutti, J. M. (2005). Pankararu. In *Enciclopédia dos Povos Indígenas no Brasil*. Instituto Socioambiental. Retrieved from http://pib .socioambiental.org/pt/povo/pankararu/print.

Baccaert, A., Navarro, C., & Um, N. (2011). *À Sombra de um Delírio Verde* [video]. Retrieved from www.thedarksideofgreen-themovie.com/.

Berger, P. B. & Luckmann, T. (2003). *A construção social da realidade: Tratado sobre a sociologia do conhecimento* [The social construction of reality: A treatise in the sociology of knowledge]. Petrópolis: Vozes.

Boesch, E. E. (1991). *Symbolic Action Theory and Cultural Psychology*. Berlin: Springer.

Boesch, E. E. (1992). Culture – individual – culture: The cycle of knowledge. In M. von Cranach, W. Doise, & P. Mugny (Eds.), *Social Representations and the Social Bases of Knowledge* (Swiss Monographs in Psychology, vol. 1, 89–95). Lewiston, NY: Hogrefe & Huber.

Brasil Constituição. (1988/2012). *Constituição da República Federativa do Brasil: texto constitucional promulgado em 5 de outubro de 1988, com as alterações adotadas pelas Emendas Constitucionais nos 1/1992 a 68/2011, pelo Decreto Legislativo no. 186/2008 e pelas*

Emendas Constitucionais de Revisão nos 1 a 6/1994. Brasília: Câmara dos Deputados, Edições Câmara.

Cornejo, C. (2015). From fantasy to imagination: A cultural history and a moral for cultural psychology. Paper presented to the Niels Bohr Lectures, University of Aalborg, Denmark.

Costa, P. E. S. (2007). Do sensível ao inteligível: O Auto de São Lourenço. Unpublished dissertation. Universidade Federal da Paraíba, Brasil.

ENEI (Encontro Nacional dos Estudantes Indígenas). (2013). Documento final do I Encontro Nacional dos Estudantes Indígenas, UFSCAR, São Carlos, Brazil.

Fernandes, R. (2007). Ensino superior para indígenas: desafios e perspectivas. Paper presented at Seminário Formação Jurídica e Povos Indígenas Desafios para uma educação superior, March 21–23, Belém, Pará, Brasil.

Gadamer, H.-G. (1954/2010). Mito e Razão. In *Hermenêutica da Obra de Arte*. São Paulo: Martins Fontes.

Gadamer, H.-G. (1981/2010). Mito e Logos. In *Hermenêutica da Obra de Arte*. São Paulo: Martins Fontes.

Guimarães, D. S. (2011). Amerindian anthropology and cultural psychology: Crossing boundaries and meeting otherness' worlds. *Culture & Psychology*, 12(2), 139–157.

Guimarães, D. S. (2012). Scientific concepts and public policies: Semiotic-cultural obstacles concerning intergroup and intercultural relationships. *Culture & Psychology*, 18(3), 345–358.

Guimarães, D. S. (2013). Self and dialogical multiplication. *Interacções*, 9, 214–242.

Guimarães, D. S. (2014). Introdução – Indígenas entre a Amazônia e São Paulo: Atravessamentos dialógicos. In R. A. Rodrigues (Ed.), *Sofrimento mental de indígenas na Amazônia*. Parintins, Brazil: Editora da Universidade Federal do Amazonas (Edua).

Guimarães, D. S. (2016a). *Amerindian Paths: Guiding Dialogues with Psychology*. Charlotte, NC: Information Age Publishing.

Guimarães, D. S. (2016b). Descending and ascending trajectories of dialogical analysis: Seventh analytic interpretation on the short story "The guerrillero." *Psicologia USP*, 27(2), 189–200.

IBGE (2012a). *Censo Demográfico 2010: Características gerais dos indígenas Resultados do universe*. Rio de Janeiro: IBGE.

IBGE (2012b). *Os indígenas no censo Demográfico 2010: Primeiras considerações com base no quesito cor ou raça*. Rio de Janeiro: IBGE.

ISA (Equipe do Programa Rio Negro do Instituto Socioambiental). (2002). Tukano. *Em Enciclopédia dos Povos Indígenas no Brasil*. Instituto Socioambiental. Retrieved from http://pib.socioambiental.org/pt/povo/tukano/print.

James, W. (1890). *The Principles of Psychology*. New York: Holt.

Krenak, A. (1998/2000). O eterno retorno do encontro. In C. A. Ricardo (Ed.), *Instituto Socioambiental: Povos indígenas no Brasil 1996/2000*. São Paulo: Instituto Socioambiental.

Macena, P. L. & Guimarães, D. S. (2016). A Psicologia Cultural na fronteira com as concepções Mbya Guarani de educação [Cultural psychology in the boundary of the Mbya Guarani conceptions of education]. In CRPSP (Ed.), *Na Fronteira da Psicologia com os Saberes Tradicionais: Práticas e Técnicas* [In the boundary of psychology and traditional knowledge: Practices and techniques] (pp. 135–147). São Paulo: CRPSP.

Marková, I. (2006). *Dialogicidade e representações sociais: As dinâmicas da mente*. Petrópolis, Brazil: Vozes.

Mead, G. H (1934). *Mind Self and Society from the Standpoint of a Social Behaviorist* (ed. by Charles W. Morris). Chicago: University of Chicago Press.

Meira, M. (2002). Baré. In *Enciclopédia dos Povos Indígenas no Brasil*. Instituto Socioambiental. Retrieved from www.indios.org.br/pt/povo/bare/print.

Monteiro, J. M. (1994). *Negros da terra: Índios e bandeirantes nas origens de São Paulo*. São Paulo: Companhia das Letras.

Moraes, H. & Guimarães, D. S. (2015). Vocational program, creative processes and the constitution of a poetic outlook on reality: A dialogue between theatrical arts and dialogical-cultural psychology. Paper presented at the SCC-Workshop. Knowledge and otherness: Disquieting experiences in the dynamics of cultural psychology, October 13–16, University of São Paulo.

Moura, M. L. & Guimarães, D. S. (2013). Social reproduction and its transformations: Relationships in educational institutions. In Y. Omi; L. P. Rodriguez-Burgos, & M. C. Peralta-Gómez. (Eds.), *Lives and Relationships: Culture in Transitions Between Social Roles* (1 edn., pp. 19–94). Charlotte, NC: Information Age Publishing.

Nigro, K. F. & Guimarães, D. S. (2016). Obscuring cannibalism in civilization: Amerindian psychology in reading today's sociocultural phenomena. In J. Valsiner, G. Marsico, N. Chaudhary, T. Sato,& V. Dazzani (Eds.), *Psychology as the Science of Human Being: The Yokohama Manifesto* (pp. 245–263). Basel: Springer.

Simão, L. M. (2010). *Ensaios Dialógicos: Compartilhamento e diferença nas relações eu outro* [Dialogical essays: sharing and difference in the I-other relationships]. São Paulo: HUCITEC.

Spink, P. K. (2003). Pesquisa de campo em psicologia social: Uma perspectiva pós-construcionista. *Psicologia & Sociedade*, 15(2), 18–42.

Stengers, I. (2002). *A invenção das ciências modernas* [The invention of modern sciences]. São Paulo: Editora 34.

UFRGS (Universidade Federal do Rio Grande do Sul). (2013). *Estudantes indígenas no ensino superior: Uma abordagem a partir da experiência na UFRGS*. Porto Alegre: Editora da UFRGS.

Valsiner, J. (1998). *The Guided Mind: A Sociogenetic Approach to Personality*. Cambridge, MA: Harvard University Press.

Venturi, G. & Bokany, V. (Eds.). (2013). *Indígenas no Brasil: demandas dos povos e percepções do opinião pública* [Indigenous in Brazil: demands of the peoples and perceptions of public opinion]. São Paulo: Editora Fundação Perseu Abramo.

Viveiros de Castro, E. B. (2004). Perspectival anthropology and the method of controlled equivocation. *Tipití: Journal of the Society for the Anthropology of Lowland South America*, 2(1):1–22.

Viveiros de Castro, E. (2005). Perspectivism and multinaturalism in indigenous America. In A. Surrallés & P. García Hierro (Eds.), *The Land Within: Indigenous Territory and the Perception of Environment* (pp. 36–73). Copenhagen: IWGIA.

Viveiros de Castro, E. (2006). A floresta de cristal: Nota sobre a ontologia dos espíritos amazônicos. *Cadernos de Campo*, 14(15), 319–338.

Viveiros de Castro, E. B. (2007). Uma figura de humano pode estar ocultando uma afecção-jaguar. *Multitudes*, 24. Retrieved from www.multitudes.net/Uma-figura-de-humano-pode-estar/.

Von Lewinski, S. (2004). *Indigenous Heritage and Intellectual Property: Genetic Resources, Traditional Knowledge and Folklore*. New York: Kluwer Law.

Wagner, R. (1981). *The Invention of Culture*. Chicago: University of Chicago Press.

Zanirato, S. H. & Ribeiro, W. C. (2007). Conhecimento tradicional e propriedade intelectual nas organizações multilaterais. *Ambiente & Sociedade*, 10(1), 39–55.

Further Reading

Albert B. & Ramos R. C. (Eds.). (2002). *Pacificando o branco: Cosmologias do contato no norte-Amazônico*. São Paulo: UNESP.

Zittoun, T. (2006). *Transitions: Development Through Symbolic Resources*. Greenwich, CT: Information Age Publishing.

32 Social Identities, Gender, and Self: Cultural Canalization in Imagery Societies

Ana Flávia do Amaral Madureira

Psychology needs culture to make sense of the human lives.

Valsiner (2012, p. 6)

Recently, I was at a beautiful beach in Brazil. Although I have lived far from the Brazilian coast, I have since childhood been fascinated with the continuous movement of the sea. Distinct from the movements of the ocean triggered by mechanical forces, they are uniquely complex, changing according to innumerous factors and interactions. Beyond that, there are more species in the oceans than on all the continents. After all, the sea is a life system!

All life systems are complex and dynamic (Fogel, Lyra, & Valsiner, 1997; Mahoney, 1998; Valsiner, 2007a). Therefore, theoretical scientific models that do not recognize these fundamental aspects of life systems are clearly limited. The mechanical models that have developed – since the emergence of the scientific revolution in Europe between the sixteenth and seventeenth centuries (Marcondes, 2000) – are unsuitable to investigating life systems through their different levels, that is, biological, sociological, and psychological levels (Valsiner, 2007a).

This is a long history of philosophers in the West struggling to deal with the complexity and dynamism of life systems. More than 2,000 years ago, on one hand, the pre-Socratic Greek philosopher Heraclitus of Ephesus (around 535–475 BC) asserted that everything is in constant flux and that the tension between opposite forces is a constant in the universe (Mahoney, 1998; Stokes, 2012). On the other hand, the pre-Socratic Greek philosopher Parmenides of Elea (around 530–460 BC) "maybe as a reaction to Heraclitus . . . tried to prove that change is impossible and reality is unique, indivisible and homogeneous" (Stokes, 2012, p. 29). For Parmenides, the change is an illusion. These philosophical assumptions that change is an illusion and that permanence is the essence of reality have deep implications for the history of sciences, including psychological science and its historical difficulty to adopt a developmental and systemic perspective in the studies of *psyche*.

However, more recently, especially in the last decades of the twentieth century, meaningful epistemological, theoretical, and methodological changes have happened in diverse scientific disciplines. For instance, in the field of physical chemistry, Ilya Prigogine[1] and Isabelle Stengers (1997) "discovered that the rational dialogue with the nature does not consist of the disenchanted flyby of a lunar world, but the exploration, always local and selective, of a complex and multiple nature" (p. 5). As a life system, we are part of nature. At the same time, we, humans, are creators and creatures of culture. After all, the fact that we are a social species (biological sociability) was fundamental to the emergence of culture (Pino, 2000).

As the image of the beautiful beach in Brazil comes again to mind, it strikes me that the continuous movement of the sea reminds me of Heraclitus of Ephesus, while the big and stable rock that I saw on the beach reminds me of Parmenides of Elea. However, this metaphor is imprecise, as stable rocks are not static entities on our planet. The rocks only seem stable for us in our too short time of life. The rocks on Earth have undergone profound changes over millions of years. Certainly geographical time is much longer than historical time. The irreversibility of time has a constructive role in nature, at different levels of analysis. Therefore, this principle should be seriously considered in psychological science, as Valsiner (2007a) emphasized.

The goal of this chapter, from a sociocultural psychology framework, is to analyze the complex relationship between self, as a dynamic and culturally contextualized system, and gender identity, as a meaningful social identity deeply connected within power relations in different societies. The formulation of a gender concept illustrates the fertile dialogue between academic production in human sciences and feminist movements as social and political movements that have a commitment to the transformation of hierarchical gender relations (Louro, 1998).

The concept of gender, as an analytical and political tool, seeks to reject the "explanations" of inequalities between men and women anchored in biological differences (Scott, 1995). Moreover, according to the historian and feminist theorist Joan Scott (1998), "when I talk about gender, I want to refer to the discourse on difference of the sexes. It does not refer only to ideas, but also to institutions, structures, daily life practices... rituals and everything that constitutes social relations" (p. 115). It is important to recognize that the differences between men and women – in diverse cultural contexts permeated by sexism – are amplified in order to maintain inequalities in public and private domains from a rigid and hierarchical perspective, as has been discussed by various contemporary authors (e.g., Bourdieu, 2005; Louro, 1998,

2004; Madureira, 2010; Oliveira & Madureira, 2014; Segato, 2003).

To analyze the complex relationship between self and gender identity from a sociocultural psychology framework, the following concepts and their articulations are explored in this chapter: (1) social identities as boundary phenomena; (2) cultural canalization of gender identities; and (3) semiotic mediation, especially the mediation through visual signs created by human beings and, more precisely, visual representations (as discussed by Santaella, 2012). It was not possible to accomplish this theoretical discussion without the deliberate transgression of rigid disciplinary boundaries that separate psychology and other sciences.

32.1 An Overview of the Central Assumptions of Sociocultural Psychology: Culture and *Psyche* Together

There is no such thing as a human nature independent of culture. Geertz (1989, p. 35)

In a world where people, social groups, and countries increasingly invest in the construction of walls (in the denotative and connotative senses), we should instead channel our efforts toward building bridges among people, countries, and different disciplines. The construction of bridges between different disciplines is an antidote to the historical tendency of modern science toward an increase in specialization of knowledge. In other words, it is to learn more and more about less and less, as criticized by the Brazilian author Rubem Alves (2012) in his interesting, didactic, and poetic book that presents an introduction to scientific philosophy.

When we seriously think about the complexity of reality (in its diverse levels: physical, biological, sociological, psychological, etc.), it makes sense to extend our horizon of knowledge. To do that, it is essential to transcend the rigid disciplinary boundaries that separate the psychologies of other sciences. More specifically, it is necessary to transcend the boundaries that separate science and art (Madureira, 2016; Moreira, 2011). From a sociocultural psychology framework, if we want to understand the complex relations between gender identities and self – which is the focus of analysis of this chapter – it is necessary to promote multiple interdisciplinary dialogues. But first, what are the fundamental assumptions of sociocultural psychology?

According to Valsiner and Rosa (2007a), the unity of sociocultural psychology comes from its contrast with nonsocial ways of looking at human beings. The emphasis on "social" permeates discourses about *psyche*, and the focus on language is, frequently, considered as the basic human feature that is both the person and the social at the same time. In this direction, the *semiotic mediation* is a fundamental explanatory principle for sociocultural psychology. After all, signs are cultural artifacts that guide, in different ways, the feelings, thoughts, and actions of each person in the world (Valsiner, 2007a). A relevant principle that presents meaningful methodological implications is the particular "forms of human psychological phenomena [that] vary across time, persons, and contexts – but the ways they are organized are universal" (Valsiner, 2007a, p. 16).

From a broad theoretical and methodological perspective, there is a continuous tension between change and stability at different levels of analysis: (1) in the biological development of each species, (2) in the cultural development of each society, and (3) in the psychological development of each person. It reminds us of the ideas by the pre-Socratic Greek philosopher Heraclitus of Ephesus, previously mentioned. It is interesting to recognize the existence of deep connections between scientific issues and philosophical assumptions, even when many scientists do not consciously or explicitly make such connections.

According to Fogel, Lyra, and Valsiner (1997, p. 3), "one of the more important aspects of dynamic systems thinking is all living systems are inherently developmental. Living systems are not rigid structures, but dynamically stable processes." Therefore, concerning the development of human *psyche*, the processes of internalization and externalization of cultural meanings are not processes of mere reproduction from an interpsychological domain to an intrapsychological domain, and vice versa (Lawrence & Valsiner, 1993; Valsiner, 2007a).

It is therefore necessary to overcome the traditional dualism (exclusive separation) between individual mental processes and collective culture. According to the immanent perspective (Demo, 2005) adopted in this chapter, culture is conceived as part of nature and not as a "transcendental entity." Throughout the phylogenesis of our species, the complex interactions between brain and culture were essential to the development of human consciousness (Geertz, 2001). Human experience, as culturally organized, is the result of a long phylogenetic history, as demonstrated by the detailed analysis carried out by Rosa (2007a, 2007b), coherent with an immanent perspective (Demo, 2005).

From a sociocultural psychology framework, culture is a central construct that makes it possible to analyze the symbolic nature of human development. Culture is not simply an "influence" on human development. Instead, culture constitutes the person and forms in a meaningful way through each person's development (Bruner, 1997, 2000; Cole, 1992; Rogoff, 2003; Shweder, 1991; Valsiner, 2007a). As Madureira and Branco (2005) emphasize, on one hand, culture makes possible the transmission of a collective legacy through the generations, and on the other hand, culture is changed through the creative actions of individuals, social groups, and political movements (e.g., feminist movements).

At the same time that culture is a structuring conceptual tool in sociocultural psychology, culture is a very difficult concept to define (Valsiner, 2007a). In social anthropology, the difficulties in defining culture are widely recognized. Diverse anthropological perspectives define "culture" in many different ways. In this chapter, I consider the *interpretative anthropological perspective* proposed by Clifford Geertz (1926–2006) as a fertile way to define culture. More precisely, Geertz (1989) adopts a semiotic conceptualization of culture. For him, "human behavior is seen as symbolic action" (p. 8). Moreover, "this suggests that there is no such thing as a human nature independent of culture" (p. 35).

This definition is coherent with sociocultural psychology in its efforts to understand the constitutive role of culture concerning the development of human *psyche* in an integrative and systemic direction. From the adoption of a semiotic conceptualization of culture, Geertz (1989), inspired by Max Weber, argues that anthropology is a science that seeks interpretations about the symbolic universe of culture. What makes Geertz's interpretative anthropological perspective a fruitful interlocutor with sociocultural psychology and its central assumptions?

Basically, the concept of culture "implies a constructive modification of the natural course of affairs" (Valsiner, 2007a, p. 19). In our daily lives, we deal with multiple cultural artifacts, such as clothes, shoes, glasses, computers, books, cars, bikes, smartphones, advertising (outdoors, television, Internet, etc.), art, science, and philosophical works. All of these introduce "constructive modifications" of the natural course of life. All of them integrate, in different proportions, two dimensions: the material and the symbolic (Pino, 2005). We ultimately live our lives in a world saturated with cultural significance. As Valsiner (2014) emphasized, we are compulsive builders of meanings.

In sum, sociocultural psychology is a heterogeneous "theoretical family" inserted in the broad context of sociogenic perspectives that defend the social genesis of human psychological development. Moreover, culture, semiotic mediation, and experience are structuring conceptual tools that

orient our theoretical view in the analysis of different subjects (Bruner, 1997; Madureira, 2012; Madureira & Branco, 2012; Rosa, 2007a, 2007b; Valsiner, 2007a; Valsiner & Rosa, 2007a, 2007b).

After this brief overview of the central assumptions of sociocultural psychology, I focus on a specific subject: social identities as boundary phenomena that connect individuals and social groups. In other words, after clarifying our general theoretical basis, we can "take off" toward new specific landscapes.

32.2 Social Identities as Boundary Phenomena: The Construction of an "Affective Bridge" between Individuals and Social Groups

My opinion is the same as yours . . . Yes, in fact, the "identity" is only revealed as something to be invented, and not to be discovered . . . The fragility and the eternally temporary condition of identity cannot be hidden. The secret was revealed. But this is a new fact, too recent. Bauman (2005, pp. 21–22, author translation)

Imagine a hypothetical world where everybody is identical, a world without any differences and ambiguity. In this dehumanized world, meaning-making processes would be impossible without the tensions and ambiguities between sameness and difference. More precisely, "human meaning, in that sense, is brought to being by difference, contrast, tension, disagreement . . . In other words, meaning is always dependent on the play between sameness and difference" (Ferreira, Salgado, & Cunha, 2006, p. 28). An essential aspect of this theoretical discussion is if differences are central to meaning-making processes, boundaries would mark these differences.

All cell membranes are boundaries that permit (or not) the transposition of some chemical substances in our bodies (Valsiner, 2007b). Thus, in biological terms, boundaries work as membranes. This metaphorical image is a promising path to study diverse relevant phenomena for psychology, such as the construction of social identities (e.g., gender identities) and the related dynamics and tensions between in-group and out-group, prejudices, and discriminatory practices (e.g., sexism) as prejudices in action (Madureira, 2007a, 2007b, 2012; Madureira & Branco, 2012).

More precisely, concerning the reproduction of *sexism* – in formal institutional practices and informal practices in daily life – a strategic domain is maintaining rigid and hierarchical symbolic boundaries between what is culturally associated with masculinity and what is culturally associated with femininity (Madureira, 2010, 2012; Oliveira & Madureira, 2014). After all, there are continuous reproductions, and also changes, of cultural meanings that configure the symbolic boundaries that delimit physical and social spaces destined for men and for women – as, for instance, bars for men and kitchens for women. The sexism culturally works to maintain these rigid and hierarchical symbolic boundaries between men and women, as if there were a "deep abyss" between them (Madureira, 2009, 2010).

As the anthropologist Rita Segato (2003) has discussed, the autonomy of women is frequently perceived as a threat to maintaining the status system in traditional societies, anchored in the criteria of gender and age. It is absolutely necessary to overcome the simplistic analyses that circumscribe the social problem of violence against women as "individual pathologies," restricted to some men, without connection with beliefs, values, and practices stimulated within the collective culture (Madureira, 2010; Segato, 2003). Therefore, public policies to combat violence against women should not ignore the fact that these issues have *clear cultural roots*.

Concerning the identity processes, along general lines, there are always symbolic boundaries that delimit – in a semipermeable or in a not permeable way – the differences between individuals and social groups (in terms of gender, social class, sexual orientation, nationality, religion, etc.). As Silva (2000, p. 82; translated by author) emphasizes,

to affirm the identity means demark boundaries, means make distinctions between what is inside and what is outside. The identity is always connected within a strong separation and distinction, supposes and, at the same time, affirms and reaffirms power relations "We" and "they" are not, in this case, only grammatical distinctions.

Some of these symbolic boundaries do not present meaningful implications in social interactions, but others present deep and worrying implications at different levels of analysis: macrosocial, interpsychological, and intrapsychological. These different levels of analysis are dynamically articulated. To illustrate how symbolic boundaries can present concrete implications for the lives of people, we can mention, again, the case of sexism.

The reproduction of sexism in daily life practices transforms semipermeable boundaries – those that symbolically mark the differences between men and women – into nonpermeable boundaries that mark the differences symbolically in a rigid way. More than simply marking the differences, what emerges is a hierarchical understanding about masculinity and femininity. The reproduction of sexism plays a strategic role in the maintenance of status quo concerning the gender relations in private and public domains. Figure 32.1 presents a didactic image of the previous discussion on social identities as boundary phenomena.

As is observed, there are deep and intricate articulations between (1) identity processes, (2) stereotypes, (3) prejudices, and (4) discriminatory practices (Galinkin & Zauli, 2011; Madureira, 2007a, 2012; Myers, 1995; Pérez-Nebra & Jesus, 2011). Beyond that, to properly study the construction of social identities

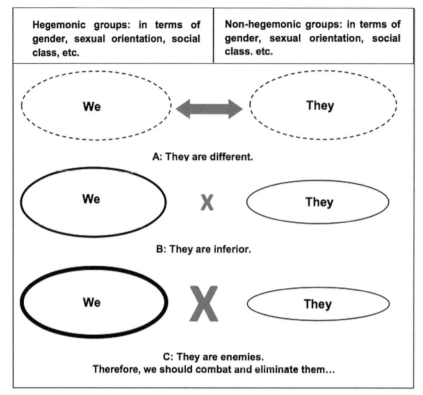

Figure 32.1 Social identities as boundary phenomena: from differences to inequalities, from inequalities to intolerance. Source: Based on Madureira (2012).

(including gender identities) and different kinds of prejudice (sexism, racism, homophobia, etc.), it is fundamental to take into account their historical-cultural bases and their affective roots (Madureira, 2007a, 2012; Madureira & Branco, 2012, 2015).

Several authors in recent years have emphasized the cultural, social, and political processes that erode the traditional references that have anchored identities, for example, religion and nation (Bauman, 2005; Galinkin & Zauli, 2011; Hall, 1998, 2000; Sawaia, 2014; Woodward, 2000). These processes present different implications, such as an increase in religious fundamentalism.

As Bauman (2005) affirms, fundamentalism promotes "*a feeling of certainty* and eliminates any doubt from the simple, easily absorbed code of behavior that is offered . . . It transmits *a com-*

fortable sensation of security" (p. 93; emphasis added; translated by author). It is not surprising to see the existence of deep connections between sexism and religious fundamentalism (in different religious traditions). In other words, we should consider seriously the affective roots of both identity processes and prejudices.

When we talk about the construction of social identities, we are talking about feelings of belonging between individuals and different groups present in society. Metaphorically, we are talking about the cultural construction of "affective bridges" that connect individuals and social groups (Madureira, 2007a, 2012). The feeling of belonging to a specific group provides a secure and familiar basis to deal with the ambiguities present in ordinary situations in daily life (Madureira, 2008). From the adoption of the principle of irreversibility of time, we are always confronted with the "unknown": the future (Valsiner, 2007a).

Surely there are many ways in which one faces the "unknown." However, in terms of general psychological processes, it is pertinent to mention the processes specified by Ernest Boesch: (1) *Heimweh* ("longing for home" – striving toward the secure and familiar) and (2) *Fernweh* ("road to the unknown" – encountering adventure and novelty, but also risks) (Valsiner, 2006). While the perception of dangers and risks is related to the promotion of the *Heimweh* process, feelings of curiosity and pleasure are related to the promotion of the *Fernweh* process. As Joerchel (2007) affirms,

according to Boesch (1998) the relations between "home," secure and the "strange, unfamiliar" is a key element in developing a self system . . . Thus, *the self concept is comprised of both the familiar, the home environment, as well as of the strange and unknown*. It is within this tension that humans develop a self concept: the secure home environment provides the base for the self confidence and self actualization, the strange and the unknown provides a platform for hopes, dreams, and desires, for potential actions, and potential self concept as well as a platform for fears and threats to the self system . . . In this respect *the construction of social barrier can be seen as defense mechanisms in reaction to a perceived threat to the self concept*. (p. 257; emphasis added)

In sum, identity processes contribute, in meaningful ways, to constructing "affective bridges" between individuals and social groups. Beyond that, identity processes offer cultural coordinates that guide the construction of subjectivity (Madureira, 2000, 2007a; Madureira & Branco, 2007, 2012) Thus multiple social ties that connect us within diverse social groups have an important role in the development of self-systems during the course of each of our lives, as, for example, our gender identities. To be a man or a woman is not a simple detail as we might think

in our sexist societies – as is discussed in the next section.

32.3 Gender Identity and Self as a Dynamic and Contextualized System

According to usage and conventions which are at last being questioned but have by no means been overcome, the social presence of a woman is different in kind from that of a man. A man's presence is dependent on the promise of power which embodies. If the promise is large and incredible, he is found to have little presence. The promised power may be moral, physical, temperamental, economic, social, sexual . . . By contrast, a woman's presence expresses her own attitude to herself, and defines what can and cannot be done to her . . . One might simplify this saying: *men act* and *women appear*. Berger (2008, pp. 39–41)

The conceptualization of identity processes as boundary phenomena is coherent within the analyses – carried out by diverse authors in the vast field of human sciences since the 1990s – that have criticized the essentialist view of identity (Bauman, 2005; Galinkin & Zauli, 2011; Hall, 1998, 2000; Louro, 1998, 2003, 2004; Madureira, 2007a, 2012; Moreira & Câmara, 2008; Pollak, 1992; Rosa, Bellelli, & Bakhurst, 2000; Rosa & Blanco, 2007; Sawaia, 2014; Silva, 2000; Woodward, 2000). According to Pollak (1992), "identity construction is a phenomenon produced in reference to others . . . Memory and identity can be perfectly negotiated, and they are not phenomena that should be understood as essences of a person or group" (p. 204). In other words, *social identities* (i.e., gender identities, national identity, social class identity, etc.) are not of essence at the "core" of individuals and social groups; instead, they are cultural and historical constructions.

Gender identities occupy a prominent place among social identities that present meaningful implications in daily life. From a sociocultural psychology framework, the articulation between gender identities and a self-system is not only an interesting theoretical subject but also a subject that presents relevant social and psychological implications. For example, the anthropologist Rita Segato (2003) emphasizes that the fight against gender violence is inseparable from the change of constitutive affection present in gender relations as to what many people consider "normal." According to the author, public policies on gender issues are fundamental, but not enough to promote "the reform of affection."

According to the historian and feminist theorist Joan Scott (1995) in her classic article on gender issues, "gender is the social organization of sexual difference. The concept [gender] is not a reflection of biological reality, but *gender constructs the meaning of this reality*" (p. 115; emphasis added; translated by author). It is important to mention that the development of the gender concept expresses the relevant exchange between the scientific enterprise and the feminist movement, which, as a social and political movement, has fought against the historical inequalities between men and women in different domains of life (Louro, 1998), as previously discussed in this chapter.

Gender, therefore, is a political and analytical tool (Louro, 1998). As a political tool, gender interdisciplinary studies seek to contribute to overcoming the historical inequalities between men and women in public and private domains of daily life. As an analytical tool, the concept of gender has contributed to developing a critical understanding of diverse phenomena from different fields in the context of human sciences over the last decades. Gender studies emphasizes the fundamental role of culture in the complex and ambiguous process of becoming men and women. Moreover, gender studies has developed diverse critical analyses about the biological essentialism present in daily life and in traditional Western biomedical models (Costa, 1999; Louro, 1998; Madureira, 2010).

In this sense, Watzlawik's (2009) study demonstrates that the concepts of masculinity and femininity, based on oversimplification and overlapping between different levels of analysis, are extremely fragile in scientific terms. In other words, to be a man or to be a woman is not a "natural fact"; instead, belonging to a gender is a cultural construction permeated with relations of power, oppression, and resistance (Foucault, 1996).

Concerning gender relations, in general, sexism corresponds to "an exclusive separation of genders, prioritizing one over the other, and associating dismissive meanings orientation to the 'other'" (Madureira, 2007b, p. 228). However, it is essential to recognize that in diverse societies, as Bourdieu (2005) has discussed, prestige, status, and autonomy are associated with masculinity. In other words, many "positive values" are socially associated with masculinity (e.g., courage, rationality, objectivity, autonomy).

Nowadays, it is not a coincidence that conservative groups, in Brazil and in various other countries around the world, defend the maintenance of the "traditional gender role" anchored in different versions of biological essentialism. If we are confronted with a "natural issue," it is not possible to promote any kind of cultural or political change. Thus we should be content with our "biological destinies" as women and as men. After all, we should respect the "laws of nature."

As a reaction against the changes that have occurred in gender relations in Western societies since the second half of the twentieth century, some important conservative segments of Brazilian society (although not only in Brazil) have defended the return to a "harmony" anchored in gender conventional standards. As Duncan, Peterson, and Winter (1997) demonstrated, there is a strong link between authoritarianism and the maintenance of a hierarchical social structure, including the hierarchical structure of gender. Nevertheless, it is extremely simplistic to affirm that the inequalities in gender relations are just the "fault of men." The maintenance of these inequalities is sustained by a complex power system that permeates all social instances (Foucault, 1996).

Therefore men and women participate, even if unintentionally, in the reproduction of sexism in daily practice. In the interfaces between gender and sexuality, the "scornful talk among women about the sexual behavior of other women is, for example, a powerful informal social control strategy concerning feminine sexuality" (Madureira, 2012, p. 585). Thus, in the studies on sexuality, it is essential to pay special attention to gender issues, permeated with cultural meanings associated with masculinity and femininity (Blackwood, 2000; Madureira, 2007b). The particular ways in which real people experience their sexuality are mediated by "gender ideologies that enable and structure differential practices from women and men" (Blackwood, 2000, p. 229).

At this moment, perhaps the reader is questioning the relation between the previous discussion on gender and the self-system? What is the relevance of this discussion for research concerned with the sociocultural psychology framework?

First, it is pertinent to mention the usefulness of the recent dialogues undertaken between sociocultural psychology and dialogical self theory (Branco & Madureira, 2008; Ferreira, Salgado, & Cunha, 2006; Hermans, 2001, 2004; Rosa, Duarte, & Gonçalves, 2008). As a "culture-inclusive" theory, dialogical self theory, proposed by Hermans (2001), was built on the ideas of William James (1842–1910) and Mikhail Bakhtin (1895–1975). More precisely, the self is conceived as a self-system, integrated by multiple I-positions that dynamically interact with the cultural context into which the individual is inserted (Hermans, 2001).

This theoretical perspective is particularly productive, for it can very well fit into the dialogical basis of sociocultural approaches. Moreover, dialogical self theory is an insightful example of the systemic approach to the issue of the self (Branco & Madureira, 2008). Basically, the self is a dynamic and cultural contextualized system. However, it is a mistake to conceive of the self as a harmonic system. As Hermans (2004, p. 13) has emphasized, "the different parts of the self [I-positions] are not only involved in communicative interchange, but also subjected to relative dominance, with some parts being more powerful or speaking with louder voices than other parts."

After all, power relations are present not only at social interactions between individuals and groups but also in the intrapsychological level of analysis. In other words, some I-positions tend to dominate other I-positions. Sometimes this dominance assumes a very rigid form, especially when some I-positions have a meaningful function in maintaining the status quo in our societies permeated by many prejudices. There are deep connections between the social hierarchies present in collective culture and power relations among different I-positions in the intrapsychological level of analysis. For example, in cultural contexts deeply permeated by sexism, it is reasonable to deduce that to be a "true" man and a "true" woman assumes vital importance, not only in ordinary social interactions but also in the interactions between different I-positions.

In these contexts, many mechanisms of cultural canalization reinforce the development of the self in a coherent way within gender stereotypes. Thus "I as a man" or "I as a woman" tends to assume a dominance over other I-positions in the self-system, regardless of the price paid in terms of physical and psychological suffering. In this sense, it is pertinent to mention that diverse authors nowadays stress that the cultural construction of hegemonic masculinity involves the constant "expulsion of oneself" of everything that can be associated with femininity and homosexuality (Bourdieu, 2005; Junqueira, 2009, 2010; Oliveira, 1998; Welzer-Lang, 2001).[2]

As previously discussed, the fight against gender violence is inseparable from the change of constitutive affection present in gender relations to what many people consider as "normal" (Segato, 2003). In a broader sense, in the promotion of gender equality, as Segato (2003) has analyzed, public policies on gender issues are fundamental, but they are not enough to promote a deep "reform of affection." In addition, sociocultural psychology can present relevant contributions for understanding culture and *psyche* in an integrated way. Among other important issues to be investigated, it is relevant to ask how gender stereotypes are promoted in ordinary cultural practice in our contemporary imagery societies.

32.4 Semiotic Mediation and Cultural Canalization of Gender Identities: The Power of Images in Contemporary Societies

In the art-form of European nude the painters and spectator-owners were usually men and the persons treated as objects, usually women. This unequal relationship is so deeply embedded in our culture that it still structures the consciousness of many women [and men too] . . . Today the attitudes and values which informed that tradition are expressed through other more widely diffused media – advertising, journalism, television. Berger (2008, p. 57)

As previously mentioned, human experiences always happen in culturally structured contexts, permeated with historically rooted beliefs, values, and practices that canalize meaning-making processes, guiding, in different ways, the thoughts, actions, and feelings of people. When we use the concept of *cultural canalization* instead of cultural determination, we intend to stress the active role of people in the meaning-making processes relative to the social world into which they are inserted and in relation to

themselves (Madureira & Branco, 2005, 2012; Madureira, 2012; Valsiner, 2007a). To understand how cultural canalization processes guide human experiences, a fundamental explanatory principle for sociocultural psychology is the principle of *semiotic mediation*.

From the sociocultural psychology framework, we consider that the semiotic processes are the basis of cultural phenomena – in both the collective and personal domains. As there are many possible combinations of icons, indexes, and symbols, verbal and visual signs present a hybrid nature that introduces great complexity into meaning-making processes, which are always immersed in the irreversible flow of time (Valsiner, 2007a). In sum, signs are cultural collective artifacts that play a fundamental role in human *psyche*.

It is necessary to clarify that the defense of the relevance of the signs, as cultural artifacts, in the research on typically human psychological functioning does not necessarily imply the conception that the relation between individuals and the social world is a purely rational undertaking mediated by signs expressed through verbal language. This conception reveals a linguistic and rationalistic reductionism concerning human *psyche*. First, because affect, cognition, and action form a complex unity that should not be overlooked by psychological science and second because verbal language is not the highest level of semiotic mediation but an intermediate level. The more abstract (and general) level of cultural mediation, related to personal values and prejudices, transcends purely verbal language (Valsiner, 2007a). In summary, it is essential to transcend the conception that semiotic mediation concerns only verbal language and rational enterprise.

Concerning the identity processes in the flow of everyday experiences, people use implicit criteria to include or exclude individuals in symbolic boundaries of a particular group. These implicit criteria are linked within the personal values system, which involves beliefs with deep affective roots and presents a cultural genesis (Branco & Madureira, 2008; Madureira, 2012). Therefore our personal beliefs are not simple individual creations. Our personal beliefs (and also our prejudices) are constructed from the "shared field" of collective culture, which is always informed by history.

In this sense, it is pertinent to mention that there is recent interest in the relations between collective memory and identity (Pollak, 1992). After all, it is on the ground of shared memories of a specific social group that social identities are constructed and, continuously, reconstructed in daily life. As Rosa, Bellelli, and Bakhurst (2000, p. 42) emphasize, "it is already common sense that identity is impossible without memory." Therefore, collective memory articulates present, past, and possible future projections (Halbwachs, 2004) and creates a "shared field" for social groups. The collective memory, shared by a specific social group, is constantly "fed by words and images" that permeate our ordinary lives.

Therefore, words and images are cultural artifacts that guide meaning-making processes by the active person in her/his life experiences. Actually, the English art critic John Berger (2008) discussed, seeing comes before words; the child looks before he can speak. Images and words – through the socialization processes of people – create a "ground of intelligibility" concerning the social word and themselves.

Thus words and images, as cultural artifacts, are conceived as psychological tools provided by collective culture (Madureira, 2016). On one hand, as cultural artifacts, words and images are different psychological tools; on the other hand, they are often complementary. For instance, to develop a detailed work of analysis and interpretation of a specific image, like a painting, we need verbal signs and their particular analytical poten-

tials. In sum, images and words are complementary "distinct realms":

> Far from being in front of a fight of titans – the verbal and the image – the linguistic expression and the visual are distinct realms, with ways of representing and meaning the reality proper of each one. They are much more complementary, so that it cannot entirely replace the other. (Santaella, 2012, p. 13, translated by author)

Throughout history, iconic signs have been used as powerful cultural artifacts to make more concrete concepts that are, in fact, extremely abstract, such as "nation," "love," "faith," and "freedom" (Chapter 22, this volume). To do that, allegorical personification and anthropomorphism of concepts have been common features of human civilization, according to Vico and as discussed by Tateo (Chapter 22, this volume). Iconic signs – in an integrated way with the narratives – are also fundamental to the cultural canalization of how we organize our memories of the past, not as a simple "neutral and objective" task but above all as a task with significant political implications (see Chapter 24, this volume). As previously mentioned, there are meaningful relations between collective memory and identity (Pollak, 1992). At the heart of this discussion, narratives and images can be used in different political ways for different purposes by different people and social groups (see Chapter 24, this volume).

Therefore, meaning-making processes involve a complex and dynamic hybridism between verbal and visual signs. Beyond that, these are embodied processes, understanding the body as "the intimate place where nature and culture meet each other" (Nightingale & Cromby, 2001, cited in Araiza & Gisbert, 2007, p. 115; translated by author). In other words, the meaning-making processes are not guided only by cognition, by "disembodied minds" devoid of feelings (Bruner, 1997, 2000; Madureira, 2007a, 2012; Valsiner,

2007a, 2012). As Le Breton (2007, p. 7) claims, "before anything, the existence is corporeal." The study of meaning making as embodied processes is, certainly, a complex challenge for sociocultural psychology. In this sense, Valsiner (2012) affirms,

The question of boundaries between person and environment has been actively disputed in the last two decades. Of course, human beings live within the boundary – circumscribed by their skin . . . The roots of this new focus on immediacy are in the resurgence of the centrality of the body in theorizing about human beings and its abstracted corollary in terms of the processes of *embodiment* of the mental processes. (Valsiner, 2012, p. 9)

Concerning gender issues, "social control penetrates in the mind through the body and its sensations" (Madureira, 2012, p. 593). Therefore, we should properly consider the cultural process of "education of vision." For thousands of years, the visual arts have followed the historical development of various societies around the world. The different artistic expressions in the domain of visual arts have formed and materialized the worldviews, beliefs, values, and feelings of people in different cultural contexts throughout history.

As Strickland (2004) discussed, art appeared about 25,000 years ago. At some time during the Ice Age, when our ancestors were still living in caves, "the Neanderthal's mentality of making instruments gave way to Cro-Magnon impulse to make images" (p. 4). We are the unique specie on our planet that produces art. This particularity is deeply linked to the human being as an excellent symbolic animal. We are compulsive builders of meaning (Valsiner, 2014), as previously mentioned in this chapter. According to the German critic and art historian Erwin Panofsky (2012, pp. 33–34), a work of art is an object produced by humans that demands "to be experienced aesthetically." In other words, the artistic object is a cultural artifact produced to create aesthetic experiences.

For Santaella (2012), however, visual arts are inserted into a wider visual territory: "the field of images as visual representations. They correspond to drawings, paintings, prints, photos, film images, television images, and holographic and infographic images (also called as 'computer images')" (p. 17; translated by author). This "image field" (visual representations) is particularly fertile for sociocultural psychology because it integrates images as cultural artifacts produced in the narrower context of the artistic universe in the same category as other images produced in the broader context of everyday cultural practices, for example, the many photos that people take with their smartphones in their daily lives or photos and drawings that appear in magazines and newspapers.

In the analysis on the historical roots of phenomena of interest by psychology and human sciences, in a broader sense, it is necessary to "educate our vision" to properly interpret cultural meanings present between the lines of, or implied in, visual representations (Santaella, 2012) produced by previous generations. In terms of gender issues, cultural meanings – which delimit what is socially expected of men and of women – are immersed in broader meaning systems established historically. The feelings of belonging to a particular gender are culturally constructed from beliefs, values, stereotypes, and prejudices that delimit, in rigid or flexible ways, the symbolic boundaries of femininity and masculinity (Madureira, 2007a, 2010, 2012).

For instance, in a previous study (Madureira, 2012), the historical roots of pejorative cultural meanings associated with the body and sexuality of women were problematized from the analysis of some elements of medieval Christian iconography, permeated by the misogyny characteristics of the social imaginary of this historical period in Europe. In the study in focus, it was possible to note the strong association between femininity and demonic forces. Aside from the figure of Mary, mother of Jesus, women would be regarded as demonic beings, dangerous, because they alienate men from the "way of salvation" (Madureira, 2012).

Therefore, the bodies and sexuality of women should be objects of strong social control to prevent the expression of the "demoniac potential" underlying femininity. Surely there are many economic, social, and cultural differences between the medieval period in Europe and our Western contemporary societies. Nevertheless, "the social imaginary in the contemporary Christian Western societies are still marked, in different ways, by archaic images about women . . . In some sense the moral dualism between Mary and Eve is still alive" (Madureira, 2012, p. 592).

Therefore, sociocultural psychology should be more attentive to the power of images in terms of cultural canalization of gender identities, especially when we recognize their pervasive impact on contemporary societies. More precisely, when we focus on the domain of images as visual representations (drawings, paintings, photographs, film and television images, computer images) (Santaella, 2012), we can deduce that we are living a true "invasion of images" in our daily lives.

Since the nineteenth century, many technological inventions have improved the impact of visual representations in the ordinary lives of humans. For example, (1) the invention of photography in the first half of the nineteenth century (Hacking, 2012), (2) the invention of cinema at the end of the nineteenth century (Kemp, 2011), (3) the invention of television in the first half of the twentieth century, (4) the expansion of the use of personal computers at the end of the twentieth century, and (5) the expansion of the use of smartphones at the beginning of the twenty-first century. Nowadays, smartphones have increasingly become extensions of the human body. People have become experts in articulating words and images (static and moving images) to express their thoughts and feelings, as illustrated, for example, by messages sent through WhatsApp in many countries around the world.

Concerning contemporary media, as Sabat (2001) analyzed, the advertising exerts a kind of "cultural pedagogy" that often has implications for the delimitation of rigid symbolic boundaries between femininity and masculinity that, unfortunately, reinforce sexism. However, *the images broadcast by the media in Western societies correspond to updates of European painting tradition that presents men as subjects and women as objects* (Berger, 2008; Loponte, 2002). More precisely, according to Berger (2008, p. 41), "men act and women appear" in the European painting tradition. The visual representations of men traditionally evolve to the incorporation of symbols of status and power (Nogueira, 1986), while women are represented as an object of masculine voyeurism (Berger, 2008; Loponte, 2002).

Note that objects are inanimate entities and as such without desires, autonomy, thoughts, and feelings – without life! For instance, it is common in advertisements of beer, widespread in Brazil, to present women – according to hegemonic body patterns – as one more object to satisfy men's desires. As if every man has heterosexual desires. As if the unique sense of a woman's life is to be an object, "property" of a powerful man to boast in social relations in daily life.

32.5 Final Remarks

We are one – by being individually unique. Valsiner (2007a, p. 18)

This chapter is the result of an effort to integrate knowledge produced in different areas beyond the disciplinary boundaries that separate psychology, other sciences, and arts. Particularly, ever since I was a teenager, I have admired the genius of intellectuals like Leonardo da Vinci (1452–1519) – intellectuals who break the rigid boundaries between science and art to create meaningful works that inspire new understandings on relevant issues about nature, culture, and about ourselves.

Each of us is individually unique. At the same time, we are part of humanity. The biological unity of our species, on one hand, and the cultural diversity of human beings, on the other hand, are fundamental for psychological science. The particular and the general are deeply connected. Since the 1990s, sociocultural psychology has invested in the construction of a more integrative and systemic view on human *psyche*. Without the establishment of interdisciplinary dialogues, this effort would be in vain. Thus the present chapter is an invitation to continue investing in the expansion of our knowledge horizons – more precisely, our knowledge horizons on gender issues, culture, and self.

In this chapter, self is conceived as a dynamic and contextualized system. In research that focuses on the development of self, it is essential to consider the role of "feelings of belonging" to specific social groups and their connections within political issues. Surely we are not on neutral political ground. Therefore, the conceptualization of social identities (e.g., gender identities) as boundary phenomena, as previously discussed, seems a fertile way to accomplish theoretical and empirical studies within a sociocultural psychology framework.

In the cultural contexts permeated by sexism, to be "a man" or to be "a woman" is not a detail. Frequently, different social practices, values, and feelings are culturally canalized to maintain the rigid symbolic boundaries that split masculinity and femininity. The transgressions of these rigid symbolic boundaries in daily life tend to trigger mechanisms of punishment against the transgressor. Critical analysis of these mechanisms is socially relevant, as, for example, in constructing prevention strategies of violence against women.

The issues focused on in this chapter are inserted into the interfaces between education and health. After all, the confrontation of sexism and other forms of prejudice in diverse educational contexts (school, family, media, etc.) is a way of contributing to the prevention of situations of violence and exclusion. In other words, it is a way of contributing to the promotion of health in a way that is coherent with the most important ethical commitment of psychology as a scientific discipline and professional field – the promotion of everyone's health and well-being.

To do so, psychology must overcome the traditional individualistic and pathological perspectives that, historically and still today, mark the discipline. We need to identify and analyze the cultural mechanisms that promote violence and suffering in many people all over the world. We live in societies that, unfortunately, feed and inflict all sorts of human suffering. More precisely, promoting suffering is lucrative in the contemporary world. It is no coincidence that one of the most lucrative industries nowadays is the pharmaceutical industry!

In the contemporary world, we observe a significant expansion of discourses anchored in hatred and intolerance toward diverse social groups in terms of gender, sexual orientation, nationality, ethnic belonging, religion, and so on. Unfortunately, this social phenomenon is present in several countries, including Brazil. Therefore, sociocultural psychology should develop theoretical and conceptual tools to face the challenges of our time, including this worrying social phenomenon. Since the 1990s, sociocultural psychology has pursued the construction of a more integrative, dynamic, contextualized, and systemic view about human *psyche*. This view has relevant social implications beyond the physical and symbolic walls that separate the academic context from everyday life.

Knowledge can be a powerful tool to promote important social change. More precisely, to promote gender equality in diverse social spheres, including interpersonal relations in the private domain, it is essential to combat, in different educational contexts, the sexist verbal and visual representations of masculinity and femininity present in our imagery contemporary societies. The study of images as cultural artifacts, including their analytical, methodological, and educational potentials (Madureira, 2016), as well as the study of visual arts history by sociocultural psychology, can offer some critical and insightful tools in this socially relevant direction.

Acknowledgments

This chapter brought some contributions from my PhD, my postdoctorate studies, and more recent reflections that I have constructed from my professional experiences as a professor at Centro Universitário de Brasília – UniCEUB (Brazil). I want to thank the National Committee for Scientific and Technological Development – CNPq (Brazil) – for the financial support of my PhD studies, including the period that I was a visiting student of the Psychology Department at Clark University (USA). I also want to thank the National Committee for Academic Support – CAPES (Brazil) for the financial support of my post-doctorate at Universidad Autónoma de Madrid (Spain). I am deeply grateful to Prof. Dr. Angela Branco (Universidade de Brasília, Brazil), Prof. Dr. Jaan Valsiner (Aalborg University, Denmark), and Prof. Dr. Alberto Rosa (Universidad Autónoma de Madrid, Spain) for their relevant theoretical contributions and for their important role in my academic trajectory.

Notes

1 Ilya Prigogine (1917–2003) was awarded a Nobel Prize for his scientific work on dissipative structures, complex systems, and irreversibility.
2 About the discussion on physical and psychological suffering involved in the construction of hegemonic masculinity, I suggest the documentary *The Mask You Live In* (dir. Jennifer Siebel Newsom, 2015), available on Netflix.

References

Alves, R. (2012). *Filosofia da Ciência: introdução ao jogo e suas regras*. São Paulo: Edições Loyola.

Araiza, A. & Gisbert, G. (2007). Transformaciones del cuerpo en psicología social. *Psicologia: Teoria e Pesquisa*, 23(1), 111–117.

Bauman, Z. (2005). *Identidade*. Rio de Janeiro: Zahar.

Blackwood, E. (2000). Culture and women's sexualities. *Journal of Social Issues*, 56(2), 223–238.

Branco, A. U. & Madureira, A. F. (2008). Dialogical self in action: The emergence of self-positions among complex emotional and cultural dimensions. *Estudios de Psicología*, 29(3), 319–332.

Berger, J. (2008). *Ways of Seeing*. London: Penguin Books.

Bourdieu, P. (2005). *A dominação masculina*. Rio de Janeiro: Bertrand Brasil.

Bruner, J. (1997). *Atos de significação*. Porto Alegre: Artes Médicas.

Bruner, J. (2000). *Cultura da Educação*. Lisboa: Edições 70.

Cole, M. (1992). Culture in development. In M. H. Bornstein & M. E. Lamb (Eds.), *Developmental Psychology: An Advanced Textbook* (pp. 731–787). Mahwah, NJ: Lawrence Erlbaum.

Costa, J. F. (1999). *Ordem médica e norma familiar*. Rio de Janeiro: Graal.

Demo, P. (2005). *Éticas multiculturais: sobre convivência humana possível*. Petrópolis, Brazil: Vozes.

Duncan, L. E., Peterson, B. E., & Winter, D. G. (1997). Authoritarianism and gender roles: Toward a psychological analysis of hegemonic relationships. *Personality and Social Psychology Bulletin*, 23(1), 193–200.

Ferreira, T., Salgado, J., & Cunha, C. (2006). Ambiguity and dialogical self: In search for a dialogical self. *Estudios de Psicología*, 27(1), 19–32.

Fogel, A., Lyra, M. C. D. P., & Valsiner, J. (1997). Introduction: Perspectives on indeterminism and development. In A. Fogel, M. C. D. P. Lyra, & J. Valsiner (Eds.), *Dynamics and Indeterminism in Developmental and Social Processes* (pp. 1–10). Mahwah, NJ: Lawrence Erlbaum.

Foucault, M. (1996). *Microfísica do poder*. Rio de Janeiro: Graal.

Galinkin, A. L. & Zauli, A. (2011). Identidade social e alteridade. In C. V. Torres & E. R Neiva (Eds.),

Psicologia Social: Principais temas e vertentes (pp. 253–261). Porto Alegre, Brazil: Artmed.

Geertz, C. (1989). *A interpretação das culturas*. Rio de Janeiro: LTC.

Geertz, C. (2001). *Nova luz sobre a antropologia*. Rio de Janeiro: Jorge Zahar.

Hacking, J. (2012). *Tudo sobre fotografia*. Rio de Janeiro: Sextante.

Halbwachs, M. (2004). *A memória coletiva*. São Paulo: Centauro.

Hall, S. (1998). *A identidade cultural na pós-modernidade*. Rio de Janeiro: DP&A.

Hall, S. (2000). Quem precisa da identidade? In T. T. Silva (Ed.), *Identidade e diferença: A Perspectiva dos estudos culturais* (pp. 103–133). Petrópolis, Brazil: Vozes.

Hermans, H. J. M. (2001). The dialogical self: Towards a theory of personal and cultural positioning. *Culture & Psychology*, 7(3), 243–282.

Hermans, H. J. M. (2004). The dialogical self: Between exchange and power. In H. J. M. Hermans & G. Dimaggio (Eds.), *The Dialogical Self in Psychotherapy* (pp. 13–28). New York: Brunner-Routledge.

Joerchel, A. C. (2007). A dance between the general and the specific: Implications for the self concept. *Integrative Psychological & Behavioral Science*, 41(3–4), 254–261.

Junqueira, R. D. (2009). Introdução – Homofobia nas escolas: Um problema de todos. In R. D. Junqueira (Eds.), *Diversidade sexual na educação: Problematizações sobre a homofobia nas escolas* (pp. 13–51). Brasília: Ministério da Educação, Secretaria de Educação Continuada, Alfabetização e Diversidade, UNESCO.

Junqueira, R. D. (2010). Currículo heteronormativo e cotidiano escolar homofóbico. *Espaço do Currículo*, 2(2), 208–230.

Kemp, P. (2011). *Tudo sobre cinema*. Rio de Janeiro: Sextante.

Lawrence, J. & Valsiner, J. (1993). Conceptual roots of internalization: From transmission to transformation. *Human Development*, 36, 150–167.

Le Breton, D. (2007). *A sociologia do corpo*. Petrópolis, Brazil: Vozes.

Loponte, L. G. (2002). Sexualidades, artes visuais e poder: Pedagogias visuais do feminino. *Estudos Feministas*, 10(2), 283–300.

Louro, G. L. (1998). *Gênero, sexualidade e educação: Uma perspectiva pós-estruturalista*. Petrópolis, Brazil: Vozes.

Louro, G. L. (2003). Currículo, gênero e sexualidade: O "normal", o "diferente" e o "excêntrico." In G. L. Louro, J. F. Neckel, & S. V. Goellner (Eds.), *Corpo, gênero e sexualidade: Um debate contemporâneo na educação* (pp. 41–52). Petrópolis, Brazil: Vozes.

Louro, G. L. (2004). *Um corpo estranho: Ensaios sobre sexualidade e teoria queer*. Belo Horizonte, Brazil: Autêntica.

Madureira, A. F. A. (2000). A construção das identidades sexuais não-hegemônicas: Gênero, linguagem e constituição da subjetividade. Master's dissertation, Instituto de Psicologia, Universidade de Brasília, Brazil.

Madureira, A. F. A. (2007a). Gênero, sexualidade e diversidade na escola: A construção de uma cultura democrática. Doctoral thesis, Instituto de Psicologia, Universidade de Brasília, Brazil.

Madureira, A. F. A. (2007b). The psychological basis of homophobia: Cultural construction of a barrier. *Integrative Psychological & Behavioral Science*, 41(3–4), 225–247.

Madureira, A. F. A. (2008). Invisible boundaries with concrete implications: Meaning making processes and symbolic boundaries. In J. Valsiner, S. Salvatore, J. Clegg, & S. Strout (Eds.), *Yearbook of Idiographic Science* (pp. 233–248). Rome: Giorgio Firera.

Madureira, A. F. A. (2009). Commentary. When stereotypes become "scientific" statements: Dealing with gender issues. *Integrative Psychological & Behavioral Science*, 43, 138–148.

Madureira, A. F. A. (2010). Gênero, sexualidade e processos identitários na sociedade brasileira: Tradição e modernidade em conflito. In A. L. Galinkin & C. Santos (Eds.), *Gênero e Psicologia Social: Interfaces* (pp. 31–63). Brasília: Tecnopolik.

Madureira, A. F. A. (2012). Belonging to gender: Social identities, symbolic boundaries and images. In J. Valsiner (Ed.), *The Oxford Handbook of Culture and Psychology* (pp. 582–601). New York: Oxford University Press.

Madureira, A. F. A. (2016). Diálogos entre a Psicologia e as Artes Visuais: As Imagens enquanto Artefatos Culturais. In J. L. Freitas & E. P. Flores (Eds.), *Arte e Psicologia: Fundamentos e Práticas* (pp. 57–82). Curitiba, Brazil: Juruá.

Madureira, A. F. A. & Branco, A. U. (2005). Construindo com o outro: uma perspectiva sociocultural construtivista do desenvolvimento humano. In M. A. Dessen & A. L. Costa Jr. (Eds.), *A ciência do desenvolvimento humano: Tendências atuais e perspectivas futuras* (pp. 90–109). Porto Alegre, Brazil: Artes Médicas.

Madureira, A. F. A. & Branco, A. U. (2007). Identidades sexuais não-hegemônicas: Processos identitários e estratégias para lidar com o preconceito. *Psicologia: Teoria e Pesquisa*, 23(1), 81–90.

Madureira, A. F. A. & Branco, A. U. (2012). As raízes histórico-culturais e afetivas do preconceito e a construção de uma cultura democrática na escola. In A. U. Branco & M. C. S. L. Oliveira (Eds.), *Diversidade e cultura da paz na escola: Contribuições da perspectiva sociocultural* (pp. 125–155). Porto Alegre, Brazil: Mediação.

Madureira, A. F. A. & Branco, A. U. (2015). Gênero, sexualidade e diversidade na escola a partir da perspectiva de professores/as. *Temas em Psicologia (Ribeirão Preto)*, 23(3), 577–591.

Mahoney, M. J. (1998). *Processos humanos de mudança: As bases científicas da psicoterapia*. Porto Alegre, Brazil: ArtMed.

Marcondes, D. (2000). *Iniciação à História da Filosofia: Dos Pré-socráticos à Wittgenstein*. Rio de Janeiro: Jorge Zahar Editor.

Moreira, A. F. B. & Câmara, M. J. (2008). Reflexões sobre currículo e identidade: Implicações para a prática pedagógica. In A. F. Moreira & V. M. Candau (Eds.), *Multiculturalismo: Diferenças culturais e práticas pedagógicas* (pp. 38–66). Petrópolis, Brazil: Vozes.

Moreira, J. (2011). A ciência da universidade e a estética, a poesia, a sapiência da vida: O lugar da pesquisa como criação. In C. Fritzen & J. Moreira, J. (Eds.), *Educação e Arte: As linguagens artísticas na formação humana* (pp. 11–26). Campinas, Brazil: Papirus.

Myers, D. G. (1995). *Psicologia Social*. México: McGraw-Hill.

Nogueira, R. (1986). Revistas masculinas ou de macho? In R. P. da Costa (Ed.), *Macho, masculino, homem: A sexualidade, o machismo e a crise de identidade do homem brasileiro* (pp. 61–63). Porto Alegre/São Paulo: L&PM.

Oliveira, M. C. S. L. & Madureira, A. F. A. (2014). Gênero e Psicologia do Desenvolvimento: Quando a ciência é utilizada como força normatizadora das identidades de gênero. *Labrys*, 26. Retrieved from www.labrys.net.br/labrys26/psy/maria%20claudia.htm.

Oliveira, P. P. (1998). Discursos sobre a masculinidade. *Estudos Feministas*, 6(1), 91–111.

Panofsky, E. (2012). *Significado nas artes visuais*. São Paulo: Perspectiva.

Pérez-Nebra, A. R. & Jesus, J. G. (2011). Preconceito, estereótipo e discriminação. In C. V. Torres & E. R. Neiva (Eds.), *Psicologia social: Principais temas e vertentes* (pp. 219–237). Porto Alegre, Brazil: ArtMed.

Pino, A. (2000). O social e o cultural na obra de Lev. S. Vygotsky. *Educação & Sociedade*, 71, 45–78.

Pino, A. (2005). *As marcas do humano: Às origens da constituição cultural da criança na perspectiva de Lev. S. Vigotski*. São Paulo: Cortez.

Pollak, M. (1992). Memória e identidade social. *Estudos Históricos*, 10(5), 200–212.

Prigogine, I. & Stengers, I. (1997). *A nova aliança: Metamorfose da ciência*. Brasília: Editora Universidade de Brasília.

Rogoff, B. (2003). *The Cultural Nature of Human Development*. New York: University Press.

Rosa, A. (2007a). Acts of psyche: Actuations as synthesis of semiosis and action. In J. Valsiner & A. Rosa (Eds.), *The Cambridge Handbook of Sociocultural Psychology* (pp. 205–237). New York: Cambridge University Press.

Rosa, A. (2007b). Dramaturgical actuations and symbolic communication: Or how beliefs make up reality. In J. Valsiner & A. Rosa (Eds.), *The Cambridge Handbook of Sociocultural Psychology* (pp. 293–317). New York: Cambridge University Press.

Rosa, A.; Bellelli, G., & Bakhurst, D. (2000). Representaciones del pasado, cultura personal e identidad nacional. In A. Rosa; G. Bellelli, & D. Bakhurst (Eds.), *Memoria colectiva e identidad nacional* (pp. 41–87). Madrid: Biblioteca Nueva.

Rosa, A. & Blanco, F. (2007). Actuations of identification in the games of identity. *Social Practice/Psychological Theorizing*. Retrieved from www.sppt-gulerce.boun.edu.tr/

Rosa, C., Duarte, F., & Gonçalves, M. (2008). Self and dialogical articulation of multifocality: Proposal of an analysis model. In J. Valsiner, S. Salvatore, J. Clegg, & S. Strout (Eds.). *Yearbook of Idiographic Science* (pp. 163–189). Rome: Giorgio Firera.

Sabat, R. (2001). Pedagogia cultural, gênero e sexualidade. *Estudos Feministas*, 9(1), 9–21.

Santaella, L. (2012). *Leitura de imagens*. São Paulo: Melhoramentos.

Sawaia, B. B. (2014). Identidade – Uma ideologia separatista? In B. B. Sawaia (Ed.), *As artimanhas da exclusão: Análise psicossocial e ética da desigualdade social* (pp. 121–129). Petrópolis, Brazil: Vozes.

Scott, J. (1995). Gênero: Uma categoria útil de análise histórica. *Educação & Realidade*, 20(2), 71–99.

Scott, J. (1998). Ponto de vista: Entrevista com Joan Wallach Scott. *Estudos Feministas*, 6(1), 114–124.

Segato, R. L. (2003). *Las estructuras elementales de la violencia: Ensayos sobre género entre la antropología, el psicoanálisis y los derechos humanos*. Buenos Aires: Universidad Nacional de Quilmas.

Shweder, R. A. (1991). *Thinking through cultures: Expeditions in cultural psychology*. Cambridge, MA: Harvard University Press.

Silva, T. T. (2000). A produção social da identidade e da diferença. In T. T. Silva (Ed.), *Identidade e diferença: A perspectiva dos estudos culturais* (pp. 73–102). Petrópolis, Brazil: Vozes.

Stokes, P. (2012). *Os 100 pensadores essenciais da filosofia: Dos pré-socráticos aos novos cientistas*. Rio de Janeiro: DIFEL.

Strickland, C. (2004). *Arte comentada: da pré-história ao pós-moderno*. Rio de Janeiro: Ediouro.

Valsiner, J. (2006). The street. Unpublished manuscript, based on invited lecture at Arquitectura 3000 in 2004, Universitat Politecnica de Catalunya, Barcelona.

Valsiner, J. (2007a). *Culture in Minds and Societies: Foundations of Cultural Psychology*. New Delhi: SAGE.

Valsiner, J. (2007b). Looking across cultural boundaries. *Integrative Psychological & Behavioral Science*, 41(3–4), 219–224.

Valsiner, J. (2012). Introduction: Culture in psychology: A renewed encounter of inquisitive minds. In J. Valsiner (Ed.), *The Oxford Handbook of Culture and Psychology* (pp. 3–24). New York: Oxford University Press.

Valsiner, J. (2014). *An Invitation to Cultural Psychology*. London: SAGE.

Valsiner, J. & Rosa, A. (2007a). Editors' Introduction – Contemporary Sociocultural Research: Uniting Culture, Society and Psychology. In J. Valsiner & A. Rosa (Eds.), *The Cambridge Handbook of Sociocultural Psychology* (pp. 1–20). New York: Cambridge University Press.

Valsiner, J. & Rosa, A. (2007b). The myth, and beyond: Ontology of psyche and epistemology of psychology. In J. Valsiner & A. Rosa (Eds.), *The Cambridge Handbook of Sociocultural Psychology* (pp. 23–39). New York: Cambridge University Press.

Watzlawik, M. S. (2009). When a man thinks he has female traits – Constructing femininity and masculinity: Methodological potentials and limitations. *Integrative Psychological & Behavioral Science*, 43(2), 126–137.

Welzer-Lang, D. (2001). A construção do masculino: Dominação das mulheres e homofobia. *Estudos Feministas*, 9(2), 460–482.

Woodward, K. (2000). Identidade e diferença: Uma introdução conceitual. In T. T. Silva (Eds.), *Identidade e diferença: A perspectiva dos estudos culturais* (pp. 7–72). Petrópolis, Brazil: Vozes.

33 The Experience of Aging: Views from Without and Within

Dieter Ferring

33.1 Introduction

Aging has become a topic of public attention due to increasing life expectancies in the industrialized societies of Asia and Europe. United Nations data from 2012 show that nine of the ten oldest populations of the world are from Europe: while Japan has the highest proportion of elderly people, Germany and Italy follow in the second and third places – followed by Bulgaria, Finland, Croatia, Greece, Latvia, Slovenia, and Malta. Combined with decreasing fertility, societies run the risk of over-aging, that is, the older part of the population are in the majority with children, adolescents, and adults in the minority. This has consequences at all levels of the socioecological context including the individual experience of aging, the effects on society, and the macro context, most notably with respect to the sustainability of public expenditures and the division and distribution of public resources.

All this has been stated quite often and several disciplines tackle the challenges associated with human aging, in particular, age-associated diseases taking a prominent position. There are losses in functional and physical status due to lifestyles and genetic programming that constitute part of each individual's profile and there are several compensatory means provided by an assistive culture that help to adapt to these. Alzheimer's disease (AD) and other neurodegenerative diseases show a heightened prevalence owing to population aging of which not much was known before the 1980s. Pharmacological research on the substances that will help to stop or, even better, prevent AD and other age-related diseases are high on the priority list across the globe. The social sciences as well as engineering sciences include aging in their theory and research, while some disciplines also develop specific approaches or even related disciplines to focus on gerontological issues, for example, geropsychology, geriatric medicine, and a sociology dedicated to the aging society. Aging, thus, has become a transversal dimension in theory and research comparable to other summative concepts such as gender or the reemerging concept of social class.

All these efforts – be they disciplinary or interdisciplinary – convey the specific meaning that age and aging represent an irreversible threat to the individual and the society. The overall meaning of both aging and the old person thus is not a positive one. Nowadays the individual person may be afraid of age-related changes and motivated to prevent, compensate, or even "deny" all changes linked to aging. Several psychological models of self-regulation described below elaborate on the various dynamics of adapting to the predominant negative age stereotype. At the societal level several phenomena reflect such a view as well: the media build up scenarios of a war on the just division of resources between generations and policymakers as well as economists, demographers, and social scientists discuss different scenarios of financing the welfare state implying that aging of societies is one if not the most important risk factor of public welfare (see some chapters in Albert & Ferring, 2013; Ferring, 2010). In this introductory statement,

I like to briefly highlight that such a view marks a change in the perception of elderly persons across human history. Being an "elder" or "elderly" already indicates such a changed view. Agricultural societies, especially, recognized the knowledge and expertise of its older members in various domains, be it sewing or healing and curing of diseases; decision makers were mostly "senior" as the Latin word "senator" stills conveys. Whole societies depended on this "wisdom" or the lack of it. With the start of the industrialization the picture began to change, given that older people (now) seem to be no longer economically productive and thus not contributing to the common good.

33.1.1 New Perspectives

So much has been written about aging that it seems imperative to not repeat and produce more of the same. This chapter bears the title "views from without and within" and I will start with the view from without highlighting some positions taken in psychological theory and research. I will focus on the lifespan models, on models analyzing aging and self-regulation, as well as conceptual "qualifiers" of aging. Following this, I will get to the individual experience and present biographical data highlighting developmental dynamics underlying the life course and offering insight into individual development. The aim of this chapter is to present a synthetic and comprehensive view on human aging combining findings from theory and research following a nomothetic quantitative approach, on the one hand, as well as an idiographic view using qualitative methods, on the other hand.

33.2 The View from Without

33.2.1 A Look at the Phenomena: From Biblical Age to Senicide

The Torah reports Methuselah to have reached 969 years of age. Abraham is told to have lived

175 years, fathering his son at the age of 99; his wife Sarah, being 10 years younger, mothered Isaac thus at the age of 89, "for her age was as nothing to God" (Genesis 25:7–10). Homer describes in his Hymns to Aphrodite, written in the seventh century BCE, that Tithonos was the lover of Eos, goddess of the dawn, who asked Zeus to make her lover immortal. The wish was granted but the goddess did not ask for eternal youth, thus, Tithonos lived forever but was eternally burdened by old age. The Pali Canon, dated 300 BCE, holds that old age, disease, and death are the three evils of suffering; aging is understood as a biological process affecting the human body and happening to everyone – even Buddha who is reported to have died at the age of 80.[1]

These few examples taken out of different cultural heritages, show that aging is a topic of historic and, certainly, prehistoric times. There seems to be the need to explain the deterioration manifesting in physical, functional, and mental impairments with advancing age that happens to all of us. Immortality or at least longevity have been desired goods – and might unrealistically be granted by the (Greek) gods – but in the end human beings are mortal and their lives have to end. This motivated further myths such as the "fountain of youth" that is a recurrent theme in human history (see Olshansky, Hayflick, & Carnes, 2002). All cultures seem to consider old age as an entity besides childhood, adolescence, and adulthood, differing by their distinctive characteristics of competences, roles, and responsibilities. Old age is distinct and different qualities are attached to it. Older people receive different evaluations in the examples given above. Tithonos may be considered the person with the greatest suffering – to live forever and age eternally. The biblical forefathers were considered important and full of power; Sarah was granted the gift of reproduction despite of her age.

While the aging process and its challenges seem to be equivocally perceived as mostly undesired life conditions in our examples here, the picture of the aging person varies across time. One explanation for differing evaluations of older adults – and already mentioned in the introduction – is offered by Cowgill and Holmes (1972) who link these differences to the transition from traditional rural-agricultural to industrial and urbanized societies. According to these authors, rural-agricultural societies value experiential knowledge since knowing when to plant what and when as well as when to prepare the harvest is crucial for life and survival. Consequently, bearers of such a knowledge are much higher appreciated in traditional societies that combine family life and production. Industrialized societies focus on the capacities of productivity (especially in the younger generation) and separate family and production of goods. Cultures of economy and production thus exert an influence on the positive or negative perception of old age in such a view. But even in rural communities, old aged persons may be considered as a burden feeding on common resources, and senicide has been reported in several societies.

The Japanese word of *ubasute* stands – according to Ogawa (2008) – for the legendary practice of abandoning older people who became unproductive and a burden to their families and leave them to die. The author uses *ubasute* as a word metaphor that describes today's "abandoning" of older adults into nursing homes separating them from their families. The phenomenon of abandoning older adults or the voluntary decision of older adults to die when resources were scarce and the life of the younger community members were at risk has been reported for several cultures. North American Indians are reported to have practices of widow suicide, female infanticide, as well as the willing abandonment of older frail adults. The Hindu practice of Sati stands for the voluntary or coerced death of the widow though independent of the widow's age.[2]

A further facet of today's "senicide" includes the phenomena of physician-assisted suicide and euthanasia. There are discussions of assisted suicide of patients diagnosed with dementia and other diagnoses (e.g., *New England Journal of Medicine*, 2013). Linked to this is a discourse about what makes life worthwhile living or – on the other hand – which conditions may render a life no longer worthy to life and may thus justify ending one's life. Both fatal as well as nonfatal diagnoses may lead to the decision to seek assisted suicide as Fischer et al. (2008) find in their analysis of assisted suicides in Switzerland. The distribution of assisted suicides across age groups shows that 252 persons out of 421 deceased persons (and thus the majority) are older than 65 years. In their analysis of 611 of assisted suicides from 31 countries all over the world, Gauthier et al. (2014) report a median age of 69 years and underline this as marking an age at high risk of malignancy or chronic disease.

33.2.2 On Aging, Death and Dying

Aging always and unchangeably includes the notion of death and the early developmental models proposed by Havighurst, Erikson, and Bühler mentioned below all include the adaptation to the finiteness of life as one developmental task of the later years. On the other side, there has been a considerable effort in psychological theory and research to arrive at and convey a positive view on aging. Successful aging, plasticity, and reserve capacity as well as adaptive mechanisms of old age are key words that mark these endeavors which are described in the following. Interestingly, the very effort of such a disciplinary discourse to create positive meaning of age and aging signifies itself a way of adaptation to the finiteness of life. I will come back to this point below.

But first, I want to point out that – when talking about the finiteness of living – one has to differ between death and the process of dying. This may be illustrated by the following statement of an older lady at the age of 83. When asked about death she told me that she is not afraid of death per se – "when it [life] ends it's ended" – but she fears dying in a non-dignified way without any form of controlling what is happening to her. This wish, which all people will certainly share, highlights the difference between the existential phenomena of death and dying. When it comes to the discourse on dying, both within social sciences as well as life sciences, I like to highlight two names here that changed or started this discourse. Elisabeth Kübler-Ross talked with dying persons and offered a book on dying and death developing a model of grief in 1969. Cecily Sanders initiated and chaired the St. Christopher's Hospice and founded the hospice movement. As Richmond (2005) writes in Sanders's obituary "more than anybody else, [she] was responsible for establishing the discipline and the culture of palliative care. She introduced effective pain management and insisted that dying people needed dignity, compassion, and respect, as well as rigorous scientific methodology in the testing of treatments" (Richmond, 2005, p. 238).

Studying dying as well as establishing conditions of dignified dying had become topics in the postwar Western world when demographic changes and over-aging were still phenomena that were hard to imagine. The postwar Western society has been described as death-denying. As Zimmerman and Rodin (2005) elaborate in their work on the denial of death, it seems that lay public as well as clinicians have taken this phenomenon for granted, while it has been increasingly questioned in the sociological literature (see Kellehear, 1984). Interestingly, death and dying are not often objects of psychological theory and research on aging. Baltes (1997), for instance, in his seminal paper on the "incomplete architecture of the human life span" never mentions death and dying, but he describes the percentage of dysfunctional inactive years of the remaining lifetime using findings by Crimmins, Hayward, and Saito (1996). He differentiates here between the "third age" as a phase of comparatively less impairments and deficits that may also be compensated, and the "fourth age" as having a height-

ened probability of losses in learning potential and cognitive plasticity and a heightened prevalence of neurodegenerative disorders and functional impairments in general.

The mortality concept that Smith (2002) links to "psychological mortality" in the fourth age implies death and dying. Smith highlights that functioning in the fourth age shows a general decline in psychological well-being and intellectual functioning and thus becomes "death-related" compared to age-related changes in the third age. She connects this to the notion of terminal decline – a phenomenon described by accelerated decline and functional breakdown five to seven years prior to death in very old age (e.g., Berg, 1996). While large data sets such as the Berlin Aging Study allow for the approximate and quantitative description of such phenomena (see also Smith & Baltes, 1993), a qualitative analysis is missing. Therefore, I take the position here that psychological theory and research on aging has widely neglected if not to say "denied" dying and death as integral parts of the life course. This may be due to the focus of predominant models that underline the potential of "successful" aging reflecting the sociocultural need for positive framing which will be part of the following section.

33.2.3 Psychology and Aging

I have described elsewhere in more detail the sequel of theory building reflecting different views on human development and aging (see Berg et al., 2008; Zittoun et al., 2013). Table 33.1 gives a selective overview of central concepts, models, and theories about human aging by listing authors, date of publication, and the title or specific key words linked to the process of human aging. When qualifying these contributions as central I refer to the echo that all these discussed models mostly stimulate psychological theory and research. Table 33.1 structures the different contribution into lifespan models, models

Table 33.1 *Overview of central concepts, models, and theories on human aging.*

Author	Year	Label/title
Lifespan models		
Bühler	1933/1959	The course of human life as a *psychological problem*
Erikson	1959	*Identity* and the life cycle
Havighurst	1961	Developmental tasks
Atchley	1972	Continuity theory
Baltes, Brim, Featherman, Lerner	1978–1990	Series on "lifespan development and behavior"
Aging and regulation		
Thomae	1970	Theory of aging and *cognitive theory* of personality
Atchley	1972	Continuity theory
Baltes & Baltes	1990	Selective optimization with compensation – a meta model
Brandtstädter & Greve	1994	Theory of assimilative-accommodative mastery
Heckhausen, Schulz	1995, 1996	Primary and secondary control – a lifespan model of successful aging
Hobfoll	1988	Theory of resource development and conservation
Carstensen	1995	Theory of socio-emotional selectivity
Heckhausen, Wrosch, & Schulz	2010	A motivational theory of lifespan development
Qualifying aging		
Havighurst	1961	Successful aging
Cumming & Henry	1961	Disengagement theory
Lemon, Bengtson, & Peterson	1972	Activity theory
Butler & Gleason	1985	Productive aging
Rowe & Kahn	1998	Successful aging
Baltes & Baltes	1990	Successful aging
Moody	2002	Conscious aging
Tornstam	2005	Positive aging and gerotranscendance
Fernández-Ballesteros	2008	Active aging
Sherman	2010	Contemplative aging
Oerlemans, Bakker, & Veenhoven	2011	Happy aging
Several authors		Healthy aging

on aging and self-regulation, as well as models that introduce qualification of the aging process as "successful," "active," and so on.

The sequence of models ranges from "disengagement" to "successful aging" if one uses their qualifiers and, thus, the message of the models or at least their summary become more "positive," that is, rendering a view on the potentials of aging with respect to being "active," "productive," or "successful" across the decades. They therefore may serve as sociocultural guidance and change the way that aging is perceived and evaluated at the individual, the micro, and the macrolevel. They may also reflect needs of the sociocultural context in identifying ways to integrate the aging experience in an increasingly aging society and thus offer a positive frame. Suffering and dying and the reflection of one's life and coming to terms with the finiteness of life are not reflected in such a view anymore.

33.2.3.1 Lifespan Models and Aging

One may start here with the early model proposed by Charlotte Bühler who divided life into five periods initiated by biological processes, the last one marked by the end of reproduction. Bühler postulated that even though age may include physical and functional decline it may also represent a "*Periode der Werkvollendung*" (p. 80), that is, a period where one accomplishes his or her "work of life." Following this, one may list the model of psychosocial crises proposed by Erikson and the model of developmental tasks by Havighurst as further theories considering age as a specific period of human development. The tension between different tendencies characterizes psychosocial crises according to Erikson asking for a solution to accomplish the next step of development. Ego integrity versus despair describe the prototypical crisis of old age. A person may thus look back on life and come to accept this as meaningful or despair about it. Erikson as well as Bühler consider biological change as well as culture as important dynamics underlying different developmental crises. Havighurst follows this logic and outlines a set of developmental tasks across the life span that reflect biological and psychosocial demands in a given sociocultural context. Later maturity covers the life time starting at the age of 60 in this model and it includes other specific tasks (e.g., adaptation to decreasing physical strength and health, the loss of loved ones, the preparation for the end of life). Havighurst highlights that old age allows for significant learning experiences even though this requires to detach oneself from old roles and taking on new ones.

All three models are in my view significant markers of psychological theories dealing with old age because they realize a lifespan approach highlighting the interplay of biological as well as sociocultural factors in defining specific topics, crises, or tasks of advancing age. Moreover, they underline room for development and in this reflect a phenomenologically valid reflection of different aging profiles of their time. Here, one can also highlight Atchley's (1972) approach which focuses development across the lifespan with respect to continuity. His fundamental proposition is immediately and intuitively evident: a person who has had an introverted youth will keep this behavior and certainly not become an outgoing extrovert in old age (Zittoun et al., 2013). A merit of this approach is that aging is considered as part of the continuous individual development and not as a categorical rupture that renders a person of a certain age as "old." Individual personality and development have to be taken into account and this opens aging to a biographical approach which I will pick up later again in this section.

But first, I would like to outline another contribution to lifespan development and aging. These two interlinked topics became particularly prominent in the 1980s which is given some focus in the book series, *Lifespan Development and Behavior*, edited by Paul B. Baltes, Orville Brim, David L. Featherman, and Richard Lerner, with other authors between 1978 and 1990. This series included 10 volumes focusing on theoretical and methodological issues with a life-course approach elaborating on a development concept that underlines the multi-causal and multidimensional nature of human development. Such a conception of lifespan development clearly differs from the conception of development in early childhood and childhood as a unidirectional process following the orthogenetic principle. Consequently, this approach sets the frame for theoretical models that elaborate the notion of plasticity in the aging process. P. B. Baltes and M. M. Baltes edited and published a volume on "successful aging" in 1990 when the last volume of *Lifespan Development and Behavior* appeared.

This book presented several views on human aging highlighting the potential of the age period described by resilience and reserve capacity (see Staudinger, Marsiske, & Baltes, 1993) as well as its special mixture of gains and losses. Aging therefore became again part of lifespan development as outlined by Bühler, Erikson, Havighurst, and other authors not mentioned here. During the 1990s, human aging became a prominent research topic not only in psychological research but also in socioeconomic and life sciences. The essence of this research was metaphorically described by P. B. Baltes as the "incomplete architecture of human ontogeny" reflecting an interplay of biology and assistive culture described by an increasing demand for culture while the biological risks (i.e., deleterious genes and dysfunctional gene expressions) increase as well and render these compensatory efforts rather fruitless (e.g., Baltes, 1997). This kind of disillusioning message was based on empirical evidence of the Berlin Aging Study showing the heightened risk for multi-morbidity and dependence in the fourth age, qualifying the changes during this period as "death-related" compared to the third age as already highlighted above.

33.2.3.2 Aging and Self-regulation

Starting point for theory and research on regulative efforts and aging is for me the notion of *differential aging* that was brought forward by Hans Thomae, author of the Bonn Longitudinal Study on Aging. This study began in 1965 with two groups born in the years 1890–1895 and 1900–1905; survivors were followed for 15 and 19 years, respectively. Thomae (1970) underlined in his theory on aging and the cognitive theory on personality that the crucial factor in determining life satisfaction in old age – as one crucial indicator for individual well-being – is not the objective but the interpretation and evaluation of age-correlated impairments and losses. The interpretation of changes depends on the one hand on needs, motives, and aspirations

of the older adult and on the other hand on the present socially shared stereotypes of old age in a given society. The essential feature for life satisfaction is the balance between individual needs and perceived reality. Thomae differentiated in later works between "aging styles" ("*Alternsstile*") and aging as fate ("*Altersschicksale*") both accentuating an active and non-deficit view of the older person. The cognitive theory of personality underlines the role that psychological processes (i.e., motivational and cognitive-evaluative processes) have on human aging in addition to biological and sociological contributions (Thomae, 1970). This approach opened the discourse for the consideration and analysis of individual adjustment processes and Table 33.1 gives an overview of some models proposed here.

The model on *selective optimization with compensation* (SOC) by Baltes and Baltes is proposed as a metamodel for the "study of successful adaptation and development across the life span" (Marsiske et al., 1995, p. 35) that may be used to describe adaptation processes in old age as well as across the life course. Several other models followed of which we can mention a few: Brandtstädter and co-workers describing *accommodative, assimilative, and immunization strategies of the aging self* or Heckhausen and Schulz's proposition of a lifespan theory of primary and secondary control based on the conceptual elaborations proposed by Rothbaum, Weisz, and Snyder (1982). Both models incorporate the functional differentiation between "changing the world" and "changing the self" that Rothbaum, Weisz, and Snyder offer. If changes occur that do not allow for direct corrective actions and thus primary control or assimilative efforts, the individual will use secondary control or accommodative and immunization strategies to regulate and change her/his needs, goals, and priorities. This is also reflected in Lazarus's differentiation between problem- and emotion-focused coping. According to this concept, emotion-focused coping predominates when stressful conditions are viewed by a person as "refractory to change," whereas problem-focused coping predominates events that are considered as "controllable by action" (Lazarus, 1993, p. 239). It seems evident that secondary control, accommodative, immunization, and emotion-centered coping become more predominant in self-regulation with advancing age and heightened risks of irreversible losses.

Carstensen and co-workers focused social interaction and networks in old age proposing a *lifespan theory of socio-emotional selectivity* determined by the predominant motives of a life period. Hobfoll's theory on *resource development and conservation* added further to aging. Baltes (2004) underlined that these last psychological models of proactive (adaptive) aging represent specific building components of the SOC model which he considered to be the holistic and integrative model. In 2010, Heckhausen, Wrosch, and Schulz came up with a further integrative model proposing a comprehensive theory of development and integrating several models mentioned up to here. The authors propose a *motivational theory of lifespan development* based on 15 propositions on adaptive developmental regulation that they group into four topics. A first class of propositions emphasizes the preference for and the advantages of primary control across the life course and, thus, underlines the adaptive value of primary control. Further propositions describe lifespan trajectories of primary and secondary control and thus "major changes in the capacity to exert primary control that are based on fundamental biological and social changes in available resources (e.g., strength, vitality, income, social status, social roles)" (Heckhausen, Wrosch, & Schulz, 2010). A third thematic group of propositions concerns the optimization of goal choice and appropriate use of control strategies, thus, describing the interplay between goal choice and disengagement and preferred control strategy. Finally, the fourth class elaborates the action phases of goal choice, goal engagement, goal disengagement,

and new goal engagement. The specific characteristics of this model lies in its action-theoretical approach highlighting the agency of the developmental actor, clearly underlining the functional priority and the individual preference for primary control efforts.

33.2.3.3 A First Summary and Conclusion

At the core of all these models is, in my understanding, the phenomenon and dynamic of adaptation to the changed life situation and, thus, the *multiple ways people use to adapt*. In this, the models take an approach that is founded in regulation theory and action theory, and in this they show several common characteristics. First, all theories postulate a change in demand structures for the aging individual, mostly illustrated by irreversible physical and functional decline and losses. These may be real changes or they may represent individual reproductions of socially shared stereotypes about human aging (Thomae, 1970). A person may thus experience a restriction of mobility by a weakening of muscles due to missing exercise; this weakening may worsen if the person perceives this an irreversible change due to aging as reflected in stereotypes about the slowly moving and clumsy elderly persons. A person may thus accept this fate and not exercise anymore, which will worsen the condition. Second, all models postulate a motivated change in action strategies motivated by changing demands and challenges serving proactive aging. One should, for instance, give up blocked goals, optimize given resources, and be selective in the choice of social partners. This implies a specific functional rationality (i.e., *Zweckrationalität*) underlying the specific behavior which is linked to "success" criteria. The rationality used here is a bounded rationality and thus subject to individual information processing. In this sense, rationality represents a "satisficing" and not an "optimal solution," that is, for the sufficient solution to a problem or challenge under specific circumstances (Simon, 1982). Third, nearly all models underline the importance or predominance of *cognitive processes that serve the goal of "changing the self" rather than "changing the world."* This shows, that the subjective reconstruction of reality is leading in taking action and is also the objective of adaptive efforts. Accommodation and not assimilation is therefore central. This also shows that some age-related changes are irreversible losses; approaches to reestablish a status quo ante are fruitless here: the loss of a loved one cannot be re-done, and also other regulative maneuvers, such as compensation, reach their limits here – the loss of a loved person cannot be compensated by loving another one. This underlines the notion of satisficing and finding a sufficient solution as the rationale underlying individual adaptation. Fourth, although all models do not neglect the macrosocial and cultural contexts as a frame of aging, they do focus on the individual, especially on cognitive processes serving adaptation. Emotional or affective needs of older adults mostly represent outcomes of such processes although they may impact or moderate cognitive processes (see Ferring & Boll, 2010). Here lies further potential for theory building. Fifth, the models emphasize processes qualified as proactive and adaptive, that all will lead to successful, optimal, or (at least) normal aging. Pathological processes cannot have a place in such a proactive conception although they represent a significant part of human ontogeny as Baltes puts it. This last point of being proactive in old age mostly indicates a further – and maybe not intended – normative message of these models illustrated in the following.

33.2.3.4 The Qualification of Aging

Table 33.1 lists some central concepts used in the description of aging – successful aging is the term that appears several times in this list, followed by the notion of activity and active aging. An evident antonym – and the only one in this list – is "disengagement." Further notions are productive and healthy aging. All the concepts imply criteria that allow a qualification of the aging process as "successful" or "productive" or "active" or "healthy" or "happy." I will not go into the details here, but like to underline the significance and the implication of these qualifiers as well as their sociocultural background.

According to the *Oxford English Dictionary*, "success" stands for the accomplishment of an aim or purpose signifying (a) the attainment of wealth, fame, or social status as well as (b) a person that achieves desired aims, or attains fame, wealth, and so on (*OED, s.v.* "success"). "Successful" thus stands for accomplishing a desired aim or result. The use of a term implicitly involves its antonym. In the denotative context of success, this includes the term of failure where it signifies (a) failure and poverty or (b) failure, flop, disaster, a nobody (with respect to a person). Success implies achievements and may in this be closely linked to protestant ethics standing for the moral value of hard work and the fulfillment of one's worldly duties as already described by Weber (1905). Is aging thus to be equaled with success or failure? Similar associations are linked to the term of "productive" and "active" which also convey a certain picture of an aging individual who is (still) active and productive and thus how an aging individual "ought" to be. The normative implications of the qualifications as "successful" or "productive" are easily at hand: aging is an achievement and can, thus, be evaluated with respect to results defining this achievement. If you do not succeed you may be considered a failure, if you are no longer productive you may no longer be a member of the productive community. Evidently, such a conception is individualistic and puts the focus on the individual neglecting the milieu and contexts of aging. It may also lead to social stigmatization contrasting the "successful copers" within the group of older adults with those being ill and disabled and thus not "successful." Such a view also promotes a perception of "the old" as weak and feeble contrasted with the younger more successful and productive groups.

This notion of "aging as a success" has not been without criticism (e.g., Moody, 2005). Other aging concepts and qualifications were put forward that may be considered as a counteraction to the aforementioned achievement-oriented approaches. Conscious aging underlines personal growth and consciousness expansion to achieve meaning while aging (Moody 2005). There is the notion of contemplative aging that elaborates spiritual needs and aspects of aging closely linked to the notion of gerotranscendence (Tornstam 2005) – another concept describing the spiritual aspect and cosmic transcendence of the aging individual which is quite close to the worldview of Zen Buddhism (see Jönson & Magnusson, 2001).

All these concepts show the motivation to describe and explain the various phenomena associated with human aging on the one hand, while, on the other hand, the multitude of "qualifications" shows that the discourse is not free of (implicit) evaluation and recommendations on how to adapt to aging in a socially accepted way. There are social values and norms involved in these concepts. The phenomenon of "youthism" and the need to stay young and attractive is one indicator of this; corrective or compensatory activities taken here include diets, exercises, cosmetics, and even surgery are used to convey the picture of a still young and attractive person. The question that arises is: what is the answer to qualifications of aging from a psychological point of view?

I like to quote Hans Thomae (1970, p. 8) here in his work on a theory on aging linked to a cognitive theory of personality:

"However no kind of classifying different ways of aging meets the great variety of interindividual differences. Defining adjustment to aging by the principle of balance between situations as it is

perceived on the one hand and motivational state or structure at the other hand, we neither have to superimpose an "ideal" or "normal" pattern of aging nor a classificatory system on the different varieties."

This statement opens the floor for a conception of aging that is linked to the individual construal of what is happening in one's life. This view not only underlines that development manifests in interindividual differences but it reflects intraindividual differences in need and motive profiles across the life course as well. Individuals try to construct meaning from the experiences in their lives and in this they integrate experiences into their theory of the self and the world (e.g., Ferring & Filipp, 2000). These individual theories depend on the experience of shaping and forming significant life events in family and social history, and on the ability to adapt to changed life situations that are integrated into the individual's behavioral program (Ferring, 2017). The individual adaptation and individual aging can thus only be understood when taking the lifespan development into consideration. An individual's biography in a given sociocultural milieu constitutes the object of study in such a view, and I would like to illustrate this in the following with some case studies.

33.3 The View from Within

33.3.1 Life Events and Melodies of Living

In a first step, I will present here short sketches of three life stories presented by older adults living in a rural area during biographic interviews.[3] All the stories illustrate that these persons structure their lives by a series of age- and history-graded events as well as – and much more important – by non-normative events. All stories illustrate as well that their lives show central topics or, to put this metaphorically, show specific "melodies" (see Zittoun et al., 2013)

Jean was born in 1928. He grew up on his father's farm; he took over the farm at the age of 26 at the end of the war and he and his growing family lived from dairy products as well as producing beef and pork. Jean died at the age of 86 in 2014 being the father of four children and five grandchildren, leaving his wife a widow at the age of 78 years. When you asked Jean about what happened in his life, he told you several things that came into his mind. He started with telling you that his "mama" died when he was seven years old. He continued with how proud he was to have four children and beautiful grandchildren, followed by stories about the war and his big family. He liked to reminisce about his family and the hard times they had during the war emphasizing that they shared everything and had to be satisfied with food that no one would eat today. He counted the losses that he experienced by telling you that all five his brothers had already died. Jean clearly was a family man.

Catherine, born in 1922, died at the age of 83 in a nursing home where she had moved at the age of 79 when she could no longer live in her big house in a rural area. When asked about her life she would talk about her husband missing in action during the war leaving her to raise the two boys. The insecurity of her husband's fate influenced – as she said – everything that she did in her life and she kept waiting for his return several years before giving up hope. She never considered marrying again. One further significant story of hers was that she missed her house that she'd built with the help of her family after the war – she felt that she had abandoned it. A further recurrent topic reveals ambivalent feelings toward her sons. On the one hand, she understood why she had to move to the nursing home, on the other hand, she expected her sons to "pay back" all she had done for them throughout her life investing everything she had to raise them and see them "well-equipped to master life." Catherine's theme was about "being abandoned" losing her husband and losing her children.

Gretchen, born in 1918, who lived to 85 years, presented herself as always being as "sly as a fox." She lived with her husband in a house that she had built during the late 1970s in the small village where she was born. She had no children and worked as a cook in private households in some larger German cities. Her private motto was to be frugal, save money, and live a modest life. She stocked diverse conserves and preserved strawberries, cherries, pears, and plums in her cellar together with wine, beer, and strong liquor without drinking this herself. Gretchen wore clothes until they became threadbare; she ate fruits from her garden and orchard even though they might already show signs of being rotten. She told that to have a "safe stock of alimentation" did her good having experienced hunger and deprivation during the war; she added as well that "life taught her" to use clothing up to the last. Interestingly, she also used this to describe her view of men – "one should consume men as they are – you cannot change them." Being very frugal in respect to herself and her husband, she gave generous gifts of money to the younger members of her large family. "To be safe and in control" was Gretchen's "melody" of life.

All these examples show that the three persons sketched here have predominant memories and apparently life themes that remain in their minds. In two cases, these are irrevocable personal losses – the mother and the spouse – experienced at different times of life. The case of Jean who was the youngest of six brothers at the age of 7 is quite dramatic and one might imagine what this did to the family in 1935. Catherine shared her loss experience with other women of her age though she showed her own personal way of coping with this life situation. She did not remarry but waited for her husband to return. The outlines that I choose to present here also indicate that the reconstruction of a life through biography is guided by the individual event history and this incorporates history- and age-graded normative events as well as critical non-normative events (see e.g., Hultsch & Plemons, 1979; Willis & Baltes, 1980).

History-graded events allow for a differentiation between birth groups and they describe the socioecological and cultural context at a given time. Age-graded events are those events that allow for a structuring of the individual life course in a given sociocultural context and in this they represent developmental talks in the sense of Havighurst's propositions. These events are age-correlated and reflect biological development as well as socioculturally shared conventions about roles and duties of the individual within society. Baptism, communion, or bar mitzvah represent such socially shared religiously motivated events; school entry, marriage, entering work life, and child birth mark another class of biologically motivated cultural events. The list of these events differs between sociocultural backgrounds, but all societies structure the human life course by a series of such age-graded events. Given this, a new class of event arises: the "nonevents" – these are age-graded events that are missing in an individual biography: a person may thus never marry, have no children, do not enter a work life, not being christened, and so on. Depending on the perceived significance of a specific event, its nonappearance will require adaptive effort by the individual, and it may mark in retrospect an important event of individual development and become part of an individual identity.

33.3.2 Conclusion: Toward a Person-centered Theory of Culturally Guided Aging in Families

Baltes and others have highlighted the importance of the three event types for shaping human development as biocultural co-constructivism where the biogenetic program and the sociocultural context interact in producing events that impact individual development. I take the position here that the influence that these events exert on individual development depends on their link to individual needs as well as the needs of the family. If an event frustrates individual and family needs, it instigates adaptive efforts of the person and the involved system. This event will be stored in individual memory following the simple principle that only those experiences are stored that are in some way linked to individual needs, be it that they impede, frustrate, or help to fulfil needs. This applies as well to the family system – family history is always a "shared experience" between members of a family reflecting the adaptation to a given socioecological and cultural context at a given time (see Ferring, 2017).

A person confronted with critical, especially non-normative, events (such as unexpected diagnosis and disease, divorce, loss of a loved one) has to integrate the experiences associated with these events into his or her model of the world and the self and there is a broad domain of literature that elaborates several models and modes of adaptation. Following the Piagetian differentiation between assimilation and accommodation, those experiences are assimilated, that is, integrated, into the individual model of the world and the self on the one hand. On the other hand, if the experience is novel and does not fit the individual frame, accommodative efforts aiming at the change of individual assumptions and concepts are required. This is elaborated by several models already mentioned in Table 33.1. Rothbaum, Weisz, and Snyder speak of primary and secondary control, Heckhausen and Schultz take this up in a lifespan perspective, and Brandtstädter and coworkers differ as well between assimilation, accommodation, and immunization. All these models indicate that the individual can change the world by some way of corrective behavior or change the self by changing individual assumptions about how the world functions (see also Janoff-Bulman, 1992, on "shattered assumptions"). All these efforts serve the function to establish meaning, which includes both purpose and goals. Meaning can be reconstructed, causally explaining why something has happened. Meaning is also teleological meaning identifying the (positive) consequences associated with a critical (negative) event. This last form is always a cognitive effort and represents a construction in a given sociocultural context. This notion underlines that culture may provide tools and means to help in the construction of meaning. What is the implication for the aging individual?

First, the aging individual is not the "aging individual" but a person with an individual biography that reflects a continuous stream of experiences integrated into the self and determining the view that a person holds on his or her life. In such an understanding, aging does not start at a specific point of time, we rather live forward as elaborated elsewhere (Zittoun et al., 2013). Second, events associated with aging pose the continuous input that a person has to integrate in his or her view of the world. Here, one may emphasize that the critical events associated with the later life course imply both losses and gains and that there is an "increasing risk of decline and decreasing potential for growth across the adult life span," as Heckhausen, Dixon, and Baltes (1989, p. 109) report from their comparison of young, middle-aged, and old adults judging development throughout adulthood. These authors highlight as well that "older adults held more elaborate conceptions about development throughout adulthood than younger adults" (Heckhausen, Dixon, and Baltes, 1989, p. 109). This last finding in particular indicates the process of constructing meaning in the face of the specific life situation associated with aging since it may stand for accommodative efforts resulting in a larger "data base" used by the older adults that allows to compare and to weigh different experiences. Third, most simple but most important, reality is always an individually constructed reality communicated and negotiated by signs within a given cultural context. This holds as well for those situations when a neurodegenerative disease such as Alzheimer's starts to have an impact on the individual (see Sabat, 2002; Ferring, 2015).

As a last point, I want to emphasize that both family and culture interact in forming development in general, including, in particular, life in advanced age. We are born into a given family that is already defined by the specific adaptive experiences of the maternal and paternal system. The family members share meanings and values linked to these experiences and this sets a frame for further development. The way a family deals with an aging person clearly depends on the values and "norms" of the family on how to deal with "their" older adults. One may show solidarity, detach oneself, be ambivalent about supporting or not, or have a conflict with the elderly persons depending on prior and shared experiences within the family (Ferring et al., 2009). Culture sets a further frame since it provides additional means of semiotic regulation and negotiating reality that may be adapted or declined by the family depending on their perceived adaptive values. In such a view, solidarity between generations may thus represent a culturally shared value but it may not be adopted if the family did not have specific adaptive experiences with practices linked to solidarity. In this, aging is a culturally shaped process in as far as a family adopts culturally shared values and practices about aging.

Notes

1 See Tilak (1989).
2 Further examples of suicide or forced suicide – if one may use this word – can be found at "The Ethics of Suicide Digital Archive" at the University of Utah, which provides reports and testimonies of suicide practices across time and cultures (http://ethicsofsuicide.lib.utah.edu/).
3 Interviews were in part performed by students as part of their training in gerontology or done in a former pilot research by myself. Jean lived in Luxembourg; he was interviewed in 2008; the two ladies lived in Germany near the Luxembourg border; they were interviewed at the age of 70 and 82.

References

Albert, I. & Ferring, D. (Eds.). (2013). *Intergenerational Relations. European Perspectives on Family and Society*. Bristol: Policy Press.

Atchley, R. C. (1972). *The Social Forces in Later Life: An Introduction to Social Gerontology*. Belmont, CA: Wadsworth.

Baltes, P. B. (1997). On the incomplete architecture of human ontogeny: Selection, optimization, and compensation as foundation of developmental theory. *American Psychologist*, 52, 366–380.

Baltes, P. B. & Baltes, M. M. (1990). Psychological perspectives on successful ageing: The model of selective optimization with compensation. In P. B. Baltes & M. M. Baltes (Eds.), *Successful Ageing: Perspectives from the Behavioral Sciences* (pp. 1–34). New York: Cambridge University Press.

Baltes, P. B. & Brim, O. G., Jr. (Eds.). (1979, 1980, 1982, 1983, 1984). *Lifespan Development and Behaviour* (vols. 2–6). New York: Academic Press.

Baltes, P. B., Featherman, D. L., & Lerner, R. M. (Eds.). (1986, 1988, 1990). *Lifespan Development and Behaviour* (vols. 7–10). New York: Academic Press.

Berg, S. (1996). Aging, behavior, and terminal decline. In J. E. Birren & K. W. Schaie (Eds.), *Handbook of the Psychology of Aging* (pp. 323 337). San Diego, CA: Academic Press.

Brandtstädter, J. & Greve, W. (1994). The ageing self: Stabilizing and protective processes. *Developmental Review*, 14, 52–80.

Bühler, C. (1933/1959). *Der menschliche Lebenslauf als psychologisches Problem* [The human life course as psychological problem]. Göttingen, Germany: Hogrefe.

Butler, R. & Gleason, H. (Eds.). (1985). *Productive Aging: Enhancing Vitality in Later Life*. New York: Springer.

Carstensen, L. L. (1995). Evidence for a life-span theory of socioemotional selectivity. *Current Directions in Psychological Science*, 4, 151–156.

Cowgill, D. O. & Holmes, L. (1972). *Aging and Modernization*. New York: Appleton-Century-Crofts.

Crimmins, E. M., Hayward, M. D., & Saito, Y. (1996). Differentials in active life expectancy in the older population of the United States. *Journals of Gerontology. Series B: Psychological Sciences and Social Sciences*, 51(3), S111-S120.

Cumming, E. & Henry, W. E. (1961). *Growing Old: The Process of Disengagement*. New York: Basic Books.

Erikson, E. H. (1959). *Identity and the Life Cycle: Selected Papers*. New York: International Universities Press.

Fernández-Ballesteros, R. (2008). *Active Aging: The Contribution of Psychology*. Göttingen, Germany: Hogrefe.

Ferring, D. (2010). Intergenerational relations in aging societies: Emerging topics in Europe. *Journal of Intergenerational Relationships*, 8(1), 101–104.

Ferring, D. (2015). Alzheimer's disease: Behavioral and social aspects. In J. D. Wright (Ed.), *International Encyclopedia of the Social & Behavioral Sciences* (2nd edn., vol. 1, pp. 584–590). Oxford: Elsevier.

Ferring, D. (2017). The family in us: Family history, family identity and self-reproductive adaptive behavior. *Integrative Psychological and Behavioral Science*, 51(1), 195–204.

Ferring, D. & Boll, T. (2010). Subjective well-being in older adults: Current state and gaps of research. In L. Bovenberg, A. Van Soest, & A. Zaidi (Eds.), *Ageing, Health and Pensions in Europe: An Economic and Social Policy Perspective* (pp. 173–205). Houndmills, UK: Palgrave Macmillan.

Ferring, D. & Filipp, S.-H. (2000). Coping as a "reality construction": On the role of attentive, comparative, and interpretative processes in coping with cancer. In J. Harvey & E. Miller (Eds.), *Loss and Trauma: General and Close Relationship Perspectives* (pp. 146–165). Philadelphia, PA: Brunner-Routledge.

Ferring, D., Michels, T., Boll, T., & Filipp, S.-H. (2009). Emotional relationship quality of adult children with ageing parents: On solidarity, conflict and ambivalence. *European Journal of Ageing*, 6(4), 253–265.

Fischer, S., Huber, C. A., Imhof, L., Mahrer-Imhof, R., Furter, M., Ziegler, S. J., & Bosshard, G. (2008). Suicide assisted by two Swiss right-to-die organisations. *Journal of Medical Ethics*, 34, 810–814.

Gauthier, S., Mausbach, J., Reisch, T., & Bartsch, C. (2014). Suicide tourism: A pilot study on the Swiss phenomenon. *Journal of Medical Ethics*, 41(8), 611–617. DOI: 10.1136/medethics-2014-102091.

Havighurst, R. J. (1961). Successful aging. *The Gerontologist*, 1, 8–13.

Heckhausen, J., Dixon, R. A., & Baltes, P. B. (1989). Gains and losses in development throughout adulthood as perceived by different adult age groups. *Developmental Psychology*, 25, 109–121.

Heckhausen, J., Wrosch, C., & Schulz, R. (2010). A motivational theory of life-span development. *Psychological Review*, 117, 32–60.

Heckhausen, J. & Schulz, R. (1995). A life-span theory of control. *Psychological Review*, 102, 284–304.

Hobfoll, S. E. (1988). *The Ecology of Stress*. New York: Hemisphere.

Hultsch, D. F. & Plemons, J. K. (1979). Life events and life-span development, In P. B. Baltes & O. G. Brim Jr. (Eds.), *Life Span Development and Behavior*. New York: Academic Press.

Janoff-Bulman, R. (1992). *Shattered Assumptions*. New York: Free Press.

Jönson, H. & Magnusson, J. A. (2001). A new age of old age? Gerotranscendence and the re-enchantment of aging. *Journal of Aging Studies*, 15, 317–331.

Kellehear, A. (1984). Are we a death-denying society? A sociological review. *Social Science and Medicine*, 18, 713–723.

Kübler-Ross, E. (1969). *On Death and Dying*. New York: Macmillan.

Lazarus, R. S. (1993). Coping theory and research: Past, present, and future. *Psychosomatic Medicine*, 55, 234–247.

Lemon, B. W., Bengtson, V. L., & Petersen, J. A. (1972). An exploration of the activity theory of aging: Activity types and life expectation among in-movers to a retirement community. *Journal of Gerontology*, 27, 511–523.

Marsiske, M., Lang, F. B., Baltes, P. B., & Baltes, M. M. (1995). Selective optimization with compensation: Life-span perspectives on successful human development. In R. Dixon & L. Bäckman (Eds.), *Compensating for Psychological Deficits and Declines: Managing Losses and Promoting Gains* (pp. 35–79). Hillsdale, NJ: Lawrence Erlbaum.

Moody, H. R. (2002). Conscious aging: A strategy for positive change in later life. In J. Ronch & J. Goldfield (Eds.) *Mental Wellness in Aging: Strength-based Approaches* (pp. 139–160). Baltimore, MD: Health Professions Press.

Moody, H. R. (2005). From successful aging to conscious aging. In M. L. Wykle, P. J. Whitehouse, & D. L. Morris (Eds.). *Successful Aging Through the Life Span: Intergenerational Issues in Health*. (pp. 55–68). New York: Springer.

New England Journal of Medicine. (2013). Physician-assisted suicide. *New England Journal of Medicine*, 368, 1450–1452. DOI: 10.1056/NEJMclde1302615.

Oerlemans, W. G. M., Bakker, A. B., & Veenhoven, R. (2011). Finding the key to happy aging: A day reconstruction study of happiness. *Journal of Gerontology. Series B: Psychological Sciences & Social Sciences*, 66B(6), 665–674.

Ogawa, T. (2008). Changing social concepts of age. In F. Coulmas, H. Conrad, A. Schad-Seiffert, & G. Vogt (Eds.), *The Demographic Challenge: A Handbook of Japan* (pp. 145–162). Leiden, Netherlands: Koninklijke Brill NV.

Olshansky, S. J., Hayflick, L., & Carnes, B. A. (2002). No truth to the fountain of youth. *Scientific American*, 286(6), 92–95.

Richmond, C. (2005). Dame Cicely Saunders. *BMJ*, 331(7510), 238.

Rothbaum, F., Weisz, J. R., & Snyder, S. S. (1982). Changing the world and changing the self: A two-process model of perceived control. *Journal of Personality and Social Psychology*, 42, 5–37.

Rowe, J. W. & Kahn, R. L. (1998). *Successful Aging*. New York: Pantheon Books.

Sabat, S. (2002). Epistemological issues in the study of insight in people with Alzheimer's. *Dementia*, 1(3), 279–293.

Schulz, R. & Heckhausen, J. (1996). A life-span model of successful aging. *American Psychologist*, 51, 702–714.

Sherman, E. (2010). *Contemplative Aging: A Way of Being in Later Life*. New York: Richard Altshuler & Associates.

Simon, H. A. (1982). Theories of bounded rationality. In H. A. Simon (Ed.), *Models of Bounded Rationality: Behavioral Economics and Business Organization* (vol. 2, pp. 408–423). Cambridge, MA: MIT Press.

Smith, J. (2002). The fourth age: A period of psychological mortality? In Max-Planck-Gesellschaft zur Förderung der Wissenschaften (Ed.), *Biomolecular Aspects of Aging: The Social and Ethical Implications* (pp. 75–88). München: Max-Planck-Gesellschaft.

Smith, J. & Baltes, P. B. (1993). Differential psychological ageing: Profiles of the old and very old. *Ageing and Society*, 13, 551–587.

Staudinger, U. M., Marsiske, M., & Baltes, P. B. (1993). Resilience and levels of reserve capacity in later adulthood: Perspectives from life-span theory. *Development and Psychopathology*, 5, 541–566.

Thomae, H. (1970). Theory of aging and cognitive theory of personality. *Human Development*, 13, 1–16. In German: Thomae, H. (1971). Die Bedeutung einer kognitiven Persönlichkeitstheorie für die Theorie des Alterns. *Zeitschrift für Gerontologie*, 4, 8–18.

Tilak. S. (1989). *Religion and Aging in the Indian Tradition*. Albany, NY: SUNY Press.

Tornstam, L. (2005). *Gerotranscendence: A Developmental Theory of Positive Aging*. New York: Springer.

Weber, M. (1905). Die protestantische Ethik und der Geist des Kapitalismus. *Archiv für Sozialwissenschaft und Sozialpolitik*, 20(1904), S1–S54; 21(1905), S1–S110 (reprinted in GARS I, 1–206).

Willis, S. L. & Baltes, P. B. (1980). Intelligence in adulthood and aging: Contemporary issues. In L. W. Poon (Ed.)., *Aging in the 1980s: Psychological Issues* (pp. 260–272). Washington, DC: American Psychological Association.

Zimmerman, C. & Rodin, G. (2005). The denial of death thesis: Sociological critique and implications for palliative care. *Palliative Medicine*, 18, 121–128.

Further Reading

Baltes, P. B. (2003). On the incomplete architecture of human ontogeny: Selection, optimization, and compensation as foundation of developmental theory. In U. M. Staudinger & U. Lindenberger (Eds.), *Understanding Human Development. Dialogues with Lifespan Psychology* (pp. 17–43). Boston: Kluwer Academic.

Baltes, P. B. & Baltes, M. M. (Eds.). (1990). *Successful Aging: Perspectives from the Behavioral Sciences*. Cambridge: Cambridge University Press.

Berg, C., Ferring, D., Knelp, N., Roth, H. J., & Weis, C. (2008). Von der praktischen Problemartikulation über diverse Theorieansätze zum dynamischen. In C. Berg, D. Ferring, & C. Weis (Eds.), *Modellversuch Sprachförderung in der frühen Kindheit: Ergebnisse eines INSIDE-Workshops* (pp. 79–91). Luxemburg: University Luxemburg.

Havighurst, R. J. & Albrecht, R. (1953). *Older People*. New York: Longmans, Green.

Hendin, H., Rutenfrans, C., & Zylics, Z. (1997). Physician-assisted suicide and euthanasia in the Netherlands: Lessons from the Dutch. *Journal of the American Medical Association*, 277, 1720–1722.

Kennedy, Q., Fung, H. H., & Carstensen, L. L. (2001). Aging, time estimation, and emotion. In S. H. McFadden & R. C. Atchley (Eds.), *Aging and the Meaning of Time: A Multidisciplinary Exploration* (pp. 51–73). New York: Springer.

Ryff, C. D. (1989). Successful aging: A developmental approach. *The Gerontologist*, 22, 209–214.

Thomae, H. (1987). Conceptualisations of responses to stress. *European Journal of Personality*, 1, 171–192.

Zittoun, T., Valsiner, J., Gonçalves, M. M., Vedeler, D., Salgado, J., & Ferring, D. (2013). *Human Development in the Life Course: Melodies of Living*. New York: Cambridge University Press.

General Conclusion

34 An Epistemological Coda: Sociocultural Psychology among the Sciences

Alberto Rosa and Jaan Valsiner

34.1 Psychology, What Is It About?

Psychology is about *psyche*.[1] It produces knowledge, methods for producing new knowledge (about psyche), and also technologies for profiting from the working of psyches and for influencing their outcomes. In addition, psychology is also a science – an institution similar to other social institutions. It is a set of corporations with rules of trade and regulations about how to carry out their businesses. Last – but not least – psychology is a sociocultural practice among many others with whom to trade products and services.

Psychology is far from having a clear figure with definite boundaries; it is a variegated assortment of discourses, methods, and practices that overlap, crisscrossing the fuzzy borders dividing its different subdisciplines. This means that, despite whatever imperialistic claims are made, no particular approach can realistically pretend to exhaust what is understood as the field of psychology. In addition, no one has either the authority or the power to set the limits of what is to be taken as psychology or to clearly demarcate its subdisciplines.

Psychology claims to be a science, even if at times what is meant by that claim is not always clear. This makes it indispensable for any contribution claiming to be part of scientific psychology, or of some of its subdisciplines, to clarify its field of study, the rules for its practice, and also the value and limits of the products it offers. Otherwise, it could not be accepted as a science of some kind. Sociocultural psychology is no exception.

This *Handbook* is made up of contributions that together offer a vista of what sociocultural psychology is like at the moment of its publication. We have reexamined the structure of the ideas reflected in the first edition back in 2007 and made major alterations. The chapters gathered here present its key concepts; they show how they can be related among themselves when stating the phenomena for its concern and the kinds of descriptions and explanations to be offered. The aim of this concluding chapter is to knit these elements together to sketch a figure of the kind of science sociocultural psychology now is, how it relates to other disciplines, and the value and limits of the knowledge it offers.

34.1.1 Psychology: A Liminal Science

It is a truism to say that psychology is a field of knowledge hinged between the natural and social sciences and the humanities. Psychology is about *psyche*, which is no other thing than a way of referring to what happens when an organism and its immediate environment encounter each other or, more restrictively, what the organism does during these encounters (behavior). This

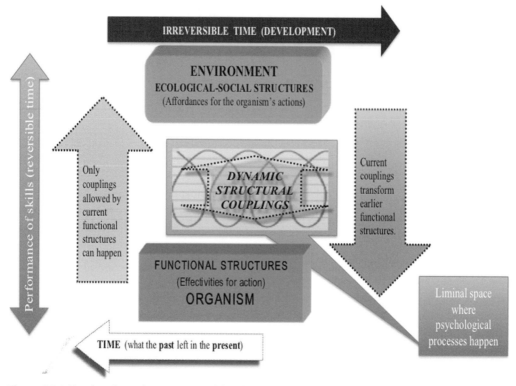

Figure 34.1 Psyche: dynamic processes arising from a spiral of circular reaction cycles.

requires us to refer to whatever processes arise in the body that contribute to shaping behavior and influence its outcome. *Psyche* is a word that does not refer to any kind of material entity but to processes interrelating material structures of different kinds: things in the environment and the assortment of organs that make up a living organism. Psyche is a Heraclitean creature rather than a Parmenidean being.

Psychology's task is to study such an ethereal subject matter to help understand its actions, so that such understanding could be of some use for improving its outcomes. In other words, psychology is about psyche, but it aims to improve the efficiency of the outcomes of the workings of the psyches of psychologists when carrying out their business and of those of the public who may profit from the products of the work of psychologists. This makes psychology a *reflective* sci-

ence that not only presents challenges but also raises interesting questions about its theoretical and methodological development (for a discussion, see Rosa, 2015).

What an individual does is certainly a result of the things he or she encounters but also of how he or she is perceived at that particular moment, of the state of activation of the agent, the task being performed at the time, the affections felt, and the abilities acquired beforehand. This makes behavior not only something that shows as movements in space but also a temporal process that involves elements that cannot be exhausted by referring to spatial (material) changes in the environment or in the body; it also has to include the dynamics of their combined changes. Figure 34.1 shows the virtual space where psychological processes appear and how circular reactions transform the shape of those interchanges in irreversible time.

The dynamics of behavior, and their transformation throughout time, can only be understood if they are (1) described in such a way that they are made to correspond with experiences of an observer (the scientist) and (2) communicated to others through some kind of understandable inscription (gestures, sounds, texts) so that such experience could be replicated and turned into shared knowledge capable of producing meaning in the addressed audience and so influence their behavior. Put differently, some kind of means of communication is needed for the sensorial awareness of phenomena to be gathered into subjective and intersubjective meaningful accounts of the experienced events, so that some kind of interobjective reality is made to appear (see Chapter 3, this volume).

Psychology, then, is not only about behavior – a vague concept declared to be "objective" by the behaviorists – but about experience, communication, understanding, and knowledge construction as well. It is concerned with how all these processes work together when individuals act within an environment, interact with each other, perform social activities, work, play, and train themselves or others in new abilities. Or they simply contemplate when they enjoy or suffer for what they believe are the events they are living, when they wonder about how to carry on with their lives, plan their future, or think about the kinds of people they or some others are and judge what they did, should have done, or shall do; and even how sometimes they manage to gather the stamina to put a resolution into effect – for good or bad.

So viewed, the task of psychology looks overwhelming. No wonder, then, that to tackle such an endeavor, a whole assortment of approaches have been developed by combining psychology's resources with others chosen from disciplines ranging from physics, chemistry, and biology to history and ethics, passing through anthropology, sociology, economics, semiotics, linguistics, and art criticism. Psychology is a science born of hybridizations.

34.1.2 Ordering the Epistemic Field of Psychology

The question, then, is how to arrange the resources at hand so that the matters to consider could be made approachable for scientific scrutiny. Figure 34.2 offers a closer look at the development of the dynamics of psyche: the encounters between the structures of an organism and its environment (see also Chapter 1, this volume).

Psychology studies the relating of organisms with their environment and, within that, gets an account of how behavior changes throughout time. Behavior (solid thick arrows in Figure 34.2) is understood as the observable spatial movements the organism performs in its environment. Such movements affect both the structures of the environment and the ongoing dynamics among the organism's organs. The affections received by the latter (dotted arrows in Figure 34.2) close the first cycle of a circular reaction and start a second by triggering a reaction in the form of a new movement. But by then, the inner equilibrium of the organism is not the same as before; these changes influence the shape of the new movement, and so on in successive cycles. The organism is constantly undergoing change. The successive reiteration of these processes makes the inner workings of the organism progressively increase its share in the agency of behavior, even if, in the eyes of the observer, only little changes in overt behavior are noticeable. How much bigger this share could get to be obviously depends on the capabilities of the structures of the organism, which nevertheless would only become functional if exercised. When they are, a set of psychological functions unfolds (irritability, orientation, sensitivity, learning, and eventually higher psychological processes, such as imagination, memory, thinking) that allows the accumulation of experience and widens the range of abilities for adjusting behavior to situational circumstances. The study of the dynamics

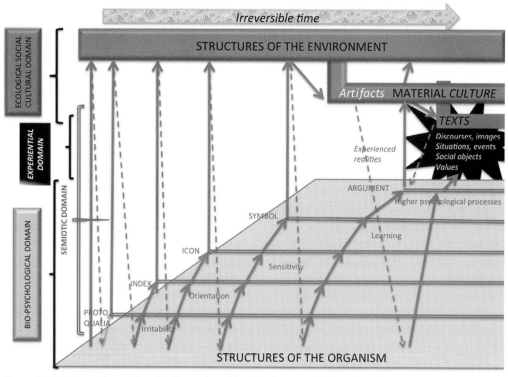

Figure 34.2 Epistemic overlaps in the study of the developmental dynamics of psyche.

relating organic structures, their psychological functions, and behavior is the field of work of disciplines laboring in the biopsychological domain.

These dynamic structural couplings not only leave a trace in the workings of the organism's structures; they also impact the structure of the environment. The organisms rearrange, transform, and sometimes dismantle the elements that make up the landscape, with the effect that the conduct has to continually readapt to the changing environmental conditions. When, in one of these cycles of mutual transformations, one particular environmental element merges with a particular configuration of behavior, with the effect of producing a change on another environmental structure, and such association becomes a permanent pattern, it can be said that artifacts and culture (the realm of the artificial) appear. When new

artifacts are used not only to operate on things but also to influence how fellow members of the group behave, artifacts begin to act as inscriptions for the direction of others, as texts of some kind, which in turn leave traces in the patterns of social interactions and in the social structure of the group. Whatever the case, the structural features of the environment (whether natural or artificial, material or social) set constraints and conditions of possibility for acting. The study of these dynamics falls within the area of work for the disciplines dealing with the ecological, social, and cultural domains and with their interactions throughout time.

Behavior, then, arises within the possibilities and constraints set by the couplings of organismic and environmental structures, which throughout time transform the inner dynamics of both kinds of structures and, consequently, change the patterns of behavior. That is why research on behavior cannot ignore the structural features of both the organism and the environment (and their changes) nor avoid the empirical consideration of how behavior changes throughout time. This means that an observer has to contemplate these changes when they happen, record what he or she then experiences, and finally produce some kind of text to communicate the observations made. Psychology, as any other science, could not exist without observers' experiences and their accumulation throughout time.

The roots. Psychology was born as a science to explain the workings of experiencing. Its primary task was conceived as the study of how a biological structure could get to know what the worldly things studied by natural sciences were really like, that is, how experiencing works to produce conscious phenomena as a result of the inner workings of the structures of the observer's organism, and also how those phenomena arrange themselves to produce the inner world of subjective experience. If empirical sciences studied worldly matters, the task of psychology was then to go into the intricacies of how empirical knowledge appears in the consciousness of an experiencer and how such an experience is capable of producing truth about the world, even if it also produces many other results. Consciousness and experience appear, then, as matters for inquiry, not only for psychology, but also for some other new disciplines. Phenomenology focuses on the description of what phenomena of consciousness are like and the kind of knowledge they produce; hermeneutics focuses on the interpretation of the meanings of texts and lived experiences of different kinds; and semiology and semiotics focus on how things can be taken as signs able to produce or convey meaning. There is little doubt that the approach taken by each of these disciplines offers knowledge worthy to be taken into account for the description, understanding, and explanation of how consciousness works and how subjective, intersubjective, and objective phenomena

can come to appear and be instrumental for shaping behavior.

The extensions. Semiotics (of a Peircean kind), when combined with a theory of action, offers formalisms useful for bridging the explanatory gaps between the aforementioned disciplines and the behavioral sciences. As Figure 34.2 shows, the affections resulting in structures of the organism produce a cascade of changes in the intraorganismic dynamics that result in refracting the reactive response in each circular reaction, influencing the subsequent overt behavior. If these intraorganismic changes are considered as also having the capability of acting as a kind of sign (index, icon, symbol, argument) of a value referred to something in the environment (presence, form, permanence, and relation, proportion, structure, or reason), then it could be said that psychological functions develop as a consequence of the iteration of cycles of semiosis actions (see Chapter 6, this volume), which eventually produce concepts about what it takes to have some kind of reality – objects, events, situations, stories – with the consequence that sometimes the outcomes of those processes produce results that only have substance within the subjective realm as a result of the fancies of imagination. This makes semiotic formalisms useful for modeling how conscious experience arises, not only as an epiphenomenon, but also as a resource for monitoring and managing behavior.

34.2 Epistemology of Sociocultural Psychology

Sociocultural psychology is concerned with how human behavior transforms the natural environment, creating artificial elements and, by so doing, making new forms of social interaction to appear, new patterns of behavior to develop, and new abilities to arise.

What distinguishes sociocultural psychology from other psychological disciplines is that it focuses on how artifacts transform social communication and activities, widening the field of experiences with phenomena referring to absent (or imagined) entities produced by artificial means, or, more specifically, how artifacts can make new kinds of experiences (both socially shared and individually felt) to appear and how these experiences affect behavior and its outcomes – changes in the environment and in the tool kit of artifacts capable of producing further structural transformations of experience, behavior, and the environment.

So viewed, the key issues of interest for sociocultural psychology are (1) to explore how artifacts play a role in shaping social interaction and communication; (2) how this influences the development of individual symbolic experiences, abilities, and resources for shaping and managing behavior; (3) to explore and record the varieties of experiences, behaviors, and abilities that show in groups and individuals with different cultural resources; and (d) how new artifacts, forms of communication, social organizations, experiences, and abilities arise as a result of these processes. All this together also produces relevant knowledge about the dynamics of historical changes. In sum, as the very name of the discipline suggests, its focus is on the dynamics among the three apexes of the triangle of society–culture–psyche, which displays many variations while keeping its basic gestalt.

The task of sociocultural psychology is triple: (1) to record these varieties, (2) to explain how the observed differences are produced, and (3) to search for the general principles governing these dynamics. This is hardly any news in science. All sciences are built on three founding pillars that make up their basic structure: *observation of phenomena, explanation of events*, and *formal explanatory principles*. The difference between one science and another is in what these pillars are made of, that is, the kinds of phenomena and events they study, the formal explanatory devices chosen as suited for the empirical material to

study, and the kinds of explanations offered. The rest of this chapter is devoted to presenting a proposal of how these three pillars can be conceived to further the development of sociocultural psychology and make it a useful cultural artifact for improving human life.

34.2.1 Sociocultural Psychology Approach on Experience and Meaning

Experience ensues as a result of the cycles of encounters between the organism and the material and social environments. Experience is also where what is taken as reality appears, where its components acquire a conscious meaning, and where the self feels concerned about what it feels and ponders what to do. Experience, then, encompasses what an individual takes to be the domains of the subjective and objective, the world where the individual believes he or she is living. Therefore experiences are always lived in the first person; they are felt as *mine*. They can also be reenacted by other people when communicated through semiotic devices of different kinds – I may get to believe that I am feeling what you are feeling when we are doing things together. But experience is also a process to be explained – it is to be described and explained in the third person, and it is an *it* to be taken as subject matter to be studied.

Experience is a key issue for sociocultural psychology. It is not only the field where realities are felt; it is also where they show as having a meaning, as having the capability of arousing for action, orienting attention, and producing attitudes, making one feel an inclination toward doing something or the anguish of not knowing what to do. Experience is made of transient and evasive phenomena of private consciousness that cannot be subjected to public scrutiny. To become something to be tackled by scientific study, it has to be disentangled in such a way that it is turned into a construct capable of having some kind of stability (reliability and validity) supported by phenomena accessible to observers.

Sociocultural psychology is interested in the study of experience because it is the domain where meaning appears, where it transforms the inner workings of psychological processes and shapes overt behavior, which in turn transforms the environment. Needed, then, is a model capable of connecting these domains that, in addition, could also link the ecological and sociocultural domains with the behavioral sciences. Such a model should also be instrumental for suggesting the kinds of phenomena to focus on and the events to be observed, while also providing formalisms able to relate phenomena and events and explain the regularities observed.

34.2.2 Bridging the Gap between Behavior, Experience, and Material Culture: A Formal Model of How Action Produces Meaningful Experiences

The formalisms of Peircean semiotics, when combined with a theory of action (González, 1997; Rosa, 2007a, 2007b), allow a conception of the dynamics of the relationships between environmental elements and the affections felt by the organism as the ground on which experience and volition grow, making signs appear and meaning develop. Such triadic relationships can be conceived as *sign-constructing actions*, able to produce series of recursive cycles, which, when reaching a stable triadic pattern (a chain of three successive semioses), can produce a *legisign* (a sign capable of representing a regularity), which in turn can produce a stable pattern of behavior – an actuation (Rosa, 2007a; Chapter 6, this volume). The resulting configuration can be modeled as a tetrahedron (the form combining three triangles in a three-dimensional figure made of four triangular planes). As Peirce's theory says, semioses are recursive in that these structures are capable of triggering the rise of new ones, which

follow the same formalism and cause series of consecutive fractal structures to arise. Such structures are useful for modeling how different kinds of signs appear, meaning develops, and action gets progressively canalized by these developing semiotic-cognitive structures (Chapter 6, this volume). The consequence is that behavior is shaped and reshaped, producing the simultaneous development of psychological functions and experiences. If at some point conflicting affects are not able to produce a behavior that efficiently solves the task, different previous patterns of the relation-affection behavior are combined in trial-and-error attempts (enacted abductions – a form of thinking in action) that end up producing a new pattern of behavior – an enactive argument.

This model offers formalisms able to explain how the cycles of action affection (see Figure 34.2) get to produce semiotic mediators (signs such as indexes, icons, symbols, and arguments) able to give meaning to the encounters with elements of the environment, to attribute value to them and make them instrumental for producing feedback loops capable of monitoring and directing behavior. This makes overt behavior the result of semiotic processes and also susceptible to be influenced by signs signaling the presence of something. Objects can then be conceived as sets of signs connected among themselves within an argument referred to a particular entity with some permanence. Arguments, then, are conceived as a kind of sign that compiles other signs into a new pattern composed following the rules of a semiotic grammar of action. So viewed, objects and behavioral patterns (habits) arise simultaneously as a result of semiotic (enactive) arguments, which, once established, can also be evoked by one of the other kinds of signs included in the argument (indexes, icons, and symbols).

This requires, first, exercising the capabilities of the body, rehearsing its movements and the sensations they produce, to explore the joy or pain they produce and relate both, so that monitoring abilities can be developed and patterns of behavior established, which in turn allows these habits so developed to be constituted as semiotic objects. It is on this basis that the most primitive kinds of (unconscious enactive) signs develop, setting into motion enactive thinking (see Chapter 11, this volume) as the ground on which instrumental operations and communicative gestures develop. This early development does not happen in a vacuum. The infant lives in a sociocultural world full of objects, animals, and people. It is through dyadic joint actions on toys (play) that communication, objects, and abilities develop together (Chapter 12, this volume).

If stable objects and habits are themselves arguments (a kind of sign), and arguments are for compiling other signs into a new one, then new (enactive) arguments (new sets of habits) are able to relate different objects within new (enactive) arguments. If this is done in such a way as to make one object serve the same purpose in another, the consequence is that the meaning of one object can be transferred to others (metonymy). If such (enactive) symbols and arguments are conventionalized within a group, meanings can be shared when using these mediational means. When this happens, the environment in which the members of that group move around is no longer only a natural ecological niche but also a cultured world populated with socially meaningful objects, in which what one does is felt as having a sense for others and oneself. It becomes an *Umwelt* – as Jakob von Uexküll called it. By then, the affections, the qualities, the gestures and voices, and the transformed environmental elements (objects and artifacts) are able to become means of communication capable of conveying meanings to others and therefore of producing shared experiences. The consequence is that cultural symbolic communication and inscriptions, rituals, and texts appear and, with them, social accumulation and transmission of experience.

Moving to convention. Social conventional signs (symbols and arguments) mark the transition from nature to culture and also from awareness to consciousness. Gestures, voices, artifacts, tokens, and inscriptions are now symbols able to evoke meanings referring to absent objects (*legisigns*). The consequence is that symbols are now capable of guiding behavior and are also a means for producing (declarative) arguments and combining them into further arguments. Social communication, through symbols and arguments, can then turn into argumentative (symbolic) thinking once the individual learns to address himself or herself, rather than another, when performing trial-and-error attempts on declarative (rather than enactive) arguments. Following Vygotsky (1934/1987), we could say that language (and any other kind of communicative code) transforms (enactive) thinking into declarative argumentation and also makes consciousness appear as an internalized version of a social dialogue among arguments and social voices as well as a resource to manage behavior according to social functions, rules, and purposes.

Arguments, then, are the key kind of sign applied for the production of purposeful behavior, personal experience, and the development of culture as well as for the mutual production of objective and subjective worlds. It is through arguments that sociocultural knowledge, either procedural or declarative, can be accumulated and transmitted – the first by learning and exercising habits, the second by engaging in social dialogues mediated through symbolic inscriptions.

Argument is an elaborated kind of sign that is shaped throughout a process, as we have sketched above and in a more detailed form in Chapter 6 (this volume). Figure 34.3 (detached and reelaborated from Figure 6.4 in Chapter 6, this volume) presents a simplified version of the semiotic properties of arguments. Argument is there presented as the apex of a tetrahedron where formal, aesthetic, and moral values intersect, at the same time that they relate to other values forming the edges of the bottom plane. Figure 34.4 unfolds the four planes of the tetrahedron delimited by

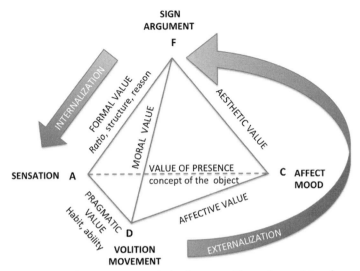

Figure 34.3 Argument: a semiotic sign compiling values arising from action and producing experiences.

edges marked by the values shared by neighboring planes.

These planes are framed by different kinds of values, which simultaneously delimitate different kinds of cultural practices, social activities, and also epistemic fields, within which particular experiences and patterns of behavior instantiate these values in particular arguments.

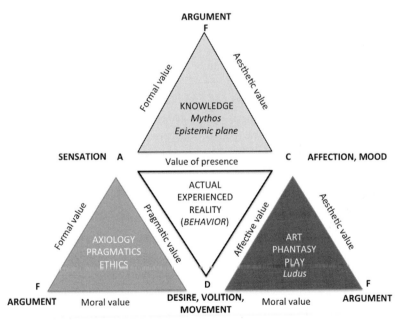

Figure 34.4 Fields of sense (and culture) arising from experience and influencing behavior.

The *axiological plane* is framed by pragmatic, moral, and formal values from where categories, such as useful or useless, good or bad, arise in relation to particular content and a particular context (the objects and situation experienced and the pattern of action then exercised), arranged according to a particular proportion of qualities and grammatical rules. It is in this plane where proportions (ratio) and rationality, rules and laws, duties and commands, are produced following the development of new ways of acting and also where habits and abilities are invoked and fostered to carry out different kinds of social tasks. This is the plane of technology, ethics, law, and politics – the realm of rules.

The *ludic plane* is where the pleasurable or harming, the good or the bad, and the beautiful or the ugly are combined to produce aesthetic sentimental arguments (emotional episodes aroused by affects and moods; Russell, 2003), or, the other way around, where sociocultural arguments are influential in producing those kinds of values in particular experiences, which in turn affect current action – either performed, perceived, or imagined – and the products that result (objects). It is the plane of imagination, play, sports, and art.

The *epistemic plane* is the site for ideas referring to what the world is believed to be like. It is made from arguments arranging the proportion of qualities sensed (sensation and perception – formal value), the sentiments felt (aesthetic values), and the ontological substances (either natural, supranatural, or fictional) believed to be behind them. Epistemic arguments shape the conceptions of objects, situations, events, stories, and epistemic discourses of different kinds (myths, stories, symbolic tokens of entities either imagined or believed real – gods, witches and fairies, mathematical functions, or scientific constructs). It is the plane where social representations and cultural knowledge nourish personal experiences and also where personal beliefs develop. It is the realm of myths, religion, history, and science – of theoretical ideas.

The fourth plane is that where actual experience is being felt in the first person. It is there where reality (either real or fictional) is actually experienced, desires arise, and actual behavior is formed, where arguments (rational, sentimental, or moral) shape experiences, desires, and behavior – in addition to giving resources and providing scaffolding for the creation of habits and the development of abilities. It is the meeting ground where psyche brings to consciousness the results of the couplings between the body, nature, and culture, where interpersonal interaction and communication happen and second person experiences can be made to appear as well as the source from which the other planes grow. It is where arguments are actually put into operation when actively performed or uttered and also the assembling plant where they are combined with others to produce new semiotic structures that increase the store of ideas that make up individual personal culture.

In sum, the formal figure of the tetrahedron is a model of how triadic semiosis flows along the edges between planes, producing new semiotic formalisms capable of offering explanations of how values, meanings, habits, experienced objects, events, abilities, and overt behavior appear. Rationality – whether pragmatic/epistemic, epistemic/ludic, or pragmatic/aesthetic – is both a product of action and a device that constrains and canalizes the production of rules of different kinds: formal epistemic-pragmatic rules on how to conceive the world and how to operate on it; norms of good taste, social manners, and canons of beauty; and also rules of fair play and for producing novelty, joy or disgust, good or harm.

Actual conscious experiences and conduct arise and can be explained through the production of arguments. A particular performance or utterance can be judged as real or faked, useful or useless, beautiful or ugly, good or bad – categories that can also be attributed to arguments. Arguments have connotations that spread from one plane to another: no argument can avoid having theoretical, pragmatic, or aesthetic features, regardless of the practice or activity from which it originated. Arguments, either performed or uttered, are always contextual; they are a product of semiotic structures previously developed but never exhaust the potential of those structures. This makes any attribution of value to an argument to be always a contextual judgment (another argument) arising from the comparison of arguments of different kinds. The attribution of truth is no exception, as it happens when relating declarative descriptions of observations (personal experiences) with hypothesis (epistemic arguments) through the use of methods (pragmatic arguments) for validation.

The tetrahedral model is itself a formal argument setting the lines along which triadic semioses link together, so that meaning coming from received sociocultural arguments can be instilled into subjective experience and behavior (internalization – downward arrow in Figure 34.3), and the other way around, how the results of individual behavior are able to produce new arguments to be added to the public domain (externalization – upward arrow in Figure 34.3).

34.2.2.1 Expanding the Model to Account for the Self-Management of Behavior

And what about me? Am I just a stage where ideas dance? Am I something real or just a figment of the imagination? Do I have something to do or say about what happens to me or about my doings? The answer to all these questions is crystal clear: yes, no, and both. The reason for such a bizarre answer lies in the possible responses to another question: of what am I made?

I, myself, am an experienced object conceived as capable of experiencing the world and myself. If I can conceive my body as an object, and myself as something whose substance my body does not exhaust, it is because the body, the consequences of what my body does, and the feelings

felt throughout time have been compiled into sets of arguments that together conceive myself as a semiotic object elaborated through the same kind of semiotic-psychological processes that shape my experience of the world. Experience presents me as a repository of knowledge, as a joyful and suffering being, and also as an agent capable of transforming elements of my environment and myself – to some extent. I also appraise the outcomes of my actions and my abilities to do so, what makes me able to represent, judge, and improve what I am like, since I also feel good or bad following the consequences of what I do.

The experiences involving the self are supported on a thick accumulation of argumentative layers: experiences of objects and situations, experiences of oneself as an object, experiences of oneself in a situation, experiences about what the situation means to me, about what to do in the situation, and how I feel about what to do, should do, or should have done. They appraise my own feelings, but they also refer to something beyond my physical comfort: they also appraise my degree of success when searching for social goals, how I played the rules, how others would assess me, what would happen to me afterward, and how I may feel by then. These are experiences that synthesize many others together and are better expressed by words that do not exist in English but do exist in German (*Erlebnis*) or in Spanish (*vivencia*), which could be dubbed by the expression *lived experience*: an experience significant for the self that also provides a life lesson. These kinds of experiences produce simultaneously memory and the self, while feeding each other (Chapter 14, this volume).

The development of the self parallels that of individual agency (Martin & Gillespie, 2010). Without the operation of the system of the self, an agent cannot be made accountable for his or her actions or the outcomes of those actions. Lived experiences act as reflective and refracting devices, as looking glasses in which the agent looks at its own figure, but also to the background, to ongoing performances and their efficacy, so that the image received shows an actor when playing. The self results from processes of reflection (Chapter 13, this volume).

The self is also a dialogical device – a continuous conversation between an *I* (*agent*) and a *you* (myself as interlocutor), in which both are and refer to a *me* (object) and which together shape the trinitarian entity the self is. It is a conversation in which commands, complaints, lamentations, and arguments are exchanged when trying to understand what happened to *me* and to ascertain what *I* should do (internal speech and symbolic reasoning; Vygotsky, 1934/1987) when moving from different *I-positions* (Chapter 27, this volume).

The operations of the system of the self within subjectivity are not only influenced by the cultural resources feeding them but are also unthinkable without them. Cultural discourses provide stories, characters, plots, and literary genres that present the perceived changes in the environmental landscapes as temporal sceneries where a drama is being performed in which one has to position oneself (Harré, 2012), so that the *agent* turns into an *actor* playing a role or becomes an *author* when improvising performances and producing new scripts. One may also go into the effort of steering one's own actions to improve one's capabilities by using materials taken from the available sociocultural tool kit. When one does so, or is capable of refraining from doing so, one can be taken as a fully accountable *person* (Rosa, 2016) – a dialogical process through which psyche gains agency on its own shaping and turns into a moral agent as a result of his or her personal participation in social life and in educational settings (Chapter 15, this volume).

The self, then, is a virtual object and a steering device that arises as an object with agency within the trajectories of experiences felt (Rosa & González, 2013; Fernández-Cid, Kriger, & Rosa, 2014, Rosa, 2016) and also as the result of a trajectory of life (Sato et al., 2007), as the protag-

onist of a story, and as a narrative self (Bruner, 2003).

34.2.2.2 Semiotic Boundaries and Growth of Meaning

Arguments are semiotic outcomes that arise from behavior. They can be stored in sociocultural repositories, such as rituals, inscriptions, and texts, and also in the shape of objects with different forms (tools, buildings, cities, or social institutions) that produce the ideas a group shares – the social representations about what things are like (Chapter 7, this volume). Sometimes the rules developed in these different realms have some coherence, but many times, they show discrepancies, causing one at times to feel confused about what one is experiencing, ambivalent about how to feel toward that, and doubtful about what to do or what one should have done (see Chapter 28, this volume).

Culture has produced throughout time a large repertoire of ready-made arguments belonging to many cultural practices, social activities, and epistemic fields. But culture is not a homogeneous whole; it is irregular and fragmented by crisscrossing fractures and cracks resulting from historical change, which disconnects some of its parts from others, at times even in contradiction. Cultural practices and professions, social groups and activities, spatial location (home or office), clock and calendar time (morning or evening; summer or winter), and age (infant, child, adult, or senior) set boundaries to the cultural materials one accesses, or will be able to access, and therefore to what one does, knows, feels, desires, or enjoys. Thus one individual can only use a fragment of the cultural wealth stored in languages and codes, in texts and discourses, in rites, sources of joy or suffering, social manners, or abilities. All this leaves a trace on the habits one acquires and the abilities to be developed or acquired while moving through the sociocultural landscape, and also on how one would conceive oneself, the life so far lived, or still to live – that

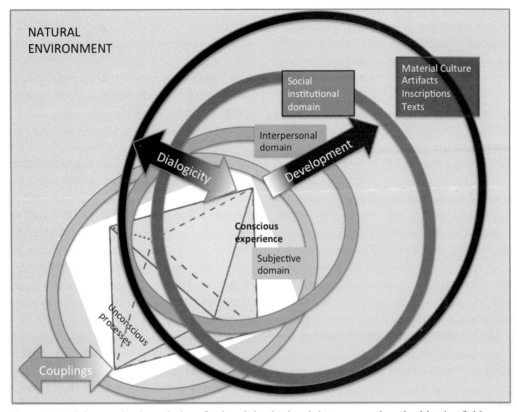

Figure 34.5 Crisscrossing boundaries of cultural, institutional, interpersonal, and subjective fields.

is, what and who one believes one should be or wants to be – and also what others are believed to be like.

Figure 34.5 shows how unconscious psychological processes (modeled by semiotic-enactive structures) arise from encounters with the environment and evolve into conscious experiences. This can only happen when elements of public culture are internalized and higher psychological processes (new semiotic structures) develop. This development requires immersion in interpersonal situations and institutions where dialogues and behavior perform the resulting diverse rules. It is through these dialogues that sociocultural symbols and arguments become operational within the personal domain, developing and producing novelty and therefore leaving a trace in the inner dynamics of the self – as in psychotherapy

(Chapter 5, this volume). The shifting shape of interpersonal spaces within the institutional fields to which one has access allows one to expand the range of personal experiences, knowledge, and abilities, producing personal development (see Chapter 16, this volume).

These different fields can also be considered as *semiospheres* (Lotman, 2005) and the borders between them as semiotic boundaries where translations between different codes cause new meanings to arise and sometimes also new symbols and arguments to be created (see Chapter 1, this volume). Cultural materials, their symbols and arguments, offer resources for the communication and constitution of experiences, which could take kaleidoscopic variations as a result of the kinds of cultural resources accessed, of the field and activity in which they are played, and also how they are refracted when processed by the semiotic-cognitive structures set into operation. Whatever the case, sociocultural semiotic resources set limits for understanding, experiencing, and acting. Beyond them are only chaos and disorder (Lotman, 2005).

34.2.2.3 Sociocultural Resources for Shaping Experiences and Behavior

The boundaries between these domains are where artifacts and signs are produced (Chapter 6, this volume) and become operational in systems of activity (Chapter 8, this volume); it is there where social representations develop and show their operation (Chapter 7, this volume) and symbolic resources are managed by individuals in the dynamics of their lives (Chapter 10, this volume) and also where innovation is produced (Chapter 9, this volume).

It is in social interaction that actions, objects, and artifacts are exchanged and where value is attributed. Value, then, becomes a kind of semiotized object according to which things of many kinds (material objects but also acts, feelings and desires, and even people) can be rated and also related to one's own self – as a property (a possession) of my own or someone else. The exchange of goods and favors is the ground on which social rules of fairness, justice, and morality develop (Chapter 17, this volume) and also where material artifacts, capable of acting as carriers of value, arise. Money is a cultural tool that not only carries economic value but is able to act as a means for the exchange of many kinds of values, contributes to shaping many social activities, and is also able to be employed for different purposes – among them, socialization (Chapter 18, this volume).

The world one believes to be leaving arises as real in consciousness when enactive, sentimental, and uttered arguments, together with feelings of selfhood, appear when encountering the environment. Such arguments require the use of cultural materials and symbolic and argumentative cultural tools that are contextually available. This makes the border between the subjective and the interpersonal realms the ground where semiotic-cognitive structures evolve and where experiences grow according to the social institutional rules of the activities in which an individual participates.

Personal lived experiences result from the workings of these processes, which also set the dynamics of imagination and make its products to appear either as belonging to collective realities (Chapter 22, this volume), as transcendent categories or entities (Chapter 19, this volume), or as religious beliefs (Chapter 20, this volume). Thus experiences can seem at first glance to sprout spontaneously from random encounters with the environment, but they can also result from crafted technologies that sociocultural institutions refined for their purposes. Art, rituals, discourses, interpersonal dialogues, and individual drillings, gathered together in carefully devised activities, are able to create religious beliefs and subjective realities capable of shaping individuals' selves and disciplining the behavior of individuals. The study of the historical unfolding of these kinds of technologies gives insights into how symbols and arguments (taken from artistic, religious, or military practices) have shaped topics that later on turned into subjects for psychological inquiry (Chapter 21, this volume).

Art and literature (objects and texts of different kinds) are material outcomes of behavior driven by lived experiences, which are also part of the environmental elements composing the cultural landscape. They provide arguments for shaping how individuals understand collective life and institutions and their changes throughout time, and the position they take when interpreting how past events are currently portrayed and understood (Chapter 24, this volume).

History and historical narratives are cultural devices that provide arguments about the doings of a group throughout time and also for producing aesthetic and moral feelings toward different groups. These make history a proficient tool for supporting feelings of collective and personal identity, for internalizing aesthetic and moral values, and therefore, instrumentally, for instilling ethnic and nationalistic ideologies or for fostering critical reflection on social life, as a defense against ideological indoctrination (Chapter 23, this volume). It is the combination of both narrative arguments and feelings of identity that makes the cultural materials encountered at a particular moment familiar or foreign, makes one feel at home or displaced, as enjoying what one feels is deserved, or missing something one believes to be deserved (Chapter 31, this volume). This makes historical accounts volatile materials able to keep conflicts alive, unless their capability for producing feelings of superiority and grievance, guilt and vengeance, is defused. This requires building a narrative of reconciliation, which often needs to change the aesthetic and moral arguments on which the groups' and their members' identities are conceived (Chapter 25, this volume). Cultural materials, together with the network of practices and institutions framing social life, provide the resources and limits within which personhood and citizenship can be conceived and also the shapes individual experience and behavior take within social and political settings (Chapters 26 and 32, this volume).

Whatever the case, neither cultural resources nor sociocultural institutions and activities can exhaust the explanation of individual experiences and behavior. Each individual psyche is a dynamic system whose inner workings produce experiences about one's own body, about others, and about one's own joyful or suffering feelings while living current events (Chapter 29, this volume). These self-reflecting experiences, when assembled with the workings of imagination on cultural material, are able to be turned into tools for shaping one's own self by setting a life project (Chapter 30, this volume) or, when producing narratives, accounting for one's past life, which adds another layer to the structures on which current experiences are framed and behavior is shaped (Chapter 33, this volume).

34.2.2.4 Capabilities and Limits of This Model

The model presented above provides basic formalisms able to account for how consecutive layers of signs, psychological functions, and patterns of experience and behavior develop from the encounters between a human organism and its environment (Maturana & Varela, 1992). These structural formalisms model the functional properties of the operation of psychological functional systems resulting from the development of assemblies of organs within the structure of the organism (Luria, 1969). The explanation of how these functional layers are generated lies in a general physical/biological principle: the capability of open systems for keeping their inner energetic balance through cyclic repetition of exchanges with their entourage (Bertalanffy, 1976; Maturana & Varela, 1992).

These formalisms result from recursive combinations of triadic semiosis into more developed structures, which replicate the form of this basic unit and produce fractal structures capable of reproducing themselves. These structures are virtual entities modeling the dynamic processes of meaning making on which psychological functions develop and increase their capability for managing the course of behavior. The model is also able to account for how both meaning and psychological processes appear as transient and contextual, while keeping the basic structural pattern (organization).

The formal semiotic structures this model provides are tools for bridging the explanatory gap between the environmental-social, bio-psychological, and experiential domains. These structures are able to model how the chain of interorgan encounters going on when adapting to environmental circumstances (the repeated shaping and reshaping of biological processes) acquires semiotic properties as signs signaling toward the psychological processes and the overt behavior to follow.

Semiotics cannot offer causal explanations of how structural couplings can change the coupling structures (which can only be provided by biochemical, anatomical, and physical causal principles) but can model how these changes can be read as signals announcing other changes to follow. This may seem trivial for the explanation of biological functions, but it is crucial for understanding how the affections produced by cultural artifacts, inscriptions, and texts are able to act as signs unleashing bodily reactions as if an environmental (absent) structure (or any kind of semiotized object) were present. It is then when semiotic formalisms show their potential for describing how biological and psychological processes and environmental (cultural) elements are capable of canalizing behavior and producing conscious experiences, thinking, and deliberation which together make the subjective realm – and also how changes in the material and social environments resulting from human behavior (artifacts, inscriptions, texts, social structures, rituals, practices, activities) can operate as extracorporeal devices for storing knowledge, directing behavior, and assessing its outcomes through the attribution of pragmatic, moral, formal, and aesthetic values.

The virtual structures that this model provides are also formal explanatory devices for describing how experiences leave a trace expanding individual abilities. The semiotic structure underlying psychological constructs, such as habits, schemas, or scripts (Rosa, 2007a, 2007b), allows these constructs to be conceived as flexible processes rather than rigid sets of associations or algorithms and is therefore able to adjust to produce understanding (new meaning) and direct behavior when interpreting the particular situations faced.

This model conceives meaning, experience, and behavior as fleeting outcomes of trajectories of experience. This makes these processes highly contextual, depending as much on the capabilities of the organism as on the social and material features of the environment in a particular moment. This makes the model suitable to account for individual developmental and (natural and cultural) ecological transformations.

The formalisms of this model allow both cultural change and psychological development to be conceived as mutually related dynamic systems. Both develop together, but without getting scrambled into a blended mix. Each feeds the other, but each evolves on a different time scale. Psychological development proceeds as the individual participates in different social settings, when joining activities carried out in particular cultural practices, and when moving from different institutional domains. Psychological development is, then, an effect of social mobility through (social, institutional, cultural) semiotic boundaries. The sociocultural environment, in turn, is transformed when the traffic between different activities produces new elements and the dynamics of particular sociocultural institutional structures and those of the sociocultural environment at large transform – what is usually called *historical change*.

This model may be useful for producing formalisms able to describe how the workings of psyche create semiotic-affective-cognitive structures capable of developing a sort of virtual operating apparatus (usually called *mind*) that mediates the production of behavioral responses and is therefore able to decouple the inner workings of the organism from the changes in the environment (Chapter 2, this volume) and to produce the rise of subjective experiences: the self and the will (Rosa, 2016; Rosa & González, 2014).

The model presented above is able to offer formal explanations, and therefore probabilistic forecasts, but it is unable to produce proper causal explanations and accurate predictions. Its potential resides in its capability for creating formal constructs for modeling processes otherwise inconceivable and also in suggesting avenues for empirical research. It is by gathering empirical evidence that flesh can be added to the bare bones of the structures the model provides. But there is something else the model provides: a heuristic device capable of pinpointing target areas for research (semiotic boundaries) and suggesting how the relationships between semiotized objects (constructs, structures, explanations) could produce some outcomes (hypothesis) so that empirical observations and experiments could be carried out. In sum, whether this model is useful for furthering psychological knowledge can only be ascertained if it proves its capabilities when put into operation for orienting and interpreting the results of empirical research, and also if the empirical research feeds the production of transformations in its formalisms.

34.3 Concluding Remarks: Sociocultural Psychology among the Sciences

Sociocultural psychology is the most hybrid among the hybrid sciences gathered under the umbrella of psychology. It dwells in and thrives on the fractures crisscrossing the sociocultural landscapes where humans live, having its raison d'être in exploring what happens to human psyches when crossing the fuzzy boundaries where meaning arises, conscious experience and ambivalence appear, and psychological processes readjust their dynamics when shaping behavior. These are matters that in some way or another are also of interest for other disciplines – semiotics, semiology, linguistics, phenomenology, hermeneutics, literary and art criticism, history, anthropology, sociology, and economics, in addition to different psychological disciplines. Sociocultural psychology can profit from the knowledge and methods these disciplines offer and also be a ground on which transactional categories and transactional codes relating to the tools of knowledge that these disciplines provide can be developed. It is by fostering cross-disciplinary hybridization that sociocultural psychology can make itself useful.

This is what the model presented above attempts to do. It offers heuristic devices able to address subjective meaning-making processes as formal structures mediating understanding and directing behavior, which can be useful in explaining how constructs coming from other psychological disciplines (awareness and attention, learning and memory, speech and thinking, affection and emotion, desires and goals, attribution, identity, self, personality, schema, script, etc.) can arise and be operational for the direction of behavior. It is by entering into dialogue with other disciplines, while putting subjective experience and meaning making in the middle, that sociocultural psychology can generate tools of knowledge for fostering psychological knowledge. But this cannot be done without borrowing phenomena and methods from neighboring disciplines, nor can it be done without taking into account how causal explanations add empirical validation to the formal explanations of the regularities observed.

This chapter has focused on presenting a model of how psyche produces experience and conduct, taking these to be described and explained in the third person. This is the stance nomothetic sciences take, and psychology is certainly among them. But can it be only a nomothetic science? Psychology is concerned with what human beings are like and why they do what they do, but the knowledge it provides is for the benefit of human beings so that they can improve their lives. That is why psychology should also be conjugated in first person singular. Psychological knowledge is not only for describing, explaining, and managing the doings of psyches but also for understanding individuals and providing them with recourses for their own management. Psychology cannot avoid being an idiographic science as well. In fact, every nomothetic perspective begins from an idiographic one.

If meaning making and personal experience are the main matters of interest for sociocultural psychology research, it cannot avoid being both a nomothetic and ideographic science. Its tools of knowledge are suitable for fertilizing both approaches and, by doing so, for increasing the validity and reliability of methods and fostering the development of psychological knowledge.

Note

1 We deliberately use this – somewhat poetic – term here, instead of the usual rationality-bound notions of "mind." *Psyche* captures the unity of the biological and the cultural, the social and the personal, and the affective and the cognitive sides of human ways of being.

References

Bertalanffy, L. von (1976). *General System Theory: Foundations, Development, Applications* (rev. edn.). New York: George Braziller.

Bruner, J. (2003). Self-making narratives. In R. Fivush & C. A. Haden (Eds.), *Autobiographical Memory and the Construction of a Narrative Self* (pp. 209–225), Mahwah, NJ: Lawrence Erlbaum.

Fernández-Cid, H., Kriger, M., & Rosa, A. (2014). Injusticia social y vivencias de la ciudadanía en jóvenes. In M. F. González & A. Rosa (Eds.), *Hacer(se) ciudadan@s: Una psicología para la democracia* (pp. 129–156). Buenos Aires: Miño y Dávila.

González, A. (1997). *Estructuras de la Praxis: Ensayo de una Filosofía Primera*. Madrid: Trotta.

Harré, R. (2012). Positioning theory: Moral dimensions of social-cultural psychology. In J. Valsiner (Ed.), *The Oxford Handbook of Culture and Psychology* (pp. 191–206). Oxford: Oxford University Press.

Lotman, J. (2005). On the semiosphere. *Sign Systems Studies*, 33(1), 206–229 (trans. by Wilma Clark). Retrieved from www.ut.ee/SOSE/sss/Lotman331.pdf.

Luria, A. R. (1969/1983). *Las Funciones Psíquicas superiores y su organización cerebral*. Barcelona: Fontanella.

Martin, J. & Gillespie, A. (2010). A neo-Meadian approach to human agency: Relating the social and the psychological in the ontogenesis of perspective-coordinating persons. *Integrative Psychological and Behavioral Science*, 44(3), 252–272. DOI: 10.1007/s12124–010–9126–7.

Maturana, H. & Varela, F. (1992). *The Tree of Knowledge: The Biological Roots of Human Understanding*. Boston: Shambhala Publications.

Rosa, A. (2007a). Acts of psyche: Actuations as synthesis of semiosis and action. In J. Valsiner & A. Rosa (Eds.), *Cambridge Handbook of Sociocultural Psychology* (pp. 205–237). New York: Cambridge University Press.

Rosa, A. (2007b). Dramaturgical actuations and symbolic communication: Or how beliefs make up reality. In J. Valsiner & A. Rosa (Eds.), *Cambridge Handbook of Sociocultural Psychology* (pp. 293–317). New York: Cambridge University Press.

Rosa, A. (2015). The reflective mind and reflexivity in psychology: Description and explanation within a psychology of experience. In G. Marsico, R. Ruggieri, & S. Salvatore (Eds.), *Reflexivity and Psychology* (Yearbook of Idiographic Science, vol. 6). Charlotte, NC: Information Age Publishing.

Rosa, A. (2016). The self rises up from lived experiences: A micro-semiotic analysis of the unfolding of trajectories of experience when performing ethics. In J. Valsiner, G. Marsico, N. Chaudhary, T. Sato, & V. Dazzani (Eds.), *Psychology as a Science of Human Being: The Yokohama Manifesto* (Annals of Theoretical Psychology, vol. 13, pp. 87–127). Cham, Switzerland: Springer.

Rosa, A. & González, F. (2013). Trajectories of experience of real life events: A semiotic approach to the dynamics of positioning. *Integrative Psychological and Behavioral Science*, 47: 395–430. DOI: 10.1007/s12124–013–9240–4.

Rosa, A. & González, F. (2014). Cultivo de psique ciudadana [Cultivating Citizen Psyches]. In M. F. González & A. Rosa (Eds.), *Hacer(se) ciudadan@s: Una psicología para la democracia*

[Making Citizens: A Psychology for Democracy] (pp. 51–87). Buenos Aires: Miño y Dávila.

Russell, J. A. (2003). Core affect and the psychological construction of emotion. *Psychological Review*, 110(1), 145–172. DOI: 10.1037/0033–295X.110.1.145.

Sato, T., Yasuda, Y., Kido, A., Arakawa, A., Mizoguchi, H., & Valsiner, J. (2007). Sampling reconsidered: Idiographic science and the analysis of personal life trajectories. In J. Valsiner & A. Rosa (Eds.). *Cambridge Handbook of Sociocultural Psychology* (pp. 82–106). New York: Cambridge University Press.

Vygotsky, L. S. (1934/1987). Thinking and speech. In R. W. Rieber & A. S. Carton (Eds.), *The Collected Works of L. S. Vygotsky. Volume 1: Problems of General Psychology* (pp. 37–285). New York: Plenum Press.

Index

abduction, 45, 195, 639
   inductive abduction, 404, 420
aboutness of symbolic resources, 184–185, 188
abstract concepts
   influence on human actions, 399–401
abstraction
   and thinking, 21–22
   constructed in collective action, 417–419
abstractive generalization
   and intensionality, 37–39
actants, 105
action
   actuations, 119–121
   and the nature of psyche, 103–104
   bodies coupling with things, 107–109
   cultural landscapes as environment for, 29
   culture as product of, 103–104
   dramatic actuations, 121
   emergent properties, 118–121
   intentional schemas, 118–119
   production of innovation, 125–127
   semiotics of, 117–118
   structure of, 117
activity as a means of surpassing adjustment, 487–488
activity theory, 248
actor network theory, 105, 154
actuations, 119–121
adaptation in living organisms, 19
Adler, Mortimer, 281
adult–child interaction
   pointing gestures, 235
   triadic rhythmic interactions, 226–227
   use of objects, 233–235
adult–infant social play, 219
aesthetic experience, 115–116
aesthetic transcendence
   defining transcendence, 351
   ecstatic power of objects, 354–357
   metaphor and standing forth in the world, 360–363
   music, 352, 358–359
   poetry, 359
   priority of the Other, 354–357
   reimagining transcendence, 363

   religious experience, 354–357
   transcendence within immanence, 357–360
   wagering on the idea of transcendence, 351–354
affective action, 117
affective bridges, 602–603
affective grounds of sensemaking, 44–45
affective register, 545–546
affects
   role in communication, 121
affordances
   creative action using material and cultural affordances, 172–174
   of objects, 107–109
   of the environment, 107
age-appropriate behavior, 564–565
aging
   adaptation to changes caused by, 622–623
   and self-regulation, 621–622
   assisted suicide, 617
   biblical age, 616
   conceptual qualifiers, 623–624
   death and dying, 617–618
   differential aging concept, 621
   effects of increasing life expectancy, 615
   euthanasia, 617
   factors influencing life-satisfaction and well-being, 621–622
   health challenges associated with, 615
   life events and melodies of living, 624–626
   lifespan models, 620–621
   methods of adaptation and coping, 621–622
   new perspectives, 616
   perceptions of, 615–616
   psychology and, 618–620
   research related to, 615
   senicide, 617
   toward a person-centered theory of culturally guided aging in families, 626–627
   ubasute tradition, 617
   view from within, 624–627
   view from without, 616–624
   views of the aging person, 616–617
agencements, 487

children's development as persons
  cultural life course, 570–571
  early work in developmental psychology, 556–557
  Stern and the experiencing person, 558–559
  through persistent imitation, 559–561
  work of Stern and Baldwin, 556–557
children's development as persons, investigation
  analysis, 563
  convergence between individual and collective meaning,
    563–567
  design and central concepts, 561–563
  duration and redundancy in development of the personal
    life course, 569–570
  imitation, 567–569
  intermediate summary of cases, 569
  multifunctional imitation in the life course, 570
  someone to copy and be copied by, 567–569
  timed and untimed living, 563–567
chimpanzees
  culture in, 235
Christianity
  source of technologies of the self, 382–383
  toward a genealogy of psychological rationality,
    390–392
citizen
  definition, 480
citizenship
  alterities in modern psytizenship, 483–484
  emergence of, 479
  emergence of the self-governing citizen, 480–483
  psychological and political aspects, 479
  role of psychology, 492–493
  see also psytizenship
climate change
  as social object, 136–138
  from science to communal discourse, 136–137
  mass media, 138
  political institutionalization and reified discourse,
    137–138
co-construction, 4, 5, 23, 87, 133, 563, 571
co-creation of artifacts, 171–172
Coe, Cati, 419
cognitive archaeology, 109
cognitive polyphasia, 55, 248
cognitive psychology
  problems related to representationalism, 63–65
cognitive revolution in psychology, 16
cognitive science of religion (CSR)
  avoiding ethical violence in research, 376–377
  enacting psychology, 370–371
  enactivism and the socio-material embeddedness of
    cognition, 371–372

  implications of interpretative speculations, 376–377
  meaning of natural, 366–367
  Mikhail Bakhtin, 374–376
  moving forward, 376–377
  non-reductive scientific naturalism, 369–374
  phenomenological naturalism, 366–367
  phenomenological naturalism and sociocultural theory,
    374–376
  religious belief, 367–369
  rethinking religious cognition, 372–374
  scientific naturalism, 367–368
  sociocultural cognition, 370–371
  sociocultural theory and embodying language, 374–376
  William James and religious belief, 368–369
cognitive theory of personality, 621
Cold War, 482
Cole, Michael, 260, 333, 486
collective action
  construction of abstraction and reification, 417–419
  influence of imaginative processes, 419–421
  use of metaphor, allegory and metonymy to inspire,
    417–419
collectivism
  children and money, 343–345
Common Core educational standards, 281
common sense, 35, 37, 41, 43, 46, 87, 88, 255, 399, 461,
    560, 584
communication, 4, 5, 17, 18, 20, 25–26, 28, 29
  and belief, 131
  intentional, 24, 25
  symbols as a product of when acting, 22–23
communication memory, 460
communication tools
  artifacts turning into, 112–114
competent baby paradigm, 226, 233
complex semiotic systems, 254–255
compliance, 58, 321
computer metaphor of the mind, 69–70
conceptualization
  leading from perception, 21
conflict ethos, 464–466
conflict theories of self-reflection, 247–249
conformity, 58, 453, 454, 465
consciousness
  emergence of, 27–28
construction of the person
  in interethnic situations, 592–593
constructivism
  approaches to subjectivity, 383
context
  importance in interpersonal psychoanalysis, 92–93
contextuality, 503

continuity and discontinuity in intergenerational
        narratives, 462–464
Cooley, Charles, 247
cooperation
    and interaction, 132–134
core–distal connectivity pattern, 215–216
corporeal turn in human sciences, 207–209
Costa, P.E.S., 585
creative cognition, 164–165
creativity, 104
    approach to the study of creative action, 174–175
    appropriation by audiences, 170
    as a dialogic process, 171–172
    co-creation of artifacts, 171–172
    creative action in actor–artifact relations, 168–169
    creative action in actor–audience relations, 171–172
    creative action in audience–artifact relations, 169–171
    creative action using material and cultural affordances,
        172–174
    creativity complex, 168
    ecologies of creating, 168
    evaluation of artifacts by audiences, 170–171
    five A's framework, 166–174
    four P's framework, 166
    interpretation of artifacts by audiences, 170
    meanings of, 163
    mediational model, 167
    role of sociocultural factors, 163–164
    sociocultural approach to study, 165–174
    theoretical roots, 164–165
    tradition of decorating eggs for Easter, 166
    user-generated content and objects, 171
Crites, Stephen, 358–359
cross-cultural psychology, 343, 344
crystallized imagination, 402
cultural affordances, 235
    creative action using, 172–174
cultural canalization
    of gender identities, 606–609
    of gender stereotypes, 605
cultural elements
    use of, 183–184
cultural experiences
    as symbolic resources, 183–184
cultural-historical activity theory (CHAT), 148–149
cultural knowledge
    from intergenerational narratives, 459–461
cultural landscapes
    environment for human action, 29
cultural life course and the development of children as
        persons, 570–571

cultural psychology
    abstractive generalization, 38–39
    approach to religion, 383–385
    as the general theory of psychology, 45–46
    as the science of sensemaking, 39–42
    contribution to a general theory of psychology, 35–36
    current developments in the field, 3
    dynamics of sensemaking, 42–45
    extensional and intensional categories, 36–37
    holism, 39
    immanent formal causation, 40
    intensionality and abstractive generalization, 37–38
    mind is sensemaking, 41–42
    mind is the process of decoupling from the environment,
        41
    mind is the psychological object, 40–41
    organizational closure, 39–40
    processual ontology, 39
    relationship to interpersonal psychoanalysis, 78–79
    sensemaking is inherently dialogical, 42
cultural tools, 333
    historical maps, 431–434
cultural uses of objects, 236
culture
    as the field distribution of possibilities, 44
    as the spirit of psyche, 28
    attitudes to money, 343–345
    dialectical study of the meaning of money, 335–337
    historical development in relation to mind (Vico),
        401–404
    nature of, 103–104
    relation to consciousness and personhood, 27–28
cyberspace, 488

dance, 25, 103, 107, 112, 117, 133, 168, 208, 212, 213,
        216, 217, 218, 219, 220, 264, 352, 358, 512, 514,
        577, 579, 583, 584
Dante, 408
de Beauvoir, Simone, 188
de Oliveira, Carlito, 587, 589, 591
death and dying, 617–618
defence systems, 80–82
Delpit, Lisa, 293
Descartes, René, 14, 70, 368
development
    crossing social borders, 312–313
development of persons
    challenges to the study of, 557–558
    elementarism, 557–558
    nondevelopmentalism, 557–558
development through overcoming ambivalence, 518–519

developmental psychology
  corporeal turn, 207–209
  future directions in movement studies, 220
  shift toward the study of movement, 208–209
Dewey, John, 15, 66, 69, 103, 114–115, 154, 481
  double psychologizing of the educational curriculum,
    281
  mutuality of mind and world, 73
  on creative perception, 170
  on creativity, 168–169, 172
  on self-reflection, 246
dialogic pedagogy
  definition, 275–276
  ecological non-instrumental dislogic pedagogies,
    294–296
  epistemological instrumental dialogic pedagogies,
    282–283
  epistemological non-instrumental dialogic pedagogies,
    287–291
  growth of interest in, 274–275
  instrumental and non-instrumental education,
    276–279
  instrumental dialogic pedagogies, 279–285
  non-instrumental dialogic pedagogies, 285–296
  ontological non-instrumental dialogic pedagogies,
    291
  social justice instrumental dialogic pedagogies,
    283–285
  types of, 276–279
  unresolved issues, 296–298
dialogical account of feelings, 512–515
dialogical nature of sensemaking, 42
dialogical perspective
  applications, 503
  approach to the human experiential mind, 503–504
  definition, 503
dialogical self theory, 605
dialogical understanding in history education, 436–438
dialogicality, 503
dialogue
  aspect of creativity, 171–172
  concept in social sciences, 274
dicent, 117
differential aging concept, 621
Dinesen, Isak, 463
discourse analysis, 72–73
discourses, 123–124
discursive practices, 400
dissociated experiences, 85–87
distanciation, 245, 251, 252, 253, 255, 256
divine, 355, 356, 360, 402, 528

"Divine Will," 387
domain-specificity of creative action, 174
Donald, Merlin, 260–261
Dostoevsky, Fyodor, 287, 294
double binds, 549
double psychologizing of the educational curriculum, 281
double-directedness of a position, 512
Down syndrome, 229, 231
dramatic actuations, 121
dreams, 27, 83, 88, 180, 182, 353, 539, 603
driving force of lack, 520
dualism
  revolt against, 70
  tendency to return to, 70–73
Duncker, K., 64
Dupré, Louis, 355–356, 357
Durkheim, Émile, 131
dynamic gestalt, 39, 46

early infancy
  breath pattern, 214–215
  core–distal connectivity pattern, 215–216
  cultural influences on motor development, 207–208
  effects of emotional deprivation, 208
  experience and body awareness, 211–214
  fundamental patterns of total body connectivity,
    214–217
  future directions in movement studies, 220
  head–tail pattern of connectivity, 216–217
  influence of social play, 207–208
  iterative movement experience, 209–211
  study of motor development and movement, 208–209
  thinking in movement, 217–219
East Asian children Pocket Money Project, 339–343
ecological non-instrumental dislogic pedagogies, 294–296
ecological psychology, 549
ecological theory of perception, 106–107
economic games, 325–326, 328–329
economic inequalities, 338–339
economic tools, 333
ecstasy, 358
Edelman, Gerald, 209
education
  crossing social borders, 312–313
  portrayals of, 523–524
  transcendent nature, 302–303
educational border zone, 309–311
  institutional borders as social membranes, 311–312
effectivities for action, 107
Egan, Kieran, 436
Ego, 503, 514

Egyptian revolution (2011), 443–444, 449–450
    irony as a mode of resistance, 452–453
    irony in images of authority figures, 450–451
    pedestrian interpretations of images produced by the
        military, 451–452
Ehrenfest, Paul, 289
Ehrenzweig, Anton, 361
elementarism, 557–558
embodied experience
    fundamental patterns of total body connectivity,
        214–217
    somatic education techniques, 211–214
embodiment
    thinking in movement, 217–219
embodiment theory, 209
embodying language, 374–376
emotion-focused coping, 621
emotional reactions
    role in communication, 121
emotions, 23
    and religious development, 385–386
enactive approach to cognition
    socio-material embeddedness of cognition, 371–372
enactive cognition theory, 18–20
enactive program, 211, 212
enactive semiosis, 118, 120
Engeström, Y., 153, 154, 248
Ensminger, J., 328
epistemic objects, 151
epistemological instrumental dialogic pedagogies,
        282–283
epistemological non-instrumental dialogic pedagogies,
        287–291
epistemology of sociocultural psychology, 637–649
Erikson, E.H., 179, 620
Estonia
    building a nation, 138–140
    collective memory work, 140–142
    historical accounts and national identity, 133–134
    national identity, 138–143
    reifying national identity as a state, 142–143
ethnic diversity in the urban context, 587–592
ethnic groups
    historical accounts and identity, 133–134
ethnic identity
    relation to history education, 428–430
ethnic reterritorialization, 576
ethnic self-affirmation, 578, 581, 582
ethnic self-identification, 575
ethos of conflict, 464–466
euthanasia, 617

Evans, Richard, 530
executive functions
    functional use of objects in the pre-language stage,
        230–233
existentials of embodied history, 542
    affective register, 545–546
    case example, 542–546
    habituation, 543
    hermeneutic repertoire, 544–545
    incorporation, 544
    intercorporeity, 543–544
expanded mediational structure (EMS), 333–334
expanded self, 335
expansive learning, 248
experience, 14, 15, 16, 17, 20–21, 23, 24, 25–26, 28,
        30–31, 103, 106, 108, 112, 114
    aesthetic, 115–116
    and body awareness, 211–214
    meaning and memory in development, 260–262
    of the world and the self, 114–116
    semiotics of behavior and, 116–125
experience and meaning
    approach of sociocultural psychology, 638–639
experience space and its constraints, 262–264
experimental psychology, 15
explanandum, 40
explanans, 40
extensional categories, 36–37

faith, 6, 353, 356, 359, 385, 386, 399, 400, 406, 530, 585,
        607
fantasy, 83, 88, 180, 183, 353, 407, 539, 568
Febvre, Lucien, 461
Fechner, Gustav, 15
feed-forward process, 559
feelings
    dialogical account of, 512–515
    driving the mind toward reflection, 23–24
Feldenkrais, Moshe, 208, 213
Feldenkrais method, 212, 215
Fernandes, Danilo, 586, 587
fiat borders, 306
field theory, 79–80, 85, 90–91
figurative schema, 131
first-person approach, 15, 28, 31, 388
Flaubert, Gustave, 187
Fogel, Alan, 213
folkpsychology, 557
forms of vitality, 218–219, 220
Foucault, Michel, 304, 381–382, 390, 470–471, 604
four levels of semiotic mediation, 186–187

fourth age, 618, 621
fragile signs, 522
Freire, Paulo, 281, 283, 284–285
Freud, Sigmund, 91, 400, 550
   internalization, 249
   theory of fantasy (imagination), 180
friendship and money, 342–343
Fromm, Erich, 78
Fromm-Reichman, Freda, 78
frontier, 30, 313, 581, 588, 591
Fuchs, T., 543, 544
functional, canonical use of objects by children, 225
functional permanence of objects, 226

Gadamer, Hans-Georg, 85
Geertz, Clifford, 72, 358, 598, 600
gender
   concept of, 598
gender equality
   insights from sociocultural psychology, 609–611
gender identities
   cultural canalization, 606–609
   semiotic mediation by images, 606–609
gender identity and self, 597–598
   as a dynamic and contextualized system, 603–606
   central assumptions of sociocultural psychology,
      598–600
   social identities as boundary phenomena, 600–603
gender relations, 604–605, 606
gender roles, 604–605
gender stereotypes, 605
Geneplore model of creativity, 169, 173
general systems theory, 18
generativity of symbolic resources, 188–189
genetic psychology, 556
genuine dialogue concept, 286–287
geropsychology, 615
Gessel, Arnold, 210
gestalt, 218, 247, 507, 549
gestalt units, 544
gestures in young children
   use in self-regulation, 230–233
Gibson, James J., 71, 106–107, 108, 550
   affordances, 173
gift exchange, 333
globalization, 488
God, 69, 130, 133, 139, 351, 352, 353, 370, 377, 385, 386,
      387, 406, 528, 557, 579, 616
Goldstein, J.A., 419
Goldstein, Kurt, 78
good me, 81, 82, 90

Grass, Günter
   adolescence and war, 531–532
   doubts over the heroic soldier propaganda, 532–535
   growing up in Nazi Germany, 527–529
   Hitler Youth and beyond, 529–531
   propaganda and the cult of Hitler, 527–529
   questions over his involvement in warfare, 532–535
   uniforms and propaganda, 529–531
Gregory, Richard, 64
Gricean maxims of good communication, 293
Griffin, Martyn, 482
group-based moral emotions, 471–473
guidance, 178, 181, 182, 189, 223, 265, 275, 279, 300,
      309, 310, 380, 510, 519, 556, 561, 619
Guimarães, D.S., 588

Habermas, Jürgen, 482
habits
   development of, 119, 120
habituation, 543
Hackney, Peggy, 213, 214, 215
Halbwachs, Maurice, 436, 459–460
handicap, 135–136, 143
Hanna, Thomas, 212
Harré, Rom, 67
Harry Potter, 562, 566–567, 568, 569
Havighurst, R.J., 620
head–tail pattern of connectivity, 216–217
Hegel, Georg
   theory of self-consciousness, 247–248
Heidbreder, E., 66
Heidegger, M., 542, 545, 546
Heraclitus of Ephesus, 597, 598
Herbart, Johann Friedrich, 15
hermeneutic philosophy, 85
hermeneutic repertoire, 544–545
hermeneutics, 352, 637
hetero-affection, 541
heuristics, 327
Hewstone, M., 67
Hexis, 548
high culture
   dialogue of, 286
hippocampus, 267
historical guilt, 471–473
historical knowledge
   from intergenerational narratives, 459–461
historical maps
   as cultural tools, 431–434
historical myths, 469
historical preexistence of the human mind, 463–464

historical representation, 133–134
historical selfhood as embodied, 540–542
historical truth
 pragmatic consequences of, 471–473
historiography
 fostering of national identity, 424–426
history
 need for youth to understand, 461–462
 politics of representing the past, 443–444
history education, 424
 and identity formation, 428–430
 approach to national identity, 427–428
 fostering of national identity, 424–426
 historical maps as cultural tools, 431–434
 ironical and dialogical understanding of nation and
  national identity, 436–438
 master narratives and their persistence, 430–431
 myths of origin and their persistence, 430–431
 relation to ethnic identity, 428–430
 sociocultural investigation of alternative pathways,
  434–436
 sociocultural views on imagining history, 426–427
history education studies
 continuities and changes, 428–430
Hitler, Adolf, 526
 cult of, 527–529
 death of, 535
holism, 39
Hollenback, J., 358
holomorphic representation, 133, 135
homeland concept, 413
Homer, 616
hospice movement, 618
human experiential mind
 defining, 504–506
 dialogic and sociocultural perspectives, 506–507
 dialogical account of feelings, 512–515
 dialogical pespective, 503–504
 first-person perspective, 507–508
 mind in motion, 511–512
 notion of position, 511–512
 perspectives within, 507–511
 phenomenology, 504–506
 relation to the self, 515
 second-person perspective, 507, 508–509
 third-person perspective, 507, 509–511
humans
 as responsive beings, 548–550
 viewed as not part of nature, 68
Hutto, D., 269
hypergeneralized signs, 404

iconic signs, 112
icons, 117
identification, 121, 143, 252, 255, 256, 304, 429, 430, 431,
  434, 435, 446, 483, 490, 491, 512
 with Other, 254
identity
 ethnic, 133–134, 142–143
 historical, 424–426
 influence of history education, 428–430
 national, 133–134, 138–143
identity construction, 140–142
ideographic, 650
ideologies, 591
Ignatius of Loyola, *Spiritual Exercises*, 386–387
 a book for building yourself, 387
 development of subjectivity through the rhetoric and
  fractal structure of the exercises, 388–390
 disciplining experience, 388–390
 giving someone the way and order, 388–390
 knowledge of the self, 388
 realising and relishing things interiorly, 388
illusion
 and poverty of the stimulus, 67–68
images
 semiotic mediation of gender identities, 606–609
imagination, 121
 and spheres of experience, 181
 as an integrative sociocultural concept, 181–183
 constraints on the use of, 192–194
 future study directions, 195
 historical perspectives on, 180–181
 loop of imagination, 181–183
 plausibility in sociocultural situations, 183
 relation to reality, 179
 role in guiding the lifecourse, 179
 role in sociocultural change, 191–192
 role in the life course, 189–191
 study methodological problems, 194–195
 symbolic resources concept, 178
 theoretical problems, 194
imagination and creativity theory, 149–150
imaginative processes, 402
 embodiment and reification of the concept of nation,
  408–417
 range of influence on human action, 419–421
imagined communities
 and national identity, 404–408
imagined landscape
 and concept of nationhood, 411–415
imagining history
 sociocultural views on, 426–427

imitation
  multifunctional imitation in the life course, 570
  personal development through persistent imitation,
    559–561
  someone to copy and be copied by, 567–569
  user-generated content and objects, 171
immanent formal causation, 40
implicatory denial, 467
incorporation, 544
indexes, 117
indexical signs, 112
indigenous people
  ethnic diversity in the urban context, 587–592
indigenous university students, 576–584
  challenges faced by, 589
  migration to the urban context, 584–587
  search for academic education, 584–587
individualism
  children and money, 343–345
inductive abduction, 404
inherent intentionality, 15
innovation
  production through action, 125–127
  user-generated content and objects, 171
institutional environment
  influence on child development, 327–329
institutionalization, 136
instrumental dialogic pedagogies, 279–285
instrumental education, 276–279
instrumentality, 153–154
  coordination of complex constellations of artefacts, 159
  failed remediation in oral health care (Finland), 155–156
  shifting multiple functions of BIM software, 157–159
intangible concepts
  influence on human actions, 399–401, 419–421
intellectualism
  fallacy of, 69
intensional categories, 36–37
intensionality
  and abstractive generalization, 37–39
intentional action
  development of, 119
intentional communication, 24, 25
intentional schemas, 118–119
intentional worlds
  semiotic constitution of, 123–125
intentionality, 15, 55, 110, 110, 120, 170, 269, 400, 504,
    505, 508, 509, 540, 541, 544, 545
interaction and cooperation, 132–134
intercorporeity, 543–544
interdisciplinary synthesis, 4

interethnic situations
  construction of the self, 575–576
  ethnic diversity in the urban context, 587–592
  multinaturalism and the construction of the person,
    589–591
  psychology and the construction of the person, 592–593
  self as the space of circulation of subjective agencies,
    591–592
intergenerational narratives
  bias in, 466–468
  breaking down literal social denials, 470–471
  building up and marginalizing the ethos of conflict,
    464–466
  contemporary effects, 458
  continuity and discontinuity, 462–464
  forms of social denial, 467
  historical guilt of descendents, 471–473
  historical preexistence of the human mind, 463–464
  literal social denial, 468–469
  memories of historical events, 459–461
  memories of past ways of living, 459–461
  natality, 463, 464
  need for youth to understand their history, 461–462
  of violence, 464–466
  parrhesia, 470–471
  pragmatic consequences of historical truth, 471–473
  reconciliation processes, 473–474
  role of group-based moral emotions, 471–473
  scaffolding children's autobiographical memories,
    458–459
  scaffolding positive family identities, 458–459
  violence from the point of view of victims, perpetrators
    and bystanders, 466–468
internalization theories of self-reflection, 249–251
interobjective architecture, 58–60
interobjectivity, 51–55
  in social research, 56
interpersonal psychoanalysis
  ability to deal with the unknown, 94–95
  approach in the consulting room, 82–83
  boundaries and regulatory mechanisms, 90–91
  considerations for the therapist, 87–89
  field theories, 90–91
  goals and growth, 93–94
  importance of context, 92–93
  origins of, 78
  relationship to cultural psychology, 78–79
  role of language, 91–92
  semiotic capacity of patients, 82
  semiotic space in the therapeutic field, 89–94
  Sullivan's modes of meaning making, 80

interpersonal psychoanalysis (*cont.*)
  systems of defence, 80–82
  work of Donnel Stern, 85–86
  work of Edgar Levenson, 83–85
  work of Harry Stack Sullivan, 79–83
  work of Phillip Bromberg, 86–87
interpretant, 117
interpretative denial, 467
intersubjectivity, 51–53
iron logic of the universal necessity, 283
ironic understanding in history education, 436–438
irony
  as a mode of resistance, 452–453
  as a tool of critique, 443
  in images of authority figures, 450–451
Islam, 383
  experience of a Swedish woman convert, 524–526

Jack, Daboma
  incident in Malta, 50–51
Jackson, Michael, 413
James, William, 15, 78, 265, 354–355, 359, 361, 373, 605
  human experiencing mind, 504–506
  on religious belief, 368–369
Jefferson, Thomas, 288
Jones, J.W., 361
Judaism, 383
Jules et Jim, 186

Kant, Immanuel, 37
Kegan, Robert, 490
kinesphere, 217
kinesthetic, 207, 212, 213, 219
Klein, Melanie, 91
Knorr-Cetina, Karin, 151
knowledge encounters, 55–58
Koenigsberg, Richard, 416
Kübler-Ross, Elisabeth, 618

Laban, Rudolph, 212, 213
Labaree, David, 278
Lacan, Jacques, 247
Lakatos, Imre, 287, 288–291
language
  embodying language, 374–376
  emergence from social symbols, 24–26
  relationship to tool use, 151–153
  role in interpersonal psychoanalysis, 91–92
language game model, 22
Latour, Bruno, 479, 492

law, 334, 360, 366, 367, 368, 369, 373, 374, 401, 461, 506
Lee, Peter, 428
legisigns, 119, 123, 639, 640
Leonardo da Vinci, 609
Leontjev, A.N., 148, 150
  cultural-historical activity theory (CHAT), 148–149
Levenson, Edgar, 83–85
Lévi-Strauss, Claude, 401
Lewin, Kurt, 79, 519, 549
life course
  duration and redundancy in development of, 569–570
  future-oriented nature, 306–307
  multifunctional imitation in, 570
  role of imagination, 189
  role of symbolic resources, 189–191
  sociocultural perspective, 178–179
  timed and untimed living, 563–567
lifespan models, 620–621
lifespan theory of socio-emotional selectivity, 622
linguistic turn in human sciences, 207
Linnell, Per, 295
literal denial, 467
literal social denial, 468–469
  breaking down, 470–471
literature, 193
Little Buddha, 186
Locke, John, 321
London, Jack, 188
loop of imagination, 181–183
Lorde, Audre, 293
Lotman, Juri, 29
Lotze, Hermann, 15
Lovejoy, Arthur, 70
Luckman, T., 590
Luria, Alexander, 3, 152

machinations, 105
machines, 104–105
Madame Bovary, 187, 188
Madureira, A.F.A., 601–602, 603, 608–609
magnet effect, 226
Malafouris, Lambros, 109–110, 118
Mamana, Silvia, 213
Mandela, Nelson, 412–413
maps
  as cultural tools, 431–434
market economy, 334, 335, 339, 341, 342, 344, 345
market exchange, 334, 335, 339, 343, 344, 345
market value, 334
marketization, 341, 344, 345–346
Marx, Karl, 13

mass media
  role in the climate change debate, 138
master narratives, 591
  and their persistence, 430–431
material affordances
  creative action using, 172–174
material culture, 104–106
material engagement theory, 118
Material Me, 335
material signs
  semiotic value, 114
Maturana, Humberto, 18–20, 371–372
McGraw, Myrtle, 210
Mead, George H., 16, 68, 78, 589 590
  concept of the significant symbol, 250
  on self-reflection, 246
  theory of the social act, 251–252
meaning, 13, 17, 20–21, 22, 23, 25, 26, 27, 29, 30, 37,
    42–43
  and memory, 263–264
  definition, 126
  distinction from sense, 538
  emerges from sensemaking, 43
meaning making
  distortion caused by anxiety, 80–82, 83
  Sullivan's modes of, 80
mediation, 17, 38
  as an epistemological barrier, 63
  by signs, 148
  four levels of semiotic mediation, 186–187
mediationism
  dominance in psychology theory, 63
  getting over it, 73–74
  problems in mainstream cognitive theory, 63–65
  problems with, 63
  tendency to return to dualism, 70–73
memory
  and meaning, 263–264
  anoetic memory, 265
  autobiographical memory, 260, 263–264, 265–267
  childhood (infantile) amnesia, 264–265, 360
  collective memory, 29, 140–142, 143, 400, 417, 425,
    444, 465, 473, 607
  declarative memory, 264–265
  embodied memory, 543
  episodic memory, 264–265, 266–267
  event memory, 459–461
  factors influencing development, 260–262
  family memories, 458–459
  making memory, 260
  nature of early memory, 264–265

procedural memory, 543
  reexperiencing, 265, 266
  semantic memory, 265
Meno dialogue, 282
Merleau-Ponty, Maurice, 211, 360, 538, 541–542
  sedimented dispositions, 548
metacanonical uses of objects, 230
meta-knowledge, 133, 144
metaphor
  and standing forth in the world, 360–363
  use to inspire collective action, 417–419
metaphysical naturalism, 366, 369
metonymy
  use to inspire collective action, 417–419
microgenesis, 104
migrants
  effects of crossing borders, 305
Miller, Arthur, 137
mimesis, 261
mimetic culture, 261
mind, 31
  art and artifacts, 110–111
  as sensemaking, 41–42
  as the process of decoupling from the environment, 41
  as the psychological object, 40–41
  historical development in relation to culture (Vico),
    401–404
mind and body duality, 15
mind of breathing, 215
mirror theories of self-reflection, 246–247
model of how action produces meaningful experiences,
    639–649
  capabilities and limitations of this model, 647–649
  self-management of behavior, 643–644
  semiotic boundaries and growth of meaning, 644–646
  sociocultural resouces for shaping experiences and
    behaviour, 646–647
  tetrahedral structure, 640–643
model of overcoming ambivalence by development,
    518–519
  extending the model, 522–526
  social context of meaning making, 535–536
modeling systems, 29
modern reflective capacity as a cultural artefact, 486
modern subjectivity
  conceptions of the self, 381–382
  genealogical approach to study, 382
  psyche as an historical object, 381–382
modernism, 72, 283
monarchy
  body of the king, 404–406

money
   as a cultural tool, 333, 345–346
   as an economic tool, 333
   bill-splitting, 336, 342–343, 344
   dialectical study of cultural meaning, 335–337
   expanded mediational structure (EMS), 333–334
   polysemic nature, 334–335
   See also children and money
monologic pedagogy, 275
mood, 118, 119, 120, 121
   affective register, 545–546
   role in communication, 121
moon, travel to, 182, 191, 192
moral, 13, 25, 28, 49
Moscovici, S., 130, 131, 132, 133, 134, 465
motivation, 15, 16, 23, 36, 82, 87
motivational theory of lifespan development, 622
motor development
   and iterative experience, 209–211
   cultural influences on early development, 207–208
   effects of early deprivation, 208
   study of, 208–209
movement
   body and perception, 107
   fundamental patterns of total body connectivity, 214–217
   future directions in developmental studies, 220
   somatic teaching, 211–213
   thinking in movement, 217–219
Muehlebach, Andrea, 489
multiculturalism, 488
multinaturalism, 589
   and the construction of the person, 589–591
Murdoch, Iris, 353–354, 356
music, 352, 358–359
music therapy, 226
Muslim women
   representations of the veil, 56, 57
mystery, 68, 105, 352, 355, 359, 363, 383, 400
mystical experience, 356, 358, 362, 363
mysticism, 361, 386
myth, 138, 139, 261, 589
   challenging, 469
   foundation myth, 143, 414, 431
   Italians, good fellows, 469
mythic culture, 261, 267
myths, 591
myths of origin and their persistence, 430–431

Nachträglich, 549
Nachträglichkeit, 550–551

naïve personalism, 557
naming
   and self-reflection, 245
narrative thinking, 217
natality, 463, 464
nation
   allegorical personification, 408–411
   defined in the remembrance of those who died for it, 415–417
   effect of delineating borders, 414–415
   embodiment and reification of the concept, 408–417
   ironical and dialogical understanding in history education, 436–438
   relationship to imagined landscape, 411–415
   unknown soldier memorials, 415–417
national identity
   and imagined communities, 404–408
   approach in history education, 427–428
   fostering through history education, 424–426
   historical accounts of Estonia, 133–134
   historical maps as cultural tools, 431–434
   influence of history education, 424
   ironical and dialogical understanding in history education, 436–438
   master narratives and their persistence, 430–431
   myths of origin, 430–431
national identity (Estonia), 138–143
   building a nation, 138–140
   collective memory work, 140–142
   reifying national identity as a state, 142–143
nationalism
   in history writing and education, 424–426
natural
   meaning in cognitive science of religion (CSR), 366–367
nature
   humans viewed as not part of, 68
Nazi Germany
   Günter Grass and the Third Reich, 529–535
   propaganda and the cult of Hitler, 527–529
   rise of, 526–527
negotiation, 30, 52, 94
Nelson, Katherine, 230
neoliberalism, 488
Neoplatonism, 386
networks, 105
Neuman, John von, 70
neuronal group selection theory, 209
neurophenomenology, 212
Nietzsche, Friedrich, 381
Nigro, K.F., 588

nomotetic, 8, 31

noncanonical use of objects by children, 225–226

nondevelopmentalism, 557–558

non-dialogic pedagogies, 275–276

non-instrumental dialogic pedagogies, 285–296

non-instrumental education, 276–279

non-reductive scientific naturalism, 369–374

normative mediator, 333

norms, 8, 105, 302, 340, 564–565, 575

not me, 90

not me experience, 82

null state, 520

number systems
  evolution of, 112–114

numerical use of objects
  development in young children, 233–235

object
  of a representamen, 117

object construction, 151

object of activity theory
  uses in studying human activities, 149–151

object relations theory, 86

objectification, 51, 54–58, 59, 148, 154
  influence of sociocultural context, 55–58

objectivity, 51–53

objects
  affordances of, 107–109
  awareness of their functional attributes, 223–225
  cultural uses, 236
  ecstatic power of, 354–357
  functional, canonical use by children, 225–226
  functional permanence of, 226
  functional uses and executive functions before language,
     230–233
  how children learn to use them according to their
     function, 225–226
  metacanonical uses, 230
  noncanonical use by children, 225–226
  numerical use in young children, 233–235
  protocanonical use by children, 225–226
  relation between symbolic and functional uses, 228–230
  rhythmic-sonorous uses, 226–228
  self-regulation through, 230–233
  use in child interaction with adults, 233–235

observer
  describing behavior, 19–20

Onfray, M., 382

ontic nature of objects, 118

ontogenesis, 104, 207, 247
  in living organisms, 19

ontological non-instrumental dialogic pedagogics, 291

ontopotentiality of symbols, 114

operation, 13, 19, 21, 22, 25, 26

ordinary life on the border, 309

organization, 38

organizational closure, 39–40

Ortega y Gasset, J., 462, 463–464, 470, 472, 473

Orwell, George, 443

ostensive gestures, 226, 231

Ostrom, Elinor, 154

Other, 30, 42, 143, 190, 360, 376, 503, 541
  dialogical dance with, 512
  generalized Other, 524
  I–Other relationships, 403
  priority in aesthetic transcendence, 354–357
  priority of, 362–363
  realm of, 360
  self-reflection via identification with, 254

ownership
  understanding in children, 319–323

Paideia proposal, 281

Paley, Vivian, 281, 283, 284, 285

Pali canon, 616

Panofsky, Erwin, 608

parataxic thinking, 80
  as a defence, 80–82

Park, Rosa Louise, 489

Parmenides of Elea, 597, 598

parrhesia, 470–471

pathic dimension, 549, 550

Pavlov, Ivan, 246

Peirce, Charles S., 15, 92, 117, 303
  on self-reflection, 245–246

Peircean Semiotics, 639

perception
  ecological theory of, 106–107
  leading to conceptualization, 21

perceptual action, 119

person, 13, 15, 17, 31

personal agency, 560

personal development through persistent imitation,
     559–561

personal dimension of experience, 538–539

personal sense, 545

personality, 557

personality suggestions, 560

personhood
  emergence of, 27–28

personified abstractions, 404–406

perspective-taking, 172

pertinentization
  ongoing process during sensemaking, 45
phenomenological naturalism, 366, 374–376
phenomenology, 15, 637
  pre-reflective, embodied experience, 539–540
Piaget, Jean, 209, 226, 228, 482
  on self-reflection, 246
planning capacitiy, 104
Plato, 14, 66, 249, 274, 417, 479
  Socratic Dialogic method, 282–283
play
  development of, 150
play and art, 111–112
Pocket Money Project, 339–343
poetry, 359
Poincaré, Henri, 164
pointing gestures, 231
political institutionalization
  climate change debate, 137–138
politics of representing the past, 443–444
  agency, 445
  Basque conflict, 443–444, 445–449
  Egyptian revolution (2011), 443–444, 449–453
  positioning, 444–445
  symbolic action and re-action, 453–455
  symbolic tools, 444–445
  theoretical framework, 444–445
polysemic nature of money, 334–335
possessions
  polysemic nature, 334–335
postmodern psytizenship from a psycho-cultural
      perspective, 486–491
postmodern transitions of psytizenship, 484–486
postmodernism, 72
power relations, 605
prejudice, 582, 602, 605
pre-reflective, embodied dimension of selfhood, 538–539
pre-reflective, embodied experience
  affective register, 545–546
  existentials of embodied history, 542–546
  future research, 552
  habituation, 543
  hermeneutic repertoire, 544–545
  historical selfhood as embodied, 540–542
  incorporation, 544
  intercorporeity, 543–544
  sedimentation of pre-reflective experiential structures,
      546–547
  sedimented experiential dispositions, 548
  turn to phenomenology, 539–540
Prigogine, Ilya, 597

private gestures in infants, 231
problem-focused coping, 621
processual ontology, 39, 46
propaganda and the cult of Hitler, 527–529
proprioception, 212, 213, 218, 219
protocanonical use of objects by children, 225–226
prototaxic thinking, 80
  as a defence, 80–82
psyche, 633
  Aristotelian view, 15
  as an historical object, 381–382
  behaviorist view, 16
  biological basis, 15
  conceptions shaped by psychology, 16
  culture as the spirit of, 28
  definition, 633–634
  distinction from spirit, 14–15
  division of, 14
  feelings drive the mind toward reflection, 23–24
  from biological processes to social behavior, 18–20
  functionalism of the American pragmatists, 15–16
  genealogical approach of cultural psychology, 383–385
  genealogical relationship to religion, 383–385
  influence of religion on the concept, 380–381
  nature of, 31, 103–104
  ontology of, 13–14
  role in the theory of evolution, 15
  sociocultural psychology view, 16
  study of developmental dynamics, 635–637
  turning things into objects, 106–109
psychoanalysis, 180
  theory on self-reflection, 247
psychogenesis and modernity, 480–483
psychological distancing theory, 248
psychological impersonalism, 557
psychological knowledge
  nature and origins of, 30–31
psychological rationality, 390–392
psychology
  as a liminal science, 633–635
  as a science, 633–637
  behaviorism, 16
  cognitive revolution, 16
  conceptions of psyche, 16
  explanatory extensions, 637
  first-person approach to the study of, 15
  fragmented state of the discipline, 35–36
  functional approaches of the German and Austrian
      schools, 15
  growth of the sociocultural perspective, 3
  need for a general theory of psychology, 35–36

ordering the epistemic field, 635–637
roots of, 637
third-person approach to the study of, 15
psychophysics, 15
psytizen carnivalization, 491–492
psytizenship
    activity as a means of surpassing adjustment, 487–488
    definition, 479–480
    empowered and dissolved psytizens, 489–491
    experience beyond decision and fragmentation, 488–489
    historico-genealogical approach, 480–484
    modern reflective capacity as a cultural artefact, 486
    postmodern psytizenship from a psycho-cultural
        perspective, 486–491
    postmodern transitions, 484–486
    psychogenesis and modernity, 480–483

queuing, 49–51

Rabbow, Paul, 386
Rancière, J., 404
rationalism of the Enlightenment, 283
reality, 130, 134, 180
    relation to imagination, 179
reciprocity
    understanding in children, 323–326
reductionism, 106
reflective modernity, 487
reification
    constructed in collective action, 417–419
reified discourse
    climate change debate, 137–138
relational psychoanalysis, 78
religion
    cultural analysis, 382–383
    cultural psychology approach, 383–385
    genealogical relationship to psyche, 383–385, 390–392
    influence of conceptions of the self, 380–381
    technologies of the self, 381–383
    see also cognitive science of religion (CSR)
religious development
    emotions and self-governance, 385–386
religious experience
    aesthetic transcendence, 354–357
religious extremism, 130
religious fundamentalism, 602
religious violence, 130
remediation, 155–156, 159
representamen, 117
representation
    as activity or process, 131–132

as product, 132–133
holomorphic, 133, 135
meanings of, 130–131
vs. object, 134–136
representationalism
    in social cognitive psychology, 65–70
    problems in cognitive psychology, 63–65
resource development and conservation theory, 622
responsiveness and personal history, 550–551
reverse action of signs, 250
revolutions, 192
rhema, 117, 123
rhythmic-sonorous uses of objects, 226–228
Ricoeur, Paul, 361–362
Rogoff, Barbara, 370
Roman Catholic culture, 490
Rorty, Richard, 487
Rosa, Alberto, 208, 599, 600
Rosch, Eleanor, 211
Rose, Nikolas, 482
Ruiz Zafon, C., 514–515
rule configuration, 154
rule constellation, 154
runaway objects, 151
rupture theories of self-reflection, 245–246

Sanders, Cecily, 618
Santaella, L., 607, 608
Sapir, Edward, 78
Sartre, Jean-Paul, 188
satisficing, 623
Scarry, Elaine, 363
scenarios, 44–45, 191, 210, 224, 229, 231, 236
Schachtel, Ernst, 360
Schiffer, Brian, 67
School of the Dialogue of Cultures, 290
science
    notion of, 13
scientific naturalism, 367–368, 369–374
Scott, Joan, 598, 604
scripts, 154, 155, 322, 454, 649
Searle, J.R., 327–328
second-person approach, 31, 208, 218, 220
sedimentation of pre-reflective experiential structures,
    546–547
sedimented experiential dispositions, 548
sedimented response registers, 551
Segato, Rita, 601, 604
selective inattention, 81
selective optimization with compensation (SOC) model,
    621

self
    and gender identity, 597–598
    as the space of circulation of subjective agencies,
        591–592
    construction of the autobiographical self, 260
    historical selfhood as embodied, 540–542
    in autobiographical memory, 267–271
    multinaturalism and the construction of the person,
        589–591
    production of, 26–27
    relation to the human experiential mind, 515
self-awareness, 540
self-consciousness theory of Hegel, 247–248
self-esteem, 80–81
self-governance
    and religious development, 385–386
self-management of behavior, 643–644
self-reflection
    complex semiotic systems, 254–255
    conflict theories, 247–249
    definition, 245
    internalization theories, 249–251
    Mead's theory of the social act, 251–252
    mirror theories, 246–247
    naming, 245
    reasons for, 255–257
    rupture theories, 245–246
    semiotic mediation, 245
    semiotic process underlying, 255–257
    social representation theory, 248
    two processes of, 252–254
    via distanciation from the self, 253
    via identification with Other, 254
self-regulation
    and aging, 621–622
    through gestures and objects, 230–233
self-states, 86–87
self story, 266
sembling, 560
semiology, 637
semiosis, 3, 117–118
semiosisaction, 639
semiospheres, 29–30, 645
semiotic boundaries and growth of meaning, 644–646
semiotic–cultural constructivism in psychology,
    575
semiotic mediation, 245, 503, 509
    influence of images on gender identities, 606–609
semiotic objects
    constitution of, 123–125
semiotic prism, 189–190, 192

semiotic resources, 185, 646
semiotic space in the therapeutic field, 89–94
semiotic tools, 508
semiotic traps, 549
semiotic value of material signs, 114
semiotics, 4, 16, 17, 29, 106, 126, 152, 164, 169, 637, 648,
    649
    border irregularities, 29–30
    of action, 117–118
    of behavior and experience, 116–125
    of self-reflection, 255
    Peircean, 639
semiotization, 30, 126
Sen, Amartya, 274
senicide, 617
Sennett, Richard, 482
sense
    distinction from meaning, 538
sensemaking
    as inherently dialogical, 42
    cultural psychology as the science of, 39–42
    mind as, 41–42
sensemaking dynamics, 42–45
    affective grounds of sensemaking, 44–45
    bivalence of meaning, 45
    culture as the field distribution of possibilities, 44
    hyperdimensionality of the distribution, 44
    meaning emerges from sensemaking, 43
    sensemaking is a field dynamics, 42–43
    sensemaking works through ongoing pertinentization,
        45
    significance in absentia (SIA), 45
    significance in praesentia (SIP), 45
    transition among signs is a habit function, 43–44
    transition among signs is the unit of analysis of
        sensemaking, 43
sensorial action, 117
sexism, 598, 600–602, 604–605
Sheets-Johnston, Maxine, 207, 218
Shotter, John, 490
Sidorkin, Alexander, 291–292, 294, 295
Sigel, I.E,
    psychological distancing theory, 248
sign transition, 42, 43
    is a habit function, 43–44
    unit of analysis of sensemaking, 43
significance in absentia (SIA), 45
significance in praesentia (SIP), 45
signs
    as internalized mediators for interaction, 20–21
    reverse action, 250

Simmel, G., 302
Skinner, B.F., 482
Skyfall, 187
Sluga, Glenda, 483
Smith, Adam
  on self-reflection, 246–247
Smith, Mark, 285
social act
  Mead's theory of, 251–252
social borders
  crossing in development and education, 312–313
social cognition, 51, 64, 67, 208, 218, 327
social cognitive psychology
  representationalism in, 65–70
social constructivism, 71, 72
social context of meaning making, 535–536
social conventional signs, 640
social denial
  forms of, 467
social engineering, 283–285, 481
social exchange
  gift exchange, 333
  money as a cultural tool, 333
social identities as boundary phenomena, 600–603
social influence, 58
social justice instrumental dialogic pedagogies,
    283–285
social membranes
  institutional borders as, 311–312
social objects
  climate change, 136–138
  national identity (Estonia), 138–143
  religious extremism, 130
  semiotic constitution of, 123–125
  social representation, 134–136
  wheelchairs, 135–136
social representation theory, 130–131, 400, 417
  behaving and acting, 131–132
  belief and communicating, 131
  individual and collective levels of analysis, 143–144
  interaction and cooperation, 132–134
  self-reflection, 248
  social objects, 134–136
social symbols
  emergence and development of, 24–26
social virtual objects, 123
social world of children, 319
socially constructed environments, 60
socially shared reality, 181
societal discourse, 131
Society of Jesus, 386, 585

sociocultural change
  role of imagination, 191–192
  role of symbolic resources, 191–192
sociocultural cognition, 370–371
sociocultural context
  influence on objectifications, 55–58
sociocultural frames of reference
  Daboma Jack incident, 50–51
sociocultural phenomena, 123
sociocultural psychology
  approach on experience and meaning, 638–639
  as a science, 633–637
  central assumptions, 598–600
  current developments in the field, 3
  definition, 16
  directions in, 8–9
  epistemology of, 637–649
  features of the sociocultural approach, 16–17
  model of how action produces meaningful experiences,
      639–649
  nature of, 31
  place among the sciences, 649–650
  structural-systemic approach, 17–18
  view of psyche, 16
sociocultural resouces
  for shaping experiences and behavior, 646–647
sociocultural theory, 148
Socrates, 274
Socratic Dialogic method, 282–283
somatic education, 215
somatic education techniques, 211
somatic teaching, 211–213
somatics, 212
soul, 14
South Park, 188
spectator theory of knowledge, 69
spheres of experience, 181
spirit, 31
  nature of, 14–15
Spiritual Exercises. See Ignatius of Loyola *Spiritual
    Exercises*
split-self, 550
statehood, 142–143
Steiner, George, 351–353, 356, 357
Stengers, Isabelle, 597
stereotypes, 582
Stern, Daniel, 218–219, 543
Stern, Donnel, 85–86
Stern, William, 556–557
  challenges to the study of development, 557–558
  the experiencing person, 558–559

Stimmung, 545
Stoicism, 386
Storr, A., 357
Straus, Erwin, 541
street art
  diversity of interactions with, 56
strong signs, 522
structural coupling, 38, 106, 116, 124, 211, 372, 373, 636,
  648
structural-systemic approach of sociocultural psychology,
  17–18
structure, 36, 38, 39, 40, 41, 42
subjectivity, 51–53, 106
Sullivan, Harry Stack, 78
  modes of meaning making, 80
  systems of defence, 80–82
  work on interpersonal psychoanalysis, 79–83
Sykes–Picot agreement (1916), 411
symbolic action and re-action, 453–455
symbolic bricolage, 184
symbolic gestures, 231
symbolic nature of humans, 13
symbolic resources, 124, 575
  aboutness, 184–185
  aboutness of, 188
  and theory of imagination, 178
  as a sociocultural concept, 183–189
  concept of, 178
  constraints on the use of, 192–194
  cultural experiences as, 183–184
  defining, 184–185
  four levels of semiotic mediation, 186–187
  future study directions, 195
  generativity, 188–189
  heuristic power of the concept, 178
  model for analyzing the use of, 185–189
  origins of the concept, 184
  plausibility, 187–188
  role in sociocultural change, 191–192
  role in the lifecourse, 189–191
  semiotic prism, 189–190, 192
  study methodological problems, 194–195
  theoretical problems, 194
  time orientation, 186
  use of cultural elements, 183–184
symbolic systems, 183
symbolic thought
  development of, 150
symbolic tools, 444–445
symbolic use of objects
  relation to functional uses, 228–230

symbols, 24–26, 117
  nature of, 112, 121
    product of communication when acting,
      22–23
sympathetic magic, 132
syntaxic thinking, 80

Tai Chi, 215
Tannaim, 274
Tartu School of semiotics, 29
technologies of the self, 381–383
terrorism, 130
texts, 29, 123–124
The Dreamers, 186
Thelen, Esther, 209–211
theology, 385
theoretic culture, 261
theory of evolution
  functions of psyche, 15
theory of mind, 65–66
theory of the ideal, 150
thinking in action, 117, 118
thinking in movement, 217–219
Third Age, 618, 621
third-person approach, 15
Thomae, Hans, 621, 624
Thompson, Clara, 78
Thompson, Evan, 211, 371–372, 373
time
  depiction of, 14
Tintin, 192
tool use
  relationship to language, 151–153
tools, 25, 104–105
  and signs, 151–152
  creative process, 109–110
  money
    as a cultural tool, 333
Toomela, Aaro, 17, 18
torpedo touch, 282
total body connectivity
  breath pattern, 214–215
  core–distal connectivity pattern, 215–216
  fundamental patterns, 214–217
  head–tail pattern of connectivity, 216–217
totalitarian regimes
  irony as a tool of critique, 443
totalitarianism, 283–285
transcendence
  defining, 351
  within immanence, 357–360

transition among signs, 42, 43
  is a habit function, 43–44
  is the unit of analysis of sensemaking, 43
transitions, 178, 184, 189, 191, 195
translation, 29, 30, 256, 336
trauma theory, 86
Trevarthen, Colwin, 210
triadic rhythmic interactions, 226–227
Truth and Reconciliation Committees, South Africa,
    466–467
Tulving, E., 264–265, 266

ubuntu tradition, 617
umbrella revolution (Hong Kong, 2014), 417–418
Umwelt, 17, 31, 108, 111, 127, 400, 640
Unheimlichkeit, 546
unknown soldier memorials, 415–417

Valsiner, Jaan, 107, 187, 208, 313, 504, 530, 538, 544,
    545, 558, 591, 597, 599, 600, 608, 609
value
  definition, 126
Varela, Francisco, 18–20, 211
Veblen, Thorsten, 296
vectors, 519, 520
Verne, Jules, 192
Vico, Giambattista, 180, 417
  axioms on the historical development of the human
    mind and and culture, 401–404
violence
  from the point of view of victims, perpetrators and
    bystanders, 466–468
  religious violence, 130
vitality forms, 215
Viveiros de Castro, E., 584, 588–589, 591–592, 593
volitional action, 117
volitive action, 119
Völkerpsychologie movement, 15
von Uekküll, Jakob, 640
Vygotsky, Lev, 3, 17, 18, 71, 148, 260, 482
  distinction between sense and meaning, 538

  internalization, 249–251
  mediation by signs, 148
  on communication, 230
  on creativity, 169, 171
  on imagination, 180–181, 182
  on the full sense of words, 520
  on the use of objects, 228
  psychological mediation, 184
  role of objects, 149–150
  signs, 333
  theory of imagination and creativity, 149–150
  theory of the sign, 249–251
  tools and signs, 151–152
  zone of proximal development, 53, 306

Wagner, Roy, 591
Waldenfels, Bernhard, 542
  agency as responsiveness, 548–551
Wartofsky, Max, 153
Watson, J.B., 66, 68
Weber, Max, 600
Weimar Germany and the rise of Nazism, 526–527
Wertsch, J.V., 123, 184, 249, 274, 426, 430, 434, 435, 436,
    437, 443, 444, 445, 453, 454
wheelchairs
  as social objects, 135–136
White, Hayden, 417
White, William Alanson, 78
Widerfahrnis, 550
Will, 387
Wineburg, Sam, 428
women
  violence against, 601
Wundt, Wilhelm, 15

Yoga, 211

Zeitverschiebung, 549
zone of free movement, 107, 544
zone of promoted action, 544
zone of proximal development, 53, 104, 306